HEARTS
TOUCHED BY
FIRE

HEARTS TOUCHED BY FIRE

THE BEST OF *BATTLES AND LEADERS OF THE CIVIL WAR*

Edited and with an Introduction by Harold Holzer

WITH CONTRIBUTIONS BY
*James M. McPherson, James I. Robertson, Jr.,
Stephen W. Sears, Craig L. Symonds,
and Joan Waugh*

THE MODERN LIBRARY

NEW YORK

IN MEMORY OF JOHN Y. SIMON,

A LEADER WHO LED BATTLES

AND KNEW THE WAR'S GREATEST GENERAL BEST OF ALL

CONTENTS

1863

1864

1865

INTRODUCTION

Harold Holzer

The most popular, influential, and enduring collection of first-person Civil War memoirs ever published could trace its origins to a good-natured interoffice debate between two young magazine editors.

In July 1883, just a few days after the twentieth anniversary of the Battle of Gettysburg, Clarence Clough Buel of *The Century Magazine* initiated a lively discussion about the war with the colleague who sat at the next desk, fellow assistant editor Robert Underwood Johnson. Both men were barely thirty. Buel was a scrappy New Yorker and alumnus of the *New York Tribune* staff; Johnson was a young *Century* veteran who could trace his roots to both a Confederate general, Bushrod Johnson, and a Union politician, Indiana governor Oliver P. Morton.

The question they argued that fateful day was: Which Civil War engagement deserved to be ranked as the bloodiest battle of them all? Buel contended that "the grewsome [sic] distinction belonged to Chickamauga,"[1] where one-third of all troops were killed or wounded in action in September 1863. Johnson insisted it was the June 1864 Union assault on Confederate breastworks at Cold Harbor, where casualty tolls reached 8,500. The two men could not agree on an answer that day (Chickamauga was in fact the costlier), but their lively discussion inspired Buel to a brainstorm: Why not let the magazine's 125,000 readers in on the conversation by offering "a series of papers on some of the great battles of the war to be written by officers in command on both sides"?[2] Johnson seconded the notion. A few days later, Buel pitched the idea to his boss, editor in chief Richard Watson Gilder.

The widely read magazine, which had begun its life as *Scribner's Monthly,* had just published two articles recalling a major prewar event—John Brown's 1859 Harpers Ferry raid—from pro-Brown and anti-Brown points of view. One piece had been authored by a proslavery "Virginian Who Witnessed the Fight," but in a great show of evenhandedness it was accompanied by a commentary provided by a self-described "Radical Abolitionist" who sympathized with it.[3] Reader response had been positive, and Buel now posited that subscribers to the 35-cent monthly would certainly embrace the idea of a modest new series—no more than eight to ten articles, he envisioned at first—on "the decisive battles" of the war itself. The articles would be written by generals, Union and Confederate alike, who had commanded the engagements two score years earlier—"or, if he were not living," Johnson proposed, by "the person most entitled to speak for him or in his place."[4] The pieces would present both sides of each major battle, guaranteeing the same scrupulous fairness that had characterized the Harpers Ferry presentations.

The editors suggested an additional rule they calculated would boost circulation nationwide, even if it obliterated a crucial aspect of war history. Politics would be eschewed. The still divisive root causes of the war would be ignored and cool-headed military history encouraged. The series, as Johnson put it, would be presented in "an unsectional way"—meaning it would focus principally on battlefield action that could be recounted and dissected, rather than on underlying issues that might more readily open old wounds. Johnson proposed "rigid enforcement of our main principle, the exclusion of political questions."[5] To guarantee widespread appeal, sectional discord would be repressed in favor of straightforward accounts focusing on strategy and tactics—exhibiting what Buel later called "strict fairness to the testimony of both sides." The articles would be marked by "good temper" and "unpartisan character," with "each side" confining "controversy to its own ranks." Union and Confederate writers alike would be urged to emphasize only "the benefit as well as the glory" of the specific events they were describing.[6] These rules enhanced the prospects of wide popular acceptance, but at the expense of burying crucial aspects of Civil War memory.

Not everyone shared Buel's enthusiasm for rehashing the late war, however free of rancor. The Century publishing company's president and business manager, Roswell Smith, initially "expressed doubt whether the project would increase the circulation of the magazine" at all.[7] Others, like Abraham Lincoln's former assistant private secretary, John Hay, firmly believed that the war had "gone by,"[8] predicting that readers would resist any efforts to churn up ancient animosities that reminded them of the painful events that had left dozens of cities ravaged and 600,000 young men dead. (Of course, Hay was at the time busy collaborating with his onetime White House colleague John G. Nicolay on a massive biography of the late president, which he intended for magazine serialization as well. He perhaps feared that the proposed new project might preempt their own.)

Buel, however, would not be dissuaded. He insisted that a Civil War series would not only interest "veterans in their own memories," but also contribute to "instructing the generation which has grown up since the War for the Union." His boss, Richard Gilder, editor since 1881, was widely known to the public at the time as both the magazine's unbilled "voice" and also as a prominent poet (Buel and Johnson dabbled in verse as well).[9] But it was likely as a Union veteran, too—he had served briefly as an emergency volunteer to repel the 1863 Confederate invasion of Pennsylvania—that Gilder "at once cordially adopted the suggestion," according to an official introduction prepared three years later. Although the *Philadelphia Times* had published a similar series in 1879, also from both Union and Confederate vantage points, Gilder insisted that "this war-series is a flank movement on all our rivals. It is a great scheme."[10] He eventually won the support of publisher Smith by stressing the project's commercial, not educational, possibilities. Ultimately, Smith too came to see the wisdom (and profitability) in expanding the reader base among the war's survivors. Enlightening the proud children of the war's veterans would provide a bonus, since they not unimportantly represented a new generation of potential subscribers. In other words, the series struck editors and publisher alike not only as a genuine public service but, more important, as a lucrative marketing bonanza.

Encouraged to proceed, Gilder assigned Johnson to lead the effort, with Buel assisting. Buel prepared an outline during his summer vacation. Johnson began contacting potential contributors. By then few inside the company doubted that the series would prove appealing. Yet it is probably fair to say that no one who signed off on the project in 1883 could have imagined the scope, size, importance, or enduring reputation that it eventually achieved.

Nor did they anticipate the setbacks that nearly derailed it before it could see the light of day. "Little did I think as a boy during the Civil War as I read the news from the front every night to my father," Johnson later remembered, "that I should some day come into close personal relations with many of the commanders on both sides whose names were then household words to us." Indeed, many of these living legends eventually became contributors. But some initially proved so reluctant to participate in the "War Series" that the enterprise nearly collapsed before it could begin.

A writer who later remembered working for Gilder recalled of his skill for tapping talent, "No other was so bent upon finding, not only new writers, but new paths for established ones."[11] But for a time, the recruitment of star contributors—an effort Gilder jokingly called "General Catching"—proved far more difficult than anyone at *The Century* had reckoned. Not surprisingly, the editors first approached the former president and undisputed hero of the Union cause, Ulysses S. Grant. But as Johnson admitted, initially "we made no progress in this flank attack upon the General's position." Still physically drained by his recent two-year-long world tour, and with recent books (by others) just beginning to rehabilitate his reputation after his disastrous second term in the White House, Grant was reluctant to contribute to new endeavors that might upset the improving equilibrium. "I do not feel now as though I could undertake the articles asked for by the *Century,*" he insisted. Besides, as he argued, his onetime military staff aide Adam Badeau had recently published an exhaustive account containing just about everything that anyone might have wanted to know about Grant's military career.[12]

Onetime Confederate general P.G.T. Beauregard was equally dismissive, telling *Century* editors he was far too busy with other projects to participate either. Union legend Philip Sheridan was planning a memoir of his own, and did not want to scoop his own recollections for the benefit of *The Century.* General William T. Sherman was certain such a project could never succeed and was "rather inclined to pooh-pooh our undertaking," Johnson lamented.[13] And the general who had surrendered to Sherman in North Carolina—Joseph E. Johnston—suspected that the project was some kind of New York plot to trample on Lost Cause glory. Editor Johnson personally wooed Johnston on visits to his Washington, D.C., home and again at his New York hotel. But he found the old general not only "suspicious of being entrapped," but also "irascible...difficult...as dry as 'the remainder biscuit after a voyage, and technical to the dotting of an *i.*'" For a time, Johnston remained "depressingly unresponsive" to the *Century*'s overtures.[14]

Response from lesser-known commanders was not much more enthusiastic. Facing a vexing predicament he labeled his "Scylla and Charybdis," Johnson encountered "reluctance" both among officers wary of speaking "of persons who are no longer living" and from those unwilling to criticize "certain persons still living." Facing all this seemingly intractable resistance, the editor grandiloquently complained that "it was at first hard steering for the Muse of History."[15] After Confederate general James Longstreet, too, declined, editor Gilder reluctantly told Johnson: "Without such names as his, Sherman's, Beauregard's...Sheridan & Grant absolutely assured we must face the issue of postponing another year."[16]

Then, just a few months later, the *Century*'s prospects dramatically rose—because Grant's suddenly plummeted. After news broke that a business partner had swindled the general out of his entire fortune, the magazine promptly renewed its invitation that he contribute, expressing "regret and sympathy" over the general's widely publicized ruin. The public, Johnson craftily told Adam Badeau, "would be glad to have its attention diverted from Grant's present troubles, and no doubt such diversion of his own mind would be welcome to him." More important, Gilder offered Grant $500 per article, and that broke the logjam. The general, who desperately needed money, abruptly folded his tent: he not only signed on, but set to work without delay, submitting a draft article on the Battle of Shiloh by June 30. "The series 'smiles' now as it never has before," Gilder exulted, certain he could now "bag" such "big flounders" as Sherman and Sheridan, too.[17]

The smiles proved short-lived. The editors read Grant's initial submission with "dismay." To Johnson, it was little more than "a copy of his dry official report of that engagement, as printed in the 'Rebellion Records,' with which we had already made ourselves familiar." So, with a proof copy in hand, Johnson went to see the general. "Without at first letting him know of its unsuitableness to the series," Johnson drew him into a lively conversation about the battle, taking copious notes as Grant fluently reminisced. Then the editor subtly ventured that such personal recollections were "typical of what was essential" for the magazine series. Johnson suggested that the Shiloh article should be just like "a talk as he would make to friends after dinner, some of whom should know all about the battle and some nothing at all." Grant "seemed astonished at this," Johnson admitted, but vowing he would try again, the general took back the article and revised it.[18]

Grant recruited biographer Badeau to approve (and edit) this and each of his subsequent contributions. Badeau likely proved helpful. Although he and Grant occasionally squabbled, the small, bespectacled former diplomat had genuine literary flair—he had once served as a theater critic—although the two later fell out, predictably, over money.[19] By July 15, the general was working on his Battle of the Wilderness reminiscence while on vacation at Long Branch, New Jersey, gamely asking Gilder if he wanted him to cover just the battle or the entire James River campaign. Perhaps half seriously, the financially strapped Grant added, "If the latter I fear I will have to *strike;* not for *higher wages;* but because I do not want to do so much work now."[20]

That summer, Grant urged Sherman to reconsider his own refusal to participate. "I hope both you and Sheridan will contribute to the series because they are to be written, in every instance, by persons who participated in the scenes described. It is better that it should be done by persons who had the largest opportunity of witnessing all that took place."[21] Ever loyal to his old commander, Sherman signed on, and so, eventually, did Admiral David Dixon Porter, General James Longstreet, and others, though Sheridan, Benjamin Butler, Winfield Scott Hancock, and a few other notables steadfastly declined. So did the late Robert E. Lee's son George Washington Custis Lee, a considerable setback for the plan. Similarly, Confederate general Jubal Early insisted he "could not write fairly for pay," adding rather ponderously: "Compensation for such hireling work was . . . a *dis*-honorarium."

Joseph E. Johnston, too, remained immune to the magazine's overtures—that is, until he came to the conclusion that contributing would give him an opportunity to lambaste his old nemesis, Jefferson Davis. He ultimately agreed to submit four articles.[22] The editors wooed additional prey relentlessly and ingeniously: if money did not do the trick, they tugged at the heartstrings. When, for example, Confederate colonel W.C.P. Breckinridge resisted the editors' initial overtures, a persistent Gilder implored: "Please don't say 'no' to our war request! This is the time for the 'unveiling of all hearts.' If the North can see the heart of the South, and the South the North's, they will love each other as never before!" Breckinridge, too, succumbed.

So did others. The famously reluctant Union general George McClellan—his character and literary style as "Corinthian" as Grant's was "Doric," remembered Johnson—became "one of the most interesting of the contributors." He was one of the most newsworthy as well: his previous five articles in the magazine had assiduously avoided the war and focused on his own world tour.[23] Now McClellan agreed to tackle the subject afresh, though unlike Joe Johnston, he avoided (or was asked by the editors to avoid) criticism of his old commander in chief, Abraham Lincoln, whom he had once dismissed as a "Gorilla."[24] Even an initially gunshy P.G.T. Beauregard finally came around after Gilder asked a mutual friend—author George Washington Cable, who had previously published in *The Century*—to intercede.[25]

These were not the only well-known writers ultimately to join the growing roster of contributors. *The Century* procured recollections by such Union luminaries as Ambrose E. Burnside, Oliver O. Howard, and Horace Porter, and Confederate history makers like Joseph Wheeler, D. H. Hill, and Edward Porter Alexander. Literary flair would be provided by Union general Lew Wallace, whose bestselling novel *Ben-Hur* had appeared in 1880.

Grant alone would contribute four separate articles to the "Battles and Leaders" series on his most important wartime campaigns, which the editors later boasted "became the foundation of his 'Personal Memoirs'"—a book that *The Century* fully expected to publish itself until Samuel Clemens interceded with a better offer, money always being Grant's chief concern. But only weeks before the hero's death from cancer in 1885, Grant's son Fred hailed the editors as "generous," telling them that "Father's connection with the *Century Magazine* has been pleasant, and he feels gratified in having done business with men who have always acted the part of gentlemen." In the end, Grant earned $4,000 for his contributions—a rate inexplicably double the editors' original offer. Longstreet took in $2,715, and Johnston, $500.[26]

The debut articles in the magazine series—Beauregard's account of the Battle of Bull Run, together with a six-page enlisted man's perspective on the same engagement by one Warren Lee Goss entitled "Recollections of a Private"—finally appeared in the November 1884 issue, a year and a half after the editors first proposed the series. Initially, it might be noted, all the accounts in the articles were to be grouped under the soporific title "Men and Events of the Civil War." But assistant editor Buel countered that "Leaders & Battles is better," persuasively arguing that " '*Battles*' is the main thing. 'Events' might seem as if we were going into, say, the condition & action of the freedmen—the Emancipation Proclamation—and other events not connected with battles." Anything that implied a concentration on toxic issues like slavery and race—however crucial and unresolved—was the last thing the editors wished to suggest. Johnson took Buel's cue, and wisely massaged the suggestion into the enduring title: "Battles and Leaders of the Civil War."

For the three years that followed, until the edition of November 1887, the recollections and reminiscences poured forth, not a dozen or so articles in total, as originally proposed, but several new articles each *month:* ninety-nine altogether (plus an array of sidebars called "Memoranda of the Civil War"). The editors may have decreed that the subjects of race and politics be ignored, but they also recognized that the "literary inexperience of men of action and sometimes their inability to make interesting records" required occasional relief. Of course, the broader contents of each issue never lacked for diversionary literature and how-to advice on a myriad of other subjects: the first edition to feature "Battles and Leaders," for example, also boasted the latest excerpt from William Dean Howells's novel *The Rise of Silas Lapham,* along with such diverse pieces as "The Chinese Theater," "Vedder's Accompaniment to the Song of Omar Khayyam," and "The Principles and Practice of House-Drainage." Nonetheless the editors also procured softer war features like Mark Twain's reminiscence "The Private History of a Campaign That Failed"; Joel Chandler Harris's "Free Joe," a fictional story replete with cringe-making "darky" dialect; and Constance Cary Harrison's home-front account of "A Virginia Girl in the First Year of the War."[27]

Not that the "War Series" itself lacked for bite and contentiousness. Though "endeavoring to hold the scales of justice evenly between the disputants" and thus "winning the respect of both," editor Johnson almost boasted that "it was not long before we found ourselves knee-deep in controversy, not across Mason and Dixon's Line, but between officers on one side or other" of particular wartime engagements. Quickly aware that every battle produced "at least four points of view"—those of the man credited with victory, the one who believes he deserves credit more, the commander blamed for defeat, and the officer blamed in turn by the losing commander—the editors commissioned, for example, varying accounts of Longstreet's delayed arrival at Gettysburg, George G. Meade's failure to pursue Lee after that battle, and the nature of Grant's near defeat on the first day at Shiloh. Even if the overall product stressed "intersectional reconciliation," its individual elements could be explosive. Once, a mere footnote criticizing "old army" General David E. Twiggs's hasty surrender of San Antonio to Texas early in the war—the source quoted Twiggs as being willing to "surrender to an old woman with a broomstick" if authorized by the state—incited one of the late general's surviving staff officers to challenge editor Johnson to a duel. "Some of these controversies were acrimonious," Johnson conceded. But he insisted that "the total result...even with these differences" constituted "a unique body of *mémoires pour servir,* as the French call materials of history."[28]

To their credit, the editors worked diligently to "shape the form, and enliven the color of the narrative[s]." Faced with a formidable problem—contributions that simply ran too long—they took up their pencils and cut. They would not guarantee any of their authors, no matter how famous, that their contributions would appear without changes. This strict policy they maintained even when a major potential author like Jefferson Davis, eager to rebut P.G.T. Beauregard's and Joseph E. Johnston's unflattering accounts of his leadership, insisted as a precondition that his words appear in print exactly as written. Eager as they were to have Davis in the fold—editors offered him seven thousand words for his recollections and assured him they would never "take the liberty of publishing part of it, or of making omissions, without first having given you our reasons and having received your permission"—they would not surrender editorial control. As Johnson wrote to Davis: "We think you will appreciate our reluctance to part with the editorial autocracy to the extent of engaging in advance to publish every word of an article on a controversial subject." Davis did not. In the end, the first and only president of the Confederacy declined to provide an article.[29]

Editors were determined from the first to get the details right. To guarantee scrupulous accuracy, Union general James B. Fry, who had served as Union provost-martial during the 1863 New York City draft riots, joined the project as an adviser and fact checker, always willing "to elucidate some obscure point, none the less if it involved controversy."[30] The editors turned for "special aid" to Colonel Robert N. Scott, editorial director of the office that had produced the Official Records of the war (and when he died, to his successor, Colonel H. M. Lazelle). While he lived, Scott even shared advance proofs of yet to be issued later volumes of the massive *Official Records of the War of the Rebellion.* Looking South as well, the editors employed General Marcus J. Wright, War Department agent for the collection of Confederate records.

From the very first article, the series also featured as accompaniment well-chosen and astutely orchestrated illustrations. Buel was determined from the start that the articles would be "better illustrated than battles and battlefields have ever been, before"[31]—beginning with accomplished sketches of a Louisiana Tiger drummer boy and a group of soldiers camped along Blackburn's Ford, followed by a portrait of Beauregard's Bull Run opponent, Union general Irvin McDowell. These pictures ushered in the practice of featuring ambitious pictures for each entry, for which the magazine tapped a dazzling array of photograph collections, artists, cartographer-draftsmen, and engravers to supply material.

To serve as principal reference models, the Massachusetts Commandery of the Loyal Legion shared its complete holdings of the Mathew Brady and Alexander Gardner photographic records of the Civil War. The editors assigned Alexander W. Drake and W. Lewis Fraser of the magazine's art department to supervise the commissioning and placement of engravings, stressing "the importance of accuracy ... in the preparation of the illustrations." Reflecting this commitment, editors asked Admiral Porter himself to review the illustrations for the articles on the battles for New Orleans.[32]

The art directors were quick to recruit the best artistic talent. Military painter Thure de Thulstrup, whose watercolors had inspired a famous series of Civil War battle chromolithographs by Boston's Louis Prang & Co., enrolled in the project. He was joined by other Prang alumni, such as marine artists Julian O. Davidson and Xanthus Smith (who had actually served on ships in the Union navy). Joining the ranks were Theodore R. Davis, wartime artist-correspondent for *Harper's Weekly*; battlefield artist Edwin Forbes, who had served as a staff artist for the rival *Frank Leslie's Illustrated Newspaper*; landscape and history painter Edward Lamson Henry; portrait and mural artist William Morris Hunt; and prolific military specialist Henry O. Ogden. The gifted Waud brothers—Alfred and William—both of whom had worked as illustrators for the picture weeklies during the war, joined the roster of contributors, too.

Nor were pro-Confederate painters ignored. The magazine featured the work of soldier-artist Allen C. Redwood (who also contributed an article on the Second Battle of Bull Run), along with that of William L. Sheppard, William Trego, Gilbert Gaul, James E. Taylor, and even Adalbert J. Volck, a Copperhead Marylander whose anti-Lincoln and pro-Confederate etchings, though famous today, had been suppressed in Union-held Baltimore throughout the war. Altogether, *The Century* engaged more than sixty engravers to produce illustrations. And the magazine spared no expense when it came to presenting maps, some of which became the first to be published of specific actions since the war itself. General Johnston himself labored over the maps of the Battle of Seven Pines, while editor Buel, "with his clairvoyant instinct for visualizing a battle," assumed overall responsibility for "supervision" of the series' hundreds of maps. All these illustrations more than lived up to the editors' boast that pictures proved "a most striking and not the least important feature of the work."[33]

The recruitment of leading writers and illustrators, the magazine's unsparing attention to editorial integrity, accuracy, and design, and perhaps, too, its bland rejection of matters of race and politics, paid off handsomely. The maiden issue of November 1883, Gilder boasted joyfully, sold "beyond anything hitherto known to us."[34] Within only six months of the series' debut, the circulation of *The Century* spiked nearly 80 percent—rising from 127,000 to 225,000. The magazine would soon claim a total readership (people then shared their magazines) of some two million per issue. Reader comments poured in and soon began appearing in their own section. Though Buel had predicted in an introductory editorial that "in popular interest as well as historical importance" the articles would "deserve wider attention than any other ever undertaken by the magazine," the editors soon admitted that they were "hardly prepared for the almost unbroken response of welcome." Accolades arrived "in the generous notice of the press...the large number of encouraging and helpful letters," and "most practical of all, in the extraordinary increase in the circulation of the magazine."[35]

To the delight of John Nicolay and the once skeptical John Hay, the public's enthusiasm for wartime history remained undiminished when their own Lincoln project began its concurrent serialization in *The Century* in 1886. From then until late 1887, *Century* readers could thus rely on the magazine to devote a major portion of each and every issue to firsthand reminiscences of both the conflict and its most famous character—literally, as promised, an unparalleled account of the battles and leaders of the Civil War. What had been originally conceived as a modest series of eight to ten articles expanded exponentially into a massive outpouring of words and images.

Understandably, the editors found it impossible to predict how long the public would remain interested in the series. Although they had launched the project believing it might continue it for one, maybe two years, by the time they detected a downturn in reader enthusiasm, they had issued multiple pieces in thirty-six consecutive monthly issues—and still had dozens of unpublished articles in reserve. But three years after it began, the serialization finally came to an end. In terms of its publishing history, however, "Battles and Leaders" was a long way from dying.

In 1888, only a year after the serialization terminated, the Century Company came out with a four-volume edition in book form, edited by Buel and Johnson, presenting all ninety-nine original illustrated *Century* articles and accompanying "Memoranda" in chronological order, from a description of Washington, D.C., on the eve of the war in 1861 to the complete text of Robert E. Lee's farewell to the Army of Northern Virginia in 1865.

But there was more. The books' allure—making the material seem fresh even to faithful magazine readers—was not only that it preserved the original memoirs in handsome binding, but that it included bonus articles in the bargain. Formerly reluctant contributors to the magazine like Jubal Early now consented to allow excerpts from their own books to be included in the bound volumes. Featured, too, were a number of articles that had originally appeared not in *The Century* but in such rival publications as the *North American Review, Southern Bivouac,* the *Philadelphia Weekly Times,* and the *Philadelphia Weekly Press.* Despite its titanic length (four thick volumes with a total of 3,090 pages, including a comprehensive index of some forty thousand items)[36], the new set sold an astounding seventy-five thousand copies. Ever since, it has remained a mother lode resource for historians, and a source of continued fascination—in all its subsequent reprints—for students of the Civil War.

A decade after the books first came off the press, in 1894, the publishers continued to mine the endlessly rich subject with a one-volume "People's Edition" they entitled *The Century War Book*. It was designed, according to its preface, to introduce wartime history to "a larger body of readers than has been reached even by the great circulations of the completer book and of *The Century Magazine*."[37] Notwithstanding the ebbs and flows in reader interest over the years, the Century Company later calculated that it profited from its *Battles and Leaders* enterprises to the tune of a breathtaking million dollars.

Perhaps Richard Watson Gilder was not overreaching when he gushed that "this war series is the most important thing, historically, I ever expect to live to see in this century."[38] Whether he meant by the word "century" the magazine or the epoch remains unclear. It is reasonable to think he may have imagined both.

But after such wide circulation, and all its subsequent editions, it is fair to ask what today—125 years after the first of these articles appeared in print and 150 years after North and South unleashed the first guns of the Civil War—constitutes the "best" of *Battles and Leaders*? How does one appraise, select, and present the essential materials from that voluminous archive that, undimmed by time, continue to endure as essential accounts of the Civil War, just as originally advertised?

Assembled in the belief that the archive more than deserves renewed attention, this collection attempts to make those choices for a new generation of readers. To help do so, the editor of this volume recruited a roster of distinguished scholars that almost rivals the list of famous authors who contributed to the original volumes: Civil War historians Craig L. Symonds, Stephen W. Sears, James M. McPherson, Joan Waugh, and James I. Robertson, Jr. Their extraordinary previous contributions include authoritative works on the land and sea war, from Union and Confederate perspectives alike, along with books on Lincoln's command leadership and the careers of Generals George B. McClellan, Ulysses S. Grant, and Stonewall Jackson—to cite but a few of their award-winning contributions to the fields of military and political history. The editor invited them to join him in selecting year-by-year highlights from the original collection, divided into the five years of the war, 1861 through 1865, and also to write individual introductions that focus on the military engagements recalled in each, with an eye to appraising the interpretations offered in the original *Battles and Leaders*.

The choices were not always easy or obvious. The leading writers of the magazine series are all included—Grant, McClellan, Beauregard, Johnston, and Longstreet, to name but a few—but so are the keen observations of lesser-known generals and staff officers such as John D. Imboden (writing on Stonewall Jackson's last campaign), Jacob D. Cox (on Antietam), Darius N. Couch (on Chancellorsville), Henry J. Hunt (the three days' fighting at Gettysburg), John Coddington Kinney (on Farragut at Mobile Bay), and Horace Porter (on Lee's surrender at Appomattox). To widen the opportunities for inclusion, the choices were selected from the four-volume book edition, not just the original magazine series. The overall result, it is hoped, is a rich and representative collection to treasure anew throughout the sesquicentennial of the American Civil War.

————

The year that the four-volume book edition of *Battles and Leaders* first appeared in print, 1888, *Century* editor Richard Watson Gilder journeyed to Gettysburg for the twenty-fifth anniversary of the monumental battle there (its twentieth anniversary, five years earlier, had inspired the original series). Here on this sacred ground he offered, as if providing a rationale in verse for the high purpose and hard work that had informed his magazine's ambitious project, a personal vision for preserving history and recognizing its heroes as a way of cementing the bonds of reunion:

Shade of our greatest, O look down to-day!
 Here the long, dread midsummer battle roared,
 And brother in brother plunged the accursed sword;—
 Here foe meets foe once more in proud array,

Yet not as once to harry and to slay,
 But to strike hands, and with sublime accord
 Weep tears heroic for the souls that soared
 Quick from earth's carnage to the starry way.

Each fought for what he deemed the people's good,
 And proved his bravery by his offered life,
 And sealed his honor with his outpoured blood....

Gilder and the editors of *The Century Magazine* sincerely believed that their extraordinary enterprise "exerted an influence in bringing about a better understanding between the soldiers" who fought one another in the Civil War, contributing significantly to a "new heritage of manhood and peace."[39] Buel and his colleagues may have overstated their contributions to sectional reconciliation—for it all but excluded the idea of extending civil rights to African Americans, failing even to properly acknowledge their battlefield sacrifices in fighting for their own freedom. (The book version at least attempted to correct the imbalance a bit by including a chapter on the "colored troops" at Petersburg.)

But Buel, Johnson, and Gilder did not overstate the venerable project's overall contribution to American history. Never before, or since, have so many firsthand accounts so vividly, dispassionately, and authoritatively described the large and small struggles of the armies and navies of blue and gray who were so determined to fight, and if necessary die, to secure their clashing visions of American freedom.

What Robert Underwood Johnson said of the series in 1923—forty years after he helped launch it—remains true today: "The work is of such a character that it simply cannot be ignored in any consideration of the Civil War, to which, in another cycle of historical study, public attention is likely to revert...."

Let the new cycle of public attention begin, with the best of *Battles and Leaders* again at its very core.

1861

INTRODUCTION

Craig L. Symonds

The first ten months of the American Civil War—from Lincoln's inauguration in March to the beginning of the first wartime winter—marked a period of experimentation and adjustment for both sides. The national government in Washington had to adjust to a wartime footing, and in Montgomery, Alabama (later in Richmond, Virginia), the breakaway states had to create a government from scratch. There were two important battles during this period: one in the Eastern Theater along the banks of Bull Run Creek near Manassas, Virginia, and one in the Western Theater at Wilson's Creek in Missouri, as well as a naval action at Port Royal, South Carolina. Each of these seemed epic at the time, though all of them were subsequently eclipsed by the unimagined fury and bloodshed of the great battles that would follow.

The essays in this first section of *Battles and Leaders of the Civil War* cover this period of experiment and adjustment. They are, of course, firsthand accounts by eyewitnesses and participants, but since they were written down some twenty years later in the 1880s, the authors also benefited from hindsight. Eyewitness accounts they may be, but they are also after-the-fact assessments, and a few of the authors used them as an opportunity to settle old scores.

The war began at Fort Sumter on April 12, 1861. Stunning as it was, the first shot was hardly a surprise to the garrison. Since the day after Christmas 1860, when Major Robert Anderson moved his men and their dependents from Fort Moultrie on Sullivan's Island out to the more isolated—and therefore more defensible—Fort Sumter, the men of the garrison knew that they were at the center of a dispute that could turn violent at any moment.

Sergeant James Chester, who rose to the rank of captain in the ensuing war, was one of those who worked tirelessly to prepare Sumter for the expected onslaught. His story provides unique insight into the ingenuity of the besieged garrison. Fort Sumter was still unfinished on December 26, and there was a lot of work to do. The soldiers put the heavy guns in place, mined the small wooden pier, erected some guns at an angle to use as mortars, and even fabricated some ersatz hand grenades in case of an attack by small boats. They created what Chester calls a "flying fougasse"—a barrel filled with small stones that had a canister of black powder at its center, making it a kind of fragmentation bomb, which they planned to roll down onto attackers. Interestingly, Chester notes that Anderson declined to place the heavy barbette guns on the highest tier of the fort. Though such guns were likely to have the greatest impact in any subsequent artillery duel, their crews would also be fully exposed to return fire, and Anderson did not want to put them at risk. Anderson not only worried about the safety of his artillerists, he hoped to avoid a confrontation altogether. As a Kentuckian, he was especially conflicted about the prospect of civil war.

In another essay, Confederate lieutenant general Stephen D. Lee (who was a mere captain in 1861 and one of Brigadier General P.G.T. Beauregard's young aides) offers a summary of the negotiations and private conversations that informed the decision to open fire. Beauregard dispatched Lee and James Chesnut (another aide) out to Sumter to ask Anderson if he would surrender. He would not, but he admitted, "Gentlemen, if you do not batter the fort to pieces about us, we shall be starved out in a few days." In Montgomery, Jefferson Davis and his advisers wanted Anderson to commit to a specific time. After a rapid exchange of telegrams, Anderson responded that he would have to evacuate by the fifteenth—in three days—unless he received supplies or reinforcements before then. Better informed than Anderson, Davis knew that supplies were already en route, and he ordered Beauregard to open fire. At about 3:30 A.M., Lee and Chesnut handed Anderson a note telling him that the batteries would open "one hour from this time."

A few minutes past 4:30 A.M. on April 12, 1861, Lee and Chesnut were in a small boat just north of Fort Sumter in Charleston Harbor. They had rowed over to Fort Johnson on James Island to deliver Beauregard's orders and were heading back to Fort Moultrie when Lee noticed the muzzle flash of a gun on James Island. He watched as the ten-inch mortar shell traced an arc across the night sky and exploded over the ramparts of Fort Sumter. That explosion, Lee writes, "woke the echoes from every nook and corner of the harbor, and in this the dead hour of the night, before dawn, that shot was a sound of alarm that brought every soldier in the harbor to his feet, and every man, woman, and child in the city of Charleston from their beds." Writing in the 1880s, Lee presents the story as a human tragedy, and his account is absent any triumphalist sentiment that may have animated others.

The onset of war prompted a surge of patriotism in both the North and South. Jacob Cox, who later became a division commander in the Union army, recalls in his essay, "At the first shot from Beauregard's guns in Charleston Harbor...men crowded to the recruiting stations to enlist for the defense of the national flag and the national union." He describes the ad hoc nature of this early mobilization in the North, which featured the election of officers, the establishment of rudimentary campsites, and the almost comical early efforts to drill the men. "The arriving regiments," he writes, "sometimes had their first taste of camp life under circumstances well calculated to dampen their ardor."

Fort Sumter had a revolutionary impact on the South as well. Lincoln's call for volunteers on April 15, which implied a federal effort to coerce the states back into the Union, provoked four more states—including Virginia—to join the Confederacy, and the rebel government moved from Montgomery to Richmond. Though there were no political parties in the South and thus no formal opposition to the government, there was personal and often bitter criticism from several quarters. One of the most vocal critics was Robert Barnwell Rhett of South Carolina, an early fire-eater who had been greatly disappointed when he had been overlooked for the presidency of the new Confederacy. Rhett died in 1876, but the editors of *The Century* invited his son, who bore the same name, to write about the formation of the Confederate government.

The younger Rhett had spent the war as the antiadministration editor of the *Charleston Mercury,* and his essay is not kind to Davis. He asserts that most of the important business of nation building in Montgomery was conducted secretly behind closed doors, and insists that the South's leaders failed to take advantage of early opportunities to improve their position. In effect, he argues, "We could have won if only..." Rhett ticks off the lost opportunities one by one: the failure to use the power of King Cotton to gain leverage with foreign powers; the failure to purchase warships from Europe (for which he blames Confederate navy secretary Stephen Mallory); and the failure to pledge low tariffs, which he insists would have prompted European governments to sign alliances with the Confederacy.

Rhett's laments are part and parcel of the Lost Cause view of the war, which was in full flower in the 1880s. But Rhett's real purpose is to malign and indict Jefferson Davis. He quotes his father, who told him in 1865: "Mr. Davis never had any policy; he drifted from the beginning to the end of the war." The clear implication is that with better leadership—presumably featuring Robert Barnwell Rhett—the South could have won.

The two pieces on the Battle of Bull Run are especially interesting, more for what they reveal about internal bickering in the upper echelons of Confederate leadership than for details of the battle itself. P.G.T. Beauregard's essay was one of the first to be published in *The Century Magazine,* appearing in November 1884. Beauregard's personal flamboyance and garrulousness are evident in his writing, which is characterized by very long sentences in even longer paragraphs (some as long as three pages). Beauregard complains that Jefferson Davis rejected his "brilliant and comprehensive" plan and forced him to remain on the defensive at Bull Run. "With 6500 men and 13 pieces of artillery," he writes, "I now awaited the onset of the enemy, who were pressing forward 20,000 strong...." Despite this, Beauregard writes, "I myself" led a movement of "such keeping and dash that the whole plateau was swept clear of the enemy."

No one who knew Beauregard was surprised by this kind of self-promotional puffery, for it had been a hallmark of the mercurial Creole general since his youth. But Beauregard not only dismissed Jefferson Davis in his essay, he also made only a fleeting reference to his own superior on the field, Confederate general Joseph E. Johnston. Touchy about such things, Johnston eagerly accepted an offer to write his own essay on the battle, hoping also to set the record straight concerning his own relationship with Jefferson Davis. The Confederate president's memoir, *Rise and Fall of the Confederate Government,* had appeared in 1881, and believing that Davis had "degraded me to the utmost of his power," Johnston was determined to respond. Instead of an essay, therefore, Johnston submitted a pedantic line-by-line rebuttal of Davis's memoir, beginning many of his paragraphs with "Mr. Davis says," followed by a quoted passage, and then a rebuttal. A number of Johnston's corrections are technical and petty, and the result is to make Johnston himself seem petty. While he was at it, Johnston took a few swipes at Beauregard, too. "An opinion seems to prevail," Johnston wrote, "that important plans of General Beauregard were executed by him. It is a mistake.... As fought, the battle was made by me." However valid, such a claim infuriated Beauregard, who then offered his own rebuttal, which appeared in the original *Battles and Leaders* volumes, and which is also included here.

The western counterpart to the Battle of Bull Run in July was the Battle of Wilson's Creek in August. As in Virginia, a Federal army advanced against a rebel position anticipating victory; as in Virginia, undisciplined but determined men shot one another down; and as in Virginia, a rebel counterattack at the right time and place drove the Federal army from the field in near panic. Confederate brigadier general Nicholas B. Pearce describes his role in the battle and gives credit for the eventual Confederate victory to the Arkansas troops he commanded. "The Arkansans in this battle were as brave, as chivalrous, and as successful as any of the troops engaged," he writes. The real value of this essay, however, is Pearce's admission that the death of the Union commander, Brigadier General Nathaniel Lyon, was very likely a major factor in the Union defeat. "In the light of the present day," Pearce writes, "it is difficult to measure the vast results had Lyon lived...."

Before Lyon was killed, and before the bulk of the Union army fell back, a Union flanking column led by German-born brigadier general Franz Sigel was roughly treated and repulsed in great disorder. Pearce notes that Sigel "made vain attempts to hold his men," but in the end he could not, and the whole column fled all the way back to Springfield. Soon afterward, Sigel's behavior at the battle became grist for the rumor mill. One rumor had it that his undisciplined men had stopped to loot houses, which was why they were surprised by the rebel counterattack; another was that Sigel himself had fled the field well ahead of his troops and arrived back in Springfield in midafternoon while most of his command was still strung out behind him on the road to Wilson's Creek.

In his essay on the battle, Sigel defends himself from these charges and describes the battle as he remembers it, though he does admit that he and his small escort were pursued by rebel cavalry "for about six miles" as they raced back to Springfield.

Only five days after the first shot at Fort Sumter, President Lincoln declared a blockade of the Southern ports. To maintain the ships of the several blockading squadrons, it was necessary to acquire some coaling stations along the Southern coast. This led to the first important naval action of the war: the seizure of Port Royal Sound off the coast of South Carolina by a squadron under Flag Officer Samuel F. Du Pont. It almost didn't happen. As navy captain Daniel Ammen notes in his essay, a furious gale nearly wrecked the fleet as it rounded Cape Hatteras heading south to Port Royal. In the end, all the warships arrived safely, though some transports were blown across the ocean and fetched up on the coast of Ireland. On November 9, Du Pont's squadron fought its way into Port Royal Sound, blasting the Confederate Fort Walker so thoroughly that the enemy abandoned its position on the coastal islands. It was the first really good war news for the North. Ammen notes, "The battle of Port Royal ... was of surpassing value in its moral and political effect, both at home and abroad. It gave us one of the finest harbors on the Atlantic sea-board, affording an admirable base for future operations...."

It did more than that, however. After watching the engagement, Robert E. Lee, who was present in South Carolina as a military adviser to President Davis, recommended that the Confederacy should abandon most of its own coast to the enemy, concentrating its resources on a handful of important port cities. Du Pont's triumph demonstrated that the balance of power between ships and forts had shifted. Steam-powered warships with heavy rifled guns proved that they could stand up to all but the strongest shore fortifications. Later in the war, Du Pont would have a falling-out with the administration over his perceived timorousness, but in the late fall of 1861, he was the first Union hero of the war, and, writing in 1887, Ammen was pleased to note the erection of a statue to Du Pont in Washington and the designation of Dupont Circle to honor his "intelligent and cheerful" commander.

Though the engagements of these early months of war seemed epic to those who fought in them—and to those who viewed them from afar—they were but a prelude to the horrible slaughter and wholesale destruction that would follow. For one thing, the armies would be larger. President Lincoln

called for 100,000 volunteers, and then 300,000 more. The Confederacy resorted to conscription—a draft—to fill its dwindling ranks. Confederates now
knew that one rebel could not in fact whip five Yanks; Union volunteers now
knew that the rebellion would not, after all, be squashed in a single summer.
The war would be neither short nor bloodless, and the scale of the conflict
would surpass anything anticipated by the leaders on either side.

CHAPTER 1

INSIDE SUMTER IN '61.

James Chester, Captain Third Artillery, U.S.A.

Toward the close of 1860, the national defenses of Charleston Harbor, consisting of Castle Pinckney, Fort Moultrie, and Fort Sumter, were garrisoned by an army of 65 men instead of the 1050 men that were required. Fort Moultrie alone, where the 65 soldiers were stationed, required 300 men for its defense, and Fort Sumter, to which they were ultimately transferred, was designed for a garrison of 650.

Fort Moultrie, at the time of which we write, was considered a rather pleasant station, Sullivan's Island being a favorite summer resort. Many of the wealthy citizens of Charleston had their summer residences there, and indeed some of them lived there all the year round. There was a large summer hotel on the beach half-way up the island, and a horse railway connected the steamboat wharf and the hotel. The military reservation stretched across the island from the front to the back beach, like a waistbelt of moderate width, and the fort looked like a big buckle at the front end. It was a brick structure, or rather an earthen structure revetted with brick. It was bastioned on the land side, and had a scarp wall perhaps fifteen feet high; but the sand had drifted against it at some points so as almost to bury its masonry. With its full complement of men it could hardly have been held against a numerous and enterprising enemy, and with 65 men it was plainly untenable.

This garrison consisted of two skeleton companies and the regimental band of the 1st Artillery. They had occupied the fort since 1857, and were fairly well acquainted in the neighborhood. Indeed, several of the men had been enlisted at the post, and were native Carolinians. As the political pot began to boil toward the close of 1860 and secession was openly discussed, the social position of the garrison became anomalous. Army officers had always been favorites in the South; and as they were discreet and agreeable, it is not surprising, perhaps, that their society continued to be sought after, even by the most outspoken

THE SOUTH-WEST OR GORGE FRONT OF FORT SUMTER, SHOWING THE GATE WHARF,
AND ESPLANADE, MACHICOULIS GALLERIES ON THE PARAPET, AND THE EFFECT
OF THE FIRE FROM CUMMING'S POINT AND FORT JOHNSON. FROM A PHOTOGRAPH.

secessionists, up to the actual commencement of hostilities. But enlisted men, even in the South, were social outcasts. It was rather surprising, therefore, to find them receiving attentions from civilians. But the fact is that the soldiers of the army were never before treated with such consideration in the South as on the eve of the rebellion.☆ The secessionists were determined to have the fort, and they wanted to get it without bloodshed. They had failed with the commissioned officers, and they had no better success with the soldiers: every enlisted man remained faithful to the Union.

The old commander of Fort Moultrie, Colonel John L. Gardner, was removed; the new one, Major Robert Anderson of Kentucky, arrived on November 21st. As a Southern man, he was expected to be reasonable. If he had scruples upon the question of qualified allegiance, he might surrender on demand, on purely professional grounds. No one doubted Major Anderson's professional ability, and of course he could see the hopelessness of his situation at

---

☆An amusing incident which illustrates this occurred during the election excitement in November, 1860. Elections in South Carolina were always peculiar. It could hardly be said that there were two parties, but there generally were two candidates for every office in the State. In such cases the candidates would each give a barbecue or feast of some kind to the voters, at which stump speeches were delivered in a somewhat florid style. The whole body of voters attended both entertainments, and it is to be feared decided rather upon the merits of the feast than the fitness of the candidate. At one of these entertainments on Sullivan's Island, the regimental band attended,—hired as an attraction,—and such soldiers as were on pass gathered around the outskirts of the crowd which surrounded the open-air supper table. The supper was over, and the speaking had begun. Everything eatable had been devoured except a remnant of ham which rested on a platter in front of the chairman—who perhaps was also the candidate—at one end of the long table. The chairman was speaking, and the audience was enthusiastic. A storm of applause had just broken out at something the speaker had said, when a soldier, who had had his eyes on the fragment of ham for some time, deliberately mounted the table at the lower end, and carefully picking his steps among the dishes, walked to the chairman's end, picked up the coveted fragment, and started on the return trip. The audacity of the man stunned the audience for a moment, but indignation soon got the better of astonishment, and the soldier was in some danger of rough treatment. But the chairman had his revolver out in a second, and holding it aloft proclaimed: "I'll shoot the first man who interferes with that soldier." And the soldier carried off the fragment. Of course he was drunk; but he could not have done the same thing without a drubbing in 1859. This anecdote—and others might be related—indicates the policy and perhaps the expectations of the secessionists in connection with the soldiers of Fort Moultrie.—J.C.

Moultrie. Moreover, he was a humane man, and would be unwilling to shed blood needlessly. But his actions clearly indicated that he would not surrender on demand. He continued defensive preparations with as much energy and zeal as his predecessor, and manifestly meant to fight. This was very discouraging to the preachers of bloodless secession, and when he transferred his command to Sumter their occupation was completely gone. Nothing but war would now get him out. Hence the efforts to get him ordered back again by President Buchanan—efforts which almost succeeded.

The transfer of Major Anderson's command from Moultrie to Sumter was neatly executed early in the evening of December 26th, 1860. It was a few minutes after sunset when the troops left Moultrie; the short twilight was about over when they reached the boats; fifteen or twenty minutes more carried them to Sumter. The workmen had just settled down to an evening's enjoyment when armed men at the door startled them. There was no parleying, no explaining; nothing but stern commands, silent astonishment, and prompt obedience. The workmen were on the wharf, outside the fort, before they were certain whether their captors were secessionists or Yankees.

Meantime the newly arrived troops were busy enough. Guards were posted, embrasures secured, and, as far as practicable, the place was put in a defensible condition against any storming-party which chagrin might drive the guard-boat people to send against it. Such an attempt was perfectly feasible. The night was very dark; the soldiers were on unknown ground and could not find their way about readily; many of the embrasures could not be closed; and there were at least a hundred willing guides and helpers already on the wharf and in a fine frame of mind for such work. But nothing was attempted, and when the soldiers felt themselves in a position to repel any attempt against them that night, two guns were fired as a signal to friends that the occupation had been successfully accomplished, and that they might proceed with their part of the programme. This was the first intimation the guard-boat people had of the transfer; and, indeed, it told them nothing, except that some soldiers must have got into Sumter. But they blew their alarm-whistle all the same, and burned blue-lights; signal-rockets were sent up from various points, and there was great excitement everywhere in the harbor until morning.

When the signal-guns were fired, the officer in charge of the two schooners which had carried provisions and ammunition to Fort Johnson (under the pretense that they were subsistence for the women and children, whom he had also carried there as a cloak) cast loose his lines and made all speed for Sumter, and the old sergeant who had been left in Moultrie for the purpose set fire to the combustibles which had been heaped around the gun-carriages, while another man spiked the guns. The garrison from the ramparts of its new nest grimly approved of the destruction of the old one.

At dawn of December 27th the men were up and ready for any emergency;

indeed, most of them had been up all night. Captain Foster had been specially busy with his former employees. Among them he found several loyal men, and also some doubtful ones who were willing to share the fortunes of the garrison. These constituted an acceptable addition to our working strength, although those classed as doubtful would have been an element of weakness in case of a fight. However, they did much good work before hostilities began, and the worst ones were weeded out before we were closely invested. Those who remained to the end were excellent men. They endured the hardships of the siege and the dangers of the bombardment without a murmur, and left Sumter with the garrison—one of them, John Swearer, severely wounded—with little besides the clothes they stood in. They were the first volunteers for the Union, but were barred from the benefits secured by legislation for the national soldiers, having never been "mustered in."

Fort Sumter was unfinished, and the interior was filled with building materials, guns, carriages, shot, shell, derricks, timbers, blocks and tackle, and coils of rope in great confusion. Few guns were mounted, and these few were chiefly on the lowest tier. The work was intended for three tiers of guns, but the embrasures of the second tier were incomplete, and guns could be mounted on the first and third tiers only.

The complete armament of the work had not yet arrived, but there were more guns on hand than we could mount or man. The first thing to be considered was immediate defense. The possibility of a sudden dash by the enemy, under cover of darkness and guided by the discharged workmen then in Charleston, demanded instant attention. It was impossible to spread 65 men over ground intended for 650, so some of the embrasures had to be bricked up. Selecting those, therefore, essential to artillery defense, and mounting guns in them, Anderson closed the rest. This was the work of many days; but we were in no immediate danger of an artillery attack. The armament of Moultrie was destroyed; its guns were spiked, and their carriages burned; and it would take a longer time to put them in condition than it would to mount the guns of Sumter.

THE SALLY-PORT OF FORT SUMTER. FROM A PHOTOGRAPH TAKEN FROM THE WHARF.

On the parade were quantities of flag-stones standing on end in masses and columns everywhere. We dared not leave them where they were, even if they had not been in the way, because mortar shells bursting among them would have made the very bomb-proofs untenable. A happy idea occurred to some one in authority, and the flag-stones were arranged two tiers high in front of the casemates, and just under the arches, thus partly closing the casemates and making excellent splinter-proofs. This arrangement, no doubt, saved the garrison from many wounds similar to that inflicted on John Swearer, for it was in passing an opening unprotected by the screen that he was struck by a fragment of shell.

Moving such immense quantities of material, mounting guns, distributing shot, and bricking up embrasures kept us busy for many weeks. But order was coming out of chaos every day, and the soldiers began to feel that they were a match for their adversaries. Still, they could not shut their eyes to the fact that formidable works were growing up around them. The secessionists were busy too, and they had the advantage of unlimited labor and material. Fort Moultrie had its armament again in position, and was receiving the framework of logs which formed the foundation for its sandbag bomb-proofs. The Stevens's Point floating battery was being made impregnable by an overcoat of railroad iron; and batteries on Morris, James, and Sullivan's islands were approaching completion. But our preparations were more advanced than theirs; and if we had been permitted to open on them at this time, the bombardment of Sumter would have had a very different termination. But our hands were tied by policy and instructions.

The heaviest guns in Sumter were three ten-inch columbiads—considered very big guns in those days. They weighed fifteen thousand pounds each, and were intended for the gorge and salient angles of the work. We found them skidded on the parade ground. Besides these there was a large number of eight-inch columbiads—more than we could mount or man—and a full supply of 42, 32, and 24-pounders, and some eight-inch sea-coast howitzers. There was an ample supply of shot and shell, and plenty of powder in the magazines, but friction primers were not abundant and cartridge-bags were scarce. The scarcity of cartridge-bags drove us to some strange makeshifts. During the bombardment several tailors were kept busy making cartridge-bags out of soldiers' flannel shirts, and we fired away several dozen pairs of woolen socks belonging to Major Anderson. In the matter of friction primers strict economy had to be observed, as we had no means of improvising a substitute.

Our first efforts in preparation were directed toward mounting the necessary guns on the lowest tier. These consisted of 42 and 32-pounders, and as the necessary trucks, gins, and tackle were on hand, the work went on rapidly. The men were in fine condition and as yet well fed; besides, they had the assistance of the engineer workmen, who soon became experts at this kind of work. Meantime a party of mechanics were making the main gate secure. This was situated at the middle of the gorge or base of the pentagon (the trace of the work was pentagonal), which was also the south-west side. It was closed by two heavy iron-studded gates, the outer a folding pair, and the inner arranged on pulleys, so that it could be raised or lowered at will. It was clear that the enemy, if he meant to bombard us, would erect batteries on Morris Island, and thus would be able to deliver an oblique fire on the gate sufficient to demolish it in a very few minutes. The gate once demolished, a night assault would become practicable.

To meet this possible emergency the main entrance was closed by a substantial brick wall, with a man-hole in the middle two feet wide and opposite to the man-hole in the gate. This wall was about six feet high, and to increase the security and sweep the wharf, an eight-inch sea-coast howitzer was mounted on its upper carriage without any chassis, so as to fire through the man-hole. The howitzer was kept loaded with double canister. To induce the belief that the folding gates were our sole dependence at this point, their outer surface was covered with iron.

The lower tier of guns being mounted, the more difficult operation of sending guns up to the third tier began. The terre-plein of the work was about fifty feet above parade level,—a considerable hoist,—but a pair of shears being already in position, and our tackle equal to the weight of eight-inch columbiads, the work went on amidst much good humor until all the guns of that caliber were in position.

We had now reached a problem more difficult to solve, namely, sending up our ten-inch columbiads. We were extremely desirous to have them—or at least two of them—on the upper tier. They were more powerful guns than any the enemy had at that time, and the only ones in our possession capable of smashing the iron-clad defenses which might be constructed against us. We had rumors that an iron-clad floating battery was being built in Charleston, which the enemy proposed to anchor in some convenient position so as to breach Sumter at his leisure. We had no faith in the penetrating power of the eight-inch guns, and if we wished to demolish this floating adversary, it was necessary that the ten-inch guns should be mounted. Besides, an iron-clad battery was well on the road to completion at Cumming's Point (twelve hundred yards from the weakest side of Sumter), which, from what we could see of it, would be impervious to any less powerful gun.

There was in the fort a large coil of very heavy rope, new, and strong enough to sustain fifteen thousand pounds, but some of the doubtful workmen had cut several strands of it at various points on the outside of the coil; at least we could account in no other way for the damage. Besides, we had no blocks large enough to receive the rope even if it had been uninjured. The rope was uncoiled and examined. The portion on the inner side of the coil was found uninjured, and a few splices gave rope enough for a triple tackle sixty feet long. The improvisation of blocks of sufficient size and strength now became the sole remaining difficulty, and it was overcome in this way: the gun-carriages of those days were made of well-seasoned oak, and one of them was cut up and the material used for the construction of blocks. When the blocks were finished the iron-clad battery was shorn of half of its terrors.

The tackle thus improvised was rigged on the shears, the first gun was rolled into position for hoisting, the sling was attached, and the windlass was manned. After carefully inspecting every knot and lashing, the officer in charge gave the word, "Heave away," and the men bent to their work steadily and earnestly, feeling, no doubt, that the battle with the iron-clad had really begun. Every eye watched the ropes as they began to take the strain, and when the gun had fairly left the skids, and there was no accident, the song which anxiety had suspended was resumed, all hands joining in the chorus, "On the plains of Mexico," with a sonorous heartiness that might well have been heard at Fort Moultrie. The gun made the vertical passage of fifty feet successfully, and was safely landed on the terre-plein. The chassis and carriage were then sent up, transported to the proper emplacement, and put in position, and the gun was mounted.

The ten-inch columbiad threw a shot weighing one hundred and twenty-eight pounds, and it was now necessary that a supply of such shot should be raised. Of course, they could have been sent up at the derrick, but that would have been a slow process, and, moreover, it would have required the derrick and the men, when they were needed for other work. So after retreat roll-call, when the day's work was over, the men were bantered by some designing sergeant as to their ability to carry a ten-inch shot up the stairway. Some of the soldiers, full of confidence and energy, shouldered a shot each and started. They accomplished the feat, and the less confident, unwilling to be outdone by comrades no bigger than themselves, shouldered a shot each and made the passage. In a few minutes sixty shot were deposited near the gun; and it became the custom to carry up a ten-inch shot after retreat—just for fun—as long as there were any to carry.

These trivial incidents serve to show the spirit and humor of the men better than any description. There never was a happier or more contented set of men in any garrison than the Sumter soldiers. There was no sulkiness among them, and no grumbling until they had to try their teeth on spun yarn as a substitute for tobacco. This occurred long before the ration was reduced, and it produced some of the loudest grumbling ever listened to.

The second ten-inch columbiad was less fortunate than its fellow. It reached the level of the terre-plein without accident, but almost at the first haul on the watch tackle to swing it in, it broke away and fell with a dull thud. There was no mirth in the faces of the men at the watch tackle as they looked over the edge of the parade wall to see how many of the men at the windlass were left. The gun had descended, breech first, like a bolt from a catapult, and had buried itself in the sand up to the trunnions; but beyond breaking the transoms of the derrick, no damage was done. The cause of the accident was easily discovered. The amateur block-maker, unwilling to weaken the blocks by too much trimming, had left their upper edges too sharp, and the strap of the upper block had been cut in consequence. In four days the derrick was repaired, and the gun safely landed on the terre-plein.

The third ten-inch columbiad was not sent up. It was mounted as a mortar on the parade, for the purpose of shelling Charleston should that become advisable. A mortar platform already existed there. A ten-inch top carriage was placed on it and the gun mounted pointing toward the city.

A laughable incident occurred in connection with this gun soon after it was mounted. Some of the officers were anxious to try how it would work, and perhaps to see how true its alignment was, and to advertise to the enemy the fact that we had at least one formidable mortar in Fort Sumter. At any rate they obtained permission from Major Anderson to try the gun with a "very small charge." So, one afternoon the gun was loaded with a blind shell, and what was considered a "very small charge" of powder. The regulation charge for the gun, as a gun, was eighteen pounds. On this occasion two pounds only were used. It was not expected that the shell would be thrown over a thousand yards, and as the bay was clear no danger was anticipated. Everything being in readiness, the gun was fired, and the eyes of the garrison followed the shell as it described its graceful curve in the direction of the city. By the time it reached the summit of its trajectory, the fact that the charge used was not a "very small" one for the

INTERIOR OF SUMTER AFTER THE SURRENDER, SHOWING THE 8-INCH COLUMBIADS PLANTED AS MORTARS, AND THE CONFEDERATE FLAG FLYING FROM THE DERRICK BY WHICH THE GUNS WERE RAISED TO THE UPPER TIER. FROM A PHOTOGRAPH.

gun fired as a mortar became painfully apparent to every observer, and fears were entertained by some that the shell would reach the city, or at least the shipping near the wharves. But fortunately it fell short, and did no damage beyond searing the secessionist guard-boat then leaving the wharf for her nightly post of observation. The guard-boat put back and Sumter was visited by a flag of truce, perhaps to find out the meaning of our performance. No doubt the explanations given were satisfactory. No more experiments for range were tried with that gun, but we knew that Charleston was within range.

Although the full armament of Sumter was not on hand, there were many more guns than places to put them. This resulted from the fact that no guns were mounted on the second tier, and because many embrasures on the first tier were bricked up. There were four unplaced eight-inch columbiads after the fort had been satisfactorily garnished with guns. But we were entirely without mortars. Perhaps this serious defect in our armament, and perhaps our success with the ten-inch gun mounted as a mortar, induced Major Anderson to mount his extra eight-inch guns in that way. Morris Island, twelve hundred yards away, was the nearest terra firma to Fort Sumter, and there the enemy would plant his most important batteries. The more searching and severe the fire that could be brought to bear upon that island, therefore, the better. So the four extra columbiads were mounted as mortars to fire in that direction. We had no carriages for the guns and no platforms. So a trench was dug in the parade at right angles to the proposed line of fire. A heavy timber was then embedded in the sand at the bottom of the trench, and another on the Morris Island side of it, in such a way that a gun resting on the one and leaning on the other would be supported at an angle of forty-five degrees. The guns were then placed in notches at equal intervals along the trench. We had no opportunity to try this novel mortar battery, but everybody was satisfied that it could have done good service.

It was expected that the walls of Fort Sumter would be able to withstand the guns which we knew the enemy possessed, but we did not anticipate importations from abroad. During the bombardment a Whitworth gun of small caliber, just received from England, was mounted in one of the Morris Island batteries, and in a few rounds demonstrated its ability to breach the work. Fortunately its supply of ammunition was limited, and the fire stopped short of an actual breach. But a few hours more of that Whitworth 12-pounder would have knocked a hole in our defenses.

A breach was not dreaded by the garrison, for, weak as it was, it could have given a good account of itself defending a breach. The greatest danger was a simultaneous attack on all sides. Sixty-four men could not be made very effective at a dozen different points. The possibility of the enemy, under cover of darkness, getting a foothold in force on the narrow bit of riprapping between tidewater and the foundation of the scarp was ever present in our minds.

The most likely place to land was the wharf, a stone structure in front of the main entrance. There an assaulting column might be formed and the main gate stormed, while the bulk of the garrison was defending the embrasures. To checkmate any such attempt, means of blowing the wharf out of existence were devised. Two five-gallon demijohns filled with powder were planted as mines, well under the wharf pavement, in such a way as to insure the total demolition of the structure by their explosion. These mines were arranged so that both should explode at the same instant. The means of firing were twofold: first, a powder-hose leading from the mines through a wooden trough buried under the pavement, and terminating in a dry well just inside the gate; second, a long lanyard connected with friction primers inserted in the corks of the powder demijohns, and extending through the trough into the well, whence it branched like a bell wire to convenient points inside the fort.

Another place offering special advantages to a storming party was the esplanade. This was a broad promenade extending the whole length of the gorge wall on the outside, and paved with immense blocks of dressed granite. As Fort Sumter was not designed to resist attack by storm, the esplanade was unswept by any fire. To remedy this defect the stone fougasse was resorted to. To the uninitiated the "fougasse" looked like a harmless pile of stones resting against the scarp wall. The only thing that would be likely to attract his attention was the bin-like inclosure of solid masonry open at the outer side, which looked like an immense dust-pan, and which he might think was a rather elaborate arrangement to hold merely a pile of stones together. There was nothing to indicate that beneath the stones, in the angle close to the scarp wall, a magazine of gunpowder lay concealed, and that behind were arrangements for firing it from the inside of the works. These harmless-looking piles of stones were mines of the deadliest kind. In addition, two eight-inch sea-coast howitzers were mounted on their upper carriages only, and placed in front of the main entrance, pointing to the right and left so as to sweep the esplanade.

The possibility of a hostile landing on the narrow strip of riprapping between the scarp wall and tide-water still remained to be provided for. Before secondary defenses were constructed, this was a continuous dead space on which a thousand men could have found a safe lodgment perfectly screened from fire and observation. The danger from such a lodgment was, that from it all our embrasures could have been assaulted at the same time. It was all-important, therefore, that the entrance by an embrasure should be made as difficult as possible. The ledge of riprapping was little more than four feet below the sills of the embrasures, and there would have been no difficulty in stepping in, if the two or three guards inside were disposed of. This fact was well known to the enemy, and we felt certain that, if he decided to attempt an assault in this way, he would consider scaling-ladders unnecessary. In order to disappoint him, therefore, we removed the riprapping in front of each embrasure to the depth of four or five feet, rolling the large stones into the water. This gave a height of eight or nine feet to the embrasure sills.

Machicoulis galleries were also erected on all the flanks and faces of the work. The machicoulis when completed looked like an immense dry-goods box, set upon the parapet so as to project over the wall some three or four feet. The beams upon which it rested extended inward to the terre-plein and were securely anchored down. But the dry-goods box was deceptive. Inside it was lined with heavy iron plates to make it bullet-proof. That portion of the bottom which projected beyond the wall was loop-holed for musketry, and a marksman in the machicoulis could shoot a man, however close he might be to the scarp wall. But musketry from the machicoulis could hardly be expected to beat off a determined assault upon the flanks and faces of the work. To meet this difficulty, hand-grenades were improvised. Shells of all sizes, from 12-pounders to 10-inch, were loaded, and the fuse-holes stopped with wooden plugs. The plugs were then bored through with a gimlet, and friction primers inserted. Behind the parapet at short intervals, and wherever it was thought they might be useful, numbers of these shell-grenades were stored under safe cover in readiness for any emergency. The method of throwing them was simple. Lanyards of sufficient length to reach to within about four feet of the riprapping were prepared, and fastened securely at the handle end near the piles of shell-grenades. To throw a grenade, the soldier lifted it on the parapet, hooked the lanyard into the eye of the friction primer, and threw the shell over the parapet. When the lanyard reached its length, the shell exploded. Thus a very few men would be more than a match for all that could assemble on the riprapping.

Another contrivance, the "flying fougasse," or bursting barrel, a device of Captain Truman Seymour, consisted of an ordinary cask or barrel filled with broken stones, and having in its center a canister of powder, sufficient to burst the barrel and scatter its contents with considerable force. A fuse connected the powder in the canister with a friction primer in the bung, and the barrel was exploded by attaching a lanyard to the eye of the primer, and letting the barrel roll over the parapet, as in the case of the shell-grenade. If one experiment can justify an opinion, the flying fougasse would have been a success. When it became known in the fort that one of the barrels was about to be fired as an experiment, the novelty of the thing attracted most of the men to the place, and the little crowd attracted the attention of the enemy. No doubt glasses were focused on the party from every battery within sight. When everything was ready the barrel was allowed to roll over the parapet, and an instant afterward a terrific explosion took place. The stones were thrown in every direction, and the surface of the water was lashed into foam for a considerable distance. The effect as seen by the secessionists must have appeared greater than it did to us, although we thought it quite satisfactory. The Charleston newspapers described the effect of the "infernal machine" as simply terrific. Only three of them were constructed, yet for moral effect an empty barrel set upon the parapet would have been just as good.

In war, plan as we may, much depends upon accident, and the moral effect of very insignificant incidents is often considerable. For this reason "Wittyman's Masterpiece" deserves to be mentioned. Wittyman was a German carpenter, not very familiar with English, and wholly ignorant of military engineering. His captain had conceived the idea that a *cheval-de-frise* across the riprapping at the salient angles of the fort would confine the enemy on whatever face he landed until he had been treated liberally with shell-grenades. So Wittyman was ordered to build a *cheval-de-frise* at the angle of the gorge nearest Morris Island. It was easy to see that Wittyman was not familiar with *chevaux-de-frise*, so the captain explained and roughly illustrated the construction. At last Wittyman seemed to grasp the idea and went to work upon it forthwith. Perhaps the work was not examined during construction, nor seen by any one but Wittyman until it was placed. But from that day forward it was the fountain of amusement for the men. No matter how sick or sad a man might be, let him look at the masterpiece and his ailments were forgotten. Not a steamer passed,—and they were passing almost every hour,—but every glass on board was leveled at the masterpiece. But it baffled every one of them. Not one could guess what it was, or what it was intended to be; and after the bombardment was over we learned, quite accidentally, that it had been set down by the enemy as a means of exploding the mines.

Any description of the siege of Sumter would be incomplete without some sort of reference to the *Star of the West* fiasco. At reveille on the 9th of January, it became generally known among the men that a large steamer flying the United States flag was off the bar, seemingly at anchor. There had been some talk among the men, based upon rumors from Charleston, that the garrison would either be withdrawn from the harbor or returned to Fort Moultrie; and there were some who believed the rumors. These believers were now confident that withdrawal had been determined on, and that the steamer off the bar was the transport come to take them away. There was no denying that appearances favored the theory, yet there was no enthusiasm. The men were beginning to feel that they were a match for their adversaries, and they were loath to leave without proving it. And, indeed, at that time Sumter was master of the situation. Moultrie had very few guns mounted,—only one, according to report,—and that fact ought to have been known to the people on the *Star of the West*. It was known officially in Washington that fourteen days previously Major Anderson had spiked the guns and burned the carriages at Moultrie, and gun-carriages cannot be replaced in two weeks when they have to be fabricated. Hence Moultrie could not have been formidable, and as soon as it should have passed the battery on Morris Island, it would have been comparatively safe.

When the *Star of the West* was seen standing in, the novelty of a steamer carrying the national flag had more attractions for the men than the breakfast table. They soon made her out to be a merchant steamer, as the walking-beam, plainly visible as she rounded into the channel, was unknown on a man-of-war. She had taken the Morris Island channel, and was approaching at a fair rate of speed. Perhaps every man in Sumter was on the ramparts, but there was no excitement. But when the blue puff of smoke from a hidden battery on Morris Island advertised the fact that she was being fired on, there was great scurrying and scampering among the men. The long roll was beaten, and the batteries were manned almost before the guns of the hidden battery had fired their second shot. As she approached, a single gun at Fort Moultrie opened at extreme long range, its shot falling over half a mile short. There seemed to be much perplexity among our officers, and Major Anderson had a conference with some of them in a room used as a laundry which opened on the terre-plein of the sea-flank. The conference was an impromptu one, as Captain Doubleday and Lieutenant Davis were not of it. But Captain Foster was there, and by his actions demonstrated his disappointment at the result. He left the laundry, bounding up the two or three steps that led to the terre-plein, smashing his hat, and muttering something about the flag, of which the words "trample on it" reached the ears of the men at the guns, and let them know that there was to be no fighting, on their part at least. Meantime the steamer had worn ship, and was standing out again, receiving the fire of the hidden battery in passing. This is about all the men saw or knew about the strange vessel at the time, although she came near enough for them to look down upon her decks and see that there were no troops visible on her.☆

With the exception of the mounting of the guns, the preparations described were chiefly intended to ward off assault. The actions of the enemy now indicated that he proposed to bombard the work at an early day. If we would meet Moultrie, and the numerous batteries which were being constructed against us, on anything like even terms, we must be prepared to shoot accurately.

Few artillerymen, without actual experience, have any idea of the difficulty of aiming a gun during a bombardment. They may be able to hit a target in ordinary practice with absolute certainty, and yet be unable to deliver a single satisfactory shot in a bombardment. The error from smoke is difficult to deal with, because it is a variable, depending upon the density of the smoke clouds which envelop your own and your adversary's batteries. (Within the writer's experience, a thin veil of fog protected a mass of army wagons—900, it was said—from the fire of some 8 or 10 guns, during a whole forenoon, although the guns were within easy range, and the wagons could be distinctly seen. Refraction saved them, every shot going over.) Then danger and its con-

---

☆The troops on the *Star of the West* consisted of 200 men, under Lieut. Charles R. Woods.—EDITORS.

sequent excitement are also disturbing elements, especially where delicate instruments have to be used. It is easier to lead a forlorn hope than to set a vernier under a heavy artillery fire. Fortunately, we had officers of experience in Sumter, and fortunately, too, we had very few instruments; one gunner's level and two old quadrants being the extent of the outfit, with perhaps some breech-sights and tangent-scales. The paucity of aiming-instruments, and perhaps the experience of some of the officers, led to the devising of instruments and methods which neither smoke nor excitement could disturb; and as some of them, in a much more perfect form, have since been adopted, the rude originals may as well be described here. Aiming cannon consists of two distinct operations: namely, alignment and elevation. In the former, according to instructions and practice, the gunner depends upon his eye and the cannon-sights. But for night firing or when the enemy is enveloped in smoke,—as he is sure to be in any artillery duel,—the eye cannot be depended on. Visual aiming in a bombardment is a delusion and a snare. To overcome this difficulty, on clear days, when all the conditions were favorable to accuracy, and we could work at our leisure, every gun in the armament was carefully aimed at all the prominent objects within its field of fire, and its position marked on the traverse circle, the index being a pointer securely fastened to the traverse fork. After this had been done, alignment became as easy as setting a watch, and could be done by night or day, by the least intelligent soldier in the garrison.

The elevation was more difficult to deal with. The ordinary method by the use of a breech-sight could not be depended on, even if there had been a sufficient supply of such instruments, because darkness or smoke would render it inapplicable or inaccurate; and the two quadrants in the outfit could not be distributed all over the fort.

Before the correct elevation to carry a shot to a given object can be determined, it is necessary to know the exact distance of the object. This was obtained from the coast-survey chart of the harbor. The necessary elevation was then calculated, or taken from the tables, and the gun elevated accordingly by means of the quadrant. The question then became, How can the gunner bring the gun to this elevation in the heat of action, and without the use of a quadrant? There was an abundance of brass rods, perhaps a quarter-inch in diameter, in the fort. Pieces of such rods, eighteen inches long, were prepared by shaping one end to fit into a socket on the cheek of

EFFECT OF THE BOMBARDMENT ON THE BARBETTE GUNS OF THE SEA FRONT OF SUMTER. FROM A PHOTOGRAPH.

the carriage, and the other into a chisel edge. They were called by the men pointing rods. A vertical line was then drawn on the right breech of the gun, and painted white. The non-commissioned officer who attended to this preparation, having carefully elevated the gun with the quadrant for a particular object, set the pointing rod in the socket, and brought its chisel end down on the vertical line. The point thus cut was marked and the initials of the object to be struck with that elevation written opposite. These arrangements, which originated with Captain Doubleday, were of great value during the bombardment.

The preparation of Sumter for defense afforded a fine field for ingenuity, because nothing connected with its equipment was complete. As another illustration of this ingenuity, the following is in point. It might become desirable to continue a bombardment into the night, and the casemates, owing to the partial closing up of the arches with flagstones, were as dark as dungeons, even on very clear nights. Lights of some kind were absolutely necessary, but there were no candles and no lamps. There was a light-house on the fort, however, and the light-keeper had several barrels of oil on hand. Small tubes of tin, to receive wicks, were made, and fitted into disks of cork sufficiently large to float them on the surface of the oil. Coffee-cups were then filled with oil and the floats laid on the surface.

Among the many incidents of the siege may be mentioned the mishap of an ice-laden Yankee schooner that strayed within range of the secession batteries; the accidental solid shot fired at Fort Sumter by an impatient secessionist in the Cumming's Point battery, and the daring generosity of McInerny, a warm-hearted and loyal Irishman, who did not "cross the broad Atlantic to become the citizen of only one Shtate," and who cheerfully risked his life and ruined his Sunday shirt by tearing a white flag from it, that he might be able to deliver in person his donation of tobacco to the besieged soldiers. There is one other incident which should find a place in these reminiscences.

Major Anderson was fully impressed with the solemn responsibilities which rested upon him when he transferred his command to Sumter. When he reached Sumter there were no halliards to the flag-staff, and as there was more pressing work on hand for several days, some time elapsed before it became possible to display the national flag. At length, however, halliards were rigged, and everything was ready for the flag. The usual method of proceeding in such a case would have been to order the sergeant of the guard to send up the flag, but it was otherwise arranged on this occasion. A dress-parade was ordered, and the little garrison formed around the flag-staff, the officers in the center. Presently Major Anderson, with Chaplain Harris of Fort Moultrie, who perhaps had been summoned for the purpose, approached the flag-staff, and the command was brought to "Attention." The flag, already bent to the halliards, was held by one officer, and another held the hoisting end of the halliards. The chaplain then, in a few words, invited those present to join with him in prayer, and Major Anderson, receiving the halliards from the officer who till that time had held them, knelt beside the chaplain, most of the officers and some of the men in the ranks following his example. Prayers being ended, all rose, and the flag of Fort Sumter was raised by Major Anderson, and the halliards secured. He then turned toward the officers and directed that the companies be dismissed. If any of those who doubted the loyalty to the Union of Major Anderson could have had but one glimpse of that impressive scene, they would have doubted no longer.

The weary waiting for war or deliverance which filled up the few weeks that intervened between the preparations and the actual bombardment developed no discontent among the men, although food and fuel were getting scarce. The latter was replenished from time to time by tearing down sheds and temporary workshops, but the former was a constantly diminishing quantity, and the men could count on their fingers the number of days between them and starvation. It was a favorite belief among the secessionists that the pinchings of hunger would arouse a spirit of mutiny among the soldiers, and compel Major Anderson to propose terms of evacuation. But no such spirit manifested itself. On the contrary, the men exhibited a devotion to their Government and the officers appointed over them which surprised their enemies, but attracted little attention from their friends./

The opening of the bombardment was a somewhat dramatic event. A relieving fleet was approaching, all unknown to the Sumter garrison, and General Beauregard, perhaps with the hope of tying Major Anderson's hands in the expected fight with that fleet, had opened negotiations with him on the 11th of April looking toward the evacuation of the fort. But Major Anderson declined to evacuate his post till compelled by hunger. The last ounce of breadstuffs had been consumed, and matters were manifestly approaching a crisis. It was evident from the activity of the enemy that something important was in the wind. That night we retired as usual. Toward half-past three on the morning of the 12th we were startled by a gun fired in the immediate vicinity of the fort, and many rose to see what was the matter. It was soon learned that a steamer from the enemy desired to communicate with Major Anderson, and a small boat under a flag of truce was received and delivered the message. Although no formal announcement of the fact was made, it became generally known among the men that in one hour General Beauregard would open his batteries on Sumter.

The men waited about for some time in expectation of orders, but received none, except an informal order to go to bed, and the information that reveille

/So faithful and true have the soldiers of the army always been that even very striking exhibitions of these qualities are not considered worthy of notice. There were military posts in 1861 which were abandoned by all the commissioned officers, at which not one of the enlisted men proved untrue. The loyalty of the latter has never been properly appreciated.—J.C.

CONFEDERATE FLOATING BATTERY IN ACTION AT THE WEST END OF SULLIVAN'S ISLAND.
Colonel Joseph A. Yates, who was a lieutenant in the attack on Fort Sumter, says in a letter accompanying the plan on page 27: "I send a rough sketch of the floating battery which I commanded; it is rough, but from my recollection it is very like her. The battery was substantially built, flat, heavily timbered on her shield, with railroad iron laid on it—two courses of rails turned inward and outward, so as to form a pretty smooth surface. The bags of sand represented on the deck were to counterweigh the guns, which were 32 and 42-pounders. She was struck many times, several shot going entirely through the shield."

would be sounded at the usual hour. This was daylight, fully two hours off, so some of the men did retire. The majority perhaps remained up, anxious to see the opening, for which purpose they had all gone on the ramparts. Except that the flag was hoisted, and a glimmer of light was visible at the guard-house, the fort looked so dark and silent as to seem deserted. The morning was dark and raw. Some of the watchers surmised that Beauregard was "bluffing," and that there would be no bombardment. But promptly at 4:30 A.M. a flash as of distant lightning in the direction of Mount Pleasant, followed by the dull roar of a mortar, told us that the bombardment had begun. The eyes of the watchers easily detected and followed the burning fuse which marked the course of the shell as it mounted among the stars, and then descended with ever-increasing velocity, until it landed inside the fort and burst. It was a capital shot. Then the batteries opened on all sides, and shot and shell went screaming over Sumter as if an army of devils were swooping around it. As a rule the guns were aimed too high, but all the mortar practice was good. In a few minutes the novelty disappeared in a realizing sense of danger, and the watchers retired to the bomb-proofs, where they discussed probabilities until reveille.

Habits of discipline are strong among old soldiers. If it had not been for orders to the contrary, the men would have formed for roll-call on the open parade, as it was their custom to do, although mortar-shells were bursting there at the lively rate of about one a minute. But they were formed under the bomb-proofs, and the roll was called as if nothing unusual was going on. They were then directed to get breakfast, and be ready to fall in when "assembly" was beaten. The breakfast part of the order was considered a grim joke, as the fare was reduced to the solitary item of fat pork, very rusty indeed. But most of the men worried down a little of it, and were "ready" when the drum called them to their work.

By this time it was daylight, and the effects of the bombardment became visible. No serious damage was being done to the fort. The enemy had concentrated their fire on the barbette batteries, but, like most inexperienced gunners, they were firing too high. After daylight their shooting improved, until at 7:30 A.M., when "assembly" was beaten in Sumter, it had become fairly good. At "assembly" the men were again paraded, and the orders of the day announced. The garrison was divided into two reliefs, and the tour of duty at the guns was to be four hours. Captain Doubleday being the senior captain, his battery took the first tour.

There were three points to be fired upon,—the Morris Island batteries, the James Island batteries, and the Sullivan's Island batteries. With these last was included the famous iron-clad floating battery, which had taken up a position off the western end of Sullivan's Island to command the left flank of Sumter. Captain Doubleday divided his men into three parties: the first, under his own immediate command, was marched to the casemate guns bearing on Morris Island; the second, under Lieutenant Jefferson C. Davis, manned the casemate guns bearing on the James Island batteries; and the third—without a commissioned officer until Dr. Crawford joined it—was marched by a sergeant✣ to the guns bearing on Sullivan's Island. The guns in the lower tier, which were the only ones used during the bombardment,—except surreptitiously without orders,—were 32 and 42-pounders, and some curiosity was felt as to the effect of such shot on the iron-clad battery. The gunners made excellent practice, but the shot were seen to bounce off its sides like peas. After battering it for about an hour and a half, no visible effect had been produced, although it had perceptibly slackened its fire, perhaps to save ammunition. But it was evident that throwing 32-pounder shot at it, at a mile range, was a waste of iron, and the attention of the gunners was transferred to Fort Moultrie.

Moultrie was, perhaps, a less satisfactory target than the iron-clad. It was

✣The non-commissioned officers in Fort Sumter were Ordnance-Sergeant James Kearney, U.S.A., Quartermaster-Sergeant William H. Hamner, 1st U.S. Artillery; Regimental Band, 1st Artillery: Sergeant James E. Galway, Corporal Andrew Smith; Company E, 1st Artillery: First Sergeant Eugene Scheibner, Sergeants Thomas Kirnan, William A. Harn, and James Chester, Corporals Owen M'Guire, Francis J. Oakes, Charles Bringhurst, and Henry Ellerbrook; Company H, 1st Artillery: First Sergeant John Renehan, Sergeants James M'Mahon, John Carmody, and John Otto, Corporal Christopher Costolan.—EDITORS.

literally buried under sand-bags, the very throats of the embrasures being closed with cotton-bales. The use of cotton-bales was very effective as against shot, but would have been less so against shell. The fact that the embrasures were thus closed was not known in Sumter till after the bombardment. It explained what was otherwise inexplicable. Shot would be

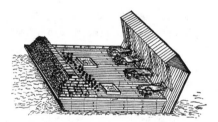

THE IRON-CLAD FLOATING BATTERY.
FROM A PLAN BY COLONEL
JOSEPH A. YATES.

seen to strike an embrasure, and the gunner would feel that he had settled one gun for certain, but even while he was receiving the congratulations of his comrades the supposed disabled gun would reply. That the cotton-bales could not be seen from Sumter is not surprising. The sand-bag casemates which covered the guns were at least eighteen feet thick, and the cotton-bale shutter was no doubt arranged to slide up and down like a portcullis inside the pile of sand-bags. The gunners of Sumter, not knowing of the existence of these shutters, directed their shot either on the embrasures for the purpose of disabling the enemy's guns, or so as to graze the sand-bag parapet for the purpose of reaching the interior of the work. The practice was very good, but the effect, for reasons already stated, was inconsiderable.

At the end of the first four hours, Doubleday's men were relieved from the guns and had an opportunity to look about them. Not a man was visible near any of the batteries, but a large party, apparently of non-combatants, had collected on the beach of Sullivan's Island, well out of the line of fire, to witness the duel between Sumter and Moultrie. Doubleday's men were not in the best of temper. They were irritated at the thought that they had been unable to inflict any serious damage on their adversary, and although they had suffered no damage in return they were dissatisfied. The crowd of unsympathetic spectators was more than they could bear, and two veteran sergeants determined to stir them up a little. For this purpose they directed two 42-pounders on the crowd, and, when no officer was near, fired. The first shot struck about fifty yards short, and, bounding over the heads of the astonished spectators, went crashing through the Moultrie House. The second followed an almost identical course, doing no damage except to the Moultrie House, and the spectators scampered off in a rather undignified manner. The Moultrie House was flying a yellow flag at the time, and the Charleston newspapers discoursed upon the barbarity of firing upon a hospital flag, forgetting, perhaps, that we also had a hospital in Sumter, which they treated to red-hot shot during the bombardment. Of course, none of the officers of Sumter knew anything about the two 42-pounder shots.

The smoke which enveloped the Confederate batteries during the first day, while not so thick as entirely to obscure them, was sufficiently so to make visual aiming extremely unreliable; and during the second day, when Sumter was on fire, nothing could be seen beyond the muzzles of our own guns. But the aiming arrangements, due to the foresight and ingenuity of Captain Doubleday, enabled us to fire with as much accuracy when we could not see the object as when we could.

Early on the first day several vessels of the fleet were observed off the bar, and orders were given to dip the flag to them. This was done, and the salute was returned, but while our flag was being hoisted after the third dip, a shell burst near the flag-staff and cut the halliards. This accident put the flag beyond our control. It ran down until the kinky halliards jammed in the pulley at the mast-head, and the flag remained at about half-staff. This has been interpreted as a signal of distress, but it was only an accident. There was no special distress in Sumter, and no signal to that effect was intended.

Major Anderson had given orders that only the casemate batteries should be manned. While this was undoubtedly prompted by a desire to save his men, it operated also, in some degree, to save the Confederates. Our most powerful batteries and all our shell guns were on the barbette tier, and, being forbidden their use, we were compelled to oppose a destructive shell fire with solid shot alone. This, especially as we had no mortars, was a great disadvantage. Had we been permitted to use our shell guns we could have set fire to the barracks and quarters in Moultrie; for, as it was, we wrecked them badly with solid shot, although we could not see them. Then the cotton-bale shutters would have been destroyed, and we could have made it much livelier generally for our adversaries. This was so apparent to the men, that one of them—a man named Carmody—stole up on the ramparts and deliberately fired every barbette gun in position on the Moultrie side of the work. The guns were already loaded and roughly aimed, and Carmody simply discharged them in succession; hence, the effect was less than it would have been if the aim had been carefully rectified. But Carmody's effort aroused the enemy to a sense of his danger. He supposed, no doubt, that Major Anderson had determined to open his barbette batteries, so he directed every gun to bear on the barbette tier of Fort Sumter, and probably believed that vigor of his fire induced Major Anderson to change his mind. But the contest was merely Carmody against the Confederate States; and Carmody had to back down, not because he was beaten, but because he was unable, single-handed, to reload his guns.

Another amusing incident in this line occurred on the Morris Island side of the fort. There, in the gorge angle, a ten-inch columbiad was mounted, *en barbette,* and as the 42-pounders of the casemate battery were making no impression on the Cumming's Point iron battery, the two veteran sergeants who had surreptitiously fired upon the spectators, as already related, determined to try a shot at the iron battery from the big gun. As this was a direct violation of orders, caution was necessary. Making sure that the major was out of the way, and that no officers were near, the two sergeants stole upstairs to the ten-inch gun. It was loaded and aimed already, they very well knew, so all they would have to do was to fire it. This was the work of a few seconds only. The gun was fired, and those in the secret down below watched the flight of the shot in great expectations of decided results. Unfortunately the shot missed; not a bad shot—almost grazing the crest of the battery—but a miss. A little less elevation, a very little, and the battery would have been smashed: so thought the sergeants, for they had great faith in the power of their gun; and they determined to try a second shot. The gun was reloaded, a feat of some difficulty for two men, but to run it "in battery" was beyond their powers. It required the united efforts of six men to throw the carriage "in gear," and the two sergeants could not budge it. Things were getting desperate around them. The secessionists had noticed the first shot, and had now turned every gun that would bear on that ten-inch gun. They were just getting the range, and it was beginning to be uncomfortable for the sergeants, who in a fit of desperation determined to fire the gun "as she was." The elevating screw was given half a turn less elevation, and the primer was inserted in the vent. Then one of the sergeants ran down the spiral stairs to see if the coast were clear, leaving his comrade in a very uncomfortable position at the end of the lanyard, and lying flat on the floor. It was getting hotter up there every second, and a perfect hurricane of shot was sweeping over the prostrate soldier. Human nature could stand it no longer. The lanyard was pulled and the gun was fired. The other sergeant was hastening up the stairway, and had almost reached the top, when he met the gun coming down, or at least trying to. Having been fired "from battery," it had recoiled over the counter-hurters, and, turning a back somersault, had landed across the head of the stairway. Realizing in a moment what had happened, and what would be to pay if they were found out, the second sergeant crept to the head of the stairway and called his comrade, who, scared almost to death,—not at the danger he was in, but at the accident,—was still hugging the floor with the lanyard in his hand. Both got safely down, swearing eternal secrecy to each other; and it is doubtful if Major Anderson ever knew how that ten-inch gun came to be dismounted. It is proper to add that the shot was a capital one, striking just under the middle embrasure of the iron battery and half covering it with sand. If it had been a trifle higher it would have entered the embrasure.

The first night of the bombardment was one of great anxiety. The fleet might send reënforcements; the enemy might attempt an assault. Both would come in boats; both would answer in English. It would be horrible to fire upon friends; it would be fatal not to fire upon enemies. The night was dark and chilly. Shells were dropping into the fort at regular intervals, and the men were tired, hungry, and out of temper. Any party that approached that night would have been rated as enemies upon general principles. Fortunately nobody ap-

A CASEMATE GUN DURING
THE CONFLAGRATION.

peared; reveille sounded, and the men oiled their appetites with the fat pork at the usual hour by way of breakfast.

The second day's bombardment began at the same hour as did the first; that is, on the Sumter side. The enemy's mortars had kept up a very slow fire all night, which gradually warmed up after daylight as their batteries seemed to awaken, until its vigor was about equal to their fire of the day before. The fleet was still off the bar—perhaps waiting to see the end. Fire broke out once or twice in the officers' quarters, and was extinguished. It broke out again in several places at once, and we realized the truth and let the quarters burn. They were firing red-hot shot. This was about 9 o'clock. As soon as Sumter was noticed to be on fire the secessionists increased the fire of their batteries to a maximum. In the perfect storm of shot and shell that beat upon us from all sides, the flag-staff was shot down, but the old flag was rescued and nailed to a new staff. This, with much difficulty, was carried to the ramparts and lashed to some chassis piled up there for a traverse.

We were not sorry to see the quarters burn. They were a nuisance. Built for fire-proof buildings, they were not fire-proof. Neither would they burn up in a cheerful way. The principal cisterns were large iron tanks immediately under the roof. These had been riddled, and the quarters below had been deluged with water. Everything was wet and burned badly, yielding an amount of pungent piney smoke which almost suffocated the garrison.

The scene inside the fort as the fire gained headway and threatened the magazine was an exciting one. It had already reached some of our stores of loaded shells and shell-grenades. These must be saved at all hazard. Soldiers brought their blankets and covered the precious projectiles, and thus the most of them were saved. But the magazine itself was in danger. Already it was full of smoke, and the flames were rapidly closing in upon it. It was evident that it must be closed, and it would be many hours before it could be opened again. During these hours the fire must be maintained with such powder as we could secure outside the magazine. A number of barrels were rolled out for this purpose, and the magazine door—already almost too hot to handle—was closed.

It was the intention to store the powder taken from the magazine in several safe corners, covering it with damp soldiers' blankets. But safe corners were hard to find, and most of the blankets were already in use covering loaded shells. The fire was raging more fiercely than ever, and safety demanded that the uncovered powder be thrown overboard. This was instantly done, and if the tide had been high we should have been well rid of it. But the tide was low, and the pile of powder-barrels rested on the riprapping in front of the embrasure. This was observed by the enemy, and some shell guns were turned upon the pile, producing an explosion which blew the gun at that embrasure clear out of battery, but did no further damage.

The fire had now enveloped the magazine, and the danger of an explosion was imminent. Powder had been carried out all the previous day, and it was more than likely that enough had sifted through the cartridge-bags to carry the fire into the powder-chamber. Major Anderson, his head erect as if on parade, called the men around him; directed that a shot be fired every five minutes; and mentioned that there was some danger of the magazine exploding. Some of the

BARBETTE
GUNS—EFFECT
OF THE RAKING
FIRE FROM FORT
MOULTRIE.

RUINS OF THE CASEMATES NEAR THE SALLY-PORT,
AND OF THE FLAG-STAFF. FROM PHOTOGRAPHS.

men, as soon as they learned what the real danger was, rushed to the door of the magazine and hurriedly dug a trench in front of it, which they kept filled with water until the danger was considered over.

It was during this excitement that ex-Senator Wigfall of Texas visited the fort. It came the turn of one of the guns on the left face of the work to fire,—we were now firing once in five minutes,—and as the cannoneer approached for the purpose of loading, he discovered a man looking in at the embrasure. The man must have raised himself to the level of the embrasure by grasping the sill with his hands. A short but lively altercation ensued between the man and the cannoneer, the man pleading to be taken in lest he should be killed with his own shot and shell. He was hauled in, Thompson, the cannoneer, first receiving his sword, to the point of which a white handkerchief was attached, not by way of surrender, but for convenience. Once inside, the bearer asked to see Major Anderson. The major was soon on the spot and opened the conversation by asking, "To what am I indebted for this visit?" The visitor replied, "I am Colonel Wigfall, of General Beauregard's staff. For God's sake, Major, let this thing stop. There has been enough bloodshed already." To which the major replied, "There has been none on my side, and besides, your batteries are still firing on me." At which Wigfall exclaimed, "I'll soon stop that," and turning to Thompson, who still held the sword under his arm, he said, pointing to the handkerchief, "Wave that out there." Thompson then handed the sword to Wigfall, saying, in substance, "Wave it yourself." Wigfall received back his sword and took a few steps toward the embrasure, when the major called him back, saying, "If you desire that to be seen you had better send it to the parapet." There was a good deal more said on the subject of the white flag both by Wigfall and the major which the writer cannot recall, but the end of it all was that a white flag was ordered to be displayed from the parapet at the request of Colonel Wigfall, and pending negotiations with him, which was instantly done, a hospital sheet being used for the purpose. Then the firing gradually ceased, and the major and his officers and Colonel Wigfall retired into the hospital bomb-proof, the only habitable room left. This was about 3 o'clock in the afternoon.

Wigfall's conference was not of long duration. He left the fort in the small boat which brought him from Morris Island, and which was manned by negroes. Shortly after his departure another small boat from Sullivan's Island, containing officers in full uniform (Wigfall wore citizen's dress with the sword), approached the fort. The officers in this boat were very much astonished and annoyed at being warned off by the sentinel, and compelled to show a white flag before they were permitted to approach. They were received by the officer of the day, who apologized for not meeting them afloat, saying that all our boats had been destroyed by shot or burned up. They were indignant at their reception, and demanded to know whether or not the fort had surrendered. What was said in reply was not distinctly heard by the writer, but it was believed to be a negative. The officer then asked what the white flag meant, and Wigfall's name was mentioned in reply. About this time Major Anderson made his appearance, and the visitors, still talking in an indignant tone, addressed themselves to him. What was said seemed to be a repetition of what had just been said to the officer of the day. The major's replies were inaudible where the writer of this stood, except when he raised his hand in a sweeping sort of gesture in the direction of Fort Moultrie, and said, "Very well, gentlemen, you can return to your batteries." They did not return, however, immediately, but were conducted into the hospital where Wigfall had been, and remained there some time. When they left we learned that there would be no more firing until General Beauregard had time to hear from his Government at Montgomery.

About 7 o'clock in the evening another white flag brought the announcement that the terms agreed upon between General Beauregard and Major Anderson had been confirmed, and that we would leave Fort Sumter the following day; which we did, after saluting our flag with fifty guns.

CHAPTER 2

THE FIRST STEP IN THE WAR.

Stephen D. Lee, Lieutenant-General, C.S.A.

In the month of December, 1860, the South itself had no more realizing sense than the North of the magnitude of events about to be entered into so lightly. Even the Southern leaders did not realize that there could be any obstacle to "peaceable secession." Many at the North were willing to "let the wayward sisters depart in peace." Only a few on either side expected that blood would be shed. When, in the first Confederate Congress at Montgomery, one prudent debater exclaimed, "What if we really have a war?" the general response was, "There will be no war." "But," he persisted, "if there *is* a war, what are our resources?" and when one man in reply expressed his conviction that if the worst came, the South could put fifty thousand men into the field, he was looked upon as an enthusiast. The expectation of "peaceable secession" was the delusion that precipitated matters in the South; and it was on this expectation, when the crisis came, that South Carolina seceded. Her first step was to organize troops and assert the sovereignty in which she believed, by the occupation of her territory.

After the evacuation of Fort Moultrie, although Major Anderson was not permitted by the South Carolina authorities to receive any large supply of provisions, yet he received a daily mail, and fresh beef and vegetables from the city of Charleston, and was unmolested at Fort Sumter. He continued industriously to strengthen the fort. The military authorities of South Carolina, and afterward of the Confederate States, took possession of Fort Moultrie, Castle Pinckney, the arsenal, and other United States property in the vicinity. They also remounted the guns at Fort Moultrie, and constructed batteries on Sullivan's, Morris, and James islands, and at other places, looking to the reduction of Fort Sumter if it should become necessary; meantime leaving no stone unturned to secure from the authorities at Washington a quiet evacuation of the fort. Several arrangements to accomplish this purpose were almost reached, but failed. Two attempts were made to reënforce and supply the garrison: one by the

FORT JOHNSON.   FORT SUMTER.   FORT MOULTRIE.
IRON-CLAD BATTERY, CUMMING'S POINT.

BURSTING OF THE SIGNAL-SHELL FROM FORT JOHNSON OVER FORT SUMTER.

steamer *Star of the West,* which tried to reach the fort, January 9th, 1861, and was driven back by a battery on Morris Island, manned by South Carolina troops; the other just before the bombardment of Sumter, April 12th. The feeling of the Confederate authorities was that a peaceful issue would finally be arrived at; but they had a fixed determination to use force, if necessary, to occupy the fort. They did not desire or intend to take the initiative, if it could be avoided. So soon, however, as it was clearly understood that the authorities at Washington had abandoned peaceful views, and would assert the power of the United States to supply Fort Sumter, General Beauregard, the commander of the Confederate forces at Charleston, in obedience to the command of his Government at Montgomery, proceeded to reduce the fort. His arrangements were about complete, and on April 11th he demanded of Major Anderson the evacuation of Fort Sumter. He offered to transport Major Anderson and his command to any port in the United States; and to allow him to move out of the fort with company arms and property, and all private property, and to salute his flag in lowering it. This demand was delivered to Major Anderson at 3:45 P.M., by two aides of General Beauregard, James Chesnut, Jr., and myself. At 4:30 P.M. he handed us his reply, refusing to accede to the demand; but added, "Gentlemen, if you do not batter the fort to pieces about us, we shall be starved out in a few days."

The reply of Major Anderson was put in General Beauregard's hands at 5:15 P.M., and he was also told of this informal remark. Anderson's reply and remark were communicated to the Confederate authorities at Montgomery. The Secretary of War, L. P. Walker, replied to Beauregard as follows:

"Do not desire needlessly to bombard Fort Sumter. If Major Anderson will state the time at which, as indicated by him, he will evacuate, and agree that in the meantime he will not use his guns against us, unless ours should be employed against Fort Sumter, you are authorized thus to avoid the effusion of blood. If this, or its equivalent, be refused, reduce the fort as your judgment decides to be most practicable."

FRANCIS W. PICKENS,
GOVERNOR OF SOUTH CAROLINA, 1861.
FROM A PHOTOGRAPH.

The same aides bore a second communication to Major Anderson, based on the above instructions, which was placed in his hands at 12:45 A.M., April 12th. His reply indicated that he would evacuate the fort on the 15th, provided he did not in the meantime receive contradictory instructions from his Government, or additional supplies, but he declined to agree not to open his guns upon the Confederate troops, in the event of any hostile demonstration on their part against his flag. Major Anderson made every possible effort to retain the aides till daylight, making one excuse and then another for not replying. Finally, at 3:15 A.M., he delivered his reply. In accordance with their instructions, the aides read it and, finding it unsatisfactory, gave Major Anderson this notification:

"FORT SUMTER, S.C., April 12, 1861, 3:20 A.M.—SIR: By authority of Brigadier-General Beauregard, commanding the Provisional Forces of the Confederate States, we have the honor to notify you that he will open the fire of his batteries on Fort Sumter in one hour from this time. We have the honor to be very respectfully, Your obedient servants, JAMES CHESNUT, JR., *Aide-de-camp.* STEPHEN D. LEE, *Captain C.S. Army, Aide-de-camp.*"

The above note was written in one of the casemates of the fort, and in the presence of Major Anderson and several of his officers. On receiving it, he was much affected. He seemed to realize the full import of the consequences, and the great responsibility of his position. Escorting us to the boat at the wharf, he cordially pressed our hands in farewell, remarking, "If we never meet in this world again, God grant that we may meet in the next."

The boat containing the two aides and also Roger A. Pryor, of Virginia, and A. R. Chisolm, of South Carolina, who were also members of General Beauregard's staff, went immediately to Fort Johnson on James Island, and the order to fire the signal gun was given to Captain George S. James, commanding the battery at that point. It was then 4 A.M. Captain James at once aroused his command, and arranged to carry out the order. He was a great admirer of

Roger A. Pryor, and said to him, "You are the only man to whom I would give up the honor of firing the first gun of the war"; and he offered to allow him to fire it. Pryor, on receiving the offer, was very much agitated. With a husky voice he said, "I could not fire the first gun of the war." His manner was almost similar to that of Major Anderson as we left him a few moments before on the wharf at Fort Sumter. Captain James would allow no one else but himself to fire the gun.☆

The boat with the aides of General Beauregard left Fort Johnson before arrangements were complete for the firing of the gun, and laid on its oars, about one-third the distance between the fort and Sumter, there to witness the firing of "the first gun of the war" between the States. It was fired from a ten-inch mortar at 4:30

FROM A PHOTOGRAPH TAKEN IN 1863.

A.M., April 12th, 1861. Captain James was a skillful officer, and the firing of the shell was a success. It burst immediately over the fort, apparently about one hundred feet above. The firing of the mortar woke the echoes from every nook and corner of the harbor, and in this the dead hour of night, before dawn, that shot was a sound of alarm that brought every soldier in the harbor to his feet, and every man, woman, and child in the city of Charleston from their beds. A thrill went through the whole city. It was felt that the Rubicon was passed. No one thought of going home; unused as their ears were to the appalling sounds, or the vivid flashes from the batteries, they stood for hours fascinated with horror. After the second shell the different batteries opened their fire on Fort Sumter, and by 4:45 A.M. the firing was general and regular. It was a hazy, foggy morning. About daylight, the boat with the aides reached

---

☆When the *Star of the West* arrived, on the 9th of January, the first shot, aimed across her bow, was fired by G. E. Haynsworth, and the second, aimed directly at her, by Cadet Horlbeek. It is claimed that before this date a hostile shot from a 4-pounder had been fired from Vicksburg by Horace Miller at a passing United States vessel, supposed to be carrying a supply of arms and ammunition to New Orleans.

—EDITORS.

SECESSION HALL, CHARLESTON, SCENE
OF THE PASSAGE OF THE ORDINANCE
OF SECESSION. FROM A PHOTOGRAPH.

Charleston, and they reported to General Beauregard.

Fort Sumter did not respond with her guns till 7:30 A.M. The firing from this fort, during the entire bombardment, was slow and deliberate, and marked with little accuracy. The firing continued without intermission during the 12th, and more slowly during the night of the 12th and 13th. No material change was noticed till 8 A.M. on the 13th, when the barracks in Fort Sumter were set on fire by hot shot from the guns of Fort Moultrie. As soon as this was discovered, the Confederate batteries redoubled their efforts, to prevent the fire being extinguished. Fort Sumter fired at little longer intervals, to enable the garrison to fight the flames. This brave action, under such a trying ordeal, aroused great sympathy and admiration on the part of the Confederates for Major Anderson and his gallant garrison; this feeling was shown by cheers whenever a gun was fired from Sumter. It was shown also by loud reflections on the "men-of-war" outside the harbor.[ψ]

About 12:30 the flag-staff of Fort Sumter was shot down, but it was soon replaced. As soon as General Beauregard heard that the flag was no longer flying, he sent three of his aides, William Porcher Miles, Roger A. Pryor, and myself, to offer, and also to see if Major Anderson would receive or needed, assistance, in subduing the flames inside the fort. Before we reached it, we saw the United States flag again floating over it, and began to return to the city.

[ψ] These vessels, part of the second expedition for the relief of Fort Sumter, were the *Baltic* (no guns), the *Pawnee* (8 9-inch guns), and the *Harriet Lane* (1 8-inch gun and 4 32-pounders). The *Pocahontas* did not arrive till the afternoon of the 13th. The expedition was in charge of Captain Gustavus V. Fox (afterward Assistant Secretary of the Navy), who had visited the fort on the 21st of March. It had been understood between Secretary Welles and Captain Fox that the movement should be supported by the *Powhatan* (1 11-inch and 10 9-inch guns); but, unknown to Mr. Welles, and perhaps without full understanding of this plan, President Lincoln had consented to the dispatch of the ship to the relief of Fort Pickens, for which destination it had sailed from New York, April 6th, under command of Lieutenant David D. Porter. This conflict of plans deprived Captain Fox of the ship which he calls the "fighting portion" of his fleet; and to this circumstance he attributed the failure of the expedition.
—EDITORS.

Before going far, however, we saw the Stars and Stripes replaced by a white flag. We turned about at once and rowed rapidly to the fort. We were directed, from an embrasure, not to go to the wharf, as it was mined, and the fire was near it. We were assisted through an embrasure and conducted to Major Anderson. Our mission being made known to him, he replied, "Present my compliments to General Beauregard, and say to him I thank him for his kindness, but need no assistance." He further remarked that he hoped the worst was over, that the fire had settled over the magazine, and, as it had not exploded, he thought the real danger was about over. Continuing, he said, "Gentlemen, do I understand you come direct from General Beauregard?" The reply was in the affirmative. He then said, "Why! Colonel Wigfall has just been here as an aide too, and by authority of General Beauregard, and proposed the same terms of evacuation offered on the 11th instant." We informed the major that we were not authorized to offer terms; that we were direct from General Beauregard, and that Colonel Wigfall, although an aide-de-camp to the general, had been detached, and had not seen the general for several days. Major Anderson at once stated, "There is a misunderstanding on my part, and I will at once run up my flag and open fire again." After consultation, we requested him not to do so, until the matter was explained to General Beauregard, and requested Major Anderson to reduce to writing his understanding with Colonel Wigfall, which he did. However, before we left the fort, a boat arrived from Charleston, bearing Major D. R. Jones, assistant adjutant-general on General Beauregard's staff, who offered substantially the same terms to Major Anderson as those offered on the 11th, and also by Colonel Wigfall, and which were now accepted.

Thus fell Fort Sumter, April 13th, 1861. At this time fire was still raging in the barracks, and settling steadily over the magazine. All egress was cut off except through the lower embrasures. Many shells from the Confederate batteries, which had fallen in the fort and had not exploded, as well as the hand-grenades used for defense, were exploding as they were reached by the fire. The wind was driving the heat and smoke down into the fort and into the casemates, almost causing suffocation. Major Anderson, his officers, and men were blackened by smoke and cinders, and showed signs of fatigue and exhaustion, from the trying ordeal through which they had passed.

It was soon discovered, by conversation, that it was a bloodless battle; not a man had been killed or seriously wounded on either side during the entire bombardment of nearly forty hours. Congratulations were exchanged on so happy a result. Major Anderson stated that he had instructed his officers only to fire on the batteries and forts, and not to fire on private property.

The terms of evacuation offered by General Beauregard were generous, and were appreciated by Major Anderson. The garrison was to embark on the

JEFFERSON DAVIS, PRESIDENT OF THE CONFEDERATE STATES OF AMERICA.
FROM A PHOTOGRAPH.

VIEW OF CUMMING'S POINT. FROM A SKETCH MADE AFTER THE BOMBARDMENT.

14th, after running up and saluting the United States flag, and to be carried to the United States fleet. A soldier killed during the salute was buried inside the fort, the new Confederate garrison uncovering during the impressive ceremonies. Major Anderson and his command left the harbor, bearing with them the respect and admiration of the Confederate soldiers.✦ It was conceded that he had done his duty as a soldier holding a most delicate trust.

This first bombardment of Sumter was but its "baptism of fire." During subsequent attacks by land and water, it was battered by the heaviest Union ar-

---

✦The officers, under General Beauregard, of the batteries surrounding Fort Sumter were:

SULLIVAN'S ISLAND, Brigadier-General R.G.M. Dunovant commanding, Lieutenant-Colonel Roswell S. Ripley, commanding the artillery: *Fire-gun Battery* (east of Fort Moultrie), Captain S. Y. Tupper; *Maffit Channel Battery* (2 guns) and *Mortar Battery No. 2* (2 10-inch mortars), Captain William Butler, Lieutenant T. A. Hugnenin; *Fort Moultrie* (30 guns), Captain W. R. Calhoun: consisting of Channel Battery, Lieutenants Thomas M. Wagner, Preston, and Sitgreaves, Sumter Battery, Lieutenants Alfred Rhett and John C. Mitchell, and Oblique Battery, Lieutenant C. W. Parker; *Mortar Battery No. 1* (2 10-inch mortars) and *Enfilade Battery* (4 guns), Captain James H. Hallonquist, Lieutenants D. G. Fleming, Jacob Valentine, and B. S. Burnet; the *Point Battery* (1 9-inch Dahlgren) and the *Floating Iron-clad Battery* (2 42-pounders and 2 32-pounders), Captain John R. Hamilton and Lieutenant Joseph A. Yates; the *Mount Pleasant Battery* (2 10-inch mortars), Captain Robert Martin, Lieutenant George N. Reynolds.

MORRIS ISLAND, Brigadier-General James Simons commanding, Lieutenant-Colonel Wilmot G. De Saussure, commanding the artillery: Major P. F. Stevens, commanding *Cumming's Point Battery* (Blakely gun, which arrived from Liverpool April 9th, Captain J. P. Thomas; 2 42-pounders, Lieutenant T. Sumter Brownfield; and 3 10-inch mortars, Lieutenants C. R. Holmes and N. Armstrong) and the *Stevens Iron-clad Battery* (3 8-inch columbiads), Captain George B. Cuthbert, Lieutenant G. L. Buist; *Trapier Battery* (3 10-inch mortars), Captain J. Gadsden King, Lieutenants W.D.H. Kirkwood, J. P. Strohecker, A. M. Huger, and E. L. Parker.

JAMES ISLAND, Major N. G. Evans commanding; *Fort Johnson* (battery of 24-pounders), Captain George S. James; *Mortar Battery,* Lieutenants W. H. Gibbes, H. S. Farley, J. E. McP. Washington, and T. B. Hayne; *Upper Battery* (2 10-inch mortars), *Lower Battery* (2 10-inch mortars), Captain S. C. Thayer.

—EDITORS.

FORT SUMTER AFTER THE BOMBARDMENT. FROM A SKETCH MADE IN APRIL, 1861.

tillery. Its walls were completely crushed, but the tons of iron projectiles imbedded in its ruins added strength to the inaccessible mass that surrounded it and made it impregnable. It was never taken, but the operations of General Sherman, after his march to the sea, compelled its evacuation, and the Stars and Stripes were again raised over it, April 14th, 1865.❧

❧Under an order from Secretary Stanton, the same flag that was lowered, April 14th, 1861, was raised again over Sumter, by Major (then General) Anderson, on April 14th, 1865, the day President Lincoln was shot. Of Major Anderson's former officers, Generals Abner Doubleday and Norman J. Hall and Chaplain Matthias Harris were present. The Rev. Henry Ward Beecher delivered an oration, and other prominent anti-slavery men attended the ceremony.—EDITORS.

CHAPTER 3

War Preparations in the North.

Jacob D. Cox, Major-General, U.S.V.

EX-GOVERNOR OF OHIO, EX-SECRETARY OF THE INTERIOR.

The wonderful outburst of national feeling in the North in the spring of 1861 has always been a thrilling and almost supernatural thing to those who participated in it. The classic myth that the resistless terror which sometimes unaccountably seized upon an army was the work of the god Pan might seem to have its counterpart in the work of a national divinity rousing a whole people, not to terror, but to a sublime enthusiasm of self-devotion. To picture it as a whole is impossible. A new generation can only approximate a knowledge of the feelings of that time by studying in detail some separate scenes of the drama that had a continent for its stage. The writer can only tell what happened under his eye. The like was happening everywhere from Maine to Kansas. What is told is simply a type of the rest./

On Friday, the twelfth day of April, 1861, the Senate of Ohio was in session, trying to go on in the ordinary routine of business, but with a sense of anxiety and strain which was caused by the troubled condition of national affairs. The

/In those opening days of the war, the National Government seemed for the moment to be subordinated to the governments of the States. A revolution in the seceding South had half destroyed the national legislature, and the national executive was left without a treasury, without an army, and without laws adequate to create these at once. At no time since the thirteen colonies declared their independence have the State governors and the State legislators found so important a field of duty as then. A little hesitation, a little lukewarmness, would have ended all. Then it was that the intense zeal and high spirit of Governor Andrew of Massachusetts led all New England, and was ready to lead the nation, as the men of Concord and Lexington had led in 1775. Then it was that Governor Morton of Indiana came to the front with a masculine energy and burly weight of character and of will which was typical of the force which the Great West could throw into the struggle.

Ohio was so situated with regard to West Virginia and Kentucky that the keystone of the Union might be said to be now west of the mountains. Governor Dennison mediated, like the statesman he was, between East and West; and Tod and Brough, following him by the will of the people in votes that ran up to majorities of near a hundred thousand, gave that vigorous support to Mr. Lincoln which showed the earnest nationality of the "war Democrats" of that day.—J.D.C.

THE AWKWARD SQUAD.

passage of "ordinances of secession" by one after another of the Southern States, and even the assembling of a provisional Confederate government at Montgomery, had not wholly destroyed the hope that some peaceful way out of our troubles would be found; yet the gathering of an army on the sands opposite Fort Sumter was really war, and if a hostile gun were fired, we knew it would mean the end of all effort at arrangement. Hoping almost against hope that blood would not be shed, and that the pageant of military array and of a secession government would pass by, we tried to give our thoughts to business; but there was no heart in it, and the "morning hour" lagged, for we could not work in earnest, and we were unwilling to adjourn.

Suddenly a senator came in from the lobby in an excited way, and, catching the chairman's eye, exclaimed, "Mr. President, the telegraph announces that the secessionists are bombarding Fort Sumter!" There was a solemn and painful hush, but it was broken in a moment by a woman's shrill voice from the spectators' seats, crying, "Glory to God!" It startled every one, almost as if the enemy were in the midst. But it was the voice of a radical friend of the slave, Abby Kelly Foster, who, after a lifetime of public agitation, believed that only through blood could his freedom be won, and who had shouted the fierce cry of joy that the question had been submitted to the decision of the sword. With most of us, the gloomy thought that civil war had begun in our own land overshadowed everything else; this seemed too great a price to pay for any good,—a scourge to be borne only in preference to yielding what was to us the very groundwork of our republicanism, the right to enforce a fair interpretation of the Constitution through the election of President and Congress.

The next day we learned that Major Anderson had surrendered, and the telegraphic news from all the Northern States showed plain evidence of a popular outburst of loyalty to the Union, following a brief moment of dismay. That was the period when the flag—*The Flag*—flew out to the wind from every housetop in our great cities, and when, in New York, wildly excited crowds marched the streets demanding that the suspected or the lukewarm should show the symbol of nationality as a committal to the country's cause. He that is not for us is against us, was the deep, instinctive feeling.

Judge Thomas M. Key of Cincinnati,ψ chairman of the Judiciary Committee, was the recognized leader of the Democratic party in the Senate, and at an early hour moved an adjournment to the following Tuesday, in order, as he said, that the senators might have the opportunity to go home and consult their constituents in the perilous crisis of public affairs. No objection was made to the adjournment, and the representatives took a similar recess. All were in a state of most anxious suspense,—the Republicans to know what initiative the Administration at Washington would take, and the Democrats to determine what course they should follow if the President should call for troops to put down the insurrection.

Before we met again, Mr. Lincoln's proclamation and call for 75,000 men for three months' service had been issued, and the great mass of the people of the North, forgetting all party distinctions, answered with an enthusiasm that swept politicians off their feet. When we met again on Tuesday morning, Judge Key, taking my arm and pacing the floor outside the railing, broke out impetuously, "Mr. Cox, the people have gone stark mad!"—"I knew they would if a blow were struck against the flag," said I, reminding him of some previous conversations we had had on the subject. He, with most of the politicians of the day, partly by sympathy with the overwhelming current of public opinion, and partly by the reaction of their own hearts against the theories which had encouraged the secessionists, determined to support the war measures of the Government and to make no factious opposition to such State legislation as might be necessary to sustain the Federal Administration.

The attitude of Mr. Key is only a type of many others, and marks one of the most striking features of the time. On the 8th of January the usual Democratic convention and celebration of the battle of New Orleans had taken place, and a series of resolutions had been passed, in which, professing to speak in the name of "200,000 Democrats of Ohio," the convention had very significantly intimated that this vast organization of men would be found in the way of any attempt to put down secession until the demands of the South in respect to slavery were complied with. A few days afterward I was returning to Columbus from my home in Trumbull county, and meeting upon the railway train with David Tod, then an active Democratic politician, but afterward one of our loyal

ψAfterward aide-de-camp and acting judge-advocate on General McClellan's staff.

"war governors," the conversation turned on the action of the convention which had just adjourned. Mr. Tod and I were personal friends and neighbors, and I freely expressed my surprise that the convention should have committed itself to what must be interpreted as a threat of insurrection in the North, if the Administration should, in opposing secession by force, follow the example of Andrew Jackson in whose honor they had assembled. He rather vehemently reasserted the substance of the resolution, saying that we Republicans would find the 200,000 Ohio Democrats in front of us, if we attempted to cross the Ohio River. My answer was, "We will give up the contest if we cannot carry your 200,000 over the heads of you leaders."

The result proved how hollow the party assertions had been, or, perhaps, I should say, how superficial was the hold of such doctrines upon the mass of men in a great political organization. At the first shot from Beauregard's guns in Charleston Harbor these men crowded to the recruiting stations to enlist for the defense of the national flag and the national union. It was a popular torrent which no leaders could resist; but many of these should be credited with the same patriotic impulse, and it made them nobly oblivious of party consistency. A few days after the surrender of Sumter, Stephen A. Douglas passed through Columbus on his way to Washington, and, in response to the calls of a spontaneous gathering of people, spoke to them from the window of his bedroom in the hotel. There had been no thought for any of the common surroundings of a public meeting. There were no torches, no music. A dark mass of men filled full the dimly lit street, and called for Douglas with an earnestness of tone wholly different from the enthusiasm of common political gatherings. He came half-dressed to his window, and, without any light near him, spoke solemnly to the people upon the terrible crisis which had come upon the nation. Men of all parties were there: his own followers to get some light as to their duty; the Breckinridge Democrats ready, most of them, repentantly to follow a Northern leader now that their Southern associates were in armed opposition to the Government; the Republicans eager to know whether so potent an influence was to be unreservedly on the side of the nation. I remember well the serious solicitude with which I listened to his opening sentences as I leaned against the railing of the State House park, trying in vain to see more than a dim outline of the man as he stood at the unlighted window. His deep, sonorous tones rolled down through the darkness from above us, an earnest, measured voice, the more solemn, the more impressive, because we could not see the speaker, and it came to us literally as "a voice in the night,"—the night of our country's unspeakable trial. There was no uncertainty in his tone; the Union must be preserved and the insurrection must be crushed; he pledged his hearty support to Mr. Lincoln's administration in doing this; other questions must stand aside till the national authority should be everywhere recognized. I do not think we greatly cheered him,—it was, rather, a deep Amen that went up from the crowd. We went home breathing more freely in the assurance we now felt that, for a time at least, no organized opposition to the Federal Government and its policy of coercion could be formidable in the North.

Yet the situation hung upon us like a nightmare. Garfield and I were lodging together at the time, our wives being kept at home by family cares, and when we reached our sitting-room, after an evening session of the Senate, we often found ourselves involuntarily groaning, "Civil war in *our* land!" The

STEPHEN A. DOUGLAS. FROM A DAGUERREOTYPE TAKEN IN 1852.

shame, the folly, the outrage, seemed too great to believe, and we half hoped to wake from it as from a dream. Among the painful remembrances of those days is the ever-present weight at the heart which never left me till I found relief in the active duties of camp life at the close of the month. I went about my duties (and I am sure most of those with whom I associated did the same) with the half-choking sense of a grief I dared not think of: like one who is dragging himself to the ordinary labors of life from some terrible and recent bereavement.

We talked of our personal duty, and though both Garfield and myself had young families, we were agreed that our activity in the organization and support of the Republican party made the duty of supporting the Government by military service come peculiarly home to us. He was, for the moment, somewhat trammeled by his half-clerical position, but he very soon cut the knot. My own path seemed unmistakably plain. He, more careful for his friend than for himself, urged upon me his doubts whether my physical strength was equal to the strain that would be put upon it. "I," said he, "am big and strong, and if my relations to the church and the college can be loosened, I shall have no excuse for not enlisting; but you are slender and will break down." It is true I then looked slender for a man six feet high; yet I had confidence in the elasticity of my constitution, and the result justified me, while it also showed how liable one is to mistake in such things. Garfield found that he had a tendency to weakness of the alimentary system, which broke him down on every campaign in which he served, and led to his retiring from the army at the close of 1863. My own health, on the other hand, was strengthened by outdoor life and exposure, and I served to the end with growing physical vigor.

When Mr. Lincoln issued his first call for troops, the existing laws made it necessary that these should be fully organized and officered by the several States. Then, the treasury was in no condition to bear the burden of war expenditures, and, till Congress could assemble, the President was forced to rely on the States for means to equip and transport their own men. This threw upon the governors and legislatures of the loyal States responsibilities of a kind wholly unprecedented. A long period of profound peace had made every military organization seem almost farcical. A few independent companies formed the merest shadow of an army, and the State militia proper was only a nominal thing. It happened, however, that I held a commission as brigadier in this State militia, and my intimacy with Governor Dennison led him to call upon me for such assistance as I could render in the first enrollment and organization of the Ohio quota. Arranging to be called to the Senate chamber when my vote might be needed, I gave my time chiefly to such military matters as the governor appointed. Although, as I have said, my military commission had been a nominal thing, and in fact I had never worn a uniform, I had not wholly neglected theoretic preparation for such work. For some years, the possibility of a war of secession had been one of the things which were forced upon the thoughts of reflecting people, and I had given some careful study to such books of tactics and of strategy as were within easy reach. I had especially been led to read military history with critical care, and had carried away many valuable ideas from that most useful means of military education. I had, therefore, some notion of the work before us, and could approach its problems with less loss of time, at least, than if I had been wholly ignorant.

My commission as brigadier-general in the Ohio quota in national service was dated the 23d of April. Just about the same time Captain George B. McClellan was requested by Governor Dennison to come to Columbus for consultation, and, by the governor's request, I met him at the railway station and took him to the State House. I think Mr. Lars Anderson (brother of Major Robert Anderson) and Mr. L'Hommedieu of Cincinnati were with him. The intimation had been given me that he would probably be made major-general of the Ohio contingent, and this, naturally, made me scan him closely. He was rather under the medium height, but muscularly formed, with broad shoulders and a well-poised head, active and graceful in motion. His whole appearance was quiet and modest, but when drawn out he showed no lack of confidence in himself. He was dressed in a plain traveling dress and wore a narrow-rimmed soft felt hat. In short, he seemed what he was, a railway superintendent in his business clothes. At the time, his name was a good deal associated with Beauregard's, and they were spoken of as young men of similar standing in the engineer corps of the army, and great things were expected of them both because of their scientific knowledge of their profession, though McClellan had been in civil life for some years. McClellan's report on the Crimean war was one of the few important memoirs our old army had produced, and was valuable enough to give a just reputation for comprehensive understanding of military organization, and the promise of ability to conduct the operations of an army.

I was present at the interview which the governor had with him. The destitution of the State of everything like military material and equipment was very plainly put, and the magnitude of the task of building up a small army out of nothing was not blinked. The governor spoke of the embarrassment he felt at every step from the lack of practical military experience in his staff, and of his desire to have some one on whom he could properly throw the details of military work. McClellan showed that he fully understood the difficulties there would be before him, and said no man could wholly master them at once, although he had confidence that if a few weeks' time for preparation were given, he would be able to put the Ohio division into reasonable form for taking the field. The command was then formally tendered and accepted. All of us who were present felt that the selection was one full of promise and hope, and that the governor had done the wisest thing practicable at the time.

The next morning McClellan requested me to accompany him to the State arsenal, to see what arms and material might be there. We found a few boxes of smooth-bore muskets which had once been issued to militia companies and had been returned rusted and damaged. No belts, cartridge-boxes, or other accouterments were with them. There were two or three smooth-bore brass field-pieces, 6-pounders, which had been honey-combed by firing salutes, and of which the vents had been worn out, bushed, and worn out again. In a heap in one corner lay a confused pile of mildewed harness which had been once used for artillery horses, but was now not worth carrying away. There had for many years been no money appropriated to buy military material or even to protect the little the State had. The Federal Government had occasionally distributed some arms which were in the hands of the independent uniformed militia, and the arsenal was simply an empty store-house. It did not take long to complete our inspection. At the door, as we were leaving the building, McClellan turned, and, looking back into its emptiness, remarked, half humorously and half sadly, "A fine stock of munitions on which to begin a great war!"

We went back to the State House where a room was assigned us, and we sat down to work. The first task was to make out detailed schedules and estimates of what would be needed to equip ten thousand men for the field. This was a unit which could be used by the governor and Legislature in estimating the appropriations needed then or subsequently. Intervals in this labor were used in discussing the general situation and plans of campaign. Before the close of the week McClellan drew up a paper embodying his own views, and forwarded it to Lieutenant-General Scott. He read it to me, and my recollection of it is that he suggested two principal lines of movement in the West: one to move eastward by the Kanawha Valley with a heavy column to coöperate with an army in front of Washington; the other to march directly southward and to open the Valley of the Mississippi. Scott's answer was appreciative and flattering, without distinctly approving his plan, and I have never doubted that the paper prepared the way for his appointment in the regular army, which followed at an early day.[*]

But in trying to give a connected idea of the first military organization of the State, I have outrun some incidents of those days which are worth recollection. From the hour the call for troops was published, enlistments began, and recruits were parading the streets continually. At the capitol the restless impulse to be doing something military seized even upon the members of the Legislature, and a good many of them assembled every evening upon the east terrace of the State House to be drilled in marching and facing by one or two of their own number who had some knowledge of company tactics. Most of the uniformed independent companies in the cities of the State immediately tendered their services and began to recruit their numbers to the hundred men re-

[*] Scott's answer was dated May 3d, and is given by General E. D. Townsend (then on Scott's staff), in his "Anecdotes of the Civil War."

quired for acceptance. There was no time to procure uniforms, nor was it desirable; for these companies had chosen their own, and would have to change it for that of the United States as soon as this could be furnished. For some days companies could be seen marching and drilling, of which part would be uniformed in some gaudy style such as is apt to prevail in holiday parades in time of peace, while another part would be dressed in the ordinary working garb of citizens of all degrees. The uniformed files would also be armed and accoutered, the others would be without arms or equipments, and as awkward a squad as could well be imagined. The material, however, was magnificent and soon began to

MAJOR-GENERAL GEORGE B. McCLELLAN. FROM A WAR-TIME PHOTOGRAPH.

take shape. The fancy uniforms were left at home, and some approximation to a simple and useful costume was made. The recent popular outburst in Italy furnished a useful idea, and the "Garibaldi uniform" of a red flannel shirt with broad falling collar, with blue trousers held by a leathern waist-belt, and a soft felt hat for the head, was extensively copied and served an excellent purpose. It could be made by the wives and sisters at home, and was all the more acceptable for that. The spring was opening and a heavy coat would not be much needed, so that with some sort of overcoat and a good blanket in an improvised knapsack, the new company was not badly provided. The warm scarlet color reflected from their enthusiastic faces as they stood in line made a picture that never failed to impress the mustering officers with the splendid character of the men.

The officering of these new troops was a difficult and delicate task, and, so far as company officers were concerned, there seemed no better way at the beginning than to let the enlisted men elect their own, as was in fact done. In most cases where entirely new companies were raised, it had been by the enthusiastic efforts of some energetic volunteers who were naturally made the commissioned officers. But not always. There were numerous examples of self-denial by men who remained in the ranks after expending much labor and money in recruiting, modestly refusing the honors, and giving way to some one supposed to have military knowledge or experience. The war in Mexico in 1846–7 had been our latest conflict with a civilized people, and to have served in it was a sure passport to confidence. It had often been a service more in name than in fact; but the young volunteers felt so deeply their own ignorance that they were ready to yield to any pretense of superior knowledge, and generously to trust themselves to any one who would offer to lead them. Hosts of charlatans and incompetents were thus put into responsible places at the beginning, but the sifting work went on fast after the troops were once in the field. The election of field-officers, however, ought not to have been allowed. Companies were necessarily regimented together of which each could have little personal knowledge of the officers of the others; intrigue and demagogy soon came into play, and almost fatal mistakes were made in selection. The evil worked its cure, but the ill effects of it were long visible.

The immediate need of troops to protect Washington caused most of the uniformed companies to be united into the first two regiments, which were quickly dispatched to the East. These off, companies began to stream in from all parts of the State. On their first arrival they were quartered wherever shelter could be had, as there were no tents or sheds to make a camp for them. Going to my evening work at the State House, as I crossed the rotunda I saw a company marching in by the south door, and another disposing itself for the night upon the marble pavement near the east entrance; as I passed on to the north hall, I saw another that had come a little earlier holding a prayer-meeting, the stone arches echoing with the excited supplications of some one who was borne out of himself by the terrible pressure of events around him, while, mingling with his pathetic, beseeching tones as he prayed for his country, came the shrill notes of the fife and the thundering din of the ubiquitous bass-drum from the company marching in on the other side. In the Senate chamber a company was quartered, and the senators were supplying them with paper and pens with which "the boys" were writing their farewells to mothers and sweethearts, whom they hardly dared hope they should see again. A similar scene was going on in the Representatives' hall, another in the Supreme Court-room. In the executive office sat the governor, the unwonted noises, when the door was opened, breaking in on the quiet, business-like air of the room,—he meanwhile dictating dispatches, indicating answers to others, receiving committees of citizens, giving directions to officers of companies and regiments, accommodating himself to the willful democracy of our institutions which insists upon seeing the man in chief command, and will not take its answer from a subordinate, until in the small hours of the night the noises were hushed, and after a brief hour of effective, undisturbed work upon the matters of chief importance, he could leave the glare of his gas-lighted office and seek a few hours' rest, only to renew his wearing labors on the morrow.

On the streets the excitement was of a rougher if not more intense character. A minority of unthinking partisans could not understand the strength and sweep of the great popular movement, and would sometimes venture to speak out their sympathy with the rebellion, or their sneers at some party friend who had enlisted. In the boiling temper of the time the quick answer was a blow; and it was one of the common incidents of the day for those who came into the State House to tell of a knock-down that had occurred here or there, when this popular punishment had been administered to some indiscreet "rebel-sympathizer."

Various duties brought young army officers of the regular service to the State capital, and others sought a brief leave of absence to come and offer their services to the governor of their native State. General Scott had planted himself firmly on the theory that the regular army must be the principal reliance for severe work, and that the volunteers could only be auxiliaries around this solid nucleus which would show them the way to perform their duty, and take the brunt of every encounter. The young regulars who asked leave to accept commissions in State regiments were therefore refused, and were ordered to their own subaltern positions and posts. There can be no doubt that the true policy would have been to encourage the whole of this younger class to enter at once the volunteer service. They would have been field-officers in the new regiments, and would have impressed discipline and system upon the organization from the beginning. The Confederates really profited by having no regular army. They gave to the officers who left our service, it is true, commissions in their so-called "provisional" army, to encourage them to expect permanent military positions if the war should end in the independence of the South; but this was only a nominal organization, and their real army was made up (as ours turned out practically to be) from the regiments of State volunteers. Less than a year afterward we changed our policy, but it was then too late to induce many of the regular officers to take regimental positions in the volunteer troops. I hesitate to declare that this was not, after all, for the best; for, although the organization of our army would have been more rapidly perfected, there are other considerations which have much weight. The army would not have been the popular thing it was, its close identification with the people's movement would have been weakened, and it, perhaps, would not so readily have melted again into the mass of the nation at the close of the war.

On the 29th of April I was ordered by McClellan to proceed next morning to Camp Dennison, near Cincinnati, where he had fixed the site for a permanent camp of instruction. I took with me one full regiment and half of another. The day was a fair one, and when about noon our railway train reached the camping ground, it seemed an excellent place for our work. The drawback was that the land was planted in wheat and corn, instead of being meadow or pasture land. Captain Rosecrans (later the well-known general) met us as McClellan's engineer officer, coming from Cincinnati with a train-load of lumber. With his compass and chain, and by the help of a small detail of men, he soon laid off the two regimental camps, and the general lines of the whole encampment for a dozen regiments. The men of the regiments shouldered the pine boards, and carried them up to the lines of the company streets which were close to the hills skirting the valley, and which opened into the parade and drill ground along the railway. Vigorous work housed all the men before night, and it was well that it did so, for the weather changed in the evening, a cold rain came on, and the next morning was a chill and dreary one. My own headquarters were in a little brick school-house of one story, and with a single aide (my only staff-officer) we bestowed ourselves for the night in the little spaces between the pupils' desks and the teacher's pulpit. The windy, cheerless night was a long one, but gave place at last to a fickle, changeable day of drifting showers and occasional sunshine, and we were roused by our first reveille in camp. A breakfast was made from some cooked provisions brought with us, and we resumed the duty of organizing and instructing the camp. With the vigorous outdoor life and the full physical and mental employment, the depression which had weighed upon me since the news of the guns at Sumter passed away, never to return.

New battalions arrived from day to day, the cantonments were built by themselves, like the first, and the business of instruction and drill was systematized. The men were not yet armed, so there was no temptation to begin too soon with the manual of the musket, and they were kept industriously employed in marching in single line, by file, in changing direction, in forming column of fours from double line, etc., before their guns were put into their hands. Each regiment was treated as a separate camp with its own chain of sentinels, and the officers of the guard were constantly busy inspecting the sentinels on post and teaching guard and picket duty theoretically to the reliefs off duty. Schools were established in each regiment for field and staff as well as for company officers, and Hardee's "Tactics" was in the hands of everybody who could procure a copy. One of the proofs of the unprecedented scale of our war preparation is found in the fact that the supply of the authorized "Tactics" was soon exhausted, making it difficult to get the means of instruction in the company schools. The arriving regiments sometimes had their first taste of camp life under circumstances well calculated to dampen their ardor. The 4th Ohio, under Colonel Lorin Andrews, president of Kenyon College, came just before a thunder-storm one evening, and the bivouac that night was as rough a one as his men were likely to experience for many a day. They made shelter by placing boards from the fence-tops to the ground, but the fields were level and soon became a mire under the pouring rain, so that they were a queer-looking lot when they crawled out in the morning. The sun was then shining bright, however, and they had better cover for their heads by the next night. The 7th Ohio, which was recruited in Cleveland and on the "Western Reserve," sent a party in advance to build some of their huts, and though they too came in a rain-storm, they were less uncomfortable than some of the others. In the course of a fortnight all the regiments of the Ohio contingent were in the camp, except the two that had been hurried to Washington. They were organized into three brigades. The brigadiers, besides myself, were Generals J. H. Bates and Newton Schleich. General Bates, who was the senior, and as such assumed command of the camp in McClellan's absence, was a graduate of West Point who had served some years in the regular army, but had resigned and adopted the profession of law. General Schleich was a Democratic senator, who had been in the State militia, and had been one of the drill-masters of the Legislative Squad, which had drilled upon the Capitol terrace. McClellan had intended to make his own headquarters in the camp; but the convenience of attending to official business in Cincinnati kept him in the city. His purpose was to make the brigade organizations permanent, and to take them as a division to the field when they were a little prepared for the work. Like many other good plans, it failed to be carried out. I was the only one of the brigadiers who remained in the service after the first enlistment for ninety days, and it was my fate to take the field with new regiments, only one of which had been in my brigade in camp. After General Bates's arrival my own hut was built on the slope of the hillside behind my brigade, close under the wooded ridge, and here for the next six weeks was my home. The morning brought its hour of business correspondence relating to the command; then came the drill, when the parade ground was full of marching companies and squads. Officers' drill followed, with sword exercise and pistol practice, and the evening was allotted to schools of theoretic tactics, outpost duty, and the like.

The first fortnight in camp was the hardest for the troops. The plowed fields became deep with mud which nothing could remove till steady good weather should allow them to be packed hard under the continued tramp of thousands of men. The organization of camp-kitchens had to be learned by the hardest experience also, and the men who had some aptitude for cooking had to be found by a slow process of natural selection, during which many an unpalatable meal had to be eaten. A disagreeable bit of information soon came to us in the proof that more than half the men had never had the contagious diseases of infancy. The measles broke out, and we had to organize a camp-hospital at once. A large barn near by was taken for this purpose, and the surgeons had their hands full of cases, which, however trivial they might seem at home, were here aggravated into dangerous illness by the unwonted surroundings, and the impossibility of securing the needed protection from exposure. The good women of Cincinnati took promptly in hand the task of providing nurses for the sick and proper diet and delicacies for hospital use. The Sisters of Charity, under the lead of Sister Anthony, a noble woman, came out in force, and their black and white robes harmonized picturesquely with the military surroundings, as they flitted about under the rough timber framing of the old barn, carrying comfort and hope from one rude couch to another.

As to supplies, hardly a man in a regiment knew how to make out a requisition for rations or for clothing, and, easy as it is to rail at "red-tape," the necessity of keeping a check upon embezzlement and wastefulness justified the staff-bureaus at Washington in insisting upon regular vouchers to support the quartermasters' and commissaries' accounts. But here, too, men were gradually found who had special talent for the work. Where everybody had to learn a new business, it would have been miraculous if grave errors had not frequently occurred. Looking back at it, the wonder is that the blunders and mishaps had not been tenfold more numerous than they were.

By the middle of May the confusion had given way to reasonable system, but we now were obliged to meet the embarrassments of reorganization for three years, under the President's second call for troops (May 3d). In every company some discontented spirits wanted to go home, and, to avoid the odium of going alone, they became mischief-makers, seeking to prevent the whole company from reënlisting. The growing discipline was relaxed or lost in the solicitations, the electioneering, the speech-making, and the other common arts of persuasion. In spite of all these discouragements, however, the daily drills and instruction went on with some approach to regularity, and our raw volunteers began to look more like soldiers. Captain Gordon Granger, of the regular army, came to muster the reënlisted regiments into the three-years service, and as he stood at the right of the 4th Ohio, looking down the line of a thousand stalwart men, all in their Garibaldi shirts (for we had not yet got our uniforms), he turned to me and exclaimed, "My God! that such men should be food for powder!" It certainly was a display of manliness and intelligence such as had hardly ever been seen in the ranks of an army. There were in camp at that time, three if not four companies in different regiments that were wholly made up of under-graduates of colleges, who had enlisted together, their officers being their tutors and professors. And where there was not so striking evidence as this of the enlistment of the best of our youth, every company

MAJOR-GENERAL GORDON GRANGER.
FROM A PHOTOGRAPH.

could still show that it was largely recruited from the best nurtured and most promising young men of the community.

Granger had been in the South-west when the secession movement began, and had seen the formation of military companies everywhere, and the incessant drilling which had been going on all winter; while we, in a strange condition of political paralysis, had been doing nothing. His information was eagerly sought by us all, and he lost no opportunity of impressing upon us the fact that the South was nearly six months ahead of us in organization and preparation. He did not conceal his belief that we were likely to find the war a much longer and more serious piece of business than was commonly expected, and that, unless we pushed hard our drilling and instruction, we should find ourselves at a disadvantage in our earlier encounters. What he said had a good effect in making officers and men take more willingly to the laborious routine of the parade ground and the regimental school; for such opinions as his soon ran through a camp, and they were commented upon by the enlisted men quite as earnestly as among the officers. Still, hope kept the upper hand, and I believe that three-fourths of us still cherished the belief that a single campaign would end the war.

Though most of our men were native Ohioans, we had in camp two regiments made up of other material. The 9th Ohio was recruited from the Germans of Cincinnati, and was commanded by Colonel Robert McCook. In camp, the drilling of the regiment fell almost completely into the hands of the adjutant, Lieutenant August Willich (afterward a general of division), and McCook, who humorously exaggerated his own lack of military knowledge, used to say that he was only "clerk for a thousand Dutchmen," so completely did the care of equipping and providing for his regiment engross his time and labor. The 10th

CAMP DENNISON, NEAR CINCINNATI.

Ohio was an Irish regiment, also from Cincinnati, and its men were proud to call themselves the "Bloody Tinth." The brilliant Lytle was its commander, and his control over them, even in the beginning of their service and near the city of their home, showed that they had fallen into competent hands. It happened, of course, that the guard-house pretty frequently contained representatives of the 10th, who, on the short furloughs that were allowed them, took a parting glass too many with their friends in the city, and came to camp boisterously drunk. But the men of the regiment got it into their heads that the 13th, which lay just opposite them across the railroad, took a malicious pleasure in filling the guard-house with the Irishmen. Some threats had been made that they would go over and "clean out" the 13th, and one fine evening these came to a head. I suddenly got orders from General Bates to form my brigade and march them at once between the 10th and 13th to prevent a collision that seemed imminent. The long-roll was beaten as if the drummers realized the full importance of the first opportunity to sound that warlike signal. We marched by the moon-light into the space between the belligerent regiments; but Lytle already had got his own men under control, and the less mercurial 13th were not disposed to be aggressive, so that we were soon dismissed, with a compliment for our promptness.

The six weeks of our stay in Camp Dennison seem like months in the retrospect, so full were they crowded with new experiences. The change came in an unexpected way. The initiative taken by the Confederates in West Virginia had to be met by prompt action, and McClellan was forced to drop his own plans and meet the exigency. The organization and equipment of the regiments for the three-years service was still incomplete, and the brigades were broken up, to take across the Ohio the regiments best prepared to go. This was discouraging to a brigade commander, for, even with veteran troops, acquaintanceship between the officer and his command is a necessary condition of confidence and a most important element of strength. My own assignment to the Great Kanawha district was one I had every reason to be content with, except that for several months I felt the disadvantage I suffered from having command of troops which I had never seen till we met in the field.

CHAPTER 4

The Confederate Government at Montgomery.

R. Barnwell Rhett

EDITOR OF THE CHARLESTON "MERCURY," 1860–62.

Twenty-six years have passed since the delegates of six States of the South that had seceded from the Union met in a convention or Provisional Congress, at the Capitol, at Montgomery, Alabama. Twenty-one years have elapsed since the close of the war between the States of the North and the eleven States of the South that entered the Confederate Government then and there organized. Most of the men who participated in the deliberations of that convention are dead, and the few now left will before long be laid away. Of the debates of that body there is no record, and the proceedings in secret session have never been published. In Washington the proceedings of the Congress of the United States were open, and at the North there was an intelligent, well-informed, powerful public opinion throughout the war. Not so at the South. Secret sessions were commenced at Montgomery, and at Richmond almost all important business was transacted away from the knowledge and thus beyond the criticism of the people. Latterly, accounts of the battles fought have been written from every standpoint; but of the course and policy of the Confederate Government, which held in its hands all the resources of the Southern people, and directed their affairs, diplomatic, financial, naval, and military, little has been said. During the war scarcely anything was known except results, and when the war terminated, the people of the South, though greatly dissatisfied, were generally as ignorant of the management of Confederate affairs as the people of the North. The arrest and long imprisonment of the President of the Confederacy made of him a representative martyr, and silenced the voice of criticism at the South. And up to this time little has been done to point out the causes of the events which occurred, or to develop the truth of history in this direction. It very well suits men at the South who opposed secession to compliment their own sagacity by assuming that the end was inevitable. Nor do men identified with the

VIEW OF MONTGOMERY, ALABAMA, SHOWING THE
STATE CAPITOL. FROM A SKETCH MADE IN 1861.

Confederacy by office, or feeling obligation for its appreciation of their personal merits, find it hard to persuade themselves that all was done that could be done in "the lost cause." And, in general, it may be an agreeable sop to Southern pride to take for granted that superior numbers alone effected the result. Yet, in the great wars of the world, nothing is so little proved as that the more numerous always and necessarily prevail. On the contrary, the facts of history show that brains have ever been more potent than brawn. The career of the Confederate States exhibits no exception to this rule. Eliminate the good sense and unselfish earnestness of Mr. Lincoln, and the great ability and practical energy of Seward and Adams, and of Stanton and Chase from the control of the affairs of the United States; conceive a management of third-rate and incompetent men in their places—will any one doubt that matters would have ended differently? To many it may be unpalatable to hear that at the South all was not done that might have been done and that cardinal blunders were made. But what is pleasing is not always true, and there can be no good excuse now for suppressing important facts or perverting history. The time has come when public attention may with propriety be directed to the realities of that momentous period at the South.

On the 20th of December, 1860, South Carolina passed unanimously the first ordinance of secession, in these words:

ALEXANDER H. STEPHENS,
VICE-PRESIDENT OF THE CONFEDERACY.
FROM A PHOTOGRAPH.

"We, the people of the State of South Carolina in convention assembled, do declare and ordain, and it is hereby declared and ordained, that the ordinance adopted by us in convention on the twenty-third day of May, in the year of our Lord one thousand seven hundred and eighty-eight, whereby the Constitution of the United States of America was ratified, and also, all Acts and parts of Acts of the General Assembly of this State, ratifying amendments of the said Constitution, are hereby repealed; and that the Union now subsisting between South Carolina and other States, under the name of 'the United States of America,' is hereby dissolved."

On her invitation, six other Southern States sent delegates to a convention in Montgomery, Alabama, for the purpose of organizing a Confederacy. On the 4th of February, 1861, this convention assembled. The material which constituted it was of a mixed character. There were members who were constitutionally timid and unfit by character and temperament to participate in such work as was on hand. Others had little knowledge of public affairs on a large scale, and had studied neither the resources of the South nor the conduct of the movement. A number of them, however, were men of ripe experience and statesmanlike grasp of the situation—men of large knowledge, with calm, strong, clear views of the policies to be pursued. Alexander H. Stephens characterized this convention as "the ablest body with which he ever served, and singularly free from revolutionary spirit."[‡]

In the organization of the convention, Howell Cobb was chosen to preside,

‡The deputies elected to meet at the Montgomery convention were: SOUTH CAROLINA, R. Barnwell Rhett, Lawrence M. Keitt, C. G. Memminger, Thomas J. Withers, Robert W. Barnwell, James Chesnut, Jr., W. Porcher Miles, and William W. Boyce; FLORIDA, Jackson Morton, James B. Owens, and J. Patton Anderson; MISSISSIPPI, Wiley P. Harris, W. S. Wilson, Walker Brooke, Alexander M. Clayton, James T. Harrison, William S. Barry, and J.A.P. Campbell; ALABAMA, Richard W. Walker, Colin J. McRae, William P. Chilton, David P. Lewis, Robert H. Smith, John Gill Shorter, Stephen F. Hale, Thomas Fearn, and Jabez L. M. Curry; GEORGIA, Robert Toombs, Martin J. Crawford, Benjamin H. Hill, Augustus R. Wright, Augustus H. Kenan, Francis S. Bartow, Engenius A. Nisbet, Howell Cobb, Thomas R. R. Cobb, and Alexander H. Stephens; LOUISIANA, John Perkins, Jr., Charles M. Conrad, Edward Sparrow, Alexander De Clonet, Duncan F. Kenner, and Henry Marshall. The Texas delegates were not appointed until February 14th.

These delegates had been appointed by the conventions of their respective States on the ground that the people had intrusted the State conventions with unlimited powers. They constituted both the convention that organized the Confederacy and its Provisional Congress. On the 8th of February the Provisional Constitution was adopted, to be in force one year. On the 9th was passed the first enactment, providing "That all the laws of the United States of America in force and in use in the Confederate States of America on the first day of November last, and not inconsistent with the Constitution of the Confederate States, be and the same are hereby continued in force until altered or repealed by the Congress." The next act, adopted February 14th, continued in office until April 1st all officers connected with the collection of customs, and the assistant treasurers, with the same powers and functions as under the Government of the United States. An act of the 25th of February declared the peaceful navigation of the Mississippi River free to the citizens of any of the States upon its borders, or upon the borders of its navigable tributaries. On the 25th of February a commission to the Government of the United States,

ROBERT TOOMBS, FIRST SECRETARY
OF STATE OF THE CONFEDERACY;
MEMBER OF THE CONFEDERATE SENATE;
BRIGADIER-GENERAL, C.S.A.
FROM A PHOTOGRAPH.

and J. J. Hooper, of Montgomery, to act as secretary. It was decided to organize a provisional government under a provisional constitution, which was adopted on the 8th of February. On the 9th a provisional President and Vice-President were elected, who were installed in office on the 18th to carry the government into effect. In regard to this election, it was agreed that when four delegations out of the six should settle upon men, the election should take place. Jefferson Davis was put forward by the Mississippi delegation and Howell Cobb by that of Georgia. The Florida delegation proposed to vote for whomsoever South Carolina should support. The South Carolina delegation offered no candidate and held no meeting to confer upon the matter. The chairman, Mr. R. Barnwell Rhett,⊕ did not call them together. Mr. Barnwell, however, was an active supporter of Mr. Davis, and it was afterward said that while in Washington in December, as a commissioner to treat for the evacuation of Fort Sumter, he had committed himself to Mr. Davis. At any rate, he was zealous. Colonel Keitt afterward stated to the writer and others in Charleston that a majority of the delegation were opposed to Mr. Davis, but that, not having compared opinions, they did not understand one another, and that Mr. Davis received the vote of

---

for the purpose of negotiating friendly relations and for the settlement of all questions of disagreement between the two governments, was appointed and confirmed. The commissioners were A. B. Roman, of Louisiana, Martin J. Crawford, of Georgia, and John Forsyth, of Alabama. An act of February 26th provided for the repeal of all laws which forbade the employment in the coasting trade of vessels not enrolled or licensed, and all laws imposing discriminating duties on foreign vessels or goods imported in them. This Provisional Congress of one House held four sessions, as follows: I. February 4th–March 16th, 1861; II. April 20th–May 22d, 1861; III. July 20th–August 22d, 1861; IV. November 18th, 1861–February 17th, 1862; the first and second of these at Montgomery, the third and fourth at Richmond, whither the Executive Department was removed late in May, 1861,—because of "the hostile demonstrations of the United States Government against Virginia," as Mr. Davis says in his "Rise and Fall of the Confederate Government."—EDITORS.

⊕Father of the writer.—EDITORS.

South Carolina, and was elected, by the casting vote of Mr. Rhett. Personally Mr. Rhett knew little of Mr. Davis. He regarded him as an accomplished man, but egotistical, arrogant, and vindictive, without depth or statesmanship. Besides this, he judged him not sufficiently in accord with the movement to lead it. His speech on the 4th of July, 1858, between New York and Boston, was reported as denunciatory of secessionists, and as comparing them to "mosquitoes around the horns of an ox, who could annoy, but could do no harm." The strong Union sentiments uttered in his New England electioneering tour, which secured to him the vote of B. F. Butler and others at the Democratic convention at Charleston, in 1860, were confirmatory of the newspaper report. As late as November 10th, 1860, after the South Carolina convention was called, Mr. Davis had written a letter, within the cognizance of Mr. Rhett, and published by himself since the war, in which he unmistakably indicated the opinion that, if South Carolina seceded, neither Georgia, nor Alabama, nor Mississippi, nor Louisiana, nor any other State would secede unless the United States Government should attempt to coerce South Carolina back into the Union, or to blockade her ports. His expectation, at that late period, apparently was that South Carolina would be left out of the Union alone, and that the United States Government would simply collect duties off the bars of her seaports; and he expressed himself "in favor of seeking to bring those [the planting States] into coöperation before asking for a popular decision upon a new policy and relation to the nations of the earth." These views did not strengthen him with Mr. Rhett for the executive head of the Southern Confederacy; nor did the published report of his shedding tears on retiring from the United States Senate after the secession of Mississippi. But Mr. Rhett's contemporary and second cousin, Mr. Barnwell, called three times to solicit his vote for Mr. Davis. The impression was produced upon his mind that he, Mr. Rhett, was the only man in the delegation opposed to Mr. Davis. In reply to objections suggested by Mr. Rhett, Mr. Barnwell said that Mr. Rhett's standard of the statesmanship requisite was higher than he might be able to get. He added that he knew Mr. Davis, and although he considered him not a man of great ability, yet he believed him just and honorable, and

LEROY POPE WALKER, FIRST
CONFEDERATE SECRETARY OF WAR.
FROM A PHOTOGRAPH.

ROBERT BARNWELL RHETT, CHAIRMAN
OF COMMITTEE ON FOREIGN AFFAIRS,
CONFEDERATE PROVISIONAL CONGRESS.
FROM A PHOTOGRAPH.

that he would utilize the best ability of the country, as Monroe and Polk and others had done, and would administer the powers intrusted to him as President, with an eye single to the interests of the Confederacy. Upon this presentment Mr. Rhett concluded to forego his own mistrust, and to give his vote for Mr. Davis, along with the rest, as he supposed. On taking the vote in the convention (February 9th) Georgia gave hers to Mr. Cobb, and the other States theirs to Mr. Davis. Georgia then changed her vote, which elected Mr. Davis unanimously. Mr. Alexander H. Stephens was chosen Vice-President.✦ Mr. Rhett was made chairman of the committee to notify the President-elect, and to present him to the convention for inauguration. This office he performed in complimentary style, reflecting the estimate of Mr. Barnwell rather than his own fears. Within six weeks the Provisional Congress found out that they had made a mistake, and that there was danger of a division into an administration and an anti-administration party, which might paralyze the Government. To avoid this, and to confer all power on the President, they resorted to secret sessions.

Mr. Davis offered the office of Secretary of State to Mr. Barnwell, but he declined it, and recommended Mr. C. G. Memminger, also of South Carolina, for the Treasury portfolio, which was promptly accorded to him. Both of these gentlemen had been coöperationists, and up to the last had opposed secession. Mr. Barnwell would not have been sent to the State convention from Beaufort but for the efforts of Edmund Rhett, an influential State senator. Of Mr. Memminger it was said that when a bill was on its passage through the Legislature of South Carolina in 1859, appropriating a sum of money for the purchase of arms, he had slipped in an amendment which had operated to prevent Governor Gist from drawing the money and procuring the arms. In Charleston he was known as an active friend of the free-school system and orphan house, a moral and charitable Episcopalian, and a lawyer, industrious, shrewd, and thrifty. As

---

✦The choice was provisional only, but was made permanent on the 6th of November, 1861, when Mr. Davis and Mr. Stephens were unanimously elected for six years. The Confederate Constitution made them ineligible to reëlection.—EDITORS.

chairman of the Committee on Ways and Means in the House of Representatives, he was familiar with the cut-and-dried plan of raising the small revenue necessary to carry on the government of South Carolina. Such was his record and experience when appointed to the cabinet of Mr. Davis. Mr. Memminger received no recommendation for this office from the South Carolina delegation; nor did the delegation from any State, so far as known, attempt to influence the President in the choice of his cabinet.

Mr. Robert Toombs, of Georgia, was appointed Secretary of State. This was in deference to the importance of his State and the public appreciation of his great mental powers and thorough earnestness, not for the active part he had taken in the State convention in behalf of secession. In public too fond of sensational oratory, in counsel he was a man of large and wise views.

Mr. Leroy Pope Walker, of Alabama, was appointed Secretary of War on the recommendation of Mr. William L. Yancey. Ambitious, without any special fitness for this post, and overloaded, he accepted the office with the understanding that Mr. Davis would direct and control its business, which he did. After differing with the President as to the number of arms to be imported, and the number of men to be placed in camp in the winter of 1861–62 (being in favor of very many more than the President), he wisely resigned.

Mr. Stephen R. Mallory, of Florida, was appointed Secretary of the Navy. He was a gentleman of unpretending manners and ordinary good sense, who had served in the Senate with Mr. Davis, and had been chairman of the Committee on Naval Affairs. With some acquaintance with officers of the United States Navy, and some knowledge of nautical matters, he had small comprehension of the responsibilities of the office. His efforts were feeble and dilatory, and he utterly failed to provide for keeping open the seaports of the Confederacy. But he was one of the few who remained in the cabinet to the end.

Mr. Judah P. Benjamin, of Louisiana, was appointed Attorney-General, and held that office until the resignation of Mr. Walker, when he was transferred to the post of Secretary of War. Upon the fall of New Orleans, public indignation compelled a change, and he was made Secretary of

HOWELL COBB, PRESIDENT OF THE
FIRST CONFEDERATE CONGRESS;
MAJOR-GENERAL, C.S.A.
FROM A PHOTOGRAPH.

STEPHEN R. MALLORY, SECRETARY
OF THE NAVY TO THE CONFEDERACY.
FROM A PHOTOGRAPH.

State. A man of great fertility of mind and resource and of facile character, he was the factotum of the President, performed his bidding in various ways, and gave him the benefit of his brains in furtherance of the views of Mr. Davis.[1]

Although a provisional government was more free to meet emergencies and correct mistakes, it was determined to proceed to the formation of a permanent government. It was apprehended that in the lapse of time and change of circumstances and of men, the cardinal points for which the South had contended, and on which the separation of sections had occurred, might be lost sight of; so it was decided to impress at once upon the new government the constitutional amendments regarded as essential. The committee, of which Mr. Rhett was chairman, agreed at its first meeting that the Constitution of the United States should be adopted, with

---

[1]Mr. Davis's reasons for the selection of the members of the first Cabinet are given in his "Rise and Fall of the Confederate Government" (New York: D. Appleton & Co., 1881), Vol. I., pp. 241–3, in these words:

"After being inaugurated, I proceeded to the formation of my Cabinet, that is, the heads of the executive departments authorized by the laws of the Provisional Congress. The unanimity existing among our people made this a much easier and more agreeable task than where the rivalries in the party of an executive have to be consulted and accommodated, often at the expense of the highest capacity and fitness. Unencumbered by any other consideration than the public welfare, having no friends to reward or enemies to punish, it resulted that not one of those who formed my first Cabinet had borne to me the relation of close personal friendship, or had political claims upon me; indeed, with two of them I had no previous acquaintance.

"It was my wish that the Hon. Robert W. Barnwell, of South Carolina, should be Secretary of State. I had known him intimately during a trying period of our joint service in the United States Senate, and he had won alike my esteem and regard. Before making known to him my wish in this connection, the delegation of South Carolina, of which he was a member, had resolved to recommend one of their number to be Secretary of the Treasury, and Mr. Barnwell, with characteristic delicacy, declined to accept my offer to him.

"I had intended to offer the Treasury Department to Mr. Toombs, of Georgia, whose knowledge on subjects of finance had particularly attracted my notice when we served together in the United States Senate. Mr. Barnwell having declined the State Department, and a colleague of his, said to be peculiarly qualified for the Treasury Department, having been recommended for it, Mr. Toombs was offered the State Department, for which others believed him to be well qualified.

only such alterations as experience had proved desirable, and to avoid latitudinarian constructions. Most of the important amendments were adopted on motion of the chairman. But the limits of this paper do not permit a specific statement of their character and scope. /

The permanent constitution was adopted on the 11th of March, 1861, and went into operation, with the permanent government, at Richmond, on the 18th of February, 1862, when the Provisional Congress expired.

Those men who had studied the situation felt great anxiety about the keeping open of the ports of the Confederacy. Much was said and published about the immediate necessity of providing gun-boats and shipping suitable for that purpose. In the winter of 1861 Mr. C. K. Prioleau, of the firm of John Fraser & Co., of Liverpool, found a fleet of ten first-class East Indiamen, available to a buyer at less than half their cost. They belonged to the East India Company, and had been built in Great Britain for armament if required, or for moving troops and carrying valuable cargoes and treasure. Four of them were vessels of great size and power and of the very first class; and there were six others, which, although smaller, were scarcely inferior for the required purpose. On surrendering their powers to the British throne, the company had these steamships for sale. Mr. Prioleau secured the refusal of this fleet. The total cost of buying, arming, and fitting out the ten ships and putting them on the Southern coast ready for action was estimated at $10,000,000, or, say, 40,000 bales of cotton. The harbor of Port Royal, selected before the war as a coaling station for the United

---

"Mr. Mallory, of Florida, had been chairman of the Committee on Naval Affairs in the United States Senate, was extensively acquainted with the officers of the navy, and for a landsman had much knowledge of nautical affairs; therefore he was selected for Secretary of the Navy.

"Mr. Benjamin, of Louisiana, had a very high reputation as a lawyer, and my acquaintance with him in the Senate had impressed me with the lucidity of his intellect, his systematic habits and capacity for labor. He was therefore invited to the post of Attorney-General.

"Mr. Reagan, of Texas, I had known for a sturdy, honest Representative in the United States Congress, and his acquaintance with the territory included in the Confederate States was both extensive and accurate. These, together with his industry and ability to labor, indicated him as peculiarly fit for the office of Postmaster-General.

"Mr. Memminger, of South Carolina, had a high reputation for knowledge of finance. He bore an unimpeachable character for integrity and close attention to duties, and, on the recommendation of the delegation from South Carolina, he was appointed Secretary of the Treasury, and proved himself entirely worthy of the trust.

"Mr. Walker, of Alabama, was a distinguished member of the bar of north Alabama, and was eminent among the politicians of that section. He was earnestly recommended by gentlemen intimately and favorably known to me, and was therefore selected for the War Department. His was the only name presented from Alabama."—EDITORS.

/One of them, offered by Mr. Rhett, and unanimously adopted, relates to civil-service reform, and is in the following words:

"The principal officer in each of the executive departments, and all persons connected with the diplomatic service, may be removed from office at the pleasure of the President. All

JUDAH P. BENJAMIN, CONFEDERATE
ATTORNEY-GENERAL UNTIL
SEPT. 17TH, 1861; SECOND SECRETARY
OF WAR; THIRD SECRETARY OF STATE.
FROM A PHOTOGRAPH.

States Navy, with 26 feet of water at mean low tide, was admirably adapted for a rendezvous and point of supply. Brunswick, Georgia, was another good harbor, fit for such a fleet. The proposal was submitted to the Government through a partner of Mr. Prioleau in Charleston, Mr. George A. Trenholm, who forwarded the proposition by his son, William L. Trenholm. Its importance was not at all comprehended, and it was rejected by the executive. Captain J. D. Bulloch, the secret naval agent in Europe, who had the *Alabama* built, states that "the Confederate Government wanted ships to cruise and to destroy the enemy's mercantile marine." It was of infinitely more importance to keep Southern ports open, but this does not seem to have been understood until too late. The opportunity of obtaining these ships was thrown away. They were engaged by the British Government.

To show the narrow spirit of those in office, an incident concerning Captain Maffit, who figured afterward in command of the *Florida,* may be mentioned. In May, after the reduction of Fort Sumter, Maffit came from Washington to offer his services, and when he met the writer was in a state of indignation and disgust. He said that after having been caressed and offered a command in the Pacific, he had sneaked away from Washington to join the Confederacy, and that he had been received by the Secretary of the Navy as if he (Maffit) had designs upon him.

The Secretary of War has stated that before the Government moved from Montgomery 360,000 men, the flower of the South, had tendered their services in the army. Only a small fraction of the number were received. The Secretary was worn out with personal applications of ardent officers, and himself stated that in May, 1861, he was constantly waylaid, in walking the back way from his

other civil officers of the executive department may be removed at any time by the President or other appointing power, when their services are unnecessary, or for dishonesty, incapacity, inefficiency, misconduct, or neglect of duty; and when so removed, the removal shall be reported to the Senate, together with the reasons therefor."

—R.B.R.

office to the Exchange Hotel, by men offering their lives in the Confederate cause.

Another instance of narrowness may be named in the case of William Cutting Heyward. He was a wealthy rice-planter and an eminently practical and efficient man, a graduate at West Point in the class with Mr. Davis. He went to Montgomery to tender a regiment. He sent in his card to the President and waited for days in the lobby without obtaining an interview, and then returned home. He finally died from exposure, performing the duties of a private in the Home Guard at Charleston. The reason alleged for not accepting more men was the want of arms, and Mr. Davis's book is an

CHRISTOPHER G. MEMMINGER,
FIRST SECRETARY OF THE TREASURY
OF THE CONFEDERACY.

apology for not procuring them. Insisting that a great war was probable, and inaugurated on the 18th of February,—there was no declaration of war before the middle of April and no efficient blockade of the ports for many months,—yet it was in May that he started Major Huse over to England with instructions to purchase 10,000 Enfield rifles! By these facts may be gauged his estimate of the emergency or of the purchasing ability of the Confederate States. The provisional constitution provided that "Congress shall appropriate no money from the Treasury unless it be asked and estimated for by the President or some one of the heads of departments, except for the purpose of paying its own expenses and contingencies." The Congress could, therefore, do nothing about the purchase of arms without a call from the executive.

But for the Treaty of Paris in 1778, made by Benjamin Franklin, Silas Deane, and Arthur Lee, with France, the independence of the thirteen original States would not have been established. It was deemed important in the Provisional Congress of the Confederate States to send commissioners abroad to negotiate for a recognition of their independence, and, in case of war with the States of the North, perhaps for assistance. The chairman of the Committee on Foreign Affairs, Mr. Rhett, reported such a resolution, which was unanimously adopted. As the treaty-making power of the Government belonged to the President, Congress could not dictate to him the limit of authority that should be conferred upon the commissioners, in the negotiations desired. But all those who had reflected upon the subject expected the President to give extensive authority for making treaties. The views held by the chairman were that the commissioners should be authorized to propose to Great Britain, France, and other European nations, upon the conditions of recognition and alliance, that the Confederate States for twenty years would agree to lay no higher duties on productions imported than fifteen or twenty per cent. *ad valorem;* that for this period, no tonnage duties would be laid on their shipping, entering or leaving Confederate ports, but such as should be imposed to keep in order the harbors and rivers; that the navigation between the ports of the Confederate States for the same time should be free to the nations entering into alliance with the Confederate States, while upon the productions and tonnage of all nations refusing to recognize their independence and enter into treaty with them, a discriminating duty of ten per cent. would be imposed. He believed, moreover, that they should be authorized to make an offensive and defensive league, with special guarantees, as was done in 1778. Here was a direct and powerful appeal to the interests of foreign nations, especially England. Would any British Minister have dared to reject a treaty offering such vast advantages to his country? And if so, when the fact became known to Parliament, could he have retained his place?

Up to September, 1862, the United States Government was committed, both by diplomatic dispatches and by the action of Congress, to the declaration that the war was made solely to preserve the Union and with the purpose of maintaining the institutions of the seceded States, unimpaired and unaltered. Hence, at this period, the issue of slavery had not been injected into diplomacy, and was no obstacle to negotiating treaties.

When Mr. Yancey received the appointment at the head of the commission, Mr. Rhett conferred with him at length, and found that the commissioner fully concurred in the views just mentioned. But he surprised Mr. Rhett by the statement that the President had given no powers whatever to make commercial treaties, or to give any special interest in Confederate trade or navigation to any foreign nations, but relied upon the idea that "Cotton is King." "Then," rejoined Mr. Rhett, "if you will take my advice, as your friend, do not accept the appointment. For you will have nothing to propose and nothing to treat about, and must necessarily fail. Demand of the President the powers essential to the success of your mission, or stay at home."

On the reassembling of the Provisional Congress in April, ascertaining that these powers had not been conferred upon the commission, Mr. Rhett prepared a resolution requesting the President to empower the commissioners to propose to European nations, as the basis of a commercial treaty, a tariff of duties for 20 years no higher than 20 per cent. *ad valorem* on their imports into the Confederate States. This he submitted to Mr. Toombs, the Secretary of State, who promptly approved it and appeared before the Committee on Foreign Affairs to urge it. It was reported, with the indorsement of the committee, to the

Congress, and was not opposed in debate; but Mr. Perkins moved, as an amendment, six years instead of twenty. As this was carried, Mr. Rhett moved to lay the resolution on the table, which was done; and this was the only effort made to appeal to the interests of foreign nations, to secure recognition of the independence of the Confederate States, or to obtain assistance. Upon his return from abroad, Mr. Yancey met Mr. Rhett and said: "You were right, sir. I went on a fool's errand." In December, 1863, at Richmond, James L. Orr, chairman of the Committee on Foreign Affairs of the Senate, said to the writer, "The Confederate States have had no diplomacy."

In March, 1863, proposals were made for a loan of $15,000,000 on 7 per cent. bonds, secured by an engagement of the Confederate Government to deliver cotton at 12 cents per pound within 6 months after peace. The loan stood in the London market at 5 per cent. premium; and the applications for it exceeded $75,000,000. In the Provisional Congress at Montgomery, Mr. Stephens proposed that the Confederate Government should purchase cotton at 8 cents per pound, paying in 8 per cent. bonds, running 20 or 30 years. He believed that 2,000,000 bales of the crop of 1860 could be obtained in that way from the planters, and that, of the crop of 1861, 2,000,000 more bales might be obtained afterward. By using this cotton as security, or shipping it abroad, he maintained the finances of the Confederate States could at once be placed on a solid basis. His plan met with much favor, but was opposed by the administration and was not carried through. Money for the long war was to be raised by loans from Confederate citizens on bonds supplemented by the issue of Treasury notes and by a duty on exported cotton.

In April, 1865, after the collapse of the Confederacy, Mr. Barnwell, who had steadfastly supported Mr. Davis in the Confederate Senate, met the writer at Greenville, S.C., where Governor Magrath had summoned the Legislature of the State to assemble. There, in conversation, Mr. Barnwell explicitly expressed his judgment in the following words: "Mr. Davis never had any policy; he drifted, from the beginning to the end of the war."

For practical regret at the issue of the secession movement, the time has long passed by. The people of the South have reconciled themselves to the restoration of the Union and to the abolishment of slavery. They have bravely and strenuously endeavored to go through the transition period of an enormous change without wreck. In complete harmony with the destinies of the Union, they are working out the future of the United States faithfully.

This is set down to prevent the suppression of important facts in history, and in justice to eminent men, now dead, who have been much misunderstood.

CHAPTER 5

Going to the Front.

RECOLLECTIONS OF A PRIVATE.

Warren Lee Goss.

Before I reached the point of enlisting, I had read and been "enthused" by General Dix's famous "shoot him on the spot" dispatch; I had attended flag-raisings, and had heard orators declaim of "undying devotion to the Union." One speaker to whom I listened declared that "human life must be cheapened"; but I never learned that he helped on the work experimentally. When men by the hundred walked soberly to the front and signed the enlistment papers, he was not one of them. As I came out of the hall, with conflicting emotions, feeling as though I should have to go finally or forfeit my birthright as an American citizen, one of the orators who stood at the door, glowing with enthusiasm and patriotism, and shaking hands effusively with those who enlisted, said to me:

"Did you enlist?" "No," I said. "Did you?"

"No; they won't take me. I have got a lame leg and a widowed mother to take care of."

I remember another enthusiast who was eager to enlist others. He declared that the family of no man who went to the front should suffer. After the war he was prominent among those who at town-meeting voted to refund the money to such as had expended it to procure substitutes. He has, moreover, been fierce and uncompromising toward the ex-Confederates since the war.

From the first I did not believe the trouble would blow over in "sixty days";‡ nor did I consider eleven dollars a month,ψ and the promised glory, large pay for the services of an able-bodied young man.

---

‡Mr. Seward, speaking in New York two days after the secession of South Carolina, said: "Sixty days' more suns will give you a much brighter and more cheerful atmosphere."

ψThe monthly pay of Union privates was: cavalry $12, artillery and infantry $11; from August 6th, 1861, $13 for all arms, and from May 1st, 1864, $16. Confederate privates received: in the cavalry and light batteries $12; in the artillery and infantry $11; increased June 9th, 1864, to $19 and $18 per month for a period of one year from that date.—Editors.

FAC-SIMILE OF THE CONCLUSION OF GENERAL DIX'S "AMERICAN FLAG" DISPATCH. ☆

It was the news that the 6th Massachusetts regiment had been mobbed by roughs on their passage through Baltimore which gave me the war fever.⁺ And yet when I read Governor John A. Andrew's instructions to have the hero martyrs "preserved in ice and tenderly sent forward," somehow, though I felt the pathos of it, I could not reconcile myself to the ice. Ice in connection with patriotism did not give me agreeable impressions of war, and when I came to think of it, the stoning of the heroic "Sixth" didn't suit me; it detracted from my desire to die a soldier's death.

☆January 18th, 1861, three days after he had entered on his duties as Secretary of the Treasury to President Buchanan, General Dix sent W. Hemphill Jones, chief clerk of one of the Treasury bureaus, to the South, for the purpose of saving the revenue-cutters at New Orleans, Mobile, and Galveston. January 29th, Mr. Jones telegraphed from New Orleans that the captain of the revenue-cutter *McClelland* refused to obey the Secretary's orders. It was seven in the evening when the dispatch was received. Immediately, Secretary Dix wrote the following reply: "Treasury Department, January 29, 1861. Tell Lieutenant Caldwell to arrest Captain Breshwood, assume command of the cutter, and obey the order I gave through you. If Captain Breshwood, after arrest, undertakes to interfere with the command of the cutter, tell Lieutenant Caldwell to consider him as a mutineer, and treat him accordingly. If any one attempts to haul down the American flag, shoot him on the spot. JOHN A. DIX, Secretary of the Treasury."—EDITORS.

⁺Concerning this encounter Colonel Edward F. Jones, of the 6th Massachusetts, says in his report:

"After leaving Philadelphia I received intimation that our passage through the city of Baltimore would be resisted. I caused ammunition to be distributed and arms loaded, and went personally through the cars, and issued the following order, viz, 'The regiment will march through Baltimore in column of sections, arms at will. You will undoubtedly be insulted, abused, and perhaps assaulted, to which you must pay no attention whatever, but march with your faces square to the front and pay no attention to the mob, even if they throw stones, bricks, or other missiles; but if you are fired upon and any one of you is hit, your officers will order you to fire. Do not fire into any promiscuous crowds, but select any man whom you may see aiming at you, and be sure you drop him.' Reaching Baltimore, horses were attached the instant that the locomotive was detached, and the cars were driven at a rapid pace across

ARRIVAL OF THE SEVENTH NEW YORK AT ANNAPOLIS, APRIL 20, 1861,
ON THE WAY TO WASHINGTON. FROM A SKETCH MADE AT THE TIME.

I lay awake all night thinking the matter over, with the "ice" and "brick-bats" before my mind. However, the fever culminated that night, and I resolved to enlist.

"Cold chills" ran up and down my back as I got out of bed after the sleepless night, and shaved, preparatory to other desperate deeds of valor. I was twenty years of age, and when anything unusual was to be done, like fighting or courting, I shaved.

---

the city. After the cars containing seven companies had reached the Washington depot the track behind them was barricaded, and the cars containing ... the following companies, viz., Company C, of Lowell, Captain Follansbee; Company D, of Lowell, Captain Hart; Company J, of Lawrence, Captain Pickering; and Company L, of Stoneham, Captain Dike, were vacated, and they proceeded but a short distance before they were furiously attacked by a shower of missiles, which came faster as they advanced. They increased their steps to double-quick, which seemed to infuriate the mob, as it evidently impressed the mob with the idea that the soldiers dared not fire or had no ammunition, and pistol-shots were numerously fired into the ranks, and one soldier fell dead. The order 'Fire' was given, and it was executed. In consequence, several of the mob fell, and the soldiers again advanced hastily. The mayor of Baltimore placed himself at the head of the column beside Captain Follansbee, and proceeded with them a short distance."

The Hon. George William Brown, then mayor of Baltimore, in his volume entitled "Baltimore and the 19th of April, 1861," thus describes the march of the soldiers after he joined the column:

"They were firing wildly, sometimes backward, over their shoulders. So rapid was the march that they could not stop to take aim. The mob, which was not very large, as it seemed to me, was pursuing with shouts and stones, and, I think, an occasional pistol-shot. The uproar was furious. I ran at once to the head of the column, some persons in the crowd shouting, 'Here comes the mayor.' I shook hands with the officer in command, Captain Follansbee, saying, as I did so, 'I am the mayor of Baltimore.' The captain greeted me cordially. I at once objected to the double-quick, which was immediately stopped. I placed myself by his side, and marched with him. He said, 'We have been attacked without provocation,' or words to that

With a nervous tremor convulsing my system, and my heart thumping like muffled drum-beats, I stood before the door of the recruiting-office, and, before turning the knob to enter, read and re-read the advertisement for recruits posted thereon, until I knew all its peculiarities. The promised chances for "travel and promotion" seemed good, and I thought I might have made a mistake in considering war so serious after all. "Chances for travel!" I must confess now, after four years of soldiering, that the "chances for travel" were no myth; but "promotion" was a little uncertain and slow.

I was in no hurry to open the door. Though determined to enlist, I was half inclined to put it off awhile; I had a fluctuation of desires; I was faint-hearted and brave; I wanted to

UNIFORM OF THE SIXTH
MASSACHUSETTS.
FROM A PHOTOGRAPH.

effect. I replied, 'You must defend yourselves.' I expected that he would face his men to the rear, and, after giving warning, would fire if necessary. But I said no more, for I immediately felt that, as mayor of the city, it was not my province to volunteer such advice. Once before in my life I had taken part in opposing a formidable riot, and had learned by experience that the safest and most humane manner of quelling a mob is to meet it at the beginning with armed resistance. The column continued its march. There was neither concert of action nor organization among the rioters. They were armed only with such stones or missiles as they could pick up, and a few pistols. My presence for a short time had some effect, but very soon the attack was renewed with greater violence. The mob grew bolder. Stones flew thick and fast. Rioters rushed at the soldiers and attempted to snatch their muskets, and at least on two occasions succeeded. With one of these muskets a soldier was killed. Men fell on both sides. A young lawyer, then and now known as a quiet citizen, seized a flag of one of the companies and nearly tore it from its staff. He was shot through the thigh, and was carried home apparently a dying man, but he survived to enter the army of the Confederacy, where he rose to the rank of captain, and he afterward returned to Baltimore, where he still lives. The soldiers fired at will. There was no firing by platoons, and I heard no order given to fire. I remember that at the corner of South street several citizens standing in a group fell, either killed or wounded. It was impossible for the troops to discriminate between the rioters and the by-standers, but the latter seemed to suffer most.... Marshal Kane, with about fifty policemen (as I then supposed, but I have since ascertained that, in fact, there were not so many), came at a run from the direction of the Camden street station, and throwing themselves in the rear of the troops, they formed a line in front of the mob, and with drawn revolvers kept it back. This was between Light and Charles streets. Marshal Kane's voice shouted, 'Keep back, men,

enlist, and yet— Here I turned the knob, and was relieved. I had been more prompt, with all my hesitation, than the officer in his duty; he wasn't in. Finally he came, and said: "What do you want, my boy?" "I want to enlist," I responded, blushing deeply with upwelling patriotism and bashfulness. Then the surgeon came to strip and examine me. In justice to myself, it must be stated that I signed the rolls without a tremor. It is common to the most of humanity, I believe, that, when confronted with actual danger, men have less fear than in its contemplation. I will, however, make one exception in favor of the first shell I heard uttering its blood-curdling hisses, as though a steam locomotive were traveling the air. With this exception I have found the actual dangers of war always less terrible face to face than on the night before the battle.

My first uniform was a bad fit: my trousers were too long by three or four inches; the flannel shirt was coarse and unpleasant, too large at the neck and too short elsewhere. The forage cap was an ungainly bag with pasteboard top and leather visor; the blouse was the only part which seemed decent; while the overcoat made me feel like a little nubbin of corn in a large preponderance of husk. Nothing except "Virginia mud" ever took down my ideas of military pomp quite so low.

After enlisting I did not seem of so much consequence as I had expected. There was not so much excitement on account of my military appearance as I deemed justly my due. I was taught my facings, and at the time I thought the drill-master needlessly fussy about shouldering, ordering, and presenting arms.

---

or I shoot!' This movement, which I saw myself, was gallantly executed, and was perfectly successful. The mob recoiled like water from a rock. One of the leading rioters, then a young man, now a peaceful merchant, tried, as he has himself told me, to pass the line, but the marshal seized him, and vowed he would shoot if the attempt was made. This nearly ended the fight, and the column passed on under the protection of the police, without serious molestation, to Camden station."

Sumner H. Needham, of Lawrence, Addison O. Whitney and Luther C. Ladd, of Lowell, and Charles A. Taylor were the killed, and thirty-six of their comrades were wounded. Twelve citizens were killed, and an unknown number were wounded. Col. Jones continues:

"As the men went into the cars I caused the blinds to the cars to be closed, and took every precaution to prevent any shadow of offense to the people of Baltimore; but still the stones flew thick and fast into the train, and it was with the utmost difficulty that I could prevent the troops from leaving the cars and revenging the death of their comrades.... On reaching Washington we were quartered at the Capitol, in the Senate Chamber."

This regiment, the 6th Massachusetts, were the first armed troops to reach Washington in response to the call of the President.

The 27th Pennsylvania Regiment (unarmed) arrived at Baltimore by the same train as the Massachusetts troops. It was attacked by a mob and obliged to remain at the President street station, from which point it was sent back the same day in the direction of Philadelphia. The same night, by order of the Board of Police Commissioners, with the concurrence of Governor Hicks and Mayor Brown, the

At this time men were often drilled in company and regimental evolutions long before they learned the manual of arms, because of the difficulty of obtaining muskets. These we obtained at an early day, but we would willingly have resigned them after carrying them for a few hours. The musket, after an hour's drill, seemed heavier and less ornamental than it had looked to be. The first day I went out to drill, getting tired of doing the same things over and over, I said to the drill-sergeant: "Let's stop this fooling and go over to the grocery." His only reply was addressed to a corporal: "Corporal, take this man out and drill him like h—l"; and the corporal did! I found that suggestions were not so well appreciated in the army as in pri-

A MOTHER'S PARTING GIFT.

vate life, and that no wisdom was equal to a drill-master's "Right face," "Left wheel," and "Right, oblique, march." It takes a raw recruit some time to learn that he is not to think or suggest, but obey. Some never do learn. I acquired it at last, in humility and mud, but it was tough. Yet I doubt if my patriotism, during my first three weeks' drill, was quite knee-high. Drilling looks easy to a spectator, but it isn't. Old soldiers who read this will remember their green recruit-hood and smile assent. After a time I had cut down my uniform so that I could see out of it, and had conquered the drill sufficiently to see through it. Then the word came: On to Washington!

Our company was quartered at a large hotel near the railway station in the town in which it had been recruited. Bunks had been fitted up within a part of the hotel but little used. We took our meals at the public table, and found fault with the style. Six months later we would have considered ourselves aristocratic to have slept in the hotel stables with the meal-bin for a dining-table. One morning there was great excitement at the report that we were going to be sent to the front. Most of us obtained a limited pass and went to see our friends

---

railways from the north were obstructed, so that the 8th Massachusetts, with General B. F. Butler, and the 7th New York were compelled to go to Annapolis by water and march thence to Washington.

—EDITORS.

for the last time, returning the same night. Many of our schoolmates came in tears to say good-bye. We took leave of them all with heavy hearts, for, lightly as I may here seem to treat the subject, it was no light thing for a boy of twenty to start out for three years into the unknown dangers of a civil war. Our mothers—God bless them!—had brought us something good to eat,—pies, cakes, doughnuts, and jellies. It was one way in which a mother's heart found utterance. The young ladies (sisters, of course) brought an invention, usually made of leather or cloth, containing needles, pins, thread, buttons, and scissors, so that nearly every recruit had an embryo tailor's shop, with the goose outside. One old lady, in the innocence of her heart, brought her son an umbrella. We did not see anything particularly laughable about it at the time, but our old drill-sergeant did. Finally we were ready to move; our tears were wiped away, our buttons were polished, and our muskets were as bright as emery paper could make them.

"Wad" Rider, a member of our company, had come from a neighboring State to enlist with us. He was about eighteen years of age, red-headed, freckled-faced, good-natured and rough, with a wonderful aptitude for crying or laughing from sympathy. Another comrade, whom I will call Jack, was honored with a call from his mother, a little woman, hardly reaching up to his shoulder, with a sweet, motherly, care-worn face. At the last moment, though she had tried hard to preserve her composure, as is the habit of New England people, she threw her arms around her boy's neck, and with an outburst of sobbing and crying, said: "My dear boy, my dear boy, what will your poor old mother do without you? You are going to fight for your country. Don't forget your mother, Jack; God bless you, God bless you!" We felt as if the mother's tears and blessing were a benediction over us all. There was a touch of nature in her homely sorrow and solicitude over her big boy, which drew tears of sympathy from my eyes as I thought of my own sorrowing mother at home. The sympathetic Wad Rider burst into tears and sobs. His eyes refused, as he expressed it, to "dry up," until, as we were moving off, Jack's mother, rushing toward him with a bundle tied like a wheat-sheaf, called out in a most pathetic voice, "Jack! Jack! you've forgotten to take your pennyroyal." We all laughed, and so did Jack, and I think the laugh helped him more than the cry did. Everybody had said his last word, and the cars were off. Handkerchiefs were waved at us from all the houses we passed; we cheered till we were hoarse, and then settled back and swung our handkerchiefs.

Just here let me name over the contents of my knapsack, as a fair sample of what all the volunteers started with. There were in it a pair of trousers, two pairs of drawers, a pair of thick boots, four pairs of stockings, four flannel shirts, a blouse, a looking-glass, a can of peaches, a bottle of cough-mixture, a button-stick, chalk, razor and strop, the "tailor's shop" spoken of above, a Bible, a small volume of Shakspere, and writing utensils. To its top was strapped a double

THE NEW YORK SEVENTH MARCHING DOWN BROADWAY, APRIL 19, 1861.

woolen blanket and a rubber one. Many other things were left behind because of lack of room in or about the knapsack.♭

On our arrival in Boston we were marched through the streets—the first march of any consequence we had taken with our knapsacks and equipments. Our dress consisted of a belt about the body, which held a cartridge-box and bayonet, a cross-belt, also a haversack and tin drinking-cup, a canteen, and, last but not least, the knapsack strapped to the back. The straps ran over, around, and about one, in confusion most perplexing to our unsophisticated shoulders, the knapsack constantly giving the wearer the feeling that he was being pulled over backward. My canteen banged against my bayonet, both tin cup and bayonet badly interfered with the butt of my musket, while my cartridge-box and haversack were constantly flopping up and down—the whole jangling like loose harness and chains on a runaway horse. As we marched into Boston Common, I involuntarily cast my eye about for a bench. But for a former experience in offering advice, I should have proposed to the captain to "chip in" and hire a team to carry our equipments. Such was my first experience in war harness. Afterward, with hardened muscles, rendered athletic by long marches and invig-

♭It is said by one of the "Monticello Guards," that most of its members started for Bull Run with a trunk and an abundant supply of fine linen shirts.—EDITORS.

FEDERAL HILL, BALTIMORE. FROM A SKETCH MADE ON THE DAY
OF THE OCCUPATION BY GENERAL BUTLER.

On the 27th of April, 1861, General B. F. Butler was assigned to the command of the Department of Annapolis, which did not include Baltimore. On the 5th of May, with two regiments and a battery of artillery, he moved from Washington to the Relay House, on the Baltimore and Ohio Railway, 7 miles from Baltimore, at the junction of the Washington branch. He fortified this position, and on the 13th entered Baltimore and occupied and fortified Federal Hill, overlooking the harbor and commanding the city. On the 15th he was followed in command of the Department by General George Cadwalader, who was succeeded on the 11th of June by General N. P. Banks, who administered the Department until succeeded by General John A. Dix, July 23d, 1861. On the 22d of May General Butler assumed command at Fort Monroe, Va.

orated by hardships, I could look back upon those days and smile, while carrying a knapsack as lightly as my heart. That morning my heart was as heavy as my knapsack. At last the welcome orders came: "Prepare to open ranks! Rear, open order, march! Right dress! Front! Order arms! Fix bayonets! Stack arms! Unsling knapsacks! In place, rest!"

The tendency of raw soldiers at first is to overload themselves. On the first long march the reaction sets in, and the recruit goes to the opposite extreme, not carrying enough, and thereby becoming dependent upon his comrades. Old soldiers preserve a happy medium. I have seen a new regiment start out with a lot of indescribable material, including sheet-iron stoves, and come back after a long march covered with more mud than baggage, stripped of everything except blankets, haversacks, canteens, muskets, and cartridge-boxes.

During that afternoon in Boston, after marching and countermarching, or, as one of our farmer-boy recruits expressed it, after "hawing and geeing" about the streets, we were sent to Fort Independence for the night for safe-keeping. A company of regulars held the fort, and the guards walked their post with an up-rightness that was astonishing. Our first impression of them was that there was a needless amount of "wheel about and turn about, and walk just so," and of saluting, and presenting arms. We were all marched to our quarters within the fort, where we unslung our knapsacks. After the first day's struggle with a knap-sack, the general verdict was, "got too much of it." At supper-time we were marched to the dining-barracks, where our bill of fare was beefsteak, coffee, wheat bread, and potatoes, but not a sign of milk or butter. It struck me as queer when I heard that the army was never provided with butter and milk.

The next day we started for Washington, by rail. We marched through New York's crowded streets without awakening the enthusiasm we thought our due; for we had read of the exciting scenes attending the departure of the New York 7th for Washington, on the day the 6th Massachusetts was mobbed in Balti-more, and also of the march of the 12th Massachusetts down Broadway on the 24th of July, when the regiment sang the then new and always thrilling lyric, "John Brown's Body." The following morning we took breakfast in Philadel-phia, where we were attended by matrons and maidens, who waited upon us with thoughtful tenderness, as if they had been our own mothers and sweet-hearts instead of strangers. They feasted us and then filled our haversacks. God bless them! If we did not quite appreciate them then, we did afterward. After embarking on the cars at Philadelphia, the waving of handkerchiefs was less and less noticeable along the route. We arrived in Baltimore late at night; Union troops now controlled the city, and we marched through its deserted streets un-molested. On our arrival at Washington the next morning, we were marched to barracks, dignified by the name of "Soldiers' Retreat," where each man received a half loaf of "soft-tack," as we had already begun to call wheat bread, with a piece of "salt junk," about as big and tough as the heel of my government shoe, and a quart of coffee,—which constituted our breakfast. Our first day in Wash-ington was spent in shaving, washing, polishing our brasses and buttons, and cleaning-up for inspection. A day or two later we moved to quarters not far from the armory, looking out on the broad Potomac, within sight of Long Bridge and the city of Alexandria.

Here and there the sound of a gun broke the serenity, but otherwise the quiet seemed inconsistent with the war preparations going on around us. In the distance, across the wide river, we could see the steeples and towers of the city of Alexandria, while up stream, on the right, was the Long Bridge. Here and there was to be seen the moving panorama of armed men, as a regiment crossed the bridge; a flash of sunlight on the polished muskets revealed them to the eye;

PENNSYLVANIA AVENUE, WASHINGTON. FROM A SKETCH MADE IN 1861.

while the white-topped army baggage-wagons filed over in constant procession, looking like sections of whitewashed fence in motion. The overgrown country village of that period, called Washington, can be described in a few words. There were wide streets stretching out from a common center like a spider's web. The Capitol, with its unfinished dome; the Patent Office, the Treasury, and the other public buildings, were in marked and classic contrast with the dilapidated, tumble-down, shabby look of the average homes, stores, groceries, and groggeries, which increased in shabbiness and dirty dilapidation as they approached the suburbs. The climate of Washington was genial, but in the winter months the mud was fearful. I have drilled in it, marched in it, and run from the provost-guard in it, and I think I appreciate it from actual and familiar knowledge. In the lower quarter of the city there was not a piece of sidewalk. Even Pennsylvania Avenue, with its side-walks, was extremely dirty; and the cavalcade of teams, artillery caissons, and baggage-wagons, with their heavy wheels, stirred the mud into a stiff batter for the pedestrian.

Officers in tinsel and gold lace were so thick on Pennsylvania Avenue that it was a severe trial for a private to walk there. The salute exacted by officers, of bringing the hand to the visor of the cap, extending the arm to its full length, and then letting it drop by the side, was tiresome when followed up with the industry required by this horde. Perhaps I exaggerate, but in a half-hour's walk on the avenue I think I have saluted two hundred officers. Brigadier-generals were more numerous there than I ever knew them to be at the front. These officers, many of whom won their positions by political wire-pulling at Washington, we privates thought the great bane of the war; they ought to have been sent to the front rank of battle, to serve as privates until they had learned the duties of a soldier. Mingled with these gaudy, useless officers were citizens in search of fat contracts, privates, "non-com's" and officers whose uniforms were well worn and faded, showing that they were from encampments and active service. Occasionally a regiment passed through the streets, on the way to camp; all surged up and down wide Pennsylvania Avenue.

The soldiers of this period were eager to collect mementoes of the war. One of my acquaintances in another regiment made sketches of the different camps he had visited around Washington, including "Brightwood" and Camp Cameron; the latter he termed "a nursery for brigadier-generals." Another friend hoarded specimens of official signatures and passes issued in Washington, conspicuous among which was a pass with the well-known John-Hancock-like signature of Drake De Kay.

Before enlisting, and while on a visit to a neighboring town, I was one evening at the village store, when the talk turned upon the duration of the war. Jim Tinkham, the clerk of the grocery store, announced his belief in a sixty days' war. I modestly asked him for more time. The older ones agreed with Jim and argued, as was common at that time, that the Government would soon blockade all the rebel ports and starve them out. Tinkham proposed to wager a supper for those present, if the rebels did not surrender before snow came that year. I accepted. Neither of us put up any money, and in the excitement of the weeks which followed I had forgotten the wager. During my first week in Wash-

THE SEVENTH NEW YORK AT CAMP CAMERON, WASHINGTON.

ington, whom should I meet but Jim Tinkham, the apostle of the sixty-day theory. He was brown with sunburn, and clad in a rusty uniform which showed service in the field. He was a veteran, for he had been at the battle of Bull Run. He confidentially declared that after getting the order to retreat at that battle, he should not have stopped short of Boston if he had not been halted by a soldier with a musket, after crossing Long Bridge.

CHAPTER 6

THE FIRST BATTLE OF BULL RUN.

P.G.T. Beauregard, General, C.S.A.

Soon after the first conflict between the authorities of the Federal Union and those of the Confederate States had occurred in Charleston Harbor, by the bombardment of Fort Sumter,—which, beginning at 4:30 A.M. on the 12th of April, 1861, forced the surrender of that fortress within thirty hours thereafter into my hands,—I was called to Richmond, which by that time had become the Confederate seat of government, and was directed to "assume command of the Confederate troops on the Alexandria line." Arriving at Manassas Junction, I took command on the 2d of June, forty-nine days after the evacuation of Fort Sumter.

Although the position at the time was strategically of commanding importance to the Confederates, the mere *terrain* was not only without natural defensive advantages, but, on the contrary, was absolutely unfavorable. Its strategic value was that, being close to the Federal capital, it held in observation the chief army then being assembled near Arlington by General McDowell, under the immediate eye of the commander-in-chief, General Scott, for an offensive movement against Richmond; and while it had a railway approach in its rear for the easy accumulation of reënforcements and all the necessary munitions of war from the southward, at the same time another (the Manassas Gap) railway, diverging laterally to the left from that point, gave rapid communications with the fertile valley of the Shenandoah, then teeming with live stock and cereal subsistence, as well as with other resources essential to the Confederates. There was this further value in the position to the Confederate army: that during the period of accumulation, seasoning, and training, it might be fed from the fat fields, pastures, and garners of Londoun, Fauquier, and the Lower Shenandoah Valley counties, which otherwise must have fallen into the hands of the enemy. But, on the other hand, Bull Run, a petty stream, was of little or no defensive

A LOUISIANA "TIGER."

strength, for it abounded in fords, and although for the most part its banks were rocky and abrupt, the side from which it would be approached offensively in most places commanded the opposite ground.

At the time of my arrival at Manassas, a Confederate army under General Joseph E. Johnston was in occupation of the Lower Shenandoah Valley, along the line of the Upper Potomac, chiefly at Harper's Ferry, which was regarded as the gateway of the valley and of one of the possible approaches to Richmond; a position from which he was speedily forced to retire, however, by a flank movement of a Federal army, under the veteran General Patterson, thrown across the Potomac at or about Martinsburg. On my other or right flank, so to speak, a Confederate force of some 2500 men under General Holmes occupied the position of Aquia Creek on the lower Potomac, upon the line of approach to Richmond from that direction through Fredericksburg. The other approach, that by way of the James River, was held by Confederate troops under Generals Huger and Magruder. Establishing small outposts at Leesburg to observe the crossings of the Potomac in that quarter, and at Fairfax Court House in observation of Arlington, with other detachments in advance of Manassas toward Alexandria on the south side of the railroad, from the very outset I was anxiously aware that the sole military advantage at the moment to the Confederates was that of holding the *interior lines*. On the Federal or hostile side were all material advantages, including superior numbers, largely drawn from the old militia organizations of the great cities of the North, decidedly better armed and equipped than the troops under me, and strengthened by a small but incomparable body of regular infantry as well as a number of batteries of regular field artillery of the highest class, and a very large and thoroughly organized staff corps, besides a numerous body of professionally educated officers in

command of volunteer regiments,†—
all precious military elements at such
a juncture.

Happily, through the foresight
of Colonel Thomas Jordan,—whom
General Lee had placed as the adjutant-general of the forces there assembled before my arrival,—arrangements
were made which enabled me to receive regularly, from private persons
at the Federal capital, most accurate
information, of which politicians high
in council, as well as War Department

ARLINGTON, THE HOME OF
GENERAL ROBERT E. LEE.

clerks, were the unconscious duets. On the 4th of July, my pickets happened
upon and captured a soldier of the regulars, who proved to be a clerk in the
adjutant-general's office of General McDowell, intrusted with the special duty
of compiling returns of his army—a work which he confessed, without reluctance, he had just executed, showing the forces under McDowell about the 1st
of July. His statement of the strength and composition of that force tallied so
closely with that which had been acquired through my Washington agencies,
already mentioned, as well as through the leading Northern news-papers (regular files of which were also transmitted to my headquarters from the Federal
capital), that I could not doubt them.

In these several ways, therefore, I was almost as well advised of the strength
of the hostile army in my front as its commander, who, I may mention, had been
a classmate of mine at West Point. Under those circumstances I had become
satisfied that a well-equipped, well-constituted Federal Army at least 50,000
strong, of all arms, confronted me at or about Arlington, ready and on the very
eve of an offensive operation against me, and to meet which I could muster
barely 18,000 men with 29 field-guns.

Previously,—indeed, as early as the middle of June,—it had become apparent to my mind that through only one course of action could there be a
well-grounded hope of ability on the part of the Confederates to encounter
successfully the offensive operations for which the Federal authorities were
then vigorously preparing in my immediate front, with so consummate a strategist and military administrator as Lieutenant-General Scott in general command at Washington, aided by his accomplished heads of the large General

---

†The professionally educated officers on the Confederate side at Bull Run included Generals Johnston,
Beauregard, Stonewall Jackson, Longstreet, Kirby Smith, Ewell, Early, Bee, D. R. Jones, Holmes, Evans,
Elzey, and Jordan, all in high positions, besides others not so prominent.—EDITORS.

Staff Corps of the United States Army. This course was to make the most enterprising, warlike use of the interior lines which we possessed, for the swift concentration at the critical instant of every available Confederate force upon the menaced position, at the risk, if need were, of sacrificing all minor places to the one clearly of major military value—there to meet our adversary so offensively as to overwhelm him, under circumstances that must assure immediate ability to assume the general offensive even upon his territory, and thus conquer an early peace by a few well-delivered blows.

My views of such import had been already earnestly communicated to the proper authorities; but about the middle of July, satisfied that McDowell was on the eve of taking the offensive against me, I dispatched Colonel James Chesnut, of South Carolina, a volunteer aide-de-camp on my staff who had served on an intimate footing with Mr. Davis in the Senate of the United States, to urge in substance the necessity for the immediate concentration of the larger part of the forces of Johnston and Holmes at Manassas, so that the moment McDowell should be sufficiently far detached from Washington, I would be enabled to move rapidly round his more convenient flank upon his rear and his communications, and attack him in reverse, or get between his forces, then separated, thus cutting off his retreat upon Arlington in the event of his defeat, and insuring as an immediate consequence the crushing of Patterson, the liberation of Maryland, and the capture of Washington.

This plan was rejected by Mr. Davis and his military advisers (Adjutant-General Cooper and General Lee), who characterized it as "brilliant and comprehensive," but essentially impracticable. Furthermore, Colonel Chesnut came back impressed with the views entertained at Richmond,—as he communicated at once to my adjutant-general,—that should the Federal army soon move offensively upon my position, my best course would be to retire behind the Rappahannock and accept battle there instead of at Manassas. In effect, it was regarded as best to sever communications between the two chief Confederate armies, that of the Potomac and that of the Shenandoah, with the inevitable immediate result that Johnston would be forced to leave Patterson in possession of the Lower Shenandoah Valley, abandoning to the enemy so large a part of the most resourceful sections of Virginia, and to retreat southward by way of the Luray Valley, pass across the Blue Ridge at Thornton's Gap and unite with me after all, but at Fredericksburg, much nearer Richmond than Manassas. These views, however, were not made known to me at the time, and happily my mind was left free to the grave problem imposed upon me by the rejection of my plan for the immediate concentration of a materially larger force,—i.e., the problem of placing and using my resources for a successful encounter behind Bull Run with the Federal army, which I was not permitted to doubt was about to take the field against me.

It is almost needless to say that I had caused to be made a thorough reconnoissance of all the ground in my front and flanks, and had made myself personally acquainted with the most material points, including the region of Sudley's Church on my left, where a small detachment was posted in observation. Left now to my own resources, of course the contingency of defeat had to be considered and provided for. Among the measures of precaution for such a result, I ordered the destruction of the railroad bridge across Bull Run at Union Mills, on my right, in order that the enemy, in the event of my defeat, should not have the immediate use of the railroad in following up their movement against Richmond—a railroad which could have had no corresponding value to us eastward beyond Manassas in any operations on our side

MAP OF THE BULL RUN CAMPAIGN.

with Washington as the objective, inasmuch as any such operations must have been made by the way of the Upper Potomac and upon the rear of that city.

Just before Colonel Chesnut was dispatched on the mission of which I have spoken, a former clerk in one of the departments at Washington, well known to him, had volunteered to return thither and bring back the latest information of the military and political situation from our most trusted friends. His loyalty to our cause, his intelligence, and his desire to be of service being vouched for, he was at once sent across the Potomac below Alexandria, merely accredited by a small scrap of paper bearing in Colonel Jordan's cipher the two words, "Trust bearer," with which he was to call at a certain house in Washington within easy rifle-range of the White House, ask for the lady of the house, and present it only to her. This delicate mission was as fortunately as it was deftly executed. In the early morning, as the newsboys were crying in the empty streets of Washington the intelligence that the order was given for the Federal army to move at once upon my position, that scrap of paper reached the hands of the one person in all that city who could extract any meaning from it. With no more delay than was necessary for a hurried breakfast and the writing in cipher by Mrs. G—— of the words, "Order issued for McDowell to march upon Manassas tonight," my agent was placed in communication with another friend, who car-

ried him in a buggy with a relay of horses as swiftly as possible down the eastern shore of the Potomac to our regular ferry across that river. Without untoward incident the momentous dispatch was quickly delivered into the hands of
a cavalry courier, and by means of relays it was in my hands between 8 and 9 o'-
clock that night. Within half an hour my outpost commanders, advised of what
was impending, were directed, at the first evidence of the near presence of the
enemy in their front, to fall back in the manner and to positions already prescribed in anticipation of such a contingency in an order confidentially communicated to them four weeks before, and the detachment at Leesburg was
directed to join me by forced marches. Having thus cleared my decks for action,
I next acquainted Mr. Davis with the situation, and ventured once more to suggest that the Army of the Shenandoah, with the brigade at Fredericksburg or
Aquia Creek, should be ordered to reënforce me,—suggestions that were at
once heeded so far that General Holmes was ordered to carry his command to
my aid, and General Johnston was given discretion to do likewise. After some
telegraphic discussion with me, General Johnston was induced to exercise this
discretion in favor of the swift march of the Army of the Shenandoah to my relief; and to facilitate that vital movement, I hastened to accumulate all possible
means of railway transport at a designated point on the Manassas Gap railroad
at the eastern foot of the Blue Ridge, to which Johnston's troops directed their
march. However, at the same time, I had submitted the alternative proposition
to General Johnston, that, having passed the Blue Ridge, he should assemble his

THE MCLEAN HOUSE, GENERAL BEAUREGARD'S HEADQUARTERS NEAR MANASSAS.
FROM A PHOTOGRAPH.

forces, press forward by way of Aldie, north-west of Manassas, and fall upon McDowell's right rear; while I, prepared for the operation, at the first sound of the conflict, should strenuously assume the offensive in my front. The situation and circumstances specially favored the signal success of such an operation. The march to the point of attack could have been accomplished as soon as the forces were brought ultimately by rail to Manassas Junction; our enemy, thus attacked so nearly simultaneously on his right flank, his rear, and his front, naturally would suppose that I had been able to turn his flank while attacking him in front, and therefore, that I must have an overwhelming superiority of numbers; and his forces, being new troops, most of them under fire for the first time, must have soon fallen into a disastrous panic. Moreover, such an operation must have resulted advantageously to the Confederates, in the event that McDowell should, as might have been anticipated, attempt to strike the Manassas Gap railway to my left, and thus cut off railway communications between Johnston's forces and my own, instead of the mere effort to strike my left flank which he actually essayed.↓

It seemed, however, as though the deferred attempt at concentration was to go for naught, for on the morning of the 18th the Federal forces were massed around Centreville, but three miles from Mitchell's Ford, and soon were seen advancing upon the roads leading to that and Blackburn's Ford. My order of battle, issued in the night of the 17th, contemplated an offensive return, particularly from the strong brigades on the right and right center. The Federal artillery opened in front of both fords, and the infantry, while demonstrating in front of Mitchell's Ford, endeavored to force a passage at Blackburn's. Their column of attack, Tyler's division, was opposed by Longstreet's forces, to the reënforcement of which Early's brigade, the reserve line at McLean's Ford, was ordered up. The Federals, after several attempts to force a passage, met a final repulse and retreated.↕ After their infantry attack had ceased, about 1 o'clock, the contest lapsed into an artillery duel, in which the Washington Artillery of New Orleans won credit against the renowned batteries of the United States regular army. A comical effect of this artillery fight was the destruction of the dinner of myself and staff by a Federal shell that fell into the fire-place of my headquarters at the McLean House.

↓"I am, however, inclined to believe he [the enemy] may attempt to turn my left flank by a movement in the direction of Vienna, Fryingpan Church, and, possibly, Gum Spring, and thus cut off Johnston's line of retreat and communication with this place [Manassas Junction] *via* the Manassas Gap railroad, while threatening my own communications with Richmond and depots of supply by the Alexandria and Orange railroad, and opening his communications with the Potomac through Leesburg and Edward's Ferry."—Extract from a letter addressed by General Beauregard to Jefferson Davis, July 11th, 1861.

↕It is denied that a serious attempt "to force a passage" was made on the 18th. This engagement was called by the Confederates the battle of Bull Run, the main fight on the 21st being known in the South as the battle of Manassas (pronounced Ma-nass'-sa).—Editors.

Our success in this first limited collision was of special prestige to my army of new troops, and, moreover, of decisive importance by so increasing General McDowell's caution as to give time for the arrival of some of General Johnston's forces. But while on the 19th I was awaiting a renewed and general attack by the Federal army, I received a telegram from the Richmond military authorities, urging me to withdraw my call on General Johnston on account of the supposed impracticability of the concentration—an abiding conviction which had been but momentarily shaken by the alarm caused by McDowell's march upon Richmond. / As this was not an order in terms, but an urgency which, notwithstanding its superior source, left me technically free and could define me as responsible for any misevent, I preferred to keep both the situation and the responsibility, and continued every effort for the prompt arrival of the Shenandoah forces, being resolved, should they come before General McDowell again attacked, to take myself the offensive. General McDowell, fortunately for my plans, spent the 19th and 20th in reconnoissances;☆ and, meanwhile, General Johnston brought 8340 men from the Shenandoah Valley, with 20 guns, and General Holmes 1265 rank and file, with 6 pieces of artillery, from Aquia Creek. As these forces arrived (most of them in the afternoon of the 20th) I placed them chiefly so as to strengthen my left center and left, the latter being weak from lack of available troops.

The disposition of the entire force was now as follows: At Union Mills Ford, Ewell's brigade, supported by Holmes's; at McLean's Ford, D. R. Jones's brigade, supported by Early's; at Blackburn's Ford, Longstreet's brigade; at Mitchell's Ford, Bonham's brigade. Cocke's brigade held the line in front and rear of Bull Run from Bonham's left, covering Lewis's, Ball's, and Island fords, to the right of Evans's demi-brigade, which covered the Stone Bridge and a farm ford about a mile above, and formed part also of Cocke's command. The Shenandoah forces were placed in reserve—Bee's and Bartow's brigades between McLean's and Blackburn's fords, and Jackson's between Blackburn's and Mitchell's fords. This force mustered 29,188 rank and file and 55 guns, of which 21,923 infantry, cavalry, and artillery, with 29 guns, belonged to my immediate forces, *i.e.*, the Army of the Potomac.

/ [TELEGRAM.]   RICHMOND, JULY 19, 1861.
GENERAL BEAUREGARD, MANASSAS, VA.

We have no intelligence from General Johnston. If the enemy in front of you has abandoned an immediate attack, and General Johnston has not moved, you had better withdraw your call upon him, so that he may be left to his full discretion. All the troops arriving at Lynchburg are ordered to join you. From this place we will send as fast as transportation permits. The enemy is advised at Washington of the projected movement of Generals Johnston and Holmes, and may vary his plans in conformity thereto.

S. COOPER, ADJUTANT-GENERAL.

☆Lack of rations, as well as the necessity for information, detained McDowell at Centreville during these two days.—EDITORS.

The preparation, in front of an ever-threatening enemy, of a wholly volunteer army, composed of men very few of whom had ever belonged to any military organization, had been a work of many cares not incident to the command of a regular army. These were increased by the insufficiency of my staff organization, an inefficient management of the quartermaster's department at Richmond, and the preposterous mismanagement of the commissary-general, who not only failed to furnish rations, but caused the removal of the army commissaries, who, under my orders, procured food from the country in front of us to keep the army from absolute want—supplies that were otherwise exposed to be gathered by the enemy. So specially severe had been the recent duties at headquarters, aggravated not a little by night alarms arising from the enemy's immediate presence, that, in the evening of the 20th, I found my chief-of-staff sunken upon the papers that covered his table, asleep in sheer exhaustion from the overstraining and almost slumberless labor of the last days and nights. I covered his door with a guard to secure his rest against any interruption, after which the army had the benefit of his usual active and provident services.

There was much in this decisive conflict about to open, not involved in any after battle, which pervaded the two armies and the people behind them and colored the responsibility of the respective commanders. The political hostilities of a generation were now face to face with weapons instead of words. Defeat to either side would be a deep mortification, but defeat to the South must turn its claim of independence into an empty vaunt; and the defeated commander on either side might expect, though not the personal fate awarded by the Carthaginians to an unfortunate commander, at least a moral fate quite similar. Though disappointed that the concentration I had sought had not been permitted at the moment and for the purpose preferred by me, and notwithstanding the nonarrival of some five thousand troops of the Shenandoah forces, my strength was now so increased that I had good hope of successfully meeting my adversary.

General Johnston was the ranking officer, and entitled, therefore, to assume command of the united forces; but as the extensive field of operations was one which I had occupied since the beginning of June, and with which I was thoroughly familiar in all its extent and military bearings, while he was wholly unacquainted with it, and, moreover, as I had made my plans and dispositions for the maintenance of the position, General Johnston, in view of the gravity of the impending issue, preferred not to assume the responsibilities of the chief direction of the forces during the battle, but to assist me upon the field. Thereupon, I explained my plans and purposes, to which he agreed.‡

---

‡See General Beauregard's postscript (page 117), and General Johnston's consideration of the same topic in the paper to follow (page 127), and his postscript (page 142).—EDITORS.

SUNDAY, July 21st, bearing the fate of the new-born Confederacy, broke brightly over the fields and woods that held the hostile forces. My scouts, thrown out in the night toward Centreville along the Warrenton Turnpike, had reported that the enemy was concentrating along the latter. This fact, together with the failure of the Federals in their attack upon my center at Mitchell's and Blackburn's fords, had caused me to apprehend that they would attempt my left flank at the Stone Bridge, and orders were accordingly issued by half-past 4 o'clock to the brigade commanders to hold their forces in readiness to move at a moment's notice, together with the suggestion that the Federal attack might be expected in that quarter. Shortly afterward the enemy was reported to be advancing from Centreville on the Warrenton Turnpike, and at half-past 5 o'clock as deploying a force in front of Evans. As their movement against my left developed the opportunity I desired, I immediately sent orders to the brigade commanders, both front and reserves, on my right and center to advance and vigorously attack the Federal left flank and rear at Centreville, while my left, under Cocke and Evans with their supports, would sustain the Federal attack in the quarter of the Stone Bridge, which they were directed to do to the last extremity. The center was likewise to advance and engage the enemy in front, and directions were given to the reserves, when without orders, to move toward the sound of the heaviest firing. The ground in our front on the other side of Bull Run afforded particular advantage for these tactics. Centreville was the apex of a triangle—its short side running by the Warrenton Turnpike to Stone Bridge, its base Bull Run, its long side a road that ran from Union Mills along the front of my other Bull Run positions and trended off to the rear of Centreville, where McDowell had massed his main forces; branch roads led up to this one from the fords between Union Mills and Mitchell's. My forces to the right of the latter ford were to advance, pivoting on that position; Bonham was in advance from Mitchell's Ford, Longstreet from Blackburn's, D. R. Jones from McLean's, and Ewell from Union Mills by the Centreville road. Ewell, as having the longest march, was to begin the movement, and each brigade was to be followed by its reserve. In anticipation of this method of attack, and to prevent accidents, the subordinate commanders had been carefully instructed in the movement by me, as they were all new to the responsibilities of command. They were to establish close communication with each other before making the attack. About half-past 8 o'clock I set out with General Johnston for a convenient position,— a hill in rear of Mitchell's Ford,—where we waited for the opening of the attack on our right, from which I expected a decisive victory by midday, with the result of cutting off the Federal army from retreat upon Washington.

Meanwhile, about half-past 5 o'clock, the peal of a heavy rifled gun was heard in front of the Stone Bridge, its second shot striking through the tent of my signal-officer, Captain E. P. Alexander; and at 6 o'clock a full rifled battery opened against Evans and then against Cocke, to which our artillery remained

TOPOGRAPHICAL MAP OF THE BULL RUN BATTLE-FIELD.

The original of this map was made for General Beauregard, soon after the battle, from actual surveys by Captain D. B. Harris, assisted by Mr. John Grant.

dumb, as it had not sufficient range to reply. But later, as the Federal skirmish-line advanced, it was engaged by ours, thrown well forward on the other side of the Run. A scattering musketry fire followed, and meanwhile, about 7 o'clock, I ordered Jackson's brigade, with Imboden's and five guns of Walton's battery, to the left, with orders to support Cocke as well as Bonham; and the brigades of Bee and Bartow, under the command of the former, were also sent to the support of the left.

At half-past 8 o'clock Evans, seeing that the Federal attack did not increase in boldness and vigor, and observing a lengthening line of dust above the trees to the left of the Warrenton Turnpike, became satisfied that the attack in his front was but a feint, and that a column of the enemy was moving around through the woods to fall on his flank from the direction of Sudley Ford. Informing his immediate commander, Cocke, of the enemy's movement, and of his own dispositions to meet it, he left 4 companies under cover at the Stone Bridge, and led the remainder of his force, 6 companies of Sloan's 4th South Carolina and Wheat's battalion of Louisiana Tigers, with 2 6-pounder howitzers, across the valley of Young's Branch to the high ground beyond it. Resting his left on the Sudley road, he distributed his troops on each side of a small copse, with such cover as the ground afforded, and looking over the open fields and a reach of the Sudley road which the Federals must cover in their approach. His two howitzers were placed one at each end of his position, and here he silently awaited the enemy now drawing near.

The Federal turning column, about 18,000 strong, with 24 pieces of artillery, had moved down from Centreville by the Warrenton Turnpike, and after passing Cub Run had struck to the right by a forest road to cross Bull Run at Sudley Ford, about 3 miles above the Stone Bridge, moving by a long circuit for the purpose of attacking my left flank. The head of the column, Burnside's brigade of Hunter's division, at about 9:45 A.M. debouched from the woods into the open fields, in front of Evans. Wheat at once engaged their skirmishers, and as the Second Rhode Island regiment advanced, supported by its splendid battery of 6 rifled guns, the fronting thicket held by Evans's South Carolinians poured forth its sudden volleys, while the 2 howitzers flung their grape-shot upon the attacking line, which was soon shattered and driven back into the woods behind. Major Wheat, after handling his battalion with the utmost determination, had fallen severely wounded in the lungs. Burnside's entire brigade was now sent forward in a second charge, supported by 8 guns; but they encountered again the unflinching fire of Evans's line, and were once more driven back to the woods, from the cover of which they continued the attack, reënforced after a time by the arrival of 8 companies of United States regular infantry, under Major Sykes, with 6 pieces of artillery, quickly followed by the remaining regiments of Andrew Porter's brigade of the same division. The contest here lasted fully an hour; meanwhile Wheat's battalion, having lost its leader, had gradually lost its organization, and Evans, though still opposing these heavy odds with undiminished firmness, sought reënforcement from the troops in his rear.

General Bee, of South Carolina, a man of marked character, whose command lay in reserve in rear of Cocke, near the Stone Bridge, intelligently applying the general order given to the reserves, had already moved toward the neighboring point of conflict, and taken a position with his own and Bartow's brigades on the high plateau which stands in rear of Bull Run in the quarter of the Stone Bridge, and overlooking the scene of engagement upon the stretch of high ground from which it was separated by the valley of Young's Branch. This plateau is inclosed on three sides by two small water-courses, which empty into Bull Run within a few yards of each other, a half mile to the south of the Stone Bridge. Rising to an elevation of quite 100 feet above the level of Bull Run at the bridge, it falls off on three sides to the level of the inclosing streams in gentle slopes, but furrowed by ravines of irregular directions and length, and studded with clumps and patches of young pine and oaks. The general direction of the crest of the plateau is oblique to the course of Bull Run in that quarter and to the Sudley and turnpike roads, which intersect each other at right angles. On the north-western brow, overlooking Young's Branch, and near the Sudley road, as the latter climbs over the plateau, stood the house of the widow Henry, while to its right and forward on a projecting spur stood the house and sheds of the free negro Robinson, just behind the turnpike, densely embowered in trees and shrubbery and environed by a double row of fences on two sides. Around the eastern and southern brow of the plateau an almost unbroken fringe of second-growth pines gave excellent shelter for our marksmen, who availed themselves of it with the most satisfactory skill. To the west, adjoining the fields that surrounded the houses mentioned, a broad belt of oaks extends directly across the crest on both sides of the Sudley road, in which, during the battle, the hostile forces contended for the mastery. General Bee, with a soldier's eye to the situation, skillfully disposed his forces. His two brigades on either side of Imboden's battery—which he had borrowed from his neighboring reserve, Jackson's brigade—were placed in a small depression of the plateau in advance of the Henry house, whence he had a full view of the contest on the opposite height across the valley of Young's Branch. Opening with his artillery upon the Federal batteries, he answered Evans's request by advising him to withdraw to his own position on the height; but Evans, full of the spirit that would not retreat, renewed his appeal that the forces in rear would come to help him hold his ground. The newly arrived forces had given the Federals such superiority at this point as to dwarf Evans's means of resistance, and General Bee, generously yielding his own better judgment to Evans's persistence, led the two brigades across the valley under the fire of the enemy's artillery, and threw them into action—1 regiment in the copse held by Colonel Evans, 2 along a fence on the

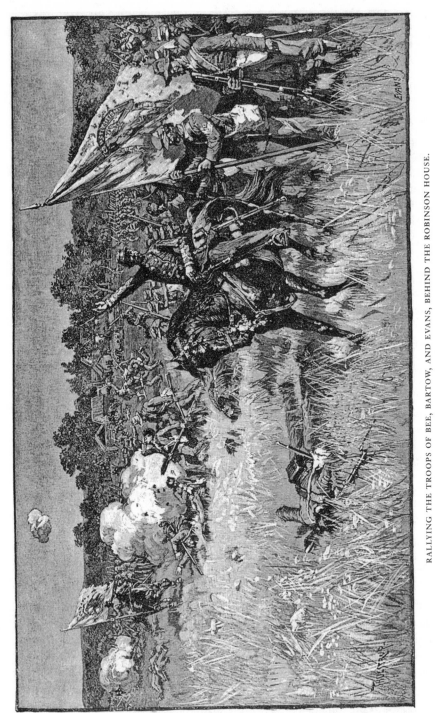

RALLYING THE TROOPS OF BEE, BARTOW, AND EVANS, BEHIND THE ROBINSON HOUSE.

right, and 2 under General Bartow on the prolonged right of this line, but extended forward at a right angle and along the edge of a wood not more than 100 yards from that held by the enemy's left, where the contest at short range became sharp and deadly, bringing many casualties to both sides. The Federal infantry, though still in superior numbers, failed to make any headway against this sturdy van, notwithstanding Bee's whole line was hammered also by the enemy's powerful batteries, until Heintzelman's division of 2 strong brigades, arriving from Sudley Ford, extended the fire on the Federal right, while its battery of 6 10-pounder rifled guns took an immediately effective part from a position behind the Sudley road. Against these odds the Confederate force was still endeavoring to hold its ground, when a new enemy came into the field upon its right. Major Wheat, with characteristic daring and restlessness, had crossed Bull Run alone by a small ford above the Stone Bridge, in order to reconnoiter, when he and Evans had first moved to the left, and, falling on some Federal scouts, had shouted a taunting defiance and withdrawn, not, however, without his place of crossing having been observed. This disclosure was now utilized by Sherman's (W. T.) and Keyes's brigades of Tyler's division; crossing at this point, they appeared over the high bank of the stream and moved into position on the Federal left. There was no choice now for Bee but to retire—a

movement, however, to be accomplished under different circumstances than when urged by him upon Evans. The three leaders endeavored to preserve the steadiness of the ranks as they withdrew over the open fields, aided by the fire of Imboden's guns on the plateau and the retiring howitzers; but the troops were thrown into confusion, and the greater part soon fell into rout across Young's Branch and around the base of the height in the rear of the Stone Bridge.

Meanwhile, in rear of Mitchell's Ford, I had been waiting with General Johnston for the sound of conflict to open in the quarter of Centreville upon the Federal left flank and rear (making allowance, however, for the delays possible to commands unused to battle), when I was chagrined to hear from General D. R. Jones that, while he had been long ready for the

A LOUISIANA "PELICAN."

movement upon Centreville, General Ewell had not come up to form on his right, though he had sent him between 7 and 8 o'clock a copy of his own order which recited that Ewell had been already ordered to begin the movement. I dispatched an immediate order to Ewell to advance; but within a quarter of an hour, just as I received a dispatch from him informing me that he had received no order to advance in the morning, the firing on the left began to increase so intensely as to indicate a severe attack, whereupon General Johnston said that he would go personally to that quarter.

After weighing attentively the firing, which seemed rapidly and heavily increasing, it appeared to me that the troops on the right would be unable to get into position before the Federal offensive should have made too much progress on our left, and that it would be better to abandon it altogether, maintaining only a strong demonstration so as to detain the enemy in front of our right and center, and hurry up all available reënforcements—including the reserves that were to have moved upon Centreville—to our left and fight the battle out in that quarter. Communicating this view to General Johnston, who approved it (giving his advice, as he said, for what it was worth, as he was not acquainted with the country), I ordered Ewell, Jones, and Longstreet to make a strong demonstration all along their front on the other side of the Run, and ordered the reserves below our position, Holmes's brigade with 6 guns, and Early's brigade, also 2 regiments of Bonham's brigade, near at hand, to move swiftly to the left. General Johnston and I now set out at full speed for the point of conflict. We arrived there just as Bee's troops, after giving way, were fleeing in disorder behind the height in rear of the Stone Bridge. They had come around between the base of the hill and the Stone Bridge into a shallow ravine which ran up to a point on the crest where Jackson had already formed his brigade along the edge of the woods. We found the commanders resolutely stemming the further flight of the routed forces, but vainly endeavoring to restore order, and our own efforts were as futile. Every segment of line we succeeded in forming was again dissolved while another was being formed; more than two thousand men were shouting each some suggestion to his neighbor, their voices mingling with the noise of the shells hurtling through the trees overhead, and all word of command drowned in the confusion and uproar. It was at this moment that General Bee used the famous expression, "Look at Jackson's brigade! It stands there like a stone wall"—a name that passed from the brigade to its immortal commander. The disorder seemed irretrievable, but happily the thought came to me that if their colors were planted out to the front the men might rally on them, and I gave the order to carry the standards forward some forty yards, which was promptly executed by the regimental officers, thus drawing the common eye of the troops. They now received easily the orders to advance and form on the line of their colors, which they obeyed with a general movement; and as General Johnston and myself rode forward shortly after with the colors of the 4th Alabama by our side, the line that had fought all morning, and had fled, routed and disordered, now advanced again into position as steadily as veterans. The 4th Alabama had previously lost all its field-officers; and noticing Colonel S. R. Gist, an aide to General Bee, a young man whom I had known as adjutant-general of South Carolina, and whom I greatly esteemed, I presented him as an able and brave commander to the stricken regiment, who cheered their new leader, and maintained under him, to the end of the day, their previous gallant behavior. We had come none too soon, as the enemy's forces, flushed with the belief of accomplished victory, were already advancing across the valley of Young's Branch and up the slope, where they had encountered for a while the fire of the Hampton Legion, which had been led forward toward the Robinson house and the turnpike in front, covering the retreat and helping materially to check the panic of Bee's routed forces.

As soon as order was restored I requested General Johnston to go back to Portici (the Lewis house), and from that point—which I considered most favorable for the purpose—forward me the reënforcements as they would come from the Bull Run lines below and those that were expected to arrive from Manassas, while I should direct the field. General Johnston was disinclined to leave the battle-field for that position. As I had been compelled to leave my chief-of-staff, Colonel Jordan, at Manassas to forward any troops arriving there, I felt it was a necessity that one of us should go to this duty, and that it was his place to do so, as I felt I was responsible for the battle. He considerately yielded to my urgency, and we had the benefit of his energy and sagacity in so directing the reënforcements toward the field, as to be readily and effectively assistant to my pressing needs and insure the success of the day.

As General Johnston departed for Portici, I hastened to form our line of battle against the on-coming enemy. I ordered up the 49th and 8th Virginia regiments from Cocke's neighboring brigade in the Bull Run lines. Gartrell's 7th Georgia I placed in position on the left of Jackson's brigade, along the belt of pines occupied by the latter on the eastern rim of the plateau. As the 49th Virginia rapidly came up, its colonel, ex-Governor William Smith, was encouraging them with cheery word and manner, and, as they approached, indicated to them the immediate presence of the commander. As the regiment raised a loud cheer, the name was caught by some of the troops of Jackson's brigade in the immediate wood, who rushed out, calling for General Beauregard. Hastily acknowledging these happy signs of sympathy and confidence, which reënforce alike the capacity of commander and troops, I placed the 49th Virginia in position on the extreme left next to Gartrell, and as I paused to say a few words to Jackson, while hurrying back to the right, my horse was killed under me by a bursting shell, a fragment of which carried away part of the heel of my boot. The Hampton Legion, which had suffered greatly, was placed on the right of Jackson's brigade, and Hunton's 8th Virginia, as it arrived, upon the right of

Hampton; the two latter being drawn somewhat to the rear so as to form with Jackson's right regiment a reserve, and be ready likewise to make defense against any advance from the direction of the Stone Bridge, whence there was imminent peril from the enemy's heavy forces, as I had just stripped that position almost entirely of troops to meet the active crisis on the plateau, leaving this quarter now covered only by a few men, whose defense was otherwise assisted solely by the obstruction of an abatis.

With 6500 men and 13 pieces of artillery, I now awaited the onset of the enemy, who were pressing forward 20,000 strong, ⊕ with 24 pieces of superior artillery and 7 companies of regular cavalry. They soon appeared over the farther rim of the plateau, seizing the Robinson house on my right and the Henry house opposite my left center. Near the latter they placed in position the two powerful batteries of Ricketts and Griffin of the regular army, and pushed forward up the Sudley road, the slope of which was cut so deep below the adjacent ground as to afford a covered way up to the plateau. Supported by the formidable lines of Federal musketry, these 2 batteries lost no time in making themselves felt, while 3 more batteries in rear on the high ground beyond the Sudley and Warrenton cross-roads swelled the shower of shell that fell among our ranks.

Our own batteries, Imboden's, Stanard's, five of Walton's guns, reënforced later by Pendleton's and Alburtis's (their disadvantage being reduced by the shortness of range), swept the surface of the plateau from their position on the eastern rim. I felt that, after the accidents of the morning, much depended on maintaining the steadiness of the troops against the first heavy onslaught, and rode along the lines encouraging the men to unflinching behavior, meeting, as I passed each command, a cheering response. The steady fire of their musketry told severely on the Federal ranks, and the splendid action of our batteries was a fit preface to the marked skill exhibited by our artillerists during the war. The enemy suffered particularly from the musketry on our left, now further reënforced by the 2d Mississippi—the troops in this quarter confronting each other at very short range. Here two companies of Stuart's cavalry charged through the Federal ranks that filled the Sudley road, increasing the disorder wrought upon that flank of the enemy. But with superior numbers the Federals were pushing on new regiments in the attempt to flank my position, and several guns, in the effort to enfilade ours, were thrust forward so near the 33d Virginia that some of its men sprang forward and captured them, but were driven back by an overpowering force of Federal musketry. Although the enemy were held well at bay, their pressure became so strong that I resolved to take the offensive, and

---

⊕According to General Fry, the Union force in the seizure of the Henry hill consisted of four brigades, a cavalry battalion, and two batteries, or (as we deduce from General Fry's statements of the strength of McDowell's forces) about 11,000 men.—EDITORS.

ordered a charge on my right for the purpose of recovering the plateau. The movement, made with alacrity and force by the commands of Bee, Bartow, Evans, and Hampton, thrilled the entire line, Jackson's brigade piercing the enemy's center, and the left of the line under Gartrell and Smith following up the charge, also, in that quarter, so that the whole of the open surface of the plateau was swept clear of the Federals.

Apart from its impressions on the enemy, the effect of this brilliant onset was to give a short breathing-spell to our troops from the immediate strain of conflict, and encourage them in withstanding the still more strenuous offensive that was soon to bear upon them. Reorganizing our line of battle under the unremitting fire of the Federal batteries opposite, I prepared to meet the new attack which the enemy were about to make, largely reënforced by the troops of Howard's brigade, newly arrived on the field. The Federals again pushed up the slope, the face of which partly afforded good cover by the numerous ravines that scored it and the clumps of young pines and oaks with which it was studded, while the sunken Sudley road formed a good ditch and parapet for their aggressive advance upon my left flank and rear. Gradually they pressed our lines back and regained possession of their lost ground and guns. With the Henry and Robinson houses once more in their possession, they resumed the offensive, urged forward by their commanders with conspicuous gallantry.

The conflict now became very severe for the final possession of this position, which was the key to victory. The Federal numbers enabled them so to extend their lines through the woods beyond the Sudley road as to outreach my left flank, which I was compelled partly to throw back, so as to meet the attack from that quarter; meanwhile their numbers equally enabled them to outflank my right in the direction of the Stone Bridge, imposing anxious watchfulness in that direction. I knew that I was safe if I could hold out till the arrival of reënforcements, which was but a matter of time; and, with the full sense of my own responsibility, I was determined to hold the line of the plateau, even if surrounded on all sides, until assistance should come, unless my forces were sooner overtaken by annihilation.

It was now between half-past 2 and 3 o'clock; a scorching sun increased the oppression of the troops, exhausted from incessant fighting, many of them having been engaged since the morning. Fearing lest the Federal offensive should secure too firm a grip, and knowing the fatal result that might spring from any grave infraction of my line, I determined to make another effort for the recovery of the plateau, and ordered a charge of the entire line of battle, including the reserves, which at this crisis I myself led into action. The movement was made with such keeping and dash that the whole plateau was swept clear of the enemy, who were driven down the slope and across the turnpike on our right and the valley of Young's Branch on our left, leaving in our final possession the Robinson and Henry houses, with most of Ricketts's and Griffin's batteries, the men of which were mostly shot down where they bravely stood by their guns. Fisher's 6th North Carolina, directed to the Lewis house by Colonel Jordan from Manassas, where it had just arrived, and thence to the field by General Johnston, came up in happy time to join in this charge on the left. Withers's 18th Virginia, which I had ordered up from Cocke's brigade, was also on hand in time to follow and give additional effect to the charge, capturing, by aid of the Hampton Legion, several guns, which were immediately turned and served upon the broken ranks of the enemy by some of our officers. This handsome work, which broke the Federal fortunes of the day, was done, however, at severe cost. The soldierly Bee, and the gallant, impetuous Bartow, whose day of strong deeds was about to close with such credit, fell a few rods back of the Henry house, near the very spot whence in the morning they had first looked forth upon Evans's struggle with the enemy. Colonel Fisher also fell at the very head of his troops. Seeing Captain Ricketts, who was badly wounded in the leg, and having known him in the old army, I paused from my anxious duties to ask him whether I could do anything for him. He answered that he wanted to be sent back to Washington. As some of our prisoners were there held under threats of not being treated as prisoners of war, I replied that that must depend upon how our prisoners were treated, and ordered him to be carried to the rear. I mention this, because the report of the Federal Committee on the Conduct of the War exhibits Captain Ricketts as testifying that I only approached him to say that he would be treated as our prisoners might be treated. I sent my own surgeons to care for him, and allowed his wife to cross the lines and accompany him to Richmond; and my adjutant-general, Colonel Jordan, escorting her to the car that carried them to that city, personally attended to the comfortable placing of the wounded enemy for the journey.

That part of the enemy who occupied the woods beyond our left and across the Sudley road had not been reached by the headlong charge which had swept their comrades from the plateau; but the now arriving reënforcements (Kershaw's 2d and Cash's 8th South Carolina) were led into that quarter. Kemper's battery also came up, preceded by its commander, who, while alone, fell into the hands of a number of the enemy, who took him prisoner, until a few moments later, when he handed them over to some of our own troops accompanying his battery. A small plateau, within the south-west angle of the Sudley and turnpike cross-roads, was still held by a strong Federal brigade—Howard's troops, together with Sykes's battalion of regulars; and while Kershaw and Cash, after passing through the skirts of the oak wood along the Sudley road, engaged this force, Kemper's battery was sent forward by Kershaw along the same road, into position near where a hostile battery had been captured, and whence it played upon the enemy in the open field.

Quickly following these regiments came Preston's 28th Virginia, which, passing through the woods, encountered and drove back some Michigan troops, capturing Brigadier-General Willcox. It was now about 3 o'clock, when another important reënforcement came to our aid—Elzey's brigade, 1700 strong, of the Army of the Shenandoah, which, coming from Piedmont by railroad, had arrived at Manassas station, 6 miles in rear of the battle-field, at noon, and had been without delay directed thence toward the field by Colonel Jordan, aided by Major T. G. Rhett, who that morning had passed from General Bonham's to General Johnston's staff. Upon nearing the vicinity of the Lewis house, the brigade was directed by a staff-officer sent by General Johnston toward the left of the field. As it reached the oak wood, just across the Sudley road, led by General Kirby Smith, the latter fell severely wounded; but the command devolved upon Colonel Elzey, an excellent officer, who was now guided by Captain D. B. Harris of the Engineers, a highly accomplished officer of my staff, still farther to the left and through the woods, so as to form an extension of the line of the preceding reënforcements. Beckham's battery, of the same command, was hurried forward by the Sudley road and around the woods into position near the Chinn house; from a well-selected point of action, in full view of the enemy that filled the open fields west of the Sudley road, it played with deadly and decisive effect upon their ranks, already under the fire of Elzey's brigade. Keyes's Federal brigade, which had made its way across the turnpike in rear of the Stone Bridge, was lurking along under cover of the ridges and a wood in order to turn my line on the right, but was easily repulsed by Latham's battery, already placed in position over that approach by Captain Harris, aided by Alburtis's battery, opportunely sent to Latham's left by General Jackson, and supported by fragments of troops collected by staff-officers. Meanwhile, the enemy had formed a line of battle of formidable proportions on the opposite height, and stretching in crescent outline, with flanks advanced, from the Pittsylvania (Carter) mansion on their left across the Sudley road in rear of Dogan's and reaching toward the Chinn house. They offered a fine spectacle as they threw forward a cloud of skirmishers down the opposite slope, preparatory to a new assault against the line on the plateau. But their right was now severely pressed by the troops that had successively arrived; the force in the south-west angle of the Sudley and Warrenton cross-roads were driven from their position, and, as Early's brigade, which, by direction of General Johnston, had swept around by the rear of the woods through which Elzey had passed, appeared on the field, his line of march bore upon the flank of the enemy, now retiring in that quarter.

This movement by my extreme left was masked by the trend of the woods from many of our forces on the plateau; and bidding those of my staff and escort around me raise a loud cheer, I dispatched the information to the several commands, with orders to go forward in a common charge. Before the full advance of the Confederate ranks the enemy's whole line, whose right was already yielding, irretrievably broke, fleeing across Bull Run by every available direction. Major Sykes's regulars, aided by Sherman's brigade, made a steady and handsome withdrawal, protecting the rear of the routed forces, and enabling many to escape by the Stone Bridge. Having ordered in pursuit all the troops on the field, I went to the Lewis house, and, the battle being ended, turned over the command to General Johnston. Mounting a fresh horse,—the fourth on that day,—I started to press the pursuit which was being made by our infantry and cavalry, some of the latter having been sent by General Johnston from Lewis's Ford to intercept the enemy on the turnpike. I was soon overtaken, however, by a courier bearing a message from Major T. G. Rhett, General Johnston's chief-of-staff on duty at Manassas railroad station, informing me of a report that a large Federal force, having pierced our lower line on Bull Run, was moving upon Camp Pickens, my depot of supplies near Manassas. I returned, and communicated this important news to General Johnston. Upon consultation it was deemed best that I should take Ewell's and Holmes's brigades, which were hastening up to the battle-field, but too late for the action, and fall on this force of the enemy, while reënforcements should be sent me from the pursuing forces, who were to be recalled for that purpose. To head off the danger and gain time, I hastily mounted a force of infantry behind the cavalrymen then

THE MAIN BATTLE-GROUND.—NO. I.

View of the Henry house, looking west from the spot where General Bee fell. The Bull Run mountains and Thoroughfare Gap appear in the distance. The Sudley road, a few rods beyond the house, under the hill, runs parallel with the rail fence (in the middle ground on the left). Just within the rail fence is where Griffin's and Ricketts's batteries were planted. Near the house stands the Union Monument, commemorating the battle.

THE MAIN BATTLE-GROUND.—NO. 2.

View of the Robinson house, looking north from the spot on the Henry plateau where General
Bee fell. At 1 P.M. this ground lay between the hostile lines, which were (roughly speaking) parallel with the sides of the picture: Confederates on the right, Union forces on the left. The foreground was between the centers of the positions.

    As these two views are taken from the same spot, the reader will best understand their relation
by holding the pages at a right angle to each other.

present, but, on approaching the line of march near McLean's Ford, which the
Federals must have taken, I learned that the news was a false alarm caught from
the return of General Jones's forces to this side of the Run, the similarity of the
uniforms and the direction of their march having convinced some nervous person that they were a force of the enemy. It was now almost dark, and too late to
resume the broken pursuit; on my return I met the coming forces, and, as they
were very tired, I ordered them to halt and bivouac for the night where they
were. After giving such attention as I could to the troops, I started for Manassas, where I arrived about 10 o'clock, and found Mr. Davis at my headquarters
with General Johnston. Arriving from Richmond late in the afternoon, Mr.
Davis had immediately galloped to the field, accompanied by Colonel Jordan.
They had met between Manassas and the battle-field the usual number of
stragglers to the rear, whose appearance belied the determined array then
sweeping the enemy before it, but Mr. Davis had the happiness to arrive in time
to witness the last of the Federals disappearing beyond Bull Run. The next
morning I received from his hand at our breakfast-table my commission, dated
July 21st, as General in the Army of the Confederate States, and after his return

to Richmond the kind congratulations of the Secretary of War and of General Lee, then acting as military adviser to the President.

It was a point made at the time at the North that, just as the Confederate troops were about to break and flee, the Federal troops anticipated them by doing so, being struck into this precipitation by the arrival upon their flank of the Shenandoah forces marching from railroad trains halted *en route* with that aim—errors that have been repeated by a number of writers, and by an ambitious but superficial French author.

There were certain sentiments of a personal character clustering about this first battle, and personal anxiety as to its issue, that gladly accepted this theory. To this may be added the general readiness to accept a sentimental or ultra-dramatic explanation—a sorcery wrought by the delay or arrival of some force, or the death or coming of somebody, or any other single magical event—whereby history is easily caught, rather than to seek an understanding of that which is but the gradual result of the operation of many forces, both of opposing design and actual collision, modified more or less by the falls of chance. The personal sentiment, though natural enough at the time, has no place in any military estimate, or place of any kind at this day. The battle of Manassas was, like any other battle, a progression and development from the deliberate counter-employment of the military resources in hand, affected by accidents, as always, but of a kind very different from those referred to. My line of battle, which twice had not only withstood the enemy's attack, but had taken the offensive and driven him back in disorder, was becoming momentarily stronger from the arrival, at last, of the reënforcements provided for; and if the enemy had remained on the field till the arrival of Ewell and Holmes, they would have been so strongly outflanked that many who escaped would have been destroyed or captured.

Though my adversary's plan of battle was a good one as against a passive defensive opponent, such as he may have deemed I must be from the respective numbers and positions of our forces, it would, in my judgment, have been much better if, with more dash, the flank attack had been made by the Stone Bridge itself and the ford immediately above it. The plan adopted, however, favored above all things the easy execution of the offensive operations I had designed and ordered against his left flank and rear at Centreville. His turning column—18,000 strong, and presumably his best troops—was thrown off by a long ellipse through a narrow forest road to Sudley Ford, from which it moved down upon my left flank, and was thus dislocated from his main body. This severed movement of his forces not only left his exposed left and rear at Centreville weak against the simultaneous offensive of my heaviest forces upon it, which I had ordered, but the movement of his returning column would have been disconcerted and paralyzed by the early sound of this heavy conflict in its rear, and it could not even have made its way back so as to be available for manœuvre before the Centreville fraction had been thrown back upon it in disorder. A new army is very liable to panic, and, in view of the actual result of the battle, the conclusion can hardly be resisted that the panic which fell on the Federal army would thus have seized it early in the day, and with my forces in such a position as wholly to cut off its retreat upon Washington. But the commander of the front line on my right, who had been ordered to hold himself in readiness to initiate the offensive at a moment's notice, did not make the move expected of him because through accident he failed to receive his own immediate order to advance.↓ The Federal commander's flanking movement, being thus uninterrupted by such a counter-movement as I had projected, was further assisted through the rawness and inadequacy of our staff organization through which I was left unacquainted with the actual state of affairs on my left. The Federal attack, already thus greatly favored, and encouraged, moreover, by the rout of General Bee's advanced line, failed for two reasons: their forces were not handled with concert of masses (a fault often made later on both sides), and the individual action of the Confederate troops was superior, and for a very palpable reason. That one army was fighting for union and the other for disunion is a political expression; the actual fact on the battle-field, in the face of cannon and musket, was that the Federal troops came as invaders, and the Southern troops stood as defenders of their homes, and further than this we need not go. The armies were vastly greater than had ever before fought on this continent, and were the largest volunteer armies ever assembled since the era of regular armies. The personal material on both sides was of exceptionally good character, and collectively superior to that of any subsequent period of the war.↓ The Confederate army was filled with generous youths who had answered the first call to arms. For certain kinds of field duty they were not as yet adapted, many of them having at first come with their baggage and servants; these they had to dispense with, but, not to offend their susceptibilities, I then exacted the least work from them, apart from military drills, even to the prejudice of important field-works, when I could not get sufficient negro labor; they "had come to fight, and not to handle the pick and shovel," and their fighting redeemed well their shortcomings as intrenchers. Before I left that gallant army, however, it had learned how readily the humbler could aid the nobler duty.

As to immediate results and trophies, we captured a great many stands of arms, batteries, equipments, standards, and flags, one of which was sent to me,

↓General R. S. Ewell.—EDITORS.

↓This battle was noteworthy for the number of participants whose names are now prominently associated with the war. On the Confederate side, besides Generals Johnston and Beauregard, were Generals Stonewall Jackson, Longstreet, Ewell, Early, J.E.B. Stuart, Kirby Smith, Wade Hampton, Fitzhugh Lee, Thomas Jordan, R. E. Rodes, F. P. Alexander, and others. On the Federal side were Generals McDowell, W. T. Sherman, Burnside, Hunter, Heintzelman, Howard, Franklin, Slocum, Keyes, Hunt, Barry, Fry, Sykes, Barnard, Wadsworth, and others.—EDITORS.

through General Longstreet, as a personal compliment by the Texan "crack shot," Colonel B. F. Terry, who lowered it from its mast at Fairfax Court House, by cutting the halyards by means of his unerring rifle, as our troops next morning reoccupied that place. We captured also many prisoners, including a number of surgeons, whom (the first time in war) we treated not as prisoners, but as guests. Calling attention to their brave devotion to their wounded, I recommended to the War Department that they be sent home without exchange, together with some other prisoners, who had shown personal kindness to Colonel Jones, of the 4th Alabama, who had been mortally wounded early in the day.

SUBSEQUENT RELATIONS OF MR. DAVIS AND THE WRITER.

The military result of the victory was far short of what it should have been. It established as an accomplished fact, on the indispensable basis of military success, the Government of the Confederate States, which before was but a political assertion; but it should have reached much further. The immediate pursuit, but for the false alarm which checked it, would have continued as far as the Potomac, but must have stopped there with no greater result than the capture of more prisoners and material. The true immediate fruits of the victory should have been the dispersion of all the Federal forces south of Baltimore and east of the Alleghanies, the liberation of the State of Maryland, and the capture of Washington, which could have been made only by the Upper Potomac. And from the high source of this achievement other decisive results would have continued to flow. From my experience in the Mexican war I had great confidence in intelligent volunteer troops, if rightly handled; and with such an active and victorious war-engine as the Confederate Army of the Potomac could have immediately been made,—reënforced, as time went, by numbers and discipline,—the Federal military power in the East could never have reached the head it took when McClellan was allowed to organize and discipline at leisure the powerful army that, in the end, wore out the South. In war one success makes another easier, and its right use is as the step to another, until final achievement. This was the use besought by me in the plan of campaign I have mentioned as presented to Mr. Davis on the 14th of July, a few days before the battle, but rejected by him as impracticable, and as rather offering opportunity to the enemy to crush us. To supply the deficiency of transportation (our vehicles being few in number, and many so poor as to break down in ordinary camp service), I myself had assigned to special duty Colonel (since Governor) James L. Kemper, of Virginia, who quickly obtained for me some two hundred good wagons, to which number I had limited him so as not to arouse again the jealousy of the President's staff. If my plan of operations for the capture of Washington had been adopted, I should have considered myself thereby authorized and free to obtain, as I readily could have done, the transportation necessary. As it was—though the difficult part of this "impracticable" plan of operations had been proven feasible, that is, the concentration of the Shenandoah forces with mine (wrung later than the eleventh hour through the alarm over the march upon Richmond, and discountenanced again nervously at the twelfth hour by another alarm as to how "the enemy may vary his plans" in consequence), followed by the decisive defeat of the main Federal forces—nevertheless the army remained rooted in the spot, although we had more than fifteen thousand troops who had been not at all or but little in the battle and were perfectly organized, while the remaining commands, in the high spirits of victory, could have been reorganized at the tap of the drum, and many with improved captured arms and equipments. I had already urged my views with unusual persistency, and acted on them against all but an express order to the contrary; and as they had been deliberately rejected in their ultimate scope by Mr. Davis as the commander-in-chief, I did not feel authorized to urge them further than their execution had been allowed, unless the subject were broached anew by himself. But there was no intimation of any such change of purpose, and the army, consistently with this inertia, was left unprovided for manœuvre with transportation for its ammunition; its fortitude, moreover, as a new and volunteer army, while spending sometimes 24 hours without food, being only less wonderful than the commissary administration at Richmond, from which such a state of affairs could proceed even two weeks after the battle of Manassas. Although certain political superstitions about not consolidating the North may then have weighed against the action I proposed, they would have been light against a true military policy, if such had existed in the head of the Government. Apart from an active material ally, such as the colonies had afield and on sea in the War of Independence with Great Britain, a country in fatal war must depend on the vigor of its warfare; the more inferior the country, the bolder and more enterprising the use of its resources, especially if its frontiers are convenient to the enemy. I was convinced that our success lay in a short, quick war of decisive blows, before the Federals, with their vast resources, could build up a great military power; to which end a concerted use of our forces, immediate and sustained, was necessary, so that, weaker though we were at all separate points, we might nevertheless strike with superior strength at some chosen decisive point, and after victory there reach for victory now made easier elsewhere, and thus sum up success. Instead of this, which in war we call concentration, our actual policy was diffusion, an inferior Confederate force at each separate point defensively confronting a superior Federal force; our power daily shrinking, that of the enemy increasing; the avowed Federal policy being that of "attrition," their bigger masses grinding our smaller, one by one, to naught. Out of this state we never emerged, when the direction of the Government was, as almost always, necessary, excepting when "Richmond" was immediately in danger.

FAIRFAX COURT HOUSE.
FROM A WAR-TIME PHOTOGRAPH.

Thus, in the fall of 1861, about three months after the battle of Manassas,—after throwing my whole force forward to Fairfax Court House, with outposts flaunting our flags on the hills in sight of Washington, in order to chafe the Federals to another battle, but without success,—I proposed that the army should be raised to an effective of 60,000 men, by drawing 20,000 for the immediate enterprise from several points along the seaboard, not even at that time threatened, and from our advanced position be swiftly thrown across the Potomac at a point which I had had carefully surveyed for that purpose, and moved upon the rear of Washington, thus forcing McClellan to a decisive engagement before his organization (new enlistments) was completed, and while our own army had the advantage of discipline and prestige—seasoned soldiers, whose term, however, would expire in the early part of the coming summer. This plan, approved by General Gustavus W. Smith (then immediately commanding General Johnston's own forces) as well as by General Johnston, was submitted to Mr. Davis in a conference at my headquarters, but rejected because he would not venture to strip those points of the troops we required. Even if those points had been captured, though none were then even threatened, they must have reverted as a direct consequence to so decisive a success. I was willing, then, should it have come to that, to exchange even Richmond temporarily for Washington. Yet it was precisely from similar combinations and elements that the army was made up, to enable it the next spring, under General Lee, to encounter McClellan at the very door of Richmond. If that which was accepted as a last defensive resort against an overwhelming aggressive army had been used in an enterprising offensive against that same army while yet in the raw, the same venture had been made at less general risk, less cost of valuable lives, and with greater certain results. The Federal army would have had no chance meanwhile to become tempered to that magnificent military machine which, through all its defeats and losses, remained sound, and was stronger, with its readily assimilating new strength, at the end of the war than ever before; the pressure would have been lifted from Kentucky and Missouri, and we should have maintained what is called an active defensive warfare, that is, should have taken and kept the offensive against the enemy, enforcing peace.

No people ever warred for independence with more relative advantages than the Confederates; and if, as a military question, they must have failed, then no country must aim at freedom by means of war. We were one in sentiment as in territory, starting out, not with a struggling administration of doubtful authority, but with our ancient State governments and a fully organized central government. As a military question, it was in no sense a civil war, but a war between two countries—for conquest on one side, for self-preservation on the other. The South, with its great material resources, its defensive means of mountains, rivers, railroads, and telegraph, with the immense advantage of the interior lines of war, would be open to discredit as a people if its failure could not be explained otherwise than by mere material contrast. The great Frederick, at the head of a little people, not only beat back a combination of several great military powers, but conquered and kept territory; and Napoleon held combined Europe at the feet of France till his blind ambition overleaped itself. It may be said that the South had no Fredericks or Napoleons; but it had at least as good commanders as its adversary. Nor was it the fault of our soldiers or people. Our soldiers were as brave and intelligent as ever bore arms; and, if only for reasons already mentioned, they did not lack in determination. Our people bore a devotion to the cause never surpassed, and which no war-making monarch ever had for his support; they gave their all—even the last striplings under the family roofs filling the ranks voided by the fall of their fathers and brothers. But the narrow military view of the head of the Government, which illustrated itself at the outset by ordering from Europe, not 100,000 or 1,000,000, but 10,000 stands of arms, as an increase upon 8000, its first estimate, was equally narrow and timid in its employment of our armies.

The moral and material forces actually engaged in the war made our success a moral certainty, but for the timid policy which—ignoring strategy as a science and boldness of enterprise as its ally—could never be brought to view the whole theater of war as one subject, of which all points were but integral parts, or to hazard for the time points relatively unimportant for the purpose of gathering for an overwhelming and rapid stroke at some decisive point; and which, again, with characteristic mis-elation, would push a victorious force directly forward into unsupported and disastrous operations, instead of using its victory to spare from it strength sufficient to secure an equally important success in another quarter. The great principles of war are truths, and the same today as in the time of Cæsar or Napoleon, notwithstanding the ideas of some thoughtless persons—their applications being but intensified by the scientific discoveries affecting transportation and communication of intelligence. These principles are few and simple, however various their deductions and application. Skill in strategy consists in seeing through the intricacies of the whole situation, and bringing into proper combination forces and influences, though seemingly unrelated, so as to apply these principles, and with boldness of decision and execution appearing with the utmost force, and, if possible, superior odds, before the enemy at some strategic, that is, decisive point. And although a sound military plan may not be always so readily conceived, yet any plan that offers decisive results, if it agree with the principles of war, is as plain and intelligible as these principles themselves, and no more to be rejected than they. There still remains, of course, the hazard of accident in execution, and the apprehension of the enemy's movements upsetting your own; but hazard may also favor as well as disfavor, and will not unbefriend the enterprising any more than the timid. It was this fear of possible consequences that kept our forces scattered in inferior relative strength at all points of the compass, each holding its bit of ground till by slow local process our territory was taken and our separate forces destroyed, or, if captured, retained by the enemy without exchange in their process of attrition. To stop the slow consumption of this passive mode of warfare I tried my part, and, at certain critical junctures, proposed to the Government active plans of operation looking to such results as I have described,—sometimes, it is true, in relation to the employment of forces not under my control, as I was the soldier of a cause and people, not of a monarch nor even of a government. Two occasions there were when certain of the most noted Federal operations, from their isolated or opportune character, might, with energy and intelligent venture on the Confederate side, have been turned into fatal disaster; among them Grant's movement in front of Vicksburg, and his change of base from the north to the south of the James River, where I was in command, in his last campaign against Richmond. I urged particularly that our warfare was sure of final defeat unless we attempted decisive strokes that might be followed up to the end, and that, even if earlier defeat might chance from the risk involved in the execution of the necessary combinations, we ought to take that risk and thereby either win or end an otherwise useless struggle. But, in addition to the radical divergence of military ideas,—the passive defensive of an intellect timid of risk and not at home in war, and the active defensive reaching for success through enterprise and boldness, according to the lessons taught us in the campaigns of the great masters,—there was a personal feeling that now gave cold hearing, or none, to any recommendations of mine. Mr. Davis's friendship, warm at the early period of the war, was changed, some time after the battle of Manassas, to a corresponding hostility from several personal causes, direct and indirect, of which I need mention but one. My report of Manassas having contained, as part of its history, a statement of the submission of the full plan of campaign for concentrating our forces, crushing successively McDowell and Patterson and capturing Washington, Mr. Davis strangely took offense thereat; and, now that events had demonstrated the practicability of that plan, he sought to get rid of his self-accused responsibility for rejecting it, by denying that any such had been submitted—an issue, for that matter, easily settled by my production of the contemporaneous report of Colonel James Chesnut, the bearer of the mission, who, moreover, at the time of this controversy was on Mr. Davis's own staff, where he remained. Mr. Davis made an endeavor to suppress the publication of my report of the battle of Manassas. The

RUINS OF THE STONE BRIDGE, LOOKING ALONG THE WARRENTON TURNPIKE
TOWARD THE BATTLE-FIELD.

This view is from a photograph taken in March, 1862, the region having been left open to the Union forces by the withdrawal of the Confederates. The Confederate battery which in the first battle of Bull Run commanded the bridge was placed on the left in the felled timber, which formed an abatis across the road. The battle was opened from beyond the small house, Van Pelt's, on the right, by the Rhode Island troops.—EDITORS.

matter came up in a secret debate in the Confederate Congress, where a host of friends were ready to sustain me; but I sent a telegram disclaiming any desire for its publication, and advising that the safety of the country should be our solicitude, and not personal ends.

Thenceforth Mr. Davis's hostility was watchful and adroit, neglecting no opportunity, great or small; and though, from motives all its opposite, it was not exposed during the war by any murmurs of mine, it bruited sometimes in certain quarters of its own force. Thus, when in January, 1862, the Western representatives expressed a desire that I should separate myself for a time from my Virginia forces and go to the defense of the Mississippi Valley from the impending offensive of Halleck and Grant, it was furthered by the Executive with inducements which I trusted,—in disregard of Senator Toombs's sagacious warning, that under this furtherance lurked a purpose to effect my downfall, urged in one of his communications through his son-in-law, Mr. Alexander, in words as impressive as they proved prophetic: "Urge General Beauregard to decline all proposals and solicitations. The Blade of Joab. *Verbum Sapienti.*" After

going through the campaign of Shiloh and Corinth, not only with those inducements unfulfilled, but with vital drawbacks from the Government, including
the refusal of necessary rank to competent subordinates to assist in organizing
my hastily collected and mostly raw troops, I was forced, the following June, in
deferred obedience to the positive order of my physicians, to withdraw from
my immediate camp to another point in my department for recovery from illness, leaving under the care of my lieutenant, General Bragg, my army, then
unmenaced and under reorganization with a view to an immediate offensive I
had purposed. In anticipation and exclusion of the receipt of full dispatches following my telegram, the latter was tortuously misread, in a manner not creditable to a school-boy and repugnant to Mr. Davis's exact knowledge of syntax,
so as to give pretext to the shocking charge that I had abandoned my army, and
a telegram was sent in naked haste directly to General Bragg, telling him to retain the permanent command of the army. The "Blade of Joab" had given its
thrust. The representatives in Congress from the West and South-west applied
to Mr. Davis in a body for my restoration; and when, disregarding his sheer pretext that I had abandoned my army, they still insisted, Mr. Davis declared that
I should not be restored *if the whole world should ask it!* This machination went to
such length that it was given out in Richmond that I had softening of the brain
and had gone crazy. So carefully was this report fostered (one of its tales being
that I would sit all day stroking a pheasant) ╱ that a friend of mine, a member of
the Confederate Congress, thought it his duty to write me a special letter respecting the device, advising me to come directly to Richmond to confound it
by my presence—a proceeding which I disdained to take. I had not only then,
but from later, still more offensive provocation, imperative cause to resign, and
would have done so but for a sense of public obligation. Indeed, in my after
fields of action the same hostility was more and more active in its various embarrassments, reckless that the strains inflicted upon me bore upon the troops
and country depending on me and relatively upon the cause, so that I often
dreaded failure more from my own Government behind me than from the
enemy in my front; and, when success came in spite of this, it was acknowledged only by some censorious official "inquiry" contrasting with the repeated
thanks of the Congress. I was, however, not the only one of the highest military
rank with whom Mr. Davis's relations were habitually unwholesome. It is an extraordinary fact that during the four years of war Mr. Davis did not call together the five generals [see page 122] with a view to determining the best

---

╱This silly tale was borrowed from an incident of Shiloh. Toward the end of the first day's battle a soldier had found a pheasant cowering, apparently paralyzed under the ceaseless din, and brought it to my
headquarters as a present to me. It was a beautiful bird, and I gave directions to place it in a cage, as I intended sending it as a pleasant token of the battle to the family of Judge Milton Brown, of Jackson, Tennessee, from whom I had received as their guest, while occupying that place, the kindest attentions; but
in the second day's conflict the poor waif was lost.—G.T.B.

military policy or settling upon a decisive plan of operations involving the whole theater of war, though there was often ample opportunity for it. We needed for President either a military man of a high order, or a politician of the first class without military pretensions, such as Howell Cobb. The South did not fall crushed by the mere weight of the North; but it was nibbled away at all sides and ends because its executive head never gathered and wielded its great strength under the ready advantages that greatly reduced or neutralized its adversary's naked physical superiority. It is but another of the many proofs that timid direction may readily go with physical courage, and that the passive defensive policy may make a long agony, but can never win a war.

POSTSCRIPT.—Since the publication of the foregoing pages in "The Century" for November, 1884, General J. E. Johnston, in the course of a paper also contributed to "The Century" [see page 121], took occasion, for the first time, to set up with positiveness and circumstantiality the claim to having exercised a controlling connection with the tactics of all the phases of the battle of the 21st of July, 1861. Respecting such a pretension I shall be content for the present to recall that, while entirely at variance with the part I have ascribed to him in relation to that field, it is logically untenable, at this day, when confronted with the records of the period. In my own official report of the battle closely contemporaneous with the events narrated—a report that was placed in his hands for perusal before transmission—it is distinctly related that for certain reasons, chiefly military, General Johnston had left in my hands for the impending conflict the command of the Confederate forces. The precise circumstances of my direct conduct of and responsibility for the battle are stated in such terms that, had I not been in actual direction of the day's operations on the part of the Confederates, General Johnston must have made the issue squarely then and there in his own official report. And all the more incumbent upon him was the making of such an issue, it seems to me, then or never, in view of the fact that the Confederate Secretary of War on the 24th of July, 1861, wrote me in these words:

> "My Dear General:
>   "Accept my congratulations for the glorious and most brilliant victory achieved by you. The country will bless and honor you for it. Believe me, dear General,
>
> > "Truly your friend,
> > "L. P. WALKER."

Further, General Lee thus addressed me:

> "My Dear General:
>   "I cannot express the joy I feel at the brilliant victory of the 21st. The skill, courage, and endurance displayed by yourself excite my highest ad-

miration. You and your troops have the gratitude of the whole country, and I offer to all my heartfelt congratulations at their success....

"Very truly yours,
"R. E. LEE."

Of the exact purport of these two letters General Johnston could not have been ignorant when he wrote his report of the battle. Nor could he have been unaware that the leading Southern newspapers had in effect attributed to me the chief direction of that battle on the Confederate side. Therefore, if it were the gross historical error which, twenty odd years after the affair, General Johnston characterizes it to be, and one that imputed to him the shirking of a duty which he could not have left unassumed without personal baseness, certainly that was the time for him by a few explicit words in his official report to dispose of so affronting an error. In that report, however, no such exigent, peremptory statement of his relation to the battle is to be found. On the other hand, upon page 57 of his "Narrative" published in 1874 (D. Appleton & Co.), may be found, I fear, the clew to the motive of his actual waiver of command in this curious paragraph:

"If the tactics of the Federals had been equal to their strategy, we should have been beaten. If, instead of being brought into action in detail, their troops had been formed in two lines, with a proper reserve, and had assailed Bee and Jackson in that order, the two Southern brigades must have been swept from the field in a few minutes; or enveloped. General McDowell would have made such a formation, probably, had he not greatly underestimated the strength of his enemy."

CONFEDERATE QUAKER GUNS.
FROM A PHOTOGRAPH.

Confederate fortifications, near Centreville, after their evacuation in the spring of 1862. The muzzle of the log was painted black and the breech was covered with brush to conceal its character from observation by balloon.

Coupled with the disquieting, ever-apprehensive tenor of his whole correspondence with the Confederate War Department, from the day he assumed command in the Valley of Virginia in May, 1861, down to the close of the struggle in 1865, the fair inference from such language as that just cited from his "Narrative" is that General Johnston came to Manassas beset with the idea that our united forces would not be able to cope with the Federal army, and that we should be beaten—a catastrophe in which he

FROM A PHOTOGRAPH TAKEN AFTER THE WAR.

was not solicitous to figure on the pages of history as the leading and responsible actor. Originally and until 1875, I had regarded it as a generous though natural act on the part of General Johnston, in such a juncture, to leave me in
command and responsible for what might occur. The history of military operations abounds in instances of notable soldiers who have found it proper to
waive chief command under similar conditions.

CHAPTER 7

RESPONSIBILITIES OF THE FIRST BULL RUN.

Joseph E. Johnston, General, C.S.A.

When the State of Virginia seceded, being a citizen of that State, I resigned my office in the United States Army; and as I had seen a good deal of military service, in the Seminole and Mexican wars and in the West, the President of the Confederacy offered me a commission in the highest grade in his army. I accepted the offer because the invasion of the South was inevitable. But I soon incurred Mr. Davis's displeasure by protesting against an illegal act of his by which I was greatly wronged.‡ Still he retained me in important positions, although his official letters were harsh. In 1864, however, he degraded me to the

---

‡The letter of protest covered nine sheets of letter-paper, and the ninth sheet (to quote from the original) sums up the matter in these words:

> "My commission is made to bear such a date that my once inferiors in the service of the United States and of the Confederate States shall be above me. But it must not be dated as of the 21st of July nor be suggestive of the victory of Manassas. I return to my first position. I repeat that my right to my rank as General is established by the Acts of Congress of the 14th of March, 1861, and the 16th of May, 1861, and not by the nomination and confirmation of the 31st of August, 1861. To deprive me of that rank it was necessary for Congress to repeal those laws. That could be done by express legislative act alone. It was not done, it could not be done, by a mere vote in secret session upon a list of nominations. If the action against which I have protested be legal, it is not for me to question the expediency of degrading one who has served laboriously from the commencement of the war on this frontier, and borne a prominent part in the only great event of that war for the benefit of persons neither of whom has yet struck a blow for this Confederacy. These views and the freedom with which they are presented may be unusual. So likewise is the occasion which calls them forth. I have the honor to be, very respectfully, your obedient servant.
>
> "J. E. JOHNSTON, GENERAL.
>
> "To His Excellency, Jefferson Davis, President of the Confederate States, Richmond."

This ninth sheet is all of the original letter that can be found by the present owner, Mrs. Bledsoe, widow of Dr. Albert T. Bledsoe, who, at the time the letter was written, was Assistant-Secretary of War. Dr. Bledsoe told his wife that President Davis handed the letter to him, with the remark that it would not go upon the official files, and that he might keep it if he liked.—EDITORS.

QUAKER GUN FOUND IN THE
CONFEDERATE WORKS AT MANASSAS.
FROM A PHOTOGRAPH.

utmost of his power by summarily removing me from a high command. Believing that he was prompted to this act by animosity, and not by dispassionate opinion, I undertake to prove this animosity by many extracts from his "Rise and Fall of the Confederacy" (D. Appleton & Co.: 1881), and my comments thereon.

Mr. Davis recites ("R. and F.," I., p. 307) the law securing to officers who might leave the United States Army to enter that of the Confederacy the same relative rank in the latter which they had in the former, provided their resignations had been offered in the six months next following the 14th of March, and then adds:

"The provisions hereof are in the view entertained that the army was of the States, not of the Government, and was to secure to officers adhering to the Confederate States the same relative rank which they had before those States had withdrawn from the Union. . . .

"How well the Government of the Confederacy observed both the letter and spirit of the law will be seen by reference to its action in the matter of appointments."

Those of the five generals were the most prominent, of course. All had resigned within the time prescribed. Their relative rank in the United States Army just before secession had been: 1st, J. E. Johnston, Brigadier-General; 2d, Samuel Cooper, Colonel; 3d, A. S. Johnston, Colonel; 4th, R. E. Lee, Lieutenant-Colonel; and 5th, G. T. Beauregard, Major. All of them but the third had had previous appointments, when, on the 31st of August, the Confederate Government announced new ones: Cooper's being dated May 16th, A. S. Johnston's May 28th, Lee's June 14th, J. E. Johnston's July 4th, and Beauregard's July 21st. So the law was violated, 1st, by disregarding existing commissions; 2d, by giving different instead of the same dates to commissions; and 3d, by not recognizing previous rank in the United States Army. The only effect of this triple violation of law was to reduce J. E. Johnston from the first to the fourth place, which, of course, must have been its object. Mr. Davis continues:

"It is a noteworthy fact that the three highest officers in rank . . . were all so indifferent to any question of personal interest that they had received their appointment before they were aware it was to be conferred" (p. 307).

This implies that the conduct described was unusual. On the contrary, it was that of the body of officers who left the United States Army to enter that of the Confederacy. It is strange that the author should disparage so many honorable men. He states ("R. and F.," I., 309) that General Lee, when ordered from Richmond to the South for the first time, asked what rank he held in the army: "So wholly had his heart and his mind been consecrated to the public service that he had not remembered, if he ever knew, of his advancement."

As each grade has its duties, an officer cannot know his duty if ignorant of his rank. Therefore General Lee always knew his rank, for he never failed in his duty. Besides, his official correspondence at the time referred to shows that he knew that he was major-general of the Virginia forces until May 25th, 1861, and a Confederate general after that date.

GENERAL SAMUEL COOPER, ADJUTANT AND INSPECTOR-GENERAL, C.S.A., RANKING OFFICER IN THE CONFEDERATE ARMY. FROM A PHOTOGRAPH.

Describing the events which immediately preceded the battle of Manassas, Mr. Davis says ("Rise and Fall," I., 340):

> "The forces there assembled [in Virginia] were divided into three armies, at positions the most important and threatened: one, under General J. E. Johnston, at Harper's Ferry, covering the valley of the Shenandoah.... Harper's Ferry was an important position both for military and political considerations.... The demonstrations of General Patterson, commanding the Federal army in that region, caused General Johnston earnestly to insist on being allowed to retire to a position nearer to Winchester."

Harper's Ferry is 22 miles east of the route into the Shenandoah Valley, and could be held only by an army strong enough to drive an enemy from the heights north and east of it. So it is anything but an important position. These objections were expressed to the Government two days after my arrival, and I suggested that being permitted to move the troops as might be necessary. All this before Patterson had advanced from Chambersburg.

On page 341, "R. and F.," Mr. Davis quotes from an official letter to me from General Cooper, dated June 13th, 1861, which began thus:

"The opinions expressed by Major Whiting in his letter to you, and on which you have indorsed your concurrence, have been duly considered. You had been heretofore instructed to exercise your discretion as to retiring from your position at Harper's Ferry."[✛]

This latter statement is incorrect. No such instructions had been given. The last instructions on the subject received by me were in General Lee's letter of June 7th.[✦] On page 341 Mr. Davis says:

"The temporary occupation [of Harper's Ferry] was especially needful for the removal of the valuable machinery and material in the armory located there."

The removal of the machinery was not an object referred to in General Cooper's letter. But the presence of our army anywhere in the Valley within a day's march of the position, would have protected that removal. That letter (page 341) was received two days after the army left Harper's Ferry to meet General McClellan's troops, believed by intelligent people of Winchester to be approaching from the west.

On page 345 Mr. Davis says it was a difficult problem to know which army, whether Beauregard's at Manassas or Johnston's in the Valley, should be reënforced by the other, because these generals were "each asking reënforcements from the other." All that was written by me on the subject is in the letter (page 345) dated July 9th:

"I have not asked for reënforcements because I supposed that the War Department, informed of the state of affairs everywhere, could best judge where the troops at its disposal are most required.... If it is proposed to strengthen us against the attack I suggest as soon to be made, it seems to me that General Beauregard might with *great expedition* furnish 5000 or 6000 men for a few days."

[✛]This letter of Major Whiting to General Johnston, and General Johnston's letter (probably referred to as the indorsement), are both dated May 28th, 1861. The phrase of General Cooper, "You had been heretofore instructed," should have read either, "You had been *theretofore* [before May 28th] instructed," or, "You *have* been heretofore [before June 13th] instructed." The latter is probably what was meant, as the only letter of instructions to General Johnston received at Harper's Ferry giving him permission to use his discretion which is to be found in the Official Records, is the one of June 7th from General Lee, in which he says: "It is hoped that you will be able to be timely informed of the approach of troops against you, and retire, provided they cannot be successfully opposed. You must exercise your discretion and judgment in this respect."—EDITORS.

[✦]"Official Records," II., 910.

Mr. Davis says, after quoting from this letter:

"As soon as I became satisfied that Manassas was the objective point of the enemy's movement, I wrote to General Johnston urging him to make preparations for a junction with General Beauregard."

There is abundant evidence that the Southern President never thought of transferring the troops in the "Valley" to Manassas until the proper time to do it came—that is, when McDowell was known to be advancing. This fact is shown by the anxiety he expressed to increase the number of those troops.[*] And General Lee, writing [from South Carolina] to Mr. Davis, November 24th, 1861 ("Official Records," II., 515), says in regard to General Beauregard's suggestion that he be reënforced from my army:

"You decided that the movements of the enemy in and about Alexandria were not sufficiently demonstrative to warrant the withdrawing of any of the forces from the Shenandoah Valley. A few days afterward, however,—I think three or four,—the reports from General Beauregard showed so clearly the enemy's purpose, that you ordered General Johnston, with his effective force, to march at once to the support of General Beauregard."

This letter is in reply to one from Mr. Davis, to the effect that statements had been widely published to show that General Beauregard's forces had been held inactive by his (Mr. Davis's) rejection of plans for vigorous offensive operations proposed to him by the general, and desiring to know of General Lee what those plans were, and why they were rejected.

"On the 17th of July, 1861," says Mr. Davis ("R. and F.," I., 346), "the following telegram was sent by the adjutant-general" to General Johnston, Winchester, Va.:

"General Beauregard is attacked. To strike the enemy a decisive blow, a junction of all your effective force will be needed. If practicable, make the movement, sending your sick and baggage to Culpeper Court House, either by railroad or by Warrenton. In all the arrangements exercise your discretion. S. COOPER, Adjutant and Inspector-General."

Mr. Davis asserts that I claim that discretion was given me by the words "all the arrangements." I claimed it from what he terms the only positive part of the

[*]See "Official Records," II., 924, 935, 940, 973, 976–977.

order, viz., "If practicable, make the movement, sending your sick to Culpeper Court House." Mr. Davis adds:

> "The sending the sick to Culpeper Court House might have been after or before the effective force had moved to the execution of the main and only positive part of the order."

"Make the movement" would have been a positive order, but "if practicable" deprived it of that character, and gave the officer receiving it a certain discretion. But, as the movement desired was made promptly, it was surely idle to discuss, twenty years after, whether the officer could lawfully have done what he *did not do.* At the time the decision of such a question might have been necessary; but, as Mr. Davis will give no more orders to generals, and as the officer concerned will execute no more, such a discussion is idle now. The use of the wagons required in the march of the army would have been necessary to remove the sick to the railroad station at Strasburg, eighteen miles distant; so this removal could *not* have been made *after* the march. There being seventeen hundred sick, this part of their transportation would have required more time than the transfer of the troops to Manassas, which was the important thing. The sick were, therefore, properly and quickly provided for in Winchester. I was the only judge of the "practicable"; and "if practicable" refers to the whole sentence—as much to sending the sick to Culpeper as to "make the movement." Still he says ("R. and F.," I., 347):

> "His [my] letters of the 12th and 15th expressed his doubts about his power to retire from before the superior force of General Patterson. Therefore, the word 'practicable' was in that connection the equivalent of 'possible.'"

It is immaterial whether "if practicable" or "if possible" was written. I was the only judge of the possibility or practicability; and, if General Patterson had not changed his position after the telegram was received, I might have thought it necessary to attack him, to "make the movement practicable." But as to my power to retire. On the 15th General Patterson's forces were half a day's march from us, and on the 12th more than a day's march; and, as Stuart's cavalry did not permit the enemy to observe us, retreat would have been easy, and I could not possibly have written to the contrary. ╱

╱Mr. Davis has a few words of praise for General Johnston, which, in this connection, will be of interest to the reader: "It gives me pleasure to state that, from all the accounts received at the time, the plans of General Johnston for masking his withdrawal to form a junction with General Beauregard were conducted with marked skill" ("R. and F.," I., 347).—Editors.

As to Mr. Davis's telegram ("R. and F.," I., 348),[☆] and the anxiety in Mr. Davis's mind lest there should be some unfortunate misunderstanding between General Beauregard and me,—my inquiry was intended and calculated to establish beyond dispute our relative positions. As a Confederate brigadier-general I had been junior to General Beauregard, but had been created general by act of Congress. But, as this had not been published to the army, it was not certain that it was known at Manassas. If it was not, the President's telegram gave the information, and prevented what he seems to have apprehended.

THE BATTLE OF BULL RUN.

On page 349, to the end of the chapter, the President describes his visit to the field of battle near Manassas. "As we advanced," he says, "the storm of battle was rolling westward." But, in fact, the fighting had ceased before he left Manassas. He then mentions meeting me on a hill which commanded a general view of the field, and proceeding farther west, where he saw a Federal "column," which a Confederate squadron charged and put to flight. But the captain in command of this squadron[♁] says in his report that the column seen was a party of our troops. Mr. Davis also dilates on the suffering of our troops for want of supplies and camp equipage, and on his efforts to have them provided for. After the battle ended, officers were duly directed by me to have food brought to the ground where the troops were to pass the night.

I was not in the conference described by Mr. Davis ("R. and F.," I., 353, 354, 355). Having left the field after 10 o'clock, and ridden in the dark slowly, it was about half-past 11 when I found the President and General Beauregard together, in the latter's quarters at Manassas. We three conversed an hour or more without referring to pursuit or an advance upon Washington. The "conference" described by him must have occurred before my arrival, and Mr. Davis may very well have forgotten that I was not present then.

But, when the President wrote, he had forgotten the subject of the conference he described; for the result, as he states it, was an order, not for pursuit by the army, but for the detail of two parties to collect wounded men and abandoned property near the field of battle. This order (pages 355, 356) is "to the same effect," Mr. Davis says, as the one he wrote, and which he terms a direction to pursue the Federal army at early dawn.

[☆]This telegram, sent in response to an inquiry from General Johnston, read as follows:

> "Richmond, July 20, 1861. General J. E. Johnston, Manassas Junction, Virginia: You are a general in the Confederate Army, possessed of the power attaching to that rank. You will know how to make the exact knowledge of Brigadier-General Beauregard, as well of the ground as of the troops and preparation, avail for the success of the object in which you coöperate. The zeal of both assures me of harmonious action. JEFFERSON DAVIS."

[♁]Captain John F. Lay. See "Official Records," II., 573.—EDITORS.

It is asserted ("R. and F.," I., 354)✦ that I left the command over both Confederate armies in General Beauregard's hands during the engagement. Such conduct would have been as base as flight from the field in the heat of battle, and would have brought upon me the contempt of every honorable soldier. It is disproved by the fact that General Beauregard was willing to serve under me there, and again in North Carolina, near the close of the war; and that he associated with me. As this accusation is published by the Southern President, and indorsed by General Beauregard, it requires my contradiction.

Instead of leaving the command in General Beauregard's hands, I assumed it over both armies immediately after my arrival on the 20th, showing General Beauregard as my warrant the President's telegram defining my position. The usual order♭ assuming command was written and sent to General Beauregard's office for distribution. He was then told that as General Patterson would no doubt hasten to join General McDowell as soon as he discovered my movement, we must attack the Federal army next morning. General Beauregard then pointed out on a map of the neighborhood the roads leading to the enemy's camp at Centreville from the different parts of our line south of the stream, and the positions of the brigades near each road; and a simple order of march, by which our troops would unite near the Federal position, was sketched. Having had neither sleep nor recumbent rest since the morning of the 17th, I begged General Beauregard to put this order of march on paper, and have the necessary copies made and sent to me for inspection in a grove, near, where I expected to be resting—this in time for distribution before night. This distribution was to be by him, the immediate commander of most of the troops. Seeing that 8 brigades were on the right of the line to Centreville, and but 1 to the left of it at a distance of 4 miles, I desired General Beauregard to have Bee's and Jackson's brigades placed in this interval near the detached brigade.

The papers were brought to me a little before sunrise next morning. They differed greatly from the order sketched the day before; but as they would have put the troops in motion if distributed, it would have been easy then to direct the course of each division. By the order sketched the day before, all our forces would have been concentrated near Centreville, to attack the Federal army. By that prepared by General Beauregard but 4 brigades were directed "to the attack of Centreville," of which one and a half had not yet arrived from the Valley, while 6 brigades were to move forward to the Union Mills and Centreville road, there to hold themselves in readiness to support the attack on Centreville, or to move, 2 to Sangster's cross-roads, 2 to Fairfax Station, and 2 to Fairfax

✦Not by Mr. Davis, but in a letter from General Thomas Jordan, quoted by Mr. Davis for another purpose.—EDITORS.
♭General J. A. Early, in his narrative of these events, says: "During the 20th, General Johnston arrived at Manassas Junction by the railroad, and that day we received the order from him assuming command of the combined armies of General Beauregard and himself."—J.E.J.

Court House. The two and a half brigades on the ground, even supported by the half brigade of the reserve also on the ground, in all probability would have been defeated by the whole Federal army before the three bodies of 2 brigades each could have come to their aid, over distances of from 3 to 5 miles. Then, if the enemy had providentially been defeated by one-sixth or one-eighth of their number, Sangster's cross-roads and Fairfax Station would have been out of their line of retreat.

Soon after sunrise on the 21st, it was reported that a large body of Federal troops was approaching on the Warrenton Turnpike. This offensive movement of the enemy would have *frustrated our plan of the day before,* if the orders for it had been delivered to the troops. It appears from the reports of the commanders of the six brigades on the right that but one of them, General Longstreet, received it. Learning that Bee's and Jackson's brigades were still on the right, I again desired General Beauregard to transfer them to the left, which he did, giving the same orders to Hampton's Legion, just arrived. These, with Cocke's brigade then near the turnpike, would necessarily receive the threatened attack.

General Beauregard then suggested that all our troops on the right should move rapidly to the left and assail the attacking Federal troops in flank. This suggestion was accepted; and together we joined those troops. Three of the four brigades of the first line, at Mitchell's, Blackburn's, and McLean's fords, reported strong bodies of United States troops on the wooded heights before them. This *frustrated the second plan.* Two Federal batteries—one in front of Bonham's brigade at Mitchell's Ford, the other before Longstreet's at Blackburn's Ford—were annoying us, although their firing was slow.

About 8 o'clock, after receiving such information as scouts could give, I left General Beauregard near Longstreet's position, and placed myself on Lookout Hill, in rear of Mitchell's Ford, to await the development of the enemy's designs. About 9 o'clock the signal officer, Captain Alexander, reported that a column of Federal troops could be seen crossing the valley of Bull Run, two miles beyond our left.

General McDowell had been instructed by his general-in-chief to pass the Confederate right and seize the railroad in our rear. But, learning that the district to be passed through was rugged and covered with woods, and therefore unfavorable to a large army, he determined, after devoting three days to reconnoissance, to operate on the open and favorable ground to his right, and turn our left. He had another object in this second plan, and an important one—that this course would place his between the two Confederate armies, and prevent their junction; and if it had been made a day or two sooner, this manœuvre would have accomplished that object.

General McDowell marched from Centreville by the Warrenton Turnpike with three divisions, sending a fourth division to deceive us by demonstrations in front of our main body. Leaving the turnpike a half mile from the Stone

Bridge, he made a long détour to Sudley Ford, where he crossed Bull Run and turned toward Manassas. Colonel Evans, who commanded fourteen companies near the Stone Bridge, discovered this manœuvre, and moved with his little force along the base of the hill north of the turnpike, to place it before the enemy near the Sudley and Manassas road. Here he was assailed by greatly superior numbers, which he resisted obstinately.

General Beauregard had joined me on Lookout Hill, and we could distinctly hear the sounds and see the smoke of the fight. But they indicated no hostile force that Evans's troops and those of Bee, Hampton, and Jackson, which we could see hurrying toward the conflict in that order, were not adequate to resist.

On reaching the broad, level top of the hill south of the turnpike, Bee, appreciating the strength of the position, formed his troops (half of his own and half of Bartow's brigade) on that ground. But seeing Evans struggling against great odds, he crossed the valley and formed on the right and a little in advance of him. Here the 5 or 6 regiments, with 6 field-pieces, held their ground for an hour against 10,000 or 12,000 United States troops,／ when, finding they were overlapped on each flank by the continually arriving enemy, General Bee fell back to the position from which he had moved to rescue Evans—crossing the valley, closely pressed by the Federal army.

Hampton with his Legion reached the valley as the retrograde movement began. Forming it promptly, he joined in the action, and contributed greatly to the orderly character of the retreat by his courage and admirable soldiership, seconded by the excellent conduct of the gentlemen composing his command. Imboden and his battery did excellent service on this trying occasion. Bee met Jackson at the head of his brigade, on the position he had first taken, and he began to re-form and Jackson to deploy at the same time.

In the mean time I had been waiting with General Beauregard on Lookout Hill for evidence of General McDowell's design. The violence of the firing on the left indicated a battle, but the large bodies of troops reported by chosen scouts to be facing our right kept me in doubt. But near 11 o'clock reports that those troops were felling trees showed that they were standing on the defensive; and new clouds of dust on the left proved that a large body of Federal troops was arriving on the field. It thus appeared that the enemy's great effort was to be against our left. I expressed this to General Beauregard, and the necessity of reënforcing the brigades engaged, and desired him to send immediate orders to Early and Holmes, of the second line, to hasten to the conflict with their

／General Fry states that these troops were Andrew Porter's and Burnside's brigades, and one regiment of Heintzelman's division. Reckoning by the estimate of strength given by General Fry these would have made a total of about 6500 men.—EDITORS.

brigades. General Bonham, who was near me, was desired to send up two regiments and a battery. I then set off at a rapid gallop to the scene of action. General Beauregard joined me without a word. Passing on the way Colonel Pendleton with two batteries, I directed him to follow with them as fast as possible.

It now seemed that a battle was to be fought entirely different in place and circumstance from the two plans previously adopted and abandoned as impracticable. Instead of taking the initiative and operating in front of our line, we were compelled to fight on the defensive more than a mile in rear of that line, and at right angles to it, on a field selected by Bee,—with no other plans than those suggested by the changing events of battle.

While we were riding forward General Beauregard suggested to me to assign him to the immediate command of the troops engaged, so that my supervision of the whole field might not be interrupted, to which I assented. So he commanded those troops under me; as elsewhere, lieutenant-generals commanded corps, and major-generals divisions, under me.

When we were near the ground where Bee was re-forming and Jackson deploying his brigade, I saw a regiment in line with ordered arms and facing to the front, but 200 or 300 yards in rear of its proper place. On inquiry I learned that it had lost all its field-officers; so, riding on its left flank, I easily marched it to its place. It was the 4th Alabama, an excellent regiment; and I mention this because the circumstance has been greatly exaggerated.

After the troops were in good battle order I turned to the supervision of the whole field. The enemy's great numerical superiority was discouraging. Yet, from strong faith in Beauregard's capacity and courage, and the high soldierly qualities of Bee and Jackson, I hoped that the fight would be maintained until I could bring adequate reënforcements to their aid. For this Holmes and Early were urged to hasten their march, and Ewell was ordered to follow them with his brigade with all speed. Broken troops were reorganized and led back into the fight with the help of my own and part of General Beauregard's staff. Cocke's brigade was held in rear of the right to observe a large body of Federal troops in a position from which Bee's right flank could have been struck in a few minutes.

After these additions had been made to our troops then engaged, we had 9 regiments of infantry, 5 batteries, and 300 cavalry of the Army of the Shenandoah, and about 2 regiments and a half of infantry, 6 companies of cavalry, and 6 field-pieces of the Army of the Potomac, holding at bay 3 divisions of the enemy. The Southern soldiers had, however, two great advantages in the contest: greater skill in the use of fire-arms, and the standing on the defensive, by which they escaped such disorder as advancing under fire produced in the ranks of their adversaries, undisciplined like themselves.

A report received about 2 o'clock from General Beauregard's office that another United States army was approaching from the north-west, and but a few miles from us, caused me to send orders to Bonham, Longstreet, and Jones to hold their brigades south of Bull Run, and ready to move.

When Bonham's two regiments appeared soon after, Cocke's brigade was ordered into action on our right. Fisher's North Carolina regiment coming up, Bonham's two regiments were directed against the Federal right, and Fisher's was afterward sent in the same direction; for the enemy's strongest efforts seemed to be directed against our left, as if to separate us from Manassas Junction.

About 3:30 o'clock, General E. K. Smith arrived with three regiments of Elzey's brigade, coming from Manassas Junction. He was instructed, through a staff-officer sent forward to meet him, to form on the left of our line, his left thrown forward, and to attack the enemy in flank. At his request I joined him, directed his course, and gave him these instructions. Before the formation was completed, he fell severely wounded, and while falling from his horse directed Colonel Elzey to take command. That officer appreciated the manœuvre and executed it gallantly and well. General Beauregard promptly seized the opportunity it afforded, and threw forward the whole line. The enemy was driven from the long-contested hill, and the tide of battle at length turned. But the first Federal line driven into the valley was there rallied on a second, the two united presenting a formidable aspect. In the mean time, however, Colonel Early had come upon the field with his brigade. He was instructed by me to make a détour to the left and assail the Federal right in flank. He reached the ground in time, accompanied by Stuart's cavalry and Beckham's battery, and made his attack with a skill and courage which routed the Federal right in a moment. General Beauregard, charging in front, made the rout complete. The Federal right fled in confusion toward the Sudley Ford, and the center and left marched off rapidly by the turnpike.

Stuart pursued the fugitives on the Sudley road, and Colonel Radford, with two squadrons which I had held in reserve near me during the day, was directed to cross Bull Run at Ball's Ford, and strike the column on the turnpike in flank. The number of prisoners taken by these parties of cavalry greatly exceeded their own numbers. But they were too weak to make a serious impression on an army, although a defeated one.

At twenty minutes before 5, when the retreat of the enemy toward Centreville began, I sent orders to Brigadier-General Bonham by Lieutenant-Colonel Lay, of his staff, who happened to be with me, to march with his own and Longstreet's brigade (which were nearest Bull Run and the Stone Bridge), by the quickest route to the turnpike, and form them across it to intercept the retreat of the Federal troops. But he found so little appearance of rout in those troops as to make the execution of his instructions seem impracticable; so the two brigades returned to their camps. When the retreat began, the body of United States troops that had passed the day on the Centreville side of Bull Run made a demonstration on the rear of our right; which was repelled by Holmes's brigade just arrived.

Soon after the firing ceased, General Ewell reported to me, saying that his brigade was about midway from its camp near Union Mills. He had ridden forward to see the part of the field on which he might be required to serve, to prepare himself to act intelligently.

The victory was as complete as one gained in an open country by infantry and artillery can be. Our cavalry pursued as far as they could effectively; but when they encountered the main column, after dispersing or capturing little parties and stragglers, they could make no impression.

General Beauregard's first plan of attack was delivered to me by his aide-de-camp, Colonel Chisolm, when I was thirty-four miles from Manassas. It was, that I should leave the railroad at Piedmont station, thirty-six miles from the enemy at Centreville, and attack him in rear, and when our artillery announced that we had begun the fight, General Beauregard would move up from Bull Run and assail the enemy on that side. I rejected the plan, because such a one would enable an officer of ordinary sense and vigor to defeat our two armies one after the other. For McDowell, by his numerical superiority, could have disposed of my forces in less than two hours; that is to say, before Beauregard could have come up, when he also could have been defeated and the campaign ended.

An opinion seems to prevail with some persons who have written about the battle, that important plans of General Beauregard were executed by him. It is a mistake; the first intention, announced to General Beauregard by me when we met, was to attack the enemy at Centreville as early as possible on the 21st. This was anticipated by McDowell's early advance. The second, to attack the Federals in flank near the turnpike with our main force, suggested by General Beauregard, was prevented by the enemy's occupation of the high ground in front of our right.

As fought, the battle was made by me; Bee's and Jackson's brigades were transferred to the left by me. I decided that the battle was to be there, and directed the measures necessary to maintain it; a most important one being the assignment of General Beauregard to the immediate command of this left, which he held. In like manner the senior officer on the right would have commanded there, if the Federal left had attacked.

These facts in relation to the battle are my defense against the accusation indorsed by General Beauregard and published by Mr. Davis.

In an account of the battle published in "The Century" for November, 1884, General Beauregard mentions offensive operations which he "had designed and ordered against his [adversary's] left flank and rear at Centreville," and censures my friend General R. S. Ewell for their failure. At the time referred to, three of

LIEUTENANT-GENERAL
RICHARD S. EWELL, C.S.A.
FROM A PHOTOGRAPH.

the four Federal divisions were near Bull Run, above the turnpike, and the fourth facing our right, so that troops of ours, going to Centreville then, if not prevented by the Federal division facing them, would have found no enemy. And General Ewell was not, as he reports, "instructed in the plan of attack"; for he says in his official report: "...I first received orders to hold myself in readiness to advance at a moment's notice. I next received a copy of an order sent to General Jones and furnished me by him, in which it was stated I had been ordered at once to proceed to his support." Three other orders, he says, followed, each contradictory of its predecessor. General Ewell knew that a battle was raging; but knew, too, that between him and it were other unengaged brigades, and that his commander was near enough to give him orders. But he had no reason to suppose that his commander desired him to move to Centreville, where there was then no enemy. There could have been no greater mistake on General Ewell's part than making the movement to Centreville.

A brief passage in my official report of this battle displeased President Davis. In referring to his telegraphic order I gave its meaning very briefly, but accurately—"directing me, if practicable, to go to [General Beauregard's] assistance, after sending my sick to Culpeper Court House." Mr. Davis objected to the word *after*. Being informed of this by a friend, I cheerfully consented to his expunging the word, because that would not affect the meaning of the sentence. But the word is still in his harsh indorsement. He also had this passage stricken out: "The delay of sending the sick, nearly seventeen hundred in number, to Culpeper, would have made it impossible to arrive at Manassas in time. They were therefore provided for in Winchester"; and substituted this: "Our sick, nearly seventeen hundred in number, were provided for in Winchester." Being ordered to send the sick to Culpeper as well as to move to Manassas, it was necessary to account for disobedience, which my words did, and which his substitute for them did not.

Mr. Davis ("R. and F.," I., 359) expresses indignation that, as he says, "among the articles abandoned by the enemy...were handcuffs, the fit appendage of a policeman, but not of a soldier." I saw none, nor did I see any one who had seen them.

Mr. Davis says (page 359): "On the night of the 22d, I held a second conference with Generals Johnston and Beauregard." I was in no conference like that of which account is given on page 360. And one that he had with me on that day proved conclusively that he had no thought of sending our army against Washington; for in it he offered me the command in West Virginia, promising to increase the forces there adequately from those around us. He says (page 361):

> "What discoveries would have been made, and what results would have ensued from the establishment of our guns upon the south bank of the river to open fire upon the capital, are speculative questions upon which it would be useless to enter."

Mr. Davis seems to have forgotten what was as well known then as now—that our army was more disorganized by victory than that of the United States by defeat; that there were strong fortifications, well manned, to cover the approaches to Washington and prevent the establishment of our guns on the south bank of the river. He knew, too, that we had no means of cannonading the capital, nor a disposition to make barbarous war. He says ("R. and F.," I., 362):

> "When the smoke of battle had lifted from the field…some…censoriously asked why the fruits of the victory had not been gathered by the capture of Washington City. Then some indiscreet friends of the generals commanding in that battle…induced the allegation that the President had prevented the generals from making an immediate and vigorous pursuit of the routed enemy."

Mr. Davis has no ground for this assertion; the generals were attacked first and most severely. It was not until the newspapers had exhausted themselves upon us that some of them turned upon him. On November 3d he wrote to me that reports were circulated to the effect that he

> "prevented General Beauregard from pursuing the enemy after the battle of Manassas, and had subsequently restrained him from advancing upon Washington City…. I call upon you, as the commanding general, and as a party to all the conferences held by me on the 21st and 22d of July, to say whether I obstructed the pursuit of the enemy after the victory at Manassas, or have ever objected to an advance or other active operation which it was feasible for the army to undertake." ("R. and F.," I., 363.)

I replied on the 10th, answering the first question in the negative, and added an explanation which put the responsibility on myself. I replied to the second question, that it had never been feasible for the army to advance farther toward

Washington than it had done, and referred to a conference at Fairfax Court House [October 1st, 1861] in reference to leading the army into Maryland, in which he informed the three senior officers that he had not the means of giving the army the strength which they considered necessary for offensive operations.

Mr. Davis was displeased by my second reply, because in his mind there was but one question in his letter. I maintain that there are two; namely, (1) Did he obstruct the pursuit of the enemy after the victory at Manassas? (2) Had he ever objected to an advance or other active operation which it was feasible for the army to undertake?

The second matter is utterly unconnected with the battle of Manassas, and as the question of advance or other active operation had been discussed nowhere by him, to my knowledge, but at the conference at Fairfax Court House, I supposed that he referred to it. He was dissatisfied with my silence in regard to the conferences which he avers took place on July 21st and 22d, the first knowledge of which I have derived from his book.

THE WITHDRAWAL FROM CENTREVILLE TO THE PENINSULA.

Mr. Davis refers ("Rise and Fall," I., 444–5) to the instructions for the reorganization of the army given by him to the three general officers whom he met in conference at Fairfax Court House on October 1st, 1861. But the correspondence urging the carrying out of the orders was carried on with Generals Beauregard and G. W. Smith (my subordinates) in that same October. He neither conversed nor corresponded with me on the subject then, the letter to me being dated May 10th, 1862. The original order was dated October 22d, 1861, to be executed "as soon as, in the judgment of the commanding general, it can be safely done under present exigencies." As the enemy was then nearer to our center than that center to either flank of our army, and another advance upon us by the Federal army was not improbable on any day, it seemed to me unsafe to make the reorganization then. From May 10th to 26th, when the President renewed the subject, we were in the immediate presence of the enemy, when reorganization would have been infinitely dangerous, as was duly represented by me. But, alluding to this conference at Fairfax Court House, he says (p. 449): "When, at that time and place, I met General Johnston for conference, he called in the two generals next in rank to himself, Beauregard and G. W. Smith." These officers were with Mr. Davis in the quarters of General Beauregard, whose guest he was, when I was summoned to him. I had not power to bring any officer into the conference. If such authority had belonged to my office, the personal relations lately established between us by the President would not have permitted me to use it.

He says (pp. 448–9): "I will now proceed to notice the allegation that I was responsible for inaction of the Army of the Potomac in the latter part of 1861 and in the early part of 1862." I think Mr. Davis is here fighting a shadow. I have never seen or heard of the "allegation" referred to; I believe that that conference attracted no public attention, and brought criticism upon no one. I have seen no notice of it in print, except the merely historical one in a publication made by me in 1874,✩ without criticism or comment.

In the same paragraph Mr. Davis expresses surprise at the weakness of the army. He has forgotten that in Richmond he was well informed of the strength of the army by periodical reports, which showed him the prevalence of epidemics which, in August and part of September, kept almost thirty per cent. of our number sick. He must have forgotten, too, his anxiety on this subject, which induced him to send a very able physician, Dr. Cartwright, to find some remedy or preventive.

He asserts also that "the generals" had made previous suggestions of a "purpose to advance into Maryland." There had been no such purpose. On the contrary, in my letter to the Secretary of War, suggesting the conference, I wrote:

> "Thus far the numbers and condition of this army have at no time justified our assuming the offensive.... The difficulty of obtaining the means of establishing a battery near Evansport‡...has given me the impression that you cannot at present put this army in condition to assume the offensive. If I am mistaken in this, and you can furnish those means, I think it important that either his Excellency the President, yourself, or some one representing you, should here, upon the ground, confer with me on this all-important question."

In a letter dated September 29th, 1861, the Secretary wrote that the President would reach my camp in a day or two for conference. He came for that object September 30th, and the next evening, *by his appointment,* he was waited on by Generals Beauregard, Gustavus W. Smith, and myself. In discussing the question of giving our army strength enough to assume the offensive in Maryland, it was proposed to bring to it from the South troops enough to raise it to the required strength. The President asked what was that strength. General Smith thought 50,000 men, General Beauregard 60,000, and I 60,000, all of us specifying soldiers like those around us. The President replied that such reënforcements could not be furnished; he could give only as many recruits as we could arm. This decided the question. Mr. Davis then proposed an expedition against Hooker's division, consisting, we believed, of 10,000 men. It was posted on the Maryland shore of the Potomac, opposite Dumfries. [See map, p. 89.]

✩See "Johnston's Narrative" (New York: D. Appleton & Co.), pp. 78, 79.
‡Evansport is on the Potomac below Alexandria, at the mouth of Quantico Creek.

"STONEWALL" JACKSON AS FIRST
LIEUTENANT OF ARTILLERY, U.S.A.
FROM A DAGUERREOTYPE TAKEN
JULY 10, 1848.

But I objected that we had no means of ferrying an equal number of men across the river in a day, even if undisturbed by ships of war, which controlled the river; so that, even if we should succeed in landing, those vessels of war would inevitably destroy or capture our party returning. This terminated the conference. Mr. Davis says, in regard to the reënforcements asked for ("R. and F.," I., 449): "I had no power to make such an addition to that army without a total disregard of the safety of other threatened positions." We had no threatened positions; and we could always discover promptly the fitting out of naval expeditions against us. And he adds (p. 451), with reference to my request for a conference in regard to reënforcements:

"Very little experience, or a fair amount of modesty without any experience, would serve to prevent one from announcing his conclusion that troops could be withdrawn from a place or places without knowing how many were there, and what was the necessity for their presence."

The refutation of this is in General G. W. Smith's memorandum of the discussion: "General Johnston said that he did not feel at liberty to express an opinion of the practicability of reducing the strength of our forces at points not within the limits of his command." On page 452 [referring to possible minor offensive operations.—EDITORS] Mr. Davis says he

"particularly indicated the lower part of Maryland, where a small force was said to be ravaging the country."

He suggested nothing so impossible. Troops of ours could not have been ferried across the broad Potomac then. We had no steamer on that river, nor could we have used one. Mr. Davis says ("R. and F.," I., 452):

"...Previously, General Johnston's attention had been called to possibilities in the Valley of the Shenandoah, and that these and other like things were not done, was surely due to other causes than 'the policy of the Administration.'"

Then he quotes from a letter to me, dated August 1st, 1861, as follows:

"... The movement of Banks⁺ will require your attention. It may be a *ruse*, but if a real movement, when your army has the requisite strength and mobility, you will probably find an opportunity, by a rapid movement through the passes, to strike him in rear or flank."

It is a matter of public notoriety that no incursion into the "Valley" worth the notice of a Confederate company was made until March, 1862. That the Confederate President should be ignorant of this is inconceivable. Mr. Davis says (p. 462):

"... I received from General Johnston notice that his position [at Centreville] was considered unsafe. Many of his letters to me have been lost, and I have thus far not been able to find the one giving the notice referred to, but the reply which is annexed clearly indicates the substance of the letter which was answered: 'General J. E. Johnston: ... Your opinion that your position may be turned whenever the enemy chooses to advance,' etc."

The sentence omitted by him after my name in his letter from which he quotes as above contains the dates of three letters of mine, in neither of which is there allusion to the safety (or reverse) of the position. They are dated 22d, 23d, and 25th of February, and contain complaints on my part of the dreadful condition of the country, and of the vast accumulation by the Government of superfluous stores at Manassas. There is another omission in the President's letter quoted, and the omission is this:

"... with your present force, you cannot secure your communications from the enemy, and may at any time, when he can pass to your rear, be compelled to retreat at the sacrifice of your siege train and army stores.... Threatened as we are by a large force on the south-east, you must see the hazard of your position, by its liability to isolation and attack in rear."

By a singular freak of the President's memory, it transferred the substance of these passages from his letter to my three.

⁺By orders dated July 19th, 1861, General N. P. Banks had been assigned to the command of the Department of the Shenandoah, relieving General Patterson in command of the army at Harper's Ferry, General Patterson being by the same orders "honorably discharged from the service of the United States," on the expiration of his term of duty.—EDITORS.

Referring again to the conference at Fairfax Court House [October 1st], Mr. Davis says (p. 464):

"Soon thereafter, the army withdrew to Centreville, a better position for defense, but not for attack, and thereby suggestive of the abandonment of an intention to advance."

The President forgets that in that conference the intention to advance was abandoned by him first. He says on the same page:

"On the 10th of March I telegraphed to General Johnston: 'Further assurance given to me this day that you shall be promptly and adequately reënforced, so as to enable you to maintain your position, and resume first policy when the roads will permit.' The first policy was to carry the war beyond our own border."

The roads then permitted the marching of armies, so we had just left Manassas.♪

On the 20th of February, after a discussion in Richmond, his Cabinet being present, the President had directed me to prepare to fall back from Manassas, and do so as soon as the condition of the country should make the marching of troops practicable. I returned to Manassas February 21st, and on the 22d ordered the proper officers to remove the public property, which was begun on the 23d, the superintendent of the railroad devoting himself to the work under the direction of its president, the Hon. John S. Barbour. The Government had collected three million and a quarter pounds of provisions there, I insisting on a supply of but a million and a half. It also had two million pounds in a meat-curing establishment near at hand, and herds of live stock besides. On the 9th of March, when the ground had become firm enough for military operations, I ordered the army to march that night, thinking then, as I do now, that the space of fifteen days was time enough in which to subordinate an army to the Commissary Department. About one million pounds of this provision was abandoned, and half as much more was spoiled for want of shelter. This loss is represented ("R. and F.," I., 468)∕ as so great as to embarrass us to the end of the war, although it was only a six days' supply for the troops then in Virginia. Ten times as much was in North Carolina railroad stations at the end of the war. Mr. Davis says (p. 467):

♪Between the 7th and 11th of March, 1862, the Confederate forces in north-eastern Virginia, under General Johnston, were withdrawn to the line of the Rappahannock. On the 11–12th Stonewall Jackson evacuated Winchester and fell back to Strasburg.—EDITORS.

∕Not by Mr. Davis, but in a statement quoted at the above page from General J. A. Early, who said, "The loss ... was a very serious one to us, and embarrassed us for the remainder of the war, as it put us at once on a running stock."—EDITORS.

"It was regretted that earlier and more effective means were not employed for the mobilization of the army,... or at least that the withdrawal was not so deliberate as to secure the removal of our ordnance, subsistence, and quartermaster's stores."

The quartermaster's and ordnance stores were brought off; and as to subsistence, the Government, which collected immediately on the frontier five times the quantity of provisions wanted, is responsible for the losses. The President suggested the time of the withdrawal himself, in the interview in his office that has been mentioned. The means taken was the only one available,—the Virginia Midland Railroad. Mr. Davis says ("R. and F.," I., 465):

"To further inquiry from General Johnston as to where he should take position, I replied that I would go to his headquarters in the field, and found him on the south bank of the river, to which he had retired, in a position possessing great natural advantages."

There was no correspondence in relation to selecting a defensive position. I was not seeking one; but, instead, convenient camping-grounds, from which my troops could certainly unite with other Confederate forces to meet McClellan's invasion. I had found and was occupying such grounds, one division being north of Orange Court House, another a mile or two south of it, and two others some six miles east of that place; a division on the south bank of the Rappahannock, and the cavalry beyond the river, and about 13,000 troops in the vicinity of Fredericksburg. Mr. Davis's narrative [of a visit to Fredericksburg at this time, the middle of March.—EDITORS] that follows is disposed of by the proof that, after the army left Manassas, the President did not visit it until about the 14th of May.☆ But such a visit, if made, could not have brought him to the conclusion that the weakness of Fredericksburg as a military position made it unnecessary to find a strong one for the army.

Mr. Davis ("R. and F.," II., 81) credits me with expecting an attack which he shows General McClellan never had in his mind:

"In a previous chapter, the retreat of our army from Centreville has been described, and reference has been made to the anticipation of the commanding general, J. E. Johnston, that the enemy would soon advance to attack that position."

☆In "The Century" magazine for May, 1885, General Johnston, to support his assertion, quoted statements by Major J. B. Washington, Dr. A. M. Fauntleroy, and Colonel E. J. Harvie, which are now omitted for want of space.—EDITORS.

This refers, I suppose, to a previous assertion ("R. and F.," I., 462), my comments upon which prove that this "anticipation" was expressed in the President's letter to me, dated February 28th, 1862. He says ("R. and F.," II., 83):

> "The withdrawal of our forces across the Rappahannock was fatal to the [Federal] programme of landing on that river and marching to Richmond before our forces could be in position to resist an attack on the capital."

This withdrawal was expressly to enable the army to unite with other Confederate troops to oppose the expected invasion. I supposed that General McClellan would march down the Potomac on the Maryland side, cross it near the mouth of Aquia Creek, and take the Fredericksburg route to Richmond. The position of Hooker, about midway between Washington and this crossing-place, might well have suggested that he had this intention.

POSTSCRIPT.—In the first paragraph of General Beauregard's postscript, it is asserted that I did not claim to have commanded in the first battle of Manassas until May, 1885, and that my official report of that action contains no such claim. It is, nevertheless, distinctly expressed in that report—thus:

> "In a brief and rapid conference, General Beauregard was assigned to the command of the left, which, as the younger officer, he claimed, while I returned to that of the whole field."

And in "Johnston's Narrative," published in 1874, it is expressed in these words, on page 49:

> "After assigning General Beauregard to the command of the troops *immediately engaged,* which he properly suggested belonged to the second in rank, not to the commander of the army, I returned to the supervision of the whole field."

So much for my not having claimed to have commanded at the "first Manassas" until May, 1885.

General Beauregard in his official report states the circumstance thus:

> "... I urged General Johnston to leave the immediate conduct of the field to me, while he, repairing to Portici, the Lewis house, should urge reënforcements forward."

This language would certainly limit his command as mine does. He did not attempt to command the army, while I did command it, and disposed of all the troops not engaged at the time of his assignment.

In his official report of the battle, General Beauregard further states:

"Made acquainted with my plan of operations and dispositions to meet the enemy, he gave them his entire approval, and generously directed their execution under my command."

The only "plan" that he offered me [to move *via* Aldie] was rejected—on the 14th, before my arrival. The battle fought was on McDowell's plan, not General Beauregard's. The proof of this is, that at its commencement little more than a regiment of Beauregard's command was on the ground where the battle was fought, and, of his 7 brigades, 1 was a mile and 6 were from 4 to 7 or 8 miles from it. The place of the battle was fixed by Bee's and Jackson's brigades, sent forward by my direction. At my request General Beauregard did write an order of march against the Federal army, finished a little before sunrise of the 21st. In it I am invariably termed commander-in-chief, and he (to command one of the wings) "second in command," or General Beauregard—conclusive proof that the troops were not "under his command."

Two letters, from General Lee and Mr. Walker, Secretary of War, are cited as evidence that General Beauregard commanded. Those gentlemen were not in a position to know if I relinquished the command. But I had this letter from General Lee:

"RICHMOND, July 24th, 1861. MY DEAR GENERAL: I almost wept for joy at the glorious victory achieved by our brave troops. The feelings of my heart could hardly be repressed on learning the brilliant share you had in its achievement. I expected nothing else, and am truly grateful for your safety...."

In conclusion, I cannot discover that my unfavorable opinion of the Federal general's tactics, quoted by General Beauregard, indicates a fear to command against him.

GENERAL EWELL AT BULL RUN.†

By Major Campbell Brown, Aide-de-Camp and Assistant Adjutant-General to General Ewell.

In General Beauregard's article on Bull Run, in "The Century" for November [1884], is this severe criticism of one of his subordinates, the late Lieutenant-General R. S. Ewell:

---

†This article appeared substantially as here printed in "The Century" for March, 1885.—EDITORS.

"Meanwhile, in rear of Mitchell's Ford, I had been waiting with General Johnston for the sound of conflict to open in the quarter of Centreville upon the Federal left flank and rear (making allowance, however, for the delays possible to commands unused to battle), when I was chagrined to hear from General D. R. Jones that, while he had been long ready for the movement upon Centreville, General Ewell had not come up to form on his right, though he had sent him between 7 and 8 o'clock a copy of his own order, which recited that Ewell had been already ordered to begin the movement. I dispatched an immediate order to Ewell to advance; but within a quarter of an hour, just as I received a dispatch from him informing me that he had received no order to advance in the morning, the firing on the left began to increase so intensely as to indicate a severe attack, whereupon General Johnston said that he would go personally to that quarter."

This contains at least three errors, so serious that they should not be allowed to pass uncorrected among the materials from which history will one day be constructed:

1. That Ewell failed to do what a good soldier would have done— namely, to move forward immediately on hearing from D. R. Jones.
2. That Beauregard was made aware of this supposed backwardness of Ewell by a message from D. R. Jones.
3. That on receiving this message he at once ordered Ewell to advance.

The subjoined correspondence,⁺ now [March, 1885] first in print, took place four days after the battle. It shows that Ewell did exactly what

⁺[CORRESPONDENCE.]
UNION MILLS, JULY 25TH, 1861.
GENERAL BEAUREGARD.

Sɪʀ: In a conversation with Major James, Louisiana 6th Regiment, he has left the impression on my mind that you think some of your orders on the 21st were either not carried out or not received by me.

My first order on that day was to hold myself in readiness to attack—this at sunrise. About 10, General Jones sent a copy of an order received by him in which it was stated that I had been ordered to cross and attack, and on receipt of this I moved on until receiving the following:

10 & 12 A.M.

On account of the difficulties of the ground in our front, it is thought advisable to fall back to our former position.

(Addressed) General Ewell.

(Sɪɢɴᴇᴅ) G.T.B.

Beauregard says he ought to have done—namely, move forward promptly; that his own staff-officer, sent to report this forward movement, carried also to headquarters the first intelligence of the failure of orders to reach him; that no such message was received from D. R. Jones as is here ascribed to him; and that the order sent back by Beauregard to Ewell was not one to advance, but to retire from an advance already begun.

It is not easy to understand these mistakes, as General Beauregard has twice given a tolerably accurate though meager account of the matter—once in his official report, and once in his biography published by Colonel Roman in 1884. Neither of these accounts can be reconciled with the later attitude.

Upon reading General Beauregard's article, I wrote to General Fitzhugh Lee, who was Ewell's assistant adjutant-general at Manassas, asking his recollection of what took place. I have liberty to make the following extracts from his reply. After stating what troops composed the brigade, he goes on:

> "These troops were all in position at daylight on the 21st July, ready for *any* duty, and held the extreme right of General Beauregard's line of battle along Bull Run, at Union Mills. As hour after hour passed, General Ewell grew impatient at not receiving any orders (beyond those to be ready to advance, which came at

---

If any other order was sent to me, I should like to have a copy of it, as well as the name of the courier who brought it.

Every movement I made was at once reported to you at the time, and this across Bull Run, as well as the advance in the afternoon, I thought were explained in my report sent in to-day.

If an order were sent earlier than the copy through General Jones, the courier should be held responsible, as neither General Holmes nor myself received it. I send the original of the order to fall back in the morning. The second advance in the afternoon and recall to Stone Bridge were in consequence of verbal orders.

My chief object in writing to you is to ask you to leave nothing doubtful in your report, both as regards my crossing in the morning and recall—and not to let it be inferred by any possibility that I blundered on that day. I moved forward as soon as notified by General Jones that I was ordered and he had been.

If there was an order sent me to advance before the one I received through General Jones, it is more than likely it would have been given to the same express.

RESPECTFULLY,
R. S. EWELL, B.G.

MANASSAS, VA., JULY 26TH, 1861.

GENERAL: Your letter of the 25th inst. is received. I do not attach the slightest blame to you for the failure of the movement on Centreville, but to the guide who did not deliver the order to move forward, sent at about 8 A.M. to General Holmes and then to you—corresponding in every respect to the one sent to Generals Jones, Bonham, and Longstreet—only their movements were subordinate to yours. Unfortunately no copy, in the hurry of the mo-

sunrise), and sent me between 9 and 10 A.M. to see General D. R. Jones, who commanded the brigade next on his left at McLean's Ford, to ascertain if that officer had any news or had received any orders from army headquarters. I found General Jones making preparations to cross Bull Run, and was told by him that, in the order he had received to do so, it was stated that General Ewell had been sent similar instructions.

"Upon my report of these facts, General Ewell at once issued the orders for his command to cross the Run and move out on the road to Centreville."

General Lee then describes the recall across Bull Run and the second advance of the brigade to make a demonstration toward Centreville, and adds that the skirmishers of Rodes's 5th Alabama Regiment, which was in advance, had actually become engaged, when we were again recalled and ordered to "move by the most direct route at once, and as rapidly as possible, for the Lewis house"—the field of battle on the left. Ewell moved rapidly, sending General Lee and another officer ahead to report and secure orders. On his arrival near the field they brought instructions to halt, when he immediately rode forward with them to General Beauregard, "and General Ewell begged General Beauregard to be allowed to go in pursuit of the enemy, but his request was refused."

---

ment, was kept of said orders; and so many guides, about a dozen or more, were sent off in different directions, that it is next to impossible to find out who was the bearer of the orders referred to. Our guides and couriers were the worst set I ever employed, whether from ignorance or over-anxiety to do well and quickly I cannot say; but many regiments lost their way repeatedly on their way toward the field of battle, and of course I can attach no more blame to their commanding officers than I could to you for not executing an order which I am convinced you did not get.

I am fully aware that you did all that could have been expected of you or your command. I merely expressed my regret that my original plan could not be carried into effect, as it would have been a most complete victory with only half the trouble and fighting.

The true cause of countermanding your forward movement after you had crossed was that it was *then* too late, as the enemy was about to annihilate our left flank, and had to be met and checked *there,* for otherwise he would have taken us in flank and rear and all would have been lost.

YOURS TRULY,

G. T. BEAUREGARD.

GENERAL R. S. EWELL, UNION MILLS, VA.

P. S. Please read the above to Major James.

N. B. The order sent you at about 8 A.M., to commence the movement on Centreville, was addressed to General Holmes and yourself, as he was to support you, but being nearer Camp Pickens, the headquarters, than Union Mills, where you were, it was to be communicated to him first, and then to you; but he has informed me that it never reached him. With

As to the real causes of the miscarriage of General Beauregard's plan of attack there need be little doubt. They are plainly stated by his immediate superior in command, General Joseph E. Johnston, in his official report, as being the "early movements of the enemy on that morning and the non-arrival of the expected troops" from Harper's Ferry. He adds: "General Beauregard afterward proposed a modification of the abandoned plan, to attack with our right, while the left stood on the defensive. This, too, became impracticable, and a battle ensued, different in place and circumstances from any previous plan on our side."

There are some puzzling circumstances connected with the supposed miscarriage of the order for our advance. The delay in sending it is unexplained. General Beauregard says it was sent "at about 8 A.M.," but D. R. Jones had received his corresponding order at 10 minutes past 7, and firing had begun at half-past 5.

The messenger was strangely chosen. It was the most important order of the day, for the movements of the army were to hinge on those of our brigade. There was no scarcity of competent staff-officers; yet it was intrusted to "a guide," presumably an enlisted man, perhaps even a citizen, whose very name was unknown.

His instructions were peculiar. Time was all-important. He was ordered not to go direct to Ewell, but first to make a détour to Holmes, who lay in reserve nearly two miles in our rear.

His disappearance is mysterious. He was never heard of after receiving the order; yet his route lay wholly within our lines, over well-beaten roads and far out of reach of the enemy.

Lastly, General Beauregard, in his official report, gives as his reason for countermanding the movement begun by Ewell at 10 o'clock, that in his judgment it would require quite three hours for the troops to get into position for attack. Had the messenger dispatched at 8 been prompt, Ewell might have had his orders by 9. But at 9 we find Beauregard in rear of Mitchell's Ford, waiting for an attack which, by his own figures, he should not have expected before 12.

It is not for me to reconcile these contradictions.

---

regard to the order sent you in the afternoon to recross the Bull Run (to march toward the Stone Bridge), it was sent you by General J. E. Johnston, as I am informed by him, for the purpose of supporting our left, if necessary.—G.T.B.

Do not publish until we know what the enemy is going to do—or reports are out—which I think will make it all right.—B.

CHAPTER 8

ARKANSAS TROOPS IN THE BATTLE OF WILSON'S CREEK.

N. B. Pearce, Brigadier-General, C.S.A.

I style this short account of my personal recollections of the battle of "Oak Hills" (as the Confederates named the engagement) as above, because I was identified with the State of Arkansas and her soldiers. I also believe that subsequent events, developed by the prominence of some of the commanders engaged in this fight, have had a tendency to obscure that just recognition which the Arkansas troops so nobly earned in this, one of the first great battles of our civil war.

The ninth day of August, 1861, found the Confederate army under General Ben. McCulloch, camped on Wilson's Creek, ten miles south of Springfield, in south-west Missouri. It consisted of a Louisiana regiment under Colonel Louis Hébert (a well-drilled and well-equipped organization, chiefly from the north part of the State); Greer's Texas regiment (mounted); Churchill's Arkansas cavalry, and McIntosh's battalion of Arkansas mounted rifles (Lieutenant-Colonel Embry), under the immediate charge of the commanding general; General Price's command of Missouri State Guards, with Bledsoe's and Guibor's batteries, and my three regiments of Arkansas infantry, with Woodruff's and Reid's batteries. More than half the Missourians were mounted, and but few of the troops in the whole command were well armed. The army numbered in all about 11,500 men,—perhaps, 6000 to 7000 of whom were in semi-fighting trim, and participated in the battle.

The Federal forces under General Nathaniel Lyon, between 5000 and 6000 strong, occupied the town of Springfield, and General McCulloch was expecting them to advance and give him battle. General McCulloch's headquarters were on the right of the Springfield road, east of Wilson's Creek, rather in advance of the center of the camp. General Price occupied a position immediately west, and in the valley of the creek, with his command mostly north of the Springfield road. I had established my headquarters on the heights east and

"BLOODY HILL," FROM THE EAST. FROM A RECENT PHOTOGRAPH.

south of Wilson's Creek and the Springfield road, with my forces occupying the elevated ground immediately adjacent.

Detailed reports as to the strength and movements of Lyon's command were momentarily expected, through spies sent out by General Price, as McCulloch relied upon the native Missourians to furnish such knowledge; but it was not until late in the afternoon that two "loyal" ladies succeeded in passing out of the Federal lines, by permission of General Lyon, and, coming in a circuitous route by Pond Springs, reached General Price's headquarters with the desired information. General McCulloch at once called a council of war of the principal officers, where it was decided, instead of waiting for the enemy, to march with the whole command, at 9 o'clock that night, and attack General Lyon at Springfield. As soon as the orders of General McCulloch had been properly published by his adjutant-general, Colonel McIntosh, the camp was thrown into a ferment of suppressed excitement. It was ordered that the advance be made in three divisions, under the separate commands of General Price, Adjutant-General McIntosh, and myself. The scene of preparation, immediately following the orders so long delayed and now so eagerly welcomed by the men, was picturesque and animating in the extreme. The question of ammunition was one of the most important and serious, and as the Ordnance Department was imperfectly organized and poorly supplied, the men scattered about in groups, to improvise, as best they could, ammunition for their inefficient arms. Here, a group would be molding bullets—there, another crowd dividing percussion-caps, and, again, another group fitting new flints to their old muskets. They had little thought then of the inequality between the discipline, arms, and accouterments of the regular United States troops they were soon to engage in battle, and their own homely movements and equipments. It was a new thing to most of them, this regular way of shooting by word of command, and it was, perhaps, the old-accustomed method of using rifle, musket, or shotgun as gamesters or marksmen that won them the battle when pressed into close quarters with the enemy. All was expectancy, and as the time sped on to 9 o'clock, the men became more and more eager to advance. What was their disappointment when, as the hour finally arrived, instead of the order to march, it was announced that General McCulloch had decided, on account of a threatened rain, which might damage and destroy much of their ammunition, to postpone the movement. The men did not "sulk in their tents," but rested on their arms in no amiable mood. This condition of uncertainty and suspense lasted well through the night, as the commanding officers were better informed than the men of the risks to be encountered, and of the probable result, in case they should make an aggressive fight against disciplined forces when only half prepared. Daybreak, on the 10th of August, found the command still at Wilson's Creek, cheerlessly waiting, many of the troops remaining in position, in line of march, on the road, and others returning to camp to prepare the morning meal.

Perhaps it was 6 o'clock when the long-roll sounded and the camp was called to arms. A few minutes before this, Sergeant Hite, of my body-guard, dashed up to my headquarters, breathless with excitement, hatless, and his horse covered with foam, exclaiming hurriedly, "General, the enemy is coming!" "Where!" said I, and he pointed in the direction of a spring, up a ravine, where he had been for water. He had been fired at, he said, by a picket of some troops advancing on the right flank. I ordered the sergeant to ride in haste to General McCulloch with this information, and proceeded to place my command in position. I was the better enabled to do this without delay, because I had on the day before, with Colonel R. H. Weightman, made a careful reconnoissance of the ground in the direction from which the enemy was said to be approaching. The colonels commanding were immediately notified, and the regiments were formed and posted so as to meet his advance. Captain Woodruff's Little Rock (Ark.) battery was ordered to occupy a hill commanding the road to Springfield, and the 3d Arkansas Infantry (Colonel John R. Gratiot) was ordered to support him. I placed Captain Reid's Fort Smith (Ark.) battery on an eminence to command the approaches to our right and rear, and gave him the 5th Arkansas Infantry (Colonel T. P. Dockery) as a support. I then advanced the 4th Arkansas Infantry (Colonel J. D. Walker) north of this battery to watch the approach down the ravine, through which Sergeant Hite had reported that the enemy was coming. Thus, the Arkansas troops under my command had all been placed in favorable position, ready for action, within a very short time after the first alarm.

While these events were taking place under my immediate notice, General McCulloch had been actively making disposition of the troops more nearly opposed to the first advance of the enemy, under General Lyon. He had posted the 3d Louisiana Infantry (Colonel Hébert) and McIntosh's 2d Arkansas Rifles (dismounted) to meet the earliest demonstration from the direction of Springfield. General Price had also been industriously engaged in placing his troops to intercept the advancing foe. General Rains's (Missouri) command had the honor of giving the first reception to the main column under General Lyon.

He was ably supported by the gallant Missouri generals, Slack, McBride, Parsons, and Clark, with their respective brigades. The fighting at this juncture— perhaps about 7 o'clock—was confined to the corn-field north of Wilson's Creek, where the Louisiana infantry, with Lieutenant-Colonel Embry's 2d Arkansas Mounted Rifles (dismounted), all under the immediate command of Colonel McIntosh, effectually charged and drove back the enemy. Simultaneously the battle opened farther west and south of Wilson's Creek, where the Missouri troops were attacked by the main column or right wing of the enemy. Totten's (Federal) battery was pushed forward, and took its first position on the side of Oak Hill, north of where the main fight afterward took place. I had directed Captain Woodruff, who was posted within easy range, to give attention to Totten, and the two batteries were soon engaged in a lively artillery duel, being well matched in skill and mettle. Lieutenant Weaver, of Woodruff's battery, was killed, and 4 of Totten's men were killed and 7 wounded in this engagement. General Lyon's right, although it had gained a temporary advantage in the early morning by surprising the Missourians, was roughly handled when they had recovered themselves. They were reënforced by Churchill's regiment, which had moved up from the extreme right, and the battle raged several hours while they held their ground. At this juncture a gallant charge was made by Greer's and Carroll's mounted regiments on Totten's battery, but it was not a complete success, as the gunners turned about and recovered their guns.

In the early morning, perhaps simultaneously with the advance of Lyon, General Sigel, commanding the left column of the advance from Springfield, came upon our right and rear, first attacking Colonel Churchill's camp, as the men were preparing for breakfast, obliging them to retreat to an adjacent wood, where they were formed in good order. The surprise resulted from the movement of the night before, when pickets had been withdrawn that were not reposted in the morning. Sigel did not wait for a fight, however, but advanced to, and had his battery unlimbered near, the Fayetteville road, west of Wilson's Creek, opposite and within range of Reid's battery as it was then in position as originally placed. Before he had discovered us, and perhaps in ignorance of our position, Reid attacked him, under my personal orders and supervision. Sigel's movement was a bold one, and we really could not tell, on his first appearance (there having been no fight with Churchill), whether he was friend or foe. An accidental gust of wind having unfurled his flag, we were no longer in doubt. Reid succeeded in getting his range accurately, so that his shot proved very effective. At this juncture, General McCulloch in person led two companies of the Louisiana infantry in a charge and captured five of the guns.☆ General Sigel was himself in command, and made vain attempts to hold his men, who were

---

☆General McCulloch's report says: "When we arrived near the enemy's battery we found that Reid's battery had opened upon it, and it was already in confusion. Advantage was taken of it, and soon the

soon in full retreat, back over the road they came, pursued by the Texas and Missouri cavalry. This was the last of Sigel for the day, as his retreat was continued to Springfield. As a precaution, however, not knowing how badly we had defeated Sigel, I immediately posted the 4th Arkansas Infantry (Colonel Walker) along the brow of the hill, commanding the road over which he had fled, which regiment remained on duty until the battle was over.

There seemed now to be a lull in the active fighting; the bloody contest in the corn-field had taken place; the fight "mit Sigel" had resulted satisfactorily to us, but the troops more immediately opposed to General Lyon had not done so well. General Price and his Missouri troops had borne the brunt of this hard contest, but had gained no ground. They had suffered heavy losses, and were running short of ammunition. I had watched anxiously for signs of victory to come from the north side of the creek, but Totten's battery seemed to belch forth with renewed vigor, and was advanced once or twice in its position. The line of battle on our left was shortening, and the fortunes of war appeared to be sending many of our gallant officers and soldiers to their death. There was no demoralization—no signs of wavering or retreat, but it was an hour of great anxiety and suspense. No one then knew what the day would bring forth. As the sun poured down upon our devoted comrades, poised and resting, as it were, between the chapters of a mighty struggle not yet completed, the stoutest of us almost weakened in our anxiety to know the outcome.

Just at this time, General Lyon appeared to be massing his men for a final and decisive movement. I had been relieved of Sigel, and Reid's battery was inactive because it could not reach Totten. This was fortunate, for my command, in a measure fresh and enthusiastic, was about to embrace an opportunity—such a one as will often win or lose a battle—by throwing its strength to the weakened line at a critical moment and winning the day. Colonel McIntosh came to me from General McCulloch, and Captain Greene from General Price, urging me to move at once to their assistance. General Lyon was in possession of Oak Hill; his lines were forward, his batteries aggressive, and his charges impetuous. The fortunes of the day were balanced in the scale, and something must be done or the battle was lost. My men were eager to go forward, and when I led the 3d Arkansas Infantry (Colonel Gratiot) and the right wing of the 5th Arkansas Infantry (Lieutenant-Colonel Neal) across the creek, and pushed rapidly up the hill in the face of the enemy, loud cheers went up from our expectant friends that betokened an enthusiasm which, no doubt, helped to win the fight. Colonel McIntosh, with two pieces of Reid's battery, and with a part of Dockery's 5th Arkansas Infantry, supported my right; the

Louisianians were gallantly charging among the guns and swept the cannoneers away. Five guns were here taken."

Federal forces occupied two lines of battle, reaching across the crest of Oak Hill; and at this juncture our troops in front were composed of the Missouri forces, under General Price (occupying the center); Texas and Louisiana troops, under General McCulloch (on the right), and my forces thrown forward (on the left), when a combined advance was ordered by General McCulloch. This proved to be the decisive engagement, and as volley after volley was poured against our lines, and our gallant boys were cut down like grass, those who survived seemed to be nerved to greater effort and a determination to win or die. At about this time (11:30 A.M.) the first line of battle before us gave way. Our boys charged the second line with a yell, and were soon in possession of the field, the enemy slowly withdrawing toward Springfield. This hour decided the contest and won for us the day. It was in our front here, as was afterward made known, that the brave commander of the Federal forces, General Lyon, was killed, gallantly leading his men to what he and they supposed was victory, but which proved (it may be because they were deprived of his enthusiastic leadership) disastrous defeat. In the light of the present day, even, it is difficult to measure the vast results had Lyon lived and the battle gone against us.

General McCulloch, myself, and our staff-officers now grouped ourselves together upon the center of the hill. Woodruff's battery was again placed in position, and Totten, who was covering the retreat of Sturgis (who had assumed command of the Federal forces after the death of General Lyon), received the benefit of his parting shots. We watched the retreating enemy through our field-glasses, *and were glad to see him go.* Our ammunition was exhausted, our men undisciplined, and we feared to risk pursuit. It was also rumored that reën-forcements were coming to the Federal army by forced marches, but it was found the next day that the disaster to the retreating army was greater than we had supposed, and a few fresh cavalry troops could doubtless have followed and captured many more stragglers and army stores. Next day the enemy evacuated Springfield, and Price, with his Missouri troops, occupied it, and had his supplies and wounded moved to that point.*

*The body of the army remained at Springfield until the beginning of General Price's march upon Lexington, on the 25th of August. A few days after the battle Pearce's brigade of Arkansas militia was disbanded on the expiration of their term of enlistment. General McCulloch moved westward with his own brigade, and then to Maysville, Arkansas, being influenced in his return by the general tenor of his instructions from the Confederate Government to avoid, if possible, operating in the State of Missouri, which had not seceded. General Price, upon being informed of his decision, issued an order re-assuming command, and the operations in the State which followed, including the capture of Lexington, were conducted with Missouri troops alone. At this time the Federal troops held the Missouri River by a cordon of military posts. The object of this line was to prevent the crossing of the river by the secessionists of north Missouri, who, to the number of 5000 or 6000, were armed and organized and desirous of joining the army of General Price in south-west Missouri. To break this blockade became the object of General Price. Of the four Federal posts, Jefferson City, Boonville, Lexington, and Kansas City, Lexington was the easiest and most important one to take. General Price left Springfield on the 25th of August, dispersed Lane's forces at Drywood, September 2d, and reached Warrensburg in pursuit of Colonel

The Arkansans in this battle were as brave, as chivalrous, and as successful as any of the troops engaged. They bore out, on many a hard-fought field later on in the struggle, the high hopes built upon their conduct here.

BRIGADIER-GENERAL W.M. Y. SLACK, C.S.A.,
MORTALLY WOUNDED AT PEA RIDGE.
FROM A PHOTOGRAPH.

MAJOR-GENERAL BEN. MCCULLOCH, C.S.A.,
KILLED IN THE BATTLE OF
PEA RIDGE, MARCH 7, 1862.
FROM A PHOTOGRAPH.

Peabody at daybreak, September 10th; Peabody getting into Lexington first, Price, after a little skirmishing with Mulligan's outpost, bivouacked within 2½ miles of Lexington. In the morning (12th) Mulligan sent out a small force which burnt a bridge in Price's path. Price then crossed to the Independence Road, and waited for his infantry and artillery. These came up in the afternoon, and Price then advanced toward Lexington, and drove Mulligan behind his defenses. There was a little skirmishing in a corn-field and in a cemetery through which Price advanced, and in the streets of Lexington, where he opened upon Mulligan with 7 pieces of artillery. Price's movement into Lexington in the afternoon of September 12th was only a reconnoissance in force. Toward dark he retired to the Fair Ground, and waited for his trains to come up, and for reënforcements that were hurrying to him from all directions, including Harris's and Green's commands from north of the Missouri.—EDITORS.

CHAPTER 9

THE FLANKING COLUMN AT WILSON'S CREEK.

Franz Sigel, Major-General, U.S.V.

On August 9th, 1861, the day before the battle at Wilson's Creek, my brigade, consisting of the 3d and 5th Missouri Infantry, commanded respectively by Lieutenant-Colonel Anselm Albert and Charles E. Salomon, and two batteries of artillery, each of 4 pieces, under the command of Lieutenants Schaefer and Schuetzenbach, was encamped on the south side of Springfield, near the Yoker-mill road. On our right was encamped the 1st Iowa Infantry, a regiment clad in militia gray. The bulk of General Lyon's forces were on the west side of the city. During the morning I sent a staff-officer to General Lyon's headquarters for orders, and on his return he reported to me that a forward movement would take place, and that we must hold ourselves in readiness to march at a moment's warning directly from our camp, toward the south, to attack the enemy from the rear. I immediately went to General Lyon, who said that we would move in the evening to attack the enemy in his position at Wilson's Creek, and that I was to be prepared to move with my brigade; the 1st Iowa would join the main column with him, while I was to take the Yokermill (Forsyth) road, then turn toward the south-west and try to gain the enemy's rear. At my request, he said that he would procure guides and some cavalry to assist me; he would also let me know the exact time when I should move. I then asked him whether, on our arrival near the enemy's position, we should attack immediately or wait until we were apprised of the fight by the other troops. He reflected a moment and then said: "Wait until you hear the firing on our side." The conversation did not last longer than about ten minutes. Between 4 and 5 o'clock in the afternoon I received the order to move at 6:30 P.M. At 6 o'clock two companies of cavalry, under Captain Eugene A. Carr and Lieutenant Charles E. Farrand, joined us, also several guides. My whole force now consisted of 8 companies of the 3d and 9 companies of the 5th Missouri (912 men), 6 pieces of artillery (85 men), and the 2 companies of cavalry (121),—in all, 1118 men.

Precisely at 6:30 o'clock the brigade moved out of its camp; after following the Yokermill road for about five miles we turned south-west into the woods, and found our way, with difficulty, to a point south of the enemy's camp, where we arrived between 11 and 12 o'clock at night. There we rested. It was a dark, cloudy night, and a drizzling rain began to fall. So far no news of our movement had reached the enemy's camp, as the cavalry in advance had arrested every person on the road, and put guards before the houses in its neighborhood.

At the first dawn of day we continued our advance for about a mile and a half, the cavalry patrols in front capturing forty men who had strolled into our line while looking for food and water, and who said that twenty regiments of Missouri, Arkansas, and Louisiana troops were encamped not far distant in the valley beyond. Moving on, we suddenly found ourselves near a hill, from which we gained a full view of the camp. We halted a few moments, when I directed four pieces of our artillery to take position on the top of the hill, commanding the camp, while the infantry, with the other two pieces and preceded by Lieutenant Farrand's cavalry company, continued its march down the road to the crossing of Wilson's Creek.

It was now 5:30 A.M. At this moment some musket-firing was heard from the north-west, announcing the approach of General Lyon's troops; I therefore ordered the four pieces to open fire against the camp, which had a "stirring" effect on the enemy, who were preparing breakfast. The surprise was complete, except that one of the enemy's cavalrymen made good his retreat from Lieutenant Farrand's dragoons and took the news of our advance to the other side (General Pearce's headquarters). I became aware of his escape, and believing that no time should be lost to lend assistance to our friends, we crossed Wilson's Creek, took down the fences at Dixon's farm, passed through it and crossed Terrel (or Tyrel) Creek. Not knowing whether it would be possible to bring all our pieces along, I left the four pieces on the hill, with a support of infantry, and continued our march until we reached the south side of the valley, which extends northward to Sharp's house, about 3000 paces, and from west to east about 1000. We took the road on the west side of the valley, along the margin of the woods, and within a fence running nearly parallel with the open fields.

During this time a large body of the enemy's cavalry, about 2500 strong, was forming across the valley, not far distant from its northern extremity; I therefore halted the column on the road, sent for the four pieces left on the other side of the creek, and, as soon as their approach was reported to me, I directed the head of our column to the right, left the road, and formed the troops in line of battle, between the road and the enemy's deserted camp,—the infantry on the left, the artillery on the right, and the cavalry on the extreme right, toward Wilson's Creek. A lively cannonade was now opened against the dense masses of the hostile cavalry, which lasted about twenty minutes, and forced the enemy to retire in disorder toward the north and into the woods. We now turned back into the road, and, advancing, made our way through a number of cattle near Sharp's house, and suddenly struck the Fayetteville road, leading north to that part of the battlefield on which General Lyon's troops were engaged. We were now on the principal line of retreat of the enemy, and had arrived there in perfect order and discipline. Up to this time we had made fifteen miles, had been constantly in motion, had had a successful engagement, and the troops felt encouraged by what they had accomplished. It is, therefore, totally false, as rumor had it after the battle, that "Sigel's men" gave themselves up to plundering the camp, became scattered, and were for this reason surprised by the "returning enemy."

When we had taken our position on the plateau near Sharp's, a cannonade was opened by me against a part of the enemy's troops, evidently forming the left of their line, confronting Lyon, as we could observe from the struggle going on in that direction. The firing lasted about 30 minutes.‡

Suddenly the firing on the enemy's side ceased, and it seemed as if we had directed our own fire against Lyon's forces. I therefore ordered the pieces to cease firing. Just at this time—it was between 9 and 10 o'clock—there was a lull in the fight on the north side, and not a gun was heard, while squads of the enemy's troops, unarmed, came streaming up the road from Skegg's Branch toward us and were captured. Meanwhile a part of McCulloch's force was advancing against us at Sharp's farm, while Reid's battery moved into position on the hill east of Wilson's Creek, and opposite our right flank, followed by some cavalry.

All these circumstances—the cessation of the firing in Lyon's front, the appearance of the enemy's deserters, and the movement of Reid's artillery and the cavalry toward the south—led us into the belief that the enemy's forces were retreating, and this opinion became stronger by the report of Dr. Melcher, who was in advance on the road to Skegg's Branch, that "Lyon's troops" were coming up the road and that we must not fire. So uncertain was I in regard to the character of the approaching troops, now only a few rods distant, that I did not trust to my own eyes, but sent Corporal Tod, of the 3d Missouri, forward to challenge them. He challenged as ordered, but was immediately shot and killed. I instantly ordered the artillery and infantry to fire. But it was too late—the artillery fired one or two shots, but the infantry, as though paralyzed, did not fire; the 3d Louisiana, which we had mistaken for the gray-clad 1st Iowa, rushed up to the plateau, while Bledsoe's battery in front and Reid's from the heights on our right flank opened with canister at point-blank against us. As a matter of

<hr>

‡Colonel Graves, commanding the First Brigade, Mo. State Guards, says in his report: "Colonel Rosser, commanding the 1st Regiment and Fourth Battalion, with Captain Bledsoe's artillery, being stationed on the extreme left, was attacked by Colonel Sigel's battery, and his men exposed to a deadly fire for thirty minutes."—F.S.

precaution I had during the last moment brought four of our pieces into battery on the right against the troops on the hill and Reid's battery; but after answering Reid's fire for a few minutes, the horses and drivers of three guns suddenly left their position, and with their caissons galloped down the Fayetteville road, in their tumultuous flight carrying panic into the ranks of the infantry, which turned back in disorder, and at the same time received the fire of the attacking line.

On our retreat the right wing, consisting mostly of the 3d Missouri Infantry and one piece of artillery, followed the road we came, while the left wing, consisting of the 5th Missouri Infantry and another piece, went down the Fayetteville road, then, turning to the right (north-west), made its way toward Little York and Springfield; on its way the latter column was joined by Lieutenant Farrand's cavalry company. Colonel Salomon was also with this column, consisting in all of about 450 men, with 1 piece and caisson. I remained with the right wing, the 3d Missouri, which was considerably scattered. I re-formed the men during their retreat into 4 companies, in all about 250 men, and, turning to the left, into the Fayetteville road, was joined by Captain Carr's company of cavalry. After considering that, by following the left wing toward Little York, we might be cut off from Springfield and not be able to join General Lyon's forces, we followed the Fayetteville road until we reached a road leading north-east toward Springfield. This road we followed. Captain Carr, with his cavalry, was leading; he was instructed to remain in advance, keep his flankers out, and report what might occur in front. One company of the 3d Missouri was at the head of our little column of infantry, followed by the piece of artillery and two caissons, behind them the remainder of the infantry, the whole flanked on each side by skirmishers. So we marched, or rather dragged along as fast as the exhausted men could go, until we reached the ford at James Fork of the White River. Carr had already crossed, but his cavalry was not in sight; it had hastened along without waiting for us;[*] a part of the infantry had also passed the creek; the piece and caissons were just crossing, when the rattling of musketry announced the presence of hostile forces on both sides of the creek. They were detachments of Missouri and Texas cavalry, under Lieutenant-Colonel Major, Captains Mabry and Russell, that lay in ambush, and now pounced upon our jaded and extended column. It was in vain that Lieutenant-Colonel Albert and myself tried to rally at least a part of them; they left the road to seek protection, or make good their escape in the woods, and were followed and hunted down by their pursuers. In this chase the greater part of our men were killed, wounded, or made prisoners, among the latter Lieutenant-Colonel Albert and

---

[*]Colonel Carr says in his official report: "It is a subject of regret with me to have left him [Sigel] behind, but I supposed all the time that he was close behind me till I got to the creek, and it would have done no good for my company to have been cut to pieces also."—EDITORS.

my orderly, who were with me in the last moment of the affray. I was not taken, probably because I wore a blue woolen blanket over my uniform and a yellowish slouch-hat, giving me the appearance of a Texas Ranger. I halted on horseback, prepared for defense, in a small strip of corn-field on the west side of the creek, while the hostile cavalrymen swarmed around and several times passed close by me. When we had resumed our way toward the north-east, we were immediately recognized as enemies, and pursued by a few horsemen, whose number increased rapidly. It was a pretty lively race for about six miles, when our pursuers gave up the chase. We reached Springfield at 4:30 in the afternoon, in advance of Sturgis, who with Lyon's troops was retreating from the battle-field, and who arrived at Springfield, as he says, at 5 o'clock. The circumstance of my arrival at the time stated gave rise to the insinuation that I had forsaken my troops after their repulse at Sharp's house, and had delivered them to their fate. Spiced with the accusation of "plunder," this and other falsehoods were repeated before the Committee on the Conduct of the War, and a letter defamatory of me was dispatched to the Secretary of War (dated February 14th, 1862, six months after the battle of Wilson's Creek). I had no knowledge of these calamnies against me until long after the war, when I found them in print.

In support of my statements, I would direct attention to my own reports on the battle and to the Confederate reports, especially to those of Lieutenant-Colonel Hyams and Captain Vigilini, of the 3d Louisiana; also to the report of Captain Carr, in which he frankly states that he abandoned me immediately before my column was attacked at the crossing of James Fork, without notifying me of the approach of the enemy's cavalry. I never mentioned this fact, as the subsequent career of General Carr, his coöperation with me during the campaigns of General Frémont, and his behavior in the battle of Pea Ridge vindicated his character and ability as a soldier and commander.

THE OPPOSING FORCES AT WILSON'S CREEK, MO.

The composition and losses of each army as here stated give the gist of all the data obtainable in the official records. K stands for killed; w for wounded; m w mortally wounded; m for captured or missing; c for captured.—EDITORS.

COMPOSITION AND LOSSES OF THE UNION ARMY.

Brig.-Gen. Nathaniel Lyon (k), Major Samuel D. Sturgis.

First Brigade, Major Samuel D. Sturgis: Regular Battalion (B, C, and D, 1st Infantry and Wood's company Rifle Recruits), Capt. Joseph B. Plummer; Battalion 2d Mo. Infantry, Major P. J. Osterhaus; F, 2d U.S. Arty., Capt. James Totten; Kansas Rangers, Capt. S. N. Wood; B, 1st U.S. Cavalry, Lieut. Charles W. Canfield. *Second Brigade,* Lieut.-Col. George L. Andrews:

Regular Battalion (B and E, 2d Infantry, Lothrop's company General Service Recruits, and Morine's company Rifle Recruits), Capt. Frederick Steele; DuBois's Battery (improvised), Lieut. John V. DuBois; 1st Mo. Infantry, Lieut.-Col. Geo. L. Andrews. *Third Brigade,* Col. Geo. W. Deitzler: 1st Kansas, Col. Geo. W. Deitzler (w), Major J. A. Halderman; 2d Kansas, Col. R. B. Mitchell (w), Lieut.-Col. Chas. W. Blair. *Missouri Volunteers. Second Brigade,* Colonel Franz Sigel: 3d Mo., Lieut.-Col. Anselm Albert; 5th Mo., Col. C. E. Salomon; I, 1st U. S. Cavalry, Capt. Eugene A. Carr; C, 2d U. S. Dragoons, Lieut. C. E. Farrand; Backof's Mo. Arty. (detachment), Lieutenants G. A. Schaefer and Edward Schuetzenbach. *Unattached Organizations:* 1st Iowa Infantry, Lieut.-Col. William H. Merritt; Wright's and Switzler's Mo. Home Guard Cavalry; detachment D, 1st U.S. Cavalry; Mo. Pioneers, Capt. J. D. Voerster.

The Union loss, as officially reported, was 223 killed, 721 wounded, and 291 missing,—total, 1235.*

COMPOSITION AND LOSSES OF THE CONFEDERATE ARMY.

Brig.-Gen. Ben. McCulloch.

MISSOURI STATE GUARD, Major-Gen. Sterling Price. RAINS'S DIVISION, Brig.-Gen. James S. Rains. *First Brigade,* Col. R. H. Weightman (m w), Col. John R. Graves: 1st Infantry, Lieut.-Col. Thomas H. Rosser; 3d Infantry, Col. Edgar V. Hurst; 4th Infantry (battalion), Major Thomas H. Murray; 5th Infantry, Col. J. J. Clarkson; Graves's Infantry, Col. John R. Graves, Major Brashear; Bledsoe's Battery, Capt. Hiram Bledsoe. *Second Brigade,* Col. Cawthon (m w). [Composition of brigade not given in the official records.] PARSON'S BRIGADE, Brig.-Gen. M. M. Parsons: Kelly's Infantry, Col. Kelly (w); Brown's Cavalry, Col. Ben. Brown (k); Guibor's Battery, Capt. Henry Guibor. CLARK'S DIVISION, Brig.-Gen. John B. Clark; Burbridge's Infantry, Col. J. Q. Burbridge (w), Major John B. Clark, Jr.; 1st Cavalry (battalion), Lieut.-Col. J. P. Major. SLACK'S DIVISION, Brig. Gen. W. Y. Slack (w); Hughes's Infantry, Col. John T. Hughes; Thornton's Infantry (battalion), Major J. C. Thornton; Rives's Cavalry, Col. B. A. Rives. MCBRIDE'S DIVISION, Brig.-Gen. James R. McBride; Wingo's Infantry; Foster's Infantry, Col. Foster (w); Campbell's Cavalry, Capt. Campbell.

ARKANSAS FORCES, Brig.-Gen. N. B. Pearce, 1st Cavalry, Col. De Rosey Carroll; Carroll's Company Cavalry, Capt. Charles A. Carroll; 3d Infantry, Col. John R. Gratiot; 4th Infantry, Col. J. D. Walker; 5th Infantry,

---

*NOTE.—Colonel Snead, with unusual facilities for ascertaining the facts, gives the losses as follows: Union, (k), 258; (w), 873; (m), 186,—total, 1317. Confederate, (k), 279; (w), 951,—total, 1230. The Union reports do not include Osterhaus's battalion, which lost (k), 15; (w), 40; and give Sigel's loss at 26 less than Colonel Snead's estimate.—EDITORS.

Col. Tom P. Dockery; Woodruff's Battery, Capt. W. E. Woodruff; Reid's Battery, Capt. J. G. Reid.

McCulloch's Brigade: 1st Ark. Mounted Riflemen, Col. T. J. Churchill; 2d Ark. Mounted Riflemen, Col. James McIntosh, Lieut.-Col. B. T. Embry; Arkansas Infantry (battalion), Lieut.-Col. Dandridge McRae; South Kansas–Texas Mounted Regiment, Col. E. Greer; 3d La. Infantry, Col. Louis Hébert.

The Confederate loss, as officially reported, was 265 killed, 800 wounded, and 30 missing,—total, 1095.*

Strength of the Opposing Forces.

The Union forces are estimated from official returns at 5400 (with 16 guns). Of these 1118 were with Sigel and 350 mounted reserve. The Confederate forces are more difficult to estimate, but Colonel Snead, General Price's adjutant-general during the battle, gives in his volume, "The Fight for Missouri" (Charles Scribner's Sons), the following estimate, which is doubtless as near the facts as it is possible to get: Price's force (Missouri State Guard), 5221; McCulloch's brigade, 2720, and Pearce's brigade, 2234,—total, 10,175 (with 15 guns).

1862

INTRODUCTION

Stephen W. Sears

As the calendar turned to 1862, the Union war effort appeared stalled on dead center. On January 10, to try to get the war moving again, President Lincoln convened a conference of his generals and advisers at the White House. "The President was greatly disturbed at the state of affairs," wrote one of his listeners, General Irvin McDowell. "Spoke of the exhausted condition of the Treasury; of the loss of public credit; of the Jacobinism in Congress; of the delicate condition of our foreign relations; of the bad news he had received...on the state of affairs in Missouri; of the want of co-operation between General Halleck and General Buell; but, more than all, the sickness of General McClellan.... To use his own expression, if something was not soon done, the bottom would be out of the whole affair...."

Clearly, Lincoln had cause to be disturbed. Of immediate concern was the illness of his general in chief, George B. McClellan, diagnosed with a serious case of typhoid fever. For almost three weeks McClellan was incommunicado; no one knew his plans, or if he had any plans, or indeed if he would survive. By McDowell's account, the president remarked, "if General McClellan did not want to use the army, he would like to '*borrow it*,' provided he could see how it could be made to do something...."

Borrowing McClellan's army was perhaps not such a far-fetched idea. It was the widespread perception, in that January of 1862, that the Army of the Potomac had sat unused at Washington for far too long. It was going on six months since McClellan had taken command after the Bull Run defeat and commenced reorganizing and training and generally breathing new life into the Union's principal army. Yet still a Confederate army under Joseph E. Johnston was encamped at Manassas, only some twenty-five miles from the capital and as menacing as ever. Further, the Rebels had closed the Potomac below Washington, and along the upper Potomac they blocked railroad and canal access to the city. McClellan's sole countermove, an attempt to clear the upper Potomac in October 1861, had been bloodily repulsed in fighting at Ball's Bluff. Washington remained encased in a near blockade, and Attorney General Edward Bates made complaint: "It isolates the Capital by closing its only outlet to the ocean, and thus makes the impression upon both parties to the contest, and especially to foreigners, that we are both weak and timid." Under this stalemate, Bates added, "the public spirit is beginning to quail." Lincoln's White House conference would at least rouse General McClellan from his sickbed, and in due course gain from him a campaign plan and a promise of action. It would be spring, however, before serious campaigning could begin in the Eastern Theater.

Just then the Western Theater appeared equally stagnant. Union forces there comprised the Department of the Missouri, under Henry Halleck, and the Department of the Ohio, under Don Carlos Buell, and neither general professed himself ready to take the offensive, separately or in combination. The president endorsed one of Halleck's excuse-filled dispatches, "It is exceedingly discouraging. As everywhere else, nothing can be done."

Yet in a remarkably short time matters in the Western Theater took an upward turn. The Union's trump card in the West proved to be its potential to seize (or hold) control of the great rivers of the Mississippi Valley—the Mississippi itself, the Ohio, and the Cumberland and the Tennessee feeding into it. A newly built Yankee gunboat fleet led the way to dramatic changes in war making on the western waters.

The Confederate commander in the West, Albert Sidney Johnston, had been assigned by Richmond to defend a vast region of Kentucky and Tennessee, from the Alleghenies west to the Mississippi. General Johnston had far too few men to adequately secure this extended line, and he had almost no naval resources. He rested his hopes on a hastily erected patchwork of fortifications designed to block the Mississippi as well as the Cumberland and Tennessee rivers, which extended deep into the western Confederacy.

To describe this riverine warfare the *Century* editors chose Rear Admiral Henry Walke, wartime commander of the *Carondelet,* the ironclad gunboat at the center of the actions he covers. Walke was a natural choice for the job, having published in 1877 his memoir *Naval Scenes and Reminiscences of the Civil War in the United States.* In his first article, "The Gun-Boats at Belmont and Fort Henry," Walke introduces James B. Eads, constructor of the gunboats, Flag Officer Andrew H. Foote, commander of the flotilla, and an aspiring brigadier general named U. S. Grant. As Walke explains, gunboats proved essential to Grant's venture at Belmont, Missouri, on the Mississippi, and, on February 6 to the taking of Fort Henry, guarding the Tennessee River just below the Kentucky border.

In Walke's second article, "The Western Flotilla," he writes of Flag Officer

Foote's abortive gunboat attack on Fort Donelson, on the Cumberland—the army's subsequent capture of Donelson is detailed in the following article— and then takes up the story of the navy's battles to open the Mississippi. Walke himself played a key role in the capture of Island No. 10, so called for being the tenth island counting south from the Ohio River's junction with the Mississippi. Island No. 10 was too formidable to be taken by bombardment, so General John Pope's army was marched around and behind the fortress; then Walke's *Carondelet* ran the Rebel river batteries in dramatic fashion to escort Pope to a blocking position that forced the enemy's surrender. Walke concludes his story with the western flotilla engaging the Confederates' riverine navy in violent mêlées that resulted, by June 1862, in clearing the Mississippi as far south as Memphis, Tennessee.

The Century scored a literary coup in its day by publishing "The Capture of Fort Donelson" by the historical novelist Lew Wallace, author of the wildly popular *Ben-Hur* (1880). Wallace, a lawyer by trade, had commanded a division in General Grant's army that took up the challenge of Donelson after Foote's gunboats failed to bombard it into submission as they had Fort Henry.

Following the capture of Donelson, General Grant took his army back down the Cumberland in transports and then up the Tennessee to Pittsburg Landing, close by the Mississippi border. At a rural meetinghouse called Shiloh, Grant waited for the army of Don Carlos Buell to join him. Twenty miles to the south, at Corinth, Mississippi, Albert Sidney Johnston was gathering every Confederate soldier he could lay hands on in the western Confederacy to try to check the Union surge that so far had made a shambles of his defenses. The consequence was the great two-day Battle of Shiloh. Grant had agreed to write several papers for *The Century*'s "War Series," and when editor R. W. Gilder read this first one, on Shiloh, he wrote his associates, "Hurrah for Grant!" He went on to say that "now that Grant has got going as a chronicler of his own battles, he might be induced to keep at it until he had made a book of his own." Indeed, that book would be Grant's famous *Personal Memoirs*, published posthumously in 1885.

Meanwhile, in the East, the opening actions of 1862 also took place on the waters, notably Virginia's Hampton Roads. The outbreak of war found the U.S. Navy's steam frigate *Merrimac* laid up for engine repairs at the Norfolk, Virginia, naval base. In abandoning the base to the Rebels, the Federals burned and scuttled the *Merrimac*. Stephen R. Mallory, the Confederacy's resourceful secretary of the navy, had the hulk raised and converted into a powerful ironclad ram, renamed CSS *Virginia*. The two naval constructors who directed the conversion, John M. Brooke and John L. Porter, tell their story here.

Intelligence on this imposing warship made its way north and started the Navy Department on a frantic search for a counter to the enemy's new weapon. At stake was maintaining the blockade of Southern ports, most immediately at

Hampton Roads. Swedish-born naval engineer John Ericsson met the challenge with the revolutionary *Monitor*, a new-from-the-keel-up armored warship featuring a revolving gun turret. Ericsson's detailed account of designing and building the *Monitor* is noticeably assertive about his creation; the ironclad's alleged failings and general unseaworthiness, he says, were due to mismanagement by others.

"The First Fight of Iron-clads" is the work of then lieutenant John Taylor Wood, in charge of the *Virginia*'s aft pivot gun during her destructive sortie against the Union blockading fleet in Hampton Roads on March 8, and then her historic duel the next day with the *Monitor*. Taylor goes on to relate the initial crimp the *Virginia* put in General McClellan's Peninsula campaign, and her fate when her base at Norfolk was seized by the Yankees.

Even before the showdown at Hampton Roads, the Union navy had made serious inroads on the coastlines of North and South Carolina, seizing bases for the blockading squadrons. The navy's most important such venture was aimed at New Orleans, the largest city in the Confederacy and the Mississippi Valley's outlet to the sea. Some sixty miles down the Mississippi from New Orleans were the city's primary guardians, Fort Jackson and Fort St. Philip, large masonry fortifications predating the war, mounting seventy-five and fifty-six cannon, respectively. Two large ironclads of the *Virginia* type were also intended for the city's defense, but they could not be completed in time.

Washington assigned Flag Officer David Glasgow Farragut the task of conquering New Orleans, and in April 1862 Farragut assembled his warship squadron off the mouth of the Mississippi. "The 'Brooklyn' at the Passage of the Forts" was written for *The Century* by John Russell Bartlett, who commanded a gun crew aboard USS *Brooklyn* the night of April 24, when in a pyrotechnic spectacular Farragut ran the Rebel batteries and captured New Orleans.

Starting in March, General McClellan finally mounted his "grand campaign" against Richmond, advancing the Army of the Potomac up the Virginia Peninsula toward the Confederate capital. To distract the Federals and keep them from reinforcing McClellan, Stonewall Jackson mounted a campaign of his own in the Shenandoah Valley. Jackson's operations, widely considered a military classic, are described here by John D. Imboden, who had commanded the 1st Virginia Partisan Rangers under Jackson.

McClellan's name was familiar to *Century* readers, he having written five articles for the magazine, all on European affairs, during the postwar years. McClellan had yet to write about his own controversial wartime command, however, and he welcomed *The Century*'s War Series as an opportunity to tell the story of the Peninsula campaign from his perspective. That perspective is predominantly self-serving, with everything that went wrong in the failed campaign blamed on the machinations of the administration in Washington, most particularly those of the secretary of war, Edwin M. Stanton. McClellan does not mention here the pivotal event in the Peninsula campaign—the accession of Robert E. Lee to command of the Army of Northern Virginia after the wounding of Joseph E. Johnston at Fair Oaks. Lee's relentless offensive in the Seven Days' Battles (June 25–July 1) demoralized McClellan and drove the larger—not the smaller, as McClellan has it—Army of the Potomac from the gates of Richmond.

Victory on the Peninsula left Lee and his army squarely between McClellan's Army of the Potomac, at Harrison's Landing on the James River, and John Pope's newly assembled Army of Virginia, on the Rappahannock River halfway between Richmond and Washington. Direction of the Union forces was now in the hands of the new general in chief, Henry Halleck, like Pope brought to Washington from the Western Theater. McClellan—and Pope as well—saw opportunity here, the chance to grind Lee between their two armies. Halleck saw here only danger, the risk of leaving Lee free to move against one or the other of the divided Union forces, and he ordered McClellan to evacuate the Peninsula and combine his army with Pope's before Washington. Lee seized the moment and brilliantly exploited it, rushing against Pope before the Army of the Potomac could seriously intervene.

Pope's "The Second Battle of Bull Run" is, like McClellan's article, self-serving, but John Pope had far more justification for thinking himself betrayed. Thanks to his delusionary overcounting of Confederate numbers, McClellan was overcautious in pulling out of the Peninsula and clearly negligent in dispatching his divisions to Pope's aid. Pope takes bitter aim at Fitz John Porter, a McClellan acolyte who was court-martialed and cashiered for disobedience of orders and misbehavior before the enemy at Second Bull Run. Twenty-four years after the event, Porter would be vindicated in a rehearing of his case, but the fact remains that both he and McClellan failed to do their proper duty to General Pope on the Second Bull Run battlefield.

James Longstreet, the highest placed of Lee's generals to survive the war, welcomed *The Century*'s invitation to write of the Confederates' attempt to exploit their victory over Pope by invading Maryland, a move fired by Lee's ambition to gain a victory on Northern soil. That ambition was enhanced when he learned that McClellan was back in command in place of Pope; having bested McClellan on the Peninsula, Lee expected to best him again in their next encounter.

At the same time that Lee was turning the tables on the Yankees in the East, Confederate forces in the West had slipped out of the Federals' grasp and were invading Kentucky. By September it appeared the war had abruptly turned 180 degrees in the South's favor.

Longstreet opens his account with the statement, "When the Second Bull Run campaign closed we had the most brilliant prospects the Confederates ever had." He favored the move into Maryland but not Lee's subsequent decision to divide his army in order to capture the Federal garrison at Harpers Ferry. Lee's decision became a fateful one, for a copy of his orders for the Harpers Ferry operation was lost, found by a Federal soldier, and passed on to General McClellan. The Lost Order represented the intelligence coup of the war, and although McClellan failed to exploit most of its promise, it did bring Lee to battle in a place he had not intended and before he was prepared. The titanic struggle along Antietam Creek in western Maryland on September 17 took the greatest one-day toll of the war, almost 23,000 total casualties. The two armies fought to mutual exhaustion, and two days later General Lee put his army on the road back to Virginia. His primary accomplishment was the capture of the 13,000-man Harpers Ferry garrison. In Longstreet's tart judgment, "The great mistake of the campaign was the division of Lee's army. If General Lee had kept his forces together, he could not have suffered defeat."

The Century commissioned Jacob D. Cox to chronicle the Union side of the Battle of Antietam, or Sharpsburg as the Confederates termed it. Cox finished the war as a major general with wide combat experience in both theaters of war. He had earlier published two well-regarded works on Sherman's operations for the publisher Scribner's "Campaigns of the Civil War" series, and for *The Century*'s War Papers he had written "War Preparations in the North." During the Maryland fighting at South Mountain and Antietam, Cox led the Kanawha Division, and under the peculiar Union command setup that he describes, he also temporarily led the Ninth Corps. Cox highlights here the piecemeal manner in which McClellan put in his forces, and he attributes the missed Union opportunity to win a decisive victory at Antietam to "McClellan's theory of the enormous superiority of Lee's numbers."

Well satisfied that he had escaped being defeated at Antietam by the imagined Confederate host, McClellan was content to see the Rebels leave Maryland, and he mounted only a brief, token pursuit. In Washington the battle was regarded as short of the victory it might have been, but at least a victory of sorts, enough for Mr. Lincoln to issue the preliminary Emancipation Proclamation. It was now a war for human freedom as well as a war for union. Antietam, the subsequent repulse of the Confederate offensive in Kentucky, and the Emancipation Proclamation combined to mark a turning point in the war.

Something over six weeks after Antietam, under peremptory orders from Washington, McClellan led the Army of the Potomac back into Virginia and pushed slowly, apparently reluctantly, toward the enemy's new position. On November 5, Lincoln issued an order relieving General McClellan of the command: "I began to fear he was playing false—that he did not want to hurt the enemy." Lincoln told his secretary, "If he let them get away I would remove him. He did so & I relieved him." To a White House visitor the president said simply that he "had tried long enough to bore with an auger too dull to take hold."

The new commander of the Army of the Potomac was Ambrose E. Burnside, who under pressure from Washington initiated a winter campaign against Lee's latest position, at Fredericksburg on the Rappahannock River. For Burnside everything went wrong from the start, and on December 13 the repeated charges he ordered against the impenetrable enemy front resulted in disaster. James Longstreet, in command of that section of the Confederate line, narrates the grim story of Fredericksburg. Before the fighting started, Longstreet's chief of artillery positioned his batteries and said, "General, we cover that ground now so well that we will comb it as with a fine-tooth comb. A chicken could not live on that field when we open on it." It was an exact prediction. Utterly defeated, Burnside fell back across the Rappahannock.

The year 1862 in the Eastern Theater closed with the battered, demoralized Army of the Potomac in winter quarters at Falmouth on the Rappahannock, apparently without prospects. In the West a savage two-day battle at Murfreesboro in Tennessee at the turn of the year left those two armies spent and without evident prospects either. And so 1862 ended as it began, with the Union war effort seemingly stalled on dead center. "Our military condition I am sorry to say, does not appear as yet to improve," Lincoln's secretary John G. Nicolay wrote to a friend on January 15, 1863. "Little disasters still tread on each other's heels. Nevertheless every point is being strained by the government, and we must continue to hope in patience."

ARMY TRANSPORTS AT THE CAIRO LEVEE. FROM A WAR-TIME SKETCH.

CHAPTER 1

THE GUN-BOATS AT BELMONT
AND FORT HENRY.

Henry Walke, Rear-Admiral, U.S.N.

At the beginning of the war, the army and navy were mostly employed in protecting the loyal people who resided on the borders of the disaffected States, and in reconciling those whose sympathies were opposed. But the defeat at Manassas and other reverses convinced the Government of the serious character of the contest, and of the necessity of more vigorous and extensive preparations for war. Our navy yards were soon filled with workmen; recruiting stations for unemployed seamen were established, and we soon had more sailors than were required for the ships that could be fitted for service. Artillerymen for the defenses of Washington being scarce, five hundred of these sailors, with a battalion of marines (for guard duty), were sent to occupy the forts on Shuter's Hill, near Alexandria. The *Pensacola* and the Potomac flotilla and the seaboard navy yards required nearly all of the remaining unemployed seamen.

While Foote was improvising a flotilla for the Western rivers he was making urgent appeals to the Government for seamen. Finally some one at the Navy Department thought of the five hundred tars stranded on Shuter's Hill, and obtained an order for their transfer to Cairo, where they were placed on the receiving ship *Maria Denning*. There they met fresh-water sailors from our great lakes, and steamboat hands from the Western rivers. Of the seamen from the East, there were Maine lumbermen, New Bedford whalers, New York liners, and Philadelphia sea-lawyers. The

FLAG-OFFICER FOOTE IN THE
WHEEL-HOUSE OF THE "CINCINNATI"
AT FORT HENRY.

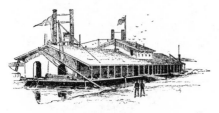

WHARF-BOAT AT CAIRO.

FROM A WAR-TIME PHOTOGRAPH.

foreigners enlisted were mostly Irish, with a few English and Scotch, French, Germans, Swedes, Norwegians, and Danes. The Northmen, considered the hardiest race in the world, melted away in the Southern sun with surprising rapidity.

On my gun-boat, the *Carondelet*, were more young men perhaps than on any other vessel in the fleet. Philadelphians were in the majority; Bostonians came next, with a sprinkling from other cities, and just enough men-o'-war's men to leaven the lump with naval discipline. The *De Kalb* had more than its share of men-o'-war's men, Lieutenant-Commander Leonard Paulding having had the first choice of a full crew, and having secured all the frigate *Sabine*'s reënlisted men who had been sent West.

During the spring and summer of 1861, Commander John Rodgers purchased, and he, with Commander Roger N. Stembel, Lieutenant S. L. Phelps, and Mr. Eads, altered, equipped, and manned, for immediate service on the Ohio and Mississippi rivers, 3 wooden gun-boats—the *Tyler*, of 6 8-inch shell-guns and 2 32-pounders; the *Lexington*, of 4 8-inch shell-guns and 2 32-pounders, and the *Conestoga*, of 4 32-pounder guns. This nucleus of the Mississippi flotilla (like the fleets of Perry, Macdonough, and Chauncey in the war of 1812) was completed with great skill and dispatch; they soon had full possession of the Western rivers above Columbus, Kentucky, and rendered more important service than as many regiments could have done. On October 12th, 1861, the *St. Louis*, afterward known as the *De Kalb*, the first of the seven iron-clad gun-boats ordered of Mr. Eads by the Government, was launched at Carondelet, near St. Louis. The other iron-clads, the *Cincinnati, Carondelet, Louisville, Mound City, Cairo*, and *Pittsburgh*, were launched soon after the *St. Louis*, Mr. Eads having pushed forward the work with most commendable zeal and energy. Three of these were built at Mound City, Ill. To the fleet of iron-clads above named were added the *Benton* (the largest and best vessel of the Western flotilla), the *Essex*, and a few smaller and partly armored gun-boats.

Flag-Officer Foote arrived in St. Louis on September 6th, and assumed command of the Western flotilla. He had been my fellow-midshipman in 1827, on board the United States ship *Natchez*, of the West India squadron, and was then a promising young officer. He was transferred to the *Hornet*, of the same squadron, and was appointed her sailing-master. After he left the *Natchez*, we never met again until February, 1861, at the Brooklyn Navy Yard, where he was the executive officer. Foote, Schenck, and myself were then the only survivors of the midshipmen of the *Natchez*, in her cruise of 1827, and now I am the only officer left.

THE GUN-BOATS "TYLER" AND "LEXINGTON"
ENGAGING THE BATTERIES OF COLUMBUS, KY., DURING THE BATTLE OF BELMONT.
AFTER A SKETCH BY REAR-ADMIRAL WALKE.

In a letter written early in January, 1862, General Polk says of the works at Columbus: "We are still quiet here. I am employed in making more and more difficult the task to take this place.... I have now, mounted and in position, all round my works, 140 cannon of various calibers, and they look not a little formidable. Besides this, I am paving the bottom of the river with submarine batteries, to say nothing of a tremendous, heavy chain across the river. I am planting mines out in the roads also."

During the cruise of 1827, while pacing the deck at night, on the lonely seas, and talking with a pious shipmate, Foote became convinced of the truth of the Christian religion, of which he was an earnest professor to the last. He rendered important service while in command of the brig *Perry,* on the coast of Africa, in 1849, in suppressing the slave-trade, and he greatly distinguished himself by his skill and gallantry in the attack upon the Barrier Forts, near Canton (1856), which he breached and carried by assault, leading the assailing column in person. He was slow and cautious in arriving at conclusions, but firm and tenacious of purpose. He has been called "the Stonewall Jackson of the Navy." He often preached to his crew on Sundays, and was always desirous of doing good. He was not a man of striking personal appearance, but there was a sailor-like heartiness and frankness about him that made his company very desirable.

Flag-Officer Foote arrived at Cairo September 12th, and relieved Commander John Rodgers of the command of the station. The first operations of the Western flotilla consisted chiefly of reconnoissances on the Mississippi, Ohio, Cumberland, and Tennessee rivers. At this time it was under the control of the War Department, and acting in coöperation with the army under General Grant, whose headquarters were at Cairo.

On the evening of the 6th of November, 1861, I received instructions from General Grant to proceed down the Mississippi with the wooden gun-boats *Tyler* and *Lexington* on a reconnoissance, and as convoy to some half-dozen transport steamers; but I did not know the character of the service expected of me until I anchored for the night, seven or eight miles below Cairo. Early the next morning, while the troops were being landed near Belmont, Missouri, opposite Columbus, Kentucky, I attacked the Confederate batteries, at the request of General Grant, as a diversion, which was done with some effect. But the superiority of the enemy's batteries on the bluffs at Columbus, both in the number and the quality of his guns, was so great that it would have been too hazardous to have remained long under his fire with such frail vessels as the *Tyler* and *Lexington*, which were only expected to protect the land forces in case of a repulse. Having accomplished the object of the attack, the gun-boats withdrew, but returned twice during the day and renewed the contest. During the last of these engagements a cannon-ball passed obliquely through the side, deck, and scantling of the *Tyler*, killing one man and wounding others. This convinced me of the necessity of withdrawing my vessels, which had been moving in a circle to confuse the enemy's gunners. We fired a few more broadsides, therefore, and, perceiving that the firing had ceased at Belmont, an ominous circumstance, I returned to the landing, to protect the army and transports. In fact, the destruction of the gun-boats would have involved the loss of our army and our depot at Cairo, the most important one in the West.

Soon after we returned to the landing-place our troops began to appear, and the officers of the gun-boats were warned by General McClernand of the approach of the enemy. The Confederates came *en masse* through a corn-field, and opened with musketry and light artillery upon the transports, which were filled or being filled with our retreating soldiers. A well-directed fire from the gun-boats made the enemy fly in the greatest confusion.

Flag-Officer Foote was at St. Louis when the battle of Belmont was fought, and made a report to the Secretary of the Navy of the part which the gun-boats took in the action, forwarding my official report to the Navy Department. The officers of the vessels were highly complimented by

MAP OF THE REGION OF
FOOTE'S OPERATIONS.

General Grant for the important aid they rendered in this battle; and in his second official report of the action he made references to my report. It was impossible for me to inform the flag-officer of the general's intentions, which were kept perfectly secret.

During the winter of 1861–62, an expedition was planned by Flag-Officer Foote and Generals Grant and McClernand against Fort Henry, situated on the eastern bank of the Tennessee River, a short distance south of the line between Kentucky and Tennessee. In January the iron-clads were brought down to Cairo, and great efforts were made to prepare them for immediate service, but only four of the iron-clads could be made ready as soon as required.

On the morning of the 2d of February the flag-officer left Cairo with the four armored vessels above named, and the wooden gun-boats *Tyler, Lexington,* and *Conestoga,* and in the evening reached the Tennessee River. On the 4th the fleet anchored six miles below Fort Henry. The next day, while reconnoitering, the *Essex* received a shot which passed through the pantry and the officers' quarters and visited the steerage.☆ On the 5th the flag-officer inspected the officers and crew at quarters, addressed them, and offered a prayer.

Heavy rains had been falling, and the river had risen rapidly to an unusual height; the swift current brought down an immense quantity of heavy driftwood, lumber, fences, and large trees, and it required all the steam-power of the *Carondelet,* with both anchors down, and the most strenuous exertions of the officers and crew, working day and night, to prevent the boat from being dragged down-stream. This adversity appeared to dampen the ardor of our crew, but when the next morning they saw a large number of white objects, which through the fog looked like polar bears, coming down the stream, and ascertained that they were the enemy's torpedoes forced from their moorings by the powerful current, they took heart, regarding the freshet as providential and as a presage of victory. The overflowing river, which opposed our progress, swept away in broad daylight this hidden peril; for if the torpedoes had not been disturbed, or had broken loose at night while we were shoving the drift-wood from our bows, some of them would surely have exploded near or under our vessels.

The 6th dawned mild and cheering, with a light breeze, sufficient to clear away the smoke. At 10:20 the flag-officer made the signal to prepare for battle,

---

☆Composition and losses of the Union fleet at Fort Henry: Flag-Officer A. H. Foote, commanding. *First Division:* Flagship *Cincinnati,* Commander R. N. Stembel: 6 32-pounders, 3 8-inch, 4 rifled army 42-pounders, 1 12-pounder boat-howitzer; *Essex,* Commander W. D. Porter: 1 32-pounder, 3 11-inch, 1 10-inch, 1 12-pounder boat-howitzer; *Carondelet,* Commander H. Walke (same armament as the *Cincinnati*); *St. Louis,* Lieut.-Commanding L. Paulding: 7 32-pounders, 2 8-inch, 4 rifled 42-pounders, 1 rifled boat-howitzer. *Second Division:* Lieut. S. L. Phelps, commanding: *Conestoga,* Lieut.-Commanding S. L. Phelps: 4 32-pounders; *Tyler,* Lieut.-Commanding William Gwin: 1 32-pounder, 6 8-inch; *Lexington,* Lieut.-Commanding J. W. Shirk: 2 32-pounders, 4 8-inch. The Union loss as officially reported was: *Cincinnati,* killed, 1; wounded, 9. *Essex,* killed, 6; wounded, 18; missing, 5. Total killed, 7; wounded, 27; missing, 5. Total, 39.—EDITORS.

and at 10:50 came the order to get under way and steam up to Panther Island, about two miles below Fort Henry. At 11:35, having passed the foot of the island, we formed in line and approached the fort four abreast,—the *Essex* on the right, then the *Cincinnati, Carondelet,* and *St. Louis.* For want of room the last two were interlocked, and remained so during the fight.

As we slowly passed up this narrow stream, not a sound could be heard nor a moving object seen in the dense woods which overhung the dark and swollen river. The gun-crews of the *Carondelet* stood silent at their posts, impressed with the serious and important character of the service before them. About noon the

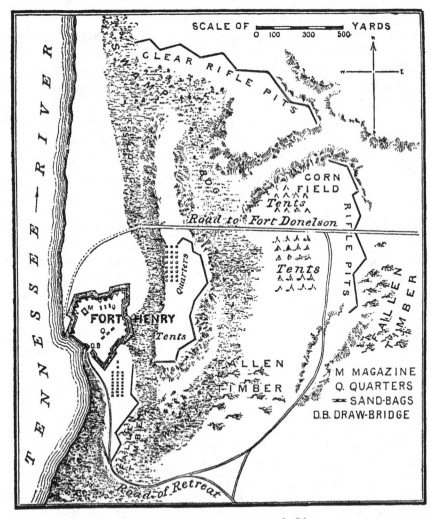

MAP OF FORT HENRY, FEBRUARY 6, 1862.

fort and the Confederate flag came suddenly into view, the barracks, the new earth-works, and the great guns well manned. The captains of our guns were men-of-war's men, good shots, and had their men well drilled.

The flag-steamer, the *Cincinnati,* fired the first shot as the signal for the others to begin. At once the fort was ablaze with the flame of her eleven heavy guns. The wild whistle of their rifle-shells was heard on every side of us. On the *Carondelet* not a word was spoken more than at ordinary drill, except when Matthew Arthur, captain of the star- board bow-gun, asked permission to fire at one or two of the enemy's re- treating vessels, as he could not at that time bring his gun to bear on the fort. He fired one shot, which passed through the upper cabin of a hospi- tal-boat, whose flag was not seen, but injured no one. The *Carondelet* was struck in about thirty places by the enemy's heavy shot and shell. Eight struck within two feet of the bow- ports, leading to the boilers, around which barricades had been built—a precaution which I always took before going into action, and which on sev- eral occasions prevented an explo- sion. The *Carondelet* fired 107 shell and solid shot; none of her officers or crew was killed or wounded.

The firing from the armored ves- sels was rapid and well sustained from the beginning of the attack, and seem- ingly accurate, as we could occasion- ally see the earth thrown in great heaps over the enemy's guns. Nor was the fire of the Confederates to be de- spised; their heavy shot broke and scattered our iron-plating as if it had been putty, and often passed com- pletely through the casemates. But our old men-of-war's men, captains of the guns, proud to show their worth in battle, infused life and courage into

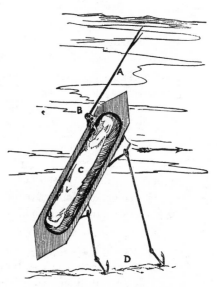

CROSS-SECTION OF A CONFEDERATE
TORPEDO FOUND IN THE
TENNESSEE RIVER.

A, iron rod armed with prongs to fasten upon the bottom of boats going up-stream and act upon B, a lever connecting with trigger to ex- plode a cap and ignite the powder. C, canvas bag containing 70 lbs. of powder. D, anchors to hold torpedo in place.

This torpedo consisted of a stout sheet- iron cylinder, pointed at both ends, about 5½ feet long and 1 foot in diameter. The iron lever was 3½ feet long, and armed with prongs to catch in the bottom of a boat. This lever was constructed to move the iron rod on the inside of the cylinder, thus acting upon the trigger of the lock to explode the cap and fire the powder. The machine was anchored, presenting the prongs in such a way that boats going down- stream should slide over them, but those com- ing up should catch.

their young comrades. When these experienced gunners saw a shot coming toward a port, they had the coolness and discretion to order their men to bow down, to save their heads.

After nearly an hour's hard fighting, the captain of the *Essex*, going below, and complimenting the First Division for their splendid execution, asked them if they did not want to rest and give three cheers, which were given with a will. But the feelings of joy on board the *Essex* were suddenly changed by a calamity which is thus described in a letter to me from James Laning, second master of the *Essex*:

"A shot from the enemy pierced the casemate just above the port-hole on the port side, then through the middle boiler, killing in its flight Acting Master's Mate S. B. Brittan, Jr., and opening a chasm for the escape of the scalding steam and water. The scene which followed was almost indescribable. The writer, who had gone aft in obedience to orders only a few moments before (and was thus providentially saved), was met by Fourth Master Walker, followed by a crowd of men rushing aft. Walker called to me to go back; that a shot from the enemy had carried away the steampipe. I at once ran to the stern of the vessel, and, looking out of the stern-port, saw a number of our brave fellows struggling in the water. The steam and hot water in the forward gun-deck had driven all who were able to get out of the ports overboard, except a few who were fortunate enough to cling to the casemate outside. When the explosion took place Captain Porter was standing directly in front of the boilers, with his aide, Mr. Brittan, at his side. He at once rushed for the port-hole on the starboard side, and threw himself out, expecting to go into the river. A seaman, John Walker, seeing his danger, caught him around the waist, and supporting him with one hand, clung to the vessel with the other, until, with the assistance of another seaman, who came to the rescue, they succeeded in getting the captain upon a narrow guard or projection which ran around the vessel, and thus enabled him to make his way outside to the after-port, where I met him. Upon speaking to him, he told me he was badly hurt, and that I must hunt for Mr. Riley, the First Master, and if he was disabled I must take command of the vessel, and man the battery again. Mr. Riley was unharmed, and already in the discharge of his duties as Captain Porter's successor. In a very few minutes after the explosion our gallant ship (which, in the language of Flag-Officer Foote, had fought most effectively through two-thirds of the engagement) was drifting slowly away from the scene of action; her commander badly wounded, a number of her officers and crew dead at their post, while many others were writhing in their last agony. As soon as the scalding steam would admit, the forward gun-deck was explored. The pilots, who were both in the pilot-house, were scalded to death. Marshall Ford, who was steering when the explosion took place, was found at his post at the wheel, standing erect, his left hand holding the spoke and his right hand grasping the signal-bell rope. A seaman named James Coffey, who was shot-man to the No. 2 gun, was on his knees, in the act of taking a shell from the box to be passed to the loader. The escaping steam and hot water had struck him square in the face, and he met death in that position. When I told Captain Porter that we were victorious, he immediately rallied, and, raising himself on his elbow, called for three cheers, and gave two himself, falling exhausted on the mattress in his effort to give the third. A seaman named Jasper P. Breas, who was badly scalded, sprang to his feet, exclaiming: 'Surrender! I must see that with my own eyes before I die.' Before any one could interfere, he clambered up two short flights of stairs to the spar-deck. He shouted 'Glory to God!' and sank exhausted on the deck. Poor Jasper died that night."

The *Essex* before the accident had fired seventy shots from her two 9-inch guns. A powder boy, Job Phillips, fourteen years of age, coolly marked down upon the casemate every shot his gun had fired, and his account was confirmed

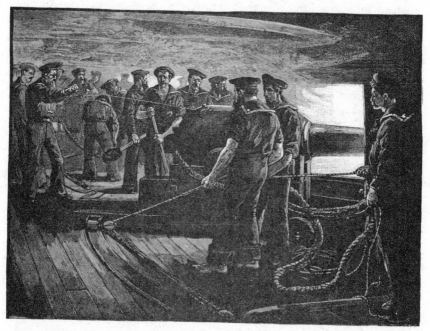

BETWEEN DECKS—SERVING THE GUNS. AFTER A SKETCH BY REAR-ADMIRAL WALKE.

by the gunner in the magazine. Her loss in killed, wounded, and missing was thirty-two.

The *St. Louis* was struck seven times. She fired one hundred and seven shots during the action. No one on board the vessel was killed or wounded.

Flag-Officer Foote during the action was in the pilot-house of the *Cincinnati,* which received thirty-two shots. Her chimneys, after-cabin, and boats were completely riddled. Two of her guns were disabled. The only fatal shot she received passed through the larboard front, killing one man and wounding several others. I happened to be looking at the flag-steamer when one of the enemy's heavy shot struck her. It had the effect, apparently, of a thunder-bolt, ripping her side-timbers and scattering the splinters over the vessel. She did not slacken her speed, but moved on as though nothing unexpected had happened.

From the number of times the gun-boats were struck, it would appear that the Confederate artillery practice, at first, at least, was as good, if not better, than ours. This, however, was what might have been expected, as the Confederate gunners had the advantage of practicing on the ranges the gun-boats would probably occupy as they approached the fort. The officers of the gun-boats, on the contrary, with guns of different caliber and unknown range, and without practice, could not point their guns with as much accuracy. To counterbalance this advantage of the enemy, the gun-boats were much better protected by their casemates for distant firing than the fort by its fresh earth-works. The Confederate soldiers fought as valiantly and as skillfully as the Union sailors. Only after a most determined resistance, and after all his heavy guns had been silenced, did General Tilghman lower his flag. The Confederate loss, as reported, was 5 killed, 11 wounded, and 5 missing. The prisoners, including the general and his staff, numbered 78 in the fort and 16 in a hospital-boat; the remainder of the garrison, a little less than 2600, having escaped to Fort Donelson.

Our gun-boats continued to approach the fort until General Tilghman, with two or three of his staff, came off in a small boat to the *Cincinnati* and surrendered the fort to Flag-Officer Foote, who sent for me, introduced me to General Tilghman, and gave me orders to take command of the fort and hold it until the arrival of General Grant.

General Tilghman was a soldierly-looking man, a little above medium height, with piercing black eyes and a resolute, intelligent expression of countenance. He was dignified and courteous, and won the respect and sympathy of all who became acquainted with him. In his official report of the battle he said that his officers and men fought with the greatest bravery until 1:50 P.M., when seven of his eleven guns were disabled; and, finding it impossible to defend the fort, and wishing to spare the lives of his gallant men, after consultation with his officers he surrendered the fort.

It was reported at the time that, in surrendering to Flag-Officer Foote, the Confederate general said, "I am glad to surrender to so gallant an officer," and that Foote replied, "You do perfectly right, sir, in surrendering, but you should have blown my boat out of the water before I would have surrendered to you." I was with Foote soon after the surrender, and I cannot believe that such a reply was made by him. He was too much of a gentleman to say anything calculated to wound the feelings of an officer who had defended his post with signal courage and fidelity, and whose spirits were clouded by the adverse fortunes of war.

When I took possession of the fort the Confederate surgeon was laboring with his coat off to relieve and save the wounded; and although the officers and crews of the gun-boats gave three hearty cheers when the Confederate flag was hauled down, the first inside view of the fort sufficed to suppress every feeling of exultation and to excite our deepest pity. On every side the blood of the dead and wounded was intermingled with the earth and their implements of war. Their largest gun, a 128-pounder, was dismounted and filled with earth by the bursting of one of our shells near its muzzle; the carriage of another was broken to pieces, and two dead men lay near it, almost covered with heaps of earth; a rifled gun had burst, throwing its mangled gunners into the water. But few of the garrison escaped unhurt.

GENERAL LLOYD TILGHMAN.
FROM A PHOTOGRAPH.

General Grant, with his staff, rode into the fort about 3 o'clock on the same day, and relieved me of the command. The general and staff then accompanied me on board the *Carondelet* (anchored near the fort), where he complimented the officers of the flotilla in the highest terms for the gallant manner in which they had captured Fort Henry. He had expected his troops to take part in a land attack, but the heavy rains had made the direct roads to the fort almost impassable.

The wooden gun-boats *Conestoga,*

Commander S. L. Phelps, *Tyler,* Lieutenant-Commander William Gwin, and *Lexington,* Lieutenant J. W. Shirk, engaged the enemy at long range in the rear of the iron-clads. After the battle they pursued the enemy's transports up the river, and the *Conestoga* captured the steamer *Eastport.* The news of the capture of Fort Henry was received with great rejoicing all over the North.*

*Following upon the capture of Fort Henry (February 6th, 1862) and of Fort Donelson (February 16th), the fortifications at Columbus on the Mississippi were evacuated February 20th. In January General Halleck reached the conclusion that the object for which General Polk had labored in fortifying Columbus had been accomplished, for on the 20th he wrote General McClellan: "Columbus cannot be taken without an immense siege-train and a terrible loss of life. I have thoroughly studied its defenses—they are very strong; but it can be turned, paralyzed, and forced to surrender." In accordance with the idea suggested in this dispatch, the Federal movement upon Forts Henry and Donelson was decided upon.

In the latter part of January General Beauregard was ordered to report to General Johnston for assignment to duty at Columbus. He arrived at Jackson, Tennessee, about the middle of February, but, being too ill to proceed to Columbus, he requested General Polk to visit him at Jackson. The fall of Forts Henry and Donelson, and the declared purpose of the Federals to push their forces up the Tennessee River, made the further occupation of Columbus a serious question. General Beauregard had sent his chief of staff, Colonel Jordan, and his engineer officer, Captain Harris, up to Columbus, and they had made such reports to him concerning the nature of the works that he was inclined to doubt their efficiency. This, together with the necessity he was under to gather as large a force as possible with which to meet the enemy's movement up the Tennessee, convinced him that Columbus should be evacuated, and the defense of the river made at Island Number Ten and Fort Pillow. These points he considered not only more defensible than Columbus, but defensible with a smaller force, which would enable him to take a part of the command then holding the river for operations in conjunction with the troops he was gathering along the line of the Memphis and Charleston railroad. When, in the conference at Jackson, Beauregard unfolded these views to General Polk, the latter was not disposed to yield a ready assent to all of them. He recognized the necessity for gathering a force for field operations. It was, indeed, exactly what he and every other prominent officer in the department had, for six months, been urging upon the authorities. He, however, questioned the advisability of giving up Columbus. The works had been accepted by Colonel Gilmer, the chief engineer of the department, an officer who subsequently became the head of the Corps of Engineers in the Confederacy. In spite of the strategical fault which might be committed in an attempt to hold it, General Polk maintained that, just at that time, the moral effect of a determined stand at Columbus would be of great service to the Confederate arms.

—DR. WM. M. POLK.

CHAPTER 2

THE WESTERN FLOTILLA AT FORT DONELSON, ISLAND NUMBER TEN, FORT PILLOW AND MEMPHIS.

Henry Walke, Rear-Admiral, U.S.N.

On the 7th of February, the day after the capture of Fort Henry, I received on board the *Carondelet* Colonels Webster, Rawlins, and McPherson, with a company of troops, and under instructions from General Grant proceeded up the Tennessee River, and completed the destruction of the bridge of the Memphis and Bowling Green Railroad.

On returning from that expedition General Grant requested me to hasten to Fort Donelson with the *Carondelet, Tyler,* and *Lexington,* and announce my arrival by firing signal guns. The object of this movement was to take possession of the river as soon as possible, to engage the enemy's attention by making formidable demonstrations before the fort, and to prevent it from being reënforced. On February 10th the *Carondelet* alone (towed by the transport *Alps*) proceeded up the Cumberland River, and on the 12th arrived a few miles below the fort.

Fort Donelson occupied one of the best defensive positions on the river. It was built on a bold bluff about 120 feet in height, on the west side of the river, where it makes a slight bend to the eastward. It had 3 batteries, mounting in all 15 guns: the lower, about twenty feet above the water; the second, about fifty feet above the water; the third, on the summit.†

---

† The armament of the fort consisted of "ten 32-pounder guns (two of them ship carronades), one 8-inch howitzer, two nondescript 9-pounders, one 10-inch Columbiad, and one rifled gun throwing a conical shell of 128 pounds." The garrison was commanded by Colonel J. E. Bailey, the artillery by Captain Joseph Dixon, and after his death by Captain Jacob Culbertson, with Captains Ross, Beaumont, and Bidwell in separate command of the guns of the lower batteries. Captain Dixon was killed in the action of the 13th with the *Carondelet* by a shot which dismounted one of his guns—"the only damage done to the batteries during the siege." (Captain Culbertson's report.)—EDITORS.

THE "CARONDELET" FIGHTING FORT DONELSON, FEBRUARY 13, 1862.
FROM A SKETCH BY REAR-ADMIRAL WALKE.

When the *Carondelet*, her tow being cast off, came in sight of the fort and proceeded up to within long range of the batteries, not a living creature could be seen. The hills and woods on the west side of the river hid part of the enemy's formidable defenses, which were lightly covered with snow; but the black rows of heavy guns, pointing down on us, reminded me of the dismal-looking sepulchers cut in the rocky cliffs near Jerusalem, but far more repulsive. At 12:50 P.M., to unmask the silent enemy, and to announce my arrival to General Grant, I ordered the bow-guns to be fired at the fort. Only one shell fell short. There was no response except the echo from the hills. The fort appeared to have been evacuated. After firing ten shells into it, the *Carondelet* dropped down the river about three miles and anchored. But the sound of her guns aroused our soldiers on the southern side of the fort into action; one report says that when they heard the guns of the *avant-courrier* of the fleet, they gave cheer upon cheer, and rather than permit the sailors to get ahead of them again, they engaged in skirmishes with the enemy, and began the battle of the three days following. On the *Carondelet* we were isolated and beset with dangers from the enemy's lurking sharp-shooters.

On the 13th a dispatch was received from General Grant, informing me that he had arrived the day before, and had succeeded in getting his army in position, almost entirely investing the enemy's works. "Most of our batteries," he said, "are established, and the remainder soon will be. If you will advance with your gun-boat at 10 o'clock in the morning, we will be ready to take advantage of any diversion in our favor."

I immediately complied with these instructions, and at 9:05, with the *Carondelet* alone and under cover of a heavily wooded point, fired 139 70-pound

EXPLOSION OF A GUN ON BOARD THE "CARONDELET" DURING THE ATTACK ON FORT DONELSON.

AFTER A SKETCH BY REAR-ADMIRAL WALKE.

and 64-pound shells at the fort. We received in return the fire of all the enemy's guns that could be brought to bear on the *Carondelet*, which sustained but little damage, except from two shots. One, a 128-pound solid, at 11:30 struck the corner of our port broadside casemate, passed through it, and in its progress toward the center of our boilers glanced over the temporary barricade in front of the boilers. It then passed over the steam-drum, struck the beams of the upper deck, carried away the railing around the engine-room and burst the steam-heater, and, glancing back into the engine-room, "seemed to bound after the men," as one of the engineers said, "like a wild beast pursuing its prey." I have preserved this ball as a souvenir of the fight at Fort Donelson. When it burst through the side of the *Carondelet*, it knocked down and wounded a dozen men, seven of them severely. An immense quantity of splinters was blown through the vessel. Some of them, as fine as needles, shot through the clothes of the men like arrows. Several of the wounded were so much excited by the suddenness of the event and the sufferings of their comrades, that they were not aware that they themselves had been struck until they felt the blood running into their shoes. Upon receiving this shot we ceased firing for a while.

After dinner we sent the wounded on board the *Alps*, repaired damages, and, not expecting any assistance, at 12:15 we resumed, in accordance with General Grant's request, and bombarded the fort until dusk, when nearly all our 10-inch and 15-inch shells were expended. The firing from the shore having ceased, we retired.

At 11:30 on the night of the 13th Flag-Officer Foote arrived below Fort Donelson with the iron-clads *St. Louis, Louisville,* and *Pittsburgh*, and the wooden gun-boats *Tyler* and *Conestoga*. On the 14th all the hard materials in the vessels, such as chains, lumber, and bags of coal, were laid on the upper decks to protect them from the plunging shots of the enemy. At 3 o'clock in the afternoon our fleet advanced to attack the fort, the *Louisville* being on the west side of the river, the *St. Louis* (flag-steamer) next, then the *Pittsburgh* and *Carondelet* on the east side of the river. The wooden gun-boats were about a thousand yards in the rear. When we started in line abreast at a moderate speed, the *Louisville* and *Pittsburgh*, not keeping up to their positions, were hailed from the flag-steamer to "steam up." At 3:30, when about a mile and a half from the fort, two shots were fired at us, both falling short. When within a mile of the fort the *St. Louis* opened fire, and the other iron-clads followed, slowly and deliberately at first, but more rapidly as the fleet advanced. The flag-officer hailed the *Carondelet*, and ordered us not to fire so fast. Some of our shells went over the fort, and almost into our camp beyond. As we drew nearer, the enemy's fire greatly increased in force and effect. But, the officers and crew of the *Carondelet* having recently been long under fire, and having become practiced in fighting, her gunners were as cool and composed as old veterans. We heard the deafening crack of the bursting shells, the crash of the solid shot, and the whizzing of fragments of shell and wood as they sped through the vessel. Soon a 128-pounder struck our anchor, smashed it into flying bolts, and bounded over the vessel, taking away a part of our smoke-stack; then another cut away the iron boat-davits as if they were pipe-stems, whereupon the boat dropped into the water. Another ripped up the iron plating and glanced over; another went through the plating and lodged in the heavy casemate; another struck the pilot-house, knocked the plating to pieces, and sent fragments of iron and splinters into the pilots, one of whom fell mortally wounded, and was taken below; another shot took away the remaining boat-davits and the boat with them; and still they came, harder and faster, taking flag-staffs and smoke-stacks, and tearing off the side armor as lightning tears the bark from a tree. Our men fought desperately, but, under the excitement of the occasion, loaded too hastily, and the port rifled gun exploded. One of the crew, in his account of the explosion soon after it occurred, said: "I was serving the gun with shell. When it exploded it knocked us all down, killing none, but wounding over a dozen men and spreading dismay and confusion among us. For about two minutes I was stunned, and at least five minutes elapsed before I could tell what was the matter. When I found out that I was more scared than hurt, although suffering from the gunpowder which I had inhaled, I looked forward and saw our gun lying on the deck, split in three pieces. Then the cry ran through the boat that we were on fire, and my duty as pump-man called me to the pumps. While I was there, two shots entered our bow-ports and killed four men and wounded several others. They were borne past me, three with their heads off. The sight almost sickened me, and I turned my head away. Our master's mate came soon after and ordered us to our quarters at the gun. I told him the gun had burst, and that we had caught fire on the upper deck from the enemy's shell. He then said: 'Never mind the fire; go to your quarters.' Then I took a station at the starboard tackle of another rifled bow-gun and remained there until the close of the fight." The carpenter and his men extinguished the flames.

When within four hundred yards of the fort, and while the Confederates were running from their lower battery, our pilot-house was struck again and another pilot wounded, our wheel was broken, and shells from the rear boats were bursting over us. All four of our boats were shot away and dragging in the water. On looking out to bring our broadside guns to bear, we saw that the other gun-boats were rapidly falling back out of line. The *Pittsburgh* in her haste to turn struck the stern of the *Carondelet,* and broke our starboard rudder, so that we were obliged to go ahead to clear the *Pittsburgh* and the point of rocks below. The pilot of the *St. Louis* was killed, and the pilot of the *Louisville* was wounded. Both vessels had their wheel-ropes shot away, and the men were prevented from steering the *Louisville* with the tiller-ropes at the stern by the shells from the rear boats bursting over them. The *St. Louis* and *Louisville,* becoming unmanageable, were compelled to drop out of battle, and the *Pittsburgh* followed;

all had suffered severely from the enemy's fire. Flag-Officer Foote was wounded while standing by the pilot of the *St. Louis* when he was killed. We were then about 350 yards from the fort.

There was no alternative for the *Carondelet* in that narrow stream but to keep her head to the enemy and fire into the fort with her two bow-guns, to prevent it, if possible, from returning her fire effectively. The enemy saw that she was in a manner left to his mercy, and concentrated the fire of all his batteries upon her. In return, the *Carondelet*'s guns were well served to the last shot. Our new acting gunner, John Hall, was just the man for the occasion. He came forward, offered his services, and with my sanction took charge of the starboard-bow rifled gun. He instructed the men to obey his warnings and follow his motions, and he told them that when he saw a shot coming he would call out "Down" and stoop behind the breech of the gun as he did so; at the same instant the men were to stand away from the bow-ports. Nearly every shot from the fort struck the bows of the *Carondelet*. Most of them were fired on the ricochet level, and could be plainly seen skipping on the water before they struck. The enemy's object was to sink the gun-boat by striking her just below the water-line. They soon succeeded in planting two 32-pound shots in her bow, between wind and water, which made her leak badly, but her compartments kept her from sinking until we could plug up the shot-holes. Three shots struck the starboard casemating; four struck the port casemating forward of the rifle-gun; one struck on the starboard side, between the water-line and plank-sheer, cutting through the planking; six shots struck the pilot-house, shattering one section into pieces and cutting through the iron casing. The smoke-stacks were riddled.

Our gunners kept up a constant firing while we were falling back; and the warning words, "Look out!" "Down!" were often heard, and heeded by nearly all the gun-crews. On one occasion, while the men were at the muzzle of the middle bow-gun, loading it, the warning came just in time for them to jump aside as a 32-pounder struck the lower sill, and glancing up struck the upper sill, then, falling on the inner edge of the lower sill, bounded on deck and spun around like a top, but hurt no one. It was very evident that if the men who were loading had not obeyed the order to drop, several of them would have been killed. So I repeated the instructions and warned the men at the guns and the crew generally to bow or stand off from the ports when a shot was seen coming.

THE GUN-BOATS AT FORT DONELSON (FEBRUARY 14, 1862)—THE LAND ATTACK IN THE DISTANCE. AFTER A SKETCH BY REAR-ADMIRAL WALKE.

But some of the young men, from a spirit of bravado or from a belief in the doctrine of fatalism, disregarded the instructions, saying it was useless to attempt to dodge a cannon-ball, and they would trust to luck. The warning words, "Look out!" "Down!" were again soon heard; down went the gunner and his men, as the whizzing shot glanced on the gun, taking off the gunner's cap and the heads of two of the young men who trusted to luck, and in defiance of the order were standing up or passing behind him. This shot killed another man also, who was at the last gun of the starboard side, and disabled the gun. It came in with a hissing sound; three sharp spats and a heavy bang told the sad fate of three brave comrades. Before the decks were well sanded, there was so much blood on them that our men could not work the guns without slipping.

MAP OF THE REGION OF THE FLOTILLA OPERATIONS.

We kept firing at the enemy so long as he was within range, to prevent him from seeing us through the smoke.

The *Carondelet* was the first in and the last out of the fight, and was more damaged than any of the other gun-boats, as the boat-carpenters who repaired them subsequently informed me. She was much longer under fire than any other vessel of the flotilla; and, according to the report of the Secretary of the Navy, her loss in killed and wounded was nearly twice as great as that of all the other gun-boats together. She fired more shot and shell into Fort Donelson than any other gun-boat, and was struck fifty-four times. These facts are given because a disposition was shown by correspondents and naval historians to ignore the services of the *Carondelet* on this and other occasions.

In the action of the 14th all of the armored vessels were fought with the greatest energy, skill, and courage, until disabled by the enemy's heavy shot. In his official report of the battle the flag-officer said: "The officers and men in this hotly contested but unequal fight behaved with the greatest gallantry and determination."⚓

⚓From the report of Captain B. G. Bidwell, "the only officer connected with the heavy batteries of Fort Donelson who was fortunate enough to escape," we take this account of the engagement:

"All was quiet until the evening of the 14th (Friday), when 4 boats came around the point, arranged themselves in line of battle, and advanced slowly, but steadily, up the river to within

Although the gun-boats were repulsed in this action, the demoralizing effect of their cannonade, and of the heavy and well-sustained fire of the *Carondelet* on the day before, must have been very great, and contributed in no small degree to the successful operations of the army on the following day.

After the battle I called upon the flag-officer, and found him suffering from his wounds. He asked me if I could have run past the fort, something I should not have ventured upon without permission.

The 15th was employed in the burial of our slain comrades. I read the Episcopal service on board the *Carondelet,* under our flag at half-mast; and the sailors bore their late companions to a lonely field within the shadows of the hills. When they were about to lower the first coffin, a Roman Catholic priest appeared, and his services being accepted, he read the prayers for the dead. As the last service was ended, the sound of the battle being waged by General Grant, like the rumbling of distant thunder, was the only requiem for our departed shipmates.

On Sunday, the 16th, at dawn, Fort Donelson surrendered and the gun-boats steamed up to Dover. After religious services the *Carondelet* proceeded back to Cairo, and arrived there on the morning of the 17th, in such a dense fog that she passed below the town unnoticed, and had great difficulty in finding the landing. There had been a report that the enemy was coming from Columbus to attack Cairo during the absence of its defenders; and while the *Carondelet* was cautiously feeling her way back and blowing her whistle, some people imagined she was a Confederate gun-boat about to land, and made hasty preparations to leave the place. Our announcement of the victory at Fort Donelson changed their dejection into joy and exultation. On the following morning an

---

200 yards of our battery, and halted, when a most incessant fire was kept up for some time. We were ordered to hold our fire until they got within range of our 32-pounders. We remained perfectly silent, while they came over about one and a half miles, pouring a heavy fire of shot and shell upon us all the time. Two more boats came around the point and threw shell at us. Our gunners were inexperienced and knew very little of the firing of heavy guns. They, however, did some excellent shooting. The rifled gun was disabled by the ramming of a cartridge while the wire was in the vent, it being left in there by a careless gunner,—being bent, it could not be got out,—but the two center boats were both disabled, the left-center (I think) by a ricochet shot entering one of the port-holes, which are tolerably large. The right-center boat was very soon injured by a ball striking her on top, and also a direct shot in the port hole, when she fell back, the two flank boats closing in behind them and protecting them from our fire in retreat. I think these two were not seriously injured. They must have fired near two thousand shot and shell at us. Our Columbiad fired about 27 times, the rifled gun very few times, and the 32-pounders about 45 or 50 rounds each. A great many of our balls took effect, being well aimed. I am confident the efficiency of the gun-boat is in the gun it carries rather than in the boat itself. We can whip them always if our men will only stand to their guns. Not a man of all ours was hurt, notwithstanding they threw grape at us. Their fire was more destructive to our works at 2 miles than at 200 yards. They over-fired us from that distance."

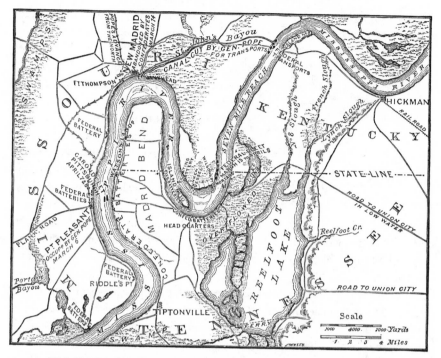

MAP OF MILITARY AND NAVAL OPERATIONS ABOUT ISLAND NUMBER TEN.
(BASED ON THE TWO MAPS BY CAPTAIN A. B. GRAY, C.S.A.,
MADE IN MARCH, 1862, AND ON OFFICIAL REPORTS.)

order congratulating the officers and men of the *Carondelet* was received from
Flag-Officer Foote.

A few days later the *Carondelet* was taken up on the ways at Mound City,
Illinois,—six or seven miles above Cairo on the Ohio River,—for repairs; and a
crowd of carpenters worked on her night and day. After the repairs were completed, she was ordered to make the experiment of backing up-stream, which
proved a laughable failure. She would sheer from one side of the river to the
other, and with two anchors astern she could not be held steady enough to fight
her bow-guns down-stream. She dragged both anchors alternately, until they
came together, and the experiment failed completely.

On the morning of the 23d the flag-officer made a reconnoissance to
Columbus, Kentucky, with four gun-boats and two mortar-boats, accompanied
by the wooden gun-boat *Conestoga*, convoying five transports. The fortifications
looked more formidable than ever. The enemy fired two guns, and sent up a
transport with the pretext, it was said, of effecting an exchange of prisoners.↓

↓The ostensible object was a request to permit the families of officers captured at Fort Donelson to pass
through the Union lines. The request was granted on the following day, but General George W. Cullum

THE MORTAR-BOATS
AT ISLAND NUMBER TEN.

But at that time, as we learned afterward from a credible source, the evacuation of the fort (which General Grant's successes at Forts Henry and Donelson had made necessary) was going on, and the last raft and barge loads of all the movable munitions of war were descending the river, which, with a large quantity previously taken away, could and would have been captured by our fleet if we had received this information in time. On the 4th of March another reconnoissance in force was made with all the gun-boats and four mortar-boats, and the fortress had still a formidable, life-like appearance, though it had been evacuated two days before.[1]

On the 5th of March, while we were descending the Mississippi in a dense fog, the flag-steamer leading, the Confederate gun-boat *Grampus,* or *Dare-devil Jack,* the sauciest little vessel on the river, suddenly appeared across our track and "close aboard." She stopped her engines and struck her colors, and we all thought she was ours at last. But when the captain of the *Grampus* saw how slowly we moved, and as no gun was fired to bring him to, he started off with astonishing speed and was out of danger before the flag-steamer could fire a gun. She ran before us yawing and flirting about, and blowing her alarm-whistle so as to announce our approach to the enemy who had now retired to Island Number Ten, a strong position sixty miles below Columbus (and of the latitude of Forts Henry and Donelson), where General Beauregard, who was now in general command of our opponents, had determined to contest the possession of the river.

On March 15th the flotilla and transports continued on their way to Island Number Ten, arriving in its vicinity about nine in the morning. The strong and muddy current of the river had overflowed its banks and carried away every

---

(General Halleck's chief of staff) and Flag-Officer Foote remonstrated with General Polk for the use made of the flag of truce.—EDITORS.

[1] On the 3d of March the evacuated works had been occupied by a scouting party of the 2d Illinois Cavalry, sent from Paducah by Brigadier-General W. T. Sherman, who had succeeded Brigadier-General Grant in command of the District of Cairo (February 14, 1862) on the assignment of General Grant to the command of the District of West Tennessee. The fact of the occupation was not known at the time of the gun-boat reconnoissance, which included a land force accompanied by General Sherman and by Brigadier-General Cullum. This detachment landed and took formal possession. In his report of the occupation, General Cullum speaks of Columbus as "the Gibraltar of the West."—EDITORS.

movable thing. Houses, trees, fences, and wrecks of all kinds were being swept rapidly down-stream. The twists and turns of the river near Island Number Ten are certainly remarkable. Within a radius of eight miles from the island it crosses the boundary line of Kentucky and Tennessee three times, running on almost every point of the compass. We were greatly surprised when we arrived above Island Number Ten and saw on the bluffs a chain of forts extending for four miles along the crescent-formed shore, with the white tents of the enemy in the rear. And there lay the island in the lower corner of the crescent, with the side fronting the Missouri shore lined with heavy ordnance, so trained that with the artillery on the opposite shore almost every point on the river between the island and the Missouri bank could be reached at once by all the enemy's batteries.

On the 17th an attack was made on the upper battery by all the iron-clads and mortar-boats. The *Benton* (flag-steamer), lashed between the *Cincinnati* and *St. Louis,* was on the east side of the river; the *Mound City, Carondelet,* and *Pittsburgh* were on the west side; the last, however, changed her position to the east side of the river before the firing began. We opened fire on the upper fort at 1:20, and by order of the flag-officer fired one gun a minute. The enemy replied promptly, and some of his shot struck the *Benton,* but, owing to the distance from which they were fired, did but little damage. We silenced all the guns in the upper fort except one. During the action one of the rifled guns of the *St. Louis* exploded, killing and wounding several of the gunners,—another proof of the truth of the saying that the guns furnished the Western flotilla were less destructive to the enemy than to ourselves.

From March 17th to April 4th but little progress was made in the reduction of the Confederate works—the gun-boats firing a few shot now and then at long range, but doing little damage. The mortar-boats, however, were daily throwing 13-inch bombs, and so effectively at times that the Confederates were driven from their batteries and compelled to seek refuge in caves and other places of safety. But it was very evident that the great object of the expedition—the reduction of the works and the capture of the Confederate forces—could not be effected by the gun-boats alone, owing to their mode of structure and to the disadvantage under which they were fought in the strong and rapid current of the Mississippi. This was the opinion not only of naval officers, but also of General Pope and other army officers.

On the 23d of March the monotony of the long and tedious investment was unfortunately varied in a very singular manner. The *Carondelet* being moored nearest the enemy's upper fort, under several large cottonwood trees, in order to protect the mortar-boats, suddenly, and without warning, two of the largest of the trees fell across her deck, mortally wounding one of the crew and severely wounding another, and doing great damage to the vessel. This was twelve days before I ran the gauntlet at Island Number Ten with the *Carondelet.*

THE "CARONDELET" RUNNING THE
CONFEDERATE BATTERIES AT ISLAND
NUMBER TEN (APRIL 4, 1862). AFTER
A SKETCH BY REAR-ADMIRAL WALKE.

To understand fully the importance of that adventure, some explanation of the military situation at and below Island Number Ten seems necessary. After the evacuation of New Madrid, which General Pope had forced by blockading the river twelve miles below, at Point Pleasant, the Confederate forces occupied their fortified positions on Island Number Ten and the eastern shore of the Mississippi, where they were cut off by impassable swamps on the land side. They were in a *cul-de-sac*, and the only way open for them to obtain supplies or to effect a retreat was by the river south of Island Number Ten. General Pope, with an army of twenty thousand men, was on the western side of the river below the island. Perceiving the defect in the enemy's position, he proceeded with great promptness and ability to take advantage of it. It was his intention to cross the river and attack the enemy from below, but he could not do this without the aid of a gun-boat to silence the enemy's batteries opposite Point Pleasant and protect his army in crossing. He wrote repeatedly to Flag-Officer Foote, urging him to send down a gun-boat past the enemy's batteries on Island Number Ten, and in one of his letters expressed the belief that a boat could pass down at night under cover of the darkness. But the flag-officer invariably declined, saying in one of his letters to General Pope that the attempt "would result in the sacrifice of the boat, her officers and men, which sacrifice I would not be justified in making."

During this correspondence the bombardment still went on, but was attended with such poor results that it became a subject of ridicule among the officers of Pope's army, one of whom (Colonel Gilmore, of Chillicothe, Ohio) is reported to have said that often when they met, and inquiry was made respecting the operations of the flotilla, the answer would generally be: "Oh! it is still bombarding the State of Tennessee at long range." And a Confederate officer said that no casualties resulted and no damage was sustained at Island Number Ten from the fire of the gun-boats.

On March 20th Flag-Officer Foote consulted his commanding officers, through Commander Stembel, as to the practicability of taking a gun-boat past the enemy's forts to New Madrid, and all except myself were opposed to the enterprise, believing with Foote that the attempt to pass the batteries would result in the almost certain destruction of the boat. I did not think so, but believed with General Pope that, under the cover of darkness and other favorable circumstances, a gun-boat might be run past the enemy's batteries, formidable as they were with nearly fifty guns. And although fully aware of the hazardous nature of the enterprise, I knew that the aid of a gun-boat was absolutely necessary to enable General Pope to succeed in his operations against the enemy, and thought the importance of this success would justify the risk of running the gauntlet of the batteries on Island Number Ten and on the left bank. The army officers were becoming impatient, and it was well known that the Confederates had a number of small gun-boats below, and were engaged in building several large and powerful vessels, of which the renowned *Arkansas* was one. And there was good reason to apprehend that these gun-boats would ascend the river and pass or silence Pope's batteries, and relieve the Confederate forces on Island Number Ten and the eastern shore of the Mississippi. That Pope and Foote apprehended this, appears from the correspondence between them.‡

The flag-officer now called a formal council of war of all his commanding officers. It was held on board the flag-steamer, on the 28th or 29th of March, and all except myself concurred in the opinion formerly expressed that the attempt to pass the batteries was too hazardous and ought not to be made. When I was asked to give my views, I favored the undertaking, and advised compliance with the requests of General Pope. When asked if I was willing to make the attempt with the *Carondelet*, I replied in the affirmative. Foote accepted my advice, and expressed himself as greatly relieved from a heavy responsibility, as he had determined to send none but volunteers on an expedition which he regarded as perilous and of very doubtful success.

Having received written orders from the flag-officer, under date of March

---

‡An interesting and important enterprise in this campaign was the sawing out, under great difficulties, of a channel, twelve miles in length, to complete a water-way for the Union transports across Madrid Bend.

—EDITORS.

30th, I at once began to prepare the *Carondelet* for the ordeal. All the loose material at hand was collected, and on the 4th of April the decks were covered with it, to protect them against plunging shot. Hawsers and chain cables were placed around the pilot-house and other vulnerable parts of the vessel, and every precaution was adopted to prevent disaster. A coal-barge laden with hay and coal was lashed to the part of the port side on which there was no iron plating, to protect the magazine. It was truly said that the *Carondelet* at that time resembled a farmer's wagon prepared for market. The engineers led the escape-steam, through the pipes aft, into the wheel-house, to avoid the puffing sound it made when blown through the smoke-stacks.

All the necessary preparations having been made, I informed the flag-officer of my intention to run the gauntlet that night, and received his approval. Colonel N. B. Buford, who commanded the land forces temporarily with the flotilla, assisted me in preparing for the trip, and on the night of the 4th brought on board Captain Hottenstein, of the 42d Illinois, and twenty-three sharp-shooters of his command, who volunteered their services, which were gratefully accepted. Colonel Buford remained on board until the last moment, to encourage us. I informed the officers and crew of the character of the undertaking, and all expressed a readiness to make the venture. In order to resist boarding parties, in case of being disabled, the sailors were well armed, and pistols, cutlasses, muskets, boarding-pikes, and hand-grenades were within reach. Hose was attached to the boilers for throwing scalding water over any who might attempt to board. If it should be found impossible to save the vessel, it was designed to sink rather than burn her.

MAJOR-GENERAL JOHN POPE.
FROM A PHOTOGRAPH TAKEN
EARLY IN THE WAR.

During the afternoon there was a promise of a clear, moonlight night, and it was determined to wait until the moon was down, and then to make the attempt, whatever the chances. Having gone so far, we could not abandon the project without an effect on the men almost as bad as failure.

At 10 o'clock the moon had gone down, and the sky, the earth, and the river were alike hidden in the black shadow of a thunder-storm, which had now spread itself over all the heavens. As the time seemed favorable, I ordered the first master to cast off. Dark clouds now rose rapidly over us and enveloped us in almost total darkness, except when the sky was lighted up by the welcome flashes of vivid lightning, to show us the perilous way we were to take. Now and then the dim outline of the landscape could be seen, and the forest bending under the roaring storm that came rushing up the river.

With our bow pointing to the island, we passed the lowest point of land without being observed, it appears, by the enemy. All speed was given to the vessel to drive her through the tempest. The flashes of lightning continued with frightful brilliancy, and "almost every second," wrote a correspondent, "every brace, post, and outline could be seen with startling distinctness, enshrouded by a bluish white glare of light, and then her form for the next minute would become merged in the intense darkness." When opposite Battery No. 2, on the mainland,/ the smoke-stacks blazed up, but the fire was soon sub-

BRIGADIER-GENERAL W. W. MACKALL, C.S.A., IN COMMAND AT ISLAND NUMBER TEN, PREVIOUSLY ASSISTANT ADJUTANT-GENERAL TO GENERAL ALBERT SIDNEY JOHNSTON. FROM A PHOTOGRAPH.

dued. It was caused by the soot becoming dry, as the escape-steam, which usually kept the stacks wet, had been sent into the wheel-house, as already mentioned, to prevent noise. With such vivid lightning as prevailed during the whole passage, there was no prospect of escaping the vigilance of the enemy, but there was good reason to hope that he would be unable to point his guns accurately. Again the smoke-stacks took fire, and were soon put out; and then the roar of the enemy's guns began, and from Batteries Nos. 2, 3, and 4 on the mainland came the continued crack and scream of their rifle-shells, which seemed to unite with the electric batteries of the clouds to annihilate us.

/The Confederate land batteries above New Madrid were ten in number—five on the eastern side of Island Number Ten; four (Batteries No. 5, 4, 3, and 2) opposite the island on the mainland, as shown on the map (p. 193), besides Battery No. 1, two miles above the island.—EDITORS.

During the dark and stormy night of April 1st Colonel George W. Roberts, of the 42d Illinois Regiment, executed a brilliant exploit. Forty picked men, in five barges, with muffled oars, left for Battery No. 1. They proceeded in silence, and were unobserved until within a few rods of the fort, when a flash of lightning discovered them to the sentries, who fired. Our men, who did not reply, were soon climbing up the slippery bank, and in three minutes more the six guns were spiked, Colonel Roberts himself spiking a huge 80-pounder pivot-gun. Some of these guns had been previously dismounted by our fleet, and were now rendered doubly useless.—H.W.

While nearing the island or some shoal point, during a few minutes of total darkness, we were startled by the order, "Hard a-port!" from our brave and skillful pilot, First Master William R. Hoel. We almost grazed the island, and it appears were not observed through the storm until we were close in, and the enemy, having no time to point his guns, fired at random. In fact, we ran so near that the enemy did not, probably could not, depress his guns sufficiently. While close under the lee of the island and during a lull in the storm and in the firing, one of our pilots heard a Confederate officer shout, "Elevate your guns!" It is probable that the muzzles of those guns had been depressed to keep the rain out, and that the officers ordered the guns elevated just in time to save us from the direct fire of the enemy's heaviest fort; and this, no doubt, was the cause of our remarkable escape.

Having passed the principal batteries, we were greatly relieved from suspense, patiently endured, however, by the officers and crew. But there was another formidable obstacle in the way—a floating battery, which was the great "war elephant" of the Confederates, built to blockade the Mississippi permanently. As we passed her she fired six or eight shots at us, but without effect. One ball struck the coal-barge, and one was found in a bale of hay; we found also one or two musket-bullets. We arrived at New Madrid about midnight with no one hurt, and were most joyfully received by our army. At the suggestion of Paymaster Nixon, all hands "spliced the main brace."

On Sunday, the 6th, after prayers and thanksgiving, the *Carondelet*, with General Gordon Granger, Colonel J. L. Kirby Smith of the 43d Ohio, and Captain Louis H. Marshall of General Pope's staff on board, made a reconnoissance twenty miles down, nearly to Tiptonville, the enemy's forts firing on her all the way down. We returned their fire, and dropped a few shells into their camps beyond. On the way back, we captured and spiked the guns of a battery of one 32-pounder and one 24-pounder, in about twenty-five minutes, opposite Point Pleasant. Before we landed to spike the guns, a tall Confederate soldier, with cool and deliberate courage, posted himself behind a large cottonwood tree, and repeatedly fired upon us, until our Illinois sharp-shooters got to work on him from behind the hammock nettings. He had two rifles, which he soon dropped, fleeing into the woods with his head down. The next day he was captured and brought into camp at Tiptonville, with the tip of his nose shot off. After the capture of this battery, the enemy prepared to evacuate his positions on Island Number Ten and the adjacent shores, and thus, as one of the historians of the civil war says, the *Carondelet* struck the blow that secured that victory.

Returning to New Madrid, we were instructed by General Pope to attack the enemy's batteries of six 64-pounders which protected his rear; and besides, another gun-boat was expected. The *Pittsburgh* (Lieutenant-Commander Thompson) ran the gauntlet without injury, during a thunder-storm, at 2 in the morning of April 7th, and arrived at 5 o'clock; but she was not ready for service, and the *Carondelet* attacked the principal batteries at Watson's Landing alone and had nearly silenced them when the *Pittsburgh* came up astern and fired nearly over the *Carondolet's* upper deck, after she and the Confederates had ceased firing. I reported to General Pope that we had cleared the opposite shores of the enemy, and were ready to cover the crossing of the river and the landing of the army. Seeing themselves cut off, the garrison at Island Number Ten surrendered to Foote on the 7th of April, the day of the Confederate repulse at Shiloh. The other Confederates retreating before Pope's advance, were nearly all overtaken and captured at 4 o'clock on the morning of the 8th; and about the same time the cavalry under Colonel W. L. Elliott took possession of the enemy's deserted works on the Tennessee shore.

The result of General Pope's operations in connection with the services of the *Carondelet* below Island Number Ten was the capture of three generals (including General W. W. Mackall, who ten days before the surrender had succeeded General John P. McCown in the command at Madrid Bend), over 5000 men, 20 pieces of heavy artillery, 7000 stand of arms, and a large quantity of ammunition and provisions, without the loss of a man on our side.

On the 12th the *Benton* (flag-steamer), with the *Cincinnati, Mound City, Cairo,* and *St. Louis,* passed Tiptonville and signaled the *Carondelet* and *Pittsburgh* to follow. Five Confederate gun-boats came up the next day and offered battle; but after the exchange of a few shots at long range they retired down the river. We followed them all the way to Craighead's Point, where they were under cover of

THE "CARONDELET" AND "PITTSBURGH" CAPTURING THE CONFEDERATE BATTERIES
BELOW NEW MADRID. AFTER A DRAWING BY REAR-ADMIRAL WALKE.

their fortifications at Fort Pillow. I was not aware at the time that we were chasing the squadron of my esteemed shipmate of the U.S. Frigates *Cumberland* and *Merrimac,* Colonel John W. Dunnington, who afterward fought so bravely at Arkansas Post.

On the 14th General Pope's army landed about six miles above Craighead's Point, near Osceola, under the protection of the gun-boats. While he was preparing to attack Fort Pillow, Foote sent his executive officer twice to me on the *Carondelet* to inquire whether I would undertake, with my vessel and two or three other gun-boats, to pass below the fort to coöperate with General Pope, to which inquiries I replied that I was ready at any time to make the attempt. But Pope and his army (with the exception of 1500 men) were ordered away, and the expedition against Fort Pillow was abandoned. Between the 14th of April and the 10th of May two or three of the mortar-boats were towed down the river and moored near Craighead's Point, with a gun-boat to protect them. They were employed in throwing 13-inch bombs across the point into Fort Pillow, two miles distant. The enemy returned our bombardment with vigor, but not with much accuracy or effect. Several of their bombs fell near the gun-boats when we were three miles from the fort.

The Confederate fleet called the "River Defense" having been reënforced, they determined upon capturing the mortar-boats or giving us battle. On the 8th three of their vessels came to the point from which the mortar-boats had thrown their bombs, but, finding none, returned. Foote had given special orders to keep up steam and be ready for battle any moment, day or night. There was so much illness at that time in the flotilla that about a third of the officers and men were under medical treatment, and a great many were unfit for duty. On the 9th of May, at his own request, our distinguished commander-in-chief, Foote, was relieved from his arduous duties. He had become very much enfeebled from the wounds received at Fort Donelson and from illness. He carried with him the sympathy and regrets of all his command. He was succeeded by Flag-Officer Charles Henry Davis, a most excellent officer.

This paper would not be complete without some account of the naval battles fought by the flotilla immediately after the retirement of Flag-Officer Foote, under whose supervision and amid the greatest embarrassments it had been built, organized, and equipped. On the morning of the 10th of May a mortar-boat was towed down the river, as usual, at 5 A.M., to bombard Fort Pillow. The *Cincinnati* soon followed to protect her. At 6:35 eight Confederate rams came up the river at full speed.✭ The *Carondelet* at once prepared for action, and slipped her hawser to the "bare end," ready for orders to "go ahead." No officer

---

✭The mortar-boat, No. 16, which was the first object of attack, was defended with great spirit by Acting-Master Gregory, who fired his mortar eleven times, reducing the charge and diminishing the elevation. (See cut, p. 206.)—EDITORS.

was on the deck of the *Benton* (flag-steamer) except the pilot, Mr. Birch, who informed the flag-officer of the situation, and passed the order to the *Carondelet*
and *Pittsburgh* to proceed without waiting for the flag-steamer. General signal
was also made to the fleet to get under way, but it was not visible on account of
the light fog.

The *Carondelet* started immediately after the first verbal order; the others,
for want of steam or some other cause, were not ready, except the *Mound City,*
which put off soon after we were fairly on our way to the rescue of the *Cincinnati*. We had proceeded about a mile before our other gun-boats left their
moorings. The rams were advancing rapidly, and we steered for the leading vessel, *General Bragg,* a brig-rigged, side-wheel steam ram, far in advance of the
others, and apparently intent on striking the *Cincinnati*. When about three-
quarters of a mile from the *General Bragg,* the *Carondelet* and *Mound City* fired on
her with their bow-guns, until she struck the *Cincinnati* on the starboard quarter, making a great hole in the shell-room, through which the water poured
with resistless force. The *Cincinnati* then retreated up the river and the *General
Bragg* drifted down, evidently disabled. The *General Price,* following the example
of her consort, also rammed the *Cincinnati*. We fired our bow-guns into the *General Price,* and she backed off, disabled also. The *Cincinnati* was again struck by
one of the enemy's rams, the *General Sumter.* Having pushed on with all speed to
the rescue of the *Cincinnati,* the *Carondelet* passed her in a sinking condition,
and, rounding to, we fired our bow and starboard broadside guns into the retreating *General Bragg* and the advancing rams, *General Jeff. Thompson, General
Beauregard,* and *General Lovell.* Heading up-stream, close to a shoal, the *Carondelet*
brought her port broadside guns to bear on the *Sumter* and *Price,* which were
dropping down-stream. At this crisis the *Van Dorn* and *Little Rebel* had run above
the *Carondelet;* the *Bragg, Jeff. Thompson, Beauregard,* and *Lovell* were below her.
The last three, coming up, fired into the *Carondelet;* she returned their fire with
her stern-guns; and, while in this position, I ordered the port rifled 50-pounder
Dahlgren gun to be leveled and fired at the center of the *Sumter.* The shot struck
the vessel just forward of her wheel-house, and the steam instantly poured out
from her ports and all parts of her casemates, and we saw her men running out
of them and falling or lying down on her deck. None of our gun-boats had yet
come to the assistance of the *Carondelet.* The *Benton* and *Pittsburgh* had probably
gone to aid the *Cincinnati,* and the *St. Louis* to relieve the *Mound City,* which had
been badly rammed by the *Van Dorn.* The smoke at this time was so dense that
we could hardly distinguish the gun-boats above us. The upper deck of the
Carondelet was swept with grape-shot and fragments of broken shell; some of the
latter were picked up by one of the sharp-shooters, who told me they were
obliged to lie down under shelter to save themselves from the grape and other
shot of the *Pittsburgh* above us, and from the shot and broken shell of the enemy
below us. Why some of our gun-boats did not fire into the *Van Dorn* and *Little*

Rebel while they were above the *Carondelet*, and prevent their escape, if possible, I never could make out.†

As the smoke rose we saw that the enemy was retreating rapidly and in great confusion. The *Carondelet* dropped down to within half a mile above Craighead's Point, and kept up a continual fire upon their vessels, which were very much huddled together. When they were nearly, if not quite, beyond gun-shot, the *Benton,* having raised sufficient steam, came down and passed the *Carondelet;* but the Confederates were under the protection of Fort Pillow before the *Benton* could reach them. Our fleet returned to Plum Point, except the *Carondelet,* which dropped her anchor on the battle-field, two miles or more below the point, and remained there two days on voluntary guard duty. This engagement was sharp, but not decisive. From the first to the last shot fired by the *Carondelet,* one hour and ten minutes elapsed. After the battle, long-range firing was kept up until the evacuation of Fort Pillow.

On the 25th seven of Colonel Ellet's rams arrived,—a useful acquisition to our fleet. During the afternoon of June 4th heavy clouds of smoke were observed rising from Fort Pillow, followed by explosions, which continued through the night; the last of which, much greater than the others, lit up the heavens and the Chickasaw bluffs with a brilliant light, and convinced us that this was the parting salute of the Confederates before leaving for the lower Mississippi. At dawn next morning the fleet was all astir to take possession of Fort Pillow, the flag-steamer leading. We found the casemates, magazines, and breastworks blown to atoms.

On our way to Memphis the enemy's steamer *Sovereign* was intercepted by one of our tugs. She was run ashore by her crew, who attempted to blow her up, but were foiled in their purpose by a boy of sixteen whom the enemy had pressed into service, who, after the abandonment of the vessel, took the extra weights from the safety-valves, opened the fire-doors and flue-caps, and put water on the fires, and, having procured a sheet, signaled the tug, which came up and took possession. It may be proper to say that on our way down the river we respected private property, and did not assail or molest any except those who were in arms against us.

The morning of the 6th of June we fought the battle of Memphis, which lasted one hour and ten minutes. It was begun by an attack upon our fleet by the enemy, whose vessels were in double line of battle opposite the city. We were then at a distance of a mile and a half or two miles above the city. Their fire continued for a quarter of an hour, when the attack was promptly met by two of our

---

†Flag-Officer Davis says in his report: "All of these vessels might easily have been captured if we had possessed the means of towing them out of action; but the steam-power of our gun-boats is so disproportionate to the bulk of the vessels that they can accomplish but little beyond overcoming the strength of the current, even when unincumbered."—EDITORS.

ram squadron, the *Queen of the West* (Colonel Charles Ellet) leading, and the *Monarch* (Lieutenant-Colonel A. W. Ellet, younger brother of the leader). These vessels fearlessly dashed ahead of our gun-boats, ran for the enemy's fleet, and at the first plunge succeeded in sinking one vessel and disabling another. The astonished Confederates received them gallantly and effectively. The *Queen of the West* and *Monarch* were followed in line of battle by the gun-boats, under the lead of Flag-Officer Davis, and all of them opened fire, which was continued from the time we got within good range until the end of the battle—two or three tugs keeping all the while a safe distance astern. The *Queen of the West* was a quarter of a mile in advance of the *Monarch,* and after having rammed one of the enemy's fleet, she was badly rammed by the *Beauregard,* which then, in company with the *General Price,* made a dash at the *Monarch* as she approached them. The *Beauregard,* however, missed the *Monarch* and struck the *General Price* instead on her port side, cutting her down to the water-line, tearing off her wheel instantly, and placing her *hors de combat.* The *Monarch* then rammed the *Beauregard,* which had been several times raked fore and aft by the shot and shell of our iron-clads, and she quickly sank in the river opposite Memphis. The *General Lovell,* after having been badly rammed by the *Queen of the West,* was struck by our shot and shell, and, at about the same time and place as the *Beauregard,* sank to the bottom so suddenly as to take a considerable number of her officers and crew down with her, the others being saved by small boats and our tugs. The *Price, Little Rebel* (with a shot-hole through her steam-chest), and our *Queen of the West,* all disabled, were run on the Arkansas shore opposite Memphis; and the *Monarch* afterward ran into the *Little Rebel* just as our fleet was passing her in pursuit of the remainder of the enemy's fleet, then retreating rapidly down the river. The *Jeff. Thompson,* below the point and opposite President's Island, was the next boat disabled by our shot. She was run ashore, burned, and blown up. The Confederate ram *Sumter* was also disabled by our shell and captured. The *Bragg* soon after shared the same fate and was run ashore, where her officers abandoned her and disappeared in the forests of Arkansas. All the Confederate rams which had been run on the Arkansas shore were captured. The *Van Dorn,* having a start, alone escaped down the river. The rams *Monarch* and *Switzerland* were dispatched in pursuit of her and a few transports, but returned without overtaking them, although they captured another steamer.

The scene at this battle was rendered most sublime by the desperate nature of the engagement and the momentous consequences that followed very speedily after the first attack. Thousands of people crowded the high bluffs overlooking the river. The roar of the cannon and shell shook the houses on shore on either side for many miles. First wild yells, shrieks, and clamors, then loud, despairing murmurs, filled the affrighted city. The screaming, plunging shell crashed into the boats, blowing some of them and their crews into fragments,

"MOUND CITY." "CARONDELET." "CINCINNATI." "PRICE." "BRAGG." "SUMTER."
MORTAR NO. 16. "VAN DORN." "LITTLE REBEL."

THE BATTLE OF FORT PILLOW, MAY 10, 1862 (LOOKING NORTH).
AFTER A SKETCH BY REAR-ADMIRAL WALKE.

and the rams rushed upon each other like wild beasts in deadly conflict. Blinding smoke hovered about the scene of all this confusion and horror; and, as the battle progressed and the Confederate fleet was destroyed, all the cheering voices on shore were silenced. When the last hope of the Confederates gave way, the lamentations which went up from the spectators were like cries of anguish.

Boats were put off from our vessels to save as many lives as possible. No serious injury was received by any one on board the United States fleet. Colonel Ellet received a pistol-shot in the leg; a shot struck the *Carondelet* in the bow, broke up her anchor and anchor-stock, and fragments were scattered over her deck among her officers and crew, wounding slightly Acting-Master Gibson and two or three others who were standing at the time on the forward deck with me. The heavy timber which was suspended at the water-line, to protect the boats from the Confederate rams, greatly impeded our progress, and it was therefore cut adrift from the *Carondelet* when that vessel was in chase of the *Bragg* and *Sumter.* The latter had just landed a number of her officers and crew, some of whom were emerging from the bushes along the bank of the river, unaware of the *Carondelet*'s proximity, when I hailed them through a trumpet, and ordered them to stop or be shot. They obeyed immediately, and by my orders were taken on board a tug and delivered on the *Benton.*

"CARONDELET."   "BENTON."   "ST. LOUIS."   "CAIRO."   "LOUISVILLE."   "QUEEN OF THE

IN THE DISTANCE CONFEDERATE FLEET ADVANCING.   WEST."   "MONARCH."

THE BATTLE OF MEMPHIS (JUNE 6, 1862), LOOKING SOUTH.
AFTER A DRAWING BY REAR-ADMIRAL WALKE.

General Jeff. Thompson, noted in partisan or border warfare, having signally failed with those rams at Fort Pillow, now resigned them to their fate. It
was said that he stood by his horse watching the struggle, and seeing at last his
rams all gone, captured, sunk, or burned, he exclaimed, philosophically, "They
are gone, and I am going," mounted his horse, and disappeared.

An enormous amount of property was captured by our squadron; and, in
addition to the Confederate fleet, we captured at Memphis six large Mississippi
steamers, each marked "C.S.A." We also seized a large quantity of cotton in
steamers and on shore, and the property at the Confederate Navy Yard, and
caused the destruction of the *Tennessee*, a large steam-ram, on the stocks, which
was to have been a sister ship to the renowned *Arkansas*. About one hundred
Confederates were killed and wounded and one hundred and fifty captured.
Chief of all results of the work of the flotilla was the opening of the Mississippi
River once for all from Cairo to Memphis, and the complete possession of
Western Tennessee by the Union forces.

CHAPTER 3

The Capture of Fort Donelson.

Lew Wallace, Major-General, U.S.V.

The village of Dover was—and for that matter yet is—what our English cousins would call the "shire-town" of the county of Stewart, Tennessee. In 1860 it was a village unknown to fame, meager in population, architecturally poor. There was a court-house in the place, and a tavern, remembered now as double-storied, unpainted, and with windows of eight-by-ten glass, which, if the panes may be likened to eyes, were both squint and cataractous. Looking through them gave the street outside the appearance of a sedgy slough of yellow backwater. The entertainment furnished man and beast was good of the kind; though at the time mentioned a sleepy traveler, especially if he were of the North, might have been somewhat vexed by the explosions which spiced the good things of a debating society that nightly took possession of the barroom, to discuss the relative fighting qualities of the opposing sections.

If there was a little of the romantic in Dover itself, there was still less of poetic quality in the country round about it. The only beautiful feature was the Cumberland River, which, in placid current from the south, poured its waters, ordinarily white and pure as those of the springs that fed it, past the village on the east. Northward there was a hill, then a small stream, then a bolder hill round the foot of which the river swept to the west, as if courteously bent on helping Hickman's Creek out of its boggy bottom and cheerless ravine. North of the creek all was woods. Taking in the ravine of the creek, a system of hollows, almost wide and deep enough to be called valleys, inclosed the town and two hills, their bluffest ascents being on the townward side. Westward of the hollows there were woods apparently interminable. From Fort Henry, twelve miles north-west, a road entered the village, stopping first to unite itself with another wagon-way, now famous as the Wynn's Ferry road, coming more directly from the west. Still another road, leading off to Charlotte and Nashville, had been cut across the low ground near the river on the south. These three

HEADQUARTERS IN THE FIELD.

highways were the chief reliances of
the people of Dover for communication with the country, and as they were more than supplemented by the
river and its boatage, the three were left the year round
to the guardianship of the winds and rains.

However, when at length the Confederate authori-
ties decided to erect a military post at Dover, the town entered but little into
consideration. The real inducement was the second hill on the north—more
properly a ridge. As it rose about a hundred feet above the level of the inlet, the
reconnoitering engineer, seeking to control the navigation of the river by a fortification, adopted it at sight. And for that purpose the bold bluff was in fact a
happy gift of nature, and we shall see presently how it was taken in hand and
made terrible.

It is of little moment now who first enunciated the idea of attacking the rebellion by way of the Tennessee River; most likely the conception was simultaneous with many minds. The trend of the river; its navigability for large
steamers; its offer of a highway to the rear of the Confederate hosts in Kentucky
and the State of Tennessee; its silent suggestion of a secure passage into the
heart of the belligerent land, from which the direction of movement could be
changed toward the Mississippi, or, left, toward Richmond; its many advantages
as a line of supply and of general communication, must have been discerned by
every military student who, in the summer of 1861, gave himself to the most
cursory examination of the map. It is thought better and more consistent with
fact to conclude that its advantages as a strategic line, so actually obtrusive of
themselves, were observed about the same time by thoughtful men on both
sides of the contest. With every problem of attack there goes a counter problem
of defense.

A peculiarity of the most democratic people in the world is their hunger
for heroes. The void in that respect had never been so gaping as in 1861. General Scott was then old and passing away, and the North caught eagerly at the
promise held out by George B. McClellan; while the South, with as much pre-

cipitation, pinned its faith and hopes on Albert Sidney Johnston. There is little doubt that up to the surrender of Fort Donelson the latter was considered the foremost soldier of all who chose rebellion for their part. When the shadow of that first great failure fell upon the veteran, President Davis made haste to reassure him of his sympathy and unbroken confidence. In the official correspondence which has survived the Confederacy there is nothing so pathetic, and at the same time so indicative of the manly greatness of Albert Sidney Johnston, as his letter in reply to that of his chief.‡

When General Johnston assumed command of the Western Department, the war had ceased to be a new idea. Battles had been fought. Preparations for battles to come were far advanced. Already it had been accepted that the North was to attack and the South to defend. The Mississippi River was a central object; if opened from Cairo to Fort Jackson (New Orleans), the Confederacy would be broken into halves, and good strategy required it to be broken. The question was whether the effort would be made directly or by turning its defended positions. Of the national gun-boats afloat above Cairo, some were formidably iron-clad. Altogether the flotilla was strong enough to warrant the theory that a direct descent would be attempted; and to meet the movement the Confederates threw up powerful batteries, notably at Columbus, Island Number Ten, Memphis, and Vicksburg. So fully were they possessed of that theory that they measurably neglected the possibilities of invasion by way of the Cumberland and Tennessee rivers. Not until General Johnston established his headquarters at Nashville was serious attention given to the defense of those streams. A report to his chief of engineers of November 21st, 1861, establishes that at that date a second battery on the Cumberland at Dover had been completed; that a work on the ridge had been laid out, and two guns mounted; and that the encampment was then surrounded by an abatis of felled timber. Later, Brigadier-General Lloyd Tilghman was sent to Fort Donelson as commandant, and on

---

‡In this letter dated Decatur, Ala., March 18th, 1862, General Johnston says in part:

"The blow [Fort Donelson] was most disastrous and almost without remedy. I therefore in my first report remained silent. This silence you were kind enough to attribute to my generosity. I will not lay claim to the motive to excuse my course. I observed silence, as it seemed to me the best way to serve the cause and the country. The facts were not fully known, discontent prevailed, and criticism or condemnation were more likely to augment than to cure the evil. I refrained, well knowing that heavy censures would fall upon me, but convinced that it was better to endure them for the present, and defer to a more propitious time an investigation of the conduct of the generals; for in the mean time their services were required and their influence useful. For these reasons Generals Floyd and Pillow were assigned to duty, for I still felt confidence in their gallantry, their energy, and their devotion to the Confederacy.... The test of merit, in my profession, with the people, is success. It is a hard rule, but I think it right. If I join this corps to the forces of Beauregard (I confess a hazardous experiment), those who are now declaiming against me will be without an argument."

—EDITORS.

January 25th he reports the batteries prepared, the entire field-works built with a trace of 2900 feet, and rifle-pits to guard the approaches were begun. The same officer speaks further of reënforcements housed in four hundred log-cabins, and adds that while this was being done at Fort Donelson, Forts Henry and Heiman, over on the Tennessee, were being thoroughly strengthened. January 30th, Fort Donelson was formally inspected by Lieutenant-Colonel Gilmer, chief engineer of the Western Department, and the final touches were ordered to be given it.

It is to be presumed that General Johnston was satisfied with the defenses thus provided for the Cumberland River. From observing General Buell at Louisville, and the stir and movement of multiplying columns under General U.S. Grant in the region of Cairo, he suddenly awoke determined to fight for Nashville at Donelson. To this conclusion he came as late as the beginning of February; and thereupon the brightest of the Southern leaders proceeded to make a capital mistake. The Confederate estimate of the Union force at that time in Kentucky alone was 119 regiments. The force at Cairo, St. Louis, and the towns near the mouth of the Cumberland River was judged to be about as great. It was also known that we had unlimited means of transportation for troops, making concentration a work of but few hours. Still General Johnston persisted in fighting for Nashville, and for that purpose divided his thirty thousand men. Fourteen thousand he kept in observation of Buell at Louisville. Sixteen thousand he gave to defend Fort Donelson. The latter detachment he himself called "the best part of his army." It is difficult to think of a great master of strategy making an error so perilous.

Having taken the resolution to defend Nashville at Donelson, he intrusted the operation to three chiefs of brigade—John B. Floyd, Gideon J. Pillow, and Simon B. Buckner. Of these, the first was ranking officer, and he was at the time under indictment by a grand jury at Washington for malversation as Secretary of War under President Buchanan, and for complicity in an embezzlement of public funds. As will be seen, there came a crisis when the recollection of the circumstance exerted an unhappy influence over his judgment. The second officer had a genuine military record; but it is said of him that he was of a jealous nature, insubordinate, and quarrelsome. His bold attempt to supersede General Scott in Mexico was green in the memories of living men. To give pertinency to the remark, there is reason to believe that a personal misunderstanding between him and General Buckner, older than the rebellion, was yet unsettled when the two met at Donelson. All in all, therefore, there is little doubt that the junior of the three commanders was the fittest for the enterprise intrusted to them. He was their equal in courage; while in devotion to the cause and to his profession of arms, in tactical knowledge, in military bearing, in the faculty of getting the most service out of his inferiors, and inspiring them with confidence in his ability,—as a soldier in all the higher meanings of the word,—he was greatly their superior.

MAP OF FORT DONELSON, AS INVESTED BY GENERAL GRANT.
BASED ON THE OFFICIAL MAP BY GENERAL J. B. MCPHERSON.

The 6th of February, 1862, dawned darkly after a thunder-storm. Pacing the parapets of the work on the hill above the inlet formed by the junction of Hickman's Creek and the Cumberland River, a sentinel, in the serviceable butternut jeans uniform of the Confederate army of the West, might that day have surveyed Fort Donelson almost ready for battle. In fact, very little was afterward done to it. There were the two water-batteries sunk in the northern face of the bluff, about thirty feet above the river; in the lower battery 9 32-pounder guns and 1 10-inch Columbiad, and in the upper another Columbiad, bored and rifled as a 32-pounder, and 2 32-pounder carronades. These guns lay between the embrasures, in snug revetment of sand in coffee-sacks, flanked right and left with stout traverses. The satisfaction of the sentry could have been nowise diminished at seeing the backwater lying deep in the creek; a more perfect ditch against assault could not have been constructed. The fort itself was of good profile, and admirably adapted to the ridge it crowned. Around it, on the landward side, ran the rifle-pits, a continuous but irregular line of logs, covered with yellow clay. From Hickman's Creek they extended far around to the little run just outside the town on the south. If the sentry thought the pits looked shallow, he was solaced to see that they followed the coping of the ascents, seventy or eighty feet in height, up which a foe must charge, and that, where they were weakest, they were strengthened by trees felled outwardly in front of them, so that the interlacing limbs and branches seemed impassable by men under fire. At points inside the outworks, on the inner slopes of the hills, defended thus from view of an enemy as well as from his shot, lay the huts and log-houses of the garrison. Here and there groups of later comers, shivering in their wet blankets, were visible in a bivouac so cheerless that not even morning fires could relieve it. A little music would have helped their sinking spirits, but there was none. Even the picturesque effect of gay uniforms was wanting. In fine, the Confederate sentinel on the ramparts that morning, taking in the whole scene, knew the jolly, rollicking picnic days of the war were over.

To make clearer why the 6th of February is selected to present the first view of the fort, about noon that day the whole garrison was drawn from their quarters by the sound of heavy guns, faintly heard from the direction of Fort Henry, a token by which every man of them knew that a battle was on. The occurrence was in fact expected, for two days before a horseman had ridden to General Tilghman with word that at 4:30 o'clock in the morning rocket signals had been exchanged with the picket at Bailey's Landing, announcing the approach of gun-boats. A second courier came, and then a third; the latter, in great haste, requesting the general's presence at Fort Henry. There was quick mounting at headquarters, and, before the camp could be taken into confidence, the general and his guard were out of sight. Occasional guns were heard the day following. Donelson gave itself up to excitement and conjecture. At noon of the 6th, as stated, there was continuous and heavy cannonading at Fort Henry, and greater excitement at Fort Donelson. The polemicists in Dover became uneasy and prepared to get away. In the evening fugitives arrived in groups, and told how the gun-boats ran straight upon the fort and took it. The polemicists hastened their departure from town. At exactly midnight the gallant Colonel Heiman marched into Fort Donelson with two brigades of infantry rescued from the ruins of Forts Henry and Heiman. The officers and men by whom they were received then knew that their turn was at hand; and at daybreak, with one mind and firm of purpose, they set about the final preparation.

Brigadier-General Pillow reached Fort Donelson on the 9th; Brigadier-General Buckner came in the night of the 11th; and Brigadier-General Floyd on the 13th. The latter, by virtue of his rank, took command.

The morning of the 13th—calm, spring-like, the very opposite of that of the 6th—found in Fort Donelson a garrison of 28 regiments of infantry: 13 from Tennessee, 2 from Kentucky, 6 from Mississippi, 1 from Texas, 2 from Alabama,

4 from Virginia. There were also present 2 independent battalions, 1 regiment of cavalry, and artillerymen for 6 light batteries, and 17 heavy guns, making a total of quite 18,000 effectives.

General Buckner's division—6 regiments and 2 batteries—constituted the right wing, and was posted to cover the land approaches to the water-batteries. A left wing was organized into six brigades, commanded respectively by Colonels Heiman, Davidson, Drake, Wharton, McCausland, and Baldwin, and posted from right to left in the order named. Four batteries were distributed amongst the left wing. General Bushrod R. Johnson, an able officer, served the general commanding as chief-of-staff. Dover was converted into a depot of supplies and ordnance stores. These dispositions made, Fort Donelson was ready for battle.

It may be doubted if General Grant called a council of war. The nearest approach to it was a convocation held on the *New Uncle Sam*, a steamboat that was afterward transformed into the gun-boat *Blackhawk*. The morning of the 11th of February, a staff-officer visited each commandant of division and brigade with the simple verbal message: "General Grant sends his compliments, and requests to see you this afternoon on his boat." Minutes of the proceedings were not kept; there was no adjournment; each person retired when he got ready, knowing that the march would take place next day, probably in the forenoon.

There were in attendance on the occasion some officers of great subsequent notability. Of these Ulysses S. Grant was first. The world knows him now; then his fame was all before him. A singularity of the volunteer service in that day was that nobody took account of even a first-rate record of the Mexican War. The battle of Belmont, though indecisive, was a much better reference. A story was abroad that Grant had been the last man to take boat at the end of that affair, and the addendum that he had lingered in face of the enemy until he was hauled aboard with the last gang-plank, did him great good. From the first his silence was remarkable. He knew how to keep his temper. In battle, as in camp, he went about quietly, speaking in a conversational tone; yet he appeared to see everything that went on, and was always intent on business. He had a faithful assistant adjutant-general, and appreciated him; he preferred, however, his own eyes, word, and hand. His aides were little more than messengers. In dress he was plain, even negligent; in partial amendment of that his horse was always a good one and well kept. At the council—calling it such by grace—he smoked, but never said a word. In all probability he was framing the orders of march which were issued that night.

Charles F. Smith, of the regular army, was also present. He was a person of superb physique, very tall, perfectly proportioned, straight, square-shouldered, ruddy-faced, with eyes of perfect blue, and long snow-white mustaches. He seemed to know the army regulations by heart, and caught a tactical mistake, whether of command or execution, by a kind of mental *coup d'œil.* He was naturally kind, genial, communicative, and never failed to answer when information was sought of him; at the same time he believed in "hours of service" regularly published by the adjutants as a rabbi believes in the Ten Tables, and to call a court-martial on a "bummer" was in his eyes a sinful waste of stationery. On the occasion of a review General Smith had the bearing of a marshal of France. He could ride along a line of volunteers in the regulation uniform of a brigadier-general,

MAJOR-GENERAL JOHN A. MCCLERNAND.
FROM A PHOTOGRAPH.

plume, chapeau, epaulets and all, without exciting laughter—something nobody else could do in the beginning of the war. He was at first accused of disloyalty, and when told of it his eyes flashed wickedly; then he laughed, and said, "Oh, never mind! They'll take it back after our first battle." And they did. At the time of the meeting on the *New Uncle Sam* he was a brigadier-general, and commanded the division which in the land operations against Fort Henry had marched up the left bank of the river against Fort Heiman.

Another officer worthy of mention was John A. McClernand, also a brigadier. By profession a lawyer, he was in his first of military service. Brave, industrious, methodical, and of unquestioned cleverness, he was rapidly acquiring the art of war.

There was still another in attendance on the *New Uncle Sam* not to be passed—a young man who had followed General Grant from Illinois, and was seeing his first of military service. No soldier in the least familiar with headquarters on the Tennessee can ever forget the slender figure, large black eyes, hectic cheeks, and sincere, earnest manner of John A. Rawlins, then assistant adjutant-general, afterward major-general and secretary of war. He had two special devotions—to the cause and to his chief. He lived to see the first triumphant and the latter first in peace as well as in war. Probably no officer of the Union was mourned by so many armies.

Fort Henry, it will be remembered, was taken by Flag-Officer Foote on the 6th of February. The time up to the 12th was given to reconnoitering the country in the direction of Fort Donelson. Two roads were discovered: one of twelve miles direct, the other almost parallel with the first, but, on account of a slight divergence, two miles longer.

By 8 o'clock in the morning, the First Division, General McClernand commanding, and the Second, under General Smith, were in full march. The infantry of this command consisted of twenty-five regiments in all, or three less than those of the Confederates. Against their six field-batteries General Grant had seven. In cavalry alone he was materially stronger. The rule in attacking fortifications is five to one; to save the Union commander from a charge of rashness, however, he had also at control a fighting quality ordinarily at home on the sea rather than the land. After receiving the surrender of Fort Henry, Flag-Officer Foote had hastened to Cairo to make preparation for the reduction of Fort Donelson. With six of his boats, he passed into the Cumberland River; and on the 12th, while the two divisions of the army were marching across to Donelson, he was hurrying, as fast as steam could drive him and his following, to a second trial of iron batteries afloat against earth batteries ashore. The *Carondelet*, Commander Walke, having preceded him, had been in position below the fort since the 12th. By sundown of the 12th, McClernand and Smith reached the point designated for them in orders.

On the morning of the 13th of February General Grant, with about twenty thousand men, was before Fort Donelson.✠ We have had a view of the army in the works ready for battle; a like view of that outside and about to go into position of attack and assault is not so easily to be given. At dawn the latter host rose up from the bare ground, and, snatching bread and coffee as best they could, fell into lines that stretched away over hills, down hollows, and through thickets, making it impossible for even colonels to see their regiments from flank to flank.

Pausing to give a thought to the situation, it is proper to remind the reader that he is about to witness an event of more than mere historical interest; he is about to see the men of the North and North-west and of the South and South-west enter for the first time into a strife of arms; on one side, the best blood of Tennessee, Kentucky, Alabama, Mississippi, and Texas, aided materially by fighting representatives from Virginia; on the other, the best blood of Illinois, Ohio, Indiana, Iowa, Missouri, and Nebraska.

We have now before us a spectacle seldom witnessed in the annals of scientific war—an army behind field-works erected in a chosen position waiting quietly while another army very little superior in numbers proceeds at leisure to place it in a state of siege. Such was the operation General Grant had before him at daybreak of the 13th of February. Let us see how it was accomplished and how it was resisted.

In a clearing about two miles from Dover there was a log-house, at the time occupied by a Mrs. Crisp. As the road to Dover ran close by, it was made the headquarters of the commanding general. All through the night of the 12th, the coming and going was incessant. Smith was ordered to find a position in front

---

✠General Grant estimates his available forces at this time at about 15,000, and on the last day at 27,000, 5000 or 6000 of whom were guarding transportation trains in the rear.—EDITORS.

of the enemy's right wing, which would place him face to face with Buckner. McClernand's order was to establish himself on the enemy's left, where he would be opposed to Pillow.

A little before dawn Birge's sharp-shooters were astir. Theirs was a peculiar service. Each was a preferred marksman, and carried a long-range Henry rifle, with sights delicately arranged as for target practice. In action each was perfectly independent. They never manœuvred as a corps. When the time came they were asked, "Canteens full?" "Biscuits for all day?" Then their only order, "All right; hunt your holes, boys." Thereupon they dispersed, and, like Indians, sought cover to please themselves behind rocks and stumps, or in hollows. Sometimes they dug holes; sometimes they climbed into trees. Once in a good location, they remained there the day. At night they would crawl out and report in camp. This morning, as I have said, the sharp-shooters dispersed early to find places within easy range of the breastworks.

The movement by Smith and McClernand was begun about the same time. A thick wood fairly screened the former. The latter had to cross an open valley under fire of two batteries, one on Buckner's left, the other on a high point jutting from the line of outworks held by Colonel Heiman of Pillow's command. Graves commanded the first (Kentucky), Maney the second (Tennessee); both were of Tennessee. As always in situations where the advancing party is ignorant of the ground and of the designs of the enemy, resort was had to skirmishers, who are to the main body what antennæ are to insects. Theirs it is to unmask the foe. Unlike sharp-shooters, they act in bodies. Behind the skirmishers, the batteries started out to find positions, and through the brush and woods, down the hollows, up the hills the guns and caissons were hauled. Nowadays it must be a very steep bluff in face of which the good artillerist will stop or turn back. At Donelson, however, the proceeding was generally slow and toilsome. The officer had to find a vantage-ground first; then with axes a road to it was hewn out; after which, in many instances, the men, with the prolongs over their shoulders, helped the horses along. In the gray of the dawn the sharp-shooters were deep in their deadly game; as the sun came up, one battery after another opened fire, and was instantly and gallantly answered; and all the time behind the hidden sharp-shooters, and behind the skirmishers, who occasionally stopped to take a hand in the fray, the regiments marched, route-step, colors flying, after their colonels.

About 11 o'clock Commander Walke, of the *Carondelet,* engaged the water-batteries. The air was then full of the stunning music of battle, though as yet not a volley of musketry had been heard. Smith, nearest the enemy at starting, was first in place; and there, leaving the fight to his sharp-shooters and skirmishers and to his batteries, he reported to the chief in the log-house, and, like an old soldier, calmly waited orders. McClernand, following a good road, pushed on rapidly to the high grounds on the right. The appearance of his column in the

LIEUT.-GENERAL SIMON B. BUCKNER,
C.S.A. FROM A PHOTOGRAPH.

valley covered by the two Confederate batteries provoked a furious shelling from them. On the double-quick his men passed through it; and when, in the wood beyond, they resumed the route-step and saw that nobody was hurt, they fell to laughing at themselves. The real baptism of fire was yet in store for them.

When McClernand arrived at his appointed place and extended his brigades, it was discovered that the Confederate outworks offered a front too great for him to envelop. To attempt to rest his right opposite their extreme left would necessitate a dangerous attenuation of his line and leave him without reserves. Over on their left, moreover, ran the road already mentioned as passing from Dover on the south to Charlotte and Nashville, which it was of the highest importance to close hermetically so that there would be no communication left General Floyd except by the river. If the road to Charlotte were left to the enemy, they might march out at their pleasure.

The insufficiency of his force was thus made apparent to General Grant, and whether a discovery of the moment or not, he set about its correction. He knew a reënforcement was coming up the river under convoy of Foote; besides which a brigade, composed of the 8th Missouri and the 11th Indiana infantry and Battery A, Illinois, had been left behind at Forts Henry and Heiman under myself. A courier was dispatched to me with an order to bring my command to Donelson. I ferried my troops across the Tennessee in the night, and reported with them at headquarters before noon the next day. The brigade was transferred to General Smith; at the same time an order was put into my hand assigning me to command the Third Division, which was conducted to a position between Smith and McClernand, enabling the latter to extend his line well to the left and cover the road to Charlotte.

Thus on the 14th of February the Confederates were completely invested, except that the river above Dover remained to them. The supineness of General Floyd all this while is to this day incomprehensible. A vigorous attack on the morning of the 13th might have thrown Grant back upon Fort Henry. Such an achievement would have more than offset Foote's conquest. The *morale* to be gained would have alone justified the attempt. But with McClernand's strong

DOVER TAVERN—GENERAL BUCKNER'S HEADQUARTERS AND THE SCENE
OF THE SURRENDER. FROM A PHOTOGRAPH TAKEN IN 1884.

division on the right, my own in the center, and C. F. Smith's on the left, the opportunity was gone. On the side of General Grant, the possession of the river was all that was wanting; with that Grant could force the fighting, or wait the certain approach of the grimmest enemy of the besieged—starvation.

It is now—morning of the 14th—easy to see and understand with something more than approximate exactness the oppositions of the two forces. Smith is on the left of the Union army opposite Buckner. My division, in the center, confronts Colonels Heiman, Drake, and Davidson, each with a brigade. McClernand, now well over on the right, keeps the road to Charlotte and Nashville against the major part of Pillow's left wing. The infantry on both sides are in cover behind the crests of the hills or in thick woods, listening to the ragged fusillade which the sharp-shooters and skirmishers maintain against each other almost without intermission. There is little pause in the exchange of shells and round shot. The careful chiefs have required their men to lie down. In brief, it looks as if each party were inviting the other to begin.

These circumstances, the sharp-shooting and cannonading, ugly as they may seem to one who thinks of them under comfortable surroundings, did in fact serve a good purpose the day in question in helping the men to forget their sufferings of the night before. It must be remembered that the weather had changed during the preceding afternoon: from suggestions of spring it turned to intensified winter. From lending a gentle hand in bringing Foote and his iron-clads up the river, the wind whisked suddenly around to the north and struck both armies with a storm of mixed rain, snow, and sleet. All night the tempest blew mercilessly upon the unsheltered, fireless soldier, making sleep impossible. Inside the works, nobody had overcoats; while thousands of those outside had marched from Fort Henry as to a summer fête, leaving coats, blankets, and knapsacks behind them in the camp. More than one stout fellow has since admitted, with a laugh, that nothing was so helpful to him that horrible night as the thought that the wind, which seemed about to turn his blood into icicles, was serving the enemy the same way; they, too, had to stand out and take the blast. Let us now go back to the preceding day, and bring up an incident of McClernand's swing into position.

About the center of the Confederate outworks there was a V-shaped hill, marked sharply by a ravine on its right and another on its left. This Colonel Heiman occupied with his brigade of five regiments—all of Tennessee but one. The front presented was about 2500 feet. In the angle of the V, on the summit of the hill, Captain Maney's battery, also of Tennessee, had been planted. Without protection of any kind, it nevertheless completely swept a large field to the left, across which an assaulting force would have to come in order to get at Heiman or at Drake, next on the south.

Maney, on the point of the hill, had been active throughout the preceding afternoon, and had succeeded in drawing the fire of some of McClernand's guns. The duel lasted until night. Next morning it was renewed with increased sharpness, Maney being assisted on his right by Graves's battery of Buckner's division, and by some pieces of Drake's on his left.

McClernand's advance was necessarily slow and trying. This was not merely a logical result of unacquaintance with the country and the dispositions of the enemy; he was also under an order from General Grant to avoid everything calculated to bring on a general engagement. In Maney's well-served guns he undoubtedly found serious annoyance, if not a positive obstruction. Concentrating guns of his own upon the industrious Confederate, he at length fancied him silenced and the enemy's infantry on the right thrown into confusion—circumstances from which he hastily deduced a favorable chance to deliver an assault. For that purpose he reënforced his Third Brigade, which was nearest the offending battery, and gave the necessary orders.

Up to this time, it will be observed, there had not been any fighting involving infantry in line. This was now to be changed. Old soldiers, rich with experience, would have regarded the work proposed with gravity; they would have shrewdly cast up an account of the chances of success, not to speak of the chances of coming out alive; they would have measured the distance to be passed, every foot of it, under the guns of three batteries, Maney's in the center, Graves's on their left, and Drake's on their right—a direct line of fire doubly crossed. Nor would they have omitted the reception awaiting them from the rifle-pits. They were to descend a hill entangled for two hundred yards with under-brush, climb an opposite ascent partly shorn of timber; make way through an abatis of tree-tops; then, supposing all that successfully accomplished, they would be at last in face of an enemy whom it was possible to reënforce with all the reserves of the garrison—with the whole garrison, if need be. A veteran would have surveyed the three regiments selected for the honorable duty with many misgivings. Not so the men themselves. They were not old soldiers. Recruited but recently from farms and shops, they accepted the assignment heartily and with youthful confidence in their prowess. It may be doubted if a man in the ranks gave a thought to the questions, whether the attack was to be supported while making, or followed up if successful, or whether it was part of a general advance. Probably the most they knew was that the immediate objective before them was the capture of the battery on the hill.

The line when formed stood thus from the right: the 49th Illinois, then the 17th, and then the 48th, Colonel Haynie. At the last moment, a question of seniority arose between Colonels Morrison and Haynie. The latter was of opinion that he was the ranking officer. Morrison replied that he would conduct the brigade to the point from which the attack was to be made, after which Haynie might take the command, if he so desired.

Down the hill the three regiments went, crashing and tearing through the undergrowth. Heiman, on the lookout, saw them advancing. Before they cleared the woods, Maney opened with shells. At the foot of the descent, in the valley, Graves joined his fire to Maney's. There Morrison reported to Haynie, who neither accepted nor refused the command. Pointing to the hill, he merely said, "Let us take it together." Morrison turned away, and rejoined his own regiment. Here was confusion in the beginning, or worse, an assault begun without a head. Nevertheless, the whole line went forward. On a part of the hillside the trees were yet standing. The open space fell to Morrison and his 49th, and paying the penalty of the exposure, he outstripped his associates. The men fell rapidly; yet the living rushed on and up, firing as they went. The battery was the common target. Maney's gunners, in relief against the sky, were shot down in quick succession. His first lieutenant (Burns) was one of the first to suffer. His second lieutenant (Massie) was mortally wounded. Maney himself was hit; still he staid, and his guns continued their punishment; and still the farmer lads and shop boys of Illinois clung to their purpose. With marvelous audacity they pushed through the abatis and reached a point within forty yards of the rifle-pits. It actually looked as if the prize were theirs. The yell of victory was rising

THE CRISP FARM—GENERAL GRANT'S HEADQUARTERS.

in their throats. Suddenly the long line of yellow breastworks before them, covering Heiman's five regiments, crackled and turned into flame. The forlorn-hope stopped—staggered—braced up again—shot blindly through the smoke at the smoke of the new enemy, secure in his shelter. Thus for fifteen minutes the Illinoisans stood fighting. The time is given on the testimony of the opposing leader himself. Morrison was knocked out of his saddle by a musket-ball, and disabled; then the men went down the hill. At its foot they rallied round their flags and renewed the assault. Pushed down again, again they rallied, and a third time climbed to the enemy. This time the battery set fire to the dry leaves on the ground, and the heat and smoke became stifling. It was not possible for brave men to endure more. Slowly, sullenly, frequently pausing to return a shot, they went back for the last time; and in going their ears and souls were riven with the shrieks of their wounded comrades, whom the flames crept down upon and smothered and charred where they lay.

Considered as a mere exhibition of courage, this assault, long maintained against odds,—twice repulsed, twice renewed,—has been seldom excelled. One hundred and forty-nine men of the 17th and 49th were killed and wounded. Haynie reported 1 killed and 8 wounded.

FRONT VIEW OF MRS. CRISP'S HOUSE.
FROM PHOTOGRAPHS TAKEN IN 1884.

There are few things connected with the operations against Fort Donelson so relieved of uncertainty as this: that when General Grant at Fort Henry became fixed in the resolution to undertake the movement, his primary object was the capture of the force to which the post was intrusted. To effect their complete environment, he relied upon Flag-Officer Foote and his gun-boats, whose astonishing success at Fort Henry justified the extreme of confidence.

Foote arrived on the 14th, and made haste to enter upon his work. The *Carondelet* (Commander Walke) had been in position since the 12th. Behind a low output of the shore, for two days, she maintained a fire from her rifled guns, happily of greater range than the best of those of the enemy.

At 9 o'clock on the 14th, Captain Culbertson, looking from the parapet of the upper battery, beheld the river below the first bend full of transports, landing troops under cover of a fresh arrival of gun-boats. The disembarkation concluded, Foote was free. He waited until noon. The captains in the batteries mistook his deliberation for timidity. The impinging of their shot on his iron armor was heard distinctly in the fort a mile and a half away. The captains began to doubt if he would come at all. But at 3 o'clock the boats took position under fire: the *Louisville* on the right, the *St. Louis* next, then the *Pittsburgh,* then the *Carondelet,* all iron-clad.

Five hundred yards from the batteries, and yet Foote was not content! In the Crimean war the allied French and English fleets, of much mightier ships, undertook to engage the Russian shore batteries, but little stronger than those at Donelson. The French on that occasion stood off 1800 yards. Lord Lyons fought his *Agamemnon* at a distance of 800 yards. Foote forged ahead within 400 yards of his enemy, and was still going on. His boat had been hit between wind and water; so with the *Pittsburgh* and *Carondelet.* About the guns the floors were slippery with blood, and both surgeons and carpenters were never so busy. Still the four boats kept on, and there was great cheering; for not only did the fire from the shore slacken; the lookouts reported the enemy running. It seemed that fortune would smile once more upon the fleet, and cover the honors of Fort Henry afresh at Fort Donelson. Unhappily, when about 350 yards off the hill a solid shot plunged through the pilot-house of the flag-ship, and carried away the wheel. Near the same time the tiller-ropes of the *Louisville* were disabled. Both vessels became unmanageable and began floating down the current. The eddies turned them round like logs. The *Pittsburgh* and *Carondelet* closed in and covered them with their hulls.

Seeing this turn in the fight, the captains of the batteries rallied their men, who cheered in their turn, and renewed the contest with increased will and energy. A ball got lodged in their best rifle. A corporal and some of his men took a log fitting the bore, leaped out on the parapet, and rammed the missile home. "Now, boys," said a gunner in Bidwell's battery, "see me take a chimney!" The flag of the boat and the chimney fell with the shot.

When the vessels were out of range, the victors looked about them. The fine form of their embrasures was gone; heaps of earth had been cast over their platforms. In a space of twenty-four feet they had picked up as many shot and shells. The air had been full of flying missiles. For an hour and a half the brave fellows had been rained upon; yet their losses had been trifling in numbers. Each gunner had selected a ship and followed her faithfully throughout the ac-

tion, now and then uniting fire on the *Carondelet*. The Confederates had behaved with astonishing valor. Their victory sent a thrill of joy through the army.
The assault on the outworks, the day before, had been a failure. With the repulse of the gun-boats the Confederates scored success number two, and the
communication by the river remained open to Nashville. The winds that blew
sleet and snow over Donelson that night were not so unendurable as they might
have been.

The night of the 14th of February fell cold and dark, and under the pitiless
sky the armies remained in position so near to each other that neither dared
light fires. Overpowered with watching, fatigue, and the lassitude of spirits
which always follows a strain upon the faculties of men like that which is the
concomitant of battle, thousands on both sides lay down in the ditches and behind logs and whatever else would in the least shelter them from the cutting
wind, and tried to sleep. Very few closed their eyes. Even the horses, after their
manner, betrayed the suffering they were enduring.

That morning General Floyd had called a council of his chiefs of brigades
and divisions. He expressed the
opinion that the post was untenable, except with fifty thousand
troops. He called attention to the
heavy reënforcements of the Federals, and suggested an immediate
attack upon their right wing to re-

THE POSITION OF THE GUN-BOATS AND THE WEST BANK.
FROM A PHOTOGRAPH TAKEN IN 1884.

Fort Donelson is in the farther distance on the extreme left—Hickman's Creek empties into the
Cumberland in the middle distance—midway are the remains of the obstructions placed in the
river by the Confederates. The upper picture, showing Isaac Williams's house, is a continuation of
the right of the lower view.

open land communication with Nashville, by way of Charlotte. The proposal was agreed to unanimously. General Buckner proceeded to make dispositions to cover the retreat, in the event the sortie should be successful. Shortly after noon, when the movement should have begun, the order was countermanded at the instance of Pillow. Then came the battle with the gun-boats.

In the night the council was recalled, with general and regimental officers in attendance. The situation was again debated, and the same conclusion reached. According to the plan resolved upon, Pillow was to move at dawn with his whole division, and attack the right of the besiegers. General Buckner was to be relieved by troops in the forts, and with his command to support Pillow by assailing the right of the enemy's center. If he succeeded, he was to take post outside the intrenchments on the Wynn's Ferry road to cover the retreat. He was then to act as rear-guard. Thus early, leaders in Donelson were aware of the mistake into which they were plunged. Their resolution was wise and heroic. Let us see how they executed it.

Preparations for the attack occupied the night. The troops for the most part were taken out of the rifle-pits and massed over on the left to the number of ten thousand or more. The ground was covered with ice and snow; yet the greatest silence was observed. It seems incomprehensible that columns mixed of all arms, infantry, cavalry, and artillery, could have engaged in simultaneous movement, and not have been heard by some listener outside. One would think the jolting and rumble of the heavy gun-carriages would have told the story. But the character of the night must be remembered. The pickets of the Federals were struggling for life against the blast, and probably did not keep good watch.

Oglesby's brigade held McClernand's extreme right. Here and there the musicians were beginning to make the woods ring with reveille, and the numbed soldiers of the line were rising from their icy beds and shaking the snow from their frozen garments. As yet, however, not a company had "fallen in." Suddenly the pickets fired, and with the alarm on their lips rushed back upon their comrades. The woods on the instant became alive.

The regiments formed, officers mounted and took their places; words of command rose loud and eager. By the time Pillow's advance opened fire on Oglesby's right, the point first struck, the latter was fairly formed to receive it. A rapid exchange of volleys ensued. The distance intervening between the works on one side and the bivouac on the other was so short that the action began before Pillow could effect a deployment. His brigades came up in a kind of echelon, left in front, and passed "by regiments left into line," one by one; however, the regiments quickly took their places, and advanced without halting. Oglesby's Illinoisans were now fully awake. They held their ground, returning in full measure the fire that they received. The Confederate Forrest

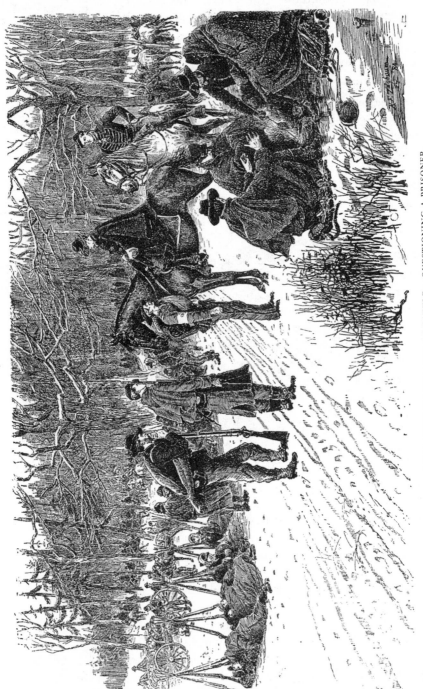

THE BIVOUAC IN THE SNOW ON THE LINE OF BATTLE—QUESTIONING A PRISONER.

rode around as if to get in their rear,[1] and it was then give and take, infantry against infantry. The semi-echelon movement of the Confederates enabled them, after an interval, to strike W.H.L. Wallace's brigade, on Oglesby's left. Soon Wallace was engaged along his whole front, now prolonged by the addition to his command of Morrison's regiments. The first charge against him was repulsed; whereupon he advanced to the top of the rising ground behind which he had sheltered his troops in the night. A fresh assault followed, but, aided by a battery across the valley to his left, he repulsed the enemy a second time. His men were steadfast, and clung to the brow of the hill as if it were theirs by holy right. An hour passed, and yet another hour, without cessation of the fire. Meantime the woods rang with a monstrous clangor of musketry, as if a million men were beating empty barrels with iron hammers.

Buckner flung a portion of his division on McClernand's left, and supported the attack with his artillery. The enfilading fell chiefly on W.H.L. Wallace. McClernand, watchful and full of resources, sent batteries to meet Buckner's batteries. To that duty Taylor rushed with his Company B; and McAllister pushed his three 24-pounders into position and exhausted his ammunition in the duel. The roar never slackened. Men fell by the score, reddening the snow with their blood. The smoke, in pallid white clouds, clung to the underbrush and tree-tops as if to screen the combatants from each other. Close to the ground the flame of musketry and cannon tinted everything a lurid red. Limbs dropped from the trees on the heads below, and the thickets were shorn as by an army of cradlers. The division was under peremptory orders to hold its position to the last extremity, and Colonel Wallace was equal to the emergency.

It was now 10 o'clock, and over on the right Oglesby was beginning to fare badly. The pressure on his front grew stronger. The "rebel yell," afterward a familiar battle-cry on many fields, told of ground being gained against him. To add to his doubts, officers were riding to him with a sickening story that their commands were getting out of ammunition, and asking where they could go for a supply. All he could say was to take what was in the boxes of the dead and wounded. At last he realized that the end was come. His right companies began to give way, and as they retreated, holding up their empty cartridge-boxes, the enemy were emboldened, and swept more fiercely around his flank, until finally they appeared in his rear. He then gave the order to retire the division.

W.H.L. Wallace from his position looked off to his right and saw but one regiment of Oglesby's in place, maintaining the right, and that was John A. Logan's 31st Illinois. Through the smoke he could see Logan riding in a gallop behind his line; through the roar in his front and the rising yell in his rear, he

---

[1] Colonel John McArthur, originally of General C. F. Smith's division, but then operating with McClernand, was there, and though at first discomfited, his men beat the cavalry off, and afterward shared the full shock of the tempest with Oglesby's troops.—L.W.

could hear Logan's voice in fierce entreaty to his "boys." Near the 31st stood W.H.L. Wallace's regiment, the 11th Illinois, under Lieutenant-Colonel Ransom. The gaps in the ranks of the two were closed up always toward the colors. The ground at their feet was strewn with their dead and wounded; at length the common misfortune overtook Logan. To keep men without cartridges under fire sweeping them front and flank would be cruel, if not impossible; and seeing it, he too gave the order to retire, and followed his decimated companies to the rear. The 11th then became the right of the brigade, and had to go in turn. Nevertheless, Ransom changed front to rear coolly, as if on parade, and joined in the general retirement. Forrest charged them and threw them into a brief confusion. The greater portion clung to their colors, and made good their retreat. By 11 o'clock Pillow held the road to Charlotte and the whole of the position occupied at dawn by the First Division, and with it the dead and all the wounded who could not get away.

Pillow's part of the programme, arranged in the council of the night before, was accomplished. The country was once more open to Floyd. Why did he not avail himself of the dearly bought opportunity, and march his army out?

Without pausing to consider whether the Confederate general could now have escaped with his troops, it must be evident that he should have made the effort. Pillow had discharged his duty well. With the disappearance of W.H.L. Wallace's brigade, it only remained for the victor to deploy his regiments into column and march into the country. The road was his. Buckner was in position to protect Colonel Head's withdrawal from the trenches opposite General Smith on the right; that done, he was also in position to cover the retreat. Buckner had also faithfully performed his task.

On the Union side the situation at this critical time was favorable to the proposed retirement. My division in the center was weakened by the dispatch of one of my brigades to the assistance of General McClernand; in addition to which my orders were to hold my position. As a point of still greater importance, General Grant had gone on board the *St. Louis* at the request of Flag-Officer Foote, and he was there in consultation with that officer, presumably uninformed of the disaster which had befallen his right. It would take a certain time for him to return to the field and dispose his forces for pursuit. It may be said with strong assurance, consequently, that Floyd could have put his men fairly *en route* for Charlotte before the Federal commander could have interposed an obstruction to the movement. The real difficulty was in the hero of the morning, who now made haste to blight his laurels. General Pillow's vanity whistled itself into ludicrous exaltation. Imagining General Grant's whole army defeated and fleeing in rout for Fort Henry and the transports on the river, he deported himself accordingly. He began by ignoring Floyd. He rode to Buckner and accused him of shameful conduct. He sent an aide to the nearest telegraph station with a dispatch to Albert Sidney Johnston, then in command

MCALLISTER'S BATTERY IN ACTION.

Captain Edward McAllister's Illinois battery did good service on the 13th. In his report he describes the manner of working the battery: "I selected a point, and about noon opened on the four-gun battery [see map, page 212] through an opening in which I could see the foe. Our fire was promptly returned with such precision that they cut our right wheel on howitzer number three in two. I had no spare wheel, and had to take one off the limber to continue the fight. I then moved all my howitzers over to the west slope of the ridge and loaded under cover of it, and ran the pieces up by hand until I could get the exact elevation. The recoil would throw the guns back out of sight, and thus we continued the fight until the enemy's battery was silenced."

of the Department, asseverating, "on the honor of a soldier," that the day was theirs. Nor did he stop at that. The victory, to be available, required that the enemy should be followed with energy. Such was a habit of Napoleon. Without deigning even to consult his chief, he ordered Buckner to move out and attack the Federals. There was a gorge, up which a road ran toward our central position, or rather what had been our central position. Pointing to the gorge and the road, he told Buckner that was his way and bade him attack in force. There was nothing to do but obey; and when Buckner had begun the movement, the wise programme decided upon the evening before was wiped from the slate.

When Buckner reluctantly took the gorge road marked out for him by Pillow, the whole Confederate army, save the detachments on the works, was virtually in pursuit of McClernand, retiring by the Wynn's Ferry road—falling back, in fact, upon my position. My division was now to feel the weight of Pillow's hand; if they should fail, the fortunes of the day would depend upon the veteran Smith.

When General McClernand perceived the peril threatening him in the morning, he sent an officer to me with a request for assistance. This request I referred to General Grant, who was at the time in consultation with Foote. Upon the turning of Oglesby's flank, McClernand repeated his request, with such a representation of the situation that, assuming the responsibility, I ordered Colonel Cruft to report with his brigade to McClernand. Cruft set out promptly. Unfortunately a guide misdirected him, so that he became involved in the retreat, and was prevented from accomplishing his object.

I was in the rear of my single remaining brigade, in conversation with Captain Rawlins, of Grant's staff, when a great shouting was heard behind me on the Wynn's Ferry road, whereupon I sent an orderly to ascertain the cause. The man reported the road and woods full of soldiers apparently in rout. An officer then rode by at full speed, shouting, "All's lost! Save yourselves!" A hurried consultation was had with Rawlins, at the end of which the brigade was put in motion toward the enemy's works, on the very road by which Buckner was pursuing under Pillow's mischievous order. It happened also that Colonel W.H.L. Wallace had dropped into the same road with such of his command as staid by their colors. He came up riding and at a walk, his leg over the horn of his saddle. He was perfectly cool, and looked like a farmer from a hard day's plowing. "Good-morning," I said. "Good-morning," was the reply. "Are they pursuing you?" "Yes." "How far are they behind?" That instant the head of my command appeared on the road. The colonel calculated, then answered: "You will have about time to form line of battle right here." "Thank you. Good-day." "Good-day."

At that point the road began to dip into the gorge; on the right and left there were woods, and in front a dense thicket. An order was dispatched to bring Battery A forward at full speed. Colonel John M. Thayer, commanding the brigade, formed it on the double-quick into line; the 1st Nebraska and the 58th Illinois on the right, and the 58th Ohio, with a detached company, on the left. The battery came up on the run and swung across the road, which had been left open for it. Hardly had it unlimbered, before the enemy appeared, and firing began. For ten minutes or thereabouts the scenes of the morning were reënacted. The Confederates struggled hard to perfect their deployments. The woods rang with musketry and artillery. The brush on the slope of the hill was mowed away with bullets. A great cloud arose and shut out the woods and the narrow valley below. Colonel Thayer and his regiments behaved with great gallantry, and the assailants fell back in confusion and returned to the intrenchments. W.H.L. Wallace and Oglesby re-formed their commands behind Thayer, supplied them with ammunition, and stood at rest waiting for orders. There was then a lull in the battle. Even the cannonading ceased, and everybody was asking, What next?

Just then General Grant rode up to where General McClernand and I were in conversation. He was almost unattended. In his hand there were some papers, which looked like telegrams. Wholly unexcited, he saluted and received the salutations of his subordinates. Proceeding at once to business, he directed them to retire their commands to the heights out of cannon range, and throw up works. Reënforcements were *en route,* he said, and it was advisable to await their coming. He was then informed of the mishap to the First Division, and that the road to Charlotte was open to the enemy.

In every great man's career there is a crisis exactly similar to that which now overtook General Grant, and it cannot be better described than as a crucial test of his nature. A mediocre person would have accepted the news as an argument for persistence in his resolution to enter upon a siege. Had General Grant done so, it is very probable his history would have been then and there concluded. His admirers and detractors are alike invited to study him at this precise juncture. It cannot be doubted that he saw with painful distinctness the effect of the disaster to his right wing. His face flushed slightly. With a sudden grip he crushed the papers in his hand. But in an instant these signs of disappointment or hesitation—as the reader pleases—cleared away. In his ordinary quiet voice he said, addressing himself to both officers, "Gentlemen, the position on the right must be retaken." With that he turned and galloped off.

Seeing in the road a provisional brigade, under Colonel Morgan L. Smith, consisting of the 11th Indiana and the 8th Missouri Infantry, going, by order of General C. F. Smith, to the aid of the First Division, I suggested that if General McClernand would order Colonel Smith to report to me, I would attempt to recover the lost ground; and the order having been given, I reconnoitered the hill, determined upon a place of assault, and arranged my order of attack. I chose Colonel Smith's regiments to lead, and for that purpose conducted them to the crest of a hill opposite a steep bluff covered by the enemy. The two regiments had been formerly of my brigade. I knew they had been admirably drilled in the Zouave tactics, and my confidence in Smith and in George F. McGinnis, colonel of the 11th, was implicit. I was sure they would take their men to the top of the bluff. Colonel Cruft was put in line to support them on the right. Colonel Ross, with his regiments, the 17th and 49th, and the 46th, 57th, and 58th Illinois, were put as support on the left. Thayer's brigade was held in reserve. These dispositions filled the time till about 2 o'clock in the afternoon, when heavy cannonading, mixed with a long roll of musketry, broke out over on the left, whither it will be necessary to transfer the reader.

The veteran in command on the Union left had contented himself with allowing Buckner no rest, keeping up a continual sharp-shooting. Early in the morning of the 14th he made a demonstration of assault with three of his regiments, and though he purposely withdrew them, he kept the menace standing, to the great discomfort of his *vis-à-vis.* With the patience of an old soldier, he waited the pleasure of the general commanding, knowing that when the time came he would be called upon. During the battle of the gun-boats he rode through his command and grimly joked with them. He who never permitted the slightest familiarity from a subordinate, could yet indulge in fatherly pleasantries with the ranks when he thought circumstances justified them. He never for a moment doubted the courage of volunteers; they were not regulars—that was all. If properly led, he believed they would storm the gates of his Satanic Majesty. Their hour of trial was now come.

From his brief and characteristic conference with McClernand and myself, General Grant rode to General C. F. Smith. What took place between them is not known, further than that he ordered an assault upon the outworks as a diversion in aid of the assault about to be delivered on the right. General Smith personally directed his chiefs of brigade to get their regiments ready. Colonel John Cook by his order increased the number of his skirmishers already engaged with the enemy.

Taking Lauman's brigade, General Smith began the advance. They were under fire instantly. The guns in the fort joined in with the infantry who were at the time in the rifle-pits, the great body of the Confederate right wing being with General Buckner. The defense was greatly favored by the ground, which subjected the assailants to a double fire from the beginning of the abatis. The men have said that "it looked too thick for a rabbit to get through." General Smith, on his horse, took position in the front and center of the line. Occasionally he turned in the saddle to see how the alignment was kept. For the most part, however, he held his face steadily toward the enemy. He was, of course, a conspicuous object for the sharp-shooters in the rifle-pits. The air around him twittered with minie-bullets. Erect as if on review, he rode on, timing the gait of his horse with the movement of the colors. A soldier said: "I was nearly scared to death, but I saw the old man's white mustache over his shoulder, and went on."

On to the abatis the regiments moved without hesitation, leaving a trail of dead and wounded behind. There the fire seemed to get trebly hot, and there some of the men halted, whereupon, seeing the hesitation, General Smith put his cap on the point of his sword, held it aloft, and called out, "No flinching now, my lads?—Here—this is the way! Come on!" He picked a path through the jagged limbs of the trees, holding his cap all the time in sight; and the effect was magical. The men swarmed in after him, and got through in the best order they could—not all of them, alas! On the other side of the obstruction they took the semblance of re-formation and charged in after their chief, who found himself then between the two fires. Up the ascent he rode; up they followed. At the last moment the keepers of the rifle-pits clambered out and fled. The four regiments engaged in the feat—the 25th Indiana, and the 2d, 7th, and 14th Iowa—planted their colors on the breastwork. Later in the day, Buckner came back with his division; but all his efforts to dislodge Smith were vain.

We left my division about to attempt the recapture of the hill, which had been the scene of the combat between Pillow and McClernand. If only on account of the results which followed that assault, in connection with the heroic performance of General C. F. Smith, it is necessary to return to it.

Riding to my old regiments,—the 8th Missouri and the 11th Indiana,—I asked them if they were ready. They demanded the word of me. Waiting a moment for Morgan L. Smith to light a cigar, I called out, "Forward it is, then!" They were directly in front of the ascent to be climbed. Without stopping for his supports, Colonel

MAJOR-GENERAL GIDEON J. PILLOW, C.S.A. FROM A PHOTOGRAPH.

Smith led them down into a broad hollow, and catching sight of the advance, Cruft and Ross also moved forward. As the two regiments began the climb, the 8th Missouri slightly in the lead, a line of fire ran along the brow of the height. The flank companies cheered while deploying as skirmishers. Their Zouave practice proved of excellent service to them. Now on the ground, creeping when the fire was hottest, running when it slackened, they gained ground with astonishing rapidity, and at the same time maintained a fire that was like a sparkling of the earth. For the most part the bullets aimed at them passed over their heads and took effect in the ranks behind them. Colonel Smith's cigar was shot off close to his lips. He took another and called for a match. A soldier ran and gave him one. "Thank you. Take your place now. We are almost up," he said, and, smoking, spurred his horse forward. A few yards from the crest of the height the regiments began loading and firing as they advanced. The defenders gave way. On the top there was a brief struggle, which was ended by Cruft and Ross with their supports.

The whole line then moved forward simultaneously, and never stopped until the Confederates were within the works. There had been no occasion to call on the reserves. The road to Charlotte was again effectually shut, and the battle-field of the morning, with the dead and wounded lying where they had fallen, was in possession of the Third Division, which stood halted within easy musket-range of the rifle-pits. It was then about half-past 3 o'clock in the afternoon. I was reconnoitering the works of the enemy preliminary to charging them, when Colonel Webster, of General Grant's staff, came to me and repeated the order to fall back out of cannon range and throw up breastworks.

"The general does not know that we have the hill," I said. Webster replied: "I give you the order as he gave it to me." "Very well," said I, "give him my compliments, and say that I have received the order." Webster smiled and rode away. The ground was not vacated, though the assault was deferred. In assuming the responsibility, I had no doubt of my ability to satisfy General Grant of the correctness of my course; and it was subsequently approved.

When night fell, the command bivouacked without fire or supper. Fatigue parties were told off to look after the wounded; and in the relief given there was no distinction made between friend and foe. The labor extended through the whole night, and the surgeons never rested. By sunset the conditions of the morning were all restored. The Union commander was free to order to a general assault next day or resort to a formal siege.

A great discouragement fell upon the brave men inside the works that night. Besides suffering from wounds and bruises and the dreadful weather, they were aware that though they had done their best they were held in a close grip by a superior enemy. A council of general and field officers was held at headquarters, which resulted in a unanimous resolution that if the position in front of General Pillow had not been reoccupied by the Federals in strength, the army should effect its retreat. A reconnoissance was ordered to make the test. Colonel Forrest conducted it. He reported that the ground was not only reoccupied, but that the enemy were extended yet farther around the Confederate left. The council then held a final session.

General Simon B. Buckner, as the junior officer present, gave his opinion first; he thought he could not successfully resist the assault which would be made by daylight by a vastly superior force. But he further remarked, that as he understood the principal object of the defense of Donelson was to cover the movement of General Albert Sidney Johnston's army from Bowling Green to Nashville, if that movement was not completed he was of opinion that the defense should be continued at the risk of the destruction of the entire force. General Floyd replied that General Johnston's army had already reached Nashville, whereupon General Buckner said that "it would be wrong to subject the army to a virtual massacre, when no good could result from the sacrifice, and that the general officers owed it to their men, when further resistance was unavailing, to obtain the best terms of capitulation possible for them."

Both Generals Floyd and Pillow acquiesced in the opinion. Ordinarily the council would have ended at this point, and the commanding general would have addressed himself to the duty of obtaining terms. He would have called for pen, ink, and paper, and prepared a note for dispatch to the commanding general of the opposite force. But there were circumstances outside the mere military situation which at this juncture pressed themselves into consideration. As this was the first surrender of armed men banded together for war upon the general government, what would the Federal authorities do with the prisoners? This question was of application to all the gentlemen in the council. It was lost to view, however, when General Floyd announced his purpose to leave with two steamers which were to be down at daylight, and to take with him as many of his division as the steamers could carry away.

General Pillow then remarked that there were no two persons in the Confederacy whom the Yankees would rather capture than himself and General Floyd (who had been Buchanan's Secretary of War, and was under indictment at Washington). As to the propriety of his accompanying General Floyd, the latter said, coolly, that the question was one for every man to decide for himself. Buckner was of the same view, and added that as for himself he regarded it as his duty to stay with his men and share their fate, whatever it might be. Pillow persisted in leaving. Floyd then directed General Buckner to consider himself in command. Immediately after the council was concluded, General Floyd prepared for his departure. His first move was to have his brigade drawn up. The peculiarity of the step was that, with the exception of one, the 20th Mississippi regiment, his regiments were all Virginians. A short time before daylight the two steamboats arrived. Without loss of time the general hastened to the river, embarked with his Virginians, and at an early hour cast loose from the shore, and in good time, and safely, he reached Nashville. He never satisfactorily explained upon what principle he appropriated all the transportation on hand to the use of his particular command.

Colonel Forrest was present at the council, and when the final resolution was taken, he promptly announced that he neither could nor would surrender his command. The bold trooper had no qualms upon the subject. He assembled his men, all as hardy as himself, and after reporting once more at headquarters, he moved out and plunged into a slough formed by backwater from the river. An icy crust covered its surface, the wind blew fiercely, and the darkness was unrelieved by a star. There was fearful floundering as the command followed him. At length he struck dry land, and was safe. He was next heard of at Nashville.

General Buckner, who throughout the affair bore himself with dignity, ordered the troops back to their positions and opened communications with General Grant, whose laconic demand of "unconditional surrender," in his reply to General Buckner's overtures, became at once a watchword of the war.

The Third Division was astir very early on the 16th of February. The regiments began to form and close up the intervals between them, the intention being to charge the breastworks south of Dover about breakfast-time. In the midst of the preparation a bugle was heard and a white flag was seen coming from the town toward the pickets. I sent my adjutant-general to meet the flag half-way and inquire its purpose. Answer was returned that General Buckner

FAC-SIMILE OF THE ORIGINAL "UNCONDITIONAL SURRENDER" DISPATCH.
(Copyright, 1885, by Charles L. Webster & Co.)

The original of the dispatch was obtained by Charles L. Webster & Co., publishers of General Grant's "Memoirs," from Dr. James K. Wallace, of Litchfield, Conn., who received it, November 28th, 1868, from his relative by marriage, General John A. Rawlins, who, as chief of staff to General Grant, had the custody, after the capture, of General Buckner's papers. General Rawlins told Dr. Wallace that it was the original dispatch. The above is an exact reproduction of the original dispatch in every particular, except that, in order to adapt it to the width of the page, the word, "Sir," has been lowered to the line beneath, and the words, "I am, sir, very respectfully," have been raised to the line above.—EDITORS.

had capitulated during the night, and was now sending information of the fact to the commander of the troops in this quarter, that there might be no further bloodshed. The division was ordered to advance and take possession of the works and of all public property and prisoners. Leaving that agreeable duty to the brigade commanders, I joined the officer bearing the flag, and with my staff rode across the trench and into the town, till we came to the door of the old tavern already described, where I dismounted. The tavern was the headquarters of General Buckner, to whom I sent my name; and being an acquaintance, I was at once admitted.

I found General Buckner with his staff at breakfast. He met me with politeness and dignity. Turning to the officers at the table, he remarked: "General Wallace, it is not necessary to introduce you to these gentlemen; you are acquainted with them all." They arose, came forward one by one, and gave their

VIEW FROM THE NATIONAL CEMETERY, WITHIN THE HEDGE ON THE RIGHT,
ACROSS TO THE HILL WHERE WERE SITUATED THE INTERIOR WORKS OF
FORT DONELSON (SEE MAP, PAGE 212). FROM A PHOTOGRAPH TAKEN IN 1884.

hands in salutation. I was then invited to breakfast, which consisted of corn bread and coffee, the best the gallant host had in his kitchen. We sat at the table about an hour and a half, when General Grant arrived and took temporary possession of the tavern as his headquarters. Later in the morning the army marched in and completed the possession.

CHAPTER 4

THE BATTLE OF SHILOH.

Ulysses S. Grant, General, U.S.A.

The battle of Shiloh, or Pittsburg Landing, fought on Sunday and Monday, the 6th and 7th of April, 1862, has been perhaps less understood, or, to state the case more accurately, more persistently misunderstood, than any other engagement between National and Confederate troops during the entire rebellion. Correct reports of the battle have been published, notably by Sherman, Badeau, and, in a speech before a meeting of veterans, by General Prentiss; but all of these appeared long subsequent to the close of the rebellion, and after public opinion had been most erroneously formed.

Events had occurred before the battle, and others subsequent to it, which determined me to make no report to my then chief, General Halleck, further than was contained in a letter, written immediately after the battle, informing him that an engagement had been fought, and announcing the result. The occurrences alluded to are these: After the capture of Fort Donelson, with over fifteen thousand effective men and all their munitions of war, I believed much more could be accomplished without further sacrifice of life.

Clarksville, a town between Donelson and Nashville, in the State of Tennessee, and on the east bank of the Cumberland, was garrisoned by the enemy. Nashville was also garrisoned, and was probably the best-provisioned depot at the time in the Confederacy. Albert Sidney Johnston occupied Bowling Green, Ky., with a large force. I believed, and my information justified the belief, that these

ON THE SKIRMISH LINE.

places would fall into our hands without a battle, if threatened promptly. I
determined not to miss this chance.
But being only a district commander,
and under the immediate orders of
the department commander, General
Halleck, whose headquarters were at
St. Louis, it was my duty to communicate to him all I proposed to do, and to
get his approval, if possible. I did so
communicate, and, receiving no reply,
acted upon my own judgment. The
result proved that my information was
correct, and sustained my judgment.

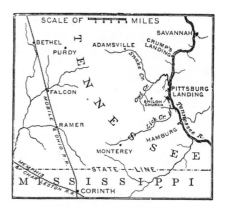

OUTLINE MAP OF THE SHILOH CAMPAIGN.

What, then, was my surprise, after so much had been accomplished by the
troops under my immediate command between the time of leaving Cairo, early
in February, and the 4th of March, to receive from my chief a dispatch of the
latter date, saying: "You will place Major-General C. F. Smith in command of
expedition, and remain yourself at Fort Henry. Why do you not obey my orders
to report strength and positions of your command?" I was left virtually in arrest
on board a steamer, without even a guard, for about a week, when I was released
and ordered to resume my command.

Again: Shortly after the battle of Shiloh had been fought, General Halleck
moved his headquarters to Pittsburg Landing, and assumed command of the
troops in the field. Although next to him in rank, and nominally in command of
my old district and army, I was ignored as much as if I had been at the most distant point of territory within my jurisdiction; and although I was in command
of all the troops engaged at Shiloh, I was not permitted to see one of the reports
of General Buell or his subordinates in that battle, until they were published by
the War Department, long after the event. In consequence, I never myself made
a full report of this engagement.

When I was restored to my command, on the 13th of March, I found it
on the Tennessee River, part at Savannah and part at Pittsburg Landing, nine
miles above, and on the opposite or western bank. I generally spent the day at
Pittsburg, and returned by boat to Savannah in the evening. I was intending to
remove my headquarters to Pittsburg, where I had sent all the troops immediately upon my reassuming command, but Buell, with the Army of the Ohio, had
been ordered to reënforce me from Columbia, Tenn. He was expected daily,
and would come in at Savannah. I remained, therefore, a few days longer than I
otherwise should have done, for the purpose of meeting him on his arrival.

General Lew Wallace, with a division, had been placed by General Smith
at Crump's Landing, about five miles farther down the river than Pittsburg, and

also on the west bank. His position I regarded as so well chosen that he was not moved from it until the Confederate attack in force at Shiloh.

The skirmishing in our front had been so continuous from about the 3d of April up to the determined attack, that I remained on the field each night until an hour when I felt there would be no further danger before morning. In fact, on Friday, the 4th, I was very much injured by my horse falling with me and on me while I was trying to get to the front, where firing had been heard. The night was one of impenetrable darkness, with rain pouring down in torrents; nothing was visible to the eye except as revealed by the frequent flashes of lightning. Under these circumstances I had to trust to the horse, without guidance, to keep the road. I had not gone far, however, when I met General W.H.L. Wallace and General (then Colonel) McPherson coming from the direction of the front. They said all was quiet so far as the enemy was concerned. On the way back to the boat my horse's feet slipped from under him, and he fell with my leg under his body. The extreme softness of the ground, from the excessive rains of the few preceding days, no doubt saved me from a severe injury and protracted

MRS. CRUMP'S HOUSE.

THE LANDING BELOW
THE HOUSE. FROM
PHOTOGRAPHS TAKEN
IN 1884.

Crump's Landing is, by river, about five miles below (north of) Pittsburg Landing. Here one of General Lew Wallace's three brigades was encamped on the morning of the battle, another brigade being two miles back, on the road to Purdy, and a third brigade half a mile farther advanced. The Widow Crump's house is about a quarter of a mile above the landing.

lameness. As it was, my ankle was very much injured; so much so, that my boot had to be cut off. During the battle, and for two or three days after, I was unable to walk except with crutches.

On the 5th General Nelson, with a division of Buell's army, arrived at Savannah, and I ordered him to move up the east bank of the river, to be in a position where he could be ferried over to Crump's Landing or Pittsburg Landing, as occasion required. I had learned that General Buell himself would be at Savannah the next day, and desired to meet me on his arrival. Affairs at Pittsburg Landing had been such for several days that I did not want to be away during the day. I determined, therefore, to take a very early breakfast and ride out to meet Buell, and thus save time. He had arrived on the evening of the 5th, but had not advised me of the fact, and I was not aware of it until some time after. While I was at breakfast, however, heavy firing was heard in the direction of Pittsburg Landing, and I hastened there, sending a hurried note to Buell, informing him of the reason why I could not meet him at Savannah. On the way up the river I directed the dispatch-boat to run in close to Crump's Landing, so that I could communicate with General Lew Wallace. I found him waiting on a boat, apparently expecting to see me, and I directed him to get his troops in line ready to execute any orders he might receive. He replied that his troops were already under arms and prepared to move.

Up to that time I had felt by no means certain that Crump's Landing might not be the point of attack. On reaching the front, however, about 8 A.M., I found that the attack on Shiloh was unmistakable, and that nothing more than a small guard, to protect our transports and stores, was needed at Crump's. Captain A. S. Baxter, a quartermaster on my staff, was accordingly directed to go back and order General Wallace to march immediately to Pittsburg, by the road nearest the river. Captain Baxter made a memorandum of his order. About 1 P.M., not hearing from Wallace, and being much in need of reënforcements, I sent two more of my staff, Colonel James B. McPherson and Captain W. R. Rowley, to bring him up with his division. They reported finding him marching toward Purdy, Bethel, or some point west from the river, and farther from Pittsburg by several miles than when he started. The road from his first position was direct, and near the river. Between the two points a bridge had been built across Snake Creek by our troops, at which Wallace's command had assisted, expressly to enable the troops at the two places to support each other in case of need. Wallace did not arrive in time to take part in the first day's fight. General Wallace has since claimed that the order delivered to him by Captain Baxter was simply to join the right of the army, and that the road over which he marched would have taken him to the road from Pittsburg to Purdy, where it crosses Owl Creek, on the right of Sherman; but this is not where I had ordered him nor where I wanted him to go. I never could see, and do not now see, why any order was necessary further than to direct him to come to Pittsburg Landing, without specifying by what route. His was one of three veteran divisions that had been in battle, and its absence was severely felt. Later in the war, General Wallace would never have made the mistake that he committed on the 6th of April, 1862. I presume his idea was that by taking the route he did, he would be able to come around on the flank or rear of the enemy, and thus perform an act of heroism that would redound to the credit of his command, as well as to the benefit of his country.[Φ]

Shiloh was a log meeting-house, some two or three miles from Pittsburg Landing, and on the ridge which divides the waters of Snake and Lick creeks, the former entering into the Tennessee just north of Pittsburg Landing, and the latter south. Shiloh was the key to our position, and was held by Sherman. His division was at that time wholly raw, no part of it ever having been in an engagement, but I thought this deficiency was more than made up by the superiority of the commander. McClernand was on Sherman's left, with troops that had been engaged at Fort Donelson, and were therefore veterans so far as Western troops had become such at that stage of the war. Next to McClernand came Prentiss, with a raw division, and on the extreme left, Stuart, with one brigade of Sherman's division. Hurlbut was in rear of Prentiss, massed, and in reserve at the time of the onset. The division of General C. F. Smith was on the right, also in reserve. General Smith was sick in bed at Savannah, some nine miles below, but in hearing of our guns. His services on those two eventful days would no doubt have been of inestimable value had his health permitted his presence. The command of his division devolved upon Brigadier-General W.H.L. Wallace, a most estimable and able officer,—a veteran, too, for he had served a year in the Mexican war, and had been with his command at Henry and Donelson.

[Φ]Since the publication in "The Century" of my article on "The Battle of Shiloh" I have received from Mrs. W.H.L. Wallace, widow of the gallant general who was killed in the first day's fight at that battle, a letter from General Lew Wallace to him, dated the morning of the 5th. At the date of this letter it was well known that the Confederates had troops out along the Mobile and Ohio railroad west of Crump's Landing and Pittsburg Landing, and were also collecting near Shiloh. This letter shows that at that time General Lew Wallace was making preparations for the emergency that might happen for the passing of reënforcements between Shiloh and his position, extending from Crump's Landing westward; and he sends the letter over the road running from Adamsville to the Pittsburg Landing and Purdy road. These two roads intersect nearly a mile west of the crossing of the latter over Owl Creek, where our right rested. In this letter General Lew Wallace advises General W.H.L. Wallace that he will send "to-morrow" (and his letter also says "April 5th," which is the same day the letter was dated and which, therefore, must have been written on the 4th) some cavalry to report to him at his headquarters, and suggesting the propriety of General W.H.L. Wallace's sending a company back with them for the purpose of having the cavalry at the two landings familiarize themselves with the road, so that they could "act promptly in case of emergency as guides to and from the different camps."

This modifies very materially what I have said, and what has been said by others, of the conduct of General Lew Wallace at the battle of Shiloh. It shows that he naturally, with no more experience than he had at the time in the profession of arms, would take the particular road that he did start upon in the absence of orders to move by a different road.

Wallace was mortally wounded in the first day's engagement, and with the change of commanders thus necessarily effected in the heat of battle, the efficiency of his division was much weakened.

The position of our troops made a continuous line from Lick Creek, on the left, to Owl Creek, a branch of Snake Creek, on the right, facing nearly south, and possibly a little west. [See map, page 244.] The water in all these streams was very high at the time, and contributed to protect our flanks. The enemy was compelled, therefore, to attack directly in front. This he did with great vigor, inflicting heavy losses on the National side, but suffering much heavier on his own.

The Confederate assaults were made with such disregard of losses on their own side, that our line of tents soon fell into their hands. The ground on which the battle was fought was undulating, heavily timbered, with scattered clearings, the woods giving some protection to the troops on both sides. There was also considerable underbrush. A number of attempts were made by the enemy to turn our right flank, where Sherman was posted, but every effort was repulsed with heavy loss. But the front attack was kept up so vigorously that, to prevent the success of these attempts to get on our flanks, the National troops were compelled several times to take positions to the rear, nearer Pittsburg Landing. When the firing ceased at night, the National line was all of a mile in rear of the position it had occupied in the morning.

In one of the backward moves, on the 6th, the division commanded by General Prentiss did not fall back with the others. This left his flanks exposed, and enabled the enemy to capture him, with about 2200 of his officers and men. General Badeau gives 4 o'clock of the 6th as about the time this capture took place. He may be right as to the time, but my recollection is that the hour was later. General Prentiss himself gave the hour as half-past five. I was with him, as I was with each of the division commanders that day, several times, and my recollection is that the last time I was with him was about half-past four, when his

---

The mistake he made, and which probably caused his apparent dilatoriness, was that of advancing some distance after he found that the firing, which would be at first directly to his front and then off to the left, had fallen back until it had got very much in rear of the position of his advance. This falling back had taken place before I sent General Wallace orders to move up to Pittsburg Landing, and, naturally, my order was to follow the road nearest the river. But my order was verbal, and to a staff-officer who was to deliver it to General Wallace, so that I am not competent to say just what order the general actually received.

General Wallace's division was stationed, the First Brigade at Crump's Landing, the Second out two miles, and the Third two and a half miles out. Hearing the sounds of battle, General Wallace early ordered his First and Third brigades to concentrate on the Second. If the position of our front had not changed, the road which Wallace took would have been somewhat shorter to our right than the River road. U.S. GRANT.

MOUNT MCGREGOR, N.Y., JUNE 21, 1885.

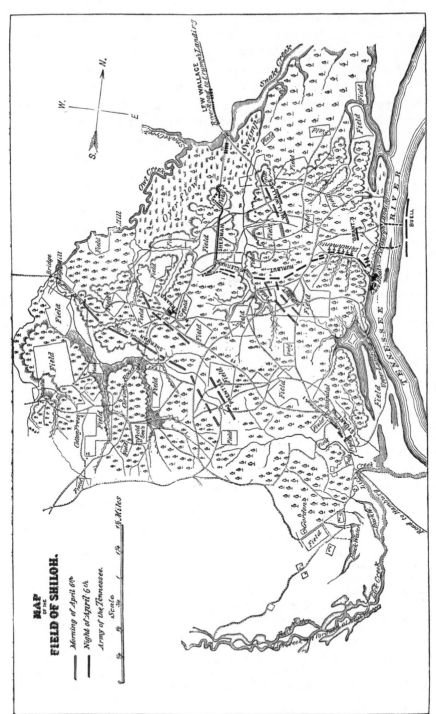

MAP
OF THE
FIELD OF SHILOH.

Morning of April 6th
Night of April 6th
Army of the Tennessee.

Scale
0   ¼   ½   ¾   1   1¼   1½ Miles

FROM GENERAL GRANT'S "MEMOIRS." BY PERMISSION OF CHARLES L. WEBSTER & CO.

division was standing up firmly, and the general was as cool as if expecting victory. But no matter whether it was four or later, the story that he and his command were surprised and captured in their camps is without any foundation whatever. If it had been true, as currently reported at the time, and yet believed by thousands of people, that Prentiss and his division had been captured in their beds, there would not have been an all-day struggle with the loss of thousands killed and wounded on the Confederate side.

With the single exception of a few minutes after the capture of Prentiss, a continuous and unbroken line was maintained all day from Snake Creek or its tributaries on the right to Lick Creek or the Tennessee on the left, above Pittsburg. There was no hour during the day when there was not heavy firing and generally hard fighting at some point on the line, but seldom at all points at the same time. It was a case of Southern dash against Northern pluck and endurance.

Three of the five divisions engaged on Sunday were entirely raw, and many of the men had only received their arms on the way from their States to the field. Many of them had arrived but a day or two before, and were hardly able to load their muskets according to the manual. Their officers were equally ignorant of their duties. Under these circumstances, it is not astonishing that many of the regiments broke at the first fire. In two cases, as I now remember, colonels led their regiments from the field on first hearing the whistle of the enemy's bullets. In these cases the colonels were constitutional cowards, unfit for any military position. But not so the officers and men led out of danger by them. Better troops never went upon a battle-field than many of these officers and men afterward proved themselves to be who fled panic-stricken at the first whistle of bullets and shell at Shiloh.

The map (facing page) used with General Grant's article on Shiloh, as first printed in "The Century" Magazine for February, 1885, was a copy of the official map which was submitted by the editors to General Grant and was approved by him. Subsequently General Grant, through his son, Colonel Frederick D. Grant, furnished the editors with a revision of the official map, agreeing in every respect with the map printed in the "Memoirs," here reproduced. In response to an inquiry by the editors for the reasons which influenced General Grant in making the substitution, Colonel Grant wrote as follows, under date of Chicago, Ill., March 20th, 1887: "Father was very ill when the map used with his article, on Shiloh, by 'The Century' Co., was submitted to him. He looked at the topography and found it about as he remembered the ground; but after you published it, he read some of the criticisms upon both the article and the map. Thus having his attention called to the subject, he revised the article, making it more *forcible,* and directed me to get for his book the map which was in the possession of Colonel Dayton, Secretary of the Society of the Army of the Tennessee, and which he had heard of or seen.

"This map proved to be more satisfactory to him than the one he had first used, as it agreed more perfectly with his statements and recollection of the positions occupied by the troops at the end of the first day's battle. Therefore, the only reason that can be assigned for General Grant's change of maps is that the one used in his book ['Memoirs'] was more *satisfactory to him,* his delicate health having prevented his thorough investigation of the map in the first place."

FIRST POSITION OF WATERHOUSE'S BATTERY.
FROM A SKETCH MADE SHORTLY AFTER THE BATTLE.

Major Ezra Taylor, General Sherman's chief of artillery, says in his report: "Captain A. C. Water-house's battery [was placed] near the left of the division [Sherman's]—four guns on the right bank of the Owl Creek [to the left and front of General Sherman's headquarters] and two guns on the left bank of Owl Creek [about 150 yards to the front]. The enemy appearing in large masses, and opening a battery to the front and right of the two guns, advanced across Owl Creek. I instructed Captain Waterhouse to retire the two guns to the position occupied by the rest of his battery, about which time the enemy appeared in large force in the open field directly in front of the position of this battery, bearing aloft, as I supposed, the American flag, and their men and officers wearing uniforms so similar to ours that I hesitated to open fire on them until they passed into the woods and were followed by other troops who wore a uniform not to be mistaken. I afterward learned that the uniform jackets worn by these troops were black. As soon as I was certain as to the character of the troops, I ordered the firing to commence, which was done in fine style and with excellent precision." Both Captain Waterhouse and Lieutenant A. R. Abbott were severely wounded.—EDITORS.

During the whole of Sunday I was continuously engaged in passing from one part of the field to another, giving directions to division commanders. In thus moving along the line, however, I never deemed it important to stay long with Sherman. Although his troops were then under fire for the first time, their commander, by his constant presence with them, inspired a confidence in officers and men that enabled them to render services on that bloody battle-field worthy of the best of veterans. McClernand was next to Sherman, and the hardest fighting was in front of these two divisions. McClernand told me on that day, the 6th, that he profited much by having so able a commander supporting him. A casualty to Sherman that would have taken him from the field

CONFEDERATE CHARGE UPON PRENTISS'S CAMP ON SUNDAY MORNING.

Of the capture of General Prentiss's camp, Colonel Francis Quinn (Twelfth Michigan Infantry) says in his official report dated April 9th: "About daylight the dead and wounded began to be brought in. The firing grew closer and closer, till it became manifest a heavy force of the enemy was upon us. The division was ordered into line of battle by General Prentiss, and immediately advanced in line about one-quarter of a mile from the tents, where the enemy were met in short-firing distance. Volley after volley was given and returned, and many fell on both sides, but their numbers were too heavy for our forces. I could see to the right and left. They were visible in line, and every hill-top in the rear was covered with them. It was manifest they were advancing, in not only one, but several lines of battle. The whole division fell back to their tents and again rallied, and, although no regular line was formed, yet from behind every tree a deadly fire was poured out upon the enemy, which held them in check for about one half-hour, when, reënforcements coming to their assistance, they advanced furiously upon our camp, and we were forced again to give way. At this time we lost four pieces of artillery. The division fell back about one half-mile, very much scattered and broken. Here we were posted, being drawn up in line behind a dense clump of bushes."—EDITORS.

that day would have been a sad one for the troops engaged at Shiloh. And how near we came to this! On the 6th Sherman was shot twice, once in the hand, once in the shoulder, the ball cutting his coat and making a slight wound, and a third ball passed through his hat. In addition to this he had several horses shot during the day.

The nature of this battle was such that cavalry could not be used in front; I therefore formed ours into line, in rear, to stop stragglers, of whom there were many. When there would be enough of them to make a show, and after they had recovered from their fright, they would be sent to reënforce some part of the line which needed support, without regard to their companies, regiments, or brigades.

On one occasion during the day, I rode back as far as the river and met General Buell, who had just arrived; I do not remember the hour, but at that time there probably were as many as four or five thousand stragglers lying under cover of the river-bluff, panic-stricken, most of whom would have been shot where they lay, without resistance, before they would have taken muskets and marched to the front to protect themselves. This meeting between General Buell and myself was on the dispatch-boat used to run between the landing and Savannah. It was brief, and related specially to his getting his troops over the river. As we left the boat together, Buell's attention was attracted by the men lying under cover of the bank. I saw him berating them and trying to shame them into joining their regiments. He even threatened them with shells from the gun-boats near by. But it was all to no effect. Most of these men afterward proved themselves as gallant as any of those who saved the battle from which they had deserted. I have no doubt that this sight impressed General Buell with the idea that a line of retreat would be a good thing just then. If he had come in by the front instead of through the stragglers in the rear, he would have thought and felt differently. Could he have come through the Confederate rear, he would have witnessed there a scene similar to that at our own. The distant rear of an army engaged in battle is not the best place from which to judge correctly what is going on in front. Later in the war, while occupying the country between the Tennessee and the Mississippi, I learned that the panic in the Confederate lines had not differed much from that within our own. Some of the country people estimated the stragglers from Johnston's army as high as twenty thousand. Of course, this was an exaggeration.

The situation at the close of Sunday was as follows: Along the top of the bluff just south of the log-house which stood at Pittsburg Landing, Colonel J. D. Webster, of my staff, had arranged twenty or more pieces of artillery facing south, or up the river. This line of artillery was on the crest of a hill overlooking a deep ravine opening into the Tennessee. Hurlbut, with his division intact, was on the right of this artillery, extending west and possibly a little north. McClernand came next in the general line, looking more to the west. His division was complete in its organization and ready for any duty. Sherman came next, his right extending to Snake Creek. His command, like the other two, was complete in its organization and ready, like its chief, for any service it might be called upon to render. All three divisions were, as a matter of course, more or less shattered and depleted in numbers from the terrible battle of the day. The division of W.H.L. Wallace, as much from the disorder arising from changes of division and brigade commanders, under heavy fire, as from any other cause, had lost its organization, and did not occupy a place in the line as a division; Prentiss's command was gone as a division, many of its members having been

CHECKING THE CONFEDERATE ADVANCE ON THE EVENING OF THE FIRST DAY.

Above this ravine, near the landing, the Federal reserve artillery was posted, and it was on this line the Confederate advance was checked, about sunset, Sunday evening. The Confederates then fell back and bivouacked in the Federal camps.

killed, wounded, or captured. But it had rendered valiant service before its final dispersal, and had contributed a good share to the defense of Shiloh.

There was, I have said, a deep ravine in front of our left. The Tennessee River was very high, and there was water to a considerable depth in the ravine. Here the enemy made a last desperate effort to turn our flank, but was repelled. The gun-boats *Tyler* and *Lexington,* Gwin and Shirk commanding, with the artillery under Webster, aided the army and effectually checked their further progress. Before any of Buell's troops had reached the west bank of the Tennessee, firing had almost entirely ceased; anything like an attempt on the part of the enemy to advance had absolutely ceased. There was some artillery firing from an unseen enemy, some of his shells passing beyond us; but I do not remember that there was the whistle of a single musket-ball heard. As his troops arrived in the dusk, General Buell marched several of his regiments part way down the face of the hill, where they fired briskly for some minutes, but I do not think a single man engaged in this firing received an injury; the attack had spent its force.

General Lew Wallace, with 5000 effective men, arrived after firing had ceased for the day, and was placed on the right. Thus night came, Wallace came, and the advance of Nelson's division came, but none—unless night—in time to be of material service to the gallant men who saved Shiloh on that first day, against large odds. Buell's loss on the 6th of April was two men killed and one wounded, all members of the 36th Indiana Infantry. The Army of the Tennessee lost on that day at least 7000 men. The presence of two or three regiments of his army on the west bank before firing ceased had not the slightest effect in preventing the capture of Pittsburg Landing.

So confident was I before firing had ceased on the 6th that the next day would bring victory to our arms if we could only take the initiative, that I visited each division commander in person before any reënforcements had reached the field. I directed them to throw out heavy lines of skirmishers in the morning as soon as they could see, and push them forward until they found the enemy, following with their entire divisions in supporting distance, and to engage the enemy as soon as found. To Sherman I told the story of the assault at Fort Donelson, and said that the same tactics would win at Shiloh. Victory was assured when Wallace arrived even if there had been no other support. The enemy received no reënforcements. He had suffered heavy losses in killed, wounded, and straggling, and his commander, General Albert Sidney Johnston, was dead. I was glad, however, to see the reënforcements of Buell and credit them with doing all there was for them to do. During the night of the 6th the remainder of Nelson's division, Buell's army, crossed the river, and were ready to advance in the morning, forming the left wing. Two other divisions; Crittenden's and McCook's, came up the river from Savannah in the transports, and were on the west bank early on the 7th. Buell commanded them in person. My command was thus nearly doubled in numbers and efficiency.

During the night rain fell in torrents, and our troops were exposed to the storm without shelter. I made my headquarters under a tree a few hundred yards back from the river-bank. My ankle was so much swollen from the fall of my horse the Friday night preceding, and the bruise was so painful, that I could get no rest. The drenching rain would have precluded the possibility of sleep, without this additional cause. Some time after midnight, growing restive under the storm and the continuous pain, I moved back to the log-house on the bank. This had been taken as a hospital, and all night wounded men were being brought in, their wounds dressed, a leg or an arm amputated, as the case might require, and everything being done to save life or alleviate suffering. The sight was more unendurable than encountering the enemy's fire, and I returned to my tree in the rain.

The advance on the morning of the 7th developed the enemy in the camps occupied by our troops before the battle began, more than a mile back from the most advanced position of the Confederates on the day before. It is known now that they had not yet learned of the arrival of Buell's command. Possibly they fell back so far to get the shelter of our tents during the rain, and also to get away from the shells that were dropped upon them by the gun-boats every fifteen minutes during the night.

The position of the Union troops on the morning of the 7th was as follows: General Lew Wallace on the right, Sherman on his left; then McClernand, and then Hurlbut. Nelson, of Buell's army, was on our extreme left, next to the river; Crittenden was next in line after Nelson, and on his right; McCook followed, and formed the extreme right of Buell's command. My old command thus formed the right wing, while the troops directly under Buell constituted the left wing of the army. These relative positions were retained during the entire day, or until the enemy was driven from the field.

In a very short time the battle became general all along the line. This day everything was favorable to the Federal side. We had now become the attacking party. The enemy was driven back all day, as we had been the day before, until finally he beat a precipitate retreat. The last point held by him was near the road leading from the landing to Corinth, on the left of Sherman and right of McClernand. About 3 o'clock, being near that point and seeing that the enemy was giving way everywhere else, I gathered up a couple of regiments, or parts of regiments, from troops near by, formed them in line of battle and marched them forward, going in front myself to prevent premature or long-range firing. At this point there was a clearing between us and the enemy favorable for charging, although exposed. I knew the enemy were ready to break, and only wanted a little encouragement from us to go quickly and join their friends who had started earlier. After marching to within musket-range, I stopped and let the troops pass. The command, *Charge,* was given, and was executed with loud cheers, and with a run, when the last of the enemy broke.

During this second day of the battle I had been moving from right to left and back, to see for myself the progress made. In the early part of the afternoon, while riding with Colonel James B. McPherson and Major J. P. Hawkins, then my chief commissary, we got beyond the left of our troops. We were moving along the northern edge of a clearing, very leisurely, toward the river above the landing. There did not appear to be an enemy to our right, until suddenly a battery with musketry opened upon us from the edge of the woods on the other side of the clearing. The shells and balls whistled about our ears very fast for about a minute. I do not think it took us longer than that to get out of range and out of sight. In the sudden start we made, Major Hawkins lost his hat. He did not stop to pick it up. When we arrived at a perfectly safe position we halted to take an account of damages. McPherson's horse was panting as if ready to drop. On examination it was found that a ball had struck him forward of the flank just back of the saddle, and had gone entirely through. In a few minutes the poor beast dropped dead; he had given no sign of injury until we came to a stop. A ball had struck the metal scabbard of my sword, just below the hilt, and broken it nearly off; before the battle was over, it had broken off entirely. There were three of us: one had lost a horse, killed, one a hat, and one a sword-scabbard. All were thankful that it was no worse.

After the rain of the night before and the frequent and heavy rains for some days previous, the roads were almost impassable. The enemy, carrying his artillery and supply trains over them in his retreat, made them still worse for troops following. I wanted to pursue, but had not the heart to order the men who had fought desperately for two days, lying in the mud and rain whenever not fighting, and I did not feel disposed positively to order Buell, or any part of his command, to pursue. Although the senior in rank at the time, I had been so only a few weeks. Buell was, and had been for some time past, a department commander, while I commanded only a district. I did not meet Buell in person until too late to get troops ready and pursue with effect; but, had I seen him at the moment of the last charge, I should have at least requested him to follow.

The enemy had hardly started in retreat from his last position, when, looking back toward the river, I saw a division of troops coming up in beautiful order, as if going on parade or review. The commander was at the head of the column, and the staff seemed to be disposed about as they would have been had they been going on parade. When the head of the column came near where I was standing, it was halted, and the commanding officer, General A. McD. McCook, rode up to where I was and appealed to me not to send his division any farther, saying that they were worn out with marching and fighting. This division had marched on the 6th from a point ten or twelve miles east of Savannah, over bad roads. The men had also lost rest during the night while crossing the Tennessee, and had been engaged in the battle of the 7th. It was not, however, the rank and file or the junior officers who asked to be excused, but the division commander.✢ I rode forward several miles the day after the battle, and found that the enemy had dropped much, if not all, of their provisions, some ammunition, and the extra wheels of their caissons, lightening their loads to enable them to get off their guns. About five miles out we found their field-

---

✢In an article on the battle of Shiloh, which I wrote for "The Century" magazine, I stated that General A. McD. McCook, who commanded a division of Buell's army, expressed some unwillingness to pursue the enemy on Monday, April 7th, because of the condition of his troops. General Badeau, in his history, also makes the same statement, on my authority. Out of justice to General McCook and his command, I must say that they left a point twenty-two miles east of Savannah on the morning of the 6th. From the heavy rains of a few days previous and the passage of trains and artillery, the roads were necessarily deep in mud, which made marching slow. The division had not only marched through this mud the day before, but it had been in the rain all night without rest. It was engaged in the battle of the second day, and did as good service as its position allowed. In fact, an opportunity occurred for it to perform a conspicuous act of gallantry which elicited the highest commendation from division commanders in the Army of the Tennessee. General Sherman, both in his memoirs and report, makes mention of this fact. General McCook himself belongs to a family which furnished many volunteers to the army. I refer to these circumstances with minuteness because I did General McCook injustice in my article in "The Century," though not to the extent one would suppose from the public press. I am not willing to do any one an injustice, and if convinced that I have done one, I am always willing to make the fullest admission.

U.S. GRANT.

MOUNT MCGREGOR, N.Y., JUNE 21, 1883.

hospital abandoned. An immediate pursuit must have resulted in the capture of a considerable number of prisoners and probably some guns.

Shiloh was the severest battle fought at the West during the war, and but few in the East equaled it for hard, determined fighting. I saw an open field, in our possession on the second day, over which the Confederates had made repeated charges the day before, so covered with dead that it would have been possible to walk across the clearing, in any direction, stepping on dead bodies, without a foot touching the ground. On our side National and Confederate were mingled together in about equal proportions; but on the remainder of the field nearly all were Confederates. On one part, which had evidently not been plowed for several years, probably because the land was poor, bushes had grown up, some to the height of eight or ten feet. There was not one of these left standing unpierced by bullets. The smaller ones were all cut down.

Contrary to all my experience up to that time, and to the experience of the army I was then commanding, we were on the defensive. We were without intrenchments or defensive advantages of any sort, and more than half the army engaged the first day was without experience or even drill as soldiers. The officers with them, except the division commanders, and possibly two or three of

FORD WHERE THE HAMBURG ROAD CROSSES LICK CREEK,
LOOKING FROM COLONEL STUART'S POSITION ON THE FEDERAL LEFT.

Lick Creek at this point was fordable on the first day of the battle, but the rains on Sunday night rendered it impassable on the second day.

the brigade commanders, were equally inexperienced in war. The result was a Union victory that gave the men who achieved it great confidence in themselves ever after.

The enemy fought bravely, but they had started out to defeat and destroy an army and capture a position. They failed in both, with very heavy loss in killed and wounded, and must have gone back discouraged and convinced that the "Yankee" was not an enemy to be despised.

After the battle I gave verbal instructions to division commanders to let the regiments send out parties to bury their own dead, and to detail parties, under commissioned officers from each division, to bury the Confederate dead in their respective fronts, and to report the numbers so buried. The latter part of these instructions was not carried out by all; but they were by those sent from Sherman's division, and by some of the parties sent out by McClernand. The heaviest loss sustained by the enemy was in front of these two divisions.

The criticism has often been made that the Union troops should have been intrenched at Shiloh; but up to that time the pick and spade had been but little resorted to at the West. I had, however, taken this subject under consideration soon after reassuming command in the field. McPherson, my only military engineer, had been directed to lay out a line to intrench. He did so, but reported that it would have to be made in rear of the line of encampment as it then ran. The new line, while it would be nearer the river, was yet too far away from the Tennessee, or even from the creeks, to be easily supplied with water from them; and in case of attack, these creeks would be in the hands of the enemy. Besides this, the troops with me, officers and men, needed discipline and drill more than they did experience with the pick, shovel, and axe. Reënforcements were arriving almost daily, composed of troops that had been hastily thrown together into companies and regiments—fragments of incomplete organizations, the men and officers strangers to each other. Under all these circumstances I concluded that drill and discipline were worth more to our men than fortifications.

General Buell was a brave, intelligent officer, with as much professional pride and ambition of a commendable sort as I ever knew. I had been two years at West Point with him, and had served with him afterward, in garrison and in the Mexican war, several years more. He was not given in early life or in mature years to forming intimate acquaintances. He was studious by habit, and commanded the confidence and respect of all who knew him. He was a strict disciplinarian, and perhaps did not distinguish sufficiently between the volunteer who "enlisted for the war" and the soldier who serves in time of peace. One system embraced men who risked life for a principle, and often men of social standing, competence, or wealth, and independence of character. The other includes, as a rule, only men who could not do as well in any other occupation. General Buell became an object of harsh criticism later, some going so far as to challenge his loyalty. No one who knew him ever believed him capable of a dishonorable

BIVOUAC OF THE FEDERAL TROOPS, SUNDAY NIGHT.

act, and nothing could be more dishonorable than to accept high rank and command in war and then betray the trust. When I came into command of the army, in 1864, I requested the Secretary of War to restore General Buell to duty.

After the war, during the summer of 1865, I traveled considerably through the North, and was everywhere met by large numbers of people. Every one had his opinion about the manner in which the war had been conducted; who among the generals had failed, how, and why. Correspondents of the press were ever on hand to hear every word dropped, and were not always disposed to report correctly what did not confirm their preconceived notions, either about the conduct of the war or the individuals concerned in it. The opportunity frequently occurred for me to defend General Buell against what I believed to be most unjust charges. On one occasion a correspondent put in my mouth the very charge I had so often refuted—of disloyalty. This brought from General Buell a very severe retort, which I saw in the New York "World" some time before I received the letter itself. I could very well understand his grievance at seeing untrue and disgraceful charges apparently sustained by an officer who, at the time, was at the head of the army. I replied to him, but not through the press. I kept no copy of my letter, nor did I ever see it in print, neither did I receive an answer.

General Albert Sidney Johnston, who commanded the Confederate forces at the beginning of the battle, was disabled by a wound in the afternoon of the first day. His wound, as I understood afterward, was not necessarily fatal, or even dangerous. But he was a man who would not abandon what he deemed an important trust in the face of danger, and consequently continued in the saddle, commanding, until so exhausted by the loss of blood that he had to be taken from his horse, and soon after died. The news was not long in reaching our side, and, I suppose, was quite an encouragement to the National soldiers. I had known Johnston slightly in the Mexican war, and later as an officer in the regular army. He was a man of high character and ability. His contemporaries at West Point, and officers generally who came to know him personally later, and who remained on our side, expected him to prove the most formidable man to meet that the Confederacy would produce. Nothing occurred in his brief command of an army to prove or disprove the high estimate that had been placed upon his military ability.↲

General Beauregard was next in rank to Johnston, and succeeded to the command, which he retained to the close of the battle and during the subsequent retreat on Corinth, as well as in the siege of that place. His tactics have been severely criticised by Confederate writers, but I do not believe his fallen chief could have done any better under the circumstances. Some of these critics claim that Shiloh was won when Johnston fell, and that if he had not fallen the army under me would have been annihilated or captured. *Ifs* defeated the Confederates at Shiloh. There is little doubt that we would have been disgracefully beaten *if* all the shells and bullets fired by us had passed harmlessly over the enemy, and *if* all of theirs had taken effect. Commanding generals are liable to be killed during engagements; and the fact that when he was shot Johnston was leading a brigade to induce it to make a charge which had been repeatedly ordered, is evidence that there was neither the universal demoralization on our side nor the unbounded confidence on theirs which has been claimed. There was, in fact, no hour during the day when I doubted the eventual defeat of the enemy, although I was disappointed that reënforcements so near at hand did not arrive at an earlier hour.

The Confederates fought with courage at Shiloh, but the particular skill claimed I could not, and still cannot, see; though there is nothing to criticise except the claims put forward for it since. But the Confederate claimants for superiority in strategy, superiority in generalship, and superiority in dash and prowess are not so unjust to the Union troops engaged at Shiloh as are many

↲In his "Personal Memoirs" General Grant says: "I once wrote that 'nothing occurred in his brief command of an army to prove or disprove the high estimate that had been placed upon his military ability'; but after studying the orders and dispatches of Johnston I am compelled to materially modify my views of that officer's qualifications as a soldier. My judgment now is that he was vacillating and undecided in his actions."

WOUNDED AND STRAGGLERS ON THE WAY TO THE LANDING,
AND AMMUNITION-WAGONS GOING TO THE FRONT.

Northern writers. The troops on both sides were American, and united they need not fear any foreign foe. It is possible that the Southern man started in with a little more dash than his Northern brother; but he was correspondingly less enduring.

The endeavor of the enemy on the first day was simply to hurl their men against ours—first at one point, then at another, sometimes at several points at once. This they did with daring and energy, until at night the rebel troops were worn out. Our effort during the same time was to be prepared to resist assaults wherever made. The object of the Confederates on the second day was to get away with as much of their army and material as possible. Ours then was to drive them from our front, and to capture or destroy as great a part as possible of their men and material. We were successful in driving them back, but not so successful in captures as if further pursuit could have been made. As it was, we captured or recaptured on the second day about as much artillery as we lost on the first; and, leaving out the one great capture of Prentiss, we took more prisoners on Monday than the enemy gained from us on Sunday. On the 6th Sherman lost 7 pieces of artillery, McClernand 6, Prentiss 8, and Hurlbut 2 batteries. On the 7th Sherman captured 7 guns, McClernand 3, and the Army of the Ohio 20.

At Shiloh the effective strength of the Union force on the morning of the 6th was 33,000. Lew Wallace brought five thousand more after nightfall. Beauregard reported the enemy's strength at 40,955. According to the custom of enumeration in the South, this number probably excluded every man enlisted as musician, or detailed as guard or nurse, and all commissioned officers,— everybody who did not carry a musket or serve a cannon. With us everybody in the field receiving pay from the Government is counted. Excluding the troops who fled, panic-stricken, before they had fired a shot, there was not a time during the 6th when we had more than 25,000 men in line. On the 7th Buell brought twenty thousand more. Of his remaining two divisions, Thomas's did not reach the field during the engagement; Wood's arrived before firing had ceased, but not in time to be of much service.

Our loss in the two-days fight was 1754 killed, 8408 wounded, and 2885 missing. Of these 2103 were in the Army of the Ohio. Beauregard reported a total loss of 10,699, of whom 1728 were killed, 8012 wounded, and 959 missing. This estimate must be incorrect. We buried, by actual count, more of the enemy's dead in front of the divisions of McClernand and Sherman alone than here reported, and four thousand was the estimate of the burial parties for the whole field. Beauregard reports the Confederate force on the 6th at over 40,000, and their total loss during the two days at 10,699; and at the same time declares that he could put only 20,000 men in battle on the morning of the 7th.

The navy gave a hearty support to the army at Shiloh, as indeed it always did, both before and subsequently, when I was in command. The nature of the ground was such, however, that on this occasion it could do nothing in aid of the troops until sundown on the first day. The country was broken and heavily timbered, cutting off all view of the battle from the river, so that friends would be as much in danger from fire from the gun-boats as the foe. But about sundown, when the National troops were back in their last position, the right of the enemy was near the river and exposed to the fire of the two gun-boats, which was delivered with vigor and effect. After nightfall, when firing had entirely ceased on land, the commander of the fleet informed himself, proximately, of the position of our troops, and suggested the idea of dropping a shell within the lines of the enemy every fifteen minutes during the night. This was done with effect, as is proved by the Confederate reports.

Up to the battle of Shiloh, I, as well as thousands of other citizens, believed that the rebellion against the Government would collapse suddenly and soon if a decisive victory could be gained over any of its armies. Henry and Donelson were such victories. An army of more than 21,000 men was captured or destroyed. Bowling Green, Columbus, and Hickman, Ky., fell in consequence, and Clarksville and Nashville, Tenn., the last two with an immense amount of stores, also fell into our hands. The Tennessee and Cumberland rivers, from their mouths to the head of navigation, were secured. But when Confederate armies were collected which not only attempted to hold a line farther south, from Memphis to Chattanooga, Knoxville and on to the Atlantic, but assumed the offensive, and made such a gallant effort to regain what had been lost, then, indeed, I gave up all idea of saving the Union except by complete conquest. Up to that time it had been the policy of our army, certainly of that portion commanded by me, to protect the property of the citizens whose territory was invaded, without regard to their sentiments, whether Union or Secession. After this, however, I regarded it as humane to both sides to protect the persons of those found at their homes but to consume everything that could be used to support or supply armies. Protection was still continued over such supplies as were within lines held by us, and which we expected to continue to hold. But such supplies within the reach of Confederate armies I regarded as contraband as much as arms or ordnance stores. Their destruction was accomplished without bloodshed, and tended to the same result as the destruction of armies. I continued this policy to the close of the war. Promiscuous pillaging, however, was discouraged and punished. Instructions were always given to take provisions and forage under the direction of commissioned officers, who should give receipts to owners, if at home, and turn the property over to officers of the quartermaster or commissary departments, to be issued as if furnished from our Northern depots. But much was destroyed without receipts to owners when it could not be brought within our lines, and would otherwise have gone to the support of secession and rebellion. This policy, I believe, exercised a material influence in hastening the end.

CHAPTER 5

SURPRISE AND WITHDRAWAL AT SHILOH.

S. H. Lockett, Colonel, C.S.A.

AT SHILOH GENERAL BRAGG'S CHIEF ENGINEER.

At the time of the battle of Shiloh I was on General Bragg's staff as his chief engineer, with the rank of captain. On the night of April 5th I accompanied him to General Johnston's headquarters, where the last council of war was held. I was not present at the meeting of the generals, but with a number of other staff-officers remained near by. We could hear the low, earnest discussion of our superiors, but could not distinguish the words spoken.

When the council closed, and General Bragg started to his own bivouac, I joined him, and received the following instructions: That as the attack would be made at daylight, the next morning at 4 o'clock I should proceed to the front along the Bark road, with Lieutenant Steel, of the engineers, and a squad of cavalry, until I came to the enemy's camp; that I should very carefully and cau-

tiously reconnoiter the camp from where I struck it toward the enemy's left flank; that I should by no means allow any firing by my little force, or do anything to attract attention; that my duty was to get all the information possible about the enemy's position and condition, and send it back by couriers from point to point, as my judgment should suggest. Those orders I carried out the next morning. Lieutenant S. M. Steel, now Major Steel, of Nashville, Tenn., had been a civil engineer and surveyor in that section of the country, had already made several daring and valuable reconnoissances of the Federal camps, and knew the country thoroughly. He was a splendid scout, and as brave a man as ever lived. Under his skillful guidance I reached in safety a point which he said was not more than a few hundred yards from the Federal camps. Here our cavalry escort and our own horses were left, and we two, leaving the road, passed down a narrow valley or gorge, got beyond the Federal pickets, and came within a few rods of a sleepy camp sentinel leaning against a tree. In front of us was a large camp as still and silent as the grave; no signs of life except a few smoldering fires of the last night's supper. Noting these facts and without disturbing the man at the tree, we returned to our cavalry squad, and I dispatched a courier to General Bragg with a note telling what I had seen. We then moved by our right flank through the woods, from a quarter to half a mile, and repeated our former manœuvre. This time we found the cooks of the camp astir preparing breakfast. While we were watching the process reveille was sounded, and I saw one or two regiments form by companies, answer to roll-call, and then disperse to their tents. Once more I returned to my cavalry and dispatched a courier.

A third time I made a descent from the hills, down a narrow hollow, still farther to our right, and saw Federal soldiers cleaning their guns and accouterments and getting ready for Sunday morning inspection. By this time firing had begun on our left, and I could see that it caused some commotion in the camps, but it was evident that it was not understood. Soon the firing became more rapid and clearer and closer, and I saw officers begin to stir out of their tents, evidently anxious to find out what it all meant. Then couriers began to arrive, and there was great bustle and confusion; the long roll was beaten; there was rapid falling in, and the whole party in front of me was so thoroughly awake and alarmed that I thought my safest course was to retreat while I could and send another courier to the rear.

How long all this took I cannot now recall, but perhaps not more than an hour and a half or two hours. When I reached my cavalry squad I knew that the battle had opened in earnest, but I determined to have one more look at the Federal position, and moved once more to the right. Without getting as near as our former positions, I had a good view of another camp with a line of soldiers formed in front of it. Meantime the Confederate troops had moved on down the hills, and I could plainly see from the firing that there was hot and heavy work on my left and in advance of my present position. I then began to fear that the division in front of me would swing around and take our forces in flank, as it was manifest that the Federal line extended farther in that direction than ours. I therefore disposed my little cavalry force as skirmishers, and sent a courier with a sketch of the ground to General Bragg, and urged the importance of having our right flank protected. How long I waited and watched at this point it is hard to say. Finally, becoming very uneasy at the state of affairs, I left Lieutenant Steel with the cavalry and rode to the left myself to make a personal report. In this ride I passed right down the line of battle of the Confederate forces, and saw some splendid duels both of artillery and infantry. Finally, as I have always thought about 11 o'clock, I came to General A. S. Johnston and his staff standing on the brow of a hill watching the conflict in their front. I rode up to General Johnston, saluted him, and said I wished to make a report of the state of affairs on our extreme right. He said he had received that report and a sketch from Captain Lockett, of the engineers. I told him I was Captain Lockett. He replied, "Well, sir, tell me as briefly and quickly as possible what you have to say." When my report was finished he said, "That is what I gathered from your note and sketch, and I have already ordered General Breckinridge to send forces to fill up the space on our right. Ride back, sir, toward the right, and you will probably meet General Breckinridge; lead him to the position you indicate, and tell him to drive the enemy he may find in his front into the river. He needs no further orders." The words are, as near as I can remember them, exactly the ones General Johnston used. I obeyed the order given, met General Breckinridge, conducted him to the place where I had left my cavalry, but found both them and the Federal division gone. I rode with General Breckinridge a few hundred yards forward, and we soon received a volley which let us know that the Federal forces had retired but a very short distance from their original position. General Breckinridge deployed Bowen's and Statham's brigades, moved them forward, and soon engaged the Federal forces. I bade the General good-day and good luck, and once more rode down the line of battle until I found General Bragg. With him I remained, excepting when carrying orders and making reconnoissances, until the close of the first day's fight.

I witnessed the various bloody and unsuccessful attacks on the "Hornets' Nest." During one of the dreadful repulses of our forces, General Bragg directed me to ride forward to the central regiment of a brigade of troops that was recoiling across an open field, to take its colors and carry them forward. "The flag must not go back again," he said. Obeying the order, I dashed through the line of battle, seized the colors from the color-bearer, and said to him, "General Bragg says these colors must not go to the rear." While I was talking to him the color-sergeant was shot down. A moment or two afterward I was almost alone on horseback in the open field between the two lines of battle. An officer came up to me with a bullet-hole in each cheek, the blood streaming from his mouth, and asked, "What are you doing with my colors, sir?" "I am obeying General Bragg's orders, sir, to hold them where they are," was my reply. "Let me have them," he said. "If any man but my color-bearer carries these colors, I am the man. Tell General Bragg I will see that these colors are in the right place. But he must attack this position in flank; we can never carry it alone from the front." It was Colonel H. W. Allen, afterward Governor Allen of Louisiana. I returned, miraculously preserved, to General Bragg, and reported Colonel Allen's words. I then carried an order to the same troops, giving the order, I think, to General

Gibson, to fall back to the fence in the rear and reorganize. This was done, and then General Bragg dispatched me to the right, and Colonel Frank Gardner (afterward Major-General) to the left, to inform the brigade and division commanders on either side that a combined movement would be made on the front and flanks of that position. The movements were made, and Prentiss was captured.

As Colonel William Preston Johnston says, that capture was a dear triumph to us—dear for the many soldiers we had lost in the first fruitless attacks, but still dearer on account of the valuable time it cost us. The time consumed in gathering Prentiss's command together, in taking their arms, in marching them to the rear, was inestimably valuable. Not only that; the news of the capture spread, and grew as it spread; many soldiers and officers believed we had captured the bulk of the Federal army, and hundreds left their positions and came to see the "captured Yanks." But after a while the Confederates were gotten into ranks, and a perfect line of battle was formed, with our left wing resting on Owl Creek and our right on the Tennessee River. General Polk was on the left, then Bragg, then Hardee, then Breckinridge. In our front only one single point was showing fight, a hill crowned with artillery. I was with General Bragg, and rode with him along the front of his corps. I heard him say over and over again, "One more charge, my men, and we shall capture them all." While this was going on a staff-officer (or rather, I think, it was one of the detailed clerks of General Beauregard's headquarters, for he wore no uniform) came up to General Bragg, and said, "The General directs that the pursuit be stopped; the victory is sufficiently complete; it is needless to expose our men to the fire of the gun-boats." General Bragg said, "My God, was a victory ever sufficiently complete?" and added, "Have you given that order to any one else?" "Yes, sir," was the reply, "to General Polk, on your left; and if you will look to the left, you will see that the order is being obeyed." General Bragg looked, and said, "My God, my God, it is too late!" and turning to me, he said, "Captain, carry that order to the troops on the right"; and to Captain Frank Parker, "You carry it to the left." In a short time the troops were all falling back—*and the victory was lost.* Captain Parker and myself were the only members of General Bragg's staff who were with him at that time. Captain Parker, I think, is still living in South Carolina, and will surely remember all that I have narrated.

In this hasty sketch I have intentionally omitted everything but the beginning and end of that day's operations, to throw what light I can upon the two great points of dispute: Was the Federal army surprised by our attack? and whose fault was it that the victory was not sufficiently complete on the first day?

In regard to the second day's fight, I will touch upon but one point. I, as a great many other staff-officers, was principally occupied in the early hours of the second day in gathering together our scattered men and getting them into some sort of manageable organization. In this duty I collected and organized a body of men about a thousand strong. They were composed of men of at least a half-dozen different regiments. The 7th Kentucky, with a tattered flag, and the 9th Arkansas were the most numerously represented. We had not one single field-officer in the command. When I reported to General Beauregard that I had the troops divided into companies, had assigned a captain to duty as lieutenant-colonel and a first lieutenant as major, he himself put me in command of them as colonel. In order that my command might have a name, I dubbed it the "Beauregard Regiment,"—a name that was received with three rousing cheers. Not long after my regiment was thus officered and christened, a message came from General Breckinridge on our extreme right that he was hard pressed, and needed reënforcements. My regiment, which was at the time just behind General Beauregard, held in reserve by his orders, was sent by him to General Breckinridge's assistance. We marched down the line of battle to the extreme right, passed beyond General Breckinridge's right, wheeled by companies into line of battle, and went in with the "rebel yell." The men on our left took up the yell and the charge, and we gained several hundred yards of ground. From this point we fought back slowly and steadily for several hours, until word came that the army was ordered to retreat, that the commands would fall back in succession from the left, and that the right wing would be the rear-guard. This order was carried out, and when night came the right wing was slowly falling back with face to the foe. We halted on the same ground we had occupied on the morning of the 6th, just before the battle began. If there was any "breaking" and "starting," as General Grant expresses it, I did not witness it.

CHAPTER 6

THE SHILOH BATTLE-ORDER AND THE WITHDRAWAL SUNDAY EVENING.

Alexander Robert Chisolm, Colonel, C.S.A.

AT SHILOH ON GENERAL BEAUREGARD'S STAFF.

In the paper published in "The Century" for February, 1885, Colonel William Preston Johnston, assuming to give the Confederate version of the campaign and battle of Shiloh, at which he was not present, has adventured material statements regarding operations on that field, which must have been based on misinformation or misunderstanding in essential particulars, as I take occasion to assert from personal knowledge acquired as an eyewitness and aide-de-camp on the staff of General Beauregard. My personal knowledge runs counter to many of his statements and deductions, but I shall here confine myself to two points.

First, I must dispute that the battle-order as promulgated was in any wise different from the one submitted by General Beauregard at his own quarters at Corinth, early in the morning of the 3d of April, to General A. S. Johnston, and which was accepted without modification or suggestion. This assertion I base on these facts: About 1 o'clock in the morning the adjutant-general of the Confederate forces, Colonel Jordan, aroused me from sleep in my tent, close by General Beauregard's chamber, and desired me to inform the general at dawn that General Johnston had agreed to his recommendation to move offensively against Pittsburg Landing early that same day, and that the circular orders to the corps commanders had been already issued by Colonel Jordan to that effect. Acting upon this request, I found that General Beauregard had already during the night made full notes on loose scraps of paper of the order of march and battle, from which he read aloud for me to copy—my copy being given to Colonel Jordan as soon as completed, as the basis of the official order which he was to frame, and did frame and issue in the name of General Johnston. And that is the order which Colonel Johnston erroneously alleges upon the posthumous authority of General Bragg to differ essentially from the plan settled upon by General Johnston for the battle. This allegation I know to be unfounded, as the order as issued varies in no wise from the notes dictated to me by General Beauregard, excepting the mere wording and some details relating to transportation and ordnance service added by Colonel Jordan; that is to say, the plan explained by General Beauregard and accepted by General Johnston at the quarters of the former.

Being limited as to space, I shall pass over a throng of facts within my personal knowledge, which would establish that General Beauregard was as actively and directly handling the Confederate forces engaged in their general conduct of the battle before the death of General Johnston as he was after that incident. I shall confine myself on this occasion to relating that after General Beauregard became cognizant of the death of General Johnston, he dispatched me to the front with orders that led to the concentration of the widely scattered and disarrayed Confederate forces, which resulted in the capture of General Prentiss and so many of his division after 5 o'clock on the 6th.

I also, later in the day, carried orders to Hardee, who was engaged on our extreme left, or Federal right, where I remained with that officer until almost dark, up to which time no orders had reached him to cease fighting. On the contrary, he was doing his best to force back the enemy in his front. As he was without any of his staff about him, for the nonce I acted as his aide-de-camp. Meantime the gun-boats were shelling furiously, and their huge missiles crushed through the branches of the trees overhead with so fearful a din, frequency, and closeness that, despite the excitement of our apparently complete victory, there was room left in our minds for some most unpleasant sensations, especially when the top of some lofty tree, cut off by a shell, would come toppling down among the men.

Possibly, had Colonel Johnston been present on the field at that last hour of the battle of the 6th, a witness of the actually fruitless efforts made to storm the last position held by the enemy upon the ridge covering the immediate landing-place, known as Pittsburg, he might be better informed why it was that that position was not carried, and be less disposed to adduce such testimony as that of General Bragg, to the effect that but for the order given by Beauregard to withdraw from action he would have carried all before him.

It so happened that I rejoined General Beauregard at a point near Shiloh Chapel (having escorted General Prentiss from the field to General Beauregard), when General Bragg rode up from the front, and I heard him say in an excited manner: "General, we have carried everything before us to the Tennessee River. I have ridden from Owl to Lick Creek, and there is none of the enemy to be seen." Beauregard quietly replied: "Then, General, do not unnecessarily expose your command to the fire of the gun-boats."

CHAPTER 7

THE PLAN AND CONSTRUCTION OF THE "MERRIMAC."

I.

John M. Brooke, Commander, C.S.N.

Early in June, 1861, the Secretary of the Navy of the Confederate States asked me to design an iron-clad. The first idea presenting itself was a shield of timber, two feet thick, plated with three or more inches of iron, inclined to the horizontal plane at the least angle that would permit working the guns; this shield, its eaves submerged to the depth of two feet, to be supported by a hull of equal length. There was nothing novel in the use of inclined iron-plating. It was apparent that to support such a shield the ends of the vessel would be so full as to prevent the attainment of speed; and that in moving *end on* even a small sea would prevent working the bow or stern gun. It then occurred to me that fineness of line, protection of hull, and buoyancy with light draught, could be obtained by extending the ends of the vessel under water *beyond the shield*, provided the shield were of sufficient length to give the requisite stability. Considering, then, the liability to the banking up of water over these submerged ends, I erected upon each a decked superstructure of ship-iron, carried up from the sides of the submerged parts to a height above water not greater than would permit free use of the guns, and of the usual form of hull above water. Water could be admitted or taken from them.

I submitted to the secretary outline drawings,—sheer, body and deck plans, with explanations,—and he approved and adopted this novel form. In reply to my suggestion that Naval-Constructor John L. Porter and Chief-Engineer William P. Williamson should be called to Richmond, that we might put the plan in execution, he replied that a practical mechanic would be sent from the Norfolk yard. This mechanic—a master ship-carpenter—came; but as he was lacking in confidence and energy, and was averse to performing unusual duty, he was permitted to return to the yard.

Messrs. Porter and Williamson were ordered to Richmond for consultation on the same general subject, and to aid in the work. They met the secretary and myself on the 23d of June, 1861. Mr. Porter brought and submitted to the secretary a model described by the latter in a report dated March 29th, 1862, to the congress of the Confederate States, as "a flat-bottomed light-draught propeller, casemated battery, with inclined iron sides and ends." The hull of this model did not extend beyond the shield. The secretary then called the attention of Messrs. Williamson and Porter to the plan proposed by me, which had been adopted by the department. The drawings were laid before them, the reasons for extending the hull under water beyond the shield were given, and both approved it. As the drawings were in pencil, the secretary directed me to make a clean drawing in ink of the plan, to be filed in the department. Messrs. Porter and Williamson were directed to ascertain if suitable engines and boilers could be obtained. Mr. Porter offered to make the clean drawing, as "being more familiar with that sort of work." Accepting the offer I went with Williamson to the Tredegar works, where we learned that there were no suitable engines in the South. Williamson then said he thought the engines of the *Merrimac* could be used, but that the vessel would necessarily draw as much water as the *Merrimac,* and it would not be worth while to build a new hull, as enough of the old hull remained to carry out the plan. Mr. Porter and I thought the draught too great, but that we could not do better. We so reported to the secretary, who concurred. That there might be official record of results of consultation, as there was of the original plan, he directed us to consider and report upon the best mode of making the *Merrimac* useful, which we did in accordance with the views above stated. Mr. Williamson and Mr. Porter returned to Norfolk, the former to adapt and repair the engines, the latter to cut the ship down, submerge her ends, etc. To me was assigned the preparation of armor, construction of guns, etc. On the 11th of July Mr. Porter submitted to the secretary drawings, based upon actual measurements of the ship and on the plan of *submerged extended ends,* which I had presented, and which had been unanimously approved. Having reference to this working plan and its details, the secretary issued the following order:

"Navy Department, Richmond, July 11, 1861. Flag-Officer F. Forrest. Sir: You will proceed with all practicable dispatch to make the changes in the form of the *Merrimac,* and to build, equip, and fit her in all respects according to the design and plans of the constructor and engineer, Messrs. Porter and Williamson....
"R. S. Mallory, Secretary of the C.S. Navy."

This and a similar order were construed by Mr. Porter to credit him with the origin of the plan, and served as a basis to a published claim after the action in Hampton Roads, which led to a call by the Confederate House of Representatives, upon the Secretary of the Navy, for information as to the origin of the plan, and to the settlement of the question by a patent, No. 100, granted me by the Confederate States, 29th July 1862. This patent is still in my possession.

LEXINGTON, VA., October, 1887.

II.

John L. Porter, Naval Constructor, Confederate States

In June, 1861, I was ordered to Richmond by Secretary Mallory, and carried up with me a model of an iron-clad for harbor defense. Soon after my arrival I was informed by the secretary that I had been sent for to confer with Chief Engineer W. P. Williamson and Lieutenant J. M. Brooke in arranging an iron-clad. We went into Engineer Williamson's office, and held a consultation, the result of which was this report to the secretary:

"Navy Department, Richmond, June 25th, 1861. Sir: In obedience to your order, we have carefully examined and considered the various plans and propositions for constructing a shot-proof steam-battery, and respectfully report that in our opinion the steam-frigate *Merrimac,* which is in such condition from the effect of fire as to be useless for any other purpose without incurring a very heavy expense in her rebuilding, can be made an efficient vessel of that character, mounting 10 heavy guns, 2 pivot and 8 broadside guns of her original battery, and from the further consideration that we cannot procure a suitable engine and boilers for any other vessel without building them, which would occupy too much time. It would appear that this is our only chance to get a suitable vessel in a short time. The bottom of the hull, boilers, and heavy and costly parts of the engine being but little injured, reduce the cost of construction to about one-third of the amount which would be required to construct such a vessel anew.

"We cannot, without further examination, make an accurate estimate of the cost of the proposed work, but think it will be about one hundred and ten thousand dollars, the most of which will be for labor, the materials being nearly all on hand in the yard, excepting the iron plating to cover the shield. The plan to be adopted in the arrangement of the shield for glancing shot, mounting guns, arranging the hull, and plating to be in accordance with the plan submitted for the approval of the department. We are, with much respect, your obedient servants,

"WILLIAM P. WILLIAMSON, Chief Engineer; JOHN M. BROOKE,
"Lieutenant; JOHN L. PORTER, Naval Constructor."

I returned immediately to the Gosport Navy Yard, and made a working drawing of the whole thing, put my shield on it, which I had in my model, and returned to the secretary, July 11th, 1861, who had the following order made out, and placed in my hands by himself:

"Navy Department,
Richmond, July 11th, 1861.

"Flag-Officer F. Forrest. Sir:

"You will proceed, with all practicable dispatch, to make the changes in the *Merrimac*, and to build, equip, and fit her in all respects according to the designs and plans of the constructor and engineer, Messrs. Porter and Williamson. As time is of the first importance in the matter, you will see that work progresses without delay to completion.

"S. R. Mallory, Secretary of the Confederate States Navy."

I came immediately back to the Navy Yard and commenced this great work, unassisted by mortal man so far as the plans and responsibilities of the hull and its workings were concerned as an iron-clad. The second letter which came from the department about this great piece of work is as follows:

"Confederate States Navy Department,
Richmond, August 18th, 1861.

"Flag-Officer F. Forrest, Commanding Navy Yard, Gosport. Sir:

"The great importance of the service expected from the *Merrimac*, and the urgent necessity of her speedy completion, induce me to call upon you to push forward the work with the utmost dispatch. Chief Engineer Williamson and Constructor Porter, severally in charge of the two respective branches of this great work, and for which they will be held personally responsible, will receive, therefore, every possible facility at the expense and delay of every other work on hand if necessary.

"Secretary S. R. Mallory, Confederate States Navy."

In April, 1846, I had been stationed in Pittsburg superintending an iron steamer, when I conceived the idea of an iron-clad, and made a model with the exact shield which I placed on the *Merrimac*. Lieutenant Brooke tried for over a week to carry out the wish of the department, but failed entirely to produce anything, whereupon I was called on by the secretary.

After I had made the plan of the *Merrimac*, and had submitted it to the department, not to Lieutenant Brooke, and when everything was fresh in the mind of the secretary, he had the order of July 11th made out and placed in my hands, to Flag-Officer Forrest, to proceed with the work with all dispatch. No man save myself had anything to do with the converting of that ship into an iron-clad,—I calculated her displacement, weight, etc., and cut her down to suit, and no man save myself knew what she would bear. Lieutenant Brooke came to the yard once while the ship was being prepared, and stated that he had tried experiments on three inches of iron and it would not stand the fire. I then told him to put on another inch, making four inches; he asked me if she would bear it. I told him she would, and the armor was changed to four inches. All the inboard plans and arrangements were made by myself, and the whole working of the ship; Lieutenant Brooke superintended the armor and guns; Engineer Williamson superintended the machinery, and John L. Porter the construction of the hull. The accompanying drawing is a correct representation of a cross-

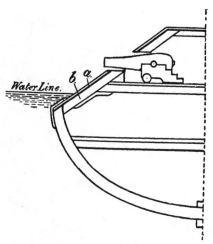

CROSS-SECTION OF "MERRIMAC."
FROM A DRAWING BY JOHN L. PORTER,
CONSTRUCTOR.

a—4 inches of iron.
b—23 inches of wood.

section amidships. She had only decks, gun and berth. Her shield sloped at an angle of 35 degrees; her rudder and propeller were well protected by a heavy fan-tail; her prow was of cast-iron securely fastened to the ship, and so well secured that though it was broken in two by striking the *Cumberland* a glancing blow, the fastenings to the vessel were not broken loose. Her deck ends were two feet below water and not awash, and the ship was as strong and well protected at her center-line as anywhere else, as her knuckle was two feet below her water-line, and her plating ran down to the knuckle and was there clamped. Her draught of water was 21 feet forward and 22 feet aft.

After the engagements of the 8th and 9th of March, 1862, I put her in the dry-dock and found she had 97 indentations on her armor from shot, 20 of which were from the 10-inch guns of the *Monitor*. Six of her top layer of plates were broken by the *Monitor's* shots, and none by those of the other vessels. None of the lower layer of plates were injured. I removed those plates and replaced them by others. Her wood-work underneath was not hurt. Her smoke-stack was full of shot-holes. She never had any boat-davits. Her pilot-house was cast solid, and was not covered with plate-iron like her shield. She had port shutters only at her four quarter port-holes. It will thus be seen that the conversion of the *Merrimac* into an iron-clad was merely accidental, and grew out of the impracticability of building an engine within the time at the disposal of the Confederacy, and no iron-clad, with submerged ends, was afterward built.

PORTSMOUTH, VA., October, 1887.

CHAPTER 8

THE BUILDING OF THE "MONITOR."

Captain John Ericsson, Inventor of the "Monitor."

The introduction of General Paixhans's brilliant invention, the shell-gun, in 1824, followed, in 1858, by the successful application of armor-plating to the steam-frigate *La Gloire,* under Napoleon III., compelled an immediate change in naval construction which startled the maritime countries of Europe, especially England, whose boasted security behind her "wooden walls" was shown to be a complete delusion. The English naval architects, however, did not overlook the fact that their French rivals, while producing a gun which rendered wooden navies almost useless, had also by their armor-plating provided an efficient protection against the destructive Paixhans shell.

Accordingly, the Admiralty without loss of time laid the keel of the *Warrior,* an armored iron steam-frigate 380 feet long, 58 feet beam, 26 feet draught, and 9200 tons displacement. The work being pushed with extraordinary vigor, this iron-clad ship was speedily launched and equipped, the admiration of the naval world.

Shortly after the adoption of armor-plating as an essential feature in the construction of vessels of war, the Southern States seceded from the Union, some of the most efficient of the United States naval officers resigning their commissions. Their loss was severely felt by the Navy Department at Washington; nor was it long before the presence of great professional skill among the officers of the naval administration of the Confederate States became manifest. Indeed, the utility of the armor-plating adopted by France and England proved to be better understood at Richmond than at Washington. While the Secretary of the Navy, Mr. Welles, and his advisers were discussing the question of armor, news reached Washington that the partly burnt and scuttled steam-frigate *Merrimac,* at the Norfolk Navy Yard, had been raised and cut down to her berth-deck, and that a very substantial structure of timber, resembling a citadel with inclined sides, was being erected on that deck.

The Navy Department at Washington early in August advertised for plans and offers for iron-clad steam-batteries to be built within a stipulated time. My attention having been thus called to a subject which I had thoroughly considered during a series of years, I was fully prepared to present plans of an impregnable steam-battery of light draught, suitable to navigate the shallow rivers and harbors of the Confederate States. Availing myself of the services of a friend who chanced to be in Washington at the time, proposals were at once sub-

CAPTAIN JOHN ERICSSON.
FROM A PHOTOGRAPH.

mitted to a board of naval officers appointed by the President; and the plans presented by my friend being rejected by the board, I immediately set out for Washington and laid the matter personally before its members, all of whom proved to be well-informed and experienced naval experts. Contrary to antici-pation, the board permitted me to present a theoretical demonstration con-cerning the stability of the new structure, doubt of which was the principal consideration which had caused the rejection of the plan presented. In less than an hour I succeeded in demonstrating to the entire satisfaction of the board ap-pointed by President Lincoln that the design was thoroughly practical, and based on sound theory. The Secretary of the Navy accordingly accepted my proposal to build an iron-clad steam-battery, and instructed me verbally to commence the construction forthwith. Returning immediately to New York, I divided the work among three leading mechanical establishments, furnishing each with detailed drawings of every part of the structure; the understanding being that the most skillful men and the best tools should be employed; also that work should be continued during night-time when practicable. The con-struction of nearly every part of the battery accordingly commenced simulta-neously, all hands working with the utmost diligence, apparently confident that their exertions would result in something of great benefit to the national cause. Fortunately no trouble or delay was met at any point; all progressed satisfacto-rily; every part sent on board from the workshops fitted exactly the place for which it was intended. As a consequence of these favorable circumstances, the battery, with steam-machinery complete, was launched in one hundred days from the laying of the keel-plate. It should be mentioned that at the moment of starting on the inclined ways toward its destined element, the novel fighting-machine was named *Monitor*.‡

Before entering on a description of this *fighting-machine* I propose to answer the question frequently asked: What circumstances dictated its size and peculiar construction?

1. The work on the *Merrimac* had progressed so far that no structure of large dimensions could possibly be completed in time to meet her.

2. The well-matured plan of erecting a citadel of considerable dimensions on the ample deck of the razed *Merrimac* admitted of a battery of heavy ordnance so formidable that no vessel of the ordinary type, of small dimensions, could withstand its fire.

3. The battery designed by the naval authorities of the Confederate States, in addition to the advantage of ample room and numerous guns, presented a formidable front to an opponent's fire by being inclined to such a degree that shot would be readily deflected. Again, the inclined sides, composed of heavy timbers well braced, were covered with two thicknesses of bar iron, ingeniously combined, well calculated to resist the spherical shot peculiar to the Dahlgren and Rodman system of naval ordnance adopted by the United States navy.

4. The shallow waters on the coast of the Southern States called for very light draught; hence the upper circumference of the propeller of the battery would be exposed to the enemy's fire unless thoroughly protected against shot of heavy caliber. A difficulty was thus presented which apparently could not be met by any device which would not seriously impair the efficiency of the propeller.

5. The limited width of the navigable parts of the Southern rivers and inlets presented an obstacle rendering manœuvring impossible; hence it would

---

‡The origin of the name *Monitor* is given in the following letter to Gustavus V. Fox, Assistant Secretary of the Navy:

"NEW-YORK, January 20th, 1862. SIR: In accordance with your request, I now submit for your approbation a name for the floating battery at Green Point. The impregnable and aggressive character of this structure will admonish the leaders of the Southern Rebellion that the batteries on the banks of their rivers will no longer present barriers to the entrance of the Union forces.

"The iron-clad intruder will thus prove a severe monitor to those leaders. But there are other leaders who will also be startled and admonished by the booming of the guns from the impregnable iron turret. 'Downing Street' will hardly view with indifference this last 'Yankee notion,' this monitor. To the Lords of the Admiralty the new craft will be a monitor suggesting doubts as to the propriety of completing those four steel-clad ships at three-and-a-half millions apiece. On these and many similar grounds I propose to name the new battery *Monitor*. Your obedient servant, J. ERICSSON."

—EDITORS.

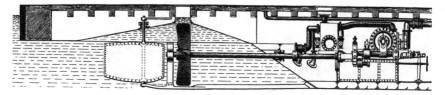

1. AFT SECTION, LONGITUDINAL PLAN THROUGH THE CENTER LINE
OF THE ORIGINAL "MONITOR."

not be practicable at all times to turn the battery so as to present a broad-side to the points to be attacked.

6. The accurate knowledge possessed by the adversary of the distance between the forts on the river-banks within range of his guns, would enable him to point the latter with such accuracy that unless every part of the sides of the battery could be made absolutely shot-proof, destruction would be certain. It may be observed that the accurate knowledge of range was an advantage in favor of the Southern forts which placed the attacking steam-batteries at great disadvantage.

7. The difficulty of manipulating the anchor within range of powerful fixed batteries presented difficulties which called for better protection to the crew of the batteries than any previously known.

Several minor points familiar to the naval artillerist and naval architect presented considerations which could not be neglected by the constructor of the new battery; but these must be omitted in our brief statement, while the foregoing, being of vital importance, have demanded special notice.

The plans above and below and on page 276 represent a longitudinal section through the center line of the battery, which, for want of space on the page, has been divided into three sections, viz., the aft, central, and forward sections, which for ready reference will be called *aft, central,* and *forward.*

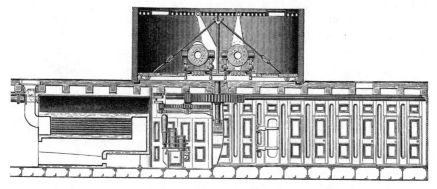

2. CENTRAL SECTION, SAME PLAN.

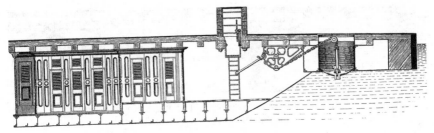

3. FORWARD SECTION, SAME PLAN.

Referring particularly to the upper and lower sections, it will be seen that the hull consists of an upper and lower body joined together in the horizontal plane not far below the water-line. The length of the upper part of the hull is 172 feet, beam 41 feet; the length of the lower hull being 122 feet, beam 34 feet. The depth from the underside of deck to the keel-plate is 11 feet 2 inches, draught of water at load-line 10 feet.

Let us now examine separately the three sectional representations.

Forward Section. The anchor-well, a cylindrical perforation of the overhanging deck, near the bow, first claims our attention. The object of this well being to protect the anchor when raised, it is lined with plate iron backed by heavy timbers, besides being protected by the armor-plating bolted to the outside of the overhang. It should be noticed that this method proved so efficient that in no instance did the anchor-gear receive any injury during the several engagements with the Confederate batteries, although nearly all of the monitors of the *Passaic* class were subjected to rapid fire at short range in upward of twenty actions. It will be remembered that the unprotected anchor of the *Merrimac* was shot away during the short battle with the *Congress* and the *Cumberland.* Having described the method of protecting the anchors, the mechanism adopted for manipulating the same remains to be explained. Referring to the illustration, it will be seen that a windlass is secured under the deck-beams near the anchor-well. The men working the handles of this mechanism were stationed in the hold of the vessel, and hence were most effectually protected against the enemy's shot, besides being completely out of sight. The Confederate artillerists were at first much surprised at witnessing the novel spectacle of vessels approaching their batteries, then stopping and remaining stationary for an indefinite time while firing, and then again departing, apparently without any intervention of anchor-gear. Our examination of this gear and the anchor-well affords a favorable opportunity of explaining the cause of Lieutenant Greene's alarm, mentioned in a statement recently published by a military journal, concerning a mysterious sound emanating from the said well during the passage of the *Monitor* from New York to Fort Monroe. Lieutenant Greene says that the sound from the anchor-well "resembled the death-groans of twenty men, and was the most dismal, awful sound [he] ever heard." Let us endeavor to trace to some physical cause this portentous sound. The reader will find, on close examination, that the chain cable which suspends the anchor passes through an aperture ("hawse-pipe") on the after side of the well, and that this pipe is very near the water-line; hence the slightest vertical depression of the bow will occasion a flow of water into the vessel. Obviously, any downward motion of the overhang will cause the air confined in the upper part of the well, when covered, to be blown through the hawse-pipe along with the admitted water, thereby producing a very discordant sound, repeated at every rise and fall of the bow during pitching. Lieutenant Greene also states that, apart from the reported sound, the vessel was flooded by the water which entered through the hawse-pipe; a statement suggesting that this flooding was the result of faulty construction, whereas it resulted from gross oversight on the part of the executive officer,—namely, in going to sea without stopping the opening round the chain-cable at the point where it passes through the side of the anchor-well.

The pilot-house is the next important object represented in the forward section of the illustration now under consideration. This structure is situated 10 feet from the anchor-well, its internal dimensions being 3 feet 6 inches long, 2 feet 8 inches wide, 3 feet 10 inches high above the plating of the deck; the sides consisting of solid blocks of wrought iron, 12 inches deep and 9 inches thick, firmly held down at the corner by 3-inch bolts passing through the iron-plated deck and deck-beams. The wheel, which by means of ordinary tiller-ropes operates the rudder, is placed within the pilot-house, its axle being supported by a bracket secured to the iron blocks as shown by the illustration. An ordinary ladder resting on the bottom of the vessel leads to the grated floor of the pilot-house. In order to afford the commanding officer and the pilot a clear view of objects before and on the sides of the vessel, the first and second iron blocks from the top are kept apart by packing pieces at the corners; long and narrow sight-holes being thereby formed extending round the pilot-house, and giving a clear view which sweeps round the entire horizon, all but that part which is hidden by the turret, hardly twelve degrees on each side of the line of keel. Regarding the adequacy of the elongated sight-hole formed between the iron blocks in the manner described, it should be borne in mind that an opening of five-eighths of an inch affords a vertical view 80 feet high at a distance of only 200 yards. More is not needed, a fact established during trials instituted by experts before the constructor delivered the vessel to the Government. Unfortunately the sight-holes were subsequently altered, the iron blocks being raised and the opening between them increased to such an extent that at sea, to quote Lieutenant Greene's report, the water entered "with such force as to knock the helmsman completely round from the wheel." It may be shown that but for the injudicious increase of the sight-holes, the commander of the *Monitor* would not have been temporarily blinded during the conflict at Hampton Roads, although he placed

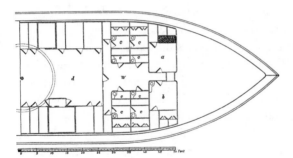

his vessel in such an extraordinary position that, according to Lieutenant Greene's report, "a shell from the enemy's gun, the muzzle not ten yards distant [from the side of the *Monitor*], struck the forward side of the pilot-house." The size of the sight-hole, after the injudicious increase, may be inferred from the re-ported fact that the blast caused by the explosion of the Confederate shell on striking the outside of the pilot-house had the power of "partly lifting the top." This "top," it should be observed, consisted of an iron plate two inches thick, let down into an appropriate groove, but not bolted down—a circumstance which called forth Lieutenant Greene's disapprobation. The object of the constructor in leaving the top plate of the pilot-house loose, so as to be readily pushed up from below, was that of affording egress to the crew in case of accident. Had the monitor *Tecumseh*, commanded by Captain T.A.M. Craven, when struck by a tor-pedo during the conflict in Mobile Bay, August 5th, 1864, been provided with a similar loose plate over the main hatch, the fearful calamity of drowning officers and crew would have been prevented. In referring to this untoward event, it should be observed that means had been provided in all the sea-going monitors to afford egress in case of injury to the hull: an opening in the turret-floor, when placed above a corresponding opening in the deck, formed a free passage to the turret, the top of which was provided with sliding hatches. Apparently the offi-cer in charge of the turret-gear of Captain Craven's vessel was not at his post, as he ought to have been during action, or else he had not been taught the imper-ative duty of placing the turret in such a position that these openings would admit of a free passage from below.[ψ]

Lieutenant Greene's report with reference to the position of the pilot-house calls for particular notice, his assertion being that he "could not fire ahead within several points of the bow." The distance between the center of the turret and the pilot-house being fifty-five feet, while the extreme breadth of the latter is only five feet, it will be found that by turning the turret through an angle of only *six degrees* from the center line of the vessel, the shot will clear the

---

[ψ]Under the circumstances of the sinking of the *Tecumseh*, the turret was no doubt being worked to meet the necessities of the battle, not to afford egress for the crew.—EDITORS.

pilot-house, a structure too substantial to suffer from the mere aërial current produced by the flight of the shot. Considering that the *Monitor*, as reported by Lieutenant Greene, was a "quick-turning vessel," the disadvantage of not being able to fire over the bow within *six degrees* of the line of keel is insignificant. Captain Coles claimed for his famous iron-clad turret-ship the advantage of an all-round fire, although the axis of his turret-guns had many times greater deviation from the line of keel than that of the *Monitor*.

The statement published by Lieutenant Greene, that the chief engineer of the vessel immediately after the engagement in Hampton Roads "suggested the clever plan of putting the pilot-house on top of the turret," is incorrect and calls for notice. The obvious device of placing the pilot-house in the center and above the turret was carefully considered before the *Monitor* turret was constructed, but could not be carried out for these reasons:

1. The turret of the battery was too light to support a structure large enough to accommodate the commanding officer, the pilot, and the steering-gear, under the severe condition of absolute impregnability against solid shot from guns of 10-inch caliber employed by the Confederates.
2. A central stationary pilot-house connected with the turret involved so much complication and additional work (see description of turret and pilot-houses further on), that had its adoption not been abandoned the *Monitor* would not have been ready to proceed to Hampton Roads until the beginning of April, 1862. The damage to the national cause which might have resulted from that delay is beyond computation.

The next important part of the battery delineated on the forward section of the illustration, namely, the quarters of the officers and crew, will now be con-

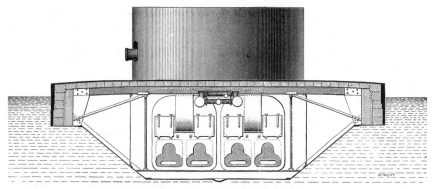

TRANSVERSE SECTION OF THE HULL OF THE ORIGINAL "MONITOR."

The diagram gives a front view of the boilers and furnaces: also a side elevation of the rotating cylindrical turret which proved impregnable against ten-inch solid shot fired with battering charges at very short range.

VIEW SHOWING THE EFFECT OF SHOT ON THE "MONITOR" TURRET.
FROM A PHOTOGRAPH TAKEN SOON AFTER THE ENGAGEMENT.

The ridges shown in the nearer port are significant of the haste with which the vessel was built. An opening of this shape is usually made by cutting three circles one above another and intersecting, and then trimming the edges to an oval. In this instance there was no time for the trimming process. Originally the armament was to be 15-inch guns, but as these could not be had in time, the 11-inch Dahlgrens were substituted.—EDITORS.

sidered; but before entering on a description it should be mentioned that in a small turret-vessel built for fighting, only one-half of the crew need be accommodated at a time, as the other half should be in and on the turret, the latter being always covered with a water-proof awning. Referring again to the forward and to part of the central section, it will be seen that the quarters extend from the transverse bulkhead under the turret to within five feet of the pilot-house, a distance of fifty feet; the forward portion, twenty-four feet in length, being occupied by the officers' quarters and extending across the battery from side to side. The height of the aft part of these quarters is 8 feet 6 inches under the deck-beams; while the height of the whole of the quarters of the crew is 8 feet 6 inches. A mere glance at the illustrations showing a side elevation and top view of internal arrangement [p. 279] gives a correct idea of the nature of the accommodations prepared for the officers and crew of the vessel which Lieutenant Greene regards as a "crude" structure, and of which he says: "Probably no ship was ever devised which was so uncomfortable for the crew." If this opinion were well founded, it would prove that submerged vessels like the monitors are unfit to live in.

Fortunately, the important question whether crews can live permanently below water-line has been set at rest by the report of the chief of the Bureau of Medicine and Surgery to the Secretary of the Navy, 1864. This minute and carefully considered report enabled the naval administration, organized by President Lincoln, to prove the healthfulness of the monitors, by the following clear presentation of the subject: "The monitor class of vessels, it is well known, have but a few inches of their hulls above the water-line, and in a heavy sea are entirely submerged. It has been doubted whether under such circumstances it would be possible long to preserve the health of the men on board, and consequently maintain the fighting material in a condition for effective service. It is gratifying, therefore, to know that an examination of the sick-reports, covering a period of over thirty months, shows that, so far from being unhealthy, there was less sickness on board the monitors than on the same number of wooden ships with an equal number of men and in similar exposed positions. The exemption from sickness upon the iron-clads in some instances is remarkable. There were on board the *Saugus,* from November 25th, 1864, to April 1st, 1865, a period of over four months, but four cases of sickness (excluding accidental injuries), and of these two were diseases with which the patients had suffered for years. On the *Montauk,* for a period of one hundred and sixty-five days prior to the 29th of May, 1865, there was but one case of disease on board. Other vessels of the class exhibit equally remarkable results, and the conclusion is reached that no wooden vessels in any squadron throughout the world can show an equal immunity from disease."

Apart from the ample size of the quarters on board the vessel, shown by the illustration, it should be mentioned that the system adopted for ventilating those quarters furnishes an abundant supply of fresh air by the following means. Two centrifugal blowers, driven by separate steam-engines, furnished seven thousand cubic feet of atmospheric air per minute by the process of suction through standing pipes on deck. Part of the air thus drawn in supported the combustion of the boiler furnaces, the remainder entering the lower part of the hull, gradually expelling the heated and vitiated air within the vessel. It has been imagined that the fresh air supplied by the blowers ought to have been conveyed to the quarters at the forward end of the vessel, by a system of conducting pipes. The laws of static balance, however, render the adoption of such a method unnecessary, since agreeably to those laws the fresh cold air, unless it be stopped by closed doors in the bulkheads, will find its way to every part of the bottom of the hull, gradually rising and expelling the upper heated strata through the hatches, and lastly through the grated top of the turret. Naval constructors who speculate on the cause of the extraordinary healthfulness of the monitors need not extend their researches beyond a thorough investigation of the system of ventilation just described.

Turret Department. The most important object delineated on the *central* section of the illustration, namely, the rotating turret, will now be considered; but before describing this essential part of the monitor system, it will be well to observe that the general belief is quite erroneous that a revolving platform, open or covered, is a novel design. So far from that being the case, this obvious device dates back to the first introduction of artillery. About 1820 the writer was taught by an instructor in fortification and gunnery that under certain conditions a position assailable from all sides should be defended by placing the guns on a turn-table. Long before building the *Monitor* I regarded the employment of a revolving structure to operate guns on board ships as a device familiar to all well-informed naval artillerists. But although constructors of revolving circular gun-platforms for naval purposes, open or covered, have a right to employ this ancient device, it will be demonstrated further on that the turret of the monitors is a distinct mechanical combination differing from previous inventions. The correctness of the assumption that revolving batteries for manipulating guns on board floating structures had been constructed nearly a century ago will be seen by the following reference to printed publications.

The "Nautical Chronicle" for 1805 contains an account of a "movable turning impregnable battery, invented by a Mr. Gillespie, a native of Scotland, who completed the model of a movable impregnable castle or battery, impervious to shot or bombs, provided with a cannon and carriage calculated to take a sure aim at any object." It is further stated that "the invention proposed will be found equally serviceable in floating batteries. Its machinery is adapted to turn the most ponderous mortars with the greatest case, according to the position of the enemy." Again, the Transactions of the Society for the Promotion of Useful Arts in the State of New York, 1807, contains an illustration representing a side elevation of a circular revolving floating battery constructed by Abraham Bloodgood. The guns of this battery, as the inventor points out, "would be more easily worked than is common, as they would not require any lateral movement." It is also stated, as a peculiar feature of this floating battery, that "its rotary motion would bring all its cannon to bear successively, as fast as they could be loaded, on objects in any direction"; and that "its circular form would cause every shot that might strike it, not near the center, to glance." Thirty-five years after the publication of the illustration and description of the circular floating revolving tower of Abraham Bloodgood, Theodore R. Timby proposed to build a tower on land for coast defense, to be composed of iron, with several floors and tiers of guns, the tower to turn on a series of friction-rollers under its base. The principal feature of Timby's "invention" was that of arranging the guns radially within the tower, and firing each gun at the instant of its coming in line with the object aimed at during the rotary motion of the tower, precisely as invented by Bloodgood. About 1865 certain influential citizens presented drawings of Timby's revolving tower to the authorities at Washington, with a view of obtaining orders to build such towers for coast defense; but the plan was found to be not only very expensive, but radically defective in principle. The slides of the gun-carriages being fixed permanently in a radial direction within the tower, the guns, of course, are directed to all points of the compass. Hence, during an attack by a hostile fleet, with many ships abreast, only one assailant can be fired at, its companions being scot-free in the dead angle formed between the effective gun and the guns on either side. In the meantime the numerous guns, distributed round the tower on the several floors, cannot be fired until their time comes during the revolution of the tower. The enemy's fleet continuing its advance, of course, calls for a change of elevation of the pieces, which, considering the constant revolution of the tower and the different altitudes above the sea of the several tiers, presents perplexing difficulties. Nothing further need be said to explain why the Government did not accept the plans for Timby's revolving towers.

The origin of rotating circular gun-platforms being disposed of, the consideration of the central section of the illustration will now be resumed. It will be seen that the turret which protects the guns and gunners of the *Monitor* consists simply of a short cylinder resting on the deck, covered with a grated iron roof provided with sliding hatches. This cylinder is composed of eight thicknesses of wrought-iron plates, each one inch thick, firmly riveted together, the inside course, which extends below the rest, being accurately faced underneath. A flat, broad ring of bronze is let into the deck, its upper face being very smooth in order to form a water-tight joint with the base of the turret without the employment of any elastic packing, a peculiar feature of the turrets of the monitors, as will be seen further on. Unfortunately, before the *Monitor* left New York for Hampton Roads, it was suggested at the Navy Yard to insert a plaited hemp rope between the base of the turret and the bronze ring, for the purpose of making the joint perfectly water-tight. As might have been supposed, the rough and uneven hemp rope did not form a perfect joint; hence during the passage a great leak was

ISAAC NEWTON, FIRST
ASSISTANT-ENGINEER OF THE
"MONITOR." FROM A MEDALLION
PORTRAIT BY LAUNT THOMPSON.

At the time of Mr. Newton's death (September 25, 1884) he had been for several years Chief Engineer of the Croton Aqueduct. The plans which have been adopted for the new aqueduct were his, both in the general features and the details.—EDITORS.

observed at intervals as the sea washed over the decks. "The water came down under the turret like a waterfall," says Lieutenant Greene in his report. It will be proper to observe in this place that the "foundering" of the *Monitor* on its way to Charleston was not caused by the "separation of the upper and lower part of the hull," as was imagined by persons who possessed no knowledge of the method adopted by the builders in joining the upper and lower hulls. Again, those who asserted that the plates had been torn asunder at the junction of the hulls did not consider that severe strain cannot take place in a structure nearly submerged. The easy motion at sea, peculiar to the monitors, was pointed out by several of their commanders. Lieutenant Greene in his report to the Secretary of the Navy, dated on board the *Monitor,* March 27th, 1862, says with reference to sea-going qualities:

> "During her passage from New York her roll was very easy and slow and not at all deep. She pitched very little and with no strain whatever."

Captain John Rodgers's report to the Secretary of the Navy, dated on board the monitor *Weehawken,* January 22d, 1863, refers specially to the easy motion of his vessel:

> "On Tuesday night, when off Chincoteague shoals, we had a very heavy gale from the E.N.E. with a very heavy sea, made confused and dangerous by the proximity of the land. The waves I measured after the sea abated; I found them twenty-three feet high. They were certainly seven feet higher in the midst of the storm. During the heaviest of the gale I stood upon the turret and admired the behavior of the vessel. She rose and fell to the waves, and I concluded that the monitor form had great sea-going qualities. If leaks were prevented no hurricane could injure her."

The true cause of the foundering of the *Monitor* was minutely explained to the writer some time after the occurrence by the engineer, a very intelligent person, who operated the centrifugal pumping-engine of the vessel at the time. According to his statement, oakum was packed under the base of the turret before going to sea, in order to make sure of a water-tight joint; but this expedient failed altogether, the sea gradually washing out the oakum in those places where it had been loosely packed, thereby permitting so large a quantity of water to enter under the turret, fully sixty-three feet in circumference, that the centrifugal pumping-engine had not sufficient power to expel it. The hull consequently filled gradually and settled, until at the expiration of about four hours the *Monitor* went to the bottom. It will be asked, in view of the preceding explanation of the construction of the monitor turrets, namely, that the smooth base of the turret forms a water-tight joint with the ring on the deck, why was oakum packed under the turret before going to Charleston? The commander of the vessel, Captain Bankhead, in his report of the foundering, adverts to the admission of water under the turret, but does not duly consider the serious character of the leak, sixty-three feet in length. Captain Bankhead evidently had not carefully investigated the matter when he attributed

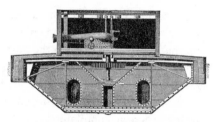

TRANSVERSE SECTION OF THE "MONITOR" THROUGH THE CENTER OF THE TURRET.

the accident to an imaginary separation of the upper and lower hull.[+] It should be observed, in justice to this officer, that having commanded the *Monitor* only during a brief period he possessed but an imperfect knowledge of his vessel, and probably knew nothing regarding the consequence of employing packing, —namely, that it might cause "water to come down under the turret like a waterfall," as previously reported by the second officer in command. It is proper to mention as a mitigating circumstance in favor of the second officer, Lieutenant Greene, that previous to the battle in Hampton Roads he had "never performed any but midshipman duty." The important question, therefore, must remain unanswered, whether in the hands of an older and more experienced executive officer the *Monitor,* like the other vessels of her type, might not have reached Charleston in safety.

Referring again to the central part of the illustration [p. 275] and the sectional representation of the turret [above], it will be found that the guns are placed across the vessel; consequently only the end of the breech and upper part of the port-hole are seen. The object of the pendulum port-stoppers suspended under the roof is to afford protection to the turret crew while loading

---

[+]Captain J. P. Bankhead says in his report:

"Found [in the morning] that the packing of oakum under and around the base had loosened somewhat from the working of the tower as the vessel pitched and rolled... towards evening the swell somewhat decreased, the bilge-pumps being found amply sufficient to keep her clear of the water that penetrated through the sight-hole of the pilot-house, hawsehole, and base of tower (all of which had been well calked previous to leaving). At 7:30 the wind hauled more to the south.... Found the vessel towed badly, yawing very much, and with the increased motion making somewhat more water around the base of the tower.... 8 P.M.; the sea about this time commenced to rise very rapidly, causing the vessel to plunge heavily, completely submerging the pilot-house, and washing over and into the turret, and at times into the blower-pipes. Observed that when she rose to the swell, the flat under-surface of the projecting armor would come down with great force, causing a considerable shock to the vessel and turret, thereby loosening still more the packing around its base.... I am firmly of the opinion that the *Monitor* must have sprung a leak somewhere in the forward part, where the hull joins on to the armor, and that it was caused by the heavy shocks received as she came down upon the sea."

—Editors.

the guns. Generally, however, the turret should be moved, and the port-holes thereby turned away from the enemy. Much time was lost during the conflict with the *Merrimac* by closing the port-stoppers in place of merely moving the turret, the latter operation being performed by a small steam-engine controlled by a single hand; while opening and closing the port-stoppers, as reported by Lieutenant Greene, required the entire gun-crew. The slow fire of the *Monitor* during the action, complained of by critics, was no doubt occasioned by an injudicious manipulation of the port-stoppers. There are occasions, however, when the turret should not be turned, in which case the port-stoppers are indispensable. The method adopted for turning the turret will be readily understood. The small steam-engine controlled by one man, before referred to, drives a double train of cog-wheels connected with the vertical axle of the turret, this axle being stepped in a bronze bearing secured to the central bulkhead of the vessel. The mechanism thus described was carefully tested before the *Monitor* left New York for Hampton Roads, and was found to move very freely, the turret being turned and the guns accurately pointed by the sailing-master without aid. The trouble reported by Lieutenant Greene regarding the manipulation of the turret was caused by inattention during the passage from New York, the working-gear having been permitted to rust for want of proper cleaning and oiling while exposed to the action of salt-water entering under the turret, from causes already explained.

Having thus briefly described the turret and its mechanism, our investigation of the central part of the sectional view of the battery will be completed by a mere reference to the steam-boilers placed aft of the turret. There are two of these boilers placed side by side, as shown in the cut on page 279. Two views being thus presented, the nature of the boilers will be understood without further explanation. It should be mentioned, however, that they proved very economical and efficient.

Aft Section. The following brief reference to this section of the sectional illustration, showing the motive engine, propeller, and rudder, will complete our description:

1. The motive engine, the construction of which is somewhat peculiar, consists of only one steam-cylinder with pistons applied at opposite ends, a steam-tight partition being introduced in the middle. The propeller-shaft has only one crank and one crank-pin, the difficulty of "passing the centers" being overcome by the expedient of placing the connecting-rods, actuated by the steam-pistons, at right angles to each other. Much space is saved within the vessel by employing only one steam-cylinder, an advantage of such importance in the short hulls of the monitors that the entire fleet built during the war was provided with engines of the stated type.

2. The propeller, being of the ordinary four-bladed type, needs no description; but the mode of protecting it against shot demands full explanation. Referring to the illustration, it will be seen that the under side of the over-hang near the stern is cut out in the middle, forming a

SINKING OF THE "MONITOR."

cavity needed to give free sweep to the propeller-blades; the slope of the cavity on either side of the propeller being considerably inclined in order to favor a free passage of the water to and from the propeller-blades.

3. The extreme beam at the forward side of the propeller-well is 31 feet, while the diameter of the propeller is only 9 feet; it will therefore be seen that the deck and side armor projects 11 feet on each side, thus protecting most effectually the propelling instrument as well as the equipoise rudder applied aft of the same. It will be readily admitted that no other vessel constructed here or elsewhere has such thorough protection to rudder and propeller as that just described.

The foregoing description of the hastily constructed steam-battery proves that, so far from being, as generally supposed, a rude specimen of naval construction, the *Monitor* displayed careful planning, besides workmanship of superior quality. Experts who examined the vessel and machinery after completion pronounced the entire structure a fine specimen of naval engineering.

The conflict in Hampton Roads, and the immediate building of a fleet of sea-going monitors by the United States Government, attracted great attention in all maritime countries, especially in the north of Europe. Admiral Lessoffsky, of the Russian navy, was at once ordered to be present during the completion and trial of our sea-going monitors. The report of this talented officer to his government being favorable, the Emperor immediately ordered a fleet of twelve vessels on the new system, to be constructed according to copies of the working-drawings from which the American sea-going monitors had been built. Sweden and Norway also forthwith laid the keels of a fleet of seven vessels of the new type, Turkey rapidly following the example of the northern European nations. It will be remembered that during the naval contest on the Danube the Russian batteries and torpedo-boats subjected the Turkish monitors to severe tests. England, in due course, adopted our turret system, discarding the turn-table and cupola.

CHAPTER 9

THE FIRST FIGHT OF IRON-CLADS.

John Taylor Wood, Colonel, C.S.A.

The engagement in Hampton Roads on the 8th of March, 1862, between the Confederate iron-clad *Virginia*, or the *Merrimac* (as she is known at the North), and the United States wooden fleet, and that on the 9th between the *Virginia* and the *Monitor*, was, in its results, in some respects the most momentous naval conflict ever witnessed. No battle was ever more widely discussed or produced a greater sensation. It revolutionized the navies of the world. Line-of-battle ships, those huge, overgrown craft, carrying from eighty to one hundred and twenty guns and from five hundred to twelve hundred men, which, from the destruction of the Spanish Armada to our time, had done most of the fighting, deciding the fate of empires, were at once universally condemned as out of date. Rams and iron-clads were in future to decide all naval warfare. In this battle old things passed away, and the experience of a thousand years of battle and breeze was forgotten. The naval supremacy of England vanished in the smoke of this fight, it is true, only to reappear some years later more commanding than ever. The effect of the news was best described by the London "Times," which said: "Whereas we had available for immediate purposes one hundred and forty-nine first-class war-ships, we have now two, these two being the *Warrior* and her sister *Ironside*. There is not now a ship in the English navy apart from these two that it would not be madness to trust to an engagement with that little *Monitor*." The Admi-

ralty at once proceeded to reconstruct the navy, cutting down a number of their largest ships and converting them into turret or broadside iron-clads.

The same results were produced in France, which had but one sea-going iron-clad, *La Gloire,* and this one, like the *Warrior,* was only protected amidships. The Emperor Napoleon promptly appointed a commission to devise plans for rebuilding his navy. And so with all the maritime powers. In this race the United States took the lead, and at the close of the war led all the others in the numbers and efficiency of its iron-clad fleet. It is true that all the great powers had already experimented with vessels partly armored, but very few were convinced of their utility, and none had been tried by the test of battle, if we except a few floating batteries, thinly clad, used in the Crimean War.

In the spring of 1861 Norfolk and its large naval establishment had been hurriedly abandoned by the Federals, why no one could tell. It is about twelve miles from Fort Monroe, which was then held by a large force of regulars. A few companies of these, with a single frigate, could have occupied and commanded the town and navy yard and kept the channel open. However, a year later, it was as quickly evacuated by the Confederates, and almost with as little reason. But of this I will speak later.

The yard was abandoned to a few volunteers, after it was partly destroyed, and a large number of ships were burnt. Among the spoils were upward of

THE BURNING OF THE FRIGATE "MERRIMAC" AND OF THE GOSPORT NAVY YARD.

twelve hundred heavy guns, which were scattered among Confederate fortifications from the Potomac to the Mississippi. Among the ships burnt and sunk was the frigate *Merrimac* of 3500 tons and 40 guns, afterward rechristened the *Virginia*, and so I will call her. During the summer of 1861 Lieutenant John M. Brooke, an accomplished officer of the old navy, who with many others had resigned, proposed to Secretary Mallory to raise and rebuild this ship as an iron-clad. His plans were approved, and orders were given to carry them out. She was raised and cut down to the old berth-deck. Both ends for seventy feet were covered over, and when the ship was in fighting trim were just awash. On the midship section, 170 feet in length, was built at an angle of 45 degrees a roof of pitch-pine and oak 24 inches thick, extending from the water-line to a height over the gun-deck of 7 feet. Both ends of the shield were rounded so that the pivot-guns could be used as bow and stern chasers or quartering. Over the gun-deck was a light grating, making a promenade about twenty feet wide. The wood backing was covered with iron plates, rolled at the Tredegar works, two inches thick and eight wide. The first tier was put on horizontally, the second up and down,—in all to the thickness of four inches, bolted through the wood-work and clinched. The prow was of cast-iron, projecting four feet, and badly secured, as events proved. The rudder and propeller were entirely unprotected. The pilot-house was forward of the smoke-stack, and covered with the same thickness of iron as the sides. The motive power was the same that had always been in the ship. Both of the engines and boilers had been condemned on her return from her last cruise, and were radically defective. Of course, the fire and sinking had not improved them. We could not depend upon them for six hours at a time. A more ill-contrived or unreliable pair of engines could only have been found in some vessels of the United States navy.

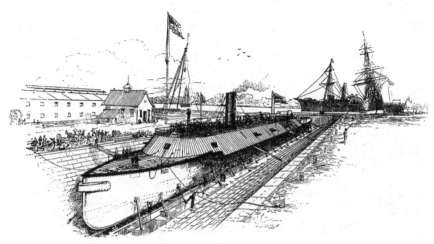

REMODELING THE "MERRIMAC" AT THE GOSPORT NAVY YARD.

Lieutenant Catesby ap R. Jones was ordered to superintend the armament, and no more thoroughly competent officer could have been selected. To his experience and skill as her ordnance and executive officer was due the character of her battery, which proved so efficient. It consisted of 2 7-inch rifles, heavily reënforced around the breech with 3-inch steel bands, shrunk on. These were the first heavy guns so made, and were the bow and stern pivots. There were also 2 6-inch rifles of the same make, and 6 9-inch smooth-bore broadside,—10 guns in all.

During the summer and fall of 1861 I had been stationed at the batteries on the Potomac at Evansport and Aquia Creek, blockading the river as far as possible. In January, 1862, I was ordered to the *Virginia* as one of the lieutenants, reporting to Commodore French Forrest, who then commanded the navy yard at Norfolk. Commodore Franklin Buchanan was appointed to the command,—an energetic and high-toned officer, who combined with daring courage great professional ability, standing deservedly at the head of his profession. In 1845 he had been selected by Mr. Bancroft, Secretary of the Navy, to locate and organize the Naval Academy, and he launched that institution upon its successful career. Under him were as capable a set of officers as ever were brought together in one ship. But of man-of-war's men or sailors we had scarcely any. The South was almost without a maritime population. In the old service the majority of officers were from the South, and all the seamen from the North.[†]

Every one had flocked to the army, and to it we had to look for a crew. Some few seamen were found in Norfolk, who had escaped from the gun-boat flotilla in the waters of North Carolina, on their occupation by Admiral Goldsborough and General Burnside. In hopes of securing some men from the army, I was sent to the headquarters of General Magruder at Yorktown, who was known to have under his command two battalions from New Orleans, among whom might be found a number of seamen. The general, though pressed for want of men, holding a long line with scarcely a brigade, gave me every facility to secure volunteers. With one of his staff I visited every camp, and the commanding officers were ordered to parade their men, and I explained to them what I wanted. About 200 volunteered, and of this number I selected 80 who had had some experience as seamen or gunners. Other commands at Richmond

---

[†] The officers of the *Merrimac* were: *Flag-Officer,* Franklin Buchanan; *Lieutenants,* Catesby ap R. Jones (executive and ordnance officer), Charles C. Simms, R. D. Minor (flag), Hunter Davidson, John Taylor Wood, J. R. Eggleston, Walter Butt; *Midshipmen,* Foute, Marmaduke, Littlepage, Craig, Long, and Rootes; *Paymaster,* James Semple; *Surgeon,* Dinwiddie B. Phillips; *Assistant-Surgeon,* Algernon S. Garnett; *Captain of Marines,* Reuben Thom; *Engineers,* H. A. Ramsey, acting chief; *Assistants,* Tynan, Campbell, Herring, Jack, and White; *Boatswain,* Hasker; *Gunner,* Oliver; *Carpenter,* Lindsey; *Clerk,* Arthur Sinclair, Jr.; *Volunteer Aides,* Lieutenant Douglas Forrest, C.S.A., Captain Thomas Kevill, detachment of Norfolk United Artillery; *Signal Corps,* Sergeant Tabb.

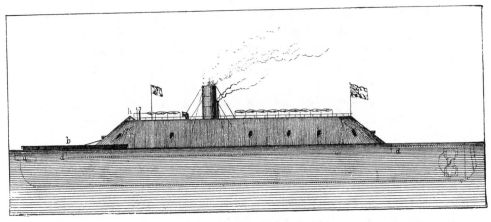

LT. R. L. BLACKFORD, DEL. MARCH 7, 1862.

THE "MERRIMAC," FROM A SKETCH MADE THE DAY BEFORE THE FIGHT.

a PROW, OF STEEL.
b WOODEN BULWARK.
h PILOT-HOUSE.
d IRON UNDER WATER.
f PROPELLER.

and Petersburg were visited, and so our crew of three hundred was made up. They proved themselves to be as gallant and trusty a body of men as any one would wish to command, not only in battle, but in reverse and retreat.

LIEUTENANT CATESBY AP R. JONES.
FROM A PHOTOGRAPH.

Notwithstanding every exertion to hasten the fitting out of the ship, the work during the winter progressed but slowly, owing to delay in sending the iron sheathing from Richmond. At this time the only establishment in the South capable of rolling iron plates was the Tredegar foundry. Its resources were limited, and the demand for all kinds of war material most pressing. And when we reflect upon the scarcity and inexperience of the workmen, and the great changes necessary in transforming an ordinary iron workshop into an arsenal in which all the machinery and tools had to be improvised, it is astonishing that so much was accomplished. The un-

FRANKLIN BUCHANAN,
ADMIRAL, C.S.N.

JOSIAH TATTNALL,
COMMODORE, C.S.N.

COMMANDERS OF THE "VIRGINIA" (OR "MERRIMAC"). FROM A PHOTOGRAPH.

finished state of the vessel interfered so with the drills and exercises that we had but little opportunity of getting things into shape. It should be remembered that the ship was an experiment in naval architecture, differing in every respect from any then afloat. The officers and the crew were strangers to the ship and to each other. Up to the hour of sailing she was crowded with workmen. Not a gun had been fired, hardly a revolution of the engines had been made, when we cast off from the dock and started on what many thought was an ordinary trial trip, but which proved to be a trial such as no vessel that ever floated had undergone up to that time. From the start we saw that she was slow, not over five knots; she steered so badly that, with her great length, it took from thirty to forty minutes to turn. She drew twenty-two feet, which confined us to a comparatively narrow channel in the Roads; and, as I have before said, the engines were our weak point. She was as unmanageable as a water-logged vessel.

It was at noon on the 8th of March that we steamed down the Elizabeth River. Passing by our batteries, lined with troops, who cheered us as we passed, and through the obstructions at Craney Island, we took the south channel and headed for Newport News. At anchor at this time off Fort Monroe were the frigates *Minnesota, Roanoke,* and *St. Lawrence,* and several gun-boats. The first two were sister ships of the *Virginia* before the war; the last was a sailing frigate of fifty guns. Off Newport News, seven miles above, which was strongly fortified and held by a large Federal garrison, were anchored the frigate *Congress,* 50 guns, and the sloop *Cumberland,* 30. The day was calm, and the last two ships were swinging lazily by their anchors. [The tide was at its height about 1:40 P.M.] Boats were hanging to the lower booms, washed clothes in the rigging. Nothing indicated that we were expected; but when we came within three-quarters of a mile, the boats were dropped astern, booms got alongside, and the *Cumberland* opened with her heavy pivots, followed by the *Congress,* the gun-boats, and the shore batteries.

COLONEL JOHN TAYLOR WOOD, LIEUTENANT ON THE "MERRIMAC." FROM AN OIL PORTRAIT.

We reserved our fire until within easy range, when the forward pivot was pointed and fired by Lieutenant Charles Simms, killing and wounding most of the crew of the after pivot-gun of the *Cumberland.* Passing close to the *Congress,* which received our starboard broadside, and returned it with spirit, we steered direct for the

Cumberland, striking her almost at right angles, under the fore-rigging on the starboard side. The blow was hardly perceptible on board the *Virginia.* Backing clear of her, we went ahead again, heading up the river, helm hard-a-starboard, and turned slowly. As we did so, for the first time I had an opportunity of using the after-pivot, of which I had charge. As we swung, the *Congress* came in range, nearly stern on, and we got in three raking shells. She had slipped her anchor, loosed her foretop-sail, run up the jib, and tried to escape, but grounded. Turning, we headed for her and took a position within two hundred yards, where every shot told. In the meantime the *Cumberland* continued the fight, though our ram had opened her side wide enough to drive in a horse and cart. Soon she listed to port and filled rapidly. The crew were driven by the advancing water to the spar-deck, and there worked her pivot-guns until she went down with a roar, the colors still flying. No ship was ever fought more gallantly.[✦] The *Congress* continued the unequal contest for more than an hour after the sinking of the *Cumberland.* Her losses were terrible, and finally she ran up the white flag.

As soon as we had hove in sight, coming down the harbor, the *Roanoke, St. Lawrence,* and *Minnesota,* assisted by tugs, had got under way, and started up from Old Point Comfort to join their consorts. They were under fire from the batteries at Sewell's Point, but the distance was too great to effect much. The first two, however, ran aground not far above Fort Monroe, and took but little part in the fight. The *Minnesota,* taking the middle or swash channel, steamed up half-way between Old Point Comfort and Newport News, when she grounded, but in a position to be actively engaged.

Previous to this we had been joined by the James River squadron, which had been at anchor a few miles above, and came into action most gallantly, passing the shore batteries at Newport News under a heavy fire, and with some loss. It consisted of the *Yorktown* (or *Patrick Henry*), 12 guns, Captain John R. Tucker; *Jamestown,* 2 guns, Lieut.-Commander J. N. Barney; and *Teaser,* 1 gun, Lieut.-Commander W. A. Webb.

As soon as the *Congress* surrendered, Commander Buchanan ordered the gun-boats *Beaufort,* Lieut.-Commander W. H. Parker, and *Raleigh,* Lieut.-Commander J. W. Alexander, to steam alongside, take off her crew, and set fire to the ship. Lieutenant Pendergrast, who had succeeded Lieutenant Smith, who had been killed, surrendered to Lieutenant Parker, of the *Beaufort.* Delivering his sword and colors, he was directed by Lieutenant Parker to return to his ship

---

[✦]According to the pilot of the *Cumberland,* A. B. Smith: "Near the middle of the fight, when the berth-deck of the *Cumberland* had sunk below water, one of the crew of the *Merrimac* came out of a port to the outside of her iron-plate roof, and a ball from one of our guns instantly cut him in two.... Finally, after about three-fourths of an hour of the most severe fighting, our vessel sank, the Stars and Stripes still waving. That flag was finally submerged, but after the hull grounded on the sands, fifty-four feet below,...our pennant was still flying from the top-mast above the waves."

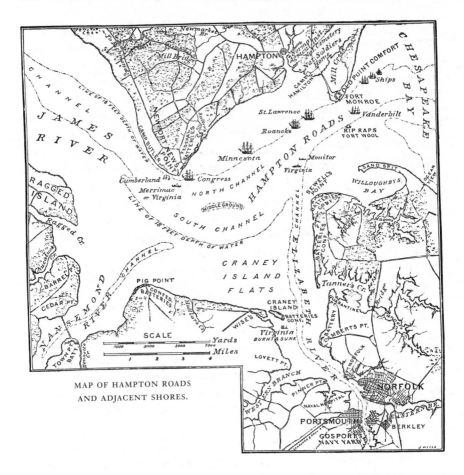

MAP OF HAMPTON ROADS
AND ADJACENT SHORES.

and have the wounded transferred as rapidly as possible. All this time the shore batteries and small-arm men were keeping up an incessant fire on our vessels. Two of the officers of the *Raleigh,* Lieutenant Tayloe and Midshipman Hutter, were killed while assisting the Union wounded out of the *Congress.* A number of the enemy's men were killed by the same fire. Finally it became so hot that the gun-boats were obliged to haul off with only thirty prisoners, leaving Lieutenant Pendergrast and most of his crew on board, and they all afterward escaped to the shore by swimming or in small boats. While this was going on, the white flag was flying at her mainmasthead. Not being able to take possession of his prize, the commodore ordered hot shot to be used, and in a short time she was in flames fore and aft. While directing this, both himself and his flag-lieutenant, Minor, were severely wounded. The command then devolved upon Lieutenant Catesby Jones.

It was now 5 o'clock, nearly two hours of daylight, and the *Minnesota* only remained. She was aground and at our mercy. But the pilots would not attempt

THE "MERRIMAC" RAMMING THE "CUMBERLAND."

the middle channel with the ebb tide and approaching night. So we returned by the south channel to Sewell's Point and anchored, the *Minnesota* escaping, as we thought, only until morning.

Our loss in killed and wounded was twenty-one. The armor was hardly damaged, though at one time our ship was the focus on which were directed at least one hundred heavy guns, afloat and ashore. But nothing outside escaped. Two guns were disabled by having their muzzles shot off. The ram was left in the side of the *Cumberland.* One anchor, the smoke-stack, and the steam-pipes were shot away. Railings, stanchions, boat-davits, everything was swept clean. The flag-staff was repeatedly knocked over, and finally a boarding-pike was used. Commodore Buchanan and the other wounded were sent to the Naval Hospital, and after making preparations for the next day's fight, we slept at our guns, dreaming of other victories in the morning.♭

But at daybreak we discovered, lying between us and the *Minnesota*, a strange-looking craft, which we knew at once to be Ericsson's *Monitor,* which had long been expected in Hampton Roads, and of which, from different sources, we had a good idea. She could not possibly have made her appearance

---

♭Lieutenant Jones reported: "It was not easy to keep a flag flying. The flag-staffs were repeatedly shot away. The colors were hoisted to the smoke-stack and several times cut down from it."—EDITORS.

LIEUTENANT GEORGE U. MORRIS,
ACTING COMMANDER OF THE
"CUMBERLAND."

In the absence of Captain Radford, the command of the *Cumberland* devolved upon the executive officer, Lieutenant Morris, from whose official report we quote the following: "At thirty minutes past three the water had gained upon us, notwithstanding the pumps were kept actively employed to a degree that, the forward-magazine being drowned, we had to take powder from the after-magazine for the ten-inch gun. At thirty-five minutes past three the water had risen to the main hatchway, and the ship canted to port, and we delivered a parting fire—each man trying to save himself by jumping overboard. Timely notice was given, and all the wounded who could walk were ordered out of the cockpit: but those of the wounded who had been carried into the sick-bay and on the berth-deck were so mangled that it was impossible to save them.... I should judge we have lost upward of one hundred men. I can only say, in conclusion, that all did their duty, and we sank with the American flag flying at the peak." When summoned to surrender, Morris replied, "Never! I'll sink alongside!"

—Editors.

at a more inopportune time for us, changing our plans, which were to destroy the *Minnesota,* and then the remainder of the fleet below Fort Monroe. She appeared but a pigmy compared with the lofty frigate which she guarded. But in her size was one great element of her success. I will not attempt a description of the *Monitor;* her build and peculiarities are well known.

After an early breakfast, we got under way and steamed out toward the enemy, opening fire from our bow pivot, and closing in to deliver our starboard broadside at short range, which was returned promptly from her 11-inch guns. Both vessels then turned and passed again still closer. The *Monitor* was firing every seven or eight minutes, and nearly every shot struck. Our ship was working worse and worse, and after the loss of the smoke-stack, Mr. Ramsey, chief engineer, reported that the draught was so poor that it was with great difficulty he could keep up steam. Once or twice the ship was on the bottom. Drawing 22 feet of water, we were confined to a narrow channel, while the *Monitor,* with only 12 feet immersion, could take any position, and always have us in range of her guns. Orders were given to concentrate our fire on the pilot-house, and with good result, as we afterward learned. More than two hours had passed, and we had made no impression on the enemy so far as we could discover, while our wounds were slight. Several times the *Monitor* ceased firing, and

THE "MERRIMAC" DRIVING THE "CONGRESS" FROM HER ANCHORAGE.

we were in hopes she was disabled, but the revolution again of her turret and the heavy blows of her 11-inch shot on our sides soon undeceived us.

Coming down from the spar-deck, and observing a division standing "at ease," Lieutenant Jones inquired:

"Why are you not firing, Mr. Eggleston?"

"Why, our powder is very precious," replied the lieutenant; "and after two hours' incessant firing I find that I can do her about as much damage by snapping my thumb at her every two minutes and a half."

Lieutenant Jones now determined to run her down or board her. For nearly an hour we manœuvred for a position. Now "Go ahead!" now "Stop!" now "Astern!" The ship was as unwieldy as Noah's ark. At last an opportunity offered. "Go ahead, full speed!" But before the ship gathered headway, the *Monitor* turned, and our disabled ram only gave a glancing blow, effecting nothing. Again she came up on our quarter, her bow against our side, and at this distance fired twice. Both shots struck about half-way up the shield, abreast of the after pivot, and the impact forced the side in bodily two or three inches. All the crews of the after guns were knocked over by the concussion, and bled from the nose or ears. Another shot at the same place would have penetrated. While alongside, boarders were called away; but she dropped astern before they could get on board. And so, for six or more hours, the struggle was kept up. At length, the

Monitor withdrew over the middle ground where we could not follow, but always maintaining a position to protect the *Minnesota.*⁄ To have run our ship ashore on a falling tide would have been ruin. We awaited her return for an hour; and at 2 o'clock P.M. steamed to Sewell's Point, and thence to the dockyard at Norfolk, our crew thoroughly worn out from the two days' fight. Although there is no doubt that the *Monitor* first retired,—for Captain Van Brunt, commanding the *Minnesota,* so states in his official report,—the battle was a drawn one, so far as the two vessels engaged were concerned. But in its general results the advantage was with the *Monitor.* Our casualties in the second day's fight were only a few wounded.

This action demonstrated for the first time the power and efficiency of the ram as a means of offense. The side of the *Cumberland* was crushed like an eggshell. The *Congress* and *Minnesota,* even with our disabled bow, would have shared the same fate but that we could not reach them on account of our great draught.

It also showed the power of resistance of two iron-clads, widely differing in construction, model, and armament, under a fire which in a short time would have sunk any other vessel then afloat.

The *Monitor* was well handled, and saved the *Minnesota* and the remainder of the fleet at Fort Monroe. But her gunnery was poor. Not a single shot struck us at the water-line, where the ship was utterly unprotected, and where one would have been fatal. Or had the fire been concentrated on any one spot, the shield would have been pierced; or had larger charges been used, the result would have been the same. Most of her shot struck us obliquely, breaking the iron of both courses, but not injuring the wood backing. When struck at right

⁄In his official report, Captain Van Brunt says of the fight, as viewed from the *Minnesota:*

"At 6 A.M. the enemy again appeared,... and I beat to quarters; but they ran past my ship and were heading for Fortress Monroe, and the retreat was beaten to enable my men to get something to eat. The *Merrimac* ran down near the Rip-Raps and then turned into the channel through which I had come. Again all hands were called to quarters, and opened upon her with my stern-guns, and made signal to the *Monitor* to attack the enemy. She immediately ran down in my wake, right within the range of the *Merrimac,* completely covering my ship, as far as was possible with her diminutive dimensions, and, much to my astonishment, laid herself right alongside of the *Merrimac,* and the contrast was that of a pigmy to a giant. Gun after gun was fired by the *Monitor,* which was returned with whole broadsides from the Rebels, with no more effect, apparently, than so many pebble-stones thrown by a child.... The *Merrimac,* finding that she could make nothing of the *Monitor,* turned her attention once more to me. In the morning she had put one eleven-inch shot under my counter, near the water-line, and now, on her second approach, I opened upon her with all my broadside-guns and ten-inch pivot—a broadside which would have blown out of water any timber-built ship in the world. She returned my fire with her rifled bow-gun, with a shell which passed through the chief engineer's state-room, through the engineers' mess-room amidships, and burst in the boatswain's room, tearing four rooms all into one, in its passage exploding two charges of powder, which set the ship on fire, but it was promptly extinguished by a party headed by my first lieutenant."

ESCAPE OF PART OF THE CREW OF THE "CONGRESS."

angles, the backing would be broken, but not penetrated. We had no solid projectiles, except a few of large windage, to be used as hot shot, and, of course, made no impression on the turret. But in all this it should be borne in mind that both vessels were on their trial trip, both were experimental, and both were receiving their baptism of fire.

On our arrival at Norfolk, Commodore Buchanan sent for me. I found him at the Naval Hospital, badly wounded and suffering greatly. He dictated a short dispatch to Mr. Mallory, Secretary of the Navy, stating the return of the ship and the result of the two days' fight, and directed me to proceed to Richmond with it and the flag of the *Congress,* and make a verbal report of the action, condition of the *Virginia,* etc.

I took the first train for Petersburg and the capital. The news had preceded me, and at every station I was warmly received, and to listening crowds was forced to repeat the story of the fight. Arriving at Richmond, I drove to Mr. Mallory's office and with him went to President Davis's, where we met Mr. Benjamin, who, a few days afterward, became Secretary of State, Mr. Seddon, afterward Secretary of War, General Cooper, Adjutant-General, and a number of others. I told at length what had occurred on the previous two days, and what changes and repairs were necessary to the *Virginia.* As to the future, I said that in the *Monitor* we had met our equal, and that the result of another engagement would be very doubtful. Mr. Davis made many inquiries as regarded the ship's draught, speed, and capabilities, and urged the completion of the repairs at as early a day as possible. The conversation lasted until near midnight. During the evening the flag of the *Congress,* which was a very large one, was brought in, and to our surprise, in unfolding it, we found it in some places saturated with blood. On this discovery it was quickly rolled up and sent to the Navy Department, where it remained during the war; it doubtless burned with that building when Richmond was evacuated.

The news of our victory was received everywhere in the South with the most enthusiastic rejoicing. Coming, as it did, after a number of disasters in the south and west, it was particularly grateful. Then again, under the circumstances, so little was expected from the navy that this success was entirely unlooked for. So, from one extreme to the other, the most extravagant anticipations were formed of what the ship could do. For instance: the blockade could be raised, Washington leveled to the ground, New York laid under contribution, and so on. At the North, equally groundless alarm was felt. As an example of this, Secretary Welles relates what took place at a Cabinet meeting called by Mr. Lincoln on the receipt of the news.☆ "'The *Merrimac,*' said Stanton, 'will change the whole character of the war; she will destroy, *seriatim,* every naval vessel; she will lay all the cities on the seaboard under contribution. I shall im-

---

☆The "news" was of the first day's battle before the *Monitor* had arrived.—EDITORS.

mediately recall Burnside; Port Royal must be abandoned. I will notify the governors and municipal authorities in the North to take instant measures to protect their harbors.' He had no doubt, he said, that the monster was at this moment on her way to Washington; and, looking out of the window, which commanded a view of the Potomac for many miles, 'Not unlikely, we shall have a shell or cannon-ball from one of her guns in the White House before we leave this room.' Mr. Seward, usually buoyant and self-reliant, overwhelmed with the intelligence, listened in responsive sympathy to Stanton, and was greatly depressed, as, indeed, were all the members."

I returned the next day to Norfolk, and informed Commodore Buchanan that he would be promoted to be admiral, and that, owing to his wound, he would be retired from the command of the *Virginia*. Lieutenant Jones should have been promoted, and should have succeeded him. He had fitted out the ship and armed her, and had commanded during the second day's fight. However, the department thought otherwise, and selected Commodore Josiah Tattnall; except Lieutenant Jones he was the best man. He had distinguished himself in the wars of 1812 and with Mexico. No one stood higher as an accomplished and chivalrous officer. While in command of the United States squadron in the East Indies, he was present as a neutral at the desperate fight at the Peiho Forts, below Pekin, between the English fleet and the Chinese, when the former lost nearly one-half of a force of twelve hundred engaged. Seeing his old friend Sir James Hope hard pressed and in need of assistance, having had four vessels sunk under him, he had his barge manned, and with his flag-

THE EXPLOSION ON THE BURNING "CONGRESS."

lieutenant, S. D. Trenchard, pulled alongside the flag-ship, through the midst of a tremendous fire, in which his coxswain was killed and several of his boat's crew were wounded. He found the gallant admiral desperately wounded, and all his crew killed or disabled but six. When he offered his services, surprise was expressed at his action. His reply was, "Blood is thicker than water."

Tattnall took command on the 29th of March. In the meantime the *Virginia* was in the dry dock under repairs. The hull four feet below the shield was covered with 2-inch iron. A new and heavier ram was strongly secured to the bow. The damage to the armor was repaired, wrought-iron port-shutters were fitted, and the rifle-guns were supplied with steel-pointed solid shot. These changes, with 100 tons more of ballast on her fan-tails, increased her draught to 23 feet, improving her resisting powers, but correspondingly decreasing her mobility and reducing her speed to 4 knots. The repairs were not completed until the 4th of April, owing to our want of resources and the difficulty of securing workmen. On the 11th we steamed down the harbor to the Roads with six gun-boats, fully expecting to meet the *Monitor* again and other vessels; for we knew their fleet had been largely reënforced, by the *Vanderbilt*, among other vessels, a powerful side-wheel steamer fitted as a ram. We were primed for a desperate tussle; but to our surprise we had the Roads to ourselves. We exchanged a few shots with the Rip-Raps batteries, but the *Monitor* with the other vessels of the fleet remained below Fort Monroe, in Chesapeake Bay, where we could not get at them except by passing between the forts.

The day before going down, Commodore Tattnall had written to Secretary Mallory, "I see no chance for me but to pass the forts and strike elsewhere, and I shall be gratified by your authority to do so." This freedom of action was never granted, and probably wisely, for the result of an

LIEUTENANT JOSEPH B. SMITH, ACTING COMMANDER OF THE "CONGRESS." FROM A PHOTOGRAPH.

According to the pilot of the "Cumberland," Lieutenant Smith was killed by a shot. His death was fixed at 4:20 P.M. by Lieutenant Pendergrast, next in command, who did not hear of it until ten minutes later. When his father, Commodore Joseph Smith, who was on duty at Washington, saw by the first dispatch from Fort Monroe that the "Congress" had shown the white flag, he said, quietly, "Joe's dead!" After speaking of the death of Lieutenant Smith, Lieutenant Pendergrast says, in his official report: "Seeing that our men were being killed without the prospect of any relief from the *Minnesota*,... not being able to get a single gun to bear upon the enemy, and the ship being on fire in several places, upon consultation with Commander William Smith we deemed it proper to haul down our colors." Lieutenant Smith's sword was sent to his father by the enemy under a flag of truce.—EDITORS.

THE "MONITOR."

THE "MERRIMAC."

THE ENCOUNTER AT SHORT RANGE.

action with the *Monitor* and fleet, even if we ran the gauntlet of the fire of the forts successfully, was more than doubtful, and any disaster would have exposed Norfolk and James River, and probably would have resulted in the loss of Richmond. For equally good reasons the *Monitor* acted on the defensive; for if she had been out of the way, General McClellan's base and fleet of transports in York River would have been endangered. Observing three merchant vessels at anchor close inshore and within the bar at Hampton, the commodore ordered Lieutenant Barney in the *Jamestown* to go in and bring them out. This was promptly and successfully accomplished, under a fire from the forts. Two were brigs loaded with supplies for the army. The capture of these vessels, within gun-shot of their fleet, did not affect its movements. As the *Jamestown* towed her prizes under the stern of the English corvette *Rinaldo,* Captain Hewett (now [1887] Vice-Admiral Sir William Hewett, commanding the Channel Squadron), then at anchor in the Roads, she was enthusiastically cheered. We remained below all day, and at night returned and anchored off Sewell's Point.

A few days later we went down again to within gun-shot of the Rip-Raps, and exchanged a few rounds with the fort, hoping that the *Monitor* would come out from her lair into open water. Had she done so, a determined effort would have been made to carry her by boarding. Four small gun-boats were ready, each of which had its crew divided into parties for the performance of certain duties after getting on board. Some were to try to wedge the turret, some to cover the pilot-house and all the openings with tarpaulins, others to scale with ladders the turret and smoke-stack, using shells, hand-grenades, etc. Even if but two of the gun-boats should succeed in grappling her, we were confident of success. Talking this over since with Captain S. D. Greene, who was the first lieutenant of the *Monitor,* and in command after Captain Worden was wounded in the pilot-house, he said they were prepared for anything of this kind and that it would have failed. Certain it is, if an opportunity had been given, the attempt would have been made.

A break-down of the engines forced us to return to Norfolk. Having completed our repairs on May 8th, and while returning to our old anchorage, we heard heavy firing, and, going down the harbor, found the *Monitor,* with the iron-clads *Galena, Naugatuck,* and a number of heavy ships, shelling our batteries at Sewell's Point. We stood directly for the *Monitor,* but as we approached they all ceased firing and retreated below the forts. We followed close down to the Rip-Raps, whose shot passed over us, striking a mile or more beyond the ship. We remained for some hours in the Roads, and finally the commodore, in a tone of deepest disgust, gave the order: "Mr. Jones, fire a gun to windward, and take the ship back to her buoy."

During the month of April, 1862, our forces, under General J. E. Johnston, had retired from the Peninsula to the neighborhood of Richmond, to defend the city against McClellan's advance by way of the Peninsula, and from time to time rumors of the possible evacuation of Norfolk reached us. On the 9th of May, while at anchor off Sewell's Point, we noticed at sunrise that our flag was not flying over the batteries. A boat was sent ashore and found them abandoned. Lieutenant Pembroke Jones was then dispatched to Norfolk, some miles distant, to call upon General Huger, who was in command, and learn the condition of affairs. He returned during the afternoon, reporting, to our great surprise, the town deserted by our troops and the navy yard on fire. This precipitate retreat was entirely unnecessary, for while the *Virginia* remained afloat, Norfolk was safe, or, at all events, was not tenable by the enemy, and James River was partly guarded, for we could have retired behind the obstructions in the channel at Craney Island, and, with the batteries at that point, could have held the place, certainly until all the valuable stores and machinery had been removed from the navy yard. Moreover, had the *Virginia* been afloat at the time of the battles around Richmond, General McClellan would hardly have retreated to James River; for, had he done so, we could at any time have closed it and rendered any position on it untenable.

Norfolk evacuated, our occupation was gone, and the next thing to be decided upon was what should be done with the ship. Two courses of action were open to us: we might have run the blockade of the forts and done some damage to the shipping there and at the mouth of the York River, provided they did not get out of our way,—for, with our great draught and low rate of speed, the enemy's transports would have gone where we could not have followed them; and the *Monitor* and other iron-clads would have engaged us with every advantage, playing around us as rabbits around a sloth, and the end would have been the certain loss of the vessel. On the other hand, the pilots said repeatedly, if the ship were lightened to eighteen feet, they could take her up James River to Harrison's Landing or City Point, where she could have been put in fighting trim again, and have been in a position to assist in the defense of Richmond. The commodore decided upon this course. Calling all hands on deck, he told them what he wished done. Sharp and quick work was necessary; for, to be successful, the ship must be lightened five feet, and we must pass the batteries at Newport News and the fleet below before daylight next morning. The crew gave three cheers, and went to work with a will, throwing overboard the ballast from the fan-tails, as well as that below,—all spare stores, water, indeed everything but our powder and shot. By midnight the ship had been lightened three feet, when, to our amazement, the pilots said it was useless to do more, that with the westerly wind blowing, the tide would be cut down so that the ship would not go up even to Jamestown Flats; indeed, they would not take the responsibility of taking her up the river at all. This extraordinary conduct of the pilots rendered some other plan immediately necessary. Moral: All officers, as far as possible, should learn to do their own piloting.

The ship had been so lifted as to be unfit for action; two feet of her hull below the shield was exposed. She could not be sunk again by letting in water without putting out the furnace fires and flooding the magazines. Never was a commander forced by circumstances over which he had no control into a more painful position than was Commodore Tattnall. But coolly and calmly he decided, and gave orders to destroy the ship; determining if he could not save his vessel, at all events not to sacrifice three hundred brave and faithful men; and that he acted wisely, the fight at Drewry's Bluff, which was the salvation of Richmond, soon after proved. She was run ashore near Craney Island, and the crew landed with their small-arms and two days' provisions. Having only two boats, it took three hours to disembark. Lieutenant Catesby Jones and myself were the last to leave. Setting her on fire fore and aft, she was soon in a blaze, and by the light of our burning ship we pulled for the shore, landing at daybreak. We marched 22 miles to Suffolk and took the cars for Richmond.

The news of the destruction of the *Virginia* caused a most profound feeling of disappointment and indignation throughout the South, particularly as so much was expected of the ship after our first success. On Commodore Tattnall the most unsparing and cruel aspersions were cast. He promptly demanded a court of inquiry, and, not satisfied with this, a court-martial, whose unanimous finding, after considering the facts and circumstances, was: "Being thus situated, the only alternative, in the opinion of the court, was to abandon and burn the ship then and there; which, in the judgment of the court, was deliberately and wisely done by order of the accused. Wherefore, the court do award the said Captain Josiah Tattnall an honorable acquittal."

It only remains now to speak of our last meeting with the *Monitor.* Arriving at Richmond, we heard that the enemy's fleet was ascending James River, and the result was great alarm; for, relying upon the *Virginia,* not a gun had been mounted to protect the city from a water attack. We were hurried to Drewry's Bluff, the first high ground below the city, seven miles distant. Here, for two days, exposed to constant rain, in bottomless mud and without shelter, on scant provisions, we worked unceasingly, mounting guns and obstructing the river. In this we were aided by the crews of small vessels which had escaped up the river before Norfolk was abandoned. The *Jamestown* and some small sailing-vessels were sunk in the channel, but, owing to the high water occasioned by a freshet, the obstructions were only partial. We had only succeeded in getting into position three thirty-twos and two sixty-fours (shell guns) and were without sufficient supply of ammunition, when on the 15th of May the iron-clad *Galena,* Commander John Rodgers, followed by the *Monitor* and three others, hove in sight. We opened fire as soon as they came within range, directing most of it on the *Galena.* This vessel was handled very skillfully. Coming up within six hundred yards of the battery, she anchored, and, with a spring from her quarter, presented her broadside; this under a heavy fire, and in a narrow river with a strong current. The *Monitor,* and others anchored just below, answered our fire deliberately; but, owing to the great elevation of the battery, their fire was in a great measure ineffectual, though two guns were dismounted and several men were killed and wounded. While this was going on, our sharp-shooters were at work on both banks. Lieutenant Catesby Jones, in his report, speaks of this service: "Lieutenant Wood, with a portion of the men, did good service as sharp-shooters. The enemy were excessively annoyed by their fire. His position was well chosen and gallantly maintained in spite of the shell, shrapnel, grape, and canister fired at them." Finding they could make no impression on our works, the *Galena,* after an action of four hours, returned down the river with her consorts. Her loss was about forty killed and wounded.‡

This was one of the boldest and best-conducted operations of the war, and one of which very little notice has been taken. Had Commander Rodgers been supported by a few brigades, landed at City Point or above on the south side, Richmond would have been evacuated. The *Virginia's* crew alone barred his way to Richmond; otherwise the obstructions would not have prevented his steaming up to the city, which would have been as much at his mercy as was New Orleans before the fleet of Farragut.

---

‡According to the official report, the loss on the *Galena* was 13 killed and 11 wounded; on the *Port Royal,* 1 wounded, and on the *Naugatuck,* 2 wounded. Total, 13 killed and 14 wounded.—EDITORS.

CHAPTER 10

FARRAGUT'S CAPTURE
OF NEW ORLEANS.

William T. Meredith, Late U.S.N.,

AND SECRETARY TO ADMIRAL FARRAGUT.

It has astonished a great many people to learn from Admiral Porter's article in "The Century" magazine [reprinted in the present work] that he was the first man to propose the opening of the Mississippi. Montgomery Blair, in the "United Service Magazine" for January, 1884, and ex-Secretary Welles, in "The Galaxy" for November, 1871, both fix the time when the discussion of the question was begun by the naval authorities, which was before the appearance of Porter on the scene at Washington. And, indeed, the importance of the great river to the South was so evident to any one who studied our coast and the South-west, that it is safe to say that the eyes of the whole nation were bent on New Orleans as a point of attack just about the time that Porter imagines he suggested it.

Why was Farragut chosen flag-officer of the squadron to attack New Orleans? The answer is that he was known as an experienced and capable officer, who was on record as having plans to capture forts with ships. He was one of the few officers of sufficient rank to command a squadron who also had the strength and vigor necessary to bear the strain of arduous duty. These were the main reasons that Mr. Welles, the Secretary, and Mr. Fox, the Assistant Secretary, had for selecting him. Besides this, his appointment met the approval of Porter, who, when consulted by the Secretary, gave his voice for Farragut. It is easy now to understand how with the lapse of time Admiral Porter has learned to think that he chose the commander of the expedition. That he could have defeated Farragut's appointment is probably true, but that he chose him is a mistake; he simply assented to the previous choice of Mr. Welles and Mr. Fox. (See articles by Welles and Blair, above referred to.)

Ex-Secretary Welles relates that the armament of the fleet had been determined, *before Farragut's appointment to the command*, after consultation with the War Department and with General McClellan, who detailed General Butler to command the land forces of the expedition. Porter, whose advice was listened to, insisted on the importance of a fleet of schooners carrying 13-inch mortars, and asserted that a bombardment of forty-eight hours would reduce Forts Jackson and St. Philip to a heap of ruins. Mr. Welles says that Mr. Fox, who was a trained naval officer, at first objected to the mortars, and advocated running by the forts with the fleet, but finally was won over by the forcible arguments of Porter, whose plan the Department fully adopted. There is evidence, given by Commander Porter himself, that he advocated bombarding the forts till they surrendered or could be captured by assault, and that he was opposed to running the fire with the fleet leaving an enemy in the rear. (See his letter on p. 312.)

The forces to attack New Orleans were fixed, measures were taken to cast thirty thousand mortar-shells, collect the fleet and transport the soldiers, before Farragut was summoned to Washington from New York. Mr. Blair says positively that he was not to be given the command until he had been subjected to a critical overhauling by the authorities. We hear of Farragut at breakfast with Mr. Blair and Mr. Fox, probably on the morning of his arrival at the capital. Mr. Fox then showed him the point of attack, the plans, and the force to be employed. Farragut said he would engage to capture New Orleans with two-thirds the naval force. Mr. Blair tells us that he was so enthusiastic and confident of success that when he went away Mr. Fox thought him over-sanguine, and was a little inclined to distrust his ability. Mr. Welles relates that after this interview Farragut was brought to him, and they entered at once into all the plans of the expedition. When they came to the mortar-flotilla, Farragut said that he placed little reliance on mortars, and that they would not have been part of his plan and advisement, but that he would take the mortar-fleet with him, as it had been adopted as part of the equipment of the fleet and might prove of more advantage than he anticipated.

At 10 o'clock on the 20th of April, while the bombardment by the mortars was at its height, the flag-ship made signal that Farragut wanted to hold a conference of commanding officers. In an hour they had all arrived excepting three, who commanded vessels detailed that day for guard duty above the fleet, and Commander Porter, who was probably too much occupied with the mortars to leave his command.

Thirteen boats trailed at the stern of the *Hartford,* while the captains waited anxiously in the cabin to hear what the flag-officer would say. A private journal kept by Commodore Bell, who led the 2d division of gun-boats in the attack, describes as follows what took place at the conference:

> "The flag-officer [Farragut] unfolded his plan of operations. Some discussion ensued, and Commander Alden read a written communication to Farragut from Porter, expressing his views as to the operations

against the forts. Having read them, Alden folded up the paper and returned it to his pocket, whereupon I [Commodore Bell] suggested the propriety of the document's being left with Farragut, and the paper was accordingly placed in his hands. It was therein stated that the boom, being a protection to the mortars against attack from above, should not be destroyed, upon which Farragut remarked that Porter had that morning assented to the boom's being broken, and again (it was stated in the communication) that the fleet should not go above the forts, as the mortar-vessels would be left unprotected. Farragut said he thought the mortars would be as well protected (with the fleet) above as below the forts, and that the coöperation of the army, which entered into the plans of both parties, could not be effectual unless some of the troops were introduced above the forts at the same time that they were below. He intended to cover their landing at the Quarantine, five miles above, they coming to the river through the bayou. Once above, the forts cut off, and his propellers intact for ascending the river to the city, if he found his ships able to cope with the enemy he would fight it out. Some of the officers considered it a hazardous thing to go above out of the reach of supplies. Farragut remarked that our ammunition was being rapidly exhausted, without a supply at hand, and that something must be done immediately. He believed in celerity."

Farragut "believed in celerity." He saw that while the ammunition was being exhausted but little impression had been made on the forts, and he felt sure that the time had come to carry out his plan of dashing boldly up the river through the fire of the forts.

The communication from Commander Porter containing his plans of attack, to which I have already alluded, and which was referred to by Commodore Bell, is as follows:

"When the ships are over the bar, guns mounted, coal-bunkers filled, sick on shore, hospital arrangements made for the wounded, the fleet should move up, mortar-fleet all in tow; the chain across the river to remain untouched for the present, or until after the mortars get their position and open their fire. It is a good defense on our side against fire-ships and rams which may be sent down the river, and our ships can so command the opening that nothing can pass down. As the mortar-vessels are somewhat helpless, they should be protected at all points by vessels of war, which should be ready at a moment's notice to repel an attack on them by rams, floating torpedoes, or fire-ships; the two latter to be towed out of the way, the rams to be run down by the heavy ships, while such vessels as the

Westfield and *Clifton* attack them end on with cannon, while gun-boats try to force them to the shore. When everything is ready for the assault, a demand for surrender should be made in language least calculated to exasperate, and of such a nature as to encourage those who might be disposed to return to their allegiance. There is evidence of a strong Union feeling in New Orleans, and everything should be done without losing by delay to prevent a counter-feeling.

"When it is evident that no surrender of the forts will be made, the mortars should open deliberate fire, keeping two shells in the air all the time, or each mortar-vessel should fire once in every ten minutes. Fort Jackson, being casemated, should receive the largest share of the bombardment, three or four vessels being employed against Fort St. Philip, firing as often as they can coolly and conveniently load and point. In the meantime preparations should be made to destroy at a moment's notice the vessels holding up the chain, or the chain itself, which can be done by applying a petard to the bobstays of the vessels or to the chain, all of which petards are prepared, and a man accustomed to the business with a galvanic battery will accompany the expedition.

"In my opinion there are two methods of attack,—one is for the vessel to run the gauntlet of the batteries by night or in a fog; the other is to attack the forts by laying the big ships close alongside of them, avoiding the casemates, firing shells, grape, and canister into the barbette, clearing the ramparts with boat-guns from the tops, while smaller and more agile vessels throw in shrapnel at shrapnel distance, clearing the parapets, and dismounting the guns in barbette.

"The larger ships should anchor with forty-five fathoms of chain with slip-ropes; the smaller vessels to keep under way and be constantly moving about, some to get above and open a cross-fire; the mortars to keep up a rapid and continuous fire, and to move up to a short range.

"The objections to running by the forts are these: It is not likely that any intelligent enemy would fail to place a chain across above the forts, and to raise such batteries as would protect them against our ships.

"Did we run the forts we should leave an enemy in our rear, and the mortar-vessels would have to be left behind. We could not return to bring them up without going through a heavy and destructive line. If the forts are run part of the mortars should be towed along which would render the progress of the vessels slow against the strong current at that point. If the forts are first captured, the moral effect would be to close the batteries on the river and open the way to New Orleans, whereas, if we don't succeed in taking them, we will have to fight our way up the river. Once having possession of the forts, New Orleans would be hermetically sealed, and we could repair damages and go up on our own terms and our own time.

"Nature points out the English Turn as the position to be strongly fortified, and it is there the enemy will most likely make his strongest stand and last effort to prevent our getting up. If this point is impassable there is solid ground there, and troops can be brought up and landed below the forts and attack them in the rear while the ships assail them in front. The result will doubtless be a victory for us. If the ships can get by the forts, and there are no obstructions above, then the plan should be to push on to New Orleans every ship that can get there, taking up as many of the mortar-fleet as can be rapidly towed. An accurate reconnoissance should be made, and every kind of attainable information provided before any movement is made.

"Nothing has been said about a combined attack of army and navy. Such a thing is not only practicable, but, if thus permitted, could be adopted. Fort St. Philip can be taken with three thousand men covered by the ships; the ditch can be filled with fascines, and the walls can be easily scaled with ladders. It can be easily attacked in front and rear."

—D. D. PORTER.

Farragut stood facing his destiny, imperishable fame or failure. He was determined to run by the forts with his ships. It was plain to him that nothing more would be accomplished by the mortars. He would not cumber his fleet during the passage by towing the mortars as Porter desired him to do. Once above the defenses, and the enemy's fleet overcome, he would either push on to New Orleans past the batteries, which he knew were at Chalmette, or cover with his guns the landing of the army through the bayou in the rear of the forts. In his heart he was determined, if events favored him, to push right on seventy-five miles up the river to New Orleans without waiting for the army. Porter's views expressed in his letter to the conference gave no support to these plans. He speaks of three methods of attack: *First,* by running the forts; *second,* bombardment by the whole fleet, mortars included, with a view to the reduction of the defenses; and *third,* a combined attack of the navy and army. The first method, which was Farragut's plan and the plan that succeeded, he strongly condemns. He feared the result of leaving an enemy in the rear. Some of the commanding officers agreed with him.

On the next day Farragut issued a General Order, which bears date one day earlier than its issuance, and is at once a reply to Porter's communication to the conference of officers and an announcement of the flag-officer's determination to challenge all objections, run the forts, conquer or be conquered.

No one can read Commodore Bell's journal and Flag-Officer Farragut's general order without seeing that there was cause for disappointment in the fleet. After a bombardment of three days the defense was still vigorous and the Confederates were undismayed. As a consequence of this Farragut had lost the little faith he ever had in mortars, and was prepared to carry out his own plans, differ as they might from the instructions of the Navy Department.

Farragut had a stupendous undertaking before him. A river with a current of three and a half miles an hour against the line of attack; two forts on opposite sides of the stream mounting 126 guns, and above them the Confederate steamers carrying 40 guns, while in the river, both above and below the forts, rafts were floating ready to be fired and cut loose on the first sign of an attempt to pass the boom. His fleet consisted of 8 steam sloops-of-war, 15 gun-boats, 1 sailing sloop, and 19 mortar-schooners. The 17 vessels which were to attempt the passage carried 166 guns and 26 howitzers. It is true that the mortar-shells were of assistance to Farragut in the passage, as they helped his own guns to distract the fire of the enemy and added to the confusion and distress in Fort Jackson. But that the passage would have been made in the darkness without the assistance of the mortars has never been seriously questioned, and is proved by Farragut's successful passage of Fort Morgan at the battle of Mobile Bay in broad daylight, which involved exactly the same principles of attack and was achieved without the use of a single mortar. The protraction of the bombardment gave the Confederates just six days more to push forward the work on the iron-clad and the fleet. Mr. Welles, in "The Galaxy," quotes a dispatch from Porter himself which shows his recognition of the fact that the Confederates were strengthening their defenses during this period. Porter says, speaking of the siege, that the enemy was "daily adding to his defense and strengthening his naval forces with iron-clad batteries."

What was the situation of affairs in Fort Jackson and Fort St. Philip about this time—the 22d of April—as shown by the testimony before the Confederate Court of Inquiry! In the two garrisons of 1100 men, 4 soldiers had been killed and 14 wounded—7 guns of the armament of 126 had been disabled. The barracks and citadel of Fort Jackson had been destroyed by fire.

There was nothing more to burn. Whenever the gun-boats approached the defenses a vigorous fire was opened on them by both forts, but when they retired the soldiers withdrew to the casemates out of reach of the mortar-fire.

And up to this time the mortar-flotilla had fired more than 13,500 shells. Porter had expected to reduce the forts to a heap of ruins in forty-eight hours, but at the end of ninety-six hours the defense was as vigorous as ever.

Did Porter believe that Farragut's passage of the forts and appearance before New Orleans would result in a speedy downfall of the defenses and the capture of the river and city? He did not, and he was very uneasy about the fleet after it passed the forts. He wondered how Farragut would return down the river to the mortar-fleet and to the army. He could not appreciate the fact that it was not necessary for him to come back; that all the defenses must soon fall, Forts Jackson and St. Philip among them, as the effect of the occupation of the river and New Orleans. He feared that Farragut was caught in a trap. He thought he would find the forts harder to take than ever, and that he would have to fight his way down the river and attack them again. All this appears in the letter of Commander Porter, which is given below. It was written to Farragut from below the forts on the morning after the passage, three days before they surrendered. The italics are not in the original:

> "MORTAR-FLOTILLA, April 25th, 1862.
>
> "Dear Sir:
>
> "Captain Boggs has arrived. I congratulate you on your victory. I witnessed your passage with great pleasure. My hopes and predictions were at last realized. You left at the forts four steamers and the famous iron-clad battery; they are mounting guns on it, and one thousand men are at work on it. She is unhurt and moves about with the stream. How fast she is I don't know. One of the steamers is iron-clad on the bow. The *McRae* is also at the fort. I sent a summons to surrender, but it was politely declined. As we have used up all the shells in the schooners, and wishing to be unhampered with the mortar-vessels, sent everything down and collected boats and spars....
>
> "They are moving all their heavy guns upon the riverside. *You will find the forts harder to take now than before unless their ammunition gives out.* I threw bombs at them all day, and tantalized them with rifle-shot, but they never fired a gun. *I hope you will open your way down, no matter what it costs.* I am sending some of the schooners down to blockade back of Fort Jackson to prevent their escaping by way of Barataria.
>
> "D. D. PORTER."

Porter overlooks the difference between his hopes and his predictions, as shown by his communication to the conference of officers, which he says are realized in this letter, and Farragut's achievement. He had opposed the plan of attack by which Farragut succeeded.

Porter's letter to the Secretary of the Navy, written before the surrender, also shows his distrust of the result of Farragut's bold ascent of the river, leaving an enemy in his rear. He says, speaking of the Confederate iron-clad below Farragut's fleet at the forts, "She mounts sixteen guns, and is almost as formidable as the *Merrimac*. This is one of the ill effects of leaving an enemy in the rear." And again, "These forts can hold out still for some time. I would suggest that the *Mystic* and *Monitor,* if they can be spared, be sent here without a moment's delay to settle the question."

On the 28th of April, three days later, the forts surrendered, and Farragut, who was then in possession of New Orleans, did not find it necessary to open his way down the river as advised by Porter, to whom the surrender must have been a surprise.

What was the immediate cause of the surrender of the forts? This is exactly the question that was asked of Colonel Edward Higgins, who had commanded Fort Jackson, by the Confederate Court of Inquiry, and his reply was: "The mutiny of the garrison." But what was the cause of the mutiny? General Duncan, who had commanded the lower defenses, including the forts, answered this in his report: "The garrison mutinied on the night of the 27th of April, giving as a reason that the city had surrendered and there was no further use in fighting." And why did the city surrender? Was it because Porter bombarded Fort Jackson 75 miles below the city, for six days, disabling, up to the night of the passage of the fleet, only 9 guns of the armament of 128, with a loss to the Confederates of less than 40 men in both garrisons?✰ Or was it be-

---

✰The following official statements made by Confederate and Union officers are given to show the condition of Fort Jackson and the garrison after the bombardment. On the 30th of April, 1862, in a letter to Adjutant-General Bridges, Colonel Edward Higgins says: "I have the honor to report that on the morning of the 27th of April a formal demand for the surrender of Forts Jackson and St. Philip was made by Commander Porter; the terms which were offered were liberal, but so strong was I in the belief that we could resist successfully any attack, either by land or by water, that the terms were at once refused. Our fort was still strong."

General Duncan, commanding all the lower Confederate defenses, says after the passage: "We are just as capable of repelling the enemy to-day as we were before the bombardment."

General Weitzel, of the United States Engineer Corps, in a report of the condition of Fort Jackson dated in May, 1862, says: "Fort St. Philip, with one or two slight exceptions, is to-day without a scratch. Fort Jackson was subjected to a torrent of 13-inch and 11-inch shells during 140 hours. To an inexperienced eye it seems as if this work were badly cut up. It is as strong to-day as when the first shell was fired at it."

Captain Harris, of the Coast Survey, whose map of the forts is published in Porter's article, says in his report after the surrender that of the "75 guns in Fort Jackson 4 guns were dismounted and 13 carriages were struck." But this was not done by the mortars alone. The fleet did its share in the passage. Granting that the injury of 11 gun-carriages permanently disabled 6 guns, the disablement of 10 guns in 75 is scarcely worth considering, with 116 guns in both forts still intact.

Comparing the losses on both sides during the bombardment and the passage of the forts, it will be seen that Farragut's loss, nearly all of which occurred in the passage of the lower defenses on the night of the final attack, was four times the Confederate list of killed and wounded at the forts during the entire siege. Does this look as if Fort Jackson had been disabled by the mortars before the final attack?

Colonel Edward Higgins on the 27th of April says: "Orders had been issued to the officers and men to retire to the casemates of the fort the moment the bombardment began; but when it became necessary to repel the attack our batteries were instantly in readiness and were at once engaged in a most terrific conflict with the enemy."

cause Farragut dashed through the fire of the forts, destroyed the Confederate fleet, and then pushed on past the Chalmette batteries 75 miles up the river, cutting off all communication, till he anchored before the city with his torn fleet?

I have taken no notice in this article of a letter written to Admiral Porter by the above-mentioned Colonel Higgins dated April 4th, 1872, ten years after the occurrence of the events which he professes to describe. This letter is useless as evidence, because it contradicts Colonel Higgins's own report to the Confederate authorities quoted here. Surely the official evidence of a man fresh from the scene of action is to be believed in preference to an account given by him ten years afterward in a letter.—W.T.M.

CHAPTER 11

Stonewall Jackson
in the Shenandoah.

John D. Imboden, Brigadier-General, C.S.A.

Soon after the battle of Bull Run Stonewall Jackson was promoted to major-general, and the Confederate Government having on the 21st of October, 1861, organized the Department of Northern Virginia, under command of General Joseph E. Johnston, it was divided into the Valley District, the Potomac District, and Aquia District, to be commanded respectively by Major-Generals Jackson, Beauregard, and Holmes. On October 28th General Johnston ordered Jackson to Winchester to assume command of his district, and on the 6th of November the War Department ordered his old "Stonewall" brigade and six thousand troops under command of Brigadier-General W. W. Loring to report to him. These, together with Turner Ashby's cavalry, gave him a force of about ten thousand men all told.

His only movement of note in the winter of 1861–62 was an expedition at the end of December to Bath and Romney, to destroy the Baltimore and Ohio railroad and a dam or two near Hancock on the Chesapeake and Ohio canal.† The weather set in to be very inclement about New Year's, with snow, rain,

---

†When Jackson took command in the Valley in November, 1861, the Union forces held Romney and occupied the north side of the Potomac in strong force. The Confederates had only a weak body of militia at Jackson's disposal, until reënforcements came from the east. After receiving the four brigades of R. B. Garnett, Wm. B. Taliaferro, William Gilham, and S. R. Anderson, Jackson moved against the Union communications along the Potomac, aiming to destroy the Chesapeake and Ohio canal. Under cover of demonstrations made against various places along the Potomac east of the objective point, a Confederate force was concentrated near Dam No. 5, December 17th, and after four days' labor a breach was made in the dam. On the 1st of January another force moved from Winchester, northward, the two columns uniting, and on the 4th instant the town of Bath was occupied, after being abandoned by a body of Union troops composed of cavalry, infantry, and artillery. Jackson followed the retreating Union troops to the river and promptly bombarded Hancock, Md., without, however, securing a surrender, and on the 7th he withdrew from the Potomac region toward Romney. On his approach the Union troops at that post evacuated without a struggle, yielding the town on January 10th. The Confederates now went into winter quarters along the south branch of the Potomac, at Romney and vicinity.—Editors.

A CONFEDERATE
OF 1862.

sleet, high winds, and intense cold. Many in Jackson's command were opposed to the expedition, and as it resulted in nothing of much military importance, but was attended with great suffering on the part of his troops, nothing but the confidence he had won by his previous services saved him from personal ruin. He and his second in command, General Loring, had a serious disagreement. He ordered Loring to take up his quarters, in January, in the exposed and cheerless village of Romney, on the south branch of the upper Potomac. Loring objected to this, but Jackson was inexorable. Loring and his principal officers united in a petition to Mr. Benjamin, Secretary of War, to order them to Winchester, or at least away from Romney. This document was sent direct to the War Office, and the Secretary, in utter disregard of "good order and discipline," granted the request without consulting Jackson. As soon as information reached Jackson of what had been done, he indignantly resigned his commission. Governor Letcher was astounded, and at once wrote Jackson a sympathetic letter, and then expostulated with Mr. Davis and his Secretary with such vigor that an apology was sent to Jackson for their obnoxious course. The orders were revoked and modified, and Jackson was induced to retain his command. This little episode gave the Confederate civil authorities an inkling of what manner of man "Stonewall" Jackson was.

In that terrible winter's march and exposure, Jackson endured all that any private was exposed to. One morning, near Bath, some of his men, having crawled out from under their snow-laden blankets, half-frozen, were cursing him as the cause of their sufferings. He lay close by under a tree, also snowed under, and heard all this; and, without noticing it, presently crawled out, too, and, shaking the snow off, made some jocular remark to the nearest men, who had no idea he had ridden up in the night and lain down amongst them. The incident ran through the little army in a few hours, and reconciled his followers to all the hardships of the expedition, and fully reëstablished his popularity.

In March Johnston withdrew from Manassas, and General McClellan collected his army of more than one hundred thousand men on the Peninsula. Johnston moved south to confront him. McClellan had planned and organized a masterly movement to capture, hold, and occupy the Valley and the Piedmont region; and if his subordinates had been equal to the task, and there had been no interference from Washington, it is probable the Confederate army would have been driven out of Virginia and Richmond captured by midsummer, 1862.

Jackson's little army in the Valley had been greatly reduced during the winter from various causes, so that at the beginning of March he did not have over 5000 men of all arms available for the defense of his district, which began to swarm with enemies all around its borders, aggregating more than ten times his own strength. Having retired up the Valley, he learned that the enemy had begun to withdraw and send troops to the east of the mountains to coöperate with McClellan. This he resolved to stop by an aggressive demonstration against Winchester, occupied by General Shields, of the Federal army, with a division of 8000 to 10,000 men.

BRIGADIER-GENERAL JOHN D. IMBODEN, C.S.A. FROM A PHOTOGRAPH.

A little after the middle of March, Jackson concentrated what troops he could, and on the 23d he occupied a ridge at the hamlet of Kernstown, four miles south of Winchester. Shields promptly attacked him, and a severe engagement of several hours ensued, ending in Jackson's repulse about dark, followed by an orderly retreat up the Valley to near Swift Run Gap in Rockingham county. The pursuit was not vigorous nor persistent.✠ Although Jackson retired before superior numbers, he had given a taste of his fighting qualities that stopped the withdrawal of the enemy's troops from the Valley.

The result was so pleasing to the Richmond government and General Johnston that it was decided to reënforce Jackson by sending General Ewell's division to him at Swift Run Gap, which reached him about the 1st of May, thus giving Jackson an aggregate force of from 13,000 to 15,000 men to open his campaign with. At the beginning of May the situation was broadly about as follows: Milroy, with about 4087 men, was on the Staunton and Parkersburg road

✠General Jackson's first announcement of the battle to General Johnston, dated March 24th, contained the following:

> "As the enemy had been sending off troops from the district, and from what I could learn were still doing so, and knowing your great desire to prevent it, and having a prospect of success, I engaged him yesterday about 3 P.M., near Winchester, and fought until dusk, but his forces were so superior to mine that he repulsed me with the loss of valuable officers and men killed and wounded; but from the obstinacy with which our troops fought and from their advantageous position I am of the opinion that his loss was greater than mine in troops, but I lost one piece of artillery and three caissons."

—Editors.

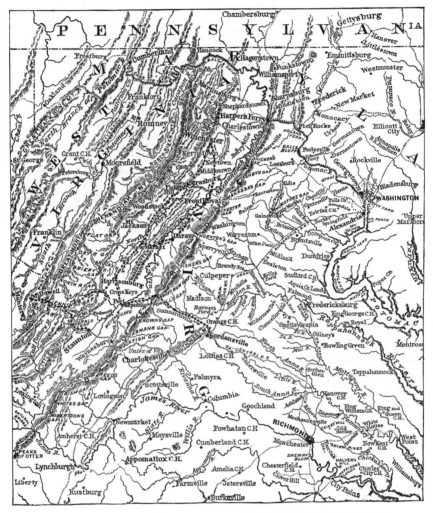

MAP OF JACKSON'S CAMPAIGN IN THE SHENANDOAH VALLEY.

The crossed line and arrows indicate Jackson's movements in the Valley. On May 6th he was at Staunton; he fought Milroy and Schenck near McDowell on May 8th; Banks at Front Royal, Newtown, and Winchester on May 23d, 24th, and 25th; Frémont at Cross Keys on June 8th; Tyler at Port Republic on June 9th.—EDITORS.

at McDowell, less than forty miles from Staunton, with Schenck's brigade of about 2500 near Franklin. The rest of Frémont's army in the mountain department was then about 30,000 men, of whom 20,000 were concentrating at Franklin, fifty miles north-west of Staunton, and within supporting distance of Milroy. Banks, who had fortified Strasburg, seventy miles north-east of Staunton by the great Valley turnpike, to fall back upon in an emergency, had pushed forward a force of 20,000 men to Harrisonburg, including Shields's division, 10,000 strong. General McDowell, with 34,000 men, exclusive of Shields's division, was at points east of the Blue Ridge, so as to be able to move either to Fredericksburg or to the Luray Valley and thence to Staunton. Not counting Colonel Miles's, later Saxton's, command, at Harper's Ferry, which was rapidly increased to 7000 men, sent from Washington and other points north of the Potomac, before the end of May, Jackson had about 80,000 men to take into account (including all Union forces north of the Rappahannock and east of the Ohio) and to keep from a junction with McClellan in front of Richmond. Not less than 65,000◆ of these enemies were in the Valley under their various commanders in May and June.

Besides Ewell's division already mentioned, General Johnston could give no further assistance to Jackson, for McClellan was right in his front with superior numbers, and menacing the capital of the Confederacy with almost immediate and certain capture. Its only salvation depended upon Jackson's ability to hold back Frémont, Banks, and McDowell long enough to let Johnston try doubtful conclusions with McClellan. If he failed in this, these three commanders of an aggregate force then reputed to be, and I believe in fact, over one hundred thousand♦ would converge and move down upon Richmond from the west as McClellan advanced from the east, and the city and its defenders would fall an easy prey to nearly, if not quite, a quarter of a million of the best-armed and best-equipped men ever put into the field by any government.

Early in May, Jackson was near Port Republic contemplating his surroundings and maturing his plans. What these latter were no one but himself knew.

Suddenly the appalling news spread through the Valley that he had fled to the east side of the Blue Ridge through Brown's and Swift Run Gaps. Only Ashby remained behind with about one thousand cavalry, scattered and moving day and night in the vicinity of McDowell, Franklin, Strasburg, Front Royal, and Luray, and reporting to Jackson every movement of the enemy. Despair was fast settling upon the minds of the people of the Valley. Jackson made no concealment of his flight, the news of which soon reached his enemies. Milroy advanced two regiments to the top of the Shenandoah Mountain, only twenty-two miles from Staunton, and was preparing to move his entire force to Staunton, to be followed by Frémont.

Jackson had collected, from Charlottesville and other stations on the Virginia Central Railroad, enough railway trains to transport all of his little army.

◆This seems to us an overestimate of the Union forces actually in the Valley during the operations of May and June. April 30th, Banks had 9178 "present for duty"; May 31st, Frémont had 14,672 (Cox and Kelley not in the Valley); McDowell's force that reached the Valley (including Shields's division, which on May 31st numbered 10,203), aggregated about 21,000. Total, 44,840. Saxton had about 7000 at Harper's Ferry, which were not engaged.—EDITORS.

♦We estimate that there were not above 80,000 Union troops in the three departments that could have been moved toward Richmond.—EDITORS.

That it was to be taken to Richmond when the troops were all embarked no one doubted. It was Sunday, and many of his sturdy soldiers were Valley men. With sad and gloomy hearts they boarded the trains at Mechum's River Station. When all were on, lo! they took a westward course, and a little after noon the first train rolled into Staunton.

News of Jackson's arrival spread like wild-fire, and crowds flocked to the station to see the soldiers and learn what it all meant. No one knew.

As soon as the troops could be put in motion they took the road leading toward McDowell, the general having sent forward cavalry to Buffalo Gap and beyond to arrest all persons going that way. General Edward Johnson, with one of Jackson's Valley brigades, was already at Buffalo Gap. The next morning, by a circuitous mountain-path, he tried to send a brigade of infantry to the rear of Milroy's two regiments on Shenandoah Mountain, but they were improperly guided and failed to reach the position in time, so that when attacked in front both regiments escaped. Jackson followed as rapidly as possible, and the following day, May 8th, on top of the Bull Pasture Mountain, three miles east of McDowell, encountered Milroy reënforced by Schenck, who commanded by virtue of seniority of commission. The conflict lasted several hours, and was severe and bloody. It was fought mainly with small-arms, the ground forbidding much use of artillery. Schenck and Milroy fled precipitately toward Franklin, to unite with Frémont. The route lay along a narrow valley hedged up by high mountains, perfectly protecting the flanks of the retreating army from Ashby's pursuing cavalry, led by Captain Sheetz. Jackson ordered him to pursue as vigorously as possible, and to guard completely all avenues of approach from the

UNION CAMP AT FRONT ROYAL. FROM A WAR-TIME SKETCH.

direction of McDowell or Staunton till relieved of this duty. Jackson buried the dead and rested his army, and then fell back to the Valley on the Warm Springs and Harrisonburg road.

The morning after the battle of McDowell I called very early on Jackson at the residence of Colonel George W. Hull of that village, where he had his headquarters, to ask if I could be of any service to him, as I had to go to Staunton, forty miles distant, to look after some companies that were to join my command. He asked me to wait a few moments, as he wished to prepare a telegram to be sent to President Davis from Staunton, the nearest office to McDowell. He took a seat at a table and wrote nearly half a page of foolscap; he rose and stood before the fireplace pondering it some minutes; then he tore it in pieces and wrote again, but much less, and again destroyed what he had written, and paced the room several times. He suddenly stopped, seated himself, and dashed off two or three lines, folded the paper, and said, "Send that off as soon as you reach Staunton." As I bade him "good-bye," he remarked: "I may have other telegrams to-day or to-morrow, and will send them to you for transmission. I wish you to have two or three well-mounted couriers ready to bring me the replies promptly."

I read the message he had given me. It was dated "McDowell," and read about thus: "Providence blessed our arms with victory at McDowell yesterday." That was all. A few days after I got to Staunton a courier arrived with a message to be telegraphed to the Secretary of War. I read it, sent it off, and ordered a courier to be ready with his horse, while I waited at the telegraph office for the reply. The message was to this effect: "I think I ought to attack Banks, but under my orders I do not feel at liberty to do so." In less than an hour a reply came, but not from the Secretary of War. It was from General Joseph E. Johnston, to whom I supposed the Secretary had referred General Jackson's message. I have a distinct recollection of its substance, as follows: "If you think you can beat Banks, attack him. I only intended by my orders to caution you against attacking fortifications." Banks was understood to have fortified himself strongly at Strasburg and Cedar Creek, and he had fallen back there. I started the courier with this reply, as I supposed, to McDowell, but, lo! it met Jackson only twelve miles from Staunton, to which point on the Harrisonburg and Warm Springs turnpike he had marched his little army, except Ashby's cavalry, which, under an intrepid leader, Captain Sheetz, he had sent from McDowell to menace Frémont, who was concentrating at Franklin in Pendleton County, where he remained in blissful ignorance that Jackson had left McDowell, till he learned by telegraph some days later that Jackson had fallen upon Banks at Front Royal and driven him through Winchester and across the Potomac.

Two hours after receiving this telegram from General Johnston, Jackson was *en route* for Harrisonburg, where he came upon the great Valley turnpike.

By forced marches he reached New Market in two days. Detachments of cavalry guarded every road beyond him, so that Banks remained in total ignorance of his approach. This Federal commander had the larger part of his force well fortified at and near Strasburg, but he kept a large detachment at Front Royal, about eight miles distant and facing the Luray or Page Valley.☆

From New Market Jackson disappeared so suddenly that the people of the Valley were again mystified. He crossed the Massanutten Mountain, and, passing Luray, hurried toward Front Royal. He sometimes made thirty miles in twenty-four hours with his entire army, thus gaining for his infantry the sobriquet of "Jackson's foot cavalry." Very early in the afternoon of May 23d he struck Front Royal. The surprise was complete and disastrous to the enemy, who were commanded by Colonel John R. Kenly. After a fruitless resistance they fled toward Winchester, twenty miles distant, with Jackson at their heels.† A large number were captured within four miles by a splendid cavalry dash of Colonel Flournoy and Lieutenant-Colonel Watts.

News of this disaster reached Banks at Strasburg, by which he learned that Jackson was rapidly gaining his rear toward Newtown. The works Banks had constructed had not been made for defense in that direction, so he abandoned them and set out with all haste for Winchester; but, *en route,* near Newtown (May 24th), Jackson struck his flank, inflicting heavy loss, and making large captures of property, consisting of wagons, teams, camp-equipage, provisions, ammunition, and over nine thousand stand of arms, all new and in perfect order, besides a large number of prisoners.⊕

Jackson now chased Banks's fleeing army to Winchester, where the latter made a stand, but after a sharp engagement with Ewell's division on the 25th he fled again, not halting till he had crossed the Potomac, congratulating himself and his Government in a dispatch that his army was at last safe in Maryland. General Saxton, with some 7000 men, held Harper's Ferry, 32 miles from Winchester. Jackson paid his respects to this fortified post, by marching a large part of his forces close to it, threatening an assault, long enough to allow all the captured property at Winchester to be sent away toward Staunton, and then returned to Winchester. His problem now was to escape the clutches of Frémont, knowing that that officer would be promptly advised by wire of what had befallen Banks. He could go back the way he came, by the Luray Valley, but that

---

☆Banks's total force now numbered 9178 present for duty as against 16,000 to 17,000 of Jackson.
—Editors.

†Colonel Kenly, in his report, says that he was attacked about 2 P.M., and that he maintained his position in front of his camp until nearly 5 o'clock, when he found that he was flanked. Retiring, he made a stand at the river in his rear, and again at the cross-road leading to Middletown. At the last point his men were run down by overwhelming numbers and captured in detachments.—Editors.

⊕Banks reports on April 30th, as present for duty, 9178; and on June 16th, 7113,—being a reduction of 2065. Jackson reports the capture in all of 3050 of Banks's men.—Editors.

ARRIVAL OF FRÉMONT'S VANGUARD ABOVE STRASBURG, IN VIEW OF JACKSON'S TRAINS MOVING TOWARD FISHER'S HILL. FROM A SKETCH MADE AT THE TIME.

would expose Staunton (the most important depot in the valley) to capture by Frémont, and he had made his plans to save it.

I had been left at Staunton organizing my recruits. On his way to attack Banks, Jackson sent me an order from New Market to throw as many men as I could arm, and as quickly as possible, into Brock's Gap, west of Harrisonburg, and into any other mountain-pass through which Frémont could reach the valley at or south of Harrisonburg. I knew that within four miles of Franklin, on the main road leading to Harrisonburg, there was a narrow defile hemmed in on both sides by nearly perpendicular cliffs, over five hundred feet high. I sent about fifty men, well armed with long-range guns, to occupy these cliffs, and defend the passage to the last extremity.

On the 25th of May, as soon as Frémont learned of Banks's defeat and retreat to the Potomac, he put his army of about 14,000 in motion from Franklin to cut off Jackson's retreat up the valley. Ashby's men were still in his front toward McDowell, with an unknown force; so Frémont did not attempt that route, but sent his cavalry to feel the way toward Brock's Gap, on the direct road to Harrisonburg. The men I had sent to the cliffs let the head of the column get well into the defile or gorge, when, from a position of perfect safety to themselves, they poured a deadly volley into the close column. The attack being unexpected, and coming from a foe of unknown strength, the Federal column halted and hesitated to advance. Another volley and the "rebel yell" from the cliffs turned them back, never to appear again. Frémont took the road to Moorefield, and thence to Strasburg, though he had been peremptorily ordered on May 24th by President Lincoln to proceed direct to Harrisonburg. It shows how close had been Jackson's calculation of chances, to state that as his rear-guard marched up Fisher's Hill, two miles from Strasburg, Frémont's advance came in sight on the mountain-side on the road from Moorefield, and a sharp skirmish took place. Jackson continued to Harrisonburg, hotly pursued by Frémont, but avoiding a conflict.

The news of Banks's defeat created consternation at Washington, and Shields was ordered to return from east of the Blue Ridge to the Luray Valley in all haste to coöperate with Frémont. Jackson was advised of Shields's approach, and his aim was to prevent a junction of their forces till he reached a point where he could strike them in quick succession. He therefore sent cavalry detachments along the Shenandoah to burn the bridges as far as Port Republic, the river being at that time too full for fording. At Harrisonburg he took the road leading to Port Republic, and ordered me from Staunton, with a mixed battery and battalion of cavalry, to the bridge over North River near Mount Crawford, to prevent a cavalry force passing to his rear.

At Cross Keys, about six miles from Harrisonburg, he delivered battle to Frémont, on June 8th, and, after a long and bloody conflict, as night closed in he was master of the field. Leaving one division—Ewell's—on the ground, to resist Frémont if he should return next day, he that night marched the rest of his army to Port Republic, which lies in the forks of the river, and made his arrangements to attack the troops of Shields's command next morning on the Lewis farm, just below the town.

On the day of the conflict at Cross Keys I held the bridge across North River at Mount Crawford with a battalion of cavalry, four howitzers, and a Parrott gun, to prevent a cavalry flank movement on Jackson's trains at Port Republic. About 10 o'clock at night I received a note from Jackson, written in pencil on the blank margin of a newspaper, directing me to report with my command at Port Republic before daybreak. On the same slip, and as a postscript, he wrote, "Poor Ashby is dead. He fell gloriously.... I know you will join with me in mourning the loss of our friend, one of the noblest men and soldiers in the Confederate army." I carried that slip of paper till it was literally worn to tatters.

VIEW OF THE BATTLE OF CROSS KEYS, FROM THE UNION POSITION,
LOOKING EAST. FROM A SKETCH MADE AT THE TIME.✝

It was early, Sunday, June 8th, when Jackson and his staff reached the bridge at Port Republic. General E. B. Tyler, who, with two brigades of Shields's division, was near by on the east side of the river, had sent two guns and a few men under a green and inefficient officer to the bridge. They arrived about the same time as Jackson, but, his troops soon coming up, the Federal officer and his supports made great haste back to the Lewis farm, losing a gun at the bridge.

✝General Ewell, the Confederate commander on the field, in his report says of the Union advance:

"The general features of the ground were a valley and a rivulet in my front, woods on both flanks, and a field of some hundreds of acres where the road crossed the center of my line, my side of the valley being more defined and commanding the other.... About 10 o'clock the enemy fell along my front with skirmishers, and shortly after posted his artillery, chiefly opposite mine. He advanced under cover on General Trimble, with a force, according to his own statement, of two brigades, which were repulsed with such signal loss that they did not make another determined effort. General Trimble had been reënforced by the 13th and 25th Virginia Regiments, Colonel J. A. Walker and Lieutenant-Colonel P. B. Duffy, of General Elzey's brigade. These regiments assisted in the repulse of the enemy. General Trimble in turn advanced and drove the enemy more than a mile, and remained on his flank ready to make the final attack.... The enemy's attack was decided by 4 P.M., it being principally directed against General Trimble, and, though from their own statement they outnumbered us on that flank two to one, it had signally failed. General Trimble's ... brigade captured one of their colors."

BATTLE OF
PORT REPUBLIC
JUNE 9, 1862.

Confederate Lines ___
Federal Lines _____

BY MAJOR JED. HOTCHKISS,
TOP. ENG. VALLEY DIST. A.N.VA.

I reached Port Republic an hour before daybreak of June 9th, and sought the house occupied by Jackson; but not wishing to disturb him so early, I asked the sentinel what room was occupied by "Sandy" Pendleton, Jackson's adjutant-general. "Upstairs, first room on the right," he replied.

Supposing he meant our right as we faced the house, I went up, softly opened the door, and discovered General Jackson lying on his face across the bed, fully dressed, with sword, sash, and boots all on. The low-burnt tallow candle on the table shed a dim light, yet enough by which to recognize him. I endeavored to withdraw without waking him. He turned over, sat up on the bed, and called out, "Who is that?"

He checked my apology with "That is all right. It's time to be up. I am glad to see you. Were the men all up as you came through camp?"

"Yes, General, and cooking."

"That's right. We move at daybreak. Sit down. I want to talk to you."

I had learned never to ask him questions about his plans, for he would never answer such to any one. I therefore waited for him to speak first. He referred very feelingly to Ashby's death, and spoke of it as an irreparable loss. When he paused I said, "General, you made a glorious winding-up of your four weeks' work yesterday."

General Frémont in his report describes the desperate fighting as follows:

"Urging vigorously forward his brigade, General Stabel encountered in the first belt of woods a strong line of skirmishers, which with hard fighting was driven out of the timber and pushed by the 8th and 45th New York over the open ground beyond the edge of the woods, where these regiments suddenly came upon the right of the enemy's main line.... Two of General Stabel's best regiments, the 27th Pennsylvania and the 41st New York, had been diverted to the right in the timber, and the shock of the entire force here was sustained by the 8th and 45th New York; and principally by the 8th, which was attacked in front and flank by four regiments.... The enemy now brought up additional artillery into the open ground on my extreme left, and General Taylor's reserve brigade [Confederate] entering the woods, the fighting continued with great severity continuously along the timber in front of our position. A Mississippi regiment, charging with yells upon Buell's battery, was gallantly met with a bayonet charge by the 27th Pennsylvania, under cover of which the battery was withdrawn. A Louisiana regiment of Taylor's brigade, undertaking a charge upon Dilger's battery, was received with a fire of canister and grape, delivered with such precision and rapidity as nearly destroyed it. Every attempt of the enemy to emerge from the cover of the woods was repulsed by artillery and counter-attacks of infantry." ...

—Editors.

He replied, "Yes, God blessed our army again yesterday, and I hope with his protection and blessing we shall do still better to-day."

Then seating himself, for the first time in all my intercourse with him, he outlined the day's proposed operations. I remember perfectly his conversation. He said: "Charley Winder [Brigadier-General commanding his old 'Stonewall' brigade] will cross the river at daybreak and attack Shields on the Lewis farm [two miles below]. I shall support him with all the other troops as fast as they can be put in line. General 'Dick' Taylor will move through the woods on the side of the mountain with his Louisiana brigade, and rush upon their left flank by the time the action becomes general. By 10 o'clock we shall get them on the run, and I'll now tell you what I want with you. Send the big new rifle-gun you have [a 12-

PENNSYLVANIA "BUCKTAILS."   COLONEL JOHNSON, MOUNTED.

THE FIRST MARYLAND (CONFEDERATE) REGIMENT AT HARRISONBURG,
JUNE 6, 1862, AND THE DEATH OF ASHBY.

In the affair of the rear-guard at Harrisonburg on the 6th of June, 1862, the 1st Maryland Regiment, Colonel (afterward General) Bradley T. Johnson, was ordered by General Ewell to charge through the woods to the left in support of the 58th Virginia, then closely engaged with the Pennsylvania 13th ("Bucktails"). They charged with a cheer, but soon began to suffer from a fire in the flank and rear. Colonel Johnson gave the command, "By the right flank, file right, march!" As soon as the colors came into line—"By the left flank, *charge!*" The right companies charged at double-quick, the left companies coming up on a run—thus changing front to the right under fire. At the same instant a volley from the enemy swept down the front files of the color company and color guard, killed the horses of General Turner Ashby and Colonel Johnson, and in a second after killed Ashby. Johnson, disentangling himself from his horse, led his regiment on, and, according to Ewell, "drove the enemy off with heavy loss," wounding and capturing their commanding officer, Lieutenant-Colonel Thomas L. Kane. General Frémont wrote that "a battalion of Colonel Kane's (Pennsylvania) regiment entered the woods under the direction of Brigadier-General [George D.] Bayard, and maintained for half an hour a vigorous attack, in which both sides suffered severely, driving the enemy." Ashby was directing when he fell not thirty yards from the enemy. Three Confederate color-sergeants were shot at one flag. As the regiment was moving into the battle of Cross Keys, June 8th, General Ewell directed Colonel Johnson to carry one of the bucktails captured from the enemy affixed to his colors as a trophy.—EDITORS.

BRIGADIER-GENERAL TURNER ASHBY,
C.S.A. FROM A PHOTOGRAPH.

pounder Parrott] to Poague [commander of the Rockbridge artillery] and let your mounted men report to the cavalry. I want you in person to take your mounted howitzers to the field, in some safe position in rear of the line, keeping everything packed on the mules, ready at any moment to take to the mountain-side. Three miles below Lewis's there is a defile on the Luray road. Shields may rally and make a stand there. If he does, I can't reach him with the field-batteries on account of the woods. You can carry your 12-pounder howitzers on the mules up the mountain-side, and at some good place unpack and shell the enemy out of the defile, and the cavalry will do the rest."

This plan of battle was carried out to the letter. I took position in a ravine about two hundred yards in rear of Poague's battery in the center of the line. General Tyler, who had two brigades of Shields's division, made a very stubborn fight, and by 9 o'clock matters began to look very serious for us. Dick Taylor had not yet come down out of the woods on Tyler's left flank.

Meanwhile I was having a remarkable time with our mules in the ravine. Some of the shot aimed at Poague came bounding over our heads, and occasionally a shell would burst there. The mules became frantic. They kicked, plunged, and squealed. It was impossible to quiet them, and it took three or four men to hold one mule from breaking away. Each mule had about three hundred pounds weight on him, so securely fastened that the load could not be dislodged by any of his capers. Several of them lay down and tried to wallow their loads off. The men held these down, and that suggested the idea of throwing them all on the ground and holding them there. The ravine sheltered us so that we were in no danger from the shot or shell which passed over us.

Just about the time our mule "circus" was at its height, news came up the line from the left that Winder's brigade near the river was giving way. Jackson rode down in that direction to see what it meant. As he passed on the brink of our ravine, his eye caught the scene, and, reining up a moment, he accosted me with, "Colonel, you seem to have trouble down there." I made some reply which drew forth a hearty laugh, and he said, "Get your mules to the mountain as soon as you can, and be ready to move."

Then he dashed on. He found his old brigade had yielded slightly to overwhelming pressure.℣ Galloping up, he was received with a cheer; and, calling out at the top of his voice, "The 'Stonewall' brigade never retreats; follow me!" led them back to their original line. Taylor soon made his appearance, and the flank attack settled the work of the day. A wild retreat began. The pursuit was vigorous. No stand was made in the defile. We pursued them eight miles. I rode back with Jackson, and at sunset we were on the battle-field at the Lewis mansion.

Jackson accosted a medical officer, and said, "Have you brought off all the wounded?" "Yes, all of ours, but not all of the enemy's." "Why not?" "Because we were shelled from across the river." "Had you your hospital flag on the field?" "Yes." "And they shelled that?" "Yes." "Well, take your men to their quarters; I would rather let them all die than have one of my men shot intentionally under the yellow flag when trying to save their wounded."✓

Frémont, hearing the noise of the battle, had hurried out from near Harrisonburg to help Tyler; but Jackson had burnt the bridge at Port Republic, after Ewell had held Frémont in check some time on the west side of the river and escaped, so that when Frémont came in sight of Tyler's battle-field, the latter's troops had been routed and the river could not be crossed.

The next day I returned to Staunton, and found General W.H.C. Whiting,

---

℣The first Confederate assault was made by Winder's (Stonewall) brigade, and was repulsed by the troops of Carroll's brigade. An incident of the counter-charge is thus described by Colonel Henry B. Kelly, C.S.A.:

"While victoriously driving back the line of the Confederate left, the advancing Federal infantry were themselves suddenly assailed in flank, on their left, by a charge of two regiments of Virginia infantry, the 44th and 58th, led by Colonel Scott."

The attack on the other flank by troops brought up from Cross Keys, by General Ewell, determined the result. Colonel Kelly says:

"At the word of command, the line moved forward, soon coming into plain view of the batteries and of the infantry of the enemy beyond the ravine, which at once opened fire on the advancing brigade. With one volley in reply, and a Confederate yell heard far over the field, the Louisianians rushed down the rough declivity and across the ravine, and carried the batteries like a flash.... By the impetus of the charge over the rough ground all formation was lost, and officers and men were all thrown into one unorganized mass around the captured guns. While this exultant crowd were rejoicing and shouting over their victory, suddenly a scathing fire of canister was poured into them by a section of Clark's battery which had been rapidly brought over from the Federal right to within two hundred yards of the position of the captured guns....

"At the outset of the attempt of the Federals to retake their batteries, Lieutenant-Colonel Peck, of the 9th Louisiana, called out to the men about the captured guns to shoot the horses, which was done. When, therefore, the Federals retook and held for a time, as they did, the ground where the guns were, they were unable, when again driven off, to take more than one gun with them for want of battery horses."—EDITORS.

✓The official references to this incident are comprised in the following.

General Jackson says in his report:

"While the forces of Shields were in full retreat, and our troops in pursuit, Frémont appeared on the opposite bank of the south fork of the Shenandoah with his army, and opened his ar-

my old commander after the fall of General Bee at Bull Run, arriving with a division of troops to reënforce Jackson. Taking him and his staff to my house as guests, General Whiting left soon after breakfast with a guide to call on Jackson at Swift Run Gap, near Port Republic, where he was resting his troops. The distance from Staunton was about twenty miles, but Whiting returned after midnight. He was in a towering passion, and declared that Jackson had treated him outrageously. I asked, "How is that possible, General, for he is very polite to every one?"

"Oh! hang him, he was polite enough. But he didn't say one word about his plans. I finally asked him for orders, telling him what troops I had. He simply told me to go back to Staunton, and he would send me orders to-morrow. I haven't the slightest idea what they will be. I believe he hasn't any more sense than my horse."

Seeing his frame of mind, and he being a guest in my house, I said little. Just after breakfast, next morning, a courier arrived with a terse order to embark his troops on the railroad trains and move to Gordonsville at once, where he would receive further orders. This brought on a new explosion of wrath. "Didn't I tell you he was a fool, and doesn't this prove it? Why, I just came through Gordonsville day before yesterday."

However, he obeyed the order; and when he reached Gordonsville he found Jackson there, and his little Valley army coming after him; a few days later McClellan was astounded to learn that Jackson was on his right flank on the Chickahominy. Shortly after the seven days' battle around Richmond, I met Whiting again, and he then said: "I didn't know Jackson when I was at your house. I have found out now what his plans were, and they were worthy of a Napoleon. But I still think he ought to have told me his plans; for if he had died McClellan would have captured Richmond. I wouldn't have known what he was driving at, and might have made a mess of it. But I take back all I said about his being a fool."

From the date of Jackson's arrival at Staunton till the battle of Port Republic was thirty-five days. He marched from Staunton to McDowell, 40 miles,

---

tillery upon our ambulances and parties engaged in the humane labors of attending to our dead and wounded, and the dead and wounded of the enemy."

Frémont says in his report of his action at Port Republic:

"Parties (Confederate) gathering the dead and wounded, together with a line of prisoners, awaiting the movements of the rebel force near by, was all, in respect to troops on either side, now to be seen. A parting salvo of carefully aimed rifle-guns, duly charged with shell, hastened the departure of the rebels with the unlucky though most gallant convoy, and the whole were speedily out of sight."

It is hardly necessary to state that intentional shelling of an ambulance and relief parties is denied by Union officers.—EDITORS.

from McDowell to Front Royal, about 110, from Front Royal to Winchester, 20 miles, Winchester to Port Republic, 75 miles, a total of 245 miles, fighting in the meantime 4 desperate battles, and winning them all.

On the 17th of June, leaving only his cavalry, under Brigadier-General B. H. Robertson, and Chew's battery, and the little force I was enlisting in the valley (which was now no longer threatened by the enemy), Jackson moved all his troops south-east, and on the 25th arrived at Ashland, seventeen miles from Richmond. This withdrawal from the valley was so skillfully managed that his absence from the scene of his late triumphs was unsuspected at Washington. On the contrary, something like a panic prevailed there, and the Government was afraid to permit McDowell to unite his forces with McClellan's lest it should uncover and expose the capital to Jackson's supposed movement on it.

Jackson's military operations were always unexpected and mysterious. In my personal intercourse with him in the early part of the war, before he had become famous, he often said there were two things never to be lost sight of by a military commander: "Always mystify, mislead, and surprise the enemy, if possible; and when you strike and overcome him, never let up in the pursuit so long as your men have strength to follow; for an army routed, if hotly pursued, becomes panic-stricken, and can then be destroyed by half their number. The other rule is, never fight against heavy odds, if by any possible manœuvring you can hurl your own force on only a part, and that the weakest part, of your enemy and crush it. Such tactics will win every time, and a small army may thus destroy a large one in detail, and repeated victory will make it invincible."

His celerity of movement was a simple matter. He never broke down his men by too-long-continued marching. He rested the whole column very often, but only for a few minutes at a time. I remember that he liked to see the men lie down flat on the ground to rest, and would say, "A man rests all over when he lies down."

CHAPTER 12

THE PENINSULAR CAMPAIGN.

George B. McClellan, Major-General, U.S.A.

In the following pages I purpose to give a brief sketch of the Peninsular campaign of 1862. As it is impossible, within the limits available, to describe even the most important battles, I shall confine myself to strategical considerations. But even this requires a rapid review of the circumstances under which, from a small assemblage of unorganized citizens, utterly ignorant of war and almost of the use of arms, was evolved that mighty Army of the Potomac, which, unshaken alike in victory and defeat, during a long series of arduous campaigns against an army most ably commanded and the equal in heroism of any that ever met the shock of battle, proved itself worthy to bear on its bayonets the honor and fate of the nation.

In July, 1861, after having secured solidly for the Union that part of western Virginia north of the Kanawha and west of the mountains, I was suddenly called to Washington on the day succeeding the first battle of Bull Run. Reaching the capital on the 26th, I found myself assigned to the command of that city and of the troops gathered around it.

All was chaos and despondency; the city was filled with intoxicated stragglers, and an attack was expected. The troops numbered less than fifty thousand, many of whom were so demoralized and undisciplined that they could not be relied upon even for defensive purposes. Moreover, the term of service

FORT MONROE—PARADE OF THE 30TH PENNSYLVANIA ARTILLERY. FROM A PHOTOGRAPH.

of a large part had already expired, or was on the point of doing so. On the Maryland side of the Potomac no troops were posted on the roads leading into the city, nor were there any intrenchments. On the Virginia side the condition of affairs was better in these respects, but far from satisfactory. Sufficient and fit material of war did not exist. The situation was difficult and fraught with danger.

The first and most pressing demand was the immediate safety of the capital and the Government. This was secured by enforcing the most rigid discipline, by organizing permanent brigades under regular officers, and by placing the troops in good defen-

MAJOR-GENERAL JOHN E. WOOL (SEE P. 344). FROM A PHOTOGRAPH.

sive positions, far enough to the front to afford room for manœuvring and to enable the brigades to support each other.

The contingency of the enemy's crossing the Potomac above the city was foreseen and promptly provided for. Had he attempted this "about three months after the battle of Manassas," he would, upon reaching "the rear of Washington," have found it covered by respectable works, amply garrisoned, with a sufficient disposable force to move upon his rear and force him to "a decisive engagement."[‡] It would have been the greatest possible good fortune for us if he had made this movement at the time in question, or even some weeks earlier. It was only for a very few days after the battle of Bull Run that the movement was practicable, and every day added to its difficulty.

Two things were at once clear: first, that a large and thoroughly organized army was necessary to bring the war to a successful conclusion; second, that Washington must be so strongly fortified as to set at rest any reasonable apprehensions of its being carried by a sudden attack, in order that the active army might be free to move with the maximum strength and on any line of operations without regard to the safety of the capital.

These two herculean tasks were entered upon without delay or hesitation. They were carried to a successful conclusion, without regard to that impatient and unceasing clamor—inevitable among a people unaccustomed to war—which finally forced the hand of the general charged with their execution. He regarded their completion as essential to the salvation of his country, and deter-

‡The words quoted are General Beauregard's.—EDITORS.

mined to accomplish them, even if sacrificed in the endeavor. Nor has he, even at this distant day, and after much bitter experience, any regret that he persisted in his determination. Washington was surrounded by a line of strong detached works, armed with garrison artillery, and secure against assault. Intermediate points were occupied by smaller works, battery epaulements, infantry intrenchments, etc. The result was a line of defenses which could easily be held by a comparatively small garrison against any assault, and could be reduced only by the slow operations of a regular siege, requiring much time and material, and affording full opportunity to bring all the resources of the country to its relief. At no time during the war was the enemy able to undertake the siege of Washington, nor, if respectably garrisoned, could it ever have been in danger from an assault. The maximum garrison necessary to hold the place against a siege from any and every quarter was 34,000 troops, with 40 field-guns; this included the requisite reserves.

With regard to the formation of the Army of the Potomac, it must suffice to say that everything was to be created from the very foundation. Raw men and officers were to be disciplined and instructed. The regular army was too small to furnish more than a portion of the general officers, and a very small portion of the staff, so that the staff-departments and staff-officers were to be fashioned mainly out of the intelligent and enthusiastic, but perfectly raw, material furnished. Artillery, small-arms, and ammunition were to be fabricated, or pur-

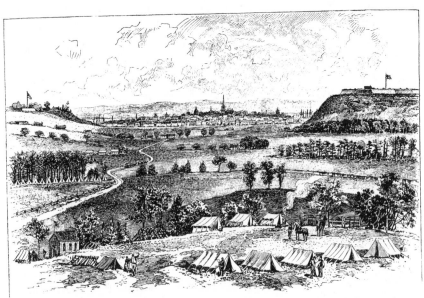

FORT ELLSWORTH.   ALEXANDRIA.   FORT LYON.

VIEW OF ALEXANDRIA FROM THE CAMP OF THE 40TH NEW YORK VOLUNTEERS.
FROM A SKETCH MADE IN NOVEMBER, 1861.

chased from abroad; wagons, ambulances, bridge trains, camp equipage, hospital stores, and all the vast *impedimenta* and material indispensable for an army in the field, were to be manufactured. So great was the difficulty of procuring small-arms that the armament of the infantry was not satisfactorily completed until the winter, and a large part of the field-batteries were not ready for service until the spring of 1862. As soon as possible divisions were organized, the formation being essentially completed in November.

On the 1st of November, upon the retirement of General Winfield Scott, I succeeded to the command of all the armies, except the Department of Virginia, which comprised the country within sixty miles of Fort Monroe. Upon assuming the general command, I found that the West was far behind the East in its state of preparation, and much of my time and large quantities of material were consumed in pushing the organization of the Western armies. Meanwhile the various coast expeditions were employed in seizing important points of the enemy's sea-board, to facilitate the prevention of blockade-running, and to cut or threaten the lines of communication near the coast, with reference to subsequent operations.

The plan of campaign which I adopted for the spring of 1862 was to push forward the armies of Generals Halleck and Buell to occupy Memphis, Nashville, and Knoxville, and the line of the Memphis and Danville Railroad, so as to deprive the enemy of that important line, and force him to adopt the circuitous routes by Augusta, Branchville, and Charleston. It was also intended to seize Washington, North Carolina, at the earliest practicable moment, and to open the Mississippi by effecting a junction between Generals Halleck and Butler. This movement of the Western armies was to be followed by that of the Army of the Potomac from Urbana, on the lower Rappahannock, to West Point and Richmond, intending, if we failed to gain Richmond by a rapid march, to cross the James and attack the city in rear, with the James as a line of supply.

So long as Mr. Cameron was Secretary of War I received the cordial support of that department; but when he resigned, the whole state of affairs changed. I had never met Mr. Stanton before reaching Washington, in 1861. He at once sought me and professed the utmost personal affection, the expression of which was exceeded only by the bitterness of his denunciation of the Government and its policy. I was unaware of his appointment as Secretary of War until after it had been made, whereupon he called to ascertain whether I desired him to accept, saying that to do so would involve a total sacrifice of his personal interests, and that the only inducement would be the desire to assist me in my work. Having no reason to doubt his sincerity, I desired him to accept, whereupon he consented, and with great effusion exclaimed: "Now we two will save the country."

On the next day the President came to my house to explain why he had appointed Mr. Stanton without consulting me; his reason being that he supposed

HEADQUARTERS OF BRIGADIER-GENERAL JOHN SEDGWICK, ON THE LEESBURG
TURNPIKE, NEAR WASHINGTON. FROM A SKETCH MADE IN JANUARY, 1862.

Stanton to be a great friend of mine, and that the appointment would naturally be satisfactory, and that he feared that if I had known it beforehand it would be said that I had dragooned him into it.

The more serious difficulties of my position began with Mr. Stanton's accession to the War Office. It at once became very difficult to approach him, even for the transaction of ordinary current business, and our personal relations at once ceased. The impatience of the Executive immediately became extreme, and I can attribute it only to the influence of the new Secretary, who did many things to break up the free and confidential intercourse that had heretofore existed between the President and myself. The Government soon manifested great impatience in regard to the opening of the Baltimore and Ohio Railroad and the destruction of the Confederate batteries on the Potomac. The first object could be permanently attained only by occupying the Shenandoah Valley with a force strong enough to resist any attack by the Confederate army then at Manassas; the second only by a general advance of the Army of the Potomac, driving the enemy back of the Rapidan. My own view was that the movement of the Army of the Potomac from Urbana would accomplish both of these objects, by forcing the enemy to abandon all his positions and fall back on Richmond. I was therefore unwilling to interfere with this plan by a premature advance, the effect of which must be either to commit us to the overland route, or to minimize the advantages of the Urbana movement. I wished to hold the enemy at Manassas to the last moment—if possible until the advance from Urbana had actually commenced, for neither the reopening of the railroad nor the destruction of the batteries was worth the danger involved.

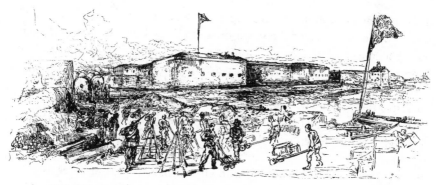

QUARTERMASTER'S DOCK, FORT MONROE. FROM A SKETCH MADE IN 1862.

The positive order of the President, probably issued under the pressure of the Secretary of War, forced me to undertake the opening of the railway. For this purpose I went to Harper's Ferry in February, intending to throw over a force sufficient to occupy Winchester. To do this it was necessary to have a reliable bridge across the Potomac—to insure supplies and prompt reënforcements. The pontoon-bridge, thrown as a preliminary, could not be absolutely trusted on a river so liable to heavy freshets; therefore it was determined to construct a canal-boat bridge. It was discovered, however, when the attempt was made, that the lift-lock from the canal to the river was too narrow for the boats by some four or five inches, and I therefore decided to rebuild the railroad bridge, and content myself with occupying Charlestown until its completion, postponing to the same time the advance to Winchester. I had fully explained my intentions to the President and Secretary before leaving Washington, providing for precisely such a contingency. While at Harper's Ferry I learned that the President was dissatisfied with my action, and on reaching Washington I laid a full explanation before the Secretary, with which he expressed himself entirely satisfied, and told me that the President was already so, and that it was unnecessary for me to communicate with him on the subject. I then proceeded with the preparations necessary to force the evacuation of the Potomac batteries. On the very day appointed for the division commanders to come to headquarters to receive their final orders, the President sent for me. I then learned that he had received no explanation of the Harper's Ferry affair, and that the Secretary was not authorized to make the statement already referred to; but after my repetition of it the President became fully satisfied with my course. He then, however, said that there was another "very ugly matter" which he desired to talk about, and that was the movement by the lower Chesapeake. He said that it had been suggested that I proposed this movement with the "traitorous" purpose of leaving Washington uncovered and exposed to attack. I very promptly objected to the coupling of any such adjective with my purposes, whereon he disclaimed any intention of conveying the idea that he expressed his own opinion, as he merely repeated the suggestions of others. I then explained the purpose and effect of fortifying Washington, and, as I thought, removed his apprehensions, but informed him that the division commanders were to be at headquarters that morning, and suggested that my plans should be laid before them that they might give their opinion as to whether the capital would be endangered; I also said that in order to leave them perfectly untrammeled I would not attend the meeting. Accordingly they met on the 8th of March and approved my plans.

On the same day was issued, without my knowledge, the order forming army corps and assigning the senior general officers to their command.⚓ My own views were that, as the command of army corps involved great responsibility and demanded ability of a high order, it was safer to postpone their formation until trial in the field had shown which general officers could best perform those vital functions. An incompetent division commander could not often jeopardize the safety of an army; while an unfit corps commander could easily lose a battle and frustrate the best-conceived plan of campaign. Of the four corps commanders, one only had commanded so much as a regiment in the field prior to the Bull Run campaign. On the next day intelligence arrived that the enemy was abandoning his positions. I crossed to the Virginia side to receive information more promptly and decide upon what should be done. During the night I determined to advance the whole army, to take advantage of any opportunity to strike the enemy, to break up the permanent camps, give the troops a little experience on the march and in bivouac, get rid of extra baggage, and test the working of the staff-departments. If this were done at all, it must be done promptly, and by moving the troops by divisions, without waiting to form the army corps. Accordingly, I telegraphed to the Secretary, explaining the state of the case and asking authority to postpone the army corps formation until the completion of the movement. The reply was an abrupt and unreasonable refusal. I again telegraphed, explaining the situation and throwing the responsibility upon the Secretary, whereupon he gave way.

Meanwhile, as far back as the 27th of February, orders had been given for collecting the transportation necessary to carry out the Urbana movement. This conclusion had been reached after full discussion. On the 27th of January had been issued the President's General War Order No. 1, directing a general movement of the land and naval forces against the enemy on the 22d of February. On

⚓First Corps, McDowell—Divisions: Franklin, McCall, and King; Second Corps, Sumner—Divisions: Richardson, Blenker, and Sedgwick; Third Corps, Heintzelman—Divisions: Porter, Hooker, and Hamilton; Fourth Corps, Keyes—Divisions: Couch, Smith, and Casey. The reserve artillery (Henry J. Hunt), the regular infantry (George Sykes), and regular cavalry (Philip St. George Cooke) and engineer troops were attached to headquarters.—EDITORS.

the 31st of January was issued the President's Special War Order No. 1, directing the Army of the Potomac to advance to the attack of Manassas on the 22d of February. The President, however, permitted me to state my objections to this order, which I did, at length, in a letter of February 3d, to the Secretary of War. As the President's order was not insisted upon, although never formally revoked, it is to be assumed that my letter produced, for a time at least, the desired effect. When Manassas had been abandoned by the enemy and he had withdrawn behind the Rapidan, the Urbana movement lost much

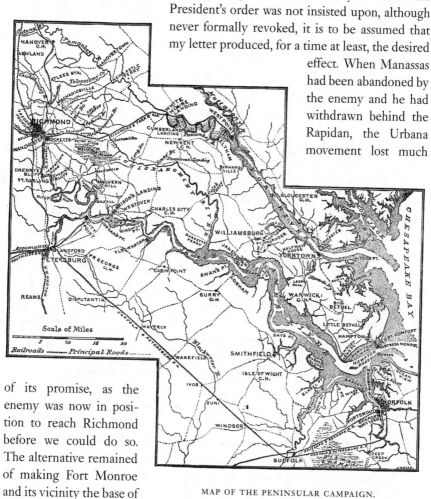

MAP OF THE PENINSULAR CAMPAIGN.

of its promise, as the enemy was now in position to reach Richmond before we could do so. The alternative remained of making Fort Monroe and its vicinity the base of operations.

The plan first adopted was to commence the movement with the First Corps as a unit, to land north of Gloucester and move thence on West Point; or, should circumstances render it advisable, to land a little below Yorktown to turn the defenses between that place and Fort Monroe. The Navy Department were confident that we could rely upon their vessels to neutralize the *Merrimac* and aid materially in reducing the batteries on the York River, either by joining in the attack or by running by them and gaining their rear. As transports arrived very slowly, especially those for horses, and the great impatience of the Government grew apace, it became necessary to embark divisions as fast as vessels arrived, and I decided to land them at Fort Monroe, holding the First Corps to the last, still intending to move it in mass to turn Gloucester. On the 17th of March the leading division embarked at Alexandria. The campaign was undertaken with the intention of taking some 145,000 troops, to be increased by a division of 10,000 drawn from the troops in the vicinity of Fort Monroe, giving a total of 155,000. Strenuous efforts were made to induce the President to take away Blenker's German division of 10,000 men. Of his own volition he at first declined, but the day before I left Washington he yielded to the non-military pressure and reluctantly gave the order, thus reducing the expected force to 145,000.

While at Fairfax Court House, on the 12th of March, I learned that there had appeared in the daily papers the order relieving me from the general command of all the armies and confining my authority to the Department of the Potomac. I had received no previous intimation of the intention of the Government in this respect. Thus, when I embarked for Fort Monroe on the 1st of April, my command extended from Philadelphia to Richmond, from the Alleghanies, including the Shenandoah, to the Atlantic; for an order had been issued a few days previous placing Fort Monroe and the Department of Virginia under my command, and authorizing me to withdraw from the troops therein ten thousand, to form a division to be added to the First Corps.

The fortifications of Washington were at this time completed and armed. I had already given instructions for the refortification of Manassas, the reopening of the Manassas Gap Railroad, the protection of its bridges by blockhouses, the intrenchment of a position for a brigade at or near the railroad crossing of the Shenandoah, and an intrenched post at Chester Gap. I left about 42,000 troops for the immediate defense of Washington, and more than 35,000 for the Shenandoah Valley—an abundance to insure the safety of Washington and to check any attempt to recover the lower Shenandoah and threaten Maryland. Beyond this force, the reserves of the Northern States were all available.

On my arrival at Fort Monroe on the 2d of April, I found five divisions of infantry, Sykes's brigade of regulars, two regiments of cavalry, and a portion of the reserve artillery disembarked. Another cavalry regiment and a part of a fourth had arrived, but were still on shipboard; comparatively few wagons had come. On the same day came a telegram stating that the Department of Virginia was withdrawn from my control, and forbidding me to form the division of ten thousand men without General Wool's sanction. I was thus deprived of the command of the base of operations, and the ultimate strength of the army was reduced to 135,000—another serious departure from the plan of campaign. Of the troops disembarked, only four divisions, the regulars, the majority of the reserve artillery, and a part of the cavalry, could be moved, in consequence of the lack of transportation. Casey's division was unable to leave Newport News until the 16th, from the impossibility of supplying it with wagons.

The best information obtainable represented the Confederate troops around Yorktown as numbering at least fifteen thousand, with about an equal force at Norfolk; and it was clear that the army lately at Manassas, now mostly near Gordonsville, was in position to be thrown promptly to the Peninsula. It was represented that Yorktown was surrounded by strong earth-works, and that the Warwick River, instead of stretching across the Peninsula to Yorktown,—as proved to be the case,—came down to Lee's Mills from the North, running parallel with and not crossing the road from Newport News to Williamsburg. It was also known that there were intrenched positions of more or less strength at Young's Mills, on the Newport News road, and at Big Bethel, Howard's Bridge, and Ship's Point, on or near the Hampton and Yorktown road, and at Williamsburg.

On my arrival at Fort Monroe, I learned, in an interview with Flag-Officer Goldsborough, that he could not protect the James as a line of supply, and that he could furnish no vessels to take an active part in the reduction of the batteries at York and Gloucester or to run by and gain their rear. He could only aid in the final attack after our land batteries had essentially silenced their fire.

I thus found myself with 53,000 men in condition to move, faced by the conditions of the problem just stated. Information was received that Yorktown was already being reënforced from Norfolk, and it was apprehended that the main Confederate army would promptly follow the same course. I therefore determined to move at once with the force in hand, and endeavor to seize a point—near the Halfway House—between Yorktown and Williamsburg, where the Peninsula is reduced to a narrow neck, and thus cut off the retreat of the Yorktown garrison and prevent the arrival of reënforcements. The advance commenced on the morning of the 4th of April, and was arranged to turn successively the intrenchments on the two roads; the result being that, on the afternoon of the 5th, the Third Corps was engaged with the enemy's outposts in front of Yorktown and under the artillery fire of the place. The Fourth Corps came upon Lee's Mills and found it covered by the unfordable line of the Warwick, and reported the position so strong as to render it impossible to execute its orders to assault. Thus, all things were brought to a stand-still, and the intended movement on the Halfway House could not be carried out. Just at this moment came a telegram, dated the 4th, informing me that the First Corps was withdrawn from my command. Thus, when too deeply committed to recede, I found that another reduction of about 43,000, including several cavalry regiments withheld from me, diminished my paper force to 92,000, instead of the 155,000 on which the plans of the campaign had been founded, and with which it was intended to operate. The number of men left behind, sick and from other causes incident to such a movement, reduced the total for duty to some 85,000, from which must be deducted all camp, depot, and train guards, escorts, and non-combatants, such as cooks, servants, orderlies, and extra-duty men in the various staff-departments, which reduced the numbers actually available for battle to some 67,000 or 68,000.

The order withdrawing the First Corps also broke up the Department of the Potomac, forming out of it the Department of the Shenandoah, under General Banks, and the Department of the Rappahannock, under General McDowell, the latter including Washington. I thus lost all control of the depots at Washington, as I had already been deprived of the control of the base at Fort Monroe and of the ground subsequently occupied by the depot at White House. The only territory remaining under my command was the paltry triangle between the departments of the Rappahannock and Virginia; even that was yet to be won from the enemy. I was thus relieved from the duty of providing for the safety of Washington, and deprived of all control over the troops in that vicinity. Instead of one directing head controlling operations which should have been inseparable, the region from the Alleghanies to the sea was parceled out among four independent commanders.

On the 3d of April, at the very moment of all others when it was most necessary to push recruiting most vigorously, to make good the inevitable losses in battle and by disease, an order was issued from the War Department discontinuing all recruiting for the volunteers and breaking up all their recruiting stations. Instead of a regular and permanent system of recruiting, whether by voluntary enlistment or by draft, a spasmodic system of large drafts was there-

VIEW FROM UNION MORTAR BATTERY NO. 4, LOOKING TOWARD
YORKTOWN,—GLOUCESTER POINT ON THE RIGHT.
FROM A SKETCH MADE APRIL 16, 1862.

after resorted to, and, to a great extent, the system of forming new regiments. The results were wasteful and pernicious. There were enough, or nearly enough, organizations in the field, and these should have been constantly maintained at the full strength by a regular and constant influx of recruits, who, by association with their veteran comrades, would soon have become efficient. The new regiments required much time to become useful, and endured very heavy and unnecessary losses from disease and in battle owing to the inexperience of the officers and men. A course more in accordance with the best-established military principles and the uniform experience of war would have saved the country millions of treasure and thousands of valuable lives.

Then, on the 5th of April, I found myself with 53,000 men in hand, giving less than 42,000 for battle, after deducting extra-duty men and other non-combatants. In our front was an intrenched line, apparently too strong for assault, and which I had now no means of turning, either by land or water. I now learned that 85,000 would be the maximum force at my disposal, giving only some 67,000 for battle. Of the three divisions yet to join, Casey's reached the front only on the 17th, Richardson's on the 16th, and Hooker's commenced arriving at Ship Point on the 10th. Whatever may have been said afterward, no one at the time—so far as my knowledge extended—thought an assault practicable without certain preliminary siege operations. At all events, my personal experience in this kind of work was greater than that of any officer under my command; and after personal reconnoissances more appropriate to a lieutenant of engineers than to the commanding general, I could neither discover nor hear of any point where an assault promised any chance of success. We were thus obliged to resort to siege operations in order to silence the enemy's artillery fire, and open the way to an assault. All the batteries would have been ready to open fire on the 5th, or, at latest, on the morning of the 6th of May, and it was determined to assault at various points the moment the heavy batteries had performed their allotted task; the navy was prepared to participate in the attack as soon as the main batteries were silenced; the *Galena,* under that most gallant and able officer, John Rodgers, was to take part in the attack, and would undoubtedly have run the batteries at the earliest possible moment; but during the night of the 3d and 4th of May the enemy evacuated his positions, regarding them as untenable under the impending storm of heavy projectiles.

Meanwhile, on the 22d of April, Franklin's division of McDowell's corps had joined me by water, in consequence of my urgent calls for reënforcements.

The moment the evacuation of Yorktown was known, the order was given for the advance of all the disposable cavalry and horse batteries, supported by infantry divisions, and every possible effort was made to expedite the movement of a column by water upon West Point, to force the evacuation of the lines at Williamsburg, and, if possible, cut off a portion of the enemy's force and trains.

The heavy storms which had prevailed recommenced on the afternoon of the 4th, and not only impeded the advance of troops by land, but delayed the movement by water so much that it was not until the morning of the 7th that the leading division—Franklin's—disembarked near West Point and took up a suitable position to hold its own and cover the landing of reënforcements. This division was attacked not long after it landed, but easily repulsed the enemy.

Meanwhile the enemy's rear-guard held the Williamsburg lines against our advance, except where Hancock broke through, until the night of the 5th, when they retired.

The army was now divided: a part at the mouth of the Pamunkey, a part at Williamsburg, and a part at Yorktown prepared to ascend the York River. The problem was to reunite them without giving the enemy the opportunity of striking either fraction with his whole force. This was accomplished on the 10th, when all the divisions were in communication, and the movement of concentration continued as rapidly as circumstances permitted, so that on the 15th the headquarters and the divisions of Franklin, Porter, Sykes, and Smith reached Cumberland Landing; Couch and Casey being near New Kent Court House, Hooker and Kearny near Roper's Church, and Richardson and Sedgwick near Eltham. On the 15th and 16th, in the face of dreadful weather and terrible roads, the divisions of Franklin, Porter, and Smith were advanced to White House, and a depot established. On the 18th the Fifth and Sixth Corps were formed, so that the organization of the Army of the Potomac was now as follows: Second Corps, Sumner—Divisions, Sedgwick and Richardson; Third Corps, Heintzelman—Divisions, Kearny and Hooker; Fourth Corps, Keyes—Divisions, Couch and Casey; Fifth Corps, F. J. Porter—Divisions, Morell and Sykes and the Reserve Artillery; Sixth Corps, Franklin—Divisions, Smith and Slocum.

WHARF, YORK RIVER.   MCCLELLAN'S HEADQUARTERS.   NELSON HOUSE.

VIEW OF MAIN STREET, YORKTOWN, THE UNION TROOPS MARCHING IN.
FROM A SKETCH MADE MAY 4, 1862.

The cavalry organization remained unchanged, and we were sadly deficient in that important arm, as many of the regiments belonging to the Army of the Potomac were among those which had been retained near Washington.

The question now arose as to the line of operations to be followed: that of the James on the one hand, and, on the other, the line from White House as a base, crossing the upper Chickahominy.

The army was admirably placed for adopting either, and my decision was to take that of the James, operating on either bank as might prove advisable, but always preferring the southern. I had urgently asked for reënforcements to come by water, as they would thus be equally available for either line of operations. The destruction of the *Merrimac* on the 11th of May had opened the James River to us, and it was only after that date that it became available. My plan, however, was changed by orders from Washington. A telegram of the 18th from the Secretary of War informed me that McDowell would advance from Fredericksburg, and directed me to extend the right of the Army of the Potomac to the north of Richmond, in order to establish communication with

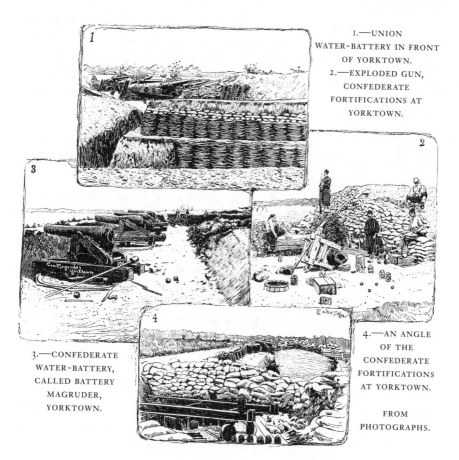

1.—UNION WATER-BATTERY IN FRONT OF YORKTOWN.
2.—EXPLODED GUN, CONFEDERATE FORTIFICATIONS AT YORKTOWN.

3.—CONFEDERATE WATER-BATTERY, CALLED BATTERY MAGRUDER, YORKTOWN.

4.—AN ANGLE OF THE CONFEDERATE FORTIFICATIONS AT YORKTOWN.

FROM PHOTOGRAPHS.

him. The same order required me to supply his troops from our depots at White House. Herein lay the failure of the campaign, as it necessitated the division of the army by the Chickahominy, and caused great delay in constructing practicable bridges across that stream; while if I had been able to cross to the James, reënforcements would have reached me by water rapidly and safely, the army would have been united and in no danger of having its flank turned, or its line of supply interrupted, and the attack could have been much more rapidly pushed.

I now proceeded to do all in my power to insure success on the new line of operations thus imposed upon me. On the 20th of May our light troops reached the Chickahominy at Bottom's Bridge, which they found destroyed. I at once ordered Casey's division to ford the stream and occupy the heights beyond, thus securing a lodgment on the right bank. Heintzelman was moved up in support of Keyes. By the 24th, Mechanicsville was carried, so that the enemy was now all together on the other side of the river. Sumner was near the railroad, on the left bank of the stream; Porter and Franklin were on the same bank near Mechanicsville.

It is now time to give a brief description of the Chickahominy. This river rises some fifteen miles north-westward of Richmond, and unites with the James about forty miles below that city. Our operations were on the part between Meadow and Bottom's bridges, covering the approaches to Richmond from the east. Here the river at its ordinary stage is some forty feet wide, fringed with a dense growth of heavy forest-trees, and bordered by low marshy lands, varying from half a mile to a mile in width. Within the limits above mentioned the firm ground, above high-water mark, seldom approaches the river on either bank, and in no place did the high ground come near the stream on both banks. It was subject to frequent, sudden, and great variations in the volume of water, and a single violent storm of brief duration sufficed to cause an overflow of the bottom-lands for many days, rendering the river absolutely impassable without long and strong bridges. When we reached the river it was found that all the bridges, except that at Mechanicsville, had been destroyed. The right bank, opposite New, Mechanicsville, and Meadow bridges, was bordered by high bluffs, affording the enemy commanding positions for his batteries, enfilading the approaches, and preventing the rebuilding of important bridges. We were thus obliged to select other less exposed points for our crossings. Should McDowell effect the promised junction, we could turn the head-waters of the Chickahominy, and attack Richmond from the north and north-west, still preserving our line of supply from White House. But with the force actually available such an attempt would expose the army to the loss of its communications and to destruction in detail; for we had an able and savage antagonist, prompt to take advantage of any error on our part. The country furnished no supplies, so that we could not afford a separation from our depots. All the information obtained showed that Richmond was intrenched, that the enemy occupied in force all the approaches from the east, that he intended to dispute every step of our advance, and that his army was numerically superior. Early on the 24th of May I received a telegram from the President, informing me that McDowell would certainly march on the 26th, suggesting that I should detach a force to the right to cut off the retreat of the Confederate force in front of Fredericksburg, and desiring me to march cautiously and safely. On the same day another dispatch came, informing me that, in consequence of Stonewall Jackson's advance down the Shenandoah, the movement of McDowell was suspended. Next day the President again telegraphed that the movement against General Banks seemed so general and connected as to show that the enemy could not intend a very desperate defense of Richmond; that he thought the time was near when I "must either attack Richmond or give up the job, and come back to the defense of Washington." I replied that all my information agreed that the mass of the enemy was still in the immediate vicinity of Richmond, ready to defend it, and that the object of Jackson's movement was probably to prevent reënforcements being sent to me. On the 26th General Stoneman, with my advanced guard, cut the Virginia Central Railroad in three places. On the same day I learned that a very considerable force of the enemy was in the vicinity of Hanover Court House, to our right and rear, threatening our communications, and in position to reënforce Jackson or oppose McDowell, whose advance was then eight miles south of Fredericksburg. I ordered General F. J. Porter to move next morning to dislodge them. He took with him his own old division, Warren's provisional brigade and Emory's cavalry brigade. His operations in the vicinity of Hanover Court House were entirely successful, and resulted in completely clearing our flank, cutting the railroads in several places, destroying bridges, inflicting a severe loss upon the enemy, and fully opening the way for the advance of McDowell's corps. As there was no indication of its immediate approach, and the position at Hanover Court House was too much exposed to be permanently held, General Porter's command was withdrawn on the evening of the 29th, and returned to its old position with the main army. The campaign had taken its present position in consequence of the assurance that I should be joined by McDowell's corps. As it was now clear that I could not count with certainty upon that force, I had to do the best I could with the means at hand.

The first necessity was to establish secure communications between the two parts of the army, necessarily separated by the Chickahominy. Richmond could be attacked only by troops on the right bank. As the expectation of the advance of McDowell was still held out, and that only by the land route, I could not yet transfer the base to the James, but was obliged to retain it on the Pamunkey, and therefore to keep on the left bank a force sufficient to protect our communications and cover the junction of McDowell. It was still permissible to believe that sufficient attention would be paid to the simplest principle of war

ST. PETER'S CHURCH,
NEAR NEW KENT COURT HOUSE.

HOTEL.   FACTORY.   RECORD OFFICE—   RUINS OF JAIL.
COURT HOUSE.

NEW KENT COURT HOUSE. FROM A SKETCH MADE MAY 19, 1862.

to push McDowell rapidly on Jackson's heels, when he made his inevitable return march to join the main Confederate army and attack our right flank. The
failure of McDowell to reach me at or before the critical moment was due to
the orders he received from Washington. The bridges over the Chickahominy
first built were swept away by the floods, and it became necessary to construct
others more solid and with long log approaches, a slow and difficult task, generally carried on by men working in the water and under fire. The work was
pushed as rapidly as possible, and on the 30th of May the corps of Heintzelman
and Keyes were on the right bank of the Chickahominy, the most advanced positions being somewhat strengthened by intrenchments; Sumner's corps was on
the left bank, some six miles above Bottom's Bridge; Porter's and Franklin's
corps were on the left bank opposite the enemy's left. During the day and night
of the 30th torrents of rain fell, inundating the whole country and threatening
the destruction of our bridges.

Well aware of our difficulties, our active enemy, on the 31st of May, made
a violent attack upon Casey's division, followed by an equally formidable one
on Couch, thus commencing the battle of Fair Oaks or Seven Pines. Heintzelman came up in support, and during the afternoon Sumner crossed the river

SECTION OF THE ENCAMPMENT OF THE ARMY OF THE POTOMAC
NEAR WHITE HOUSE, VA. PROCESS REPRODUCTION OF A PHOTOGRAPH.

"We were now [middle of May] encamped [near White House] on the old Custis place, at present
owned by General Fitzhugh Lee of the Rebel cavalry service. On every side of us were immense
fields of wheat, which, but for the presence of armies, promised an abundant harvest.... It was
marvelous that such quiet could exist where a hundred thousand men were crowded together, yet
almost absolute stillness reigned throughout the vast camp during the whole of this pleasant Sabbath."—from George T. Stevens's "Three Years in the Sixth Corps." The picture represents the
space occupied by about one brigade.—EDITORS.

with great difficulty, and rendered such efficient service that the enemy was
checked. In the morning his renewed attacks were easily repulsed, and the
ground occupied at the beginning of the battle was more than recovered; he had
failed in the purpose of the attack. The ground was now so thoroughly soaked
by the rain, and the bridges were so much injured, that it was impracticable to
pursue the enemy or to move either Porter or Franklin to the support of the
other corps on the south bank. Our efforts were at once concentrated upon the
restoration of the old and the building of new bridges.

On the 1st of June the Department of Virginia, including Fort Monroe, was
placed under my command. On the 2d the Secretary telegraphed that as soon
as Jackson was disposed of in the Shenandoah, another large body of troops
would be at my service; on the 5th, that he intended sending a part of General
McDowell's force as soon as it could return from Front Royal (in the Shenandoah Valley, near Manassas Gap, and about one hundred and fifteen miles north-
west of Richmond), probably as many as I wanted; on the 11th, that McCall's
force had embarked to join me on the day preceding, and that it was intended
to send the residue of General McDowell's force to join me as speedily as pos-

sible, and that it was clear that a strong force was operating with Jackson for the purpose of preventing the forces there from joining me.

On the 26th the Secretary telegraphed that the forces of McDowell, Banks, and Frémont would be consolidated as the Army of Virginia, and would operate promptly in my aid by land.

Fortunately for the Army of the Potomac, however, I entertained serious doubts of the aid promised by the land route, so that, on the 18th, I ordered a number of transports, with supplies of all kinds, to be sent up the James, under convoy of the gun-boats, so that I might be free to cut loose from the Pamunkey and move over to the James, should circumstances enable me or render it desirable to do so.

The battle of Fair Oaks was followed by storms of great severity, continuing until the 20th of June, and adding vastly to the difficulties of our position, greatly retarding the construction of the bridges and of the defensive works regarded as necessary to cover us in the event of a repulse, and making the ground too difficult for the free movements of troops.

On the 19th Franklin's corps was transferred to the south side of the Chickahominy, Porter's corps, reënforced by McCall's division (which, with a few additional regiments, had arrived on the 12th and 13th), being left alone on the north side.

This dangerous distribution was necessary in order to concentrate sufficient force on the south side to attack Richmond with any hope of success; and, as I was still told that McDowell would arrive by the overland route, I could not yet change the base to the James.

It was not until the 25th that the condition of the ground and the completion of the bridges and intrenchments left me free to attack. On that day the first step was taken, in throwing forward the left of our picket-line, in face of a strong opposition, to gain ground enough to enable Sumner and Heintzelman to support the attack to be made next day by Franklin on the rear of Old Tavern. The successful issue of this attack would, it was supposed, drive the enemy from his positions on the heights overlooking Mechanicsville, and probably enable us to force him back into his main line of works. We would then be in position to reconnoiter the lines carefully, determine the points of attack, and take up a new base and line of supply if expedient.

During the night of the 24th information arrived confirming the anticipation that Jackson was moving to attack our right and rear, but I persisted in the operation intended for the 25th, partly to develop the strength of the enemy opposite our left and center, and with the design of attacking Old Tavern on the 26th, if Jackson's advance was so much delayed that Porter's corps would not be endangered.

Late in the afternoon of the 25th, Jackson's advance was confirmed, and it was rendered probable that he would attack next day. All hope of the advance of

McDowell's corps in season to be of any service had disappeared; the dangerous position of the army had been faithfully held to the last moment. After deducting the garrisons in rear, the railroad guards, non-combatants, and extra-duty men, there were not more than 75,000 men for battle. The enemy, with a force larger than this, the strong defenses of Richmond close at hand in his rear, was free to strike on either flank. I decided then to carry into effect the long-considered plan of abandoning the Pamunkey and taking up the line of the James.

The necessary orders were given for the defense of the depots at the White House to the last moment and its final destruction and abandonment; it was also ordered that all possible stores should be pushed to the front while communications were open.

The ground to the James had already been reconnoitered with reference to this movement.

During the night of the 26th Porter's siege-guns and wagon-trains were brought over to the south side of the Chickahominy. During the afternoon of that day his corps had been attacked in its position on Beaver Dam Creek, near Mechanicsville, and the enemy repulsed with heavy losses on their part. It was now clear that Jackson's corps had taken little or no part in this attack, and that his blow would fall farther to the rear. I therefore ordered the Fifth Corps to fall back and take position nearer the bridges, where the flanks would be more secure. This was skillfully effected early on the 27th, and it was decided that this corps should hold its position until night. All the corps commanders on the south side were on the 26th directed to be prepared to send as many troops as they could spare in support of Porter on the next day. All of them thought the enemy so strong in their respective fronts as to require all their force to hold their positions.✩

✩Soon after the appearance of General McClellan's article the following letter was received from the daughter of General Heintzelman:

"In 'The Century' for May, 1885, General McClellan has an article, 'The Peninsular Campaign,' in which there are one or two misstatements in regards to the Third Corps, commanded by General Heintzelman. Fortunately my father's papers, which are in my possession, contain replies to both allegations,—one in the handwriting of General Heintzelman's adjutant-general, and the other the rough draft of a letter addressed to General Lorenzo Thomas, then Adjutant-General of the army. General McClellan says [see above]:

"'All the corps commanders on the south side were on the 26th directed to be prepared to send as many troops as they could spare in support of Porter on the next day. All of them thought the enemy so strong in their respective fronts as to require all their force to hold their positions.'

"Upon the demand for troops General Heintzelman replied as follows:

"'HEADQUARTERS THIRD CORPS, 4 P.M., JUNE 26, 1862.
GENERAL MARCY, CHIEF OF STAFF:

"'I think I can hold the intrenchments with four brigades for twenty-four hours; that would leave two (2) brigades available for service on the other side of the

Shortly after noon on the 27th the attack commenced upon Porter's corps, in its new position near Gaines's Mill, and the contest continued all day with great vigor.

The movements of the enemy were so threatening at many points on our center and left as to indicate the presence of large numbers of troops, and for a long time created great uncertainty as to the real point of his main attack. General Porter's first call for reënforcement and a supply of axes failed to reach me; but, upon receiving a second call, I ordered Slocum's division to cross to his support. The head of the division reached the field at 3:30 and immediately went into action. At about 5 P.M. General Porter reported his position as critical, and the brigades of French and Meagher—of Richardson's division—were ordered to reënforce him, although the fearless commander of the Second Corps, General Sumner, thought it hazardous to remove them from his own threatened front. I then ordered the reserve of Heintzelman to move in support of Sumner, and a brigade of Keyes's corps to headquarters for such use as might be required. Smith's division, left alone when Slocum crossed to the aid of Porter, was so seriously threatened that I called on Sumner's corps to send a brigade to its support.

French and Meagher reached the field before dusk, just after Porter's corps had been forced by superior numbers to fall back to an interior position nearer the bridges, and, by their steady attitude, checked all further progress of the enemy and completed the attainment of the purpose in view, which was to hold the left bank of the river until dark, so that the movement to the James might be safely commenced. The siege-guns, material, and trains on the left bank were

---

river, but the men are so tired and worn out that I fear they would not be in a condition to fight after making a march of any distance....

S. P. HEINTZELMAN, BRIGADIER-GENERAL.'

"This is far from being a statement that all his forces were required to hold his own lines. "General McClellan says [see p. 359]:

" 'Meanwhile, through a misunderstanding of his orders, and being convinced that the troops of Sumner and Franklin at Savage's Station were ample for the purpose in view, Heintzelman withdrew his troops during the afternoon, crossed the swamp at Brackett's Ford, and reached the Charles City road with the rear of his column at 10 P.M.'

"When the same statement was first made in 1863, General Heintzelman wrote the following letter:

" 'HEADQUARTERS DEFENSES OF WASHINGTON, APRIL 11TH, 1863. GENERAL L. THOMAS, ADJUTANT-GENERAL, U.S.A., WASHINGTON.
GENERAL:
    I find in the "New York Tribune" of the 8th of April a "Preliminary Report of the Operations of the Army of the Potomac, since June 25th, 1862," made by General G. B. McClellan....

all safe, and the right wing was in close connection with the rest of the army. The losses were heavy, but the object justified them, or rather made them necessary. At about 6 o'clock next morning the rear-guard of regulars crossed to the south side and the bridges were destroyed.

I now bent all my energies to the transfer of the army to the James, fully realizing the very delicate nature of a flank march, with heavy trains, by a single road, in face of an active enemy, but confident that I had the army well in hand and that it would not fail me in the emergency. I thought that the enemy would not anticipate that movement, but would assume that all my efforts would be directed to cover and regain the old depots; and the event proved the correctness of this supposition. It seemed certain that I could gain one or two days for the movement of the trains, while he remained uncertain as to my intentions; and that was all I required with such troops as those of the Army of the Potomac.

During the night of the 27th I assembled the corps commanders at headquarters, informed them of my intentions, and gave them their orders. Keyes's corps was ordered to move at once, with its trains, across White Oak Swamp, and occupy positions on the farther side, to cover the passage of the remainder of the army. By noon of the 28th this first step was accomplished. During the 28th Sumner, Heintzelman, and Franklin held essentially their old positions; the trains converged steadily to the White Oak Swamp and crossed as rapidly as possible, and during this day and the succeeding night Porter followed the movement of Keyes's corps and took position to support it.

" 'In a paragraph commencing "On the 28th Porter's corps was also moved across the White Oak Swamp," etc., is the following:

> "They were ordered to hold this position until dark, then to fall back across the swamp and rejoin the rest of the army. This order was not fully carried out, nor was the exact position I designated occupied by the different divisions concerned."

" 'I was furnished with a map marked in red with the positions we should occupy.

" 'As I had the fortified lines thrown up some time before by the troops in my command, I had no difficulty in knowing where to go, and I did occupy these lines. General Sumner's were more indefinite, and he occupied a position in advance of the one designated. This left a space of half a mile unoccupied, between his right and Franklin's left. In the morning I was informed that some rebels were already at or near Dr. Trent's house, where General McClellan's headquarters had been; I sent and found this to be the case. General Franklin had also called at my headquarters and told me that the enemy were repairing the bridges of the Chickahominy, and would soon cross in force. About 1 P.M. I saw some of our troops filing into the fields between Dr. Trent's house and Savage's Station, and a few moments later Generals Franklin and W. F. Smith came to me and reported the enemy approaching, and urged me to ride to General Sumner and get him to fall back and close this gap. I rode briskly to the front, and on the Williamsburg

Early on the 28th, when Franklin's corps was drawing in its right to take a more concentrated position, the enemy opened a sharp artillery fire and made at one point a spirited attack with two Georgia regiments, which were repulsed by the two regiments on picket.

Sumner's and Heintzelman's corps and Smith's division of Franklin's were now ordered to abandon their intrenchments, so as to occupy, on the morning of the 29th, a new position in rear, shorter than the old and covering the crossing of the swamp. This new line could easily be held during the day, and these troops were ordered to remain there until dark, to cover the withdrawal of the rest of the trains, and then cross the swamp and occupy the positions about to be abandoned by Keyes's and Porter's corps. Meanwhile Slocum's division had been ordered to Savage's Station in reserve, and, during the morning, was ordered across the swamp to relieve Keyes's corps. This was a critical day; for the crossing of the swamp by the trains must be accomplished before its close, and their protection against attack from Richmond must be assured, as well as communication with the gun-boats.

A sharp cavalry skirmish on the Quaker road indicated that the enemy was alive to our movement, and might at any moment strike in force to intercept the march to the James. The difficulty was not at all with the movement of the troops, but with the immense trains that were to be moved virtually by a single road, and required the whole army for their protection. With the exception of the cavalry affair on the Quaker road, we were not troubled during this day south of the swamp, but there was severe fighting north of it. Sumner's corps evacuated their works at daylight and fell back to Allen's farm, nearly two miles west of Savage's Station, Heintzelman being on their left. Here Sumner was fu-

---

road, where it passed between my two divisions, met General Sumner's troops falling back. He wished me to turn back with him to arrange for ulterior operations, but as my right flank was entirely uncovered by these movements, I declined until after I had seen my division commanders and given them orders how to fall back. On my return there was some difficulty in finding General Sumner, and when found he informed me he had made his arrangements. I returned to my command, and on the way found the ground filled with troops, more than could be used to any advantage, and if the enemy planted a few batteries of artillery on the opposite side of the railroad, they would have been cut in pieces.

"'An aide to General McClellan having reported to me the day before to point out to me a road across the White Oak Swamp, opening from the left flank of my position of the fortified lines, I did not hesitate to retreat by that road, and left at 3 P.M. General Smith, of Franklin's corps, having sent to the rear all his batteries earlier in the day, I, at his request, let him have two of mine (Osborn's and Bramhall's), and they did good service that afternoon in checking and defeating the rebel attack.

"'My remaining would have been no aid to General Sumner, as he already had more troops than he could defile through the narrow road in his rear, and the road I took covered his left flank.

riously attacked three times, but each time drove the enemy back with much loss.

Soon afterward Franklin, having only one division with him, ascertained that the enemy had repaired some of the Chickahominy bridges and was advancing on Savage's Station, whereupon he posted his division at that point and informed Sumner, who moved his corps to the same place, arriving a little after noon. About 4 P.M. Sumner and Franklin—three divisions in all—were sharply attacked, mainly by the Williamsburg road; the fighting continued until between 8 and 9 P.M., the enemy being at all times thoroughly repulsed, and finally driven from the field.

Meanwhile, through a misunderstanding of his orders, and being convinced that the troops of Sumner and Franklin at Savage's Station were ample for the purpose in view, Heintzelman withdrew his troops during the afternoon, crossed the swamp at Brackett's Ford, and reached the Charles City road with the rear of his column at 10 P.M.

Slocum reached the position of Keyes's corps early in the afternoon, and, as soon as the latter was thus relieved, it was ordered forward to the James, near Malvern Hill, which it reached, with all its artillery and trains, early on the 30th. Porter was ordered to follow this movement and prolong the line of Keyes's corps to our right. The trains were pushed on in rear of these corps and massed under cover of the gun-boats as fast as they reached the James, at Haxall's plantation. As soon as the fighting ceased with the final repulse of the enemy, Sumner and Franklin were ordered to cross the swamp; this was effected during the night, the rear-guard crossing and destroying the bridge at 5 A.M. on the 30th. All the troops and trains were now between the swamp and

---

"'Before dark the advance of my corps was across the swamp, and by 10 P.M. the rear was over, with but little molestation from the enemy. I immediately sought General McClellan, and reported to him what I had done, and this is the first intimation I have had that my conduct was not entirely satisfactory.

"'To hold my position till dark, by which time I was to receive orders, would have been impossible. After Generals Franklin and Sumner had fallen back, my right flank and rear were uncovered, and by a road which passed entirely in my rear; and beyond my right flank my only line of retreat would have been cut off, and I would have lost my entire corps. I did not know where General McClellan was, and it was, therefore, impossible to report to him for orders.

"'When General Birney reached Fisher's Ford, the enemy were there, but not in force; they soon arrived in force, and he had to take another road more to our left. Had we been a little later they would have been in possession, and our retreat by this road cut off.

S. P. HEINTZELMAN.'

"I trust that you will be able to find space for these letters.

—MARY L. HEINTZELMAN."

—EDITORS.

CAPTAIN LE CLERC.   COMTE DE PARIS.   CAPTAIN MOHAIN.
DUC DE CHARTRES.   PRINCE DE JOINVILLE.

THE ORLÉANS PRINCES AND SUITE AT DINNER. FROM A PHOTOGRAPH.

General McClellan contributed an article to "The Century" magazine for February, 1884, on "The Princes of the House of Orléans," in which he spoke as follows of the services of the Comte de Paris and his brother, the Duc de Chartres:

"In August, 1861, the two brothers, accompanied by the Prince de Joinville, sailed for New York. Toward the close of September they arrived in Washington, and the young Princes at once received authority from the President to enter the army as aides-de-camp, being permitted to serve without taking the oath of allegiance, and without pay; it was also understood that they should be permitted to leave the service should family or political exigencies require it. They were borne on the army register as Louis Philippe d'Orléans and Robert d'Orléans, additional aides-de-camp in the regular army, with the rank of captain, and were assigned to the staff of the major-general commanding the Army of the Potomac. The Prince de Joinville accepted no rank, and simply accompanied headquarters, on the invitation of the general commanding, as an amateur and friend. The position held by these "young gentlemen"—as the Prince de Joinville always designated them—was not free from difficulties.

the James, and the first critical episode of the movement was successfully accomplished.

The various corps were next pushed forward to establish connection with Keyes and Porter, and hold the different roads by which the enemy could advance from Richmond and strike our line of march. I determined to hold the positions now taken until the trains had all reached a place of safety, and then concentrate the army near the James, where it could enjoy a brief rest after the fatiguing battles and marches through which it was passing, and then renew the advance on Richmond.

General Franklin, with Smith's division of his own corps, Richardson's of the Second, and Naglee's brigade were charged with the defense of the White Oak Swamp crossing. Slocum held the ground thence to the Charles City road; Kearny from that road to the Long Bridge road; McCall on his left; Hooker thence to the Quaker road; Sedgwick at Nelson's farm, in rear of McCall and Kearny. The Fifth Corps was at Malvern Hill, the Fourth at Turkey Bridge. The trains moved on during this day, and at 4 P.M. the last reached Malvern Hill and kept on to Haxall's, so that the most difficult part of the task was accomplished, and it only remained for the troops to hold their ground until nightfall, and then continue the march to the positions selected near Malvern Hill.

The fighting on this day (June 30th) was very severe, and extended along the whole line. It first broke out between 12 and 1, on General Franklin's command, in the shape of a fierce artillery fire, which was kept up through the day and inflicted serious losses. The enemy's infantry made several attempts to

---

Princes who might at any time be called upon to assume their places in the government of a great nation, yet serving in the army of a republic whose cause was not regarded with very friendly eyes by the existing government of their own country, they had many contradictions to reconcile, many embarrassments to overcome. Connected by family ties with so many of the royal families of Europe, always received by them as of royal rank, the elder regarded by so many in France as the rightful heir to the throne, they could never lose sight of the dignity of their position, while it was at the same time necessary for them to perform their duties in a subordinate grade, and to win the confidence and friendship of their new comrades, who were sure to weigh men by their personal qualities and abilities, not by their social position across the Atlantic. Their task was accomplished with complete success, for they gained the full confidence, respect, and regard of their commander and their comrades. From the moment they entered the service, they were called upon to perform precisely the same duties and in precisely the same manner as their companions on the personal staff of their commander....

"Their conduct was characterized by an innate love for a soldier's life, by an intense desire to perfect themselves in the profession of arms by actual experience of war on a large scale, and by unswerving devotion to duty. Not only this, their heads and hearts were with us in our hour of trial, and I believe that, next to their own France, they most loved this country, for which they so freely and so often exposed their lives on the field of battle.

"Soon after the beginning of the peninsular campaign, the Princes were strongly urged by their friends at home to return at once to England, partly to receive the large numbers of their adherents expected to attend the Exhibition of 1862, and partly because the French ex-

cross near the old bridge and below, but was in every case thrown back. Franklin held his position until after dark, and during the night fell back to Malvern. At half-past 2 Slocum's left was attacked in vain on the Charles City road. At about 3 McCall was attacked, and, after 5 o'clock, under the pressure of heavy masses, he was forced back; but Hooker came up from the left, and Sedgwick from the rear, and the two together not only stopped the enemy, but drove him off the field.

At about 4 P.M. heavy attacks commenced on Kearny's left, and three ineffectual assaults were made. The firing continued until after dark. About midnight Sumner's and Heintzelman's corps and McCall's division withdrew from the positions they had so gallantly held, and commenced their march to Malvern, which they reached unmolested soon after daybreak. Just after the rear of the trains reached Malvern, about 4 P.M., the enemy attacked Porter's corps, but were promptly shaken off.

Thus, on the morning of July 1st, the army was concentrated at Malvern, with the trains at Haxall's, in rear. The supplies which had been sent from White House on the 18th were at hand in the James.

After consultation with Commodore Rodgers, I decided that Harrison's Landing was a better position for the resting-place of the army, because the channel passed so close to City Point as to enable the enemy to prevent the passage of transports if we remained at Malvern. It was, however, necessary to accept battle where we were, in order to give ample time for the trains to reach Harrison's, as well as to give the enemy a blow that would check his farther pursuit.

Accordingly, the army was carefully posted on the admirable position of Malvern Hill, with the right thrown back below Haxall's. The left was the natural point of attack, and there the troops were massed and the reserve artillery placed, while full preparations were made to frustrate any attempt to turn our right. Early in the forenoon the army was concentrated and ready for battle, in a position of unusual strength—one which, with such troops as held it, could justly be regarded as impregnable. It was, then, with perfect confidence that I awaited the impending battle.

----

pedition to Mexico had greatly strained the relations between this country and France. They persisted in remaining with the army until the close of the Seven Days, and left only when assured that the immediate resumption of the attack on Richmond was improbable. Had the prompt receipt of reënforcements rendered a new advance practicable, it is certain that no considerations would have withdrawn them from the field until the completion of the operations against Richmond. Although warmly attached to them and very unwilling to lose their services, their commander fully recognized the imperative nature of the reasons for their departure, and entirely acquiesced in the propriety of their prompt return to Europe."

Soon after the termination of the war, the Comte de Paris began his extensive "History of the Civil War in America," the first volume of the American edition being issued in 1875.—EDITORS.

The enemy began feeling the position between 9 and 10 A.M., and at 3 P.M. made a sharp attack upon Couch's division, which remained lying on the ground until the enemy were within close range, when they rose and delivered a volley which shattered and drove back their assailants in disorder. At 4 P.M. the firing ceased for a while, and the lull was availed of to rectify the position and make every preparation for the approaching renewal of the attack. It came at 6 P.M., opened by the fire of all their artillery and followed by desperate charges of infantry advancing at a run. They were always repulsed with the infliction of fearful loss, and in several instances our infantry awaited their approach within a few yards, poured in a single volley, and then dashed forward with the bayonet. At 7 P.M. the enemy was accumulating fresh troops, and the brigades of Meagher and Sickles were sent from Sumner's and Heintzelman's corps to reënforce Porter and Couch; fresh batteries were moved forward from the reserve artillery and the ammunition was replenished.

The enemy then repeated his attacks in the most desperate style until dark, but the battle ended with his complete repulse, with very heavy losses, and without his even for one moment gaining a foothold in our position. His frightful losses were in vain. I doubt whether, in the annals of war, there was ever a more persistent and gallant attack, or a more cool and effective resistance.

Although the result of this bloody battle was a complete victory on our part, it was necessary, for the reasons already given, to continue the movement to Harrison's, whither the trains had been pushed during the night of the 30th of June and the day of the 1st of July. Immediately after the final repulse the orders were given for the withdrawal of the army. The movement was covered by Keyes's corps. So complete was the enemy's discomfiture, and so excellent the conduct of the rear-guard, that the last of the trains reached Harrison's after dark on the 3d, without loss and unmolested by the enemy.

This movement was now successfully accomplished, and the Army of the Potomac was at last in a position on its true line of operations, with its trains intact, no guns lost save those taken in battle, when the artillerists had proved their heroism and devotion by standing to their guns until the enemy's infantry were in the midst of them.

During the "Seven Days" the Army of the Potomac consisted of 143 regiments of infantry, 55 batteries, and less than 8 regiments of cavalry, all told. The opposing Confederate army consisted of 187 regiments of infantry, 79 batteries, and 14 regiments of cavalry. The losses of the two armies from June 25th to July 2d were:☆

☆Tables of the "Opposing Forces" of the "Seven Days," made from the fullest revised data of the War Records office, will show that the Army of the Potomac consisted of 150 regiments of infantry; 2 regiments and 1 battalion of engineers; 1 regiment of heavy or siege artillery; 58 batteries; and 10 regiments of cavalry. The Confederate forces consisted of 173 regiments and 12 battalions of infantry; 71 batteries;

CONFEDERATE BATTERY AT MATHIAS POINT, OR BUDD'S FERRY, ON THE POTOMAC.
FROM A SKETCH MADE IN FEBRUARY, 1862.

	Killed.	Wounded.	Missing.	Total.
Confederate Army	2,823	13,703	3,223	19,749
Army of the Potomac	1,734	8,062	6,053	15,849

The Confederate losses in killed and wounded alone were greater than the total losses of the Army of the Potomac in killed, wounded, and missing.

No praise can be too great for the officers and men who passed through these seven days of battle, enduring fatigue without a murmur, successfully meeting and repelling every attack made upon them, always in the right place at the right time, and emerging from the fiery ordeal a compact army of veterans, equal to any task that brave and disciplined men can be called upon to undertake. They needed now only a few days of well-earned repose, a renewal of ammunition and supplies, and reënforcements to fill the gaps made in their ranks by so many desperate encounters, to be prepared to advance again, with entire confidence, to meet their worthy antagonists in other battles. It was, however, decided by the authorities at Washington, against my earnest remonstrances, to abandon the position on the James, and the campaign. The Army of the Potomac was accordingly withdrawn, and it was not until two years later that it again found itself under its last commander at substantially the same point on the bank of the James. It was as evident in 1862 as in 1865 that there was the true defense of Washington, and that it was on the banks of the James that the fate of the Union was to be decided.

---

and 12 regiments of cavalry. General McClellan correctly estimates the Union loss, but the Confederate loss, according to the revised returns, was: killed, 3286; wounded, 15,909; missing, 940. Total, 20,135.—EDITORS.

CHAPTER 13

THE SECOND BATTLE OF BULL RUN.[‡]

John Pope, Major-General, U.S.A.

Early in June, 1862, I was in command of the army corps known as the "Army of the Mississippi," which formed the left wing of the army engaged in operations against Corinth, Miss., commanded by General Halleck. A few days after Corinth was evacuated I went to St. Louis on a short leave of absence from my command, and while there I received a telegram from Mr. Stanton, Secretary of War, requesting me to come to Washington immediately. I at once communicated the fact to General Halleck by telegraph, and received a reply from him strongly objecting to my leaving the army which was under his command. I quite concurred with him both as to his objections to my going to Washington for public reasons and as to the unadvisability of such a step on personal considerations. I was obliged, however, to go, and I went accordingly, but with great reluctance and against the urgent protests of my friends in St. Louis, and subsequently of many friends in the Army of the West.

When I reached Washington the President was absent at West Point, but I reported in person to Secretary Stanton. I had never seen him before, and his peculiar appearance and manners made a vivid impression on me. He was short and stout. His long beard, which hung over his breast, was slightly tinged with gray even at that time, and he had the appearance of a man who had lost much sleep and was tired both in body and mind. Certainly, with his large eye-glasses and rather disheveled appearance, his presence was not imposing. Although he was very kind and civil to me, his manner was abrupt and his speech short and rather dictatorial. He entered at once on the business in hand, seemingly without the least idea that any one should object to, or be reluctant to agree to, his views and purposes. He was surprised, and, it seemed to me, not well pleased, that I did not assent to his

[‡]Accompanying General Beauregard's paper on the First Battle of Bull Run (p. 85) are maps and many pictures of interest with reference to the second battle.—EDITORS.

PICKETING THE RAPIDAN.

plans with effusion; but went on to unfold them in the seeming certainty that they must be submitted to. He informed me that the purpose was to unite the armies under McDowell, Frémont, and Banks, all three of whom were my seniors in rank, and to place me in general command. These armies were scattered over the northern part of Virginia, with little or no communication or concert of action with one another; Frémont and Banks being at Middletown, in the Shenandoah Valley, and McDowell's corps widely separated, King's division at Fredericksburg, and Ricketts's at and beyond Manassas Junction.

The general purpose at that time was to demonstrate with the army toward Gordonsville and Charlottesville and draw off as much as possible of the force in front of General McClellan, who then occupied the line of the Chickahominy, and to distract the attention of the enemy in his front so as to reduce as far as practicable the resistance opposed to his advance on Richmond.

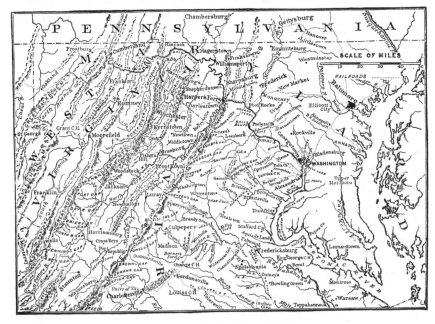

OUTLINE MAP OF THE CAMPAIGN.

It became apparent to me at once that the duty to be assigned to me was in the nature of a forlorn-hope, and my position was still further embarrassed by the fact that I was called from another army and a different field of duty to command an army of which the corps commanders were all my seniors in rank. I therefore strongly urged that I be not placed in such a position, but be permitted to return to my command in the West, to which I was greatly attached and with which I had been closely identified in several successful operations on the

VIEW IN CULPEPER DURING THE OCCUPATION BY POPE. FROM A PHOTOGRAPH.

The building with the ball and vane is the Court House, in which Confederate prisoners were confined.

Mississippi. It was not difficult to forecast the delicate and embarrassing position in which I should be placed, nor the almost certainly disagreeable, if not unfortunate, issue of such organization for such a purpose.

It would be tedious to relate the conversations between the President, the Secretary of War, and myself on this subject. Sufficient to say that I was finally informed that the public interests required my assignment to this command, and that it was my duty to submit cheerfully. An order from the War Department was accordingly issued organizing the Army of Virginia, to consist of the army corps of McDowell, Banks, and Frémont, and placing me in command.

One result of this order was the very natural protest of General Frémont against being placed under the command of his junior in rank, and his request to be relieved from the command of his corps.[φ]

It was equally natural that the subordinate officers and the enlisted men of those corps should have been ill-pleased at the seeming affront to their own officers, involved in calling an officer strange to them and to the country in which they were operating, and to the character of the service in which they were engaged, to supersede well-known and trusted officers who had been with them from the beginning, and whose reputation was so closely identified with their own. How far this feeling prevailed among them, and how it influenced their actions, if it did so at all, I am not able to tell; but it is only proper for me to say (and it is a pleasure as well as a duty to say it) that Generals McDowell and Banks never exhibited to me the slightest feeling on the subject either in their conversation or acts. Indeed, I think it would be hard to find officers more faithful to their duty or more deeply interested in the success of the army. To Gen-

---

[φ]This request was complied with, and on the 29th of June, 1862, General Franz Sigel assumed command of the First Corps.—EDITORS.

eral McDowell especially is due my gratitude for his zeal and fidelity in what was and ought to have been considered a common cause, the success of the Union Army.

Knowing very well the difficulties and embarrassments certain to arise from all these sources, and the almost hopeless character of the service demanded of me, I, nevertheless, felt obliged, in deference to the wish of the President and Secretary of War, to submit; but I entered on this command with great reluctance and serious forebodings.

On the 27th of June, accordingly, I assumed command of the Army of Virginia, which consisted of the three corps above named, which numbered as follows: Frémont's corps, 11,500; Banks's corps, 8000, and McDowell's corps, 18,500,—in all, 38,000 men.[*] The cavalry numbered about 5000, but most of it was badly organized and armed, and in poor condition for service. These forces were scattered over a wide district of country, not within supporting distance of one another, and some of the brigades and divisions were badly organized and in a more or less demoralized condition. This was especially the case in the army corps of General Frémont, as shown in the report of General Sigel which was sent me when he had assumed command of it.

My first object was, therefore, to bring the three corps of the army together, or near enough together to be within supporting distance of one another, and to put them in as efficient a condition for active service as was possible with the time and means at my disposal. When I assumed this command, the troops under General Stonewall Jackson had retired from the valley of the Shenandoah to Richmond, so there was not at that time any force of the enemy of any consequence within several days' march of my command. I accordingly sent orders to General Sigel to move forward, cross the Shenandoah at Front Royal, and, pursuing the west side of the Blue Ridge to Luray, and then crossing it at Thornton's Gap, take post at Sperryville. At the same time I directed General Banks to cross the Shenandoah at Front Royal and proceed by way of Chester Gap to Little Washington. Ricketts's division of McDowell's corps, then at and beyond Manassas Junction, was ordered to move forward to Waterloo Bridge, where the turnpike from Warrenton to Sperryville crosses the Rappahannock, there known as Hedgman's River. In deference to the wishes of the Govern-

---

[*]On the 27th of June, according to the "Official Records," the strength of the Army of Virginia appears to have been about as follows: Headquarters, 200; Sigel's corps (Frémont's), 13,200; Banks's, 12,100; McDowell's, 19,300; cavalry, 5800. Total of the three army corps, 44,600, or 6600 more than General Pope's estimate; aggregate, 50,600, or 7600 more than General Pope's estimate. On the 31st of July the consolidated report showed 46,858 "effectives." An error in the report of Banks's corps reduced this aggregate to 40,358. After the battle of Cedar Mountain, and when he had been reënforced by Reno (7000), Pope estimated his force at barely 40,000. With this force were 25 field-batteries numbering about 150 guns.—EDITORS.

ment, and much against my opinion, King's division of the same corps was kept at Fredericksburg. The wide separation of this division from the main body of the army not only deprived me of its use when, as became plain afterward, it was much needed, but left us exposed to the constant danger that the enemy might interpose between us.

The partial concentration of the corps so near to the Blue Ridge and with open communications with the Shenandoah Valley seemed to me best to fulfill the object of covering that valley from any movements from the direction of Richmond with any force less than the army under my command. The position was one also which gave most favorable facilities for the intended operations toward Gordonsville and Charlottesville.

At the date of my orders for this concentration of the army under my command,[*] the Army of the Potomac under General McClellan occupied both banks of the Chickahominy, and it was hoped that his advance against Richmond, so long delayed, might be facilitated by vigorous use of the Army of Virginia.

During the preparation for the march of the corps of Banks and Sigel toward Sperryville and Little Washington, began the series of battles which preceded and attended the retreat of General McClellan from the Chickahominy toward Harrison's Landing.

When first General McClellan began to intimate by his dispatches that he designed making this retreat toward the James River, I suggested to the President the impolicy of such a movement, and the serious consequences that would be likely to result from it; I urged upon him that he send orders to General McClellan, if he were unable to maintain his position on the Chickahominy, and were pushed by superior forces of the enemy, to mass his whole force on the north side of that stream, even at the risk of losing some of his material of war, and endeavor to retire in the direction of Hanover Court House, but in no event to retreat farther south than the White House on the Pamunkey River. I told the President that by the movement to the James River the whole army of the enemy would be interposed between General McClellan and myself, and that they would then be able to strike in either direction as might seem most advantageous to them; that this movement would leave entirely unprotected, except so far as the small force under my command could protect it, the whole region in front of Washington, and that it would therefore be impossible to send him any of my troops without putting it in the power of the enemy to

---

[*]The President's order constituting the Army of Virginia is dated June 26th. On that day the second of the Seven Days' battles referred to in the next paragraph began with Lee's attack on McClellan's right near Mechanicsville. General Pope took command on the 27th; on that day was fought the battle of Gaines's Mill, and the march to the James began that night.—EDITORS.

FROM A PHOTOGRAPH TAKEN SINCE THE WAR.

exchange Richmond for Washington; that to them the loss of Richmond would be comparatively a small loss, while to us the loss of Washington would be almost a fatal blow. I was so impressed with these opinions that I several times urged them upon the attention of the President and the Secretary of War.

The soundness of these views can be easily tested by subsequent facts.

RETREAT OF THE UNION TROOPS ACROSS THE RAPPAHANNOCK AT RAPPAHANNOCK STATION. AFTER A SKETCH MADE AT THE TIME.

The enemy actually did choose between the danger of losing Richmond and the chance of capturing Washington.[#] Stonewall Jackson's corps was detached from Lee's army confronting McClellan at Harrison's Landing early in July, and on the 19th of that month was concentrated at Gordonsville in my front; while Stuart's cavalry division, detached from Lee's army about the same time, was at or near Fredericksburg watching our movements from that direction. On the 13th of August Longstreet's whole corps was dispatched to join Jackson at Gordonsville, to which place he had fallen back from Cedar Mountain, and the head of Longstreet's corps had joined Jackson at that place on August 15th. These forces were commanded by Lee in person, who was at Gordonsville on that day. The first troops of the Army of the Potomac which left Harrison's Landing moved out from that place

---

[#]General Lee says in his report dated April 18th, 1863:

"To meet the advance of the latter [Pope] ... General Jackson, with his own and Ewell's divisions, was ordered to proceed toward Gordonsville on July 13th. Upon reaching that vicinity he ascertained that the force under General Pope was superior to his own, but the uncertainty that then surrounded the designs of McClellan rendered it inexpedient to reënforce him from the army at Richmond.... Assistance was promised should the progress of General Pope put it in our power to strike an effectual blow without withdrawing the troops too long from the defense of the capital. The army at Westover [Harrison's Landing], continuing to manifest no intention of resuming active operations, and General Pope's advance having reached the Rapidan, General A. P. Hill, with his division, was ordered on July 27th to join General Jackson. At the same time, in order to keep McClellan stationary, or, if possible, to cause him to withdraw, General D. H. Hill, commanding south of James River, was directed to threaten his communications."

And in his report, dated June 8th, 1863:

"The victory at Cedar Run [August 9th] effectually checked the progress of the enemy for the time, but it soon became apparent that his army was being largely increased. The corps of Major-General Burnside from North Carolina, which had reached Fredericksburg [August 4th and 5th], was reported to have moved up the Rappahannock a few days after the battle, to unite with General Pope, and a part of General McClellan's army was believed to have left Westover for the same purpose. It therefore seemed that active operations on the James were no longer contemplated, and that the most effectual way to relieve Richmond

on August 14th, / at which date there was nothing of Lee's army, except D. H. Hill's corps, left in front of McClellan or near to him. Hill's corps could have opposed but little effective resistance to the advance of the Army of the Potomac upon Richmond.

It seems clear, then, that the views expressed to the President and Secretary of War, as heretofore set forth, were sound, and that the enemy had left McClellan to work his will on Richmond, while they pushed forward against the small army under my command and to the capture of Washington. This movement of Lee was, in my opinion, in accordance with true military principle, and was the natural result of McClellan's retreat to Harrison's Landing, which completely separated the Army of the Potomac from the Army of Virginia and left the entire force of the enemy interposed between them.

The retreat of General McClellan to Harrison's Landing was, however, continued to the end. During these six days of anxiety and apprehension Mr. Lincoln spent much of his time in the office of the Secretary of War, most of that time reclining on a sofa or lounge. The Secretary of War was always with him, and from time to time his Cabinet officers came in. Mr. Lincoln himself appeared much depressed and wearied, though occasionally, while waiting for telegrams, he would break into some humorous remark, which seemed rather a protest against his despondent manner than any genuine expression of enjoyment. He spoke no unkind word of any one, and appeared to be anxious him-

---

from any danger of attack from that quarter would be to reënforce General Jackson and advance upon General Pope."

—EDITORS.

/On the 30th of July General Halleck ordered General McClellan to send away his sick as rapidly as possible. On the 3d of August General Halleck telegraphed: "It is determined to withdraw your army from the Peninsula to Aquia Creek. You will take immediate measures to effect this.... Your material and transportation should be removed first." General McClellan protested against the movement, as did Generals Dix, Burnside, and Sumner. General Halleck replied to General McClellan that he saw no alternative. "There is no change of plans." "I ... have taken the responsibility ... and am to risk my reputation on it."

The movement of the sick began at once. Between the 1st of August, when the order was received, and the 16th, when the evacuation of Harrison's Landing was completed, 14,159 were sent away, many of them necessarily to the North. The first troops arrived at Aquia within seven days, and the last of the infantry within 26 days, after the receipt of the order.

(The original movement of the Army of the Potomac, from Alexandria to Fort Monroe, had taken 37 days, and Mr. Tucker, who had superintended its transport, said of it: "I confidently submit that for economy and celerity this expedition is without a parallel on record.")

In the terms of General Halleck's order of August 3d, there were to be transported first the 14,159 sick; next all the material of the army, and the transportation, embracing 3100 wagons, 350 ambulances, 13,000 horses and mules; then 89,407 officers and men, 360 guns, and 13,000 artillery and cavalry horses, together with the baggage and stores in use; but in order to hasten the movement this routine was not rigidly observed, and the movement of Peck's division (ordered to move last) of 7581 men and 10 guns was countermanded by General Halleck.—EDITORS.

self to bear all the burden of the situation; and when the final result was reported he rose with a sorrowful face and left the War Department.

A day or two after General McClellan reached the James River I was called before the President and his Cabinet to consult upon means and movements to relieve him. I do not know that it would be proper even at this day for me to state what occurred or what was said during this consultation, except so far as I was myself directly concerned. General McClellan was calling for reënforcements, and stating that "much over rather than under one hundred thousand men" were necessary before he could resume operations against Richmond. I had not under my command one-half that force.

I stated to the President and Cabinet that I stood ready to undertake any movement, however hazardous, to relieve the Army of the Potomac. Some suggestions which seemed to me impracticable were made, and much was said which under the circumstances will not bear repetition.

I stated that only on one condition would I be willing to involve the army under my command in direct operations against the enemy to relieve the Army of the Potomac. That condition was, that such peremptory orders be given to General McClellan, and in addition such measures taken in advance as would render it certain that he would make a vigorous attack on the enemy with his whole force the moment he heard that I was engaged.

In face of the extraordinary difficulties which existed and the terrible responsibility about to be thrown on me, I considered it my duty to state plainly to the President that I could not risk the destruction of my army in such a movement as was suggested if it were left to the discretion of General McClel-

THE BATTLE OF CEDAR MOUNTAIN—VIEW FROM THE UNION LINES.
FROM A SKETCH MADE AT THE TIME.

The picture shows the artillery duel and deployment of troops before the main attack toward the right, in the middle distance.

lan or any one else to withhold the vigorous use of his whole force when my attack was made.

The whole plan of campaign for the army under my command was necessarily changed by the movement of the Army of the Potomac to Harrison's Landing. A day or two after General McClellan had reached his position on James River I addressed him a letter stating to him my position, the disposition of the troops under my command, and what was required of them, and requesting him in all good faith and earnestness to write me freely and fully his views, and to suggest to me any measures which he thought desirable to enable me to coöperate with him, and offering to render any assistance in my power to the operations of the army under his command. I stated to him that I was very anxious to assist him in his operations, and that I would undertake any labor or run any risk for that purpose. I therefore requested him to feel no hesitation in communicating freely with me, as he might rest assured that any suggestions he made would meet all respect and consideration from me, and that, so far as was within my power, I would carry out his wishes with all energy and all the means at my command. In reply to this communication I received a letter from General McClellan very general in its terms and proposing nothing toward the accomplishment of the purpose I suggested to him.

It became very apparent, therefore, considering the situation in which the Army of the Potomac and the Army of Virginia were placed in relation to each other and the absolute necessity of harmonious and prompt coöperation between them, that some military superior both of General McClellan and myself should be placed in general command of all the operations in Virginia, with power to enforce joint action between the two armies within that field of operations. General Halleck was accordingly called to Washington and assigned to the command-in-chief of the army,☆ though Mr. Stanton was opposed to it and used some pretty strong language to me concerning General Halleck and my action in the matter. They, however, established friendly relations soon after General Halleck assumed command.

The reasons which induced me, in the first instance, to ask to be relieved from the command of the Army of Virginia, as heretofore set forth, were

☆The first step toward calling General Halleck to Washington appears in the President's telegram of July 24 asking if he could not come "for a flying visit." On the 6th, Governor Sprague was sent to him at Corinth, on a confidential mission, arriving there on the 10th. Meanwhile the President had visited General McClellan and received from his hands the Harrison's Bar letter. On the 11th, General Halleck was appointed General-in-chief. Mr. Chase says in his diary (see "Life and Public Services of S. P. Chase," by J. W. Schuckers, p. 447) that he and Mr. Stanton "proposed to the President to send Pope to the James and give [Ormsby M.] Mitchel the command of the front of Washington.... The President was not prepared for anything so decisive, and sent for Halleck and made him Commander-in-chief." Secretary Welles says ("Lincoln and Seward," p. 191): "Pope also... uniting with Stanton and General Scott in advising that McClellan should be superseded and Halleck placed in charge of military affairs at Washington."—EDITORS.

greatly intensified by the retreat of General McClellan to James River and the bitter feelings and controversies which it occasioned, and I again requested the President to relieve me from the command and permit me to return to the West. The utter impossibility of sending General McClellan anything like the reënforcements he asked for, the extreme danger to Washington involved in sending him even a fraction of the small force under my command, and the glaring necessity of concentrating these two armies in some judicious manner and as rapidly as possible, resulted in a determination to withdraw the Army of the Potomac from the James River and unite it with the Army of Virginia. The question of the command of these armies when united was never discussed in my presence, if at all, and I left Washington with the natural impression that when this junction was accomplished General Halleck would himself assume the command in the field. Under the changed condition of things brought about by General McClellan's retreat to James River, and the purpose to withdraw his army and unite it with that under my command, the campaign of the Army of Virginia was limited to the following objects:

1. To cover the approaches to Washington from any enemy advancing from the direction of Richmond, and to oppose and delay its advance to the last extremity, so as to give all the time possible for the withdrawal of the Army of the Potomac from the James River.
2. If no heavy forces of the enemy moved north, to operate on their lines of communication with Gordonsville and Charlottesville, so as to force Lee to make heavy detachments from his force at Richmond and facilitate to that extent the withdrawal of the Army of the Potomac.

Halleck was of the opinion that the junction of the two armies could be made on the line of the Rappahannock, and my orders to hold fast to my communications with Fredericksburg, through which place McClellan's army was to make its junction with the Army of Virginia, were repeated positively.

The decision of the enemy to move north with the bulk of his army was promptly made and vigorously carried out, so that it became apparent, even before General McClellan began to embark his army, that the line of the Rappahannock was too far to the front. That fact, however, was not realized by Halleck until too late for any change which could be effectively executed.

Such was the organization of the Army of Virginia, and such its objects and the difficulties with which it was embarrassed from the very beginning. This rather long preface appears to me to be essential to any sufficient understanding of the second battle of Bull Run, and why and how it was fought.

It is also necessary as a reply to a statement industriously circulated at the time and repeated again and again for obvious purposes, until no doubt it is generally believed, that I had set out to capture Richmond with a force suffi-

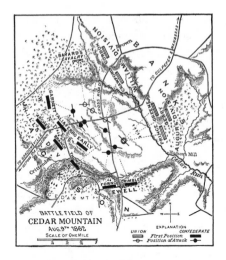

BATTLE FIELD OF
CEDAR MOUNTAIN
AUG.9TH 1862
SCALE OF ONE MILE

EXPLANATION
UNION   CONFEDERATE
First Position
Position of Attack

NOTE ON THE BATTLE OF CEDAR MOUN-
TAIN: On the 13th of July, the regular command of Jackson, consisting of the divisions of
Ewell and Winder, marched from Mechanicsville, on the Chickahominy, under orders to
dispute the advance of Pope's army south of
the Rapidan. The column reached Gordonsville on the 19th, and Jackson, on learning that
Pope's forces outnumbered his own, remained
inactive until reënforced early in August by the
division of A. P. Hill. Pope was now on the
Upper Rappahannock, with the corps of Banks
and Sigel, the former at Culpeper, the latter
at Sperryville. The outposts of infantry and
cavalry under Generals S. W. Crawford and
George D. Bayard were along the Rapidan,
covering the approaches to Culpeper and
Sperryville [see map, p. 366]. On the 8th Bayard's pickets discovered the enemy crossing at
Barnett's Ford in large force, and retired along the Orange Court House road toward Culpeper.

Jackson's object was to strike Banks at Culpeper before the latter could be reënforced. On Jackson's approach, Pope ordered Banks's corps forward to Cedar Mountain, about eight miles beyond
Culpeper, where it arrived in detachments, being in hand by noon of the 9th, in two divisions,
numbering about 8000 men, under Generals C. C. Angur and A. S. Williams. General J. B. Ricketts's division, of McDowell's corps, was coming up as support. The Confederate divisions of Generals C. S. Winder and R. S. Ewell were now disposed along the northern base of the mountain, the
brigades of General I. R. Trimble, Colonel H. Forno, and General J. A. Early, of Ewell's division,
on the right, with those of General W. B. Taliaferro and Lieutenant Colonel T. S. Garnett, of
Winder's division, on the left, and Winder's "Stonewall" brigade, under Colonel C. A. Ronald, in
reserve. The brigades of Generals L. O'B. Branch, J. L. Archer, and E. C. Thomas, of A. P. Hill's division, were within call, the entire command under Jackson on the field, numbering at least 20,000.
The Confederates opened the battle, sending forward Early and Taliaferro at 3 o'clock, but moving with caution.

Banks's line was formed in the valley of Cedar Run, and overlapped the Confederate left.
Geary and Prince, advancing, encountered Early and Taliaferro on the broad cultivated plateau

cient for the purpose, and that the falling back from the Rapidan was unexpected by the Government, and a great disappointment to it. The whole campaign was, and perhaps is yet, misunderstood because of the false impressions
created by this statement.

Under the orders heretofore referred to, the concentration of the three
corps of the Army of Virginia (except King's division of McDowell's corps) was
completed, Sigel's corps being at Sperryville, Banks's at Little Washington, and
Ricketts's division of McDowell's corps at Waterloo Bridge. I assumed the command in person July 29th, 1862.

As this paper is mainly concerned with the second battle of Bull Run, I
shall not recount any of the military operations beyond the Rappahannock, nor
give any account of the battle of Cedar Mountain [see above] and the skirmishes which followed.

south of the Culpeper road, while Crawford closed in from the north on the enemy's left. The advantage was with Banks. At 6 o'clock the battle was at its height: Garnett struck the flank of Crawford, and the fresh brigades of Hill's division were led against Prince and Geary. The extreme right of Banks's line, the brigade of General G. H. Gordon (Williams's division), now charged up to the point where Crawford had gone in, and General G. S. Greene's brigade (Angur's division) moved to the aid of Prince and Geary. Meanwhile, Banks's artillery having been forced back by the guns on the mountain-sides, Ewell threw forward his brigades on the right, Thomas (Hill's division) came forward into the gap between Early and Forno, and the battle was decided by the repulse everywhere of Banks's troops. The last charge was made by Bayard's cavalry on the extreme Union right. The advance of Branch brought fresh muskets against Bayard, and the successes of Jackson all along the line closed the day. After dark Banks withdrew to his first position north of Cedar Creek and was there met by Ricketts's division and by General Pope in person.

The journal of General L. O'B. Branch, written August 13th, contains the following description of the battle: "General Jackson came to me and told me his left was beaten and broken, and the enemy was turning him and he wished me to advance. I was already in line of battle and instantly gave the order, 'Forward, march.' I had not gone 100 yards through the woods before we met the celebrated Stonewall Brigade, utterly routed and fleeing as fast as they could run. After proceeding a short distance farther we met the enemy pursuing. My brigade opened upon them and quickly drove the enemy back from the woods into a large field. Following up to the edge of the field, I came in view of large bodies of the enemy, and having a very fine position, I opened upon them with great effect. The enemy's cavalry attempted to charge us in two columns, but the fire soon broke them and sent them fleeing across the field in every direction. The infantry then retreated also. Advancing into the field, I halted near the middle of it, in doubt which direction to take. Just at that moment General Jackson came riding up from my rear alone. I reported my brigade as being solid, and asked for orders. My men recognized him and raised a terrific shout as he rode along the line with his hat off. He evidently knew how to appreciate a brigade that had gone through a hot battle and was then following the retreating enemy without having broken its line of battle, and remained with me ... until the pursuit ceased."

General S. W. Crawford gives this account of the flank movement attempted by his brigade: "Onward these regiments charged, driving the enemy's infantry back through the wood beyond.... But the reserves of the enemy were at once brought up and thrown upon the broken ranks. The field-officers had all been killed, wounded, or taken prisoners; the support I looked for did not arrive, and my gallant men, broken, decimated by that fearful fire, that unequal contest, fell back again across the space, leaving most of their number upon the field." Crawford's brigade lost 494 killed or wounded, and 373 missing, out of a total of 1767 engaged.—EDITORS.

It is only necessary to say that the course of these operations made it plain enough that the Rappahannock was too far to the front, and that the movements of Lee were too rapid and those of McClellan too slow to make it possible, with the small force I had, to hold that line, or to keep open communication with Fredericksburg without being turned on my right flank by Lee's whole army and cut off altogether from Washington.

On the 21st of August, being then at Rappahannock Station, my little army confronted by nearly the whole force under General Lee, which had compelled the retreat of McClellan to Harrison's Landing, I was positively assured that two days more would see me largely enough reënforced by the Army of the Potomac to be not only secure, but to assume the offensive against Lee, and I was instructed to hold on "and fight like the devil."

I accordingly held on till the 26th of August, when, finding myself to be

CHARGE OF UNION CAVALRY UPON THE CONFEDERATE ADVANCE NEAR
BRANDY STATION, AUGUST 20, 1862. FROM A SKETCH MADE AT THE TIME.

outflanked on my right by the main body of Lee's army, while Jackson's corps
having passed Salem and Rectortown the day before were in rapid march in the
direction of Gainesville and Manassas Junction, and seeing that none of the
reënforcements promised me were likely to arrive, I determined to abandon the
line of the Rappahannock and communications with Fredericksburg, and concentrate my whole force in the direction of Warrenton and Gainesville, to
cover the Warrenton pike, and still to confront the enemy rapidly marching to
my right.‡

Stonewall Jackson's movement on Manassas Junction was plainly seen and
promptly reported, and I notified General Halleck of it. He informed me on the

‡Reynolds's division of Porter's corps, having arrived at Aquia on August 13th and 20th, joined General
Pope on the 22d, and was assigned to McDowell's corps. General Porter reported to General Burnside
(who had arrived at Aquia on August 5th with about 12,000 men from North Carolina) for orders on the
21st. Being pushed out toward the Upper Rappahannock to connect with Reno, his advance under
Morell, on the 24th, found Reno and Reynolds gone; no troops of General Pope's were to be seen or
heard of (except one company of cavalry, afterward discovered, which had been left to guard Kelly's
ford), nor were any orders from General Pope or any information as to his whereabouts received by
General Porter or General Burnside until the 26th. So far as appears, no information of this movement
was communicated to General Halleck. On the 24th, in reply to General McClellan's inquiry from Falmouth, 9:40 P.M., "Please inform me exactly where General Pope's troops are.... Up to what point is the
Orange and Alexandria railroad now available? Where are the enemy in force?" General Halleck
telegraphed: "You ask me for information which I cannot give. I do not know either where General Pope
is or where the enemy in force is. These are matters which I have all day been most anxious to ascertain."—EDITORS.

23d of August that heavy reënforcements would begin to arrive at Warrenton Junction on the next day (24th), and as my orders still held me to the Rappahannock I naturally supposed that these troops would be hurried forward to me with all speed. Franklin's corps especially, I asked, should be sent rapidly to Gainesville. I also telegraphed Colonel Herman Haupt, chief of railway transportation, to direct one of the strongest divisions coming forward, and to be at Warrenton Junction on the 24th, to be put in the works at Manassas Junction. A cavalry force had been sent forward to observe the Thoroughfare Gap early on the morning of the 26th, but nothing was heard from it.[♱]

On the night of August 26th Jackson's advance, having passed Thoroughfare Gap, struck the Orange and Alexandria railroad at Manassas Junction, and made it plain to me that all of the reënforcements and movements of the troops promised me had altogether failed.[↓] Had Franklin been even at Centreville, or had Cox's and Sturgis's divisions been as far west as Bull Run on that day, the movement of Jackson on Manassas Junction would not have been practicable.

As Jackson's movement on Manassas Junction marks the beginning of the second battle of Bull Run, it is essential to a clear understanding of subsequent operations to give the positions of the army under my command on the night of August 26th, as also the movements and operations of the enemy as far as we knew them.

From the 18th until the night of the 26th of August the troops had been marching and fighting almost continuously. As was to be expected under such circumstances, the effective force had been greatly diminished by death, by wounds, by sickness, and by fatigue.[♪]

Heintzelman's corps, which had come up from Alexandria, was at Warrenton Junction, and numbered, as he reported to me, less than eight thousand men,[☆] but it was without wagons, without artillery, without horses even for the

[♱]General Pope's orders of the 25th disposed his troops on the line of the Rappahannock, from Waterloo to Kelly's Ford, as for an advance toward the Rapidan. Reno was ordered back to Kelly's Ford to resume communication with the forces under Burnside at Falmouth.—Editors.

[↓]The first information appears to have been received in a communication between the telegraph operators at Pope's headquarters and at Manassas Junction, dated 8:20 P.M., on August 26th. From this time until the 30th all direct communication between General Pope and Washington remained cut off, and nothing was heard of him except *via* Falmouth.—Editors.

[♪]August 18th, skirmishes at Rapidan Station and on Clark's Mountain, near Orange Court House; 20th, skirmishes at Raccoon Ford, Stevensburg, Brandy Station, Rappahannock Station, and near Kelly's Ford; 21st, skirmishes along the Rappahannock, at Kelly's, Beverly (or Cunningham's), and Freeman's Fords; 22d, actions at Freeman's Ford and Hazel River, and skirmishes along the Rappahannock; 23d, engagement at Rappahannock Station, action at Beverly Ford, and skirmish at Fant's Ford, 23d and 24th, actions at Sulphur (or Warrenton) Springs; 24th and 25th, actions at Waterloo Bridge; 25th, skirmish at Sulphur Springs; 26th, skirmishes at Bristoe Station, Bull Run Bridge, Gainesville, Haymarket, Manassas Junction, and Sulphur Springs.—Editors.

[☆]Heintzelman's infantry (effectives) numbered 15,011 on the 10th of August, and the full corps, replenished by six new regiments, reported 16,000 for duty September 10th. There are no intermediate reports.—Editors.

field-officers, and with only forty rounds of ammunition to the man. The corps of General F. J. Porter consisted of about ten thousand men, and was by far the freshest if not the best in the army. He had made very short and deliberate marches from Fredericksburg, and his advance division, mainly troops of the regular army under Sykes, had arrived at Warrenton Junction by eleven o'clock on the morning of the 27th, Morell's division of the same corps arriving later in the same day.

I saw General F. J. Porter at Warrenton Junction about 11 o'clock on the morning of the 27th. Sykes's division of his corps was encamped near; Morell's was expected in a few hours. I had seen General Porter at West Point while we were both cadets, but I think I never had an acquaintance with him there, nor do I think I ever met him afterward in the service except for about five minutes in Philadelphia in 1861, when I called at his office for a pass, which was then required to go to Washington via Annapolis. This, I think, was the first and only time I ever met him previous to the meeting at Warrenton Junction. He had so high a reputation in the army and for services since the outbreak of the war, that I was not only curious to see him, but was exceedingly glad that he had joined the army under my command with a corps which I knew to be one of the most effective in the service. This feeling was so strong that I expressed it warmly and on several occasions. He appeared to me a most gentlemanlike man, of a soldierly and striking appearance. I had but little conversation with him, as I was engaged, as he was, in writing telegrams. He seemed to me to exhibit a listlessness and indifference not quite natural under the circumstances, which, however, it is not unusual for men to assume in the midst of dangers and difficulties, merely to impress one with their superior coolness.

The troops were disposed as follows: McDowell's corps and Sigel's corps were at Warrenton under general command of General McDowell, with Banks's corps at Fayetteville as a reserve. Reno's corps was directed upon the Warrenton turnpike to take post three miles east of Warrenton. Porter's corps was near Bealeton Station moving slowly toward Warrenton Junction; Heintzelman at Warrenton Junction, with very small means to move in any direction.

Up to this time I had been placed by the positive orders of General Halleck much in the position of a man tied by one leg and fighting with a person much his physical superior and free to move in any direction. The following telegrams will explain exactly the situation as heretofore indicated:

"August 25th, 1862.

"Major-General Halleck:

"Your dispatch just received. Of course I shall be ready to recross the Rappahannock at a moment's notice. You will see from the positions taken that each army corps is on the best roads across the river. You wished forty-eight hours to assemble the forces from the Peninsula behind the

Rappahannock, and four days have passed without the enemy yet being permitted to cross. I don't think he is yet ready to do so. In ordinarily dry weather the Rappahannock can be crossed almost anywhere, and these crossing-places are best protected by concentrating at central positions to strike at any force which attempts to cross. I had clearly understood that you wished to unite our whole forces before a forward movement was begun, and that I must take care to keep united with Burnside on my left, so that no movement to separate us could be made. This withdrew me lower down the Rappahannock than I wished to come. I am not acquainted with your views, as you seem to suppose, and would be glad to know them so far as my own position and operations are concerned. I understood you clearly that, at all hazards, I was to prevent the enemy from passing the Rappahannock. This I have done, and shall do. I don't like to be on the defensive if I can help it, but must be so as long as I am tied to Burnside's forces, not yet wholly arrived at Fredericksburg. Please let me know, if it can be done, what is to be my own command, and if I am to act independently against the enemy. I certainly understood that, as soon as the whole of our forces were concentrated, you designed to take command in person, and that, when everything was ready, we were to move forward in concert. I judge from the tone of your dispatch that you are dissatisfied with something. Unless I know what it is, of course I can't correct it. The troops arriving here come in fragments. Am I to assign them to brigades and corps? I would suppose not, as several of the new regiments coming have been assigned to army corps directly from your office. In case I commence offensive operations I must know what forces I am to take and what you wish left, and what connection must be kept up with Burnside. It has been my purpose to conform my operations to your plans, yet I was not informed when McClellan evacuated Harrison's Landing, so that I might know what to expect in that direction; and when I say these things in no complaining spirit I think that you know well that I am anxious to do everything to advance your plans of campaign. I understood that this army was to maintain the line of the Rappahannock until all the forces from the Peninsula had united behind that river. I have done so. I understood distinctly that I was not to hazard anything except for this purpose, as delay was what was wanted.

"The enemy this morning has pushed a considerable infantry force up opposite Waterloo Bridge, and is planting batteries, and long lines of his infantry are moving up from Jeffersonville toward Sulphur Springs. His whole force, as far as can be ascertained, is massed in front of me, from railroad crossing of Rappahannock around to Waterloo Bridge, their main body being opposite Sulphur Springs.

"JOHN POPE, Major-General."

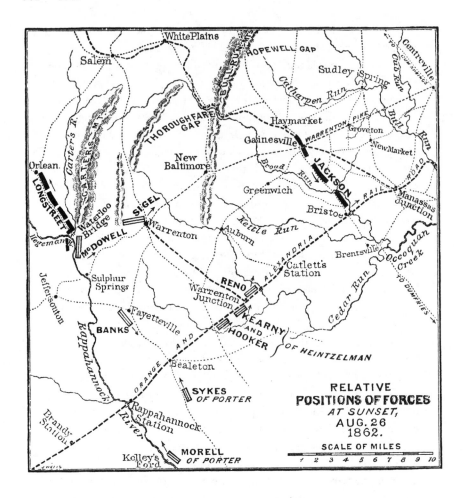

RELATIVE
POSITIONS OF FORCES
AT SUNSET,
AUG. 26
1862.

SCALE OF MILES

U.S. MILITARY TELEGRAPH.
(RECEIVED AUG. 26TH, 1862, FROM WAR DEP'T, 11:45 A.M.)

"Major-General Pope:—

"Not the slightest dissatisfaction has been felt in regard to your operations on the Rappahannock. The main object has been accomplished in getting up troops from the Peninsula, although they have been greatly delayed by storms. Moreover, the telegraph has been interrupted, leaving us for a time ignorant of the progress of the evacuation.... If possible to attack the enemy in flank, do so, but the main object now is to ascertain his position. Make cavalry excursions for that purpose, especially toward Front Royal. If possible to get in his rear, pursue with vigor.

"H. W. HALLECK, General-in-Chief."

The movements of the enemy toward my right forced me either to abandon the line of the Rappahannock and the communications with Fredericksburg, or to risk the loss of my army and the almost certain loss of Washington. Of course between these two alternatives I could not hesitate in a choice. I considered it my duty, at whatever sacrifice to my army and myself, to retard, as far as I could, the movement of the enemy toward Washington, until I was certain that the Army of the Potomac had reached Alexandria.

The movement of Jackson presented the only opportunity which had offered to gain any success over the superior forces of the enemy. I determined, therefore, on the morning of the 27th of August to abandon the line of the Rappahannock and throw my whole force in the direction of Gainesville and Manassas Junction, to crush any force of the enemy that had passed through Thoroughfare Gap, and to interpose between Lee's army and Bull Run. Having the interior line of operations, and the enemy at Manassas being inferior in force, it appeared to me, and still so appears, that with even ordinary promptness and energy we might feel sure of success.

In the meantime heavy forces of the enemy still confronted us at Waterloo Bridge,/ while his main body continued its march toward our right, following the course of Hedgman's River (the Upper Rappahannock). I accordingly sent orders, early on the 27th of August, to General McDowell to move rapidly on Gainesville by the Warrenton pike with his own corps, reënforced by Reynolds's division and Sigel's corps. I directed Reno, followed by Kearny's division of Heintzelman's corps, to move on Greenwich, so as to reach there that night, to report thence at once to General McDowell, and to support him in operations against the enemy which were expected near Gainesville. With Hooker's division of Heintzelman's corps I moved along the railroad toward Manassas Junction, to reopen our communications and to be in position to coöperate with the forces along the Warrenton pike.

On the afternoon of that day a severe engagement took place between Hooker's division and Ewell's division of Jackson's corps, near Bristoe Station, on the railroad. Ewell was driven back along the railroad, but at dark still confronted Hooker along the banks of Broad Run. The loss in this action was about three hundred killed and wounded on each side. Ewell left his dead, many of his wounded, and some of his baggage on the field.↓

I had not seen Hooker for many years, and I remembered him as a very handsome young man, with florid complexion and fair hair, and with a figure agile and graceful. As I saw him that afternoon on his white horse riding in rear of his line

/On the afternoon of August 26th, Longstreet's corps moved to Hinson's Mill Ford, six miles above, leaving R. H. Anderson's division (about 6000 effectives) at Waterloo Bridge.—Editors.
↓This engagement is known as Kettle Run. The Confederate force consisted of Early's brigade, with two regiments of Forno's, two of Lawton's, and Brown's and Johnson's batteries. After disputing Hooker's advance for some hours, Ewell withdrew under fire.—Editors.

THE REAR OF THE COLUMN. FROM A WAR-TIME SKETCH.

of battle, and close up to it, with the excitement of battle in his eyes, and that gallant and chivalric appearance which he always presented under fire, I was struck with admiration. As a corps commander, with his whole force operating under his own eye, it is much to be doubted whether Hooker had a superior in the army.

The railroad had been torn up and the bridges burned in several places just west of Bristoe Station. I therefore directed General Banks, who had reached Warrenton Junction, to cover the railroad trains at that place until General Porter marched, and then to run back the trains toward Manassas as far as he could and rebuild the railroad bridges. Captain Merrill of the Engineers was also directed to repair the railroad track and bridges toward Bristoe. This work was done by that accomplished officer as far east as Kettle Run on the 27th, and the trains were run back to that point next morning.

At dark on the 27th Hooker informed me that his ammunition was nearly exhausted, only five rounds to the man being on hand. Before this time it had become apparent that Jackson, with his whole force, was south of the Warrenton pike and in the immediate neighborhood of Manassas Junction.

McDowell reached his position at Gainesville during the night of the 27th, and Kearny and Reno theirs at Greenwich. It was clear on that night that we had completely interposed between Jackson and the enemy's main body, which was still west of the Bull Run range, and in the vicinity of White Plains.

In consequence of Hooker's report, and the weakness of the small division which he commanded, and to strengthen my right wing moving in the direction of Manassas, I sent orders to Porter at dark, which reached him at 9 P.M., to move forward from Warrenton Junction at 1 A.M. that night, and to report to me at Bristoe Station by daylight next morning (August 28th).

There were but two courses left to Jackson by this sudden movement of the army. He could not retrace his steps through Gainesville, as that place was occupied by McDowell with a force equal if not superior to his own. To retreat through Centreville would carry him still farther away from the main body of Lee's army. It was possible, however, to mass his whole force at Manassas Junction and assail our right (Hooker's division), which had fought a severe battle that afternoon, and was almost out of ammunition. Jackson, with A. P. Hill's division, retired through Centreville. Thinking it altogether within the probabilities that he might adopt the other alternative, I sent the orders above mentioned to General Porter. He neither obeyed them nor attempted to obey them,☆ but afterward gave as a reason for not doing so that his men were tired, the night was too dark to march, and that there was a wagon train on the road toward Bristoe. The distance was nine miles along the railroad track, with a wagon road on each side of it most of the way; but his corps did not reach Bristoe Station until 10:30 o'clock next morning, six hours after daylight; and the moment he found that the enemy had left our front he asked to halt and rest his corps. Of his first reason for not complying with my orders, it is only necessary to say that Sykes's division had reached Warrenton Junction at 11 o'clock on the morning of the 27th, and had been in camp all day. Morell's division arrived later in the day at Warrenton Junction, and would have been in camp for at least eight hours before the time it was ordered to march. The marches of these two divisions from Fredericksburg had been extremely deliberate, and involved but little more exercise than is needed for good health. The diaries of these marches make Porter's claim of fatigue ridiculous. To compare the condition of this corps and its marches with those of any of the troops of the Army of Virginia is a sufficient answer to such a pretext. The impossibility of marching on account of the darkness of that night finds its best answer in the fact that nearly every other division of the army, and the whole of Jackson's corps, marched during the greater part of the night in the immediate vicinity of Porter's corps, and from nearly every point of the compass. The plea of darkness and of the obstruction of a wagon train along the road will strike our armies with some surprise in the light of their subsequent experience of night marches. The railroad track itself was clear and entirely practicable for the march of infantry.

☆Porter marched about 3 A.M., instead of at 1, as ordered. The leading brigade lit candles to look for the road. On the Confederate side Colonel Henry Forno, 5th Louisiana, reports: "After 12 o'clock at night of the 27th, the brigade was put in motion with orders to follow General Early, but owing to the darkness I was unable to find him." Two orders addressed by Pope at Bristoe to McDowell at Gainesville fell into the hands of A. P. Hill, at Centreville. Some of the Confederates (Jackson, Trimble, and Stuart) mention the darkness of the night of the 26th; and General McDowell lost his way from this cause on the night of the 28th.—EDITORS.

According to the testimony of Colonel Myers, quartermaster in charge of the train, the train was drawn off the roads and parked after dark that night; and even if this had not been the case, it is not necessary to tell any officer who served in the war that the infantry advance could easily have pushed the wagons off the road to make way for the artillery. Colonel Myers also testified that he could have gone on with his train that night, and that he drew off the road and parked his train for rest and because of the action of Hooker's division in his front, and not because he was prevented from continuing his march by darkness or other obstacles.

At 9 o'clock on the night of the 27th, satisfied of Jackson's position, I sent orders to General McDowell at Gainesville to push forward at the earliest dawn of day upon Manassas Junction, resting his right on the Manassas Gap Railroad and extending his left to the east. I directed General Reno at the same time to march from Greenwich, also direct on Manassas Junction, and Kearny to move from the same place upon Bristoe Station. This move of Kearny was to strengthen my right at Bristoe and unite the two divisions of Heintzelman's corps.‡

Jackson began to evacuate Manassas Junction during the night (the 27th) and marched toward Centreville and other points of the Warrenton pike west of that place, and by 11 o'clock next morning was at and beyond Centreville and north of the Warrenton pike.⊕ I arrived at Manassas Junction shortly after the last of Jackson's force had moved off, and immediately pushed forward Hooker, Kearny, and Reno upon Centreville,⊕ and sent orders to Porter to come forward to Manassas Junction. I also wrote McDowell the situation and directed him to call back to Gainesville any part of his force which had moved in the direction of Manassas Junction, and march upon Centreville along the Warrenton pike with the whole force under his command to intercept the retreat of Jackson toward Thoroughfare Gap. With King's division in advance, McDowell, marching toward Centreville, encountered late in the afternoon the advance of Jackson's corps retreating toward Thoroughfare

---

‡General Pope's orders of the 27th for the movements of the 28th directed his whole army upon Manassas. Full information of these dispositions reached General A. P. Hill early the next morning, through the captured orders.—EDITORS.

⊕At this time Jackson's command was concentrated near Groveton. General Pope says in his report: "I reached Manassas Junction... about 12 o'clock... less than an hour after Jackson, in person, had retired." Jackson was, however, on the old "battle-field of Manassas" at 8 A.M., as appears from the order of that date to A. P. Hill, and about noon when he sent orders to Taliaferro to attack the Federal troops (evidently Reynolds), supposed to be marching on Centreville, but actually moving from Gainesville to Manassas under Pope's first orders. Jackson says: "My command had hardly concentrated north of the turnpike before the enemy's advance reached the vicinity of Groveton from the direction of Warrenton." In the sketch on p. 387, Meade's brigade and Cooper's battery are seen deploying for action.—EDITORS.

⊕At 1:20 or 2 P.M. Pope repeated his orders sent "a few minutes ago" to McDowell to march toward Gum Springs, distant 20 miles in the direction of Aldie Gap. The note sent "a few minutes ago," reached McDowell at 3:15 P.M. The orders to march on Centreville were dated 4:15 P.M., and McDowell appears to have received the second while preparing to execute the first.—EDITORS.

COLLISION ON THURSDAY, AUGUST 28, BETWEEN REYNOLDS'S DIVISION
AND JACKSON'S RIGHT WING.

The view is from the north side of the turnpike (from a war-time sketch), east of Gainesville, and looking toward Groveton. The smoke along the woods indicates the position of the Confederates, who fell back toward Groveton, while Reynolds turned off to the right toward Manassas. During the battles of Friday and Saturday (the 29th and 30th), the lines were nearly reversed. Jackson was then to the left, looking south toward Manassas, and Longstreet's lines, facing like Reynolds's in the above picture, but extending farther to the right, and confronting McDowell and Porter (see maps, pp. 392 and 403).—EDITORS.

Gap.‖ Late in the afternoon, also, Kearny drove the rear-guard of Jackson out of Centreville and occupied that place with his advance beyond it toward Gainesville. A very severe engagement occurred between King's division and Jackson's forces near the village of Groveton on the Warrenton pike, which was terminated by the darkness, both parties maintaining their ground. ⁄ The

‖Jackson says: "Dispositions were promptly made to attack the enemy, based upon the idea that he would continue to press forward upon the turnpike toward Alexandria; but as he did not appear to advance in force, and there was reason to believe that his main body was leaving the road and inclining toward Manassas Junction, my command was advanced through the woods, leaving Groveton on the left, until it reached a commanding position near Brawner's house. By this time it was sunset; but as his column appeared to be moving by, with its flank exposed, I determined to attack at once, which was vigorously done by the divisions of Taliaferro and Ewell."—EDITORS.

⁄King's division (which had not been at Gainesville on the night of the 27th, but near Buckland Mills, and was consequently near the Warrenton pike instead of at Manassas, when, by General Pope's 4:15 P.M. order, the army was directed upon Centreville instead of upon Manassas) encountered Jackson's forces in position as stated in the preceding note about 5:30 P.M. Gibbon's brigade, with two regiments of Doubleday's (the 56th Pennsylvania and 76th New York), contended against Taliaferro's division and two brigades (Lawton's and Trimble's) of Ewell's division. General Jackson says:

"The batteries of Wooding, Poague, and Carpenter were placed in position in front of Starke's brigade, and above the village of Groveton, and, firing over the heads of our skirmishers,

conduct of this division in this severe engagement was admirable, and reflects the utmost credit both upon its commanders and the men under their command. That this division was not reënforced by Reynolds☆ and Sigel‡ seems unaccountable. The reason given, though it is not satisfactory, was the fact that General McDowell had left the command just before it encountered the enemy, and had gone toward Manassas Junction, where he supposed me to be, in order to give me some information about the immediate country in which we were operating, and with which, of course, he was much more familiar from former experience than I could be.✢ I had left Manassas Junction, however, for Centreville. Hearing the sound of the guns indicating King's engagement with

---

poured a heavy fire of shot and shell upon the enemy. This was responded to by a very heavy fire from the enemy, forcing our batteries to select another position. By this time Taliaferro's command, with Lawton's and Trimble's brigades on his left, was advanced from the woods to the open field, and was now moving in gallant style until it reached an orchard on the right of our line and was less than 100 yards from a large force of the enemy. The conflict here was fierce and sanguinary. Although largely reënforced, the Federals did not attempt to advance, but maintained their ground with obstinate determination. Both lines stood exposed to the discharges of musketry and artillery until about 9 o'clock, when the enemy slowly fell back, yielding the field to our troops. The loss on both sides was heavy, and among our wounded were Major-General Ewell and Brigadier-General Taliaferro."

Gibbon's brigade lost 133 killed, 539 wounded, 79 missing, total, 751, "or considerably over one-third of the command." King held his ground until 1 A.M. on the 29th, when, being without support, without communication with either of the generals in command over him, and without orders since those of 4:15 P.M., he marched to Manassas Junction.—EDITORS.

☆Reynolds, ordered to march *en échelon* on King's right, was moving toward Manassas (see note to picture, p. 387), when, at 5 P.M., he received McDowell's order, based on Pope's of 4:15, to march on Centreville. He turned off at Bethlehem Church and took the Sudley Springs road toward the Warrenton pike. General Reynolds says:

"About this time heavy cannonading was heard both to our front and left, the former supposed to be from Sigel's corps, and the latter from King's division, which had taken the Warrenton pike from Gainesville. I sent word to the column to hasten its march, and proceeded to the left at once myself in the direction of the firing, arriving on the field just before dark, and found that Gibbon's brigade, of King's division, was engaged with the enemy, with Doubleday's and Patrick's brigades in the vicinity. After the firing ceased I saw General King, who, determining to maintain his position, I left about 9 o'clock P.M. to return to my division, promising to bring it up early in the morning to his support. Before leaving, however, I heard the division moving off, and I learned from General Hatch that it was moving by Gainesville toward Manassas. I then returned to my own division, which I reached at daylight."

—EDITORS.

‡Sigel was ordered to move at 2:45 A.M. and to march *en échelon* on Reynolds's right. His advance appears to have reached Manassas about noon. He states that during the afternoon he was ordered by General Pope to march by New Market on Centreville, and arrived on the field of the First Bull Run, near the Henry house (see p. 392), too late to take part in King's engagement.—EDITORS.

✢According to General McDowell, this was "after putting these divisions in motion (under the 4:15 P.M. order) and going with Reynolds's division to near Manassas"; and in compliance with General Pope's request of 1:20 or 2 P.M., viz., "Give me your views fully; you know the country much better than I do." General McDowell found Reynolds at daybreak on the 29th.—EDITORS.

the enemy, McDowell set off to rejoin his command, but lost his way, and I first heard of him next morning at Manassas Junction. As his troops did not know of his absence, there was no one to give orders to Sigel and Reynolds.

The engagement of King's division was reported to me about 10 o'clock at night near Centreville. I felt sure then, and so stated, that there was no escape for Jackson. On the west of him were McDowell's corps (I did not then know that he had detached Ricketts's),/ Sigel's corps, and Reynolds's division, all under command of McDowell. On the east of him, and with the advance of Kearny nearly in contact with him on the Warrenton pike, were the corps of Reno and Heintzelman. Porter was supposed to be at Manassas Junction, where he ought to have been on that afternoon.

I sent orders to McDowell (supposing him to be with his command), and also direct to General King, several times during that night and once by his own staff-officer, to hold his ground at all hazards, to prevent the retreat of Jackson toward Lee, and that at daylight our whole force from Centreville and Manassas would assail him from the east, and he would be crushed between us. I sent orders also to General Kearny at Centreville to move forward cautiously that night along the Warrenton pike; to drive in the pickets of the enemy, and to keep as closely as possible in contact with him during the night, resting his left on the Warrenton pike and throwing his right to the north, if practicable, as far as the Little River pike, and at daylight next morning to assault vigorously with his right advance, and that Hooker and Reno would certainly be with him shortly after daylight. I sent orders to General Porter, who I supposed was at Manassas Junction, to move upon Centreville at dawn, stating to him the position of our forces, and that a severe battle would be fought that morning (the 29th).

With Jackson at and near Groveton, with McDowell on the west, and the rest of the army on the east of him, while Lee, with the mass of his army, was still west of Thoroughfare Gap, the situation for us was certainly as favorable as the most sanguine person could desire, and the prospect of crushing Jackson, sandwiched between such forces, were certainly excellent. There is no doubt, had General McDowell been with his command when King's division of his corps became engaged with the enemy, he would have brought forward to its support both Sigel and Reynolds, and the result would have been to hold the ground west of Jackson at least until morning brought against him also the forces moving from the direction of Centreville.

To my great disappointment and surprise, however, I learned toward day-

/In the exercise of his discretion McDowell, then commanding two corps, sent Ricketts to Thoroughfare Gap on the morning of the 28th, to delay Longstreet's advance, notwithstanding General Pope's orders to move on Manassas with his whole command. But for this, the movement on Manassas as ordered in the morning, as well as the movement on Centreville as ordered in the afternoon, would have left no troops except Buford's broken-down cavalry between Longstreet and Jackson, or between Longstreet and Pope's left.—EDITORS.

light the next morning (the 29th) that King's division had fallen back toward Manassas Junction, and that neither Sigel nor Reynolds had been engaged or had gone to the support of King. The route toward Thoroughfare Gap had thus been left open by the wholly unexpected retreat of King's division, due to the fact that he was not supported by Sigel and Reynolds, and an immediate change was necessary in the disposition of the troops under my command. Sigel and Reynolds were near Groveton, almost in contact with Jackson; Ricketts had fallen back toward Bristoe from Thoroughfare Gap, after offering (as might have been expected) ineffectual resistance to the passage of the Bull Run range by very superior forces; King had fallen back to Manassas Junction; Porter was at Manassas Junction or near there; Reno‡ and Hooker near Centreville; Kearny at Centreville and beyond toward Groveton; Jackson near Groveton with his whole corps; Lee with the main army of the enemy, except three brigades of Longstreet which had passed Hopewell Gap, north of Thoroughfare Gap.

The field of battle was practically limited to the space between the old railroad grade from Sudley to Gainesville if prolonged across the Warrenton pike and the Sudley Springs road east of it. The railroad grade indicates almost exactly the line occupied by Jackson's force, our own line confronting it from left to right.

The ridge which bounded the valley of Dawkins's Branch on the west, and on which were the Hampton Cole and Monroe houses, offered from the Monroe house a full view of the field of battle from right to left, and the Monroe house being on the crest of the ridge overlooked and completely commanded the approach to Jackson's right by the Warrenton turnpike. To the result of the battle this ridge was of the last importance, and, if seized and held by noon, would absolutely have prevented any reënforcement of Jackson's right from the direction of Gainesville. The northern slope of this ridge was held by our troops near the Douglass house, near which, also, the right of Jackson's line rested. The advance of Porter's corps at Dawkins's Branch was less than a mile and a half from the Monroe house, and the road in his front was one of several which converged on that point.

The whole field was free from obstacles to movement of troops and nearly so to manœuvres, with only a few eminences, and these of a nature to have been seized and easily held by our troops even against very superior numbers. The ground was gently undulating and the water-courses insignificant, while the intersecting system of roads and lanes afforded easy communication with all parts of the field. It would be difficult to find anywhere in Virginia a more perfect field of battle than that on which the second battle of Bull Run was fought.

---

‡Reno appears not to have been at Centreville at this time, since General Pope's headquarters "near Bull Run" were between him and Centreville at 3 A.M. on the 30th.—EDITORS.

About daylight, therefore, on the 29th of August, almost immediately after I received information of the withdrawal of King's division toward Manassas Junction, I sent orders to General Sigel, in the vicinity of Groveton, to attack the enemy vigorously at daylight and bring him to a stand if possible.☆ He was to be supported by Reynolds's division. I instructed Heintzelman‡ to push forward from Centreville toward Gainesville on the Warrenton pike at the earliest dawn with the divisions of Kearny and Hooker, and gave orders also to Reno with his corps to follow closely in their rear. They were directed to use all speed, and as soon as they came up with the enemy to establish communication with Sigel, and to attack vigorously and promptly. I also sent orders to General Porter⸸ at Manassas Junc-

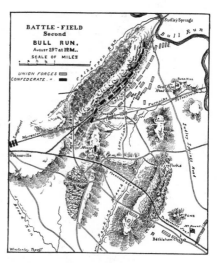

RELATIVE POSITION AT NOON,
FRIDAY, AUGUST 29TH.

This map represents General Pope's view of the situation at noon, August 29th, with Longstreet placed at Gainesville; whereas, according to General Longstreet and others, he was at that hour on Jackson's right and confronting Porter.—EDITORS.

tion to move forward rapidly with his own corps and King's division of McDowell's corps, which was there also, upon Gainesville by the direct route from Manassas Junction to that place. I urged him to make all possible speed, with the purpose that he should come up with the enemy or connect himself with the left of our line near where the Warrenton pike is crossed by the road from Manassas Junction to Gainesville.

Shortly after sending this order I received a note from General McDowell, whom I had not been able to find during the night of the 28th, dated Manassas Junction, requesting that King's division be not taken from his command. I im-

---

☆These orders to Sigel are not found in the "Official Records," but they correspond with the orders given to Kearny and Heintzelman at 9:50 and 10 P.M., on the 28th. General Sigel says he received them during the night, made his preparations at night, and "formed in order of battle at daybreak." Such of the subordinate reports as mention the time, as well as the reports of Generals McDowell and Reynolds, tend to confirm General Sigel's statement.—EDITORS.

‡These orders to Heintzelman are dated 10 P.M., August 28th; similar orders to Kearny direct are dated 9:50 P.M.—EDITORS.

⸸At 3 A.M. on the 29th, General Pope ordered Porter, then at Bristoe, to "move upon Centreville at the first dawn of day." In the order of the 29th to Porter, "Push forward with your corps and King's division, which you will take with you upon Gainesville," the hour is not noted, but General Pope testified on the Porter court-martial that he sent it between 8 and 9 A.M. Porter appears to have received it about 9:30. —EDITORS.

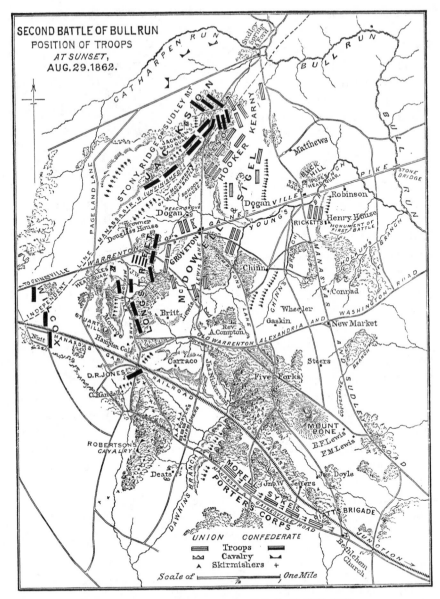

SECOND BATTLE OF BULL RUN
POSITION OF TROOPS
AT SUNSET,
AUG. 29. 1862.

UNION   CONFEDERATE
Troops
Cavalry
Skirmishers +

Scale of One Mile

RELATIVE POSITIONS AT SUNSET, FRIDAY, AUGUST 29TH.

At noon of that day Porter's corps was in much the same position as at sunset. According to General Pope, at noon Porter, with very little resistance to overcome, might have occupied the hill of the Monroe and Hampton Cole houses, a position of great importance. But, according to other authorities, Longstreet was in position between Jackson and Porter by noon. At that hour the right of the Union army was arrayed in continuous line in front of Jackson from a point on the turnpike three-quarters of a mile west of Groveton to the point where the Sudley Springs road crosses the unfinished railroad which was Jackson's stronghold. The map above illustrates the situation at the time of the greatest success on the right, when Jackson's left had been turned upon itself by Kearny's, Reno's, and Hooker's divisions.—EDITORS.

mediately sent a joint order, addressed to Generals McDowell and Porter,[✦] repeating the instructions to move forward with their commands toward Gainesville, and informing them of the position and movements of Sigel and Heintzelman.

Sigel attacked the enemy at daylight on the morning of the 29th about a mile east of Groveton, where he was joined by the divisions of Hooker and Kearny. Jackson fell back,[♦] but was so closely pressed by these forces that he was obliged to make a stand. He accordingly took up his position along and behind the old railroad embankment extending along his entire front, with his left near Sudley Springs and his right just south of the Warrenton pike. His batteries, some of them of heavy caliber, were posted behind the ridges in the open ground, while the mass of his troops were sheltered by woods and the railroad embankment.

I arrived on the field from Centreville about noon, and found the opposing forces confronting each other, both considerably cut up by the severe action in which they had been engaged since daylight. Heintzelman's corps (the divisions of Hooker and Kearny) occupied the right of our line toward Sudley Springs. Sigel was on his left, with his line extending a short distance south of the Warrenton pike, the division of Schenck occupying the high ground to the left (south) of the pike. The extreme left was held by Reynolds. Reno's corps had reached the field and the most of it had been pushed forward into action, leaving four regiments in reserve behind the center of the line of battle. Immediately after I reached the ground, General Sigel reported to me that his line was weak, that the divisions of Schurz and Steinwehr were much cut up and ought to be drawn back from the front. I informed him that this was impossible, as there were no troops to replace them, and that he must hold his ground; that I would not immediately push his troops again into action, as the corps of McDowell and Porter were moving forward on the road from Manassas Junction to Gainesville, and must very soon be in position to fall upon the enemy's right flank and possibly on his rear. I rode along the front of our line and gave the same information to Heintzelman and Reno. I shall not soon forget the bright and confident face and the alert and hearty manner of that most accomplished and loyal soldier, General J. L. Reno. From first to last in this campaign he was always cheerful and ready; anxious to anticipate if possible, and prompt

---

[✦]This joint order refers to the one just cited as having been sent "an hour and a half ago," under which Porter was marching toward Gainesville when McDowell joined him near Manassas Junction. After receiving the joint order, General McDowell again joined Porter, at the front, and showed him a dispatch just received from Buford, dated 9:30 A.M., and addressed to Ricketts. It appears to have escaped notice that this dispatch was forwarded by Ricketts to McDowell at 11:30 A.M., which fixes the time of the meeting between Generals McDowell and Porter at the front as *after* 11:30.—EDITORS.

[♦]Not mentioned by Jackson or any of the subordinate commanders of either army. Jackson appears to have received the attack in position as stated by General Pope in the next sentence.—EDITORS.

to execute with all his might, the orders he received. He was short in stature and upright in person, and with a face and manner so bright and engaging at all times, but most especially noticeable in the fury of battle, that it was both a pleasure and a comfort to see him. In his death, two weeks afterward, during the battle of South Mountain, when he led his troops with his usual gallantry and daring, the Government lost one of its best and most promising officers. Had he lived to see the end of the war, he would undoubtedly have attained one of the highest, if not the very highest position in the army. His superior abilities were unquestioned, and if he lacked one single element that goes to make a perfect soldier, certainly it was not discovered before his death.

The troops were permitted to rest for a time, and to resupply themselves with ammunition. From 1:30 to 4 o'clock P.M. very severe conflicts occurred repeatedly all along the line, and there was a continuous roar of artillery and small-arms, with scarcely an intermission. About two o'clock in the afternoon three discharges of artillery were heard on the extreme left of our line or right of the enemy's, and I for the moment, and naturally, believed that Porter and McDowell had reached their positions and were engaged with the enemy. I heard only three shots, and as nothing followed I was at a loss to know what had become of these corps, or what was delaying them, as before this hour they should have been, even with ordinary marching, well up on our left. Shortly afterward I received information that McDowell's corps was advancing to join the left of our line by the Sudley Springs road, and would probably be up within two hours [about 4 P.M.—Editors]. At 4:30 o'clock I sent a peremptory order to General Porter, who was at or near Dawkins's Branch, about four or five miles distant from my headquarters, to push forward at once into action on the enemy's right, and if possible on his rear, stating to him generally the condition of things on the field in front of me. At 5:30 o'clock, when General Porter should have been going into action in compliance with this order, I directed Heintzelman and Reno to attack the enemy's left. The attack was made promptly and with vigor and persistence, and the left of the enemy was doubled back toward his center. After a severe and bloody action of an hour Kearny forced the position on the left of the enemy and occupied the field of battle there.

By this time General McDowell had arrived on the field, and I pushed his corps, supported by Reynolds, forward at once into action along the Warrenton pike toward the enemy's right, then said to be falling back. This attack along the pike was made by King's division near sunset; but, as Porter made no movement whatever toward the field, Longstreet, who was pushing to the front, was able to extend his lines beyond King's left with impunity, and King's attack did not accomplish what was expected, in view of the anticipated attack which Porter was ordered to make, and should have been making at the same time.

From 5 o'clock in the day until some time after dark the fighting all along our lines was severe and bloody, and our losses were very heavy. To show clearly the character of the battle on the 29th, I embody extracts from the official reports of General Lee, of General T. J. Jackson, and of Longstreet and Hill, who commanded the enemy's forces on that day. I choose the reports of the officers commanding against us for several reasons, but especially to show Longstreet's movements and operations on the afternoon of the 29th of August, when, it is alleged, he was held in check by Porter. General Lee says:

"Generals Jones and Wilcox bivouacked that night [28th] east of the mountain; and on the morning of the 29th the whole command resumed the march, the sound of cannon at Manassas announcing that Jackson was already engaged. Longstreet entered the turnpike near Gainesville, and, moving down toward Groveton, the head of his column came upon the field in rear of the enemy's left, which had already opened with artillery upon Jackson's right, as previously described. He immediately placed some of his batteries in position, but before he could complete his dispositions to attack, the enemy withdrew; not, however, without loss from our artillery. Longstreet took position on the right of Jackson, Hood's two brigades, supported by Evans, being deployed across the turnpike, at right angles to it. These troops were supported on the left by three brigades

THE BATTLE OF GROVETON, AUGUST 29TH, AS SEEN FROM CENTREVILLE.
FROM A SKETCH MADE AT THE TIME.

under General Wilcox, and by a light force on the right under General Kemper. D. R. Jones's division formed the extreme right of the line, resting on the Manassas Gap railroad. The cavalry guarded our right and left flanks; that on the right being under General Stuart in person. After the arrival of Longstreet the enemy changed his position and began to concentrate opposite Jackson's left, opening a brisk artillery fire, which was responded to with effect by some of General A. P. Hill's batteries. Colonel Walton placed a part of his artillery upon a commanding position between the lines of Generals Jackson and Longstreet, by order of the latter, and engaged the enemy vigorously for several hours. Soon afterward General Stuart reported the approach of a large force from the direction of Bristoe Station, threatening Longstreet's right. The brigades under General Wilcox were sent to reënforce General Jones, but no serious attack was made, and after firing a few shots the enemy withdrew. While this demonstration was being made on our right, a large force advanced to assail the left of Jackson's position, occupied by the division of General A. P. Hill. The attack was received by his troops with their accustomed steadiness, and the battle raged with great fury. The enemy was repeatedly repulsed, but again pressed on to the attack with fresh troops. Once he succeeded in penetrating an interval between General Gregg's brigade, on the extreme left, and that of General Thomas, but was quickly driven back with great slaughter by the 14th South Carolina regiment, then in reserve, and the 49th Georgia, of Thomas's brigade. The contest was close and obstinate: the combatants sometimes delivering their fire at ten paces. General Gregg, who was most exposed, was reënforced by Hays's brigade under Colonel Forno, and successfully and gallantly resisted the attacks of the enemy, until, the ammunition of his brigade being exhausted, and all his field-officers but two killed or wounded, it was relieved, after several hours of severe fighting, by Early's brigade and the 8th Louisiana regiment. General Early drove the enemy back, with heavy loss, and pursued about two hundred yards beyond the line of battle, when he was recalled to the position of the railroad where Thomas, Pender, and Archer had firmly held their ground against every attack. While the battle was raging on Jackson's left, General Longstreet ordered Hood and Evans to advance, but before the order could be obeyed Hood was himself attacked, and his command at once became warmly engaged. General Wilcox was recalled from the right and ordered to advance on Hood's left, and one of Kemper's brigades, under Colonel Hunton, moved forward on his right. The enemy was repulsed by Hood after a severe contest, and fell back, closely followed by our troops. The battle continued until 9 P.M., the enemy retreating until he reached a strong position, which he held with a large force.

The darkness of the night put a stop to the engagement, and our troops remained in their advanced position until early next morning, when they were withdrawn to their first line. One piece of artillery, several stands of colors, and a number of prisoners were captured. Our loss was severe in this engagement; Brigadier-Generals Field and Trimble, and Colonel Forno, commanding Hays's brigade, were severely wounded, and several other valuable officers killed or disabled whose names are mentioned in the accompanying reports."

General Jackson in his report, dated April 27th, 1863, says:

"My troops on this day were distributed along and in the vicinity of the cut of an unfinished railroad (intended as a part of the track to connect the Manassas road directly with Alexandria), stretching from the Warrenton turnpike in the direction of Sudley's Mill. It was mainly along the excavation of this unfinished road that my line of battle was formed on the 29th: Jackson's division, under Brigadier-General Starke, on the right; Ewell's division, under Brigadier-General Lawton, in the center; and Hill's division on the left. In the morning, about 10 o'clock, the Federal artillery opened with spirit and animation upon our right, which was soon replied to by the batteries of Poague, Carpenter, Dement, Brockenbrough, and Latimer, under Major [L. M.] Shumaker. This lasted for some time, when the enemy moved around more to our left, to another point of attack. His next effort was directed against our left. This was vigorously repulsed by the batteries of Braxton, Crenshaw, and Pegram. About 2 o'clock P.M. the Federal infantry, in large force, advanced to the attack of our left, occupied by the division of General Hill. It pressed forward in defiance of our fatal and destructive fire with great determination, a portion of it crossing a deep cut in the railroad track, and penetrating in heavy force an interval of nearly 175 yards, which separated the right of Gregg's from the left of Thomas's brigade. For a short time Gregg's brigade, on the extreme left, was isolated from the main body of the command. But the 14th South Carolina regiment, then in reserve, with the 49th Georgia, left of Colonel Thomas, attacked the exultant enemy with vigor and drove them back across the railroad track with great slaughter."

General Longstreet says in his report, dated October 10th, 1862:

"Early on the 29th [August] the columns [that had passed Thoroughfare and Hopewell Gaps] were united, and the advance to join General Jackson was resumed. The noise of battle was heard before we reached

THE HALT ON THE LINE OF BATTLE. FROM A WAR-TIME SKETCH.

Gainesville. The march was quickened to the extent of our capacity. The excitement of battle seemed to give new life and strength to our jaded men, and the head of my column soon reached a position in rear of the enemy's left flank, and within easy cannon-shot.

"On approaching the field some of Brigadier-General Hood's batteries were ordered into position, and his division was deployed on the right and left of the turnpike, at right angles with it, and supported by Brigadier-General Evans's brigade. Before these batteries could open, the enemy discovered our movements and withdrew his left. Another battery (Captain Stribling's) was placed upon a commanding position to my right, which played upon the rear of the enemy's left and drove him entirely from that part of the field. He changed his front rapidly, so as to meet the advance of Hood and Evans.

"Three brigades, under General Wilcox, were thrown forward to the support of the left; and three others, under General Kemper, to the support of the right of these commands. General D. R. Jones's division was placed upon the Manassas Gap railroad to the right, and *en échelon* with regard to the last three brigades. Colonel Walton placed his batteries in a commanding position between my line and that of General Jackson, and engaged the enemy for several hours in a severe and successful artillery duel. At a late hour in the day Major-General Stuart reported the approach of the enemy in heavy columns against my extreme right. I withdrew General Wilcox, with his three brigades, from the left, and placed his command in position to support Jones in case of an attack against my right. After some few shots the enemy withdrew his forces, moving them around toward his front, and about 4 o'clock in the afternoon began to press forward against General Jackson's position. Wilcox's brigades were moved back to their former position, and Hood's two brigades, supported by Evans, were quickly pressed forward to the attack. At the same time Wilcox's three brigades made a like advance, as also Hunton's brigade, of Kemper's command.

"These movements were executed with commendable zeal and ability. Hood, supported by Evans, made a gallant attack, driving the enemy back till 9 o'clock at night. One piece of artillery, several regimental standards, and a number of prisoners were taken. The enemy's entire force was found to be massed directly in my front, and in so strong a position that it was not deemed advisable to move on against his immediate front; so the troops were quietly withdrawn at 1 o'clock the following morning. The wheels of the captured piece were cut down, and it was left on the ground. The enemy seized that opportunity to claim a victory, and the Federal commander was so imprudent as to dispatch his Government, by telegraph, tidings to that effect. After withdrawing from the attack, my troops were placed in the line first occupied, and in the original order."

General A. P. Hill says in his report, dated February 25th, 1863:

"Friday morning, in accordance with orders from General Jackson, I occupied the line of the unfinished railroad, my extreme left resting near Sudley Ford, my right near the point where the road strikes the open field, Gregg, Field, and Thomas in the front line; Gregg on the left and Field on the right; with Branch, Pender, and Archer as supports....

"The evident intention of the enemy this day was to turn our left and overwhelm Jackson's corps before Longstreet came up, and to accomplish this the most persistent and furious onsets were made, by column after column of infantry, accompanied by numerous batteries of artillery. Soon my reserves were all in, and up to 6 o'clock my division, assisted by the Louisiana brigade of General Hays, commanded by Colonel Forno, with a heroic courage and obstinacy almost beyond parallel, had met and repulsed six distinct and separate assaults, a portion of the time the majority of the men being without a cartridge....

"The enemy prepared for a last and determined attempt. Their serried masses, overwhelming superiority of numbers, and bold bearing

COLLECTING
THE WOUNDED.

In his "Recollections of a Private" [see
"The Century" magazine for January, 1886]
Warren Lee Goss says: "At the end of the first
day's battle, August 29th, so soon as the fighting
ceased, many sought without orders to rescue comrades lying wounded between the opposing lines. There
seemed to be an understanding between the men of both armies
that such parties were not to be disturbed in their mission of mercy. After the failure of the attempt of Grover and Kearny to carry the railroad embankment, the Confederates followed their
troops back and formed a line in the edge of the woods. When the fire had died away along the
darkling woods, little groups of men from the Union lines went stealthily about, bringing in the
wounded from the exposed positions. Blankets attached to poles or muskets often served as
stretchers to bear the wounded to the ambulances and surgeons. There was a great lack here of organized effort to care for our wounded. Vehicles of various kinds were pressed into service. The
removal went on during the entire night, and tired soldiers were roused from their slumbers by the
plaintive cries of comrades passing in the comfortless vehicles. In one instance a Confederate and
a Union soldier were found cheering each other on the field. They were put into the same Virginia
farm-cart and sent to the rear, talking and groaning in fraternal sympathy."

made the chances of victory to tremble in the balance; my own division exhausted by seven hours' unremitted fighting, hardly one round per man remaining, and weakened in all things save its unconquerable spirit. Casting about for help, fortunately it was here reported to me that the brigades of Generals Lawton and Early were near by, and, sending to them, they promptly moved to my front at the most opportune moment, and this last charge met the same disastrous fate that had befallen those preceding. Having received an order from General Jackson to endeavor to avoid a general engagement, my commanders of brigades contented themselves with repulsing the enemy and following them up but a few hundred yards."

General J.E.B. Stuart says in his report, dated February 28th, 1863:

"I met with the head of General Longstreet's column between Hay Market and Gainesville, and there communicated to the commanding general General Jackson's position and the enemy's. I then passed the cavalry through the column so as to place it on Longstreet's right flank, and advanced directly toward Manassas, while the column kept directly down the pike to join General Jackson's right. I selected a fine position for a battery on the right, and one having been sent to me, I fired a few shots at the enemy's supposed position, which induced him to shift his position. General Robertson, who, with his command, was sent to reconnoiter farther down the road toward Manassas, reported the enemy in his front. Upon repairing to that front, I found that Rosser's regiment was engaged with the enemy to the left of the road, and Robertson's vedettes had found the enemy approaching from the direction of Bristoe Station toward Sudley. The prolongation of his line of march would have passed through my position, which was a very fine one for artillery as well as observation, and struck Longstreet in flank. I waited his approach long enough to ascertain that there was at least an army corps, at the same time keeping detachments of cavalry dragging brush down the road from the direction of Gainesville, so as to deceive the enemy,—a ruse which Porter's report shows was successful,—and notified the commanding general, then opposite me on the turnpike, that Longstreet's flank and rear were seriously threatened, and of the importance to us of the ridge I then held. Immediately upon the receipt of that intelligence, Jenkins's, Kemper's, and D. R. Jones's brigades, and several pieces of artillery were ordered to me by General Longstreet, and, being placed in position fronting Bristoe, awaited the enemy's advance. After exchanging a few shots with rifle-pieces this corps withdrew toward Manassas, leaving artillery and supports to hold the position until night. Brigadier-General Fitz Lee returned to the vicinity of Sudley, after a very successful expedition, of which his official report has not been received, and was instructed to coöperate with Jackson's left. Late in the afternoon the artillery on this commanding ridge was, to an important degree, auxiliary to the attack upon the enemy, and Jenkins's brigade repulsed the enemy in handsome style at one volley, as they advanced across a corn-field. Thus the day ended, our lines having considerably advanced."

What would have been the effect of the application on the enemy's right at, or any time after, 4 o'clock that afternoon of ten or twelve thousand effective men who had not been in battle at all, I do not myself consider doubtful.

In this battle the Fifth Corps, under General F. J. Porter, took no part whatever, but remained all day in column, without even deploying into line of battle or making any effort in force to find out what was in their front. That General Porter knew of the progress of the battle on his right, and that he believed the Union army was being defeated, is shown by his own dispatches to McDowell, several times repeated during the day. That subjoined will be sufficient:

"Generals McDowell and King:

"I found it impossible to communicate by crossing the woods to Groveton. The enemy are in great force on this road, and as they appear to have driven our forces back, the fire of the enemy having advanced and ours retired, I have determined to withdraw to Manassas. I have attempted to communicate with McDowell and Sigel, but my messengers have run into the enemy. They have gathered artillery and cavalry and infantry, and the advancing masses of dust show the enemy coming in force. I am now going to the head of the column to see what is passing and how affairs are going, and I will communicate with you. Had you not better send your train back?

"F. J. PORTER, Major-General."

Not the artillery only, but the volleys of musketry in this battle were also plainly heard on their right and front by the advance of Porter's troops much of the day. In consequence of his belief that the army on his right was being defeated, as stated in more than one of these dispatches, he informed General McDowell that he intended to retire to Manassas, and advised McDowell to send back his trains in the same direction.

For this action, or non-action, he has been on the one hand likened to Benedict Arnold, and on the other favorably compared with George Washington. I presume he would not accept the first position, and probably would hardly lay claim to the second. Certainly I have not the inclination, even had I

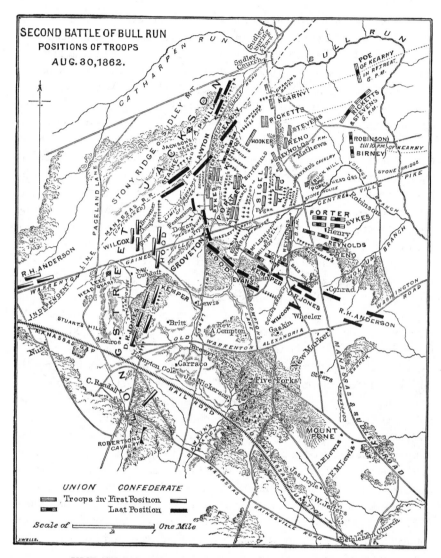

FIRST AND LAST POSITIONS IN THE FIGHTING OF AUGUST 30TH.

During the assault by Porter's corps and King's division, Jackson's forces were behind the unfinished railway. When that assault failed, the Unionists north of the turnpike were attacked by the
brigades of Featherston and Pryor (of Wilcox), which were acting with some of Jackson's troops
and with one brigade of Hood. Wilcox, with his own proper brigade, passed far to the right
and fought his way to an advanced position, after Evans and D. R. Jones had compelled Sigel and
McDowell to loosen their hold on and west of Bald Hill. [NOTE—Tower, Milroy, and McLean,
on the map, should be placed more to the east on and near Bald Hill.] At dark the Confederates
were somewhat in advance of the positions indicated on the map.—EDITORS.

the power, to assign him to either or to any position between the two; and if he were alone concerned in the question, I should make no comment at all on the subject at this day. Many others than himself and the result of a battle, however, are involved in it, and they do not permit silence when the second battle of Bull Run is discussed. Without going into the merits of the case, which has been obscured and confused by so many and such varied controversies, I shall confine myself to a bare statement of the facts as they are known to me personally, or communicated officially by officers of rank and standing, and by the official reports of both armies engaged in the battle. General Porter was tried by court-martial a few months after the battle and was cashiered. The reasons given by him at the time for his failure to go into action, or take any part in the battle, were: first, that he considered himself under General McDowell's orders, who told him that they were too far to the front for a battle; and, second, that the enemy was in such heavy force in his front that he would have been defeated had he attacked. General McDowell stated before the court-martial that, so far from saying that they were too far to the front for battle, he directed General Porter before leaving him to put his corps into the action where he was, and that he (McDowell) would move farther to the right and go into the battle there. Upon Porter remarking that he could not go in there without getting into a fight, McDowell replied, "I thought that was what we came here for."

General J.E.B. Stuart, who commanded the cavalry in Lee's army, tells in his official report above quoted precisely what was in General Porter's front, and what means he took to produce upon General Porter the impression that there were heavy forces in front of him and advancing toward him. General Porter certainly made no reconnoissance in force to ascertain whether or not there was a heavy force in his front; and Stuart's report makes it quite certain that, at the time referred to by him, Porter could easily have moved forward from Dawkins's Branch and seized the ridge on which are the Hampton Cole and Monroe houses, from which he would have had a complete view of the field from right to left. Not only this, but his occupation of that ridge would have connected him closely with our left and absolutely prevented Longstreet from forming on Jackson's right until he had dislodged Porter, which would have occupied him too long to have permitted the effective use of his troops for any other purpose, and certainly for the advance which he subsequently made against our left. Longstreet now asserts that he was in front of Porter with part of his corps at some indefinite hour of the day, variously fixed, but according to him by 11 o'clock in the morning, about the time that Porter's corps reached Dawkins's Branch. He further asserts, somewhat extravagantly, that if Porter had attacked he (Longstreet) would have annihilated him. He seems to have thought it a simple matter to annihilate an army corps of ten or twelve thousand men, much of which was composed of regular troops, but perhaps his statement to that effect would hardly be accepted by military men. If such an assertion made by a corps commander of one army is sufficient reason for a corps commander of the opposing army not to attack, even under orders to do so, it is hard to see how any general commanding an army could direct a battle at all; and certainly if such assertions as Longstreet's are considered reliable, there would have been no battle fought in our civil war, since they could easily have been had from either side in advance of any battle that was fought.

It seems pertinent to ask why General Longstreet did not annihilate Porter's corps during the day if it were so easily in his power to do so. It is also proper to suggest that it would have required a long time and all of his force to do this annihilating business on such a corps as Porter's; and in that case, what would have become of Jackson's right deprived of Longstreet's active support, which barely enabled Jackson to hold the ground that afternoon, Longstreet himself falling back at least a mile from our front at 1 o'clock that night after several hours of severe fighting?

I shall not discuss the various statements concerning the time of Long-street's arrival on the field. That he may have been there in person at the hour he mentions is of course possible; but that his corps was with him, that it was in line of battle at any such hour, or was in any such condition to fight as Porter was, can neither be truthfully asserted nor successfully maintained. Whatever Porter supposed to be Longstreet's position, however, in no respect touches his obligation to move forward under the circumstances and force Longstreet to develop what he really had, which he (Porter) certainly did not know and had taken no measures to know. The severe fighting on his right, which he heard and interpreted into a defeat for the Union army, did not permit him to rest idle on the field with his troops in column and with no sufficient effort even to find out anything of the field in front of him.

If a mere impression that the enemy is in heavy force and that an attack or further advance might be hazardous is a sufficient reason for a corps commander to keep out of a battle, raging in his hearing, especially when he thinks that his friends are being defeated, it is extremely difficult to see how any army commander would venture to engage in battle at all, unless he could ascertain in advance and keep himself acquainted during the day with the impressions of his corps commanders about the propriety of going into the battle. Certainly Porter did not know at that time that Longstreet was in his front, and his non-action was based on fancy, and not on any fact that he knew.

But wherever Longstreet was in the morning, it is certain that at 4 o'clock that day, or about 4 o'clock, according to his own official report, he withdrew the larger part of his force and advanced to Jackson's right flank to resist the last attack of the Union army on Jackson's line, and that for several hours he was engaged in a severe battle on our left, utterly ignoring Porter and presenting his

MONUMENT TO THE UNION SOLDIERS
WHO FELL AT GROVETON AUGUST 28, 29,
AND 30, 1862. FROM A PHOTOGRAPH
TAKEN SOON AFTER THE MONUMENT
WAS ERECTED IN 1865.

This view is taken from the edge of the railway cut, looking toward the Union lines. The shaft is of brown sandstone, and in design and material is like the monument erected on the Henry hill at the same time. The shot and shell that were fixed with mortar to the base and to the top of the shaft, and every vestige of the inclosing fence, have been carried off by relic-hunters. In May, 1884, the monument was partly hidden by the four evergreens which were planted at the corners. The field behind the railway cut and behind the embankment, east of the cut, was even then strewn with the tins of cartridge-boxes, rusty camp utensils, and bits of broken accouterments.—EDITORS.

right flank to Porter's attack during that whole time. He seems also to have entirely forgotten that he was "held in check," as he was good-natured enough to say he was years afterward. During these long hours General Porter still remained idle with his corps in column, and many of them lying on the ground, for ease of position probably, as they were not under fire.

Taking the enemy's own account of the battle that afternoon, which lasted several hours, and its result, it is not unreasonable to say that, if General Porter had attacked Longstreet's right with ten or twelve thousand men while the latter was thus engaged, the effect would have been conclusive. Porter's case is the first I have ever known, or that I find recorded in military history, in which the theory has been seriously put forth that the hero of a battle is the man who keeps out of it. With this theory in successful operation, war will be stripped of most of its terrors, and a pitched battle need not be much more dangerous to human life than a militia muster.

When the battle ceased on the 29th of August, we were in possession of the field on our right, and occupied on our left the position held early in the day, and had every right to claim a decided success. What that success might have been, if a corps of twelve thousand men who had not been in battle that day had been thrown against Longstreet's right while engaged in the severe fight that afternoon, I need not indicate. To say that General Porter's non-action during that whole day was wholly unexpected and disappointing, and that it provoked severe comment on all hands, is to state the facts mildly.

Every indication during the night of the 29th and up to 10 o'clock on the morning of the 30th pointed to the retreat of the enemy from our front. Paroled prisoners of our own army, taken on the evening of the 29th, who came into our lines on the morning of the 30th, reported the enemy retreating during the whole night in the direction of and along the Warrenton pike (a fact since confirmed by Longstreet's report).☆ Generals McDowell and Heintzelman, who reconnoitered the position held by the enemy's left on the evening of the 29th, also confirmed this statement. They reported to me the evacuation of these positions by the enemy, and that there was every indication of their retreat in the direction of Gainesville. On the morning of the 30th, as may be easily believed, our troops, who had been marching and fighting almost continuously for many days, were greatly exhausted. They had had little to eat for two days, and artillery and cavalry horses had been in harness and under the saddle for ten days, and had been almost out of forage for the last two days. It may be readily imagined how little these troops, after such severe labors and hardships, were in condition for further active marching and fighting. On the 28th I had telegraphed General Halleck our condition, and had begged of him to have rations and forage sent forward to us from Alexandria with all speed; but about daylight on the 30th I received a note from General Franklin, written by direction of General McClellan, informing me that rations and forage would be loaded into the available wagons and cars at Alexandria as soon as I should send back a cavalry escort to guard the trains. Such a letter, when we were fighting the enemy and when Alexandria was full of troops, needs no comment. Our cavalry was well-nigh broken down completely, and certainly we were in no condition to spare troops from the front, nor could they have gone to Alexandria and returned within the time by which we must have had provisions and forage or have fallen back toward supplies; nor am I able to understand of what use cavalry could be to guard railroad trains. It was not until I received this letter that I began to be hopeless of any successful issue to our operations; but I felt it to be my duty, notwithstanding the broken-down condition of the forces under my command, to hold my position. I had received no sort of information of any troops coming forward to reënforce me since the 24th, and did not expect on the morning of the 30th that any assistance would reach me from the direction of Washington, but I determined again to give battle to the enemy and delay as long as possible his farther advance toward Washington. I accordingly prepared to renew the engagement.

General Porter, with whose non-action of the day before I was naturally dissatisfied, had been peremptorily ordered that night to report to me in person with his corps, and arrived on the field early in the morning. His corps had been reënforced by Piatt's brigade of Sturgis's division, and was estimated to be about twelve thousand strong; but in some hitherto unexplained manner one

---

☆According to General Longstreet's and other Confederate reports, their troops withdrew at night to their line of battle of the day, occupying the same positions and in the same order. General Pope's orders for the 30th directed that the corps of McDowell, Heintzelman, and Porter, with the necessary cavalry, should move "forward in pursuit of the enemy," and "press him vigorously all day." The command of the pursuit was assigned to General McDowell.—EDITORS.

brigade‡ of his (Porter's) corps had straggled off from the corps and appeared at Centreville during the day. With this straggling brigade was General Morell, commander of the division to which it belonged.

This brigade remained at Centreville all day, in sight and sound of the battle in which the corps to which it belonged was engaged, but made no move to join it or to approach the field of battle. On the contrary, the brigade commander made requisition for ten thousand pairs of shoes on one of my aides-de-camp who was at Centreville in charge of the headquarters train. The troops under General Sturgis and General A. Sanders Piatt had followed this brigade by a misunderstanding of the situation; but the moment they found themselves away from the battle these two officers, with true soldierly spirit, passed Morell and brought their commands to the field and into the battle, where they rendered gallant and distinguished services.

Between 12 and 2 o'clock during the day I advanced Porter's corps, supported by King's division of McDowell's corps, and supported also on their left by Sigel's corps and Reynolds's division, to attack the enemy along the Warrenton pike. At the same time the corps of Heintzelman and Reno on our right were directed to push forward to the left and front toward the pike and attack the enemy's left flank. For a time Ricketts's division of McDowell's corps was placed in support of this movement. I was obliged to assume the aggressive or to fall back, as from want of provisions I was not able to await an attack from the enemy or the result of any other movement he might make.

Every moment of delay increased the odds against us, and I therefore pushed forward the attack as rapidly as possible. Soon after Porter advanced to attack along the Warrenton pike and the assault was made by Heintzelman and Reno on the right, it became apparent that the enemy was massing his forces as fast as they arrived on the right of Jackson, and was moving forward to force our left. General McDowell was therefore directed to recall Ricketts's division from our right, and put it so as to strengthen our left thus threatened.

Porter's corps was repulsed after some severe fighting, and began to retire, and the enemy advancing to the assault, our whole line was soon furiously engaged. The main attack of the enemy was made against our left, but was met with stubborn resistance by the divisions of Schenck and Reynolds, and the brigade of Milroy, who were soon reënforced on the left by Ricketts's division. The action was severe for several hours, the enemy bringing up heavy reserves and pouring mass after mass of his troops on our left. He was able also to present at least an equal force all along our line of battle. Porter's corps was halted and re-formed, and as soon as it was in condition it was pushed forward to the

‡Griffin's brigade. Griffin testified that he was ordered by General Morell to follow Sykes, who was supposed to have gone to Centreville. Griffin moved thence toward the battle-field about 5 P.M. He found the road blocked, and the bridge over Cub Run broken.—EDITORS.

support of our left, where it rendered distinguished service, especially the brigade of regulars under Colonel (then Lieutenant-Colonel) Buchanan.

McLean's brigade of Schenck's division, which was posted in observation on our left flank, and in support of Reynolds, became exposed to the attack of the enemy on our left when Reynolds's division was drawn back to form line to support Porter's corps, then retiring from their attack, and it was fiercely assailed by Hood and Evans, in greatly superior force. This brigade was commanded in person by General Schenck, the division commander, and fought with supreme gallantry and tenacity. The enemy's attack was repulsed several times with severe loss, but he returned again and again to the assault.

It is needless for me to describe the appearance of a man so well known to the country as General R. C. Schenck. I have only to say that a more gallant and devoted soldier never lived, and to his presence and the fearless exposure of his person during these attacks is largely due the protracted resistance made by this brigade. He fell, badly wounded, in the front of his command, and his loss was deeply felt and had a marked effect on the final result in that part of the field.

Tower's brigade of Ricketts's division was pushed forward to his support, and the brigade was led by General Tower in person with conspicuous gallantry. The conduct of these two brigades and their commanders in plain view of our whole left was especially distinguished, and called forth hearty and enthusiastic cheers. Their example was of great service, and seemed to infuse new spirit into the troops that witnessed their intrepid conduct.

I have always considered it a misfortune to the country that in this action General Tower received a severe wound which disabled him from active service. He is a man of very superior abilities, zealous, and full of spirit and *élan*, and might easily have expected to serve his country in a much higher position than the one that he held on that field.

Reno's corps was withdrawn from our right center late in the afternoon and thrown into action on our left, where the assaults of the enemy were persistent and unintermitting. Notwithstanding the disadvantages under which we labored, our troops held their ground with the utmost firmness and obstinacy. The loss on both sides was heavy. By dark our left had been forced back half or three-fourths of a mile, but still remained firm and unbroken and still held the Warrenton pike on our rear, while our right was also driven back equally far, but in good order and without confusion. At dark the enemy took possession of the Sudley Springs road, and was in position to threaten our line of communication *via* stone bridge. After 6 o'clock in the evening I learned, accidentally, that Franklin's corps had arrived at a point about 4 miles east of Centreville, or 12 miles in our rear, and that it was only about 8000 strong.

The result of the battle of the 30th convinced me that we were no longer able to hold our position so far to the front, and so far away from the absolute

THE RETREAT OVER THE STONE BRIDGE, SATURDAY EVENING, AUGUST 30TH. ☆

necessaries of life, suffering, as were men and horses, from fatigue and hunger, and weakened by the heavy losses in battle. About 8 o'clock in the evening, therefore, I sent written orders to the corps commanders to withdraw leisurely to Centreville, and stated to them what route each should pursue and where they should take position at and near Centreville. General Reno, with his corps,

☆Captain William H. Powell, of the 4th Regular Infantry, in a letter to "The Century," dated Fort Omaha, Nebraska, March 12th, 1885, thus describes the retreat upon Washington and McClellan's reception by his old army:

"The last volley had been fired, and as night fell upon us the division of regulars of Porter's corps was ordered to retire to Centreville. It had fought hard on the extreme left to preserve the line of retreat by the turnpike and the stone bridge. We were gloomy, despondent, and about 'tired out'; we had not had a change of clothing from the 14th to the 31st of August, and had been living, in the words of the men, on 'salt horse,' 'hard-tack,' and 'chicory juice.' As we filed from the battle-field into the turnpike leading over the stone bridge, we came upon a group of mounted officers, one of whom wore a peculiar style of hat which had been seen on the field that day, and which had been the occasion of a great deal of comment in the ranks. As we passed these officers, the one with the peculiar hat called out in a loud voice:

"'What troops are these?'

"'The regulars,' answered somebody.

"'Second Division, Fifth Corps,' replied another.

"'God bless them! they saved the army,' added the officer, solemnly. We learned that he was General Irvin McDowell.

"As we neared the bridge we came upon confusion. Men singly and in detachments were mingled with sutlers' wagons, artillery, caissons, supply wagons, and ambulances, each striving to get ahead of the other. Vehicles rushed through organized bodies, and broke the columns into fragments. Little detachments gathered by the roadside, after crossing the bridge, crying out the numbers of their regiments as a guide to scattered comrades.

was ordered to take post to cover this movement. The withdrawal was made slowly, quietly, and in good order, no attempt whatever being made by the enemy to obstruct our movement. A division of infantry, with its batteries, was posted to cover the crossing of Cub Run.

The exact losses in this battle I am unable to give, as the reports from corps commanders only indicated the aggregate losses since August 22d, but they were very heavy.

Before leaving the field I sent orders to General Banks, at Bristoe Station, where the railroad was broken, to destroy the cars and such of the stores as he could not take off in the wagon trains, and join me at Centreville. I had previously sent him instructions to bring off from Warrenton Junction and Bristoe Station all of the ammunition and all of the sick and wounded who could bear transportation, throwing personal baggage and property out of the regimental trains, if necessary, for the purpose.

At no time during the 29th, 30th, or 31st of August was the road between Bristoe and Centreville interrupted by the enemy. The orders will show conclusively that every arrangement was made in the minutest detail for the security of our wagon train and supplies; and General Banks's subsequent report to me is positive that none of the wagons or mules were lost. I mention this matter merely to answer the wholly unfounded statements made at the time, and repeated often since, of our loss of wagons, mules, and supplies.

I arrived personally at Centreville about 9 or 10 o'clock that night [the

---

"And what a night it was! Dark, gloomy, and beclouded by the volumes of smoke which had risen from the battle-field. To our disgust with the situation was added the discomfort of a steady rain setting in after nightfall. With many threats to reckless drivers, and through the untiring efforts of our officers,—not knowing how, when, or where we should meet the enemy again,—we managed to preserve our organization intact, keeping out of the road as much as possible, in order to avoid mingling with others. In this way we arrived at Centreville some time before midnight, and on the morning of the 31st of August we were placed in the old Confederate earth-works surrounding that village to await developments.

"It was Sunday. The morning was cold and rainy; everything bore a look of sadness in unison with our feelings. All about were the *disjecta membra* of a shattered army; here were stragglers plodding through the mud, inquiring for their regiments; little squads, just issuing from their shelterless bivouac on the wet ground; wagons wrecked and forlorn; half-formed regiments, part of the men with guns and part without; wanderers driven in by the patrols; while every one you met had an unwashed, sleepy, downcast aspect, and looked as if he would like to hide his head somewhere from all the world.

"During the afternoon of Sept. 1st, a council of war was held in the bivouac of the regular division, at which I noticed all the prominent generals of that army. It was a long one, and apparently not over-pleasant, if one might judge of it by the expressions on the faces of the officers when they separated. The information it developed, however, was that the enemy was between the Army of the Potomac and Washington; that Kearny was then engaged with him at Chantilly, and that we must fall back toward the defenses of the city. Dejection disappeared, activity took the place of immobility, and we were ready again to renew the contest.

30th]. The next morning the various corps were posted in the old intrench-ments in and around Centreville, and ammunition trains and some supplies were brought up during the day and distributed. We spent that whole day rest-ing the men and resupplying them with ammunition and provisions as far as our means permitted.

Franklin's corps arrived at Centreville late on the afternoon of the 30th; Sumner's the next day. What was then thought by the Government of our oper-ations up to this time is shown in the subjoined dispatch:

> WASHINGTON, August 31st, 1862. 11 A.M.
> My Dear General: You have done nobly. Don't yield another inch if you can avoid it. All reserves are being sent forward.... I am doing all I can for you and your noble army. God bless you and it....
>
> H. W. HALLECK, General-in-chief.

The enemy's cavalry appeared in front of Cub Run that morning, but made no attempt to attack. Our cavalry, under Buford and Bayard, was completely broken down, and both of these officers reported to me that not five horses to the company could be forced into a trot. No horses whatever had reached us for remounts since the beginning of operations. It was impracticable, therefore, to use the cavalry as cavalry to cover our front with pickets or to make reconnois-sances of the enemy's front.

This paper would be incomplete indeed did it fail to contain some short, if

---

But who was to be our leader? and where were we to fight? Those were the questions that sprang to our lips. We had been ordered to keep our camp-fires burning brightly until 'tat-too'; and then, after the rolls had been called, we stole away—out into a gloomy night, made more desolate by the glare of dying embers. Nothing occurred to disturb our march; we ar-rived at Fairfax Court House early on the morning of the 2d of September. At this point we were turned off on the road to Washington, and went into bivouac. Here all sorts of rumors reached us; but, tired out from the weary night march, our blankets were soon spread on the ground, and we enjoyed an afternoon and night of comparative repose.

"About 4 o'clock on the next afternoon, from a prominent point, we descried in the dis-tance the dome of the Capitol. We would be there at least in time to defend it! Darkness came upon us and still we marched. As the night wore on, we found at each halt that it was more and more difficult to arouse the men from the sleep into which they would fall appar-ently as soon as they touched the ground. During one of these halts, while Colonel Buchanan, the brigade commander, was resting a little off the road, some distance in advance of the head of the column, it being starlight, two horsemen came down the road toward us. I thought I observed a familiar form, and, turning to Colonel Buchanan, said:

"'Colonel, if I did not know that General McClellan had been relieved of all command, I should say that he was one of that party,' adding immediately, 'I do really believe it is he!'

"'Nonsense,' said the colonel; 'what would General McClellan be doing out in this lonely place, at this time of night, without an escort?'

"The two horsemen passed on to where the men of the column were lying, standing, or sitting, and were soon lost in the shadowy gloom. But a few moments had elapsed, however,

entirely insufficient, tribute to that most gallant and loyal soldier, John Buford. I remember very well how surprised I was when I was first placed in command of the Army of Virginia that General Buford, then only a major in the inspector-general's department, reported to me for duty as inspector. I asked him how he could possibly remain in such a position while a great war was going on, and what objections he could have (if he had any) to being placed in a command in the field. He seemed hurt to think I could have even a doubt of his wish to take the field, and told me that he had tried to get a command, but was without influence enough to accomplish it. I went at once to the Secretary of War and begged him to have Major Buford appointed a brigadier-general of volunteers and ordered to report to me for service. The President was good enough to make the appointment, and certainly a better one was never made. Buford's coolness, his fine judgment, and his splendid courage were known of all men who had to do with him; but besides, and in addition to these high qualities, he acquired in a few months, through his presence and manner, an influence over men as remarkable as it was useful. His quiet dignity, covering a fiery spirit and a military sagacity as far-reaching as it was accurate, made him in the short period of his active service one of the most respected and trusted officers in the service. His death, brought about by disease contracted during the months of active service and constant exposure, was widely lamented in the army.

On the morning of the 1st of September I directed General Sumner to push forward a reconnoissance toward Little River pike, which enters the Warrenton pike at Fairfax, with two brigades, to ascertain if the enemy was making any movement toward our right by that road. The enemy was found moving again slowly toward the right, heavy columns moving along the Little River pike in the direction of Fairfax. This movement had become so developed by the afternoon of that day, and was so evidently directed to turn our right, that I made the necessary disposition of troops to fight a battle between the Little River pike and the road from Fairfax to Centreville. General Hooker was sent early in the afternoon to Fairfax Court House, and directed to concentrate all

---

when Captain John D. Wilkins, of the 3d Infantry (now colonel of the 5th) came running toward Colonel Buchanan, crying out:

"'Colonel! Colonel! General McClellan is here!'

"The enlisted men caught the sound! Whoever was awake aroused his neighbor. Eyes were rubbed, and those tired fellows, as the news passed down the column, jumped to their feet, and sent up such a hurrah as the Army of the Potomac had never heard before. Shout upon shout went out into the stillness of the night; and as it was taken up along the road and repeated by regiment, brigade, division, and corps, we could hear the roar dying away in the distance. The effect of this man's presence upon the Army of the Potomac—in sunshine or rain, in darkness or in daylight, in victory or defeat—was electrical, and too wonderful to make it worth while attempting to give a reason for it. Just two weeks from this time this defeated army, under the leadership of McClellan, won the battles of South Mountain and Antietam, having marched ten days out of the two weeks in order to do it."

MAJOR-GENERAL PHILIP KEARNY.
FROM A PHOTOGRAPH.

the troops in that vicinity and to push forward to Germantown with his advance. I instructed McDowell to move along the road from Centreville toward Fairfax Court House, as far as Difficult Creek, and to connect on his right with Hooker. Reno was directed to push forward north of the road to Centreville, and in the direction of Chantilly, toward the flank of the enemy's advance; Heintzelman's corps to support Reno. Just before sunset the enemy attacked us toward our right, but was met by Hooker, McDowell, and Reno, and by Kearny's division of Heintzelman's corps. A very severe action was fought in the midst of a terrific thunder-storm, and was only ended by the darkness. The enemy was driven back entirely from our front, and did not again renew his attack upon us.

In this short but severe action the army lost two officers of the highest capacity and distinction, whose death caused general lamentation in the army and country. The first was Major-General Philip Kearny, killed in advance of his division and while commanding it. There have been few such officers as Kearny in our own or any other army. In war he was an enthusiast, and he never seemed so much at home and so cheerful and confident as in battle. Tall and lithe in figure, with a most expressive and mobile countenance, and a manner which inspired confidence and zeal in all under his command, no one could fail to admire his chivalric bearing and his supreme courage. He seemed to think that it was his mission to make up the shortcomings of others, and in proportion as these shortcomings were made plain, his exertions and exposure were multiplied. He was a great and most accomplished soldier, and died as he would himself have wished to die, and as became his heroic character, at the head of his troops and in the front of the battle.

General Isaac I. Stevens, who was killed at the same time and nearly on the same ground, was an officer in many respects contrasted to Kearny. He was short and rather stout, with a swarthy complexion and very bright dark eyes. He was a man of very superior abilities and of marked skill and courage. His extreme political opinions before the war, ardently asserted, as was his habit in all matters which interested him, made it somewhat difficult for him to secure such a position in the army as one of his capacity might well have expected. The prejudice against him on this account was soon shown to be utterly groundless, for a more zealous and faithful officer never lived. His conduct in the battle in which he lost his life, and in every other operation of the campaign, was marked by high intelligence and the coolest courage, and his death in the front of battle ended too soon a career which would have placed him among the foremost officers of the war. As an officer of engineers before the war, and as Governor of, and delegate to Congress from Washington Territory, he was always a man of note, and possessed the abilities and the force to have commanded in time any position to which he might have aspired. The loss of these two officers was a heavy blow to the army, not so much perhaps because of their soldierly capacity as because of their well-known and unshakable fidelity to duty, and their entire loyalty to their comrades in arms.

MAJOR-GENERAL ISAAC I. STEVENS.
FROM A PHOTOGRAPH.

On the morning of the 2d of September the army was posted behind Difficult Creek from Flint Hill to the Alexandria pike. The enemy disappeared from our front, moving toward the Upper Potomac with no attempt to force our position. And here the second battle of Bull Run may be said to terminate. On that day I received orders from General Halleck to take position in the intrenchments in front of Washington, with a view to reorganizing the army and eliminating such of the discordant elements in it as had largely caused the misfortunes of the latter part of that campaign.

The transactions at Alexandria and Washington City during these eventful days, as also at Centreville during part of them, are as closely connected with these battles, and had nearly as much to do with their results, as any part of the operations in the field; but they demand more space than is accorded to this article. The materials to write a complete account of these matters are at hand, and it is quite probable that the course of events may yet make their publication necessary.

There are other matters which, although not important, seem not out of place in this paper. A good deal of cheap wit has been expended upon a fanciful story that I published an order or wrote a letter or made a remark that my "headquarters would be in the saddle." It is an expression harmless and innocent enough, but it is even stated that it furnished General Lee with the basis for the only joke of his life. I think it due to army tradition, and to the comfort of those who have so often repeated this ancient joke in the days long before the civil war, that these later wits should not be allowed with impunity to poach on this well-tilled manor. This venerable joke I first heard when a cadet at West Point, and it was then told of that gallant soldier and gentleman, General W. J. Worth, and I presume it could be easily traced back to the Crusades and beyond. Certainly I never used this expression or wrote or dictated it, nor does any such expression occur in any order of mine; and as it has perhaps served its time and effected its purpose, it ought to be retired.

I thus conclude for the present this account of the second battle of Bull Run. The battle treated of, as well as the campaign which preceded it, have been, and no doubt still are, greatly misunderstood. Probably they will remain during this generation a matter of controversy, into which personal feeling and prejudice so largely enter that dispassionate judgment cannot now be looked for.

I submit this article to the public judgment with all confidence that it will be fairly considered, and as just a judgment passed upon it as is possible at this time. I well understood, as does every military man, how difficult and how thankless was the task imposed on me, and I do not hesitate to say that I would gladly have avoided it if I could have done so consistent with duty.

To confront with a small army greatly superior forces, to fight battles without the hope of victory, but only to gain time by delaying the forward movement of the enemy, is a duty the most hazardous and the most difficult that can be imposed upon any general or any army. While such operations require the highest courage and endurance on the part of the troops, they are unlikely to be understood or appreciated, and the results, however successful in view of the object aimed at, have little in them to attract public commendation or applause.

At no time could I have hoped to fight a successful battle with the superior forces of the enemy which confronted me, and which were able at any time to outflank and bear my small army to the dust. It was only by constant movement, incessant watchfulness, and hazardous skirmishes and battles, that the forces under my command were saved from destruction, and that the enemy was embarrassed and delayed in his advance until the army of General McClellan was at length assembled for the defense of Washington.

I did hope that in the course of these operations the enemy might commit some imprudence, or leave some opening of which I could take such advantage as to gain at least a partial success. This opportunity was presented by the advance of Jackson on Manassas Junction; but although the best dispositions possible in my view were made, the object was frustrated by causes which could not have been foreseen, and which perhaps are not yet completely known to the country.

CHAPTER 14

THE INVASION OF MARYLAND.

James Longstreet, Lieutenant-General, C.S.A.

When the Second Bull Run campaign closed we had the most brilliant prospects the Confederates ever had. We then possessed an army which, had it been kept together, the Federals would never have dared attack. With such a splendid victory behind us, and such bright prospects ahead, the question arose as to whether or not we should go into Maryland. General Lee, on account of our short supplies, hesitated a little, but I reminded him of my experience in Mexico, where sometimes we were obliged to live two or three days on green corn. I told him we could not starve at that season of the year so long as the fields were loaded with "roasting ears." Finally he determined to go on, and accordingly crossed the river and went to Frederick City. On the 6th of September some of our cavalry, moving toward Harper's Ferry, became engaged with some of the Federal artillery near there. General Lee proposed that I should organize a force, and surround the garrison and capture it. I objected, and urged that our troops were worn with marching and were on short rations, and that it would be a bad idea to divide our forces while we were in the enemy's country, where he could get information, in six or eight hours, of any movement we might make. The Federal army, though beaten at the Second Manassas, was not disorganized, and it would certainly come out to look for us, and we should guard against being caught in such a condition. Our army consisted of a superior quality of soldiers, but it was in no condition to divide in the enemy's country. I urged that we should keep it well in hand, recruit our strength, and get up supplies, and then we could do anything we pleased. General Lee made no reply to this, and I supposed the Harper's Ferry scheme was abandoned. A day or two after we had reached Frederick City, I went up to General Lee's tent and found the front walls closed. I inquired for the general, and he, recognizing my voice, asked me to come in. I went in and found Jackson there. The two were discussing the move against Harper's Ferry, both heartily approving it. They had gone so far that it seemed useless for me to offer any further opposition, and I only suggested that Lee should use his entire army in the move instead of sending off a large portion of it to Hagerstown as he intended to do. General Lee so far changed the wording of his order as to require me to halt at Boons-boro' with General D. H. Hill; Jackson being ordered to Harper's Ferry *via* Bolivar Heights, on the south side; McLaws by the Maryland Heights on the north, and Walker, *via* Loudoun Heights, from the south-east. This was afterward changed, and I was sent on to Hagerstown, leaving D. H. Hill alone at South Mountain.

The movement against Harper's Ferry began on the 10th. Jackson made a wide, sweeping march around the Ferry, passing the Potomac at Williamsport, and moving from there on toward Martinsburg, and turning thence upon Harper's Ferry to make his attack by Bolivar Heights. McLaws made a hurried march to reach Maryland Heights before Jackson could get in position, and succeeded in doing so. With Maryland Heights in our possession the Federals could not hold their position there. McLaws put 200 or 300 men to each piece of his artillery and carried it up the heights, and was in position when Jackson came on the heights opposite. Simultaneously Walker appeared upon Loudoun Heights, south of the Potomac and east of the Shenandoah, thus completing the combination against the Federal garrison. The surrender of the Ferry and the twelve thousand Federal troops there was a matter of only a short time.

If the Confederates had been able to stop with that, they might have been well contented with their month's campaign. They had had a series of successes and no defeats; but the division of the army to make this attack on Harper's Ferry was a fatal error, as the subsequent events showed.

While a part of the army had gone toward Harper's Ferry I had moved up to Hagerstown. In the meantime Pope had been relieved and McClellan was in command of the army, and with ninety thousand refreshed troops was marching forth to avenge the Second Manassas. The situation was a very serious one for us. McClellan was close upon us. As we moved out of Frederick he came on and occupied that place, and there he came across a lost copy of the order assigning position to the several commands in the Harper's Ferry move.

This "lost order" has been the subject of much severe comment by Virginians who have written of the war. It was addressed to D. H. Hill, and they charged that its loss was due to him, and that the failure of the campaign was the result of the lost order. As General Hill has proved that he never received the order at his headquarters it must have been lost by some one else.‡ Ordinar-

---

‡The following is the text of the "lost order" as quoted by General McClellan in his official report:

"SPECIAL ORDERS. }
No. 191.   }

HEADQUARTERS, ARMY }
OF NORTHERN VIRGINIA. }
September 9th, 1862.   }

ily, upon getting possession of such an order, the adversary would take it as a *ruse de guerre,* but it seems that General McClellan gave it his confidence, and made his dispositions accordingly. He planned his attack upon D. H. Hill under the impression that I was there with 12 brigades, 9 of which were really at Hagerstown, while R. H. Anderson's division was on Maryland Heights with General McLaws. Had McClellan exercised due diligence in seeking information from his own resources, he would have known better the situation at South Mountain and could have enveloped General D. H. Hill's division on the afternoon of the 13th, or early on the morning of the 14th, and then turned upon McLaws at Maryland Heights, before I could have reached either point. As it was, McClellan, after finding the order, moved with more confidence on toward South Mountain, where D. H. Hill was stationed as a Confederate rear-guard with five thousand men under his command. As I have stated, my command was at Hagerstown, thirteen miles farther on. General Lee was with me, and on the night of the 13th we received information that McClellan was at the foot of South Mountain with his great army. General Lee ordered me to march back to the mountain early the next morning. I suggested that, instead of meeting McClellan there, we withdraw Hill and unite my forces and Hill's at Sharpsburg, at the same time explaining that Sharpsburg was a strong defensive position from which we could strike the flank or rear of any force that might be sent to the relief of Harper's Ferry. I endeavored to show him that by making a forced march to Hill my troops would be in an exhausted condition and could not make a proper battle. Lee listened patiently enough, but did not change his

---

"The army will resume its march to-morrow, taking the Hagerstown road. General Jackson's command will form the advance, and after passing Middletown, with such portions as he may select, take the route toward Sharpsburg, cross the Potomac at the most convenient point, and by Friday night take possession of the Baltimore and Ohio Railroad, capture such of the enemy as may be at Martinsburg, and intercept such as may attempt to escape from Harper's Ferry.

"General Longstreet's command will pursue the same road as far as Boonsboro', where it will halt with the reserve, supply, and baggage trains of the army.

"General McLaws, with his own division and that of General R. H. Anderson, will follow General Longstreet; on reaching Middletown he will take the route to Harper's Ferry, and by Friday morning possess himself of the Maryland Heights and endeavor to capture the enemy at Harper's Ferry and vicinity.

"General Walker, with his division after accomplishing the object in which he is now engaged, will cross the Potomac at Check's ford, ascend its right bank to Lovettsville, take possession of Loudoun Heights, if practicable, by Friday morning, Keyes's ford on his left, and the road between the end of the mountain and the Potomac on his right. He will, as far as practicable, coöperate with General McLaws and General Jackson in intercepting the retreat of the enemy.

"General D. H. Hill's division will form the rear-guard of the army, pursuing the road taken by the main body. The reserve artillery, ordnance, and supply trains, etc., will precede General Hill.

"General Stuart will detach a squadron of cavalry to accompany the commands of Gen-

THE OLD LUTHERAN CHURCH, SHARPSBURG. FROM A WAR-TIME PHOTOGRAPH.

The church stands at the east end of the village, on Main street, and was a Federal hospital after the battle. Burnside's skirmishers gained a hold in the first cross-street below the church, where there was considerable fighting. On the hill in the extreme distance Main street becomes the Shepherdstown road, by which the Confederates retreated.—EDITORS.

plans, and directed that I should go back the next day and make a stand at the mountain. After lying down, my mind was still on the battle of the next day, and I was so impressed with the thought that it would be impossible for us to do anything at South Mountain with the fragments of a worn and exhausted army, that I rose and, striking a light, wrote a note to General Lee, urging him to order Hill away and concentrate at Sharpsburg. To that note I got no answer,

---

erals Longstreet, Jackson, and McLaws, and, with the main body of the cavalry, will cover the route of the army and bring up all stragglers that may have been left behind.

"The commands of Generals Jackson, McLaws, and Walker, after accomplishing the objects for which they have been detached, will join the main body of the army at Boonsboro' or Hagerstown.

"Each regiment on the march will habitually carry its axes in the regimental ordnance wagons, for use of the men at their encampments, to procure wood, etc. By command of General R. E. Lee.

"R. H. CHILTON, ASSISTANT ADJUTANT-GENERAL.

"MAJOR-GENERAL D. H. HILL, Commanding Division."

Comparison of the above with the copy of the order as printed among the Confederate Correspondence ("Official Records," Volume XIX., Part II., p. 603) shows that the latter contains two paragraphs, omitted above. In the first paragraph the officers and men of Lee's army are prohibited from visiting Frederickstown except on written permission; and in the second paragraph directions are given for the transportation of the sick and disabled to Winchester.—EDITORS.

and the next morning I marched as directed, leaving General Toombs, as ordered by General Lee, at Hagerstown to guard our trains and supplies.

We marched as hurriedly as we could over a hot and dusty road, and reached the mountain about 3 o'clock in the afternoon, with the troops much scattered and worn. In riding up the mountain to join General Hill I discovered that everything was in such disjointed condition that it would be impossible for my troops and Hill's to hold the mountain against such forces as McClellan had there, and wrote a note to General Lee, in which I stated that fact, and cautioned him to make his arrangements to retire that night. We got as many troops up as we could, and by putting in detachments here and there managed to hold McClellan in check until night, when Lee ordered the withdrawal to Sharpsburg.

On the afternoon of the 15th of September my command and Hill's crossed the Antietam Creek, and took position in front of Sharpsburg, my command filing into position on the right of the Sharpsburg and Boonsboro' turnpike, and D. H. Hill's division on the left. Soon after getting into position we found our left, at Dunker Church, the weak point, and Hood, with two brigades, was changed from my right to guard this point, leaving General D. H. Hill between the parts of my command.

LEE'S HEADQUARTERS IN SHARPSBURG. FROM A PHOTOGRAPH.

This house, which was the residence of Jacob H. Grove, is noted in Sharpsburg as the place where Lee held a conference with Longstreet and D. H. Hill. But Lee's headquarters tents were pitched in a small grove on the right of the Shepherdstown road, just outside the town.—EDITORS.

That night, after we heard of the fall of Harper's Ferry, General Lee ordered Stonewall Jackson to march to Sharpsburg as rapidly as he could come. Then it was that we should have retired from Sharpsburg and gone to the Virginia side of the Potomac.

The moral effect of our move into Maryland had been lost by our discomfiture at South Mountain, and it was then evident we could not hope to concentrate in time to do more than make a respectable retreat, whereas by retiring before the battle we could have claimed a very successful campaign.

On the forenoon of the 15th, the blue uniforms of the Federals appeared among the trees that crowned the heights on the eastern bank of the Antietam. The number increased, and larger and larger grew the field of blue until it seemed to stretch as far as the eye could see, and from the tops of the mountains down to the edges of the stream gathered the great army of McClellan. It was an awe-inspiring spectacle as this grand force settled down in sight of the Confederates, then shattered by battles and scattered by long and tiresome marches. On the 16th Jackson came and took position with part of his command on my left. Before night the Federals attacked my left and gave us a severe fight, principally against Hood's division, but we drove them back, holding well our

THE SUNKEN ROAD, OR "BLOODY LANE."
FROM A PHOTOGRAPH TAKEN
SINCE THE WAR.

This view is from the second bend in the lane, looking toward the Hagerstown pike, the Dunker Church wood appearing in the background. In the foreground Richardson crossed to the left into the corn-field near Piper's house. The house in the middleground, erected since the war, marks the scene of French's hard fight after passing Roulette's house.—EDITORS.

ground. After nightfall Hood was relieved from the position on the left, ordered to replenish his ammunition, and be ready to resume his first position on my right in the morning. General Jackson's forces, who relieved Hood, were extended to our left, reaching well back toward the Potomac, where most of our cavalry was. Toombs had joined us with two of his regiments, and was placed as guard on the bridge on my right. Hooker, who had thrown his corps against my left in the afternoon, was reënforced by the corps of Sumner and Mansfield. Sykes's division was also drawn into position for the impending battle. Burnside was over against my right, threatening the passage of the Antietam at that point. On the morning of the 17th the Federals were in good position along the Antietam, stretching up and down and across it to our left for three miles. They had a good position for their guns, which were of the most approved make and metal. Our position overcrowned theirs a little, but our guns were inferior and our ammunition was very imperfect.

Back of McClellan's line was a high ridge upon which was his signal station overlooking every point of our field. D. R. Jones's brigades of my command deployed on the right of the Sharpsburg pike, while Hood's brigades awaited orders. D. H. Hill was on the left extending toward the Hagerstown-Sharpsburg pike, and Jackson extended out from Hill's left toward the Potomac. The battle opened heavily with the attacks of the corps of Hooker, Mansfield, and Sumner against our left center, which consisted of Jackson's right and D. H. Hill's left. So severe and persistent were these attacks that I was obliged to send Hood to support our center. The Federals forced us back a little, however, and held this part of our position to the end of the day's work. With new troops and renewed efforts McClellan continued his attacks upon this point from time to time, while he brought his forces to bear against other points. The line swayed forward and back like a rope exposed to rushing currents. A force too heavy to be withstood would strike and drive in a weak point till we could collect a few fragments, and in turn force back the advance till our lost ground was recovered. A heroic effort was made by D. H. Hill, who collected some fragments and led a charge to drive back and recover our lost ground at the center. He soon found that his little band was too much exposed on its left flank and was obliged to abandon the attempt. Thus the battle ebbed and flowed with terrific slaughter on both sides.

The Federals fought with wonderful bravery and the Confederates clung to their ground with heroic courage as hour after hour they were mown down like grass. The fresh troops of McClellan literally tore into shreds the already ragged army of Lee, but the Confederates never gave back.

I remember at one time they were surging up against us with fearful numbers. I was occupying the left over by Hood, whose ammunition gave out. He retired to get a fresh supply. Soon after the Federals moved up against us in great masses.

We were under the crest of a hill occupying a position that ought to have been held by from four to six brigades. The only troops there were Cooke's regiment of North Carolina infantry, and they were without a cartridge. As I rode along the line with

THE SUNKEN ROAD, LOOKING EAST FROM ROULETTE'S LANE. FROM A PHOTOGRAPH TAKEN IN 1885.

CONFEDERATE DEAD (OF D. H. HILL'S DIVISION) IN THE SUNKEN ROAD.
FROM A PHOTOGRAPH.

my staff I saw two pieces of the Washington Artillery (Miller's battery), but there were not enough men to man them. The gunners had been either killed or wounded. This was a fearful situation for the Confederate center. I put my staff-officers to the guns while I held their horses. It was easy to see that if the Federals broke through our line there, the Confederate army would be cut in two and probably destroyed, for we were already badly whipped and were only holding our ground by sheer force of desperation. Cooke sent me word that his ammunition was out. I replied that he must hold his position as long as he had a man left. He responded that he would show his colors as long as there was a man alive to hold them up. We loaded up our little guns with canister and sent a rattle of hail into the Federals as they came up over the crest of the hill.

That little battery shot harder and faster, with a sort of human energy, as though it realized that it was to hold the thousands of Federals at bay or the battle was lost. So warm was the reception we gave them that they dodged back behind the crest of the hill. We sought to make them believe we had many batteries before them. As the Federals would come up they would see the colors of the North Carolina regiment waving placidly and then would receive a shower of canister. We made it lively while it lasted. In the meantime General Chilton, General Lee's chief of staff, made his way to me and asked, "Where are the troops you are holding your line with?" I pointed to my two pieces and to Cooke's regi-

ROULETTE'S
FARM.

1.—View of
William
Roulette's farm-house. 2.—Roulette's spring-
house, in which Confederate prisoners were
confined during the battle. 3.—Roulette's
spring, a copious fountain which refreshed
many thirsty soldiers of both armies.

ment, and replied, "There they are; but that regiment hasn't a cartridge."

Chilton's eyes popped as though they would come out of his head; he struck spurs to his horse and away he went to General Lee. I suppose he made some remarkable report, although I did not see General Lee again until night. After a little a shot came across the Federal front, plowing the ground in a parallel line. Another and another, each nearer and nearer their line. This enfilade fire, so distressing to soldiers, was from a battery on D. H. Hill's line, and it soon beat back the attacking column.

Meanwhile, R. H. Anderson and Hood came to our support and gave us more confidence. It was a little while only until another assault was made against D. H. Hill, and extend-ing far over toward our left, where McLaws and Walker were supporting Jackson. In this desperate effort the lines seemed to swing back and forth for many minutes, but at last they settled down to their respective positions, the Confed-erates holding with a desperation which seemed to say, "We are here to die."

Meantime General Lee was over toward our right, where Burnside was try-ing to cross to the attack. Toombs, who had been assigned as guard at that point, did handsome service. His troops were footsore and worn from marching, and he had only four hundred men to meet the Ninth Corps. The little band fought bravely, but the Federals were pressing them slowly back. The delay that Toombs caused saved that part of the battle, however, for at the last moment A. P. Hill came in to reënforce him, and D. H. Hill discovered a good place for a battery and opened with it. Thus the Confederates were enabled to drive the Federals back, and when night settled down the army of Lee was still in posses-sion of the field. But it was dearly bought, for thousands of brave soldiers were dead on the field and many gallant commands were torn as a forest in a cyclone. It was heart-rending to see how Lee's army had been slashed by the day's fighting.

Nearly one-fourth of the troops who went into the battle were killed or wounded. We were so badly crushed that at the close of the day ten thousand fresh troops could have come in and taken Lee's army and everything it had. But McClellan did not know it, and [apparently] feared, when Burnside was pressed back, that Sharpsburg was a Confederate victory, and that he would have to retire. As it was, when night settled down both armies were content to stay where they were.

AFTER THE BATTLE—POSITION
OF THE CONFEDERATE BATTERIES
IN FRONT OF DUNKER CHURCH.
FROM A PHOTOGRAPH.

During the progress of the battle of Sharpsburg General Lee and I were riding along my line and D. H. Hill's, when we received a report of movements of the enemy and started up the ridge to make a reconnoissance. General Lee and I dismounted, but Hill declined to do so. I said to Hill, "If you insist on riding up there and drawing the fire, give us a little interval so that we may not be in the line of the fire when they open upon you." General Lee and I stood on the top of the crest with our glasses, looking at the movements of the Federals on the rear left. After a moment I turned my glass to the right—the Federal left. As I did so, I noticed a puff of white smoke from the mouth of a cannon. "There is a shot for you," I said to General Hill. The gunner was a mile away, and the cannon-shot came whisking through the air for three or four seconds and took off the front legs of the horse that Hill sat on and let the animal down upon his stumps. The horse's head was so low and his croup so high that Hill was in a most ludicrous position. With one foot in the stirrup he made several efforts to get the other leg over the croup, but failed. Finally we prevailed upon him to try the other end of the horse, and he got down. He had a third horse shot under him before the close of the battle. That shot at Hill was the second best shot I ever saw. The best was at Yorktown. There a Federal officer came out in front of our line, and sitting down to his little platting table began to make a map. One of our officers carefully sighted a gun, touched it off, and dropped a shell into the hands of the man at the little table.‡

When the battle was over and night was gathering, I started to Lee's headquarters to make my report. In going through the town I passed a house that

‡Major Alfred A. Woodhull, Surgeon, U.S.A., wrote from David's Island, N.Y., July 16th, 1886:

"General Longstreet's 'best shot' was undoubtedly the shell that shattered the plane table that First Lieutenant Orlando G. Wagner, Topographical Engineer, was using in front of Yorktown, when he was mortally wounded, precisely as described. He died April 21st, 1862.

"Early on the morning of September 17th, 1862 (about 8 or 9 o'clock), I was standing near the guns of Captain Stephen H. Weed, 5th Artillery, when a small group came in sight, directly in our front, about a mile away. There was no firing of any importance at that time on our left, and Captain Weed, who was a superb artillerist himself, aimed and fired at the single mounted man and struck the horse. I witnessed the shot, and have no doubt it was the one General Longstreet commemorates as the 'second best.' My recollection is that the horse was gray, and I had the impression that the party was somewhat to the left (south) of

FIELD-HOSPITALS AT
CAPTAIN SMITH'S BARNS,
NEAR SHARPSBURG. FROM
A PHOTOGRAPH.

These pictures, according to a letter received by the editors from Dr. Samuel Sexton (8th Ohio), represent two field-hospitals established for the use of French's division at Antietam. The upper one was in charge of Dr. Sexton, who sent back the wounded men under his care at the front to this place during the battle, and afterward organized a hospital for all of the wounded soldiers found there,—utilizing for that purpose Captain Smith's barns, and erecting, besides, a number of shelters (shown in the cut) out of Virginia split-rails, set up on end in two parallel rows, meeting at the top, where they were secured. The sheds thus made were afterward thatched with straw, and could accommodate about 10 or 15 men each.

The lower picture shows an adjacent hospital for wounded Confederate prisoners, which was in charge of Dr. Anson Hurd of the 14th Indiana, who is seen standing on the right.

had been set afire and was still burning. The family was in great distress, and I stopped to do what I could for them. By that I was detained until after the other officers had reached headquarters and made their reports. My delay caused some apprehension on the part of General Lee that I had been hurt; in fact, such a report had been sent him. When I rode up and dismounted he seemed much relieved, and, coming to me very hurriedly for one of his dignified manner, threw his arms upon my shoulders and said:

"Here is my old war-horse at last."

When all the reports were in, General Lee decided that he would not be prepared the next day for offensive battle, and would prepare only for defense, as we had been doing.

The next day [the 18th] the Federals failed to advance, and both armies remained in position. During the day some of the Federals came over under a flag

---

the turnpike. General Longstreet kindly writes me that he cannot now recall the hour, but that there was little firing at the time, and that the place 'was about twenty feet from the Boonsboro' pike, north.'"

—Editors.

of truce to look after their dead and wounded. The following night we withdrew, passing the Potomac with our entire army. After we had crossed, the Federals made a show of pursuit, and a force of about fifteen hundred crossed the river and gave a considerable amount of trouble to the command under Pendleton. A. P. Hill was sent back with his division, and attacked the Federals who had crossed the river in pursuit of us. His lines extended beyond theirs, and he drove them back in great confusion. Some sprang over the bluffs of the river and were killed; some were drowned and others were shot.[↓]

Proceeding on our march, we went to Bunker Hill, where we remained for several days. A report was made of a Federal advance, but it turned out to be only a party of cavalry and amounted to nothing. As soon as the cavalry retired we moved back and camped around Winchester, where we remained until some time in October. Our stragglers continued to come in until November, which shows how many we had lost by severe marches.

The great mistake of the campaign was the division of Lee's army. If General Lee had kept his forces together, he could not have suffered defeat. At Sharpsburg he had hardly 37,000 men,[♭] who were in poor condition for battle, while McClellan had about 87,000, who were fresh and strong.

[↓]Major Alfred A. Woodhull, Surgeon, U.S.A., wrote from David's Island, N.Y., July 21st, 1886, concerning this movement:

> "Early Saturday, September 20th, Major Charles S. Lovell, 10th Infantry, crossed to reconnoiter with the Second Brigade (regulars), of Sykes's division, and other troops followed. On our ascent to the plateau we passed some abandoned artillery, but met with no opposition until nearly a mile from the bank, where a long infantry line was confronted unexpectedly. Major Lovell had been informed that cavalry was to cross before us at daylight, but we were then found to be in advance, and the cavalry which was to feel the way was in our rear, and being useless was at once withdrawn. The overlapping size of the advancing force in front, its manifest effort to envelop our left flank as well, and the probability of its extension beyond our right, compelled an immediate return, which was effected with steadiness, while skirmishing. Infantry reënforcements that had crossed the river were simultaneously withdrawn, but on the right the 118th Pennsylvania, known as the "Corn Exchange" regiment, suffered severely, especially in one wing, where it was said at the time that there was a misapprehension of orders. When our men were in the stream there were dropping shots, but there was no direct infantry fire of importance. A fierce Union artillery fire was kept up to cover the retreat of our right, which indeed lost heavily. But there was no such slaughter as the Confederate reports announced (I think A. P. Hill put it at 3000, and said the Potomac was blue with the Yankee dead). Had the cavalry really been in advance, the reconnoissance could have been accomplished with comparative ease. I was a medical officer attached to the infantry, and, acting as an aide for Major Lovell, had opportunity to witness what is here stated."
>
> —Editors.

[♭]This was Lee's estimate as stated to me at the time. It is much above the estimate of those who have since written of this campaign. Colonel Charles Marshall, in his evidence in the Fitz-John Porter case, gives our forces at the Second Manassas on August 29th as 50,000, not including artillery or cavalry. R. H. Anderson joined me on the night of August 29th, with over 4000.—J.L.

Lee says officially that "Antietam was fought with less than 40,000 men on our side."—Editors.

BLACKFORD'S, OR BOTELER'S, FORD, FROM THE MARYLAND SIDE.
FROM A RECENT PHOTOGRAPH.

This picture, taken from the tow-path of the Chesapeake and Ohio Canal, shows the ford below Shepherdstown by which Lee's army retreated after Antietam, the cliff on the Virginia side being the scene of the disaster to the 118th Pennsylvania, or Corn Exchange, regiment. When Porter's corps arrived at the Potomac in pursuit, on September 19th, Confederate artillery on the cliffs disputed the passage. A small Union force, under General Griffin, moved across the river in face of a warm fire, and, scaling the heights, captured several pieces of artillery. This attacking party was recalled during the night. Next morning, the 20th, two brigades of Sykes's division crossed and gained the heights on the left by the cement mill, while one brigade of Morell's division advanced to the right toward Shepherdstown and ascended the heights by way of the ravine. The 118th Pennsylvania formed beyond the crest and abreast of the dam. Soon the Confederates attacked with spirit. The Union forces were withdrawn without much loss, except to the 118th Pennsylvania, which was a new regiment, numbering 737 men, and had been armed, as it proved, with defective rifles. They made a stout resistance, until ordered to retreat, when most of the men fled down the precipitous face of the bluff and thence across the river, some crossing on the dam, the top of which was then dry. They were also under fire in crossing; and out of 362 in killed, wounded, and captured at this place, the 118th Pennsylvania lost 269.

The next year, when on our way to Gettysburg, there was the same situation of affairs at Harper's Ferry, but we let it alone.

General Lee was not satisfied with the result of the Maryland campaign, and seemed inclined to attribute the failure to the Lost Dispatch; though I believe he was more inclined to attribute the loss of the dispatch to the fault of a courier or to other negligence than that of the officer to whom it was directed.

Our men came in so rapidly after the battle that renewed hope of gathering his army in great strength soon caused Lee to look for other and new prospects, and to lose sight of the lost campaign. But at Sharpsburg was sprung the keystone of the arch upon which the Confederate cause rested. Jackson was quite satisfied with the campaign, as the Virginia papers made him the hero of Harper's Ferry, although the greater danger was with McLaws, whose service was the severer and more important. Lee lost nearly 20,000 by straggling in this campaign,—almost twice as many as were captured at Harper's Ferry.

The battle casualties of Jackson's command from the Rappahannock to the Potomac, according to the "Official Records," were 4629, while mine, including those of R. H. Anderson's division, were 4725, making in all, 9354. That taken from the army of 55,000 at the Second Manassas left a force of 45,646 moving across the Potomac. To that number must be added the forces that joined us; namely, D. H. Hill with 5000, McLaws with 4000, and Walker with 2000. Thus Lee's army on entering Maryland was made up of nearly 57,000 men, exclusive of artillery and cavalry. As we had but 37,000 at Sharpsburg, our losses in the several engagements after we crossed the Potomac, *including stragglers,* reached nearly 20,000. Our casualties in the affairs of the Maryland campaign, including Sharpsburg, were 13,964. Estimating the casualties in the Maryland campaign preceding Sharpsburg at 2000, it will be seen that we lost at Sharpsburg 11,000 to 12,000. Only a glance at these figures is necessary to impress one with the number of those who were unable to stand the long and rapid marches, and fell by the wayside, viz., 8000 to 9000. The Virginians who have written of the war have often charged the loss of the Maryland campaign to "laggards." It is unkind to apply such a term to our soldiers, who were as patient, courageous, and chivalrous as any ever marshaled into phalanx. Many were just out of the hospitals, and many more were crippled by injuries received in battle. They were marching without sufficient food or clothing, with their muskets, ammunition, provisions, and in fact their all, packed upon their backs. They struggled along with bleeding feet, tramping rugged mountain roads through a heated season. Such soldiers should not be called "laggards" by their countrymen. Let them have their well-earned honors though the fame of others suffer thereby.

CHAPTER 15

THE BATTLE OF ANTIETAM.

Jacob D. Cox, Major-General, U.S.V.

It was not till some time past noon of the 15th of September that, the way being clear for the Ninth Corps at South Mountain, we marched through Fox's gap to the Boonsboro' and Sharpsburg turnpike, and along this road till we came up in rear of Sumner's command. Hooker's corps, which was part of the right wing (Burnside's), had been in the advance, and had moved off from the turnpike to the right near Keedysville. I was with the Kanawha Division, assuming that my temporary command of the corps ended with the battle on the mountain. When we approached the line of hills bordering the Antietam, we received orders to turn off the road to the left, and halted our battalions closed in mass. It was now about 3 o'clock in the afternoon. McClellan, as it seemed, had just reached the field, and was surrounded by a group of his principal officers, most of whom I had never seen before. I rode up with General Burnside, dismounted, and was very cordially greeted by General McClellan. He and Burnside were evidently on terms of most intimate friendship and familiarity. He introduced me to the officers I had not known before, referring pleasantly to my service with him in Ohio and West Virginia, putting me upon an easy footing with them in a very agreeable and genial way.

We walked up the slope of the ridge before us, and looking westward from its crest the whole field of the coming battle was before us. Immediately in front the Antietam wound through the hollow, the hills rising gently on both sides. In the background on our left was the village of Sharpsburg, with fields inclosed by stone fences in front of it. At its right was a bit of wood (since known as the West Wood), with the little Dunker Church standing out white and sharp against it. Farther to the right and left the scene was closed in by wooded ridges with open farm lands between, the whole making as pleasing and prosperous a landscape as can easily be imagined. We made a large group as we stood upon the hill, and it was not long before we attracted the enemy's attention. A puff of

NORTH OF THE DUNKER CHURCH—A UNION CHARGE THROUGH THE CORN-FIELD.

white smoke from a knoll on the right of the Sharpsburg road was followed by the screaming of a shell over our heads. McClellan directed that all but one or two should retire behind the ridge, while he continued the reconnoissance, walking slowly to the right. I noted with satisfaction the cool and business-like air with which he made his examination under fire. The Confederate artillery was answered by a battery, and a lively cannonade ensued on both sides, though without any noticeable effect. The enemy's position was revealed, and he was evidently in force on both sides of the turnpike in front of Sharpsburg, covered by the undulations of the rolling ground which hid his infantry from our sight.

UNION SIGNAL STATION ON ELK MOUNTAIN, FIVE OR SIX MILES SOUTH-EAST OF SHARPSBURG. FROM A PHOTOGRAPH.

The examination of the enemy's position and the discussion of it continued till near the close of the day. Orders were then given for the Ninth Corps to move to the left, keeping off the road, which was occupied by other troops. We moved through fields and farm lands, an hour's march in the dusk of the evening, going into bivouac about a mile south of the Sharpsburg bridge, and in rear of the hills bordering the Antietam.

On Tuesday, September 16th, we confidently expected a battle, and I kept with my division. In the afternoon I saw General Burnside, and learned from him that McClellan had determined to let Hooker make a movement on our extreme right to turn Lee's position. Burnside's manner in speaking of this implied that he thought it was done at Hooker's solicitation and through his desire, openly evinced, to be independent in command.

I urged Burnside to assume the immediate command of the corps and allow me to lead only my own division. He objected that as he had been announced as commander of the right wing of the army composed of two corps (his own and Hooker's), he was unwilling to waive his precedence or to assume that Hooker was detached for anything more than a temporary purpose. I pointed out that Reno's staff had been granted leave of absence to take the body of their chief to Washington, and that my division staff was too small for corps duty; but he met this by saying that he would use his staff for this purpose and help me in every way he could, till the crisis of the campaign should be over.

The 16th passed without serious fighting, though there was desultory cannonading and picket firing. It was hard to restrain our men from showing themselves on the crest of the long ridge in front of us, and whenever they did so they drew the fire from some of the enemy's batteries, to which ours would re-

DOUBLEDAY'S DIVISION OF HOOKER'S CORPS CROSSING THE UPPER FORDS
OF THE ANTIETAM. FROM A SKETCH MADE AT THE TIME.

spond. In the afternoon McClellan reconnoitered the line of the Antietam near us, Burnside being with him. As the result of this we were ordered to change our positions at nightfall, staff-officers being sent to guide each division to its new camp. Rodman's division went half a mile to the left, where a country road led to a ford in a great bend in the Antietam curving deeply into the enemy's side of the stream.‡ Sturgis's division was placed on the sides of the road leading to the stone bridge, since known as Burnside's Bridge (below the Sharpsburg bridge). Willcox's was put in reserve in rear of Sturgis. My own division was divided, Seammon's brigade going with Rodman, and Crook's going with Sturgis. Crook was ordered to take the advance in crossing the bridge, in case we should be ordered to attack. This selection was made by Burnside himself, as a compliment to the division for the vigor of its assault at South Mountain. While we were moving, we heard Hooker's guns far off on the right and front, and the cannonade continued an hour or more after it became dark.

The morning of Wednesday, the 17th, broke fresh and fair. The men were astir at dawn, getting breakfast and preparing for a day of battle. The artillery opened on both sides as soon as it was fairly light, and the positions which had been assigned us in the dusk of the evening were found to be exposed in some places to the direct fire of the Confederate guns, Rodman's division suffering more than the others. Fairchild's brigade alone reported thirty-six casualties before they could find cover. It was not till 7 o'clock that orders came to advance toward the creek as far as could be done without exposing the men to unnecessary loss. Rodman was directed to acquaint himself with the situation of the ford in front of him, and Sturgis to seek the best means of approach to the stone bridge. All were then to remain in readiness to obey further orders.

When these arrangements had been made, I rode to the position Burnside had selected for himself, which was upon a high knoll north-east of the Burnside Bridge, near a hay-stack which was a prominent landmark. Near by was Benjamin's battery of 20-pounder Parrotts, and a little farther still to the right, on the same ridge, General Sturgis had sent in Durell's battery. These were exchanging shots with the enemy's guns opposite, and had the advantage in range and weight of metal.

Whatever the reason, McClellan had adopted a plan of battle which practically reduced Sumner and Burnside to the command of one corps each, while Hooker had been sent far off on the right front, followed later by Mansfield, but without organizing the right wing as a unit so that one commander could give

‡The information obtained from the neighborhood was that no fords of the Antietam were passable at that time, except one about half-way between the two upper bridges and another less than half a mile below Burnside's Bridge. We, however, found during the engagement another ford a short distance above Burnside's Bridge. The inquiry and reconnoissance for the fords was made by engineer officers of the general staff, and our orders were based on their reports.—J.D.C.

his whole attention to handling it with vigor. In his preliminary report, made before he was relieved from command, McClellan says:

> "The design was to make the main attack upon the enemy's left—at least to create a diversion in favor of the main attack, with the hope of something more, by assailing the enemy's right—and, as soon as one or both of the flank movements were fully successful, to attack their center with any reserve I might then have in hand."

McClellan's report covering his whole career in the war, dated August 4th, 1863 (and published February, 1864, after warm controversies had arisen and he had become a political character), modifies the above statement in some important particulars. It says:

> "My plan for the impending general engagement was to attack the enemy's left with the corps of Hooker and Mansfield, supported by Sumner's, and if necessary by Franklin's, and as soon as matters looked favorably there to move the corps of Burnside against the enemy's extreme right upon the ridge running to the south and rear of Sharpsburg, and having carried their position, to press along the crest toward our right, and whenever either of these flank movements should be successful, to advance our center with all the forces then disposable."

The opinion I got from Burnside as to the part the Ninth Corps was to take was fairly consistent with the design first quoted, viz., that when the attack by Sumner, Hooker, and Franklin should be progressing favorably, we were "to create a diversion in favor of the main attack, with the hope of something more." It would also appear probable that Hooker's movement was at first intended to be made by his corps alone, taken up by Sumner's two corps as soon as he was ready to attack, and shared in by Franklin if he reached the field in time, thus making a simultaneous oblique attack from our right by the whole army except Porter's corps, which was in reserve, and the Ninth Corps, which was to create the "diversion" on our left and prevent the enemy from stripping his right to reënforce his left. It is hardly disputable that this would have been a better plan than the one actually carried out. Certainly the assumption that the Ninth Corps could cross the Antietam alone at the only place on the field where the Confederates had their line immediately upon the stream which must be crossed under fire by two narrow heads of column, and could then turn to the right along the high ground occupied by the hostile army before that army had been broken or seriously shaken elsewhere, is one which would hardly be made till time had dimmed the remembrance of the actual positions of Lee's divisions upon the field.

THE SHARPSBURG
BRIDGE OVER THE
ANTIETAM. FROM
A WAR-TIME
PHOTOGRAPH.

The evidence that the plan did not originally include the wide separation of two corps to the right, to make the extended turning movement, is found in Hooker's incomplete report, and in the wide interval in time between the marching of his corps and that of Mansfield. Hooker was ordered to cross the Antietam at about 2 o'clock in the afternoon of the 16th by the bridge in front of Keedysville and the ford below it. He says that after his troops were over and in march, he rode back to McClellan, who told him that he might call for reën-forcements and that when they came they should be under his command. Some-what later McClellan rode forward with his staff to observe the progress making, and Hooker again urged the necessity of reënforcements. Yet Sumner did not receive orders to send Mansfield to support Hooker till evening, and the Twelfth Corps marched only half an hour before midnight, reaching its bivouac, about a mile and a half in rear of that of Hooker, at 2 A.M. of the 17th. Sumner was also ordered to be in readiness to march with the Second Corps an hour before day, but his orders to move did not reach him till nearly half-past 7 in the morning.

By this time, Hooker had fought his battle, had been repulsed, and later in the morning was carried wounded from the field. Mansfield had fallen before his corps was deployed, and General Alpheus S. Williams who succeeded him was fighting a losing battle at all points but one—where Greene's division held the East Wood.

After crossing the Antietam, Hooker had shaped his course to the westward, aiming to reach the ridge upon which the Hagerstown turnpike runs, and which is the dominant feature of the landscape. This ridge is some two miles distant from the Antietam, and for the first mile of the way no resistance was met. However, Hooker's progress had been observed by the enemy, and Hood's two brigades were taken from the center and passed to the left of D. H. Hill. Here they occupied an open wood (since known as the East Wood), north-east of the Dunker Church. Hooker was now trying to approach the Confederate positions, Meade's division of the Pennsylvania Reserves being in the advance. A sharp skirmishing combat ensued and artillery was also brought into action on both sides, the engagement continuing till after dark. On our side Seymour's brigade had been chiefly engaged, and had felt the enemy so vigorously that Hood supposed he had repulsed a serious effort to take the wood. Hooker was, however, aiming to pass quite beyond the flank, and kept his other divisions north of the hollow beyond the wood, and upon the ridge which reaches the turnpike near the largest reëntrant bend of the Potomac, which is here only half a mile distant. Here he bivouacked upon the northern slopes of the ridge, Doubleday's division resting with its right upon the turnpike, Ricketts's division upon the left of Doubleday, and Meade covering the front of both with the skirmishers of Seymour's brigade. Between Meade's skirmishers and the ridge were the farm-house and barn of J. Poffenberger on the east of the road, where Hooker made his own quarters for the night. Half a mile farther in front was the farm of D. R. Miller, the dwelling on the east, and the barn surrounded by stacks on the west of the road.✛ Mans-

GERMAN REFORMED CHURCH IN KEEDYSVILLE, USED AS A UNION HOSPITAL. FROM A PHOTOGRAPH TAKEN IN 1886.

✛Hooker's unfinished report says he slept in the barn of D. R. Miller, but he places it on the east of the road, and the spot is fully identified as Poffenberger's by General Gibbon, who commanded the right brigade, and by Major Rufus R. Dawes (afterward Brevet Brigadier-General), both of whom subsequently visited the field and determined the positions.—J.D.C.

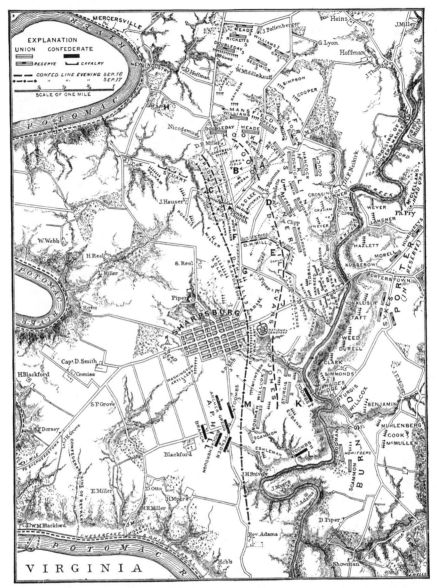

THE FIELD OF ANTIETAM.

On the afternoon of September 16th, Hooker's corps crossed at the two fords and the bridge north of McClellan's headquarters.

A. From near sunset till dark Hooker engaged Hood's division (of Longstreet's corps) about the "East Wood," marked A on the map. Hood was relieved by two brigades of Jackson's corps, which was in and behind the Dunker Church wood (or West Wood), C.

B. At dawn on the 17th, Hooker and Jackson began a terrible contest which raged in and about the famous corn-field, B, and in the woods, A and C. Jackson's reserves regained the corn-field. Hartsuff's brigade, of Hooker's corps, and Mansfield's corps charged through the corn-field into the Dunker Church wood, General Mansfield being mortally wounded in front of the East Wood.

field's corps, marching as it did late in the night, kept farther to the right than Hooker's, but moved on a nearly parallel course and bivouacked upon the farm of another J. Poffenberger near the road which, branching from the Hagerstown turnpike at the Dunker Church, intersects the one running from Keedysville through Smoketown to the same turnpike about a mile north of Hooker's position.

On the Confederate side, Hood's division had been so severely handled that it was replaced by Jackson's (commanded by J. R. Jones), which, with Ewell's, had been led to the field from Harper's Ferry by Jackson, reaching Sharpsburg in the afternoon of the 16th. These divisions were formed on the left of D. H. Hill and almost at right angles to his line, crossing the turnpike and facing northward. Hood's division, on being relieved, was placed in reserve near the Dunker Church, and spent part of the night in cooking rations, of which its supply had been short for a day or two. The combatants on both sides slept upon their arms, well knowing that the dawn would bring bloody work.

When day broke on Wednesday morning, the 17th, Hooker, looking south from the Poffenberger farm along the turnpike, saw a gently rolling landscape,

---

Jackson, with the aid of Hood, and a part of D. H. Hill's division, again cleared the Dunker Church wood. J. G. Walker's division, taken from the extreme right of the Confederate line, charged in support of Jackson and Hood.

C. Sumner's corps formed line of battle in the center, Sedgwick's division facing the East Wood, through which it charged over the corn-field again, and through Dunker Church wood to the edge of the fields beyond. McLaws's division (of Longstreet's corps), just arrived from Harper's Ferry, assisted in driving out Sedgwick, who was forced to retreat northward by the Hagerstown pike.

D. About the time that Sedgwick charged, French and Richardson, of Sumner's corps, dislodged D. H. Hill's line from Roulette's house.

E. Hill re-formed in the sunken road, since known as the "Bloody Lane," where his position was carried by French and Richardson, the latter being mortally wounded in the corn-field, E.

F. Irwin and Brooks, of Franklin's corps, moved to the support of French and Richardson. At the point F, Irwin's brigade was repelled.

G. D. H. Hill, reënforced by R. H. Anderson's division of Longstreet's corps, fought for the ground about Piper's house.

H. Stuart attempted a flank movement north of the Dunker Church wood, but was driven back by the thirty guns under Doubleday.

J. Pleasonton, with a part of his cavalry and several batteries, crossed the Boonsboro' bridge as a flank support to Richardson, and to Burnside on the south. Several battalions of regulars from Porter's corps came to his assistance and made their way well up to the hill which is now the National Cemetery.

K. Toombs (of Longstreet) had defended the lower bridge until Burnside moved Rodman and Seammon to the fords below.

L. Then Toombs hurried south to protect the Confederate flank. Sturgis and Crook charged across the Burnside Bridge and gained the heights. Toombs was driven away from the fords.

M. After 3 o'clock, Burnside's lines, being re-formed, completed the defeat of D. R. Jones's division (of Longstreet), and on the right gained the outskirts of Sharpsburg. Toombs, and the arriving brigades of A. P. Hill, of Jackson's corps, saved the village and regained a part of the lost ground.—EDITORS.

THE PRY HOUSE, GENERAL McCLELLAN'S
HEADQUARTERS AT THE BATTLE
OF ANTIETAM. FROM A PHOTOGRAPH
TAKEN IN 1886.

of which the commanding point was the Dunker Church, whose white brick walls appeared on the west side of the road backed by the foliage of the West Wood, which came toward him, filling a slight hollow which ran parallel to the turnpike, with a single row of fields between. Beyond the Miller house and barns, the ground dipped into a little depression. Beyond this was seen a large corn-field between the East Wood and the turnpike, rising again to the higher level. There was, however, another small dip beyond, which could not be seen from Hooker's position; and on the second ridge, near the church, and extending across the turnpike eastward into the East Wood, could be seen the Confederate line of gray, partly sheltered by piles of rails taken from the fences. They seemed to Hooker to be at the farther side of the corn-field and at the top of the first rise of ground beyond Miller's. It was plain that the high ground about the little white church was the key of the enemy's position, and if that could be carried Hooker's task would be well done.

The Confederates opened the engagement by a rapid fire from a battery near the East Wood as soon as it was light, and Hooker answered the challenge by an immediate order for his line to advance. Doubleday's division was in two lines, Gibbon's and Phelps's brigades in front, supported by Patrick and Hofmann. Gibbon had the right and guided upon the turnpike. Patrick held a small wood in his rear, which is upon both sides of the road a little north of Miller's house. Some of Meade's men were supposed to be in the northernmost extension of the West Wood, and thus to cover Gibbon's right flank as he advanced. Part of Battery B, 4th United States Artillery (Gibbon's own battery), was run forward to Miller's barn and stack-yard on the right of the road, and fired over the heads of the advancing regiments. Other batteries were similarly placed more to the left. The line moved swiftly forward through Miller's orchard and kitchen garden, breaking through a stout picket fence on the near side, down into the moist ground of the hollow, and up through the corn, which was higher than their heads, and shut out everything from view. At the southern side of the field they came to a low fence, beyond which was an open field, at the farther side of which was the enemy's line. But Gibbon's right, covered by the corn, had outmarched the left, which had been exposed to a terrible fire, and the direction taken had been a little oblique, so that the right wing of the 6th Wisconsin, the flanking regiment, had crossed the turnpike and was suddenly assailed by a sharp fire from the West Wood on its flank. They swung back into the road, lying down along the high, stout post-and-rail fence, keeping up their fire by shooting between the rails. Leaving this little band to protect their right, the main line, which had come up on the left, leaped the fence at the south edge of the corn-field and charged across the open at the enemy in front. But the concentrated fire of artillery and musketry was more than they could bear. Men fell by scores and hundreds, and the thinned lines gave way and ran for the shelter of the corn. They were rallied in the hollow on the north side of the field. The enemy had rapidly extended his left under cover of the West Wood, and now made a dash at the right flank and at Gibbon's exposed guns. His men on the right faced by that flank and followed him bravely, though with little order, in a dash at the Confederates, who were swarming out of the wood. The gunners double-charged the cannon with canister, and under a terrible fire of both artillery and rifles the enemy broke and sought shelter.

Patrick's brigade had come up in support of Gibbon, and was sent across the turnpike into the West Wood to cover that flank. They pushed forward, the enemy retiring, until they were in advance of the principal line in the corn-field, upon which the Confederates were now advancing. Patrick faced his men to the left, parallel to the edge of the wood and to the turnpike, and poured his fire into the flank of the enemy, following it by a charge through the field and up to the fence along the road. Again the Confederates were driven back, but only to push in again by way of these woods, forcing Patrick to resume his original line of front and to retire to the cover of a ledge at right angles to the road near Gibbon's guns.

Farther to the left Phelps's and Hofmann's brigades had had similar experience, pushing forward nearly to the Confederate lines, and being driven back with great loss when they charged over open ground against the enemy. Ricketts's division entered the edge of the East Wood; but here, at the salient angle, where D. H. Hill and Lawton joined, the enemy held the position stubbornly, and the repulse of Doubleday's division made Ricketts glad to hold even the edge of the East Wood, as the right of the line was driven back.

It was now about 7 o'clock, and Mansfield's corps (the Twelfth) was approaching, for that officer had called his men to arms at the first sound of Hooker's battle and had marched to his support. The corps consisted of two divisions, Williams's and Greene's. It contained a number of new and undrilled regiments, and in hastening to the field in columns of battalions in mass, proper intervals for deployment had not been preserved, and time was necessarily lost before the troops could be put in line. General Mansfield fell mortally wounded before the deployment was complete, and the command devolved on General Williams. Williams had only time to take the most general directions from Hooker, when the latter also was wounded.[+] The Twelfth Corps attack seems to have been made obliquely to that of Hooker, and facing more to the westward, for General Williams speaks of the post-and-rail fences along the turnpike being a great obstruction in their front. Greene's division, on his left, moved along the ridge leading to the East Wood, taking as the guide for his extreme left the line of the burning house of Mumma, which had been set on fire by D. H. Hill's men. Doubleday, in his report, notices this change of direction of Williams's division, which had relieved him, and says Williams's brigades were swept away by a fire from their left and front, from behind rocky ledges they could not see.[♭] Our officers were deceived in part as to the extent and direction of the enemy's line by the fact that the Confederate cavalry commander, Stuart, had occupied a commanding hill west of the pike and beyond our right flank, and from this position, which, in fact, was considerably detached from the Confederate line, he used his batteries with such effect as to produce the belief that a continuous line extended from this point to the Dunker Church.[/] Our true lines of attack were convergent ones, the right sweeping southward along the pike and through the narrow strip of the West Wood, while the division which drove the enemy from the East Wood should move upon the commanding ground around the church. This error of direction was repeated with disastrous effect a little later, when Sumner came on the ground with Sedgwick's corps.

When Mansfield's corps came on the field, Meade, who succeeded

---

[+]Of the early morning fight in the corn-field, General Hooker says in his report:

"We had not proceeded far before I discovered that a heavy force of the enemy had taken possession of a corn-field (I have since learned about a thirty-acre field), in my immediate front, and from the sun's rays falling on their bayonets projecting above the corn could see that the field was filled with the enemy, with arms in their hands, standing apparently at 'support arms.' Instructions were immediately given for the assemblage of all of my spare batteries near at hand, of which I think there were five or six, to spring into battery on the right of this field, and to open with canister at once. In the time I am writing every stalk of corn in the northern and greater part of the field was cut as closely as could have been done with a knife, and the slain lay in rows precisely as they had stood in their ranks a few moments before.

"It was never my fortune to witness a more bloody, dismal battlefield. Those that escaped fled in the opposite direction from our advance, and sought refuge behind the trees, fences, and stone ledges nearly on a line with the Dunker Church, etc., as there was no resisting this torrent of death-dealing missives.... The whole morning had been one of unusual animation to me and fraught with the grandest events. The conduct of my troops was sublime, and the occasion almost lifted me to the skies, and its memories will ever remain near me. My command followed the fugitives closely until we had passed the corn-field a quarter of a mile or more, when I was removed from my saddle in the act of falling out of it from loss of blood, having previously been struck without my knowledge."

—EDITORS.

[♭]Both in the West and East Wood and on the ground south of the East Wood the Confederates were protected by outcroppings of rocks, which served as natural breastworks.—EDITORS.

[/]Stuart says he had batteries from all parts of Jackson's command, and mentions Poague's, Pegram's, and Carrington's, besides Pelham's which was attached to the cavalry. He also says he was supported part of the time by Early's brigade; afterward by one regiment of it, the 13th Virginia.—EDITORS.

SUMNER'S ADVANCE—FRENCH'S DIVISION CLOSING IN UPON ROULETTE'S BARNS
AND HOUSE—RICHARDSON'S DIVISION CONTINUING THE LINE FAR TO THE LEFT.
FROM A SKETCH MADE AT THE TIME.

Hooker,[1] withdrew the First Corps to the ridge north of Poffenberger's, where it had bivouacked the night before. It had suffered severely, having lost 2470 in killed and wounded, but it was still further depleted by straggling, so that Meade reported less than 7000 men with the colors that evening. Its organization was preserved, however, and the story that it was utterly dispersed was a mistake.

Greene's division, on the left of the Twelfth Corps, profited by the hard fighting of those who had preceded it, and was able to drive the enemy quite out of the East Wood and across the open fields between it and the Dunker Church. Greene even succeeded, about the time of Sumner's advance, in getting a foothold about the Dunker Church itself, which he held for some time.[*] But the fighting of Hooker's and Mansfield's men, though lacking unity of force and of purpose, had cost the enemy dear. J. R. Jones, who commanded Jackson's division, had been wounded; Starke, who succeeded Jones, was killed; Lawton, who followed Starke, was wounded. Ewell's division, commanded by

[1]The order assigning Meade to command is dated 1:25 P.M.—EDITORS.
[*]Until he was driven out, about 1:30, according to Generals Williams and Greene.—EDITORS.

MAJOR-GENERAL ISRAEL B. RICHARDSON.
FROM A PHOTOGRAPH.

Referring in his report to the incidents accompanying General Richardson's fall, General Caldwell says: "The enemy made one more effort to break my line, and this time the attack was made in the center. Colonel Barlow [General Francis C.], hearing firing to his left, on our old front, immediately moved to the left and formed in line with the rest of the brigade. The whole brigade then moved forward in line, driving the enemy entirely out of the cornfield [see E on the map] and through the orchard beyond, the enemy firing grape and canister from two brass pieces in the orchard to our front, and shell and spherical case-shot from a battery on our right. While leading his men forward under the fire, Colonel Barlow fell dangerously wounded by a grape-shot in the groin. By command of General Richardson I halted the brigade, and, drawing back the line, re-formed it near the edge of the corn-field. It was now 1 o'clock P.M. Here we lay exposed to a heavy artillery fire, by which General Richardson was severely wounded. The fall of General Richardson (General Meagher having been previously borne from the field) left me in command of the division, which I formed in line, awaiting the enemy's attack. Not long after, I was relieved of the command by General Hancock, who had been assigned to the command of the division by General McClellan." General Richardson was carried to Pry's house, McClellan's headquarters, where he died November 3d.—EDITORS.

Early, had suffered hardly less. Hood was sent back into the fight to relieve Lawton, and had been reënforced by the brigades of Ripley, Colquitt, and McRae (Garland's), from D. H. Hill's division. When Greene reached the Dunker Church, therefore, the Confederates on that wing had suffered more fearfully than our own men. Nearly half their numbers were killed and wounded, and Jackson's famous "Stonewall" division was so completely disorganized that only a handful of men under Colonels Grigsby and Stafford remained and attached themselves to Early's command. Of the division under Early, his own brigade was all that retained much strength, and this, posted among the rocks in the West Wood and vigorously supported by Stuart's horse artillery on the flank, was all that covered the left of Lee's army. Could Hooker and Mansfield have attacked together,—or, still better, could Sumner's Second Corps have marched before day and united with the first onset,—Lee's left must inevitably have been crushed long before the Confederate divisions of McLaws, Walker, and A. P. Hill could have reached the field. It is this failure to carry out any intelligible plan which the historian must regard as the unpardonable military fault on the National side. To account for the hours between 4 and 8 on that morning, is the most serious responsibility of the National commander.

Sumner's Second Corps was now approaching the scene of action, or rather two divisions of it—Sedgwick's

SCENE AT THE RUINS OF MUMMA'S HOUSE AND BARNS.
FROM A SKETCH MADE AT THE TIME.

These buildings were fired early in the morning by D. H. Hill's men, who feared they would become a point of vantage to the Union forces. The sketch was made after the advance of French to the sunken road. Presumably, the battery firing upon the Confederate line to the right of that road is the First Rhode Island Light Artillery; for Captain John A. Tompkins, of Battery A. says, in his report, that he placed his pieces on a knoll "directly in front of some burning ruins," and opened fire upon a battery in front. "At 9:30," he continues, "the enemy appeared upon my right front with a large column, apparently designing to charge the battery. I was not aware of their approach until the head of the column gained the brow of a hill about sixty yards from the right gun of the battery. The pieces were immediately obliqued to the right and a sharp fire of canister opened upon them, causing them to retire in confusion, leaving the ground covered with their dead and wounded, and abandoning one of their battle-flags, which was secured by a regiment which came up on my right after the enemy had retreated. The enemy now opened a fire upon us from a battery in front, and also from one on the right near the white school-house [Dunker Church]. Two guns were directed to reply to the battery on the right, while the fire of the rest was directed upon the guns in front, which were silenced in about twenty minutes, and one of their caissons blown up." At noon, Tompkins was relieved by Battery G.—EDITORS.

and French's—Richardson's being still delayed ↓ till his place could be filled by Porter's troops, the strange tardiness in sending orders being noticeable in regard to every part of the army. Sumner met Hooker, who was being carried from the field, and the few words he could exchange with the wounded general were enough to make him feel the need of haste, but not sufficient to give him any clear idea of the position.

↓ Sumner says Richardson came about an hour later. Howard, who succeeded Sedgwick, says his division moved "about 7." French says he followed "about 7:30." Hancock, who succeeded Richardson, says that officer received his orders "about 9:30."—EDITORS.

Both Sedgwick and French marched their divisions by the right flank, in three columns, a brigade in each column, Sedgwick leading. They crossed the Antietam by Hooker's route, but did not march as far to the north-west as Hooker had done. When the center of the corps was opposite the Dunker Church, and nearly east of it, the change of direction was given; the troops faced to their proper front and advanced in line of battle in three lines, fully deployed, and 60 or 70 yards apart, Sumner himself being in rear of Sedgwick's first line, and near its left. When they approached the position held by Greene's division at Dunker Church, French kept on so as to form on Greene's left, while Sedgwick, under Sumner's immediate lead, diverged somewhat to the right, passing through the East Wood, crossing the turnpike on the right of Greene and of the Dunker Church, and plunged into the West Wood. At this point there were absolutely no Confederate troops in front of them. Early was farther to the right, opposing Williams's division of the Twelfth Corps, and now made haste under cover of the woods to pass around Sedgwick's right and to get in front of him to oppose his progress. This led to a lively skirmishing fight in which Early was making as great a demonstration as possible, but with no chance of solid success. At this very moment, however, McLaws's and Walker's divisions came upon the field, marching rapidly from Harper's Ferry. Walker charged headlong upon the left flank of Sedgwick's lines, which were soon thrown into confusion, and McLaws, passing by Walker's left, also threw his division diagonally upon the already broken and retreating lines of Sumner. Taken at such a disadvantage, these had never a chance; and in spite of the heroic bravery of Sumner and Sedgwick, with most of their officers (Sedgwick being severely wounded), the division was driven off to the north with terrible losses, carrying along in the rout part of Williams's men of the Twelfth Corps, who had been holding Early at bay. All these troops were rallied at the ridge on the Poffenberger farm, where Hooker's corps had already taken position. Here some thirty batteries of both corps were concentrated, and, supported by the organized parts of all three of the corps which had fought upon this part of the field, easily repulsed all efforts of Jackson and Stuart to resume the aggressive or to pass between them and the Potomac. Sumner himself did not accompany the routed troops to this position, but as soon as it was plain that the division could not be rallied, he galloped off to put himself in communication with French and with the headquarters of the army and try to retrieve the misfortune. From the flag-station east of the East Wood he signaled to McClellan: "Reënforcements are badly wanted. Our troops are giving way." It was between 9 and 10 o'clock when Sumner entered the West Wood, and in fifteen minutes, or a little more, the one-sided combat was over.[b]

---

[b]Sumner's principal attack was made, as I have already indicated, at right angles to that of Hooker. He had thus crossed the line of Hooker's movement both in the latter's advance and retreat. Greene's divi-

The enemy now concentrated upon Greene at the Dunker Church, and after a stubborn resistance he too was driven back across the turnpike and the open ground to the edge of the East Wood. Here, by the aid of several batteries gallantly handled, he defeated the subsequent effort to dislodge him. French had come up on his left, and both his batteries and the numerous ones on the Poffenberger hill swept the open ground and the corn-field over which Hooker had fought, and he was able to make good his position. The enemy was content to regain the high ground near the church, and French's attack upon D. H. Hill was now attracting their attention.

The battle on the extreme right was thus ended before 10 o'clock in the morning, and there was no more serious fighting north of the Dunker Church. French advanced on Greene's left, over the open farm lands, and after a fierce combat about the Roulette and Clipp farm buildings, drove D. H. Hill's division from them. Richardson's division came up on French's left soon after, and foot by foot, field by field, from hill to hill and from fence to fence, the enemy was pressed back, till after several hours of fighting the sunken road, since known as "Bloody Lane," was in our hands, piled full of the Confederate dead who had defended it with their lives. Richardson had been mortally wounded, and Hancock had been sent from Franklin's corps to command the division. Barlow had been conspicuous in the thickest of the fight, and after a series of brilliant actions was carried off desperately wounded. On the Confederate side equal courage had been shown and a magnificent tenacity exhibited. But it is not my purpose to describe the battle in detail. I limit myself to such an outline as may make clear my interpretation of the larger features of the engagement and its essential plan.

The head of Franklin's corps (the Sixth) had arrived about 10 o'clock and taken the position near the Sharpsburg Bridge which Sumner had occupied. Before noon Smith's and Slocum's divisions were ordered to Sumner's assistance, and early in the afternoon Irwin and Brooks, of Smith, advanced to the

---

sion was the only part of the Twelfth Corps troops he saw, and he led Sedgwick's men to the right of these. Ignorant, as he necessarily was, of what had occurred before, he assumed that he formed on the extreme right of the Twelfth Corps, and that he fronted in the same direction as Hooker had done. This misconception of the situation led him into another error. He had seen only a few stragglers and wounded men of Hooker's corps on the line of his own advance, and hence concluded that the First Corps was completely dispersed and its division and brigade organizations broken up. He not only gave this report to McClellan at the time, but reiterated it later in his statement before the Committee on the Conduct of the War. The truth was that he had marched westward more than half a mile south of the Poffenberger hill, where Meade was with the sadly diminished but still organized First Corps, and half that distance south of the Miller farm buildings, near which Williams's division of the Twelfth Corps held the ground along the turnpike till they were carried away in the disordered retreat of Sedgwick's men toward the right. Sedgwick had gone in, therefore, between Greene and Williams, of the Twelfth Corps, and the four divisions of the two corps alternated in their order from left to right, thus: French, Greene, Sedgwick, Williams.—J.D.C.

charge and relieved Greene's division and part of French's, holding the line from Bloody Lane by the Clipp, Roulette, and Mumma houses to the East Wood and the ridge in front. Here Smith and Slocum remained till Lee retreated, Smith's division repelling a sharp attack. French and Richardson's battle may be considered as ended at 1 or 2 o'clock.

It seems to me very clear that about 10 o'clock in the morning was the great crisis in this battle. The sudden and complete rout of Sedgwick's division was not easily accounted for, and with McClellan's theory of the enormous superiority of Lee's numbers, it looked as if the Confederate general had massed overwhelming forces on our right. Sumner's notion that Hooker's corps was utterly dispersed was naturally accepted, and McClellan limited his hopes to holding on at the East Wood and the Poffenberger hill where Sedgwick's batteries were massed and supported by the troops that had been rallied there. Franklin's corps as it came on the field was detained to support the threatened

CHARGE OF IRWIN'S BRIGADE (SMITH'S DIVISION) AT THE DUNKER CHURCH.
FROM A SKETCH MADE AT THE TIME.

General Wm. F. Smith, commanding the Second Division of Franklin's corps, went to the assistance of French. On getting into position, for the most part to the right of French, General Smith, in his report, says: "Finding that the enemy were advancing, I ordered forward the Third Brigade (Colonel Irwin's), who, passing through the regular battery then commanded by Lieutenant Thomas (Fourth Artillery), charged upon the enemy and drove them gallantly until abreast the little church at the point of woods, the possession of which had been so fiercely contested. At this point a severe flank fire from the woods was received." The brigade rallied behind the crest of a slope, and remained in an advanced position until the next day.—EDITORS.

GENERAL VIEW OF THE BATTLE OF ANTIETAM. FROM A SKETCH MADE AT THE TIME.

This sketch was made on the hill behind McClellan's headquarters, which is seen in the hollow on the left. Sumner's corps is seen in line of battle in the middleground, and Franklin's is advancing in column to his support. The smoke in the left background is from a bursting Confederate caisson. The column of smoke is from the burning house and barn of S. Mumma, who gave the ground on which the Dunker Church stands, and after whom, in the Confederate reports, the church is frequently called "St. Mumma's." On the right is the East Wood, in which is seen the smoke of the conflict between Mansfield and Jackson. —EDITORS.

right center, and McClellan determined to help it further by a demonstration upon the extreme left by the Ninth Corps. At this time, therefore (10 A.M.), he gave his order to Burnside to try to cross the Antietam and attack the enemy, thus creating a diversion in favor of our hard-pressed right./ Facts within my own recollection strongly sustain this view that the hour was 10 A.M. I have mentioned the hill above the Burnside Bridge where Burnside took his posi-

/Here, in regard to the time at which Sumner was ordered to march to Hooker's support, is a disputed question of fact. In his official report, McClellan says he ordered Burnside to make this attack at 8 o'clock, and from the day that the latter relieved McClellan in command of the army, and especially after the battle of Fredericksburg, a hot partisan effort was made to hold Burnside responsible for the lack of complete success at Antietam as well as for the repulse upon the Rappahannock. I think I understand the limitations of Burnside's abilities as a general, but I have had, ever since the battle itself, a profound conviction that the current criticisms upon him in relation to the battle of Antietam were unjust. Burnside's official report declares that he received the order to advance at 10 o'clock. This report was dated on the 30th of September, within two weeks of the battle, and at a time when public discussion of the incomplete results of the battle was animated. It was made after he had in his hands my own report as his immediate subordinate, in which I had given about 9 o'clock as my remembrance of the time. As I directed the details of the action at the bridge in obedience to this order, it would have been easy for him to have accepted the hour named by me, for I should have been answerable for any delay in execution after that time. But he believed he knew the time at which the order came to him upon the hill-top

GENERAL MCCLELLAN RIDING THE LINE OF BATTLE AT ANTIETAM.
FROM A SKETCH MADE AT THE TIME.

The troops were Hooker's and Sedgwick's, and the time about 11 A.M. of September 17th. General McClellan rode his black horse, "Daniel Webster," which, on account of the difficulty of keeping pace with him, was better known to the staff as "that devil Dan."   —EDITORS.

tion, and to which I went after the preliminary orders for the day had been issued. There I remained until the order of attack came, anxiously watching what we could see at the right, and noting the effect of the fire of the heavy guns of Benjamin's battery. From that point we could see nothing that occurred beyond the Dunker Church, for the East and West Woods, with farm-houses and orchards between, made an impenetrable screen. But as the morning wore on we saw lines of troops advancing from our right upon the other side of the Antietam, and engaging the enemy between us and the East Wood. The Confederate lines facing them now rose into view. From our position we looked, as it were, down between the opposing lines as if they had been the sides of a street, and as the fire opened we saw wounded men carried to the rear and stragglers mak-

overlooking the field, and no officer in the whole army has a better established reputation for candor and freedom from any wish to avoid full personal responsibility for his acts. It was not till quite lately that I saw a copy of his report or learned its contents, although I enjoyed his personal friendship down to the time of his death. He was content to have stated the fact as he knew it, and did not feel the need of debating it. Several circumstances have satisfied me that his accuracy in giving the hour was greater than my own. McClellan's preliminary report (dated October 16th, 1862) explicitly states that the order to Burnside to attack was "communicated to him at 10 o'clock A.M." This exact agreement with General Burnside would ordinarily be conclusive in itself.—J.D.C.

ing off. Our lines halted, and we were tortured with anxiety as we speculated whether our men would charge or retreat. The enemy occupied lines of fences and stone-walls, and their batteries made gaps in the National ranks. Our long-range guns were immediately turned in that direction, and we cheered every well-aimed shot. One of our shells blew up a caisson close to the Confederate line. This contest was going on, and it was yet uncertain which would succeed, when one of McClellan's staff☆ rode up with an order to Burnside. The latter turned to me, saying we were ordered to make our attack. I left the hill-top at once to give personal supervision to the movement ordered, and did not return to it, and my knowledge by actual vision of what occurred on the right ceased. The manner in which we had waited, the free discussion of what was occurring under our eyes and of our relation to it, the public receipt of the order by Burnside in the usual and business-like form, all forbid the supposition that this was any reiteration of a former order. It was immediately transmitted to me without delay or discussion, further than to inform us that things were not going altogether well on the right, and that it was hoped our attack would be of assistance to that wing. If then we can determine whose troops we saw engaged, we shall know something of the time of day; for there has been a general agreement reached as to the hours of movement during the forenoon on the right. The official map settles this. No lines of our troops were engaged in the direction of Bloody Lane and the Roulette farm-house, and between the latter and our station on the hill, till French's division made its attack. We saw them distinctly on the hither side of the farm buildings, upon the open ground, considerably nearer to us than the Dunker Church or the East Wood. In number we took them to be a corps. The place, the circumstances, all fix it beyond controversy that they were French's men, or French's and Richardson's. No others fought on that part of the field until Franklin went to their assistance at noon or later. The incident of their advance and the explosion of the caisson was illustrated by the pencil of the artist, Forbes, on the spot [see p. 449], and placed by him at the time Franklin's head of column was approaching from Rohrersville, which was about 10 o'clock.♪

McClellan truly said, in his original report, that the task of carrying the bridge in front of Burnside was a difficult one. The depth of the valley and the

---

☆Colonel D. B. Sackett, who says he got the order from McClellan about 9 o'clock.—EDITORS.

♪It will not be wondered at, therefore, if to my mind the story of the 8 o'clock order is an instance of the way in which an erroneous memory is based upon the desire to make the facts accord with a theory. The actual time must have been as much later than 9 o'clock as the period during which, with absorbed attention, we had been watching the battle on the right,—a period, it is safe to say, much longer than it seemed to us. The judgment of the hour, 9 o'clock, which I gave in my report, was merely my impression from passing events, for I hastened at once to my own duties without thinking to look at my watch, while the cumulative evidence seems to prove conclusively that the time stated by Burnside, and by McClellan himself in his original report, is correct.—J.D.C.

shape of its curve made it impossible to reach the enemy's position at the bridge by artillery fire from the hill-tops on our side. Not so from the enemy's position, for the curve of the valley was such that it was perfectly enfiladed near the bridge by the Confederate batteries at the position now occupied by the national cemetery. [See map, p. 438.] The Confederate defense of the passage was intrusted to D. R. Jones's division of four brigades, which was the one Longstreet himself had disciplined and led till he was assigned to a larger command. Toombs's brigade was placed in advance, occupying the defenses of the bridge itself and the wooded slopes above, while the other brigades supported him, covered by the ridges which looked down upon the valley. The division batteries were supplemented by others from the reserve, and the valley, the bridge, and the ford below were under the direct and powerful fire of shot and shell from the Confederate cannon. Toombs speaks in his report in a characteristic way of his brigade holding back Burnside's corps; but his force, thus strongly supported, was as large as could be disposed of at the head of the bridge, and abundantly large for resistance to any that could be brought against it. Our advance upon the bridge could only be made by a narrow column, showing a front of eight men at most. But the front which Toombs deployed behind his defenses was three or four hundred yards both above and below the bridge. He himself says in his report:

> "From the nature of the ground on the other side, the enemy were compelled to approach mainly by the road which led up the river for near three hundred paces parallel with my line of battle and distant therefrom from fifty to a hundred and fifty feet, thus exposing his flank to a destructive fire the most of that distance."

Under such circumstances, I do not hesitate to affirm that the Confederate position was virtually impregnable to a direct attack over the bridge, for the column approaching it was not only exposed at pistol-range to the perfectly covered infantry of the enemy and to two batteries which were assigned to the special duty of supporting Toombs, and which had the exact range of the little valley with their shrapnel, but if it should succeed in reaching the bridge its charge across it must be made under a fire plowing through its length, the head of the column melting away as it advanced, so that, as every soldier knows, it could show no front strong enough to make an impression upon the enemy's breastworks, even if it should reach the other side. As a desperate sort of diversion in favor of the right wing, it might be justifiable; but I believe that no officer or man who knew the actual situation at that bridge thinks a serious attack upon it was any part of McClellan's original plan. Yet, in his detailed official report, instead of speaking of it as the difficult task the original report had called it, he treats it as little different from a parade or march across, which might have been done in half an hour.

Burnside's view of the matter was that the front attack at the bridge was so difficult that the passage by the ford below must be an important factor in the task; for if Rodman's division should succeed in getting across there, at the bend in the Antietam, he would come up in rear of Toombs, and either the whole of D. R. Jones's division would have to advance to meet Rodman, or Toombs must abandon the bridge. In this I certainly concurred, and Rodman was ordered to push rapidly for the ford. It is important to remember, however, that Walker's Confederate division had been posted during the earlier morning to hold that part of the Antietam line, and it was probably from him that Rodman suffered the first casualties which occurred in his ranks. But, as we have seen, Walker had been called away by Lee only an hour before, and had made the hasty march by the rear of Sharpsburg, to fall upon Sedgwick. If, therefore, Rodman had been

THE CHARGE ACROSS THE BURNSIDE BRIDGE. FROM A SKETCH MADE AT THE TIME.

In his report General Sturgis describes as follows the charge across the bridge:

"Orders arrived from General Burnside to carry the bridge at all hazards. I then selected the Fifty-first New York and the Fifty-first Pennsylvania from the Second Brigade, and directed them to charge with the bayonet. They started on their mission of death full of enthusiasm, and, taking a route less exposed than the regiments [Second Maryland and Sixth New Hampshire] which had made the effort before them, rushed at a double-quick over the slope leading to the bridge and over the bridge itself, with an impetuosity which the enemy could not resist; and the Stars and Stripes were planted on the opposite bank at 1 o'clock P.M., amid the most enthusiastic cheering from every part of the field from where they could be seen."

sent to cross at 8 o'clock, it is safe to say that his column fording the stream in the face of Walker's deployed division would never have reached the farther bank,—a contingency that McClellan did not consider when arguing long afterward the favorable results that might have followed an earlier attack. As Rodman died upon the field, no full report for his division was made, and we only know that he met with some resistance from both infantry and artillery; that the winding of the stream made his march longer than he anticipated, and that, in fact, he only approached the rear of Toombs's position from that direction about the time when our last and successful charge upon the bridge was made, between noon and 1 o'clock.

The attacks at Burnside's Bridge were made under my own eye. Sturgis's division occupied the center of our line, with Crook's brigade of the Kanawha Division on his right front, and Willcox's division in reserve, as I have already stated. Crook's position was somewhat above the bridge, but it was thought that by advancing part of Sturgis's men to the brow of the hill they could cover the advance of Crook, and that the latter could make a straight dash down the hill to our end of the bridge. The orders were accordingly given, and Crook advanced, covered by the 11th Connecticut (of Rodman), under Colonel Kingsbury, deployed as skirmishers. In passing over the spurs of the hills, Crook came out on the bank of the stream above the bridge and found himself under a heavy fire. He faced the enemy and returned the fire, getting such cover for his men as he could and trying to drive off or silence his opponents. The engagement was one in which the Antietam prevented the combatants from coming to close quarters, but it was none the less vigorously continued with musketry fire. Crook reported that his hands were full, and that he could not approach closer to the bridge. But later in the contest, and about the time that the successful charge at the bridge was made, he got five companies of the 28th Ohio over by a ford above. Sturgis ordered forward an attacking column from Nagle's brigade, supported and covered by Ferrero's brigade, which took position in a field of corn on one of the lower slopes of the hill opposite the head of the bridge. The whole front was carefully covered with skirmishers, and our batteries on the heights overhead were ordered to keep down the fire of the enemy's artillery. Nagle's effort was gallantly made, but it failed, and his men were forced to seek cover behind the spur of the hill from which they had advanced. We were constantly hoping to hear something from Rodman's advance by the ford, and would gladly have waited for some more certain knowledge of his progress, but at this time McClellan's sense of the necessity of relieving the right was such that he was sending reiterated orders to push the assault. Not only were these forwarded to me, but to give added weight to my instructions Burnside sent direct to Sturgis urgent messages to carry the bridge at all hazards. I directed Sturgis to take two regiments from Ferrero's brigade, which had not been engaged, and make a column by moving them by the flank, the one left in front and the other right in front, side by side, so that when they passed the bridge they could turn to left and right, forming line as they advanced on the run. He chose the 51st New York, Colonel Robert B. Potter, and the 51st Pennsylvania, Colonel John F. Hartranft (both names afterward greatly distinguished), and both officers and men were made to feel the necessity of success. At the same time Crook succeeded in bringing a light howitzer of Simmonds's mixed battery down from the hill-tops, and placed it where it had a point-blank fire on the farther end of the bridge. The howitzer was one we had captured in West Virginia, and had been added to the battery, which was partly made up of heavy rifled Parrott guns. When everything was ready, a heavy skirmishing fire was opened all along the bank, the howitzer threw in double charges of canister, the two regiments charged up the road in column with fixed bayonets, and in scarcely more time than it takes to tell it, the bridge was passed and Toombs's brigade fled through the woods and over the top of the hill. The charging regiments were advanced in line to the crest above the bridge as soon as they were deployed, and the rest of Sturgis's division, with Crook's brigade, were immediately brought over to strengthen the line. These were soon joined by Rodman's division with Seammon's brigade, which had crossed at the ford, and whose presence on that side of the stream had no doubt made the final struggle of Toombs's men less obstinate than it would otherwise have been, the fear of being taken in rear having always a strong moral effect upon even the best of troops. It was now about 1 o'clock, and nearly three hours had been spent in a bitter and bloody contest across the narrow stream. The successive efforts to carry the bridge had been made as closely following each other as possible. Each had been a fierce combat, in which the men, with wonderful courage, had not easily accepted defeat, and even when not able to cross the bridge had made use of the walls at the end, the fences, and every tree and stone as cover, while they strove to reach with their fire their well-protected and nearly concealed opponents. The lulls in the fighting had been short, and only to prepare new efforts. The severity of the work was attested by our losses, which, before the crossing was won, exceeded five hundred men and included some of our best officers, such as Colonel Kingsbury, of the 11th Connecticut; Lieutenant-Colonel Bell, of the 51st Pennsylvania, and Lieutenant-Colonel Coleman, of the 11th Ohio, two of them commanding regiments. The proportion of casualties to the number engaged was much greater than common, for the nature of the task required that comparatively few troops should be exposed at once, the others remaining under cover.

Our first task was to prepare to hold the height we had gained against the return assault of the enemy which we expected, and to reply to the destructive fire from the enemy's abundant artillery. The light batteries were brought over and distributed in the line. The men were made to lie down behind the crest to save them from the concentrated artillery fire which the enemy opened upon

BURNSIDE'S ATTACK UPON SHARPSBURG. FROM A SKETCH MADE AT THE TIME.

In this attack Willcox's division (the right of the line) charged into the village. Colonel Fairchild, commanding a brigade in Rodman's division, on the left of the line (which included Hawkins's Zouaves, seen at the stone-wall in the picture), describes as follows in his report the advance upon Sharpsburg after the hill above the bridge had been gained: "We continued to advance to the opposite hill under a tremendous fire from the enemy's batteries, up steep embankments. Arriving near a stone fence, the enemy—a brigade composed of South Carolina and Georgia regiments—opened on us with musketry. After returning their fire I immediately ordered a charge, which the whole brigade gallantly responded to, moving with alacrity and steadiness. Arriving at the fence, behind which the enemy were awaiting us, receiving their fire, losing large numbers of our men, we charged over the fence, dislodging them and driving them from their positions down the hill toward the village, a stand of regimental colors belonging to a South Carolina regiment being taken by Private Thomas Hare, Company D, 89th New York Volunteers, who was afterward killed. We continued to pursue the enemy down the hill. Discovering that they were massing fresh troops on our left, I went back and requested General Rodman to bring up rapidly the Second Brigade to our support, which he did, they engaging the enemy, he soon afterward falling badly wounded.... The large force advancing on our left flank compelled us to retire from the position, which we could have held had we been properly supported."

us as soon as Toombs's regiments succeeded in reaching their main line. But McClellan's anticipation of an overwhelming attack upon his right was so strong that he determined still to press our advance, and sent orders accordingly. The ammunition of Sturgis's and Crook's men had been nearly exhausted, and it was imperative that they should be freshly supplied before entering into another engagement. Sturgis also reported his men so exhausted by their efforts as to be unfit for an immediate advance. On this I sent to Burnside the request that Willcox's division be sent over, with an ammunition train, and that Sturgis's division be replaced by the fresh troops, remaining, however, on the west side of the stream as support to the others. This was done as rapidly as was practicable, where everything had to pass down the steep hill road and through so narrow a defile as the bridge. Still, it was 3 o'clock before these changes and further preparations could be made. Burnside had personally striven to hasten them, and had come over to the west bank to consult and to hurry matters, and took his share of personal peril, for he came at a time when the ammunition wagons were delivering cartridges, and the road where they were, at the end of the bridge, was in the range of the enemy's constant and accurate fire. It is proper to mention this because it has been said that he did not cross the stream. The criticisms made by McClellan as to the time occupied in these changes and movements will not seem forcible, if one will compare them with any similar movements on the field; such as Mansfield's to support Hooker, or Sumner's or Franklin's to reach the scene of action. About this, however, there is fair room for difference of opinion; what I personally know is that it would have been folly to advance again before Willcox had relieved Sturgis, and that as soon as the fresh troops reported and could be put in line, the order to advance was given. McClellan is in accord with all other witnesses in declaring that when the movement began, the conduct of the troops was gallant beyond criticism.

Willcox's division formed the right, Christ's brigade being north and Welsh's brigade south of the road leading from the bridge to Sharpsburg. Crook's brigade of the Kanawha Division supported Willcox. Rodman's division formed on the left, Harland's brigade having the position on the flank, and Fairchild's uniting with Willcox at the center. Seammon's brigade of the Kanawha Division was the reserve for Rodman on the extreme left. Sturgis's division remained and held the crest of the hill above the bridge. About half the batteries of the divisions accompanied the movement, the rest being in position on the hill-tops east of the Antietam. The advance necessarily followed the high ground toward Sharpsburg, and as the enemy made strongest resistance toward our right, the movement curved in that direction, the six brigades of D. R. Jones's Confederate division being deployed diagonally across our front, holding the stone fences and crests of the cross ridges and aided by abundant artillery, in which arm the enemy was particularly strong. The battle was a fierce one from the moment Willcox's men showed themselves on the open ground. Christ's brigade, taking advantage of all the cover the trees and inequalities of surface gave them, pushed on along the depression in which the road ran, a section of artillery keeping pace with them in the road. The direction of movement brought all the brigades of the first line in échelon, but Welsh soon fought his way up beside Christ, and they, together, drove the enemy successively from the fields and farm-yards till they reached the edge of the village. Upon the elevation on the right of the road was an orchard in which the shattered and diminished force of Jones made a final stand, but Willcox concentrated his artillery fire upon it, and his infantry was able to push forward and occupy it. They now partly occupied the town of Sharpsburg, and held the high ground commanding it on the south-east, where the national cemetery now is. The struggle had been long and bloody. It was half-past 4 in the afternoon, and ammunition had again run low, for the wagons had not been able to accompany the movement. Willcox paused for his men to take breath again, and to fetch up some cartridges; but meanwhile affairs were taking a serious turn on the left.

As Rodman's division went forward, he found the enemy before him seemingly detached from Willcox's opponents, and occupying ridges upon his left front, so that he was not able to keep his own connection with Willcox in the swinging movement to the right. Still, he made good progress in the face of stubborn resistance, though finding the enemy constantly developing more to his left, and the interval between him and Willcox widening. In fact his movement became practically by column of brigades. The view of the field to the south was now obstructed by fields of tall Indian corn, and under this cover Confederate troops approached the flank in line of battle. Seammon's officers in the reserve saw them as soon as Rodman's brigades écheloned, as these were toward the front and right. This hostile force proved to be A. P. Hill's division of six brigades, the last of Jackson's force to leave Harper's Ferry, and which had reached Sharpsburg since noon. Those first seen by Seammon's men were dressed in the National blue uniforms which they had captured at Harper's Ferry, and it was assumed that they were part of our own forces till they began to fire. Seammon quickly changed front to the left, drove back the enemy before him, and occupied a line of stone fences, which he held until he was withdrawn from it. Harland's brigade was partly moving in the corn-fields. One of his regiments was new, having been organized only three weeks, and the brigade had somewhat lost its order and connection when the sudden attack came. Rodman directed Colonel Harland to lead the right of the brigade, while he himself attempted to bring the left into position. In performing this duty he fell mortally wounded, and the brigade broke in confusion after a brief effort of its right wing to hold on. Fairchild, also, now received the fire on his left, and was forced to fall back and change front.

Being at the center when this break occurred on the left, I saw that it would be impossible to continue the movement to the right, and sent instant orders to Willcox and Crook to retire the left of their line, and to Sturgis to come forward into the gap made in Rodman's. The troops on the right swung back in perfect order; Seammon's brigade hung on at its stone-wall with unflinching tenacity till Sturgis had formed on the curving hill in rear of them, and Rodman's had found refuge behind. Willcox's left, then united with Sturgis and Seammon, was withdrawn to a new position on the left flank of the whole line. That these manœuvres on the field were really performed in good order is demonstrated by the fact that, although the break in Rodman's line was a bad one, the enemy was not able to capture many prisoners, the whole number of missing, out of the 2340 casualties which the Ninth Corps suffered in the battle, being 115, which includes wounded men unable to leave the field. The enemy were not lacking in bold efforts to take advantage of the check we had received, but were repulsed with severe punishment, and as the day declined were content to entrench themselves along the line of the road leading from Sharpsburg to the Potomac at the mouth of the Antietam, half a mile in our front. The men of the Ninth Corps lay that night upon their arms, the line being one which rested with both flanks near the Antietam, and curved outward upon the rolling hilltops which covered the bridge and commanded the plateau between us and the enemy. With my staff I lay upon the ground behind the troops, holding our horses by the bridles as we rested, for our orderlies were so exhausted that we could not deny them the same chance for a little broken slumber.

The conduct of the battle on the left has given rise to several criticisms, among which the most prominent has been that Porter's corps, which lay in reserve, was not put in at the same time with the Ninth Corps. McClellan answered this by saying that he did not think it prudent to divest the center of all reserve troops.‡ No doubt a single strong division marching beyond the left flank of the Ninth Corps would have so occupied A. P. Hill's division that our movement into Sharpsburg could not have been checked, and, assisted by the advance of Sumner and Franklin on the right, apparently would have made certain the complete rout of Lee. As troops are put in reserve, not to diminish the army, but to be used in a pinch, I am deeply convinced that McClellan's refusal

---

‡General Thomas M. Anderson, in 1886 Lieutenant-Colonel of the 9th Infantry, U.S.A., wrote to the editors in that year:

"At the battle of Antietam I commanded one of the battalions of Sykes's division of regulars, held in reserve on the north of Antietam creek near the stone bridge. Three of our battalions were on the south side of the creek, deployed as skirmishers in front of Sharpsburg. At the time A. P. Hill began to force Burnside back upon the left, I was talking with Colonel Buchanan, our brigade commander, when an orderly brought him a note from Captain (now Colonel) Blunt, who was the senior officer with the battalions of our brigade beyond the creek. The note, as I remember, stated in effect that Captain Dryer, commanding the 4th Infantry, had ridden into the enemy's lines, and upon returning had reported that there were but one Confederate battery and two regiments in front of Sharpsburg, connecting the wings of Lee's army.* Dryer was one of the coolest and bravest officers in our service, and on his report Blunt asked instructions. We learned afterward that Dryer proposed that he, Blunt, and Brown, commanding the 4th, 12th, and 14th Infantries, should charge the enemy in Sharpsburg instanter. But Blunt preferred asking for orders. Colonel Buchanan sent the note to Sykes, who was at the time talking with General McClellan and Fitz-John Porter, about a

---

*General Fitz-John Porter writes to say that no such note as "Captain Dryer's report" was seen by him, and that no such discussion as to the opportunity for using the "reserve" took place between him and General McClellan. General Porter says that nearly all of his Fifth Corps (according to McClellan's report, 12,900 strong), instead of being idle at that critical hour, had been sent to reënforce the right and left wings, leaving of the Fifth Corps to defend the center a force "not then four thousand strong," according to General Porter's report.—EDITORS.

PRESIDENT LINCOLN IN GENERAL
MCCLELLAN'S TENT AT ANTIETAM AFTER
THE BATTLE. FROM A PHOTOGRAPH.

to use them on the left was the result of his continued conviction through all the day after Sedgwick's defeat, that Lee was overwhelmingly superior in force, and was preparing to return a crushing blow upon our right flank. He was keeping something in hand to cover a retreat, if that wing should be driven back. Except in this way, also, I am at a loss to account for the inaction of our right during the whole of our engagement on the left. Looking at our part of the battle as only a strong diversion to prevent or delay Lee's following up his success against Hooker and the rest, it is intelligible. I certainly so understood it at the time, as my report witnesses, and McClellan's preliminary report supports this view. If he had been impatient to have our attack delivered earlier, he had reason for double impatience that Franklin's fresh troops should assail Lee's left simultaneously with ours, unless he regarded action there as hopeless, and looked upon our movement as a sort of forlorn-hope to keep Lee from following up his advantages.

But even these are not all the troublesome questions requiring an answer. Couch's division had been left north-east of Maryland Heights to observe Jackson's command, supposed still to be in Harper's Ferry. Why could it not have come up on our left as well as A. P. Hill's division, which was the last of the Confederate troops to leave the Ferry, there being nothing to observe after it was gone? Couch's division, coming with equal pace with Hill's on the other side of the river, would have answered our needs as well as one from Porter's corps. Hill came, but Couch did not. Yet even then, a regiment of horse watch-

---

hundred and fifty yards from us. They were sitting on their horses between Taft's and Weed's batteries a little to our left. I saw the note passed from one to the other in the group, but could not, of course, hear what was said.

"We received no orders to advance, however, although the advance of a single brigade at the time (sunset) would have cut Lee's army in two.

"After the war, I asked General Sykes why our reserves did not advance upon receiving Dryer's report. He answered that he remembered the circumstance very well and that he thought McClellan was inclined to order in the Fifth Corps, but that when he spoke of doing so Fitz-John Porter said: 'Remember, General! I command the last reserve of the last Army of the Republic.'"

At this time Sykes and Griffin, of Porter's corps, had been advanced, and part of their troops were actively engaged.—EDITORS.

ing that flank and scouring the country as we swung it forward would have developed Hill's presence and enabled the commanding general either to stop our movement or to take the available means to support it; but the cavalry was put to no such use; it occupied the center of the whole line, only its artillery being engaged during the day. It would have been invaluable to Hooker in the morning as it would have been to us in the afternoon. McClellan had marched from Frederick City with the information that Lee's army was divided, Jackson being detached with a large force to take Harper's Ferry. He had put Lee's strength at 120,000 men. Assuming that there was still danger that Jackson might come upon our left with a large force, and that Lee had proven strong enough without Jackson to repulse three corps on our right and right center, McClellan might have regarded his own army as divided also for the purpose of meeting both opponents, and his cavalry would have been upon the flank of the part with which he was attacking Lee; Porter would have been in position to help either part in an extremity, or to cover a retreat, and Burnside would have been the only subordinate available to check Lee's apparent success. Will any other hypothesis intelligibly account for McClellan's dispositions and orders? The error in the above assumption would be that McClellan estimated Lee's troops at nearly double their actual numbers, and that what was taken for proof of Lee's superiority in force on the field was a series of partial reverses which resulted directly from the piecemeal and disjointed way in which McClellan's morning attacks had been made.

The same explanation is the most satisfactory one that I can give for the inaction of Thursday, the 18th of September. Could McClellan have known the desperate condition of most of Lee's brigades he would have known that his own were in much better case, badly as they had suffered. I do not doubt that most of his subordinates discouraged the resumption of the attack, for the rooted belief in Lee's preponderance of numbers had been chronic in the army during the whole year. That belief was based upon the inconceivably mistaken reports of the secret service organization, accepted at headquarters, given to the War Department at Washington as a reason for incessant demands of reënforcements, and permeating downward through the whole organization till the error was accepted as truth by officers and men, and became a factor in their morale which can hardly be over-estimated. The result was that Lee retreated unmolested on the night of the 18th, and that what might have been a real and decisive success was a drawn battle in which our chief claim to victory was the possession of the field.

The Ninth Corps occupied its position on the heights west of the Antietam without further molestation, except an irritating picket firing, till the Confederate army retreated. But the position was one in which no shelter from the weather could be had; nor could any cooking be done; and the troops were short of rations. Late in the afternoon of Thursday, Morell's division of Porter's

GENERAL MCCLELLAN AND PRESIDENT LINCOLN AT ANTIETAM. FROM A PHOTOGRAPH.

The Proclamation of Emancipation was published September 22d, three days after the withdrawal of Lee to Virginia, and was communicated to the army officially on September 24th.

On October 1st President Lincoln visited the army to see for himself if it was in no condition to pursue Lee into Virginia. General McClellan says in his general report: "His Excellency the President honored the Army of the Potomac with a visit, and remained several days, during which he went through the different encampments, reviewed the troops, and went over the battle-fields of South Mountain and Antietam. I had the opportunity during this visit to describe to him the operations of the army since the time it left Washington, and gave him my reasons for not following the enemy after he crossed the Potomac." In "McClellan's Own Story" he says that the President "more than once assured me that he was fully satisfied with my whole course from the beginning: that the only fault he could possibly find was, that I was too prone to be sure that every-

corps was ordered to report to Burnside to relieve the picket line and some of the regiments in the most exposed position. One brigade was sent over the Antietam for this purpose,^ψ and a few of the Ninth Corps regiments were enabled to withdraw far enough to cook some rations of which they had been in need for twenty-four hours. Harland's brigade of Rodman's division had been taken to the east side of the stream on the evening of the 17th to be reorganized.

thing was ready before acting, but that my actions were all right when I started. I said to him that I thought a few experiments with those who acted before they were ready would probably convince him that in the end I consumed less time than they did."

After the President's return to Washington, October 5th, Halleck telegraphed to McClellan under date of October 6th: "The President directs that you cross the Potomac and give battle to the enemy or drive him south," etc.

On October 7th McClellan, in "General Orders No. 163," referred to the Proclamation of Emancipation. He warned the army of the danger to military discipline of heated political discussions, and reminded them that the "remedy for political errors, if any are committed, is to be found only in the action of the people at the polls." On October 5th General McClellan had said, in a letter to his wife, "Mr. Aspinwall [W. H., of New York] is decidedly of the opinion that it is my duty to submit to the President's proclamation and quietly continue doing my duty as a soldier. I presume he is right, and am at least sure that he is honest in his opinion. I shall surely give his views full consideration." —Editors.

ψPorter in his report says that Morell took the place of the whole Ninth Corps. In this he is entirely mistaken, as the reports from Morell's division show.—J.D.C.

CHAPTER 16

THE BATTLE OF FREDERICKSBURG.

James Longstreet, Lieutenant-General, C.S.A.

In the early fall of 1862, a distance of not more than thirty miles lay between the Army of the Potomac and the Army of Northern Virginia. A state of uncertainty had existed for several weeks succeeding the battle of Sharpsburg, but the movements that resulted in the battle of Fredericksburg began to take shape when on the 5th of November the order was issued removing General McClellan from command of the Federal forces.

The order assigning General Burnside to command was received at General Lee's headquarters, then at Culpeper Court House, about twenty-four hours after it reached Warrenton, though not through official courtesy. General Lee, on receiving the news, said he regretted to part with McClellan, "for," he added, "we always understood each other so well. I fear they may continue to make these changes till they find some one whom I don't understand."

The Federal army was encamped around Warrenton, Virginia, and was soon divided into three grand divisions, whose commanders were Generals Sumner, Hooker, and Franklin.

Lee's army was on the opposite side of the Rappahannock River, divided into two corps, the First commanded by myself and the Second commanded by General T. J. (Stone-

CONFEDERATE PICKET WITH
BLANKET-CAPOTE AND RAW-HIDE
MOCCASINS.

wall) Jackson. At that time the Confederate army extended from Culpeper Court House (where the First Corps was stationed) on its right across the Blue Ridge down the Valley of Virginia to Winchester. There Jackson was encamped with the Second Corps, except one division which was stationed at Chester Gap on the Blue Ridge Mountains.

About the 18th or 19th of November, we received information through our scouts that Sumner, with his grand division of more than thirty thousand men, was moving toward Fredericksburg. Evidently he intended to surprise us and cross the Rappahannock before we could offer resistance. On receipt of the information, two of my divisions were ordered down to meet him. We made a forced march and arrived on the hills around Fredericksburg about 3 o'clock on the afternoon of the 21st. Sumner had already arrived, and his army was encamped on Stafford Heights, overlooking the town from the Federal side. Before I reached Fredericksburg, General Patrick, provost-marshal-general, crossed the river under a flag of truce and put the people in a state of great excitement by delivering the following letter:

"HEADQUARTERS OF THE ARMY OF THE POTOMAC,
"November 21st, 1862.

"TO THE MAYOR AND COMMON COUNCIL OF FREDERICKSBURG. GENTLEMEN: Under cover of the houses of your city, shots have been fired upon the troops of my command. Your mills and manufactories are furnishing provisions and the material for clothing for armed bodies in rebellion against the Government of the United States. Your railroads and other means of transportation are removing supplies to the depots of such troops. This condition of things must terminate, and by direction of General Burnside I accordingly demand the surrender of your city into my hands, as the representative of the Government of the United States, at or before 5 o'clock this afternoon. Failing in an affirmative reply to this demand by the hour indicated, sixteen hours will be permitted to elapse for the removal from the city of women and children, the sick and wounded and aged, etc., which period having expired I shall proceed to shell the town. Upon obtaining possession of the city every necessary means will be taken to preserve order and secure the protective operation of the laws and policy of the United States Government. I am, very respectfully, your obedient servant,

"E. V. SUMNER,
"Brevet Major-General, U.S. Army,
"Commanding Right Grand Division."

While the people were in a state of excitement over the receipt of this demand for the surrender of their town, my troops appeared upon the heights opposite those occupied by the Federals. The alarmed non-combatants heard of my arrival and immediately sent to me the demand of the Federal general. I stated to the town authorities that I did not care to occupy the place for military purposes and that there was no reason why it should be shelled by the Federal army. We were there to protect ourselves against the advance of the enemy, and could not allow the town to be occupied by the Federals. The mayor sent to General Sumner a satisfactory statement of the situation and was notified that the threatened shelling would not take place, since the Confederates did not purpose to make the town a base of military operations.

Before my troops reached the little city, and before the people of Fredericksburg knew that any part of the Confederate army was near, there was great excitement over the demand for surrender. No people were in the place except aged and infirm men, and women and children. That they should become alarmed when the surrender of the town was demanded by the Federals was quite natural, and a number proceeded with great haste to board a train then ready to leave. As the train drew out, Sumner's batteries on Stafford Heights opened fire on it, adding to the general terror, but fortunately doing no serious damage. The spectacle was nothing, however, to what we witnessed a short time after. About the 26th or 27th it became evident that Fredericksburg would be the scene of a battle, and we advised the people who were still in the town to prepare to leave, as they would soon be in danger if they remained. The evacuation of the place by the distressed women and helpless men was a painful sight. Many were almost destitute and had nowhere to go, but, yielding to the cruel necessities of war, they collected their portable effects and turned their backs on the town. Many were forced to seek shelter in the woods and brave the icy November nights to escape the approaching assault from the Federal army.

Very soon after I reached Fredericksburg the remainder of my corps arrived from Culpeper Court House, and as soon as it was known that all the Army of the Potomac was in motion for the prospective scene of battle Jackson was drawn down from the Blue Ridge. In a very short time the Army of Northern Virginia was face to face with the Army of the Potomac.

When Jackson arrived he objected to the position, not that he feared the result of the battle, but because he thought that behind the North Anna was a point from which the most fruitful results would follow. He held that we would win a victory at Fredericksburg, but it would be a fruitless one to us, whereas at North Anna, when we drove the Federals back, we could give pursuit to advantage, which we could not do at Fredericksburg. General Lee did not entertain the proposition, however, and we continued our preparations to meet the enemy at the latter place.✩

✩That General Lee was not quite satisfied with the place of battle is shown by a dispatch to the Richmond authorities on the second day after the battle, when it was uncertain what Burnside's next move

At a point just above the town, a range of hills begins, extending from the river edge out a short distance and bearing around the valley somewhat in the form of a crescent. On the opposite side are the noted Stafford Heights, then occupied by the Federals. At the foot of these hills flows the Rappahannock River. On the Confederate side nestled Fredericksburg, and around it stretched the fertile bottoms from which fine crops had been gathered and upon which the Federal troops were to mass and give battle to the Confederates. On the Confederate side nearest the river was Taylor's Hill, and south of it the now famous Marye's Hill; next, Telegraph Hill, the highest of the elevations on the Confederate side (later known as Lee's Hill, because during the battle General Lee was there most of the time), where I had my headquarters in the field; next was a declination through which Deep Run Creek passed on its way to the Rappahannock River; and next was the gentle elevation at Hamilton's Crossing, not dignified with a name, upon which Stonewall Jackson massed thirty thousand men. It was upon these hills that the Confederates made their preparations to receive Burnside whenever he might choose to cross the Rappahannock. The Confederates were stationed as follows: On Taylor's Hill next to the river and forming my left, R. H. Anderson's division; on Marye's Hill, Ransom's and McLaws's divisions; on Telegraph Hill, Pickett's division; to the right and about Deep Run Creek, Hood's division, the latter stretching across Deep Run Bottom.

On the hill occupied by Jackson's corps were the divisions of A. P. Hill, Early, and Taliaferro, that of D. H. Hill being in reserve on the extreme right. To the Washington Artillery, on Marye's Hill, was assigned the service of advising the army at the earliest possible moment of the Federal advance. General Barksdale, with his Mississippi brigade, was on picket duty in front of Fredericksburg on the night of the advance.

The hills occupied by the Confederate forces, although over-crowned by the heights of Stafford, were so distant as to be outside the range of effective fire by the Federal guns, and, with the lower receding grounds between them, formed a defensive series that may be likened to natural bastions. Taylor's Hill, on our left, was unassailable; Marye's Hill was more advanced toward the town, was of a gradual ascent and of less height than the others, and we considered it

---

would be. In that dispatch he says; "Should the enemy cross at Port Royal in force, before I can get this army in position to meet him, I think it more advantageous to retire to the Annas and give battle, than on the banks of the Rappahannock. My design was to have done so in the first instance. My purpose was changed not from any advantage in this position, but from an unwillingness to open more of our country to depredation than possible, and also with a view of collecting such forage and provisions as could be obtained in the Rappahannock Valley. With the numerous army opposed to me, and the bridges and transportation at its command, the crossing of the Rappahannock, where it is narrow and winding as in the vicinity of Fredericksburg, can be made at almost any point without molestation. It will, therefore, be more advantageous to us to draw him farther away from his base of operations."—Editors.

the point most assailable, and guarded it accordingly. The events that followed proved the correctness of our opinion on that point. Lee's Hill, near our center, with its rugged sides retired from Marye's and rising higher than its companions, was comparatively safe.

This was the situation of the 65,000 Confederates massed around Fredericksburg, and they had twenty-odd days in which to prepare for the approaching battle.

The Federals on Stafford Heights carefully matured their plans of advance and attack. General Hunt, chief of artillery, skillfully posted 147 guns to cover the bottoms upon which the infantry was to form for the attack, and at the same time play upon the Confederate batteries as circumstances would allow. Franklin and Hooker had joined Sumner, and Stafford Heights held the Federal army, 116,000 strong, watching the plain where the bloody conflict was soon to be. In the meantime the Federals had been seen along the banks of the river, looking for the most available points for crossing. President Lincoln had been down with General Halleck, and it had been suggested by the latter to cross at Hoop-pole Ferry, about 28 or 30 miles below Fredericksburg. We discovered the movement, however, and prepared to meet it, and Burnside abandoned the idea and turned his attention to Fredericksburg, under the impression that many of our troops were down at Hoop-pole, too far away to return in time for this battle.[*]

The soldiers of both armies were in good fighting condition, and there was every indication that we would have a desperate battle. We were confident that Burnside could not dislodge us, and patiently awaited the attack.

On the morning of the 11th of December, 1862, an hour or so before daylight, the slumbering Confederates were awakened by a solitary cannon thundering on the heights of Marye's Hill. Again it boomed, and instantly the aroused Confederates recognized the signal of the Washington Artillery and knew that the Federal troops were preparing to cross the Rappahannock to give us the expected battle. The Federals came down to the river's edge and began the construction of their bridges, when Barksdale opened fire with such effect that they were forced to retire. Again and again they made an effort to cross, but each time they were met and repulsed by the well-directed bullets of the Mississippians. This contest lasted until 1 o'clock, when the Federals, with angry desperation, turned their whole available force of artillery on the little city, and sent down from the heights a perfect storm of shot and shell, crushing the houses with a cyclone of fiery metal. From our position on the heights we saw the batteries hurling an avalanche upon the town whose only offense was that near its edge in a snug retreat nestled three thousand Confederate hornets that

---

[*] It is more than probable that Burnside accepted the proposition to move by Hoop-pole Ferry for the purpose of drawing some of our troops from the points he had really selected for his crossing.—J.L.

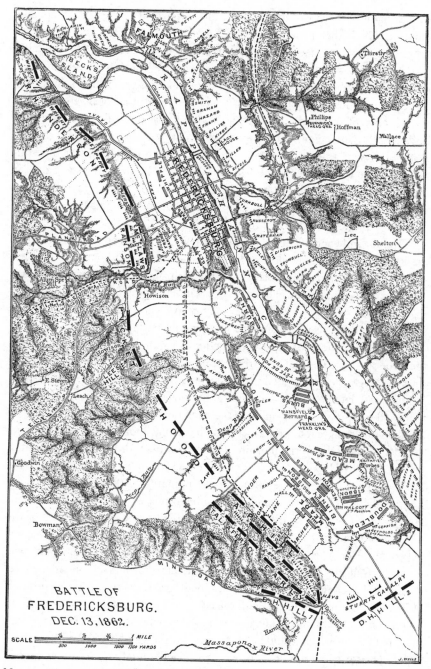

BATTLE OF
FREDERICKSBURG.
DEC. 13, 1862.

SCALE

NOTE.—The batteries which had position on the outskirts of the town in rear of Sumner's attack were Waterman's, Kusscrow's, Kirby's, Hazard's, Frank's, Arnold's, Phillips's, and Dickenson's. In placing the Union artillery, we have followed an official map made under direction of General Henry J. Hunt, chief of artillery.—EDITORS.

were stinging the Army of the Potomac into a frenzy. It was terrific, the pandemonium which that little squad of Confederates had provoked. The town caught fire in several places, shells crashed and burst, and solid shot rained like hail. In the midst of the successive crashes could be heard the shouts and yells of those engaged in the struggle, while the smoke rose from the burning city and the flames leaped about, making a scene which can never be effaced from the memory of those who saw it. But, in the midst of all this fury, the little brigade of Mississippians clung to their work. At last, when I had everything in readiness, I sent a peremptory order to Barksdale to withdraw, which he did, fighting as he retired before the Federals, who had by that time succeeded in landing a number of their troops. The Federals then constructed their pontoons without molestation, and during the night and the following day the grand division of Sumner passed over into Fredericksburg.

About a mile and a half below the town, where the Deep Run empties into the Rappahannock, General Franklin had been allowed without serious opposition to throw two pontoon-bridges on the 11th, and his grand division passed over and massed on the level bottoms opposite Hamilton's Crossing, thus placing himself in front of Stonewall Jackson's corps. The 11th and 12th were thus spent by the Federals in crossing the river and preparing for battle.

Opposite Fredericksburg, the formation along the river-bank was such that the Federals were concealed in their approaches, and, availing themselves of this advantage, they succeeded in crossing and concealing the grand division of Sumner and, later, a part of Hooker's grand division in the city of Fredericksburg, and so disposing of Franklin in the open plain below as to give out the impression that the great force was with the latter and about to oppose Jackson.

Before daylight on the morning of the eventful 13th I rode to the right of my line held by Hood's division. General Hood was at his post in plain hearing of the Federals south of Deep Run, who were marching their troops into position for the attack. The morning was cold and misty, and everything was obscured from view, but so distinctly did the mist bear to us the sounds of the moving Federals that Hood thought the advance was against him. He was relieved, however, when I assured him that the enemy, to reach him, would have to put himself in a pocket and be subjected to attack from Jackson on one side, Pickett and McLaws on the other, and Hood's own men in front. The position of Franklin's men on the 12th, with the configuration of the ground, had left no doubt in my mind as to Franklin's intentions. I explained all this to Hood, assuring him that the attack would be on Jackson. At the same time I ordered Hood, in case Jackson's line should be broken, to wheel around to his right and strike in on the attacking bodies, telling him that Pickett, with his division, would be ordered to join in the flank movement. These orders were given to both division generals, and at the same time they were advised that I would be attacked near my left center, and that I must be at that point to meet my part of the battle.

They were also advised that my position was so well defended I could have no other need of their troops. I then returned to Lee's Hill, reaching there soon after sunrise.

Thus we stood at the eve of the great battle. Along the Stafford Heights 147 guns were turned upon us, and on the level plain below, in the town, and hidden on the opposite bank ready to cross, were assembled nearly 100,000 men, eager to begin the combat. Secure on our hills, we grimly awaited the onslaught. The valley, the mountain-tops, everything was enveloped in the thickest fog, and the preparations for the fight were made as if under cover of night. The mist brought to us the sounds of the preparation for battle, but we were blind to the movements of the Federals. Suddenly, at 10 o'clock, as if the elements were taking a hand in the drama about to be enacted, the warmth of the sun brushed the mist away and revealed the mighty panorama in the valley below.

Franklin's 40,000 men, reënforced by two divisions of Hooker's grand division, were in front of Jackson's 30,000. The flags of the Federals fluttered gayly, the polished arms shone brightly in the sunlight, and the beautiful uniforms of the buoyant troops gave to the scene the air of a holiday occasion rather than the spectacle of a great army about to be thrown into the tumult of battle. From my place on Lee's Hill I could see almost every soldier Franklin had, and a splendid array it was. But off in the distance was Jackson's ragged infantry, and beyond was Stuart's battered cavalry, with their soiled hats and yellow butternut suits, a striking contrast to the handsomely equipped troops of the Federals.

About the city, here and there, a few soldiers could be seen, but there was no indication of the heavy masses that were concealed by the houses. Those of Franklin's men who were in front of Jackson stretched well up toward Lee's Hill, and were almost within reach of our best guns, and at the other end they stretched out to the east until they came well under the fire of Stuart's horse artillery under Major John Pelham, a brave and gallant officer, almost a boy in years. As the mist rose, the Confederates saw the movement against their right near Hamilton's Crossing. Major Pelham opened fire upon Franklin's command and gave him lively work, which was kept up until Jackson ordered Pelham to retire. Franklin then advanced rapidly to the hill where Jackson's troops had been stationed, feeling the woods with shot as he progressed. Silently Jackson awaited the approach of the Federals until they were within good range, and then he opened a terrific fire which threw the Federals into some confusion. The enemy again massed and advanced, pressing through a gap between Archer and Lane. This broke Jackson's line and threatened very serious trouble. The Federals who had wedged themselves in through that gap came upon Gregg's brigade, and then the severe encounter ensued in which the latter general was mortally wounded. Archer and Lane very soon received reënforcements and, rallying, joined in the counter-attack and recovered their lost ground. The concentration of Taliaferro's and Early's divisions against this at-

THE SUNKEN ROAD UNDER MARYE'S HILL. FROM A PHOTOGRAPH TAKEN IN 1884.

In the background is seen the continuation of Hanover street, which on the left ascends the hill to the Marye Mansion. The little square field lies in the fork made by the former road and the Telegraph road (see map, p. 469). Nearly all that remained in 1884 of the famous stone-wall is seen in the right of the picture. The horses are in the road, which is a continuation of the street south of Hanover street, and on which is the brick house mentioned in General Couch's article. The house in which General Cobb died would be the next object in the right of the picture if the foreground were extended. And beyond that house, following the Telegraph road south, there was, at the time of the battle, a long stretch of stone-wall (see map, p. 469), little if any of which was to be seen in 1881, the stone having been used for the gatehouse of the National Cemetery.

In his official report General Kershaw, who succeeded General Cobb, thus describes the situation during the battle in that part of the road seen in the picture: "The road is about 25 feet wide, and is faced by a stone-wall about 4 feet high on the city side. The road having been cut out of the side of the hill, in many places this last wall is not visible above the surface of the ground. The ground falls off rapidly to almost a level surface, which extends about 150 yards, then, with another abrupt fall of a few feet, to another plain which extends some 200 yards, and then falls off abruptly into a wide ravine, which extends along the whole front of the city and discharges into Hazel Run. I found, on my arrival, that Cobb's brigade, Colonel McMillan commanding, occupied our entire front, and my troops could only get into position by doubling on them. This was accordingly done, and the formation along most of the line during the engagement was consequently four deep. As an evidence of the coolness of the command, I may mention here that, notwithstand-

tack was too much for it, and the counter-attack drove the Federals back to the railroad and beyond the reach of our guns on the left. Some of our troops following up this repulse got too far out, and were in turn much discomfited when left to the enemy's superior numbers, and were obliged to retire in poor condition. A Federal brigade advancing under cover of Deep Run was discovered at this time and attacked by regiments of Pender's and Law's brigades, the former of A. P. Hill's and the latter of Hood's division; and, Jackson's second line advancing, the Federals were forced to retire. This series of demonstrations and attacks, the partial success and final discomfiture of the Federals, constitute the hostile movements between the Confederate right and the Federal left.

HOUSE BY THE STONE-WALL, IN WHICH GENERAL COBB DIED. FROM A WAR-TIME PHOTOGRAPH.

I have described, in the opening of this article, the situation of the Confederate left. In front of Marye's Hill is a plateau, and immediately at the base of the hill there is a sunken road known as the Telegraph road. On the side of the road next to the town was a stone-wall, shoulder-high, against which the earth was banked, forming an almost unapproachable defense. It was impossible for

ing that their fire was the most rapid and continuous I have ever witnessed, not a man was injured by the fire of his comrades.... In the meantime line after line of the enemy deployed in the ravine, and advanced to the attack at intervals of not more than fifteen minutes until about 4:30 o'clock, when there was a lull of about a half hour, during which a mass of artillery was placed in position in front of the town and opened upon our position. At this time I brought up Colonel De Saussure's regiment. Our batteries on the hill were silent, having exhausted their ammunition, and the Washington Artillery were relieved by a part of Colonel Alexander's battalion. Under cover of this artillery fire, the most formidable column of attack was formed, which, about 5 o'clock, emerged from the ravine and, no longer impeded by our artillery, impetuously assailed our whole front. From this time until after 6 o'clock the attack was continuous, and the fire on both sides terrific. Some few, chiefly officers, got within 30 yards of our lines, but in every instance their columns were shattered by the time they got within 100 paces. The firing gradually subsided, and by 7 o'clock our pickets were established within thirty yards of those of the enemy.

"Our chief loss after getting into position in the road was from the fire of sharp-shooters, who occupied some buildings on my left flank in the early part of the engagement, and were only silenced by Captain [W.] Wallace, of the 2d Regiment, directing the continuous fire of one company upon the buildings. General Cobb, I learn, was killed by a shot from that quarter. The regiments on the hill suffered most, as they were less perfectly covered."—Editors.

COBB'S AND KERSHAW'S TROOPS BEHIND THE STONE-WALL.

the troops occupying it to expose more than a small portion of their bodies. Behind this stone-wall I had placed about twenty-five hundred men, being all of General T.R.R. Cobb's brigade, and a portion of the brigade of General Kershaw, both of McLaws's division. It must now be understood that the Federals, to reach what appeared to be my weakest point, would have to pass directly over this wall held by Cobb's infantry.

An idea of how well Marye's Hill was protected may be obtained from the following incident: General E. P. Alexander, my engineer and superintendent of artillery, had been placing the guns, and in going over the field with him before the battle, I noticed an idle cannon. I suggested that he place it so as to aid in covering the plain in front of Marye's Hill. He answered: "General, we cover that ground now so well that we will comb it as with a fine-tooth comb. A chicken could not live on that field when we open on it."

A little before noon I sent orders to all my batteries to open fire through the streets or at any points where the troops were seen about the city, as a diversion in favor of Jackson. This fire began at once to develop the work in hand for myself. The Federal troops swarmed out of the city like bees out of a hive, coming in double-quick march and filling the edge of the field in front of Cobb. This was just where we had expected attack, and I was prepared to meet it. As the troops massed before us, they were much annoyed by the fire of our batteries. The field was literally packed with Federals from the vast number of troops that had been massed in the town. From the moment of their appearance began the most fearful carnage. With our artillery from the front, right, and left tearing through their ranks, the Federals pressed forward with almost invincible determination, maintaining their steady step and closing up their broken ranks. Thus resolutely they marched upon the stone fence behind which quietly waited the Confederate brigade of General Cobb. As they came within reach of this brigade, a storm of lead was poured into their advancing ranks and they were swept from the field like chaff before the wind. A cloud of smoke shut out the scene for a moment, and, rising, revealed the shattered fragments recoiling from their gallant but hopeless charge. The artillery still plowed through their retreating ranks and searched the places of concealment into which the troops had plunged. A vast number went pell-mell into an old railroad cut to escape fire from the right and front. A battery on Lee's Hill saw this and turned its fire into the entire length of the cut, and the shells began to pour down upon the Federals with the most frightful destruction. They found their position of refuge more uncomfortable than the field of the assault.

Thus the right grand division of the Army of the Potomac found itself repulsed and shattered on its first attempt to drive us from Marye's Hill. Hardly was this attack off the field before we saw the determined Federals again filing out of Fredericksburg and preparing for another charge. The Confederates under Cobb reserved their fire and quietly awaited the approach of the enemy.

The Federals came nearer than before, but were forced to retire before the well-directed guns of Cobb's brigade and the fire of the artillery on the heights. By that time the field in front of Cobb was thickly strewn with the dead and dying Federals, but again they formed with desperate courage and renewed the attack and again were driven off. At each attack the slaughter was so great that by the time the third attack was repulsed, the ground was so thickly strewn with dead that the bodies seriously impeded the approach of the Federals. General Lee, who was with me on Lee's Hill, became uneasy when he saw the attacks so promptly renewed and pushed forward with such persistence, and feared the Federals might break through our line. After the third charge he said to me: "General, they are massing very heavily and will break your line, I am afraid." "General," I replied, "if you put every man now on the other side of the Potomac on that field to approach me over the same line, and give me plenty of ammunition, I will kill them all before they reach my line. Look to your right; you are in some danger there, but not on my line."

I think the fourth time the Federals charged, a gallant fellow came within one hundred feet of Cobb's position before he fell. Close behind him came some few scattering ones, but they were either killed or they fled from certain death.[*] This charge was the only effort that looked like actual danger to Cobb, and after it was repulsed I felt no apprehension, assuring myself that there were enough of the dead Federals on the field to give me half the battle. The anxiety shown by General Lee, however, induced me to bring up two or three brigades, to be on hand, and General Kershaw, with the remainder of his brigade, was ordered down to the stone-wall, rather, however, to carry ammunition than as a reënforcement for Cobb. Kershaw dashed down the declivity and arrived just in time to succeed Cobb, who, at this juncture, fell from a wound in the thigh and died in a few minutes from loss of blood.

A fifth time the Federals formed and charged and were repulsed. A sixth time they charged and were driven back, when night came to end the dreadful carnage, and the Federals withdrew, leaving the battle-field literally heaped with the bodies of their dead. Before the well-directed fire of Cobb's brigade, the Federals had fallen like the steady dripping of rain from the eaves of a house. Our musketry alone killed and wounded at least 5000; and these, with the slaughter by the artillery, left over 7000 killed and wounded before the foot of Marye's Hill. The dead were piled sometimes three deep, and when morning broke, the spectacle that we saw upon the battle-field was one of the most dis-

[*]In his official report General Lafayette McLaws says: "The body of one man, believed to be an officer, was found within about thirty yards of the stone-wall, and other single bodies were scattered at increased distances until the main mass of the dead lay thickly strewn over the ground at something over one hundred yards off, and extending to the ravine, commencing at the point where our men would allow the enemy's column to approach before opening fire, and beyond which no organized body of men was able to pass."—EDITORS.

tressing I ever witnessed. The charges had been desperate and bloody, but utterly hopeless. I thought, as I saw the Federals come again and again to their death, that they deserved success if courage and daring could entitle soldiers to victory.

During the night a Federal strayed beyond his lines and was taken up by some of my troops. On searching him, we found on his person a memorandum of General Burnside's arrangements, and an order for the renewal of the battle the next day. This information was sent to General Lee, and immediately orders were given for a line of rifle-pits on the top of Marye's Hill for Ransom, who had been held somewhat in reserve, and for other guns to be placed on Taylor's Hill.

We were on our lines before daylight, anxious to receive General Burnside again. As the gray of the morning came without the battle, we became more anxious; yet, as the Federal forces retained position during the 14th and 15th, we were not without hope. There was some little skirmishing, but it did not amount to anything. But when the full light of the next morning revealed an abandoned field, General Lee turned to me, referring in his mind to the dispatch I had captured and which he had just re-read, and said: "General, I am losing confidence in your friend General Burnside." We then put it down as a *ruse de guerre.* Afterward, however, we learned that the order had been made in good faith but had been changed in consequence of the demoralized condition of the grand divisions in front of Marye's Hill. During the night of the 15th the Federal troops withdrew, and on the 16th our lines were reëstablished along the river.☆

I have heard that, referring to the attack at Marye's Hill while it was in progress, General Hooker said: "There has been enough blood shed to satisfy any reasonable man, and it is time to quit." I think myself it was fortunate for Burnside that he had no greater success, for the meeting with such discomfiture gave him an opportunity to get back safe. If he had made any progress, his loss would probably have been greater.

☆General Lee explained officially, as follows, why he expected the attack would be resumed:

> "The attack on the 13th had been so easily repulsed, and by so small a part of our army, that it was not supposed the enemy would limit his efforts to an attempt which, in view of the magnitude of his preparations and the extent of his force, seemed to be comparatively insignificant.
>
> "Believing, therefore, that he would attack us, it was not deemed expedient to lose the advantages of our position and expose the troops to the fire of his inaccessible batteries beyond the river by advancing against him; but we were necessarily ignorant of the extent to which he had suffered, and only became aware of it when, on the morning of the 16th, it was discovered that he had availed himself of the darkness of night, and the prevalence of a violent storm of wind and rain, to recross the river. The town was immediately reoccupied and our position on the river-bank resumed."

—Editors.

CONFEDERATE WORKS ON WILLIS'S HILL, NOW THE SITE OF THE NATIONAL CEMETERY.
FROM A WAR-TIME PHOTOGRAPH.

Such was the battle of Fredericksburg as I saw it. It has been asked why we did not follow up the victory. The answer is plain. It goes without saying that the battle of the First Corps, concluded after nightfall, could not have been changed into offensive operations. Our line was about three miles long, extending through woodland over hill and dale. An attempt at concentration to throw the troops against the walls of the city at that hour of the night would have been little better than madness. The Confederate field was arranged for defensive battle. Its abrupt termination could not have been anticipated, nor could any skill have marshaled our troops for offensive operations in time to meet the emergency. My line was long and over broken country,—so much so that the troops could not be promptly handled in offensive operations. Jackson's corps was in mass, and could he have anticipated the result of my battle, he would have been justified in pressing Franklin to the river when the battle of the latter was lost. Otherwise, pursuit would have been as unwise as the attack he had just driven off. The Federal batteries on Stafford Heights were effectively posted to protect their troops against our advance, and Franklin would have been in good defensive position against attack on the next day. It is well known that after driving off attacking forces, if immediate pursuit can be made so that the victors can go along with the retreating forces pell-mell, it is well enough to do so; but the attack should be immediate. To follow a success by counter-attack against the enemy in position is problematical. In the case of the armies at Fredericksburg it would have been, to say the least, very hazardous to give counter-attack, the Federal position being about as strong as ours from which we had driven them back. Attempts to break up an army by following on its line of retreat are hazardous and rarely successful, while movements against the flanks and rear increase the demoralization and offer better opportunities for great results. The condition of a retreating army may be illustrated by a little incident witnessed thirty years ago on the western plains of Texas. A soldier of my regiment essayed to capture a rattlesnake. Being pursued, the reptile took refuge in a prairie-dog's hole, turning his head as he entered it, to defend the sally-port. The soldier, coming up in time, seized the tail as it was in the act of passing under cover, and at the same instant the serpent seized the index finger of the soldier's hand. The result was the soldier lost the use of his finger. The wise serpent made a successful retreat. The rear of a retreating army is always its best guarded point.

During the attack upon General Jackson, and immediately after his line was broken, General Pickett rode up to General Hood and suggested that the moment was at hand for the movement anticipated by my orders, and requested that it be executed. Hood did not agree, so the opportunity was allowed to pass. Had Hood sprung to the occasion we would have enveloped Franklin's command, and might possibly have marched it into the Confederate camp. Hood commanded splendid troops, quite fresh and eager for occasion to give renewed assurances of their mettle.

It has been reported that the troops attacking Marye's Hill were intoxicated, having been plied with whisky to nerve them to the desperate attack. That can hardly be true. I know nothing of the facts, but no sensible commander will allow his troops strong drink upon going into battle. After a battle is over, the soldier's gill is usually allowed if it is at hand. No troops could have displayed greater courage and resolution than was shown by those brought against Marye's Hill. But they miscalculated the wonderful strength of the line behind the stone fence. The position held by Cobb surpassed courage and resolution, and was occupied by those who knew well how to hold a comfortable defense.

After the retreat, General Lee went to Richmond to suggest other operations, but was assured that the war was virtually over, and that we need not harass our troops by marches and other hardships. Gold had advanced in New York to two hundred, and we were assured by those at the Confederate capital that in thirty or forty days we would be recognized and peace proclaimed. General Lee did not share in this belief.

I have been asked if Burnside could have been victorious at Fredericksburg. Such a thing was hardly possible. Perhaps no general could have accomplished more than Burnside did, and it was possible for him to have suffered greater loss. The battle of Fredericksburg was a great and unprofitable sacrifice of human life made, through the pressure from the rear, upon a general who should have known better and who doubtless acted against his judgment. If I had been in General Burnside's place, I would have asked the President to allow me to resign rather than execute his order to force the passage of the river and march the army against Lee in his stronghold.

Viewing the battle after the lapse of more than twenty years, I may say, however, that Burnside's move might have been made stronger by throwing two of his grand divisions across at the mouth of Deep Run, where Franklin crossed with his grand division and six brigades of Hooker's. Had he thus placed Hooker and Sumner, his sturdiest fighters, and made resolute assault with them in his attack on our right, he would in all probability have given us trouble. The partial success he had at that point might have been pushed vigorously by such a force and might have thrown our right entirely from position, in which event the result would have depended on the skillful handling of the forces. Franklin's grand division could have made sufficient sacrifice at Marye's Hill and come as near success as did Sumner's and two-thirds of Hooker's combined. I think, however, that the success would have been on our side, and it might have been followed by greater disaster on the side of the Federals; still they would have had the chance of success in their favor, while in the battle as it was fought it can hardly be claimed that there was even a chance.

Burnside made a mistake from the first. He should have gone from Warrenton to Chester Gap. He might then have held Jackson and fought me, or have held me and fought Jackson, thus taking us in detail. The doubt about the matter was whether or not he could have caught me in that trap before we could concentrate. At any rate, that was the only move on the board that could have benefited him at the time he was assigned to the command of the Army of the Potomac. By interposing between the corps of Lee's army he would have secured strong ground and advantage of position. With skill equal to the occasion, he should have had success. This was the move about which we felt serious apprehension, and we were occupying our minds with plans to meet it when the move toward Fredericksburg was reported. General McClellan, in his report of August 4th, 1863, speaks of this move as that upon which he was studying when the order for Burnside's assignment to command reached him.

When Burnside determined to move by Fredericksburg, he should have moved rapidly and occupied the city at once, but this would only have forced us back to the plan preferred by General Jackson.

1863

INTRODUCTION

James M. McPherson

The year 1863 opened on a profoundly pessimistic note for supporters of the Union cause. Morale in Union armies and among the Northern public was at a low point. When President Abraham Lincoln had learned of the Union defeat in the battle of Fredericksburg on December 13, 1862, he said: "If there is a worse place than Hell, I am in it." At the dawn of the new year, news of the bloody repulse of General William T. Sherman's attack on the Yazoo River bluffs just north of Vicksburg arrived in Washington. Early that New Year's morning, Lincoln met with Generals Ambrose E. Burnside and Henry W. Halleck plus Secretary of War Edwin M. Stanton to discuss what to do with Burnside's Army of the Potomac in the aftermath of Fredericksburg. Lincoln turned aside Burnside's offer to resign and also rejected his suggestion that the president should get rid of some other generals as well. Lincoln urged general in chief Halleck to return with Burnside to Fredericksburg and decide on a strategy for the next campaign. "If in such a difficulty you do not help," Lincoln wrote Halleck, "you fail me precisely in the point for which I sought your assistance.... Your military skill is useless to me, if you will not do this." When the general in chief read this letter, he promptly submitted his resignation. Lincoln apologized and refused to accept the resignation.

Depressed by his experiences that morning, the president repaired to the public rooms of the White House, where he endured the traditional New Year's Day reception. After this three-hour ordeal of handshaking, he went to his office to sign the Emancipation Proclamation. His hand was sore and shaking so badly that he had to wait for a while before he could pen a firm and unwavering signature. "I never in my life felt more certain that I was doing right than I do in signing this paper," he told the small group that had gathered to witness the occasion. "If my name ever goes into history it will be for this act, and my whole soul is in it."

Of course Lincoln's name did go into history, as much for this act as for anything else he did. But the Emancipation Proclamation would have little effect unless Union armies won the war. Prospects for that victory never appeared darker than on the first day of 1863. And things would get worse before they got better. On January 20, Burnside launched an initially promising movement against the Confederate Army of Northern Virginia at Fredericksburg, but the heavens opened and heavy rain bogged down the Army of the Potomac in what became notorious as the Mud March. Burnside had to abort the movement; morale plunged even lower; and Lincoln replaced Burnside with Joseph Hooker. The new commander reorganized the army and raised its morale, but winter turned into spring before Hooker was ready to move.

In the West, General Ulysses S. Grant renewed the campaign against Vicksburg, key to control of the entire Mississippi Valley. But during February and March, Grant's Army of the Tennessee seemed mired in the endless swamps and bayous that protected three sides of the Confederate defenses at Vicksburg. Only on the east, away from the Mississippi River, was there high ground suitable for an attack on these defenses. Grant's problem was to move his army, supplies, and transportation across the river to that high ground. As he made several apparently false starts in this effort, disease and exposure took a toll on his troops. False rumors of excessive drinking, which had dogged Grant for years, began to circulate again. But Lincoln resisted pressure to remove him from command. "What I want," the president reportedly said, "is generals who will fight battles and win victories. Grant has done this, and I propose to stick by him."

Lincoln's faith in Grant would soon pay off. But as winter turned into spring, the antiwar wing of the Democratic Party in the North (called Peace Democrats by themselves and Copperheads by the Republicans) stepped up their campaign for a cease-fire and peace negotiations. Efforts to restore the Union by war had failed, they declared, and they seemed to be gaining many adherents to that view. Peace Democrats also attacked the Emancipation Proclamation as unconstitutional, "wicked, inhuman, and unholy."

Defeatism in the North was an anguish of the spirit caused by military defeat. In contrast, Southerners were buoyed up by military success but were suffering from hyperinflation and shortages. The tightening Union naval blockade, weaknesses and imbalances in the Confederate economy, the escape of slaves to Union lines, and enemy occupation of some of the South's best agricultural areas put increasing strains on the Southern economy. Despite the conversion of hundreds of thousands of acres from cotton to food crops and forage, food was scarce in parts of the South because of the deterioration of railroads and the priority given to army shipments. A drought in the summer of 1862 had made matters worse. Even the middle class suffered, especially in Richmond, where the population had more than doubled since the start of the war. "The shadow of the gaunt form of famine is upon us," wrote a War Department clerk in Richmond in March. "I have lost twenty pounds, and my wife and children are emaciated." The rats in his kitchen were so hungry that they nibbled bread crumbs from his daughter's hand, "as tame as kittens. Perhaps we shall have to eat them!" Bread riots in Richmond and elsewhere during the spring of 1863 testified to the desperate situation, which was not alleviated until the 1863 crops began to mature in the summer.

This unrest in the South coincided with the beginning of major military campaigns on three fronts. At Charleston, South Carolina, a powerful Union naval fleet of nine new ironclads attacked the forts defending the city on April 7. They were decisively repulsed by Confederate artillery that damaged all of them and sank one. Combined operations by the Union navy and army captured some forts during the next several months, but Charleston's main defenses held and the city remained defiant. In Mississippi and Virginia, however, initial Union efforts seemed more promising. In mid-April, Grant launched a campaign that would soon put Vicksburg under siege. The Union river fleet ran downriver past the Confederate batteries at Vicksburg with minimal losses. The Northern infantry slogged down the Louisiana side of the river while Colonel Benjamin Grierson's Union cavalry brigade distracted Confederate defenders of Vicksburg with a spectacular raid through the whole state of Mississippi. In early May, as he would recall in *The Century,* Grant crossed his entire army to the east bank of the river 40 miles below Vicksburg. During the next three weeks the Federals marched 180 miles, won five battles, and penned up 32,000 Confederate troops and 3,000 civilians in Vicksburg between the Union army on land and the gunboats on the river.

Grant had cut loose from his base and from the telegraph for the initial stages of this campaign, so news of his victories was delayed. Meanwhile, after a promising start, the North received little but bad news from Virginia. At the end of April, General Hooker began his campaign against General Robert E. Lee's Army of Northern Virginia. Instead of crossing the Rappahannock River directly in the face of Confederate defenses at Fredericksburg, as Burnside had done the previous December, Hooker sent two-thirds of his troops on a rapid march upriver to cross at lightly defended fords and come at Lee from the flank and rear. This maneuver, which Darius Couch described in his contribution to the *Century* collection, put Lee's 60,000 men in a vise between 70,000 Union troops advancing toward a crossroads mansion named Chancellorsville, ten miles in Lee's rear, and 40,000 across the river in his front. Lee's only apparent choices were to retreat toward Richmond, which would expose his army to possible attacks on both flanks, or to face his troops about to meet the larger threat from Chancellorsville, which would risk an attack on his rear from the Union force that could then cross the Rappahannock at Fredericksburg.

Lee was not known as "the Gray Fox" for nothing. As he had done before, he took a bold risk and divided his army, leaving General Jubal Early with only 10,000 men to hold the trenches at Fredericksburg and taking the rest toward Chancellorsville. There, the second-growth forest of scrub oaks and pines intertwined with thick undergrowth, known as the Wilderness, would neutralize the superior numbers and artillery of the Union forces.

Confounded by Lee's moves, Hooker yielded the initiative he had so successfully seized. On May 1 he drew back into a defensive position around Chancellorsville. Lee immediately took advantage of this withdrawal. On May 2 he sent his famous corps commander Stonewall Jackson with 28,000 troops on a long march through the thick woods around Hooker's front to attack him in the flank. This dangerous maneuver worked because Hooker thought that Jackson's march was a retreat. Shortly after 5:00 P.M. on May 2 he learned otherwise. Jackson's men burst from the woods in a screaming attack on the Union right that rolled it up like a wet leaf. Riding ahead to reconnoiter in the moonlight, Jackson was shot by his own men, who mistook him and his staff for Union cavalry. James Power Smith recalled the unexpected turn of events for *The Century*. Surgeons amputated Jackson's arm. When Lee heard this news, he said that Jackson "had lost his left arm; but I have lost my right arm." Nevertheless, the Confederate attack pressed forward on May 3, and by May 6 had forced all of the Union army to retreat again to the north bank of the Rappahannock.

Although grieved by Jackson's death on May 10 from pneumonia, which he had contracted after his wounding, Confederates celebrated the victory at Chancellorsville as Lee's greatest triumph yet. When Lincoln received word of the outcome at Chancellorsville, his face turned "ashen," according to a newspaper reporter who was present. "My God, my God," the president exclaimed. "What will the country say?" It said plenty, nearly all of it bad. Copperheads stepped up their denunciations of the war as a failure. Republicans in Congress were stunned. When the influential senator Charles Sumner of Massachusetts learned the news of Chancellorsville, he lamented: "Lost, lost, all is lost."

But all was not lost. Reports of Grant's success in Mississippi soon trickled in. To relieve the pressure on Vicksburg and in Middle Tennessee as well as to follow up his victory at Chancellorsville, Lee persuaded President Jefferson Davis to authorize an invasion of the North. Another victory on the scale of Chancellorsville, they hoped, might force the Lincoln administration to sue for peace. The invasion would also allow Lee to subsist his army on the rich Pennsylvania countryside. He believed that both the Army of the Potomac and the Northern people were demoralized and ready to give up. He also considered his own army invincible. "They will go anywhere and do anything if properly led," Lee wrote in June 1863. So he led them into Pennsylvania, a move that in retrospect became known as the high tide of the Confederacy.

The Army of the Potomac was not as demoralized by its defeats as Lee believed. Nor was his own army invincible. On July 1, advance units of the two armies collided a mile west of a Pennsylvania town named Gettysburg. The unit commanders on both sides sent couriers pounding down the roads to summon reinforcements. Because Gettysburg was the hub of a dozen roads radiating to all points of the compass, the reinforcements poured in and the fighting escalated. Over the next three days the largest battle in the history of the Western Hemisphere, and one of the most important in the history of the United States, took place in and around that small town. Henry J. Hunt's vivid reports chronicled the complex battle for *Battles and Leaders of the Civil War*. Confederate attacks broke the Union lines on the first day and drove them back to a defensive position along three hills and a connecting ridge south of Gettysburg. On July 2, Confederate assaults on both flanks of this position bent but did not break the Union lines as desperate fighting in once quiet locales made such places as the Peach Orchard, Wheatfield, Devil's Den, Little Round Top, Culp's Hill, and Cemetery Hill famous down the ages.

Lee planned to give the enemy the coup de grâce on July 3. He planned a three-pronged attack: a renewal of the assault on Culp's Hill that had been stalled by a stubborn Union defense and by darkness the night before; an attack on the Union center along Cemetery Ridge spearheaded by General George Pickett's fresh division of Virginians; and a strike against the Union rear by cavalry commander Jeb Stuart, whose jaded horsemen, absent from the army for a week on a raid, were to sweep in from the east as Pickett's men were piercing the Union line from the west. All three parts of this plan failed. Northern troops punished the attackers at Culp's Hill; Union cavalry stopped Stuart's troopers three miles from the main battlefield; and the center of the Army of the Potomac held firm against Pickett's Charge and killed, wounded, or captured half of the 13,000 Confederate troops who participated in that charge.

Union general George Gordon Meade, who had replaced Hooker on June 28, fought a superb defensive battle at Gettysburg. But he did not counterattack against Lee's shattered army, which retreated on July 4 weaker by more than 25,000 men who were killed, wounded, or captured in the battle and on the retreat. The Confederates finally crossed the Potomac into Virginia on July 14. Lincoln was upset by Meade's failure to follow up his great victory with a knockout blow. "My dear general," wrote Lincoln in a letter to Meade that he decided not to send, "I do not believe you appreciate the magnitude of the misfortune involved in Lee's escape. He was within your easy grasp, and to have closed upon him would, in connection with our other late successes, have ended the war. As it is, the war will be prolonged indefinitely."

Whether Lincoln's censure of Meade (which the general never saw) was justified continues to be a matter of debate among historians—just as it was in *Battles and Leaders of the Civil War*. In any event, foremost among the "other late successes" to which the president referred was the capture of Vicksburg and the army that had held it. After a siege of almost seven weeks, the starving defenders surrendered to Grant on the Fourth of July, the same day the Army of Northern Virginia began its weary retreat from Gettysburg. On receiving word of Vicksburg's surrender, the Confederate garrison of 7,000 men at Port Hudson, which had experienced a similar siege of seven weeks, also capitulated. The Mississippi River was now under complete Union control and the Confederacy was split in twain. President Lincoln, having recovered from his disappointment, praised General Grant for his success at Vicksburg and declared, "The Father of Waters goes unvexed to the sea."

Despite the vicious antidraft riots in New York City during the third week of July, the twin victories at Gettysburg and Vicksburg caused Northern spirits to soar. "Copperheads are palsied and dumb for the moment at least," wrote a New York Republican. "Government is strengthened four-fold at home and abroad." Southern morale sank in proportion to the rise in Northern confidence. "Events have succeeded one another with disastrous rapidity," wrote Josiah Gorgas, chief of ordnance for Confederate armies. "One brief month ago we were apparently at the point of success. Lee was in Pennsylvania... Vicksburg seemed to laugh all Grant's efforts to scorn.... Now the picture is just as sober as it was bright then."

The other principal Union army, General William S. Rosecrans's Army of the Cumberland, also sprang into action at the end of June. In a brief and almost bloodless campaign, Rosecrans maneuvered General Braxton Bragg's Confederate Army of Tennessee out of its namesake state and occupied Chattanooga on September 9. But then Bragg turned on Rosecrans. Reinforced by parts of two divisions from the Army of Northern Virginia under General James Longstreet, Bragg counterattacked at Chickamauga Creek, ten miles south of Chattanooga, on September 19. In one of the hardest-fought battles of the war, whose casualties of 35,000 to both sides were second only to Gettysburg's 48,000, the Confederates scored a breakthrough on the Union right on September 20 and sent part of the Army of the Cumberland reeling back to Chattanooga. Only a determined stand by the rest of the army under General George Thomas saved Union forces from a rout. For his leadership, Thomas was known ever after as the Rock of Chickamauga.

This battle temporarily reversed the summer's momentum of Union success. Bragg laid siege to the crippled Army of the Cumberland in Chattanooga. Confederate war clerk John B. Jones wrote exultantly in his diary that "the effects of this great victory will be electrical. The whole South will be filled again with patriotic fervor, and in the North there will be a corresponding depression."

But Lincoln and Stanton moved quickly to redeem the situation. They ordered two small corps from the Army of the Potomac to Chattanooga to reinforce Union troops there, now under the command of Thomas. The president also sent Grant to Chattanooga to take command of the combined forces, which soon included four divisions from the Army of the Tennessee under Sherman.

Grant welded these troops from three armies into a unit and attacked the Confederate besiegers at Lookout Mountain and Missionary Ridge on November 24–25. In the most successful frontal assault of the war—successful beyond Grant's expectations—divisions from the Army of the Cumberland that had been humiliated at Chickamauga two months earlier now stormed up Missionary Ridge and routed the enemy. Union forces stood poised in northern Georgia as winter came on, ready to launch an offensive against Atlanta in the spring.

When he heard the news from Chattanooga, John B. Jones, recently so elated by the outcome at Chickamauga, now lamented this "incalculable disaster." Another Southern official wrote of "calamity…defeat…utter ruin." And a third wrote a discouraged diary entry: "I have never actually despaired of the cause [but now] steadfastness is yielding to a sense of hopelessness."

In Washington, by contrast, President Lincoln's annual message to Congress on December 8 noted that although the year had begun with "dark and doubtful days," now "the crisis which threatened to divide the friends of the Union is past." This optimistic statement turned out to be premature. More dark and doubtful days lay ahead before the victorious end at Appomattox. But the great battles of 1863, and particularly the Union victories at Gettysburg, Vicksburg, and Chattanooga, proved to be crucial turning points in the war. As Lincoln said in his dedicatory address at the cemetery for Union soldiers in Gettysburg on November 19, 1863, those brave men had given "the last full measure of devotion" so that "this nation, under God…shall not perish from the earth" but instead "shall have a new birth of freedom."

FIRST · SECOND · FIFTH · THIRD · CAVALRY · SIXTH · NINTH · ELEVENTH · TWELFTH

CORPS BADGES OF THE ARMY OF THE POTOMAC UNDER HOOKER.

CHAPTER 1

THE CHANCELLORSVILLE CAMPAIGN.[†]

Darius N. Couch, Major-General, U.S.V.

In the latter part of January, 1863, the Army of the Potomac under Burnside was still occupying its old camps on the left bank of the Rappahannock, opposite Fredericksburg. After the failures under Burnside it was evident that the army must have a new commander. For some days there had been a rumor that Hooker had been fixed upon for the place, and on the 26th of January it was confirmed. This appointment, undoubtedly, gave very general satisfaction to the army, except perhaps to a few, mostly superior officers, who had grown up with it, and had had abundant opportunities to study Hooker's military character; these believed that Mr. Lincoln had committed a grave error in his selection. The army, from its former reverses, had become quite disheartened and almost sulky; but the quick, vigorous measures now adopted and carried out with a firm hand had a magical effect in toning up where there had been demoralization and inspiring confidence where there had been mistrust. Few changes were made in the heads of the general staff departments, but for his chief-of-staff Hooker applied for Brigadier-General Charles P. Stone, who, through some untoward influence at Washington, was not given to him. This was a mistake of the war dignitaries, although the officer finally appointed to the office, Major-General Daniel Butterfield, proved himself very efficient. Burnside's system of dividing the army into three grand divisions was set aside, and the novelty was introduced of giving to each army corps a distinct badge, an idea which was very popular with officers and men.[⚓]

[†]Reprinted with permission from the "Philadelphia Times."—EDITORS.

[⚓]This idea originated with General Butterfield, who not only instituted the badges, but devised them in detail. As organized by Hooker the First Corps was commanded by Reynolds; the Second by Couch; the Third by Sickles; the Fifth by Meade; the Sixth by Sedgwick; the Eleventh by Howard; the Twelfth by Slocum, and the cavalry corps by Stoneman. In each corps the badge of the First Division was red; of the Second Division, white; of the Third Division, blue. After the battle of Chickamauga (Sept. 19th and

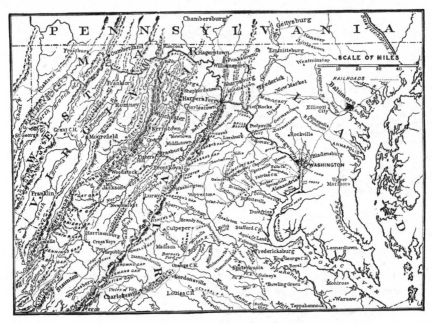

OUTLINE MAP OF THE CHANCELLORSVILLE CAMPAIGN.

Some few days after Mr. Lincoln's visit to the army in April I was again thrown with the President, and it happened in this wise. My pickets along the river were not only on speaking terms with those of the enemy on the other side of the river, but covertly carried on quite a trade in exchanging coffee for tobacco, etc. This morning it was hallooed over to our side: "You have taken Charleston," which news was sent to headquarters. Mr. Lincoln hearing of it wished me to come up and talk the matter over. I went and was ushered into a side tent, occupied only by himself and Hooker. My entrance apparently interrupted a weighty conversation, for both were looking grave. The President's manner was kindly, while the general, usually so courteous, forgot to be conventionally polite. The Charleston rumor having been briefly discussed, Mr. Lincoln remarked that it was time for him to leave. As he stepped toward the general, who had risen from his seat, as well as myself, he said: "I want to impress upon you two gentlemen in your next fight,"—and turning to me he completed the sentence,—"put in all of your men"—in the long run a good military maxim.

The weather growing favorable for military operations, on April 12th were commenced those suggestive preliminaries to all great battles, clearing out the

20th, 1863), the Eleventh and Twelfth corps were sent west, and on April 4th, 1864, they were consolidated to form the new Twentieth Corps, which retained the star of the Twelfth for a badge. The old Twentieth lost its designation Sept. 28th, 1863.—EDITORS.

hospitals, inspecting arms, looking after ammunition, shoeing animals, issuing provisions, and making every preparation necessary to an advance. The next day, the 13th, Stoneman was put in motion at the head of ten thousand finely equipped and well organized cavalry to ascend the Rappahannock and, swinging around, to attack the Confederate cavalry wherever it might be found, and "Fight! fight! fight!" At the end of two days' march Stoneman found the river so swollen by heavy rains that he was constrained to hold up, upon which Hooker suspended his advance until the 27th. This unexpected delay of the cavalry seemingly deranged Hooker's original plan of campaign. He had hoped that Stoneman would have been able to place his horsemen on the railroad between Fredericksburg and Richmond, by which Lee received his supplies, and make a wreck of the whole structure, compelling that general to evacuate his stronghold at Fredericksburg and vicinity and fall back toward Richmond.

I estimate the grand total of Hooker's seven corps at about 113,000 men ready for duty, although the data from which the conclusion is arrived at are not strictly official. This estimate does not include the cavalry corps of not less than 11,000 duty men, nor the reserve artillery, the whole number of guns in the army being 400. Lee's strength in and around Fredericksburg was placed at between 55,000 and 60,000, not including cavalry. It is not known if Hooker's information concerning the Confederate force was reliable, but Peck, operating in front of Norfolk, notified him that two of Lee's divisions under Longstreet were on the south side of the James. The hour was, therefore, auspicious for Hooker to assume the offensive, and he seized it with a boldness which argued

THE RIGHT WING OF HOOKER'S ARMY CROSSING THE RAPPAHANNOCK AT KELLY'S FORD.
FROM A WAR-TIME SKETCH.

well for his fitness to command. The aim was to transfer his army to the south side of the river, where it would have a manœuvring footing not confronted by intrenched positions. On the 27th of April the Eleventh and Twelfth corps were set in motion for Kelly's Ford, twenty-five miles up the Rappahannock, where they concentrated on the evening of the 28th, the Fifth, by reason of its shorter marching distance, moving on the 28th. The object of the expedition was unknown to the corps commanders until communicated to them after their arrival at the ford by the commanding general in person.✦ The Eleventh Corps crossed the Rappahannock, followed in the morning by the Twelfth and Fifth corps— the two former striking for Germanna Ford, a crossing of the Rapidan, the latter for Ely's Ford, lower down the same stream. Both columns, successfully effecting crossings with little opposition from the enemy's pickets, arrived that evening, April 30th, at the point of concentration, Chancellorsville. It had been a brilliantly conceived and executed movement.

In order to confound Lee, orders were issued to assemble the Sixth, Third, and First corps under Sedgwick at Franklin's Crossing and Pollock's Mill, some three miles below Fredericksburg, on the left, before daylight of the morning of the 29th, and throw two bridges across and hold them. This was done under a severe fire of sharp-shooters. The Second Corps, two divisions, marched on the 28th for Banks's Ford, four miles to the right; the other division, Gibbon's, occupying Falmouth, near the river-bank, was directed to remain in its tents, as they were in full view of the enemy, who would readily observe their withdrawal. On the 29th the two divisions of the Second Corps reached United States Ford, held by the enemy; but the advance of the right wing down the river uncovered it, whereupon a bridge of pontoons was thrown across and the corps reached Chancellorsville the same night as the Fifth, Eleventh, and Twelfth. The same day, the 30th, Sedgwick was instructed to place a corps across the river and make a demonstration upon the enemy's right, below Fredericksburg, and the Third Corps received orders to join the right wing at Chancellorsville, where the commanding general arrived the same evening, establishing his headquarters at the Chancellor House, which, with the adjacent grounds, is Chancellorsville. All of the army lying there that night were in exuberant spirits at the success of their general in getting "on the other side" without fighting for a position. As I rode into Chancellorsville that night the general hilarity pervading the camps was particularly noticeable; the soldiers, while chopping wood and lighting fires, were singing merry songs and indulging in peppery camp jokes.

✦General Hooker sent for me on the night of the 27th to ride over to his headquarters, where he explained to me, as next in rank, his plan of campaign. He informed me that, under certain contingencies, the right wing would be placed at my command. Although anticipating the narrative, I may say I think it was a signal misfortune to our arms that he did not delay joining that wing until the morning of May 1st, when he would have found Banks's Ford in our possession.—D.N.C.

The position at Chancellorsville not only took in reverse the entire system of the enemy's river defenses, but there were roads leading from it directly to his line of communication. [See map, p. 492.] But in order to gain the advantages now in the commanding general's grasp he had divided his army into two wings, and the enemy, no ordinary enemy, lay between them. The line of communication connecting the wings was by way of United States Ford and twenty miles long. It was of vital importance that the line be shortened in order to place the wings within easy support of each other. The possession of Banks's Ford, foreshadowed in the instructions given to Slocum, would accomplish all that at present could be wished.

There were three roads over which the right wing could move upon Fredericksburg: the Orange turnpike, from the west, passed through Chancellorsville, and was the most direct; the United States Ford road, crossing the former at Chancellorsville, became the Plank road, bent to the left and united with the turnpike five miles or so from Chancellorsville; the third road fell back from Chancellorsville toward the Rappahannock, passed along by Banks's Ford, six miles distant, and continued to Fredericksburg. That wing was ready for the advance at an early hour in the morning of May 1st, but somehow things dragged; the order defining the movement, instead of being issued the previous night, was not received by the corps commanders, at least by me, until hours after light. Meade was finally pushed out on the left over the Banks's Ford and turnpike roads, Slocum and Howard on the right along the Plank road, the left to be near Banks's Ford by 2 P.M., the right at the junction of its line of movement with the turnpike at 12 M. No opposition was met, excepting that the division marching over the turnpike came upon the enemy two or three miles out, when the sound of their guns was heard at Chancellorsville, and General Hooker ordered me to take Hancock's division and proceed to the support of those engaged. After marching a mile and a half or so I came upon Sykes, who commanded, engaged at the time in drawing back his advance to the position he then occupied. Shortly after Hancock's troops had got into a line in front, an order was received from the commanding general "to withdraw both divisions to Chancellorsville." Turning to the officers around me, Hancock, Sykes, Warren, and others, I told them what the order was, upon which they all agreed with me that the ground should not be abandoned, because of the open country in front and the commanding position. An aide, Major J. B. Burt, dispatched to General Hooker to this effect, came back in half an hour with positive orders to return. Nothing was to be done but carry out the command, though Warren suggested that I should disobey, and then he rode back to see the general. In the meantime Slocum, on the Plank road to my right, had been ordered in, and the enemy's advance was between that road and my right flank. Sykes was first to move back, then followed by Hancock's regiments over the same road. When all but two of the latter had withdrawn, a third order came to me, brought by one

FROM A PHOTOGRAPH.

J. Hooker

of the general's staff: "Hold on until 5 o'clock." It was then perhaps 2 P.M. Disgusted at the general's vacillation and vexed at receiving an order of such tenor, I replied with warmth unbecoming in a subordinate: "Tell General Hooker he is too late, the enemy are already on my right and rear. I am in full retreat."

The position thus abandoned was high ground, more or less open in front, over which an army might move and artillery be used advantageously; moreover, were it left in the hands of an enemy, his batteries, established on its crest and slopes, would command the position at Chancellorsville. Everything on the whole front was ordered in. General Hooker knew that Lee was apprised of his presence on the south side of the river, and must have expected that his enemy would be at least on the lookout for an advance upon Fredericksburg. But it was of the utmost importance that Banks's Ford should fall into our hands, therefore the enemy ought to have been pressed until their strength or weakness was developed; it would then have been time enough to run away.

Mott's Run, with a considerable brushy ravine, cuts the turnpike three-fourths of a mile east of Chancellorsville. Two of Hancock's regiments, under Colonel Nelson A. Miles, subsequently the Indian fighter, were directed to occupy the ravine. Continuing my way through the woods toward Chancellorsville, I came upon some of the Fifth Corps under arms. Inquiring for their commanding officer, I told him that in fifteen minutes he would be attacked. Before finishing the sentence a volley of musketry was fired into us from the direction of the Plank road. This was the beginning of the battle of Chancellorsville. Troops were hurried into position, but the observer required no wizard to tell him, as they marched past, that the high expectations which had animated them only a few hours ago had given place to disappointment. Proceeding to the Chancellor House, I narrated my operations in front to Hooker, which were seemingly satisfactory, as he said: "It is all right, Couch, I have got Lee just where I want him; he must fight me on my own ground." The retrograde movement had prepared me for something of the kind, but to hear from his own lips that the advantages gained by the successful marches of his lieutenants were to culminate in fighting a defensive battle in that nest of thickets was too much, and I retired from his presence with the belief that my commanding general was a whipped man. The army was directed to intrench itself. At 2 A.M. the corps commanders reported to General Hooker that their positions could be held; at least so said Couch, Slocum, and Howard.

Until after dark on May 1st the enemy confined his demonstrations to finding out the position of our left with his skirmishers. Then he got some guns upon the high ground which we had abandoned as before mentioned, and cannonaded the left of our line. There were not many casualties, but that day a shell severely wounded the adjutant-general of the Second Corps, now General F. A. Walker. Chancellorsville was a strategic point to an offensive or retreating army, as roads diverged from it into every part of Virginia; but for a defensive position it was bad, particularly for such an army as Hooker had under him, which prided itself upon its artillery, which was perhaps equal to any in the world. There were no commanding positions for artillery, and but little open country to operate over; in fact, the advantages of ground for this arm were mainly with the attacking party.

During the 29th and 30th the enemy lay at Fredericksburg observing Sedg-wick's demonstrations on the left, entirely unconscious of Hooker's successful crossing of the right wing, until midday of the latter date, but that night Lee formed his plan of operations for checking the farther advance of the force which had not only turned the left flank of his river defenses but was threaten-ing his line of communication with Richmond as well as the rear of his center at Fredericksburg. Stonewall Jackson, who was watching Sedgwick, received in-structions to withdraw his corps, march to the left, across the front of Hooker's intrenched position, until its right flank was attained, and assault with his col-umn of 22,000 men, while his commanding general would, with what force he could spare, guard the approaches to Fredericksburg.

On the morning of May 2d our line had become strong enough to resist a front attack unless made in great force; the enemy had also been hard at work on his front, particularly that section of it between the Plank road and turnpike. Sedgwick, the previous night, had been ordered to send the First Corps (Reynolds's) to Chancellorsville. At 7 A.M. a sharp cannonade was opened on our left, followed by infantry demonstrations of no particular earnestness. Two hours later the enemy were observed moving a mile or so to the south and front of the center, and later the same column was reported to the commander of the Eleventh Corps by General Devens, whose division was on the extreme right flank. At 9:30 A.M. a circular directed to Generals Slocum and Howard called at-tention to this movement and to the weakness of their flanks.

At 11 A.M. our left was furiously cannonaded by their artillery, established on the heights in front of Mott's Run, followed by sharp infantry firing on the fronts of the Second and Twelfth corps. As time flew along and no attack came from the enemy seen moving in front, Hooker conceived that Lee was retreat-ing toward Gordonsville. There was color for this view, as the main road from Fredericksburg to that point diverged from the Plank road two miles to the left of Chancellorsville, and passed along his front at about the same distance. Hooker therefore jumped at the conclusion that the enemy's army was moving into the center of Virginia. But instead of the hostile column being on the Gor-donsville road in retreat, it was Stonewall's corps moving on an interior neigh-borhood road, about one mile distant, and in search of our right flank and rear. At 2 P.M. I went into the Chancellor House, when General Hooker greeted me with the exclamation: "Lee is in full retreat toward Gordonsville, and I have sent out Sickles to capture his artillery." I thought, without speaking it: "If your conception is correct, it is very strange that only the Third Corps should be sent in pursuit." Sickles received orders at 1 P.M. to take two divisions, move to his front and attack, which he did, capturing some hundreds of prisoners. The country on the front being mostly wooded enabled the enemy to conceal his movements and at the same time hold Sickles in check with a rear-guard, which made such a show of strength that reënforcements were called for and furnished. In the meantime Jackson did not for a moment swerve from his purpose, but steadily moved forward to accomplish what he had undertaken.

It was about 5:30 in the evening when the head of Jackson's column found itself on the right and rear of the army, which on that flank consisted of the Eleventh Corps, the extreme right brigade receiving its first intimation of danger from a volley of musketry fired into their rear, followed up so impetuously that no efficient stand could be made by the brigades of the corps that successively attempted to resist the enemy's charge. When General Hooker found out what that terrific roar on his right flank meant he quickly mounted and flew across the open space to meet the onset, passing on his way stampeded pack-mules, officers' horses, caissons, with men and horses running for their lives. Gathering up such troops as were nearest to the scene of action, Berry's division from the Third Corps, some from the Twelfth, Hays's brigade of the Second, and a portion of the Eleventh, an effectual stand was made. Pleasonton, who was returning from the front, where he had been operating with Sickles (at the time Jackson attacked), taking in the state of things, rapidly moved his two regiments of cavalry and a battery to the head and right flank of the enemy's advance columns, when, making a charge and bringing up his own guns, with others of the Eleventh and Third Corps, he was enabled to punish them severely.

Pickets had been thrown out on Howard's flank, but not well to the right and rear. I suspect that the prime reason for the surprise was that the superior officers of the right corps had been put off their guard by adopting the conjecture of Hooker, "Lee's army is in full retreat to Gordonsville," as well as by expecting the enemy to attack precisely where ample preparations had been made to receive him. It can be emphatically stated that no corps in the army, surprised as the Eleventh was at this time, could have held its ground under similar circumstances.

At half-past two that afternoon the Second Corps' lines were assaulted by artillery and infantry. Just previous to Jackson's attack on the right a desperate effort was made by Lee's people to carry the left at Mott's Run, but the men who held it were there to stay. Hooker, desiring to know the enemy's strength in front of the Twelfth Corps, advanced Slocum into the thicket, but that officer found the hostile line too well defended for him to penetrate it and was forced to recall the attacking party. When night put an end to the fighting of both combatants, Hooker was obliged to form a new line for his right flank perpendicular to the old one and barely half a mile to the right of Chancellorsville. Sickles was retired, with the two columns, from his advanced position in the afternoon to near where Pleasonton had had his encounter, before mentioned, some distance to the left of the new line of our right flank and close up to the enemy. The situation was thought to be a very critical one by General Hooker, who had simply a strong body in front of the enemy, but without supports, at least near enough to be used for that purpose. At the same time it was a menace

STAMPEDE OF THE ELEVENTH CORPS ON THE PLANK ROAD.

to Jackson's right wing or flank. Before midnight some of the latter's enterprising men pushed forward and actually cut off Sickles's line of communication.
When this news was carried to Hooker it caused him great alarm, and preparations were at once made to withdraw the whole front, leaving General Sickles
to his fate; but that officer showed himself able to take care of his rear, for he ordered after a little while a column of attack, and communication was restored
at the point of the bayonet.

The situation of Jackson's corps on the morning of May 3d was a desperate
one, its front and right flank being in the presence of not far from 25,000 men,
with the left flank subject to an assault of 30,000, the corps of Meade and
Reynolds, by advancing them to the right, where the thicket did not present an
insurmountable obstacle. It only required that Hooker should brace himself up
to take a reasonable, common-sense view of the state of things, when the success gained by Jackson would have been turned into an overwhelming defeat.
But Hooker became very despondent. I think that his being outgeneraled by
Lee had a good deal to do with his depression. After the right flank had been established on the morning of the 3d by Sickles getting back into position our line
was more compact, with favorable positions for artillery, and the reserves were
well in hand. Meade had been drawn in from the left and Reynolds had arrived
with the First Corps. The engineers had been directed on the previous night to
lay out a new line, its front a half mile in rear of Chancellorsville, with the
flanks thrown back,—the right to the Rapidan, a little above its junction with

the Rappahannock, the left resting on the latter river. The Eleventh Corps, or at least that portion which formed line of battle, was withdrawn from the front and sent to the rear to reorganize and get its scattered parts together, leaving the following troops in front: one division of the Second Corps on the left from Mott's Run to Chancellorsville, the Twelfth Corps holding the center and right flank, aided by the Third Corps and one division of the Second Corps (French's), on the same flank; the whole number in front, according to my estimate, being 37,000 men. The First and Fifth corps in reserve numbered 30,000, and, placing the number of reliable men in the Eleventh Corps at 5000, it will be seen that the reserves nearly equaled those in line of battle in front.

After the day's mishaps Hooker judged that the enemy could not have spared so large a force to move around his front without depleting the defenses of Fredericksburg. Accordingly, at 9 P.M., an imperative order was sent to the commander of the left wing to cross the river at Fredericksburg, march upon Chancellorsville, and be in the vicinity of the commanding general at daylight. But Sedgwick was already across the river and three miles below Fredericksburg. It was 11 P.M., May 2d, when he got the order, and twelve or fourteen miles had to be marched over by daylight. The night was moonlit, but any officer who has had experience in making night marches with infantry will understand the vexatious delays occurring even when the road is clear; but when, in addition, there is an enemy in front, with a line of fortified heights to assault, the problem which Sedgwick had to solve will be pronounced impossible of solution. However, that officer set his column in motion by flank, leaving one division that lay opposite the enemy, who were in force to his left. The marching column, being continually harassed by skirmishers, did not arrive at Fredericksburg until daylight. The first assault upon the heights behind the town failed. Attempts to carry them by flank movements met with no success. Finally a second storming party was organized, and the series of works were taken literally at the point of the bayonet, though at heavy loss. It was then 11 A.M. The column immediately started for Chancellorsville, being more or less obstructed by the enemy until its arrival near Salem Heights, 5 or 6 miles out, where seven brigades under Early, six of which had been driven from the defenses of Fredericksburg, made a stand in conjunction with supports sent from Lee's army before Chancellorsville. This was about the middle of the afternoon, when Sedgwick in force attacked the enemy. Though at first successful, he was subsequently compelled to withdraw those in advance and look to his own safety by throwing his own flanks so as to cover Banks's Ford, the friendly proximity of which eventually saved this wing from utter annihilation.

At about 5 A.M., May 3d, fighting was begun at Chancellorsville, when the Third (Sickles's) Corps began to retire to the left of our proper right flank, and all of that flank soon became fiercely engaged, while the battle ran along the whole line. The enemy's guns on the heights to our left, as well as at every point

STAYING JACKSON'S ADVANCE, SATURDAY EVENING, MAY 2, WITH ARTILLERY PLACED
ACROSS THE PLANK ROAD. FROM A WAR-TIME SKETCH.

on the line where they could be established, were vigorously used, while a full
division threw itself on Miles at Mott's Run. On the right flank our guns were
well handled, those of the Twelfth Corps being conspicuous, and the opposing
lines of infantry operating in the thicket had almost hand-to-hand conflicts,
capturing and recapturing prisoners. The enemy appeared to know what he
was about, for pressing the Third Corps vigorously he forced it back, when he
joined or rather touched the left of Lee's main body, making their line continuous from left to right. Another advantage gained by this success was the possession of an open field, from which guns covered the ground up to the Chancellor
House. Upon the south porch of that mansion General Hooker stood leaning
against one of its pillars, observing the fighting, looking anxious and much
careworn. After the fighting had commenced I doubt if any orders were given
by him to the commanders on the field, unless, perhaps, "to retire when out of
ammunition." None were received by me, nor were there any inquiries as to
how the battle was going along my front. On the right flank, where the fighting
was desperate, the engaged troops were governed by the corps and division
leaders. If the ear of the commanding general was, as he afterward stated,
strained to catch the sound of Sedgwick's guns, it could not have heard them in
the continuous uproar that filled the air around him; but as Sedgwick, who was
known as a fighting officer, had not appeared at the time set—daylight—nor for
some hours after, it was conclusive evidence that he had met with strong opposition, showing that all of Lee's army was not at Chancellorsville, so that the
moment was favorable for Hooker to try his opponent's strength with every
available man. Moreover, the left wing might at that very time be in jeopardy,

therefore he was bound by every patriotic motive to strike hard for its relief. If he had remembered Mr. Lincoln's injunction ("Gentlemen, in your next fight put in all of your men"), the face of the day would have been changed and the field won for the Union arms.

Not far from 8:30 A.M. the headquarters pennants of the Third and Twelfth corps suddenly appeared from the right in the open field of Chancellorsville; then the Third began to fall back, it was reported, for want of ammunition, followed by that portion of the Twelfth fighting on the same flank, and the division of the Second Corps on its right. It is not known whether any efforts were made to supply the much-needed ammunition to the Third as well as the Twelfth Corps, whose ammunition was nearly used up when it retired. My impression is that the heads of the ordnance, as well as of other important departments, were not taken into the field during this campaign, which was most unfortunate, as the commanding general had enough on his mind without charging it with details.

The open field seized by Jackson's old corps after the Third Corps drew off was shortly dotted with guns that made splendid practice through an opening in the wood upon the Chancellor House, and everything else, for that matter, in that neighborhood. Hooker was still at his place on the porch, with nothing between him and Lee's army but Geary's division of the Twelfth and Hancock's division and a battery of the Second Corps. But Geary's right was now turned, and that flank was steadily being pressed back along his intrenched line to the

THE 29TH PENNSYLVANIA (OF KANE'S BRIGADE, GEARY'S DIVISION, TWELFTH CORPS) IN THE TRENCHES UNDER ARTILLERY FIRE, MAY 3.

junction of the Plank road and the turnpike, when a cannon-shot struck the pillar against which Hooker was leaning and knocked him down. A report flew around that he was killed. I was at the time but a few yards to his left, and, dismounting, ran to the porch. The shattered pillar was there, but I could not find him or any one else. Hurrying through the house, finding no one, my search was continued through the back yard. All the time I was thinking, "If he is killed, what shall I do with this disjointed army?" Passing through the yard I came upon him, to my great joy, mounted, and with his staff also in their saddles. Briefly congratulating him on his escape—it was no time to blubber or use soft expressions—I went about my own business. This was the last I saw of my commanding general in front. The time, I reckon, was from 9:15 to 9:30 A.M., I think nearer the former than the latter. He probably left the field soon after his hurt, but he neither notified me of his going nor did he give any orders to me whatever. Having some little time before this seen that the last stand would be about the Chancellor House, I had sent to the rear for some of the Second Corps batteries, which had been ordered there by the commanding general, but word came back that they were so jammed in with other carriages that it was impossible to extricate them. General Meade, hearing of my wants, kindly sent forward the 5th Maine battery belonging to his corps. It was posted in rear of the Chancellor House, where the United States Ford road enters the thicket. With such precision did the artillery of Jackson's old corps play upon this battery that all of the officers and most of the non-commissioned officers and men were killed or wounded. The gallant Kirby, whose guns could not be brought up, was mortally wounded in the same battery ∕ of which I had for the time placed him in command, and my horse was killed under me while I was trying to get some men to train a gun on the flank of the force then pushing Geary's division. The enemy, having 30 pieces in position on our right, now advanced some of his guns to within 500 or 600 yards of the Chancellor House, where there were only four of Pettit's Second Corps guns to oppose them, making a target of that building and taking the right of Hancock's division in reverse, a portion of which had been withdrawn from its intrenchments and thrown back to the left to meet the enemy should he succeed in forcing Mott's Run. This flank was stoutly held by Colonel Miles, who, by the bye, had been carried off the field, shot through the body. Lee by this time knew well enough, if he had not known before, that the game was sure to fall into his hands, and accordingly plied every gun and rifle that could be brought to bear on us. Still everything was firmly held excepting Geary's right, which was slowly falling to pieces, for the enemy

∕The 5th Maine battery, Capt. G. F. Leppien, belonged to the First Corps. Captain Leppien and Lieutenants G. T. Stevens and A. B. Twitchell were wounded, Capt. Leppien mortally. Lieut. E. Kirby was the proper commander of Battery I, 1st U.S. Artillery, Second Corps. The 5th Maine lost 6 men killed and 19 wounded; 43 horses were disabled, and the guns were hauled off by hand.—EDITORS.

had his flank and there was no help for it. Riding to Geary's left, I found him there dismounted, with sword swinging over his head, walking up and down, exposed to a severe infantry fire, when he said: "My division can't hold its place; what shall I do?" To which I replied: "I don't know, but do as we are doing; fight it out."

It was not then too late to save the day. Fifty pieces of artillery, or even forty, brought up and run in front and to the right of the Chancellor House, would have driven the enemy out of the thicket, then forcing back Geary's right, and would have neutralized the thirty guns to the right which were pounding us so hard. But it is a waste of words to write what might have been done. Hooker had made up his mind to abandon the field, otherwise he would not have allowed the Third and part of the Twelfth Corps to leave their ground for want of ammunition. A few minutes after my interview with Geary a staff-officer from General Hooker rode up and requested my presence with that general. Turning to General Hancock, near by, I told him to take care of things and rode to the rear. The Chancellor House was then burning, having been fired in several places by the enemy's shells.

At the farther side of an open field, half a mile in the rear of Chancellorsville, I came upon a few tents (three or four) pitched, around which, mostly dismounted, were a large number of staff-officers. General Meade was also present, and perhaps other generals. General Hooker was lying down I think in

SECOND LINE OF UNION DEFENSE AT THE JUNCTION OF THE ROADS TO ELY'S
AND UNITED STATES FORDS. FROM A WAR-TIME SKETCH.

a soldier's tent by himself. Raising himself a little as I entered, he said: "Couch, I turn the command of the army over to you. You will withdraw it and place it in the position designated on this map," as he pointed to a line traced on a field-sketch. This was perhaps three-quarters of an hour after his hurt. He seemed rather dull, but possessed of his mental faculties. I do not think that one of those officers outside of the tent knew what orders I was to receive, for on stepping out, which I did immediately on getting my instructions, I met Meade close by, looking inquiringly as if he expected that finally he would receive the order for which he had waited all that long morning, "to go in." Colonel N. H. Davis broke out: "We shall have some fighting now." These incidents are mentioned to show the temper of that knot of officers. No time was to be lost, as only Hancock's division now held Lee's army. Dispatching Major John B. Burt with orders for the front to retire, I rode back to the thicket, accompanied by Meade, and was soon joined by Sickles, and after a little while by Hooker, but he did not interfere with my dispositions. Hancock had a close shave to withdraw in safety, his line being three-fourths of a mile long, with an exultant enemy as close in as they dared, or wished, or chose to be, firing and watching. But everything was brought off, except five hundred men of the Second Corps who, through the negligence of a lieutenant charged by Hancock with the responsibility of re-tiring the force at Mott's Run, were taken prisoners. However, under the cir-cumstances, the division was retired in better shape than one could have anticipated. General Sickles assisted in getting men to draw off the guns of the Maine battery before spoken of. General Meade wished me to hold the strip of thicket in rear of Chancellorsville, some six hundred yards in front of our new line of defense. My reply was: "I shall not leave men in this thicket to be shelled out by Lee's artillery. Its possession won't give us any strength. Yonder [point-ing to the rear] is the line where the fighting is to be done." Hooker heard the conversation, but made no remarks. Considerable bodies of troops of different corps that lay in the brush to the right were brought within the lines, and the battle of Chancellorsville was ended. My pocket diary, May 3d, has the follow-ing: "Sickles opened at about 5 A.M. Orders sent by me at 10 for the front to re-tire; at 12 M. in my new position"; the latter sentence meaning that at that hour my corps was in position on the new or second line of defense.

As to the charge that the battle was lost because the general was intoxi-cated, I have always stated that he probably abstained from the use of ardent spirits when it would have been far better for him to have continued in his usual habit in that respect. The shock from being violently thrown to the ground, to-gether with the physical exhaustion resulting from loss of sleep and the anxiety of mind incident to the last six days of the campaign, would tell on any man. The enemy did not press us on the second line, Lee simply varying the monot-ony of watching us by an occasional cannonade from the left, a part of his army having been sent to Salem Church to resist Sedgwick. Sedgwick had difficulty in maintaining his ground, but held his own by hard fighting until after midnight, May 4th–5th, when he recrossed at Banks's Ford.

Some of the most anomalous occurrences of the war took place in this campaign. On the night of May 2d the commanding general, with 80,000 men in his wing of the army, directed Sedgwick, with 22,000, to march to his relief. While that officer was doing this on the 3d, and when it would be expected that every effort would be made by the right wing to do its part, only one-half of it was fought (or rather half-fought, for its ammunition was not replenished), and then the whole wing was withdrawn to a place where it could not be hurt, leaving Sedgwick to take care of himself.

At 12 o'clock on the night of the 4th–5th General Hooker assembled his corps commanders in council. Meade, Sickles, Howard, Reynolds, and myself were present; General Slocum, on account of the long distance from his post, did not arrive until after the meeting was broken up. Hooker stated that his instructions compelled him to cover Washington, not to jeopardize the army, etc. It was seen by the most casual observer that he had made up his mind to retreat. We were left by ourselves to consult, upon which Sickles made an elaborate argument, sustaining the views of the commanding general. Meade was in favor of fighting, stating that he doubted if we could get off our guns. Howard was in favor of fighting, qualifying his views by the remark that our present situation was due to the bad conduct of his corps, or words to that effect. Reynolds, who was lying on the ground very much fatigued, was in favor of an advance. I had similar views to those of Meade as to getting off the guns, but said I "would favor an advance if I could designate the point of attack." Upon collecting the suffrages, Meade, Reynolds, and Howard voted squarely for an advance, Sickles and myself squarely no; upon which Hooker informed the council that he should take upon himself the responsibility of retiring the army to the other side of the river. As I stepped out of the tent Reynolds, just behind me, broke out, "What was the use of calling us together at this time of night when he intended to retreat anyhow?"

On the morning of May 5th, corps commanders were ordered to cut roads, where it was necessary, leading from their positions to the United States Ford. During the afternoon there was a very heavy rainfall. In the meantime Hooker had in person crossed the river, but, as he gave orders for the various corps to march at such and such times during the night, I am not aware that any of his corps generals knew of his departure. Near midnight I got a note from Meade informing me that General Hooker was on the other side of the river, which had risen over the bridges, and that communication was cut off from him. I immediately rode over to Hooker's headquarters and found that I was in command of the army, if it had any commander. General Hunt, of the artillery, had brought the information as to the condition of the bridges, and from the reports there seemed to be danger of losing them entirely. After a short conference with

Meade I told him that the recrossing would be suspended, and that "we would stay where we were and fight it out," returning to my tent with the intention of enjoying what I had not had since the night of the 30th ultimo—a good sleep; but at 2 A.M., communication having been reëstablished, I received a sharp message from Hooker, to order the recrossing of the army as he had directed, and everything was safely transferred to the north bank of the Rappahannock.

In looking for the causes of the loss of Chancellorsville, the primary ones were that Hooker expected Lee to fall back without risking battle. Finding himself mistaken he assumed the defensive, and was outgeneraled and became demoralized by the superior tactical boldness of the enemy.

CHAPTER 2

STONEWALL JACKSON'S LAST BATTLE.

*The Rev. James Power Smith, Captain and Assistant
Adjutant-General, C.S.A.*

At daybreak on the morning of the 29th of April, 1863, sleeping in our tents at corps headquarters, near Hamilton's Crossing, we were aroused by Major Samuel Hale, of Early's staff, with the stirring news that Federal troops were crossing the Rappahannock on pontoons under cover of a heavy fog. General Jackson had spent the night at Mr. Yerby's hospitable mansion near by, where Mrs. Jackson [his second wife] had brought her infant child for the father to see. He was at once informed of the news, and promptly issued to his division commanders orders to prepare for action.

At his direction I rode a mile across the fields to army headquarters, and finding General Robert E. Lee still slumbering quietly, at the suggestion of Colonel Venable, whom I found stirring, I entered the general's tent and awoke him. Turning his feet out of his cot he sat upon its side as I gave him the tidings from the front. Expressing no surprise, he playfully said: "Well, I thought I heard firing, and was beginning to think it was time some of you young fellows were coming to tell me what it was all about. Tell your good general that I am sure he knows what to do. I will meet him at the front very soon."

It was Sedgwick who had crossed, and, marching along the river front to

STONEWALL JACKSON'S CAP.

Major Jed. Hotchkiss, who owns the "old gray cap," writes that Jackson wore it through the Valley, Seven Days, and Second Manassas campaigns. At Frederick City, in the Antietam campaign, he bought a soft hat for his general, who, at Fredericksburg, gave him the cap as a souvenir.—EDITORS.

LEE AND JACKSON IN COUNCIL ON THE NIGHT OF MAY 1.

impress us with his numbers, was now intrenching his line on the river road, under cover of Federal batteries on the north bank.

All day long we lay in the old lines of the action of December preceding, watching the operation of the enemy. Nor did we move through the next day, the 30th of April. During the forenoon of the 29th General Lee had been informed by General J.E.B. Stuart of the movement in force by General Hooker across the Rappahannock upon Chancellorsville; and during the night of Thursday, April 30th, General Jackson withdrew his corps, leaving Early and his division with Barksdale's brigade to hold the old lines from Hamilton's Crossing along the rear of Fredericksburg.

By the light of a brilliant moon, at midnight, that passed into an early dawn of dense mist, the troops were moved, by the Old Mine road, out of sight of the enemy, and about 11 A.M. of Friday, May 1st, they reached Anderson's position, confronting Hooker's advance from Chancellorsville, near the Tabernacle Church on the Plank road. To meet the whole Army of the Potomac, under Hooker, General Lee had of all arms about 60,000 men. General Longstreet, with part of his corps, was absent below Petersburg. General Lee had two divisions of Longstreet's corps, Anderson's and McLaws's, and Jackson's corps, consisting of four divisions, A. P. Hill's, D. H. Hill's, commanded by Rodes, Trimble's, commanded by Colston, and Early's; and about 170 pieces of field-artillery. The divisions of Anderson and McLaws had been sent from Fredericksburg to meet Hooker's advance from Chancellorsville; Anderson on Wednesday, and McLaws (except Barksdale's brigade, left with Early) on Thursday. At the Tabernacle Church, about four miles east of Chancellorsville, the opposing forces met and brisk skirmishing began. On Friday, Jackson, reaching Anderson's position, took command of the Confederate advance, and urged on his skirmish line under Brigadier-General Ramseur with great vigor. How the muskets rattled along a front of a mile or two, across the unfenced fields, and through the woodlands! What spirit was imparted to the line, and what cheers rolled along its length, when Jackson, and then Lee himself, appeared riding abreast of the line along the Plank road! Slowly but steadily the line advanced, until at night-fall all Federal pickets and skirmishers were driven back upon the body of Hooker's force at Chancellorsville.

Here we reached a point, a mile and a half from Hooker's lines, where a road turns down to the left toward the old Catherine Furnace; and here at the fork of the roads General Lee and General Jackson spent the night, resting on the pine straw, curtained only by the close shadow of the pine forest. A little after night-fall I was sent by General Lee upon an errand to General A. P. Hill, on the old stone turnpike a mile or two north; and returning some time later with information of matters on our right, I found General Jackson retired to rest, and General Lee sleeping at the foot of a tree, covered with his army cloak. As I aroused the sleeper, he slowly sat up on the ground and said, "Ah, Captain, you have returned, have you? Come here and tell me what you have learned on the right." Laying his hand on me he drew me down by his side, and, passing his arm around my shoulder, drew me near to him in a fatherly way that told of his warm and kindly heart. When I had related such information as I had secured for him, he thanked me for accomplishing his commission, and then said he regretted that the young men about General Jackson had not relieved him of annoyance, by finding a battery of the enemy which had harassed our advance, adding that the young men of that day were not equal to what they were when he was a young man. Seeing immediately that he was jesting and disposed to rally me, as he often did young officers, I broke away from the hold on me which he tried to retain, and, as he laughed heartily through the stillness of the night, I went off to make a bed of my saddle-blanket, and, with my head in my saddle, near my horse's feet, was soon wrapped in the heavy slumber of a wearied soldier.

Some time after midnight I was awakened by the chill of the early morning hours, and, turning over, caught a glimpse of a little flame on the slope above me, and sitting up to see what it meant, I saw, bending over a scant fire of twigs, two men seated on old cracker boxes and warming their hands over the little fire. I had but to rub my eyes and collect my wits to recognize the figures of Robert E. Lee and Stonewall Jackson. Who can tell the story of that quiet coun-

Near 3 P.m.
May 2, 1863

General,

The enemy has made a stand at Chancellor's which is about 2 miles from Chancellorsville. I hope as soon as practicable to attack.

I trust that an Ever Kind Providence will bless us with great success.

Respectfully

T. J. Jackson
Lt. Genl.

Genl. R. E. Lee

The leading division is up & the next two appear to be well closed.

T. J. J.

cil of war between two sleeping armies? Nothing remains on record to tell of plans discussed, and dangers weighed, and a great purpose formed, but the story of the great day so soon to follow.

It was broad daylight, and the thick beams of yellow sunlight came through the pine branches, when some one touched me rudely with his foot, saying: "Get up, Smith, the general wants you!" As I leaped to my feet the rhythmic click of the canteens of marching infantry caught my ear. Already in motion! What could it mean? In a moment I was mounted and at the side of the general, who sat on his horse by the roadside, as the long line of our troops cheerily, but in silence as directed, poured down the Furnace road. His cap was pulled low over his eyes, and, looking up from under the visor, with lips compressed, indicating the firm purpose within, he nodded to me, and in brief and rapid utterance, without a superfluous word, as though all were distinctly formed in his mind and beyond question, he gave me orders for our wagon and ambulance trains. From the open fields in our rear, at the head of the Catharpin road, all trains were to be moved upon that road to Todd's Tavern, and thence west by interior roads, so that our troops would be between them and the enemy at Chancellorsville. My orders having been delivered and the trains set in motion, I returned to the site of our night's bivouac, to find that General Jackson and his staff had followed the marching column.

Slow and tedious is the advance of a mounted officer who has to pass, in narrow wood roads through dense thickets, the packed column of marching infantry, to be recognized all along the line and good-naturedly chaffed by many a gay-spirited fellow: "Say, here's one of Old Jack's little boys, let him by, boys!" in the most patronizing tone. "Have a good breakfast this morning, sonny?" "Better hurry up, or you'll catch it for getting behind." "Tell Old Jack we're all a-comin'." "Don't let him begin the fuss till we get thar!" And so on, until about 3 P.M., after a ride of ten miles of tortuous road, I found the general, seated on a stump by the Brock road, writing this dispatch, which, through the courtesy of the Virginia State Library, is here given in fac-simile. [See p. 512.]

The place here mentioned as Chancellor's was also known as Dowdall's Tavern. It was the farm of the Rev. Melzi Chancellor, two miles west

LIEUTENANT-GENERAL THOMAS JONATHAN JACKSON, C.S.A. FROM A PHOTOGRAPH TAKEN IN WINCHESTER, VA., IN 1862.

of Chancellorsville, and the Federal force found here and at Talley's, a mile farther west, was the Eleventh Corps, under General Howard. General Fitz Lee, with cavalry scouts, had advanced until he had view of the position of Howard's corps, and found them unsuspicious of attack.

Reaching the Orange Plank road, General Jackson himself rode with Fitz Lee to reconnoiter the position of Howard, and then sent the Stonewall brigade of Virginia troops, under Brigadier-General Paxton, to hold the point where the Germanna Plank road obliquely enters the Orange road. Leading the main column of his force farther on the Brock road to the old turnpike, the head of the column turned sharply eastward toward Chancellorsville. About a mile had been passed, when he halted and began the disposition of his forces to attack Howard. Rodes's division, at the head of the column, was thrown into line of battle, with Colston's forming the second line and A. P. Hill's the third, while the artillery under Colonel Stapleton Crutchfield moved in column on the road, or was parked in a field on the right. The well-trained skirmishers of Rodes's division, under Major Eugene Blackford, were thrown to the front. It must have been between 5 and 6 o'clock in the evening, Saturday, May 2d, when these dispositions were completed. Upon his stout-built, long-paced little sorrel, General Jackson sat, with visor low over his eyes and lips compressed, and with his watch in his hand. Upon his right sat General Robert E. Rodes, the very picture of a soldier, and every inch all that he appeared. Upon the right of Rodes sat Major Blackford.

"Are you ready, General Rodes?" said Jackson.

"Yes, sir!" said Rodes, impatient for the advance.

"You can go forward then," said Jackson.

A nod from Rodes was order enough for Blackford, and then suddenly the woods rang with the bugle call, and back came the responses from bugles on the right and left, and the long line of skirmishers, through the wild thicket of undergrowth, sprang eagerly to their work, followed promptly by the quick steps of the line of battle. For a moment all the troops seemed buried in the depths of the gloomy forest, and then suddenly the echoes waked and swept the country for miles, never failing until heard at the headquarters of Hooker at Chancellorsville—the wild "rebel yell" of the long Confederate lines.

Never was assault delivered with grander enthusiasm. Fresh from the long winter's waiting, and confident from the preparation of the spring, the troops were in fine condition and in high spirits. The boys were all back from home or sick leave. "Old Jack" was there upon the road in their midst; there could be no mistake and no failure. And there were Rodes and A. P. Hill. Had they not seen and cheered, as long and as loud as they were permitted, the gay-hearted Stuart and the long-bearded Fitz Lee on his fiery charger? Was not Crutchfield's array of brass and iron "dogs of war" at hand, with Poague and Palmer, and all the rest, ready to bark loud and deep with half a chance?

STONEWALL JACKSON'S "OLD SORREL."

This picture is from a photograph taken at the Maryland State Fair at Hagerstown, in 1884. At that time "Old Sorrel" was thought to be about thirty-four years old. At the fair, relic-hunters plucked away much of his mane and tail.—EDITORS.

Alas! for Howard and his unformed lines, and his brigades with guns stacked, and officers at dinner or asleep under the trees, and butchers deep in the blood of beeves! Scattered through field and forest, his men were preparing their evening meal. A little show of earth-work facing the south was quickly taken by us in reverse from the west. Flying battalions are not flying buttresses for an army's stability. Across Talley's fields the rout begins. Over at Hawkins's hill, on the north of the road, Carl Schurz makes a stand, soon to be driven into the same hopeless panic. By the quiet Wilderness Church in the vale, leaving wounded and dead everywhere, by Melzi Chancellor's, on into the deep thicket again, the Confederate lines pressed forward,—now broken and all disaligned by the density of bush that tears the clothes away; now halting to load and deliver a volley upon some regiment or fragment of the enemy that will not move as fast as others. Thus the attack upon Hooker's flank was a grand success, beyond the most sanguine expectation.

The writer of this narrative, an aide-de-camp of Jackson's, was ordered to remain at the point where the advance began, to be a center of communication between the general and the cavalry on the flanks, and to deliver orders to detachments of artillery still moving up from the rear. A fine black charger, with

STONEWALL JACKSON GOING FORWARD ON THE PLANK ROAD
IN ADVANCE OF HIS LINE OF BATTLE.

elegant trappings, deserted by his owner and found tied to a tree, became mine only for that short and eventful night-fall; and about 8 P.M., in the twilight, thus comfortably mounted, I gathered my couriers about me and went forward to find General Jackson. The storm of battle had swept far on to the east and become more and more faint to the ear, until silence came with night over the fields and woods. As I rode along that old turnpike, passing scattered fragments of Confederates looking for their regiments, parties of prisoners concentrating under guards, wounded men by the roadside and under the trees at Talley's and Chancellor's, I had reached an open field on the right, a mile west of Chancellorsville, when, in the dusky twilight, I saw horsemen near an old cabin in the field. Turning toward them, I found Rodes and his staff engaged in gathering the broken and scattered troops that had swept the two miles of battle-field. "General Jackson is just ahead on the road, Captain," said Rodes; "tell him I will be here at this cabin if I am wanted." I had not gone a hundred yards before I heard firing, a shot or two, and then a company volley upon the right of the road, and another upon the left. A few moments farther on I met Captain Murray Taylor, an aide of A. P. Hill's, with tidings that Jackson and Hill were wounded, and some around them killed, by the fire of their own men. Spurring my horse into a sweeping gallop, I soon passed the Confederate line of battle, and, some three or four rods on its front, found the general's horse beside a pine sapling on the left, and a rod beyond a little party of men caring for a wounded officer. The story of the sad event is briefly told, and, in essentials, very much as it came to me from the lips of the wounded general himself, and in everything confirmed and completed by those who were eye-witnesses and near companions.

When Jackson had reached the point where his line now crossed the turnpike, scarcely a mile west of Chancellorsville, and not half a mile from a line of Federal troops, he had found his front line unfit for the farther and vigorous advance he desired, by reason of the irregular character of the fighting, now right, now left, and because of the dense thickets, through which it was impossible to preserve alignment. Division commanders found it more and more difficult as the twilight deepened to hold their broken brigades in hand. Regretting the necessity of relieving the troops in front, General Jackson had ordered A. P. Hill's division, his third and reserve line, to be placed in front. While this change was being effected, impatient and anxious, the general rode forward on the turnpike, followed by two or three of his staff and a number of couriers and signal sergeants. He passed the swampy depression and began the ascent of the hill toward Chancellorsville, when he came upon a line of the Federal infantry lying on their arms. Fired at by one or two muskets (two musket-balls from the enemy whistled over my head as I came to the front), he turned and came back toward his line, upon the side of the road to his left. As he rode near to the Confederate troops, just placed in position and ignorant that he was in the front, the left company begin firing to the front, and two of his party fell from their saddles dead—Captain Boswell, of the Engineers, and Sergeant Cunliffe, of the Signal Corps. Spurring his horse across the road to his right, he was met by a second volley from the right company of Pender's North Carolina brigade. Under this volley, when not two rods from the troops, the general received three balls at the same instant. One penetrated the palm of his right hand and was cut out that night from the back of his hand. A second passed around the wrist of the left arm and out through the left hand. A third ball passed through the left arm half-way from shoulder to elbow. The large bone of the upper arm was splintered to the elbow-joint, and the wound bled freely. His horse turned quickly from the fire, through the thick bushes which swept the cap from the general's head, and scratched his forehead, leaving drops of blood to stain his face. As he lost his hold upon the bridle-rein, he reeled from the saddle, and was caught by the arms of Captain Wilbourn, of the Signal Corps. Laid upon the ground, there came at once to his succor General A. P. Hill and members of his staff. The writer reached his side a minute after, to find General Hill holding the head and shoulders of the wounded chief. Cutting open the coat-sleeve from wrist to shoulder, I found the wound in the upper arm, and with my handkerchief I bound the arm above the wound to stem the flow of blood. Couriers were sent for Dr. Hunter McGuire, the surgeon of the corps and the general's trusted friend, and for an ambulance. Being outside of our lines, it was urgent that he should be moved at once. With difficulty litter-bearers were brought from the line near by, and the general was placed upon the litter and carefully raised to the shoulder, I myself bearing one corner. A moment after, artillery from the Federal side was opened upon us; great broadsides thundered over the woods; hissing shells searched the dark thickets through, and shrapnels swept the road along which we moved. Two or three steps farther, and the litter-bearer at my side was struck and fell, but, as the litter turned, Major Watkins Leigh, of Hill's staff, happily caught it. But the fright of the men was so great that we were obliged to lay the litter and its burden down upon the road. As the litter-bearers ran to the cover of the trees, I threw myself by the general's side and held him firmly to the ground as he attempted to rise. Over us swept the rapid fire of shot and shell—grape-shot striking fire upon the flinty rock of the road all around us, and sweeping from their feet horses and men of the artillery just moved to the front. Soon the firing veered to the other side of the road, and I sprang to my feet, assisted the general to rise, passed my arm around him, and with the wounded man's weight thrown heavily upon me, we forsook the road. Entering the woods, he sank to the ground from exhaustion, but the litter was soon brought, and again rallying a few men, we essayed to carry him farther, when a second bearer fell at my side. This time, with none to assist, the litter careened, and the general fell to the ground, with a groan of deep pain. Greatly alarmed, I sprang to his head, and, lifting his head as a stray beam of moonlight came through clouds and leaves, he opened his eyes and wearily said: "Never mind me, Captain, never mind me." Raising him again to his feet, he was accosted by Brigadier-General Pender: "Oh, General, I hope you are not seriously wounded. I will have to retire my troops to re-form them, they are so much broken by this fire." But Jackson, rallying his strength, with firm voice said: "You must hold your ground, General Pender; you must hold your ground, sir!" and so uttered his last command on the field.

Again we resorted to the litter, and with difficulty bore it through the bush, and then under a hot fire along the road. Soon an ambulance was reached, and stopping to seek some stimulant at Chancellor's (Dowdall's Tavern), we were found by Dr. McGuire, who at once took charge of the wounded man. Passing back over the battle-field of the afternoon, we reached the Wilderness store, and then, in a field on the north, the field-hospital of our corps under Dr. Harvey Black. Here we found a tent prepared, and after midnight the left arm was amputated near the shoulder, and a ball taken from the right hand.

All night long it was mine to watch by the sufferer, and keep him warmly wrapped and undisturbed in his sleep. At 9 A.M., on the next day, when he aroused, cannon firing again filled the air, and all the Sunday through the fierce battle raged, General J.E.B. Stuart commanding the Confederates in Jackson's place. A dispatch was sent to the commanding general to announce formally his disability,—tidings General Lee had received during the night with profound grief. There came back the following note:

> "GENERAL: I have just received your note, informing me that you were wounded. I cannot express my regret at the occurrence. Could I have directed events, I should have chosen, for the good of the country, to have been disabled in your stead. I congratulate you upon the victory which is due to your skill and energy. Most truly yours, R. E. LEE, GENERAL."

When this dispatch was handed to me at the tent, and I read it aloud, General Jackson turned his face away and said, "General Lee is very kind, but he should give the praise to God."

The long day was passed with bright hopes for the wounded general, with tidings of success on the battle-field, with sad news of losses, and messages to and from other wounded officers brought to the same infirmary.

On Monday the general was carried in an ambulance, by way of Spotsylvania Court House, to most comfortable lodging at Chandler's, near Guinea's Station, on the Richmond, Fredericksburg and Potomac railroad. And here, against our hopes, notwithstanding the skill and care of wise and watchful surgeons, attended day and night by wife and friends, amid the prayers and tears of all the Southern land, thinking not of himself, but of the cause he loved, and for the troops who had followed him so well and given him so great a name, our chief sank, day by day, with symptoms of pneumonia and some pains of pleurisy, until, at 3:15 P.M. on the quiet of the Sabbath afternoon, May 10th, 1863, he raised himself from his bed, saying, "No, no, let us pass over the river,

STONEWALL JACKSON'S GRAVE, LEXINGTON, VA. FROM A PHOTOGRAPH.

and rest under the shade of the trees"; and, falling again to his pillow, he passed away, "over the river, where, in a land where warfare is not known or feared, he rests forever 'under the trees.'"

His shattered arm was buried in the family burying-ground of the Ellwood place—Major J. H. Lacy's—near his last battle-field.

His body rests, as he himself asked, "in Lexington, in the Valley of Virginia." The spot where he was so fatally wounded in the shades of the Wilderness is marked by a large quartz rock, placed there by the care of his chaplain and friend, the Rev. Dr. B. T. Lacy, and the latter's brother, Major Lacy.

Others must tell the story of Confederate victory at Chancellorsville. It has been mine only, as in the movement of that time, so with my pen now, to follow my general himself. Great, the world believes him to have been in many elements of generalship; he was greatest and noblest in that he was good, and, without a selfish thought, gave his talent and his life to a cause that, as before the God he so devoutly served, he deemed right and just.

CHAPTER 3

LEE'S INVASION OF PENNSYLVANIA.

James Longstreet, Lieutenant-General, C.S.A.

One night in the spring of 1863 I was sitting in my tent opposite Suffolk, Virginia, when there came in a slender, wiry fellow about five feet eight, with hazel eyes, dark hair and complexion, and brown beard. He wore a citizen's suit of dark material, and except for his stooping shoulders was well formed and evidently a man of great activity. He handed me a note from Mr. Seddon, Secretary of War. That was my first meeting with the famous scout, Harrison, who in his unpretending citizen's dress passed unmolested from right to left through the Federal army, visited Washington City, ate and drank with the Federal officers, and joined me at Chambersburg with information more accurate than a force of cavalry could have secured.

While my command was at Suffolk, engaged in collecting supplies from the eastern coasts of Virginia and North Carolina, General Burnside was relieved and General Hooker put in command of the Federal Army of the Potomac. General Lee was not expecting Hooker to move so early, and gave me no warning until the Federals moved out to turn his left by Chancellorsville. He then sent urgent demand for me, but it so happened that all my trains were down on the eastern coasts, and I could not move my troops without leaving the trains to the enemy. I made haste to get them back as quickly as possible, and the moment we got them within our lines I pulled up from around Suffolk, and, re-crossing the Blackwater, started back on my march to join General Lee at Fredericksburg. Before we got to Richmond, however, we received dispatches announcing the Confederate success. But with these tidings of victory came the sad intelligence that General Stonewall Jackson was seriously wounded, a piece of news that cast a deep gloom over the army.

On the 9th of May I joined General Lee at his headquarters at Fredericksburg. At our first meeting we had very little conversation; General Lee merely stated that he had had a severe battle, and the army had been very much bro-

UNION CAVALRY SCOUTING IN FRONT OF THE CONFEDERATE ADVANCE.

ken up. He regarded the wound accidently inflicted on Jackson as a terrible calamity. Although we felt the immediate loss of Jackson's services, it was supposed he would rally and get well. He lingered for several days, one day reported better and the next worse, until at last he was taken from us to the shades of Paradise. The shock was a very severe one to men and officers, but the full extent of our loss was not felt until the remains of the beloved general had been sent home. The dark clouds of the future then began to lower above the Confederates.

General Lee at that time was confronted by two problems: one, the finding of a successor for Jackson, another, the future movements of the Army of Northern Virginia. After considering the matter fully he decided to reorganize his army, making three corps instead of two. I was in command of the First Corps, and he seemed anxious to have a second and third corps under the command of Virginians. To do so was to overlook the claims of other generals who had been active and very efficient in the service. He selected General Ewell to command the Second, and General A. P. Hill for the Third Corps. General Ewell was entitled to command by reason of his rank, services, and ability. Next in rank was a North Carolinian, General D. H. Hill, and next a Georgian, General Lafayette McLaws, against whom was the objection that they were not Virginians.‡

‡General D. H. Hill was the superior of General A. P. Hill in rank, skill, judgment, and distinguished services. He had served with the army in Virginia, on the Peninsula in the battles of Williamsburg, Seven Pines, and the Seven Days' battles around Richmond. In the Maryland campaign he made the battle of South Mountain alone from morning till late in the afternoon, with five thousand against a large part of McClellan's army. He also bore the brunt of the battle of Sharpsburg. He came, however, not from Virginia but from North Carolina, and had just been detailed for service in that State.

Next in rank after General D. H. Hill was General Lafayette McLaws, who had served with us continuously from the Peninsular campaign. His attack on Maryland Heights in the campaign of 1862

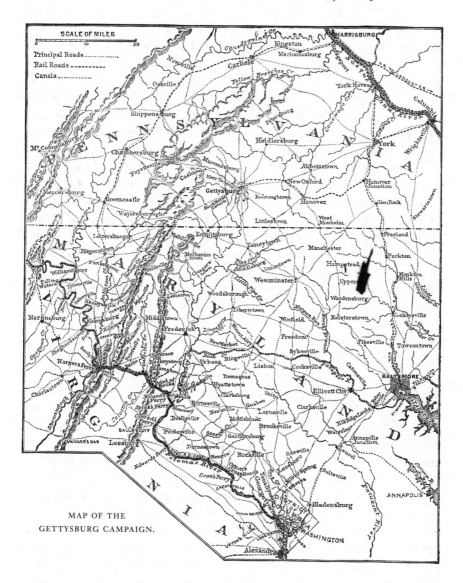

MAP OF THE
GETTYSBURG CAMPAIGN.

---

was the crowning point in the capture of Harper's Ferry with its garrison and supplies. With Maryland Heights in our hands Harper's Ferry was untenable. Without Maryland Heights in our possession Jackson's forces on the south side of the Potomac could not have taken the post. At Fredericksburg McLaws held the ground at Marye's Hill with 5000 men (his own and Ransom's division) against 40,000, and put more than double his defending forces *hors de combat,* thus making, for his numbers, the best battle of the war. General McLaws was not in vigorous health, however, and was left to command his division in the campaign. He called on General Lee to know why his claims had been overlooked, but I do not know that Lee gave him satisfactory reasons.—J.L.

In reorganizing his army, General Lee impaired to some extent the *morale* of his troops, but the First Corps, dismembered as it was, still considered itself, with fair opportunities, invincible, and was ready for any move warranted by good judgment.

While General Lee was reorganizing his army he was also arranging the new campaign. Grant had laid siege to Vicksburg, and Johnston was concentrating at Jackson to drive him away. Rosecrans was in Tennessee and Bragg was in front of him. The force Johnston was concentrating at Jackson gave us no hope that he would have sufficient strength to make any impression upon Grant, and even if he could, Grant was in position to reënforce rapidly and could supply his army with greater facility. Vicksburg was doomed unless we could offer relief by strategic move. I proposed to send a force through east Tennessee to join Bragg and also to have Johnston sent to join him, thus concentrating a large force to move against Rosecrans, crush out his army, and march against Cincinnati. That, I thought, was the only way we had to relieve Vicksburg. General Lee admitted the force of my proposition, but finally stated that he preferred to organize a campaign into Maryland and Pennsylvania, hoping thereby to draw the Federal troops from the southern points they occupied. After discussing the matter with him for several days, I found his mind made up not to allow any of his troops to go west. I then accepted his proposition to make a campaign into Pennsylvania, provided it should be offensive in strategy but defensive in tactics, forcing the Federal army to give us battle when we were in strong position and ready to receive them. One mistake of the Confederacy was in pitting force against force. The only hope we had was to outgeneral the Federals. We were all hopeful and the army was in good condition, but the war had advanced far enough for us to see that a mere victory without decided fruits was a luxury we could not afford. Our numbers were less than the Federal forces, and our resources were limited while theirs were not. The time had come when it was imperative that the skill of generals and the strategy and tactics of war should take the place of muscle against muscle. Our purpose should have been to impair the *morale* of the Federal army and shake Northern confidence in the Federal leaders. We talked on that line from day to day, and General Lee, accepting it as a good military view, adopted it as the key-note of the campaign. I suggested that we should have all the details and purposes so well arranged and so impressed upon our minds that when the critical moment should come, we could refer to our calmer moments and know we were carrying out our original plans. I stated to General Lee that if he would allow me to handle my corps so as to receive the attack of the Federal army, I would beat it off without calling on him for help except to guard my right and left, and called his attention to the battle of Fredericksburg as an instance of defensive warfare, where we had thrown not more than five thousand troops into the fight and had beaten off two-thirds of the Federal army with great loss to them and slight loss to my own troops. I also

GENERAL ROBERT E. LEE.
FROM A PHOTOGRAPH TAKEN AFTER THE WAR.

called his attention to Napoleon's instructions to Marmont at the head of an invading army.

A few days before we were ready to move, General Lee sent for General Ewell to receive his orders. I was present at the time and remarked that if we were ever going to make an offensive battle it should be done south of the Potomac—adding that we might have an opportunity to cross the Rappahannock near Culpeper Court House and make a battle there. I made this suggestion in order to bring about a discussion which I thought would give Ewell a better idea of the plan of operations. My remark had the desired effect and we talked over the possibilities of a battle south of the Potomac. The enemy would be on our right flank while we were moving north. Ewell's corps was to move in advance to Culpeper Court House, mine to follow, and the cavalry was to move along on our right flank to the east of us. Thus, by threatening his rear we could draw Hooker from his position on Stafford Heights opposite Fredericksburg. Our movements at the beginning of the campaign were necessarily slow in order that we might be sure of having the proper effect on Hooker.

Ewell was started off to the valley of Virginia to cross the mountains and move in the direction of Winchester, which was occupied by considerable forces under Milroy. I was moving at the same time east of the Blue Ridge with Stuart's cavalry on my right so as to occupy the gaps from Ashby on to Harper's Ferry. Ewell, moving on through the valley, captured troops and supplies at Winchester, and passed through Martinsburg and Williamsport into Maryland. As I moved along the eastern slope of the Blue Ridge we heard from day to day of the movements of Hooker's army, and that he had finally abandoned his position on Stafford Heights, and was moving up the Potomac in the direction of Washington. Upon receipt of that information, A. P. Hill was ordered to draw off from Fredericksburg and follow the movements of General Ewell, but to cross the Potomac at Shepherdstown. When Hill with his troops and well-supplied trains had passed my rear, I was ordered to withdraw from the Blue Ridge, pass over to the west of the Shenandoah and follow the movements of the other troops, only to cross the Potomac at Williamsport. I ordered General Stuart, whom I considered under my command, to occupy the gaps with a part of his cavalry and to follow with his main force on my right, to cross the Potomac at Shepherdstown, and move on my right flank. Upon giving him this order, he informed me that he had authority from General Lee to occupy the gaps with a part of his cavalry, and to follow the Federal army with the remainder. At the same time he expressed his purpose of crossing the river east of the Blue Ridge and trying to make way around the right of the Federal army; so I moved my troops independent of the cavalry, and, following my orders, crossed at Williamsport, came up with A. P. Hill in Maryland, and moved on thence to Chambersburg.

CONFEDERATES AT A FORD.

Before we left Fredericksburg for the campaign into Maryland and Pennsylvania, I called up my scout, Harrison, and, giving him all the gold he thought
he would need, told him to go to Washington City and remain there until he
was in possession of information which he knew would be of value to us, and directed that he should then make his way back to me and report. As he was leaving, he asked where he would find me. That was information I did not care to
impart to a man who was going directly to the Federal capital. I answered that
my command was large enough to be found without difficulty. We had reached
Chambersburg on the 27th of June and were remaining there to give the troops
rest, when my scout straggled into the lines on the night of June 28th. He told
me he had been to Washington and had spent his gold freely, drinking in the sa-
loons and getting upon confidential terms with army officers. In that way he had
formed a pretty good idea of the general movements of the Federal army and
the preparation to give us battle. The moment he heard Hooker had started
across the Potomac he set out to find me. He fell in with the Federal army before reaching Frederick—his plan being to walk at night and stop during the

day in the neighborhood of the troops. He said there were three corps near Frederick when he passed there, one to the right and one to the left, but he did not succeed in getting the position of the other. This information proved more accurate than we could have expected if we had been relying upon our cavalry. I sent the scout to report to General Lee, who was near, and suggested in my note that it might be well for us to begin to look to the east of the Blue Ridge. Meade was then in command of the Federal army, Hooker having been relieved.

The two armies were then near each other, the Confederates being north and west of Gettysburg, and the Federals south and south-east of that memorable field. On the 30th of June we turned our faces toward our enemy and marched upon Gettysburg. The Third Corps, under Hill, moved out first and my command followed. We then found ourselves in a very unusual condition: we were almost in the immediate presence of the enemy with our cavalry gone. Stuart was undertaking another wild ride around the Federal army. We knew nothing of Meade's movements further than the report my scout had made. We did not know, except by surmise, when or where to expect to find Meade, nor whether he was lying in wait or advancing. The Confederates moved down the Gettysburg road on June 30th, encountered the Federals on July 1st, and a severe engagement followed. The Federals were driven entirely from the field and forced back through the streets of Gettysburg to Cemetery Hill, which had been previously selected as a Federal rallying-point and was occupied by a reserve force of the Eleventh Corps.

CHAPTER 4

THE FIRST DAY AT GETTYSBURG.

Henry J. Hunt, Brevet Major-General, U.S.A.,

CHIEF OF ARTILLERY OF THE ARMY OF THE POTOMAC.

The battles of Fredericksburg and Chancellorsville raised the confidence of the Confederate Army of Northern Virginia to such a height as to cause its subordinate officers and soldiers to believe that, as opposed to the Army of the Potomac, they were equal to any demand that could be made upon them. Their belief in the superiority of the Southerner to the Northerner as a fighter was no longer, as at the beginning of the war, a mere provincial conceit, for it was now supported by signal successes in the field. On each of these two occasions the Army of the Potomac had been recently reorganized under a new general, presumably abler than his predecessor and possessing the confidence of the War Department, and the results were crowning victories for the Confederates. Yet at Fredericksburg defeat was not owing to any lack of fighting qualities on the part of the Federal soldiers, but rather to defective leadership.

At Chancellorsville both qualities were called in question. In none of the previous battles between these armies had the disparity of numbers been so great. The Federal general had taken the initiative, his plan of operations was excellent, and his troops were eager for battle. The Confederates could at first oppose but a portion of their inferior force to the attack of greatly superior numbers, and the boast of the Federal commander, that "the Army of Northern Virginia was the legitimate property of the Army of the Potomac," seemed in a fair way to be justified, when at first contact the advantages already gained were thrown away by the assumption of a timid, defensive attitude. Lee's bold offensive, which followed immediately on this exhibition of weakness, the consequent rout of a Federal army-corps, and the subsequent retreat of the whole army, a large portion of which had not been engaged, confirmed the exultant Confederates in their conviction—which now became an article of faith—that both in combat and in generalship the superiority of the Southerner was fully established. The Federal soldiers returned from Chancellorsville to their

BUFORD'S CAVALRY OPPOSING THE CONFEDERATE ADVANCE UPON GETTYSBURG.

camps on the northern bank of the Rappahannock, mortified and incensed at finding themselves, through no fault of their own, in the condition of having in an offensive campaign lost the battle without fighting, except when the enemy forced it upon them.

Yet in this battle the Northern soldier fought well. Under the circumstances no men could have withstood such a sudden attack as that made by "Stonewall" Jackson on the flank and rear of the Eleventh Corps; but as soon as Jackson encountered troops in condition for action, his pursuit was checked and he was brought to a stand. The panic did not extend beyond the routed corps, nor to all of that, for its artillery and so much of its infantry as could form a proper line did their duty, and the army, far from being "demoralized" by this mishap, simply ridiculed the corps which, from its supposed want of vigilance, had allowed itself to be surprised in a position in which it could not fight. The surprise itself was not the fault of the troops, and in subsequent battles the corps redeemed its reputation. Both armies were composed in the main of Americans, and there was little more difference between their men than might be found between those of either army at different periods, or under varying circumstances; for although high bounties had already brought into the Federal ranks an inferior element which swelled the muster-rolls and the number of stragglers, "bounty jumping"‡ had not as yet become a regular business.

The morale of the Confederate army was, however, much higher at this time than that of its adversary. It was composed of men not less patriotic, many of whom had gone into the war with reluctance, but who now felt that they were defending their homes. They were by this time nearly all veterans, led by officers having the confidence of their Government, which took pains to inspire

---

‡This term was applied to the practice of enlisting and securing bounty money, and then, either deserting outright, or shirking the serious work of the field.—EDITORS.

its soldiers with the same feeling. Their successes were extolled and magnified, their reverses palliated or ignored. Exaggerations as to the relative numbers of the troops had been common enough on both sides, but those indulged in at the South had been echoed, sometimes suggested, in the North by a portion of the press and people, so that friends and enemies united in inspiring in the Confederate soldier a belief in himself and a contempt for his enemy. In the Army of the Potomac it was different; the proportion of veterans was much smaller; a cessation of recruiting at the very beginning of active operations, when men were easily obtainable to supply losses in existing regiments, had been followed, as emergencies arose, by new levies, for short periods of service, and in new organizations which could not readily be assimilated by older troops. Moreover, there were special difficulties. The Army of the Potomac was not in favor at the War Department. Rarely, if ever, had it heard a word of official

commendation after a success, or of sympathy or encouragement after a defeat. From the very beginning its camps had been filled with imputations and charges against its leaders, who were accused on the streets, by the press, in Congress, and even in the War Department itself, and after victories as well as after defeats, not only of incapacity or misconduct, but sometimes of "disloyalty" to their superiors, civil and military, and even to the cause for which they fought. These accusations were followed or accompanied by frequent changes of commanders of the army, of army-corps, and even of divisions. Under such circumstances, but little confidence could be felt by the troops, either in the wisdom of a war office which seemed to change its favorites with the caprice of a coquette, or in the capacity of new generals who followed each other in such rapid succession. But it is due to that patient and sorely tried army, to say that the spirit of both officers and men was of the best, and their devotion to duty unconquerable. The army itself had

GENERAL MEADE IN THE FIELD.
FROM A PHOTOGRAPH.

originally been so admirably disciplined and tempered, that there always remained to it a firm self-reliance and a stern sense of duty and of honor that was proof against its many discouragements. In battle it always acquitted itself well and displayed the highest soldierly qualities, no matter who commanded it or whence he came. Chancellorsville furnishes no exception to this assertion, nor evidence of inferiority of the Northern to the Southern soldier, but it does furnish striking illustrations of Napoleon's well-known saying, "In war *men* are nothing, *a man* is everything."

General Lee, who felt great confidence in his own troops, and overrated the effects of successive reverses on the Federal soldiers, now resolved to assume the offensive, for he knew that to remain on the defensive would in the end force him back on Richmond. He determined, therefore, in case the Army of the Potomac could not be brought to action under favorable circumstances in Virginia, to transfer, if permitted, the field of operations to Northern soil, where a victory promptly followed up might give him possession of Baltimore or Washington, and perhaps lead to the recognition of the Confederacy by foreign powers. The valley of the Shenandoah offered a safe line of operations; the Federal troops occupying it were rather a bait than an obstacle, and to capture or destroy them seemed quite practicable to one who controlled absolutely all Confederate troops within the sphere of his operations. The sharp lesson he had administered the previous year had not been heeded by the Federal War Office; an opportunity now offered to repeat it, and he took his measures accordingly. In case his Government would not consent to a bolder offensive, he could at least clear the valley of Virginia of the enemy,—a distinct operation, yet a necessary preliminary to an invasion of the North. This work was assigned to Lieutenant-General Ewell, an able officer, in every way qualified for such an enterprise.

In anticipation of the new campaign, Lee's army was strengthened and reorganized into three army-corps of three divisions each. Each division consisted of four brigades, except Rodes's and Anderson's, which had five each, and Pickett's, which had three at Gettysburg,—in all, thirty-seven infantry brigades. The cavalry were the select troops of the Confederacy. Officers and men had been accustomed all their lives to the use of horses and arms, "and to the very end the best blood in the land rode after Stuart, Hampton, and the Lees." They were now organized as a division, under Major-General J.E.B. Stuart, consisting of the six brigades of Hampton, Robertson, Fitzhugh Lee, Jenkins, W. E. Jones, and W.H.F. Lee, and six batteries of horse-artillery under Major R. F. Beckham. To these should be added Imboden's command, a strong brigade of over 2000 effective horsemen and a battery of horse-artillery, which had been operating in the mountain country and was now near Staunton, awaiting orders. The artillery had recently received an excellent organization under its commandant-in-chief, General Pendleton. It consisted, besides the horse-artillery, of fifteen so-called "battalions," each of four batteries, with one lieutenant-colonel and a major. To each army-corps were attached five battalions, one for each division and two as a reserve, the whole under a colonel as chief of artillery. The total number of batteries was 69, of guns 287, of which 30 were with the cavalry. With few exceptions the batteries were of four guns each. The army was commanded by a full general, each army-corps, except the artillery, by a lieutenant-general, each division by a major-general, each brigade, except two, by brigadier-generals. Nearly all these officers were veterans of proved ability and many had served in the Mexican war.

In the Army of the Potomac the discharge of 58 regiments had reduced its strength since Chancellorsville by 25,000 effectives, partly replaced by 5 brigades numbering less than 12,000 men. At the battle of Gettysburg the 7 army-corps consisted of 19 infantry divisions, 7 of which had 2 brigades, 11 had 3, and 1 had 4; in all 51 brigades. The army and army-corps were commanded by major-generals, the divisions by 3 major-generals and 16 brigadier-generals, the infantry brigades by 22 brigadier-generals and 29 colonels. The average strength of army-corps and divisions was about half that of the Confederates, a fact that should be kept in mind, or the terms will be misleading. The cavalry had been raised under disadvantages. Men accustomed to the use of both horses and arms were comparatively few in the North and required training in everything that was necessary to make a trooper. The theater of war was not considered favorable for cavalry, and it was distributed to the various headquarters for escort duty, guards, and orderlies. It was not until 1863 that it was united under General Pleasonton in a corps consisting of three weak divisions, Buford's, D. McM. Gregg's, and Duffié's, afterward consolidated into two, Stahel's cavalry, which joined at Frederick, June 28th, becoming the third division. The corps was then organized as follows: First Division, Buford: brigades, Gamble, Devin, Merritt; Second Division, Gregg: brigades, McIntosh, Huey, J. Irvin Gregg; Third Division, Kilpatrick: brigades, Farnsworth, Custer. The divisions and three of the brigades were commanded by brigadier-generals, the other five brigades by colonels. To the cavalry were attached Robertson's and Tidball's brigades of horse-artillery. Under excellent chiefs and the spirit created by its new organization, the Federal cavalry soon rivaled that of the Confederates.

The field-artillery was in an unsatisfactory condition. The high reputation it had gained in Mexico was followed by the active and persistent hostility of the War Department, which almost immediately dismounted three-fourths of its authorized batteries. Congress in 1853 made special provision for remounting them as schools of instruction for the whole arm, a duty which the War Department on shallow pretexts evaded. Again in 1861 Congress amply provided for the proper organization and command of the artillery in the field, but as there was no chief nor special administration for the arm, and no regulations for its government, its organization, control, and direction were left to the fancies of the various army commanders. General officers were practically denied it, and in 1862 the War Department announced in orders that field-officers of artillery were an unnecessary expense and their muster into service forbidden. Promotion necessarily ceased, and such able artillerists as Hays, DeRussy, Getty, Gibbon, Griffin, and Ayres could only receive promotion by transfer to the infantry or cavalry. No adequate measures were taken for the supply of recruits, and the batteries were frequently dependent on the troops to which they were attached for men enough to work their guns in battle. For battery-draft they were often glad to get the refuse horses after the ambulance and quartermasters' trains were supplied. Still, many of the batteries attained a high degree of excellence, due mainly to the self-sacrifice, courage, and intelligence of their own officers and men.

On taking command of the army, General Hooker had transferred the military command of the artillery to his own headquarters, to be resumed by the chief of artillery only under specific orders and for special occasions, which resulted in such mismanagement and confusion at Chancellorsville that he consented to organize the artillery into brigades. This was a decided improvement, which would have been greater if the brigade commanders had held adequate rank. As it was, there was no artillery commandant-in-chief for months before the battle of Gettysburg, and of the 14 brigades 4 were commanded by field-officers, 9 by captains, and 1 by a lieutenant, taken from their batteries for the purpose. The number of field-batteries at Gettysburg was 65, of guns 370, of which 212 were with the infantry, 50 with the cavalry, 108 in the reserve. The disadvantages under which the artillery labored all through the war, from want of proper regulations, supervision, and command, were simply disgraceful to our army administration from the close of the Mexican to that of the Civil war, and caused an unnecessary expenditure of both blood and treasure.

It will be perceived by comparison that the organization of the Army of the Potomac was at this period in every way inferior to that of its adversary. The army-corps and divisions were too numerous and too weak. They required too many commanders and staffs, and this imposed unnecessary burdens on the general-in-chief, who was often compelled to place several army-corps under the commander of one of them, thus reproducing the much-abused "grand divisions" of Burnside, under every possible disadvantage. Had the number of infantry corps been reduced to four at most, and the divisions to twelve, the army would have been more manageable and better commanded, and the artillery, without any loss, but rather a gain of efficiency, would have been reduced by a dozen or fifteen batteries.

———

Early in June Lee's army began to move, and by the 8th Longstreet's and Ewell's corps had joined Stuart's cavalry at Culpeper. A. P. Hill's corps was left in ob-

MAJOR-GENERAL JOHN F. REYNOLDS.

FROM A PHOTOGRAPH.

The uniform is that of a field-officer in the regular infantry. Early in the war General Reynolds was Lieutenant-Colonel of the 14th United States Infantry, and was made Brigadier-General of Volunteers in September, 1861.—EDITORS.

servation at Fredericksburg; and so skillfully were the changes concealed that Hooker, believing that all the enemy's infantry were still near that town, ordered Pleasonton to beat up Stuart's camps at Culpeper, and get information as to the enemy's position and proposed movements. For these purposes he gave Pleasonton two small brigades of infantry, 3000 men under Generals Ames and Russell, which carried his total force to 10,981. They were echeloned along the railroad, which crosses the river at Rappahannock Station, and runs thence ten miles to Culpeper. About midway is Brandy Station, a few hundred yards north of which is Fleetwood Hill. Dividing his force equally, Pleasonton ordered Buford and Ames to cross at Beverly Ford, and Gregg, Duffié, and Russell at Kelly's Ford. All were to march to Brandy Station, Duffié being thrown out to Stevensburg, seven miles east of Culpeper, to watch the Fredericksburg road. Then the whole force was to move on Culpeper. On the 8th, General Lee, having sent Jenkins's brigade as Ewell's advance into the valley, reviewed the other 5 brigades of Stuart, 10,292 combatants, on the plains near Brandy Station. After the review they were distributed in the neighborhood with a view to crossing the Rappahannock on the 9th, Stuart establishing his headquarters at Fleetwood. Accident had thus disposed his forces in the most favorable manner to meet Pleasonton's converging movements.

At daybreak Buford crossed and drove the enemy's pickets from the ford back to the main body, near St. James's church. Stuart, on the first report of the crossing, sent Robertson's brigade toward Kelly's to watch that ford, and Colonel M. C. Butler's 2d South Carolina to Brandy Station. He himself took the command at the church, where he was attacked by Buford. At Brandy Station W.H.F. Lee was wounded, and Colonel Chambliss took command of his brigade. Meantime Gregg had crossed at Kelly's Ford, and Duffié, leading, took a southerly road, by which he missed Robertson's brigade. Learning that Duffié's advance had reached Stevensburg and that Buford was heavily engaged, Gregg pushed direct for Brandy Station, sending orders to Duffié to follow his movement. Stuart, notified of his approach, had sent in haste some artillery and two of Jones's regiments to Fleetwood, and Colonel Butler started at once for Stevensburg, followed soon after by Wickham's 4th Virginia. On their approach two squadrons of the 6th Ohio, in occupation of the place, fell back skirmishing. Duffié sent two regiments to their aid, and after a severe action, mainly with the 2d South Carolina, reoccupied the village. In this action Colonel Butler lost a leg, and his lieutenant-colonel, Hampton, was killed.

On Gregg's arrival near Brandy Station the enemy appeared to be in large force, with artillery, on and about Fleetwood Hill. He promptly ordered an attack; the hill was carried, and the two regiments sent by Stuart were driven back. Buford now attacked vigorously and gained ground steadily, for Stuart had to reënforce his troops at Fleetwood from the church. In the struggles that followed, the hill several times changed masters; but as Duffié did not make his appearance, Gregg was finally overmatched and withdrew, leaving three of his guns, two of them disabled, in the enemy's hands, nearly all of their horses being killed and most of their cannoneers *hors de combat*. There were some demonstrations of pursuit, but the approach of Buford's reserve brigade stopped them. Duffié finally came up and Gregg reported to Pleasonton, informing him of the approach of Confederate infantry from Culpeper. Pleasonton, who had captured some important dispatches and orders, now considered his mission accomplished, and ordered a withdrawal of his whole command. This was effected leisurely and without molestation. Gregg recrossed at Rappahannock Station, Buford at Beverly Ford, and at sunset the river again flowed between the opposing forces. Stuart reports his losses at 485, of whom 301 were killed or wounded. Pleasonton reports an aggregate loss (exclusive of Duffié's, which would not exceed 25) of 907, of whom 421 were killed or wounded. In nearly all the previous so-called "cavalry" actions, the troops had fought as dismounted dragoons. This was in the main a true cavalry battle, and enabled the Federals to dispute the superiority hitherto claimed by, and conceded to, the Confederate cavalry. In this respect the affair was an important one. It did not, however, delay Lee's designs on the valley; he had already sent Imboden toward Cumberland to destroy the railroad and canal from that place to Martinsburg.

Milroy's Federal division, about 9000 strong, occupied Winchester, with McReynolds's brigade in observation at Berryville. Kelley's division of about 10,000 men was at Harper's Ferry, with a detachment of 1200 infantry and a battery under Colonel B. F. Smith at Martinsburg. On the night of June 11th, Milroy received instructions to join Kelley, but, reporting that he could hold Winchester, was authorized to remain there. Ewell, leaving Brandy Station June 10th, reached Cedarville *via* Chester Gap on the evening of the 12th, whence he detached Jenkins and Rodes to capture McReynolds, who, discovering their approach, withdrew to Winchester. They then pushed on to Martinsburg, and on the 14th drove out the garrison. Smith's infantry crossed the Potomac at Shepherdstown, and made its way to Maryland Heights; his artillery retreated by the Williamsport road, was pursued, and lost five guns.

Meanwhile Ewell, with Early's and Edward Johnson's divisions, marched direct on Winchester. Arriving in the neighborhood on the evening of the 13th, he ordered Early on the 14th to leave a brigade in observation on the south of the town, move his main force under cover of the hills to the north-western side, and seize the outworks which commanded the main fort. He also ordered Johnson to deploy his division on the east of the town, so as to divert attention from Early. This was so successfully done that the latter placed, unperceived, twenty guns and an assaulting column in position, and at 6 P.M., by a sudden attack, carried the outworks, driving the garrisons into the body of the place. This capture was a complete surprise, and Milroy called a council of war, which decided on an immediate retreat, abandoning the artillery and wagons. Ewell had anticipated this, and ordered Johnson to occupy with a brigade a position on the Martinsburg pike, north of Winchester. The retreat commenced at 2 A.M. of the 15th, and after proceeding three or four miles, the advance encountered Johnson's troops, attacked vigorously, and at first successfully, but, the enemy receiving reënforcements, a hard fight ensued in which the Federals lost heavily. The retreat was then continued; the troops separated in the darkness, one portion reaching Harper's Ferry, another crossing the Potomac at Hancock. On the 15th Ewell crossed the river, occupied Hagerstown and Sharpsburg, and sent Jenkins's cavalry to Chambersburg to collect supplies. On the 17th the garrison of Harper's Ferry was removed to Maryland Heights, and the valley of the Shenandoah was cleared of Federal troops. In these brilliant operations General Lee claims for Ewell the capture of 4000 prisoners and small-arms, 28 pieces of artillery, 11 colors, 300 loaded wagons, as many horses, and a considerable quantity of stores of all descriptions, the entire Confederate loss, killed, wounded, and missing, being 269.

These operations indicate on the part of General Lee either contempt for his opponent, or a belief that the chronic terror of the War Department for the safety of Washington could be safely relied upon to paralyze his movements,— or both. On no other reasonable hypothesis can we account for his stretching his army from Fredericksburg to Williamsport, with his enemy concentrated on one flank, and on the shortest road to Richmond.

General Hooker's instructions were to keep always in view the safety of Washington and Harper's Ferry, and this necessarily subordinated his operations to those of the enemy. On June 5th he reported that in case Lee moved *via* Culpeper toward the Potomac with his main body, leaving a corps at Fredericksburg, he should consider it his duty to attack the latter, and asked if that would be within the spirit of his instructions. In reply he was warned against such a course, and its dangers to Washington and Harper's Ferry were pointed out. On June 10th, learning that Lee was in motion, and that there were but few troops in Richmond, he proposed an immediate march on that place, from which, after capturing it, he could send the disposable part of his force to any threatened point north of the Potomac, and was informed that Lee's army, and not Richmond, was his true objective. Had he taken Richmond, Peck's large force at Suffolk and Keyes's 10,000 men[1] in the Peninsula might have been utilized, and Hooker's whole army set free for operations against Lee.

[1] The forces referred to consisted (January 1st, 1863) of three brigades and some unassigned commands at Suffolk, under General John J. Peck, and two brigades, and three cavalry commands—also unassigned, stationed at Yorktown, Gloucester Point, and Williamsburg, under General E. D. Keyes. The troops under Peck belonged to the Seventh Corps. Keyes's command was known as the Fourth Corps. Both were included in the Department of Virginia, commanded by General John A. Dix, with headquarters at Fort Monroe.

While Lee was invading the North an expedition was sent by General Dix from White House to the South Anna River and Bottom's Bridge to destroy Lee's communications and threaten Richmond. —EDITORS.

As yet an invasion of the North had not been definitely fixed upon. On June 8th, the day before the engagement at Brandy Station, Lee, in a confidential letter to Mr. Seddon, Confederate Secretary of War, stated that he was aware of the hazard of taking the aggressive, yet nothing was to be gained by remaining on the defensive; still, if the department thought it better to do so, he would adopt that course. Mr. Seddon replied, June 10th, the date of Hooker's proposal to march on Richmond, concurring in General Lee's views. He considered aggressive action indispensable, that "all attendant risks and sacrifices must be incurred," and adds, "I have not hesitated, in coöperating with your plans, to leave this city almost defenseless." General Lee now had full liberty of action, with the assured support of his Government,—an immense advantage over an opponent who had neither.

As soon as Hooker learned from Pleasonton that a large infantry force was at Culpeper, he extended his right up the Rappahannock, and when informed of Ewell's move toward the valley, being forbidden to attack A. P. Hill at Fredericksburg or to spoil Lee's plans by marching to Richmond, he moved his army, on the night of June 13th, toward the line of the Orange and Alexandria Railroad, and occupied Thoroughfare Gap in advance of it. On the 15th Longstreet left Culpeper, keeping east of the Blue Ridge and so covering its gaps. Hill left Fredericksburg on the 14th, and reached Shepherdstown *via* Chester Gap on the 23d. Stuart's cavalry had been thrown out on Longstreet's right to occupy the passes of the Bull Run mountains and watch Hooker's army.

PENNSYLVANIA COLLEGE, GETTYSBURG. FROM A PHOTOGRAPH.

The cupola was first used by Union officers, and then by Confederate, as a station for observation and signals. During the withdrawal of the First and Eleventh corps through the town to Cemetery Hill, there was hard fighting in the college grounds.—EDITORS.

On the 17th he encountered, near Aldie, a portion of Pleasonton's command; a fierce fight ensued, which left the Federals in possession of the field. During the four following days there was a succession of cavalry combats; those of the 19th near Middleburg, and of the 21st near Upperville, were especially well contested, and resulted in the retreat of Stuart through Ashby's Gap. Longstreet had already withdrawn through the gaps and followed Hill to the Potomac. Imboden, his work of destruction completed, had taken post at Hancock. Longstreet and Hill crossed the Potomac on the 24th and 25th and directed their march on Chambersburg and Fayetteville, arriving on the 27th. Stuart had been directed to guard the mountain passes until the Federal army crossed the river, and, according to General Lee's report, "to lose no time in placing his command on the right of our [Confederate] column as soon as he should perceive the enemy moving northward," in order to watch and report his movements. According to Stuart's report, he was authorized to cross between the Federal army and Washington, and directed after crossing to proceed with all dispatch to join Early in Pennsylvania.

General Lee so far had been completely successful; his army was exultant, and he lost no time in availing himself of his advantages. On the 21st he ordered Ewell to take possession of Harrisburg; and on the 22d Ewell's whole corps was on the march, Rodes's and Johnson's divisions *via* Chambersburg to Carlisle, which they reached on the 27th, and Early *via* Greenwood and Gettysburg to York, with orders from Ewell to break up the Northern Central Railroad, destroy the bridge across the Susquehanna at Wrightsville, and then rejoin the main body at Carlisle. Early entered York on the 28th, and sent Gordon's brigade, not to destroy but to secure possession of the bridge, which would enable him to operate upon Harrisburg from the rear; but a small militia force under Colonel Frick, retreating from Wrightsville across the bridge, after an unsuccessful attempt to destroy one of its spans, set fire to and entirely destroyed that fine structure, Gordon's troops giving their aid to the citizens to save the town from the flames. On the 29th Ewell received orders from General Lee to rejoin the army at Cashtown; the next evening, 30th, his reserve artillery and trains, with Johnson's division as an escort, were near Chambersburg, and Ewell with Early's and Rodes's, near Heidlersburg. Thus suddenly ended Ewell's Harrisburg expedition. One object was to collect supplies, and contributions were accordingly levied. Much damage was done to roads and bridges, but the prompt advance of the Army of the Potomac made this useless to the Confederates.

Before committing his army to an invasion of the North, General Lee recommended the proper steps to cover and support it. In a letter of June 23d, addressed to President Davis, he states that the season was so far advanced as to stop further Federal operations on the Southern coast, and that Confederate troops in that country and elsewhere were now disposable. He proposed, there-

THE LUTHERAN SEMINARY. THE UPPER PICTURE FROM A WAR-TIME PHOTOGRAPH.

Both pictures show the face of the seminary toward the town, and in the right-hand view is seen the Chambersburg Pike. On the first day, Buford and Reynolds used the cupola for observations; thereafter it was the chief signal-station and observatory for the Confederates.—EDITORS.

fore, that an army should as soon as possible be organized at Culpeper, as "the well-known anxiety of the Northern Government for the safety of its capital would induce it to retain a large force for its defense, and thus relieve the opposition to our advance"; and suggested that General Beauregard be placed in command, "as his presence would give magnitude even to a small demonstration." On the 25th he wrote twice to Mr. Davis urging the same views. The proposition embarrassed Mr. Davis, who could not see how, with the few troops under his hand, it could be carried out. In fact, although General Lee had pointed out the means, the proposition came too late, as the decisive battle took

GETTYSBURG FROM OAK HILL. FROM A PHOTOGRAPH.

Oak Hill is a mile north-west of Gettysburg, and the view here is south-east, showing Stevens Hall (named after Thaddeus Stevens), the preparatory department of the Pennsylvania College on the left; then Culp's Hill; then Pennsylvania College, and, to the right of its cupola, the observatory on Cemetery Hill.

place much earlier than was expected. This correspondence, however, with that between Lee and Mr. Seddon, shows that Hooker's project to capture Richmond by a *coup-de-main* was feasible. It was not now a question of "swapping queens." Washington was safe, being well fortified and sufficiently garrisoned, or with available troops within reach, without drawing on Hooker; and to take Richmond and scatter the Confederate Government was the surest way to ruin Lee's army—"his true objective."

On the first appearance of danger of invasion, Pennsylvania's vigilant governor, Curtin, warned the people of the State and called out the militia. General Couch was sent to Harrisburg to organize and command them, but disbelief in the danger—due to previous false alarms—caused delays until the fugitives from Milroy's command, followed by Jenkins's cavalry, roused the country. Defensive works were then thrown up at Harrisburg and elsewhere, and local forces were raised and moved toward the enemy.

Early in June Hooker represented in strong terms the necessity of having one commander for all the troops whose operations would have an influence on those of Lee's army, and in reply was informed by Halleck that any movements he might suggest for other commands than his own would be ordered *if practicable*. Misunderstandings and confusion naturally resulted, and authority was given Hooker from time to time to exercise control over the troops of Heintzelman, commanding the Department of Washington, and of Schenck, commanding the Middle Department, followed, June 24th, by orders specifically placing the troops in Harper's Ferry and its vicinity at his disposal.

Disregarding Ewell's movements, Hooker conformed his own to those of the enemy's main body, and crossed the Potomac at Edwards's Ferry on the 25th and 26th of June. On the 27th three army-corps under Reynolds occupied Middletown and the South Mountain passes. The Twelfth Corps was near Harper's Ferry, and the three other corps at or near Frederick. Hooker now ordered the Twelfth Corps to march early on the 28th to Harper's Ferry, there to be joined by its garrison from Maryland Heights, in order to cut Lee's communications with Virginia, and in conjunction with Reynolds to operate on his rear. General Halleck, however, objected to the abandonment of the Heights, notwithstanding Hooker's representations that the position was utterly useless for any purpose; whereupon Hooker abandoned his project, and finding now that he was "not allowed to manœuvre his own army in the presence of the enemy," asked to be relieved from his command. He had encountered some of the difficulties which had beset a predecessor whom he had himself mercilessly criticised, and promptly succumbed to them. His request was complied with, and Major-General George G. Meade was appointed his successor, this being the fifth change of commanders of the army in front of Washington in ten months. Meade was an excellent officer of long service, who had always proved equal to his position, whether as a specialist or a commander of troops. Many welcomed his advent—some regretted Hooker's departure. All thought the time for the change unfortunate, but accepted loyally, as that army ever did, the leader designated by the President, and gave Meade their hearty support. He was succeeded in the command of the Fifth Corps by Major-General George Sykes, a veteran of the Mexican war and a distinguished soldier.

GENERAL LEE'S HEADQUARTERS
ON THE CHAMBERSBURG PIKE.
FROM A WAR-TIME PHOTOGRAPH.

When General Meade assumed command, June 28th, the best information placed Longstreet at Chambersburg, A. P. Hill between that place and Cashtown, and Ewell in occupation of Carlisle, York, and the country between them, threatening Harrisburg. Unacquainted with Hooker's plans and views, he determined at once to move on the main line from Frederick to Harrisburg, extending his wings as far as compatible with a ready concentration, in order to force Lee to battle before he could cross the Susquehanna. With this view he spent the day in ascertaining the position of his army, and brought up his cavalry, Buford to his left, Gregg to his right, and Kilpatrick to the front. Directing French to occupy Frederick with seven thousand men of the garrison of Harper's Ferry, he put his army in motion early on the morning of the 29th. Kilpatrick reached Littlestown that night; and on the morning of the 30th the rear of his division, while passing through Hanover, was attacked by a portion of Stuart's cavalry. Stuart, availing himself of the discretion allowed him, had left Robertson's and Jones's brigades to guard the passes of the Blue Ridge, and on the night of the 24th, with those of Hampton, Fitzhugh Lee, and Chambliss, had started to move round the Army of the Potomac, pass between it and Centreville into Maryland, and so rejoin Lee; but the movements of that army forced him so far east that he was compelled to ford the Potomac near Seneca [20 miles above Washington], on the night of the 27th. Next morning, learning that Hooker had already crossed the river, he marched north by Rockville, where he captured a wagon train. Paroling his prisoners and taking the train with him, he pushed on—through Westminster, where he had a sharp action with a squadron of Delaware horse—to Union Mills, and encamped there on the 29th. During the night, he learned that the Federal army was still between him and Lee on its march north, and his scouts reported its cavalry in strong force at Littlestown, barring his direct road to Gettysburg; wherefore, on the morning of the 30th he moved across country to Hanover, Chambliss in front and Hampton in rear of his long train of two hundred wagons, with Fitzhugh Lee well out on his left flank. About 10 A.M. Chambliss, reaching Hanover,

NORTH-EAST CORNER OF THE
MCPHERSON WOODS, WHERE
GENERAL REYNOLDS WAS KILLED.
FROM A PHOTOGRAPH.

found Kilpatrick passing through the town and attacked him, but was driven out before Hampton or Lee could come to his support. Stuart's men and horses were now nearly worn out; he was encumbered with a large captured train; a junction with some part of Lee's army was a necessity, and he made a night march for York, only to learn that Early had left the day before. Pushing on to Carlisle, he found that Ewell was gone, and the place occupied by a militia force under General W. F. Smith.✦ His demand of a surrender was refused; he threw a few shells into the town and burned the Government barracks. That night he learned that Lee's army was concentrating at Gettysburg, and left for that place next day. Thus ended a raid which greatly embarrassed Lee, and by which the services of three cavalry brigades were, in the critical period of the campaign, exchanged for a few hundred prisoners and a wagon train.

Hearing nothing from Stuart, and therefore believing that Hooker was still south of the Potomac, Lee, on the afternoon of the 28th, ordered Longstreet and A. P. Hill to join Ewell at Harrisburg; but late that night one of Longstreet's scouts came in and reported that the Federal army had crossed the river, that Meade had relieved Hooker and was at Frederick. Lee thereupon changed the rendezvous of his army to Cashtown, which place Heth reached on the 29th. Next day Heth sent Pettigrew's brigade on to Gettysburg, nine miles, to procure a supply of shoes. Nearing this place, Pettigrew discovered the advance of a large Federal force and returned to Cashtown. Hill immediately notified Generals Lee and Ewell, informing the latter that he would advance next morning on Gettysburg. Buford, sending Merritt's brigade to Mechanicstown as guard to his trains, had early on the morning of the 29th crossed into and moved up the Cumberland valley *via* Boonsboro' and Fairfield with those of Gamble and Devin, and on the afternoon of Tuesday, June 30th, under instructions from Pleasonton, entered Gettysburg, Pettigrew's brigade withdrawing on his approach.

✦General Smith commanded the First Division, Department of the Susquehanna, and was charged with the protection of Harrisburg.—EDITORS.

From Gettysburg, near the eastern base of the Green Ridge, and covering all the upper passes into the Cumberland valley, good roads lead to all important points between the Susquehanna and the Potomac. It is therefore an important strategic position. On the west of the town, distant nearly half a mile, there is a somewhat elevated ridge running north and south, on which stands the "Lutheran Seminary." This ridge is covered with open woods through its whole length, and is terminated nearly a mile and a half north of the seminary by a commanding knoll, bare on its southern side, called Oak Hill. From this ridge the ground slopes gradually to the west, and again rising forms another ridge about 500 yards from the first, upon which, nearly opposite the seminary, stand McPherson's farm buildings. The second ridge is wider, smoother, and lower than the first, and Oak Hill, their intersection, has a clear view of the slopes of both ridges and of the valley between them. West of McPherson's ridge Willoughby Run flows south into Marsh Creek. South of the farm buildings and directly opposite the seminary, a wood borders the run for about 300 yards, and stretches back to the summit of McPherson's ridge. From the town two roads run: one south-west to Hagerstown *via* Fairfield, the other north-westerly to Chambersburg *via* Cashtown. The seminary is midway between them, about 300 yards from each. Parallel to and 150 yards north of the Chambersburg pike, is the bed of an unfinished railroad, with deep cuttings through

CONFEDERATE DEAD ON THE FIELD OF THE FIRST DAY. FROM A PHOTOGRAPH.

the two ridges. Directly north of the town the country is comparatively flat and open: on the east of it, Rock Creek flows south. On the south, and overlooking it, is a ridge of bold, high ground, terminated on the west by Cemetery Hill and on the east by Culp's Hill, which, bending to the south, extends half a mile or more and terminates in low grounds near Spangler's Spring. Culp's Hill is steep toward the east, is well wooded, and its eastern base is washed by Rock Creek.

Impressed by the importance of the position, Buford, expecting the early return of the enemy in force, assigned to Devin's brigade the country north, and to Gamble's that west of the town; sent out scouting parties on all the roads to collect information, and reported the condition of affairs to Reynolds. His pickets extended from below the Fairfield road, along the eastern bank of Willoughby Run, to the railroad cut, then easterly some 1500 yards north of the town, to a wooded hillock near Rock Creek.

On the night of June 30th Meade's headquarters and the Artillery Reserve were at Taneytown; the First Corps at Marsh Run, the Eleventh at Emmitsburg, Third at Bridgeport, Twelfth at Littlestown, Second at Uniontown, Fifth at Union Mills, Sixth and Gregg's cavalry at Manchester, Kilpatrick's at Hanover. A glance at the map will show at what disadvantage Meade's army was now placed. Lee's whole army was nearing Gettysburg, while Meade's was scattered over a wide region to the east and south of that town.

Meade was now convinced that all designs on the Susquehanna had been abandoned; but as Lee's corps were reported as occupying the country from Chambersburg to Carlisle, he ordered, for the next day's moves, the First and Eleventh corps to Gettysburg, under Reynolds, the Third to Emmitsburg, the Second to Taneytown, the Fifth to Hanover, and the Twelfth to Two Taverns,

UNION DEAD NEAR MCPHERSON'S WOODS. FROM A PHOTOGRAPH.

directing Slocum to take command of the Fifth in addition to his own. The Sixth Corps was left at Manchester, thirty-four miles from Gettysburg, to await orders. But Meade, while conforming to the current of Lee's movement, was not merely drifting. The same afternoon he directed the chiefs of engineers and artillery to select a field of battle on which his army might be concentrated, whatever Lee's lines of approach, whether by Harrisburg or Gettysburg,—indicating the general line of Pipe Creek as a suitable locality. Carefully drawn instructions were sent to the corps commanders as to the occupation of this line, should it be ordered; but it was added that developments might cause the offensive to be assumed from present positions. These orders were afterward cited as indicating General Meade's intention not to fight at Gettysburg. They were, under any circumstances, wise and proper orders,

JOHN L. BURNS, "THE OLD HERO OF GETTYSBURG."‡ FROM A PHOTOGRAPH TAKEN SOON AFTER THE BATTLE.

‡I have seen it stated in an account of Burns, that he was an old regular soldier who had served in the Florida war.—H.J.H.

Sergeant George Eustice, of Company F, 7th Wisconsin Volunteers, in a letter from Gilroy, Santa Clara County, California, gives this account of John Burns's action in the ranks of that regiment:

"It must have been about noon when I saw a little old man coming up in the rear of Company F. In regard to the peculiarities of his dress, I remember he wore a swallow-tailed coat with smooth brass buttons. He had a rifle on his shoulder. We boys began to poke fun at him as soon as he came amongst us, as we thought no civilian in his senses would show himself in such a place. Finding that he had really come to fight I wanted to put a cartridge-box on him to make him look like a soldier, telling him he could not fight without one. Slapping his pantaloons-pocket, he replied, 'I can get my hands in here quicker than in a box. I'm not used to them new-fangled things.' In answer to the question what possessed him to come out there at such a time, he replied that the rebels had either driven away or milked his cows, and that he was going to be even with them. About this time the enemy began to advance. Bullets were flying thicker and faster, and we hugged the ground about as close as we could. Burns got behind a tree and surprised us all by not taking a double-quick to the rear. He was as calm and collected as any veteran on the ground. We soon had orders to get up and move about a hundred yards to the right, when we were engaged in one of the most stubborn contests I ever experienced. Foot by foot we were driven back to a point near the seminary, where we made a stand, but were finally driven through the town to Cemetery Ridge. I never saw John Burns

and it would probably have been better had he concentrated his army behind Pipe Creek rather than at Gettysburg; but events finally controlled the actions of both leaders.

At 8 A.M., July 1st, Buford's scouts reported Heth's advance on the Cashtown road,✛ when Gamble's brigade formed on McPherson's Ridge, from the Fairfield road to the railroad cut; one section of Calef's battery A, 2d United States, near the left of his line, the other two across the Chambersburg or Cashtown pike. Devin formed his disposable squadrons from Gamble's right toward Oak Hill, from which he had afterward to transfer them to the north of the town to meet Ewell. As Heth advanced, he threw Archer's brigade to the right, Davis's to the left of the Cashtown pike, with Pettigrew's and Brockenbrough's brigades in support. The Confederates advanced skirmishing heavily with Buford's dismounted troopers. Calef's battery, engaging double the number of its own guns, was served with an efficiency worthy of its former reputation as "Duncan's battery" in the Mexican war, and so enabled the cavalry to hold their long line for two hours. When Buford's report of the enemy's advance reached Reynolds, the latter, ordering Doubleday and Howard to follow, hastened toward Gettysburg with Wadsworth's small division (two brigades, Meredith's and Cutler's) and Hall's 2d Maine battery. As he approached he heard the sound of battle, and directing the troops to cross the fields toward the firing, galloped himself to the seminary, met Buford there, and both rode to the front, where the cavalry, dismounted, were gallantly holding their ground against heavy odds. After viewing the field, he sent back to hasten up Howard, and as

---

after our movement to the right, when we left him behind his tree, and only know that he was true blue and grit to the backbone, and fought until he was three times wounded."

In his official report, General Doubleday says:

"My thanks are specially due to a citizen of Gettysburg named John Burns, who, although over seventy years of age, shouldered his musket and offered his services to Colonel Wister, 150th Pennsylvania Volunteers. Colonel Wister advised him to fight in the woods, as there was more shelter there; but he preferred to join our line of skirmishers in the open fields. When the troops retired, he fought with the Iron Brigade [Meredith's]. He was wounded in three places."—EDITORS.

✛The opening of the battle on the Chambersburg road, on July 1st, is thus described by Captain Newel Cheney, of the 9th N.Y. Cavalry, in a paper prepared for the Gettysburg Monument Commission of New York:

"Colonel William Sackett, commanding the 9th N.Y. Cavalry, was brigade officer of the day and in charge of the brigade picket-line made up of details from each regiment of Devin's brigade (9th N.Y., 6th N.Y., 4th N.Y., and 17th Pa.) the night of June 30th, and extending from the south side of the Chambersburg road, on the east side of Willoughby Run, northerly and eastwardly across the Mummasburg, Carlisle, and Harrisburg roads. He had his headquarters on the Chambersburg road, near the Lutheran Seminary. The advanced picket put on the Chambersburg road near Willoughby Run consisted of a corporal and three men, relieved every two hours, with orders not to fire on any one approaching from the front, but to notify the pickets in each direction and the reserve. No one approached from the front until

the enemy's main line was now advancing to the attack, directed Doubleday, who had arrived in advance of his division, to look to the Fairfield road, sent Cutler with three of his five regiments north of the railroad cut, posted the other two under Colonel Fowler, of the 14th New York, south of the pike, and replaced Calef's battery by Hall's, thus relieving the cavalry. Cutler's line was hardly formed when it was struck by Davis's Confederate brigade on its front and right flank, whereupon Wadsworth, to save it, ordered it to fall back to Seminary Ridge. This order not reaching the 147th New York, its gallant major, Harney, held that regiment to its position until, having lost half its numbers, the order to retire was repeated. Hall's battery was now imperiled, and it withdrew by sections, fighting at close canister range and suffering severely. Fowler thereupon changed his front to face Davis's brigade, which held the cut, and with Dawes's 6th Wisconsin—sent by Doubleday to aid the 147th New York—charged and drove Davis from the field. The Confederate brigade suffered severely, losing all its field-officers but two, and a large proportion of its men killed and captured, being disabled for further effective service that day. In the meantime Archer's Confederate brigade had occupied McPherson's wood, and as the regiments of Meredith's "Iron Brigade" came up, they were sent forward by Doubleday, who fully recognized the importance of the position, to dislodge Archer. At the entrance of the wood they found Reynolds in person, and, animated by his presence, rushed to the charge, struck successive heavy blows, outflanked and turned the enemy's right, captured General Archer and a large portion of his brigade, and pursued the remainder across Willoughby Run.

---

daylight next morning, July 1st, when Corporal Alphouse Hodges, of Company F., 9th N.Y. Cavalry, was on this post with three men. At daylight he saw men approaching along the road, nearly a mile away, across Willoughby Run. Acting on his orders, he immediately sent his men to notify the line and the reserve, while he advanced across the Run till near enough to see that those approaching were the enemy, when he turned back, and as he did so the enemy fired at him. He retired to the Run, and from behind the abutments of the bridge fired several shots back at the enemy. These are supposed to be the first shots fired from our side on the morning of July 1st at Gettysburg, and occurred about 5:30 A.M., as near as Hodges can remember. When he fell back from the bridge to the higher ground, he found Colonel Sackett had formed a skirmish-line of the whole of his picket force, which, as I have said, consisted of detachments from the different regiments of the (Devin's) brigade. Here the advance of the enemy was first seriously disputed by this skirmish-line, which they held till after Hall's battery (2d Maine) came up and took position on the right of the Chambersburg road in rear of this skirmish-line and fired.... The First Brigade of Buford's division (Colonel Gamble's) coming up on the left of the road, the line of the Second Brigade, still under command of Colonel Sackett, moved farther to the right and occupied the line from the Chambersburg road to the Mummasburg road. That portion of the 9th Cavalry which had remained in camp received orders to water their horses by squadrons in Rock Creek about 7 A.M. As soon as they had watered, they saddled up and proceeded out on the Mummasburg road to the skirmish-line on Oak Ridge. The first squadron, under Captain Hanley (afterward Lieutenant-Colonel), was the first to reach the line, and he immediately ordered Lieutenant A.C. Robertson (afterward Captain) with twenty men to advance down the road into

MAJOR-GENERAL ABNER DOUBLEDAY. FROM
A PHOTOGRAPH.

Wadsworth's small division had thus won decided successes against superior numbers, but it was at grievous cost to the army and the country, for Reynolds, while directing the operations, was killed in the wood by a sharp-shooter. It was not, however, until by his promptitude and gallantry he had determined the decisive field of the war, and had opened brilliantly a battle which required three days of hard fighting to close with a victory. To him may be applied in a wider sense than in its original one, Napier's happy enlogium on Ridge: "No man died on that field with more glory than he, yet many died, and there was much glory."

After the repulse of Davis and Archer, Heth's division was formed in line mostly south of the Cashtown pike, with Pender's in second line, Pegram's and McIntosh's artillery (nine batteries) occupying all the commanding positions west of Willoughby Run. Doubleday reëstablished his former lines, Meredith holding McPherson's wood. Soon after, Rowley's and Robinson's divisions (two brigades each) and the four remaining batteries of the corps arrived. Rowley's division was thrown forward, Stone's brigade to the interval between Meredith and Cutler, and Biddle's

---

the woods, where he found the enemy's line near the residence of N. Hoffman. Finding the enemy had a strong line, he retired to a position a little back of the residence of J. Forney, from behind which some of the enemy were firing at him. He dismounted his men and drove the enemy from behind Forney's buildings, then fell back to the stone wall on the ridge, where the balance of the regiment were formed dismounted. Here the regiment held their ground for some time while the enemy approached on their hands and knees through the wheat-field in front. Daniel Cornish, of Company F, getting sight of a rebel not far away in the field, fired and killed him. The regiment cheered, and the enemy, evidently thinking our men would charge on them, hastily withdrew out of the wheat-field. As they fell back one man stopped behind a tree in the field near the road, and Perry Nichols, of Company F, advanced and captured him. This is said to be the first prisoner captured. He was immediately taken to Buford's headquarters, and gave the first information we received from the enemy's side. It was during this skirmish that Cyrus W. James, Company G, 9th N.Y. Cavalry, was killed by a rebel bullet, and he is said to have been the first man killed that morning on our side."—Editors.

with Cooper's battery to occupy the ridge between the wood and the Fairfield road. Reynolds's battery replaced Hall's, and Calef's rejoined Gamble's cavalry, now in reserve. Robinson's division was halted near the base of Seminary Ridge. By this time, near noon, General Howard arrived, assumed command, and directed General Schurz, commanding the Eleventh Corps, to prolong Doubleday's line toward Oak Hill with Schimmelfennig's and Barlow's divisions and three batteries, and to post Steinwehr's division and two batteries on Cemetery Hill, as a rallying-point. By 1 o'clock, when this corps was arriving, Buford had reported Ewell's approach by the Heidlersburg road, and Howard called on Sickles at Emmitsburg and Slocum at Two Taverns for aid, to which both these officers promptly responded. It was now no longer a question of prolonging Doubleday's line, but of protecting it against Ewell whilst engaged in front with Hill. Schurz's two divisions, hardly 6000 effectives, accordingly formed line on the open plain half a mile north of the town. They were too weak to cover the ground, and a wide interval was left between the two corps, covered only by the fire of Dilger's and Wheeler's batteries (ten guns) posted behind it.

That morning, whilst on the march to Cashtown, Ewell received Hill's no-

ASSAULT OF BROCKENBROUGH'S CONFEDERATE BRIGADE (HETH'S DIVISION)
UPON THE STONE BARN OF THE MCPHERSON FARM.

The line of the stone barn was held by Stone's brigade, Pennsylvania Bucktails (Doubleday's division), its right resting on the Chambersburg pike (the left of the picture) and its left on the McPherson woods, where a part of Archer's Confederate brigade of Heth's division was captured by Meredith's brigade.—EDITORS.

CONFEDERATE DEAD GATHERED FOR BURIAL NEAR THE MCPHERSON WOODS.
FROM PHOTOGRAPHS.

tice that his corps was advancing to Gettysburg, upon which he turned the heads of his own columns to that point. Reporting the change by a staff-officer to General Lee, Ewell was instructed that if the Federals were in force at Gettysburg a general battle was not to be brought on until the rest of the army was up. Approaching Gettysburg, Rodes, guided by the sounds of battle, followed the prolongation of Seminary Ridge; Iverson's, Daniel's, and Ramseur's brigades on the western, O'Neal's and Doles's on the eastern slope. Ewell, recognizing the importance of Oak Hill, ordered it to be occupied by Carter's artillery battalion, which immediately opened on both the Federal corps, enfilading Doubleday's line. This caused Wadsworth again to withdraw Cutler to Seminary Ridge, and Reynolds's battery was posted near McPherson's house, under partial cover. Stone therefore placed two of his three regiments on the Cashtown pike, so as to face Oak Hill. This left an interval between Stone and Cutler, through which Cooper and Reynolds could fire with effect, and gave to these lines a cross-fire on troops entering the angle between them. Robinson now sent his two brigades to strengthen Cutler's right. They took post behind the stone walls of a field, Paul's brigade facing west, Baxter's north. Rodes, regarding this advance as a menace, gave orders at 2:30 P.M. to attack. Iverson, sweeping round to his left, engaged Paul, who prolonged Cutler's line, and O'Neal attacked Baxter. The repulse of O'Neal soon enabled Baxter to turn upon Iverson. Cutler also attacked him in flank, and after losing 500 men killed and wounded, 3 of Iverson's regiments surrendered. General Robinson reports the capture of 1000 prisoners and 3 colors; General Paul was severely wounded, losing both eyes. Meanwhile Daniel's brigade advanced directly on Stone, who maintained his lines against this attack and also Brockenbrough's, of Hill's corps, but was soon severely wounded. Colonel Wister, who succeeded him, met the same fate, and Colonel

LIEUTENANT BAYARD WILKESON HOLDING HIS BATTERY
(G, 4TH UNITED STATES ARTILLERY) TO ITS WORK IN AN EXPOSED POSITION.

The death of Lieutenant Bayard Wilkeson, who commanded Battery G, Fourth U.S. Artillery, was one of the most heroic episodes of the fight. He was but nineteen years old and was the son of Samuel Wilkeson, who, as correspondent of the "New-York Times," was at Meade's headquarters during the fight. Young Wilkeson, by his fearless demeanor, held his battery in an exposed position on the Union right. General John B. Gordon, finding it impossible to advance his Confederate division in the face of Wilkeson's fire, and realizing that if the officer on the horse could be disposed of the battery would not remain, directed two batteries of his command to train every gun upon him. Wilkeson was brought to the ground, desperately wounded, and his horse was killed. He was carried by the Confederates to the Alms House (or dragged himself there—the accounts differ), where he died that night. Just before he expired, it is said, he asked for water; a canteen was brought to him; as he took it a wounded soldier lying next to him begged, "For God's sake give me some!" He passed the canteen untouched to the man, who drank every drop it contained. Wilkeson smiled on the man, turned slightly, and expired.—EDITORS.

Dana took command of the brigade. Ramseur, who followed Daniel, by a conversion to the left, now faced Robinson and Cutler with his own brigade, the remnant of Iverson's, and one regiment of O'Neal's, his right connecting with Daniel's left, and the fighting became hot. East of the ridge, Doles's brigade had been held in observation, but about 3:30 P.M., on the advance of Early, he sent his skirmishers forward and drove those of Devin—who had gallantly held the enemy's advance in check with his dismounted troopers—from their line and its hillock on Rock Creek. Barlow, considering this an eligible position for his own right, advanced his division, supported by Wilkeson's battery, and seized it. This made it necessary for Schurz to advance a brigade of Schimmelfennig's division to connect with Barlow, thus lengthening his already too extended line.

The arrival of Early's division had by this time brought an overwhelming force on the flank and rear of the Eleventh Corps. On the east of Rock Creek, Jones's artillery battalion, within easy range, enfiladed its whole line and took it in reverse, while the brigades of Gordon, Hays, and Avery in line, with Smith's in reserve, advanced about 4 P.M. upon Barlow's position, Doles, of Rodes's division, connecting with Gordon. An obstinate and bloody contest ensued, in which Barlow was desperately wounded, Wilkeson killed, and the whole corps forced back to its original line, on which, with the aid of Coster's brigade and Heckman's battery, drawn from Cemetery Hill, Schurz endeavored to rally it and cover the town. The fighting here was well sustained, but the Confederate force was overpowering in numbers, and the troops retreated to Cemetery Hill, Ewell entering the town about 4:30 P.M. These retrograde movements had uncovered the flank of the First Corps and made its right untenable.

Meanwhile, that corps had been heavily engaged along its whole line; for, on the approach of Rodes, Hill attacked with both his divisions. There were thus opposed to the single disconnected Federal line south of the Cashtown pike two solid Confederate ones which outflanked their left a quarter of a mile or more. Biddle's small command, less than a thousand men, after a severe contest, was gradually forced back. In McPherson's wood and beyond, Meredith's and Dana's brigades repeatedly repulsed their assailants, but as Biddle's retirement uncovered their left, they too fell back to successive positions from which they inflicted heavy losses, until finally all three reached the foot of Seminary Ridge, where Colonel Wainwright, commanding the corps artillery, had planted twelve guns south of the Cashtown pike, with Stewart's battery, manned in part by men of the Iron Brigade, north of it. Buford had already thrown half of Gamble's dismounted men south of the Fairfield road. Heth's division had suffered so severely that Pender's had passed to its front, thus bringing fresh troops to bear on the exhausted Federal line.

It was about 4 P.M. when the whole Confederate line advanced to the final attack. On their right Gamble held Lane's brigade for some time in check, Per-

THE LINE OF DEFENSE AT THE CEMETERY GATE-HOUSE. FROM A PHOTOGRAPH.

rin's and Scales's suffered severely, and Scales's was broken up, for Stewart, swinging half his guns, under Lieutenant Davison, upon the Cashtown pike, raked it. The whole corps being now heavily pressed and its right uncovered, Doubleday gave the order to fall back to Cemetery Hill, which was effected in comparatively good order, the rear, covered by the 7th Wisconsin, turning when necessary to check pursuit. Colonel Wainwright, mistaking the order, had clung with his artillery to Seminary Hill, until, seeing the infantry retreating to the town, he moved his batteries down the Cashtown pike until lapped on both sides by the enemy's skirmishers, at close range, when they were compelled to abandon one gun on the road, all its horses being killed. The Eleventh Corps also left a disabled gun on the field. Of the troops who passed through the town, many, principally men of the Eleventh Corps, got entangled in the streets, lost their way, and were captured.

On ascending Cemetery Hill, the retreating troops found Steinwehr's division in position covered by stone fences on the slopes, and occupying by their skirmishers the houses in front of their line. As they arrived they were formed, the Eleventh Corps on the right, the First Corps on the left of Steinwehr. As the batteries came up, they were well posted by Colonels Wainwright and Osborn, and soon a formidable array of artillery was ready to cover with its fire all the approaches. Buford assembled his command on the plain west of Cemetery Hill, covering the left flank and presenting a firm front to any attempt at pursuit. The First Corps found a small reënforcement awaiting it, in the 7th Indiana, part of the train escort, which brought up nearly five hundred fresh men. Wadsworth met them and led them to Culp's Hill, where, under direction of

Captain Pattison of that regiment, a defensive line was marked out. Their brigade (Cutler's) soon joined them; wood and stone were plentiful, and soon the right of the line was solidly established.

Nor was there wanting other assurance to the men who had fought so long that their sacrifices had not been in vain. As they reached the hill they were received by General Hancock, who arrived just as they were coming up from the town, under orders from General Meade to assume the command. His person was well known; his presence inspired confidence, and it implied also the near approach of his army-corps. He ordered Wadsworth at once to Culp's Hill to secure that important position, and aided by Howard, by Warren who had also just arrived from headquarters, and by others, a strong line, well flanked, was soon formed.

General Lee, who from Seminary Hill had witnessed the final attack, sent Colonel Long, of his staff, a competent officer of sound judgment, to examine the position, and directed Ewell to carry it if practicable, renewing, however, his previous warning to avoid bringing on a general engagement until the army was all up. Both Ewell, who was making some preparations with a view to attack, and Long found the position a formidable one, strongly occupied and not accessible to artillery fire. Ewell's men were indeed in no condition for an immediate assault. Of Rodes's eight thousand, nearly three thousand were *hors de combat.* Early had lost over five hundred, and had but two brigades disposable, the other two having been sent on the report of the advance of Federal troops, probably the Twelfth Corps, then near by, to watch the York road. Hill's two divisions had been very roughly handled, and had lost heavily, and he withdrew them to Seminary Hill as Ewell entered the town, leaving the latter with not more than eight thousand men to secure the town and the prisoners. Ewell's absent division (Edward Johnson's) was expected soon, but it did not arrive until near sunset, when the Twelfth Corps and Stannard's Vermont brigade were also up, and the Third Corps was arriving. In fact an assault by the Confederates was not practicable before 5:30 P.M., and after that the position was perfectly secure. For the first time that day the Federals had the advantage of position, and sufficient troops and artillery to occupy it, and Ewell would not have been justified in attacking without the positive orders of Lee, who was present, and wisely abstained from giving them.

CHAPTER 5

THE SECOND DAY AT GETTYSBURG.

Henry J. Hunt, Brevet Major-General, U.S.A.,

CHIEF OF ARTILLERY, A.P.

On June 30th, at Taneytown, General Meade received information that the enemy was advancing on Gettysburg, and corps commanders were at once instructed to hold their commands in readiness to march against him. The next day, July 1st, Meade wrote to Reynolds that telegraphic intelligence from Couch, and the movements reported by Buford, indicated a concentration of the enemy's army either at Chambersburg or at some point on a line drawn from that place through Heidlersburg to York. Under these circumstances, Meade informed Reynolds that he had not yet decided whether it was his best policy to move to attack before he knew more definitely Lee's point of concentration. He seems, however, soon to have determined not to advance until the movements or position of the enemy gave strong assurance of success, and if the enemy took the offensive, to withdraw his own army from its actual positions and form line of battle behind Pipe Creek, between Middleburg and Manchester. The considerations probably moving him to this are not difficult to divine. Examination of the maps will show that such a line would cover Baltimore and Washington in all directions from which Lee could advance, and that Westminster, his base, would be immediately behind him, with short railroad communication to Baltimore. It would, moreover, save much hard marching, and restore to the ranks the thousands of stragglers who did not reach Gettysburg in time for the battle.

From Westminster—which is in Parr's Ridge, the eastern boundary of the valley of the Monocacy—good roads led in all directions, and gave the place the same strategic value for Meade that Gettysburg had for Lee. The new line could not be turned by Lee without imminent danger to his own army, nor could he afford to advance upon Baltimore or Washington, leaving the Army of the Potomac intact behind and so near him;—that would be to invite the fate of Burgoyne. Meade, then, could safely select a good "offensive-defensive line"

HALL'S BATTERY ON THE FIRST DAY RESISTING THE CONFEDERATE ADVANCE
ON THE CHAMBERSBURG ROAD.

behind Pipe Creek and establish himself there, with perfect liberty of action in all directions. Without magazines or assured communications, Lee would have to scatter his army more or less in order to subsist it, and so expose it to Meade; or else keep it united, and so starve it, a course which Meade could compel by simple demonstrations. There would then be but two courses for Lee,—either to attack Meade in his chosen position or to retreat without a battle. The latter, neither the temper of his army nor that of his Government would probably permit. In case of a defeat Meade's line of retreat would be comparatively short, and easily covered, whilst Lee's would be for two marches through an open country before he could gain the mountain passes. As Meade believed Lee's army to be at least equal to his own, all the elements of the problem were in favor of the Pipe Creek line. But Meade's orders for July 1st, drawing his corps toward the threatened flank, carried Reynolds to Gettysburg, and Buford's report hastened this movement. Reynolds, who probably never received the Pipe Creek circular, was eager for the conflict, and his collision with Heth assuming the dimensions of a battle, caused an immediate concentration of both armies at Gettysburg. Prior to this, the assembling of Meade's army behind Pipe Creek would have been easy, and all fears of injuring thereby the *morale* of his troops were idle; the Army of the Potomac was of "sterner stuff" than that implies. The battle of July 1st changed the situation. Overpowered by numbers, the First and Eleventh corps had, after hard fighting and inflicting as well as incurring heavy losses, been forced back to their reserve, on Cemetery Hill, which they still held. To have withdrawn them now would have been a retreat, and might have discouraged the Federal, as it certainly would have elated the Confederate troops; especially as injurious reports unjust to both the corps named had been circulated. It would have been to acknowledge a defeat when there was no defeat. Meade therefore resolved to fight at Gettysburg. An ominous dispatch from General Halleck to Meade, that afternoon, suggesting that whilst his tactical arrangements were good, his strategy was at fault, that he was too far

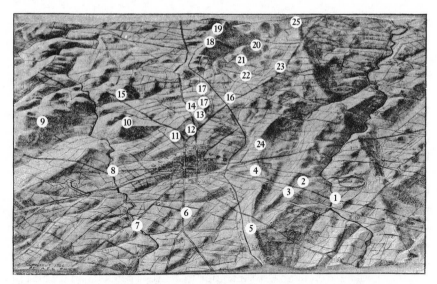

RELIEF MAP OF THE BATTLE-FIELD OF GETTYSBURG, LOOKING SOUTH. FROM A
PHOTOGRAPH OF A RELIEF MAP BY AMBROSE E. LEHMAN, C.E.

1. Chambersburg pike bridge over Willoughby Creek—beginning of the battle of the first day.
2. McPherson's farm and woods. 3. Railway cuts. 4. Seminary. 5. Oak Hill. 6. Carlisle Road. 7. Harrisburg Road bridge over Rock Creek. 8. Hanover Road. 9. Wolf Hill. 10. Culp's Hill. 11. East Cemetery Hill. 12. Cemetery Hill. 13. Ziegler's Grove. 14. Meade's headquarters on the Taneytown Road. 15. Slocum's headquarters on Power's Hill. 16. Codori's. 17. Cemetery Ridge. 18. Little Round Top. 19. Round Top. 20. Devil's Den. 21. Wheat-field. 22. Trostle's farm. 23. Peach Orchard. 24. Seminary Ridge. 19 to 23. About extreme right of Longstreet's line.

east, that Lee might attempt to turn his left, and that Frederick was preferable as a base to Westminster, may have confirmed Meade in this decision.

In pursuance of his instructions, I had that morning (July 1st) reconnoitered the country behind Pipe Creek for a battle-ground. On my return I found General Hancock at General Meade's tent. He informed me that Reynolds was killed, that a battle was going on at Gettysburg, and that he was under orders to proceed to that place. His instructions were to examine it and the intermediate country for a suitable field, and if his report was favorable the troops would be ordered forward. Before the receipt that evening of Hancock's written report from Cemetery Hill, which was not very encouraging, General Meade received from others information as to the state of affairs at the front, set his troops in motion toward Gettysburg, afterward urged them to forced marches, and under his orders I gave the necessary instructions to the Artillery Reserve and Park for a battle there. The move was, under the circumstances, a bold one, and Meade, as we shall see, took great risks. We left Taneytown toward 11 P.M., and reached Gettysburg after midnight. Soon after, General Meade, accompanied by General Howard and myself, inspected our lines so far as then occupied, after which he directed me to examine them again in the morning, and to see that the artillery was properly posted. He had thus recognized my "command" of the artillery; indeed, he did not know it had been suspended. I resumed it, therefore, and continued it to the end of the battle.

At the close of July 1st Johnson's and Anderson's divisions of the Confederate army were up. Ewell's corps now covered our front from Benner's Hill to the Seminary, his line passing through the town—Johnson on the left, Early in the center, Rodes on the right. Hill's corps occupied Seminary Ridge, and during the next morning extended its line from the Seminary south nearly to the Peach Orchard on the Emmitsburg road; Trimble—*vice* Pender, wounded—on the left; Anderson on the right; Pettigrew—*vice* Heth, wounded—in reserve. Of Longstreet's corps, McLaws's division and Hood's—except Law's brigade not yet up—camped that night on Marsh Creek, four miles from Gettysburg. His Reserve Artillery did not reach Gettysburg until 9 A.M. of the 2d. Pickett's division had been left at Chambersburg as rear-guard, and joined the corps on the night of the 2d.

It had not been General Lee's intention to deliver a general battle whilst so far from his base, unless attacked, but he now found himself by the mere force of circumstances committed to one. If it must take place, the sooner the better. His army was now nearly all on the ground, and delay, whilst it could not improve his own position, would certainly better that of his antagonist. Longstreet, indeed, urged General Lee instead of attacking to turn Meade's left, and by interposing between him and Washington and threatening his communication, to force him to attack the Confederate army in position; but General Lee probably saw that Meade would be under no such necessity; would have no great difficulty in obtaining supplies, and—disregarding the clamor from Washington—could play a waiting game, which it would be impossible for Lee to maintain in the open country. He could not advance on Baltimore or Washington with Meade in his rear, nor could his army subsist itself in a hostile region which would soon swarm with additional enemies. His communications could be cut off, for his recommendation to assemble even a small army at Culpeper to cover them and aid him had not been complied with.

A battle was a necessity to Lee, and a defeat would be more disastrous to Meade, and less so to himself, at Gettysburg than at any point east of it. With the defiles of the South Mountain range close in his rear, which could be easily held by a small force, a safe retreat through the Cumberland Valley was assured, so that his army, once through these passes, would be practically on the banks of the Potomac, at a point already prepared for crossing. Any position east of Gettysburg would deprive him of these advantages. It is more probable that General Lee was influenced by cool calculation of this nature than by hot blood, or that the opening success of a chance battle had thrown him off his balance. Whatever his reasons, he decided to accept the gage of battle offered by Meade, and to attack as soon as practicable. Ewell had made arrangements to

GENERAL MEADE'S HEADQUARTERS ON THE TANEYTOWN ROAD.
FROM A WAR-TIME PHOTOGRAPH.

General Meade arrived at Cemetery Hill at one o'clock in the morning of July 2d, and after day-light established his headquarters in a small farm-house on the Taneytown road, little more than an eighth of a mile east of Hancock's line of battle, which was the Union center. In the afternoon of July 2d, headquarters became the target of a heavy artillery fire which caused a scattering of officers and staffs and the headquarters signal corps. During the terrific cannonade which preceded Pickett's charge on July 3d, Meade's headquarters received a still greater storm of shot and shell, with the same result.—EDITORS.

take possession of Culp's Hill in the early morning, and his troops were under arms for the purpose by the time General Meade had finished the moonlight inspection of his lines, when it was ascertained by a reconnoitering party sent out by Johnson, that the hill was occupied, and its defenders on the alert; and further, from a captured dispatch from General Sykes to General Slocum, that the Fifth Corps was on the Hanover road only four miles off, and would march at 4 A.M. for Culp's Hill. Johnson thereupon deferred his attack and awaited Ewell's instructions.

General Lee had, however, during the night determined to attack the Federal left with Longstreet's corps, and now instructed Ewell, as soon as he heard Longstreet's guns, to make a diversion in his favor, to be converted, if opportunity offered, into a real attack.

Early on the morning of July 2d, when nearly all the Confederate army had reached Gettysburg or its immediate vicinity, a large portion of the Army of the Potomac was still on the road. The Second Corps and Sykes, with two divisions of the Fifth, arrived about 7 A.M., Crawford's division not joining until noon; Lockwood's brigade—two regiments from Baltimore—at 8; De Trobriand's and Burling's brigades of the Third Corps, from Emmitsburg, at 9, and the Artillery Reserve and its large ammunition trains from Taneytown at 10:30 A.M. Sedgwick's Sixth Corps, the largest in the army, after a long night march from Manchester, thirty-four miles distant, reached Rock Creek at 4 P.M. The rapidity with which the army was assembled was creditable to it and to its commander. The heat was oppressive, the long marches, especially the night marches, were trying and had caused much straggling.

All this morning Meade was busily engaged personally or by his staff in rectifying his lines, assigning positions to the commands as they came up, watching the enemy, and studying the field, parts of which we have described in general terms. Near the western base of Cemetery Hill is Ziegler's Grove. From this grove the distance nearly due south to the base of Little Round Top is a mile and a half. A well-defined ridge known as Cemetery Ridge follows this line from Ziegler's for 900 yards to another small grove, or clump of trees, where it turns sharply to the east for 200 yards, then turns south again, and continues in a direct line toward Round Top, for 700 yards, to George Weikert's. So far the ridge is smooth and open, in full view of Seminary Ridge opposite, and distant from 1400 to 1600 yards. At Weikert's, this ridge is lost in a large body of rocks, hills, and woods, lying athwart the direct line to Round Top, and forcing a bend to the east in the Taneytown road. This rough space also stretches for a quarter of a mile or more *west* of this direct line, toward Plum Run. Toward the south it sinks into low marshy ground which reaches to the base of Little Round Top, half a mile or more from George Weikert's. The west side of this broken ground was wooded through its whole extent from north to south. Between this wood and Plum Run is an open cleared space 300 yards wide—a continuation of the open country in front of Cemetery Ridge; Plum Run flows southeasterly toward Little Round Top, then makes a bend to the south-west, where it receives a small stream or "branch" from Seminary Ridge. In the angle between these streams is Devil's Den, a bold, rocky height, steep on its eastern face, and prolonged as a ridge to the west. It is 500 yards due west of Little Round Top, and 100 feet lower. The northern extremity is composed of huge rocks and bowlders, forming innumerable crevices and holes, from the largest of which the hill derives its name. Plum Run valley is here marshy but strewn with similar bowlders, and the slopes of the Round Tops are covered with them. These afforded lurking-places for a multitude of Confederate sharp-shooters whom, from the difficulties of the ground, it was impossible to dislodge, and who were opposed by similar methods on our part; so that at the close of the battle these hiding-places, and especially the "Den" itself, were filled with dead and wounded men. This kind of warfare was specially destructive to Hazlett's battery on Round Top, as the cannoneers had to expose themselves in firing, and in one case three were shot in quick succession, before the fourth succeeded in discharging the piece. A cross-road connecting the Taneytown and

Emmitsburg roads runs along the northern base of Devil's Den. From its Plum Run crossing to the Peach Orchard is 1100 yards. For the first 400 yards of this distance, there is a wood on the north and a wheat-field on the south of the road, beyond which the road continues for 700 yards to the Emmitsburg road along Devil's Den ridge, which slopes on the north to Plum Run, on the south to Plum Branch. From Ziegler's Grove the Emmitsburg road runs diagonally

MAJOR-GENERAL DANIEL E. SICKLES. FROM A WAR-TIME PHOTOGRAPH.

across the interval between Cemetery and Seminary ridges, crossing the latter two miles from Ziegler's Grove. From Peach Orchard to Ziegler's is nearly a mile and a half. For half a mile the road runs along a ridge at right angles to that of Devil's Den, which slopes back to Plum Run. The angle at the Peach Orchard is thus formed by the intersection of two bold ridges, one from Devil's Den, the other along the Emmitsburg road. It is distant about 600 yards from the wood which skirts the whole length of Seminary Ridge and covers the movement of troops between it and Willoughby Run, half a mile beyond. South of the Round Top and Devil's Den ridge the country is open, and the principal obstacles to free movement are the fences—generally of stone—which surround the numerous fields.

As our troops came up they were assigned to places on the line: the Twelfth Corps, General A. S. Williams,—*vice* Slocum, commanding the right wing,—to Culp's Hill, on Wadsworth's right; Second Corps to Cemetery Ridge—Hays's and Gibbon's divisions, from Ziegler's to the clump of trees, Caldwell's to the short ridge to its left and rear. This ridge had been occupied by the Third Corps, which was now directed to prolong Caldwell's line to Round Top, relieving Geary's division, which had been stationed during the night on the extreme left, with two regiments at the base of Little Round Top. The Fifth Corps was placed in reserve near the Rock Creek crossing of the Baltimore pike; the Artillery Reserve and its large trains were parked in a central position on a cross-road from the Baltimore pike to the Taneytown road; Buford's cavalry, except Merritt's brigade (then at Emmitsburg), was near Round Top, from which point it was ordered that morning to Westminster, thus uncovering our left flank; Kilpatrick's and Gregg's divisions were well out on the right flank, from which, after a brush with Stuart on the evening of the 2d, Kilpatrick was sent next morning to replace Buford, Merritt being also ordered up to our left.

The morning was a busy and in some respects an anxious one; it was believed that the whole Confederate army was assembled, that it was equal if not superior to our own in numbers, and that the battle would commence before our troops were up. There was a gap in Slocum's line awaiting a division of infantry, and as some demonstrations of Ewell about daylight indicated an immediate attack at that point, I had to draw batteries from other parts of the line—for the Artillery Reserve was just then starting from Taneytown—to cover it until it could be properly filled. Still there was no hostile movement of the enemy, and General Meade directed Slocum to hold himself in readiness to attack Ewell with the Fifth and Twelfth, so soon as the Sixth Corps should arrive. After an examination Slocum reported the ground as unfavorable, in which Warren concurred and advised against an attack there. The project was then abandoned, and Meade postponed all offensive operations until the enemy's intentions should be more clearly developed. In the meantime he took precautionary measures. It was clearly now to his advantage to fight the battle where he was, and he had some apprehension that Lee would attempt to turn his flank and threaten his communications,—just what Longstreet had been advising. In this case it might be necessary to fall back to the Pipe Creek line, if possible, or else to follow Lee's movement into the open country. In either case, or in that of a forced withdrawal, prudence dictated that arrangements should be made in advance, and General Meade gave instructions for examining the roads and communications, and to draw up an order of movement, which General Butterfield, the chief-of-staff, seems to have considered an order absolute for the withdrawal of the army without a battle.

These instructions must have been given early in the morning, for General Butterfield states that it was on his arrival from Taneytown, which place he left at daylight. An order was drawn up accordingly, given to the adjutant-general, and perhaps prepared for issue in case of necessity to corps commanders; but it was not recorded nor issued, nor even a copy of it preserved. General Meade declared that he never contemplated the issue of such an order unless contingencies made it necessary; and his acts and dispatches during the day were in accordance with his statement. There is one circumstance pertaining to my own duties which to my mind is conclusive, and I relate it because it may have contributed to the idea that General Meade intended to withdraw from Gettysburg. He came to me that morning before the Artillery Reserve had arrived, and, therefore, about the time that the order was in course of preparation, and informed me that one of the army corps had left its whole artillery ammunition train behind it, and that others were also deficient, notwithstanding his orders on that subject. He was very much disturbed, and feared that, taking into account the large expenditure of the preceding day by the First and Eleventh corps, there would not be sufficient to carry us through the battle. This was not the first nor the last time that I was called upon to meet deficiencies under such circumstances, and I was, therefore, prepared for this, having directed General Tyler, commanding the Artillery Reserve, whatever else he might leave behind, to bring up every round of ammunition in his trains, and I knew he would not fail me. Moreover, I had previously, on my own responsibility, and unknown to General Hooker, formed a special ammunition column attached to the Artillery Reserve, carrying twenty rounds per gun, over and above the authorized amount, for every gun in the army, in order to meet such emergencies. I was, therefore, able to assure General Meade that there would be enough ammunition for the battle, but none for idle cannonades, the besetting sin of some of our commanders. He was much relieved, and expressed his satisfaction. Now, had he had at this time any intention of withdrawing the army, the first thing to get rid of would have been this Artillery Reserve and its large trains, which were then blocking the roads in our rear; and he would surely have told me of it.

UNION BREASTWORKS ON LITTLE ROUND TOP—BIG ROUND TOP IN THE DISTANCE.
FROM WAR-TIME PHOTOGRAPHS.

Still, with the exception of occasional cannonading, and some skirmishing near the Peach Orchard, the quiet remained unbroken, although Lee had determined upon an early attack on our left. He says in his detailed report that our line extended "upon the high ground along the Emmitsburg road, with a steep ridge [Cemetery] in rear, which was also occupied"; and in a previous "outline" report he says: "In front of General Longstreet the enemy held a position [the salient angle at the Peach Orchard] from which, if he could be driven, it was thought our artillery could be used to advantage in assailing the more elevated ground beyond, and thus enable us to gain the crest of the ridge." It would appear from this that General Lee mistook the few troops on the Peach Orchard ridge in the morning for our main line, and that by taking it and sweeping up the Emmitsburg road under cover of his batteries, he expected to "roll up" our lines to Cemetery Hill. That would be an "oblique order of battle," in which the attacking line, formed obliquely to its opponent, marches directly forward, constantly breaking in the *end* of his enemy's line and gaining his rear. General Longstreet was ordered to form the divisions of Hood and McLaws on Anderson's right, so as to envelop our left and drive it in. These divisions were only three miles off at daylight, and moved early, but there was great delay in forming them for battle, owing principally to the absence of Law's brigade, for which it would have been well to substitute Anderson's fresh division, which could have been replaced by Pettigrew's, then in reserve. There seems to have been no good reason why the attack should not have been made by 8 or 9 A.M. at the latest, when the Federal Third Corps was not yet all up, nor Crawford's division, nor the Artillery Reserve, nor the Sixth Corps, and our lines were still very incomplete. This is one of the cheap criticisms after all the facts on both sides are known; but it is apt for its purpose, as it shows how great a risk Meade took in abandoning his Pipe Creek line for Gettysburg on the chances of Lee's army not yet being assembled; and also, that there was no lack of boldness and decision on Meade's part. Indeed, his course, from the hour that he took command, had been marked by these qualities.

A suggestive incident is worth recording here. In the course of my inspection of the lines that morning, while passing along Culp's Hill, I found the men hard at work intrenching, and in such fine spirits as at once to attract attention. One of them finally dropped his work, and, approaching me, inquired if the reports just received were true. On asking what he referred to, he replied that twice word had been passed along the line that General McClellan had been assigned to the command of the army, and the second time it was added that he was on the way to the field and might soon be expected. He continued, "The boys are all jubilant over it, for they know that if *he* takes command everything will go right." I have been told recently by the commander of a Fifth Corps battery that during the forced march of the preceding night the same report ran through that corps, excited great enthusiasm amongst the men, and renewed their vigor. It was probably from this corps—just arrived—that the report had spread along the line.✝

On my return to headquarters from this inspection General Meade told me that General Sickles, then with him, wished me to examine a new line, as he thought that assigned to him was not a good one, especially that he could not use his artillery there. I had been as far as Round Top that morning, and had noticed the unfavorable character of the ground, and, therefore, I accompanied Sickles direct to the Peach Orchard, where he pointed out the ridges, already described, as his proposed line. They commanded all the ground behind, as well as in front of them, and together constituted a favorable position for *the enemy* to hold. This was one good reason for our taking possession of it. It would, it is true, in our hands present a salient angle, which generally exposes both its sides to enfilade fires; but here the ridges were so high that each would serve as

✝Lieutenant O. S. Barrett, in a pamphlet sketch of the "Old Fourth Michigan Infantry" (Detroit, 1888), relates a similar occurrence in the Second Corps. He says:

"We arrived at Hanover, Pennsylvania, on the afternoon of July 1st. . . . An aide-de-camp came riding along, saying, 'Boys, keep up good courage, McClellan is in command of the army again.' Instantly the space above was filled with the hats and caps of the gratified soldiers. . . . I knew this was untrue myself, but it served its purpose, as intended."—EDITORS.

a "traverse" for the other, and reduce that evil to a minimum. On the other hand it would so greatly lengthen our line—which in any case must rest on Round Top, and connect with the left of the Second Corps—as to require a larger force than the Third Corps alone to hold it, and it would be difficult to occupy and strengthen the angle if the enemy already held the wood in its front. At my instance General Sickles ordered a reconnoissance to ascertain if the wood was occupied.

About this time a cannonade was opened on Cemetery Hill, which indicated an attack there, and as I had examined the Emmitsburg Ridge, I said I would not await the result of the reconnoissance but return to headquarters by way of Round Top, and examine that part of the proposed line. As I was leaving, General Sickles asked me if he should move forward his corps. I answered, "Not on my authority; I will report to General Meade for his instructions." I had not reached the wheat-field when a sharp rattle of musketry showed that the enemy held the wood in front of the Peach Orchard angle.

As I rode back a view from that direction showed how much farther Peach Orchard was to the front of the direct line than it appeared from the orchard itself. In fact there was a third line between them, which appeared, as seen from the orchard, to be continuous with Cemetery Ridge, but was nearly six hundred yards in front of it. This is the open ground east of Plum Run already described, and which may be called the Plum Run line. Its left where it crosses the run abuts rather on Devil's Den than Round Top; it was commanded by the much higher Peach Orchard crests, and was therefore not an eligible line to occupy, although it became of importance during the battle.

As to the other two lines, the choice between them would depend on circumstances. The direct short line through the woods, and including the Round Tops, could be occupied, intrenched, and made impregnable to a front attack. But, like that of Culp's Hill, it would be a purely defensive one, from which, owing to the nature of the ground and the enemy's commanding position on the ridges at the angle, an advance in force would be impracticable. The salient line proposed by General Sickles, although much longer, afforded excellent positions for our artillery; its occupation would cramp the movements of the enemy, bring us nearer his lines, and afford us facilities for taking the offensive. It was in my judgment tactically the better line of the two, provided it were strongly occupied, for it was the only one on the field from which we could have passed from the defensive to the offensive with a prospect of decisive results. But General Meade had not, until the arrival of the Sixth Corps, a sufficient number of troops at his disposal to risk such an extension of his lines; it would have required both the Third and the Fifth corps, and left him without any reserve. Had he known that Lee's attack would be postponed until 4 P.M., he might have occupied this line in the morning; but he did not know this, expected an attack at any moment, and, in view of the vast interests involved, adopted a defensive policy, and ordered the occupation of the *safe* line. In taking risks, it would not be for his army alone, but also for Philadelphia, Baltimore, and Washington. Gettysburg was not a good strategical position for us, and the circumstances under which our army was assembled limited us tactically to a strictly defensive battle. But even a strictly defensive battle gained here would be, in its results, almost as valuable as an offensive one with a brilliant victory, since it would necessarily be decisive as to both the campaign and the invasion, and its moral effect abroad and at home, North and South, would be of vast importance in a political as well as a military sense. The additional risks of an offensive battle were out of all proportion to the prospective gains. The decision then to fight a defensive rather than an offensive battle, to look rather to solid than to brilliant results, was wise.

After finishing my examination I returned to headquarters and briefly reported to General Meade that the proposed line was a good one in itself, that it offered favorable positions for artillery, but that its relations to other lines were such that I could not advise it, and suggested that he examine it himself before ordering its occupation. He nodded assent, and I proceeded to Cemetery Hill.

The cannonade there still continued; it had been commenced by the enemy, and was accompanied by some movements of troops toward our right. As soon as I saw that it would lead to nothing serious, I returned direct to the Peach Orchard, knowing that its occupation would require large reënforcements of artillery. I was here met by Captain Randolph, the corps chief of artillery, who informed me that he had been ordered to place his batteries on the

WEED'S POSITION ON LITTLE ROUND TOP, LOOKING IN THE DIRECTION
OF THE PEACH ORCHARD. FROM A WAR-TIME SKETCH.

GENERAL G. K. WARREN AT THE SIGNAL STATION ON LITTLE ROUND TOP.
FROM A SKETCH MADE AT THE TIME.

new line. Seeing Generals Meade and Sickles, not far off, in conversation, and supposing that General Meade had consented to the occupation, I sent at once to the reserve for more artillery, and authorized other general officers to draw on the same source. Here, perhaps, I may be allowed to say *en passant* that this large reserve, organized by the wise forethought of General McClellan, sometimes threatened with destruction, and once actually broken up, was often, as at Malvern Hill, and now at Gettysburg, an invaluable resource in the time of greatest need. When in 1864, in the Rapidan campaign, it was "got rid of," it reconstituted itself, without orders, and in a few weeks, through the necessities of the army, showing that "principles vindicate themselves."

When I arrived Birney's division was already posted on the crest, from Devil's Den to the Peach Orchard, and along the Emmitsburg road, Ward's brigade on the left, Graham's at the angle, De Trobriand's connecting them by a thin line. Humphreys's division was on Graham's right, near the Emmitsburg road, Carr's brigade in the front line, about the Smith house, Brewster's in second line. Burling's, with the exception of Sewell's 5th New Jersey Regiment, then in skirmish order at the front, was sent to reënforce Birney. Seeley's battery, at first posted on the right, was soon after sent to the left of the Smith house, and replaced on the right by Turnbull's from the Artillery Reserve. Randolph had ordered Smith's battery, 4th New York, to the rocky hill at the Devil's Den; Winslow's to the wheat-field. He had placed Clark on the crest looking south, and his own ("E," 1st Rhode Island) near the angle, facing west. The whole corps was, however, too weak to cover the ground, and it was too late for Meade to withdraw it. Sykes's Fifth Corps had already been ordered up and was momentarily expected. As soon as fire opened, which was just as he arrived on the ground, General Meade also sent for Caldwell's division from Cemetery Ridge, and a division of the Twelfth Corps from Culp's, and soon after for troops from the Sixth Corps. McGilvery's artillery brigade soon arrived from the reserve, and Bigelow's, Phillips's, Hart's, Ames's, and Thompson's batteries had been ordered into position on the crests, when the enemy opened from a long line of guns, stretching down to the crossing of the Emmitsburg pike. Smith's position at Devil's Den gave him a favorable oblique fire on a part of this line, and as he did not reply I proceeded to the Den. Finding the acclivity steep and rocky, I dismounted and tied my horse to a tree before crossing the valley. My rank, brigadier-general, the command being that of a lieutenant-general, gave me a very small and insufficient staff, and even this had been recently cut down. The inspector of artillery, Lieutenant-Colonel Warner, adjutant-general, Captain Craig, my only aide, Lieutenant Bissell, my one orderly, and even the flag-bearer necessary to indicate my presence to those seeking me, were busy conveying orders or messages, and I was alone; a not infrequent and an awkward thing for a general who had to keep up communications with every part of a battle-field and with the general-in-chief. On climbing to the summit, I found that Smith had just got his guns, one by one, over the rocks and chasms, into an excellent position. After pointing out to me the advancing lines of the enemy, he opened, and very effectively. Many guns were immediately turned on him, relieving so far the rest of the line. Telling

TROSTLE'S FARM, THE SCENE OF THE FIGHTING BY BIGELOW'S NINTH
MASSACHUSETTS BATTERY. FROM A WAR-TIME PHOTOGRAPH.

TROSTLE'S HOUSE, SCENE OF THE FIGHTING OF BIGELOW'S BATTERY.
FROM A WAR-TIME PHOTOGRAPH.

him that he would probably lose his battery, I left to seek infantry supports, very doubtful if I would find my horse, for the storm of shell bursting over the place was enough to drive any animal wild. On reaching the foot of the cliff, I found myself in a plight at once ludicrous, painful, and dangerous. A herd of horned cattle had been driven into the valley between Devil's Den and Round Top, from which they could not escape. A shell had exploded in the body of one of them, tearing it to pieces; others were torn and wounded. All were *stampeded*, and were bellowing and rushing in their terror, first to one side and then to the other, to escape the shells that were bursting over them and among them. Cross I must, and in doing so I had my most trying experience of that battle-field. Luckily the poor beasts were as much frightened as I was, but their rage was subdued by terror, and they were good enough to let me pass through scot-free, but "badly demoralized." However, my horse was safe, I mounted, and in the busy excitement that followed almost forgot my scare.

It was not until about 4 P.M. that Longstreet got his two divisions into position in two lines, McLaws's on the right of Anderson's division of Hill's corps, and opposite the Peach Orchard; Hood's on the extreme Confederate right and crossing the Emmitsburg road. Hood had been ordered, keeping his left on that road, to break in the end of our line, supposed to be at the orchard; but perceiving that our left was "refused" (bent back toward Devil's Den), and noticing the importance of Round Top, he suggested to Longstreet that the latter be turned and attacked. The reply was that General Lee's orders were to attack along the Emmitsburg road. Again Hood sent his message and received the same reply, notwithstanding which he directed Law's brigade upon Round Top, in which movement a portion of Robertson's brigade joined; the rest of the division was thrown upon Devil's Den and the ridge between it and the Peach Orchard. The first assaults were repulsed, but after hard fighting, McLaws's division being also advanced, toward 6 o'clock the angle was broken in, after a resolute defense and with great loss on both sides. In the meantime three of Anderson's brigades were advancing on Humphreys, and the latter received orders from Birney, now in command of the corps (Sickles having been severely wounded soon after 6 o'clock near the Trostle house), to throw back his left, form an oblique line in his rear, and connect with the right of Birney's division, then retiring. The junction was not effected, and Humphreys, greatly outnumbered, slowly and skillfully fell back to Cemetery Ridge, Gibbon sending two regiments and Brown's Rhode Island battery to his support. But the enemy was strong and covered the whole Second Corps front, now greatly weakened by detachments. Wilcox's, Perry's, and Wright's Confederate brigades pressed up to the ridge, outflanking Humphreys's right and left, and Wright broke through our line and seized the guns in his front, but was soon driven out, and not being supported they all fell back, about dusk, under a heavy artillery fire.

As soon as Longstreet's attack commenced, General Warren was sent by General Meade to see to the condition of the extreme left. The duty could not have been intrusted to better hands. Passing along the lines he found Little Round Top, the key of the position, unoccupied except by a signal station. The enemy at the time lay concealed, awaiting the signal for assault, when a shot fired in their direction caused a sudden movement on their part which, by the gleam of reflected sunlight from their bayonets, revealed their long lines outflanking the position. Fully comprehending the imminent danger, Warren sent to General Meade for a division.[1] The enemy was already advancing when, noticing the approach of the Fifth Corps, Warren rode to meet it, caused

---

[1]Before the Committee on the Conduct of the War General Warren testified that he went to Little Round Top "by General Meade's direction." In a letter dated July 13th, 1872, General Warren says:

> "Just before the action began in earnest, on July 2d, I was with General Meade, near General Sickles, whose troops seemed very badly disposed on that part of the field. At my suggestion, General Meade sent me to the left to examine the condition of affairs, and I continued on till I reached Little Round Top. There were no troops on it, and it was used as a signal station. I saw that this was the key of the whole position, and that our troops in the woods in front of it could not see the ground in front of them, so that the enemy would come upon them before they would be aware of it. The long line of woods on the west side of the Emmitsburg road (which road was along a ridge) furnished an excellent place for the enemy to form out of sight, so I requested the captain of a rifle battery just in front of Little Round Top to fire a shot into these woods. He did so, and as the shot went whistling through the air the sound of it reached the enemy's troops and caused every one to look in the direction of it. This motion revealed to me the glistening of gun-barrels and bayonets of the enemy's line of battle, already formed and far outflanking the position of any of our troops; so that the line of his advance from his right to Little Round Top was unopposed. I have been particular in telling this, as the discovery was intensely thrilling to my feelings, and almost appalling. I immediately sent a hastily written dispatch to General Meade to send a division at least to me, and General Meade directed the Fifth Army Corps to take position there. The battle was already beginning to rage at the Peach Orchard, and before a single man reached Round Top the

Weed's and Vincent's brigades and Hazlett's battery to be detached from the latter and hurried them to the summit. The passage of the six guns through the roadless woods and amongst the rocks was marvelous. Under ordinary circumstances it would have been considered an impossible feat, but the eagerness of the men to get into action with their comrades of the infantry, and the skillful driving, brought them without delay to the very summit, where they went immediately into battle. They were barely in time, for the enemy were also climbing the hill. A close and bloody hand-to-hand struggle ensued, which left both Round Tops in our possession. Weed and Hazlett were killed, and Vincent was mortally wounded—all young men of great promise. Weed had served with much distinction as an artillerist in the Peninsular, Second Bull Run, and Antietam campaigns, had become chief of artillery of his army corps, and at Chancellorsville showed such special aptitude and fitness for large artillery commands that he was immediately promoted from captain to brigadier-general and transferred to the infantry. Hazlett was killed whilst bending over his former chief, to receive his last message. Lieutenant Rittenhouse efficiently commanded the battery during the remainder of the battle.

The enemy, however, clung to the woods and rocks at the base of Round Top, carried Devil's Den and its woods, and captured three of Smith's guns, who, however, effectively deprived the enemy of their use by carrying off all the implements.

The breaking in of the Peach Orchard angle exposed the flanks of the batteries on its crests, which retired firing, in order to cover the retreat of the infantry. Many guns of different batteries had to be abandoned because of the destruction of their horses and men; many were hauled off by hand; all the batteries lost heavily. Bigelow's 9th Massachusetts made a stand close by the Trostle house in the corner of the field through which he had retired fighting with

---

whole line of the enemy moved on us in splendid array, shouting in the most confident tones. While I was still all alone with the signal officer, the musket-balls began to fly around us, and he was about to fold up his flags and withdraw, but remained, at my request, and kept waving them in defiance. Seeing troops going out on the Peach Orchard road, I rode down the hill, and fortunately met my old brigade. General Weed, commanding it, had already passed the point, and I took the responsibility to detach Colonel O'Rorke, the head of whose regiment I struck, who, on hearing my few words of explanation about the position, moved at once to the hill-top. About this time First Lieutenant Charles E. Hazlett of the Fifth Artillery, with his battery of rifled cannon, arrived. He comprehended the situation instantly and planted a gun on the summit of the hill. He spoke to the effect that though he could do little execution on the enemy with his guns, he could aid in giving confidence to the infantry, and that his battery was of no consequence whatever compared with holding the position. He staid there till he was killed. I was wounded with a musket-ball while talking with Lieutenant Hazlett on the hill, but not seriously; and, seeing the position saved while the whole line to the right and front of us was yielding and melting away under the enemy's fire and advance, I left the hill to rejoin General Meade near the center of the field, where a new crisis was at hand."

—Editors.

prolonges fixed. Although already much cut up, he was directed by McGilvery to hold that point at all hazards until a line of artillery could be formed in front of the wood beyond Plum Run; that is, on what we have called the "Plum Run line." This line was formed by collecting the serviceable batteries, and fragments of batteries, that were brought off, with which, and Dow's Maine battery fresh from the reserve, the pursuit was checked. Finally some twenty-five guns formed a solid mass, which unsupported by infantry held this part of the line, aided General Humphreys's movements, and covered by its fire the abandoned guns until they could be brought off, as all were, except perhaps one. When, after accomplishing its purpose, all that was left of Bigelow's battery was withdrawn, it was closely pressed by Colonel Humphreys's 21st Mississippi, the only Confederate regiment which succeeded in crossing the run. His men had entered the battery and fought hand-to-hand with the cannoneers; one was killed whilst trying to spike a gun, and another knocked down with a handspike whilst endeavoring to drag off a prisoner. The battery went into action with 104 officers and men. Of the four battery officers one was killed, another mortally, and a third, Captain Bigelow, severely wounded. Of 7 sergeants, 2 were killed and 4 wounded; or a total of 28 men, including 2 missing; and 65 out of 88 horses were killed or wounded. As the battery had sacrificed itself for the safety of the line, its work is specially noticed as typical of the service that artillery is not infrequently called upon to render, and did render in other instances at Gettysburg besides this one.

When Sickles was wounded General Meade directed Hancock to take command of the Third as well as his own corps, which he again turned over to Gibbon. About 7:15 P.M. the field was in a critical condition. Birney's division

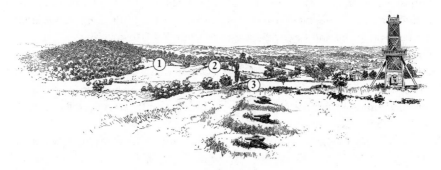

CULP'S HILL.

VIEW OF CULP'S HILL FROM THE POSITION OF THE BATTERIES NEAR
THE CEMETERY GATE. FROM PHOTOGRAPHS.

1. Position of Stevens's 5th Maine Battery which enfiladed Early's division in the charge upon East Cemetery Hill. 2. Left of the line of field-works on Culp's Hill. 3. Position of the 33d Massachusetts behind the fence of a lane where the left of the Confederate charge was repulsed.

—EDITORS.

EARLY'S CHARGE ON THE EVENING OF JULY 2 UPON EAST CEMETERY HILL.

was now broken up; Humphreys's was slowly falling back, under cover of McGilvery's guns; Anderson's line was advancing. On its right, Barksdale's brigade, except the 21st Mississippi, was held in check only by McGilvery's artillery, to whose support Hancock now brought up Willard's brigade of the Second Corps. Placing the 39th New York in reserve, Willard with his other three regiments charged Barksdale's brigade and drove it back nearly to the Emmitsburg road, when he was himself repulsed by a heavy artillery and infantry fire, and fell back to his former position near the sources of Plum Run. In this affair Willard was killed and Barksdale mortally wounded. Meanwhile the 21st Mississippi crossed the run from the neighborhood of the Trostle house, and drove out the men of Watson's battery ("I," 5th United States), on the extreme left of McGilvery's line, but was in turn driven off by the 39th New York, led by Lieutenant Peeples of the battery, musket in hand, who thus recovered his guns, Watson being severely wounded.

Birney's division once broken, it was difficult to stem the tide of defeat. Hood's and McLaws's divisions—excepting Barksdale's brigade—compassed the Devil's Den and its woods, and as the Federal reënforcements from other corps came piecemeal, they were beaten in detail until by successive accretions they greatly outnumbered their opponents, who had all the advantages of position, when the latter in turn retired, but were not pursued. This fighting was confined almost wholly to the woods and wheat-field between the Peach Orchard and Little Round Top, and the great number of brigade and regimental commanders, as well as of inferior officers and soldiers, killed and wounded on both sides, bears testimony to its close and desperate character. General Meade was on the ground active in bringing up and putting in reënforcements, and in doing so had his horse shot under him. At the close of the day the Confederates held the base of the Round Tops, Devil's Den, its woods, and the Emmitsburg road, with skirmishers thrown out as far as the Trostle house; the Federals had the two Round Tops, the Plum Run line, and Cemetery Ridge. During the night the Plum Run line, except the wood on its left front (occupied by McCandless's brigade, Crawford's division, his other brigade being on Big Round Top), was abandoned; the Third Corps was massed to the left and rear of Caldwell's division, which had reoccupied its short ridge, with McGilvery's artillery on its crest. The Fifth Corps remained on and about Round Top, and a division [Ruger's] which had been detached from the Twelfth Corps returned to Culp's Hill.

When Longstreet's guns were heard, Ewell opened a cannonade, which after an hour's firing was overpowered by the Federal artillery on Cemetery Hill. Johnson's division then advanced, and found only one brigade—Greene's—of the Twelfth Corps in position, the others having been sent to the aid of Sickles at the Peach Orchard. Greene fought with skill and determination for two or three hours, and, reënforced by seven or eight hundred men of the First and Eleventh corps, succeeded in holding his own intrenchments, the enemy taking possession of the abandoned works of Geary and Ruger. This brought Johnson's troops near the Baltimore pike, but the darkness prevented their seeing or profiting by the advantage then within their reach. When Ruger's division returned from Round Top, and Geary's from Rock Creek, they found

CONFEDERATE SKIRMISHERS AT THE FOOT OF CULP'S HILL.

Johnson in possession of their intrenchments, and immediately prepared to drive him out at daylight.

It had been ordered that when Johnson engaged Culp's Hill, Early and Rodes should assault Cemetery Hill. Early's attack was made with great spirit, by Hoke's and Avery's brigades, Gordon's being in reserve; the hill was ascended through the wide ravine between Cemetery and Culp's hills, a line of infantry on the slopes was broken, and Wiedrich's Eleventh Corps and Ricketts's reserve batteries near the brow of the hill were overrun; but the excellent position of Stevens's 12-pounders at the head of the ravine, which enabled him to sweep it, the arrival of Carroll's brigade sent unasked by Hancock,—a happy inspiration, as this line had been weakened to send supports both to Greene and Sickles,—and the failure of Rodes to coöperate with Early, caused the attack to miscarry. The cannoneers of the two batteries, so summarily ousted, rallied and recovered their guns by a vigorous attack—with pistols by those who had them, by others with handspikes, rammers, stones, and even fence-rails—the "Dutchmen" showing that they were in no way inferior to their "Yankee" comrades, who had been taunting them ever since Chancellorsville. After an hour's desperate fighting the enemy was driven out with heavy loss, Avery being among the killed. At the close of this second day a consultation of corps commanders was held at Meade's headquarters. I was not present, although summoned, but was informed that the vote was unanimous to hold our lines and to await an attack for at least one day before taking the offensive, and Meade so decided.

CHAPTER 6

THE THIRD DAY AT GETTYSBURG.

Henry J. Hunt, Brevet Major-General, U.S.A.,
Chief of Artillery, A.P.

In view of the successes gained on the second day, General Lee resolved to renew his efforts. These successes were:

1st. *On the right,* the lodgment at the bases of the Round Tops, the possession of Devil's Den and its woods, and the ridges on the Emmitsburg road, which gave him the coveted positions for his artillery.

2d. *On the left,* the occupation of part of the intrenchments of the Twelfth Corps, with an outlet to the Baltimore pike, by which all our lines could be taken in reverse.

3d. *At the center,* the partial success of three of Anderson's brigades in penetrating our lines, from which they were expelled only because they lacked proper support. It was thought that better concert of action might have made good a lodgment here also.

Both armies had indeed lost heavily, but the account in that respect seemed in favor of the Confederates, or at worst balanced. Pickett's and Edward Johnson's divisions were fresh, as were Posey's and Mahone's brigades of R. H. Anderson's, and William Smith's brigade of Early's division. These could be depended upon for an assault; the others could be used as supports, and to follow up a success. The artillery was almost intact. Stuart had arrived with his cavalry, excepting the brigades of Jones and Robertson, guarding the communications; and Imboden had also come up. General Lee, therefore, directed the renewal of operations both on the right and left. Ewell had been ordered to attack at daylight on July 3d, and during the night reënforced Johnson with Smith's, Daniel's, and O'Neal's brigades. Johnson had made his preparations, and was about moving, when at dawn Williams's artillery opened upon him,

HAND-TO-HAND FOR RICKETTS'S GUNS ON THE EVENING OF THE SECOND DAY.

preparatory to an assault by Geary and Ruger for the recovery of their works. The suspension of this fire was followed by an immediate advance by both sides. A conflict ensued which lasted with varying success until near 11 o'clock, during which the Confederates were driven out of the Union intrenchments by Geary and Ruger, aided by Shaler's brigade of the Sixth Corps. They made one or two attempts to regain possession, but were unsuccessful, and a demonstration to turn Johnson's left caused him to withdraw his command to Rock Creek. At the close of the war the scene of this conflict was covered by a forest of dead

STEUART'S BRIGADE RENEWING THE CONFEDERATE ATTACK ON CULP'S HILL,
MORNING OF THE THIRD DAY.

trees, leaden bullets proving as fatal to them as to the soldiers whose bodies were thickly strewn beneath them.

Longstreet's arrangements had been made to attack Round Top, and his orders issued with a view to turning it, when General Lee decided that the assault should be made on Cemetery Ridge by Pickett's and Pettigrew's divisions, with part of Trimble's. Longstreet formed these in two lines—Pickett on the right, supported by Wilcox; Pettigrew on the left, with Lane's and Scales's brigades under Trimble in the second line. Hill was ordered to hold his line with the remainder of his corps,—six brigades,—give Longstreet assistance if required, and avail himself of any success that might be gained. Finally a powerful artillery force, about one hundred and fifty guns, was ordered to prepare the way for the assault by cannonade. The necessary arrangements caused delay, and before notice of this could be received by Ewell, Johnson, as we have seen, was attacked, so that the contest was over on the left before that at the center was begun. The hoped-for concert of action in the Confederate attacks was lost from the beginning.

On the Federal side Hancock's corps held Cemetery Ridge with Robinson's division, First Corps, on Hays's right in support, and Doubleday's at the angle between Gibbon and Caldwell. General Newton, having been assigned to the command of the First Corps, *vice* Reynolds, was now in charge of the ridge

THE 29TH PENNSYLVANIA FORMING LINE OF BATTLE ON CULP'S HILL
AT 10 A.M., JULY 3.

held by Caldwell. Compactly arranged on its crest was McGilvery's artillery, forty-one guns, consisting of his own batteries, reënforced by others from the Artillery Reserve. Well to the right, in front of Hays and Gibbon, was the artillery of the Second Corps under its chief, Captain Hazard. Woodruff's battery was in front of Ziegler's Grove; on his left, in succession, Arnold's Rhode Island, Cushing's United States, Brown's Rhode Island, and Rorty's New York. In the fight of the preceding day the two last-named batteries had been to the front and suffered severely. Lieutenant T. Fred Brown was severely wounded, and his command devolved on Lieutenant Perrin. So great had been the loss in men and horses that they were now of four guns each, reducing the total number in the corps to twenty-six. Daniels's battery of horse artillery, four guns, was at the angle. Cowan's 1st New York battery, six rifles, was placed on the left of Rorty's soon after the cannonade commenced. In addition, some of the guns on Cemetery Hill, and Rittenhouse's on Little Round Top, could be brought to bear, but these were offset by batteries similarly placed on the flanks of the enemy, so that on the Second Corps line, within the space of a mile, were 77 guns to oppose nearly 150. They were on an open crest plainly visible from all parts of the opposite line. Between 10 and 11 A.M., everything looking favorable at Culp's Hill, I crossed over to Cemetery Ridge, to see what might be going on at other points. Here a magnificent display greeted my eyes. Our whole front for two miles was covered by batteries already in line or going into position. They stretched—apparently in one unbroken mass—from opposite the town to the Peach Orchard, which bounded the view to the left, the ridges of which were planted thick with cannon. Never before had such a sight been witnessed on this continent, and rarely, if ever, abroad. What did it mean? It might possibly be to hold that line while its infantry was sent to aid Ewell, or to guard against a counter-stroke from us, but it most probably meant an assault on our center, to be preceded by a cannonade in order to crush our batteries and shake our infantry; at least to cause us to exhaust our ammunition in reply, so that the assaulting troops might pass in good condition over the half mile of open ground which was beyond our effective musketry fire. With such an object the cannonade would be long and followed immediately by the assault, their whole army being held in readiness to follow up a success. From the great extent of ground occupied by the enemy's batteries, it was evident that all the artillery on our west front, whether of the army corps or the reserve, must concur as a *unit*, under the chief of artillery, in the defense. This is provided for in all well-organized armies by special rules, which formerly were contained in our own army regulations, but they had been condensed in successive editions into a few short lines, so obscure as to be virtually worthless, because, like the rudimentary toe of the dog's paw, they had become, from lack of use, mere survivals—unintelligible except to the specialist. It was of the first importance to subject the enemy's infantry, from the first moment of their advance, to such a cross-fire of our artillery as would break their formation, check their impulse, and drive them back, or at least bring them to our lines in such condition as to make them an easy prey. There was neither time nor necessity for reporting this to General Meade, and beginning on the right, I instructed the chiefs of artillery and battery commanders to withhold their fire for fifteen or twenty minutes after the cannonade commenced, then to concentrate their fire with all possible accuracy on those batteries which were most destructive to us—but slowly, so that when the enemy's ammunition was exhausted, we should have sufficient left to meet the assault. I had just given these orders to the last battery on Little Round Top, when the signal-gun was fired, and the enemy opened with all his guns. From that point the scene was indescribably grand. All their batteries were soon covered with smoke, through which the flashes were incessant, whilst the air seemed filled with shells, whose sharp explosions, with the hurtling of their fragments, formed a running accompaniment to the deep roar of the guns. Thence I rode to the Artillery Reserve to order fresh batteries and ammunition to be sent up to the ridge as soon as the cannonade ceased; but both the reserve and the train had gone to a safer place. Messengers, however, had been left to receive and convey orders, which I sent by them; then I returned to the ridge. Turning into the Taneytown pike, I saw evidence of the necessity under which the reserve had "decamped," in the remains of a dozen exploded caissons, which had been placed under cover of a hill, but which the shells had managed to search out. In fact, the fire was more dangerous behind the ridge than on its crest, which I soon reached at the position occupied by General Newton behind McGilvery's batteries, from which we had a fine view as all our own guns were now in action.

Most of the enemy's projectiles passed overhead, the effect being to sweep all the open ground in our rear, which was of little benefit to the Confederates— a mere waste of ammunition, for everything here could seek shelter. And just here an incident already published may be repeated, as it illustrates a peculiar feature of civil war. Colonel Long, who was at the time on General Lee's staff, had a few years before served in my mounted battery expressly to receive a course of instruction in the use of field-artillery. At Appomattox we spent several hours together, and in the course of conversation I told him I was not satisfied with the conduct of this cannonade which I had heard was under his direction, inasmuch as he had not done justice to his instruction; that his fire, instead of being concentrated on the point of attack, as it ought to have been, and as I expected it would be, was scattered over the whole field. He was amused at the criticism and said: "I remembered my lessons at the time, and when the fire became so scattered, wondered what you would think about it!"

I now rode along the ridge to inspect the batteries. The infantry were lying down on its reverse slope, near the crest, in open ranks, waiting events. As I passed along, a bolt from a rifle-gun struck the ground just in front of a man of the front rank, penetrated the surface and passed under him, throwing him "over and over." He fell behind the rear rank, apparently dead, and a ridge of earth where he had been lying reminded me of the backwoods practice of "barking" squirrels. Our fire was deliberate, but on inspecting the chests I found that the ammunition was running low, and hastened to General Meade to advise its immediate cessation and preparation for the assault which would certainly follow. The headquarters building, immediately behind the ridge, had been abandoned, and many of the horses of the staff lay dead. Being told that the general had gone to the cemetery, I proceeded thither. He was not there, and on telling General Howard my object, he concurred in its propriety, and I rode back along the ridge, ordering the fire to cease. This was followed by a cessation of that of the enemy, under the mistaken impression that he had silenced our guns, and almost immediately his infantry came out of the woods and formed for the assault. On my way to the Taneytown road to meet the fresh batteries which I had ordered up, I met Major Bingham, of Hancock's staff, who informed me that General Meade's aides were seeking me with orders to "cease firing"; so I had only anticipated his wishes. The batteries were found and brought up, and Fitzhugh's, Weir's, and Parsons's were put in near the clump of trees. Brown's and Arnold's batteries had been so crippled that they were now withdrawn, and Brown's was replaced by Cowan's. Meantime the enemy advanced, and McGilvery opened a destructive oblique fire, reënforced by that of Rittenhouse's six rifle-guns from Round Top, which were served with remarkable accuracy, enfilading Pickett's lines. The Confederate approach was magnificent, and excited our admiration; but the story of that charge is so well known that I need not dwell upon it further than as it concerns my own command. The steady fire from McGilvery and Rittenhouse, on their right, caused Pickett's men to "drift" in the opposite direction, so that the weight of the assault fell upon the positions occupied by Hazard's batteries. I had counted on an artillery cross-fire that would stop it before it reached our lines, but, except a few shots here and there, Hazard's batteries were silent until the enemy came within canister range. They had unfortunately exhausted their long range projectiles during the cannonade, under the orders of their corps commander, and it was too late to replace them. Had my instructions been followed here, as they were by McGilvery, I do not believe that Pickett's division would have reached our line. We lost not only the fire of one-third of our guns, but the resulting cross-fire, which would have doubled its value. The prime fault was in the obscurity of our army regulations as to the artillery, and the absence of all regulations as to the proper relations of the different arms of service to one another. On this occasion it cost us much blood, many lives, and for a moment endangered the integrity of our line if not the success of the battle. Soon after Pickett's repulse, Wilcox's, Wright's, and Perry's brigades were moved forward, but under the fire of the fresh batteries in Gibbon's front, of McGilvery's and Rit-

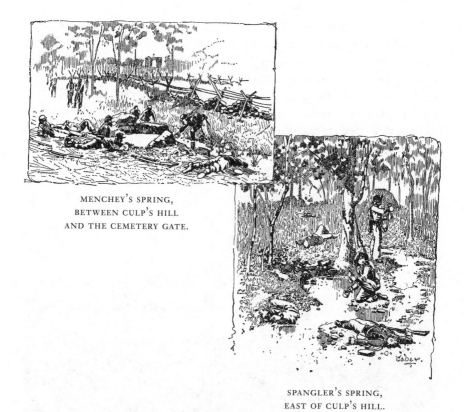

MENCHEY'S SPRING,
BETWEEN CULP'S HILL
AND THE CEMETERY GATE.

SPANGLER'S SPRING,
EAST OF CULP'S HILL.

tenhouse's guns and the advance of two regiments of Stannard's Vermont brigade, they soon fell back. The losses in the batteries of the Second Corps were very heavy. Of the five battery commanders and their successors on the field, Rorty, Cushing, and Woodruff were killed, and Milne was mortally and Sheldon severely wounded at their guns. So great was the destruction of men and horses, that Cushing's and Woodruff's United States, and Brown's and Arnold's Rhode Island batteries were consolidated to form two serviceable ones.

The advance of the Confederate brigades to cover Pickett's retreat showed that the enemy's line opposite Cemetery Ridge was occupied by infantry. Our own line on the ridge was in more or less disorder, as the result of the conflict, and in no condition to advance a sufficient force for a counter-assault. The largest bodies of organized troops available were on the left, and General Meade now proceeded to Round Top and pushed out skirmishers to feel the enemy in its front. An advance to the Plum Run line, of the troops behind it, would have brought them directly in front of the numerous batteries which crowned the Emmitsburg Ridge, commanding that line and all the intervening ground; a farther advance, to the attack, would have brought them under additional heavy flank fires. McCandless's brigade, supported by Nevin's, was, however, pushed forward, under cover of the woods, which protected them from the fire of all these batteries; it crossed the Wheat-field, cleared the woods, and had an encounter with a portion of Benning's brigade, which was retiring. Hood's and McLaws's divisions were falling back under Longstreet's orders to their strong position, resting on Peach Orchard and covering Hill's line. It needs but a moment's examination of the official map to see that our troops on the left

PICKETT'S CHARGE, I.—LOOKING DOWN THE UNION LINES
FROM THE "CLUMP OF TREES."

General Hancock and staff are seen in the left center of the picture.—This and the two pictures that follow are from the Cyclorama of Gettysburg, by permission of the National Panorama Company.

PICKETT'S CHARGE, II.—THE MAIN COLLISION TO THE RIGHT
OF THE "CLUMP OF TREES." FROM THE CYCLORAMA OF GETTYSBURG.

In this hand-to-hand conflict General Armistead, of Pickett's Division, was killed, and General Webb, of Gibbon's Division, was wounded.

were locked up. As to the center, Pickett's and Pettigrew's assaulting divisions had formed no part of A. P. Hill's line, which was virtually intact. The idea that there must have been "a gap of at least a mile" in that line, made by throwing forward these divisions, and that a prompt advance from Cemetery Ridge would have given us the line, or the artillery in front of it, was a delusion. A prompt counter-charge after a combat between two small bodies of men is one thing; the change from the defensive to the offensive of an army, after an engagement at a single *point*, is quite another. *This* was not a "Waterloo defeat" with a fresh army to follow it up, and to have made such a change to the offensive, on the assumption that Lee had made no provision against a reverse, would have been rash in the extreme. An advance of 20,000 men from Cemetery Ridge in the face of the 140 guns then in position would have been stark madness; an immediate advance from any point, in force, was simply impracticable, and before due preparation could have been made for a change to the offensive, the favorable moment—had any resulted from the repulse—would have passed away.

Whilst the main battle was raging, sharp cavalry combats took place on both flanks of the army. On the left the principal incident was an attack made by order of General Kilpatrick on infantry and artillery in woods and behind stone fences, which resulted in considerable losses, and especially in the death of General Farnsworth, a gallant and promising officer who had but a few days before been appointed brigadier-general and had not yet received his commission. On the right an affair of some magnitude took place between Stuart's command of four and Gregg's of three brigades; but Jenkins's Confederate brigade was soon thrown out of action from lack of ammunition, and two only of Gregg's were engaged. Stuart had been ordered to cover Ewell's left and was proceeding toward the Baltimore pike, where he hoped to create a diversion in aid of the Confederate infantry, and in case of Pickett's success to fall upon the retreating Federal troops. From near Cress's Ridge, two and a half miles east of Gettysburg, Stuart commanded a view of the roads in rear of the Federal lines. On its northern wooded end he posted Jackson's battery, and took possession of the Rummel farm-buildings, a few hundred yards distant. Hampton and Fitzhugh Lee were on his left, covered by the wood, Jenkins and Chambliss on the right, along the ridge. Half a mile east on a low parallel ridge, the southern part of which bending west toward Cress's Ridge furnished excellent positions for artillery, was the Federal cavalry brigade of McIntosh, who now sent a force toward Rummel's, from which a strong body of skirmishers was thrown to meet them, and the battery opened. McIntosh now demanded reënforcements, and Gregg, then near the Baltimore pike, brought him Custer's brigade and Pen-

PICKETT'S CHARGE, III.—(CONTINUATION OF THE PICTURE ON P. 587).
FROM THE GETTYSBURG CYCLORAMA.

nington's and Randol's batteries. The artillery soon drove the Confederates out of Rummel's, and compelled Jackson's Virginia battery to leave the ridge. Both sides brought up reënforcements and the battle swayed from side to side of the interval. Finally the Federals were pressed back, and Lee and Hampton, emerging from the wood, charged, swords in hand, facing a destructive artillery fire— for the falling back of the cavalry had uncovered our batteries. The assailants were met by Custer's and such other mounted squadrons as could be thrown in; a *mêlée* ensued, in which Hampton was severely wounded and the charge repulsed. Breathed's and McGregor's Confederate batteries had replaced Jackson's, a sharp artillery duel took place, and at nightfall each side held substantially its original ground. Both sides claim to have held the Rummel house. The advantage was decidedly with the Federals, who had foiled Stuart's plans. Thus the battle of Gettysburg closed as it had opened, with a very creditable cavalry battle.

General Lee now abandoned the attempt to dislodge Meade, intrenched a line from Oak Hill to Peach Orchard, started all his *impedimenta* to the Potomac in advance, and followed with his army on the night of July 4th, *via* Fairfield. This compelled Meade to take the circuitous routes through the lower passes; and the strategic advantage to Lee and disadvantage to Meade of Gettysburg were made manifest.

General Meade has been accused of slowness in the pursuit. The charge is not well founded; he lost no time in commencing, or vigor in pushing, it. As early as the morning of the 4th he ordered French at Frederick to seize and hold the lower passes, and he put all the cavalry except Gregg's and McIntosh's brigades in motion to harass the enemy's anticipated retreat, and to destroy his trains and bridges at Williamsport. It stormed heavily that day, and the care of the wounded and burial of the dead proceeded whilst the enemy's line was being reconnoitered. As soon, on the 5th, as it was certain that Lee was retreating, Gregg was started in pursuit on the Chambersburg pike, and the infantry— now reduced to a little over 47,000 effectives, short of ammunition and supplies—by the lower passes. The Sixth Corps taking the Hagerstown road, Sedgwick reported the Fairfield pass fortified, a large force present, and that a fight could be had; upon which, on the 6th, Meade halted the rest of the infantry and ordered two corps to his support, but soon learning that although the pass could be carried it would cause too much delay, he resumed the march, leaving McIntosh and a brigade of the Sixth Corps to follow the enemy through the Fairfield pass. On the evening of the 4th—both armies being still in position at Gettysburg—Kilpatrick had a sharp encounter with the enemy in Monterey pass, and this was followed by daily cavalry combats on the different routes, in which much damage was done to trains and many captures of wagons, caissons, and prisoners effected. On the 5th, whilst Lee was moving through the passes, French destroyed the pontoon-bridge at Falling Waters. On the 6th—as Meade was leaving Gettysburg—Buford attacked at Williamsport and Kilpatrick toward Hagerstown, on his right, but as Imboden's train guard was strong, Stuart was up, and Longstreet close by, they had to withdraw. [See p. 603.] The enemy proceeded to construct a new bridge and intrench a strong line covering Williamsport and Falling Waters. There were heavy rains on the 7th and 8th, but the infantry corps reached Middleton on the morning of the 9th, received supplies, crossed the mountains that day, and at its close the right was at Boonsboro', and the left at Rohrersville, on the roads to Hagerstown and Williamsport. By this time the Potomac was swollen and impassable. On the 10th Meade continued his advance, and received information that the enemy had occupied a line extending from near Falling Waters, through Downsville to Funkstown, which he was intrenching. This at 1 P.M. he reported to Halleck, informing him at the same time that his cavalry had driven that of Lee to within a mile of Funkstown, and that he would next day move cautiously until he had developed the enemy's force and position. Halleck, at 9 P.M., sent him a cipher dispatch as follows:

"I think it will be best for you to postpone a general battle till you can concentrate all your forces and get up your reserves and reënforcements; I will push on the troops as fast as they arrive. It would be well to have staff-officers at the Monocacy, to direct the troops arriving where to go, and to see that they are properly fitted out. They should join you by forced marches. Beware of partial combats. Bring up and hurl upon the enemy all your forces, good and bad."

Meade, fully alive to the importance of striking Lee before he could cross the Potomac, disregarded this, advanced on the 11th, and on the 12th pushed forward reconnoissances to feel the enemy. After a partial examination made by himself and his chiefs of staff and of engineers, which showed that its flanks could not be turned, and that the line, so far as seen by them, presented no vulnerable points, he determined to make a demonstration in force on the next morning, the 13th, supported by the whole army, and to attack if a prospect of success offered. On assembling his corps commanders, however, he found their opinion so adverse that he postponed it for further examination, after which he issued the order for the next day, the 14th. On advancing that morning, it was found that the enemy had abandoned his line and crossed the river, partly by fording, partly by a new bridge.

A careful survey of the enemy's intrenched line after it was abandoned justified the opinion of the corps commanders against an attack, as it showed that an assault would have been disastrous to us. It proved also that Meade in overriding that opinion did not shrink from a great responsibility, notwithstanding his own recent experience at Gettysburg, where all the enemy's attacks on even partially intrenched lines had failed. If he erred on this occasion it was on the side of temerity.

But the hopes and expectations excited by the victory of Gettysburg were as unreasonable as the fears that had preceded it; and great was the disappointment that followed the "escape" of Lee's army. It was promptly manifested, too, and in a manner which indicates how harshly and unjustly the Army of the Potomac and its commanders were usually judged and treated; and what trials the latter had to undergo whilst subjected to the meddling and hectoring of a distant superior, from which they were not freed until the general-in-chief accompanied them in the field. On the day following Lee's withdrawal, before it was possible that all the circumstances could be known, three dispatches passed between the respective headquarters.

First. Halleck to Meade, July 14th (in part):

"I need hardly say to you that the escape of Lee's army without another battle has created great dissatisfaction in the mind of the President, and it will require an active and energetic pursuit on your part to remove the impression that it has not been sufficiently active heretofore."

Second. Meade to Halleck, July 14th:

"Having performed my duty conscientiously and to the best of my ability, the censure of the President conveyed in your dispatch of 1 P.M. this day, is, in my judgment, so undeserved that I feel compelled most respectfully to ask to be immediately relieved from the command of this army."

Third. Halleck to Meade, July 14th:

"My telegram stating the disappointment of the President at the escape of Lee's army was not intended as a censure, but as a stimulus to an active pursuit. It is not deemed a sufficient cause for your application to be relieved."☆

☆At the end of July the following letters passed between Halleck and Meade:

"[UNOFFICIAL.] HEADQUARTERS OF THE ARMY, WASHINGTON, JULY 28TH, 1863. MAJOR-GENERAL MEADE, ARMY OF THE POTOMAC, WARRENTON, VA. GENERAL: I take this method of writing you a few words which I could not well communicate in any other way. Your fight at Gettysburg met with universal approbation of all military men here. You handled your troops in that battle as well, if not better, than any general has handled his army during the war. You brought all your forces into action at the right time and place, which no commander of the Army of the Potomac has done before. You may well be proud of that battle. The President's order or proclamation of July 4th showed how much he appreciated your success. And now a few words in regard to subsequent events. You should not have been surprised or vexed at the President's disappointment at the escape of Lee's army. He had exam-

CONFEDERATE PRISONERS ON THE BALTIMORE PIKE. FROM A WAR-TIME SKETCH.

Whatever the object of these dispatches of General Halleck, they are perfectly consistent with a determination on the part of the War Department to discredit under all circumstances the Army of the Potomac and any commander identified with it,—and that was the effect in this case.

---

ined into all the details of sending you reënforcements to satisfy himself that every man who could possibly be spared from other places had been sent to your army. He thought that Lee's defeat was so certain that he felt no little impatience at his unexpected escape. I have no doubt, General, that you felt the disappointment as keenly as any one else. Such things sometimes occur to us without any fault of our own. Take it all together, your short campaign has proved your superior generalship, and you merit, as you will receive, the confidence of the Government and the gratitude of the country. I need not assure you, General, that I have lost none of the confidence which I felt in you when I recommended you for the command. Very respectfully, your obedient servant, H. W. HALLECK."

"[UNOFFICIAL.] HEADQUARTERS, A.P., JULY 31, 1863. MAJOR-GENERAL HALLECK, GENERAL-IN-CHIEF. MY DEAR GENERAL: I thank you most sincerely and heartily for your kind and generous letter of the 28th inst., received last evening. It would be wrong in me to deny that I feared there existed in the minds both of the President and yourself an idea that I had failed to do what another would and could have done in the withdrawal of Lee's army. The expression you have been pleased to use in a letter, *to wit,* a feeling of disappointment, is one that I cheerfully accept and readily admit was as keenly felt by myself as any one. But permit me, dear General, to call your attention to the distinction between disappointment and dissatisfaction. The one was a natural feeling in view of the momentous consequences that would have resulted from a *successful* attack, but does not necessarily convey with it any censure. I could not view the use of the latter expression in any other light than as intending to convey an expression of opinion on the part of the President, that I had failed to do what I might and should have done. Now let me say in the frankness which characterizes your let-

The losses of both armies were very large. The revised returns show for the Army of the Potomac: killed, 3072; wounded, 14,497; missing, 5434,—total, 23,003; and for the Army of Northern Virginia: killed, 2592; wounded, 12,709; missing, 5150,—total, 20,451. But the returns for the latter army are not complete; some commands are not reported, and in others the regimental show larger losses than do the brigade returns from which the foregoing numbers are compiled.

As to the comparative strength of the two armies on the field of battle, we have no satisfactory data. The last Confederate return was for May 31st, showing "Present for duty, under arms," 59,484, infantry. The morning report of the Army of the Potomac for June 30th shows "Present for duty, equipped," 77,208, infantry. Neither return is worth much except as a basis for guessing; the long marches, followed by the forced ones of July 1–2, of the Army of the Potomac left thousands of stragglers on the roads. These totals are of little importance; they would have been of some significance had the larger army been defeated; but it was not. At the "points of contact" the Confederates were almost always the stronger. On July 1st 18,000 Federal combatants contended against at least 25,000 Confederates, and got the worst of it. On July 2d Longstreet's 15,000 overcame Sickles's 10,000, and had to halt when a larger force was opposed to them. Williams's Twelfth Corps retook its works from a larger body of Ewell's troops, for at the contested point they were opposed by an inferior number; and then held them, for Johnson's superior force was as much hampered here by the nature of the ground as was Meade's on the left, the evening before. In many re-

---

ter, that perhaps the President was right. If such was the case, it was my duty to give him an opportunity to replace me by one better fitted for the command of the army. It was, I assure you, with such feelings that I applied to be relieved. It was not from any personal considerations, for I have tried in this whole war to forget all personal considerations, and I have always maintained they should not for an instant influence any one's action. Of course you will understand that I do not agree that the President was right—and I feel sure when the true state of the case comes to be known, however natural and great may be the feeling of disappointment, that no blame will be attached to any one. Had I attacked Lee the day I proposed to do so, and in the ignorance that then existed of his position, I have every reason to believe the attack would have been unsuccessful and would have resulted disastrously. This opinion is founded on the judgment of numerous distinguished officers, after inspecting Lee's vacated works and position. Among these officers I could name Generals Sedgwick, Wright, Slocum, Hays, Sykes, and others.

The idea that Lee had abandoned his lines early in the day that he withdrew, I have positive intelligence is not correct, and that not a man was withdrawn until after dark. I mention these facts to remove the impression which newspaper correspondents have given the public; that it was only necessary to advance to secure an easy victory. I had great responsibility thrown on me: on one side were the known and important fruits of victory, and on the other, the equally important and terrible consequences of a defeat. I considered my position at Williamsport very different from that at Gettysburg. When I left Frederick it was with the firm determination to attack and fight Lee without regard to time or place as soon as I could come in contact with him. But, after defeating him and requiring him to abandon his

spects the Confederates had the advantage: they had much better ground for their artillery; they were fresher; they were all veterans; they were better organized; they were commanded by officers who had been selected for their experience and abilities, and in whom they had implicit confidence. These were enormous advantages, sufficient to counterbalance the difference of numbers, which, if any existed, was small; and whilst all the Confederate army, except here and there a brigade, were fought to the utmost, the strongest Federal corps (the Sixth) was hardly in action, the total loss of its eight brigades being but two hundred and forty-two killed, wounded, and missing. But the Southerners were subjected here to the disadvantages that the Northerners had to contend with in Virginia: they were surrounded by enemies, not friends who supplied them with aid and information; and they were not by choice, but by necessity, the assailants on the chosen ground of their opponents.

Right gallantly did they act their part, and their failure carried no discredit with it. Their military honor was not tarnished by their defeat, nor their spirit lowered, but their respect for their opponents was restored to what it had been before Fredericksburg and Chancellorsville.

---

schemes of invasion, I did not think myself justified in making a blind attack, simply to prevent his escape, and running all the risks attending such a venture. Now, as I said before, in this perhaps I erred in judgment, for I take this occasion to say to you, and through you to the President—that I have no pretensions to any superior capacity for the post he has assigned me to—that all I can do is to exert my utmost efforts and do the best I can; but that the moment those who have a right to judge my actions think or feel satisfied either that I am wanting, or that another would do better, that moment I earnestly desire to be relieved, not on my own account, but on account of the country and the cause. You must excuse so much egotism, but your kind letter in a measure renders it necessary. I feel, General, very proud of your good opinion, and assure you I shall endeavor in the future to continue to merit it. Reciprocating the kind feeling you have expressed, I remain, General, most truly and respectfully yours, GEORGE G. MEADE, Major-General."

—EDITORS.

CHAPTER 7

The Confederate Retreat from Gettysburg.

John D. Imboden, Brigadier-General, C.S.A.

During the Gettysburg campaign, my command—an independent brigade of cavalry—was engaged, by General Lee's confidential orders, in raids on the left flank of his advancing army, destroying railroad bridges and cutting the canal below Cumberland wherever I could—so that I did not reach the field till noon of the last day's battle. I reported direct to General Lee for orders, and was assigned a position to aid in repelling any cavalry demonstration on his rear. None of a serious character being made, my little force took no part in the battle, but were merely spectators of the scene, which transcended in grandeur any that I beheld in any other battle of the war.

When night closed the struggle, Lee's army was repulsed. We all knew that the day had gone against us, but the full extent of the disaster was only known in high quarters. The carnage of the day was generally understood to have been frightful, yet our army was not in retreat, and it was surmised in camp that with to-morrow's dawn would come a renewal of the struggle. All felt and appreciated the momentous consequences to the cause of Southern independence of final defeat or victory on that great field.

It was a warm summer's night; there were few camp-fires, and the weary soldiers were lying in groups on the luxuriant grass of the beautiful meadows, discussing the events of the day, speculating on the morrow, or watching that our horses did not straggle off while browsing. About 11 o'clock a horseman came to summon me to General Lee. I promptly mounted and, accompanied by Lieutenant George W. McPhail, an aide on my staff, and guided by the courier who brought the message, rode about two miles toward Gettysburg to where half a dozen small tents were pointed out, a little way from the roadside to our left, as General Lee's headquarters for the night. On inquiry I found that he was not there, but had gone to the headquarters of General A. P. Hill, about half a mile nearer to Gettysburg. When we reached the place indicated,

"CARRY ME BACK TO OLE VIRGINNY."

a single flickering candle, visible from the road through the open front of a common wall-tent, exposed to view Generals Lee and Hill seated on camp-stools with a map spread upon their knees. Dismounting, I approached on foot. After exchanging the ordinary salutations General Lee directed me to go back to his headquarters and wait for him. I did so, but he did not make his appearance until about 1 o'clock, when he came riding alone, at a slow walk, and evidently wrapped in profound thought.

When he arrived there was not even a sentinel on duty at his tent, and no one of his staff was awake. The moon was high in the clear sky and the silent scene was unusually vivid. As he approached and saw us lying on the grass under a tree, he spoke, reined in his jaded horse, and essayed to dismount. The effort to do so betrayed so much physical exhaustion that I hurriedly rose and stepped forward to assist him, but before I reached his side he had succeeded in alighting, and threw his arm across the saddle to rest, and fixing his eyes upon the ground leaned in silence and almost motionless upon his equally weary horse,—the two forming a striking and never-to-be-forgotten group. The moon shone full upon his massive features and revealed an expression of sadness that I had never before seen upon his face. Awed by his appearance I waited for him to speak until the silence became embarrassing, when, to break it and change the silent current of his thoughts, I ventured to remark, in a sympathetic tone, and in allusion to his great fatigue:

"General, this has been a hard day on you."

He looked up, and replied mournfully:

"Yes, it has been a sad, sad day to us," and immediately relapsed into his thoughtful mood and attitude. Being unwilling again to intrude upon his reflections, I said no more. After perhaps a minute or two, he suddenly straightened up to his full height, and turning to me with more animation and excitement of manner than I had ever seen in him before, for he was a man of wonderful equanimity, he said in a voice tremulous with emotion:

"I never saw troops behave more magnificently than Pickett's division of Virginians did to-day in that grand charge upon the enemy. And if they had been supported as they were to have been,—but, for some reason not yet fully explained to me, were not,—we would have held the position and the day would have been ours." After a moment's pause he added in a loud voice, in a tone almost of agony, "Too bad! *Too bad!* OH! TOO BAD!"[†]

I shall never forget his language, his manner, and his appearance of mental suffering. In a few moments all emotion was suppressed, and he spoke feelingly of several of his fallen and trusted officers; among others of Brigadier-Generals Armistead, Garnett, and Kemper of Pickett's division. He invited me into his tent, and as soon as we were seated he remarked:

"We must now return to Virginia. As many of our poor wounded as possible must be taken home. I have sent for you, because your men and horses are fresh and in good condition, to guard and conduct our train back to Virginia. The duty will be arduous, responsible, and dangerous, for I am afraid you will be harassed by the enemy's cavalry. How many men have you?"

"About 2100 effective present, and all well mounted, including McClanahan's six-gun battery of horse artillery."

"I can spare you as much artillery as you require," he said, "but no other troops, as I shall need all I have to return safely by a different and shorter route than yours. The batteries are generally short of ammunition, but you will probably meet a supply I have ordered from Winchester to Williamsport. Nearly all the transportation and the care of all the wounded will be intrusted to you. You

---

[†]Of interest in this connection is a letter written by General Lee to Mr. Davis from Camp Orange on the 8th of August, 1863, and first printed in "A Piece of Secret History," by Colonel C. C. Jones, Jr., in "The Century" (old series) for February, 1876. In this letter General Lee speaks in the highest terms of his army, and says, in part:

"... We must expect reverses, even defeats. They are sent to teach us wisdom and prudence, to call forth greater energies, and to prevent our falling into greater disasters. Our people have only to be true and united, to bear manfully the misfortunes incident to war, and all will come right in the end.

"I know how prone we are to censure, and how ready to blame others for the nonfulfillment of our expectations. This is unbecoming in a generous people, and I grieve to see its expression. The general remedy for the want of success in a military commander is his removal. This is natural, and in many instances proper. For, no matter what may be the ability of the officer, if he loses the confidence of his troops, disaster must sooner or later ensue.

"I have been prompted by these reflections more than once since my return from Penna. to propose to your Exc'y the propriety of selecting another commander for this army. I have seen and heard of expressions of discontent in the public journals at the result of the expedition. I do not know how far this feeling extends in the army. My brother officers have been too kind to report it, and so far the troops have been too generous to exhibit it. It is fair, however, to suppose that it does exist, and success is so necessary to us that nothing should be risked to secure it. I therefore, in all sincerity, request your Exc'y to take measures to supply my place. I do this with the more earnestness because no one is more aware than myself of my inability for the duties of my position. I cannot even accomplish what I myself desire. How can I fulfill the expectations of others? ...

will recross the mountain by the Chambersburg road, and then proceed to Williamsport by any route you deem best, and without a halt till you reach the river. Rest there long enough to feed your animals; then ford the river, and do not halt again till you reach Winchester, where I will again communicate with you."

After a good deal of conversation about roads, and the best disposition of my forces to cover and protect the vast train, he directed that the chiefs of his staff departments should be waked up to receive, in my presence, his orders to collect as early next day as possible all the wagons and ambulances which I was to convoy, and have them in readiness for me to take command of them. His medical director [Dr. Lafayette Guild] was charged to see that all the wounded who could bear the rough journey should be placed in the empty wagons and ambulances. He then remarked to me that his general instructions would be sent to me in writing the following morning. As I was about leaving to return to my camp, as late, I think, as 2 A.M., he came out of his tent to where I was about to mount, and said in an undertone: "I will place in your hands by a staff-officer, to-morrow morning, a sealed package for President Davis, which you will retain in your possession till you are across the Potomac, when you will de-tail a reliable commissioned officer to take it to Richmond with all possible dis-patch and deliver it into the President's own hands. And I impress it on you that, whatever happens, this package must not fall into the hands of the enemy. If un-fortunately you should be captured, destroy it at the first opportunity."

On the morning of July 4th my written instructions, and a large official en-velope addressed to President Davis, were handed to me by a staff-officer.

It was apparent by 9 o'clock that the wagons, ambulances, and wounded could not be collected and made ready to move till late in the afternoon. Gen-eral Lee sent to me eight Napoleon guns of the famous Washington Artillery of New Orleans, under the immediate command of Major Eshleman, one of the best artillery officers in the army, a four-gun battery under Captain Tanner, and a Whitworth under Lieutenant Pegram. Hampton's cavalry brigade, then under command of Colonel P.M.B. Young, with Captain James F. Hart's four-gun bat-tery of horse artillery, was ordered to cover the rear of all trains moving under my convoy on the Chambersburg road. These 17 guns and McClanahan's 6 guns gave us 23 pieces in all for the defense of the trains.

Shortly after noon of the 4th the very windows of heaven seemed to have opened. The rain fell in blinding sheets; the meadows were soon overflowed,

---

"I have no complaints to make of any one but myself. I have received nothing but kind-ness from those above me, and the most considerate attention from my comrades and com-panions in arms. To your Excellency I am specially indebted for uniform kindness and consideration. You have done everything in your power to aid me in the work committed to my charge, without omitting anything to promote the general welfare...."

GOOD-BYE!

and fences gave way before the raging streams. During the storm, wagons, ambulances, and artillery carriages by hundreds—nay, by thousands—were assembling in the fields along the road from Gettysburg to Cashtown, in one confused and apparently inextricable mass. As the afternoon wore on there was no abatement in the storm. Canvas was no protection against its fury, and the wounded men lying upon the naked boards of the wagon-bodies were drenched. Horses and mules were blinded and maddened by the wind and water, and became almost unmanageable. The deafening roar of the mingled sounds of heaven and earth all around us made it almost impossible to communicate orders, and equally difficult to execute them.

About 4 P.M. the head of the column was put in motion near Cashtown, and began the ascent of the mountain in the direction of Chambersburg. I remained at Cashtown giving directions and putting in detachments of guns and troops at what I estimated to be intervals of a quarter or a third of a mile. It was found from the position of the head of the column west of the mountain at dawn of the 5th—the hour at which Young's cavalry and Hart's battery began the ascent of the mountain near Cashtown—that the entire column was seventeen miles long when drawn out on the road and put in motion. As an advance-guard I had placed the 18th Virginia Cavalry, Colonel George W. Imboden, in front with a section of McClanahan's battery. Next to them, by request, was placed an ambulance carrying, stretched side by side, two of North Carolina's most distinguished soldiers, Generals Pender and Scales, both badly wounded, but resolved to bear the tortures of the journey rather than become prisoners. I shared a little bread and meat with them at noon, and they waited patiently for hours for the head of the column to move. The trip cost poor Pender his life. General Scales appeared to be worse hurt, but stopped at Winchester, recovered, and fought through the war.

After dark I set out from Cashtown to gain the head of the column during the night. My orders had been peremptory that there should be no halt for any cause whatever. If an accident should happen to any vehicle, it was immediately to be put out of the road and abandoned. The column moved rapidly, considering the rough roads and the darkness, and from almost every wagon for many miles issued heart-rending wails of agony. For four hours I hurried forward on my way to the front, and in all that time I was never out of hearing of the groans and cries of the wounded and dying. Scarcely one in a hundred had received adequate surgical aid, owing to the demands on the hard-working surgeons from still worse cases that had to be left behind. Many of the wounded in the wagons had been without food for thirty-six hours. Their torn and bloody clothing, matted and hardened, was rasping the tender, inflamed, and still oozing wounds. Very few of the wagons had even a layer of straw in them, and all were without springs. The road was rough and rocky from the heavy washings of the preceding day. The jolting was enough to have killed strong men, if long exposed to it. From nearly every wagon as the teams trotted on, urged by whip and shout, came such cries and shrieks as these:

"O God! why can't I die?"

"My God! will no one have mercy and kill me?"

"Stop! Oh! for God's sake, stop just for one minute; take me out and leave me to die on the roadside."

"I am dying! I am dying! My poor wife, my dear children, what will become of you?"

Some were simply moaning; some were praying, and others uttering the most fearful oaths and execrations that despair and agony could wring from them; while a majority, with a stoicism sustained by sublime devotion to the cause they fought for, endured without complaint unspeakable tortures, and even spoke words of cheer and comfort to their unhappy comrades of less will or more acute nerves. Occasionally a wagon would be passed from which only low, deep moans could be heard. No help could be rendered to any of the sufferers. No heed could be given to any of their appeals. Mercy and duty to the many forbade the loss of a moment in the vain effort then and there to comply with the prayers of the few. On! On! we *must* move on. The storm continued, and the darkness was appalling. There was no time even to fill a canteen with water for a dying man; for, except the drivers and the guards, all were wounded and utterly helpless in that vast procession of misery. During this one night I realized more of the horrors of war than I had in all the two preceding years.

And yet in the darkness was our safety, for no enemy would dare attack where he could not distinguish friend from foe. We knew that when day broke upon us we should be harassed by bands of cavalry hanging on our flanks. Therefore our aim was to go as far as possible under cover of the night. Instead of going through Chambersburg, I decided to leave the main road near Fairfield after crossing the mountains, and take "a near cut" across the country to Greencastle, where daybreak on the morning of the 5th of July found the head of our column. We were now twelve or fifteen miles from the Potomac at Williamsport, our point of crossing into Virginia.

Here our apprehended troubles began. After the advance—the 18th Virginia Cavalry—had passed perhaps a mile beyond the town, the citizens to the number of thirty or forty attacked the train with axes, cutting the spokes out of ten or a dozen wheels and dropping the wagons in the streets. The moment I heard of it I sent back a detachment of cavalry to capture every citizen who had been engaged in this work, and treat them as prisoners of war. This stopped the trouble there, but the Union cavalry began to swarm down upon us from the fields and cross-roads, making their attacks in small bodies, and striking the column where there were few or no guards, and thus creating great confusion. I had a narrow escape from capture by one of these parties—of perhaps fifty men that I tried to drive off with canister from two of McClanahan's guns that were close at hand. They would perhaps have been too much for me, had not Colonel Imboden, hearing the firing, turned back with his regiment at a gallop, and by the suddenness of his movement surrounded and caught the entire party.

To add to our perplexities still further, a report reached me a little after sunrise, that the Federals in large force held Williamsport. I did not fully credit this, and decided to push on. Fortunately the report was untrue. After a great deal of desultory fighting and harassments along the road during the day, nearly the whole of the immense train reached Williamsport on the afternoon of the 5th. A part of it, with Hart's battery, came in next day, General Young having halted and turned his attention to guarding the road from the west with his cavalry. We took possession of the town to convert it into a great hospital for the thousands of wounded we had brought from Gettysburg. I required all the families in the place to go to cooking for the sick and wounded, on pain of having their kitchens occupied for that purpose by my men. They readily complied. A large number of surgeons had accompanied the train, and these at once pulled off their coats and went to work, and soon a vast amount of suffering was mitigated. The bodies of a few who had died on the march were buried. All this be-

THE RETREAT FROM GETTYSBURG.

came necessary because the tremendous rains had raised the river more than ten feet above the fording stage of water, and we could not possibly cross then. There were two small ferry-boats or "flats" there, which I immediately put into requisition to carry across those of the wounded, who, after being fed and having their wounds dressed, thought they could walk to Winchester. Quite a large number were able to do this, so that the "flats" were kept running all the time.

Our situation was frightful. We had probably ten thousand animals and nearly all the wagons of General Lee's army under our charge, and all the wounded, to the number of several thousand, that could be brought from Gettysburg. Our supply of provisions consisted of a few wagon-loads of flour in my own brigade train, a small lot of fine fat cattle which I had collected in Pennsylvania on my way to Gettysburg, and some sugar and coffee procured in the same way at Mercersburg.

The town of Williamsport is located in the lower angle formed by the Potomac with Conococheague Creek. These streams inclose the town on two sides, and back of it about one mile there is a low range of hills that is crossed by four roads converging at the town. The first is the Greencastle road leading down the creek valley; next the Hagerstown road; then the Boonsboro' road; and lastly the River road.

Early on the morning of the 6th I received intelligence of the approach from Frederick of a large body of cavalry with three full batteries of six rifled guns. These were the divisions of Generals Buford and Kilpatrick, and Huey's brigade of Gregg's division, consisting, as I afterward learned, of 23 regiments of cavalry, and 18 guns, a total force of about 7000 men.

I immediately posted my guns on the hills that concealed the town, and dismounted my own command to support them—and ordered as many of the wagoners to be formed as could be armed with the guns of the wounded that we had brought from Gettysburg. In this I was greatly aided by Colonel J. L. Black of South Carolina, Captain J. F. Hart commanding a battery from the same State, Colonel William R. Aylett of Virginia, and other wounded officers. By noon about 700 wagoners were organized into companies of 100 each and officered by wounded line-officers and commissaries and quartermasters,—about 250 of these were given to Colonel Aylett on the right next the river,—about as many under Colonel Black on the left, and the residue were used as skirmishers. My own command proper was held well in hand in the center.

The enemy appeared in our front about half-past one o'clock on both the Hagerstown and Boonsboro' roads, and the fight began. Every man under my command understood that if we did not repulse the enemy we should all be captured and General Lee's army be ruined by the loss of its transportation, which at that period could not have been replaced in the Confederacy. The fight began with artillery on both sides. The firing from our side was very rapid, and seemed to make the enemy hesitate about advancing. In a half hour J. D. Moore's battery ran out of ammunition, but as an ordnance train had arrived from Winchester, two wagon-loads of ammunition were ferried across the river and run upon the field behind the guns, and the boxes tumbled out, to be broken open with axes. With this fresh supply our guns were all soon in full play again. As the enemy could not see the supports of our batteries from the hill-tops, I moved the whole line forward to his full view, in single ranks, to show a long front on the Hagerstown approach. My line passed our guns fifty or one hundred yards, where they were halted awhile, and then were withdrawn behind the hill-top again, slowly and steadily.

Leaving Black's wagoners and the Marylanders on the left to support Hart's and Moore's batteries, Captain Hart having been put in command by Colonel Black when he was obliged to be elsewhere, I moved the 18th Virginia Cavalry and 62d Virginia Mounted Infantry rapidly to the right, to meet and repel five advancing regiments (dismounted) of the enemy. My three regiments, with Captain John H. McNeill's Partisan Rangers and Aylett's wagoners, had to sustain a very severe contest. Hart, seeing how hard we were pressed on the right, charged the enemy's right with his little command, and at the same time Eshleman with his eight Napoleons advanced four hundred yards to the front, and got an enfilading position, from which, with the aid of McClanahan's battery, he poured a furious fire into the enemy's line. The 62d and Aylett, supported by the 18th Cavalry, and McNeill, charged the enemy who fell back sullenly to their horses.

Night was now rapidly approaching, when a messenger from Fitzhugh Lee arrived to urge me to "hold my own," as he would be up in a half hour with three thousand fresh men. The news was sent along our whole line, and was received with a wild and exultant yell. We knew then that the field was won, and slowly pressed forward. Almost at the same moment we heard distant guns on the enemy's rear and right on the Hagerstown road. They were Stuart's, who was approaching on that road, while Fitzhugh Lee was coming on the Greencastle road. That settled the contest. The enemy broke to the left and fled by the Boonsboro' road. It was too dark to follow. When General Fitzhugh Lee joined me with his staff on the field, one of the enemy's shells came near striking him. General Lee thought it came from Eshleman's battery, till, a moment later, he saw a blaze from its gun streaming away from us.

We captured about 125 of the enemy who failed to reach their horses. I could never ascertain the loss on either side. I estimated ours at about 125. The wagoners fought so well that this came to be known as "the wagoners' fight." Quite a number of them were killed in storming a farm from which sharpshooters were rapidly picking off Eshleman's men and horses.

My whole force engaged, wagoners included, did not exceed three thousand men. The ruse practiced by showing a formidable line on the left, then withdrawing it to fight on the right, together with our numerous artillery, 23 guns, led to the belief that our force was much greater.

By extraordinary good fortune we had thus saved all of General Lee's trains. A bold charge at any time before sunset would have broken our feeble lines, and then we should all have fallen an easy prey to the Federals. The next day our army arrived from Gettysburg, and the country is familiar with the way it escaped across the Potomac on the night of the 13th of July.

It may be interesting to repeat one or two facts to show the peril in which the army was till the river could be bridged. Over four thousand prisoners taken at Gettysburg were ferried across the river by the morning of the 9th, and I was ordered with a single regiment, the 62d Virginia, to guard them to Staunton and send them on to Richmond. When the general assigned me to this duty he expressed an apprehension that before I could reach Winchester the Federal cavalry would cross at Harper's Ferry, intercept and capture my guard and release the prisoners. Before we had left the river I had an interview with him at his headquarters near Hagerstown, in which he expressed great impatience at the tardiness in building rude pontoons at the river, and calling in Colonel James L. Corley, his chief quartermaster, told him to put Major John A. Harman in charge of the work; remarking that without Harman's extraordinary energy to conduct the work, the pontoons would not be done for several days. Harman took charge that day, and by tearing down warehouses on the canal got joists to build boats with, and in twenty-four hours had enough of them ready to float down to Falling Waters and construct a bridge. As we were talking General Longstreet came into the tent, wet and muddy, and was cordially greeted by General Lee in this wise: "Well, my old war-horse, what news do you bring us from the front?" That cordial greeting between chief and lieutenant is a sufficient answer, in my mind, to the statements of alleged ill feeling between the two men growing out of affairs at Gettysburg. It has been said that if "Stonewall" Jackson had been in command at Gettysburg, Longstreet would have been shot. This is a monstrous imputation upon General Lee, no less than upon Longstreet, and utterly without foundation, in my opinion. They were surely cordial on the 9th of July, 1863.

Before I had gone two miles on my anxious march toward Winchester a courier overtook me with a note from General Lee directing me to return immediately to his headquarters. I halted my column, hurried back, was ferried over the river, and galloped out on the Hagerstown road to where I had parted from the general that morning. He had left with his staff to ride toward Hagerstown, where a heavy artillery fire indicated an attack by the enemy in considerable force. When I overtook him he said that he understood I was familiar with the fords of the Potomac from Williamsport to Cumberland, and with the roads to them. I replied that I was. He then called up one of his staff, either General Long or General Alexander, I think, and directed him to write down my answers to his questions, and required me to name and describe ford after ford all the way up to Cumberland, and to describe minutely their character, and the roads and surrounding country on both sides of the river, and directed me, after I had given him all the information I could, to send to him my brother and his regiment, the 18th Virginia Cavalry, to act as an advance and guide if he should require it. He did not say so, but I felt that his situation was precarious in the extreme. When about to dismiss me, referring to the freshet in the river he laughingly said: "You know this country well enough to tell me whether it ever quits raining about here? If so, I should like to see a clear day soon." I did not see him again till he left the Shenandoah Valley for the east side of the Blue Ridge.

CHAPTER 8

THE VICKSBURG CAMPAIGN.

Ulysses S. Grant, General, U.S.A.

It is generally regarded as an axiom in war that all great armies moving in an enemy's country should start from a base of supplies, which should be fortified and guarded, and to which the army is to fall back in case of disaster. The first movement looking to Vicksburg and the force defending it as an objective was begun early in November, 1862, and conformed to this axiom. It followed the line of the Mississippi Central Railroad, with Columbus, Kentucky, as a base, and soon after it started, a coöperating column was moved down the Mississippi River on transports, with Memphis as its base. Both these movements failing, the entire Army of the Tennessee was transferred to the neighborhood of Vicksburg, and landed on the opposite or western bank of the river at Milliken's Bend. The Mississippi flows through a low alluvial bottom many miles in

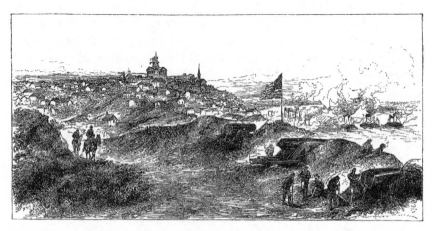

VICKSBURG FROM THE NORTH—AFTER THE SURRENDER.
FROM A SKETCH MADE AT THE TIME.

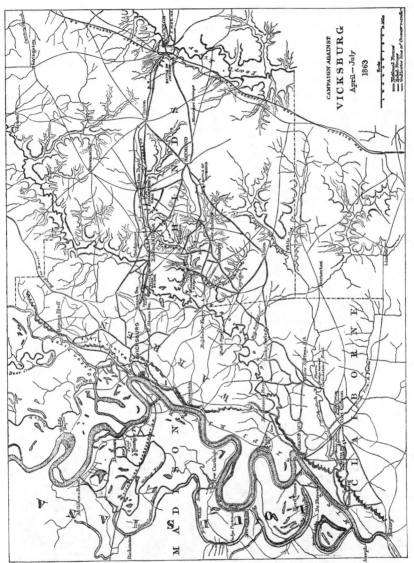

FROM GENERAL BADEAU'S "MILITARY HISTORY OF ULYSSES S. GRANT": D. APPLETON & CO., N.Y.

width, and is very tortuous in its course, running to all points of the compass, sometimes within a few miles. This valley is bounded on the east side by a range of high land rising in some places more than two hundred feet above the bottom. At points the river runs up to the bluffs, washing their base. Vicksburg is built on the first high land on the eastern bank below Memphis, and four hundred miles from that place by the windings of the river.

The winter of 1862–63 was unprecedented for continuous high water in the Mississippi, and months were spent in ineffectual efforts to reach high land above Vicksburg from which we could operate against that stronghold, and in making artificial waterways through which a fleet might pass, avoiding the batteries to the south of the town, in case the other efforts should fail.

In early April, 1863, the waters of the Mississippi having receded sufficiently to make it possible to march an army across the peninsula opposite Vicksburg, I determined to adopt this course, and moved my advance to a point below the town. It was necessary, however, to have transports below, both for the purpose of ferrying troops over the river and to carry supplies. These had necessarily to run the batteries. Under the direction of Admiral Porter this was successfully done. On the 29th, Grand Gulf, the first bluff south of Vicksburg on the east side of the river, and about fifty miles below, was unsuccessfully attacked by the navy. The night of the same day the batteries of that place were run by the navy and transports, again under the direction of Admiral Porter, and on the following day the river was crossed by the troops, and a landing effected at Bruinsburg, some nine miles below.

FUNERAL ON THE LEVEE AT THE DUCKPORT CANAL, APRIL, 1863.
FROM A WAR-TIME SKETCH.

I was now in the enemy's country, with a vast river and the stronghold of Vicksburg between me and my base of supplies. I had with me the Thirteenth Corps, General McClernand commanding, and two brigades of Logan's division of the Seventeenth Corps, General McPherson commanding; in all not more than twenty thousand men to commence the campaign with. These were soon reënforced by the remaining brigade of Logan's division and by Crocker's division of the Seventeenth Corps. On the 7th of May I was further reënforced by Sherman with two divisions of his, the Fifteenth Corps. My total force was then about thirty-three thousand men. The enemy occupied Grand Gulf, Vicksburg, Haynes's Bluff, and Jackson, with a force of nearly sixty thousand men. My first problem was to capture Grand Gulf to use as a base, and then if possible beat the enemy in detail outside the fortifications of Vicksburg. Jackson is fifty miles east of Vicksburg, and was connected with it by a railroad. Haynes's Bluff is eleven miles north, and on the Yazoo River, which empties into the Mississippi some miles above the town.

Bruinsburg is two miles from high ground. The bottom at that point is higher than most of the low land in the valley of the Mississippi, and a good road leads to the bluff. It was natural to expect the garrison from Grand Gulf to come out to meet us, and prevent, if they could, our reaching this solid base. Bayou Pierre enters the Mississippi just above Bruinsburg; and as it is a navigable stream, and was high at the time, in order to intercept us they had to go by Port Gibson, the nearest point where there was a bridge to cross upon. This more than doubled the distance from Grand Gulf to the high land back of Bruinsburg. No time was to be lost in securing this foothold. Our transportation was not sufficient to move all the army across the river at one trip or even two. But the landing of the Thirteenth Corps and one division of the Seventeenth was effected during the day, April 30th, and early evening. McClernand was advanced as soon as ammunition and two days' rations (to last five) could be issued to his men. The bluffs were reached an hour before sunset, and McClernand was pushed on, hoping to reach Port Gibson and save the bridge spanning the Bayou Pierre before the enemy could get there; for crossing a stream in the presence of an enemy is always difficult. Port Gibson, too, is the starting-point of roads to Grand Gulf, Vicksburg, and Jackson.

McClernand's advance met the enemy about five miles south of Port Gibson at Thompson's plantation. There was some firing during the night, but nothing rising to the dignity of a battle until daylight. The enemy had taken a strong natural position with most of the Grand Gulf garrison, numbering about seven or eight thousand men, under General Bowen. His hope was to hold me in check until reënforcements under Loring could reach him from Vicksburg; but Loring did not come in time to render much assistance south of Port Gibson. Two brigades of McPherson's corps followed McClernand as fast as rations and ammunition could be issued, and were ready to take position upon the

REAR-ADMIRAL PORTER'S FLOTILLA PASSING THE VICKSBURG BATTERIES, NIGHT OF
APRIL 16, 1863, THE FLAG-SHIP "BENTON" LEADING, FOLLOWED BY THE "LOUISVILLE,"
"LAFAYETTE," "GENERAL PRICE," "MOUND CITY," "PITTSBURGH," "CARONDELET," AND
"TUSCUMBIA"; AND THE TRANSPORTS "HENRY CLAY," "FOREST QUEEN," AND
"SILVERWARE." FROM A WAR-TIME SKETCH.

battle-field whenever the Thirteenth Corps could be got out of the way.

The country in this part of Mississippi stands on edge, as it were, the roads running along the ridges except when they occasionally pass from one ridge to another. Where there are no clearings, the sides of the hills are covered with a very heavy growth of timber, and with undergrowth, and the ravines are filled with vines and canebrakes, almost impenetrable. This makes it easy for an inferior force to delay, if not defeat, a far superior one.

Near the point selected by Bowen to defend, the road to Port Gibson divides, taking two ridges, which do not diverge more than a mile or two at the widest point. These roads unite just outside the town. This made it necessary for McClernand to divide his force. It was not only divided, but it was separated by a deep ravine of the character above described. One flank could not reenforce the other except by marching back to the junction of the roads. McClernand put the divisions of Hovey, Carr, and A. J. Smith upon the right-hand branch, and Osterhaus on the left. I was on the field by 10 A.M., and inspected both flanks in person. On the right the enemy, if not being pressed back, was at least not repulsing our advance. On the left, however, Osterhaus was not faring so well. He had been repulsed, with some loss. As soon as the road could be cleared of McClernand's troops I ordered up McPherson, who was close upon

REAR-ADMIRAL PORTER'S FLOTILLA ARRIVING BELOW VICKSBURG ON
THE NIGHT OF APRIL 16, 1863—IN THE FOREGROUND GENERAL W. T. SHERMAN
GOING IN A YAWL TO THE FLAG-SHIP "BENTON."

the rear of the Thirteenth Corps with two brigades of Logan's division. This
was about noon. I ordered him to send one brigade (General John E. Smith's
was selected) to support Osterhaus, and to move to the left and flank the enemy
out of his position. This movement carried the brigade over a deep ravine to a
third ridge, and when Smith's troops were seen well through the ravine Osterhaus was directed to renew his front attack. It was successful and unattended by
heavy loss. The enemy was sent in full retreat on their right, and their left followed before sunset.

While the movement to our left was going on, McClernand, who was with
his right flank, sent me frequent requests for reënforcements, although the force
with him was not being pressed. I had been upon the ground, and knew it did
not admit of his engaging all the men he had. We followed up our victory until
night overtook us, about two miles from Port Gibson; then the troops went into
bivouac for the night.

We started next morning [May 2d] for Port Gibson as soon as it was light
enough to see the road. We were soon in the town, and I was delighted to find
that the enemy had not stopped to contest our crossing further at the bridge,
which he had burned. The troops were set to work at once to construct a bridge
across the South Fork of the Bayou Pierre. At this time the water was high, and
the current rapid. What might be called a raft-bridge was soon constructed
from material obtained from wooden buildings, stables, fences, etc., which sufficed for carrying the whole army over safely. Colonel James H. Wilson, a member of my staff, planned and superintended the construction of this bridge,

going into the water and working as hard as any one engaged. Officers and men generally joined in this work. When it was finished the army crossed, and marched eight miles beyond to the North Fork that day. One brigade of Logan's division was sent down the stream to occupy the attention of a rebel battery which had been left behind, with infantry supports, to prevent our repairing the burnt railroad bridge. Two of his brigades were sent up the bayou to find a crossing, and to reach the North Fork to repair the bridge there. The enemy soon left when he found we were building a bridge elsewhere. Before leaving Port Gibson we were reënforced by Crocker's division, McPherson's corps, which had crossed the Mississippi at Bruinsburg and come up without stopping, except to get two days' rations. McPherson still had one division west of the Mississippi River guarding the road from Milliken's Bend to the river below until Sherman's command should relieve it.

When the movement from Bruinsburg commenced we were without a wagon-train. The train, still west of the Mississippi, was carried around, with proper escort, by a circuitous route from Milliken's Bend to Hard Times, seventy or more miles below, and did not get up for some days after the battle of Port Gibson. My own horses, headquarters' transportation, servants, mess-chest, and everything except what I had on, were with this train. General A. J. Smith happened to have an extra horse at Bruinsburg, which I borrowed, with a saddle-tree without upholstering further than stirrups. I had no other for nearly a week.

It was necessary to have transportation for ammunition. Provisions could be taken from the country; but all the ammunition that can be carried on the person is soon exhausted when there is much fighting. I directed therefore, immediately on landing, that all the vehicles and draught animals, whether horses, mules, or oxen, in the vicinity should be collected and loaded to their capacity with ammunition. Quite a train was collected during the 30th, and a motley train it was. In it could be found fine carriages, loaded nearly to the tops with boxes of cartridges that had been pitched in promiscuously, drawn by mules with plow-harness, straw-collars, rope lines, etc.; long-coupled wagons, with racks for carrying cotton bales, drawn by oxen, and everything that could be found in the way of transportation on a plantation, either for use or pleasure. The making out of provision returns was stopped for the time. No formalities were to retard our progress until a position was secured, when time could be spared to observe them.[✠]

[✠]"It was at Port Gibson I first heard through a Southern paper of the complete success of Colonel Benjamin H. Grierson, who was making a raid through central Mississippi [from La Grange, Tennessee, to Baton Rouge, Louisiana]. He had started from La Grange, April 17th, with three regiments of about 1700 men. On the 21st he had detached Colonel Hatch with one regiment to destroy the railroad between Columbus and Macon and then return to La Grange. Hatch had a sharp fight with the enemy at Columbus and retreated along the railroad, destroying it at Okolona and Tupelo, and arriving in La

During the night of the 2d of May the bridge over the North Fork was repaired, and the troops commenced crossing at 5 the next morning. Before the leading brigade was over, it was fired upon by the enemy from a commanding position; but they were soon driven off. It was evident that the enemy was covering a retreat from Grand Gulf to Vicksburg. Every commanding position from this (Grindstone) crossing to Hankinson's Ferry, over the Big Black, was occupied by the retreating foe to delay our progress. McPherson, however, reached Hankinson's Ferry before night, seized the ferry-boat, and sent a detachment of his command across and several miles north on the road to Vicksburg. When the junction of the road going to Vicksburg with the road from Grand Gulf to Raymond and Jackson was reached, Logan, with his division, was turned to the left toward Grand Gulf. I went with him a short distance from this junction. McPherson had encountered the largest force yet met since the battle of Port Gibson, and had a skirmish nearly approaching a battle; but the road Logan had taken enabled him to come up on the enemy's right flank, and they soon gave way. McPherson was ordered to hold Hankinson's Ferry, and the road back to Willow Springs, with one division; General McClernand who was now in the rear was to join in this, as well as to guard the line back down the bayou. I did not want to take the chances of having an enemy lurking in our rear.

MAJOR-GENERAL ANDREW J. SMITH.
FROM A PHOTOGRAPH.

On the way from the junction to Grand Gulf, where the road comes into the one from Vicksburg to the same place, six or seven miles out, I learned that the last of the enemy had retreated past that place on their way to Vicksburg. I left Logan to make the proper disposition of his troops for the night, while I rode into the town with an escort of about twenty cavalry. Admiral Porter had already arrived with his fleet. The enemy had abandoned his heavy guns and evacuated the place.

When I reached Grand Gulf, May 3d, I had not been with my baggage since the 27th of April, and, consequently, had had no change of under-

Grange April 26th. Grierson continued his movement with about 1000 men, breaking the Vicksburg and Meridian railroad and the New Orleans and Jackson railroad, arriving at Baton Rouge May 2d. This raid was of great importance, for Grierson had attracted the attention of the enemy from the main movement against Vicksburg."—From "Personal Memoirs of U. S. Grant."

clothing, no meal except such as I could pick up sometimes at other headquarters, and no tent to cover me. The first thing I did was to get a bath, borrow some fresh underclothing from one of the naval officers, and get a good meal on the flag-ship. Then I wrote letters to the general-in-chief informing him of our present position, dispatches to be telegraphed from Cairo, orders to General Sullivan, commanding above Vicksburg, and gave orders to all my corps commanders. About 12 o'clock at night I was through my work, and started for Hankinson's Ferry, arriving there before daylight. While at Grand Gulf I heard from Banks, who was on the Red River,✦ and he said that he could not be at Port Hudson before the 10th of May, and then with only fifteen thousand men. Up to this time my intention had been to secure Grand Gulf as a base of supplies, detach McClernand's corps to Banks, and coöperate with him in the reduction of Port Hudson.

The news from Banks forced upon me a different plan of campaign from the one intended. To wait for his coöperation would have detained me at least a month. The reënforcements would not have reached 10,000 men, after deducting casualties and necessary river-guards, at all high points close to the river, for over 300 miles. The enemy would have strengthened his position and been reënforced by more men than Banks could have brought. I therefore determined to move independently of Banks, cut loose from my base, destroy the rebel force in rear of Vicksburg, and invest or capture the city.

Grand Gulf was accordingly given up as a base, and the authorities at Washington were notified. I knew well that Halleck's caution would lead him to disapprove this course; but it was the only one that gave any chance of success. The time it would take to communicate with Washington and get a reply would be so great that I could not be interfered with until it was demonstrated whether my plan was practicable. Even Sherman, who afterward ignored bases of supplies other than what were afforded by the country while marching through four States of the Confederacy, with an army more than twice as large as mine at this time, wrote me from Hankinson's Ferry, advising me of the impossibility of supplying our army over a single road. He urged me to "stop all troops till your army is partially supplied with wagons, and then act as quick as possible; for this road will be jammed, as sure as life." To this I replied: "I do not calculate upon the possibility of supplying the army with full rations from Grand Gulf. I know it will be impossible without constructing additional roads. What I do expect is to get up what rations of hard bread, coffee, and salt we can, and make the country furnish the balance." We started from Bruinsburg with an average of about two days' rations, and received no more from our own supplies

---

✦Banks reached Alexandria on the 7th of May, and was acting in concert with Farragut's and Porter's fleet to control the waters of Red River.—EDITORS.

for some days; abundance was found in the meantime. A delay would give the enemy time to reënforce and fortify.

McClernand's and McPherson's commands were kept substantially as they were on the night of the 2d, awaiting supplies to give them three days' rations in haversacks. Beef, mutton, poultry, and forage were found in abundance. Quite a quantity of bacon and molasses was also secured from the country, but bread and coffee could not be secured in quantity sufficient for all the men. Every plantation, however, had a run of stone, propelled by mule-power, to grind corn for the owners and their slaves. All these were kept running while we were stopping day and night, and when we were marching, during the night, at all plantations covered by the troops. But the product was taken by the troops nearest by; so that the majority of the command was destined to go without bread until a new base was established on the Yazoo, above Vicksburg.

While the troops were awaiting the arrival of rations, I ordered reconnoissances made by McClernand and McPherson, with a view of leading the enemy to believe that we intended to cross the Big Black and attack the city at once.

On the 6th Sherman arrived at Grand Gulf, and crossed his command that night and the next day. Three days' rations had been brought up from Grand Gulf for the advanced troops, and were issued. Orders were given for a forward movement the next day. Sherman was directed to order up Blair, who had been left behind to guard the road from Milliken's Bend to Hard Times with two brigades.

The quartermaster at Young's Point was ordered to send 200 wagons with General Blair, and the commissary was to load them with hard bread, coffee, sugar, salt, and 100,000 pounds of salt meat.

On the 3d Hurlbut, who had been left at Memphis, was ordered to send four regiments from his command to Milliken's Bend to relieve Blair's division, and on the 5th he was ordered to send Lauman's division in addition, the latter to join the army in the field. The four regiments were to be taken from troops near the river, so that there would be no delay.

During the night of the 6th McPherson drew in his troops north of the Big Black and was off at an early hour on the road to Jackson, via

MAJOR-GENERAL RICHARD J. OGLESBY.
FROM A PHOTOGRAPH.

Rocky Springs, Utica, and Raymond. That night he and McClernand were both at Rocky Springs, ten miles from Hankinson's Ferry. McPherson remained there during the 8th, while McClernand moved to Big Sandy and Sherman marched from Grand Gulf to Hankinson's Ferry. The 8th McPherson moved to a point within a few miles of Utica; McClernand and Sherman remained where they were. On the 10th McPherson moved to Utica; Sherman to Big Sandy,— McClernand was still at Big Sandy. The 11th McClernand was at Five Mile Creek; Sherman at Auburn; McPherson five miles advanced from Utica. May 12th McClernand was at Fourteen Mile Creek; Sherman at Fourteen Mile Creek; McPherson at Raymond, after a battle.▌

Up to this point our movements had been made without serious opposition. My line was now nearly parallel with the Jackson and Vicksburg Railroad, and about seven miles south of it. The right was at Raymond, eighteen miles from Jackson, McPherson commanding; Sherman in the center on Fourteen Mile Creek, his advance thrown across; McClernand to the left, also on Fourteen Mile Creek, advance across, and his pickets within two miles of Edwards's Station, where the enemy had concentrated a considerable force, and where they undoubtedly expected us to attack. McClernand's left was on the Big Black. In all our moves, up to this time, the left had hugged the Big Black closely, and all the ferries had been guarded to prevent the enemy throwing a force on our rear.

McPherson encountered the enemy, 5000 strong, with 2 batteries, under General Gregg, about 2 miles out of Raymond. This was about 2 P.M. Logan was in advance with one of his brigades. He deployed and moved up to engage the enemy. McPherson ordered the road in rear to be cleared of wagons, and the

▌"After McPherson crossed the Big Black at Hankinson's Ferry, Vicksburg could have been approached and besieged by the south side. It is not probable, however, that Pemberton would have permitted a close besiegement. The broken nature of the ground would have enabled him to hold a strong defensible line from the river south of the city to the Big Black, retaining possession of the railroad back to that point. It was my plan, therefore, to get to the railroad east of Vicksburg, and approach from that direction. Accordingly McPherson's troops that had crossed the Big Black were withdrawn, and the movement east, to Jackson, commenced.

"As has been stated before, the country is very much broken, and the roads generally confined to the tops of the hills. The troops were moved one (sometimes two) corps at a time, to reach designated points out parallel to the railroad, and only from six to ten miles from it. McClernand's corps was kept with its left flank on the Big Black guarding all the crossings. Fourteen Mile Creek, a stream substantially parallel with the railroad, was reached, and crossings effected by McClernand and Sherman with slight loss. McPherson was to the right of Sherman, extending to Raymond. The cavalry was used in this advance in reconnoitering to find the roads; to cover our advances, and to find the most practicable routes from one command to another, so they could support each other in case of an attack. In making this move I estimated Pemberton's movable force at Vicksburg at about eighteen thousand men, with smaller forces at Haynes's Bluff and Jackson. It would not be possible for Pemberton to attack me with all his troops at one place, and I determined to throw my army between his and fight him in detail. This was done with success, but I found afterward that I had entirely under-estimated Pemberton's strength."—From "Personal Memoirs of U. S. Grant.," C. L. Webster & Co.

balance of Logan's division, and Crocker's, which was still farther in rear, to come forward with all dispatch. The order was obeyed with alacrity. Logan got his division in position for assault before Crocker could get up, and attacked with vigor, carrying the enemy's position easily, sending Gregg flying from the field, not to appear against our front again until we met at Jackson.

In this battle McPherson lost 66 killed, 339 wounded, and 37 missing,— nearly or quite all from Logan's division. The enemy's loss was 100 killed, 305 wounded, besides 415 taken prisoners.

I regarded Logan and Crocker as being as competent division commanders as could be found in or out of the army, and both equal to a much higher command. Crocker, however, was dying of consumption when he volunteered. His weak condition never put him on the sick-report when there was a battle in prospect, as long as he could keep on his feet. He died not long after the close of the Rebellion.

When the news reached me of McPherson's victory at Raymond about sundown, my position was with Sherman. I decided at once to turn the whole column toward Jackson and capture that place without delay./

Accordingly, all previous orders given during the day for movements on the 13th were annulled by new ones. McPherson was ordered at daylight to move on Clinton, ten miles from Jackson. Sherman was notified of my determination to capture Jackson and work from there westward. He was ordered to start at four in the morning and march to Raymond. McClernand was ordered to march with three divisions by Dillon's to Raymond. One was left to guard the crossing of the Big Black. On the 10th I received a letter from Banks, on the Red River, asking reënforcements. Porter had gone to his assistance, with a part of his fleet, on the 3d, and I now wrote to him describing my position and declining to send any troops. I looked upon side movements, as long as the enemy held Port Hudson and Vicksburg, as a waste of time and material. General Joseph E. Johnston arrived at Jackson in the night of the 13th, from Tennessee, and immediately assumed command of all the Confederate troops in Mississippi. I knew he was expecting reënforcements from the south and east. On the 6th I had written to General Halleck, "Information from the other side leaves me to believe the enemy are bringing forces from Tullahoma."

/"Pemberton was now on my left, with, as I supposed, about 18,000 men; in fact, as I learned afterward, with nearly 50,000. A force was also collected on my right at Jackson, the point where all the railroads communicating with Vicksburg connect. All the enemy's supplies of men and stores would come by that point. As I hoped in the end to besiege Vicksburg I must first destroy all possibility of aid. I therefore determined to move swiftly toward Jackson, destroy or drive any force in that direction, and then turn upon Pemberton. But by moving against Jackson I uncovered my own communication. So I finally decided to have none—to cut loose altogether from my base and move my whole force eastward. I then had no fears for my communications, and if I moved quickly enough could turn upon Pemberton before he could attack me in the rear."—From "Personal Memoirs of U. S. Grant.," C. L. Webster & Co.

Up to this time my troops had been kept in supporting distances of each other as far as the nature of the country would admit. Reconnoissances were constantly made from each corps to enable them to acquaint themselves with the most practicable routes from one to another in case a union became necessary.

McPherson reached Clinton with the advance early on the 13th, and immediately set to work destroying the railroad. Sherman's advance reached Raymond before the last of McPherson's command had got out of the town. McClernand withdrew from the front of the enemy, at Edwards's Station, with much skill and without loss, and reached his position for the night in good order. On the night of the 13th McPherson was ordered to march at early dawn upon Jackson, only fifteen miles away. Sherman was given the same order; but he was to move by the direct road from Raymond to Jackson, which is south of the road McPherson was on, and does not approach within two miles of it at the point where it crossed the line of intrenchments which at that time defended the city. McClernand was ordered to move one division of his command to Clinton, one division a few miles beyond Mississippi Springs,—following Sherman's line,—and a third to Raymond. He was also directed to send his siege-guns, four in number, with the troops going by Mississippi Springs. McClernand's position was an advantageous one, in any event. With one division at Clinton, he was in position to reënforce McPherson at Jackson rapidly if it became necessary. The division beyond Mississippi Springs was equally available to reënforce Sherman. The one at Raymond could take either road. He still had two other divisions farther back now that Blair had come up, available within a day at Jackson. If this last command should not be wanted at Jackson, they were already one day's march from there on their way to Vicksburg, and on three different roads leading to the latter city. But the most important consideration in my mind was to have a force confronting Pemberton if he should come out to attack my rear. This I expected him to do; as shown farther on, he was directed by Johnston to make this very move.

I notified General Halleck that I should attack the State capital on the 14th. A courier carried the dispatch to Grand Gulf, through an unprotected country.

Sherman and McPherson communicated with each other during the night, and arranged to reach Jackson at the same hour. It rained in torrents during the night of the 13th and the fore part of the day of the 14th. The roads were intolerable, and in some places on Sherman's line, where the land was low, they were covered more than a foot deep with water. But the troops never murmured. By 9 o'clock Crocker, of McPherson's corps, who was now in advance, came upon the enemy's pickets and speedily drove them in upon the main body. They were outside of the intrenchments, in a strong position, and proved to be the troops that had been driven out of Raymond. Johnston had been reënforced during the night by Georgia and South Carolina regiments, so that his force amounted to eleven thousand men, and he was expecting still more.

Sherman also came upon the rebel pickets some distance out from the town, but speedily drove them in. He was now on the south and south-west of Jackson, confronting the Confederates behind their breastworks; while McPherson's right was nearly two miles north, occupying a line running north and south across the Vicksburg Railroad. Artillery was brought up and reconnoissances made preparatory to an assault. McPherson brought up Logan's division, while he deployed Crocker's for the assault. Sherman made similar dispositions on the right. By 11 A.M. both were ready to attack. Crocker moved his division forward, preceded by a strong skirmish line. These troops at once encountered the enemy's advance and drove it back on the main body, when they returned to their proper regiment, and the whole division charged, routing the enemy completely and driving him into this main line. This stand by the enemy was made more than two miles outside of his main fortifications. McPherson followed up with his command until within range of the guns of the enemy from their intrenchments, when he halted to bring his command into line, and reconnoiter to determine the next move. It was now about noon.

While this was going on, Sherman was confronting a rebel battery which enfiladed the road on which he was marching—the Mississippi Springs road—and commanded a bridge spanning the stream over which he had to pass. By detaching right and left the stream was forced, and the enemy flanked and speedily driven within the main line. This brought our whole line in front of the enemy's line of works, which was continuous on the north, west, and south sides, from the Pearl River north of the city to the same river south. I was with Sherman. He was confronted by a sufficient force to hold us back. Appearances did not justify an assault where we were. I had directed Sherman to send a force to the right, and to reconnoiter as far as to the Pearl River. This force—Tuttle's division—not returning, I rode to the right with my staff, and soon found that the enemy had left that part of the line. Tuttle's movement or McPherson's pressure had, no doubt, led Johnston to order a retreat, leaving only the men at the guns to retard us while he was getting away. Tuttle had seen this, and, passing through the lines without resistance, came up in rear of the artillerists confronting Sherman, and captured them, with ten pieces of artillery. I rode immediately to the State House, where I was soon followed by Sherman. About the same time McPherson discovered that the enemy was leaving his front, and advanced Crocker, who was so close upon the enemy that they could not move their guns or destroy them. He captured seven guns, and, moving on, hoisted the National flag over the Confederate capital of Mississippi. Stevenson's brigade was sent to cut off the Confederate retreat, but was too late or not expeditious enough.

Our loss in this engagement was: McPherson, 36 killed, 229 wounded, 3 missing; Sherman, 6 killed, 22 wounded, and 4 missing. The enemy lost 845 killed, wounded, and captured. Seventeen guns fell into our hands, and the enemy destroyed by fire their storehouses, containing a large amount of commissary stores. On this day Blair reached New Auburn and joined McClernand's Fourth Division. He had with him two hundred wagons loaded with rations, the only commissary supplies received during the entire campaign. I slept that night in the room that Johnston had occupied the night before.

About 4 in the afternoon I sent for the corps commanders, and directed the disposition to be made of their troops. Sherman was to remain in Jackson until he destroyed that place as a railroad center and manufacturing city of military supplies. He did the work most effectually. Sherman and I went together into a manufactory which had not ceased work on account of the battle, nor for the entrance of Yankee troops. Our presence did not seem to attract the attention of either the manager, or of the operatives (most of whom were girls). We looked on awhile to see the tent-cloth which they were making roll out of the looms, with C.S.A. woven in each bolt. There was an immense amount of cotton in bales stacked outside. Finally I told Sherman I thought they had done work enough. The operatives were told they might leave and take with them what cloth they could carry. In a few minutes cotton and factory were in a blaze. The proprietor visited Washington, while I was President, to get his pay for this property, claiming that it was private. He asked me to give him a statement of the fact that his property had been destroyed by National troops, so that he might use it with Congress where he was pressing, or proposed to press, his claim. I declined.

On the night of the 13th Johnston sent the following dispatch to Pemberton at Edwards's Station:

> "I have lately arrived, and learn that Major-General Sherman is between us with four divisions at Clinton. It is important to establish communication, that you may be reënforced. If practicable, come up in his rear at once. To beat such a detachment would be of immense value. All the troops you can quickly assemble should be brought. Time is all-important."

This dispatch was sent in triplicate by different messengers. One of the messengers happened to be a loyal man, who had been expelled from Memphis some months before, by Hurlbut, for uttering disloyal and threatening sentiments. There was a good deal of parade about this expulsion, ostensibly as a warning to those who entertained the sentiments he expressed; but Hurlbut and the expelled man understood each other. He delivered his copy of Johnston's dispatch to McPherson, who forwarded it to me.

Receiving this dispatch on the 14th, I ordered McPherson to move promptly in the morning back to Bolton, the nearest point where Johnston could reach the road. Bolton is about twenty miles west of Jackson. I also informed McClernand of the capture of Jackson, and sent him the following orders:

> "It is evidently the design of the enemy to get north of us and cross the Big Black, and beat us into Vicksburg. We must not allow them to do this. Turn all your forces toward Bolton Station, and make all dispatch in getting there. Move troops by the most direct road from wherever they may be on the receipt of this order."

And to Blair I wrote:

> "Their design is evidently to cross the Big Black and pass down the peninsula between the Big Black and Yazoo rivers. We must beat them. Turn your troops immediately to Bolton: take all the trains with you. Smith's division, and any other troops now with you, will go to the same place. If practicable, take parallel roads, so as to divide your troops and train."

Johnston stopped on the Canton road, only six miles north of Jackson, the night of the 14th. He sent from there to Pemberton dispatches announcing the loss of Jackson, and the following dispatch [given here in part.—EDITORS]:

> "Can he [Grant] supply himself from the Mississippi? Can you not cut him off from it, and above all, should he be compelled to fall back for want of supplies, beat him? As soon as the reënforcements are all up, they must be united to the rest of the army. I am anxious to see a force assembled that may be able to inflict a heavy blow upon the enemy."

The concentration of my troops was easy, considering the character of the country. McPherson moved along the road parallel with and near the railroad. Of McClernand's command one division (Hovey's) was on the road McPherson had to take, but with a start of four miles; one (Osterhaus's) was at Raymond, on a converging road that intersected the other near Champion's Hill; one (Carr's) had to pass over the same road with Osterhaus's, but, being back at Mississippi Springs, would not be detained thereby; the fourth (Smith's, with Blair's division) was near Auburn, with a different road to pass over. McClernand faced about and moved promptly. His cavalry from Raymond seized Bolton by half-past 9 in the morning, driving out the enemy's pickets and capturing several men.

The night of the 15th Hovey was at Bolton; Carr and Osterhaus were about three miles south, but abreast, facing west; Smith was north of Raymond, with Blair in his rear.

McPherson's command, with Logan in front, had marched at 7 o'clock, and by 4 reached Hovey and went into camp. Crocker bivouacked just in Hovey's rear on the Clinton road. Sherman, with two divisions, was in Jackson, completing the destruction of roads, bridges, and military factories. I rode in person out to Clinton. On my arrival I ordered McClernand to move early in the morning on Edwards's Station, cautioning him to watch for the enemy, and not to bring on an engagement unless he felt very certain of success.

I naturally expected that Pemberton would endeavor to obey the orders of his superior, which I have shown were to attack us at Clinton. This, indeed, I knew he could not do, but I felt sure he would make the attempt to reach that point. It turned out, however, that he had decided his superior's plans were impracticable, and consequently determined to move south from Edwards's Station, and get between me and my base. I, however, had no base, having abandoned it more than a week before. On the 15th Pemberton had actually marched south from Edwards's Station; but the rains had swollen Baker's Creek, which he had to cross, so much that he could not ford it, and the bridges were washed away. This brought him back to the Jackson road, on which there was a good bridge over Baker's Creek. Some of his troops were marching until midnight to get there. Receiving here early on the 16th a repetition of his order to join Johnston at Clinton, he concluded to obey, and sent a dispatch to his chief, informing him of the route by which he might be expected.

About 5 o'clock in the morning (16th) two men who had been employed on the Jackson and Vicksburg Railroad were brought to me. They reported that they had passed through Pemberton's army in the night, and that it was still marching east. They reported him to have 80 regiments of infantry and 10 batteries; in all about 25,000 men.

I had expected to leave Sherman at Jackson another day in order to complete his work. But, getting the above information, I sent him orders to move with all dispatch to Bolton, and to put one division, with an ammunition train, on the road at once, with directions to its commander to march with all possible speed until he came up to our rear. Within an hour after receiving this order, Steele's division was on the road. At the same time I dispatched to Blair, who was near Auburn, to move with all speed to Edwards's Station. McClernand was directed to embrace Blair in his command for the present. Blair's division was a part of the Fifteenth Army Corps (Sherman's); but as it was on its way to join its corps, it naturally struck our left first, now that we had faced about and were moving west. The Fifteenth Corps, when it got up, would be on our extreme right. McPherson was directed to get his trains out of the way of the troops, and to follow Hovey's division as closely as possible. McClernand had two roads, about three miles apart, converging at Edwards's Station, over which to march his troops. Hovey's division of his corps had the advance on a third road (the Clinton) still farther north. McClernand was directed to move Blair's and A. J. Smith's divisions by the southernmost of these roads, and Osterhaus and Carr by the middle road. Orders were to move cautiously, with skirmishers in the front to feel for the enemy. Smith's division, on the most southern road, was the first to encounter the enemy's pickets, who were speedily driven in. Osterhaus, on the middle road, hearing the firing, pushed his skirmishers forward, found the enemy's pickets, and forced them back to the main line. About the same time Hovey encountered the enemy on the northern or direct wagon road from Jackson to Vicksburg. McPherson was hastening up to join Hovey, but was embarrassed by Hovey's trains occupying the roads. I was still back at Clinton. McPherson sent me word of the situation and expressed the wish that I was up. By 7:30 I was on the road and proceeded rapidly to the front, ordering all trains that were in front of troops off the road. When I arrived Hovey's skirmishing amounted almost to a battle.

McClernand was in person on the middle road, and had a shorter distance to march to reach the enemy's position than McPherson. I sent him word by a staff-officer to push forward and attack. These orders were repeated several times without apparently expediting McClernand's advance.

Champion's Hill, where Pemberton had chosen his position to receive us, whether taken by accident or design, was well selected. It is one of the highest points in that section, and commanded all the ground in range. On the east side of the ridge, which is quite precipitous, is a ravine, running first north, then westerly, terminating at Baker's Creek. It was grown up thickly with large trees and undergrowth, making it difficult to penetrate with troops, even when not defended. The ridge occupied by the enemy terminated abruptly where the ravine turns westerly. The left of the enemy occupied the north end of this ridge. The Bolton and Edwards's Station road turns almost due south at this point, and ascends the ridge, which it follows for about a mile, then, turning west, descends by a gentle declivity to Baker's Creek, nearly a mile away. On the west side the slope of the ridge is gradual, and is cultivated from near the summit to the creek. There was, when we were there, a narrow belt of timber near the summit, west of the road.

From Raymond there is a direct road to Edwards's Station, some three miles west of Champion's Hill. There is one also to Bolton. From this latter road there is still another, leaving it about three and a half miles before reaching Bolton, and leading direct to the same station. It was along these two roads that three divisions of McClernand's corps, and Blair, of Sherman's, temporarily under McClernand, were moving. Hovey, of McClernand's command, was with McPherson, farther north on the road from Bolton, direct to Edwards's Station. The middle road comes into the northern road at the point where the latter turns to the west, and descends to Baker's Creek; the southern road is still several miles south and does not intersect the others until it reaches Edwards's Station. Pemberton's lines covered all these roads and faced east. Hovey's line, when it first drove in the enemy's pickets, was formed parallel to that of the enemy, and confronted his left.

By eleven o'clock the skirmishing had grown into a hard-contested battle. Hovey alone, before other troops could be got to assist him, had captured a battery of the enemy. But he was not able to hold his position, and had to abandon the artillery. McPherson brought up his troops as fast as possible—Logan in front—and posted them on the right of Hovey and across the flank of the enemy. Logan reënforced Hovey with one brigade from his division; with his other two he moved farther west to make room for Crocker, who was coming up as rapidly as the roads would admit. Hovey was still being heavily pressed, and was calling on me for more reënforcements. I ordered Crocker, who was now coming up, to send one brigade from his division. McPherson ordered two batteries to be stationed where they nearly enfiladed the enemy's line, and they did good execution.

From Logan's position now a direct forward movement would carry him over open fields in rear of the enemy and in a line parallel with them. He did make exactly this move, attacking, however, the enemy through the belt of woods covering the west slope of the hill for a short distance. Up to this time I had kept my position near Hovey, where we were the most heavily pressed; but about noon I moved with a part of my staff by our right, around, until I came up with Logan himself. I found him near the road leading down to Baker's Creek. He was actually in command of the only road over which the enemy could retreat; Hovey, reënforced by two brigades from McPherson's command, confronted the enemy's left; Crocker, with two brigades, covered their left flank; McClernand, two hours before, had been within two and a half miles of their center with two divisions, and two divisions—Blair's and A. J. Smith's—were confronting the rebel right; Ransom, with a brigade of McArthur's division, of the Seventeenth Corps (McPherson's), had crossed the river at Grand Gulf a few days before and was coming up on their right flank. Neither Logan nor I knew that we had cut off the retreat of the enemy. Just at this juncture a messenger came from Hovey, asking for more reënforcements. There were none to spare. I then gave an order to move McPherson's command by the left flank around to Hovey. This uncovered the Confederate line of retreat, which was soon taken advantage of by the enemy.☆

☆Dr. William M. Beach of London, Ohio, sends to the editors this anecdote of General Grant:

"At the time of the Vicksburg campaign I was the Assistant Surgeon of the 78th Ohio Regiment: but I had been detailed by J. H. Boncher, Medical Director of the 17th Army Corps, as the Division Hospital Director of Logan's division. I had a regular service of men and wagons; and at the battle of Champion's Hill—when my division had been assigned to its position—I chose an abandoned farm-house and its surroundings as a proper place to establish our hospital, and immediately proceeded in its preparation. My position was in the rear of our left wing, and not far in the rear of Hovey's right wing. About the time I was fairly ready to receive the wounded the line had advanced across an open field, and had swung to the right and front

During all this time Hovey, reënforced as he was by a brigade from Logan and another from Crocker, and by Crocker gallantly coming up with two other brigades on his right, had made several assaults, the last one about the time the road was opened to the rear. The enemy fled precipitately. This was between 3 and 4 o'clock. I rode forward, or rather back, to where the middle road intersects the north road, and found the skirmishers of Carr's division just coming in. Osterhaus was farther south, and soon after came up with skirmishers advanced in like manner. Hovey's division, and McPherson's two divisions with him, had marched and fought from early dawn, and were not in the best condition to follow the retreating foe. I sent orders to Osterhaus to pursue the enemy, and to Carr, whom I saw personally, I explained the situation, and directed him to pursue vigorously as far as the Big Black, and to cross it if he could, Osterhaus to follow him. The pursuit was continued until after dark.

The battle of Champion's Hill lasted about four hours of hard fighting, preceded by two or three hours of skirmishes, some of which rose almost to the dignity of battle. Every man of Hovey's division and of McPherson's two divisions was engaged during the battle. No other part of my command was engaged at all, except that (as described before). Osterhaus's and A. J. Smith's had encountered the rebel advanced pickets as early as 7:30. Their positions were admirable for advancing upon the enemy's line. McClernand, with two divisions, was within a few miles of the battle-field long before noon, and in easy hearing. I sent him repeated orders by staff-officers fully competent to explain to him the situation. These traversed the road separating us, without escort, and directed him to push forward, but he did not come.‡ Instead of this he sent orders to Hovey, who belonged to his corps, to join on to his right flank. Hovey was bearing the brunt of the battle at the time. To obey the order he would have had to pull out from the front of the enemy and march back as far as McClernand had to advance to get into battle, and substantially over the same ground. Of course, I did not permit Hovey to obey the order of his intermediate superior.

---

nearly a quarter of a mile. The steady roar of battle had rolled from Hovey's front by this time to that of Logan's, who was steadily advancing, and where the sound of the conflict was now simply *terrific.* Grant and his staff, coming from the left, dismounted at the front gate, within twenty feet of where I was standing. He had scarcely dismounted, when,—more clearly and distinctly hearing the fury of the contest on our right,—leisurely taking his cigar from his mouth, he turned slowly to one of his staff and said, '*Go down to Logan and tell him he is making history to-day.*' "

—Editors.

‡"It is true, in front of McClernand there was a small force of the enemy, and posted in a good position behind a ravine, obstructing his advance; but if he had moved to the right by the road my staff-officers had followed, the enemy must either have fallen back or been cut off."

—From "Personal Memoirs of U. S. Grant," C. L. Webster & Co.

We had in this battle about fifteen thousand men actually engaged. This excludes those that did not get up—all of McClernand's command except Hovey. Our loss was 410 killed, 1844 wounded, and 187 missing. Hovey alone lost twelve hundred killed, wounded, and missing,—one-third of his division.

Had McClernand come up with reasonable promptness, or had I known the ground as I did afterward, I cannot see how Pemberton could have escaped with any organized force. As it was he lost over 3000 killed and wounded, and about 3000 captured in battle and in pursuit. Loring's division, which was the right of Pemberton's line, was cut off from the retreating army, and never got back into Vicksburg. Pemberton himself fell back that night to the Big Black River. His troops did not stop before midnight, and many of them left before the general retreat commenced, and no doubt a good part of them returned to their homes. Logan alone captured 1300 prisoners and 11 guns. Hovey captured 300, under fire, and about 700 in all, exclusive of 500 sick and wounded, whom he paroled, thus making 1200.

McPherson joined in the advance as soon as his men could fill their cartridge-boxes, leaving one brigade to guard our wounded. The pursuit was continued as long as it was light enough to see the road. The night of the 16th of May found McPherson's command bivouacked from two to six miles west of the battle-field, along the line of the road to Vicksburg. Carr and Osterhaus were at Edwards's Station, and Blair was about three miles south-east. Hovey remained on the field where his troops had fought so bravely and bled so freely. Much war material abandoned by the enemy was picked up on the battle-field, among it thirty pieces of artillery. I pushed through the advancing column with my staff, and kept in advance until after night. Finding ourselves alone we stopped and took possession of a vacant house. As no troops came up we moved back a mile or more, until we met the head of the column just going into bivouac on the road. We had no tents, so we occupied the porch of a house which had been taken for a rebel hospital, and which was filled with wounded and dying who had been brought from the battle-field we had just left.

While a battle is raging one can see his enemy mowed down by the thousand and the ten thousand, with great composure. But after the battle these scenes are distressing, and one is naturally disposed to do as much to alleviate the suffering of an enemy as of a friend.

We were now assured of our position between Johnston and Pemberton, without the possibility of a junction of their forces. Pemberton might indeed have made a night march to the Big Black, crossed the bridge there, and, by moving north on the west side, have eluded us, and finally returned to Johnston. But this would have given us Vicksburg. It would have been his proper move, however, and the one Johnston would have made had he been in Pemberton's place. In fact, it would have been in conformity with Johnston's orders to Pemberton.

Sherman left Jackson with the last of his troops about noon on the 16th, and reached Bolton, twenty miles west, before halting. His rear-guard did not get in until 2 A.M. the 17th, but renewed their march by daylight. He paroled his prisoners at Jackson, and was forced to leave his own wounded,—in care of surgeons and attendants however. At Bolton he was informed of our victory. He was directed to commence the march early next day, and to diverge from the road he was on, to Bridgeport, on the Big Black River, some eleven miles above where we expected to find the enemy. Blair was ordered to join him there with the pontoon train as early as possible.

This movement brought Sherman's corps together, and at a point where I hoped a crossing of the Big Black might be effected, and Sherman's corps used to flank the enemy out of his position in our front, and thus open a crossing for the remainder of the army. I informed him that I would endeavor to hold the enemy in my front while he crossed the river.

The advanced division, Carr's (McClernand's corps), resumed the pursuit at 3:30 A.M. on the 17th, followed closely by Osterhaus; McPherson bringing up the rear with his corps. As I expected, the enemy was found in position on the Big Black. The point was only six miles from that where my advance had rested for the night, and was reached at an early hour. Here the river makes a turn to the west, and has washed close up to the high land. The east side is a low bottom, sometimes overflowed at very high water, but was cleared and in cultivation. A bayou runs irregularly across this low land, the bottom of which,

GENERAL BLAIR'S DIVISION CROSSING BIG BLACK RIVER. FROM A WATER-COLOR.

however, is above the surface of the Big Black at ordinary stages. When the river is full, water runs through it, converting the point of land into an island. The bayou was grown up with timber, which the enemy had felled into the ditch. All this time there was a foot or two of water in it. The rebels had constructed a parapet along the inner bank of this bayou, by using cotton bales from the plantation close by and throwing dirt over them. The whole was thoroughly commanded from the height west of the river. At the upper end of the bayou there was a strip of uncleared land, which afforded a cover for a portion of our men. Carr's division was deployed on our right, Lawler's brigade forming his extreme right, and reaching through these woods to the river above. Osterhaus's division was deployed to the left of Carr, and covered the enemy's entire front. McPherson was in column on the road, the head close by, ready to come in whenever he could be of assistance.

While the troops were standing as here described, an officer from Banks's staff ⸭ came up and presented me with a letter from General Halleck, dated the 11th of May. It had been sent by the way of New Orleans to Banks to forward to me. It ordered me to return to Grand Gulf, and to coöperate from there with Banks, against Port Hudson, and then to return with our combined forces to besiege Vicksburg. I told the officer that the order came too late, and that Halleck would not give it then if he knew our position. The bearer of the dispatch insisted that I ought to obey the order, and was giving arguments to support his position, when I heard great cheering to the right of our line, and, looking in that direction, saw Lawler, in his shirt-sleeves, leading a charge upon the enemy. I immediately mounted my horse and rode in the direction of the charge, and saw no more of the officer who delivered the dispatch, I think not even to this day.

The assault was successful. But little resistance was made. The enemy fled from the west bank of the river, burning the bridge behind them, leaving the men and guns on the east side to fall into our hands. Many tried to escape by swimming the river. Some succeeded and some were drowned in the attempt. Eighteen guns were captured, and 1751 prisoners. Our loss was 39 killed, 237 wounded, and 3 missing. The enemy probably lost but few men except those captured and drowned. But for the successful and complete destruction of the bridge, I have but little doubt that we should have followed the enemy so closely as to prevent his occupying his defenses around Vicksburg.

As the bridge was destroyed and the river was high, new bridges had to be built. It was but little after 9 o'clock A.M. when the capture took place. As soon as work could be commenced, orders were given for the construction of three

---

⸭Brigadier-General William Dwight, afterward of Banks's staff. According to Banks, Dwight reported that Grant said "he would give me 5000 men, but that I should not wait for them."—EDITORS.

bridges. One was taken charge of by Lieutenant Peter C. Hains, of the Engineer Corps, one by General McPherson himself, and one by General Ransom, a most gallant and intelligent volunteer officer. My recollection is that Hains built a raft-bridge; McPherson a pontoon, using cotton bales in large numbers for pontoons; and that Ransom felled trees on opposite banks of the river, cutting only on one side of the tree, so that they would fall with their tops interlacing in the river, without the trees being entirely severed from their stumps. A bridge was then made with these trees to support the roadway. Lumber was taken from buildings, cotton-gins, and wherever found, for this purpose. By 8 o'clock on the morning of the 18th all three bridges were complete and the troops were crossing.

Sherman reached Bridgeport about noon of the 17th, and found Blair with the pontoon train already there. A few of the enemy were intrenched on the west bank, but they made little resistance, and soon surrendered. Two divisions were crossed that night, and the third the following morning.

On the 18th I moved along the Vicksburg road in advance of the troops, and as soon as possible joined Sherman. My first anxiety was to secure a base of supplies on the Yazoo River above Vicksburg. Sherman's line of march led him to the very point on Walnut Hills occupied by the enemy the December before, when he was repulsed. Sherman was equally anxious with myself. Our impatience led us to move in advance of the column, and well up with the advanced skirmishers. There were some detached works along the crest of the hill. These were still occupied by the enemy, or else the garrison from Haynes's Bluff had not all got past on their way to Vicksburg. At all events, the bullets of the enemy whistled by thick and fast for a short time. In a few minutes Sherman had the pleasure of looking down from the spot coveted so much by him the December before,—on the ground where his command lay so helpless for offensive action [Chickasaw Bayou]. He turned to me, saying that up to this minute he had felt no positive assurance of success. This, however, he said, was the end of one of the greatest campaigns in history, and I ought to make a report of it at once. Vicksburg was not yet captured, and there was no telling what might happen before it was taken; but whether captured or not, this was a complete and successful campaign. I do not claim to quote Sherman's language, but the substance only. My reason for mentioning this incident will appear farther on.

McPherson, after crossing the Big Black, came into the Jackson and Vicksburg road which Sherman was on, but to his rear. He arrived at night near the lines of the enemy, and went into camp. McClernand moved by the direct road near the railroad to Mount Albans, and then turned to the left, and put his troops on the road from Baldwin's Ferry to Vicksburg. This brought him south of McPherson. I now had my three corps up to the works built for the defense of Vicksburg on three roads,—one to the north, one to the east, and one to the south-east of the city. By the morning of May 19th the investment was as complete as my limited number of troops would allow. Sherman was on the right and covered the high ground from where it overlooked the Yazoo as far south-east as his troops would extend. McPherson joined on to his left, and occupied ground on both sides of the Jackson road. McClernand took up the ground to his left, and extended as far toward Warrenton as he could, keeping a continuous line.

On the 19th there was constant skirmishing with the enemy while we were getting into better position. The enemy had been much demoralized by his defeats at Champion's Hill and the Big Black, and I believed would not make much effort to hold Vicksburg. Accordingly at 2 o'clock I ordered an assault. It resulted in securing more advanced positions for all our troops, where they were fully covered from the fire of the enemy.

The 20th and 21st were spent in strengthening our position, and in making roads in rear of the army, from Yazoo River, or Chickasaw Bayou. Most of the army had now been for three weeks with only five days' rations issued by the commissary. They had an abundance of food, however, but began to feel the want of bread. I remember, that in passing around to the left of the line on the 21st, a soldier, recognizing me, said in rather a low voice, but yet so that I heard him, "*Hard-tack.*" In a moment the cry was taken up all along the line, "*Hard-tack! Hard-tack!*" I told the men nearest to me that we had been engaged ever since the arrival of the troops in building a road over which to supply them with everything they needed. The cry was instantly changed to cheers. By the night of the 21st all the troops had full rations issued to them. The bread and coffee were highly appreciated.

I now determined on a second assault. Johnston was in my rear, only fifty miles away, with an army not much inferior in numbers to the one I had with me, and I knew he was being reënforced. There was danger of his coming to the assistance of Pemberton, and, after all, he might defeat my anticipations of capturing the garrison, if, indeed, he might not prevent the capture of the city. The immediate capture of Vicksburg would save sending me the reënforcements, which were so much wanted elsewhere, and would set free the army under me to drive Johnston from the State. But the first consideration of all was: the troops believed they could carry the works in their front, and would not have worked so patiently in the trenches if they had not been allowed to try.

The attack was ordered to commence on all parts of the line at 10 o'clock A.M. on the 22d with a furious cannonading from every battery in position. All the corps commanders set their time by mine, so that all might open the engagement at the same minute. The attack was gallant, and portions of each of the three corps succeeded in getting up to the very parapets of the enemy, and in planting their battle-flags upon them; but at no place were we able to enter.

General McClernand reported that he had gained the enemy's intrenchments at several points, and wanted reënforcements. I occupied a position from which I believed I could see as well as he what took place in his front, and I did not see the success he reported. But his request for reënforcements being repeated, I could not ignore it, and sent him Quinby's division of the Seventeenth Corps. Sherman and McPherson were both ordered to renew their assaults as a diversion in favor of McClernand. This last attack only served to increase our casualties, without giving any benefit whatever. As soon as it was dark, our troops that had reached the enemy's line and had been obliged to remain there for security all day, were withdrawn, and thus ended the last assault on Vicksburg.

I now determined upon a regular siege,—to "out-camp the enemy," as it were, and to incur no more losses. The experience of the 22d convinced officers and men that this was best, and they went to work on the defenses and approaches with a will. With the navy holding the river the investment of Vicksburg was complete. As long as we could hold our position, the enemy was limited in supplies of food, men, and munitions of war, to what they had on hand. These could not last always.

The crossing of troops at Bruinsburg commenced April 30th. On the 18th of May the army was in rear of Vicksburg. On the 19th, just twenty days after the crossing, the city was completely invested and an assault had been made: five distinct battles—besides continuous skirmishing—had been fought and won by the Union forces; the capital of the State had fallen, and its arsenals, military manufactories, and everything useful for military purposes had been destroyed; an average of about 180 miles had been marched by the troops engaged; but 5 days' rations had been issued, and no forage; over 6000 prisoners had been captured, and as many more of the enemy had been killed or wounded; 27 heavy cannon and 61 field-pieces had fallen into our hands; 250 miles of the river, from Vicksburg to Port Hudson, had become ours. The Union force that had crossed the Mississippi River up to this time was less than 43,000 men. One division of these—Blair's—only arrived in time to take part in the battle of Champion's Hill, but was not engaged there; and one brigade—Ransom's—of McPherson's corps reached the field after the battle. The enemy had at Vicksburg, Grand Gulf, Jackson, and on the roads between these places, over sixty thousand men. They were in their own country, where no rear-guards were necessary. The country is admirable for defense, but difficult to conduct an offensive campaign in. All their troops had to be met. We were fortunate, to say the least, in meeting them in detail: at Port Gibson, 7000 or 8000; at Raymond, 5000; at Jackson, from 8000 to 11,000; at Champion's Hill, 25,000; at the Big Black, 4000. A part of those met at Jackson were all that were left of those encountered at Raymond. They were beaten in detail by a force smaller than their own, upon their own ground. Our loss up to this time was:

	Killed.	Wounded.	Missing.
Port Gibson	131	719	25
South Fork, Bayou Pierre		1	
Skirmishes, May 3d	1	9	
Fourteen Mile Creek	6	24	
Raymond	66	339	37
Jackson	42	251	7
Champion's Hill	410	1844	187
Big Black	39	237	3
Bridgeport		1	
Total [In all, 4379]	695	3425	259

Of the wounded many were but slightly so, and continued on duty. Not half of them were disabled for any length of time.[+]

After the unsuccessful assault on the 22d, the work of the regular siege began. Sherman occupied the right, starting from the river above Vicksburg; McPherson the center (McArthur's division now with him); and McClernand the left, holding the road south to Warrenton. Lauman's division arrived at this time and was placed on the extreme left of the line.

In the interval between the assaults of the 19th and 22d, roads had been completed from the Yazoo River and Chickasaw Bayou, around the rear of the army, to enable us to bring up supplies of food and ammunition; ground had been selected and cleared, on which the troops were to be encamped, and tents and cooking utensils were brought up. The troops had been without these from the time of crossing the Mississippi up to this time. All was now ready for the pick and spade. With the two brigades brought up by McArthur, which reached us in rear of Vicksburg, and Lauman's division brought from Memphis, and which had just arrived, we had now about forty thousand men for the siege. Prentiss and Hurlbut were ordered to send forward every man that could be spared. Cavalry especially was wanted to watch the fords along the Big Black, and to observe Johnston. I knew that Johnston was receiving reënforcements from Bragg, who was confronting Rosecrans in Tennessee. Vicksburg was so important to the enemy that I believed he would make the most strenuous efforts to raise the siege, even at the risk of losing ground elsewhere.

My line was more than fifteen miles long, extending from Haynes's Bluff to Vicksburg, thence south to Warrenton. The line of the enemy was about seven. In addition to this, having an enemy at Canton and Jackson, in our rear, who was being constantly reënforced, we required a second line of defense facing the

[+]The revised statements (unpublished "Official Records," Vol. XXIV., part I., p. 167) show that the aggregate Union losses, including the above, from May 1st to July 4th, were: killed, 1514; wounded, 7395; captured or missing, 453,—total, 9362.—EDITORS.

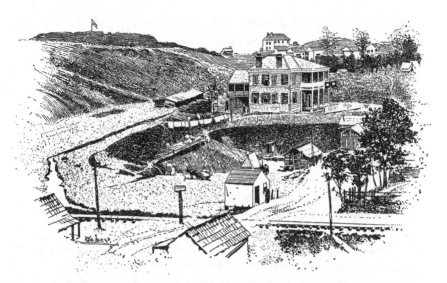

HEADQUARTERS OF THE UNION SIGNAL CORPS, VICKSBURG.
FROM A WAR-TIME PHOTOGRAPH.

other way. I had not troops enough under my command to man these. But General Halleck appreciated the situation, and, without being asked, forwarded reënforcements with all possible dispatch.

The ground about Vicksburg is admirable for defense. On the north it is about two hundred feet above the Mississippi River at the highest point, and very much cut up by the washing rains; the ravines were grown up with cane and underbrush, while the sides and tops were covered with a dense forest. Farther south the ground flattens out somewhat, and was in cultivation. But here, too, it was cut by ravines and small streams. The enemy's line of defense followed the crest of a ridge, from the river north of the city, eastward, then southerly around to the Jackson road, full three miles back of the city; thence in a south-westerly direction to the river. Deep ravines of the description given lay in front of these defenses.

As there is a succession of gullies, cut out by rains, along the side of the ridge, the line was necessarily very irregular. To follow each of these spurs with intrenchments, so as to command the slopes on either side, would have lengthened their line very much. Generally, therefore, or in many places, their line would run from near the head of one gully nearly straight to the head of another, and an outer work, triangular in shape, generally open in the rear, was thrown up on the point; with a few men in this outer work they commanded the approaches to the main line completely.

The work to be done to make our position as strong against the enemy as his was against us, was very great. The problem was also complicated by our wanting our line as near that of the enemy as possible. We had but four engineer officers with us. Captain F. E. Prime, of the Engineer Corps, was the chief, and the work at the beginning was mainly directed by him. His health soon gave out, when he was succeeded by Captain Cyrus B. Comstock, also of the Engineer Corps. To provide assistants on such a long line, I directed that all officers who had been graduated at West Point, where they had necessarily to study military engineering, should, in addition to their other duties, assist in the work.

The chief quartermaster and the chief commissary were graduates. The chief commissary, now the commissary-general of the army [General Robert Macfeely], begged off, however, saying that there was nothing in engineering that he was good for, unless he would do for a sap-roller. As soldiers require rations while working in the ditches as well as when marching and fighting, and we would be sure to lose him if he was used as a sap-roller, I let him off. The general is a large man,—weighs two hundred and twenty pounds, and is not tall.

We had no siege-guns except six 32-pounders, and there were none in the West to draw from. Admiral Porter, however, supplied us with a battery of navy-guns, of large caliber, and with these, and the field-artillery used in the campaign, the siege began. The first thing to do was to get the artillery in batteries, where they would occupy commanding positions; then establish the camps, under cover from the fire of the enemy, but as near up as possible; and then construct rifle-pits and covered ways, to connect the entire command by the shortest route. The enemy did not harass us much while we were constructing our batteries. Probably their artillery ammunition was short; and their infantry was kept down by our sharp-shooters, who were always on the alert and ready to fire at a head whenever it showed itself above the rebel works.

In no place were our lines more than six hundred yards from the enemy. It was necessary, therefore, to cover our men by something more than the ordinary parapet. To give additional protection sand-bags, bullet-proof, were placed along the tops of the parapets, far enough apart to make loop-holes for musketry. On top of these, logs were put. By these means the men were enabled to walk about erect when off duty, without fear of annoyance from sharp-shooters. The enemy used in their defense explosive musket-balls, thinking, no doubt, that, bursting over the men in the trenches, they would do some execution; but I do not remember a single case where a man was injured by a piece of one of the shells. When they were hit, and the ball exploded, the wound was terrible. In these cases a solid ball would have hit as well. Their use is barbarous, because they produce increased suffering without any corresponding advantage to those using them.

The enemy could not resort to the method we did to protect their men, because we had an inexhaustible supply of ammunition to draw upon, and used it freely. Splinters from the timber would have made havoc among the men behind.

There were no mortars with the besiegers, except what the navy had in front of the city; but wooden ones were made by taking logs of the toughest wood that could be found, boring them out for six or twelve pounder shells, and binding them with strong iron bands. These answered as coehorns, and shells were successfully thrown from them into the trenches of the enemy.

The labor of building the batteries and intrenching was largely done by the pioneers, assisted by negroes who came within our lines and who were paid for their work, but details from the troops had often to be made. The work was pushed forward as rapidly as possible, and when an advanced position was secured and covered from the fire of the enemy, the batteries were advanced. By the 30th of June there were 220 guns in position, mostly light

WOODEN COEHORN ON GRANT'S LINES.
FROM A SKETCH MADE AT THE TIME.

field-pieces, besides a battery of heavy guns belonging to, manned, and commanded by the navy. We were now as strong for defense against the garrison of Vicksburg as they were against us. But I knew that Johnston was in our rear, and was receiving constant reënforcements from the east. He had at this time a larger force than I had prior to the battle of Champion's Hill.

As soon as the news of the arrival of the Union army behind Vicksburg reached the North, floods of visitors began to pour in. Some came to gratify curiosity; some to see sons or brothers who had passed through the terrible ordeal; members of the Christian and Sanitary Commissions came to minister to the wants of the sick and the wounded. Often those coming to see a son or brother would bring a dozen or two of poultry. They did not know how little the gift would be appreciated; many soldiers had lived so much on chickens, ducks, and turkeys, without bread, during the march, that the sight of poultry, if they could get bacon, almost took away their appetite. But the intention was good.

Among the earliest arrivals was the Governor of Illinois [Yates], with most of the State officers. I naturally wanted to show them what there was of most interest. In Sherman's front the ground was the most broken and most wooded, and more was to be seen without exposure. I therefore took them to Sherman's headquarters and presented them. Before starting out to look at the lines—possibly while Sherman's horse was being saddled—there were many questions asked about the late campaign, about which the North had been so imperfectly informed. There was a little knot about Sherman and around me, and I heard Sherman repeating in the most animated manner what he had said to me, when

POSITION OF QUINBY'S DIVISION OF MCCLERNAND'S CORPS. FROM A LITHOGRAPH.

On the ridge in the background are Confederate forts connected by breastworks, and on the right is pictured the blowing up, June 25th, of the Confederate works on the Jackson road, in front of General Logan's division. The Union rifle-pits are at the farther edge of the ravine, in which the troops were protected. On the left is Battery Archer, 2 siege-guns; center, 12th Wisconsin Battery; right, 6th Wisconsin Battery. The trees in front of the explosion mark the scene of the conference between Grant and Pemberton.

we first looked down from Walnut Hills upon the land below, on the 18th of May, adding: "Grant is entitled to every bit of the credit for the campaign; I opposed it. I wrote him a letter about it." But for this speech it is not likely that Sherman's opposition would have ever been heard of. His untiring energy and great efficiency during the campaign entitled him to a full share of all the credit due for its success. He could not have done more if the plan had been his own.

On the 26th of May I sent Blair's division up the Yazoo to drive out a force of the enemy supposed to be between the Big Black and the Yazoo. The country was rich, and full of supplies of both fruit and forage. Blair was instructed to take all of it. The cattle were to be driven in for the use of our army, and the food and forage to be consumed by our troops or destroyed by fire; all bridges were to be destroyed, and the roads rendered as nearly impassable as possible. Blair went forty-five miles, and was gone almost a week. His work was effectually done. I requested Porter at this time to send the Marine brigade—a floating nondescript force which had been assigned to his command, and which proved very useful— up to Haynes's Bluff to hold it until reënforcements could be sent.

On the 26th I also received a letter from Banks, asking me to reënforce him with ten thousand men at Port Hudson. Of course I could not comply with his

On May 25th General Grant wrote to General Banks that it seemed to him advisable to collect as large a force at Vicksburg as possible, and says, "I would be pleased, General, to have you come, with such force as you are able to spare." In the same letter General Grant makes this statement:

"When I commenced writing this it was my intention to propose sending you, if you will furnish transportation, 8000 or 10,000 men to coöperate with you on Port Hudson; but, whilst

request, nor did I think he needed them. He was in no danger of an attack by the garrison in his front, and there was no army organizing in his rear to raise the siege. On the 3d of June a brigade from Hurlbut's command arrived, General Nathan Kimball commanding./ It was sent to Mechanicsburg, some miles north-east of Haynes's Bluff, and about midway between the Big Black and the Yazoo. A brigade of Blair's division and twelve hundred cavalry had already, on Blair's return from up the Yazoo, been sent to the same place—with instructions to watch the crossings of the Big Black River, to destroy the roads in his (Blair's) front, and to gather or destroy all supplies.

On the 7th of June our little force of colored and white troops across the Mississippi, at Milliken's Bend, were attacked by about three thousand men from Richard Taylor's Trans-Mississippi command. With the aid of the gunboats these were speedily repelled. I sent Mower's brigade over with instructions to drive the enemy beyond the Tensas bayou; and we had no further trouble in that quarter during the siege. This was the first important engagement of the war in which colored troops were under fire.☆ These were very raw, having all been enlisted since the beginning of the siege, but they behaved well.

On the 8th of June a full division arrived from Hurlbut's command, under General Sooy Smith. It was sent immediately to Haynes's Bluff, and General C. C. Washburn was assigned to the general command at that point.

On the 11th a strong division arrived from the Department of the Missouri under General Herron, which was placed on our left. This cut off the last possible chance of communication between Pemberton and Johnston, as it enabled Lauman to close up on McClernand's left, while Herron intrenched from Lanman to the water's edge. At this point the water recedes a few hundred yards from the high land. Through this opening, no doubt, the Confederate commanders had been able to get messengers under cover of night.

---

writing, a courier came in from my cavalry, stating that a force of the enemy are now about thirty miles north-east of here.... At present, therefore, I do not deem it prudent to send off any men I have, or even safe...."

On May 23d, 1863, General Halleck wrote to General Banks:

"I assure you that the Government is exceedingly disappointed that you and General Grant are not acting in conjunction. It thought to secure that object by authorizing you to assume the entire command as soon as you and General Grant could unite."

In Halleck's instructions, dated November 9th, 1862, General Banks was authorized "to assume control of any military forces from the Upper Mississippi which may come within your command.... You will exercise superior authority as far as you may ascend the river...."—EDITORS.

/General Kimball was wounded at Fredericksburg, and on recovering was assigned to the command of a division in the West.—EDITORS.

☆Colored troops had been under fire on the 27th of May at Port Hudson.—EDITORS.

POSITION OF LOGAN'S DIVISION OF MCPHERSON'S CORPS. FROM A LITHOGRAPH.

In the middle-ground is seen the main line of works, which on the right ascends the hill to the White House at the end of the curtain of trees. On the ridge to the left of the White House is the Union sap leading to the exploding mine under the Confederate fort near the Jackson road. Between the Union and Confederate lines, a little to the left of the center, are the trees that mark the conference between Grant and Pemberton.

On the 14th General Parke arrived with two divisions of Burnside's corps,‡ and was immediately dispatched to Haynes's Bluff. These latter troops— Herron's and Parke's—were the reënforcements already spoken of, sent by Halleck in anticipation of their being needed. They arrived none too soon.

I now had about seventy-one thousand men. More than half were disposed of across the peninsula, between the Yazoo, at Haynes's Bluff, and the Big Black, with the division of Osterhaus watching the crossings of the latter river farther south and west, from the crossing of the Jackson road to Baldwin's Ferry, and below.

There were eight roads leading into Vicksburg, along which and the immediate sides of which our work was specially pushed and batteries advanced; but no commanding point within range of the enemy was neglected.

On the 17th I received a letter from General Sherman and on the 18th one from McPherson, saying that their respective commands had complained to them of a fulsome congratulatory order published by General McClernand to

‡These troops came from the Department of the Ohio (Burnside), June 14th to 17th, having been transferred from the Army of the Potomac in the previous March. After Vicksburg they returned to Burnside's command and took part in the East Tennessee campaign.—EDITORS.

the Thirteenth Corps, which did great injustice to the other troops engaged in the campaign.

This order had been sent north and published, and now papers containing it had reached our camps. The order had not been heard of by me, and certainly not by troops outside of McClernand's command, until brought in this way. I at once wrote McClernand, directing him to send me a copy of this order. He did so, and I at once relieved him from the command of the Thirteenth Army Corps, and ordered him back to Springfield, Illinois. The publication of his order in the press was in violation of War Department orders and also of mine.

On the 22d of June positive information was received that Johnston had crossed the Big Black River for the purpose of attacking our rear, to raise the siege and release Pemberton. The correspondence between Johnston and Pemberton shows that all expectation of holding Vicksburg had by this time passed from Johnston's mind. I immediately ordered Sherman to the command of all the forces from Haynes's Bluff to the Big Black River. This amounted now to quite half the troops about Vicksburg. Besides these, Herron's and A. J. Smith's divisions were ordered to hold themselves in readiness to reënforce Sherman. Haynes's Bluff had been strongly fortified on the land side, and on all commanding points from there to the Big Black, at the railroad crossing, batteries had been constructed. The work of connecting by rifle-pits, where this was not already done, was an easy task for the troops that were to defend them.

We were now looking west, besieging Pemberton, while we were also looking east to defend ourselves against an expected siege by Johnston. But as against the garrison of Vicksburg we were as substantially protected as they were against us. When we were looking east and north we were strongly fortified, and on the defensive. Johnston evidently took in the situation and wisely, I think, abstained from making an assault on us, because it would simply have inflicted loss on both sides without accomplishing any result.

We were strong enough to have taken the offensive against him; but I did not feel disposed to take any risk of loosing our hold upon Pemberton's army, while I would have rejoiced at the opportunity of defending ourselves against an attack by Johnston.

From the 23d of May the work of fortifying and pushing forward our position nearer to the enemy had been steadily progressing. At three points on the Jackson road in front of Ransom's brigade a sap was run up to the enemy's parapet, and by the 25th of June we had it undermined and the mine charged. The enemy had countermined, but did not succeed in reaching our mine. At this particular point the hill on which the rebel work stands rises abruptly. Our sap ran close up to the outside of the enemy's parapet. In fact, this parapet was also our protection. The soldiers of the two sides occasionally conversed pleasantly across this barrier; sometimes they exchanged the hard bread of the Union soldiers for the tobacco of the Confederates; at other times the enemy threw over

THE FIGHT IN THE CRATER AFTER THE EXPLOSION OF THE UNION MINE UNDER THE
CONFEDERATE FORT ON THE JACKSON ROAD, JUNE 25, 1863. FROM A LITHOGRAPH.
To the right and left are seen part of the approaches from the main Union line at the White House.

hand-grenades, and often our men, catching them in their hands, returned them.

Our mine had been started some distance back down the hill, consequently when it had extended as far as the parapet it was many feet below it. This caused the failure of the enemy in his search to find and destroy it. On the 25th of June, at 3 o'clock, all being ready, the mine was exploded. A heavy artillery fire all along the line had been ordered to open with the explosion. The effect was to blow the top of the hill off and make a crater where it stood. The breach was not sufficient to enable us to pass a column of attack through. In fact, the enemy, having failed to reach our mine, had thrown up a line farther back, where most of the men guarding that point were placed. There were a few men, however, left at the advance line, and others working in the counter-mine, which was still being pushed to find ours. All that were there were thrown into the air, some of them coming down on our side, still alive. I remember one colored man, who had been under ground at work, when the explosion took place, who was thrown to our side. He was not much hurt, but was terribly frightened. Some one asked him how high he had gone up. "Dunno, Massa, but t'ink 'bout t'ree mile," was the reply. General Logan commanded at this point, and took this colored man to his quarters, where he did service to the end of the siege.

As soon as the explosion took place the crater was seized upon by two regiments of our troops who were near by, under cover, where they had been placed for the express purpose. The enemy made a desperate effort to expel them, but failed, and soon retired behind the new line. From here, however, they threw hand-grenades, which did some execution. The compliment was returned by our men, but not with so much effect. The enemy could lay their grenades on the parapet, which alone divided the contestants, and then roll them down upon us; while from our side they had to be thrown over the parapet, which was at considerable elevation. During the night we made efforts to secure our position in the crater against the missiles of the enemy, so as to run trenches along the outer base of their parapet, right and left; but the enemy continued throwing their grenades, and brought boxes of field ammunition (shells) the fuses of which they would light with port-fires, and throw them by hand into our ranks. We found it impossible to continue this work. Another mine was consequently started, which was exploded on the 1st of July, destroying an entire rebel redan, killing and wounding a considerable number of its occupants, and leaving an immense chasm where it stood. No attempt to charge was made this time, the experience of the 25th admonishing us. Our loss in the first affair was about thirty killed and wounded. The enemy must have lost more in the two explosions than we did in the first. We lost none in the second.

From this time forward the work of mining and of pushing our position nearer to the enemy was prosecuted with vigor, and I determined to explode no more mines until we were ready to explode a number at different points and assault immediately after. We were up now at three different points, one in front of each corps, to where only the parapet of the enemy divided us.

At this time an intercepted dispatch from Johnston to Pemberton informed me that Johnston intended to make a determined attack upon us, in order to relieve the garrison of Vicksburg. I knew the garrison would make no forcible effort to relieve itself. The picket lines were so close to each other—where there was space enough between the lines to post pickets—that the men could converse. On the 21st of June I was informed, through this means, that Pemberton was preparing to escape, by crossing to the Louisiana side under cover of night; that he had employed workmen in making boats for that purpose; that the men had been canvassed to ascertain if they would make an assault on the "Yankees" to cut their way out; that they had refused, and almost mutinied, because their commander would not surrender and relieve their sufferings, and had only been pacified by the assurance that boats enough would be finished in a week to carry them all over. The rebel pickets also said that houses in the city had been pulled down to get material to build these boats with. Afterward this story was verified. On entering the city we found a large number of very rudely constructed boats.

All necessary steps were at once taken to render such an attempt abortive. Our pickets were doubled; Admiral Porter was notified so that the river might

IN THE SAPS BETWEEN THE WHITE HOUSE
AND THE VICKSBURG CRATER, JULY 2, 1863.
FROM A SKETCH MADE AT THE TIME.

be more closely watched; material was collected on the west bank of the river to be set on fire and light up the river if the attempt was made; and batteries were established along the levee crossing the peninsula on the Louisiana side. Had the attempt been made, the garrison of Vicksburg would have been drowned or made prisoners on the Louisiana side. General Richard Taylor was expected on the west bank to coöperate in this movement, I believe, but he did not come, nor could he have done so with a force sufficient to be of service. The Mississippi was now in our possession from its source to its mouth, except in the immediate front of Vicksburg and Port Hudson. We had nearly exhausted the country, along a line drawn from Lake Providence to opposite Bruinsburg. The roads west were not of a character to draw supplies over for any considerable force.

By the 1st of July our approaches had reached the enemy's ditch at a number of places. At ten points we could move under cover to within from five to 100 yards of the enemy. Orders were given to make all preparations for assault on the 6th of July. The debouches were ordered widened, to afford easy egress, while the approaches were also to be widened to admit the troops to pass through four abreast. Plank and sand-bags, the latter filled with cotton packed in tightly, were ordered prepared, to enable the troops to cross the ditches.

On the night of the 1st of July Johnston was between Brownsville and the Big Black, and wrote Pemberton from there that about the 7th of the month an attempt would be made to create a diversion to enable him to cut his way out. Pemberton was a prisoner before this message reached him.

On July 1st Pemberton, seeing no hope of outside relief, addressed the following letter to each of his four division commanders:

"Unless the siege of Vicksburg is raised, or supplies are thrown in, it will become necessary very shortly to evacuate the place. I see no prospect of the former, and there are many great, if not insuperable, obstacles in the way of the latter. You are, therefore, requested to inform me with as little delay as possible as to the condition of your troops, and their ability to make the marches and undergo the fatigues necessary to accomplish a successful evacuation."

Two of his generals suggested surrender, and the other two practically did the same; they expressed the opinion that an attempt to evacuate would fail. Pemberton had previously got a message to Johnston suggesting that he should try to negotiate with me for a release of the garrison with their arms. Johnston replied that it would be a confession of weakness for him to do so; but he authorized Pemberton to use his name in making such an arrangement.

On the 3d, about 10 o'clock A.M., white flags appeared on a portion of the rebel works. Hostilities along that part of the line ceased at once. Soon two persons were seen coming toward our lines bearing a white flag. They proved to be General Bowen, a division commander, and Colonel Montgomery, aide-de-camp to Pemberton, bearing the following letter to me:

"I have the honor to propose an armistice for —— hours, with the view to arranging terms for the capitulation of Vicksburg. To this end, if agreeable to you, I will appoint three commissioners, to meet a like number to be named by yourself, at such place and hour to-day as you may find convenient. I make this proposition to save the further effusion of blood, which must otherwise be shed to a frightful extent, feeling myself fully able to maintain my position for a yet indefinite period. This communication will be handed you, under a flag of truce, by Major-General John S. Bowen."

It was a glorious sight to officers and soldiers on the line where these white flags were visible, and the news soon spread to all parts of the command. The troops felt that their long and weary marches, hard fighting, ceaseless watching by night and day in a hot climate, exposure to all sorts of weather, to diseases, and, worst of all, to the gibes of many Northern papers that came to them, saying all their suffering was in vain, Vicksburg would never be taken, were at last at an end, and the Union sure to be saved.

Bowen was received by General A. J. Smith, and asked to see me. I had been a neighbor of Bowen's in Missouri, and knew him well and favorably before the war; but his request was refused. He then suggested that I should meet Pemberton. To this I sent a verbal message saying that if Pemberton desired it I would meet him in front of McPherson's corps, at 3 o'clock that afternoon. I also sent the following written reply to Pemberton's letter:

"Your note of this date is just received, proposing an armistice for several hours, for the purpose of arranging terms of capitulation through commissioners to be appointed, etc. The useless effusion of blood you propose stopping by this course can be ended at any time you may choose, by the unconditional surrender of the city and garrison. Men who have shown so much endurance and courage as those now in Vicksburg will always challenge the respect of an adversary, and I can assure you will be treated with all the respect due to prisoners of war. I do not favor the proposition of appointing commissioners to arrange the terms of capitulation, because I have no terms other than those indicated above."

At 3 o'clock Pemberton appeared at the point suggested in my verbal message, accompanied by the same officers who had borne his letter of the morning. Generals Ord, McPherson, Logan, A. J. Smith, and several officers of my staff accompanied me. Our place of meeting was on a hill-side within a few hundred feet of the rebel lines. Near by stood a stunted

FIRST CONFERENCE BETWEEN GRANT AND PEMBERTON, JULY 3, 1863.
FROM A SKETCH MADE AT THE TIME.

Grant and Pemberton met near the tree and went aside to the earth-work, where they sat in conference. To their right is a group of four, including General John S. Bowen, C.S.A., General A. J. Smith, General James B. McPherson, and Colonel L. M. Montgomery. Under the tree are Chief-of-Staff John A. Rawlins, Assistant Secretary of War Charles A. Dana, and Theodore R. Davis, special artist, who made the above and many other sketches of the Vicksburg siege, in this work
—EDITORS.

oak-tree, which was made historical by the event. It was but a short time before the last vestige of its body, root, and limb had disappeared, the fragments being taken as trophies. Since then the same tree has furnished as many cords of wood, in the shape of trophies, as "The True Cross."

Pemberton and I had served in the same division during a part of the Mexican war. I knew him very well, therefore, and greeted him as an old acquaintance. He soon asked what terms I proposed to give his army if it surrendered. My answer was the same as proposed in my reply to his letter. Pemberton then

GENERAL GRANT.

MASTER FRED S. GRANT.

CHARLES A. DANA,
ASSISTANT SECRETARY OF WAR.

UNION HEADQUARTERS, JULY 3. GENERAL GRANT RECEIVING GENERAL PEMBERTON'S
MESSAGE. FROM A SKETCH MADE AT THE TIME.

In his "Personal Memoirs" (C. L. Webster & Co.) General Grant says: "On leaving Bruinsburg for the front I left my son Frederick, who had joined me a few weeks before, on board one of the gunboats asleep, and hoped to get away without him until after Grand Gulf should fall into our hands; but on waking up he learned that I had gone, and being guided by the sound of the battle raging at Thompson's Hill—called the battle of Port Gibson—found his way to where I was. He had no horse to ride at the time, and I had no facilities for even preparing a meal. He therefore foraged around the best he could until we reached Grand Gulf. Mr. C. A. Dana, then an officer of the War Department, accompanied me on the Vicksburg campaign and through a portion of the siege. He was in the same situation as Fred so far as transportation and mess arrangements were concerned. The first time I call to mind seeing either of them, after the battle, they were mounted on two enormous horses, grown white from age, equipped with dilapidated saddles and bridles. Our trains arrived a few days later, after which we were all perfectly equipped. My son accompanied me throughout the campaign and siege, and caused no anxiety either to me or to his mother, who was at home. He looked out for himself and was in every battle of the campaign. His age, then not quite thirteen, enabled him to take in all he saw, and to retain a recollection of it that would not be possible in more mature years."

said, rather snappishly, "The conference might as well end," and turned abruptly as if to leave. I said, "Very well." General Bowen, I saw, was very anxious that the surrender should be consummated. His manners and remarks while Pemberton and I were talking showed this. He now proposed that he and one of our generals should have a conference. I had no objection to this, as nothing could be made binding upon me that they might propose. Smith and Bowen accordingly had a conference, during which Pemberton and I, moving some distance away toward the enemy's lines, were in conversation. After a while Bowen suggested that the Confederate army should be allowed to march out, with the honors of war, carrying their small-arms and field-artillery. This was promptly and unceremoniously rejected. The interview here ended, I agreeing, however, to send a letter giving final terms by 10 o'clock that night. I had sent word to Admiral Porter soon after the correspondence with Pemberton had commenced, so that hostilities might be stopped on the part of both army and navy. It was agreed on my parting with Pemberton that they should not be renewed until our correspondence should cease.

When I returned to my headquarters I sent for all the corps and division commanders with the army immediately confronting Vicksburg. (Half the army was from eight to twelve miles off, waiting for Johnston.) I informed them of the contents of Pemberton's letters, of my reply, and the substance of the interview, and was ready to hear any suggestion; but would hold the power of deciding entirely in my own hands. This was the nearest to a "council of war" I ever held. Against the general and almost unanimous judgment of the council I sent the following letter:

"In conformity with agreement of this afternoon I will submit the following proposition for the surrender of the city of Vicksburg, public stores, etc. On your accepting the terms proposed I will march in one division as a guard, and take possession at 8 A.M. to-morrow. As soon as rolls can be made out and paroles be signed by officers and men, you will be allowed to march out of our lines, the officers taking with them their side-arms and clothing; and the field, staff, and cavalry officers one horse each. The rank and file will be allowed all their clothing, but no other property. If these conditions are accepted, any amount of rations you may deem necessary can be taken from the stores you now have, and also the necessary cooking-utensils for preparing them. Thirty wagons also, counting two-horse or mule teams as one, will be allowed to transport such articles as cannot be carried along. The same conditions will be allowed to all sick and wounded officers and soldiers as fast as they become able to travel. The paroles for these latter must be signed, however, whilst officers present are authorized to sign the roll of prisoners."

By the terms of the cartel then in force, prisoners captured by either army were required to be forwarded, as soon as possible, to either Aiken's Landing below Dutch Gap, on the James River, or to Vicksburg, there to be exchanged, or paroled until they could be exchanged. There was a Confederate Commissioner at Vicksburg, authorized to make the exchange. I did not propose to take him prisoner, but to leave him free to perform the functions of his office. Had I insisted upon an unconditional surrender, there would have been over thirty-odd thousand men to transport to Cairo, very much to the inconvenience of the army on the Mississippi; thence the prisoners would have had to be transported by rail to Washington or Baltimore; thence again by steamer to Aiken's—all at very great expense. At Aiken's they would have to be paroled, because the Confederates did not have Union prisoners to give in exchange. Then again Pemberton's army was largely composed of men whose homes were in the south-west; I knew many of them were tired of the war and would get home just as soon as they could. A large number of them had voluntarily come into our lines during the siege and requested to be sent north where they could get employment until the war was over and they could go to their homes.

Late at night I received the following reply to my last letter:

"I have the honor to acknowledge the receipt of your communication of this date, proposing terms of capitulation for this garrison and post. In the main, your terms are accepted; but, in justice both to the honor and spirit of my troops manifested in the defense of Vicksburg, I have to submit the following amendments, which, if acceded to by you, will perfect the agreement between us. At 10 o'clock A.M. to-morrow I propose to evacuate the works in and around Vicksburg, and to surrender the city and garrison under my command, by marching out with my colors and arms, stacking them in front of my present lines, after which you will take possession. Officers to retain their side-arms and personal property, and the rights and property of citizens to be respected."

This was received after midnight; my reply was as follows:

"I have the honor to acknowledge the receipt of your communication of 3d July. The amendment proposed by you cannot be acceded to in full. It will be necessary to furnish every officer and man with a parole signed by himself, which, with the completion of the roll of prisoners, will necessarily take some time. Again, I can make no stipulations with regard to the treatment of citizens and their private property. While I do not propose to cause them any undue annoyance or loss, I cannot consent to leave myself under any restraint by stipulations. The property which officers will be allowed to take with them will be as stated in my proposition of last evening: that is, officers will be allowed their private baggage and side-arms, and mounted officers one horse each. If you mean by your proposition for each brigade to march to the front of the lines now occupied by it, and stack arms at 10 o'clock A.M., and then return to the inside and there remain as prisoners until properly paroled, I will make no objection to it. Should no notification be received of your acceptance of my terms by 9 o'clock A.M., I shall regard them as having been rejected, and shall act accordingly. Should these terms be accepted, white flags should be displayed along your lines to prevent such of my troops as may not have been notified from firing upon your men."

Pemberton promptly accepted these terms.

During the siege there had been a good deal of friendly sparring between the soldiers of the two armies, on picket and where the lines were close together. All rebels were known as "Johnnies"; all Union troops as "Yanks." Often "Johnny" would call, "Well, Yank, when are you coming into town?" The reply was sometimes: "We propose to celebrate the 4th of July there." Sometimes it would be: "We always treat our prisoners with kindness and do not want to hurt them"; or, "We are holding you as prisoners of war while you are feeding yourselves." The garrison, from the commanding general down, undoubtedly expected an assault on the 4th. They knew from the temper of their men it would be successful when made, and that would be a greater humiliation than to surrender. Besides it would be attended with severe loss to them.

The Vicksburg paper, which we received regularly through the courtesy of the rebel pickets, said prior to the 4th, in speaking of the "Yankee" boast that they would take dinner in Vicksburg that day, that the best receipt for cooking rabbit was, "First ketch your rabbit." The paper at this time, and for some time previous, was printed on the plain side of wall paper. The last was issued on the 4th and announced that we had "caught our rabbit."

I have no doubt that Pemberton commenced his correspondence on the 3d for the twofold purpose; first, to avoid an assault, which he knew would be successful, and second, to prevent the capture taking place on the great national holiday,—the anniversary of the Declaration of American Independence. Holding out for better terms, as he did, he defeated his aim in the latter particular.

At the 4th, at the appointed hour, the garrison of Vicksburg marched out of their works, and formed line in front, stacked arms, and marched back in good order. Our whole army present witnessed this scene without cheering.

Logan's division, which had approached nearest the rebel works, was the first to march in, and the flag of one of the regiments of his division was soon floating over the court-house. Our soldiers were no sooner inside the lines than the two armies began to fraternize. Our men had had full rations from the time the siege commenced to the close. The enemy had been suffering, particularly toward the last. I myself saw our men taking bread from their haversacks and giving it to the enemy they had so recently been engaged in *starving out*. It was accepted with avidity and with thanks.

Pemberton says in his report: "If it should be asked why the 4th of July was selected as the day for surrender, the answer is obvious. I believed that upon that day I should obtain better terms. Well aware of the vanity of our foe, I knew they would attach vast importance to the entrance, on the 4th of July, into the stronghold of the great river, and that, to gratify their national vanity, they would yield then what could not be extorted from them at any other time." This does not support my view of his reasons for selecting the day he did for surrendering. But it must be recollected that his first letter asking terms was received about 10 o'clock, A.M., July 3d. It then could hardly be expected that it would take 24 hours to effect a surrender. He knew that Johnston was in our rear for the purpose of raising the siege, and he naturally would want to hold out as long as he could. He knew his men would not resist an assault, and one was expected on the 4th. In our interview he told me he had rations enough to hold out some time—my recollection is two weeks. It was this statement that induced me to insert in the terms that he was to draw rations for his men from his own supplies.

On the 3d, as soon as negotiations were commenced, I notified Sherman, and directed him to be ready to take the offensive against Johnston, drive him out of the State, and destroy his army if he could. Steele and Ord were directed at the same time to be in readiness to join Sherman as soon as the surrender took place. Of this Sherman was notified.

I rode into Vicksburg with the troops, and went to the river to exchange congratulations with the navy upon our joint victory. At that time I found that many of the citizens had been living under-ground. The ridges upon which Vicksburg is built, and those back to the Big Black, are composed of a deep yellow clay, of great tenacity. Where roads and streets are cut through, perpendicular banks are left, and stand as well as if composed of stone. The magazines of the enemy were made by running passage-ways into this clay at places where there were deep cuts. Many citizens secured places of safety for their families by carving out rooms in these embankments. A door-way in these cases would be cut in a high bank, starting from the level of the road or street, and after running in a few feet a room of the size required was carved out of the clay, the dirt being removed by the door-way. In some instances I saw where two rooms were cut out, for a single family, with a door-way in the clay wall separating them. Some of these were carpeted and furnished with considerable elaboration. In these the occupants were fully secure from the shells of the navy, which were dropped into the city, night and day, without intermission. [See "Naval Operations," p. 655.]

I returned to my old headquarters outside in the afternoon, and did not move them into the town until the 6th. On the afternoon of the 4th I sent Captain William M. Dunn, of my staff, to Cairo, the nearest point where the telegraph could be reached, with a dispatch to the general-in-chief. It was as follows:

> "The enemy surrendered this morning. The only terms allowed is their parole as prisoners of war. This I regard as a great advantage to us at this moment. It saves, probably, several days in the capture, and leaves troops and transports ready for immediate service. Sherman, with a large force, moves immediately on Johnston, to drive him from the State. I will send troops to the relief of Banks, and return the Ninth Army Corps to Burnside."

At the same time I wrote to General Banks informing him of the fall, and sending him a copy of the terms, also saying I would send him all the troops he wanted to insure the capture of the only foothold the enemy now had on the Mississippi River. General Banks had a number of copies of this letter printed, or at least a synopsis of it, and very soon a copy fell into the hands of General Gardner, who was then in command of Port Hudson. Gardner at once sent a letter to the commander of the National forces, saying that he had been informed of the surrender of Vicksburg and telling how the information reached him. He added that if this was true it was useless for him to hold out longer. General Banks gave him assurances that Vicksburg had been surrendered, and General Gardner surrendered unconditionally on the 9th of July.[1] Port Hudson, with nearly 6000 prisoners, 51 guns, and 5000 small-arms and other stores, fell into the hands of the Union forces. From that day on, the river remained under National control.

Pemberton and his army were kept in Vicksburg until the whole could be paroled. The paroles were in duplicate, by organization (one copy for each, National and Confederate), signed by the commanding officers of the companies or regiments. Duplicates were also made for each soldier, and signed by each individually, one to be retained by the soldier signing, and one to be retained by us. Several hundred refused to sign their paroles, preferring to be sent north as prisoners to being sent back to fight again. Others again kept out of the way, hoping to escape either alternative.

Pemberton appealed to me in person to compel these men to sign their paroles, but I declined. It also leaked out that many of the men who had signed their paroles intended to desert and go to their homes as soon as they got out of our lines. Pemberton, hearing this, again appealed to me to assist him. He

[1]See article on Port Hudson, to follow.—Editors.

wanted arms for a battalion, to act as guards in keeping his men together while being marched to a camp of instruction, where he expected to keep them until exchanged. This request was also declined. It was precisely what I expected and hoped that they would do. I told him, however, I would see that they marched beyond our lines in good order. By the 11th, just one week after the surrender, the paroles were completed, and the Confederate garrison marched out. Many deserted; fewer of them were ever returned to the ranks to fight again than would have been the case had the surrender been unconditional and the prisoners been sent to the James River to be paroled.

As soon as our troops took possession of the city, guards were established along the whole line of parapet, from the river above to the river below. The prisoners were allowed to occupy their old camps behind the intrenchments. No restraint was put upon them, except by their own commanders. They were rationed about as our own men, and from our supplies. The men of the two armies fraternized as if they had been fighting for the same cause. When they passed out of the works they had so long and so gallantly defended, between lines of their late antagonists, not a cheer went up, not a remark was made that would give pain. I believe there was a feeling of sadness among the Union soldiers at seeing the dejection of their late antagonists.

The day before the departure the following order was issued:

"Paroled prisoners will be sent out of here to-morrow. They will be authorized to cross at the railroad-bridge and move from there to Edwards's Ferry, / and on by way of Raymond. Instruct the commands to be orderly and quiet as these prisoners pass, to make no offensive remarks, and not to harbor any who fall out of ranks after they have passed."

On the 8th a dispatch was sent from Washington by Halleck, saying:

"I fear your paroling the prisoners at Vicksburg without actual delivery to a proper agent, as required by the seventh article of the cartel, may be construed into an absolute release, and that the men will immediately be placed in the ranks of the enemy. Such has been the case elsewhere. If these prisoners have not been allowed to depart, you will detain them until further orders."

Halleck did not know that they had already been delivered into the hands of Major Watts, Confederate Commissioner for the Exchange of Prisoners.

At Vicksburg 31,600 prisoners were surrendered, together with 172 cannon, about 60,000 muskets, and a large amount of ammunition. The small-arms

/ Meant Edwards's Station.—U.S.G.

of the enemy were far superior to the bulk of ours. Up to this time our troops at the west had been limited to the old United States flint-lock muskets changed into percussion, or the Belgian musket imported early in the war—almost as dangerous to the person firing it as to the one aimed at—and a few new and improved arms. These were of many different calibers, a fact that caused much trouble in distributing ammunition during an engagement. The enemy had generally new arms, which had run the blockade, and were of uniform caliber. After the surrender I authorized all colonels, whose regiments were armed with inferior muskets, to place them in the stack of captured arms, and replace them with the latter. A large number of arms, turned in to the ordnance department as captured, were these arms that had really been used by the Union army in the capture of Vicksburg.

In this narrative I have not made the mention I should like of officers, dead and alive, whose services entitle them to special mention. Neither have I made that mention of the navy which its services deserve. Suffice it to say, the close of the siege found us with an army unsurpassed, in proportion to its numbers, taken as a whole, officers and men. A military education was acquired which no other school could have given. Men who thought a company was quite enough for them to command properly, at the beginning, would have made good regimental or brigade commanders; most of the brigade commanders were equal to the command of a division, and one, Ransom, would have been equal to the command of a corps at least. Logan and Crocker ended the campaign fitted to command independent armies.

General F. P. Blair joined me at Milliken's Bend, a full-fledged general, without having served in a lower grade. He commanded a division in the campaign. I had known Blair in Missouri, where I had voted against him in 1858 when he ran for Congress. I knew him as a frank, positive, and generous man, true to his friends even to a fault, but always a leader. I dreaded his coming. I knew from experience that it was more difficult to command two generals desiring to be leaders, than it was to command one army, officered intelligently, and with subordination. It affords me the greatest pleasure to record now my agreeable disappointment in respect to his character. There was no man braver than he, nor was there any who obeyed all orders of his superior in rank with more unquestioning alacrity. He was one man as a soldier, another as a politician.

The navy, under Porter, was all it could be, during the entire campaign. Without its assistance the campaign could not have been successfully made with twice the number of men engaged. It could not have been made at all, in the way it was, with any number of men, without such assistance. The most perfect harmony reigned between the two arms of the service. There never was a request made, that I am aware of, either of the flag-officer or any of his subordinates, that was not promptly complied with.

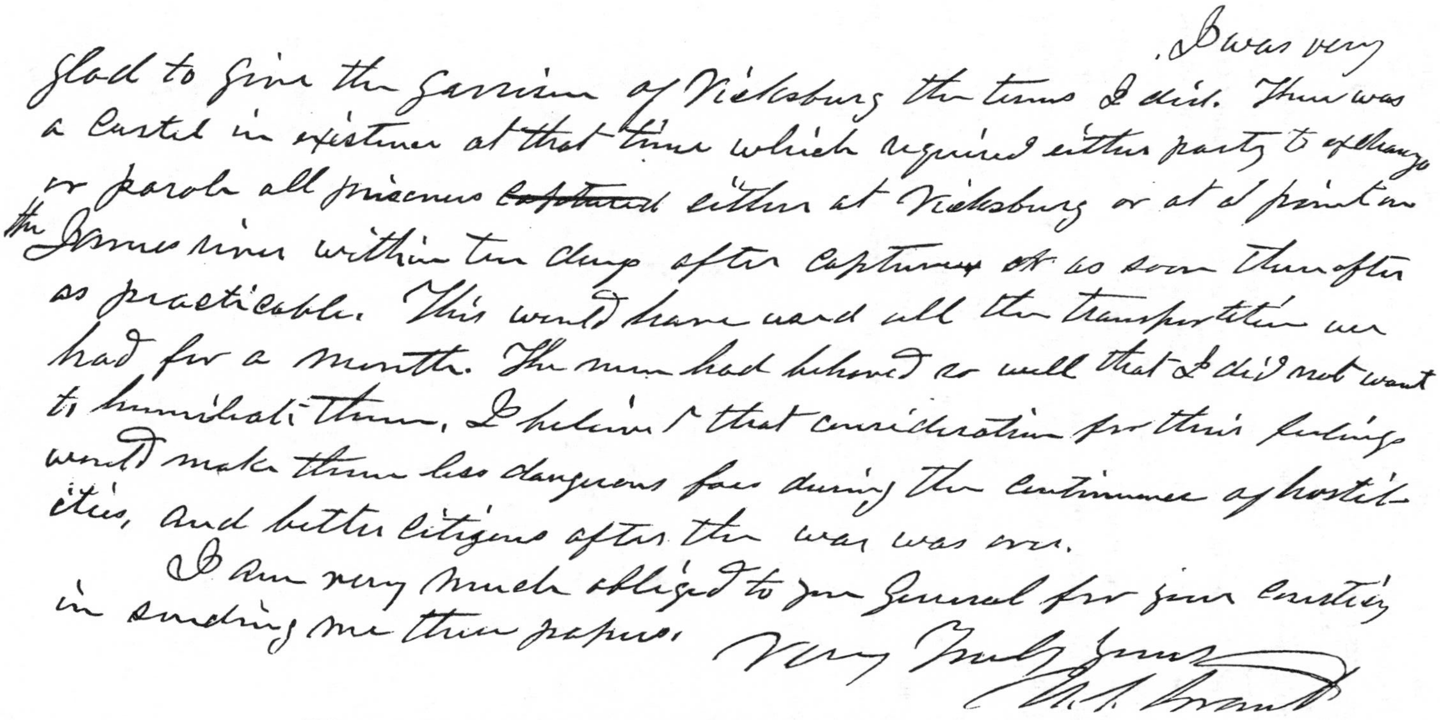

Glad to give the garrison of Vicksburg the times of their surrender. There was
a desire in certain quarters at that time which required either parole or exchange
or parole all prisoners captured either at Vicksburg or at other points in
the same river within the time kept after capturing off to arm them. Thought
as practicable. This would have used all the transportation we
had for a month. The men had believed as well that I did not want
to humiliate them. I believe that consideration for their feelings
would make them less dangerous when during the continuance of hostilities, and better citizens after the war was over.

I am very much obliged to you General for your courtesy
in sending me these papers.

Very truly yours
U. S. Grant

. It was very

FROM A LETTER TO GEN. MARCUS J. WRIGHT, C.S.A., DATED NEW YORK, NOV. 30, 1884.

The campaign of Vicksburg was suggested and developed by circumstances. The elections of 1862 had gone against the prosecution of the war: voluntary enlistments had nearly ceased, and the draft had been resorted to; this was resisted, and a defeat, or backward movement, would have made its execution impossible. A forward movement to a decisive victory was necessary. Accordingly I resolved to get below Vicksburg, unite with Banks against Port Hudson, and make New Orleans a base; and, with that base and Grand Gulf as a starting-point, move our combined forces against Vicksburg. Upon reaching Grand Gulf, after running its batteries and fighting a battle, I received a letter from Banks informing me that he could not be at Port Hudson under ten days, and then with only fifteen thousand men. The time was worth more than the reënforcements; I therefore determined to push into the interior of the enemy's country.

With a large river behind us, held above and below by the enemy, rapid movements were essential to success. Jackson was captured the day after a new commander had arrived, and only a few days before large reënforcements were expected. A rapid movement west was made; the garrison of Vicksburg was met in two engagements and badly defeated, and driven back into its stronghold and there successfully besieged.

CHAPTER 9

NAVAL OPERATIONS IN THE VICKSBURG CAMPAIGN.

Professor James Russell Soley, U.S.N.

By the 1st of July, 1862, the Mississippi had been traversed by the fleet of Davis from Cairo down, and by that of Farragut from the Passes up, and the only point where the Confederates retained a strong foothold was at Vicksburg. The objects of the river operations were to establish communication from the Ohio to the Gulf, and to cut off the important supplies drawn by the Confederacy from Arkansas, Louisiana, and Texas. The commanders of the Mississippi squadron during this period were, first, Charles Henry Davis, and later, David D. Porter, the transfer of the command taking place October 15th, 1862. The operations of the navy at this time were unique in maritime warfare in the energy and originality with which complex conditions were met.

After the defeat of Montgomery's flotilla at Memphis, on the 6th of June, by the combined forces of Flag-Officer Davis and Colonel Ellet, the Mississippi squadron remained at Memphis for three weeks. Immediately after the battle Davis had formed the project of sending a force up the Arkansas and White rivers to cut off the Confederate gun-boats which were supposed to have taken refuge there, among them the *Van Dorn*, the only vessel remaining of Montgomery's flotilla. Davis did not know that the *Van Dorn* had made her way into the Yazoo. There were, however, two Confederate gun-boats in White River, the *Maurepas* and *Pontchartrain*, which had previously been in the flotilla of Hollins at Island Number Ten—the former under Lieutenant Joseph Fry and the latter under Lieutenant John W. Dunnington.

On the 10th Davis received a telegram from General Halleck urging him to open communication by way of Jacksonport with General Curtis, then moving through Arkansas toward the Mississippi. Davis accordingly altered his plan, and directed that the expedition should confine its operations to the White River. The force detached for the purpose was composed of the iron-clads *Mound City* and *St. Louis,* and the wooden gun-boats *Conestoga* and *Tyler,* under Commander A. H. Kilty, of the *Mound City,* and the 46th Indiana, Colonel Graham N. Fitch. Ascending the White River, the expedition arrived on the evening of the 16th in the neighborhood of St. Charles, ninety miles from the mouth.

Anticipating this movement, Hindman had taken steps to obstruct the channel at this point, where the first bluffs touch the river. One hundred men, under Captain A. M. Williams, C.S. Engineers, were the only force which could be spared for the defense of the place, and their only arms were thirty-five Enfield rifles which Hindman had impounded at Memphis. Lieutenant Dunnington had placed two rifled 32-pounders in battery on the bluffs, and had manned them with part of the crew of the *Pontchartrain.* Finally, Fry had stationed the *Maurepas* in the river below.

The approach of Kilty's gun-boats was first discovered on the afternoon of June 16th. Expecting an immediate attack, Fry placed the *Maurepas* across the stream and prepared to defend her. Finding that the gun-boats remained below, Fry now landed his guns and settled his ship, sinking her across the channel. Two transports also were sunk, and the imperfect obstruction thus created was completed about daylight. During the night a small rifled Parrott gun was placed in position four hundred yards below Dunnington's battery, under Midshipman F. M. Roby. Two rifled Parrott 8-pounders were also moved up soon after daylight, and placed near Roby's gun, and the three guns were manned by the crew of the *Maurepas,* and fought personally by Fry, the senior officer present. Below this second battery Captain Williams was stationed with his thirty-five men, those without arms having been sent to the rear. He was presently reënforced by the 12-pounder howitzer from the *Maurepas,* manned by some of her crew. The total force under Fry's command comprised the men with Williams, and 79 seamen from the two gun-boats,—in all, 114 persons, to resist the attack of Fitch's Indiana regiment, and four gun-boats, two of them ironclads. Rarely has it happened to such a feeble force to accomplish so much by a determined resistance.

Early on the morning of June 17th the troops landed about two miles below the bluffs. At half-past 8 the gun-boats advanced to the attack, the *Mound City* ahead, followed closely by the *St. Louis,* the *Lexington* and the *Conestoga* bringing up the rear. They moved slowly, endeavoring to discover the enemy's position, but in total ignorance of the whereabouts of his guns, which were covered by the trees and bushes on the bluffs. About 9 o'clock Williams's men were engaged by Fitch's skirmishers. The firing disclosed the enemy's advanced position, and the gun-boats opened a heavy fire of grape and shell upon it, compelling Williams to fall back. Fry's battery of four light guns, manned by the crew of the *Maurepas,* now became engaged with the gun-boats. At 10 Dunnington opened with his rifled 32-pounders. Kilty had now to some extent made out the location of the Confederate guns, and, moving up, replied with a rapid fire, aimed carefully in what was supposed to be the direction of the batteries, the vessel taking a position at point-blank range from both of them. At the same time Fitch sent word to him that the troops were ready to storm the batteries, unless he desired to silence them with the gun-boats. Kilty, unfortunately for himself and his crew, gallantly decided on the latter course.

The *Mound City* had been in position less than half an hour, about 600 yards from the batteries, when one of the 32-pounder rifle shot, directed by the skillful and experienced eye of Lieutenant Dunnington, penetrated the port casemate of the *Mound City* just forward of the armor, or, as Colonel Fitch rather comically described it in his report, "the larboard forequarter of the gun-boat," and, after killing 8 men at the gun, struck the steam-drum, and went through it directly fore and aft. At the time, the *Mound City* was turning her wheel over slowly, and, being in slack water, the wheel kept on turning until the steam was exhausted, and the boat slowly forged ahead, running her nose directly under the battery. Lieutenant Blodgett immediately ran up in the *Conestoga*, with great gallantry, and making fast to the *Mound City*, towed her away from the bank and out of action. Fitch, seeing the catastrophe, and apprehensive lest another fortunate shot from the enemy should deprive him of his support afloat, gave the signal to cease firing, and assaulted the works simultaneously in front and in flank. They were quickly carried; Dunnington and Williams made good their retreat, but Fry, who was badly wounded, was taken prisoner with about thirty of his men. General Hindman reported the Confederate loss as 6 killed, 1 wounded, and 8 missing.

The scene on board the *Mound City*, upon the explosion of the steam-drum, was beyond description. The gun-deck was at once filled with scalding steam, and many of the crew were instantly killed,—literally cooked alive. Others, in an agony of pain, jumped into the water, where they were shot at by sharpshooters from the bluff, under orders from Dunnington and Williams. The boats from the other vessels put off at once to the rescue, and were riddled with shot while picking up their comrades. Out of 175 officers and men on board the *Mound City*, only 23 answered to their names at the roll-call that evening, and these were men and boys that were in the shell-room and magazine when the explosion took place. The only officers unhurt were Dominy, the first master, and McElroy, the gunner. Eighty-two men perished in the casemate, 43 were killed in the water or drowned, and 25 were severely wounded. The latter, among whom was the gallant Kilty, were sent at once to Memphis in the *Conestoga*. The *Mound City* remained at St. Charles, under First Master John H. Duble, of the *Conestoga*, with a crew of one hundred of Fitch's men, her injuries being temporarily repaired.

The expedition continued up White River as far as Crooked Point Cut-off, 63 miles above St. Charles, where the gun-boats were compelled to turn back by the falling of the water. Halleck and Grant meantime had decided to increase Fitch's command by the addition of two regiments, which sailed for White River on the 26th of June, under convoy of the *Conestoga*. Commander John A. Winslow, of *Kearsarge-Alabama* fame, who was at this time in command of the forces afloat in White River, was ordered to give additional convoy as far up as the state of the water would permit. The bulk of the naval force was then withdrawn, the *Lexington* remaining to support Fitch in his subsequent operations up the river. Curtis reached Helena on the 13th of July without communicating with the gun-boats.

During the months of May and June, 1862, Farragut's fleet had been slowly working up from New Orleans, receiving the surrender of the principal cities on the way, and having an occasional encounter with the Confederate batteries along the river. None of the latter were at this time of any great importance, although those at Grand Gulf inflicted some damage on two of the gun-boats which attacked them on June 9th. No serious obstruction, however, to the passage of the river from Cairo to the sea now existed, except at Vicksburg.

The advance division of Farragut's squadron under Commander Lee in the *Oneida* had summoned Vicksburg to surrender on the 18th of May, but had met with a refusal. Farragut, arriving soon after, held a consultation with General Williams, who commanded a small detachment of Butler's army, and the two came to the conclusion that they had not enough men to make an attempt on Vicksburg with any hope of success, and Farragut went back to New Orleans.

Soon after, Farragut received pressing instructions from the Navy Department to attack Vicksburg, and in consequence returned up the river with his squadron, the mortar-boats under Porter, and 3000 troops under Williams. On the night of the 26th of June Porter placed his mortar-boats in position, nine on the eastern and eight on the western bank, the latter, as at New Orleans, being dressed with bushes to prevent an accurate determination of their position. The next day they opened upon Vicksburg. On the 28th Farragut passed the batteries with all the vessels of his fleet, except the *Brooklyn*, *Katahdin*, and *Kennebec*, which dropped back, owing to a too rigid adherence to their original orders. No impression of any consequence was made on the forts, nor were the ships materially injured, notwithstanding the great advantage which the forts possessed in their plunging fire. The *Hartford* was principally damaged by the battery above the town, which was able to rake a passing ship in a position from which the latter could not reply. Farragut, in his report of July 2d, sums up the situation with the phrase:

"The forts can be passed, and we have done it, and can do it again as often as may be required of us. It will not, however, be an easy matter for us to do more than silence the batteries for a time, as long as the enemy has a large force behind the hills to prevent our landing and holding the place."

While Farragut with the Western Gulf Squadron, so called, was passing the batteries at Vicksburg, the Mississippi flotilla was still at Memphis, except the rams now commanded by Lieutenant-Colonel Alfred W. Ellet, which had left Memphis about the 20th, and arrived above Vicksburg on the afternoon of the 24th. Here Ellet opened communication with Farragut across the neck of land opposite Vicksburg. Farragut replied, suggesting the coöperation of Davis's iron-clads. Davis received this message at Memphis on the 28th, and the next day started down the river. During the interval, Ellet's audacity was rewarded by another extraordinary success. Taking the *Monarch* and the *Lancaster,* the latter under Charles Rivers Ellet, a mere boy nineteen years of age, he steamed fifty miles up the Yazoo River. Ellet was in perfect ignorance of what he might find there, whether batteries, gun-boats, or torpedoes. His rams carried no armament. As a matter of fact there were at the time in the river two of Hollins's former fleet, the *Polk* and the *Livingston,* and the last of Montgomery's vessels, the *Van Dorn.* These were tied up abreast of a battery at Liverpool Landing, and above them was a barrier made from a raft. The *Arkansas* was at Yazoo City above the barrier, completing her preparations. The officer in charge at Liverpool Landing, Commander Robert F. Pinkney, on the approach of the rams set fire to his three gun-boats, and the purpose of Ellet's visit being thus easily accomplished, he withdrew again to the Mississippi.☆

Davis arrived above Vicksburg on the 1st of July, and joined Farragut with four gun-boats and six mortar-boats. The fleets remained here at anchor for several days, while the army was attempting to make a cut-off across the neck of the land opposite Vicksburg, and thus create a new channel out of range of the batteries on the bluffs. During this time Porter continued his daily bombardment. Beyond this nothing was attempted, there being no force of troops to make it worth while.

While matters were in this condition, it was resolved between the two flag-officers that a detachment of gun-boats should make a reconoissance in force up the Yazoo River. The shoalness and narrowness of the stream led them to take vessels of the upper squadron in preference to those of the lower, and the following were selected: the *Carondelet,* Commander Henry Walke; *Tyler,* Lieutenant William Gwin, and *Queen of the West.* The *Arkansas,* an armored ram with a heavy battery, was known to be up the river, and Farragut in his report mentions her as one of the objects of investigation.

The engagement that followed has been the subject of much discussion. The *Queen of the West,* which had no weapons except her ram and the muskets of

☆Lieutenant-Colonel Alfred W. Ellet soon after received a brigadier-general's commission, with instructions to organize and equip the Mississippi Marine Brigade for future work in patrolling the river. He also received commissions for such of his men as he chose to recommend. Charles Rivers Ellet, though but nineteen years of age, received a colonel's commission, and succeeded to the command of the ram fleet which his father, Charles Ellet, Jr., had created.—EDITORS.

THE CONFEDERATE RAM "ARKANSAS" RUNNING THROUGH THE UNION FLEET
AT VICKSBURG, JULY 15, 1862.

the sharp-shooters, and possibly a borrowed howitzer, immediately proceeded down the river. The *Tyler*, a very vulnerable wooden gun-boat, also retreated, placing herself under the protection of the *Carondelet*. The latter therefore became the principal antagonist of the Confederate ram. It now became a question for Walke of the *Carondelet* to decide whether he would advance to meet the *Arkansas* bows on, trusting to the skillful management of the helm to avoid a ram-thrust, or would retreat, engaging her with his stern guns. He chose the latter course.‡

‡In a note to the editors Admiral Walke states:

"When the *Tyler* was passing the *Carondelet*, I hailed the commander of the *Tyler*, and ordered him to go down to our fleet and report the arrival of the *Arkansas*; but the *Tyler* ran under the protection of the *Carondelet*. The latter, while advancing, fired several rounds of her bow-guns and all her starboard broadside guns at the *Arkansas*, which, returning the fire, raked the *Carondelet* from stem to stern, striking her forward three times. One shot glanced on the forward plating, one went through it and broke up, one from forward passed through the officers' rooms on the starboard side, and through the captain's cabin. Being a stern-wheel boat, the *Carondelet* required room and time to turn around. To avoid being sunk immediately, she turned and retreated. I was not such a simpleton as to 'take the bull by the horns,' to be fatally rammed, and sacrifice my command through fear of the criticisms of any man, or the vaunting opinion of much less experienced officers. If I had continued fighting, bows on, in that narrow river, a collision, which the enemy desired, would have been inevitable, and would have sunk the *Carondelet* in a few minutes."

The *Arkansas* was decidedly the superior vessel. Apart from the fact that she was larger, and had at the beginning of the contest somewhat greater speed, she had a more efficient battery, and a far more complete and impenetrable armor protection. Indeed the Eads gun-boats, of which the *Carondelet* was one, were by no means fully armored, their two and one-half inch plating on the casemate covering only the forward end and that part of the sides abreast of the machinery. The stern was not armored at all. The side armor had no heavy backing, and such as it was could only ward off a shot directly abeam. It was by no means a complete protection to the boilers, as was shown in the catastrophe at St. Charles. The *Arkansas* on the other hand had three inches of railroad iron surrounding her casemate, with a heavy backing of timber and cotton bales. She had, besides, her ram, which experience had shown was a weapon much to be dreaded. However, the position adopted by Walke was the one which, by exposing his weakest point, gave the enemy the benefit of his superiority. The *Carondelet,* instead of presenting her armored bow, armed with three rifled guns, 30, 50, and 70 pounders, presented her unarmored stern, armed with two smooth-bore 32-pounders. That she escaped total destruction in the running fight of an hour or so that ensued with the two 8-inch guns in the *Arkansas*'s bow is little short of a miracle. Walke made a very good fight of it, and both he and Gwin of the *Tyler,* who pluckily supported the *Carondelet,* inflicted much injury on their antagonist, riddling her smoke-stack so as nearly to destroy her speed, wounding her captain twice, damaging her wheel, and killing her Yazoo pilot. When near the mouth of the river, the *Carondelet*'s steering gear was disabled and she ran in close to the bank, where the water was too shoal for the *Arkansas* to follow her. The latter, therefore, passed her, the two vessels exchanging broadsides, and the *Arkansas* continued on her course to Vicksburg.

Her approach caught the two flag-officers fairly napping. Notwithstanding their knowledge of her presence in the Yazoo, and the heavy firing that had been heard for more than an hour, there was, out of the combined fleet of twenty vessels or thereabouts, but one that had steam up, the captured ram *General Bragg,* and she did nothing. The *Arkansas* dashed boldly through the mass of clustered vessels, receiving the broadside of each ship as she passed, and delivering her fire rapidly in return. Her audacity was rewarded by success, for though she was badly battered, she was neither stopped nor disabled. On the other hand, her shot, penetrating the boiler of the ram *Lancaster,* used up that vessel and caused considerable loss of life among her crew. The *Benton,* Davis's flagship, got under way after Brown had passed, and followed him "at her usual snail's pace," to borrow Davis's phrase, without overtaking him. In a few minutes the *Arkansas* was under the guns of Vicksburg.

A week before, on the 7th of July, Farragut had written to the department that he hoped "soon to have the pleasure of recording the combined attack by army and navy, for which we all so ardently long." In the course of the week that had elapsed these hopes had been pretty well extinguished. The canal had turned out a failure, and the prospect that a considerable force of troops would arrive had been growing every day more remote. Before the *Arkansas* made her appearance, therefore, Farragut had already been meditating a return down the river, and the falling of the water and the prevalence of sickness in his crews admonished him to hasten. He also wished to damage the *Arkansas* in the rush by, so as to recover in some measure the prestige lost through her successful passage of the fleet. Preparations were therefore made for the descent on that very afternoon.

Already on the 10th Porter had left his station below Vicksburg with twelve of his mortar-boats, which were to be sent round to the James River. Most of the gun-boats of the mortar-flotilla went with him to tow the schooners down. The force that remained was composed of six mortar-schooners, under Commander W. B. Renshaw, with the ferry-boat *Westfield.* On the afternoon of the 15th these were moved up into position on the west bank of the river (with the exception of one, the *Sidney C. Jones,* which had run on shore and was blown up), and by half-past 3 they were engaged with the batteries. Davis, in the river above, also stationed three of his vessels, the *Benton, Louisville,* and *Cincinnati,* in position to attack the upper batteries, and to aid in covering Farragut's passage. Toward 7 in the evening the fleet got under way, consisting of the four sloops, the *Hartford, Richmond, Oneida,* and *Iroquois,* four gun-boats, and the ram *Sumter,* which Davis had lent for the special purpose of attacking the *Arkansas.* The fleet made a gallant dash past the batteries, meeting with little loss, but the attack on the *Arkansas* was a failure, for she had shifted her position and could not be readily distinguished by the flashes of the guns. A single 11-inch shot, however, reached the ram and inflicted very serious injury, especially to the engine.

Early on the morning of the 22d, Farragut's reunited squadron being now at anchor below Vicksburg, another attempt was made on the *Arkansas.* While the upper and the lower fleets were drawing the fire of the batteries in their neighborhood, the *Essex,* under Commodore William D. Porter, started down the river, followed by the *Queen of the West,* Lieutenant-Colonel A. W. Ellet. The crew of the *Arkansas* was small, but they were skillfully handled. The assailants tried to ram her in succession, but as each came on the beak of the Confederate was turned toward them, and they only succeeded in giving a glancing blow, and, sheering off, ran on the bank. Extricating themselves with difficulty, they withdrew as rapidly as they could from their perilous position, the *Essex* going below and the *Queen,* temporarily disabled, resuming her station with the upper squadron. One shot from the *Essex* did serious damage on board the *Arkansas.*

The *Essex* and *Sumter* were now permanently detained below Vicksburg. Shortly after the last engagement Farragut sailed down the river with Williams and his troops. Davis had expected Farragut's departure, but he had relied on the occupation by the land forces of the point opposite Vicksburg, by which he communicated with his vessels below. As these had now departed, nothing could be gained by staying longer in the neighborhood. Davis accordingly withdrew to Helena, and for the next four months Vicksburg was left unmolested.

Williams remained at Baton Rouge, with the *Essex, Kineo, Katahdin,* and *Sumter,* while Farragut continued to New Orleans with the rest of his fleet. At daylight on the 5th of August, Baton Rouge was unsuccessfully attacked by the Confederates under General John C. Breckinridge, and on the 6th the *Arkansas* was destroyed. The remaining events of the summer of 1862 were of little importance. Early in August a reconnoissance showed that the White River had fallen three feet and was impracticable for gun-boats. Later in the month a more important expedition was sent down the river. It was composed of the *Benton, Mound City,* and *Bragg,* together with four of Ellet's rams, the *Switzerland, Monarch, Samson,* and *Lioness,* all under Lieutenant-Commander Phelps, with a detachment of troops under Colonel Charles R. Woods. At Milliken's Bend, thirty miles above Vicksburg, the Confederate transport steamer *Fairplay* was captured, loaded with a heavy cargo of arms and ammunition. The gun-boats then penetrated far up the Yazoo River, and two of the rams even ascended the Sunflower for twenty miles. When the expedition returned to Helena, it had destroyed or captured a vast quantity of military supplies. It taught the Confederates a lesson, however, and it was a long time before the Federal fleet could again enter the Yazoo with impunity.

The experience of the gun-boats in the White River showed the necessity of obtaining light-draught vessels for service in the uncertain channels of the tributaries of the Mississippi, and each additional operation in these rivers confirmed the impression. As early as the 27th of June Davis had urgently recommended this step, and his recommendations, sustained by the earnest appeals of other officers, resulted in the creation of the "tin-clads," or "light-draughts," which during the next year performed invaluable service.

On the 15th of October Davis was relieved of this command, having been appointed Chief of the Bureau of Navigation at the Navy Department. He was succeeded by Porter. Two important and much-needed changes in organization took place about this time, the first being the formal transfer of the squadron on the 1st of October from the War Department, under which it had first come into existence, to the Navy Department, which henceforth exercised exclusive direction of it. The second was the order of the Secretary of War of November 8th, directing Ellet to report "for orders and duty" to Porter. These two changes made the vessels in the Mississippi for the first time a homogeneous naval force, and swept away all the complications of command which had hitherto vexed and harassed its commander-in-chief.

Porter, as acting rear-admiral, assumed command of the Mississippi squadron at the naval depot at Cairo, which was now the headquarters. He received from Davis intact the squadron as it had come from Foote—the *Benton*, the seven Eads iron-clads, and the three Rodgers gun-boats. He had also Ellet's nine rams and several very valuable captured vessels, including the *Eastport*, and Montgomery's rams captured at Memphis—the *Bragg, Pillow, Price*, and *Little Rebel*. The only vessels that had been withdrawn were the *Essex* and *Sumter*, now in the river below Vicksburg. Porter was also getting at this very time an accession to his force in the new tin-clads,—the *Brilliant, Rattler, Romeo, Juliet, Marmora, Signal*, and others,—and an equally important accession of iron-clads, the *Lafayette* and *Choctaw*, altered steam-boats of great power, and the newly (and rather badly) constructed boats, *Chillicothe, Indianola*, and *Tuscumbia*.

On the 21st of November Porter issued orders from Cairo to Captain Henry Walke, then in command of the gun-boats patrolling the river below Helena, to enter the Yazoo and destroy the batteries as far up as possible. Accordingly, on the 11th of December the *Marmora* and *Signal* entered the river for twenty miles. They found that in the interval since Phelps's raid in August, the Confederates had been by no means idle. The channel was full of scows and floats, indicating torpedoes, one of which exploded near the *Signal*, while another was discharged by musket-balls from the *Marmora*. Next day, as the river was rising, the light-draughts went in again, supported by two iron-clads, the *Cairo*, Lieutenant-Commander T. O. Selfridge, and the *Pittsburgh*, Lieutenant Hoel. The *Queen of the West* also went in. About a dozen miles up, the *Cairo* was struck by two torpedoes, one exploding under her bow, the other under her quarter. She sank in twelve minutes, disappearing completely save the tops of her smoke-stacks. The discipline of the crew was perfect, the men remaining at quarters until they were ordered away, and no lives were lost. Several torpedoes were removed before the expedition returned to the mouth of the river.

The object of both these expeditions was to prepare for the attack on Chickasaw Bluffs. On December 23d, Porter, who had now come down from Cairo, went up the Yazoo with the *Benton, Tyler*, and *Lexington*, three tin-clads, and two rams. By three days' incessant labor, under musketry fire from the banks, the fleet worked up to a point within range of the enemy's heavy batteries at Haynes's Bluff, whose fire the *Benton* sustained for two hours. The ship was not much damaged, but her commander, Gwin, one of the best officers in the squadron, was mortally wounded.

After the failure of the army at that point (December 29th) came the expedition against Arkansas Post. The vessels detailed by Porter for this movement were the iron-clads *De Kalb*, Lieutenant-Commander John G. Walker, *Louisville*, Lieutenant-Commander Elias K. Owen, and *Cincinnati*, Lieutenant George M. Bache; the ram *Monarch*, Colonel C. R. Ellet; the gun-boats *Black Hawk*, Lieutenant-Commander K. R. Breese, and *Tyler*, Lieutenant-Commander James W. Shirk; and the tin-clads *Rattler*, Lieutenant-Commander Watson Smith, and *Glide*, Lieutenant S. E. Woodworth. McClernand's force, comprising Sherman's and Morgan's corps, accompanied the fleet in transports. As a feint the vessels ascended the White River, crossing over to the Arkansas by the cut-off. On the 9th of January the army landed three miles below the fort.

Fort Hindman was a square bastioned work, standing at a bend of the river, sufficiently high to command the surrounding country. It was commanded by Lieutenant Dunnington, who had done such good service at St. Charles, and defended by troops under General Churchill. On the side facing the river were three casemates, two of them at the angles containing each a 9-inch gun, and the intermediate one an 8-inch. On the opposite side the approaches were defended by a line of trenches a mile in length, beginning at the fort and terminating in an impassable swamp. In the main work and in the trenches were mounted fourteen lighter pieces, several of them rifled. Two or three outlying works were built on the levee below the fort, but these were exposed to an enfilading fire from the gun-boats, and at the first attack by the latter were promptly abandoned.

On the afternoon and night of the 10th, the army marched up past the abandoned outworks, and took position about one thousand yards from the fort. On the afternoon of the same day the three iron-clads advanced to within 300 or 400 yards of the fort and opened with their heavy guns. When they had become hotly engaged, Porter moved up the *Black Hawk* and the *Lexington,* together with the light-draughts, which threw in a destructive fire of shrapnel and rifle-shells. When the guns on the river-side had been partly silenced, Lieutenant-Commander Smith in the *Rattler* was ordered to pass the fort and enfilade it, which he did in a very gallant and handsome manner. The *Rattler* suffered somewhat, being raked by a heavy shell, and having her cabin knocked to pieces. After passing the fort she was entangled in the snags above and obliged to return. As night came on and the troops were not yet in position, the vessels were withdrawn, and tied up to the bank below.

The next day at 1 o'clock the army was reported ready, and the fleet moved up to a second attack. The same disposition was made of the vessels. All of the casemate-guns were silenced, No. 3, which was in the casemate assigned to the *Cincinnati,* being reduced to a complete wreck. At the same time the troops gradually advanced, and were just preparing for a final assault, when white flags were run up all along the works. Lieutenant Dunnington surrendered to Porter, and General Churchill to McClernand.

On the 30th of January Grant assumed command of the army before Vicksburg. The enemy's right flank rested on the Yazoo Valley, a vast tract of partly overflowed country, oval in shape, two hundred miles long, and intersected by innumerable streams and bayous. This oval valley was bounded by the Mississippi on the west, and on the north, east, and south by what was in reality one long stream, known in its successive parts as the Coldwater, Tallahatchie, and Yazoo rivers. The bounding streams made the valley almost an island, the only break in their continuity being at the northern end of the valley, at Yazoo Pass, a bayou which had formerly connected the Coldwater with the Mississippi, but which had been closed by the erection of a levee several years before. The greater part of the valley was impassable for troops, and the streams were deemed impassable for vessels. The district was a rich storehouse of Confederate supplies, which were carried in small vessels through obscure passages and channels to Yazoo City, and thence to Vicksburg. At Yazoo City also, protected from assault by torpedoes and by the forts at Haynes's Bluff, was a large navy-yard, where several gun-boats were in course of erection.

Porter's plan was to cut the levee at Yazoo Pass, thus restoring the entrance and raising the water in the rivers, and by this means to get in the rear of Yazoo City before the enemy could prepare his defenses. Involving, as it did, a circuit of some two hundred miles through the tributary streams in the enemy's country, it was an audacious and original conception, but still a sagacious piece of naval strategy.

General Grant adopted the plan, and on the 2d of February the work of cutting the levee was begun by Colonel James Harrison Wilson of the Engineers. On the evening of the 3d a mine was exploded in the remaining portion of the embankment, and the waters of the Mississippi rushed through in a torrent, cutting a passage forty yards wide, and sweeping everything before them. The difference in the levels was eight or nine feet, and some days elapsed before the new entrance was practicable for vessels. The first reconnoissance developed the fact that the Confederates had already been vigilant enough to block the way to the Coldwater by felling trees on the banks of the Pass. The removal of these occasioned a further delay of two weeks, when time was of great importance.

The naval expedition, which was commanded by Lieutenant-Commander Watson Smith, was composed of two iron-clads, the *Chillicothe*, Lieutenant-Commander James P. Foster, and the *DeKalb*, Lieutenant-Commander John G. Walker, and the tin-clads *Rattler*, *Forest Rose*, *Romeo*, *Marmora*, *Signal*, and *Petrel*. To these were added two vessels of the ram fleet, the *Fulton* and *Lioness*. The only troops at first ordered to accompany the vessels were four thousand men comprising the division under Brigadier-General L. F. Ross, which, being delayed by the want of boats, only left Helena on the 23d, arriving a week later at the Coldwater. Meantime, as the feasibility of the project became more apparent, Grant enlarged his plan, and McPherson's corps, about 30,000 men, was ordered up, but, owing to delays, only a small part of this force under Brigadier-General I. F. Quinby took part in the movement.

On the 28th of February Smith's flotilla reached the Coldwater. Notwithstanding the work which had been done by the army pioneers in removing obstructions, the progress of the flotilla had been excessively slow,—hardly more than three miles a day. The tortuous windings of the stream, which imposed the

THE "BLACKHAWK,"
ADMIRAL PORTER'S FLAG-SHIP,
VICKSBURG, 1863.

utmost caution on the vessels navigating them in a swift current, and the over-hanging branches of the dense growth of trees lining the banks, which damaged the smoke-stacks and light upper works, made the passage slow and difficult, and caused a number of mishaps. There appears to be little doubt, however, that if the gun-boats had been pushed they might have got on considerably faster, perhaps with a saving of three or four days. In the Coldwater they made better time, though still moving slowly, and they only reached the Tallahatchie on the 6th of March. After four days more of rather dilatory navigation, they arrived at the junction of the Tallahatchie and the Yazoo. The transports were close behind them.

The Confederates had put to the fullest use the time given them by Smith's dilatory advance. A hastily constructed work of earth and cotton bales, called Fort Pemberton, was thrown up at the junction of the Tallahatchie and Yazoo, and though barely completed when the gun-boats arrived, it was armed and garrisoned, and in condition to receive them. The old *Star of the West*, of Fort Sumter fame, was sunk in the river as an obstruction. The *Chillicothe* and *DeKalb* attacked the fort on three different days, but their guns alone were not enough to reduce it, and the troops under Ross could find no firm ground for a landing. The *Chillicothe* was badly racked by the enemy's fire, showing plainly her defective construction. Smith, who had started on the expedition in failing health, was now sent back in the *Rattler* (he died shortly after), and the command of the vessels fell to Foster of the *Chillicothe*. Finding that nothing more could be accomplished, Foster decided to return. On the way back he met General Quinby's troops descending the Tallahatchie, and at that officer's request steamed down again to Fort Pemberton. On the 5th of April the expedition withdrew, and on the 10th arrived in the Mississippi, about two months after it had started.

About the middle of March, before the Yazoo Pass expedition returned, Porter decided to try another route, through a series of narrow streams and bayous which made a circuitous connection between the Mississippi and the Sunflower, a tributary of the Yazoo River. Steele's Bayou was a sluggish stream which entered the Mississippi a few miles above the mouth of the Yazoo. Black Bayou, which was little better than a narrow ditch, connected Steele's Bayou with Deer Creek, a tortuous river with a difficult and shallow channel. A second lateral bayou, called Rolling Fork, connected Deer Creek with the Sunflower. From Rolling Fork the way was easy, but the difficulties of reaching that point were such that no commander with less than Porter's indefatigable energy and audacious readiness to take risks that promised a bare chance of success, would have ventured on the expedition.

The flotilla, consisting of the remaining five Eads gun-boats, the *Carondelet*, *Cincinnati, Louisville, Mound City*, and *Pittsburgh*, started on the 14th of March, Porter commanding in person, while a coöperating detachment of troops under Sherman marched through the swamps. After overcoming obstacles that would have been insurmountable to almost any other commander, it arrived early at Rolling Fork. Here Porter was attacked by a small force, which was evidently only the advance-guard of a large army on its way up from Vicksburg. Sherman could not come to his assistance, being himself entangled in the swamp. At the same time Porter learned that detached parties of the enemy were felling trees in his rear, which would shortly render the bayous impassable, and place his five iron-clads in a position from which they could not be extricated. Under these circumstances, he wisely abandoned all thought of farther advance, and after dropping down Deer Creek until he fell in with the army, he succeeded, notwithstanding the additional obstructions which had been placed in the rivers, in retracing his course; and on the 24th of March, after almost incredible difficulties, his iron-clads arrived safe in the Mississippi.

While the two expeditions were at work in the Yazoo Valley, a series of detached operations had been going on below Vicksburg. The portion of the river that was virtually held by the enemy, from Vicksburg to Port Hudson, included the outlet of the Red River, by which provisions and stores from Louisiana and Texas, arms and ammunition from the Rio Grande, and detachments of men, were forwarded through the trans-Mississippi country. On the 2d of February Porter sent the *Queen of the West,* under Colonel Charles R. Ellet, to the Red River. Her passage of the Vicksburg batteries alone and by daylight—for her start had been delayed for necessary repairs—was made in the true Ellet fashion. She was struck thrice before she got abreast of the town. At this point she turned and delivered a ram-thrust at the enemy's steamer *Vicksburg,* which lay at one of the wharves, and damaged her badly; a second attempt to ram was prevented by a conflagration in the cotton bales which Ellet had placed around his deck. These were quickly pitched overboard, the ram dashed past the lower batteries, and though struck a dozen times by the enemy's shot, in an hour or two she was ready for active operations and started down the river.

For once the Confederates were fairly taken by surprise, and before they knew of his approach, Ellet had run down one hundred miles to the Red River and pounced upon three heavily laden store-ships. These were burned, and the *Queen,* ascending again until near Vicksburg, coaled from a barge which Porter had set adrift the night before, and which had passed the batteries without mishap. A tender was also found in the *De Soto,* a little ferry-boat captured by the army. With her the *Queen* started on February 10th on a second raid, burning and destroying as occasion offered. Without meeting any serious opposition, this novel expedition proceeded down the Mississippi, up the Red River, down the Atchafalaya, and back again, then farther up the Red River. The Confederate ram *Webb,* which was regarded as its most dangerous antagonist, was nowhere to be seen. But the catastrophe was coming. On the 14th, some fifty miles from the river-mouth, Ellet captured a transport, the *Era No.* 5. Leaving her at this point, the *Queen* hastened up again, followed by the *De Soto,* but in rounding a bend of the river she ran aground under a 4-gun battery, whose fire made havoc with her, finally cutting her steam-pipe. Part of the crew made for the *De Soto* in a boat, and the remainder, Ellet among them, jumped overboard on cotton bales, and drifted down the stream. Upon reaching the *Era,* the *De Soto,* which had lost her rudder, was burned, the floating contingent was picked up, and the prize, now manned by the crews of the abandoned vessels, made her way to the Mississippi.

Shortly before this Porter had sent down the iron-clad *Indianola,* under Lieutenant-Commander George Brown, to support Ellet in his isolated position. She had passed Vicksburg and Warrenton at night without a scratch, and descending the river met the *Era* coming up. Both vessels continued on their way, the *Era* to Vicksburg, and the *Indianola* to the mouth of Red River, where she lay for three days. She then moved up toward Vicksburg, the two coal barges which she had brought with her being lashed alongside. While she was working slowly up, the Confederates, who had meantime repaired the *Queen*, fitted out an expedition composed of their prize, together with the *Webb* and two cotton-clad steamers. These followed the *Indianola* and overtook her a short distance below Warrenton. Engaging her at night, which gave them peculiar advantages, they succeeded in ramming her seven times, disabling her steering gear, and opening at last one great hole in her side. The Union vessel, reduced to a sinking condition, was then run ashore and surrendered.

A day or two later, Porter, whose buoyancy of spirit never deserted him, set adrift from his anchorage a dummy-monitor, constructed out of a coal-barge surmounted by barrels. The incident was in the nature of a stupendous joke, but it had very practical results. The dummy passed the Vicksburg batteries under a terrific fire. When the *Queen of the West*, acting as a picket to the grounded *Indianola*, saw this new antagonist coming she only stopped to give the alarm, and fled down the river. The supposed monitor stuck fast a mile or two above the *Indianola*, but the Confederate officer in charge of the work on board the latter did not wait for an attack, but set fire to the recent prize, which was in great part destroyed.

Less than three weeks after, on the 14th of March, Farragut ran the batteries at Port Hudson.☆ Most of his fleet, including the *Richmond, Monongahela,*

☆In a letter to the editors Rear-Admiral T. A. Jenkins says, in reference to Farragut's plan of an attack on Port Hudson:

"The great importance, not to say necessity, of coöperation by a part of the military forces, in so far, at the least, as to cause a diversion upon the enemy's rear, was decided upon, whereupon the commanding general (Banks) was conferred with with great frequency, until at last in the early part of March, 1863, it was arranged that a considerable force (8000 or 10,000) of all arms should rendezvous at Baton Rouge, preparatory to moving to the rear of the Port Hudson works, a little time before the vessels should move from Poplar Island, which lay just out of range of the Port Hudson heavy guns. After a review of the military forces at Baton Rouge, and after Admiral Farragut had attended to the minutest details of inspection of the vessels,—the removal of the sick, the necessary changes of officers and men, and last, but most difficult at that time, the employment of a sufficient number of competent river pilots,—the vessels got under way in their usual order of steaming, led by the *Hartford,* and stood up to Poplar Island, where the *Essex* and the bomb-vessels were lying. During a brief stay here, the commanders of the vessels were called on board and their instructions were repeated to them. Every contingency, even the most minute, every casualty that could or might happen, was discussed, and proposed remedies pointed out. On the night of the 14th of March, at dark, everything was prepared for a quiet, and it was hoped unperceived, movement of the vessels up the river. Near the last moment before the actual firing commenced, Admiral Farragut's attention was called to an approaching river steamer with flaring lights

Genesee, and *Kineo,* failed to get through, and the *Mississippi* was burnt;‡ but the *Hartford* and *Albatross* made the passage, and, coming up to Vicksburg, communicated with the vessels above. At Farragut's request, General Ellet sent two of his rams, the *Lancaster* and *Switzerland,* to join the *Hartford.* The *Lancaster* was sunk in passing the batteries, but the *Switzerland* managed to get through. From this time the Union forces retained control of the mouth of the Red River and the adjacent waters of the Mississippi.

The navy was now called upon to coöperate with General Grant's plan of attacking Vicksburg by the left and rear. Porter rapidly made his preparations to descend the river, and on the night of April 16th started with seven of his iron-clads, the *Benton, Lafayette,* and *Tuscumbia,* and the Eads gun-boats *Carondelet, Louisville, Mound City,* and *Pittsburgh.* The ram *General Price* and three transports laden with stores accompanied the fleet. The passage was one of the most brilliant and successful of the many dashes of this kind that were made on the river. Some of the vessels lost the coal-barges which they carried alongside, and all met with various mischances and damages, but the only casualty of importance was the sinking of one of the transports. About a week later six more transports ran the batteries. Of these also one was sunk.

From now on to the fall of Vicksburg, for over two months, Porter was in command of three detached fleets, acting from three distinct bases of operation—one the squadron which had remained above Vicksburg, and which was now to operate along the Yazoo River, the second that which had passed the batteries and was occupied with the river from Vicksburg 25 miles or more to Grand Gulf, and the third the vessels in Red River. Porter moved from one to the other as occasion required. His first duty lay at Grand Gulf, which was

---

and steam-whistles blowing. He was calm, but the lights and noise of the little steamer ruffled him a good deal. He saw at once that the enemy's attention had been specially called to him and his little squadron. The commander of the steamer came within speaking distance, reporting that General Banks's army was within 'five miles of the rear of the Port Hudson works.' That was all. The *Hartford* moved up against a current of three to five knots, while her greatest speed was not exceeding seven knots. The noise and flaring lights of the messenger steamer had evidently put the enemy on both sides of the river on the alert, for a shot from one of the enemy's lower batteries soon whistled harmlessly overhead, and, as if by magic, at the next moment the piles of pine-knots placed on the right bank of the river blazed up, illuminating for a time the entire breadth of the river, making the dark hulls of the vessels as they passed between the immense piles of burning pine a target for the Port Hudson gunners. The smoke of the guns in battery and on shipboard soon obscured these lights, and the darkness of Erebus and the noises of Prandemonium followed and continued, until the *Hartford,* with her little cockle-shell consort (the *Albatross*) anchored out of range of the enemy's guns, abreast of a huge pine-knot fire, to which the rebels before leaving added a small wooden building."

‡The *Mississippi* passed the lower batteries, but, running at high speed, struck on the spit opposite Port Hudson. Failing after half an hour to get her off, and being under fire of three batteries, Captain McIaneton Smith had the sick and wounded taken off with the crew, and then set fire to the ship. At 3 A.M. she floated off, drifting through the fleet, and half an hour later blew up.—EDITORS.

really the southern extremity of the Vicksburg forts. The batteries were well armed, and one hundred or more feet above the river. On the 29th of April the seven iron-clads of the lower fleet engaged them for four hours, silencing them, but not destroying the guns. As the elevation of the batteries made it impossible for the fleet to capture them, the army was landed lower down the river, which resulted in the evacuation of Grand Gulf on the 3d of May.[*]

As Grant advanced into the interior, Porter turned his attention to the Red River. For the last fortnight Farragut had been blockading the river with the *Hartford* and *Albatross,* a service of great importance in view of the active operations on foot along the river, and at the end of that time he was joined by a detached force of gun-boats which had been operating in the Teche, and which had reached Red River through the Atchafalaya. Banks was then moving against Alexandria, and a light squadron was formed to go up and coöperate with him. At this juncture Porter arrived with three iron-clads, and with these and a part of Farragut's detached squadron he steamed up to Alexandria, where Banks arrived on May 7th. After clearing out the Red River and its tributary the Black, and destroying much property, the expedition returned, Banks going to Port Hudson and Porter returning to his old station above Vicksburg.

The Yazoo River now became for a short time the central point of Porter's operations. Nothing had been done there since December except a demonstration during the attack of April 29–30 on Grand Gulf, which, though conducted with spirit and gallantry, was really only a feint to prevent the enemy from reënforcing his works below Vicksburg. In the fortnight that had elapsed, how-

---

[*]Rear-Admiral Henry Walke writes as follows to the editors regarding this engagement, in which he commanded the *Lafayette:*

"To one approaching Grand Gulf on the river from the northward, six miles above, Bald Head presents a very formidable appearance. Rising abruptly 180 feet, surrounded by hills higher still, and with the wide gulf beneath, it is not unlike a little Gibraltar, as it is called. Here the river turns due west, and the principal fortification was on the Point of Rocks, a precipitous bluff about fifty feet high, at the foot of Bald Head. Three-quarters of a mile east of it is the mouth of Big Black River, which was defended with two 8-inch Columbiads. Here the gulf is about a mile and a half wide, and two hundred yards north or in front of the Point of Rocks there is a shoal which becomes an island at low water. The lower fort of heavy guns was three-quarters of a mile west of Bald Head and four hundred yards from the river, and sixty feet above the river at its ordinary level. The battery on the Point of Rocks mounted two 100-pounder rifles, one 64-pounder shell gun, and one 30-pounder rifle. A sunken road connected this fort with the batteries below. Seven or eight guns of smaller and various caliber were mounted on high points between them. The lower fort mounted one 100-pounder rifle, two 8-inch shell guns, and two 32-pounders.

"The fleet, under Rear-Admiral Porter, got into line at 7:30 A.M. of the 29th, steaming down to the Grand Gulf batteries, the *Pittsburgh,* Lieutenant W. R. Hoel, leading; then the *Louisville,* Lieutenant-Commander E. K. Owen; *Carondelet,* Lieutenant J. M. Murphy; *Mound City,* Lieutenant-Commander Byron Wilson (attacking the lower batteries); *Lafayette,* Captain Henry Walke; *Benton* (flag-ship), Lieutenant J. A. Greer, and *Tuscumbia,* Lieutenant-Commander J. W. Shirk; steaming slowly with a current of five or six knots, 150 yards apart

UPPER BATTERIES "LOUISVILLE." "PITTSBURGH."
"MOUND CITY."
MIDDLE AND LOWER BATTERIES.
"TRENTON." "TUSCUMBIA." "CARONDELET." "LAFAYETTE."

BATTLE OF GRAND GULF (SECOND POSITION).

ever, Grant's environment of the town on the east had cut off Haynes's Bluff and the whole Yazoo Valley above it. Porter immediately sent up the *De Kalb, Choctaw,* and four light-draughts under Lieutenant-Commander K. R. Breese to open communication. Pushing on to Haynes's Bluff, the *De Kalb,* Lieutenant-Commander John G. Walker, in advance, it was found that evacuation had al-

---

and 100 yards from the shore, except the *Lafayette,* which rounded to above the fort on the Point of Rocks, ran into the shoal water, and took a flanking position 600 yards north-east from it. The battle was commenced by the leading gun-boat, *Pittsburgh,* at 7:55 A.M.; the other gun-boats followed in succession four minutes after. All the gun-boats fired into the upper fort with their bow and broadside guns as they passed up or down. The *Pittsburgh* rounded to opposite the battery of light guns half-way between the upper and lower batteries; the *Louisville* next below, the *Carondelet* next, opposite the lower battery, and the *Mound City* just below the lower battery. The flag-steamer *Benton* and the *Tuscumbia* gallantly opened fire close under the Point of Rocks at 8:15 with their bow and broadside guns, rounded to, heading up the river, the enemy firing on them with musketry. At 9 a shell entered the *Benton's* starboard quarter, setting her on fire; it was soon extinguished. At 9:05 a shell from No. 5 gun carried away the enemy's flag-staff; at 10 the admiral made signal for the *Lafayette* to assist the boats below; at 10:10 the *Benton* was caught in the eddy; in turning around she dropped fifteen hundred yards and then ran into shore to turn around with her head up stream; continuing the engagement, she steamed up to the batteries on the bluffs again. At 12:25 the *Benton* went up the river to communicate with General Grant, who was on a tug above with three of McClernand's divisions on transports.

"In the engagement the *Benton* fired 347 shot and shell, and was struck 47 times, nearly

ready begun, and the small force left in the works hastily abandoned them. The fortifications were of great strength and covered a large area. On the 20th Walker with the *De Kalb* and *Choctaw* and three of the light-draughts, steamed up to Yazoo City. The work of destruction, begun by the retreating enemy, was completed by the gun-boats. The navy-yard, a large and well-equipped establishment, and the only one now remaining to the Confederates, with its mills and machine-shops and its stores of lumber, was burned, as were also three formidable vessels then in course of construction. A second expedition under Walker, a few days later, struck out into the tributary streams, the Sunflower, Rolling Fork, and the smaller bayous, burning the transports that had taken refuge there. Several steamers were sunk by the enemy on Walker's approach, and three were captured and burnt by his vessels. Navigation in the Yazoo Valley was broken up, and the destruction of military supplies and provisions was enormous.

During Grant's assault on the 22d of May, the fleet below Vicksburg kept up a heavy fire on the hill and water batteries, and during the siege the mortar-boats were incessantly at work, shelling the city and the batteries. From time to time the gun-boats joined in the bombardment, notably on May 27th and June 20th. On the first of these occasions, the *Cincinnati,* Lieutenant George M. Bache, engaged alone the battery on Fort Hill, the principal work above Vicksburg, while the other iron-clads, under Commander Woodworth, were similarly occupied below. The fire from the upper battery was too much for the *Cincinnati,* which sank not far from the shore, losing a considerable number of

---

every shot penetrating her iron plating. The *Tuscumbia,* following the *Benton,* engaged the upper batteries until noon. She was obliged to drop out of action about noon, and landed about four miles below Grand Gulf, having been struck by shot, shell, grape, and shrapnel eighty-one times, two shells having exploded inside her turret. As the *Lafayette* approached the upper battery at 8:15 A.M., ahead of the *Benton* and *Tuscumbia,* she fired 11-inch and 9-inch shell into it, but in turning to take her position on the other side of the port, she was whirled around so quickly between the swift current and the counter-current, that her gunners could not get good aim with broadside guns, but as soon as she turned her 100-pounder rifles on the battery in a flanking position in the eddy, every shell seemed to strike the mark; but even there it was difficult to hold her steady for good aim. After firing 35 rounds, about 9 A.M. her 11-inch bow guns were turned upon the fort and fired with such precision that we expected to silence it, as their fire was dying away. This was the position our whole squadron should have taken, but it was not known that that part of the gulf was navigable. The heaviest guns of the enemy could point to the northward and westward, but not to the eastward, where the *Lafayette* was exempt from that terrible battering which the *Benton* and *Tuscumbia* received, while they were revolving at the mercy of the currents, in constant danger of running ashore.

"At 9:20 A.M. the admiral made a preconcerted signal for the *Lafayette* to go to the assistance of the gun-boats at the lower batteries, thinking no doubt that his two heaviest vessels could silence the upper fort. This move was not after the lower batteries were silenced (as has been stated), but about two hours before. The *Lafayette* proceeded immediately with all speed and rounded to about 10 A.M. opposite the lower battery. She joined battle with the

her crew. On the second occasion three heavy guns mounted on scows were placed in position on the point opposite Vicksburg, where they did good execution under Lieutenant-Commander F. M. Ramsay, enfilading the rifle-pits in front of Sherman's position and rendering them untenable. The lower squadron also took part in this bombardment. In addition to the work of the squadron afloat, when the army called for siege-guns thirteen heavy cannon were landed from the gun-boats and placed in position in the rear of Vicksburg, where they were constantly and efficiently worked by naval crews, first under Selfridge, and later under Walker. At the same time the squadron was engaged in the duty of patrolling the rivers, keeping open lines of communication, convoying transports, and coöperating with troops in beating off the enemy at detached points.

On the 25th of May Banks, who had returned with his army from Alexandria, had invested Port Hudson, which had been subjected for several nights previous to a bombardment from the *Essex* and the mortar flotilla, under Commander Caldwell. During the month of June a naval battery of 9-inch guns, under Lieutenant-Commander Edward Terry of the *Richmond*, rendered efficient service in the siege operations. On the 9th of July Port Hudson surrendered and the Mississippi was now clear of obstructions to its mouth.

Besides the main operations at Vicksburg and Port Hudson, the navy had been occupied from time to time in detached bodies at other points. A cut-off, at the mouth of the Arkansas, ingeniously made by Selfridge in April, had contributed materially to the facility of operations at that place. In May Lieutenant-Commander Wilson in the *Mound City* effectually destroyed a water-battery at Warrenton. In June an attack was made on Milliken's Bend by Confederate troops from Arkansas under Taylor, and the garrison was driven from their works to the levee. At this critical moment Ramsay, in the *Choctaw*, turned his guns on the successful assailants, and though unable to see the enemy on account of the intervening bank, he hailed the troops on shore to as-

---

gun-boats there, firing her 11-inch shell from her bow guns into it and to bring her head up stream and her starboard side guns to bear on it quickly. The pilot ran her low into the bank of the river under the fort. She continued firing with the starboard broadside guns within five hundred yards of the lower fort, and with the other gun-boats continued firing on the lower batteries, enfilading the upper fort until 11:30, when the lower batteries were silenced, and all the gun-boats, except the *Pittsburgh*, steamed close to and passed the Point of Rocks (which had not been silenced), raking it with their bow guns. The *Benton* had just then gone up the river.

"The remainder of the squadron continued firing on the upper fort. The *Lafayette* took her former position, flanking the fort. The *Louisville, Mound City,* and *Carondelet* steamed around in a circle, firing as they bore in front of the fort. The *Pittsburgh* remained in her original position, raking it with her bow guns from the west. The enemy, thus involved, fought desperately to the last; their guns, ceasing one by one at long intervals, were at last silent; whereupon the admiral made signal for his squadron to follow his motions. But the fort, as if to give us notice that it was not silenced, fired the last gun after we had started to go up the river."

certain their position; and so well placed were the hundred or more shell and shrapnel that he fired that the Confederates were soon in full retreat.

Finally, on the 4th of July, the day of the fall of Vicksburg, General Holmes made his attack on Helena with a force of about 8000 men, then garrisoned by 4000 under B. M. Prentiss. The enemy had placed batteries in opposition above and below the town, and, making a spirited attack in front, succeeded in carrying a portion of the outlying works. The garrison fought stubbornly, but were heavily outnumbered. The wooden gun-boat *Tyler*, under Lieutenant-Commander James M. Prichett, had been covering the approach by the old town road, but seeing the strategic points of the enemy's position, Prichett with masterly skill placed his vessel where her bow and stern guns could reach the batteries above and below, while her broadside enfiladed the ravines down which the enemy was pouring in masses. The gun-boat's rapid discharge of shrapnel and shell told heavily upon the Confederates, who, after sustaining it for a time, fled in disorder, Prentiss's men pursuing them with the bayonet. The destructive fire of the *Tyler* caused an unusually severe loss.

The fall of Vicksburg was followed by successful gun-boat raids, one in July under Selfridge in the Red, Black, and Tensas rivers, the other in August under Bache in the White River. General Herron and Lieutenant-Commander Walker also proceeded up the Yazoo and retook Yazoo City, but with the loss of the *De Kalb*, destroyed by torpedoes near Yazoo City. The vessel sank in fifteen minutes, but all hands were saved. Porter accepted the misfortune with that true understanding of the business of war which had been the secret of so much of his success—that without taking risks you cannot achieve results.

CHAPTER 10

The Capture of Port Hudson.

Richard B. Irwin, Lieutenant-Colonel,
Assistant Adjutant-General, U.S.V.

General Banks arrived in New Orleans on the 14th of December, 1862, with the advance of a fleet of transports from New York and Hampton Roads, bringing reënforcements for the Department of the Gulf.‡ On the 15th he took command of the department, Butler then formally taking leave of the troops. His orders were to move up the Mississippi, in order to open the river, in coöperation with McClernand's column from Cairo. Banks was to take command of the combined forces as soon as they should meet.

On the 16th General Grover, with 12 regiments and a battery, without disembarking at New Orleans, accompanied by two batteries and two troops of cavalry from the old force, and convoyed by a detachment of Farragut's fleet under Captain James Alden, of the *Richmond*, was sent to occupy Baton Rouge. The next morning the town was evacuated by the small Confederate detachment which had been posted there, and General Grover quietly took possession. The town was held without opposition until the war ended.

An attempt followed to occupy Galveston, apparently under importunity from Brigadier-General Andrew J. Hamilton, and in furtherance of the policy that had led the Government to send him with the expedition as military governor of Texas. This resulted on the 1st of January in a military and naval disaster in which three companies of the 42d Massachusetts regiment, under Colonel Isaac S. Burrell, were taken prisoners by the Confederates under Magruder.ψ

---

‡These reënforcements finally included 39 regiments of infantry (of which 22 were 9-months' men), six batteries of artillery, and one battalion of cavalry.

ψOn the 21st of December three companies of the 42d Massachusetts, under Colonel Isaac S. Burrell, were dispatched from New Orleans, without disembarking. Holcomb's 2d Vermont battery was sent with them but, waiting for its horses to arrive, did not go ashore. Burrell landed at Kuhn's wharf on the 24th, took nominal possession of the town, but really occupied only the wharf itself, protected by barri-

Weitzel, who was occupying the La Fourche, was strengthened so as to enable him to make the district safe in view of the projected operations on the Mississippi; a strong work was constructed at Donaldsonville commanding the head of the bayou; and intrenchments were thrown up at Brashear City to prevent, with the aid of the navy, any approach of the enemy from the direction of Berwick Bay. On the 14th of January, having crossed the bay, Weitzel ascended the Teche, accompanied by the gun-boats *Calhoun, Estrella,* and *Kinsman,* under Lieutenant-Commander Buchanan, forced the Confederates to destroy the gun-boat *Cotton,* and took 50 prisoners, with a loss of 6 killed and 27 wounded. Among the dead was Buchanan, who was succeeded by Lieutenant-Commander A. P. Cooke.

After providing for the garrisons and the secure defense of New Orleans, Banks organized his available forces in four divisions, commanded by Major-General C. C. Augur and Brigadier-Generals Thomas W. Sherman, William H. Emory, and Cuvier Grover. Each division was composed of three brigades with three field-batteries, and there were also two battalions and six troops of cavalry, numbering about 700 effectives, and a regiment of heavy artillery, the 1st Indiana (21st Infantry) to man the siege train. The veteran regiments that had served in the department from the beginning were distributed so as to leaven the mass and to furnish brigade commanders of some experience; of the eight colonels commanding brigades, all but two belonged to these regiments. The whole force available for active operations was about 25,000. Two-thirds were,

---

cades and the 32 guns of the fleet under Commander W. B. Renshaw. Major-General J. B. Magruder, who had been barely a month in command of the district of Texas, had directed his attention as soon as he arrived to the defenseless condition of the coast, menaced as it was by the blockading fleet; thus it happened that Burrell's three companies found themselves confronted by two brigades (Scurry's and Sibley's, under Colonel Reily), an artillery regiment, 14 heavy guns, and 14 field-pieces. Magruder had also caused two improvised gun-boats to be equipped under an old California steamboat man, Captain Leon Smith; these were the *Bayou City,* Captain Henry Lubbock, and *Neptune,* Captain Sangster. Early in the morning of the 1st of January Magruder, having perfected his plans, under cover of a heavy artillery fire, assaulted the position of the 42d Massachusetts with two storming parties of 300 and 500 men respectively, led by Colonels Green, Bagby, and Cook, with the remainder of the troops under Brigadier-General W. R. Scurry in support. A sharp fight followed, but the defenders had the concentrated fire of the fleet to protect them; the scaling-ladders proved too short to reach the wharf, and as day began to break the assailants were about to draw off, when suddenly the Confederate gun-boats appeared on the scene, and in a few moments turned the defeat into a signal victory. The *Neptune* was disabled and sunk by the *Harriet Lane;* the *Harriet Lane* herself was boarded and captured by the *Bayou City;* the *Westfield* ran aground and was blown up by her gallant commander, and soon the white flag, first displayed on the *Harriet Lane,* was flying from all the fleet. Thereupon Burrell surrendered. The Confederates ceased firing on him as soon as they perceived his signal; but the navy, observing that the firing on shore went on for some time, notwithstanding the naval truce, thought it had been violated; accordingly the *Clifton, Owasco,* and *Saxon* put to sea, preceded by the army transport steamers, the *Saxon,* which had brought the three unlucky companies of the 42d, and the *Mary A. Boardman,* with Holcomb's 2d Vermont battery still aboard. The Confederates lost 26 killed and 117 wounded; the Union troops 5 killed and 15 wounded.

—R.B.I.

MAGRUDER'S MEN BOARDING THE "HARRIET LANE" AT GALVESTON.
SEE PREVIOUS PAGE.

however, new levies, and of these, again, half were nine-months' men; some were armed with guns that refused to go off, others did not know the simplest evolutions, while in one instance (afterward handsomely redeemed) the colonel was actually unable to disembark his men except by the novel command, "Break ranks, boys, and get ashore the best way you can!"

The cavalry was poor, except the six old companies, and was quite insufficient in numbers. Of land and water transportation, both indispensable to any possible operation, there was barely enough for the movement of a single division. In Washington, Banks had been led to expect that he would find in the depots, or in the country, all material required for moving his army; yet the supplies in the depots barely sufficed for the old force of the department, while the country could furnish very little at best, and nothing at all until it should be occupied. Banks had finally to send his chief quartermaster back to Washington before these deficiencies could be supplied.

Again, Banks had not been informed until he reached New Orleans that the Confederates held in force any fortified place below Vicksburg, yet Port Hudson, 135 miles above New Orleans, was found strongly intrenched, with 21 heavy guns in position, and a garrison of 12,000 men—increased to 16,000 before Banks could have brought an equal number to the attack.

Banks could not communicate with the commander of the northern col-

SHARP-SHOOTERS OF THE 75TH N.Y.
VOLUNTEERS PICKING OFF THE GUNNERS
OF THE CONFEDERATE GUN-BOAT
"COTTON," IN THE ACTION AT
BAYOU TECHE, LA., JANUARY 14, 1863.
FROM A SKETCH MADE AT THE TIME.

umn, and knew practically nothing of its movements.

Under these conditions, all concert between the coöperating forces was rendered impossible from the start, and it became inevitable that the expectations of the Government that Banks would go against Vicksburg immediately on landing in Louisiana should be doomed to disappointment.

The Confederate occupation of Port Hudson had completely changed the nature of the problem confided to General Banks for solution, for he had now to choose among three courses, each involving an impossibility: to carry by assault a strong line of works, three miles long, impregnable on either flank and defended by 16,000 good troops; to lay siege to the place, with the certainty that it would be relieved from Mississippi and the prospect of losing his siege train in the venture; to leave Port Hudson in his rear and go against Vicksburg, thus sacrificing his communications, putting New Orleans in peril, and courting irreparable and almost inevitable disaster as the price of the remote chance of achieving a great success. No word came from Grant or McClernand.

Meanwhile Banks was trying to find a way of turning Port Hudson on the west by means of the Atchafalaya, the mouth of Red River, and the net-work of bayous, interlacing and intersecting one another, that connect the Atchafalaya with the Mississippi, in time of flood overflowing and fertilizing, at other seasons serving as highways for the whole region between the two rivers. The Mississippi was unusually high, the narrow and tortuous bayous were swollen and rapid; the levees, nearly everywhere neglected since the outbreak of the war, had in some places been cut by the Confederates; a large area of the country was under water; while great rafts of drift-logs added to the difficulty of navigation occasioned by the scarcity of suitable steamers and skilled pilots. Every attempt to penetrate the bayous having failed, Banks was just turning his attention to the preparations for gaining the same end by a movement from Berwick Bay by the Atchafalaya or Teche, when the news came that two of Ellet's rams, the *Queen of the West* and *Indianola*, after successfully running the batteries of Vicksburg, had been captured by the Confederates. These gun-boats must therefore be reck-

RETURN OF A FORAGING PARTY OF THE 24TH CONNECTICUT VOLUNTEERS
TO BATON ROUGE. FROM A SKETCH MADE AT THE TIME.

oned with in any movement on or beyond the Atchafalaya, while their presence above Port Hudson as a hostile force, in place of the reënforcement expected from Admiral Porter, greatly increased the anxiety Admiral Farragut had for some time felt to pass the batteries of Port Hudson with part of his fleet, control the long reach above, and cut off the Confederate supplies from the Red River country. General Banks fell in with the admiral's plans, and, concentrating 17,000 men at Baton Rouge, moved to the rear of Port Hudson on the 14th of March, with the divisions of Augur, Emory, and Grover, for the purpose of coöperating with the fleet by dividing the attention of the garrison and gaining a flank fire of artillery on the lower batteries on the bluff. The field-returns showed 12,000 men in line after providing for detachments and for holding Baton Rouge. Admiral Farragut had intended to pass the batteries on the 15th, in the gray of the morning, but at the last moment saw reason to change this plan and moved to the attack before midnight. In a naval affair like this the coöperation of the army could not have been very effective at best; the change of hour left us little more than spectators and auditors of the battle between the ships and the forts. The *Hartford* and *Albatross* passed up comparatively uninjured, but in the smoke and darkness the rest of the fleet could not go by, and the *Mississippi*, stranding, was set on fire and blown up—the grandest display of fireworks I ever witnessed, and the costliest. [See p. 671.]

This gave the navy command of the mouth of Red River, and, accordingly, Banks at once reverted to the execution of his former plan,—a turning movement by the Atchafalaya. That involved disposing of Taylor's force of about 4000 or 5000 men encamped and intrenched on the Teche below Franklin. Our force was so much stronger than Taylor's as to suggest the idea of capturing him in his position, by getting in his rear, simultaneously with a front attack; and this was particularly to be desired, as otherwise he might retire indefinitely into the vast open country behind him and return at his leisure at some inopportune moment. So perfectly was the movement masked that Taylor was actually preparing to attack the force in his front (Weitzel) when the main army began crossing Berwick Bay.

Weitzel crossed on the 9th; Emory followed; they then bivouacked on the west bank to wait for Grover's movement. So few were the facilities that it took Grover two days to embark. Six hours more were lost by a dense fog, and four by the stranding of the *Arizona*. When the proposed landing-place at Madame Porter's plantation was reached after dark, the road was found to be under water and impassable, but a practicable way was discovered six miles farther up the lake, at McWilliams's plantation. There the landing began early on the 13th,

MARCH OF THE NINETEENTH ARMY CORPS BY THE BAYOU SARA ROAD TOWARD PORT HUDSON, SATURDAY, MARCH 14, 1863. FROM A SKETCH MADE AT THE TIME.

and with great difficulty, owing to the shallowness of the water, was completed by 4 o'clock in the afternoon. Favored by the woods and undergrowth, which concealed their numbers, Vincent's 2d Louisiana and Reily's 4th Texas Cavalry, with a section of Cornay's battery, delayed the advance until Dwight's brigade, supported by two regiments of Birge's and by Closson's battery, went out and drove them away. At 6 the division took up the line of march to the Teche and bivouacked at nightfall on Madame Porter's plantation, five miles distant.

Meanwhile Banks had moved Emory and Weitzel slowly up the Teche, seeking to hold Taylor's forces in position until Grover could gain their rear. Taylor fell back behind the intrenched lines below Centreville known as Fort Bisland, and there a brisk engagement took place on the 13th, Banks only seeking to gain a good position on both sides of the bayou, and to occupy the enemy's attention, while he listened in vain for Grover's guns, which were to have been the signal for a direct and determined attack in front.

At night, knowing that Grover's movement must certainly have been seen and reported during his passage up Grand Lake and surmising some miscarriage, Banks gave orders to carry the works by assault at daylight. However, early in the night, Taylor ordered his whole force to fall back on Franklin; the sounds of the movement were heard, and toward daylight reconnoitering parties discovered the evacuation. Banks's whole force at once moved in pursuit.

Early in the morning Taylor met Grover advancing against his line of retreat, which here follows the great bow of the Teche, known as Irish Bend, struck Birge's brigade in flank, forced Grover to develop, and with the assistance of the *Diana*⁺ held him just long enough to make good the retreat.

Taylor had made a gallant fight and had extricated himself cleverly. His reports show his whole force to have been 5000. Grover had about the same. We lost at Bisland 40 killed and 184 wounded,—total, 224; at Irish Bend, 49 killed, 274 wounded, 30 missing,—total, 353. The losses of the Confederates are not reported, but they destroyed their two gun-boats and all their transport steamers except one, which we captured, and their troops began to disperse soon after passing Franklin. We captured many prisoners on the march. Their gun-boats came down the Atchafalaya too late to dispute Grover's landing, were defeated by our flotilla, under Lieutenant-Commander A. P. Cooke, and the *Queen of the West* was destroyed. On the 20th Butte-à-la-Rose, with sixty men and two heavy guns, surrendered to Cooke, and the same day Banks occupied Opelousas.

Here he received his first communication from General Grant, dated before Vicksburg, March 23d, and sent through Admiral Farragut. This opened a correspondence, the practical effect of which was to cause General Banks to

---

⁺A Union gun-boat captured by the Confederates and afterward set on fire and destroyed by them, as mentioned above.—EDITORS.

conform his movements to the expectation that General Grant would send an army corps to Bayou Sara to join in reducing Port Hudson.

Banks moved on to Alexandria, on the Red River, to push Taylor farther out of the way. Taylor retired toward Shreveport. On the 14th of May the whole command marched on Simsport, crossed the Atchafalaya, and moved to Bayou Sara, where the advance of the army crossed the Mississippi on the night of the 23d and moved immediately to the rear of Port Hudson.

There communication was made with Augur's two brigades, which had established themselves in position on the 21st, after a brisk engagement, known as the battle of Plains Store,[1] just in time, apparently, to prevent the evacuation, which had been ordered by General Johnston and afterward countermanded by President Davis. With Augur we found T. W. Sherman and two brigades from New Orleans.

When the investment was completed on the 26th, we had about 14,000 men of all arms in front of the works, and behind them the Confederates had about 7000, under Major-General Frank Gardner. Part of the garrison (three brigades, as it proved) was known to have gone to succor Vicksburg, and all reports, apparently confirmed by the comparative feebleness of the attack on Augur at Plains Store, indicated a reduction even greater than had actually taken place. Nothing was known, of course, of the phenomenal success of Grant's operations, nor could it have been surmised, while his precarious position in the event of a defeat or even a serious check was obvious enough; the magnitude of the Confederate forces in Mississippi and the energy habitual to their commanders everywhere, added an additional reason against delay. Finally the troops themselves, elated by their success in the Teche campaign, were in the best of spirits for an immediate attack. For these reasons General Banks, with the full concurrence of all his commanders, save one, ordered a general assault to be made on the morning of the 27th of May.

Early in the morning Weitzel, who commanded the right wing on this day, moved to the attack in two lines, Dwight at first leading, and steadily drove the Confederates in his front into their works. Thus unmasked, the Confederate artillery opened with grape and canister, but our batteries, following the infantry as closely as possible, soon took commanding positions within 200 and 300 yards of the works that enabled them to keep down the enemy's fire. The whole fight took place in a dense forest of magnolias, mostly amid a thick undergrowth, and among ravines choked with felled or fallen timber, so that it was difficult not only to move but even to see; in short, in the phrase of the day, the affair was "a gigantic bush-whack." Soon after Weitzel's movement began Grover, on his left, moved to the attack at two points, but only succeeded in gaining and holding commanding positions within about two hundred yards of

[1] Augur lost 15 killed, 71 wounded, 14 missing,—total, 100; the Confederates, 89.

the works. This accomplished, and no sound of battle coming from his left, Grover determined to wait where he was for the attack that had been expected in that quarter, or for further orders, and Weitzel conformed his action to Grover's: properly in both cases, although it was afterward made apparent that had Weitzel continued to press his attack a few minutes longer he would probably have broken through the Confederate defense and taken their whole line in reverse. To make a diversion, Dwight caused the two colored regiments on the extreme right to form for the attack; they had hardly done so when the extreme left of the Confederate line opened on them, in an exposed position, with artillery and musketry and forced them to abandon the attempt with great loss. In Augur's front the Confederate works were in full view, but the intervening plain was obstructed by tangled abatis of huge trees felled with their great branches spread as if to receive us with open arms, and these obstructions were commanded by the fire of nearly a mile of the works. His movement had therefore been meant for a demonstration, mainly in aid of Sherman, to be converted into a real attack if circumstances should favor; but as the morning wore away and no sound came from Sherman, General Banks rode to the left and gave fresh orders for that assault; then, returning to the center about two o'clock, he ordered Augur to attack simultaneously. At the word Chapin's brigade moved forward with great gallantry, but was soon caught and cruelly punished in the impassable abatis. Sherman gallantly led his division on horseback, surrounded by his full staff, likewise mounted, but though the ground in his front was less difficult than that which Augur had to traverse, it was very exposed, and the for-

OPENING OF THE NAVAL ATTACK ON PORT HUDSON, MARCH 13, 1863.

mation was, moreover, broken by three parallel lines of fence. No progress was possible, and when night fell the result was that we had gained commanding positions, yet at a fearful cost.

The next day a regular siege was begun. Grover was assigned to the command of the right wing, embracing his own and Paine's divisions and Weitzel's brigade; while Dwight was given command of Sherman's division, raised to three brigades by transferring regiments. From left to right, from this time, the lines were held in the order of Dwight, Augur, Paine, Grover, and Weitzel.

On the 14th of June, time still pressing, the lines being everywhere well advanced, the enemy's artillery effectually controlled by ours, every available man having been brought up, and yet our force growing daily less by casualties and sickness, Taylor menacing our communications on the west bank of the Mississippi, and the issue of Grant's operations before Vicksburg in suspense, Banks ordered a second assault to be delivered simultaneously at daybreak on the left and center, preceded by a general cannonade of an hour's duration. Dwight's attack on the left was misdirected by its guides and soon came to naught. Paine attacked with great vigor at what proved to be the strongest point of the whole work, the priest-cap near the Jackson road. He himself almost instantly fell severely wounded at the head of his division, and this attack also ended in a disastrous repulse, our men being unable to cross the crest just in front of the work, forming a natural glacis so swept by the enemy's fire that in examining the position afterward I found this grass-crowned knoll shaved bald, every blade cut down to the roots as by a hoe.

Our loss in the two assaults was nearly 4000, including many of our best and bravest officers. The heat, especially in the trenches, became almost insupportable, the stenches quite so, the brooks dried up, the creek lost itself in the pestilential swamp, the springs gave out, and the river fell, exposing to the tropical sun a wide margin of festering ooze. The illness and mortality were enormous. The labor of the siege, extending over a front of seven miles, pressed so severely upon our numbers, far too weak for such an undertaking, that the men were almost incessantly on duty; and as the numbers for duty diminished, of course the work fell the more heavily upon those that remained. From first to last we had nearly 20,000 men of all arms engaged before Port Hudson, yet the effective strength of infantry and artillery at no time exceeded 13,000, and at the last hardly reached 9000, while even of these every other man might well have gone on the sick-report if pride and duty had not held him to his post.

Meanwhile Taylor with his forces, reorganized and reënforced until they again numbered four or five thousand, had crossed the Atchafalaya at Morgan's Ferry and Berwick Bay, surprised and captured the garrisons at Brashear City and Bayou Bœuf almost without resistance, menaced Donaldsonville, carried havoc and panic through the La Fourche, and finally planted batteries on the

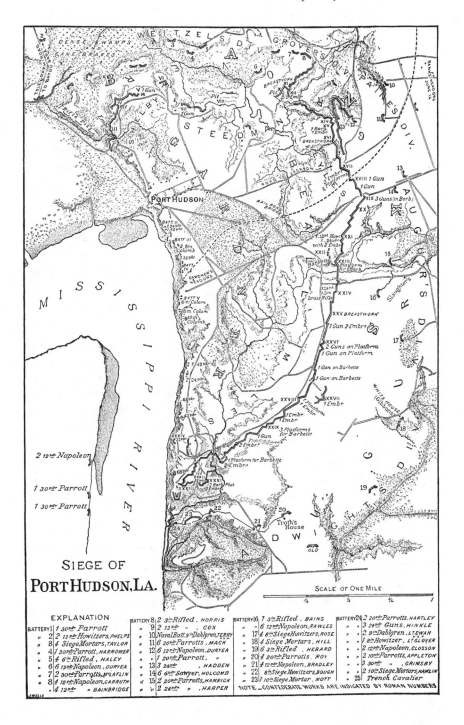

SIEGE OF
PORT HUDSON, LA.

SCALE OF ONE MILE

EXPLANATION

BATTERY		BATTERY		BATTERY		BATTERY	
1	1 30-pr Parrott	8	2 3-in Rifled, NORRIS	16	7 3-in Rifled, BAINS	24	2 20-pr Parrotts, HARTLEY
" 2	2 12-pr Howitzers, PHELPS	" 9	2 12-pr " , COX	" 17	6 12-pr Napoleon, RAWLES	"	3 24-pr Guns, HINKLE
" 3	4 Siege Mortars, TAYLOR	10	Naval Batt. 9-in Dahlgren, TERRY	18	8-in Siege Howitzers, ROSE	"	2 9-in Dahlgren, LT SWAN
" 4	1 30-pr Parrott, HARROWER	" 11	6 20-pr Parrotts, MACK	" 18	4 Siege Mortars, HILL	"	1 8-in Howitzer, LT GLOVER
" 5	4 6-in Rifled, HALEY	" 12	6 12-pr Napoleon, DURYEA	" 19	6 3-in Rifled, HEBARD	"	2 12-pr Napoleon, CLOSSON
" 6	6 12-pr Napoleon, DURYEA	"	1 20-pr Parrott, "	20	4 20-pr Parrotts, ROY	"	2 10-pr Parrotts, APPLETON
" 7	2 30-pr Parrotts, McLAFLIN	13	3 24-pr " , HADDEN	21	4 12-pr Napoleon, BRADLEY	"	3 30-pr " , GRIMSBY
" 8	4 12-pr Napoleon, CARRUTH	14	6 6-pr Sawyer, HOLCOMB	22	8-in Siege Howitzers, BOUGH	"	2 10-in Siege Mortars, HAMLIN
"	4 12-pr " BAINBRIDGE	" 15	2 20-pr Parrotts, HAMRICK	23	1 10-in Siege Mortar, MOTT	25	French Cavalier
		"	2 24-pr " , HARPER				

NOTE.—CONFEDERATE WORKS ARE INDICATED BY ROMAN NUMBERS

Mississippi to cut off our communication with New Orleans. At Donald-sonville, however, an assault by about 1500 Texans was repulsed by about 200 men, including convalescents, under Major J. D. Bullen, 28th Maine, ⁄ and at La Fourche Crossing Taylor's forces suffered another check at the hands of a de-tachment under Lieutenant-Colonel Albert Stickney, 47th Massachusetts. Oth-erwise Taylor, whose operations were conducted with marked skill and vigor, had everything his own way. In New Orleans great was the excitement when it was known that the Confederate forces were on the west bank within a few miles of the city; but fortunately the illness that had deprived Emory's division of its commander in the field had given New Orleans a commander of a courage and firmness that now, as always, rose with the approach of danger, with whom difficulties diminished as they drew near, and whose character had earned the respect of the inhabitants. Still by the 4th of July things were at such a pass that General Emory plainly told General Banks he must choose between Port Hudson and New Orleans. However, Banks was convinced that Port Hud-son must be in his hands within three days.

His confidence was justified. At last on the 7th of July, when the sap-head was within 16 feet of the priest-cap, and a storming party of 1000 volunteers had been organized, led by the intrepid Birge, and all preparations had been made for springing two heavily charged mines, word came from Grant that Vicksburg had surrendered. Instantly an aide was sent to the "general-of-the-trenches" bearing duplicates in "flimsy" of a note from the adjutant-general an-nouncing the good news. One of these he was directed to toss into the Confederate lines. Some one acknowledged the receipt by calling back, "That's another damned Yankee lie!" Once more the cheers of our men rang out as the word passed, and again the forest echoed with the strains of the "Star-spangled Banner" from the long-silent bands. Firing died away, the men began to mingle in spite of everything, and about 2 o'clock next morning came the long, gray envelope that meant *surrender.*

Formalities alone remained; these were long, but the articles were signed on the afternoon of the 8th; a moment later a long train of wagons loaded with rations for the famished garrison moved down the Clinton road, and on the morning of the 9th a picked force of eight regiments, under Brigadier-General George L. Andrews, marched in with bands playing and colors flying; the Con-federates stacked arms and hauled down their flag, and the National ensign floated in its stead. By General Banks's order, General Gardner's sword was re-turned to him in the presence of his men in recognition of the heroic defense—a worthy act, well merited.

⁄Aided by the gun-boats *Princess Royal,* Commander M. B. Woolsey, and *Winona,* Lieutenant-Commander A. W. Weaver.

But, stout as the defense had been, the besiegers had on their part displayed some of the highest qualities of the soldier; among these valor in attack, patient endurance of privation, suffering, and incredible toil, and perseverance under discouragement. And to defenders and besiegers it is alike unjust to say, even though it has been said by the highest authority, that Port Hudson surrendered only because Vicksburg had fallen. The simple truth is that Port Hudson surrendered because its hour had come. The garrison was literally starving. With less than 3000 famished men in line, powerful mines beneath the salients, and a last assault about to be delivered at 10 paces, what else was left to do?

With the post there fell into our hands 6340 prisoners, 20 heavy guns, 31 field-pieces, about 7500 muskets, and two river steamers.* Many of the guns were ruined, some had been struck over and over again, and the depots and magazines were empty. The garrison also lost about 500 prisoners or deserters before the surrender, and about 700 killed and wounded. Our loss was 707 killed, 3336 wounded, 319 missing,—total, 4362.

The army was greatly assisted by Admiral Farragut's fleet above and below Port Hudson, and directly by two fine batteries forming part of the siege-works, manned by seamen under Lieutenant-Commander Edward Terry.

While the ceremonies of capitulation were going on, Weitzel led Augur's division aboard the transports and hastened to Donaldsonville to drive Taylor out of the La Fourche. Grover followed. On the 13th, at Koch's plantation, Green and Major suddenly fell upon Weitzel's advance, composed of Dudley's brigade and Dwight's under Colonel Joseph S. Morgan, and handled them roughly. We lost 50 killed, 223 wounded, 186 missing,—total, 465,—as well as 2 guns, while Green's loss was 3 killed and 30 wounded. As the gun-boats could not be got round to Berwick Bay in time to cut off Taylor, he crossed Berwick Bay on the 21st with all his spoils that he could carry away and took post on the lower Teche, until in September the Nineteenth Corps, reorganized and placed under the command of Franklin, once more advanced into the Teche country and drove him back toward Opelousas.

After the fall of Vicksburg and Port Hudson, Grant sent Herron's division, and the Thirteenth Corps under Ord, to report to Banks. Banks went to Vicksburg to consult with Grant, and Grant came to New Orleans; together they agreed with Admiral Farragut in urging an immediate attack on Mobile. This was the only true policy; success would have been easy and must have influenced powerfully the later campaigns that centered about Chattanooga and At-

---

* *Starlight* and *Red Chief,* found aground in Thompson's Creek, floated and brought into the river by the ingenuity and skill of Major Joseph Bailey, 4th Wisconsin, whose success here led to its repetition on the Red River the next year, when Admiral Porter's fleet was rescued.—R.B.I.

THE BAGGAGE TRAIN OF GENERAL AUGUR'S DIVISION CROSSING BAYOU MONTECINO
ON THE MARCH TO PORT HUDSON. FROM A SKETCH MADE AT THE TIME.

lanta; but for reasons avowedly political rather than military, the Government ordered, instead, an attempt to "plant the flag at some point in Texas." The unaccountable failure at Sabine Pass followed,‡ then the occupation of the Texan coast by the Thirteenth Corps. So the favorable moment passed and 1863 wore away.

‡In September a detachment of the Nineteenth Corps, under Franklin, convoyed by the navy, was sent by sea to effect a landing at Sabine Pass, and thence operate against Houston and Galveston; but the gun-boats meeting with a disaster in an encounter with the Confederate batteries, the expedition returned to New Orleans without having accomplished anything.—R.B.I.

CHAPTER 11

CHICKAMAUGA–THE GREAT BATTLE
OF THE WEST.‡

Daniel H. Hill, Lieutenant-General, C.S.A.

On the 13th of July, 1863, while in charge of the defenses of Richmond and Pe-tersburg and the Department of North Carolina, I received an unexpected order to go West. I was seated in a yard of a house in the suburbs of Richmond (the house belonging to Mr. Poe, a relative of the poet), when President Davis, dressed in a plain suit of gray and attended by a small escort in brilliant uni-form, galloped up and said: "Rosecrans is about to advance upon Bragg; I have found it necessary to detail Hardee to defend Mississippi and Alabama. His corps is without a commander. I wish you to command it." "I cannot do that," I replied, "as General Stewart ranks me." "I can cure that," answered Mr. Davis, "by making you a lieutenant-general. Your papers will be ready to-morrow. When can you start?" "In twenty-four hours," was the reply. Mr. Davis gave his views on the subject, some directions in regard to matters at Chattanooga, and then left in seemingly good spirits.✤

‡At the beginning of the Civil War I was asked the question, "Who of the Federal officers are most to be feared?" I replied: "Sherman, Rosecrans, and McClellan. Sherman has genius and daring, and is full of resources. Rosecrans has fine practical sense, and is of a tough, tenacious fiber. McClellan is a man of tal-ents, and his delight has always been in the study of military history and the art and science of war." Grant was not once thought of. The light of subsequent events thrown upon the careers of these three great soldiers has not changed my estimate of them; but I acquiesce in the verdict which has given greater renown to some of their comrades. It was my lot to form a more intimate acquaintance with the three illustrious officers who I foresaw would play an important part in the war. I fought against McClel-lan from Yorktown to Sharpsburg (Antietam), I encountered Rosecrans at Chickamauga, and I surren-dered to Sherman at Greensboro, N.C.—each of the three commanding an army.—D.H.H.

✤His cheerfulness was a mystery to me. Within a fortnight the Pennsylvania campaign had proved abortive. Vicksburg and Port Hudson had fallen, and Federal gun-boats were now plying up and down the Mississippi, cutting our communications between the east and west. The Confederacy was cut in two, and the South could readily be beaten in detail by the concentration of Federal forces, first on one side of the Mississippi and then on the other. The end of our glorious dream could not be far off. But I was as cheerful at that interview as was Mr. Davis himself. The bitterness of death had passed with me

CONFEDERATE LINE OF BATTLE IN THE CHICKAMAUGA WOODS.

The condition of our railroads even in 1863 was wretched, so bad that my staff and myself concluded to leave our horses in Virginia and resupply ourselves in Atlanta. On the 19th of July I reported to General Bragg at Chattanooga. I had not seen him since I had been the junior lieutenant in his battery of artillery at Corpus Christi, Texas, in 1845. The other two lieutenants were George H. Thomas and John F. Reynolds. We four had been in the same mess there. Reynolds had been killed at Gettysburg twelve days before my new assignment. Thomas, the strongest and most pronounced Southerner of the four, was now Rosecrans's lieutenant. It was a strange casting of lots that three messmates of Corpus Christi should meet under such changed circumstances at Chickamauga.

My interview with General Bragg at Chattanooga was not satisfactory. He was silent and reserved and seemed gloomy and despondent. He had grown prematurely old since I saw him last, and showed much nervousness. His relations with his next in command (General Polk) and with some others of his

before our great reverses on the 4th of July. The Federals had been stunned by the defeat at Chancellorsville, and probably would not have made a forward movement for months. A corps could have been sent to General Joe Johnston, Grant could have been crushed, and Vicksburg, "the heart of the Confederacy," could have been saved. The drums that beat for the advance into Pennsylvania seemed to many of us to be beating the funeral march of the dead Confederacy. Our thirty days of mourning were over before the defeat of Lee and Pemberton. Duty, however, was to be done faithfully and unflinchingly to the last. The calmness of our Confederate President may not have been the calmness of despair, but it may have risen from the belief, then very prevalent, that England and France would recognize the Confederacy at its last extremity, when the Northern and Southern belligerents were both exhausted. Should the North triumph, France could not hope to retain her hold upon Mexico. Besides, the English aristocracy, as is well known, were in full sympathy with the South.—D.H.H.

subordinates were known not to be pleasant. His many retreats, too, had alienated the rank and file from him, or at least had taken away that enthusiasm which soldiers feel for the successful general, and which makes them obey his orders without question, and thus wins for him other successes. The one thing that a soldier never fails to understand is victory, and the commander who leads him to victory will be adored by him whether that victory has been won by skill or by blundering, by the masterly handling of a few troops against great odds, or by the awkward use of overwhelming numbers. Long before Stonewall Jackson had risen to the height of his great fame, he had won the implicit confidence of his troops in all his movements. "Where are you going?" one inquired of the "foot cavalry" as they were making the usual stealthy march to the enemy's rear. "We don't know, but old Jack does," was the laughing answer. This trust was the fruit of past victories, and it led to other and greater achievements.

I was assigned to Hardee's old corps, consisting of Cleburne's and Stewart's divisions, and made my headquarters at Tyner's Station, a few miles east of Chattanooga on the Knoxville railroad. The Federals soon made their appearance at Bridgeport, Alabama, and I made arrangements to guard the crossings of the Tennessee north of Chattanooga.✦ On Fast Day, August 21st, while religious services were being held in town, the enemy appeared on the opposite side of the river and began throwing shells into the houses.✸ Rev. B. M. Palmer, D.D., of New Orleans, was in the act of prayer when a shell came hissing near the church. He went on calmly with his petition to the Great Being "who rules in the armies of heaven and among the inhabitants of earth," but at its close, the preacher, opening his eyes, noticed a perceptible diminution of his congregation. Some women and children were killed and wounded by the shelling. Our pickets and scouts had given no notice of the approach of the enemy. On Sunday, August 30th, we learned through a citizen that McCook's corps had crossed at Caperton's Ferry, some thirty-five miles below Chattanooga, the movement having begun on the 29th. Thomas's corps was also crossing at or near the same point.

The want of information at General Bragg's headquarters was in striking contrast with the minute knowledge General Lee always had of every operation in his front, and I was most painfully impressed with the feeling that it was

---

✦A regiment was placed at Sivley's Ford, another at Blythe's Ferry, farther north, and S.A.M. Wood's brigade was quartered at Harrison, in supporting distance of either point. The railroad upon which Rosecrans depended for his supplies ran south of Chattanooga, and had he crossed the river above the town he would have been separated many miles from his base and his depot. But he probably contemplated throwing a column across the Tennessee to the north of the town to cut off Buckner at Knoxville from a junction with Bragg, and inclose him between that column and the forces of Burnside which were pressing toward Knoxville.—D.H.H.

Buckner's division was promptly withdrawn south of the Hiawassee.—EDITORS.

✸Colonel J. T. Wilder, who led the reconnoissance, says: "The enemy opened fire upon the command from their batteries, which was replied to by Captain Lilly's 18th Indiana battery."—EDITORS.

to be a hap-hazard campaign on our part./ Rosecrans had effected the crossing of the river (Thomas's corps) and had occupied Will's Valley, between Sand and Lookout mountains, without opposition, and had established his headquarters at Trenton. Lookout Mountain now interposed to screen all the enemy's movements from our observation.☆

On the 7th of September Rosecrans sent McCook to cross Lookout Mountain at Winston's Gap, forty-six miles south of Chattanooga, and to occupy Alpine, east of the mountains. Thomas was ordered to cross the mountain at Stevens's and Cooper's gaps, some twenty-five miles from Chattanooga, and to occupy McLemore's Cove on the east, a narrow valley between Lookout and Pigeon mountains. Pigeon Mountain is parallel to the former, not so high and rugged, and does not extend so far north, ending eight miles south of Chattanooga. Crittenden was left in Will's Valley to watch Chattanooga.

General Bragg had had some inclosed works constructed at Chattanooga, and the place could have been held by a division against greatly superior forces. By holding Chattanooga in that way, Crittenden's corps would have been neutralized, and a union between Rosecrans and Burnside would have been impossible. Moreover, the town was the objective point of the campaign, and to lose it was virtually to lose all east Tennessee south of Knoxville. If Bragg knew at the time of the prospective help coming to him from the Army of Northern Virginia, it was of still more importance to hold the town, that he might be the more readily in communication with Longstreet on his arrival. Under similar circumstances General Lee detached Early's division to hold the heights of Fredericksburg, and neutralized Sedgwick's corps, while he marched to attack Hooker at Chancellorsville. Bragg, however, may have felt too weak to spare even one division from his command. Whatever may have been his motive, he completely abandoned the town by the 8th, and Crittenden took possession of it next day. My corps,‡ consisting of Breckinridge's and Cleburne's divisions, had led in the withdrawal, and was halted at Lafayette, twenty-two miles from, and almost south of, Chattanooga, and east of Pigeon Mountain, which separates it from McLemore's Cove, into which the columns of Thomas began to

/My sympathies had all been with Bragg. I knew of the carping criticisms of his subordinates and the cold looks of his soldiers, and knew that these were the natural results of reverses, whether the blame lay with the commander or otherwise. I had felt, too, that this lack of confidence or lack of enthusiasm, whichever it might be, was ominous of evil for the impending battle. But ignorance of the enemy's movements seemed a still worse portent of calamity.—D.H.H.

☆General Bragg had said petulantly a few days before the crossing into Will's Valley: "It is said to be easy to defend a mountainous country, but mountains hide your foe from you, while they are full of gaps through which he can pounce upon you at any time. A mountain is like the wall of a house full of rat-holes. The rat lies hidden at his hole, ready to pop out when no one is watching. Who can tell what lies hidden behind that wall?" said he, pointing to the Cumberland range across the river.—D.H.H.

‡Breckinridge's division of my corps had come up from Mississippi and was substituted for Stewart's, sent to Knoxville to join Buckner.—D.H.H.

pour on the 9th. I placed Breckinridge in charge of the Reserve Artillery and the wagon-train at Lafayette, while Cleburne was sent to hold the three gaps in Pigeon Mountain, Catlett's on the north, Dug in the center, and Blue Bird on the south. Cleburne pitched his tent by the road leading to the center gap. Notwithstanding the occupation of Chattanooga, Rosecrans did not attempt to concentrate his forces there, but persisted in pushing two of his corps to our left and rear.

As the failure of Bragg to beat Rosecrans in detail has been the subject of much criticism, it may be well to look into the causes of the failure. So far as the commanding general was concerned, the trouble with him was: first, lack of knowledge of the situation; second, lack of personal supervision of the execution of his orders. No general ever won a permanent fame who was wanting in these grand elements of success, knowledge of his own and his enemy's condition, and personal superintendence of operations on the field.[*]

The failure to attack Negley's division in the cove on September 10th[†] was owing to Bragg's ignorance of the condition of the roads, the obstructions at Dug Gap, and the position of the enemy. He attributed the failure to make the attack on the same force on the 11th to the major-general [Hindman] who had it in charge,—whether justly or unjustly, I do not know.[‡] All day of the 11th my signal corps and scouts at Blue Bird Gap reported the march of a heavy column to our left and up the cove. These reports were forwarded to the commanding general, but were not credited by him.

On the morning of the 13th I was notified that Polk was to attack Crittenden at Lee and Gordon's Mills, and the Reserve Artillery and baggage trains

---

[*]Invidious critics have attributed many of Stonewall Jackson's successes to lucky blunders, or at best to happy inspirations at the moment of striking. Never was there a greater mistake. He studied carefully (shall I add prayerfully?) all his own and his adversary's movements. He knew the situation perfectly, the geography and the topography of the country, the character of the officers opposed to him, the number and material of his troops. He never joined battle without a thorough personal reconnoissance of the field. That duty he trusted to no engineer officer. When the time came for him to act, he was in the front to see that his orders were carried out, or were modified to suit the ever-shifting scenes of battle. —D.H.H.

[†]Thomas's corps, after crossing at Bridgeport, Shell Mound, and Caperton's Ferry, arrived, September 4th, near Trenton, in Will's Valley (east of Sand Mountain). On the 6th Negley's division, with Baird's supporting, reached Johnson's Crook, and on the 10th crossed Missionary Ridge into McLemore's Cove. On the 11th Negley and Baird retired to Stevens's Gap after feeling the enemy in front of Dug Gap, in Pigeon Mountain. Meantime Davis's and Johnson's divisions of McCook's corps crossing the Tennessee at Caperton's Ferry passed over Sand Mountain and seized Winston's Gap, while Sheridan's division, moving via Trenton, was close at hand. On the 10th McCook's three divisions were at Alpine. Crittenden's corps by September 4th was across the Tennessee (at Bridgeport, Shell Mound, and Battle Creek). On the 9th Wood's division occupied Chattanooga, and Palmer and Van Cleve marched to Rossville. On the 10th Crittenden, leaving Wagner's brigade to occupy Chattanooga, pursued the enemy toward Dalton and Ringgold. Wood reached Lee and Gordon's Mills on the 11th, and Crittenden was now ordered to close up his whole force on Wood.—EDITORS.

[‡]The Comte de Paris states that Bragg sent word to Hindman, at 11 A.M. September 11th, to retire if he deemed it not prudent to attack.—EDITORS.

were specially intrusted to my corps. Breckinridge guarded the roads leading south from Lafayette, and Cleburne guarded the gaps in Pigeon Mountain. The attack was not made at Lee and Gordon's Mills, and this was the second of the lost opportunities. Bragg in his official report, speaking of this failure, quotes his first order to Polk to attack, dated 6 P.M. September 12th, Lafayette, Ga.:

> "GENERAL: I inclose you a dispatch from General Pegram. This presents you a fine opportunity of striking Crittenden in detail, and I hope you will avail yourself of it at daylight to-morrow. This division crushed, and the others are yours. We can then turn again on the force in the cove. Wheeler's cavalry will move on Wilder so as to cover your right. I shall be delighted to hear of your success."

This order was twice repeated at short intervals, the last dispatch being:

> "The enemy is approaching from the south—and it is highly important that your attack in the morning should be quick and decided. Let no time be lost."

The rest of the story is thus told by General Bragg:

> "At 11 P.M. a dispatch was received from the general [Polk] stating that he had taken up a strong position for defense, and requesting that he should be heavily reënforced. He was promptly ordered not to defer his attack,— his force being already numerically superior to the enemy,—and was reminded that his success depended upon the promptness and rapidity of his movements. He was further informed that Buckner's corps would be moved within supporting distance the next morning. Early on the 13th I proceeded to the front, ahead of Buckner's command, to find that no advance had been made upon the enemy and that his forces [the enemy's] had formed a junction and recrossed the Chickamauga. Again disappointed, immediate measures were taken to place our trains and limited supplies in safe positions,

ALEXANDER'S BRIDGE FROM THE CONFEDERATE SIDE OF THE CHICKAMAUGA LOOKING UPSTREAM.
FROM A PHOTOGRAPH TAKEN IN 1884.

when all our forces were concentrated along the Chickamauga threatening the enemy in front."

During the active operations of a campaign the post of the commander-in-chief should be in the center of his marching columns, that he may be able to give prompt and efficient aid to whichever wing may be threatened. But whenever a great battle is to be fought, the commander must be on the field to see that his orders are executed and to take advantage of the ever-changing phases of the conflict. Jackson leading a cavalry fight by night near Front Royal in the pursuit of Banks, Jackson at the head of the column following McClellan in the retreat from Richmond to Malvern Hill, presents a contrast to Bragg sending, from a distance of ten miles, four consecutive orders for an attack at daylight, which he was never to witness.

Surely in the annals of warfare there is no parallel to the coolness and nonchalance with which General Crittenden marched and counter-marched for a week with a delightful unconsciousness that he was in the presence of a force of superior strength. On the 11th we find him with two divisions (Van Cleve's and Palmer's) at Ringgold, twenty miles from Chattanooga, and with his third (Thomas J. Wood's), ten miles from Ringgold, at Lee and Gordon's Mills, where it remained alone and unsupported, until late in the day of the 12th. Crittenden was at the mills with his whole corps on the 13th and morning of the 14th, moving back to Missionary Ridge during the 14th all his divisions except Wood's, which remained all that day. Crittenden seemed to think that so long as the bridge there was held, there was no danger of the rebels passing to his rear on the road toward Chattanooga, though there were other bridges and several good fords over the Chickamauga at other points. It was to the isolation of Wood that Bragg refers in his order dated Lafayette, 6 P.M., on the 12th. Captain Polk (in the Southern Historical Society papers) says:

> "General Bragg, in his official report of the battle of Chickamauga, charges General Polk with the failure to crush Crittenden's forces in their isolated position at Ringgold. It will be noted, however, that General Polk was ordered to take position at a particular spot,—Rock Spring,—thence, if not attacked, to advance by daylight of the 13th of September, and assume the offensive against the opposing forces, which were expected from the way of Ringgold. But Crittenden was at Gordon's Mills behind the Chickamauga on the evening of the 12th. The order was simply impracticable."

The concentration at Rock Spring, seven miles south-west from Ringgold and four and a half miles south-east from Lee and Gordon's Mills, was apparently to interpose between Crittenden's columns, and to strike in detail whichever should present itself. But General Crittenden, unaware, apparently, of his danger, crossed the Chickamauga at the mills, and united with Wood about nightfall on the 12th. General Polk discovered that there was a large force in front of him on the night of the 12th, and not a single division, and hence he thought only of a defensive attitude. It is probable that, from his long experience of Bragg's ignorance of the situation, he was skeptical in regard to the accuracy of the general's information on the present occasion. Bragg certainly did not know of the union of Crittenden's forces in the afternoon and night of the 12th. But, even with that knowledge, he would have acted wisely in falling upon the combined forces on the 13th and 14th.

The truth is, General Bragg was bewildered by "the popping out of the rats from so many holes." The wide dispersion of the Federal forces, and their confrontal of him at so many points, perplexed him, instead of being a source of congratulation that such grand opportunities were offered for crushing them one by one. He seems to have had no well-organized system of independent scouts, such as Lee had, and such as proved of inestimable service to the Germans in the Franco-Prussian war. For information in regard to the enemy, apparently he trusted alone to his very efficient cavalry. But the Federal cavalry moved with infantry supports, which could not be brushed aside by our cavalry. So General Bragg only learned that he was encircled by foes, without knowing who they were, what was their strength, and what were their plans. His enemy had a great advantage over him in this respect. The negroes knew the country well, and by dividing the numbers given by them by three, trustworthy information could be obtained. The waning fortunes of the Confederacy were developing a vast amount of "latent unionism" in the breasts of the original secessionists—those fiery zealots who in '61 proclaimed that "one Southerner could whip three Yankees." The negroes and the fire-eaters with "changed hearts" were now most excellent spies.

The 13th of September was a day of great anxiety to me at Lafayette, in charge of the Reserve Artillery and the wagons trains, with only two weak divisions, less than nine thousand strong, to protect them. During the 11th and 12th my signal corps on Pigeon Mountain had been constantly reporting the march of a heavy column to our left and rear. These reports were communicated by me to the commanding general, and were discredited by him. At 8 A.M. on the 13th Lieutenant Baylor came to my camp with a note from General Wharton, of the cavalry, vouching for the lieutenant's entire trustworthiness. Lieutenant Baylor told me that McCook had encamped the night before at Alpine, twenty miles from Lafayette, toward which his march was directed. Our cavalry pickets had been driven in on the Alpine road the afternoon before, and had been replaced by infantry. Soon after the report by Lieutenant Baylor, a brisk fire opened upon the Alpine road, two miles from Lafayette. I said to my staff, as we galloped toward the firing, "It is to be South Mountain over again." This referred to the defense, on the 14th of September, 1862, of the passes of that mountain by my gallant division, reduced by fighting and marching to five thousand men. We learned, on reaching the Alpine road, that General Daniel Adams's skirmishers had been attacked by two regiments of cavalry, which were repulsed. General Adams said to me, "The boldness of the cavalry advance convinces me that an infantry column is not far off." Lucius Polk's brigade was brought down from Pigeon Mountain, and every disposition was made to celebrate appropriately the next day—the anniversary of South Mountain. But that was not to be. General McCook (Federal) had been ordered to Summerville, eleven miles south of Lafayette on the main road to Rome, Ga. But he had become cautious after hearing that Bragg was not making the hot and hasty retreat that Rosecrans had supposed. He therefore ordered his wagon-train back to the top of Lookout Mountain, and remained all day of the 13th at Alpine. His cavalry had taken some prisoners from General Adams, and he thus learned certainly that Bragg had been reënforced. At midnight on the 13th McCook received the order to hurry back to join Thomas [in McLemore's Cove]. Then began the race of life and death, the crossing back over Lookout Mountain, the rapid exhausting march north through Lookout Valley, and the junction at last at Stevens's Gap on the 17th. The contemporary accounts represent McCook's march as one of fatigue and suffering.

General Bragg returned to Lafayette on the afternoon of the 13th, and I communicated to him verbally that night the report of Lieutenant Baylor. He replied excitedly, "Lieutenant Baylor lies. There is not an infantry soldier of the enemy south of us." The next morning he called his four corps commanders, Polk, Buckner, W.H.T. Walker, and myself, together, and told us that McCook was at Alpine, Crittenden at Lee and Gordon's Mills, and Thomas in McLemore's Cove. McCook was at that very time making that famous march, estimated by Rosecrans at fifty-seven miles, to join Thomas at Stevens's Gap. But the Confederate commander did not know of this withdrawal, and possibly the fear of an attack in his rear by McCook kept him from falling upon Thomas and Crittenden in his front. The nightmare upon Bragg for the next three days was due, doubtless, to his uncertainty about the movements of his enemy, and to the certainty that there was not that mutual confidence between him and some of his subordinates that there ought to be between a chief and his officers to insure victory. Bragg's want of definite and precise information had led him more than once to issue "impossible" orders, and therefore those intrusted with their execution got in the way of disregarding them. Another more serious trouble with him was the disposition to find a scapegoat for every failure and disaster. This made his officers cautious about

striking a blow when an opportunity presented itself, unless they were protected by a positive order. ╱

In reference to the long intervals between battles in the West, I once said to
General Patton Anderson, "When two armies confront each other in the East,
they get to work very soon; but here you look at one another for days and weeks
at a time." He replied with a laugh, "Oh, we out here have to crow and peck
straws awhile before we use our spurs." The crowing and pecking straws were
now about over. On the 13th Rosecrans awoke from his delusion that Bragg was
making a disorderly retreat, and issued his orders for the concentration of his
army in McLemore's Cove. Granger's corps came up from Bridgeport, occupied Rossville on the 14th, and remained there until the battle of the 20th.
Rossville is at the gap in Missionary Ridge through which runs the road from
Chattanooga to Lafayette and Rome, Ga. General Rosecrans had felt it to be of
vital importance to hold this gap at all hazards, in case of a disaster to his arms.
On the 16th Rosecrans had his forces well in hand, extending from Lee and
Gordon's Mills to Stevens's Gap, in a line running from east to south-west some
eleven miles long. On the same day Bragg, with headquarters still at Lafayette,
held the gaps in Pigeon Mountain, and the fords to Lee and Gordon's Mills.
Each commander was in position, on the 17th, to turn the left flank of his
adversary,—Bragg by crossing the Chickamauga at points north of Lee and
Gordon's Mills; but by this he risked fighting with his back to the river,—a hazardous situation in case of defeat. He risked too, to some extent, his trains,
which had yet to be moved toward Ringgold and Dalton. His gain, in case of a
decided victory, would be the cutting off of Rosecrans from Chattanooga, and
possibly the recapture of that place. Rosecrans could have flanked Bragg by
crossing at the Mills and at the fords between that place and Catlett's. This
would have cut off Bragg from Rome certainly, and from Dalton in case of his
advance upon Chattanooga, or else would have compelled him to come out and
fight upon ground selected by his antagonist. The risk to Rosecrans was an in-
secure line of retreat in case of defeat, and possibly the loss of Chattanooga. But
he had Granger's corps to hold the fortifications of Chattanooga, and he held
also the gaps in Lookout Mountain. Bragg showed superior boldness by taking
the initiative. Rosecrans determined to act upon the defensive. He says that he
knew on the 17th that Bragg would try to seize the Dry Valley and Rossville
roads—the first on the west and the second on the east of Missionary Ridge. He
thus divined the plan of his enemy twelve hours before Bragg's order was issued. Therefore Rosecrans, on the afternoon of the 17th, ordered McCook to
take the place of Thomas at Pond Spring, Thomas to relieve the two divisions

---

╱General Lee sought for no vicarious victim to atone for his *one* disaster. "I alone am to blame; the order
for attack was mine," said he, after the repulse of the assault upon Cemetery Ridge at Gettysburg. Lee
and Bragg were cast in different molds.—D.H.H.

of Crittenden at Crawfish Springs, and Crittenden to take these divisions and extend them to the left of Wood at Lee and Gordon's, so as to protect the road to Chattanooga. McCook's corps reached its position at dark, Crittenden's near midnight. Thomas marched all night uninterruptedly, and the head of his columns reached the Widow Glenn's (Rosecrans's headquarters) at daylight on the 19th.

On the 18th Bragg issued, from Leet's tan-yard, his order for battle:

"1. [Bushrod] Johnson's column (Hood's), on crossing at or near Reed's Bridge, will turn to the left by the most practicable route, and sweep up the Chickamauga toward Lee and Gordon's Mills.

"2. Walker, crossing at Alexander's Bridge, will unite in this move and push vigorously on the enemy's flank and rear in the same direction.

"3. Buckner, crossing at Tedford's Ford, will join in the movement to the left, and press the enemy up the stream from Polk's front at Lee and Gordon's.

"4. Polk will press his forces to the front of Lee and Gordon's Mills, and if met by too much resistance to cross will bear to the right and cross at Dalton's Ford or at Tedford's, as may be necessary, and join the attack wherever the enemy may be.

"5. Hill will cover our left flank from an advance of the enemy from the cove, and, by pressing the cavalry in his front, ascertain if the enemy is reënforcing at Lee and Gordon's Mills, in which event he will attack them in flank.

"6. Wheeler's cavalry will hold the gaps in Pigeon Mountain, and cover our rear and left, and bring up stragglers.

"7. All teams, etc., not with troops should go toward Ringgold and Dalton beyond Taylor's Ridge. All cooking should be done at the trains; rations when cooked will be forwarded to the troops.

"8. The above movement will be executed with the utmost promptness, vigor, and persistence."

Had this order been issued on any of the four preceding days, it would have found Rosecrans wholly unprepared for it, with but a single infantry division (Wood's) guarding the crossings of the Chickamauga, and that at one point only, Lee and Gordon's—the fords north of it being watched by cavalry. Even if the order had been given twenty-four hours earlier, it must have been fatal to Rosecrans in the then huddled and confused grouping of his forces.

All that was effected on the 18th was the sending over of Walker's small corps of a little more than 5000 men near Alexander's Bridge, and Bushrod Johnson's division of 3600 men at Reed's Bridge, farther north. These troops drove off Wilder's mounted infantry from the crossings immediately south of

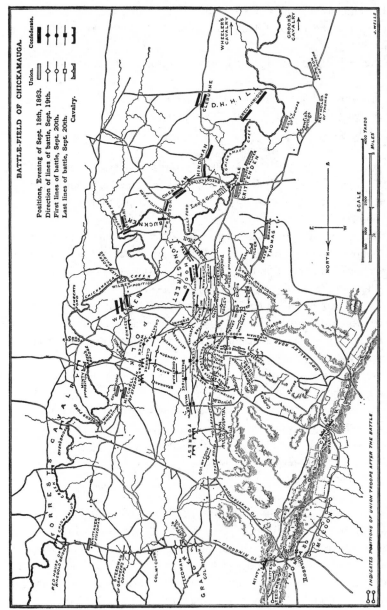

BATTLE-FIELD OF CHICKAMAUGA.

Positions, Evening of Sept. 18th, 1863.
Direction of lines of battle, Sept. 19th.
First lines of battle, Sept. 20th.
Last lines of battle, Sept. 20th.

Confederate.

Union.

Cavalry.

INDICATES POSITIONS OF UNION TROOPS AFTER THE BATTLE

THIS MAP IS BASED UPON THE OFFICIAL REPORTS, THE OFFICIAL TOPOGRAPHICAL MAP COMPILED BY EDWARD RUGER
UNDER THE DIRECTION OF COLONEL W. E. MERRILL, CHIEF ENGINEER DEPARTMENT OF THE CUMBERLAND,
AND THE MAPS OF CAPTAIN WALTER J. MORRIS OF GENERAL LEONIDAS POLK'S STAFF.—EDITORS.

them, so as to leave undisputed passage for Bragg's infantry, except in the neighborhood of Lee and Gordon's. On the night of the 18th Bragg's troops were substantially as follows: Hill's corps on the extreme left, with center at Glass's Mill; Polk's at Lee and Gordon's; Buckner's at Byram's Ford; Hood's at Tedford's Ford.☆ During the night Cheatham's division of Polk's corps was detached, moved down the Chickamauga, and crossed at Hunt's Ford about 7 A.M. on the 19th. On that morning the Federal line of battle ran, in the main, parallel to the Chattanooga road from Lee and Gordon's to beyond Kelly's farm, and consisted of the divisions of Wood, Van Cleve, and Palmer of Crittenden's corps, and Baird's and Brannan's of Thomas's corps, in the order named from right to left. Negley and Reynolds, commanders under Thomas, had not come up at the opening of the battle of the 19th. The leading division (R. W. Johnson's) of McCook's corps reached Crawfish Springs at an early hour that day, and the divisions of Davis and Sheridan soon followed. It is about five miles from Crawfish Springs to Kelly's farm.

Soon after getting into position at Kelly's after his night march, General Thomas was told by Colonel Daniel McCook, commanding a brigade of the Reserve Corps, that there were no rebel troops west of the Chickamauga, except one brigade that had crossed at Reed's Bridge the afternoon before, and which could easily be captured, as he (McCook) had burned the bridge behind the rebels. Thomas ordered Brannan to take two brigades and make a reconnoissance on the road to Reed's Bridge, and place a third brigade on the road to Alexander's Bridge. This order took the initiative away from Bragg, and put it in the hands of Thomas with his two divisions in line to crush the small Confederate force west of the river, and then with *his* supports, as they came, beat, in detail, the *Confederate* supports, delayed, as they must be, by the crossings and the distances to march. Croxton's brigade, of Brannan's division, met Forrest's cavalry on the Reed's Bridge road, and drove it back on the infantry—two small brigades under Ector and Wilson. These advanced with the "rebel yell," pushed Croxton back, and ran over his battery, but were in turn beaten back by Brannan's and Baird's forces. Baird now began the readjustment of his lines, and during the confusion of the movement Liddell's (Confederate) division, two thousand strong, struck the brigades of Scribner and King, and drove them in disorder, capturing Loomis's battery, commanded by Lieutenant Van Pelt. Bush's Indiana battery was captured at the same time. The defeat had become a panic, and Baird's and Brannan's men were going pell-mell to the rear, when the victorious Liddell found himself in the presence of a long line of Federal troops overlapping both flanks of his little force. These were the troops of Brannan's reorganized division on his right, and of the freshly arrived division of

---

☆Hood's division, about 5000, was the only part of Longstreet's corps in the action of the 19th.
　　　　　　　　　　　　　　　　　　　　　　　　　　　　　　　　—D.H.H.

R. W. Johnson from McCook. Liddell extricated himself skillfully, losing heavily, however, and being compelled to abandon his captured guns. It was by Rosecrans's own order, at 10:15 A.M., that R. W. Johnson had been hurried forward five miles from Crawfish Springs, just in time to save the Federal left from a grave disaster. At 11 A.M. Bragg ordered Cheatham to the relief of Liddell, but he reached the ground after Johnson—too late to drive Brannan as well as Baird off the field. Cheatham's veteran division of seven thousand men advanced gallantly, driving the enemy before it, when it was in its turn hurled back by an attacking column which Thomas had organized after the defeat of Liddell and the arrival of two fresh divisions, viz., Palmer's of Crittenden's corps and Reynolds, of his own corps.

Unfortunately for the Confederates, there was no general advance, as there might have been along the whole line—an advance that must have given a more decisive victory on the 19th than was gained on the 20th. It was desultory fighting from right to left, without concert, and at inopportune times. It was the sparring of the amateur boxer, and not the crushing blows of the trained pugilist. From daylight on the 19th until after midday, there was a gap of two miles between Crittenden and Thomas, into which the Confederates could have poured, turning to right or left, and attacking in flank whichever commander was least prepared for the assault. As Cheatham was falling back, A. P. Stewart's division of Buckner's corps, 3400 strong, attacked Palmer's division of Crittenden's corps, which was flanking Cheatham, drove it back, and marching forward met Van Cleve's division of the same corps hastening to the assistance of Thomas, and hurled it back also. Hood, with his own division and Bushrod Johnson's, moved at 2:30 P.M., and gained for a time a most brilliant success, crushing the right center of the Federal army, capturing artillery, and seizing the Chattanooga road. The three Confederate divisions, after their first triumphs, had to encounter the four fresh divisions of Wood, Davis, Sheridan, and Negley, and were in turn driven back to the east of the road.

Stewart had recaptured the battery lost by Cheatham's division, twelve pieces of Federal artillery, over two hundred prisoners, and several hundred rifles. Hood and Bushrod Johnson had met with a similar success at first, but, of course, three divisions could not stand the combined attack of six.

On our extreme left a good deal of demonstrating had been done by the Federals on the 17th and 18th; infantry had been crossed over at Owen's Ford, and threats made at Glass's Mill. On the 19th I ordered an attack at the latter place. Slocomb's battery had a bloody artillery duel with one on the west of the river, and, under cover of the artillery fire, Helm's brigade of Breckinridge's division was crossed over, and attacked Negley's infantry and drove it off. Riding over the ground with Breckinridge, I counted eleven dead horses at the Federal battery, and a number of dead infantrymen that had not been removed. The clouds of dust rolling down the valley revealed the precipitate retirement of the foe, not on account of our pressure upon him, but on account of the urgency of the order to hurry to their left. This was the time to have relieved the strain upon our right by attacking the Federal right at Lee and Gordon's. My veteran corps, under its heroic division commanders, Breckinridge and Cleburne, would have flanked the enemy out of his fortifications at this point, and would by their brilliant onset have confounded Rosecrans in his purpose of massing upon his left; but Bragg had other plans.‡

At 3 p.m. I received an order to report to the commander-in-chief at Tedford's Ford, to set Cleburne's division in motion to the same point, and to relieve Hindman at Gordon's with Breckinridge's division. Cleburne had six miles to march over a road much obstructed with wagons, artillery, and details of soldiers. He got into position on the extreme right after sundown. Thomas had, in the meanwhile, moved Brannan from his left to his right, and was retiring Baird and R. W. Johnson to a better position, when Cleburne, with Cheatham upon his left, moved upon them "in the gloaming" in magnificent style, capturing three pieces of artillery, a number of caissons, two stand of colors, and three hundred prisoners. The contest was obstinate, for a time, on our left, where log breastworks were encountered; and here that fine soldier, Brigadier-General Preston Smith, of Cheatham's division, lost his life. Discovering that our right extended beyond the enemy, I threw two batteries in advance of our fighting line and almost abreast of that of the enemy. These caused a hasty abandonment of the breastworks and a falling back of some half a mile. This ended the contest for the day.

General Rosecrans made a very natural mistake about our overwhelming numbers. But it *was* a big mistake. The South, from patriotic pride, still kept up its old military organizations, for how could it merge together divisions and brigades around which clustered such glorious memories? But the waste of war had reduced them to mere skeleton divisions and brigades. My corps at Chickamauga was but little more than one-third of the size of my division at Yorktown, and so it was through the whole Southern army. Captain W. M. Polk, from data furnished him by General Marcus J. Wright, has given an estimate of the numbers in the respective corps and divisions of the two armies; he concludes that the Federals had 45,855 and the Confederates 33,897 in the battle of the 19th.

I witnessed some of the heaviest fighting on the afternoon of the 19th, and never saw so little straggling from the field. I saw but one deserter from Hood's ranks, and not one from Cleburne's. The divisions of Hindman, Breckinridge, and Preston had not been put into the fight, and two brigades of McLaws's

---

‡The great commander is he who makes his antagonist keep step with him. Thomas, like the grand soldier he was, by attacking first, made Bragg keep step with him. He who begins the attack assumes that he is superior to his enemy, either in numbers or in courage, and therefore carries with him to the assault all the moral advantage of his assumed superiority.—D.H.H.

(Kershaw's and Humphreys's) were expected next day. Rosecrans had put in all but two of his brigades. The outlook seemed hopeful for the Confederates. Longstreet arrived at 11 P.M. on the 19th.[✤]

Soon after, General Bragg called together some of his officers and ventured upon that hazardous experiment, a change of organization in face of the enemy. He divided his army into two wings; he gave to Polk the right wing, consisting of the corps of Hill and Walker, and the division of Cheatham,—comprising in all 18,794 infantry and artillery, with 3500 cavalry under Forrest; to Longstreet he gave the left wing, consisting of the corps of Buckner and Hood, and the division of Hindman,—22,849 infantry and artillery, with 4000 cavalry under Wheeler. That night Bragg announced his purpose of adhering to his plan of the 19th for the 20th, viz., successive attacks from right to left, and he gave his wing commanders orders to begin at daylight. I left Cleburne, after his fight, at 11 P.M., and rode with Captains Coleman and Reid five miles to Tedford's Ford, where the orders for the day announced that Bragg's headquarters would be, that I might get instructions for the next day. On the way I learned from some soldiers that Breckinridge was coming up from Lee and Gordon's. I sent Captain Reid to him to conduct him to Cleburne's right. General Polk, however, as wing commander, gave General Breckinridge permission to rest his weary men, and took him to his own headquarters. It was after 2 o'clock when General Breckinridge moved off under the guidance of Captain Reid, and his division did not get into position until after sunrise. Captain Coleman and myself reached the ford after midnight, only to learn that Bragg was not there. Some time after the unsuccessful search, my other staff-officers came up, and my chief-of-staff gave me a message from General Polk that my corps had been put under his command, and that he wished to see me at Alexander's Bridge. He said not a word to any of them about an attack at daylight, nor did he to General Breckinridge, who occupied the same room with him that night. I have by me written statements from General Breckinridge and the whole of my staff to that effect. General Polk had issued an order for an attack at daylight, and had sent a courier with a copy, but he had failed to find me. I saw the order for the first time nineteen years afterward in Captain Polk's letter to the Southern Historical Society. At 3 A.M. on the 20th I went to Alexander's Bridge, but not finding the courier who was to be posted there to conduct me to General Polk, I

[✤]While lying on the Rapidan in August, after that disastrous day at Gettysburg, Longstreet had suggested to General Lee the reënforcing of Bragg. The general went to Richmond, and after a time got the consent of the Confederate authorities to send Longstreet, without artillery or cavalry, with the much reduced divisions of McLaws and Hood. Lee followed Longstreet to his horse to see him off, and as he was mounting said, "General, you must beat those people." (Lee always called the Federals "those people.") Longstreet said, "General, if you will give your orders that the enemy, when beaten, shall be destroyed, I will promise to give you victory, if I live; but I would not give the life of a single soldier of mine for a barren victory." Lee replied, "The order has been given and will be repeated."—D.H.H.

sent Lieutenant Morrison, aide-de-camp, to hunt him up and tell him I could be found on the line of battle, which I reached just after daylight, before Breckinridge had got into position. Neither of my division commanders had heard anything of the early attack, and cooked rations were being distributed to our men, many of whom had not eaten anything for twenty-four hours. At 7:25 an order was shown me from General Polk, directed to my major-generals, to begin the attack. I sent a note to him that I was adjusting my line, and that my men were getting their rations. Polk soon after came up, and assented to the delay. Still nothing was said of the daylight attack. Bragg rode up at 8 A.M. and inquired of me why I had not begun the attack at daylight. I told him that I was hearing then for the first time that such an order had been issued and had not known whether we were to be the assailants or the assailed. He said angrily, "I found Polk after sunrise sitting down reading a newspaper at Alexander's Bridge, two miles from the line of battle, where he ought to have been fighting."

However, the essential preparations for battle had not been made up to this hour and, in fact, could not be made without the presence of the commander-in-chief. The position of the enemy had not been reconnoitered, our line of battle had not been adjusted, and part of it was at right angles with the rest; there was no cavalry on our flanks, and no order had fixed the strength or position of the reserves. My corps had been aligned north and south, to be parallel

GENERAL THOMAS'S BIVOUAC AFTER THE FIRST DAY'S BATTLE.

to the position of the enemy. Cheatham's division was at right angles to my line, and when adjusted was found to be exactly behind Stewart's, and had therefore to be taken out after the battle was begun, and placed in reserve. Kershaw's brigade of Longstreet's corps was also out of place, and was put in reserve.

Rosecrans in person made a careful alignment of his whole line in the morning, arranging it so as to cover the Rossville (Chattanooga) and the Dry Valley roads. It began four hundred yards east of the Rossville road, on a crest which was occupied from left to right by Baird's division (Thomas's corps), R. W. Johnson's division (McCook's), Palmer's division (Crittenden's), and Reynolds's division (Thomas's). These four divisions became isolated during the day, and the interest of the battle centers largely in them. They lay behind substantial breastworks of logs,[†] in a line running due south and bending back toward the road at each wing. "Next on the right of Reynolds," says a Federal newspaper account, "was Brannan's division of Thomas's corps, then Negley's of the same corps, its right making a crotchet to the rear. The line across the Chattanooga road toward Missionary Ridge was completed by Sheridan's and Davis's divisions of McCook's corps: Wood's and Van Cleve's divisions of Crittenden's corps were in reserve at a proper distance." The line from Reynolds extended in a south-westerly direction. Minty's cavalry covered the left and rear at Missionary Mills; Mitchell's and Wilder's cavalry covered the extreme right. Rosecrans's headquarters were at Widow Glenn's house.

The Confederate line ran at the outset from north to south, Hill's corps on the right, next Stewart's division, Hood in reserve, then Bushrod Johnson's, then Hindman's on the extreme left, Preston's in reserve. After the fighting had actually begun, Walker's and Cheatham's divisions and Kershaw's brigade were taken out and put in reserve. Wheeler's cavalry covered our left, and Forrest had been sent, at my request, to our right. The Confederates were confronted with eight Federal divisions protected generally by breast-works. The battle can be described in a few words. The Confederate attack on the right was mainly unsuccessful because of the breastworks, but was so gallant and persistent that Thomas called loudly for reënforcements, which were promptly sent, weakening the Federal right, until finally a gap was left. This gap Longstreet entered. Discovering, with the true instinct of a soldier, that he could do more by

---

[†]The ringing of axes in our front could be heard all night.—D.H.H.

These breastworks were described as follows by William F. G. Shanks, war correspondent of the "New York Herald":

> "General Thomas had wisely taken the precaution to make rude works about breast-high along his whole front, using rails and logs for the purpose. The logs and rails ran at right angles to each other, the logs keeping parallel to the proposed line of battle and lying upon the rails until the proper height was reached. The spaces between these logs were filled with rails, which served to add to their security and strength. The spade had not been used."

—EDITORS.

turning to the right, he disregarded the order to wheel to the left and wheeled the other way, striking the corps of Crittenden and McCook in flank, driving them with their commanders and the commanding general off the field.[1] Thomas, however, still held his ground, and, though ordered to retreat, strongly refused to do so until nightfall, thus saving the Federals from a great disaster. Longstreet, then, was the organizer of victory on the Confederate side, and Thomas the savior of the army on the other side.

Longstreet did not advance until noon, nor did he attack the breastworks on the Federal left (Thomas's position) at all, though Federal writers at the time supposed that he did. Those assaults were made first by the divisions of Breckinridge and Cleburne of Hill's corps, and then by the brigades of Gist, Walthall, Govan, and others sent to their assistance. Stewart began his brilliant advance at 11 A.M., and before that time Thomas began his appeals for help.

Breckinridge moved at 9:30 A.M., and Cleburne fifteen minutes later, according to the order for attack. Forrest dismounted Armstrong's division of cavalry to keep abreast of Breckinridge, and held Pegram's division in reserve. Breckinridge's two right brigades, under Adams and Stovall, met but little opposition, but the left of Helm's brigade encountered the left of the breastworks, and was badly cut up. The heroic Helm was killed, and his command repulsed. His brigade, now under the command of that able officer, Colonel J. H. Lewis, was withdrawn. The simultaneous advance of Cleburne's troops would have greatly relieved Helm, as he was exposed to a flank as well as a direct fire. General Breckinridge suggested, and I cordially approved the suggestion, that he should wheel his two brigades to the left, and get in rear of the breastworks. These brigades had reached the Chattanooga road, and their skirmishers had pressed past Cloud's house, where there was a Federal field-hospital. The wheeling movement enabled Stovall to gain a point beyond the retired flank of the breastworks, and Breckinridge says in his report, "Adams had advanced still farther, being actually in rear of his intrenchments. A good supporting line to my division at this moment would probably have produced decisive results." Federal reënforcements had, however, come up. Adams was badly wounded and fell into the enemy's hands, and the two brigades were hurled back. Beatty's brigade of Negley's division had been the first to come to Baird's assistance. General Thomas says:

> "Beatty, meeting with greatly superior numbers, was compelled to fall
> back until relieved by the fire of several regiments of Palmer's reserve,

---

[1] General Bushrod Johnson was the first to enter the gap with his division and, with the coolness and judgment for which he was always distinguished, took in the situation at a glance and began the flank movement to the right. General Longstreet adopted the plan of his lieutenant, and made his other troops conform to Bushrod Johnson's movement.—D.H.H.

THE SINK-HOLE NEAR WIDOW GLENN'S HOUSE. FROM A RECENT PHOTOGRAPH.

This sink-hole contained the only water to be had in the central part of the battle-field. Colonel Wilder's brigade of mounted infantry at one time gained the pool after a hard contest and quenched their thirst. In the water were lying dead men and horses that had been wounded and had died while drinking.

> which I had ordered to the support of the left, being placed in position by General Baird, and which, with the coöperation of Van Derveer's brigade ⁄ of Brannan's division, and a portion of Stanley's brigade of Negley's division, drove the enemy entirely from Baird's left and rear."

Here was quite a sensation made by Breckinridge's two thousand men. American troops cannot stand flank and rear attacks. While Breckinridge was thus alarming Thomas for his left, Cleburne was having a bloody fight with the forces behind the breastworks. From want of alignment before the battle, Deshler's brigade had to be taken out that it might not overlap Stewart. L. E. Polk's brigade soon encountered the enemy behind his logs, and after an obstinate contest was driven back. Wood's (Confederate) brigade on the left had almost reached Poe's house (the burning house) on the Chattanooga road, when he was subjected to a heavy enfilading and direct fire, and driven back with great loss.

⁄General Adams was captured by Van Derveer's men.—D.H.H.

Cleburne withdrew his division four hundred yards behind the crest of a hill. The gallant young brigadier Deshler was killed while executing the movement, and his brigade then fell into the able hands of Colonel R. Q. Mills. The fierce fight on our right lasted until 10:30 A.M. It was an unequal contest of two small divisions against four full ones behind fortifications. Surely, there were never nobler leaders than Breckinridge and Cleburne, and surely never were nobler troops led on a more desperate "forlorn-hope"—against odds in numbers and superiority in position and equipment. But their unsurpassed and unsurpassable valor was not thrown away. Before a single Confederate soldier had come to their relief, Rosecrans ordered up other troops to the aid of Thomas, in addition to those already mentioned. At 10:10 A.M. he ordered McCook to be ready at 10:30; Sheridan's division to support Thomas.

General McCook says that he executed the order and marched the men at double-quick. This weakening of his right by Rosecrans to support his left was destined soon to be his ruin. So determined had been the assaults of Breckinridge and Cleburne, that, though repulsed and badly punished, they were not pursued by the enemy, who did not venture outside of his works.

At 11 A.M. Stewart's division advanced under an immediate order from Bragg. His three brigades under Brown, Clayton, and Bate advanced with Wood of Cleburne's division, and, as General Stewart says, "pressed on past the cornfield in front of the burnt house, two or three hundred yards beyond the Chattanooga road, driving the enemy within his line of intrenchments.... Here they encountered a fresh artillery fire on front and flank, heavily supported by infantry, and had to retire."

This was the celebrated attack upon Reynolds and Brannan which led directly to the Federal disaster. In the meantime our right was preparing to renew the attack. I proposed to the wing commander, Polk, to make a second advance, provided fresh troops were sent forward, requesting that the gap in Breckinridge's left, made by the withdrawal of Helm, should be filled by another brigade. General J. K. Jackson's was sent for that purpose, but unfortunately took its position too far in rear to engage the attention of the enemy in front, and every advance on our right during the remainder of the day was met with flank and cross fire from that quarter. Gist's brigade and Liddell's division of Walker's corps reported to me. Gist immediately attacked with great vigor the log-works which had repulsed Helm so disastrously, and he in turn was driven back. Liddell might have made as great an impression by moving on the Chattanooga road as Breckinridge had done, but his strong brigade (Walthall's) was detached, and he advanced with Govan's alone, seized the road for the second time that day, and was moving behind the breastworks, when, a column of the enemy appearing on his flank and rear, he was compelled to retreat.

This was simultaneous with the advance of Stewart. The heavy pressure on Thomas caused Rosecrans to support him by sending the divisions of Negley and Van Cleve and Brannan's reserve brigade. In the course of these changes, an order to Wood, which Rosecrans claims was misinterpreted, led to a gap being left into which Longstreet stepped with the eight brigades (Bushrod Johnson's original brigade and McNair's, Gregg's, Kershaw's, Law's, Humphreys's, Benning's, and Robertson's) which he had arranged in three lines to constitute his grand column of attack. Davis's two brigades, one of Van Cleve's, and Sheridan's entire division were caught in front and flank and driven from the field. Disregarding the order of the day, Longstreet now gave the order to wheel to the right instead of the left, and thus take in reverse the strong position of the enemy. Five of McCook's brigades were speedily driven off the field. He estimates their loss at forty per cent. Certainly that flank march was a bloody one. I have never seen the Federal dead lie so thickly on the ground, save in front of the sunken wall at Fredericksburg.

But that indomitable Virginia soldier, George H. Thomas,☆ was there and was destined to save the Union army from total rout and ruin, by confronting with invincible pluck the forces of his friend and captain in the Mexican war. Thomas had ridden to his right to hurry up reënforcements, when he discovered a line advancing, which he thought at first was the expected succor from Sheridan, but he soon heard that it was a rebel column marching upon him. He chose a strong position on a spur of Missionary Ridge, running east and west, placed upon it Brannan's division with portions of two brigades of Negley's; Wood's division (Crittenden's) was placed on Brannan's left. These troops, with such as could be rallied from the two broken corps, were all he had to confront the forces of Longstreet, until Steedman's division of Granger's corps came to his relief about 3 P.M. Well and nobly did Thomas and his gallant troops hold their own against foes flushed with past victory and confident of future success. His new line was nearly at right angles with the line of log-works on the west side of the Rossville road, his right being an almost impregnable wall-like hill, his left nearly an inclosed fortification. Our only hope of success was to get in his rear by moving far to our right, which overlapped the Federal left.

Bushrod Johnson's three brigades in Longstreet's center were the first to fill the gap left by Wood's withdrawal from the Federal right; but the other five brigades under Hindman and Kershaw moved promptly into line as soon as space could be found for them, wheeled to the right, and engaged in the murderous flank attack. On they rushed, shouting, yelling, running over batteries, capturing trains, taking prisoners, seizing the headquarters of the Federal commander, at the Widow Glenn's, until they found themselves facing the new Federal line on Snodgrass Hill. Hindman had advanced a little later than the

---

☆Bragg had great respect and affection for the first lieutenant of his battery. The tones of tenderness with which he spoke of "Old Tom" are still remembered by me.—D.H.H.

center, and had met great and immediate success. The brigades of Deas and Manigault charged the breastworks at double-quick, rushed over them, drove Laiboldt's Federal brigade of Sheridan's division off the field down the Rossville road; then General Patton Anderson's brigade of Hindman, having come into line, attacked and beat back the forces of Davis, Sheridan, and Wilder‡ in their front, killed the hero and poet General Lytle, took 1100 prisoners, 27 pieces of artillery, commissary and ordnance trains, etc. Finding no more resistance on his front and left, Hindman wheeled to the right to assist the forces of the center. The divisions of Stewart, Hood, Bushrod Johnson, and Hindman came together in front of the new stronghold of the Federals. [See map, p. 702.]

It was now 2:30 P.M. Longstreet, with his staff, was lunching on sweet-potatoes. A message came just then that the commanding general wished to see him. He found Bragg in rear of his lines, told him of the steady and satisfactory progress of the battle, that sixty pieces of artillery had been reported captured (though probably the number was over-estimated), that many prisoners and stores had been taken, and that all was going well. He then asked for additional troops to hold the ground gained, while he pursued the two broken corps down the Dry Valley road and cut off the retreat of Thomas. Bragg replied that there was no more fight in the troops of Polk's wing, that he could give Longstreet no reënforcements, and that his headquarters would be at Reed's Bridge. He seems

---

‡James Burns, 39th Indiana Mounted Infantry, writes to the editors from Harper, Kansas:

"Wilder's brigade, with Colonel T. J. Harrison's 39th Indiana Mounted Infantry regiment, which was ordered to report to Colonel Wilder about 9 o'clock A.M. of the 20th of September, was stationed on a hill about one-third of a mile in the rear of the line of battle,—the 39th on the left of the brigade. A few minutes after 11 o'clock A.M. the brigade was ordered to advance across the valley where the ammunition train was stationed, and up the hill to the support of Captain Lilly's battery, and to hold the hill at all hazards until the train was got out of the way. My company, 'A,' 39th Indiana, was in advance, and on reaching the brow of the hill Major Evans gave the commands, '39th Indiana on left into line'; 'Fire at will.' At a distance of less than fifty yards six solid lines of gray were coming with their hats down, their bayonets at a charge, and the old familiar rebel yell. Our first volley did not check their advance, but as volley after volley from our Spencer rifles followed, with scarce a second's intermission, and regiment after regiment came on left into line on our right, and poured the same steady, deadly fire into their fast-thinning ranks, they broke and fled.

"Colonel Wilder and Colonel Harrison rode along our lines, directing that if they charged us again, no shot must be fired until the word of command was given. In a few moments those lines of gray once more emerged from the sheltering timber on the opposite side of the field, and steadily, as if on parade, they advanced to the charge till the line had reached to the point at which they broke before, when the command 'Fire' was given, and again they broke and fled in wild confusion. Three times more did those brave men advance at a charge, and each time were they hurled back. A lieutenant of the 17th Indiana went down with a few men under cover of the fire of the brigade, and brought in the flag of an Alabama regiment. We then received orders to move off, remount and guard the ammunition train to Chattanooga, which we did successfully."

not to have known that Cheatham's division and part of Liddell's had not been in action that day.ᛏ

Some of the severest fighting had yet to be done after 3 P.M. It probably never happened before for a great battle to be fought to its bloody conclusion with the commanders of each side away from the field of conflict. But the Federals were in the hands of the indomitable Thomas, and the Confederates were under their two heroic wing commanders Longstreet and Polk. In the lull of the strife I went with a staff-officer to examine the ground on our left. One of Helm's wounded men had been overlooked, and was lying alone in the woods, his head partly supported by a tree. He was shockingly injured.ᛧ

Hindman and Bushrod Johnson organized a column of attack upon the front and rear of the stronghold of Thomas. It consisted of the brigades of Deas, Manigault, Gregg, Patton, Anderson, and McNair. Three of the brigades, Johnson says, had each but five hundred men, and the other two were not strong. Deas was on the north side of the gorge through which the Crawfish road crosses, Manigault across the gorge and south, on the crest parallel to the Snodgrass Hill, where Thomas was. The other three brigades extended along the crest with their faces north, while the first two faced east. Kershaw, with his own and Humphreys's brigade, was on the right of Anderson and was to coöperate in the movement. It began at 3:30 P.M. A terrific contest ensued. The bayonet was used, and men were killed and wounded with clubbed muskets. A little after 4, the enemy was reënforced, and advanced, but was repulsed by Anderson and Kershaw.

ᛏGeneral Longstreet wrote to me in July, 1884:

> "It is my opinion that Bragg thought at 3 P.M. that the battle was lost, though he did not say so positively. I asked him at that time to reënforce me with a few troops that had not been so severely engaged as mine, and to allow me to go down the Dry Valley road, so as to interpose behind Thomas and cut off his retreat to Chattanooga, at the same time pursuing the troops that I had beaten back from my front. His reply, as well as I can remember, was that he had no troops except my own that had any fight left in them, and that I should remain in the position in which I then was. After telling me this, he left me, saying, 'General, if anything happens, communicate with me at Reed's Bridge.' In reading Bragg's report, I was struck with his remark that the morning after the battle 'he found the ever-vigilant General Liddell feeling his way to find the enemy.' Inasmuch as every one in his army was supposed to know on the night of the battle that we had won a complete victory, it seemed to me quite ludicrous that an officer should be commended for his vigilance the next morning in looking for the enemy in his immediate presence. I know that I was then laying a plan by which we might overhaul the enemy at Chattanooga or between that point and Nashville. It did not occur to me on the night of the 20th to send Bragg word of our complete success. I thought that the loud huzzas that spread over the field just at dark were a sufficient assurance and notice to any one within five miles of us.... Rosecrans speaks particularly of his apprehension that I would move down the Dry Valley road."

—D.H.H.

ᛧHe belonged to Von Zinken's regiment, of New Orleans, composed of French, Germans, and Irish. I said to him: "My poor fellow, you are badly hurt. What regiment do you belong to?" He replied: "The

General Bushrod Johnson claims that his men were surely, if slowly, gaining ground at all points, which must have made untenable the stronghold of Thomas. Relief was, however, to come to our men, so hotly engaged on the left, by the advance of the right. At 3 P.M. Forrest reported to me that a strong column was approaching from Rossville, which he was delaying all he could. From prisoners we soon learned that it was Granger's corps. We were apprehensive that a flank attack, by fresh troops, upon our exhausted and shattered ranks might prove fatal. Major-General Walker strongly advised falling back to the position of Cleburne, but to this I would not consent, believing that it would invite attack, as we were in full view.❦ Cheatham's fine division was sent to my assistance by the wing commander. But Granger, who had gallantly marched without orders to the relief of Thomas, moved on "to the sound of the firing, attacked with vigor and broke our line."╱ Rosecrans thus describes the timely help afforded by Granger to the sorely beset Thomas:

> "Arrived in sight, Granger discovered at once the peril and the point of danger—the gap—and quick as thought he directed his advance brigade upon the enemy. General Steedman, taking a regimental color, led the column. Swift was the charge and terrible the conflict, but the enemy was broken. A thousand of our brave men killed and wounded paid for its possession."

Longstreet was determined to send Preston with his division of three brigades under Gracie, Trigg, and Kelly, aided by Robertson's brigade of Hood's division, to carry the heights—the main point of defense. His troops were of the best material and had been in reserve all day; but brave, fresh, and strong as they were, it was with them alternate advance and retreat, until success was assured by a renewal of the fight on the right. At 3:30 P.M. General Polk sent an

---

Fifth Confederit, and a dammed good regiment it is." The answer, though almost ludicrous, touched me as illustrating the *esprit de corps* of the soldier—his pride in and his affection for his command. Colonel Von Zinken told me afterward that one of his desperately wounded Irishmen cried out to his comrades, "Charge them, boys; they have cha-ase (cheese) in their haversacks." Poor Pat, he has fought courageously in every land in quarrels not his own.—D.H.H.

❦Major-General Walker claims that he proposed to me to make an advance movement with his whole corps, and complains that his command was disintegrated by sending it in by brigades. General Walker did propose, as he says, to fall back and align upon Cleburne, when we saw Granger's corps approaching on our right, and I did refuse to permit this, believing that a withdrawal in full view of Granger would invite an attack upon our flank, and this might be fatal to troops more or less demoralized by the bloody repulse which they had sustained. The proposal to advance with his whole corps was never heard by me, and was, at best, impossible, as two of his five brigades had been detached, the one by Polk and the other by myself, to fill gaps in the line.—D.H.H.

╱According to the official returns the entire loss during the afternoon in Steedman's two brigades (including 613 captured or missing) was 1787. A Federal writer says that of the eight staff-officers of Brig.-Gen. Whitaker "three were killed, three wounded, and one killed or captured."—D.H.H.

order to me to assume command of the attacking forces on the right and renew the assault. Owing to a delay in the adjustment of our lines, the advance did not begin until 4 o'clock. The men sprang to their arms with the utmost alacrity, though they had not heard of Longstreet's success, and they showed by their cheerfulness that there was plenty of "fight in them." Cleburne ran forward his batteries, some by hand, to within three hundred yards of the enemy's breast-works, pushed forward his infantry, and carried them. General J. K. Jackson, of Cheatham's division, had a bloody struggle with the fortifications in his front, but had entered them when Cheatham with two more of his brigades, Maney's and Wright's, came up. Breckinridge and Walker met with but little opposition until the Chattanooga road was passed, when their right was unable to overcome the forces covering the enemy's retreat. As we passed into the woods west of the road, it was reported to me that a line was advancing at right angles to ours. I rode to the left to ascertain whether they were foes or friends, and soon recognized General Buckner. The cheers that went up when the two wings met were such as I had never heard before, and shall never hear again.

Preston gained the heights a half hour later, capturing 1000 prisoners and 4500 stand of arms. But neither right nor left is entitled to the laurels of a complete triumph. It was the combined attack which, by weakening the enthusiasm of the brave warriors who had stood on the defense so long and so obstinately, won the day.

Thomas had received orders after Granger's arrival to retreat to Rossville, but, stout soldier as he was, he resolved to hold his ground until nightfall. An hour more of daylight would have insured his capture. Thomas had under him all the Federal army, except the six brigades which had been driven off by the left wing.☆

Whatever blunders each of us in authority committed before the battles of the 19th and 20th, and during their progress, the great blunder of all was that of not pursuing the enemy on the 21st. The day was spent in burying the dead and gathering up captured stores. Forrest, with his usual promptness, was early in the saddle, and saw that the retreat was a rout. Disorganized masses of men were

☆In regard to the relative strength of the two armies, Colonel Archer Anderson says:

"From an examination of the original returns in the War Department, I reckon, in round numbers, the Federal infantry and artillery on the field at 59,000, and the Confederate infantry and artillery at 55,000. The Federal cavalry, about 10,000 strong, was outnumbered by the Confederates by 1000 men. Thus speak the returns. Perhaps a deduction of 5000 men from the reported strength of each army would more nearly represent the actual strength of the combatants. But in any case it is, I think, certain that Rosecrans was stronger in infantry and artillery than Bragg by at least 4000 men."

The Federal estimate of their loss, in captured or missing, is below the mark by 1000, if the Confederate claim of the capture of 6500 prisoners is correct. The Confederates also claim to have taken 51 pieces of artillery, 15,000 stand of arms, and a large amount of ordnance stores, camp-equipage, etc.—D.H.H.

hurrying to the rear; batteries of artillery were inextricably mixed with trains of wagons; disorder and confusion pervaded the broken ranks struggling to get on. Forrest sent back word to Bragg that "every hour was worth a thousand men." But the commander-in-chief did not know of the victory until the morning of the 21st, and then he did not order a pursuit. Rosecrans spent the day and the night of the 21st in hurrying his trains out of town. A breathing-space was allowed him; the panic among his troops subsided, and Chattanooga—the objective point of the campaign—was held. There was no more splendid fighting in '61, when the flower of the Southern youth was in the field, than was displayed in those bloody days of September, '63. But it seems to me that the *élan* of the Southern soldier was never seen after Chickamauga—that brilliant dash which had distinguished him was gone forever. He was too intelligent not to know that the cutting in two of Georgia meant death to all his hopes. He knew that Longstreet's absence was imperiling Lee's safety, and that what had to be done must be done quickly. The delay in striking was exasperating to him; the failure to strike after the success was crushing to all his longings for an independent South. He fought stoutly to the last, but, after Chickamauga, with the sullenness of despair and without the enthusiasm of hope. That "barren victory" sealed the fate of the Southern Confederacy.

CHAPTER 12

CHATTANOOGA.

Ulysses S. Grant, General, U.S.A.

After the fall of Vicksburg I urged strongly upon the Government the propriety of a movement against Mobile. General Rosecrans had been at Murfreesboro', Tennessee, with a large and well-equipped army from early in the year 1863, with Bragg confronting him with a force quite equal to his own at first, considering that it was on the defensive. But after the investment of Vicksburg, Bragg's army was largely depleted to strengthen Johnston, in Mississippi, who was being reënforced to raise the siege. I frequently wrote to General Halleck suggesting that Rosecrans should move against Bragg. By so doing he would either detain the latter's troops where they were, or lay Chattanooga open to capture. General Halleck strongly approved the suggestion, and finally wrote me that he had repeatedly ordered Rosecrans to advance, but that the latter had constantly failed to comply with the order,✛ and at last, after having held a

---

✛In an article in "The Century" magazine for May, 1887, General Rosecrans says:

"Since our forces in rear of Vicksburg would be endangered by General Joseph E. Johnston, if he should have enough troops, we must not drive Bragg out of middle Tennessee until it shall be too late for his command to reënforce Johnston's. Bragg's army is now, apparently, holding this army in check. It is the most important service he can render to his cause. The Confederate authorities know it. They will not order, nor will Bragg venture to send away any substantial detachments. The news that Vicksburg could not hold out over two or three weeks having reached us, we began our movements to dislodge Bragg from his intrenched camp on the 24th of June, 1863. It rained for seventeen consecutive days. The roads were so bad that it required four days for Crittenden's troops to march seventeen miles. Yet, on the 4th of July, we had possession of both the enemy's intrenched camps, and by the 7th, Bragg's army was in full retreat over the Cumberland Mountains into Sequatchie valley, whence he proceeded to Chattanooga, leaving us in full possession of middle Tennessee and of the damaged Nashville and Chattanooga railway, with my headquarters at Winchester, fifty miles from our starting-point, Murfreesboro'. This movement was accomplished in fifteen days, and with a loss of only 586 killed and wounded."

—Editors.

council of war, replied, in effect, that it was a military maxim "not to fight two decisive battles at the same time." If true, the maxim was not applicable in this case. It would be bad to be defeated in two decisive battles fought the same day, but it would not be bad to win them. I, however, was fighting no battle, and the siege of Vicksburg had drawn from Rosecrans's front so many of the enemy that his chances of victory were much greater than they would be if he waited until the siege was over, when these troops could be returned. Rosecrans was ordered to move against the army that was detaching troops to raise the siege. Finally, on the 24th of June, he did move, but ten days afterward Vicksburg surrendered, and the troops sent from Bragg were free to return.↓ It was at this time that I recommended to the general-in-chief the movement against Mobile. I knew the peril the Army of the Cumberland was in, being depleted continually not only by ordinary casualties, but also by having to detach troops to hold its constantly extending line over which to draw supplies, while the enemy in front was as constantly being strengthened. Mobile was important to the enemy, and, in the absence of a threatening force, was guarded by little else than artillery. If threatened by land and from the water at the same time, the prize would fall easily, or troops would have to be sent to its defense. Those troops would necessarily come from Bragg.

My judgment was overruled, however, and the troops under my command were dissipated over other parts of the country where it was thought they could render the most service. Four thousand were sent to Banks, at New Orleans; five thousand to Schofield, to use against Price, in Arkansas; the Ninth Corps back to Kentucky; and finally, in August, the whole of the Thirteenth Corps to Banks. I also sent Ransom's brigade to Natchez, to occupy that point, and to relieve Banks from guarding any part of the river above what he had guarded before the fall of Port Hudson. Ransom captured a large amount of ammunition and about five thousand beef cattle that were crossing the river going east for the rebel armies. At this time the country was full of deserters from Pemberton's army, and it was reported that many had also left Johnston. These avowed they would never go back to fight against us again. Many whose homes were west of the river went there, and others went North to remain until they could return with security.

Soon it was discovered in Washington that Rosecrans was in trouble and required assistance. The emergency was now too immediate to allow us to give this assistance by making an attack in the rear of Bragg upon Mobile. It was, therefore, necessary to reënforce directly, and troops were sent from every available point. On the 13th of September Halleck telegraphed me to send all

---

↓Late in August the divisions of Breckinridge and W.H.T. Walker were transferred from Mississippi to Bragg's army, and the brigades of Gregg and McNair followed early in September. These troops were engaged at Chickamauga.—EDITORS.

available forces to Memphis, and thence east along the Memphis and Charleston railroad to coöperate with Rosecrans. This instruction was repeated two days later, but I did not get even the first until the 23d of the month. As fast as transports could be provided all the troops except a portion of the Seventeenth Corps were forwarded under Sherman, whose services up to this time demonstrated his superior fitness for a separate command.♭ I also moved McPherson, with most of the troops still about Vicksburg, eastward, to compel the enemy to keep back a force to meet him. Meanwhile Rosecrans had very skillfully manœuvred Bragg south of the Tennessee River, and through and beyond Chattanooga. If he had stopped and intrenched, and made himself strong there, all would have been right, and the mistake of not moving earlier partially compensated. But he pushed on, with his forces very much scattered, until Bragg's troops from Mississippi began to join him./ Then Bragg took the initiative. Rosecrans had to fall back in turn, and was able to get his army together at Chickamauga, some miles south-east of Chattanooga, before the main battle was brought on. The battle was fought on the 19th and 20th of September, and Rosecrans was badly defeated, with a heavy loss in artillery, and some sixteen thousand men killed, wounded, and captured. The corps under Major-General George H. Thomas stood its ground, while Rosecrans, with Crittenden and McCook, returned to Chattanooga. Thomas returned also, but later, and with his troops in good order. Bragg followed and took possession of Missionary Ridge, overlooking Chattanooga. He also occupied Lookout Mountain, west of the town, which Rosecrans had abandoned, and with it his control of the river and river road as far back as Bridgeport. The National troops were now strongly intrenched in Chattanooga Valley, with the Tennessee River behind them, the enemy occupying commanding heights to the east and west, with a

---

♭In his "Personal Memoirs" (C. L. Webster & Co.) General Grant says:

"Soon after negotiations were opened with General Pemberton for the surrender of the city, I notified Sherman, whose troops extended from Haynes's Bluff on the left to the crossing of the Vicksburg and Jackson road over the Big Black on the right, and directed him to hold his command in readiness to advance and drive the enemy from the State as soon as Vicksburg surrendered.... Johnston heard of the surrender of Vicksburg almost as soon as it occurred, and immediately fell back on Jackson. On the 8th of July Sherman was within ten miles of Jackson, and on the 11th was close up to the defenses of the city and shelling the town. The siege was kept up until the morning of the 17th, when it was found that the enemy had evacuated during the night. The weather was very hot, the roads dusty, and the water bad. Johnston destroyed the roads as he passed, and had so much the start that pursuit was useless; but Sherman sent one division, Steele's, to Brandon, fourteen miles east of Jackson.... Sherman was ordered back to Vicksburg, and his troops took much the same position they had occupied before—from the Big Black to Haynes's Bluff."

—Editors.

/Bragg was also reënforced by Longstreet, from the Army of Northern Virginia.—Editors.

strong line across the valley, from mountain to mountain, and Chattanooga Creek for a large part of the way in front of their line.

On the 29th of September Halleck telegraphed me the above results, and directed all the forces that could be spared from my department to be sent to Rosecrans, suggesting that a good commander like Sherman or McPherson should go with the troops; also that I should go in person to Nashville to superintend the movement. Long before this dispatch was received Sherman was already on his way, and McPherson also was moving east with most of the garrison of Vicksburg. I at once sent a staff-officer to Cairo, to communicate, in my name, directly with the Government, and to forward me any and all important dispatches without the delays that had attended the transmission of previous ones. On the 3d of October a dispatch was received at Cairo ordering me to move with my staff and headquarters to that city, and report from there my arrival. This dispatch reached me on the 10th. I left Vicksburg the same day, reached Columbus *en route* for Cairo on the 16th, and reported my arrival at once. The reply to my telegram from Cairo, announcing my arrival at that point, came on the morning of the 17th, directing me to proceed immediately to the Galt House, Louisville, Kentucky, where I would meet an officer of the War Department with my instructions. I left Cairo within an hour after the receipt of this dispatch, going by rail by the way of Indianapolis, Indiana. Just as the train I was on was starting out of the depot at Indianapolis, a messenger came running up to stop it, saying the Secretary of War was coming into the station and wanted to see me. I had never met Mr. Stanton up to that time, though we had held frequent conversations over the wires, the year before, when I was in Tennessee. Occasionally, at night, he would order the wires between the War Department and my headquarters to be connected, and we would hold a conversation for an hour or two. On this occasion the secretary was accompanied by Governor Brough, of Ohio, whom I had never met, though he and my father had been old acquaintances. Mr. Stanton dismissed the special train that had brought him to Indianapolis and accompanied me to Louisville.

Up to this time no hint had been given me of what was wanted after I left Vicksburg, except the suggestion in one of Halleck's dispatches that I had better go to Nashville and superintend the operation of the troops sent to relieve Rosecrans. Soon after we had started, the secretary handed me two orders, saying that I might take my choice of them. The two were identical in all but one particular. Both created the Military Division of the Mississippi, giving me the command, composed of the Departments of the Ohio, the Cumberland, and the Tennessee, and all the territory from the Alleghanies to the Mississippi River, north of Banks's command in the south-west. One order left the department commanders as they were, while the other relieved Rosecrans and assigned Thomas to his place. I accepted the latter. We reached Louisville after

THE ARMY OF THE CUMBERLAND IN FRONT OF CHATTANOOGA. FROM A LITHOGRAPH.
The picture shows the intrenchments occupied by three divisions of Thomas's corps. In the fore-ground is seen Fort Grose, manned on the left of the picture by the 24th Ohio and on the right by the 36th Indiana, guns of the First Ohio Battery being in the inclosures. Fort Negley is at the end of the line of works seen in the middle-ground, Lookout Mountain being in the distance.
—Editors.

night, and, if I remember rightly, in a cold, drizzling rain. The Secretary of War told me afterward that he caught a cold on that occasion from which he never expected to recover.

A day was spent in Louisville, the secretary giving me the military news at the capital, and talking about the disappointment at the results of some of the campaigns. By the evening of the day after our arrival all matters of discussion seemed exhausted, and I left the hotel to spend the evening away, both Mrs. Grant (who was with me) and myself having relations living in Louisville. In the course of the evening Mr. Stanton received a dispatch from Mr. C. A. Dana [an officer of the War Department], then in Chattanooga, informing him that unless prevented Rosecrans would retreat, and advising peremptory orders against his doing so. A retreat at that time would have been a terrible disaster. It would not only have been the loss of a most important strategic position to us, but it would have been attended with the loss of all the artillery still left with the Army of the Cumberland, and the annihilation of that army itself, either by capture or demoralization.

All supplies for Rosecrans had to be brought from Nashville. The railroad between this base and the army was in possession of the Government up to Bridgeport, the point at which the road crosses to the south side of the Tennessee River; but Bragg, holding Lookout and Raccoon mountains west of Chattanooga, commanded the railroad, the river, and the shortest and best wagon roads both south and north of the Tennessee, between Chattanooga and Bridgeport. The distance between these two places is but twenty-six miles by rail; but owing to this position of Bragg all supplies for Rosecrans had to be hauled by a circuitous route, north of the river, and over a mountainous country, increasing the distance to over sixty miles. This country afforded but little food for his animals, nearly ten thousand of which had already starved, and none were left to draw a single piece of artillery or even the ambulances to convey the sick. The men had been on half rations of hard bread for a considerable time, with but few other supplies, except beef driven from Nashville across the country. The region along the road became so exhausted of food for the cattle that by the time they reached Chattanooga they were much in the condition of the few animals left alive there, "on the lift." Indeed, the beef was so poor that the soldiers were in the habit of saying, with a faint facetiousness, that they were living on half rations of hard bread and "beef dried on the hoof." Nothing could be transported but food, and the troops were without sufficient shoes or other clothing suitable for the advancing season. What they had was well worn. The fuel within the Federal lines was exhausted, even to the stumps of trees. There were no teams to draw it from the opposite bank, where it was abundant. The only means for supplying fuel, for some time before my arrival, had been to cut trees from the north bank of the river, at a considerable distance up the stream, form rafts of it, and float it down with the current, effecting a landing on the south side, within our lines, by the use of paddles or poles. It would then be carried on the shoulders of the men to their camps. If a retreat had occurred at this time it is not probable that any of the army would have reached the railroad as an organized body, if followed by the enemy.

On the receipt of Mr. Dana's dispatch Mr. Stanton sent for me. Finding that I was out, he became nervous and excited, inquiring of every person he met, including guests of the house, whether they knew where I was, and bidding them find me and send me to him at once. About 11 o'clock I returned to the hotel, and on my way, when near the house, every person met was a messenger from the secretary, apparently partaking of his impatience to see me. I hastened to the room of the secretary and found him pacing the floor rapidly, in a dressing-gown. Saying that the retreat must be prevented, he showed me the dispatch. I immediately wrote an order assuming command of the Military Division of the Mississippi, and telegraphed it to General Rosecrans. I then telegraphed to him the order from Washington assigning Thomas to the command of the Army of the Cumberland; and to Thomas that he must hold Chattanooga at all hazards, informing him at the same time that I would be at the front as soon as possible. A prompt reply was received from Thomas, saying, "We will hold the town till we starve." I appreciated the force of this dispatch later when I witnessed the condition of affairs which prompted it. It looked, indeed, as if but two courses were open: one to starve, the other to surrender or be captured.

On the morning of the 20th of October I started by train with my staff, and proceeded as far as Nashville. At that time it was not prudent to travel beyond that point by night, so I remained in Nashville until the next morning. Here I met for the first time Andrew Johnson, Military Governor of Tennessee. He delivered a speech of welcome. His composure showed that it was by no means his maiden effort. It was long, and I was in torture while he was delivering it, fearing something would be expected from me in response. I was relieved, however, the people assembled having apparently heard enough. At all events they commenced a general hand-shaking, which, although trying where there is so much of it, was a great relief to me in this emergency.

From Nashville I telegraphed to Burnside, who was then at Knoxville,☆ that important points in his department ought to be fortified, so that they could be held with the least number of men; to Porter at Cairo, that Sherman's advance had passed Eastport, Miss. [see p. 731], and that rations were probably on their way from St. Louis by boat for supplying his army, and requesting him to send a gun-boat to convoy them; and to Thomas, suggesting that large parties should be put at work on the wagon road then in use back to Bridgeport.

On the morning of the 21st we took the train for the front, reaching Stevenson, Alabama, after dark. Rosecrans was there on his way north. He came into my car, and we held a brief interview in which he described very clearly the situation at Chattanooga, and made some excellent suggestions as to what should be done. My only wonder was that he had not carried them out. We then proceeded to Bridgeport, where we stopped for the night. From here we took horses and made our way by Jasper and over Waldron's Ridge to Chattanooga. There had been much rain and the roads were almost impassable from mud knee-deep in places, and from washouts on the mountain-sides. I had been on crutches since the time of my fall in New Orleans,‡ and had to be carried over places where it was not safe to cross on horseback. The roads were strewn with the débris of broken wagons and the carcasses of thousands of starved mules and horses. At Jasper, some ten or twelve miles from Bridgeport, there was a halt. Howard had his headquarters there. From this point I telegraphed Burnside to make every effort to secure 500 rounds of ammunition for his artillery and small-arms. We stopped for the night at a little hamlet some ten or twelve miles farther on. The next day we reached Chattanooga, a little before dark. I

☆General Burnside assumed command of the Department of the Ohio, succeeding General H. G. Wright, on the 25th of March, 1863.—EDITORS.

‡In August General Grant went to New Orleans to confer with Banks about coöperating in movements that had been ordered west of the Mississippi. During the visit his horse fell, severely injuring him.
—EDITORS.

went directly to Thomas's headquarters, and remained there a few days until I could establish my own.

During the evening most of the general officers called in to pay their respects and to talk about the condition of affairs. They pointed out on the maps the line marked with a red or blue pencil which Rosecrans had contemplated falling back upon. If any of them had approved the move, they did not say so to me. I found General W. F. Smith occupying the position of chief engineer of the Army of the Cumberland. I had known Smith as a cadet at West Point, but had no recollection of having met him after my graduation, in 1843, up to this time. He explained the situation of the two armies and the topography of the country so plainly that I could see it without an inspection. I found that he had established a saw-mill on the banks of the river, by utilizing an old engine found in the neighborhood; and by rafting logs from the north side of the river above had got out the lumber and completed pontoons and roadway plank for a second bridge, one flying-bridge being there already. He was also rapidly getting out the materials for constructing the boats for a third bridge. In addition to this he had far under way a steamer for plying between Chattanooga and Bridgeport whenever he might get possession of the river. This boat consisted of a scow made of the plank sawed out at the mill, housed in, with a stern-wheel attached which was propelled by a second engine taken from some shop or factory.

I telegraphed to Washington this night, notifying Halleck of my arrival, and asking to have Sherman assigned to the command of the Army of the Tennessee, headquarters in the field. The request was at once complied with.

The next day, the 24th, I started out to make a personal inspection, taking Thomas and Smith with me, besides most of the members of my personal staff. We crossed to the north side of the river, and, moving to the north of detached spurs of hills, reached the Tennessee, at Brown's Ferry, some three miles below Lookout Mountain, unobserved by the enemy. Here we left our horses back from the river and approached the water on foot. There was a picket station of the enemy, on the opposite side, of about twenty men, in full view, and we were within easy range. They did not fire upon us nor seem to be disturbed by our presence. They must have seen that we were all commissioned officers. But, I suppose, they looked upon the garrison of Chattanooga as prisoners of war, feeding or starving themselves, and thought it would be inhuman to kill any of them except in self-defense. That night I issued orders for opening the route to Bridgeport—a "cracker line," as the soldiers appropriately termed it. They had been so long on short rations that my first thought was the establishment of a line over which food might reach them.

Chattanooga is on the south bank of the Tennessee, where that river runs nearly due west. It is at the northern end of a valley five or six miles in width through which runs Chattanooga Creek. To the east of the valley is Missionary Ridge, rising from five to eight hundred feet above the creek, and terminating somewhat abruptly a half-mile or more before reaching the Tennessee. On the west of the valley is Lookout Mountain, 2200 feet above tide-water. Just below the town, the Tennessee makes a turn to the south and runs to the base of Lookout Mountain, leaving no level ground between the mountain and river. The Memphis and Charleston railroad passes this point, where the mountain stands nearly perpendicular. East of Missionary Ridge flows the South Chickamauga River; west of Lookout Mountain is Lookout Creek; and west of that, the Raccoon Mountain. Lookout Mountain at its northern end rises almost perpendic-

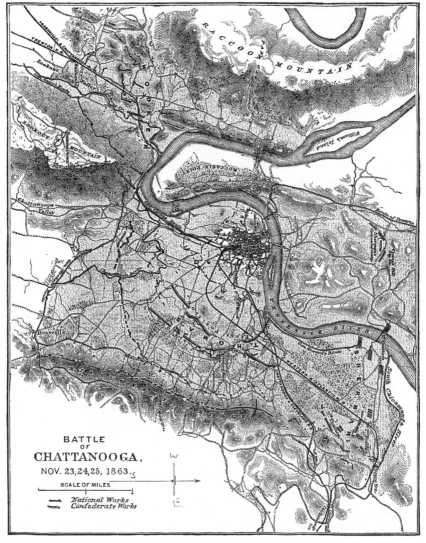

REPRODUCED BY PERMISSION FROM "THE MILITARY HISTORY OF ULYSSES S. GRANT," BY GENERAL ADAM BADEAU. (N.Y. D. APPLETON & CO.)

ularly for some distance, then breaks off in a gentle slope of cultivated fields to near the summit, where it ends in a palisade thirty or more feet in height. On the gently sloping ground, between the upper and lower palisades, there is a single farm-house, which is reached by a wagon road from the valley to the east.

The intrenched line of the enemy commenced on the north end of Missionary Ridge and extended along the crest for some distance south, thence across Chattanooga Valley to Lookout Mountain. Lookout Mountain was also fortified and held by the enemy, who also kept troops in Lookout Valley and on Raccoon Mountain, with pickets extending down the river so as to command the road on the north bank and render it useless to us. In addition to this there was an intrenched line in Chattanooga Valley extending from the river east of the town to Lookout Mountain, to make the investment complete. Besides the fortifications on Missionary Ridge there was a line at the base of the hill, with occasional spurs of rifle-pits half-way up the front. The enemy's pickets extended out into the valley toward the town, so far that the pickets of the two armies could converse. At one point they were separated only by the narrow creek which gives its name to the valley and town, and from which both sides drew water. The Union lines were shorter than those of the enemy.

Thus the enemy, with a vastly superior force, was strongly fortified to the east, south, and west, and commanded the river below. Practically the Army of the Cumberland was besieged. The enemy, with his cavalry north of the river, had stopped the passing of a train loaded with ammunition and medical supplies. The Union army was short of both, not having ammunition enough for a day's fighting.

Long before my coming into this new field, General Halleck had ordered parts of the Eleventh and Twelfth corps, commanded respectively by Generals Howard and Slocum, Hooker in command of the whole, from the Army of the Potomac, to reënforce Rosecrans. It would have been folly to have sent them to Chattanooga to help eat up the few rations left there. They were consequently left on the railroad, where supplies could be brought them. Before my arrival Thomas ordered their concentration at Bridgeport.

General W. F. Smith had been so instrumental in preparing for the move which I was now about to make, and so clear in his judgment about the manner of making it, that I deemed it but just to him that he should have command of the troops detailed to execute the design, although he was then acting as a staff-officer, and was not in command of troops.

On the 24th of October, after my return to Chattanooga, the following details were made: General Hooker, who was now at Bridgeport, was ordered to cross to the south side of the Tennessee and march up by Whiteside's and Wauhatchie to Brown's Ferry. General Palmer, with a division of the Fourteenth Corps, Army of the Cumberland, was ordered to move down the river on the north side, by a back road, until opposite Whiteside's, then cross and hold the road in Hooker's rear after he had passed. Four thousand men were at the same time detailed to act under General Smith directly from Chattanooga. Eighteen hundred of them, under General Hazen, were to take sixty pontoon-boats and, under cover of night, float by the pickets of the enemy at the north base of Lookout, down to Brown's Ferry, then land on the south side and capture or drive away the pickets at that point. Smith was to march with the remainder of the detail, also under cover of night, by the north bank of the river, to Brown's Ferry, taking with him all the material for laying the bridge, as soon as the crossing was secured.

On the 26th Hooker crossed the river at Bridgeport and commenced his eastward march. At 3 o'clock on the morning of the 27th Hazen moved into the stream with his sixty pontoons and eighteen hundred brave and well-equipped men. Smith started enough in advance to be near the river when Hazen should arrive. There are a number of detached spurs of hills north of the river at Chattanooga, back of which is a good road parallel to the stream, sheltered from view from the top of Lookout. It was over this road Smith marched. At 5 o'clock Hazen landed at Brown's Ferry, surprised the picket-guard and captured most of it. By 7 o'clock the whole of Smith's force was ferried over and in possession of a height commanding the ferry. This was speedily fortified while a detail was laying the pontoon-bridge. By 10 o'clock the bridge was laid, and our extreme right, now in Lookout Valley, was fortified and connected with the rest of the army. The two bridges over the Tennessee River,—a flying one at Chattanooga

HAZEN'S MEN LANDING FROM PONTOON-BOATS AT BROWN'S FERRY (SEE MAP, P. 726).
FROM A WAR-TIME SKETCH.

and the new one at Brown's Ferry,—with the road north of the river, covered from both the fire and the view of the enemy, made the connection complete. Hooker found but slight obstacles in his way, and on the afternoon of the 28th emerged into Lookout Valley at Wauhatchie. Howard marched on to Brown's Ferry, while Geary, who commanded a division in the Twelfth Corps, stopped three miles south. The pickets of the enemy on the river below were cut off and soon came in and surrendered.

The river was now open to us from Lookout Valley to Bridgeport. Between Brown's Ferry and Kelley's Ferry the Tennessee runs through a narrow gorge in the mountains, which contracts the stream so much as to increase the current beyond the capacity of an ordinary steamer to stem. To get up these rapids, steamers must be cordelled, that is, pulled up by ropes from the shore. But there is no difficulty in navigating the stream from Bridgeport to Kelley's Ferry. The latter point is only eight miles from Chattanooga, and connected with it by a good wagon road, which runs through a low pass in the Raccoon Mountain on the south side of the river to Brown's Ferry, thence on the north side to the river opposite Chattanooga. There were several steamers at Bridgeport, and abundance of forage, clothing, and provisions.

On the way to Chattanooga I had telegraphed back to Nashville for a good supply of vegetables and small rations, which the troops had been so long deprived of. Hooker had brought with him from the east a full supply of land transportation. His animals had not been subjected to hard work on bad roads without forage, but were in good condition. In five days from my arrival at Chattanooga the way was open to Bridgeport, and, with the aid of steamers and Hooker's teams, in a week the troops were receiving full rations. It is hard for any one not an eye-witness to realize the relief this brought. The men were soon reclothed and well fed; an abundance of ammunition was brought up, and a cheerfulness prevailed not before enjoyed in many weeks. Neither officers nor men looked upon themselves any longer as doomed. The weak and languid appearance of the troops, so visible before, disappeared at once. I do not know what the effect was on the other side, but assume it must have been correspondingly depressing. Mr. Davis had visited Bragg but a short time before, and must have perceived our condition to be about as Bragg described it in his subsequent report. "These dispositions," he said, "faithfully sustained, insured the enemy's speedy evacuation of Chattanooga, for want of food and forage. Possessed of the shortest route to his depot and the one by which reënforcements must reach him, we held him at our mercy, and his destruction was only a question of time." But the dispositions were not "faithfully sustained," and I doubt not that thousands of men engaged in trying to "sustain" them now rejoice that they were not.

There was no time during the rebellion when I did not think, and often say, that the South was more to be benefited by defeat than the North. The latter had the people, the institutions, and the territory to make a great and prosperous nation. The former was burdened with an institution abhorrent to all civilized peoples not brought up under it, and one which degraded labor, kept it in ignorance, and enervated the governing class. With the outside world at war with this institution, they could not have extended their territory. The labor of the country was not skilled, nor allowed to become so. The whites could not toil without becoming degraded, and those who did were denominated "poor white trash." The system of labor would have soon exhausted the soil and left the people poor. The non-slaveholders would have left the country, and the small slaveholder must have sold out to his more fortunate neighbors. Soon the slaves would have outnumbered the masters, and, not being in sympathy with them, would have risen in their might and exterminated them. The war was expensive to the South as well as to the North, both in blood and treasure; but it was worth all it cost.

The enemy was surprised by the movement which secured to us a line of supplies. He appreciated its importance, and hastened to try to recover the line from us. His strength on Lookout Mountain was not equal to Hooker's command in the valley below. From Missionary Ridge he had to march twice the distance we had from Chattanooga, in order to reach Lookout Valley. But on the night of the 28th–29th [of October] an attack was made on Geary, at Wauhatchie, by Longstreet's corps. When the battle commenced, Hooker ordered Howard up from Brown's Ferry. He had three miles to march to reach Geary. On his way he was fired upon by rebel troops from a foot-hill to the left of the road, and from which the road was commanded. Howard turned to the left, and charged up the hill, and captured it before the enemy had time to intrench, taking many prisoners. Leaving sufficient men to hold this height, he pushed on to reënforce Geary. Before he got up, Geary had been engaged for about three hours against a vastly superior force. The night was so dark that the men could not distinguish one another except by the light of the flashes of their muskets. In the darkness and uproar Hooker's teamsters became frightened, and deserted their teams. The mules also became frightened, and, breaking loose from their fastenings, stampeded directly toward the enemy. The latter no doubt took this for a charge, and stampeded in turn. By 4 o'clock in the morning the battle had entirely ceased, and our "cracker line" was never afterward disturbed.[Φ]

[Φ]Major J. L. Coker, of Darlington, South Carolina, says of General Grant's description of this fighting in Lookout Valley:

> "The engagement of Wauhatchie, or Lookout Valley, was of minor importance; but it is well to have errors corrected. General Geary's Federal division was not attacked by Longstreet's corps, but by Jenkins's South Carolina brigade, commanded by Colonel (afterward General) John Bratton. No other troops fired a shot at Geary's men that night. The battle lasted about one hour and a half, and was brought to a close on account of General Howard's advance threatening Bratton's rear, and not by a Confederate stampede caused by a 'mule-charge' in the dark. When the order to retire was received, the brigade was withdrawn in good order. The

In securing possession of Lookout Valley, Smith lost one man killed and four or five wounded. The enemy lost most of his pickets at the ferry by capture. In the night engagement of the 28th–29th Hooker lost 416 killed and wounded. I never knew the loss of the enemy, but our troops buried over 150 of his dead, and captured more than 100.

Having got the Army of the Cumberland in a comfortable position, I now began to look after the remainder of my new command. Burnside was in about as desperate a condition as the Army of the Cumberland had been, only he was not yet besieged. He was a hundred miles from the nearest possible base, Big South Fork of the Cumberland River, and much farther from any railroad we had possession of. The roads back were over mountains, and all supplies along the line had long since been exhausted. His animals, too, had been starved, and their carcasses lined the road from Cumberland Gap, and far back toward Lexington, Kentucky. East Tennessee still furnished supplies of beef, bread, and forage, but it did not supply ammunition, clothing, medical supplies, or small rations, such as coffee, sugar, salt, and rice.

Stopping to organize his new command, Sherman had started from Memphis for Corinth on the 11th of October. His instructions required him to repair the road in his rear in order to bring up supplies. The distance was about 330 miles through a hostile country. His entire command could not have maintained the road if it had been completed. The bridges had all been destroyed by the enemy and much other damage done; a hostile community lived along the road; guerrilla bands infested the country, and more or less of the cavalry of the enemy was still in the west. Often Sherman's work was destroyed as soon as completed, though he was only a short distance away.

The Memphis and Charleston road strikes the Tennessee River at Eastport, Mississippi. Knowing the difficulty Sherman would have to supply himself from Memphis, I had previously ordered supplies sent from St. Louis on small steamers, to be convoyed by the navy, to meet him at Eastport. These he got. I now ordered him to discontinue his work of repairing roads, and to move on with his whole force to Stevenson, Alabama, without delay. This order was borne to Sherman by a messenger who paddled down the Tennessee in a canoe, and floated over Muscle Shoals; it was delivered at Inka on the 27th. In this Sherman was notified that the rebels were moving a force toward Cleveland,

---

writer, acting assistant adjutant-general on Colonel Bratton's staff, was wounded and taken from the field at the close of the battle, and did not observe any disorder. General Howard was opposed by a small force, and made such progress that Jenkins's brigade was in danger of being cut off from the crossing over Lookout Creek. They were ordered out when they seemed to be getting the better of General Geary, who was surprised by the night attack, and no doubt thought himself 'greatly outnumbered,' and reported himself attacked by a corps instead of a brigade."

—Editors.

east Tennessee, and might be going to Nashville, in which event his troops were in the best position to beat them there. Sherman, with his characteristic promptness, abandoned the work he was engaged upon and pushed on at once. On the 1st of November he crossed the Tennessee at Eastport, and that day was in Florence, Alabama, with the head of column, while his troops were still crossing at Eastport, with Blair bringing up the rear.

Sherman's force made an additional army, with cavalry, artillery, and trains, all to be supplied by the single-track road from Nashville. All indications pointed also to the probable necessity of supplying Burnside's command, in east Tennessee, 25,000 more, by the same road. A single track could not do this. I therefore gave an order to Sherman to halt General G. M. Dodge's command of eight thousand men at Athens, and subsequently directed the latter to arrange his troops along the railroad from Decatur, north toward Nashville, and to rebuild that road. The road from Nashville to Decatur passes over a broken country, cut up with innumerable streams, many of them of considerable width, and with valleys far below the road-bed. All the bridges over these had been destroyed and the rails taken up and twisted by the enemy. All the locomotives and cars not carried off had been destroyed as effectually as they knew how to destroy them. All bridges and culverts had been destroyed between Nashville and Decatur, and thence to Stevenson, where the Memphis and

VIEW OF CHATTANOOGA AND MOCCASIN POINT FROM THE SIDE
OF LOOKOUT MOUNTAIN. FROM A PHOTOGRAPH.

Charleston and the Nashville and Chattanooga roads unite. The rebuilding of this road would give us two roads as far as Stevenson over which to supply the army. From Bridgeport, a short distance farther east, the river supplements the road.

General Dodge, besides being a most capable soldier, was an experienced railroad builder. He had no tools to work with except those of the pioneers—axes, picks, and spades. With these he was able to intrench his men and protect them against surprises by small parties of the enemy. As he had no base of supplies until the road could be completed back to Nashville, the first matter to consider, after protecting his men, was the getting in of food and forage from the surrounding country. He had his men and teams bring in all the grain they could find, or all they needed, and all the cattle for beef, and such other food as could be found. Millers were detailed from the ranks to run the mills along the line of the army; when these were not near enough to the troops for protection, they were taken down and moved up to the line of the road. Blacksmith shops, with all the iron and steel found in them, were moved up in like manner. Blacksmiths were detailed and set to work making the tools necessary in railroad and bridge building. Axemen were put to work getting out timber for bridges, and cutting fuel for the locomotives when the road should be completed; carbuilders were set to work repairing the locomotives and cars. Thus every branch of railroad-building, making tools to work with, and supplying the workingmen with food, was all going on at once, and without the aid of a mechanic or laborer except what the command itself furnished. But rails and cars the men could not make without material, and there was not enough rolling stock to keep the road we already had worked to its full capacity. There were no rails except those in use. To supply these deficiencies I ordered eight of the ten engineers General McPherson had at Vicksburg to be sent to Nashville, and all the cars he had, except ten. I also ordered the troops in west Tennessee to points on the river and on the Memphis and Charleston road, and ordered the cars, locomotives, and rails from all the railroads, except the Memphis and Charleston, to Nashville. The military manager of railroads, also, was directed to furnish more rolling stock, and, as far as he could, bridge material. General Dodge had the work assigned him finished within forty days after receiving his orders. The number of bridges to rebuild was 182, many of them over deep and wide chasms. The length of road repaired was 182 miles.

The enemy's troops, which it was thought were either moving against Burnside or were going to Nashville, went no farther than Cleveland. Their presence there, however, alarmed the authorities at Washington, and on account of our helpless condition at Chattanooga caused me much uneasiness. Dispatches were constantly coming, urging me to do something for Burnside's relief; calling attention to the importance of holding east Tennessee; saying the President was much concerned for the protection of the loyal people in that section, etc. We had not at Chattanooga animals to pull a single piece of artillery, much less a supply train. Reënforcements could not help Burnside, because he had neither supplies nor ammunition sufficient for them; hardly indeed bread and meat for the men he had. There was no relief possible for him, except by expelling the enemy from Missionary Ridge and about Chattanooga.

On the 4th of November Longstreet left our front with about 15,000 troops, besides Wheeler's cavalry, 5000 more, to go against Burnside.✦ The situation seemed desperate, and was more exasperating because nothing could be done until Sherman should get up. The authorities at Washington were now more than ever anxious for the safety of Burnside's army, and plied me with dispatches faster than ever, urging that something should be done for his relief. On the 7th, before Longstreet could possibly have reached Knoxville, I ordered Gen. Thomas peremptorily to attack the enemy's right so as to force the return of the troops that had gone up the valley. I directed him to take mules, officers' horses, or animals wherever he could get them, to move the necessary artillery. But he persisted in the declaration that he could not move a single piece of artillery, and could not see how he could possibly comply with the order. Nothing was left to be done but to answer Washington dispatches as best I could, urge Sherman forward, although he was making every effort to get forward, and encourage Burnside to hold on, assuring him that in a short time he would be relieved. All of Burnside's dispatches showed the greatest confidence in his ability to hold his position as long as his ammunition should hold out. He even suggested the propriety of abandoning the territory he held south and west of Knoxville, so as to draw the enemy farther from his base, and to make it more difficult for him to get back to Chattanooga when the battle should begin. Longstreet had a railroad as far as London; but from there to Knoxville he had to rely on wagon trains. Burnside's suggestion, therefore, was a good one, and it was adopted. On the 14th I telegraphed him:

> "Sherman's advance has reached Bridgeport. His whole force will be ready to move from there by Tuesday at furthest. If you can hold Longstreet in check until he gets up, or, by skirmishing and falling back, can avoid serious loss to yourself, and gain time, I will be able to force the enemy back from here, and place a force between Longstreet and Bragg that must inevitably make the former take to the mountain-passes by every available road, to get to his supplies. Sherman would have been here before this but for the high water in Elk River driving him some thirty miles up the river to cross."

✦In the course of the preparation of this paper we asked General Grant, whether the detachment of Longstreet for the attack on Knoxville was not, in his opinion, a great mistake on the part of Bragg. He replied in the affirmative; and when it was further presumed that Bragg doubtless thought his position impregnable, the Victor of Chattanooga answered, with a shrewd look that accented the humor of his words: "Well, it *was* impregnable."—EDITORS.

VIEW OF LOOKOUT MOUNTAIN FROM THE HILL TO THE NORTH, WHICH WAS GENERAL HOOKER'S POSITION DURING THE BATTLE
ON THE MOUNTAIN, NOVEMBER 24, 1863: FROM A WAR-TIME PHOTOGRAPH.

The military road winding over the north slope of Lookout was built after Hooker captured the mountain.

Longstreet, for some reason or other, stopped at London until the 13th. That being the terminus of his railroad communications, it is probable he was directed to remain there awaiting orders.♭ He was in a position threatening Knoxville, and at the same time where he could be brought back speedily to Chattanooga. The day after Longstreet left London, Sherman reached Bridgeport in person, and proceeded on to see me that evening, the 14th, and reached Chattanooga the next day.

My orders for the battle were all prepared in advance of Sherman's arrival, except the dates, which could not be fixed while troops to be engaged were so far away. The possession of Lookout Mountain was of no special advantage to us now. Hooker was instructed to send Howard's corps to the north side of the Tennessee, thence up behind the hills on the north side, and to go into camp opposite Chattanooga; with the remainder of the command Hooker was, at a time to be afterward appointed, to ascend the western slope between the upper and lower palisades, and so get into Chattanooga Valley.

The plan of battle was for Sherman to attack the enemy's right flank, form a line across it, extend our left over South Chickamauga River, so as to threaten or hold the railroad in Bragg's rear,∕ and thus force him either to weaken his lines elsewhere or lose his connection with his base at Chickamauga Station. Hooker was to perform like service on our right. His problem was to get from Lookout Valley to Chattanooga Valley in the most expeditious way possible; cross the latter valley rapidly to Rossville, south of Bragg's line on Missionary Ridge, form line there across the ridge, facing north, with his right flank extended to Chickamauga Valley east of the ridge, thus threatening the enemy's rear on that flank and compelling him to reënforce this also. Thomas, with the Army of the Cumberland, occupied the center, and was to assault while the enemy was engaged with most of his forces on his two flanks.

To carry out this plan, Sherman was to cross the Tennessee at Brown's Ferry and move east of Chattanooga to a point opposite the north end of Missionary Ridge, and to place his command back of the foot-hills out of sight of the enemy on the ridge. There are two streams called Chickamauga emptying into the Tennessee River east of Chattanooga: North Chickamauga, taking its rise in Tennessee, flowing south and emptying into the river some seven or eight miles east; while the South Chickamauga, which takes its rise in Georgia, flows northward, and empties into the Tennessee some three or four miles above the town. There were now 116 pontoons in the North Chickamauga River, their presence there being unknown to the enemy.

♭In his history, the Comte de Paris says Longstreet was delayed "by the necessity of collecting provisions and organizing his trains."—Editors.
∕A bridge was thrown across the South Chickamauga Creek, at its mouth, and a brigade of cavalry was sent across it. That brigade caused the bridge across the Holston River to be burned by the enemy and thus cut off General Longstreet's forces from coming back to General Bragg.—Editors.

At night a division was to be marched up to that point, and at 2 o'clock in the morning moved down with the current, thirty men in each boat. A few were to land east of the mouth of the South Chickamauga, capture the pickets there, and then lay a bridge connecting the two banks of the river. The rest were to land on the south side of the Tennessee, where Missionary Ridge would strike it if prolonged, and a sufficient number of men to man the boats were to push to the north side to ferry over the main body of Sherman's command, while those left on the south side intrenched themselves.☆ Thomas was to move out from his lines facing the ridge, leaving enough of Palmer's corps to guard against an attack down the valley. Lookout Valley being of no present value to us, and being untenable by the enemy if we should secure Missionary Ridge, Hooker's orders were changed. His revised orders brought him to Chattanooga by the established route north of the Tennessee. He was then to move out to the right to Rossville.‡

The next day after Sherman's arrival I took him, with Generals Thomas and Smith and other officers, to the north side of the river and showed them the ground over which Sherman had to march, and pointed out generally what he was expected to do. I, as well as the authorities in Washington, was still in a great state of anxiety for Burnside's safety. Burnside himself, I believe, was the only one who did not share in this anxiety. Nothing could be done for him, however, until Sherman's troops were up. As soon, therefore, as the inspection was over, Sherman started for Bridgeport to hasten matters, rowing a boat himself, I believe, from Kelley's Ferry. Sherman had left Bridgeport the night of the 14th, reached Chattanooga the evening of the 15th, made the above-described

---

☆This was not, however, the original plan to which Sherman assented, which was to march at once for the north end of the ridge.—EDITORS.

‡Hooker's position in Lookout Valley was absolutely essential to us so long as Chattanooga was besieged. It was the key to our line for supplying the army. But it was not essential after the enemy was dispersed from our front, or even after the battle for this purpose was begun. Hooker's orders, therefore, were designed to get his force past Lookout Mountain and Chattanooga Valley, and up to Missionary Ridge. By crossing the north face of Lookout the troops would come into Chattanooga Valley in rear of the line held by the enemy across the valley, and would necessarily force its evacuation. Orders were accordingly given to Hooker to march by this route. But days before the battle began the advantages as well as disadvantages of this plan of action were all considered. The passage over the mountain was a difficult one to make in the face of an enemy. It might consume so much time as to lose us the use of the troops engaged in it at other points where they were more wanted. After reaching Chattanooga Valley, the creek of the same name, quite a formidable stream to get an army over, had to be crossed.

I was perfectly willing that the enemy should keep Lookout Mountain until we got through with the troops on Missionary Ridge. By marching Hooker to the north side of the river, thence up the stream and recrossing at the town, he could be got in position at any named time; when in this new position he would have Chattanooga Creek behind him; and the attack on Missionary Ridge would unquestionably have caused the evacuation by the enemy of his line across the valley and on Lookout Mountain. Hooker's order was changed accordingly. As explained elsewhere, the original order had to be reverted to because of a flood in the river rendering the bridge at Brown's Ferry unsafe for the passage of troops at the exact juncture when it was wanted to bring all the troops together against Missionary Ridge.
—U.S.G.

inspection the morning of the 16th, and started back the same evening to hurry up his command, fully appreciating the importance of time.

His march was conducted with as much expedition as the roads and season would admit of. By the 20th he was himself at Brown's Ferry with head of column, but many of his troops were far behind, and one division, Ewing's, was at Trenton, sent that way to create the impression that Lookout was to be taken from the south. Sherman received his orders at the ferry, and was asked if he could not be ready for the assault the following morning. News had been received that the battle had been commenced at Knoxville. Burnside had been cut off from telegraphic communication. The President, the Secretary of War, and General Halleck were in an agony of suspense. My suspense was also great, but more endurable, because I was where I could soon do something to relieve the situation. It was impossible to get Sherman's troops up for the next day. I then asked him if they could not be got up to make the assault on the morning of the 22d, and ordered Thomas to move on that date. But the elements were against us. It rained all the 20th and 21st. The river rose so rapidly that it was difficult to keep the pontoons in place.

General Orlando B. Willcox, a division commander under Burnside, was at this time occupying a position farther up the valley than Knoxville,—about Maynardsville,—and was still in telegraphic communication with the North. A dispatch was received from him, saying that he was threatened from the east. The following was sent in reply:

> "If you can communicate with General Burnside, say to him that our attack on Bragg will commence in the morning. If successful, such a move will be made as, I think, will relieve east Tennessee, if he can hold out. Longstreet passing through our lines to Kentucky need not cause alarm. He would find the country so bare that he would lose his transportation and artillery before reaching Kentucky, and would meet such a force before he got through that he could not return."

Meantime Sherman continued his crossing, without intermission, as fast as his troops could be got up. The crossing had to be effected in full view of the enemy on the top of Lookout Mountain. Once over, the troops soon disappeared behind the detached hills on the north side, and would not come to view again, either to watchmen on Lookout Mountain or Missionary Ridge, until they emerged between the hills to strike the bank of the river. But when Sherman's advance reached a point opposite the town of Chattanooga, Howard, who, it will be remembered, had been concealed behind the hills on the north side, took up his line of march to join the troops on the south side. His crossing was in full view both from Missionary Ridge and the top of Lookout, and the enemy, of course, supposed these troops to be Sherman's. This enabled Sherman to get to his assigned position without discovery.

On the 20th, when so much was occurring to discourage,—rains falling so heavily as to delay the passage of troops over the river at Brown's Ferry, and threatening the entire breaking of the bridge; news coming of a battle raging at Knoxville; of Willcox being threatened by a force from the east,—a letter was received from Bragg which contained these words:

"As there may still be some non-combatants in Chattanooga, I deem it proper to notify you that prudence would dictate their early withdrawal."

Of course I understood that this was a device intended to deceive; but I did not know what the intended deception was. On the 22d, however, a deserter came in who informed me that Bragg was leaving our front, and on that day Buckner's division was sent to reënforce Longstreet, at Knoxville, and another division started to follow, but was recalled. The object of Bragg's letter no doubt was in some way to detain me until Knoxville could be captured, and his troops there be returned to Chattanooga.

During the night of the 21st the rest of the pontoon-boats, completed, one hundred and sixteen in all, were carried up to and placed in North Chickamauga. The material for the roadway over these was deposited out of view of the enemy within a few hundred yards of the bank of the Tennessee where the north end of the bridge was to rest.

Hearing nothing from Burnside, and hearing much of the distress in Washington on his account, I could no longer defer operations for his relief. I determined therefore to do on the 23d, with the Army of the Cumberland, what had been intended to be done on the 24th.

The position occupied by the Army of the Cumberland had been made very strong for defense during the months it had been besieged. The line was about a mile from the town, and extended from Citico Creek, a small stream running near the base of Missionary Ridge and emptying into the Tennessee about two miles below the mouth of the South Chickamauga, on the left, to Chattanooga Creek on the right. All commanding points on the line were well fortified and well equipped with artillery. The important elevations within the line had all been carefully fortified and supplied with a proper armament. Among the elevations so fortified was one to the east of the town, named Fort Wood. It owed its importance chiefly to the fact that it lay between the town and Missionary Ridge, where most of the strength of the enemy was. Fort Wood had in it twenty-two pieces of artillery, most of which would reach the nearer points of the enemy's line. On the morning of the 23d Thomas, according to instructions, moved Granger's corps of two divisions, Sheridan and T. J. Wood commanding, to the foot of Fort Wood, and formed them into line as if going on parade—Sheridan on the right, Wood to the left, extending to or near Citico Creek. Palmer, commanding the Fourteenth Corps, held that part of our line facing south and south-west. He supported Sheridan with one division, Baird's, while his other division, under [R. W.] Johnson, remained in the trenches, under arms, ready to be moved to any point. Howard's corps was moved in rear of the center. The picket lines were within a few hundred yards of each other. At 2 o'clock in the afternoon all were ready to advance. By this time the clouds had lifted so that the enemy could see from his elevated position all that was going on. The signal for advance was given by a booming of cannon from Fort Wood and other points on the line. The rebel pickets were soon driven back upon the main guards, which occupied minor and detached heights between the main ridge and our lines. These too were carried before halting, and before the enemy had time to reënforce their advance guards. But it was not without loss on both sides. This movement secured to us a line fully a mile in advance of the one we occupied in the morning, and one which the enemy had occupied up to this time. The fortifications were rapidly turned to face the other way. During the following night they were made strong. We lost in this preliminary action about eleven hundred killed and wounded, while the enemy probably lost quite as heavily, including the prisoners that were captured. With the exception of the firing of artillery, kept up from Missionary Ridge and Fort Wood until night closed in, this ended the fighting for the day.

The advantage was greatly on our side now, and if I could only have been

BRIDGING LOOKOUT CREEK PREPARATORY TO THE ASSAULT BY HOOKER.
FROM A WAR-TIME SKETCH.

THE BATTLE OF LOOKOUT MOUNTAIN. FROM A PAINTING LENT
BY CAPTAIN W. L. STORK.

This picture shows the Union troops fighting in the woods near the cliffs of Point Lookout.

Early in October, 1863, Jefferson Davis visited Lookout Mountain with General Bragg. As they approached the edge of the cliff, General Bragg, with a wave of the hand, alluded to "the fine view"; whereupon Major Robert W. Wooley, who had little faith in the military outlook, exclaimed to a brother officer, but so that all could hear: "Yes, it's a fine view, but a —— bad prospect."

—Editors.

assured that Burnside could hold out ten days longer I should have rested more easy. But we were doing the best we could for him and the cause.

By the night of the 23d Sherman's command was in a position to move, though one division (Osterhaus's) had not yet crossed the river at Brown's Ferry. The continuous rise in the Tennessee had rendered it impossible to keep the bridge at that point in condition for troops to cross; but I was determined to move that night, even without this division. Accordingly, orders were sent to Osterhaus to report to Hooker if he could not cross by 8 o'clock on the morning of the 24th. Because of the break in the bridge, Hooker's orders were again changed, but this time only back to those first given to him.

General W. F. Smith had been assigned to duty as chief engineer of the military division. To him was given the general direction of moving troops by the boats from North Chickamauga, laying the bridge after they reached their position, and, generally, all the duties pertaining to his office of chief engineer. During the night General Morgan L. Smith's division was marched to the point where the pontoons were, and the brigade of Giles A. Smith was selected for the delicate duty of manning the boats and surprising the enemy's pickets on the south bank of the river. During this night, also, General J. M. Brannan, chief of artillery, moved forty pieces of artillery belonging to the Army of the Cumberland, and placed them on the north side of the river so as to command the ground opposite, to aid in protecting the approach to the point where the south end of the bridge was to rest. He had to use Sherman's artillery horses for this purpose, Thomas having none.

At 2 o'clock in the morning, November 24th, Giles A. Smith pushed out from the North Chickamauga with his 116 boats, each loaded with 30 brave and well-armed men. The boats, with their precious freight, dropped down quietly with the current to avoid attracting the attention of any one who could convey information to the enemy, until arriving near the mouth of South Chickamauga. Here a few boats were landed, the troops debarked, and a rush was made upon the picket-guard known to be at that point. The guard was surprised, and twenty of their number captured. The remainder of the troops effected a landing at the point where the bridge was to start, with equally good results. The work of ferrying over Sherman's command from the north side of the Tennessee was at once commenced, using the pontoons for the purpose. A steamer was also brought up from the town to assist. The rest of M. L. Smith's division came first, then the division of John E. Smith. The troops as they landed were put to work intrenching their position. By daylight the two entire divisions were over, and well covered by the works they had built.

The work of laying the bridge on which to cross the artillery and cavalry was now begun. The ferrying over the infantry was continued with the steamer and the pontoons, taking the pontoons, however, as fast as they were wanted to put in their place in the bridge. By a little past noon the bridge was completed, as well as one over the South Chickamauga, connecting the troops left on that side with their comrades below, and all the infantry and artillery were on the south bank of the Tennessee.

Sherman at once formed his troops for assault on Missionary Ridge. By 1 o'clock he started, with M. L. Smith on his left, keeping nearly the course of Chickamauga River; J. E. Smith next, to the right and a little in the rear; then Ewing, still farther to the right, and also a little to the rear of J. E. Smith's command, in column ready to deploy to the right if an enemy should come from that direction. A good skirmish line preceded each of these columns. Soon the foot of the hill was reached; the skirmishers pushed directly up, followed closely by their supports. By half-past 3 Sherman was in possession of the height, without having sustained much loss. A brigade from each division was now brought up, and artillery was dragged to the top of the hill by hand. The enemy did not seem to have been aware of this movement until the top of the hill was gained. There had been a drizzling rain during the day, and the clouds were so low that Lookout Mountain and the top of Missionary Ridge were obscured from the view of persons in the valley. But now the enemy opened fire upon their assailants, and made several attempts with their skirmishers to drive them away, but without avail. Later in the day a more determined attack was made, but this, too, failed, and Sherman was left to fortify what he had gained.

Sherman's cavalry took up its line of march soon after the bridge was completed, and by half-past three the whole of it was over both bridges, and on its way to strike the enemy's communications at Chickamauga Station. All of Sherman's command was now south of the Tennessee. During the afternoon General Giles A. Smith was severely wounded and carried from the field.

Thomas having done on the 23d what was expected of him on the 24th, there was nothing for him to do this day, except to strengthen his position. Howard, however, effected a crossing of Citico Creek and a junction with Sherman, and was directed to report to him. With two or three regiments of his command, he moved in the morning along the banks of the Tennessee and reached the point where the bridge was being laid. He went out on the bridge as far as it was completed from the south end, and saw Sherman superintending the work from the north side, moving himself south as fast as an additional boat was put in and the roadway put upon it. Howard reported to his new chief across the chasm between them, which was now narrow and in a few minutes was closed.

While these operations were going on to the east of Chattanooga, Hooker was engaged on the west. He had three divisions: Osterhaus's, of the Fifteenth Corps, Army of the Tennessee; Geary's, Twelfth Corps, Army of the Potomac; and Cruft's, Fourteenth Corps, Army of the Cumberland. Geary was on the right at Wauhatchie, Cruft at the center, and Osterhaus near Brown's Ferry. These troops were all west of Lookout Creek. The enemy had the east bank of

THE FIGHT EAST OF THE PALISADES ON LOOKOUT MOUNTAIN.
FROM A WAR-TIME SKETCH.

the creek strongly picketed and intrenched, and three brigades of troops in the rear to reënforce them if attacked. These brigades occupied the summit of the mountain. General Carter L. Stevenson was in command of the whole. Why any troops except artillery, with a small infantry guard, were kept on the mountain-top, I do not see. A hundred men could have held the summit— which is a palisade for more than thirty feet down—against the assault of any number of men from the position Hooker occupied.

The side of Lookout Mountain confronting Hooker's command was rugged, heavily timbered, and full of chasms, making it difficult to advance with troops, even in the absence of an opposing force. Farther up the ground becomes more even and level, and was in cultivation. On the east side the slope is much more gradual, and a good wagon road, zigzagging up it, connects the town of Chattanooga with the summit.

Early in the morning of the 24th Hooker moved Geary's division, supported by a brigade of Cruft's, up Lookout Creek, to effect a crossing. The remainder of Cruft's division was to seize the bridge over the creek, near the crossing of the railroad. Osterhaus was to move up to the bridge and cross it. The bridge was seized by Grose's brigade after a slight skirmish with the picket guarding it. This attracted the enemy so that Geary's movement farther up was not observed. A heavy mist obscured him from the view of the troops on the top of the mountain. He crossed the creek almost unobserved, and captured the picket of over forty men on guard near by. He then commenced ascending the mountain directly in his front. By this time the enemy was seen coming down from their camp on the mountain slope, and filing into their rifle-pits to contest the crossing of the bridge. By 11 o'clock the bridge was complete. Osterhaus was up, and after some sharp skirmishing the enemy was driven away, with considerable loss in killed and captured.

While the operations at the bridge were progressing, Geary was pushing up the hill over great obstacles, resisted by the enemy directly in his front, and in face of the guns on top of the mountain. The enemy, seeing their left flank and rear menaced, gave way and were followed by Cruft and Osterhaus. Soon these were up abreast of Geary, and the whole command pushed up the hill, driving the enemy in advance. By noon Geary had gained the open ground on the north slope of the mountain with his right close up to the base of the upper palisade, but there were strong fortifications in his front. The rest of the command coming up, a line was formed from the base of the upper palisade to the mouth of Chattanooga Creek.

Thomas and I were on the top of Orchard Knob. Hooker's advance now made our line a continuous one. It was in full view extending from the Tennessee River, where Sherman had crossed, up Chickamauga River to the base of Missionary Ridge, over the top of the north end of the ridge, to Chattanooga Valley, then along parallel to the ridge a mile or more, across the valley to the mouth of Chattanooga Creek, thence up the slope of Lookout Mountain to the foot of the upper palisade. The day was hazy, so that Hooker's operations were not visible to us except at moments when the clouds would rise. But the sound of his artillery and musketry was heard incessantly. The enemy on his front was partially fortified, but was soon driven out of his works. At 2 o'clock the clouds, which had so obscured the top of Lookout all day as to hide whatever was going on from the view of those below, settled down and made it so dark where Hooker was as to stop operations for the time. At 4 o'clock Hooker reported his position as impregnable. By a little after 5, direct communication was established, and a brigade of troops was sent from Chattanooga to reënforce him. These troops had to cross Chattanooga Creek, and met with some opposition, but soon overcame it, and by night the commander, General Carlin, reported to Hooker and was assigned to his left. I now telegraphed to Washington:

> "The fight to-day progressed favorably. Sherman carried the end of Missionary Ridge, and his right is now at the tunnel, and his left at Chickamauga Creek. Troops from Lookout Valley carried the point of the mountain, and now hold the eastern slope and a point high up. Hooker re-

ports two thousand prisoners taken, besides which a small number have fallen into our hands, from Missionary Ridge."

The next day the President replied:

"Your dispatches as to fighting on Monday and Tuesday are here. Well done. Many thanks to all. Remember Burnside."

Halleck also telegraphed:

"I congratulate you on the success thus far of your plans. I fear that Burnside is hard pushed, and that any further delay may prove fatal. I know you will do all in your power to relieve him."

The division of Jefferson C. Davis, Army of the Cumberland, had been sent to the North Chickamauga to guard the pontoons as they were deposited in the river, and to prevent all ingress or egress by citizens. On the night of the 24th his division, having crossed with Sherman, occupied our extreme left, from the upper bridge over the plain to the north base of Missionary Ridge. Firing continued to a late hour in the night, but it was not connected with an assault at any point.

At 12 o'clock at night, when all was quiet, I began to give orders for the next day, and sent a dispatch to Willcox to encourage Burnside. Sherman was directed to attack at daylight. Hooker was ordered to move at the same hour, and endeavor to intercept the enemy's retreat, if he still remained; if he had gone, then to move directly to Rossville and operate against the left and rear of the force on Missionary Ridge. Thomas was not to move until Hooker had reached Missionary Ridge. As I was with him on Orchard Knob, he would not move without further orders from me.

The morning of the 25th opened clear and bright, and the whole field was in full view from the top of Orchard Knob. It remained so all day. Bragg's headquarters were in full view, and officers—presumably staff-officers—could be seen coming and going constantly.

The point of ground which Sherman had carried on the 24th was almost disconnected from the main ridge occupied by the enemy. A low pass, over which there is a wagon road crossing the hill, and near which there is a railroad tunnel, intervenes between the two hills. The problem now was to get to the latter. The enemy was fortified on the point, and back farther, where the ground was still higher, was a second fortification commanding the first. Sherman was out as soon as it was light enough to see, and by sunrise his command was in motion. Three brigades held the hill already gained. Morgan L. Smith moved along the east base of Missionary Ridge; Loomis along the west base, supported

by two brigades of John E. Smith's division; and Corse with his brigade was between the two, moving directly toward the hill to be captured. The ridge is
steep and heavily wooded on the east side, where M. L. Smith's troops were advancing, but cleared and with a more gentle slope on the west side. The troops
advanced rapidly and carried the extreme end of the rebel works. Morgan L.
Smith advanced to a point which cut the enemy off from the railroad bridge and
the means of bringing up supplies by rail from Chickamauga Station, where the
main depot was located. The enemy made brave and strenuous efforts to drive
our troops from the position we had gained, but without success. The contest
lasted for two hours. Corse, a brave and efficient commander, was badly
wounded in this assault. Sherman now threatened both Bragg's flank and his
stores, and made it necessary for him to weaken other points of his line to
strengthen his right. From the position I occupied I could see column after column of Bragg's forces moving against Sherman; every Confederate gun that
could be brought to bear upon the Union forces was concentrated upon him.
J. E. Smith, with two brigades, charged up the west side of the ridge to the support of Corse's command, over open ground, and in the face of a heavy fire of
both artillery and musketry, and reached the very parapet of the enemy. He lay
here for a time, but the enemy coming with a heavy force upon his right flank,
he was compelled to fall back, followed by the foe. A few hundred yards
brought Smith's troops into a wood, where they were speedily re-formed, when
they charged and drove the attacking party back to his intrenchments.

Seeing the advance, repulse, and second advance of J. E. Smith from the position I occupied, I directed Thomas to send a division to reënforce him. Baird's
division was accordingly sent from the right of Orchard Knob. It had to march
a considerable distance, directly under the eyes of the enemy, to reach its position.☆ Bragg at once commenced massing in the same direction. This was what
I wanted. But it had now got to be late in the afternoon, and I had expected before this to see Hooker crossing the ridge in the neighborhood of Rossville, and
compelling Bragg to mass in that direction also.

The enemy had evacuated Lookout Mountain during the night, as I expected he would. In crossing the valley he burned the bridges over Chattanooga
Creek, and did all he could to obstruct the roads behind him. Hooker was off
bright and early, with no obstructions in his front but distance and the destruction above named. He was detained four hours in crossing Chattanooga Creek,
and thus was lost the immediate advantages I expected from his forces. His
reaching Bragg's flank and extending across it was to be the signal for Thomas's

---

☆Concerning this movement General Baird writes as follows: "I was ordered to report to General Sherman to reënforce his command. I marched the distance, about two miles to the rear of his position, and
sent an officer to report to him, but I immediately received orders to return and form on the left of the
line which was to assault Missionary Ridge. I reached there, and got my troops in position, just as the gun
was fired directing the assault."—EDITORS.

BAIRD'S DIVISION FIGHTING FOR THE CREST OF MISSIONARY RIDGE.
FROM THE ATLANTA CYCLORAMA.

assault of the ridge. But Sherman's condition was getting so critical that the assault for his relief could not be delayed any longer.

Sheridan's and Wood's divisions had been lying under arms from early in the morning, ready to move the instant the signal was given. I now directed Thomas to order the charge at once.‡ I watched eagerly to see the effect, and became impatient at last that there was no indication of any charge being made. The center of the line which was to make the charge was near where Thomas and I stood together, but concealed from our view by the intervening forest. Turning to Thomas to inquire what caused the delay, I was surprised to see General Thomas J. Wood, one of the division commanders who were to make the charge, standing talking to him. I spoke to General Wood, asking him why he had not charged, as ordered an hour before. He replied very promptly that this was the first he had heard of it, but that he had been ready all day to move at a moment's notice. I told him to make the charge at once. He was off in a moment, and in an incredibly short time loud cheering was heard, and he and Sheridan were driving the enemy's advance before them toward Missionary Ridge. The Confederates were strongly intrenched on the crest of the ridge in

---

‡In this order authority was given for the troops to re-form after taking the first line of rifle-pits preparatory to carrying the ridge.—U.S.G.

front of us, and had a second line half-way down and another at the base. Our men drove the troops in front of the lower line of rifle-pits so rapidly, and followed them so closely, that rebel and Union troops went over the first line of works almost at the same time. Many rebels were captured and sent to the rear under the fire of their own friends higher up the hill. Those that were not captured retreated, and were pursued. The retreating hordes being between friends and pursuers, caused the enemy to fire high, to avoid killing their own men. In fact, on that occasion the Union soldier nearest the enemy was in the safest position. Without awaiting further orders or stopping to re-form, on our troops went to the second line of works; over that and on for the crest—thus effectually carrying out my orders of the 18th for the battle and of the 24th for this charge. I watched their progress with intense interest. The fire along the rebel line was terrific. Cannon and musket balls filled the air; but the damage done was in small proportion to the ammunition used.[⚓] The pursuit continued until the crest was reached, and soon our men were seen climbing over the Confederate barrier at different points in front of both Sheridan's and Wood's divisions. The retreat of the enemy along most of his line was precipitate, and the panic so great that Bragg and his officers lost all control over their men. Many were captured and thousands threw away their arms in their flight.

Sheridan pushed forward until he reached the Chickamauga River at a point above where the enemy had crossed. He met some resistance from troops occupying a second hill in rear of Missionary Ridge, probably to cover the retreat of the main body and of the artillery and trains. It was now getting dark, but Sheridan, without halting on that account, pushed his men forward up this second hill slowly and without attracting the attention of the men placed to defend it, while he detached to the right and left to surround the position. The enemy discovered the movement before these dispositions were complete, and beat a hasty retreat, leaving artillery, wagon trains, and many prisoners in our hands. To Sheridan's prompt movement the Army of the Cumberland and the nation are indebted for the bulk of the capture of prisoners, artillery, and small-arms that day. Except for his prompt pursuit, so much in this way would not have been accomplished.

[⚓]Captain Benjamin F. Hegler, of Attica, Indiana, who was second in command of the 15th Indiana in the assault on Missionary Ridge, writes to the editors:

"General Grant says of the assault on Missionary Ridge that 'the fire along the rebel line was terrific. Cannon and musket balls filled the air; but the damage done was in small proportion to the ammunition used.' The inference might be that the assault, though brilliant, was after all a rather harmless diversion. The 15th Indiana, of Sheridan's division, started up the ridge just to the left of Bragg's headquarters with 337 officers and men, and lost 202 killed and wounded, in just forty-five minutes, the time taken to advance from the line of works at the foot of the ridge and to carry the crest. This report I made officially to General Sheridan near Chickamauga Creek the morning after the battle."

While the advance up Missionary Ridge was going forward, General Thomas, with his staff, General Gordon Granger, commander of the corps, making the assault, and myself and staff, occupied Orchard Knob, from which the entire field could be observed. The moment the troops were seen going over the last line of rebel defenses I ordered Granger to join his command, and mounting my horse I rode to the front. General Thomas left about the same time. Sheridan, on the extreme right, was already in pursuit of the enemy east of the ridge. Wood, who commanded the division to the left of Sheridan, accompanied his men on horseback, but did not join Sheridan in the pursuit. To the left, in Baird's front, where Bragg's troops had massed against Sherman, the resistance was more stubborn, and the contest lasted longer. I ordered Granger to follow the enemy with Wood's division, but he was so much excited, and kept up such a roar of musketry, in the direction the enemy had taken, that by the time I could stop the firing the enemy had got well out of the way. The enemy confronting Sherman, now seeing everything to their left giving way, fled also. Sherman, however, was not aware of the extent of our success until after nightfall, when he received orders to pursue at daylight in the morning.

Hooker, as stated, was detained at Chattanooga Creek by the destruction of

THE CONFEDERATE LINE OPPOSED TO BAIRD'S DIVISION ON MISSIONARY RIDGE.
FROM THE ATLANTA CYCLORAMA.

the bridges at that point. He got his troops over, with the exception of the artillery, by fording the stream, at a little after 3 o'clock. Leaving his artillery to follow when the bridges should be reconstructed, he pushed on with the remainder of his command. At Rossville he came upon the flank of a division of the enemy, which soon commenced a retreat along the ridge. This threw them on Palmer. They could make but little resistance in the position they were caught in, and as many of them as could do so escaped. Many, however, were captured. Hooker's position during the night of the 25th was near Rossville, extending east of the ridge. Palmer was on his left, on the road to Graysville.

During the night I telegraphed to Willcox that Bragg had been defeated, and that immediate relief would be sent to Burnside if he could hold out; to Halleck I sent an announcement of our victory, and informed him that forces would be sent up the valley to relieve Burnside.

Before the battle of Chattanooga opened I had taken measures for the relief of Burnside the moment the way should be clear. Thomas was directed to have the little steamer that had been built at Chattanooga loaded to its capacity with rations and ammunition. Granger's corps was to move by the south bank of the Tennessee River to the mouth of the Holston, and up that to Knoxville, accompanied by the boat. In addition to the supplies transported by boat, the men were to carry forty rounds of ammunition in their cartridge-boxes, and four days' rations in haversacks.

In the battle of Chattanooga, troops from the Army of the Potomac, from the Army of the Tennessee, and from the Army of the Cumberland participated. In fact, the accidents growing out of the heavy rains and the sudden rise in the Tennessee River so mingled the troops that the organizations were not kept together, under their respective commanders, during the battle. Hooker, on the right, had Geary's division of the Twelfth Corps, Army of the Potomac; Osterhaus's division of the Fifteenth Corps, Army of the Tennessee; and Cruft's division of the Army of the Cumberland. Sherman had three divisions of his own army, Howard's corps from the Army of the Potomac, and Jeff. C. Davis's division of the Army of the Cumberland. There was no jealousy— hardly rivalry. Indeed I doubt whether officers or men took any note at the time of this intermingling of commands. All saw a defiant foe surrounding them, and took it for granted that every move was intended to dislodge him, and it made no difference where the troops came from so that the end was accomplished.

The victory at Chattanooga was won against great odds, considering the advantage the enemy had of position; and was accomplished more easily than was expected by reason of Bragg's making several grave mistakes: first, in sending away his ablest corps commander, with over 20,000 troops; second, in sending away a division of troops on the eve of battle; third, in placing so much of a force on the plain in front of his impregnable position.

It was known that Mr. Davis had visited Bragg on Missionary Ridge a short time before my reaching Chattanooga. It was reported and believed that he had come out to reconcile a serious difference between Bragg and Longstreet, and finding this difficult to do planned the campaign against Knoxville, to be conducted by the latter general. I had known both Bragg and Longstreet before the war, the latter very well. We had been three years at West Point together, and, after my graduation, for a time in the same regiment. Then we served together in the Mexican war. I had known Bragg in Mexico, and met him occasionally subsequently. I could well understand how there might be an irreconcilable difference between them.

Bragg was a remarkably intelligent and well-informed man, professionally and otherwise. He was also thoroughly upright. But he was possessed of an irascible temper, and was naturally disputatious. A man of the highest moral character and the most correct habits, yet in the old army he was in frequent trouble. As a subordinate he was always on the lookout to catch his commanding officer infringing upon his prerogatives; as a post commander he was equally vigilant to detect the slightest neglect, even of the most trivial order.

I heard in the old army an anecdote characteristic of General Bragg. On one occasion, when stationed at a post of several companies, commanded by a field-officer, he was himself commanding one of the companies and at the same time acting post quartermaster and commissary. He was a first lieutenant at the time, but his captain was detached on other duty. As commander of the company he made a requisition upon the quartermaster—himself—for something he wanted. As quartermaster he declined to fill the requisition, and indorsed on the back of it his reason for so doing. As company commander he responded to this, urging that his requisition called for nothing but what he was entitled to, and that it was the duty of the quartermaster to fill it. As quartermaster he still persisted that he was right. In this condition of affairs Bragg referred the whole matter to the commanding officer of the post. The latter, when he saw the nature of the matter referred, exclaimed: "My God, Mr. Bragg, you have quarreled with every officer in the army, and now you are quarreling with yourself."

Longstreet was an entirely different man. He was brave, honest, intelligent, a very capable soldier, subordinate to his superiors, just and kind to his subordinates, but jealous of his own rights, which he had the courage to maintain. He was never on the lookout to detect a slight, but saw one as soon as anybody when intentionally given.

It may be that Longstreet was not sent to Knoxville for the reason stated, but because Mr. Davis had an exalted opinion of his own military genius, and thought he saw a chance of "killing two birds with one stone." On several occasions during the war he came to the relief of the Union army by means of his *superior military genius.*

I speak advisedly when I say Mr. Davis prided himself on his military capacity. He says so himself virtually, in his answer to the notice of his nomination to the Confederate Presidency. Some of his generals have said so in their writings since the downfall of the Confederacy. Whatever the cause or whoever is to blame, grave mistakes were made at Chattanooga, which enabled us, with the undaunted courage of the troops engaged, to gain a great victory, under the most trying circumstances presented during the war, much more easily than could otherwise have been attained. If Chattanooga had been captured, east Tennessee would have followed without a struggle. It would have been a victory to have got the army away from Chattanooga safely. It was manifold greater to defeat, and nearly destroy, the besieging army.

In this battle the Union army numbered in round figures about 60,000 men; we lost 752 killed, and 4713 wounded and 350 captured or missing. The rebel loss was much greater in the aggregate, as we captured, and sent North to be rationed there, over 6100 prisoners. Forty pieces of artillery, over seven thousand stand of small-arms, and many caissons, artillery wagons, and baggage wagons fell into our hands. The probabilities are that our loss in killed was the heavier, as we were the attacking party. The enemy reported his loss in killed at 361; but as he reported his missing at 4146, while we held over 6000 of them as prisoners, and there must have been hundreds, if not thousands, who deserted, but little reliance can be placed in this report. There was certainly great dissatisfaction with Bragg,⁺ on the part of the soldiers, for his harsh treatment of them, and a disposition to get away if they could. Then, too, Chattanooga following in the same half-year with Gettysburg in the East, and Vicksburg in the West, there was much the same feeling in the South at this time that there had been in the North the fall and winter before. If the same license had been allowed the people and the press in the South that was allowed in the North, Chattanooga would probably have been the last battle fought for the preservation of the Union.

Bragg's army now being in full retreat, the relief of Burnside's position at Knoxville was a matter for immediate consideration. Sherman marched with a portion of the Army of the Tennessee, and one corps of the Army of the Cumberland, toward Knoxville; but his approach caused Longstreet to abandon the siege long before these troops reached their destination. Knoxville was now relieved; the anxiety of the President was removed, and the loyal portion of the North rejoiced over the double victory: the raising of the siege of Knoxville and the victory at Chattanooga.

⁺General Bragg was succeeded by General Hardee December 2d, 1863, and the latter by General Polk December 23d. General Johnston assumed command December 27th. On February 24th, 1864, General Bragg, "under the direction of the President, was *charged with the conduct of military operations in the armies of the Confederacy.*" In November, 1864, he was placed in command of the Department of North Carolina. In February, 1865, he came under General J. E. Johnston's command again, and so remained till the surrender. General Bragg died Sept. 27th, 1876.—Editors.

1864

INTRODUCTION

Joan Waugh

In early 1864, President Abraham Lincoln turned to General Ulysses S. Grant to win the war. By March, Grant formulated a national military strategy with the defeat of Generals Robert E. Lee's and Joseph E. Johnston's armies as the centerpiece. Grant would direct the Army of the Potomac with Major General George G. Meade. His plan was simple and straightforward: force the Army of Northern Virginia out into the open and defeat them in battle, and then, "On to Richmond." General William T. Sherman was ordered to advance south with three Western armies from Chattanooga to Atlanta. Once Atlanta was taken, Grant expected Sherman to strike out into the Southern heartland. General Philip H. Sheridan was tapped to head the Cavalry Corps in the Army of the Potomac, revitalizing that arm of the military.

Other Union armies were directed to coordinate attacks at the same time. In the West, Grant ordered General Nathaniel P. Banks to take Mobile, Alabama, while the Army of the James, led by General Benjamin F. Butler, threatened Richmond from the South. General Franz Sigel received orders to move up the Shenandoah Valley, cutting Lee's communications lines and attacking Richmond from the east. Grant explained, "Before this time these various armies had acted separately and independently of each other, giving the enemy an opportunity, often, of depleting one command not pressed, to reinforce another more actively engaged. I determined to stop this." Grant brought all possible Northern manpower and resource superiority to bear on defeating the Confederates with his plan for armies acting in concert.

The Overland Campaign commenced when the approximately 120,000-strong Army of the Potomac crossed the Rapidan River in Virginia to engage Lee's estimated 64,000 Confederates in the first week of May 1864. The early movements of the Overland Campaign saw the unraveling of the Union strategy. Grant's attempt to move swiftly through a thick patch of brush and trees known locally as the Wilderness was foiled on May 5 as Lee blocked his way and commenced a fight. Grant responded with an attack exploiting a weakness in Lee's position. Fighting resumed the following day but ended in stalemate. In his recollection for *Battles and Leaders*, Lieutenant Colonel Charles S. Venable recalled a dangerous moment during the battle when a courageous Lee rallied retreating soldiers to stand and fight. "Lee's presence at the front aroused his men to great enthusiasm," Venable stated, adding: "He was a superb figure as he sat on his spirited gray with the light of battle on his face. His presence was an inspiration." The two-day Battle of the Wilderness resulted in 18,000 Federal and 12,000 Confederate casualties. A shock for Lee came when Grant declined retreat, as so many Union commanders had done before, instead slipping around Lee's right flank.

Grant moved south from the Wilderness and toward Spotsylvania Court House, where Lee's men erected a line of strong earthworks. The Battle of Spotsylvania raged back and forth for several days. The Confederates fought off repeated Union assaults behind a defensive position known as the "Mule Shoe." On May 12, the Federals broke through a part of Lee's formation, but the Southerners stood their ground for twenty-two hours in what came to be called the "Bloody Angle." In a riveting account of the bloodletting, Union soldier G. Norton Galloway wrote: "So continuous and heavy was our fire that the head logs of the breastworks were cut and torn until they resembled hickory brooms." On May 20, after days of constant fighting, Grant turned southeast again, but Lee thwarted the Union army's leftward thrusts toward Richmond at North Anna River (May 23–27), Totopotomoy Creek (May 26–30), and Bethesda Church (May 31–June 1).

The spring of 1864 was one of Lee's finest moments, when he switched from his favored aggressive style to one of defensive warfare, forcing Grant into a war of attrition. Confederate general E. M. Law expressed awe for the feats of his commander at this time. "General Lee held so completely the admiration and confidence of his men," Law explained, "that his conduct of a campaign was rarely criticized." Weakened by illness, handicapped by the deaths or injuries of his principal lieutenants, and faced with a much larger opponent, Lee adapted brilliantly. He knew that the Confederacy's best hopes rested on Northern political demoralization once the high cost of these battles was widely known. In turn, Lincoln's reelection chances might be dashed, and a Democratic administration open to Southern independence would bring the participants to a conference table.

By month's end, the Federals reached a crossroads northeast of Richmond called Cold Harbor, where 59,000 well-entrenched Rebels faced 108,000 Federals across a seven-mile front. On June 3, Grant's massive early morning frontal assault on Confederate lines failed miserably. The campaign's previous battles were inconclusive, but Cold Harbor was a victory for Lee. That day saw some 7,000 Federal casualties (to less than 1,500 for the Rebels), shattered three Union corps, and ended a month of incessant campaigning for both armies. The Union had suffered 50,000 losses and the Confederacy 32,000—41 percent of Grant's forces and 50 percent of Lee's. Those losses were terrible for a South unable to replenish its armies, but also a blow for the Northern morale needed to finish the war.

Grant flanked Lee one last time, crossing the James River and heading toward Petersburg. If Union troops could seize that vital communications and rail center, nearby Richmond would fall. On June 12, the army marched to the river and crossed a 2,100-foot-long pontoon bridge in a movement that caught Lee off guard. On June 16, the entire Union army was on the south bank. Moving swiftly, the Federals were closing in on Petersburg, defended by a ten-mile line of strongly built fortifications around the city. From June 15 to 18, the Federal forces, numbering around 63,000, threatened to overwhelm the much less numerous Confederate defenders, but several Union assaults failed to capture the Petersburg works. The Confederates quickly brought in reinforcements, making their defensive position even more formidable. General Lee arrived on June 18 to oversee operations. Grant, realizing that continued frontal attacks would be useless, ordered his men to "use the spade." The Overland Campaign had ended, and the siege of Petersburg had begun.

The stalled military situation held huge consequences for the fate of the Lincoln administration. At this point, only victories in the field could sustain the Republicans in the fall elections. Butler's, Banks's, and Sigel's campaigns had all failed. Reports from Georgia brought little relief. Sherman's campaign began on May 7, featuring an almost continuous movement south in the face of weak resistance by Johnston. The biggest clash occurred at Kennesaw Mountain, Georgia, on June 27, where Sherman ordered a massed infantry assault against a strongly fortified position. One of Sherman's corps commanders, General O. O. Howard, assessed the Kennesaw battle for the *Century* series: "Our losses in this assault were heavy indeed, and our gain was nothing. We realized now, as never before, the futility of direct assaults upon intrenched lines already well prepared and well manned." After Kennesaw, Sherman pushed ever closer to Atlanta. In early July, the Federals arrived at the city gates, and like Grant in front of Petersburg, Sherman laid siege. Stalemate of the two biggest Federal armies excited Northern dissatisfaction with the war's costs.

Back in Virginia, Grant sought to cut Lee's lines of supply at Petersburg, ordering his soldiers to build a trench system around the Rebel line of defensive fortifications. By late June, the Confederates had approximately 50,000 (the number would rise to 66,000) men to 112,000 for the Union. From his headquarters at City Point on the James River, Grant presided over a vast logistical operation that kept the supplies flowing in to the troops in the field. In July and August, Grant extended his lines around the city, sending units out to cut the major railroad connections. Lee dispatched mobile forces to stop the Union's forays, and many battles took place away from the siege area.

Federal forces badly mishandled a chance to end the Petersburg stalemate in the ill-starred attack that came to be known as the Battle of the Crater on July 30, 1864. Soldiers from the 48th Pennsylvania had tunneled five hundred feet under the Confederate works, packing the tunnel with four tons of black powder. When the powder was detonated, the blast created a huge gap in the Confederate lines. Union major William H. Powell recalled looking with astonishment at "an enormous hole in the ground about 30 feet deep, 60 feet wide, and 170 feet long." Yet gross Federal incompetence failed to secure a success. Black troops in Union general Ambrose E. Burnside's Ninth Corps played an important role in the battle. Specially trained to lead the assault, they were pulled at the last minute due to political considerations, but still supported the attack. Brigadier General Henry Goddard Thomas witnessed the sorry affair, concluding: "Thus ended in disaster what had first promised to be a grand success." The debacle claimed 504 killed, 1,881 wounded, and 1,413 missing. An investigation followed, with one officer cashiered and one forced to retire.

Lee hoped to draw the Federals away from Petersburg and Richmond. His strategy worked, courtesy of Confederate general Jubal A. Early, who carried out a monthlong campaign culminating in an advance toward Washington, D.C. Two Early victories, at Lynchburg on June 18–19 and at Monocacy on July 9, resulted in Grant's detaching the Sixth Corps from Petersburg and rushing it north. Early and his small army of 14,000 arrived at the outskirts of the Northern capital on July 11, alarming the citizenry. Early described what happened next: "I determined to make an assault on the enemy's works at daylight the next morning. But during the night a dispatch was received...that two corps had arrived from General Grant's army.... As soon as it was light enough to see, I rode to the front, and found the parapet lined with troops. I had, therefore, reluctantly to give up all hopes of capturing Washington."

Early demonstrated the shockingly porous nature of Union defenses, prompting Grant to give Philip Sheridan the command of a newly created Army of the Shenandoah with orders to defeat Early and lay waste to the countryside. Sheridan carried out Grant's orders with a vengeance, destroying huge parts of the valley's capacity to feed the Southern army. This destruction was called "the burning" by the area's inhabitants. The Union cavalry played a vital role in the campaign. Cavalry commander Wesley Merritt defended those actions, recording that "the cavalry was deployed across the valley, burning, destroying or taking away everything of value...to the enemy. It was a severe measure, and appears severer now in the lapse of time; but it was necessary as a measure of war." Within a short period, Sheridan notched victories against Jubal Early at Third Winchester on September 19, Fisher's Hill on September 22, and Cedar Creek on October 19. With the last of his three victories, Sheridan had fulfilled Grant's instructions to end the Confederate presence in the valley. Now Sheridan could unite his forces with Grant's along the Petersburg-Richmond front. Northern morale rose while Confederate spirits fell dramatically.

Two Federal naval victories in 1864 mitigated the disappointment of the seemingly endless ground campaigns. On June 19 the war sloop USS *Kearsarge* defeated the famed Rebel raider CSS *Alabama* off the coast of France in the Battle of Cherbourg. Writing for *Battles and Leaders,* the Union ship's surgeon, John M. Browne, recounted the war of wits between the Confederate captain, Raphael Semmes, and the newly appointed Union captain, John Winslow. Brown pinpointed the exact moment it became clear to the men that the Federal sloop's superior gunnery had had its intended outcome: "The effect upon the enemy was readily perceived," observed Brown, "and nothing could restrain the enthusiasm of our men. Cheer succeeded cheer; caps were thrown in the air or overboard...sanguine of victory, the men were shouting, as each projectile took effort: 'That is a good one!'"

The second Union naval success carried an even greater lift for Northerners at a critical time. On August 5, Admiral David G. Farragut seized control of Mobile Bay in Alabama, bringing an end to Confederate shipbuilding in that city and disabling the port's ability to offer a friendly harbor for Southern ships avoiding the Union blockade. Lieutenant John Coddington Kinney described the war's greatest naval hero as he prepared for attack: "He was sixty-three years old, of medium height...with an expression combining overflowing kindliness with iron will and invincible determination, and with eyes [that] in emergency, could flash fire and fury." Farragut's triumph closed the last remaining major Confederate port on the Gulf of Mexico and boosted Lincoln's prospects for a fall victory. It was followed shortly by more good news for the Union from the two major theaters of war.

The Democrats' midsummer expectations for certain electoral victory were permanently dashed as Grant's strategy finally paid handsome dividends. Dissatisfied with Johnston's proclivity for giving up Georgia's territory, Davis replaced him with General John Bell Hood. Hurling his forces against the Federals at the Battle of Peachtree Creek on July 20, at the Battle of Atlanta on July 22, and at the Battle of Ezra Church on July 28, Hood sustained huge casualties with nothing gained. Sherman tightened his hold on Atlanta, forcing Hood to abandon it on September 1–2. On September 2, the city surrendered to Sherman, prompting wild celebrations throughout the North and, along with positive tidings from the Shenandoah Valley, assuring Lincoln of a second term and the continuance of Grant's relentless campaigns. Confederate citizens knew that they were now facing a dire scenario.

Jefferson Davis vowed to fight on, spurring Sherman's famous "March to the Sea." Detaching General George H. Thomas to protect Tennessee from the depredations of Hood's army, Sherman left Atlanta on November 16 and began his storied campaign through Georgia to the port city of Savannah. General Howard captured the esprit de corps of Sherman's army at the beginning of their journey: "Behold now," Howard declared, "this veteran army thus reorganized and equipped, with moderate baggage and a few days' supply of small rations, but with plenty of ammunition, ready to march anywhere Sherman might lead." Sherman and his force of 62,000 marched three hundred miles across the state—almost uncontested—living off the land and in some cases inflicting unauthorized damage to personal property. Captain Daniel Oakey of the 2nd Massachusetts remembered his unit's role, describing a rough and ready group of soldiers "who were expected to make fifteen miles a day; to corduroy the road when necessary; to destroy such property as was designed by our corps commander, and to consume everything eatable by man or beast." Crushing civilian and material support for the Confederacy, Sherman's troops arrived at Savannah's outskirts by December 17, and Confederate defenders led by General William J. Hardee abandoned the city on December 21. On the next day, Sherman sent a telegram to President Lincoln, offering him the city as a Christmas present.

The biggest campaigns of late 1864 took place in other areas of the Western Theater. While Sherman occupied Atlanta, John Bell Hood attempted to distract his old foe by threatening Union supply lines in Chattanooga. Explaining his strategy for the move on Tennessee, Hood remarked, "I decided to operate at the earliest moment possible in the rear of Sherman, as I became more and more convinced of our inability successfully to resist an advance of the Federal army." When Sherman did not follow him, Hood and his Army of Tennessee struck out for Nashville, hoping to recapture that city for the Confederacy. On November 30, 1864, the aggressive-minded commander hurled his forces against General John M. Schofield's Army of the Ohio at Franklin, losing 6,000 men in the effort. Hood then moved his army outside Nashville, where George Thomas was waiting for him. On December 15–16, Thomas unleashed a devastating blow to Hood, effectively ending the Confederate presence in Tennessee. Staffer Charles P. Stone penned a tribute to his commander, praising "the heroic courage and the tremendous force of one man, whose name will yet rank among the great captains of all time."

Eighteen sixty-four, the year of "total war," closed on a grim note for the Confederates. With Lincoln's reelection in November, the North had demonstrated the will to continue the fight to the finish. Union victory was only a matter of time.

CHAPTER 1

FROM THE WILDERNESS TO COLD HARBOR.

E. M. Law, Major-General, C.S.A.

On the 2d of May, 1864, a group of officers stood at the Confederate signal station on Clark's Mountain, Virginia, south of the Rapidan, and examined closely through their field-glasses the position of the Federal army then lying north of the river in Culpeper county. The central figure of the group was the commander of the Army of Northern Virginia, who had requested his corps and division commanders to meet him there. Though some demonstrations had been made in the direction of the upper fords, General Lee expressed the opinion that the Federal army would cross the river at Germanna or Ely's. Thirty-six hours later General Meade's army, General Grant, now commander-in-chief, being with it, commenced its march to the crossings indicated by General Lee.

The Army of the Potomac, which had now commenced its march toward Richmond, was more powerful in numbers than at any previous period of the war. It consisted of three corps: the Second (Hancock's), the Fifth (Warren's), and the Sixth (Sedgwick's); but the Ninth (Burnside's) acted with Meade throughout the campaign. Meade's army was thoroughly equipped, and provided with every appliance of modern warfare. On the other hand, the Army of Northern Virginia had gained little in numbers during the winter just passed, and had never been so scantily supplied with food and clothing. The equipment as to arms was well enough for men who knew how to use them, but commissary and quartermasters' supplies were lamentably deficient. A new pair of shoes or an overcoat was a luxury, and full rations would have astonished the stomachs of Lee's ragged Confederates. But they took their privations cheerfully, and complaints were seldom heard. I recall an instance of one hardy fellow whose trousers were literally "worn to a frazzle" and would no longer adhere to his legs even by dint of the most persistent patching. Unable to buy, beg, or borrow another pair, he wore instead a pair of thin cotton drawers. By nursing these carefully he managed to get through the winter. Before the cam-

WATERING HORSES IN THE RAPIDAN.

paign opened in the spring a small lot of clothing was received, and he was the first man of his regiment to be supplied.

I have often heard expressions of surprise that these ragged, barefooted, half-starved men would fight at all. But the very fact that they remained with their colors through such privations and hardships was sufficient to prove that they would be dangerous foes to encounter upon the line of battle. The *morale* of the army at this time was excellent, and it moved forward confidently to the grim death-grapple in the wilderness of Spotsylvania with its old enemy, the Army of the Potomac.

General Lee's headquarters were two miles north-east of Orange Court House; of his three corps, Longstreet's was at Gordonsville, Ewell's was on and near the Rapidan, above Mine Run, and Hill's on his left, higher up the stream. When the Federal army was known to be in motion, General Lee prepared to move upon its flank with his whole force as soon as his opponent should clear the river and begin the march southward. The route selected by General Grant led entirely around the right of Lee's position on the river above. Grant's passage of the Rapidan was unopposed, and he struck boldly out on the direct road to Richmond. Two roads lead from Orange Court House down the Rapidan toward Fredericksburg. They follow the general direction of the river, and are almost parallel to each other, the "Old turnpike" nearest the river, and the "Plank road" a short distance south of it. The route of the Federal army lay directly across these two roads, along the western borders of the famous Wilderness.

About noon on the 4th of May, Ewell's corps was put in motion on and toward the Orange turnpike, while A. P. Hill, with two divisions, moved parallel with him on the Orange Plank road. The two divisions of Longstreet's corps encamped near Gordonsville were ordered to move rapidly across the country and follow Hill on the Plank road. Ewell's corps was the first to find itself in the presence of the enemy. As it advanced along the turnpike on the morning of the

UNION TROOPS CROSSING THE RAPIDAN AT GERMANNA FORD, MAY 4, 1864.
FROM A SKETCH MADE AT THE TIME.

5th, the Federal column was seen crossing it from the direction of Germanna Ford. Ewell promptly formed line of battle across the turnpike, and communicated his position to General Lee, who was on the Plank road with Hill. Ewell was instructed to regulate his movements by the head of Hill's column, whose progress he could tell by the firing in its front, and not to bring on a general engagement until Longstreet should come up. The position of Ewell's troops, so near the flank of the Federal line of march, was anything but favorable to a preservation of the peace, and a collision soon occurred which opened the campaign in earnest.

General Warren, whose corps was passing when Ewell came up, halted, and turning to the right made a vigorous attack upon Edward Johnson's division, posted across the turnpike. J. M. Jones's brigade, which held the road, was driven back in confusion.‡ Steuart's brigade was pushed forward to take its place.

‡Major Jed. Hotchkiss, Topographical Engineer of the Confederate Second Corps, who witnessed this movement and mapped it at the time, writes to the editors:

"The attack was made by Jones, *not* by Warren. Early in the day Jones drove the Federal flanking videttes back very near Wilderness Run; then, having developed the Federal march, Jones fell back about two miles, and took position where the Flat Run road, from the Ger-

Rodes's division was thrown in on Johnson's right, south of the road, and the line, thus reëstablished, moved forward, reversed the tide of battle, and rolled back the Federal attack. The fighting was severe and bloody while it lasted. At some points the lines were in such close proximity in the thick woods which covered the battle-field that when the Federal troops gave way several hundred of them, unable to retreat without exposure to almost certain death, surrendered themselves as prisoners.

Ewell's entire corps was now up—Johnson's division holding the turnpike, Rodes's division on the right of it, and Early's in reserve. So far Ewell had been engaged only with Warren's corps, but Sedgwick's soon came up from the river and joined Warren on his right. Early's division was sent to meet it. The battle extended in that direction, with steady and determined attacks upon Early's front, until nightfall. The Confederates still clung to their hold on the Federal flank against every effort to dislodge them.

When Warren's corps encountered the head of Ewell's column on the 5th of May, General Meade is reported to have said: "They have left a division to fool us here, while they concentrate and prepare a position on the North Anna." If the stubborn resistance to Warren's attack‡ did not at once convince him of his mistake, the firing that announced the approach of Hill's corps along the Plank road, very soon afterward, must have opened his eyes to the bold strategy of the Confederate commander. General Lee had deliberately chosen this as his battle-ground. He knew this tangled wilderness well, and appreciated fully the advantages such a field afforded for concealing his great inferiority of force and for neutralizing the superior strength of his antagonist. General Grant's bold movement across the lower fords into the Wilderness, in the execution of his plan to swing past the Confederate army and place himself between it and Richmond, offered the expected opportunity of striking a blow upon his flank while his troops were stretched out on the line of march. The wish for such an opportunity was doubtless in a measure "father to the thought" expressed by General Lee three days before, at the signal station on Clark's Mountain.

Soon after Ewell became engaged on the Old turnpike, A. P. Hill's advance struck the Federal outposts on the Plank road at Parker's store, on the outskirts of the Wilderness. These were driven in and followed up to their line of battle, which was so posted as to cover the junction of the Plank road with the Stevensburg and Brock roads, on which the Federal army was moving toward Spotsyl-

---

manna road, intersects the old turnpike, but keeping his skirmishers engaged. It was not until *afternoon* that Warren turned his right and drove him back about one-quarter mile; Battle's brigade, of Rodes's division, who was in support, then moved forward, but was confused by Jones's retreating men and also forced back; then Gordon's brigade, of Early's division, which had been formed facing south-east, its left on the turnpike, advanced and drove back the Federal advance and reëstablished the line as first held by Jones."

vania. The fight began between Getty's division of the Sixth Corps and Heth's division, which was leading A. P. Hill's column. Hancock's corps, which was already on the march for Spotsylvania by way of Chancellorsville, was at once recalled, and at 4 o'clock in the afternoon was ordered to drive Hill "out of the Wilderness." Cadmus Wilcox's division went to Heth's support, and Poague's battalion of artillery took position in a little clearing on the north side of the Plank road, in rear of the Confederate infantry. But there was little use for artillery on such a field. After the battle was fairly joined in the thickets in front, its fire might do as much damage to friend as to foe; so it was silent. It was a desperate struggle between the infantry of the two armies, on a field whose physical aspects were as grim and forbidding as the struggle itself. It was a battle of brigades and regiments rather than of corps and divisions. Officers could not see the whole length of their commands, and could tell whether the troops on their right and left were driving or being driven only by the sound of the firing. It was a fight at close quarters too, for as night came on, in those tangled thickets of stunted pine, sweet-gum, scrub-oak, and cedar, the approach of the opposing lines could be discerned only by the noise of their passage through the underbrush or the flashing of their guns. The usually silent Wilderness had suddenly become alive with the angry flashing and heavy roar of the musketry, mingled with the yells of the combatants as they swayed to and fro in the gloomy thickets. Among the killed were General Alexander Hays, of Hancock's corps, and General J. M. Jones, of Ewell's.

When the battle closed at 8 o'clock, General Lee sent an order to

CONFEDERATE LINE WAITING ORDERS IN THE WILDERNESS.

Longstreet to make a night march, so as to arrive upon the field at daylight the next morning. The latter moved at 1 A.M. of the 6th, but it was already daylight when he reached the Plank road at Parker's store, three miles in rear of Hill's battle-field.✦ During the night the movements of troops and preparations for battle could be heard on the Federal line, in front of Heth's and Wilcox's divisions, which had so far sustained themselves against every attack by six divisions under General Hancock. But Heth's and Wilcox's men were thoroughly worn out. Their lines were ragged and irregular, with wide intervals, and in some places fronting in different directions. In the expectation that they would be relieved during the night, no effort was made to rearrange and strengthen them to meet the storm that was brewing.

As soon as it was light enough to see what little could be seen in that dark forest, Hancock's troops swept forward to the attack. The blow fell with greatest force upon Wilcox's troops south of the Orange Plank road. They made what front they could and renewed the fight, until, the attacking column overlapping the right wing, it gave way, and the whole line "rolled up" from the right and retired in disorder along the Plank road as far as the position of Poague's artillery, which now opened upon the attacking force. The Federals pressed their advantage and were soon abreast of the artillery on the opposite side, their bullets flying across the road among the guns where General Lee himself stood. For a while matters looked very serious for the Confederates. General Lee, after sending a messenger to hasten the march of Longstreet's troops and another to prepare the trains for a movement to the rear, was assisting in rallying the disordered troops and directing the fire of the artillery, when the head of Longstreet's corps appeared in double column, swinging down the Orange Plank road at a trot. In perfect order, ranks well closed, and no stragglers, those splendid troops came on, regardless of the confusion on every side, pushing their steady way onward like "a river in the sea" of confused and troubled human waves around them. Kershaw's division took the right of the road, and, coming into line under a heavy fire, moved obliquely to the right (south) to meet the Federal left, which had "swung round" in that direction. The Federals were checked in their sweeping advance and thrown back upon their front line of breastworks, where they made a stubborn stand. But Kershaw, urged on by Longstreet, charged with his whole command, swept his front, and captured the works.

Nearly at the same moment Field's division took the left of the road, with Gregg's brigade in front, Benning's behind it, Law's next, and Jenkins's following. As the Texans in the front line swept past the batteries where General Lee was standing, they gave a rousing cheer for "Marse Robert," who spurred his

---

✦The right of Ewell's corps formed a junction with the left of A. P. Hill's at a point about half-way between Parker's store and the Orange turnpike on the afternoon of the 5th.—EDITORS.

CAPTURE OF A PART OF THE BURNING UNION BREASTWORKS ON THE BROOK ROAD
ON THE AFTERNOON OF MAY 6. FROM A SKETCH MADE AT THE TIME.

horse forward and followed them in the charge. When the men became aware
that he was "going in" with them, they called loudly to him to go back. "We
won't go on unless you go back," was the general cry. One of the men dropped
to the rear, and taking the bridle turned the general's horse around, while General Gregg came up and urged him to do as the men wished. At that moment a
member of his staff (Colonel Venable) directed his attention to General
Longstreet, whom he had been looking for, and who was sitting on his horse
near the Orange Plank road. With evident disappointment General Lee turned
off and joined General Longstreet.

The ground over which Field's troops were advancing was open for a short
distance, and fringed on its farther edge with scattered pines, beyond which
began the Wilderness. The Federals [Webb's brigade of Hancock's corps] were
advancing through the pines with apparently resistless force, when Gregg's
eight hundred Texans, regardless of numbers, flanks, or supports, dashed directly upon them. There was a terrific crash, mingled with wild yells, which settled down into a steady roar of musketry. In less than ten minutes one-half of
that devoted eight hundred were lying upon the field dead or wounded; but
they had delivered a staggering blow and broken the force of the Federal advance. Benning's and Law's brigades came promptly to their support, and the
whole swept forward together. The tide was flowing the other way. It ebbed and
flowed many times that day, strewing the Wilderness with human wrecks. Law's
brigade captured a line of log breastworks in its front, but had held them only a
few moments when their former owners [Webb's brigade] came back to claim

them. The Federals were driven back to a second line several hundred yards beyond, which was also taken. This advanced position was attacked in front and on the right from across the Orange Plank road, and Law's Alabamians "advanced backward" without standing on the order of their going, until they reached the first line of logs, now in their rear. As their friends in blue still insisted on claiming their property and were advancing to take it, they were met by a countercharge and again driven beyond the second line. This was held against a determined attack, in which the Federal General Wadsworth was shot from his horse as he rode up close to the right of the line on the Plank road. The position again becoming untenable by reason of the movements of Federal troops on their right, Law's men retired a second time to the works they had first captured. And so, for more than two hours, the storm of battle swept to and fro, in some places passing several times over the same ground, and settling down at length almost where it had begun the day before.

About 10 o'clock it was ascertained that the Federal left flank rested only a short distance south of the Orange Plank road, which offered a favorable opportunity for a turning movement in that quarter. General Longstreet at once moved Mahone's, Wofford's, Anderson's, and Davis's brigades, the whole under General Mahone, around this end of the Federal line. Forming at right angles to it, they attacked in flank and rear, while a general advance was made in front. So far the fight had been one of anvil and hammer. But this first display of tactics at once changed the face of the field. The Federal left wing was rolled up in confusion toward the Plank road and then back upon the Brock road.

This partial victory had been a comparatively easy one. The signs of demoralization and even panic among the troops of Hancock's left wing, who had been hurled back by Mahone's flank attack, were too plain to be mistaken by the Confederates, who believed that Chancellorsville was about to be repeated. General Longstreet rode forward and prepared to press his advantage. Jenkins's fresh brigade was moved forward on the Plank road to renew the attack, supported by Kershaw's division, while the flanking column was to come into position on its right. The latter were now in line south of the road and almost parallel to it. Longstreet and Kershaw rode with General Jenkins at the head of his brigade as it pressed forward, when suddenly the quiet that had reigned for some moments was broken by a few scattering shots on the north of the road, which were answered by a volley from Mahone's line on the south side. The firing in their front, and the appearance of troops on the road whom they failed to recognize as friends through the intervening timber, had drawn a single volley, which lost to them all the fruits of the splendid work they had just done. General Jenkins was killed and Longstreet seriously wounded by our own men. The troops who were following them faced quickly toward the firing and were about to return it; but when General Kershaw called out, "They are friends!" every musket was lowered, and the men dropped upon the ground to avoid the fire.

The head of the attack had fallen, and for a time the movements of the Confederates were paralyzed. Lee came forward and directed the dispositions for a new attack, but the change of commanders after the fall of Longstreet, and the resumption of the thread of operations, occasioned a delay of several hours, and then the tide had turned, and we received only hard knocks instead of victory. When at 4 o'clock an attack was made upon the Federal line along the Brock road, it was found strongly fortified and stubbornly defended. The log breastworks had taken fire during the battle, and at one point separated the combatants by a wall of fire and smoke which neither could pass. Part of Field's division captured the works in their front, but were forced to relinquish them for want of support. Meanwhile Burnside's corps, which had reënforced Hancock during the day, made a vigorous attack on the north of the Orange Plank road. Law's (Alabama) and Perry's (Florida) brigades were being forced back, when, Heth's division coming to their assistance, they assumed the offensive, driving Burnside's troops beyond the extensive line of breastworks constructed previous to their advance.

The battles fought by Ewell on the Old turnpike and by A. P. Hill on the Plank road, on the 5th of May, were entirely distinct, no connected line existing between them. Connection was established with Ewell's right by Wilcox's division, after it had been relieved by Longstreet's troops on the morning of the 6th. While the battle was in progress on the Orange Plank road, on the 6th, an unsuccessful attempt was made to turn Ewell's left next the river, and heavy as-

BREASTWORKS OF HANCOCK'S CORPS ON THE BROOK ROAD—MORNING OF MAY 7.
FROM A SKETCH MADE AT THE TIME.

saults were made upon the line of Early's division. So persistent were these attacks on the front of Pegram's brigade, that other troops were brought up to its support, but the men rejected the offer of assistance.

Late in the day General Ewell ordered a movement against the Federal right wing, similar to that by which Longstreet had "doubled up" Hancock's left in the morning. Two brigades, under General John B. Gordon, moved out of their works at sunset, and lapping the right of Sedgwick's corps [the Sixth] made a sudden and determined attack upon it.⧫ Taken by surprise, the Federals were driven from a large portion of their works with the loss of six hundred prisoners,—among them Generals Seymour and Shaler. Night closed the contest, and with it the battle of the Wilderness.

When Lee's army appeared on the flank of the Federal line of march on the 5th of May, General Grant had at once faced his adversary and endeavored to push him out of the way. Grant's strongest efforts had been directed to forcing back the Confederate advance on the Orange Plank road, which, if successful, would have enabled him to complete his plan of "swinging past" that army and placing himself between it and Richmond. On the other hand, Lee's principal effort had been to strike the head of Grant's column a crushing blow where it crossed the Plank road, in order to force it from its route and throw it in confusion back into the Wilderness. Both attempts had failed. What advantages had been gained by the two days' fighting remained with the Confederates. They held a position nearer the Federal line of march than when the battle began, and had inflicted losses incomparably heavier than they had themselves sustained. Both sides were now strongly intrenched, and neither could well afford to attack. And so the 7th of May was spent in skirmishing, each waiting to see what the other would do. That night the race for Spotsylvania began. General Lee had been informed by "Jeb" Stuart of the movement of the Federal trains southward during the afternoon. After dark the noise of moving columns along the Brock road could be heard, and it was at once responded to by a similar movement on the part of Lee. The armies moved in parallel columns separated only by a short interval. Longstreet's corps (now commanded by R. H. Anderson) marched all night and arrived at Spotsylvania at 8 o'clock on the morning of the 8th, where the ball was already in motion. Stuart had thrown his cavalry across the Brock road to check the Federal advance, and as the Federal cavalry

---

⧫In this movement General Early was in command, and all of his division shared in the attack except Johnston's brigade, which was to the west of Flat Run. The Confederate brigades confronting Sedgwick on the east of the run were Gordon's, Pegram's, and Hays's. Gordon, on the left, began the movement against Sedgwick's right, and Hays and Pegram followed up the attack. According to General A. A. Humphreys ("The Virginia Campaign of 1864 and 1865," New York: Charles Scribner's Sons), "General Early drew back his brigades and formed a new line in front of his old. During the night an entirely new line was taken up by the Sixth Corps, its front and right thrown back—a change which the right of the Fifth Corps conformed to."—EDITORS.

had failed to dislodge him, Warren's corps had been pushed forward to clear the way. Kershaw's, Humphreys's, and Law's brigades were at once sent to Stuart's assistance. The head of Warren's column was forced back and immediately commenced intrenching. Spotsylvania Court House was found occupied by Federal cavalry and artillery, which retired without a fight. The Confederates had won the race.

The troops on both sides were now rapidly arriving. Sedgwick's corps joined Warren's, and in the afternoon was thrown heavily against Anderson's right wing, which, assisted by the timely arrival of Ewell's corps, repulsed the attack with great slaughter. Hill's corps (now under command of General Early) did not arrive until the next morning, May 9th. General Lee's line now covered Spotsylvania Court House, with its left (Longstreet's corps) resting on the Po River, a small stream which flows on the south-west; Ewell's corps in the center, north of the Court House; and Hill's on the right, crossing the Fredericksburg road. These positions were generally maintained during the battles that followed, though brigades and divisions were often detached from their proper commands and sent to other parts of the field to meet pressing emergencies.

No engagement of importance took place on the 9th, which was spent in intrenching the lines and preparing places of refuge from the impending storm. But the 10th was "a field-day." Early in the morning it was found that Hancock's corps had crossed the Po above the point where the Confederate left rested, had reached the Shady Grove road, and was threatening our rear, as well as the trains which were in that direction on the Old Court House road leading to Louisa Court House. General Early was ordered from the right with Mahone's and Heth's divisions, and, moving rapidly to the threatened quarter, attacked Hancock's rear division as it was about to recross the Po—driving it, with severe loss, through the burning woods in its rear, back across the river.

Meanwhile General Grant was not idle elsewhere. He had commenced his efforts to break through the lines confronting him. The first assault was made upon Field's division of Longstreet's corps and met with a complete and bloody repulse. Again at 3 o'clock in the afternoon, the blue columns pressed forward to the attack, and were sent back torn and bleeding, leaving the ground covered with their dead and wounded. Anticipating a renewal of the assaults, many of our men went out in front of their breastworks, and, gathering up the muskets and cartridge-boxes of the dead and wounded, brought them in and distributed them along the line. If they did not have repeating-rifles, they had a very good substitute—several loaded ones to each man. They had no reserves, and knew that if they could not sufficiently reduce the number of their assailants to equalize matters somewhat before they reached the works, these might become untenable against such heavy and determined attacks.

A lull of several hours succeeded the failure of the second attack, but it was only a breathing spell preparatory to the culminating effort of the day. Near sunset our skirmishers were driven in and the heavy, dark lines of attack came into view, one after another, first in quick time, then in a trot, and then with a rush toward the works. The front lines dissolved before the pitiless storm that met them, but those in the rear pressed forward, and over their dead and dying comrades reached that portion of the works held by the Texas brigade. These gallant fellows, now reduced to a mere handful by their losses in the Wilderness, stood manfully to their work. Their line was bent backward by the pressure, but they continued the fight in rear of the works with bayonets and clubbed muskets. Fortunately for them, Anderson's brigade had cleared its own front, and a portion of it turned upon the flank of their assailants, who were driven out, leaving many dead and wounded inside the works.

While this attack was in progress on Field's line, another, quite as determined, was made farther to the right, in front of Rodes's division of Ewell's corps. Doles's brigade was broken and swept out of its works with the loss of three hundred prisoners. But as the attacking force poured through the gap thus made, Daniel's brigade on one side and Steuart's on the other drew back from their lines and fell upon its flanks, while Battle's and Johnston's brigades were hurried up from the left and thrown across its front. Assailed on three sides at once, the Federals were forced back to the works, and over them, whereupon they broke in disorderly retreat to their own lines.

The next day was rainy and disagreeable, and no serious fighting took place. There were movements, however, along the Federal lines during the day that indicated a withdrawal from the front of Longstreet's corps. Late in the afternoon, under the impression that General Grant had actually begun another flanking movement, General Lee ordered that all the artillery on the left and center that was "difficult of access" should be withdrawn from the lines, and that everything should be in readiness to move during the night if necessary. Under this order, General Long, Ewell's chief of artillery, removed all but two batteries from the line of General Edward Johnson's division, for the reason given, that they were "difficult of access." Johnson's division held an elevated point somewhat advanced from the general line, and known as "the salient" [or "Bloody Angle"; see map], the breastworks there making a considerable angle, with its point toward the enemy. This point had been held because it was a good position for artillery, and if occupied by the enemy would command portions of our line. Such projections on a defensive line are always dangerous if held by infantry alone, as an attack upon the point of the angle can only be met by a diverging fire; or if attacked on either face, the troops holding the other face, unless protected by traverses or by works in rear (as were some of the Confederates), are more exposed than those on the side attacked. But with sufficient artillery, so posted as to sweep the sides of the angle, such a position may be

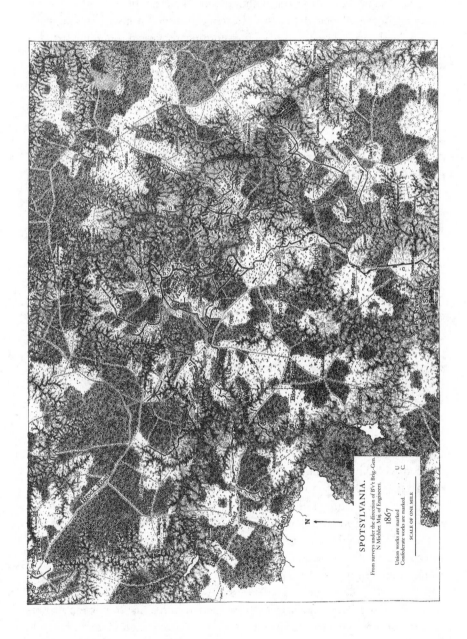

SPOTSYLVANIA.

From surveys under the direction of Bv't Brig.-Gen.
N Michler, Maj. of Engineers.

1867

Union works are marked . . . . U
Confederate works are marked C

SCALE OF ONE MILE

very strong. To provide against contingencies, a second line had been laid off and partly constructed a short distance in rear, so as to cut off this salient.

After the artillery had been withdrawn on the night of the 11th, General Johnson discovered that the enemy was concentrating in his front, and, convinced that he would be attacked in the morning, requested the immediate return of the artillery that had been taken away. The men in the trenches were kept on the alert all night and were ready for the attack, when at dawn on the morning of the 12th a dense column emerged from the pines half a mile in the front of the salient and rushed to the attack. They came on, to use General Johnson's words, "in great disorder, with a narrow front, but extending back as far as I could see." Page's battalion of artillery, which had been ordered back to the trenches at 4 o'clock in the morning, was just arriving and was not in position to fire upon the attacking column, which offered so fair a mark for artillery. The guns came only in time to be captured. The infantry in the salient fought as long as fighting was of any use; but deprived of the assistance of the artillery, which constituted the chief strength of the position, they could do little to check the onward rush of the Federal column, which soon overran the salient, capturing General Johnson himself, 20 pieces of artillery, and 2800 men— almost his entire division. The whole thing happened so quickly that the extent of the disaster could not be realized at once. Hancock's troops, who made the assault, had recovered their formation, and, extending their lines across the works on both sides of the salient, had resumed their advance, when Lane's brigade of Hill's corps, which was immediately on the right of the captured works, rapidly drew back to the unfinished line in rear, and poured a galling fire upon Hancock's left wing, which checked its advance and threw it back with severe loss. General Gordon, whose division (Early's) was in reserve and under orders to support any part of the line about the salient, hastened to throw it in front of the advancing Federal column. As the division was about to charge, General Lee rode up and joined General Gordon, evidently intending to go forward with him. Gordon remonstrated, and the men, seeing his intention, cried out, "General Lee to the rear!" which was taken up all along the line. One of the men respectfully but firmly took hold of the general's bridle and led his horse to the rear, and the charge went on. The two moving lines met in the rear of the captured works, and after a fierce struggle in the woods the Federals were forced back to the base of the salient. But Gordon's division did not cover their whole front. On the left of the salient, where Rodes's division had connected with Johnson's, the attack was still pressed with great determination. General Rodes drew out Ramseur's brigade from the left of his line (a portion of Kershaw's division taking its place), and sent it to relieve the pressure on his right and restore the line between himself and Gordon. Ramseur swept the trenches the whole length of his brigade, but did not fill the gap, and his right was exposed to a terrible fire from the works still held by the enemy. Three brigades from Hill's corps were ordered up. Perrin's, which was the first to arrive, rushed forward through a fearful fire and recovered a part of the line on Gordon's left. General Perrin fell dead from his horse just as he reached the works. General Daniel had been killed, and Ramseur painfully wounded, though remaining in the trenches with his men. Rodes's right being still hard pressed, Harris's (Mississippi) and McGowan's (South Carolina) brigades were or-

SPOTSYLVANIA COURT HOUSE.

SPOTSYLVANIA TAVERN, NEAR THE COURT HOUSE.

BOTH FROM WAR-TIME PHOTOGRAPHS.

dered forward and rushed through the blinding storm into the works on Ramseur's right. The Federals still held the greater part of the salient, and though the Confederates were unable to drive them out, the Federals could get no farther. Hancock's corps, which had made the attack, had been reënforced by Russell's and Wheaton's divisions of the Sixth Corps and one-half of Warren's corps, as the battle progressed. Artillery had been brought up on both sides, the Confederates using every piece that could be made available upon the salient. Before 10 o'clock General Lee had put in every man that could be spared for the restoration of his broken center. It then became a matter of endurance with the men themselves. All day long and until far into the night the battle raged with unceasing fury, in the space covered by the salient and the adjacent works. Every attempt to advance on either side was met and repelled from the other. The hostile battle-flags waved over different portions of the same works, while the men fought like fiends for their possession. [See "Hand-to-Hand Fighting at Spotsylvania," to follow.]

During the day diversions were made on both sides, to relieve the pressure in the center. An attack upon Anderson's (Longstreet's) corps by Wright's Sixth Corps (Sedgwick hav-

VIEWS OF CONFEDERATE INTRENCHMENTS AT SPOTSYLVANIA. FROM WAR-TIME PHOTOGRAPHS.

ing been killed on the 9th) was severely repulsed, while, on the other side of the salient, General Early, who was moving with a part of Hill's corps to strike the flank of the Federal force engaged there, met and defeated Burnside's corps, which was advancing at the same time to attack Early's works.

———

While the battle was raging at the salient, a portion of Gordon's division was busily engaged in constructing in rear of the old line of intrenchments a new and shorter one, to which Ewell's corps retired before daylight on the 13th. Never was respite more welcome than the five days of comparative rest that followed the terrible battle of the 12th to our wearied men, who had been marching and fighting almost without intermission since the 4th of May. Their comfort was materially enhanced, too, by the supply of coffee, sugar, and other luxuries to which they had long been strangers, obtained from the haversacks of the Federal dead. It was astonishing into what close places a hungry Confederate would go to get something to eat. Men would sometimes go out under a severe fire, in the hope of finding a full haversack. It may seem a small matter to the readers of war history; but to the *makers* of it who were in the trenches, or on the march, or engaged in battle night and day for weeks without intermission, the supply of the one article of coffee, furnished by the Army of the Potomac to the Army of Northern Virginia, was *not* a small matter, but did as much as any other material agency to sustain the spirits and bodily energies of the men, in a campaign that taxed both to their utmost limit. Old haversacks gave place to better ones, and tin cups now dangled from the accouterments of the Confederates, who at every rest on the march or interval of quiet on the lines could be seen gathered around small fires, preparing the coveted beverage.

In the interval from the 12th to the 18th our army was gradually moving east to meet corresponding movements on the other side. Longstreet's corps was shifted from the left to the extreme right, beyond the Fredericksburg road. Ewell's corps still held the works in rear of the famous salient, when on the morning of the 18th a last effort was made to force the lines of Spotsylvania at the only point where previous efforts had met with even partial success. This was destined to a more signal failure than any of the others. Under the fire of thirty pieces of artillery, which swept all the approaches to Ewell's line, the attacking force⁄ was broken and driven back in disorder before it came well within reach of the muskets of the infantry. After the failure of this attack, the "sidling" movement, as the men expressed it, again began, and on the afternoon of the 19th Ewell's corps was thrown round the Federal left wing to ascertain the extent of this movement. After a severe engagement, which lasted until

⁄ The attacking column consisted of the Second and Sixth corps, the Second Corps leading.—Editors.

night, Ewell withdrew, having lost about nine hundred men in the action. This seemed a heavy price to pay for information that might have been otherwise obtained, but the enemy had suffered more severely, and General Grant was delayed in his turning movement for twenty-four hours. He however got the start in the race for the North Anna; Hancock's corps, leading off on the night of the 20th, was followed rapidly by the remainder of his army.

On the morning of the 21st Ewell's corps moved from the left to the right of our line, and later on the same day it was pushed southward on the Telegraph road, closely followed by Longstreet's corps.☆ A. P. Hill brought up the rear that night, after a sharp "brush" with the Sixth Corps, which was in the act of retiring from its lines. Lee had the inside track this time, as the Telegraph road on which he moved was the direct route, while Grant had to swing round on the arc of a circle of which this was the chord. About noon on the 22d the head of our column reached the North Anna, and that night Lee's army lay on the south side of the river. We had won the second heat and secured a good night's rest besides, when the Federal army appeared on the other side in the forenoon of the 23d.

Warren's corps crossed the river that afternoon without opposition at Jericho Ford, four miles above the Chesterfield bridge on the Telegraph road; but as it moved out from the river it met Cadmus Wilcox's division of Hill's corps, and a severe but indecisive engagement ensued, the confronting lines intrenching as usual. Meanwhile a small earth-work, that had been built the year before, covering the approaches to the bridge on the Telegraph road and now held by a small detachment from Kershaw's division, was attacked and carried by troops of Hancock's corps, the Confederates retiring across the river with the loss of a few prisoners.

It did not seem to be General Lee's purpose to offer any serious resistance to Grant's passage of the river at the points selected. His lines had been retired from it at both these points, but touched it at Ox Ford, a point intermediate between them. Hancock's corps, having secured the Chesterfield bridge, crossed over on the morning of the 24th, and, extending down the river, moved out until it came upon Longstreet's and Ewell's corps in position and ready for battle. The Sixth Corps (General Wright) crossed at Jericho Mill and joined Warren. The two wings of Grant's army were safely across the river, but there was no connection between them. Lee had only thrown back his flanks and let them in on either side, while he held the river between; and when General Grant attempted to throw his center, under Burnside, across between the ford and the bridge, it was very severely handled and failed to get a foothold on the south

---

☆Swinton and others state that Longstreet moved on the night of the 20th, followed by Ewell. This is an error.—E.M.L.

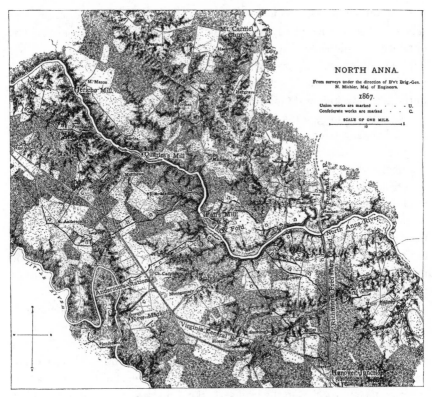

NORTH ANNA.

From surveys under the direction of B'v't Brig.-Gen.
N. Michler, Maj. of Engineers.

1867.

Union works are marked . . . . U.
Confederate works are marked . . . C.

SCALE OF ONE MILE.

OX FORD IS OTHERWISE KNOWN AS ANDERSON BRIDGE AND FORD.
ANDERSON'S STATION IS VERDON, AND THE CH. CADY HOUSE IS J. ANDERSON'S.

side. A detachment from Warren's corps was sent down on the south side to help Burnside across,‡ but was attacked by Mahone's division, and driven back with heavy loss, narrowly escaping capture. General Grant found himself in what may be called a military dilemma. He had cut his army in two by running it upon the point of a wedge. He could not break the point, which rested upon the river, and the attempt to force it out of place by striking on its sides must of necessity be made without much concert of action between the two wings of his army, neither of which could reënforce the other without crossing the river twice; while his opponent could readily transfer his troops, as needed, from one wing to the other, across the narrow space between them.

The next two days were consumed by General Grant in fruitless attempts to find a vulnerable point in our lines. The skirmishers were very active, often

---

‡Crittenden's division of Burnside's corps forded the river on the 24th at Quarles's Mill, between Ox Ford and Jericho Mill, and connected with Warren's left. Potter's division of this corps was with Hancock, leaving only one division, O. B. Willcox's, at Ox Ford.—EDITORS.

forcing their way close up to our works. The line of my brigade crossed the Richmond and Fredericksburg railroad. It was an exposed point, and the men stationed there, after building their log breastwork, leant their muskets against it and moved out on one side, to avoid the constant fire that was directed upon it. As I was passing that point on one occasion, the men called to me, "Stoop!" At the same moment I received a more forcible admonition from the whiz of a minie-ball close to my head. Turning quickly, I caught a glimpse of something blue disappearing behind a pile of earth that had been thrown out from the railroad cut some distance in front. Taking one of the muskets leaning against the works I waited for the reappearance of my friend in blue, who had taken such an unfair advantage of me. He soon appeared, rising cautiously behind his earth-work, and we both fired at the same moment, neither shot taking effect. This time my friend didn't "hedge," but commenced reloading rapidly, thinking, I suppose, that I would have to do the same. But he was mistaken; for, taking up another musket, I fired at once, with a result at which both of us were equally surprised, he probably at my being able to load so quickly, and I at hitting the mark. He was found there, wounded, when my skirmishers were pushed forward.

On the morning of May 27th General Grant's army had disappeared from our front. During the night it had "folded its tents like the Arab and as quietly stolen away," on its fourth turning movement since the opening of the cam-

JERICHO MILLS—UNION ENGINEER CORPS AT WORK.
FROM A WAR-TIME PHOTOGRAPH.

paign. The Army of the Potomac was already on its march for the Pamunkey River at Hanovertown, where the leading corps crossed on the morning of the 27th. Lee moved at once to head off his adversary, whose advance column was now eight miles nearer Richmond than he was. In the afternoon of the 28th, after one of the severest cavalry engagements of the war, in which Hampton and Fitz Lee opposed the advance of Sheridan at Hawes's Shop, the infantry of both armies came up and again confronted each other along the Totopotomoy. Here the Confederate position was found too strong to be attacked in front with any prospect of success, and again the "sidling" movements began—this time toward Cold Harbor.

Sheridan's cavalry had taken possession of Cold Harbor on the 31st, and had been promptly followed up by two corps of infantry.[*] Longstreet's and a part of Hill's corps, with Hoke's and Breckinridge's divisions,[†] were thrown across their front. The fighting began on the Cold Harbor line, late in the afternoon of the 1st of June, by a heavy attack upon the divisions of Hoke and Kershaw. Clingman's brigade on Hoke's left gave way, and Wofford's on Kershaw's right, being turned, was also forced back; but the further progress of the attack was checked and the line partly restored before night. By the morning of the 2d of June the opposing lines had settled down close to each other, and everything promised a repetition of the scenes at Spotsylvania.

Three corps of Grant's army (General W. F. Smith's Eighteenth Corps having arrived from Drewry's Bluff) now confronted the Confederate right wing at Cold Harbor, while the other two looked after Early's (Ewell's) corps near Bethesda Church. In the afternoon of June 2d, General Early, perceiving a movement that indicated a withdrawal of the Federal force in his front, attacked Burnside's corps while it was in motion, striking also the flank of Warren's corps, and capturing several hundred prisoners. This was accomplished with small loss, and had the effect of preventing the coöperation of these two corps in the attack at Cold Harbor the next day.

Early in the morning of the 2d I was ordered to move with my own and Anderson's brigades, of Field's division, "to reënforce the line on the right," exercising my own discretion as to the point where assistance was most needed. After putting the troops in motion I rode along the line, making a personal inspection as I went. Pickett's division, the first on our right, held a strong position along the skirt of a wood, with open fields in front, and needed no strengthening. The left of Kershaw's division, which was the next in order, was equally strong; but on calling at General Kershaw's quarters I was informed of

---

[*]The Sixth and Eighteenth corps reached Cold Harbor on the 1st of June.—EDITORS.

[†]Breckinridge came from the Valley and joined Lee's army at the North Anna [Hanover Junction] with about 2700 men. Hoke had just arrived from Petersburg. Pickett's division, which had been serving in the Department of North Carolina, had also joined its corps at the North Anna.—E.M.L.

THE PENNSYLVANIA RESERVES RESISTING A CONFEDERATE ATTACK NEAR
THE BETHESDA CHURCH, JUNE 2. FROM A SKETCH MADE AT THE TIME.

the particulars of the attack upon his own and Hoke's divisions the evening before, and requested by him to place my troops as a support to his right wing,
which had been thrown back by the attack. On examining the line I found it
bent sharply back at almost a right angle, the point of which rested upon a body
of heavy woods. The works were in open ground and were ill-adapted to resist
an attack. The right face of the angle ran along a slope, with a small marshy
stream behind and higher ground in front. The works had evidently been built
just where the troops found themselves at the close of the fight the previous
evening.

Convinced that under such assaults as we had sustained at Spotsylvania
our line would be broken at that point, I proposed to cut off the angle by building a new line across its base, which would throw the marshy ground in our
front and give us a clear sweep across it with our fire from the slope on the other
side. This would not only strengthen but shorten the line considerably, and I
proposed to General Kershaw to build and occupy it with my two brigades that
night.

Meanwhile the enemy was evidently concentrating in the woods in front,
and every indication pointed to an early attack. Nothing could be done upon
the contemplated line during the day, and we waited anxiously the coming of
night. The day passed without an attack. I was as well satisfied that it would
come at dawn the next morning as if I had seen General Meade's order directing it. That no mistake should be made in the location of the works, I procured
a hatchet, and accompanied by two members of my staff, each with an armful
of stakes, went out after dark, located the line, and drove every stake upon it.
The troops were formed on it at once, and before morning the works were finished. Artillery was placed at both ends of the new line, abreast of the infantry.
General Kershaw then withdrew that portion of his division which occupied

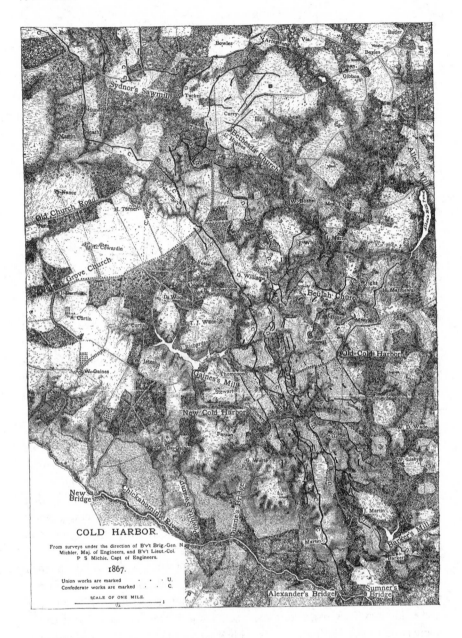

COLD HARBOR.

From surveys under the direction of B'v't Brig.-Gen N.
Michler, Maj. of Engineers, and B'v't Lieut.-Col.
P S Michie, Capt of Engineers.

1867.

Union works are marked · · · · U.
Confederate works are marked · · · C.

SCALE OF ONE MILE.

the salient, the men having leveled the works as far as possible before leaving them.

Our troops were under arms and waiting, when with the misty light of early morning the scattering fire of our pickets, who now occupied the abandoned works in the angle, announced the beginning of the attack. As the assaulting column swept over the old works a loud cheer was given, and it rushed on into the marshy ground in the angle. Its front covered little more than the line of my own brigade of less than a thousand men; but line followed line until the space inclosed by the old salient became a mass of writhing humanity, upon which our artillery and musketry played with cruel effect. I had taken position on the slope in rear of the line and was carefully noting the firing of the men, which soon became so heavy that I feared they would exhaust the car-

THE TAVERN AT NEW COLD HARBOR, HANOVER COUNTY, VIRGINIA, AS IT APPEARED IN 1864, NOT LONG AFTER GENERAL GRANT'S CHANGE OF POSITION.

tridges in their boxes before the attack ceased. Sending an order for a supply of ammunition to be brought into the lines, I went down to the trenches to regulate the firing. On my way I met a man, belonging to the 15th Alabama regiment of my brigade, running to the rear through the storm of bullets that swept the hill. He had left his hat behind in his retreat, was crying like a big baby, and was the bloodiest man I ever saw. "Oh, General," he blubbered out, "I am dead! I am killed! Look at this!" showing his wound. He was a broad, fat-faced fellow, and a minie-ball had passed through his cheek and the fleshy part of his neck, letting a large amount of blood. Finding it was only a flesh-wound, I told him to go on; he was not hurt. He looked at me doubtfully for a second as if questioning my veracity or my surgical knowledge, I don't know which; then, as if satisfied with my diagnosis, he broke into a broad laugh, and, the tears still running down his cheeks, trotted off, the happiest man I saw that day.

On reaching the trenches, I found the men in fine spirits, laughing and talking as they fired. There, too, I could see more plainly the terrible havoc made in the ranks of the assaulting column. I had seen the dreadful carnage in front of Marye's Hill at Fredericksburg, and on the "old railroad cut" which Jackson's men held at the Second Manassas; but I had seen nothing to exceed this. It was not war; it was murder. When the fight ended, more than a thousand men lay in front of our works either killed or too badly wounded to leave the field.♭ Among them were some who were not hurt, but remained among the dead and wounded rather than take the chances of going back under that merciless fire. Most of these came in and surrendered during the day, but were fired on in some instances by their own men (who still held a position close in our front) to

♭From the close range of the artillery and musketry, there must have been a much greater proportion of these than usual. I estimated the whole loss of the Eighteenth Corps, which made the attack, at between 4000 and 5000.—E.M.L. [The "Official Records" show that the losses of that corps at Cold Harbor aggregated 3019.—EDITORS.]

prevent them from doing so. The loss in my command was fifteen or twenty, most of them wounded about the head and shoulders, myself among the number. Our artillery was handled superbly during the action. Major Hamilton, chief of artillery of Kershaw's division, not only coöperated with energy in strengthening our line on the night of June 2d, but directed the fire of his guns with great skill during the attack on the 3d, reaching not only the front of the attacking force, but its flanks also, as well as those of the supporting troops.

While we were busy with the Eighteenth Corps on the center of the general line, the sounds of battle could be heard both on the right and left, and we knew from long use what that meant. It was a general advance of Grant's whole army. Early's corps below Bethesda Church was attacked without success. On our right, where the line extended toward the Chickahominy, it was broken at one point, but at once restored by Finegan's (Florida) brigade, with heavy loss to Hancock's troops who were attacking there. The result of the action in the center, which has been described, presents a fair picture of the result along the entire line—a grand advance, a desperate struggle, a bloody and crushing repulse. Before 8 o'clock A.M. on the 3d of June the battle of Cold Harbor was over, and with it Grant's "overland campaign" against Richmond.

When General Grant was appointed to the command of the Union armies and established his headquarters with the Army of the Potomac, we of the Army of Northern Virginia knew very little about his character and capacity as a commander. Even "old army" officers, who were supposed to know all about any one who had ever been in the army before the war, seemed to know as little as anybody else. The opinion was pretty freely expressed, however, that his Western laurels would wither in the climate of Virginia. His name was associated with Shiloh, where it was believed that he had been outgeneraled and badly beaten by Albert Sidney Johnston, and saved by Buell. The capture of Vicksburg and the battle of Chattanooga, which gave him a brilliant reputation at the North, were believed by the Confederates to be due more to the weakness of the forces opposed to him and the bad generalship of their commanders than to any great ability on his part. That he was bold and aggressive, we all knew, but we believed that it was the boldness and aggressiveness that arise from the consciousness of strength, as he had generally managed to fight his battles with the advantage of largely superior numbers. That this policy of force would be pursued when he took command in Virginia, we had no doubt; but we were not prepared for the unparalleled stub-

EXTREME RIGHT OF THE
CONFEDERATE LINE, COLD HARBOR.
FROM A WAR-TIME PHOTOGRAPH.

bornness and tenacity with which he persisted in his attacks under the fearful losses which his army sustained at the Wilderness and at Spotsylvania. General Grant's method of conducting the campaign was frequently discussed among the Confederates, and the universal verdict was that he was no strategist and that he relied almost entirely upon the brute force of numbers for success. Such a policy is not characteristic of a high order of generalship, and seldom wins unless the odds are overwhelmingly on the side of the assailant. It failed in this instance, as shown by the result at Cold Harbor, which necessitated an entire change in the plan of campaign. What a part at least of his own men thought about General Grant's methods was shown by the fact that many of the prisoners taken during the campaign complained bitterly of the "useless butchery" to which they were subjected, some going so far as to prophesy the destruction of their army. "He fights!" was the pithy reply of President Lincoln to a deputation of influential politicians who urged his removal from the command of the army. These two words embody perfectly the Confederate idea of General Grant at that time. If, as the mediæval chroniclers tell us, Charles Martel (the Hammer) gained that title by a seven days' continuous battle with the Saracens at Tours, General Grant certainly entitled himself to a like distinction by his thirty days' campaign from the Wilderness to Cold Harbor.

General Lee held so completely the admiration and confidence of his men that his conduct of a campaign was rarely criticised. Few points present themselves in his campaign from the Wilderness to Cold Harbor upon which criticism can lay hold, when all the circumstances are considered. His plan of striking the flank of Grant's army as it passed through the Wilderness is above criticism. Fault can be found only with its execution. The two divisions of Longstreet at Gordonsville, and Anderson's division of Hill's corps left on the Upper Rapidan, were too widely separated from the rest of the army, and, as the event proved, should have been in supporting distance of A. P. Hill on the Orange Plank road on the afternoon of the 5th of May. That Lee did not strike Grant a damaging blow when he had him at such disadvantage on the North Anna may seem strange to those who had witnessed his bold aggressiveness at the Wilderness and on other fields. He was ill and confined to his tent at the time; but, as showing his purpose had he been able to keep the saddle, he was heard to say, as he lay prostrated by sickness, "We must strike them a blow; we must never let them pass us again."∕ Whatever General Lee did, his men thought it the best that could be done under the circumstances. Their feeling toward him is well illustrated by the remark of a "ragged rebel" who took off his hat to the general as he was passing and received a like courteous salute in return: "God bless Marse Robert! I wish he was emperor of this country and I was his carriage-driver."

∕Statement of Colonel Venable of General Lee's staff.—E.M.L.

The results of the "overland campaign" against Richmond, in 1864, cannot be gauged simply by the fact that Grant's army found itself within a few miles of the Confederate capital when it ended. It might have gotten there in a much shorter time and without any fighting at all. Indeed, one Federal army under General Butler was already there, threatening Richmond, which was considered by the Confederates much more secure after the arrival of the armies of Lee and Grant than it had been before. Nor can these results be measured only by the losses of the opposing armies on the battle-field, except as they affected the *morale* of armies themselves; for their losses were about proportional to their relative strength. So far as the Confederates were concerned, it would be idle to deny that they (as well as General Lee himself) were disappointed at the result of their efforts in the Wilderness on the 5th and 6th of May, and that General Grant's constant "hammering" with his largely superior force had, to a certain extent, a depressing effect upon both officers and men. "It's no use killing these fellows; a half-dozen take the place of every one we kill," was a common remark in our army. We knew that our resources of men were exhausted, and that the vastly greater resources of the Federal Government, if brought fully to bear, even in this costly kind of warfare, must wear us out in the end. The question with us (and one often asked at the time) was, "How long will the people of the North, and the army itself, stand it?" We heard much about the demoralization of Grant's army, and of the mutterings of discontent at home with the conduct of the campaign, and we verily believed that their patience would soon come to an end.

A RABBIT IN A CONFEDERATE CAMP.

So far as the fighting qualities of our men were concerned, they were little if at all impaired by the terrible strain that had been put upon them. Had General Lee so ordered, they would have attacked the Federal army, after the battle of Cold Harbor, with the same courage, though perhaps more quiet, that they had displayed on entering the campaign thirty days before. The Army of Northern Virginia was so well seasoned and tempered that, like the famous Toledo blade, it could be bent back and doubled upon itself, and then spring again into perfect shape.

It may justly be said of both armies that in this terrible thirty days' struggle their courage and endurance was superb. Both met "foemen worthy of their steel," and battles were fought such as could only have occurred between men of kindred race, and nowhere else than in America.

CHAPTER 2

HAND-TO-HAND FIGHTING
AT SPOTSYLVANIA.

G. Norton Galloway.

General Hancock's surprise and capture of the larger portion of Edward Johnson's division, and the capture of the salient "at Spotsylvania Court House on the 12th of May, 1864, accomplished with the Second Corps," have been regarded as one of the most brilliant feats of that brilliant soldier's career; but without the substantial assistance of General Wright, grand old John Sedgwick's worthy successor, and the Sixth Corps, a defeat as bitter as his victory was sweet would have been recorded against the hero of that day.

The storm which had set in early in the afternoon of the 11th of May continued with great severity, and but little rest was obtained during the night. Soon after dark, however, a remarkable change in the weather took place, and it became raw and disagreeable; the men gathered in small groups about half-drowned fires, with their tents stretched about their shoulders, while some hastily pitched the canvas on the ground, and sought shelter beneath the rumpled and dripping folds. Others rolled themselves up, and lay close to the simmering logs, eager to catch a few moments' sleep; many crouched about, without any shelter whatever, presenting a pitiable sight.

Throughout the day some skirmishing and sharp-shooting had occurred, but this had been of a spasmodic character, and had elicited no concern. About dusk the Sixth Corps moved to a position on the right and rear of the army. The stormy night was favorable to Hancock's movement, and about 10 o'clock he put his troops in motion, marching to a point on the left of the Sixth Corps' former position in the neighborhood of the Brown house, massing his troops in that vicinity.

General Grant's orders to Hancock were to assault at daylight on the 12th in coöperation with Burnside on his left, while Wright and Warren were held in readiness to assault on his right. The Confederate army was composed of three

STRUGGLING FOR THE WORKS AT THE "BLOODY ANGLE."

corps—Longstreet (now R. H. Anderson) on their left, Ewell in the center, and
A. P. Hill (now under Early) on the right. The point to be assaulted was a salient
of field-works on the Confederate center, afterward called the "Bloody Angle."
It was held by General Edward Johnson's division. Here the Confederate line
broke off at an angle of ninety degrees, the right parallel, about the length of a
small brigade, being occupied by General George H. Steuart's regiments.‡ This
point was a part or continuation of the line of works charged and carried by
General Upton on May 10th, and was considered to be the key to Lee's position.

Just as the day was breaking, Barlow's and Birney's divisions of Hancock's
corps pressed forward upon the unsuspecting foe, and leaping the breastworks
after a hand-to-hand conflict with the bewildered enemy, in which guns were
used as clubs, possessed themselves of the intrenchments. Over three thousand
prisoners were taken, including General Johnson and General Steuart. Twenty
Confederate cannon became the permanent trophies of the day, twelve of them
belonging to Page and eight to Cutshaw.

Upon reaching the second line of Lee's works, held by Wilcox's division,
who by this time had become apprised of the disaster to their comrades, Hancock met with stern resistance, as Lee in the meantime had been hurrying
troops to Ewell from Hill on the right and Anderson on the left, and these were

‡Steuart occupied only part of the right parallel; Jones, Stafford, and Hays were on his left, and Lane was
on his right in that parallel.—EDITORS.

sprung upon our victorious lines with such an impetus as to drive them hastily back toward the left of the salient.[☥]

As soon as the news of Hancock's good and ill success reached army head-quarters, the Sixth Corps—Upton's brigade being in advance—was ordered to move with all possible haste to his support. At a brisk pace we crossed a line of intrenchments a short distance in our front, and, passing through a strip of timber, at once began to realize our nearness to the foe. It was now about 6 o'clock, and the enemy, reënforced, were making desperate efforts to regain what they had lost. Our forces were hastily retiring at this point before the concentrated attack of the enemy, and these with our wounded lined the road. We pressed forward and soon cleared the woods and reached an insidious fen, covered with dense marsh grass, where we lay down for a few moments await-ing orders. I cannot imagine how any of us survived the sharp fire that swept over us at this point—a fire so keen that it split the blades of grass all about us, the minies moaning in a furious concert as they picked out victims by the score.

The rain was still falling in torrents and held the country about in obscu-rity. The command was soon given to my regiment, the 95th Pennsylvania Vol-unteers, Captain Macfarlain commanding,—it being the advance of Upton's brigade,—to "rise up," whereupon with hurrahs we went forward, cheered on by Colonel Upton, who had led us safe through the Wilderness. It was not long before we reached an angle of works constructed with great skill. Immediately in our front an abatis had been arranged consisting of limbs and branches inter-woven into one another, forming footlocks of the most dangerous character. But there the works were, and over some of us went, many never to return. At this moment Lee's strong line of battle, hastily selected for the work of retrieving ill fortune, appeared through the rain, mist, and smoke. We received their bolts, losing nearly one hundred of our gallant 95th. Colonel Upton saw at once that this point must be held at all hazards; for if Lee should recover the angle, he would be enabled to sweep back our lines right and left, and the fruits of the morning's victory would be lost. The order was at once given us to lie down and commence firing; the left of our regiment rested against the works, while the right, slightly refused, rested upon an elevation in front. And now began a des-perate and pertinacious struggle.

[☥]Of the Union troops on the left of Hancock, General Grant ("Personal Memoirs," p. 231) says:

> "Burnside on the left had advanced up east of the salient to the very parapet of the enemy. Potter, commanding one of his divisions, got over, but was not able to remain there.... Burn-side accomplished but little on our left of a positive nature, but negatively a great deal. He kept Lee from reënforcing his center from that quarter."

—Editors.

Under cover of the smoke-laden rain the enemy was pushing large bodies of troops forward, determined at all hazards to regain the lost ground. Could we hold on until the remainder of our brigade should come to our assistance? Regardless of the heavy volleys of the enemy that were thinning our ranks, we stuck to the position and returned the fire until the 5th Maine and the 121st New York of our brigade came to our support, while the 96th Pennsylvania went in on our right; thus reënforced, we redoubled our exertions. The smoke, which was dense at first, was intensified by each discharge of artillery to such an extent that the accuracy of our aim became very uncertain, but nevertheless we kept up the fire in the supposed direction of the enemy. Meanwhile they were crawling forward under cover of the smoke, until, reaching a certain point, and raising their usual yell, they charged gallantly up to the very muzzles of our pieces and reoccupied the Angle.

Upon reaching the breastwork, the Confederates for a few moments had the advantage of us, and made good use of their rifles. Our men went down by the score; all the artillery horses were down; the gallant Upton was the only mounted officer in sight. Hat in hand, he bravely cheered his men, and begged them to "hold this point." All of his staff had been either killed, wounded, or dismounted.

At this moment, and while the open ground in rear of the Confederate works was choked with troops, a section of Battery C, 5th United States Artillery, under Lieutenant Richard Metcalf,[*] was brought into action and in-

---

[*] This is, I believe, the only instance in the history of the war of a battery charging on breastworks. It was commanded by Lieutenant James Gillies, and was attached to the Second Corps. Sergeant William E. Lines, one of only two survivors of the section that went in on that day, and who commanded the right gun, has given the writer the following facts relative to the matter:

"After the capture of the Confederate works, we were put in position just under the hill near the small pine-trees so much spoken of. We fired a few rounds of solid shot. Of course we could not see the Confederate line, but we elevated our guns so as to clear our own infantry. While we were waiting, a staff-officer with a Sixth Corps badge rode up to Lieutenant Gillian, and I could see they had some argument or dispute, for the officer soon went away. Directly another officer rode up to Gillian, and the same sort of colloquy took place, the officer evidently wanting Gillian to do something that the latter would not do. This officer rode away. In a very short time General Wright, who then commanded the Sixth Corps, rode up to Gillian, and had a moment's conversation with him. Lieutenant Metcalf then came over to the first section, and gave the command, 'Limber the guns,' 'drivers mount,' 'cannoneers mount,' 'caissons rear,' and away we went, up the hill, past our infantry, and into position. The staff-officer who led us was shot before we got into position. I have often thought it was owing to that fact that we got so close to the enemy's works. We were a considerable distance in front of our infantry, and of course artillery could not live long under such a fire as the enemy were putting through there. Our men went down in short order. The left gun fired nine rounds. I fired fourteen with mine, and was assisted in the last four rounds by an officer of a Vermont regiment, and by another from the 95th Pennsylvania, both of whom were shot. The effect of our canister upon the Confederates was terrible: they were evidently

UPTON'S BRIGADE AT THE "BLOODY ANGLE." AFTER DRAWINGS BY A PARTICIPANT.

creased the carnage by opening at short range with double charges of canister. This staggered the apparently exultant enemy. In the maze of the moment these guns were run up by hand close to the famous Angle, and fired again and again, and they were only abandoned when all the drivers and cannoneers had fallen. The battle was now at white heat.

trying to strengthen their first line from the second when we opened on them, and you can imagine the execution at that distance. When Lieutenant Metcalf and myself could no longer serve the guns, we withdrew. Our section went into action with twenty-three men and one officer—Lieutenant Metcalf. The only ones who came out sound were the lieutenant and myself. Every horse was killed, seven of the men were killed outright, sixteen wounded; the gun-carriages were so cut with bullets as to be of no further service.... Twenty-seven balls passed through the lid of the limber-chest while Number Six was getting out ammunition, and he was wounded in the face and neck by the fragments of wood and lead. The sponge-bucket on my gun had thirty-nine holes in it, being perforated like a sieve. The force of the balls can be imagined when I say that the bucket was made of one-eighth-inch iron. One curious circumstance on the morning we captured the works [May 12th] was, that musketry shots seemed to make such a slight noise; instead of the sharp *bing* of the shot, it was a dull *thud*. This may have been an important aid to our success, as the [first] firing of the enemy's skirmishers did not alarm their men in the breastworks."

—G.N.G.

It is also claimed that a section of Brown's Rhode Island battery was run up to the breastworks in a similar manner.—EDITORS.

The rain continued to fall, and clouds of smoke hung over the scene. Like leeches we stuck to the work, determined by our fire to keep the enemy from rising up. Captain John D. Fish, of Upton's staff, who had until this time performed valuable service in conveying ammunition to the gunners, fell, pierced by a bullet. This brave officer seemed to court death as he rode back and forth between the caissons and cannoneers with stands of canister under his "gum" coat. "Give it to them, boys! I'll bring you the canister," said he; and as he turned to cheer the gunners, he fell from his horse, mortally wounded. In a few moments the two brass pieces of the 5th Artillery, cut and hacked by the bullets of both antagonists, lay unworked with their muzzles projecting over the enemy's works, and their wheels half sunk in the mud. Between the lines and near at hand lay the horses of these guns, completely riddled. The dead and wounded were torn to pieces by the canister as it swept the ground where they had fallen. The mud was half-way to our knees, and by our constant movement the fallen were almost buried at our feet. We now backed off from the breastwork a few yards, abandoning for a while the two 12-pounders, but still keeping up a fusillade. We soon closed up our shattered ranks and the brigade settled down again to its task. Our fire was now directed at the top of the breastworks, and woe be to the head or hand that appeared above it. In the meantime the New Jersey brigade, Colonel W. H. Penrose, went into action on our right, and the Third Brigade, General Eustis's, was hard at work. The Vermont brigade, under Colonel Lewis A. Grant, which had been sent to Barlow's assistance, was now at the Angle, and General Wheaton's brigade was deep in the struggle. The Second and Third Divisions of the Sixth Corps were also ready to take part. It will thus be seen that we had no lack of men for the defense or capture of this position, whichever it may be termed.

The great difficulty was in the narrow limits of the Angle, around which we were fighting, which precluded the possibility of getting more than a limited number into action at once. At one time our ranks were crowded in some parts four deep by reënforcements. Major Henry P. Truefitt, commanding the 119th Pennsylvania, was killed, and Captain Charles P. Warner, who succeeded him, was shot dead. Later in the day Major William Ellis, of the 49th New York, who had excited our admiration, was shot through the arm and body with a ramrod during one of the several attempts to get the men to cross the works and drive off the enemy. Our losses were frightful. What remained of many different regiments that had come to our support had concentrated at this point, and had planted their tattered colors upon a slight rise of ground close to the Angle, where they staid during the latter part of the day.

To keep up the supply of ammunition pack mules were brought into use, each animal carrying three thousand rounds. The boxes were dropped close behind the troops engaged, where they were quickly opened by the officers or file-closers, who served the ammunition to the men. The writer fired four hundred rounds of ammunition, and many others as many or more. In this manner a continuous and rapid fire was maintained, to which for a while the enemy replied with vigor.

Finding that we were not to be driven back, the Confederates began to use more discretion, exposing themselves but little, using the loop-holes in their works to fire through, and at times placing the muzzles of their rifles on the top logs, seizing the trigger and small of the stock, and elevating the breech with one hand sufficiently to reach us. During the day a section of Cowan's battery took position behind us, sending shell after shell close over our heads, to explode inside the Confederate works. In like manner Coehorn mortars eight hundred yards in our rear sent their shells with admirable precision gracefully curving over us. Sometimes the enemy's fire would slacken, and the moments would become so monotonous that something had to be done to stir them up. Then some resolute fellow would seize a fence-rail or piece of abatis, and, creeping close to the breastworks, thrust it over among the enemy, and then drop on the ground to avoid the volley that was sure to follow. A daring lieutenant in one of our left companies leaped upon the breastworks, took a rifle that was handed to him, and discharged it among the foe. In like manner he discharged another, and was in the act of firing a third shot when his cap flew up in the air, and his body pitched headlong among the enemy.

On several occasions squads of disheartened Confederates raised pieces of shelter-tents above the works as a flag of truce; upon our slacking fire and calling to them to come in, they would immediately jump the breastworks and surrender. One party of twenty or thirty thus signified their willingness to submit; but owing to the fact that their comrades occasionally took advantage of the cessation to get a volley into us, it was some time before we concluded to give them a chance. With leveled pieces we called to them to come in. Springing upon the breastworks in a body, they stood for an instant panic-stricken at the terrible array before them; that momentary delay was the signal for their destruction. While we, with our fingers pressing the trigger, shouted to them to jump, their troops, massed in the rear, poured a volley into them, killing or wounding all but a few, who dropped with the rest and crawled in under our pieces, while we instantly began firing.

The battle, which during the morning raged with more or less violence on the right and left of this position, gradually slackened, and attention was concentrated upon the Angle. So continuous and heavy was our fire that the head logs of the breastworks were cut and torn until they resembled hickory brooms. Several large oak-trees, which grew just in the rear of the works, were completely gnawed off by our converging fire, and about 3 o'clock in the day fell among the enemy with a loud crash.[*]

Toward dusk preparations were made to relieve us. By this time we were nearly exhausted, and had fired three to four hundred rounds of ammunition per man. Our lips were incrusted with powder from "biting cartridge." Our shoulders and hands were coated with mud that had adhered to the butts of our rifles.[/]

The troops of the Second Corps, who were to relieve us, now moved up, took our position, and opened fire as we fell back a short distance to rearrange our shattered ranks and get something to eat, which we were sadly in need of. When darkness came on we dropped from exhaustion.

About midnight, after twenty hours of constant fighting, Lee withdrew from the contest at this point, leaving the Angle in our possession. Thus closed the battle of the 12th of May.

On the 13th, early in the day, volunteers were called for to bury the dead. The writer volunteered to assist, and with the detail moved to the works near the Angle, in front of which we buried a number of bodies near where they fell. We were exposed to the fire of sharp-shooters, and it was still raining. We cut the name, company, and regiment of each of the dead on the lids of ammunition-boxes which we picked up near by. The inscriptions were but feebly executed, for they were done with a pocket-knife. This work ended, we went close up where we had fought on Thursday and viewed the "Bloody Angle."

A momentary gleam of sunshine through the gloom of the sky seemed to add a new horror to the scene. Hundreds of Confederates, dead or dying, lay piled over one another in those pits. The fallen lay three or four feet deep in some places, and, with but few exceptions, they were shot in and about the head. Arms, accouterments, ammunition, cannon, shot and shell, and broken foliage were strewn about. With much labor a detail of Union soldiers buried the dead by simply turning the captured breastworks upon them. Thus had these unfortunate victims unwittingly dug their own graves.[☆] The trenches were nearly full of muddy water. It was the most horrible sight I had ever witnessed.

The enemy's defenses at this point were elaborately constructed of heavy

---

[*]The stump of one of these trees is preserved in Washington. In his official report, Brigadier-General Samuel McGowan, who commanded a brigade in Wilcox's Confederate division, says: "To give some idea of the intensity of the fire, an oak-tree twenty-two inches in diameter, which stood just in rear of the right of the brigade, was cut down by the constant scaling of musket-balls, and fell about 12 o'clock Thursday night, injuring by its fall several soldiers in the 1st South Carolina regiment."—EDITORS.

[/]Our pieces at times would become choked with burnt powder, and would receive the cartridge but half way. This fact, however, did not interfere with their discharge.—G.N.G.

[☆]The Confederate General McGowan officially says: "The trenches on the right in the 'Bloody Angle' ran with blood and had to be cleared of the dead bodies more than once."—EDITORS.

timber, banked with earth to the height of about four feet; above this was placed what is known as a head log, raised just high enough to enable a musket to be inserted between it and the lower work. Pointed pine and pin-oak formed an abatis, in front of which was a deep ditch. Shelves ran along the inside ledges of these works (a series of square pits) and along their flank traverses which extended to the rear; upon these shelves large quantities of "buck and ball" and "minie" cartridges were piled ready for use, and the guns of the dead and wounded were still pointing through the apertures, just as the men had fallen from them.

UNION HOSPITAL AT ALSOP'S FARM-HOUSE, NEAR THE BROCK ROAD.
FROM A WAR-TIME PHOTOGRAPH.

CHAPTER 3

SHERIDAN'S RICHMOND RAID.

Theo. F. Rodenbough, Brevet Brigadier-General, U.S.A.

The Army of the Potomac had been hibernating on the left bank of the Rapidan River, when as the season for active operations was about to open (April, 1864) there arrived a lieutenant-general commanding and a chief of cavalry. The one was not unknown to fame; the other was almost an entire stranger to his new command.

During the first two years of the war the Union cavalry lacked the paternal care essential to its proper development. Its first father was General Hooker, who organized a multitude of detachments into a compact army corps of 12,000 horsemen; transforming that which had been a by-word and a reproach into a force that, by its achievements in war, was ultimately to effect a radical change in the armament and use of mounted troops by the great military powers.

The winter of 1863–64 brought little rest to the cavalry. While the artillery and infantry were comfortably quartered, the cavalry was "hutted" three miles in front of the infantry picket lines, and a part was distributed as escorts and or-

UNHORSED TROOPERS RETURNING FROM SHERIDAN'S RAID.

derlies at infantry headquarters. Although the infantry maintained a picket line of its own, where it was useless, the cavalry was compelled to keep up a chain of videttes sixty miles in length, besides the necessary patrol duty and reconnoissances. Upon his arrival, Grant seems to have noted this maladministration and to have taken steps to correct it. For a chief of his cavalry, he told the President, he "wanted the very best man in the army," and few will deny that he got that man.

I remember Sheridan's arrival at the headquarters of the Cavalry Corps. We all thought a commander might have been selected from home material. One or two things that he did, however, met with warm approval. He set about reforming the abuses above referred to. On one occasion he was about to send a staff-officer to demand the immediate return to the corps of a small regiment which had been acting as "body-guard" for an infantry general. The officer, desiring for certain reasons to secure a modification of the order, sounded General Sheridan, who simply turned to him and in a low but distinct tone said: "Give my compliments to General X. and say that I have been placed in command of the cavalry of this army, and by —— I want it *all.*"

The 15,000 "paper strength" of the corps was sifted to 12,424 effectives. There were three divisions, subdivided into seven brigades. General A.T.A. Torbert was assigned to command the First Division, with General G. A. Custer, Colonel T. C. Devin, and General Wesley Merritt as brigade commanders; General D. McM. Gregg to the Second Division, with General H. E. Davies and Colonel J. Irvin Gregg to brigades; General J. H. Wilson to the Third Division, with Colonels J. B. McIntosh and G. H. Chapman to brigades. To each division were attached two batteries of horse artillery, with the same number as a reserve.

Sheridan's lieutenants were well chosen. Torbert had already distinguished himself as an infantry commander; Gregg had come from the regular cavalry and possessed the confidence of the whole corps for good judgment and coolness; Wilson, promoted from the corps of engineers, was very quick and impetuous; Merritt was a pupil of the Cooke-Buford school, with cavalry virtues well proportioned, and to him was given the Reserve Brigade of regulars—the Old Guard. Custer was the meteoric *sabreur;* McIntosh, the last of a fighting race; Devin, the "Old War Horse"; Davies, polished, genial, gallant; Chapman, the student-like; Irvin Gregg, the steadfast. There were, besides, Graham, Williston, Butler, Fitzhugh, Du Pont, Pennington, Clark, Randolph, Brewerton, Randol, Dennison, Martin, all tried men of the horse artillery.

The campaign was opened May 3d–4th, 1864, with the crossing of the Rapidan River by the army in two columns: one (Hancock's corps), preceded by Gregg's cavalry division, at Ely's Ford; the other (Warren and Sedgwick), led by Wilson, at Germanna Ford. The enemy's pickets were brushed away, the pontoons laid down, and the troops and immense trains were moved to the south side, apparently before Lee had realized the fact. On the second day Warren was attacked and Wilson found himself, for the time, separated from our infantry and confronted near Todd's tavern by a strong force of cavalry under Hampton, which engaged Wilson vigorously and after some fighting began to press him back. The opportune reënforcement of two regiments from Gregg turned the tables, and the enemy was driven beyond Corbin's Bridge. From the start Lee's cavalry was aggressive, and by its ceaseless activity in that densely wooded region reminded one of a swarm of bees suddenly disturbed by strange footsteps. On the 7th a more determined effort was made by Stuart to get on the left and rear of Meade, tempted by the rich prize of four thousand wagons. Torbert and Gregg were pitted against Hampton and Fitz Lee. The fight lasted from 4 P.M. until after dark, the field remaining in possession of the Union force; it was renewed early on the 8th, and after an obstinate struggle, in which the losses were heavy on both sides,—especially in officers,—the Confederates gave it up and retired sullenly. This was a cavalry affair, although in sight of the infantry of both armies. The curious blending of tragic and commonplace elements in war was illustrated during the hottest of the fight on the second day. It was raging about a small farm-house apparently deserted; shells were bursting in the yard, especially around the old-fashioned "pole" well, bullets were pattering on the shingles, dead and wounded men and horses made the place a slaughter-house. As Captain Leoser, 2d United States Cavalry, was advancing his skirmishers near the house, the cellar door was slowly lifted and a harsh-featured woman poked her head out, looked at the well and then at the captain, and threw an empty bucket at him with the curt remark, "Yank, I reckon you kin tote me a pail o' water," and promptly disappeared.

General Grant states in his "Memoirs" that on the 8th of May he gave Sheridan verbal orders to start on an independent expedition toward Richmond.[†] But he does not mention an incident that may have precipitated that movement. It happened that on the 8th of May Grant, Meade, and Sheridan were together at army headquarters. Meade seemed somewhat anxious about his trains, and said something to which Sheridan took exception. Meade instantly remarked, "No, I don't mean that," and put his hand, in friendly fashion, on Sheridan's shoulder. The cavalry general moved aside impatiently and replied with spirit, "If I am permitted to cut loose from this army I'll draw Stuart after me, and whip him, too." This was the principal object of the Richmond raid; the damage to the enemy was only incidental.

A few hours were spent in preparation. The command was stripped of all impediments, such as unserviceable animals, wagons, and tents. The necessary ammunition train, two ambulances to a division, a few pack-mules for baggage, three days' rations and a half-day's forage carried on the saddle, comprised the

---

[†]"Memoirs," Vol. II., p. 158.

MAJOR-GENERAL GEORGE A. CUSTER.
FROM A PHOTOGRAPH.

outfit. Torbert being disabled, Merritt assumed command of his division, and Gibbs of the Reserve Brigade. On the 9th of May, 1864, at 6 A.M., this magnificent body of 10,000 horsemen moved out on the Telegraph Road leading from Fredericksburg to Richmond. According to a Southern authority it took four hours at a brisk pace to pass a given point; to those who viewed it from behind barred windows and doors it was like the rush of a mighty torrent.

The column as it stood, "fours" well closed up, was thirteen miles long. It had been moving at a walk for two hours before the enemy caught up, and Wickham's brigade began to harass Sheridan's rear. It made no difference in the progress of the Union column, although numerous little brushes occurred. In one of these the 1st North Carolina Cavalry charged our rear-guard, consisting of the 6th Ohio Cavalry and a section of the 6th New York Battery. In the mêlée a Confederate officer cut his way through the column to the rear piece; placing his hand on the gun he exclaimed, "This is my piece." "Not by a d——d sight," replied a cannoneer, as with a well-planted blow of his fist he knocked the would-be captor off his horse and took him prisoner.

Passing through Chilesburg late in the afternoon, the leading brigade of Merritt's division (Custer's) took the trot and charged into Beaver Dam Station, on the Virginia Central Railroad, at an opportune moment. Two trains of cars carrying wounded and prisoners from Spotsylvania were about to start for Richmond. In a moment 378 Union captives rent the air with their cheers; the guard accompanying the trains escaped, leaving their arms behind, together with a large quantity of small-arms from the battle-field. After reserving certain articles, the torch was applied to the trains and buildings, with 1,500,000 rations and medical stores for Lee's army. The railroad track and telegraph were destroyed for some distance, the work being continued throughout the night while the main body rested. By the morning of the 10th Stuart had concentrated a large force, and about breakfast-time he announced the fact by sending a few shells into Gregg's camp. A skirmish ensued, and the march was resumed to Ground Squirrel bridge over the South Anna River, where all bivouacked. Even during the night the enemy buzzed about us, evidently trying to wear us out. On the 11th, at 3 A.M., Davies moved to Ashland and, not without a severe encounter with Mun-

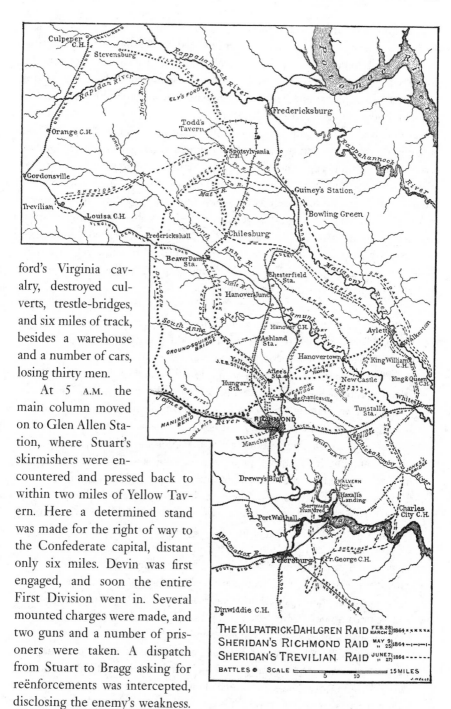

THE KILPATRICK-DAHLGREN RAID FEB.28, MARCH 2, 1864 ××××××
SHERIDAN'S RICHMOND RAID MAY 9, 25, 1864 —⊢—⊢—⊢—
SHERIDAN'S TREVILIAN RAID JUNE 7, 27, 1864 --------
BATTLES ● SCALE 5 10 15 MILES

ford's Virginia cavalry, destroyed culverts, trestle-bridges, and six miles of track, besides a warehouse and a number of cars, losing thirty men.

At 5 A.M. the main column moved on to Glen Allen Station, where Stuart's skirmishers were encountered and pressed back to within two miles of Yellow Tavern. Here a determined stand was made for the right of way to the Confederate capital, distant only six miles. Devin was first engaged, and soon the entire First Division went in. Several mounted charges were made, and two guns and a number of prisoners were taken. A dispatch from Stuart to Bragg asking for reënforcements was intercepted, disclosing the enemy's weakness.

Under the circumstances the Confederates are entitled to the greatest credit for the pertinacity and pluck displayed. Finally Wilson with part of his division was put in on Merritt's left, and the line, advancing, broke the enemy's grip and the fight was won. At this moment Stuart received his death-wound by a pistol-shot in the abdomen. Deep in the hearts of all true cavalrymen, North and South, will ever burn a sentiment of admiration mingled with regret for this knightly soldier and generous man. Sheridan had succeeded in his purpose, but he had found a foeman worthy of his steel.

If defeated at this point the enemy was not annihilated. Richmond was awakening to its peril; and, aware of the weakness of the garrison, the Confederate authorities felt very uneasy. As when the Germans approached Paris or when Early menaced Washington, a general call to arms was made. But Nature seemed rather favorable to defensive operations. For three days it had rained more or less, and a little rain in the region of the Chickahominy is known to go a great way toward making a mortar-bed of the roads and meadows. About midnight the column moved forward in the order: Wilson, Merritt, Gregg. Captain Field, 4th United States Artillery (then serving with Fitzhugh's battery), writes of the experience of Wilson's command:

"We marched all night, virtually. The halts were frequent and exasperating. It was so dark that we could only follow the cavalry by putting a bugler on a white horse directly in rear of the regiment in front of us, with orders to move on as soon as they did. Finally, whether the bugler fell asleep waiting or we fell asleep while watching the white horse, it happened that we found a gap of unknown dimensions in front of us and started at a trot to close it. I know of nothing which creates such an appalling sense of loneliness as the fact of being left behind in an enemy's country at night. It was a swampy region: the hoofs and the wheels made little or no sound. Once the deep blackness was pierced by a jet of vivid flame, and a sharp explosion on the road showed that we had sprung one of the torpedoes which had been to some extent planted there. While in doubt as to the road, we came upon a man wrapped in a blue overcoat standing near a gate, who told us that General Sheridan had left him to show us the way. Of course we followed his directions and entered the gate. It was evident that we were very near the city, as we could see the lights and hear the dogs barking. The road became less plainly marked and seemed to lead into extensive pleasure grounds, and finally we brought up on the edge of a large fish-pond. At that moment half a dozen flashes came from what seemed to be an embankment, and we found that we were in a regular trap and immediately under the fire of one of the outworks of the city. The guide who had given us the direction was either a deserter or a rebel in our uniform, and had deliberately misled us. He received the reward of his treachery, for Colonel McIntosh, who had from the first suspected him, kept him near him, and when their guns opened blew out his brains with a pistol."

About this time General Sheridan and staff, riding in rear of Wilson's division, hearing the firing, became convinced that the head of the column had passed the point where he had intended to turn in the direction of Mechanicsville. He sent off several of his staff to strike the road, which seemed as easily found as the proverbial needle in a haystack. But Captain F. C. Newhall *did* find the needle, and Merritt was sent down to Meadow Bridge to cover a crossing. In the meanwhile, as day broke, part of Wilson's command, including Fitzhugh's battery, found itself within the outer line of fortifications and threatened from all sides. South of them lay Richmond and its garrison; on the east a struggle for the bridge was going on between Merritt and an unknown force; while in a northerly direction, in rear of the main column, Gregg was standing off a force under Gordon. It was the tightest place in which the corps ever found itself. Fitzhugh had just ordered his caissons to go down as near the bridge as he could get, as our only avenue of escape appeared to be in that direction, when upon the scene came the sturdy presence of Sheridan. He hailed Fitzhugh, "Hullo, Charley! What are you doing with your caissons?" Fitzhugh explained that if hard pressed he wanted them out of the way. With a hearty laugh Sheridan replied, "Pushed *hard!* Why, what do you suppose we have in front of us? A lot of department clerks from Richmond, who have been forced into the ranks. I could capture Richmond, if I wanted, but I can't hold it; and the prisoners tell me that every house in the suburbs is loopholed, and the streets barricaded. It isn't worth the men it would cost; but I'll stay here all day to show these fellows how much I care for them, and go when I get ready. Send for your caissons and take it easy." As Captain Field says, "It was a little thing, but here was the spirit that burned so high at Winchester."

The enemy had torn up the bridge, and were in some force on the opposite bank. Merritt dismounted all but three regiments, and Custer charged his men over the railroad bridge to cover the reconstruction, driving the enemy back some distance. As soon as the flooring was down the mounted force under Colonel Gibbs crossed. Gregg and Wilson covered the crossing of the ammunition and ambulance trains, and after a brisk affair with a brigade of infantry and cavalry under General Gordon, followed Merritt, to their common satisfaction. A small but enterprising Virginia newsboy had managed to slip into our lines with the morning papers, full of the alleged barbarities of the vandal horde. He seemed utterly indifferent to the horrors of war, crossed the bridge with the cavalry, and found his first Yankee customer in Lieutenant Whitehead, who eagerly exchanged a quarter for a Richmond "Inquirer," which he sent to General Sheridan.

As soon as the head of our column turned toward the James it lost interest as an objective for the enemy. They were glad to watch us at a respectful distance, now that their beloved capital was once more safe. By way of Bottom's Bridge the corps moved to Malvern Hill and Haxall's, where much-needed supplies were procured from Butler's army; many of us exchanged our mud-stained garments for blue flannel shirts from the gun-boats lying in the James, and for the nonce became horse-marines. On the 21st Sheridan, continuing his march to rejoin Grant, crossed the Pamunkey near White House, on the ruins of the railroad bridge, after six hours' work at repairing it, two regiments at a time working as pioneers. The only incident of the crossing was the fall of a pack-mule from the bridge, from a height of thirty feet. The mule turned a somersault, struck an abutment, disappeared under water, came up and swam ashore without disturbing his pack. On the 23d the corps encamped at Aylett's, and at 5 P.M. I was sent with my regiment, 2d United States Cavalry, accompanied by Captains Wadsworth and Goddard of the staff, to open communication with the army, the sound of whose guns had been heard early in the day. After a forty-mile night march we had the good fortune to find General Grant near Chesterfield Station, where on the 25th the Cavalry Corps also reported, having fully performed its allotted task. It had deprived Lee's army, for the time, of its "eyes and ears," damaged his communications, destroyed an immense quantity of supplies, killed the leader of his cavalry, saved to our Government the subsistence of ten thousand horses and men for three weeks, perfected the *morale* of the cavalry corps, and produced a moral effect of incalculable value to the Union cause. Sheridan's casualties on the raid were 625 men killed or wounded, and 300 horses.

The Cavalry Corps returned in time to take part in an important flanking movement by the army, which in the meantime had fought the battle of Spotsylvania and had moved by the left to the North Anna River. On the 26th of May the army was posted on the north bank of that stream, with our left resting near Chesterfield bridge. Our infantry was now cautiously transferred from the right by the rear around the left of the line south of the river, crossing by Hanover Ferry. Sheridan, with Gregg's and Torbert's divisions, was to precede the infantry on the left, while Wilson's division threatened the enemy's left at Little River. On the 27th Torbert crossed at Hanover Ferry after some resistance by the enemy's cavalry, and pushed on to Hanover Town, where he bivouacked, having captured sixty prisoners. Having secured the desired position, Grant directed Sheridan to regain the touch with Lee's main army. To this end Gregg was sent in the direction of Hanover Court House, but was opposed at Hawes's Shop by the enemy's dismounted cavalry (including a brigade of South Carolina troops with long-range rifles) in an intrenched position. General Gregg writes:

"In the shortest possible time both of my brigades were hotly engaged. Every available man was put into the fight, which had lasted some hours.

HENRY E. DAVIES, JR.   PHILIP H. SHERIDAN.   A.T.A. TORBERT.

      D. MCM. GREGG.   WESLEY MERRITT.   JAMES H. WILSON.

SHERIDAN AND SOME OF HIS GENERALS. FAC-SIMILE OF A PHOTOGRAPH TAKEN IN 1864.

Neither party would yield an inch. Through a staff-officer of General Sheridan I sent him word as to how we stood, and stated that with some additional force I could destroy the equilibrium and go forward. Soon General Custer reported with his brigade. This he dismounted and formed on a road leading to the front and through the center of my line. In column of platoons, with band playing, he advanced. As arranged, when the head of his column reached my line all went forward with a tremendous yell, and the contest was of short duration. We went right over the rebels, who resisted with courage and desperation unsurpassed. Our success cost the Second Division 256 men and officers, killed and wounded. This fight has always been regarded by the Second Division as one of its severest."

General Grant adds:

"But our troops had to bury the dead, and found that more Confederate than Union soldiers had been killed."

A number of prisoners were taken by Gregg. On the 29th of May a reconnoissance in force was ordered to locate the enemy's line. We could easily find his cavalry,—too easily sometimes,—but the main Army of Northern Virginia seemed to have hidden itself, and Grant's infantry moved cautiously to the left and front. Sheridan was charged with the protection of our left while the general movement lasted. On the 30th Hancock and Warren discovered the enemy in position. Torbert was attacked by the Confederate cavalry near Old Church, at 2 P.M., and fought until 5 P.M., when he succeeded in pressing the enemy toward Cold Harbor. Wilson had been sent to the right to cut the Virginia Central, and occupied Hanover Court House after a sharp skirmish with Young's cavalry. On the 31st Torbert saddled up at 2 A.M.; he moved toward Old Cold Harbor at 5 A.M., found the enemy's cavalry in position, and drove them three miles upon their infantry. Retiring leisurely in search of a suitable camping-ground, Sheridan was directed by Grant to return to Cold Harbor and "hold it at all hazards." So at 10 P.M., weary and disgusted, having been on duty for eighteen hours, we moved back and reoccupied the old rifle-pits—at least, part of the force did. The remainder were massed in rear, lying down in front of their jaded horses, bridle-rein on arm, and graciously permitted to doze. At 5 A.M., as things remained quiet in front, coffee was prepared and served to the men as they stood to horse. Officers' packs appeared in an adjoining field, and the mess-cooks managed to broil a bone, butter a hoe-cake, and boil more coffee, and although the command remained massed the surroundings seemed more peaceful. My fourth cup of coffee was in hand when a few shots were heard in front, causing a general pricking up of ears. Soon skirmishers' compliments began to come our way and drop among the packs. Our line in the rifle-pits was at once reënforced. An amusing scene met the eye where the pack-mules had been standing: the ground was covered with the débris of officers' light baggage and mess-kits, mules were braying and kicking, and drivers were yelling, when, suddenly, jackasses, mules, and contrabands made for the rear, encountering on the way the corps commander and staff, who only by turning into a convenient farm-yard escaped the deluge.

The center of the line was occupied by the Reserve Brigade (Merritt's): six hundred dismounted men of the 1st and 2d United States, 6th Pennsylvania, and 1st New York Dragoons, armed with Sharps breech-loading carbines—excepting the 1st New York, which had Spencer magazine carbines (seven-shooters). The brigade was posted on the crest of a ravine, with timber in front and rear, excepting opposite the regiment on the left where there was a clearing, and on the right which rested on a swamp. The enemy kept up a desultory fire until 8 A.M., when a compact mass of infantry, marching steadily and silently, company front, was reported moving through the timber upon our position. This timber consisted of large trees with but little undergrowth. Our men were not aware of the character of the force about to attack us. But the *morale* of the corps was so good and their confidence in Sheridan so great that when the order "to hold at all hazards" was repeated they never dreamed of leaving the spot. Foreseeing a great expenditure of ammunition, some of the cavalry-men piled even their pistol-cartridges by their sides where they would be handy. On came the gray-coated foe, armed with Austrian muskets with sword-bayonets. These, flashing through the trees, caught the eye of a little Irish corporal of the 2d Cavalry, who exclaimed in astonishment, "Howly Mother! here they come wid sabers on fut!"

For a moment the skirmishers redoubled their fire, the enemy took the double-quick, and as they charged us the rebel yell rang through the forest. Then a sheet of flame came from the cavalry line, and for three or four minutes the din was deafening. The repeating carbines raked the flank of the hostile column while the Sharps single-loaders kept up a steady rattle. The whole thing was over in less than five minutes; the enemy, surprised, stunned, and demoralized, withdrew more quickly than they came, leaving their dead and wounded. We did not attempt to follow, but sent out parties to bring in the badly wounded, who were menaced with a new danger as the woods were now on fire. From prisoners we found that the attack was made by part of Kershaw's division (reported to be 1500 strong), and that they had advanced confidently, being told that "there was nothing in their front but cavalry." The tremendous racket we made hastened the approach of the Sixth Corps on its way to relieve us. To them we cheerfully gave place, having taken the initiative in what was destined to be, before the sun went down, the bloody and historic battle of Cold Harbor.

CHAPTER 4

GENERAL LEE IN THE WILDERNESS CAMPAIGN.

Charles S. Venable, Lieutenant-Colonel, C.S.A.,
of General Lee's Staff.

During the winter of 1863–64 General Lee's headquarters were near Orange Court House. They were marked by the same bare simplicity and absence of military form and display which always characterized them. Three or four tents of ordinary size, situated on the steep hillside, made the winter home of himself and his personal staff. It was without sentinels or guards. He used during the winter every exertion for filling up the thin ranks of his army and for obtaining the necessary supplies for his men. There were times in which the situation seemed to be critical in regard to the commissariat. The supplies of meat were brought mainly from the States south of Virginia, and on some days the Army of Northern Virginia had not more than twenty-four hours' rations ahead. On one occasion the general received by mail an anonymous communication from a private soldier containing a very small slice of salt pork, carefully packed between two oak chips, and accompanied by a letter saying that this was the daily ration of meat, and that the writer having found it impossible to live on it had been, though he was a gentleman, reduced by the cravings of hunger to the necessity of stealing. The incident gave the commanding general great pain and anxiety, and led to some strong interviews and correspondence with the Commissary Department. During the winter General Lee neglected no interest of his soldiers. He consulted with their chaplains and attended their meetings, in which plans for the promotion of special religious services among the men were discussed and adopted.

While he was accessible at all times, and rarely had even one orderly before his tent, General Lee had certain wishes which his aides-de-camp knew well they must conform to. They did not allow any friend of soldiers condemned by court-martial (when once the decree of the court had been confirmed by him) to reach his tent for personal appeal, asking reprieve or remission of sentence. He said that with the great responsibilities resting on him he could not bear the pain and distress of such applications, and to grant them when the judge advocate-general had attested the fairness and justice of the court's decision would be a serious injury to the proper discipline of the army. Written complaints of officers as to injustice done them in regard to promotion he would sometimes turn over to an aide-de-camp, with the old-fashioned phrase, "'Suage him, Colonel, 'suage him"; meaning thereby that a kind letter should be written in reply. But he disliked exceedingly that such disappointed men should be allowed to reach his tent and make complaints in person. On one occasion during the winter an officer came with a grievance and would not be satisfied without an interview with the commanding general. He went to the general's tent and remained some time. Immediately upon his departure General Lee came to the adjutant's tent with flushed face, and said warmly, "Why did you permit that man to come to my tent and make me show my temper?" The views which prevail with many as to the gentle temper of the

UNIFORM OF THE MARYLAND
GUARD, C.S.A.

great soldier, derived from observing him in domestic and social life, in fondling of children, or in kind expostulation with erring youths, are not altogether correct. No man could see the flush come over that grand forehead and the temple veins swell on occasions of great trial of patience and doubt that Lee had the high, strong temper of a Washington, and habitually under the same strong control. Cruelty he hated. In that same early spring of 1864 I saw him stop when in full gallop to the front (on report of a demonstration of the enemy against his lines) to denounce scathingly and threaten with condign punishment a soldier who was brutally beating an artillery horse.

The quiet camp-life at Orange had been broken in upon for a brief season in November by Meade's Mine-Run campaign. In this General Lee, finding that Meade failed to attack the Confederate lines, made arrangements on the night of December 1st to bring on a general battle on the next morning by throwing two divisions against the Federal left, held by Warren's corps, which had been found by a close cavalry reconnoissance to present a fair occasion for successful attack. He had hoped to deal a severe blow to Meade's army, and felt very keenly his failure to carry out his designs. When he discovered that Meade had withdrawn, he exclaimed in the presence of his generals, "I am too old to command this army; we should never have permitted these people to get away." Some who were standing by felt that in his heart he was sighing for that great "right arm" which he threw around Hooker at Chancellorsville. Both armies returned quietly to winter quarters and rested until May 4th, when Lee marched out in the early morning to meet the Federal army which had moved under its new commander, at midnight on the 3d, to turn his right flank. He took with him Ewell's corps (less two brigades which had been detached for duty elsewhere during the winter) and two divisions of Hill's corps—with artillery and cavalry—leaving Longstreet with two divisions at Gordonsville (Pickett's being absent below Richmond), Longstreet's third division and Anderson's division of Hill's corps, on the Rapidan heights, to follow him on the next day.

On the morning of the 5th General Lee, though generally reticent at table on military affairs, spoke very cheerfully of the situation, having learned that Grant was crossing at Germanna Ford and moving into the Wilderness. He expressed his pleasure that the Federal general had not profited by General Hooker's Wilderness experiences, and that he seemed inclined to throw away to some extent the immense advantage which his great superiority in numbers in every arm of the service gave him. On the 5th Ewell marched on the old turnpike, and Hill on the Plank road, and the cavalry on a road still farther to the right into the Wilderness. Lee rode with Hill at the head of his column. He was at the front in the skirmish at Parker's Store and moved with the advance to the field on the edge of the forest which became the scene of the great conflict on the Plank road. Riding on in advance of the troops, the party, consisting of Generals Lee, Hill, and Stuart and their staff-officers, dismounted and sat under the shade of the trees, when a party of the enemy's skirmishers deployed from a grove of old-field pines on the left, thus revealing the close proximity of Grant's forces, and the ease of concealing movements in the Wilderness.

Hill's troops were soon up and in line, and then began on the Plank road a fierce struggle, nearly simultaneously with that of Ewell's forces on the old turnpike. Thus was inaugurated a contest of many battles, in which the almost daily deadly firing did not cease for eleven long months.

Heth's and Wilcox's divisions, under Lee's eye, maintained themselves well against the heavy assault of the Federal forces which greatly outnumbered them; Ewell's corps did good work on the old turnpike in its contest with Warren's corps, and Rosser's cavalry on the right had driven Wilson back. Lee slept on the field not far from his line of battle, sending orders to Longstreet to make a night march and reach the front by daybreak on the 6th.

On that morning serious disaster seemed imminent. Longstreet did not arrive in time to reënforce Lee's line of battle in the position it held at the close of the engagement of the preceding evening. Hancock's well-planned attack on our right forced the two Confederate divisions from their position, and it seemed at one moment that they would sweep the field. Lee gave orders to get his wagon trains ready for a movement in retreat, and sent an aide to quicken the march of Longstreet's two divisions. These came soon, a little after sunrise, at double-quick, in parallel columns, down the Plank road. Lee was in the midst of Hill's sullenly retreating troops, aiding in rallying them, and restoring confidence and order, when Longstreet's men came gallantly in and re-formed the line of battle under his eye. Lee's presence at the front aroused his men to great enthusiasm. He was a superb figure as he sat on his spirited gray with the light of battle on his face. His presence was an inspiration. The retreating columns turned their faces bravely to the front once more, and the fresh divisions went forward under his eye with splendid spirit. It was on this occasion that the men of the Texas brigade (always favorites of the general), discovering that he was riding with them into the charge, shouted to him that they would not go on unless he went back. The battle line was restored early in the morning. Soon afterward, Anderson's division, which had been left on the Rapidan heights, arrived on the ground; and a successful assault, which carried everything before it, was made on Grant's left. The Federal troops were driven back, with heavy loss, to their intrenchments on the Brock road. Longstreet's wounding, and the necessary delay in the change of commanders,‡ caused loss of time in attacking them in this position. An attack made in the afternoon failed, after some partial successes, to gain possession of the Federal breastworks. The rumor which General Grant mentions in his "Memoirs," and to which he seems to have given credence, that "Lee's men were in confusion after this attack, and that his efforts failed to restore order," was without foundation in fact. On the same afternoon, of the 6th, a successful flank assault was made by Gordon, with three brigades of Ewell's corps, the results of which were not so great as hoped for, because night put a stop to his further successful rolling up of Sedgwick's line.

The Wilderness fighting closed with the night of the 6th of May.

Lee's grand tactics in these two days of battle had been a superb exhibition of military genius and skill in executing his plan of throwing his little army boldly against his opponent, where his great inferiority in numbers would place him at the least disadvantage; where manœuvring of large bodies was most difficult, and where superiority in cavalry and artillery counted almost for nothing.

---

‡R. H. Anderson was taken from Hill's corps to command Longstreet's, and Mahone assumed command of Anderson's division.—Editors.

MAJOR-GENERAL G.W.C. LEE, C.S.A.
FROM A PHOTOGRAPH.

The failure to push rapidly the successful movement in which Longstreet was wounded was a serious disappointment to General Lee. I believe his daring spirit conceived the signal defeat of Grant's army, and the driving it back across the Rapidan, as a possibility within his immediate grasp. One thing remarkable in the position of the Confederate lines in these engagements is worthy of note, namely, the large gap between Ewell's right and Longstreet and Hill's left. I had occasion, on being sent with orders to General Ewell on the 6th, to ride across this lonesome interval of half a mile or more, and to meet or see no one, except two Federal soldiers, who had found it easier to desert to the front than to the rear.

The quiet on the 7th told Lee that Grant would move on around his left. When Grant did move, the Confederate general, with that firm reliance upon the steadfast courage of his men in fighting against odds which had never failed him, and in the consequent ability of a small body of his troops to hold superior forces in check until he could come to their support, sent Anderson with Longstreet's two divisions to support Stuart's cavalry in holding Spotsylvania Court House until he could come up with the rest of his army. This mutual confidence between the general and his men was a striking feature of the campaign, and, indeed, a prime necessity for any possibility of success. General Grant sent troops to occupy Spotsylvania Court House, but retained Hancock's corps to guard against the contingency of another attack from Lee in the Wilderness. Lee had evidently won the respect of his foes when, with his smaller force, reduced by two days' hard fighting, he could employ one part of his infantry to aid in checking the movement of

MAJOR-GENERAL STEPHEN D. RAMSEUR,
C.S.A. FROM A PHOTOGRAPH.

the Army of the Potomac on Spotsylvania Court House, and at the same time threaten its rear in the Wilderness. Meanwhile General Grant was sending to Washington for reënforcements.

Lee sent an aide-de-camp with Anderson under orders to keep him constantly advised, and, following with the main body of his army, took up his position on the Spotsylvania lines in the afternoon of the 8th. And Grant again found himself in a position which required hard fighting and in which he could not use to great advantage his superiority in numbers and equipment.

The Spotsylvania campaign of twelve days was marked by almost daily combats. It was General Lee's habit in those days of physical and mental trial to retire about 10 or 11 at night, to rise at 3 A.M., breakfast by candle-light, and return to the front, spending the entire day on the lines. The 9th of May was spent by both armies mainly in strengthening their positions by throwing up intrenchments. The day was marked, however, by the death of General Sedgwick, who was killed by a Confederate sharp-shooter. He was much liked and respected by his old West Point comrades in the Confederate army, and his death was a real sorrow to them. Early on the morning of the 10th Hancock's corps made an effort to pass around Lee's left wing and gain a position on his flank and rear. This was repulsed by Early, commanding Hill's corps (Hill being ill). Almost simultaneously came fierce assaults on Lee's left wing, which were repulsed with terrible slaughter. These were renewed again in the afternoon with the same result. The heaviest assault was made at 5 o'clock by Hancock and Warren, and again repulsed; again reorganized and hurled at Lee's lines only to meet with a still more bloody reception. In one of these attacks a small portion of the Confederate line was taken, but held for a short time only by the assailants. It was pitiful to see and hear the bravest of these brave men who had got up nearest to the Confederate lines as they lay the next day groaning with the pangs of thirst and pains of death, when to relieve them was impossible, on account of the active sharp-shooting of the Federal riflemen. One fair-haired New York youth lay thus twenty-four hours near the Confederate intrenchments before he was relieved from his sufferings by death, every effort to bring him in having been rendered unavailing by the sharp fire which his would-be rescuers met at the hands of his comrades, ignorant of their kind intentions. About the same hour at which these last assaults were made, there was a heavy attack by the Sixth Corps on Ewell's front, near Lee's headquarters for the day, about 200 yards in rear of Doles's brigade, which captured and held a portion of the lines for a short time. This attack was repulsed and the line recaptured by Gordon, the men and officers, as in the Wilderness, again beseeching Lee to go to the rear, and shouting their promises to retake the line if he would only go back.

The 11th of May was a comparatively quiet day, as there were no regular assaults on the Confederate lines. But on that day the gallant J.E.B. Stuart met his death in an engagement with Sheridan, whom he had followed up from Spotsylvania and boldly attacked with greatly inferior numbers near Richmond. Stuart's loss was greatly mourned by General Lee,⁺ who prized him highly both as a skillful soldier of splendid courage and energy, and a hearty, joyous, loving friend.

On the 12th, before dawn, came Hancock's famous assault on a weak salient in Ewell's front—the sole appreciable success in attack of all the hard fighting by the Federal troops since they crossed the Rapidan. The threatening attitude of Hancock's attacking column, as indicated by the noise of the preparations going on in front of the salient during the night, had not been communicated to General Lee. The announcement of the disaster was the first news which came to him of this movement of the enemy. He galloped forward in the darkness of the morning and learned the extent of it from those engaged in rallying the remnants of Edward Johnson's division and in making arrangements to check Hancock. The occasion aroused all the combative energies of his soldier nature, and he rode forward with his columns toward the captured angle. His generals expostulated with him, and his men cried him back shouting their promises to retake the lines. The advance of Hancock's troops, after his successful assault, was checked by the brigades of Hill's corps, under Early, which held the lines on the right of the salient, and by Ewell's troops on the left of it.

A line of battle was formed making the base of the triangle of the salient, and the work on the retrenchment (which had been begun the day before as a new line to remedy this weak point in the lines) was pushed rapidly forward. During the day General Lee sent three brigades and a number of batteries of artillery to reënforce Rodes's division, on which fell the main task of holding the enemy in check and recovering, if practicable, the salient and the eighteen pieces of Confederate artillery which lay silent between the opposing lines (having arrived too late in the morning for effective use against Hancock's assault). In that narrow space of the salient captured before dawn raged the fiercest battle of the war. Lee's position during the day was near Early's lines, where he observed, from time to time, the movements of the Federal troops in aid of Hancock's attack, and counter-movements of Early's troops. He was with the artillery when it broke Burnside's assault. Lee was present dictating notes and orders in the midst of his guns. At one time he rode at the head of Harris's Mississippi brigade, which by his orders I was guiding down in column to the assistance of Rodes. The men marched steadily on until they noticed that Lee at their head was riding across a space swept by the artillery fire of the enemy. Then were renewed the same protesting shouts of "Go back, General Lee," and the same promises to do their duty. The firing in the battle of the salient did not

⁺The news of Stuart's fall reached General Lee on the 19th.—C.S.V.

cease until far into the night. Hancock had been compelled to retire behind the lines which he had captured, holding them as breastworks for the protection of his troops. The Confederate front at the close covered four of the eighteen pieces of artillery. Lee's retrenchment in rear of our battle-line (which rendered the salient a useless capture) had been completed. The wearied and worn Confederate battalions were withdrawn to this line late at night, but the four recovered guns, after being dragged off, were left hopelessly stuck in a swamp outside of the new lines, and became Hancock's trophies after all. General Grant did not leave Hancock unaided in this fight, having sent the Sixth and Fifth corps to his support. He expected much from Burnside also, but Early's counter-movements in part prevented the realization of these hopes. I have gone into some detail in this brief sketch of the battle of the salient, because, as perhaps the fiercest struggle of the war, it is illustrative of the valor of the troops on both sides.

On the 18th an attack was made on Early's left and easily repulsed, though some of the assailants reached the breastworks. On the 19th Ewell was sent to the north side of the Ny to threaten Grant's communications. He met some Federal reënforcements, and, being without artillery (finding the ground impracticable for it), he regained his position on the south side of that stream with some loss. Hampton's cavalry brigade and battery of horse artillery proved of great assistance in his withdrawal from his hazardous position.

The battles of Spotsylvania Court House closed with the 19th of May. It gives a clearer idea of the nature of this tremendous contest to group by days and count its various combats from the beginning of the campaign: On May 5th, three; on May 6th, four; on May 8th, two; on May 10th, five; on May 12th, repeated assaults during twenty hours in salient and two combats on another part of the line; May 18th, one; May 19th, one. It is no wonder that on these fields the Confederate ordnance officers gathered more than 120,000 pounds of lead, which was recast in bullets and did work again before the campaign of 1864 was closed.

Lee, discovering that Grant had set out on the 20th of May on his flanking movement southward, immediately marched so as to throw his army between the Federal forces and Richmond. He crossed the North Anna on the 21st. General Grant arrived on the 23d. Lee would gladly have compelled battle in his position there. He was anxious now to strike a telling blow, as he was convinced that General Grant's men were dispirited by the bloody repulses of their repeated attacks on our lines. Lee had drawn Pickett and Breckinridge to him. But in the midst of the operations on the North Anna he succumbed to sickness, against which he had struggled for some days. As he lay in his tent he would say, in his impatience, "We must strike them!" "We must never let them pass us again!" "We must strike them!" He had reports brought to him constantly from the field. But Lee ill in his tent was not Lee at the front. He was much disappointed in not securing larger results from the attack which prevented the junction of Hancock's and Warren's columns after they had crossed the North Anna.

On May 26th Grant withdrew his army from its rather critical position on the south side of the North Anna, and moved again to the east, down the Pamunkey, which he crossed on the 28th, to find Lee confronting him on the Totopotomoy. Grant had received reënforcements from Washington, and had drawn Smith's corps from Butler in Bermuda Hundred. This corps reached him at Cold Harbor on June 1st. On the 30th the Confederate forces were in line of battle, with the left at Atlee's Station confronting the Federal army. General Lee was still sick, and occupied a house at night for the first time during the campaign. As one of his trusted lieutenants has well said: "In fact, nothing but his own determined will kept him in the field; and it was then rendered more evident than ever that he was the head and front, the very life and soul of his army." Grant declined general battle and drew eastward; and after several lesser combats, with no serious results, the two armies confronted one another on the 3d of June at Cold Harbor. In these days Lee had drawn to himself Hoke's division from Beauregard, and had been reënforced by Finegan's Florida brigade and Keitt's South Carolina regiment.

The days from May 30th to June 2d were anxious ones for General Lee. For while General Grant had easy and safe communication with Petersburg and Bermuda Hundred, and commanded all the Federal troops north and south of Richmond, he commanded only the Army of Northern Virginia and was compelled to communicate his "suggestions" to General Beauregard through General Bragg and the War Department at Richmond. This marred greatly the unity, secrecy, and celerity of action so absolutely essential to success. That he considered this separation of commands, and the consequent circuitous mode of communication with its uncertain results, a very grave matter is plain from the telegrams which he sent at this time. General Beauregard had telegraphed from Chester (half-way between Richmond and Petersburg), on May 30th, 5:15 P.M., as follows:

> "War Department must determine when and what troops to order from here. I send to General Bragg all information I obtain relative to movement of enemy's troops in front."

This called forth the following telegrams:[†]

[†]The first dispatch is from the original in possession of General T. F. Rodenbough. The dispatch to Jefferson Davis is from the original in possession of the Massachusetts Commandery of the Loyal Legion.—EDITORS.

"ATLEE'S, 7½ P.M., 30th May, 1864.

"GENERAL G. T. BEAUREGARD, HANCOCK'S HOUSE:

"If you cannot determine what troops you can spare, the Department cannot. The result of your delay will be disaster. Butler's troops will be with Grant to-morrow.

"R. E. LEE."

"ATLEE'S, 7½ P.M., 30th May, 1864.

"HIS EXCELLENCY JEFFERSON DAVIS, Richmond:

"General Beauregard says the Department must determine what troops to send from him. He gives it all necessary information. The result of this delay will be disaster. Butler's troops (Smith's Corps) will be with Grant to-morrow. Hoke's division at least should be with me by light to-morrow.

"R. E. LEE."

INDORSEMENT.

"OPERATOR: Read last sentence 'by light to-morrow.'"

"C.S.V.,
"A.A.G."

The battle of the 3d of June was a general assault by Grant along a front nearly six miles in length, and a complete and bloody repulse at all points, except at one weak salient on Breckinridge's line, which the brave assailants occupied for a short time only to be beaten back in a bloody hand-to-hand conflict on the works. The Federal losses were naturally, under the circumstances, very large, and those of the Confederates very small. The dead and dying lay in front of the Confederate lines in triangles, of which the apexes were the bravest men who came nearest to the breastworks under the withering, deadly fire. The battle lasted little more than one brief hour, beginning between 5 and 6 A.M. The Federal troops spent the remainder of the day in strengthening their own lines in which they rested quietly. Lee's troops were in high spirits. General Early, on the 6th and 7th of June, made two efforts to attack Grant's forces on his right flank and rear, but found him thoroughly protected with intrenchments. On the 12th General Hampton met Sheridan at Trevilian and turned him back from his march to the James River and Lynchburg. General Grant lay in his lines until the night of June 12th.

On that night he moved rapidly across the peninsula. The overland campaign north of the James was at an end.

Except in the temporary driving back of Lee's right on the morning of May 6th before the arrival of Longstreet's divisions, the brief occupation of Rodes's front on May 10th, Hancock's morning assault on May 12th, and a few minor

At Lees 7½ P.M. 3 0 May '64

Genl G T Beauregard
Hancocks House —

If you cannot determine what troops be you
Can spare the Dept cannot — The result will
be disaster of your delay will be disaster —
Butters troops will be with Grant tomorrow

2 7/3 40 Chd

R E Lee

A CALL FOR REËNFORCEMENTS.

events, the campaign had been one series of severe and bloody repulses of Federal attacks. The campaign on the Confederate side was an illustration of Lee's genius, skill, and boldness, and as well of the steadiness, courage, and constancy of his greatly outnumbered forces, and of their sublime faith in their great commander.

After the battle of Cold Harbor, Lee felt strong enough to send Breckinridge toward the valley to meet Hunter's expedition, and on the 13th to detach Early with the Second Corps, now numbering some eight thousand muskets and twenty-four pieces of artillery, to join Breckinridge; he also restored Hoke's division to Beauregard.

When Grant set out for the James, Lee threw a corps of observation between him and Richmond. Grant moved his troops rapidly in order to capture Petersburg by a *coup de main*. Smith's corps was in front of the advanced lines of Petersburg on the morning of the 15th. The first brigade of Hoke's division reached Beauregard on the evening of the 15th. On the night of the 15th Lee tented on the south side of the James, near Drewry's Bluff. On the 16th and 17th, his troops coming up, he superintended personally the recapture of Beauregard's Bermuda Hundred line, which he found to be held very feebly by the forces of General Butler, who had taken possession of them on the withdrawal of Bushrod Johnson's division by Beauregard to Petersburg on the 16th. On the 17th a very pretty thing occurred, in these lines, of which I was an eye-witness, and which evinced the high spirit of Lee's men, especially of a division which had been with him throughout the campaign, beginning at the Wilderness, namely, Field's division of Longstreet's corps. After the left of Beauregard's evacuated line had been taken up, there remained a portion the approach to which was more formidable. The order had been issued to General Anderson commanding the corps to retake this portion of the lines by a joint assault of Pickett's and Field's divisions. Soon afterward the engineers, upon a careful reconnoissance, decided that a good line could be occupied without the loss of life which might result from this recapture. The order to attack was therefore withdrawn by General Lee. This rescinding order reached Field but did not reach Pickett. Pickett's division began its assault under the first order. The men of Field's division, hearing the firing and seeing Pickett's men engaged, leaped from their trenches,—first the men, then the officers and flag-bearers,—rushed forward and were soon in the formidable trenches, which were found to be held by a very small force. On the 15th, 16th, and 17th battle raged along the lines of intrenchments and forts east of Petersburg, between Grant's forces and Beauregard's troops, who made a splendid defense against enormous odds. About dark on the 17th grave disaster to the Confederates seemed imminent, when Gracie's brigade of Alabamians, just returned from Chaffin's Bluff on the north side of the James, gallantly leaped over the works and drove the assailants back, capturing a thousand or more prisoners. Hoke, too, on his part of the lines, had easily repulsed Smith's assaults. This battle raged until near midnight. Meantime Beauregard's engineers were preparing an interior line, to which his wearied troops fell back during the night. A renewal of the attack on the lines held by the Confederate troops on the night of the 17th had been ordered by Grant along his whole front for an early hour on the 18th. But the withdrawal of the Confederates to interior lines necessarily caused delay, and, when the attack was made at noon, Lee and two of his divisions, Kershaw's and Field's, had reached the Petersburg lines. The attack made no impression on the lines, which were held until the evacuation on April 2d, 1865.

To some military critics General Lee seemed not to have taken in the full force of Beauregard's urgent telegrams in those critical days of June. But it must be remembered how easy it was for General Grant to make a forced march on Richmond from the north side of the James, accompanied by a strong feint on the Petersburg lines. Then, too, any strategist will see that Petersburg, cut off from Richmond by an enemy holding the railroad between the two cities (or holding an intrenched line so near it as to make its use hazardous), would not have been a very desirable possession. The fact is, that the defense of Richmond against an enemy so superior in numbers to the defending army, and in possession of the James River to City Point as a great water-way to its base of supplies, was surrounded with immense difficulties. And, in fact, in sending back Hoke's division to Beauregard, and in approving that general's withdrawing of Bushrod Johnson's division from the Bermuda Hundred line to Petersburg, Lee thereby sent him more reënforcements by far than he sent to Rodes on the 12th of May at Spotsylvania, when that general was holding the base of the salient against Hancock and Wright and Warren. Besides this, Lee had already detached

BELLE PLAIN, POTOMAC CREEK, A UNION BASE OF SUPPLIES.
FROM A PHOTOGRAPH TAKEN IN 1864.

Breckinridge's division and Early's corps to meet Hunter at Lynchburg. And, after all, the result showed that Lee's reliance on his men to hold in check attacking forces greatly superior in numbers did not fail him in this instance; that he was bold to audacity was a characteristic of his military genius.

The campaign of 1864 now became the siege of Petersburg. On the night of June 18th Hunter retreated rapidly from before Lynchburg toward western Virginia, and Early, after a brief pursuit, marched into Maryland, and on July 11th his advance was before the outer defenses of Washington.

CHAPTER 5

THE BATTLE OF THE PETERSBURG CRATER.

William H. Powell, Major, U.S.A.

By the assaults of June 17th and 18th, 1864, on the Confederate works at Petersburg, the Ninth Corps, under General Burnside, gained an advanced position beyond a deep cut in the railroad, within 130 yards of the enemy's main line and confronting a strong work called by the Confederates Elliott's Salient, and sometimes Pegram's Salient. In rear of that advanced position was a deep hollow. A few days after gaining this position Lieutenant-Colonel Henry Pleasants, who had been a mining engineer and who belonged to the 48th Pennsylvania Volunteers, composed for the most part of miners from the upper Schuylkill coal region, suggested to his division commander, General Robert B. Potter, the possibility of running a mine under one of the enemy's forts in front of the deep hollow. This proposition was submitted to General Burnside, who approved of the measure, and work was commenced on the 25th of June. If ever a man labored under disadvantages, that man was Colonel Pleasants. In his testimony before the Committee on the Conduct of the War, he said:

> "My regiment was only about four hundred strong. At first I employed but
> a few men at a time, but the number was increased as the work progressed,

THE APPROACH TO THE CRATER AS SEEN FROM A POINT SOUTH-EAST
OF THE MOUTH OF THE MINE. FROM A SKETCH MADE IN 1864.

until at last I had to use the whole regiment—non-commissioned officers and all. The great difficulty I had was to dispose of the material got out of the mine. I found it impossible to get any assistance from anybody; I had to do all the work myself. I had to remove all the earth in old cracker-boxes; I got pieces of hickory and nailed on the boxes in which we received our crackers, and then iron-clad them with hoops of iron taken from old pork and beef barrels.... Whenever I made application I could not get anything, although General Burnside was very favorable to it. The most important thing was to ascertain how far I had to mine, because if I fell short of or went beyond the proper place, the explosion would have no practical effect. Therefore I wanted an accurate instrument with which to make the necessary triangulations. I had to make them on the farthest front line, where the enemy's sharp-shooters could reach me. I could not get the instrument I wanted, although there was one at army headquarters, and General Burnside had to send to Washington and get an old-fashioned theodolite, which was given to me.... General Burnside told me that General Meade and Major Duane, chief engineer of the Army of the Potomac, said the thing could not be done—that it was all clap-trap and nonsense; that such a length of mine had never been excavated in military operations, and could not be; that I would either get the men smothered, for want of air, or crushed by the falling of the earth; or the enemy would find it out and it would amount to nothing. I could get no boards or lumber supplied to me for my operations. I had to get a pass and send two companies of my own regiment, with wagons, outside of our lines to rebel saw-mills, and get lumber in that way, after having previously got what lumber I could by tearing down an old bridge. I had no mining picks furnished me, but had to take common army picks and have them straightened for my mining picks.... The only officers of high rank, so far as I learned, that favored the enterprise were General Burnside, the corps commander, and General Potter, the division commander."

On the 23d of July Colonel Pleasants had the whole mine ready for the placing of the powder. With proper tools and instruments it could have been done in one-third or one-fourth of the time. The greatest delay was occasioned by taking out the material, which had to be carried the whole length of the gallery. Every night the pioneers of Colonel Pleasants's regiment had to cut bushes to cover the fresh dirt at the mouth of the gallery; otherwise the enemy could have observed it from trees inside his own lines.

The main gallery was $510\frac{8}{10}$ feet in length. The left lateral gallery was thirty-seven feet in length and the right lateral thirty-eight feet. The magazines, eight in number, were placed in the lateral galleries—two at each end a few feet apart in branches at nearly right angles to the side galleries, and two more in each of the side galleries similarly placed by pairs, situated equidistant from each other and the end of the galleries.

It had been the intention of General Grant to make an assault on the enemy's works in the early part of July; but the movement was deferred in consequence of the work on the mine, the completion of which was impatiently awaited. As a diversion Hancock's corps and two divisions of cavalry had crossed to the north side of the James at Deep Bottom and had threatened Richmond. A part of Lee's army was sent from Petersburg to checkmate this move, and when the mine was ready to be sprung Hancock

BREVET BRIGADIER-GENERAL
HENRY PLEASANTS.
FROM A PHOTOGRAPH.

was recalled in haste to Petersburg. When the mine was ready for the explosives General Meade requested General Burnside to submit a plan of attack. This was done in a letter dated July 26th, 1864, in which General Burnside said:

"It is altogether probable that the enemy are cognizant of the fact that we are mining, because it is mentioned in their papers, and they have been heard at work on what are supposed to be shafts in close proximity to our galleries. But the rain of night before last has, no doubt, much retarded their work. We have heard no sound of workmen in them either yesterday or to-day; and nothing is heard by us in the mine but the ordinary sounds of work on the surface above. This morning we had some apprehension that the left lateral gallery was in danger of caving in from the weight of the batteries above it and the shock of their firing. But all possible precautions have been taken to strengthen it, and we hope to preserve it intact. The placing of the charges in the mine will not involve the necessity of making a noise. It is therefore probable that we will escape discovery if the mine is to be used within two or three days. It is, nevertheless, highly important, in my opinion, that the mine should be exploded at the earliest possible moment consistent with the general interests of the campaign.... But it may not be improper for me to say that the advantages reaped from the work would be but small if it were exploded without any coöperative movement.

"My plan would be to explode the mine just before daylight in the morning or at about 5 o'clock in the afternoon; mass the two brigades of

the colored division in rear of my first line, in columns of division,—
'double-columns closed in mass,'—the head of each brigade resting on the
front line, and, as soon as the explosion has taken place, move them forward, with instructions for the divisions to take half distance, and as soon
as the leading regiments of the two brigades pass through the gap in the
enemy's line, the leading regiment of the right brigade to come into line
perpendicular to the enemy's line by the 'right companies on the right
into line, wheel,' the left companies on the right into line, and proceed at
once down the line of the enemy's works as rapidly as possible; and the
leading regiment of the left brigade to execute the reverse movement to
the left, moving up the enemy's line. The remainder of the columns to
move directly toward the crest in front as rapidly as possible, diverging in
such a way as to enable them to deploy into column of regiments, the right
column making as nearly as possible for Cemetery Hill; these columns to
be followed by the other divisions of the corps as soon as they can be
thrown in. This would involve the necessity of relieving these divisions by
other troops before the movement, and of holding columns of other
troops in readiness to take our place on the crest, in case we gain it, and
sweep down it. It would, in my opinion, be advisable, if we succeed in
gaining the crest, to throw the colored division right into the town. There
is a necessity for the coöperation, at least in the way of artillery, by the
troops on our right and left. Of the extent of this you will necessarily be
the judge. I think our chances of success, in a plan of this kind, are more
than even."

With a view of making the attack, the division of colored troops, under
General Edward Ferrero, had been drilling for several weeks, General Burnside
thinking that they were in better condition to head a charge than either of the
white divisions. They had not been in any very active service. On the other
hand, the white divisions had performed very arduous duties since the beginning of the campaign, and before Petersburg had been in such proximity to the

MOUTH OF THE MINE.

enemy that no man could raise his head above the parapets without being fired at. They had been in the habit of using every possible means of covering themselves from the enemy's fire.

General Meade objected to the use of the colored troops, on the ground, as he stated, that they were a new division and had never been under fire, while this was an operation requiring the very best troops. General Burnside, however, insisted upon his programme, and the question was referred to General Grant, who confirmed General Meade's views, although he subsequently said in his evidence before the Committee on the Conduct of the War:

> "General Burnside wanted to put his colored division in front, and I believe if he had done so it would have been a success. Still I agreed with General Meade as to his objections to that plan. General Meade said that if we put the colored troops in front (we had only one division) and it should prove a failure, it would then be said, and very properly, that we were shoving these people ahead to get killed because we did not care anything about them. But that could not be said if we put white troops in front."

The mine was charged with only 8000 pounds of powder, instead of 14,000, as asked for, the amount having been reduced by order of General Meade; and while awaiting the decision of General Grant on the question of the colored troops, precise orders for making and supporting the attack were issued by General Meade.

In the afternoon of the 29th of July, Generals Potter and O. B. Willcox met together at General Burnside's headquarters, to talk over the plans of the attack, based upon the idea that the colored troops would lead the charge, and while there the message was received from General Meade that General Grant disapproved of that plan, and that General Burnside must detail one of his white divisions to take the place of the colored division. This was the first break in the original plan. There were then

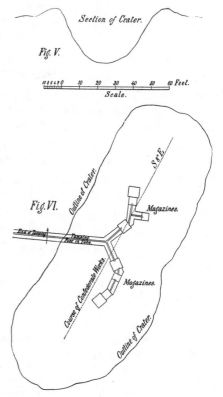

DIAGRAM OF THE CRATER.

scarcely twelve hours, and half of these at night, in which to make this change—and no possible time in which the white troops could be familiarized with the duties expected of them in connection with the assault.

General Burnside was greatly disappointed by this change; but he immediately sent for General Ledlie, who had been in command of the First Division only about six weeks. Upon his arrival General Burnside determined that the three commanders of his white divisions should "pull straws," and Ledlie was (as he thought) the unlucky victim. He, however, took it good-naturedly, and, after receiving special instructions from General Burnside, proceeded with his brigade commanders to ascertain the way to the point of attack. This was not accomplished until after dark on the evening before the explosion.

The order of attack, as proposed by General Burnside, was also changed by direction of General Meade with the approval of General Grant. Instead of moving down to the right and left of the crater of the mine, for the purpose of driving the enemy from their intrenchments, and removing to that extent the danger of flank attacks, General Meade directed that the troops should push at once for the crest of Cemetery Hill.

The approaches to the Union line of intrenchments at this particular point were so well covered by the fire of the enemy that they were cut up into a network of covered ways almost as puzzling to the uninitiated as the catacombs of Rome.†

Upon General Ledlie's return from the front orders were issued, and the division was formed at midnight. Shortly afterward it advanced through the covered ways, and was in position some time before daybreak, behind the Union breastworks, and immediately in front of the enemy's fort, which was to be blown up. The orders were that Ledlie's division should advance first, pass over the enemy's works, and charge to Cemetery Hill, four hundred yards to the right, and approached by a slope comparatively free from obstacles; as soon as the First Division should leave the works, the next division (Willcox's) was to advance to the left of Cemetery Hill, so as to protect the left flank of the First Division; and the next division (Potter's) was to move in the same way to the right of Cemetery Hill. The Ninth Corps being out of the way, it was intended that the Fifth and Eighteenth corps should pass through and follow up the movement.

At 3:30 A.M. Ledlie's division was in position, the Second Brigade, Colonel E. G. Marshall, in front, and that of General W. F. Bartlett behind it, the men

---

†The writer of this article was serving as judge-advocate of Ledlie's division, and also performed the duties of aide-de-camp to General Ledlie at the time of the explosion. When the orders were published for the movement he and Lieutenant George M. Randall, also of the regular army, and aide-de-camp to General Ledlie, were informed that they must accompany the advance troops in the attack, but that the volunteer staff would remain with General Ledlie, all of whom did so during the entire engagement, in or near a bomb-proof within the Union lines.—W.H.P.

CARRYING POWDER TO THE MINE. FROM A SKETCH MADE AT THE TIME.

and officers in a feverish state of expectancy, the majority of them having been awake all night. Daylight came slowly, and still they stood with every nerve strained prepared to move forward the instant an order should be given. Four o'clock arrived, officers and men began to get nervous, having been on their feet four hours; still the mine had not been exploded. General Ledlie then directed me to go to General Burnside and report to him that the command had been in readiness to move since 3:30 A.M., and to inquire the cause of the delay of the explosion. I found General Burnside in rear of the fourteen-gun battery, delivered my message, and received the reply from the general information that there was some trouble with the fuse dying out, but that an officer had gone into the gallery to ignite it again, and that the explosion would soon take place.[φ]

I returned immediately, and just as I arrived in rear of the First Division

[φ]Sergeant Henry Rees entered the mine and found that the fuse had died out at the first splicing. He cut the fuse above the charred portion; on his way out for materials he met Lieutenant Jacob Douty, who assisted in making a fresh splice, which was a success.—EDITORS.

the mine was sprung. It was a magnificent spectacle, and as the mass of earth went up into the air, carrying with it men, guns, carriages, and timbers, and spread out like an immense cloud as it reached its altitude, so close were the Union lines that the mass appeared as if it would descend immediately upon the troops waiting to make the charge. This caused them to break and scatter to the rear, and about ten minutes were consumed in re-forming for the attack.⁺ Not much was lost by this delay, however, as it took nearly that time for the cloud of dust to pass off. The order was then given for the advance. As no part of the Union line of breastworks had been removed (which would have been an arduous as well as hazardous undertaking), the troops clambered over them as best they could. This in itself broke the ranks, and they did not stop to re-form, but pushed ahead toward the crater, about 130 yards distant, the débris from the explosion having covered up the abatis and *chevaux-de-frise* in front of the enemy's works.

Little did these men anticipate what they would see upon arriving there: an enormous hole in the ground about 30 feet deep, 60 feet wide, and 170 feet long, filled with dust, great blocks of clay, guns, broken carriages, projecting timbers, and men buried in various ways—some up to their necks, others to their waists, and some with only their feet and legs protruding from the earth. One of these near me was pulled out, and proved to be a second lieutenant of the battery which had been blown up. The fresh air revived him, and he was soon able to walk and talk. He was very grateful and said that he was asleep when the explosion took place, and only awoke to find himself wriggling up in the air; then a few seconds afterward he felt himself descending, and soon lost consciousness.

The whole scene of the explosion struck every one dumb with astonishment as we arrived at the crest of the débris. It was impossible for the troops of the Second Brigade to move forward in line, as they had advanced; and, owing to the broken state they were in, every man crowding up to look into the hole, and being pressed by the First Brigade, which was immediately in rear, it was equally impossible to move by the flank, by any command, around the crater. Before the brigade commanders could realize the situation, the two brigades became inextricably mixed, in the desire to look into the hole.

However, Colonel Marshall yelled to the Second Brigade to move forward, and the men did so, jumping, sliding, and tumbling into the hole, over the débris of material, and dead and dying men, and huge blocks of solid clay. They were followed by General Bartlett's brigade. Up on the other side of the crater they climbed, and while a detachment stopped to place two of the dismounted guns of the battery in position on the enemy's side of the crest of the crater, a portion of the leading brigade passed over the crest and attempted to re-form. In doing

---

⁺Immediately following the explosion the heavy guns along the line opened a severe fire.—W.H.P.

THE CHARGE TO THE CRATER. FROM A SKETCH MADE AT THE TIME.

so members of these regiments were killed by musket-shots from the rear, fired by the Confederates who were still occupying the traverses and intrenchments to the right and left of the crater. These men had been awakened by the noise and shock of the explosion, and during the interval before the attack had recovered their equanimity, and when the Union troops attempted to re-form on the enemy's side of the crater, they had faced about and delivered a fire into the backs of our men. This coming so unexpectedly caused the forming line to fall back into the crater.

Had General Burnside's original plan, providing that two regiments should sweep down inside the enemy's line to the right and left of the crater, been sanctioned, the brigades of Colonel Marshall and General Bartlett could and would have re-formed and moved on to Cemetery Hill before the enemy realized fully what was intended; but the occupation of the trenches to the right and left by the enemy prevented re-formation, and there being no division, corps, or army commander present to give orders to other troops to clear the trenches, a formation under fire from the rear was something no troops could accomplish.

After falling back into the crater a partial formation was made by General Bartlett and Colonel Marshall with some of their troops, but owing to the precipitous walls the men could find no footing except by facing inward, digging their heels into the earth, and throwing their backs against the side of the crater, or squatting in a half-sitting, half-standing posture, and some of the men were shot even there by the fire from the enemy in the traverses. It was at this juncture that Colonel Marshall requested me to go to General Ledlie and explain the condition of affairs, which he knew that I had seen and understood perfectly well. This I did immediately.

While the above was taking place the enemy had not been idle. He had brought a battery from his left to bear upon the position, and as I started on my errand the crest of the crater was being swept with canister. Special attention was given to this battery by our artillery, but for some reason or other the enemy's guns could not be silenced. Passing to the Union lines under this storm of canister, I found General Ledlie and a part of his staff ensconced in a protected angle of the works. I gave him Colonel Marshall's message, explained to him the situation, and Colonel Marshall's reasons for not being able to move forward. General Ledlie then directed me to return at once and say to Colonel Marshall and General Bartlett that it was General Burnside's order that they should move forward immediately. This message was delivered. But the firing on the crater now was incessant, and it was as heavy a fire of canister as was ever poured continuously upon a single objective point. It was as utterly impracticable to re-form a brigade in that crater as it would be to marshal bees into line after upsetting the hive; and equally as impracticable to re-form outside of the crater, under the severe fire in front and rear, as it would be to hold a dress parade in front of a charging enemy. Here, then, was the second point of advantage lost by the fact that there was no person present with authority to change the programme to meet the circumstances. Had a prompt attack of the troops to the right and left of the crater been made as soon as the leading brigade had passed into the crater, or even fifteen minutes afterward, clearing the trenches and diverting the fire of the enemy, success would have been inevitable, and particularly would this have been the case on the left of the crater, as the small fort immediately in front of the Fifth Corps was almost, if not entirely, abandoned for a while after the explosion of the mine, the men running away from it as if they feared that it was to be blown up also.

Whether General Ledlie informed General Burnside of the condition of affairs as reported by me I do not know; but I think it likely, as it was not long after I had returned to the crater that a brigade of the Second Division (Potter's) under the command of Brigadier-General S. G. Griffin advanced its skirmishers and followed them immediately, directing its course to the right of the crater. General Griffin's line, however, overlapped the crater on the left, where two or three of his regiments sought shelter in the crater. Those on the right passed over the trenches, but owing to the peculiar character of the enemy's works, which were not single, but complex and involuted and filled with pits, traverses, and bomb-proofs, forming a labyrinth as difficult of passage as the crater itself, the brigade was broken up, and, meeting the severe fire of canister,

CRATER.   MUSEUM.

THE CONFEDERATE SIDE OF THE CRATER, LOOKING TOWARD THE UNION LINES. FROM A SKETCH MADE IN 1886,
TAKEN FROM THE ROAD BACK OF THE CRATER, AND NEARLY HALF-WAY TO THE CEMETERY CREST.
ON THE LEFT IS THE SWALE WHERE MAHONE'S TROOPS FORMED
FOR THE COUNTER-CHARGE.

also fell back into the crater, which was then full to suffocation. Every organization melted away, as soon as it entered this hole in the ground, into a mass of human beings clinging by toes and heels to the almost perpendicular sides. If a man was shot on the crest he fell and rolled to the bottom of the pit.

From the actions of the enemy, even at this time, as could be seen by his moving columns in front, he was not exactly certain as to the intentions of the Union commander; he appeared to think that possibly the mine explosion was but a feint and that the main attack would come from some other quarter. However, he massed some of his troops in a hollow in front of the crater, and held them in that position.

Meantime General Potter, who was in rear of the Union line of intrenchments, being convinced that something ought to be done to create a diversion and distract the enemy's attention from this point, ordered Colonel Zenas R. Bliss, commanding his First Brigade, to send two of his regiments to support General Griffin, and with the remainder to make an attack on the right. Subsequently it was arranged that the two regiments going to the support of General Griffin should pass into the crater, turn to the right, and sweep down the enemy's lines. Colonel Bliss was partly successful, and obtained possession of some 200 or 300 yards of the line, and one of the regiments advanced to within 20 or 30 yards of the battery whose fire was so severe on the troops; but it could make no further headway for lack of support—its progress being impeded by slashed timber, while an unceasing fire of canister was poured into the men. They therefore fell back to the enemy's traverses and intrenchments.

At the time of ordering forward Colonel Bliss's command General Potter wrote a dispatch to General Burnside, stating that it was his opinion, from what he had seen, and from the reports he had received from subordinate officers, that too many men were being forced in at this one point; that the troops there were in confusion, and it was absolutely necessary that an attack should be made from some other point of the line, in order to divert the enemy's attention and give time to straighten out our line. To that dispatch he never received an answer. Orders were, however, being constantly sent to the three division commanders of the white troops to push the men forward as fast as could be done, and this was, in substance, about all the orders that were received by them during the day up to the time of the order for the withdrawal.

When General Willcox came with the Third Division to support the First, he found the latter and three regiments of his own, together with the regiments of Potter's Second Division which had gone in on the right, so completely filling up the crater that no more troops could be got in there, and he therefore ordered an attack with the remainder of his division on the works of the enemy to the left of the crater. This attack was successful, so far as to carry the intrenchments for about 150 yards; but they were held only for a short time.

Previous to this last movement I had again left the crater and gone to Gen-

THE CRATER, AS SEEN FROM THE UNION SIDE. FROM A SKETCH MADE AT THE TIME.

In October, 1887, Major James C. Colt, of Cheraw, South Carolina, wrote as follows with regard to this picture, and the Confederate battery, under his command, bearing on the crater:

"I am satisfied that I made that sketch of the crater. I had sent the sketch home after the battle, and had given some of the officers on the lines copies. It was made when I was in front of the Federal lines under the flag of truce for burying the dead. One gun that was blown up by the explosion fell between the lines, as represented in the sketch.

"My guns [Colt's battalion] were all upon the front line up to the time of the explosion of the mine. After that time one of my batteries was placed upon a second line, upon the Jerusalem plank-road immediately in rear of the crater. I also had a mortar-battery between the crater and the cemetery, about 150 yards in rear of the battery that was so effective on the day of the explosion. This battery [Wright's], where I was during the engagement, was just across the ravine to our left of the crater and just in rear of our infantry line, about three hundred yards distant from the crater. It was erected there to defend Elliott's salient. It bore directly upon the crater, and was the only battery which could reach the Federal troops in advancing to our lines and after they occupied the crater. It commanded the ground from the Federal main line to the Jerusalem plank-road in rear of the crater. General Potter was unable to silence it, or even to do us any serious injury, because he could not fire directly upon its front. From this position, which was very elevated, I had a view of the whole field from the Federal main line to the ridge or plank-road. I saw all the movements of the Federal troops from the beginning to the end of the fight. I remember particularly being struck with the gallantry of one of the Federal officers, with a flag in one hand and waving his sword in the other, mounting our works."

eral Ledlie, and had urged him to try to have something done on the right and left of the crater—saying that every man who got into the trenches to the right or left of it used them as a means of escape to the crater, and the enemy was re-occupying them as fast as our men left. All the satisfaction I received was an order to go back and tell the brigade commanders to get their men out and press forward to Cemetery Hill. This talk and these orders, coming from a commander sitting in a bomb-proof inside the Union lines, were disgusting. I returned again to the crater and delivered the orders, which I knew beforehand could not possibly be obeyed; and I told General Ledlie so before I left him. Upon my return to the crater I devoted my attention to the movements of the enemy, who was evidently making dispositions for an assault.

About two hours after the explosion of the mine (7 o'clock) and after I had returned to the crater for the third time, General Edward Ferrero, commanding the colored division of the Ninth Corps, received an order to advance his division, pass the white troops which had halted, and move on to carry the crest of Cemetery Hill at all hazards. General Ferrero did not think it advisable to move his division in, as there were three divisions of white troops already huddled together, and he so reported to Colonel Charles G. Loring, of General Burnside's staff. Loring requested Ferrero to wait until he could report to General Burnside. General Ferrero declined to wait, and then Colonel Loring gave him an order, in General Burnside's name, to halt without passing over the Union works, which order he obeyed. Colonel Loring went off to report to General Burnside, came back, and reported that the order was peremptory for the colored division to advance at all hazards.

The division then started in, moved by the left flank, under a most galling fire, passed around the crater on the crest on the débris, and all but one regiment passed beyond the crater. The fire upon them was incessant and severe, and many acts of personal heroism were done here by officers and men. Their drill for this object had been unquestionably of great benefit to them, and had they led the attack, fifteen or twenty minutes from the time the débris of the explosion had settled would have found them at Cemetery Hill, before the enemy could have brought a gun to bear on them.

But the leading brigade struck the enemy's force, which I had previously reported as massed in front of the crater, and in a sharp little action the colored troops captured some two hundred prisoners and a stand of colors, and recaptured a stand of colors belonging to a white regiment of the Ninth Corps. In this almost hand-to-hand conflict the colored troops became somewhat disorganized, and some twenty minutes were consumed in re-forming; then they made the attempt to move forward again. But, unsupported, subjected to a galling fire from batteries on the flanks, and from infantry fire in front and partly on the flank, they broke up in disorder and fell back to the crater, the majority passing on to the Union line of defenses, carrying with them a number of the white troops who were in the crater and in the enemy's intrenchments. ⁄

⁄A field-officer of one of the colored regiments [Lieutenant-Colonel John A. Bross] seized a stand of United States colors as he saw his men faltering when they first met the withering fire of the enemy, and mounting the very highest portion of the crest of the crater waved the colors zealously amid the storm of shot and canister. The gallant fellow was soon struck to the earth.

Had any one in authority been present when the colored troops made their charge, and had they been supported, even at that late hour in the day, there would have been a possibility of success; but when they fell back and broke up in disorder, it was the closing scene of the tragedy. The rout of the colored troops was followed up by a feeble attack from the enemy, more in the way of a reconnoissance than a charge; but the attack was repulsed by the troops in the crater and in the intrenchments connected therewith, and the Confederates retired.

It was now evident that the enemy did not fear a demonstration from any other quarter, as they began to collect their troops for a decisive assault. On observing this I left the crater and reported to General Ledlie, whom I found seated in a bomb-proof with General Ferrero, that some means ought to be devised for withdrawing the mass of men from the crater without exposing them to the terrific fire which was kept up by the enemy; that if some shovels and picks could be found, the men in an hour could open a covered way by which they could be withdrawn; that the enemy was making every preparation for a determined assault on the crater, and, disorganized as the troops were, they could make no permanent resistance. Not an implement of any kind could be found; indeed, the proposition was received with disfavor. Matters remained *in statu quo* until about 2 P.M., when the enemy's anticipated assault was made.

About 9:30 A.M. General Meade had given positive orders to have the troops withdrawn from the crater. To have done so under the severe fire of the enemy would have produced a stampede, which would have endangered the Union lines, and might possibly have communicated itself to the troops that were massed in rear of the Ninth Corps. General Burnside thought, for these and other reasons, that it would be possible to leave his command there until nightfall, and then withdraw it. There was no means of getting food or water to them, for which they were suffering. The midsummer sun caused waves of moisture produced by the exhalation from this mass to rise above the crater. Wounded men died there begging piteously for water, and soldiers extended their tongues to dampen their parched lips until their tongues seemed to hang from their mouths. Finally, the enemy, having taken advantage of our inactivity to

---

While this was taking place an amusing occurrence happened in the crater. As the colored column was moving by the left flank around the edge of the crater to the right, the file-closers, on account of the narrowness of the way, were compelled to pass through the mass of white men inside the crater. One of these file-closers was a massively built, powerful, and well-formed sergeant, stripped to the waist—his coal-black skin shining like polished ebony in the strong sunlight. As he was passing up the slope to emerge on the enemy's side of the crest he came across one of his own black fellows, who was lagging behind his company, evidently with the intention of remaining inside the crater, out of the way of the bullets. He was accosted by the sergeant with "None ob yo' d—n skulkin', now," with which remark he seized the culprit with one hand, and, lifting him up in his powerful grasp by the waist-band of his trousers, carried him to the crest of the crater, threw him over on the enemy's side, and quickly followed.—W.H.P.

mass his troops, was seen to emerge from the swale [see cut, p. 833] between the hill on which the crater was situated and that of the cemetery. On account of this depression they could not be seen by our artillery, and hence no guns were brought to bear upon them. The only place where they could be observed was from the crater. But there was no serviceable artillery there, and no infantry force sufficiently organized to offer resistance when the enemy's column pressed forward. All in the crater who could possibly hang on by their elbows and toes lay flat against its conical wall and delivered their fire; but not more than a hundred men at a time could get into position, and these were only armed with muzzle-loading guns, and in order to re-load they were compelled to face about and place their backs against the wall.

The enemy's guns suddenly ceased their long-continued and uninterrupted fire on the crater, and the advancing column charged in the face of feeble resistance offered by the Union troops. At this stage they were perceived by our artillery, which opened a murderous fire, but too late. Over the crest and into the crater they poured, and a hand-to-hand conflict ensued. It was of short duration, however; crowded as our troops were, and without organization, resistance was vain. Many men were bayoneted at that time—some probably that would not have been, except for the excitement of battle. About 87 officers[*] and 1652 men of the Ninth Corps were captured, the remainder retiring to our own lines, to which the enemy did not attempt to advance.

In the engagements of the 17th and 18th of June, in order to obtain the position held by the Ninth Corps at the time of the explosion, the three white divisions lost 29 officers and 348 men killed; 106 officers and 1851 men wounded; and 15 officers and 554 men missing,—total, 2903. From the 20th of June to the day before the crater fight of July 30th these same divisions lost in the trenches 12 officers and 231 men killed; 44 officers and 851 men wounded; and 12 men missing,—total, 1150. These casualties were caused by picket and shell firing, and extended pretty evenly over the three divisions. The whole of General Willcox's division was on the line for thirty days or more without relief. General Potter's and General Ledlie's divisions had slight reliefs, enabling those officers to draw some of their men off at intervals for two or three days at a time.

In the engagement of July 30th the four divisions of the Ninth Corps had 52 officers and 376 men killed; 105 officers and 1556 men wounded; and 87 officers and 1652 men captured,—total, 3828.

---

[*]Among the captured was General William F. Bartlett. Earlier in the war he had lost a leg, which he replaced with one of cork. While he was standing in the crater, a shot was heard to strike with the peculiar thud known to those who have been in action, and the general was seen to totter and fall. A number of officers and men immediately lifted him, when he cried out, "Put me any place where I can sit down." "But you are wounded, General, aren't you?" was the inquiry. "My leg is shattered all to pieces," said he. "Then you can't sit up," they urged; "you'll have to lie down." "Oh, no!" exclaimed the general, "*it's only my cork leg that's shattered!*"—W.H.P.

It was provided in General Meade's order for the movement that the cavalry corps should make an assault on the left. Two divisions of the cavalry were over at Deep Bottom. They could not cross the river until after the Second Corps had crossed, so that it was late in the day before they came up. Indeed, the head of the column did not appear before the of-

SIDES AND EDGE OF TWO BULLETS THAT MET POINT TO POINT AT THE CRATER— THE SIDES FROM PHOTOGRAPHS OF THE ORIGINAL IN MAJOR GRIFFITH'S MUSEUM AT THE CRATER.

fensive operations had been suspended. As General James H. Wilson had been ordered to be in readiness, and in view of the unavoidable delay of General Sheridan, orders were sent to Wilson not to wait for General Sheridan, but to push on himself to the Weldon railroad. But the length of the march prevented success; so no attack was made by the cavalry, except at Lee's Mills, where General Gregg, encountering cavalry, drove them away in order to water his horses. The Fifth Corps and the Eighteenth Corps remained inert during the day, excepting Turner's division of the Tenth Corps (temporarily attached to the Eighteenth), which made an attempt on the right of the crater, but it happened to be just at the time that the colored troops broke up; so his command was thrown into confusion, and fell back to the trenches.

THE SIEGE OF PETERSBURG—I. SHARP-SHOOTERS ON THE LINE OF THE EIGHTEENTH CORPS. 2. BIVOUAC OF THE FIFTH CORPS IN THE RIFLE-PITS. FROM SKETCHES MADE AT THE TIME.

In this affair the several efforts made to push troops forward to Cemetery Hill were as futile in their results as the dropping of handfuls of sand into a running stream to make a dam. With the notable exception of General Robert B. Potter, there was not a division commander in the crater or connecting lines, nor was there a corps commander on the immediate scene of action; the result being that the subordinate commanders attempted to carry out the orders issued prior to the commencement of the action, when the first attack developed the fact that a change of these plans was absolutely necessary.[*]

[*] A revised table that has been prepared for publication in the "Official Records" shows the loss of the Ninth Corps to have been 50 officers and 423 men killed, 124 officers and 1522 men wounded, and 79 officers and 1277 men captured or missing—3475. The total loss at the mine (including Turner's division of the Tenth Corps) was 504 killed, 1881 wounded, and 1413 captured or missing—3798. General Mahone states that the number of prisoners taken was 1101. The loss in Lee's army is not fully reported. Elliott's brigade lost 677, and that was probably more than half of the casualties on the Confederate side.—EDITORS.

CHAPTER 6

The Duel Between the "Alabama" and the "Kearsarge."

John M. Browne, Surgeon of the "Kearsarge."

On Sunday, the 12th of June, 1864, the *Kearsarge*, Captain John A. Winslow, was lying at anchor in the Scheldt, off Flushing, Holland. The cornet suddenly appeared at the fore, and a gun was fired. These were unexpected signals that compelled absent officers and men to return to the ship. Steam was raised, and as soon as we were off, and all hands called, Captain Winslow gave the welcome news of a telegram from Mr. Dayton, our minister to France, announcing that the *Alabama* had arrived the day previous at Cherbourg; hence the urgency of departure, the probability of an encounter, and the expectation of her capture or destruction. The crew responded with cheers. The succeeding day witnessed the arrival of the *Kearsarge* at Dover for dispatches, and the day after (Tuesday) her appearance off Cherbourg, where we saw the Confederate flag flying within the breakwater. As we approached, officers and men gathered in groups on deck, and looked intently at the "daring rover" that had been able for two years to escape numerous foes and to inflict immense damage on our commerce. She was a beautiful specimen of naval architecture. The surgeon went on shore and obtained *pratique* (permission to visit the port) for boats. Owing to the neutrality limitation, which would not allow us to remain in the harbor longer than twenty-four hours, it was inexpedient to enter the port. We placed a vigilant watch by turns at each of the harbor entrances, and continued it to the moment of the engagement.

On Wednesday Captain Winslow

paid an official visit to the French admiral commanding the maritime district, and to the United States commercial agent, bringing on his return the unanticipated news that Captain Semmes had declared his intention to fight. At first the assertion was barely credited, the policy of the *Alabama* being regarded as opposed to a conflict, and to escape rather than to be exposed to injury, perhaps destruction; but the doubters were half convinced when the so-called challenge was known to read as follows:

"C.S.S. 'ALABAMA,' CHERBOURG, June 14th, 1864.
"To A. BONFILS, Esq., CHERBOURG.
"Sir:

"I hear that you were informed by the U.S. Consul that the *Kearsarge* was to come to this port solely for the prisoners landed by me, and that she was to depart in twenty-four hours. I desire you to say to the U.S. Consul that my intention is to fight the *Kearsarge* as soon as I can make the necessary arrangements. I hope these will not detain me more than until tomorrow evening, or after the morrow morning at furthest. I beg she will not depart before I am ready to go out.

"I have the honor to be, very respectfully,
"Your obedient servant,
"R. SEMMES, Captain."

This communication was sent by Mr. Bonfils, the Confederate States Commercial Agent, to Mr. Liais, the United States Commercial Agent, with a request that the latter would furnish a copy to Captain Winslow for his guidance. There was no other challenge to combat. The letter that passed between the commercial agents *was* the challenge about which so much has been said. Captain Semmes informed Captain Winslow through Mr. Bonfils of his intention to fight; Captain Winslow informed Captain Semmes through Mr. Liais that he came to Cherbourg to fight, and had no intention of leaving. He made no other reply.

Captain Winslow assembled the officers and discussed the expected battle. It was probable the two ships would engage on parallel lines, and the *Alabama* would seek neutral waters in event of defeat; hence the necessity of beginning the action several miles from the breakwater. It was determined not to surrender, but to fight until the last, and, if need be, to go down with colors flying. Why Captain Semmes should imperil his ship was not understood, since he would risk all and expose the cause of which he was a selected champion to a needless disaster, while the *Kearsarge,* if taken or destroyed, could be replaced. It was therefore concluded that he would fight because he thought he would be the victor.

Preparations were made for battle, with no relaxation of the watch. Thursday passed; Friday came; the *Kearsarge* waited with ports down, guns pivoted to starboard, the whole battery loaded, and shell, grape, and canister ready to use in any mode of attack or defense; yet no *Alabama* appeared. French pilots came on board and told of unusual arrangements made by the enemy, such as the hurried taking of coals, the transmission of valuable articles to the shore, such as captured chronometers, specie, and the bills of ransomed vessels; and the sharpening of swords, cutlasses, and boarding-pikes. It was reported that Captain Semmes had been advised not to give battle; that he replied he would prove to the world that his ship was not a privateer, intended only for attack upon merchant vessels, but a true man-of-war; further, that he had consulted French officers, who all asserted that in his situation they would fight. Certain newspapers declared that he ought to improve the opportunity afforded by the presence of the enemy to show that his ship was not a "corsair," to prey upon defenseless merchantmen, but a real ship-of-war, able and willing to fight the "Federal" waiting outside the harbor. It was said the *Alabama* was swift, with a superior crew, and it was known that the ship, guns, and ammunition were of English make.

A surprise by night was suggested, and precautionary means were taken; everything was well planned and ready for action, but still no *Alabama* came. Meanwhile the *Kearsarge* was cruising to and fro off the breakwater. A message was brought from Mr. Dayton, our minister to Paris, by his son, who with difficulty had obtained permission from the French admiral to visit the *Kearsarge*. Communication with either ship was prohibited, but the permission was given upon the promise of Mr. Dayton to return on shore directly after the delivery of the message. Mr. Dayton expressed the opinion that Captain Semmes would not fight, though acknowledging the prevalence of a contrary belief in Cherbourg. He was told that, in the event of battle, if we were successful the colors would be displayed at the mizzen as the flag of victory. He went on shore with the intention of leaving for Paris without delay. In taking leave of the French admiral the latter advised Mr. Dayton to remain over night, and mentioned the fixed purpose of Captain Semmes to fight on the following day, Sunday; and he gave the intelligence that there could be no further communication with the *Kearsarge*. Mr. Dayton passed a part of Saturday night trying to procure a boat to send off the acquired information, but the vigilance along the coast made his efforts useless. He remained, witnessed the battle, telegraphed the result to Paris, and was one of the first to go on board and offer congratulations.

At a supper in Cherbourg on Saturday night, several officers of the *Alabama* met sympathizing friends, the coming battle being the chief topic of conversation. Confident of victory, they proclaimed the intent to sink the "Federal" or gain a "corsair." They rose with promises to meet the following night to repeat

THE CREW OF THE "KEARSARGE" AT QUARTERS. FROM A PHOTOGRAPH.

the festivity as victors, were escorted to the boat, and departed with cheers and best wishes for a successful return.‡

Sunday, the 19th, came; a fine day, atmosphere somewhat hazy, little sea, light westerly wind. At 10 o'clock the *Kearsarge* was near the buoy marking the line of shoals to the eastward of Cherbourg, at a distance of about three miles from the entrance. The decks had been holystoned, the bright work cleaned, the guns polished, and the crew were dressed in Sunday suits. They were inspected at quarters and dismissed to attend divine service. Seemingly no one thought of the enemy so long awaited and not appearing, speculation as to her coming had nearly ceased. At 10:20 the officer of the deck reported a steamer approaching from Cherbourg,—a frequent occurrence, and consequently it created no surprise. The bell was tolling for service when some one shouted, "She's coming, and heading straight for us!" Soon, by the aid of a glass, the officer of the deck made out the enemy and shouted, "The *Alabama!*" and calling down the ward-room hatch repeated the cry, "The *Alabama!*" The drum beat to general quarters; Captain Winslow put aside the prayer-book, seized the trumpet, ordered the ship about, and headed seaward. The ship was cleared for action, with the battery pivoted to starboard.

The *Alabama* approached from the western entrance, escorted by the French iron-clad frigate *Couronnet* flying the pennant of the commandant of the

‡This incident, and others pertaining to the *Alabama,* were told the writer by the officers who were taken prisoners.—J.M.B.

port, followed in her wake by a small fore-and-aft-rigged steamer, the *Deerhound,* flying the flag of the Royal Mersey Yacht Club. The commander of the frigate had informed Captain Semmes that his ship would escort him to the limit of the French waters. The frigate, having convoyed the *Alabama* three marine miles from the coast, put down her helm, and steamed back into port without delay.

The steam-yacht continued on, and remained near the scene of action.

Captain Winslow had assured the French admiral that in the event of an engagement the position of the ship should be far enough from shore to prevent a violation of the law of nations. To avoid a question of jurisdiction, and to avert an escape to neutral waters in case of retreat, the *Kearsarge* steamed to sea, followed by the enemy, giving the appearance of running away and being pursued. Between six and seven miles from the shore the *Kearsarge,* thoroughly ready, at 10:50 wheeled, at a distance of one and a quarter miles from her opponent, presented the starboard battery, and steered direct for her, with the design of closing or of running her down. The *Alabama* sheered and presented her starboard battery. More speed was ordered, the *Kearsarge* advanced rapidly, and at 10:57 received a broadside of solid shot at a range of about eighteen hundred yards. This broadside cut away a little of the rigging, but the shot mostly passed over or fell short. It was apparent that Captain Semmes intended to fight at long range.

The *Kearsarge* advanced with increased speed, receiving a second and part of a third broadside with similar effect. Captain Winslow wished to get at short range, as the guns were loaded with five-second shell. Arrived within nine hundred yards, the *Kearsarge,* fearing a fourth broadside, and apprehensive of a raking, sheered and broke her silence with the starboard battery. Each ship was now pressed under a full head of steam, the position being broadside, both employing the starboard guns.

Captain Winslow, fearful that the enemy would make for the shore, determined with a port helm to run under the *Alabama's* stern for raking, but was prevented by her sheering and keeping her broadside to the *Kearsarge,* which forced the fighting on a circular track, each ship, with a strong port helm, steaming around a common center, and pouring its fire into its opponent a quarter to half a mile away. There was a current setting to westward three knots an hour.

The action was now fairly begun. The *Alabama* changed from solid shot to shell.⧾ A shot from an early broadside of the *Kearsarge* carried away the spanker-gaff of the enemy, and caused his ensign to come down by the run. This incident was regarded as a favorable omen by the men, who cheered and went with increased confidence to their work. The fallen ensign reappeared at the mizzen. The *Alabama* returned to solid shot, and soon after fired both shot and shell to the end. The firing of the *Alabama* was rapid and wild, getting better near the

---

⧾Commander Kell says the *Alabama* began with shell.—EDITORS.

REAR-ADMIRAL JOHN A. WINSLOW, CAPTAIN OF THE "KEARSARGE."
FROM A PHOTOGRAPH TAKEN SOON AFTER THE FIGHT,
IN POSSESSION OF PAYMASTER-GENERAL J. A. SMITH, U.S.N.

close; that of the *Kearsarge* was deliberate, accurate, and almost from the beginning productive of dismay, destruction, and death.✦ The *Kearsarge* gunners had been cautioned against firing without direct aim, and had been advised to point

✦Captain Semmes in his official report says: "The firing now became very hot, and the enemy's shot and shell soon began to tell upon our hull, knocking down, killing, and disabling a number of men in different parts of the ship."—J.M.B.

the heavy guns below rather than above the water-line, and to clear the deck of the enemy with the lighter ones. Though subjected to an incessant storm of shot and shell, they kept their stations and obeyed instructions.

The effect upon the enemy was readily perceived, and nothing could restrain the enthusiasm of our men. Cheer succeeded cheer; caps were thrown in the air or overboard; jackets were discarded; sanguine of victory, the men were shouting, as each projectile took effect: "That is a good one!" "Down, boys!" "Give her another like the last!" "Now we have her!" and so on, cheering and shouting to the end.

After the *Kearsarge* had been exposed to an uninterrupted cannonade for eighteen minutes, a 68-pounder Blakely shell passed through the starboard bulwarks below the main rigging, exploded upon the quarter-deck, and wounded three of the crew of the after pivot-gun. With these exceptions, not an officer or man received serious injury. The three unfortunate men were speedily taken below, and so quietly was the act done that at the termination of the fight a large number of the men were unaware that any of their comrades were wounded. Two shots entered the ports occupied by the thirty-twos, where several men were stationed, one taking effect in the hammock-netting, the other going through the opposite port, yet none were hit. A shell exploded in the hammock-netting and set the ship on fire; the alarm calling for fire-quarters was sounded, and men who had been detailed for such an emergency put out the fire, while the rest staid at the guns.

It is wonderful that so few casualties occurred on board the *Kearsarge*, considering the number on the *Alabama*—the former having fired 173 shot and shell, and the latter nearly double that number. The *Kearsarge* concentrated her fire, and poured in the 11-inch shells with deadly effect. One penetrated the coal-bunker of the *Alabama*, and a dense cloud of coal-dust arose. Others struck near the water-line between the main and mizzen masts, exploded within board, or, passing through, burst beyond. Crippled and torn, the *Alabama* moved less quickly and began to settle by the stern, yet did not slacken her fire, but returned successive broadsides without disastrous result to us.

Captain Semmes witnessed the havoc made by the shells, especially by those of our after pivot-gun, and offered a reward to any one who would silence it. Soon his battery was turned upon this particular offending gun. It was in vain, for the work of destruction went on. We had completed the seventh rotation on the circular track and had begun the eighth, when the *Alabama*, now settling, sought to escape by setting all available sail (fore-trysail and two jibs), left the circle amid a shower of shot and shell, and headed for the French waters; but to no purpose. In winding, the *Alabama* presented the port battery, with only two guns bearing, and showed gaping sides, through which the water washed. The *Kearsarge* pursued, keeping on a line nearer the shore, and with a few well-directed shots hastened the sinking. Then the *Alabama* was at our mercy. Her colors were struck, and the *Kearsarge* ceased firing. I was told by our prisoners that two of the junior officers swore they would never surrender, and in a mutinous spirit rushed to the two port guns and opened fire upon the *Kearsarge*. Captain Winslow, amazed at this extraordinary conduct of an enemy who had hauled down his flag in token of surrender, exclaimed, "He is playing us a trick; give him another broadside." Again the shot and shell went crashing through her sides, and the *Alabama* continued to settle by the stern. The *Kearsarge* was laid across her bows for raking, and in position to use grape and canister.

A white flag was then shown over the stern of the *Alabama* and her ensign was half-masted, union down. Captain Winslow for the second time gave orders to cease firing. Thus ended the fight, after a duration of one hour and two minutes. Captain Semmes, in his report, says: "Although we were now but four hundred yards from each other, the enemy fired upon me five times after my colors had been struck. It is charitable to suppose that a ship-of-war of a Christian nation could not have done this intentionally." He is silent as to the renewal by the *Alabama* of the fight after his surrender—an act which, in Christian warfare, would have justified the *Kearsarge* in continuing the fire until the *Alabama* had sunk beneath the waters.

Boats were now lowered from the *Alabama*. Her master's-mate, Fullam, an Englishman, came alongside the *Kearsarge* with a few of the wounded, reported the disabled and sinking condition of his ship, and asked for assistance. Captain Winslow inquired, "Does Captain Semmes surrender his ship?" "Yes," was the reply. Fullam then solicited permission to return with his boat and crew to assist in rescuing the drowning, pledging his word of honor that when this was

THE ELEVEN-INCH FORWARD PIVOT-GUN ON THE "KEARSARGE," IN ACTION.

done he would come on board and surrender. Captain Winslow granted the request. With less generosity he could have detained the officer and men, supplied their places in the boat from his ship's company, secured more prisoners, and afforded equal aid to the distressed. The generosity was abused, as the sequel shows. Fullam pulled to the midst of the drowning, rescued several officers, went to the yacht *Deerhound*, and cast his boat adrift, leaving a number of men struggling in the water.

It was now seen that the *Alabama* was settling fast. The wounded, and the boys who could not swim, were sent away in the quarter-boats, the waist-boats having been destroyed. Captain Semmes dropped his sword into the sea and jumped overboard with the remaining officers and men.

Coming under the stern of the *Kearsarge* from the windward, the *Deerhound* was hailed, and her commander requested by Captain Winslow to run down and assist in picking up the men of the sinking ship. Or, as her owner, Mr. John Lancaster, reported: "The fact is, that when we passed the *Kearsarge* the captain cried out, 'For God's sake, do what you can to save them'; and that was my warrant for interfering in any way for the aid and succor of his enemies." The *Deerhound* was built by the Lairds at the same time and in the same yard with the *Alabama*. Throughout the action she kept about a mile to the windward of the contestants. After being hailed she steamed toward the *Alabama*, which sank almost immediately after. This was at 12:24. The *Alabama* sank in forty-five fathoms of water, at a distance of about four and a half miles from the breakwater, off the west entrance. She was severely hulled between the main and mizzen masts, and settled by the stern; the mainmast, pierced by a shot at the very last, broke off near the head and went over the side, the bow lifted high from the water, and then came the end. Suddenly assuming a perpendicular position, caused by the falling aft of the battery and stores, straight as a plumb-line, stern first, she went down, the jib-boom being the last to appear above water. Thus sank the terror of merchantmen, riddled through and through, and as she disappeared to her last resting-place there was no cheer; all was silent.

The yacht lowered her two boats, rescued Captain Semmes (wounded in the hand by broken iron rigging), First Lieutenant Kell, twelve officers, and twenty-six men, leaving the rest of the survivors to the two boats of the *Kearsarge*. Apparently aware that the forty persons he had rescued would be claimed, Mr. Lancaster steamed away as fast as he coul, direct for Southampton, without waiting for such surgical assistance as the *Kearsarge* might render. Captain Winslow permitted the yacht to secure his prisoners, anticipating their subsequent surrender. Again his confidence was misplaced, and he afterward wrote: "It was my mistake at the moment that I could not recognize an enemy who, under the garb of a friend, was affording assistance." The aid of the yacht, it is presumed, was asked in a spirit of chivalry, for the *Kearsarge*, comparatively uninjured, with but three wounded, and a full head of steam, was in condition to engage a second enemy. Instead of remaining at a distance of about four hundred yards from the *Alabama,* and from this position sending two boats, the other boats being injured, the *Kearsarge* by steaming close to the settling ship, and in the midst of the defeated, could have captured all—Semmes, officers, and men. Captain Semmes says: "There was no appearance of any boat coming to me from the enemy after the ship went down. Fortunately, however, the steam-yacht *Deerhound,* owned by a gentleman of Lancashire, England, Mr. John Lancaster, who was himself on board, steamed up in the midst of my drowning men, and rescued a number of both officers and men from the water. I was fortunate enough myself thus to escape to the shelter of the neutral flag, together with about forty others, all told. About this time the *Kearsarge* sent one, and then, tardily, another boat."

This imputation of inhumanity is contradicted by Mr. Lancaster's assertion that he was requested to do what he could to save "the poor fellows who were struggling in the water for their lives."

The *Deerhound* edged to the leeward and steamed rapidly away. An officer approached Captain Winslow and reported the presence of Captain Semmes and many officers on board the English yacht. Believing the information authentic, as it was obtained from the prisoners, he suggested the expediency of firing a shot to bring her to, and asked permission. Captain Winslow declined, saying "it was impossible; the yacht was simply coming round." Meanwhile the *Deerhound* increased the distance from the *Kearsarge;* another officer spoke to him in similar language, but with more positiveness. Captain Winslow replied that no Englishman who carried the flag of the Royal Yacht Squadron could so act. The *Deerhound* continued her flight, and yet another officer urged the necessity of firing a shot. With undiminished confidence Captain Winslow refused, saying the yacht was "simply coming round," and would not go away without communicating. The escape of the yacht and her coveted prize was manifestly regretted. The famed *Alabama,* "a formidable ship, the terror of American commerce, well armed, well manned, well handled," was destroyed, "sent to the bottom in an hour," but her commander had escaped; the victory seemed already lessened. It was held by the Navy Department that Captain Semmes violated the usages of war in surrendering to Captain Winslow through the agency of one of his officers and then effecting an escape during the execution of the commission; that he was a prisoner of the United States Government from the moment he sent the officer to make the surrender.[*]

---

[*]The controversy in reference to the *Deerhound* is summarized thus in a letter to the editors from Professor James Russell Soley, U.S.N.:

"A neutral ship, in general, could have no right to take part in hostilities even to the extent of rescuing the drowning sailors of a belligerent, their situation being a part and a consequence of the battle. In the case of the *Deerhound,* however, the interference was directly authorized

The wounded of the survivors were brought on board the *Kearsarge* for surgical attendance. Seventy men, including five officers (Surgeon F. L. Galt, acting paymaster, Second Lieutenant J. D. Wilson, First Assistant-Engineer M. J. Freeman, Third Assistant-Engineer Pundt, and Boatswain McCloskey), were saved by the *Kearsarge*'s boats and a French pilot-boat. Another pilot-boat saved Second Lieutenant Armstrong and some men, who were landed at Cherbourg. Lieutenant Wilson was the only officer who delivered up his sword. He refused to go on board the *Deerhound,*

SEAMAN WILLIAM GOUIN, MORTALLY WOUNDED ON THE "KEARSARGE."

and because of his honorable conduct Captain Winslow on taking his parole gave him a letter of recommendation. Our crew fraternized with their prisoners, and shared their clothes, supper, and grog with them. The conduct of the *Alabama*'s Assistant-Surgeon Llewellyn, son of a British rector, deserves mention. He was unremitting in attention to the wounded during battle, and after the surrender superintended their removal to the boats, refusing to leave the ship while one remained. This duty performed, being unable to swim, he attached two empty shell-boxes to his waist as a life-preserver and jumped overboard. Nevertheless, he was unable to keep his head above water.

When the *Kearsarge* was cleared for action every man on the sick-list went to his station. The *Kearsarge* had three wounded, of whom one died in the hospital a few days after the fight. This was William Gouin, ordinary seaman, whose behavior during and after battle was worthy of the highest praise. Stationed at the after pivot-gun he was seriously wounded in the leg by the explo-

---

by Captain Winslow's request, addressed to Mr. Lancaster, and, therefore, the latter committed no breach of neutrality in taking the prisoners on board. Once on board the English yacht, however, they were as free as air. So far from its being the obligation of the *Deerhound* to surrender them, the obligation was exactly the other way. Their surrender would have been as gross a violation of neutrality toward the Confederates as their unauthorized rescue would have been toward the Union Government. Captain Winslow was therefore perfectly right in refusing to detain the *Deerhound,* since the conduct of the yacht was the necessary and logical consequence of his own act. The point where he was clearly in the wrong was in making the request in the first place. What he should have done, as Surgeon-General Browne clearly intimates, was to have steamed up close to the sinking *Alabama,* and saved her people himself, instead of remaining four hundred yards off."

It will be noticed that this statement leaves untouched the question of the right of a prisoner to escape after surrender and before delivering himself up.—Editors.

CLOSE OF THE COMBAT—THE "KEARSARGE" GETTING INTO POSITION
TO RAKE THE "ALABAMA."

sion of a shell; in agony, and exhausted from the loss of blood, he dragged himself to the forward hatch, concealing the severity of his injury, so that his comrades might not leave their stations for his assistance; fainting, he was lowered to the care of the surgeon, and when he revived he greeted the surgeon with a smile, saying, "Doctor, I can fight no more, and so come to you, but it is all right; I am satisfied, for we are whipping the *Alabama*"; and afterward, "I will willingly lose my leg or my life, if it is necessary." Lying upon his mattress, he paid attention to the progress of the fight, so far as could be known by the sounds on the deck, his face showing satisfaction whenever the cheers of his shipmates were heard; with difficulty he waved his hand over his head, and joined in each cheer with a feeble voice. When a wounded shipmate on either side of him complained, he reproved him, saying, "Am I not worse hurt than you! and I am satisfied, for we are whipping the *Alabama*." Directly after the enemy's wounded were brought on board he desired the surgeon to give him no further attention, for he was "doing well," requesting that all aid be given to "the poor fellows of the *Alabama*." In the hospital he was patient and resigned, and happy in speaking of the victory. "This man, so very interesting by his courage and resignation," wrote the French surgeon-in-chief, "received general sympathy; all desired his recovery and lamented his death." At a dinner given by loyal Americans in Paris to Captain Winslow and two of his officers, a telegram was received announcing the death of Gouin. His name was honorably mentioned, his behavior eulogized, and his memory drunk in silence.

At 3:10 P.M. the *Kearsarge* anchored in Cherbourg harbor close by the ship-of-war *Napoléon*, and was soon surrounded by boats of every description filled with excited and inquisitive people. Ambulances, by order of the French admiral, were sent to the landing to receive the wounded, and thence they were

THE BOAT FROM THE "ALABAMA" ANNOUNCING THE SURRENDER
AND ASKING FOR ASSISTANCE.
The picture shows shot-marks in the thin deal covering of the chain armor amidships.

taken to the Hôpital de la Marine, where arrangements had been made for their reception. Dr. Galt and all the prisoners except four officers were paroled and sent on shore before sunset. Secretary Welles soon after expressed his disapprobation of this action.

An incident that occasioned gratification was the coincidence of the lowering of the enemy's colors by an early shot from the *Kearsarge*, already mentioned, and the unfolding of the victorious flag by a shot from the *Alabama*. The *Kearsarge*'s colors were "stopped" at the mizzen, that they might be displayed if the ensign were carried away, and to serve as the emblem of victory in case of success. A shot from the last broadside of the *Alabama* passed high over the *Kearsarge*, carried away the halyards of the colors, stopped at the mizzen, and in so doing pulled sufficiently to break the stop, and thereby unfurled the tri-umphant flag.

The *Kearsarge* received twenty-eight shot and shell, of which thirteen were in the hull, the most efficient being abaft the mainmast. A 100-pounder rifle shell entered at the starboard quarter and lodged in the stern-post. The blow shook the ship from stem to stern. Luckily the shell did not explode, otherwise the result would have been serious, if not fatal. A 32-pounder shell entered for-ward of the forward pivot port, crushing the waterways, raising the gun and car-riage, and lodged, but did not explode, else many of the gun's crew would likely have been injured by the fragments and splinters. The smoke-pipe was perfo-rated by a rifle shell, which exploded inside and tore a ragged hole nearly three feet in diameter, and carried away three of the chain guys. Three boats were shattered. The cutting away of the rigging was mostly about the mainmast. The spars were left in good order. A large number of pieces of burst shell were gath-ered from the deck and thoughtlessly thrown overboard. During the anchorage in Cherbourg harbor no assistance was received from shore except that ren-dered by a boiler-maker in patching up the smoke-stack, every other repair being made by our own men.

Captain Semmes in his official report says:

> "At the end of the engagement it was discovered, by those of our officers who went alongside the enemy's ship with the wounded, that her midship section on both sides was thoroughly iron-coated. The planking had been ripped off in every direction by our shot and shell, the chain broken and indented in many places, and forced partly into the ship's side. The enemy was heavier than myself, both in ship, battery, and crew; but I did not know until the action was over that she was also iron-clad."

The ships were well matched in size, speed, armament, and crew, showing a likeness rarely seen in naval battles.[+] The number of the ship's company of the *Kearsarge* was 163. That of the *Alabama*, from the best information, was esti-mated at 150.

The chain plating was made of one hundred and twenty fathoms of sheet-chains of one-and-seven-tenths inch iron, covering a space amidships of forty-nine and one-half feet in length by six feet two inches in depth, stopped up and

	Alabama.		Kearsarge.
[+]Length over all	220 ft.	..	232 ft.
Length at water-line	210 ft.	..	196½ ft.
Beam	32 ft.	..	33 ft.
Depth	17 ft.	..	16½ ft.
2 Engines apiece, each of	300 h.p.	..	400 h.p.
Tonnage	1040	..	1061

down to eye-bolts with marlines, secured by iron dogs, and employed for
the purpose of protecting the engines
when the upper part of the coal-
bunkers was empty, as happened during the action. The chains were
concealed by one-inch deal-boards as
a finish. The chain plating was struck
by a 32-pounder shot in the starboard
gangway, which cut the chain and
bruised the planking; and by a 32-
pounder shell, which broke a link of
the chain, exploded, and tore away a
portion of the deal covering. Had the
shot been from the 100-pounder rifle
the result would have been different,
though without serious damage, because the shot struck five feet above
the water-line, and if sent through the
side would have cleared the machinery and boilers. It is proper therefore
to assert that in the absence of the
chain armor the result would have
been nearly the same, notwithstanding the common opinion at the time
that the *Kearsarge* was an "iron-clad"

THE SHELL IN THE STERN-POST
OF THE "KEARSARGE."

The charge was withdrawn from the shell,
which was boxed in, and in that condition it remained for months, until the ship reached
Boston, where, when the vessel was repaired, a
section of the stern-post containing the embedded shell was cut away and sent to the Navy
Department, and was finally deposited in the
Ordnance Museum, at the Navy Yard, Washington.—J.M.B.

contending with a wooden ship. The chains were fastened to the ship's sides
more than a year previous to the fight, while at the Azores. It was the suggestion
of the executive officer, Lieutenant-Commander James S. Thornton, to hang
the sheet-chain (or spare anchor-cable) over the sides, so as to protect the midship section, he having served with Admiral Farragut in passing the forts to
reach New Orleans, and having observed its benefit on that occasion. The work
was done in three days, at a cost for material not exceeding seventy-five dollars.
In our visit to European ports, the use of sheet-chains for protective purposes
had attracted notice and caused comment. It is strange that Captain Semmes did
not know of the chain armor; supposed spies had been on board and had been
shown through the ship, as there was no attempt at concealment; the same pilot
had been employed by both ships, and had visited each during the preparation
for battle. The *Alabama* had bunkers full of coal, which brought her down in the
water. The *Kearsarge* was deficient in seventy tons of coal of her proper supply,
but the sheet-chains stowed outside gave protection to her partly-filled bunkers.

The battery of the *Kearsarge* consisted of seven guns: two 11-inch pivots, smooth bore, one 30-pounder rifle, and four light 32-pounders; that of the *Alabama* of eight guns: one 68-pounder pivot, smooth bore, one 100-pounder pivot rifle, and six heavy 32-pounders. Five guns were fought by the *Kearsarge* and seven by the *Alabama*, each with the starboard battery. Both ships had made thirteen knots an hour under steam; at the time of the battle the *Alabama* made ten knots. The masts of the *Kearsarge* were low and small; she never carried more than top-sail yards, depending upon her engines for speed. The greater size and height of the masts of the *Alabama* and the heaviness of her rig (barque) gave the appearance of a larger vessel than her antagonist.

Most of the line officers of the *Kearsarge* were from the merchant service, and of the crew only eleven men were of foreign birth. Most of the officers of the *Alabama* were formerly officers in the United States Navy; nearly all the crew were English, Irish, and Welsh, a few of whom were said to belong to the "Royal Naval Reserve." Captain Semmes said, "Mr. Kell, my first lieutenant, deserves great credit for the fine condition in which the ship went into action with regard to her battery, magazine, and shell-rooms"; and he assuredly had confidence in the speed and strength of his ship, as shown by the eagerness and dash with which he opened the fight. The prisoners declared that the best practice during the action was by the gunners who had been trained on board the *Excellent* in Portsmouth harbor. The Blakely rifle was the most effective gun. The *Alabama* fought bravely until she could no longer fight or float.

The contest was decided by the superiority of the 11-inch Dahlgrens, especially the after-pivot, together with the coolness and accuracy of aim of the gunners of the *Kearsarge,* and notably by the skill of William Smith, the captain of the after-pivot, who in style and behavior was like Long Tom Coffin in Cooper's "Pilot."

To the disparagement of Captain Winslow it has been said that Lieutenant-Commander Thornton commanded the ship during the action. This is not true. Captain Winslow, standing on the horse-block abreast the mizzen-mast, fought his ship gallantly and, as is shown by the result, with excellent judgment. In an official report he wrote:

"It would seem almost invidious to particularize the conduct of any one man or officer, in which all had done their duty with a fortitude and coolness which cannot be too highly praised, but I feel it due to my executive officer, Lieutenant-Commander Thornton, who superintended the working of the battery, to particularly mention him for an example of coolness and encouragement of the men while fighting which contributed much toward the success of the action."

This Sunday naval duel was fought in the presence of more than 15,000 spectators, who, upon the heights of Cherbourg, the breakwater, and rigging of men-of-war, witnessed "the last of the *Alabama*." Among them were the captains, their families, and crews of two merchant ships burnt by the daring cruiser a few days before her arrival at Cherbourg, where they were landed in a nearly destitute condition. Many spectators were provided with spy-glasses and camp-stools. The *Kearsarge* was burning Newcastle coals, and the *Alabama* Welsh coals, the difference in the amount of smoke enabling the movements of each ship to be distinctly traced. An excursion train from Paris arrived in the morning, bringing hundreds of pleasure-seekers, who were unexpectedly favored with the spectacle of a sea-fight. A French gentleman at Boulogne-sur-Mer assured me that the fight was the conversation of Paris for more than a week.

Note.—Twelve Confederate cruisers figured in the so-called "*Alabama* Claims" settlement with England. Named in the order of the damage inflicted by each, these cruisers were: the *Alabama, Shenandoah, Florida, Tallahassee, Georgia, Chickamauga, Sumter, Nashville, Retribution, Jeff. Davis, Sallie,* and *Boston.* The actual losses inflicted by the *Alabama* ($7,050,293.76, according to claims for ships and cargoes filed up to March 15th, 1872) were only about $400,000 greater than those inflicted by the *Shenandoah.* The sum total of the claims filed against the twelve cruisers for ships and cargoes, up to March 15th, 1872, was $19,782,917.60, all but about six millions of it being charged to the account of the *Alabama* and *Shenandoah.*

On May 8th, 1871, the Treaty of Washington was concluded, in accordance with which a Tribunal of Arbitration was appointed, which assembled at Geneva. It consisted of Count Frederick Sclopis, named by the King of Italy; Mr. Jacob Staempfli, named by the President of the Swiss Confederation; Viscount d'Itajuba, named by the Emperor of Brazil; Mr. Charles Francis Adams, named by the President of the United States; and Sir Alexander Cockburn, named by the Queen of Great Britain. The Counsel of Great Britain was Sir Roundell Palmer (afterward Lord Selborne). The United States was represented by William M. Evarts, Caleb Cushing, and Morrison R. Waite. Claims were made by the United States for indirect and national losses, as well as for the actual private losses represented by nearly twenty millions on ships and cargoes.

The Tribunal decided that England was in no way responsible for the $1,781,915.43 of losses inflicted by the *Tallahassee, Georgia, Chickamauga, Nashville, Retribution, Jeff. Davis, Sallie, Boston,* and *Sumter;* and on September 14th, 1872, it awarded $15,500,000 damages for actual losses of ships and cargoes and interest, on account of the *Alabama,* the *Florida* and her tenders, and the *Shenandoah* after she left Melbourne.—Editors.

CHAPTER 7

THE COLORED TROOPS
AT PETERSBURG.

Henry Goddard Thomas, Brevet Major-General, U.S.V.

East of Petersburg, on high ground, protruding like the ugly horn of a rhinoceros, stood the Confederate earthwork, fortified as a battery, which we undermined and exploded July 30th, 1864. It did a good deal of goring before we destroyed it. Its position enabled the garrison to throw a somewhat enfilading fire into our lines, under which many fell, a few at a time.

For some time previous to the explosion of the mine it was determined by General Burnside that the colored division‡ should lead the assault. The general tactical plan had been given to the brigade commanders (Colonel Sigfried and myself), with a rough outline map of the ground, and directions to study the front for ourselves. But this latter was impracticable except in momentary glimpses. The enemy made a target of every head that appeared above the work, and their marksmanship was good. The manner of studying the ground was this: Putting my battered old hat on a ramrod and lifting it above the rampart just enough for them not to discover that no man was under it, I drew their fire; then stepping quickly a few paces one side, I took a hasty observation.

‡There was but one division of colored troops in the Army of the Potomac—the Fourth Division of the Ninth Corps, organized as follows:

Brigadier-General Edward Ferrero, commanding division. *First Brigade,* Colonel Joshua K. Sigfried (of the 48th Penn.): 27th U.S. colored troops, Lieutenant-Colonel Charles J. Wright; 30th U.S. colored troops, Colonel Delevan Bates; 39th U.S. colored troops, Colonel Ozora P. Stearns; 43d U.S. colored troops, Lieutenant-Colonel H. Seymour Hall. *Second Brigade,* Colonel Henry Goddard Thomas, 19th U.S. colored troops: 19th U.S. colored troops, Lieutenant-Colonel Joseph G. Perkins; 22d U.S. colored troops, Colonel Cleaveland J. Campbell; battalion of six companies 26th U.S. colored troops, Lieutenant-Colonel Charles S. Russell; 29th U.S. colored troops, Lieutenant-Colonel John A. Brons; 31st U.S. colored troops, Lieutenant-Colonel W.E.W. Ross.

This made a division of only nine regiments, divided into two brigades, yet it was numerically a large division. The regiments were entirely full, and a colored deserter was a thing unknown. On the day of the action the division numbered 4300, of which 2000 belonged to Sigfried's brigade and 2300 to mine.—H.G.T.

We were all pleased with the compliment of being chosen to lead in the assault. Both officers and men were eager to show the white troops what the colored division could do. We had acquired confidence in our men. They believed us infallible. We had drilled certain movements, to be executed in gaining and occupying the crest. It is an axiom in military art that there are times when the ardor, hopefulness, and enthusiasm of new troops, not yet rendered doubtful by reverses or chilled by defeat, more than compensate, in a dash, for training and experience. General Burnside, for this and other reasons, most strenuously urged his black division for the advance. Against his most urgent remonstrance he was overruled. About 11 P.M., July 29th, a few hours before the action, we were officially informed that the plan had been changed, and our division would not lead.

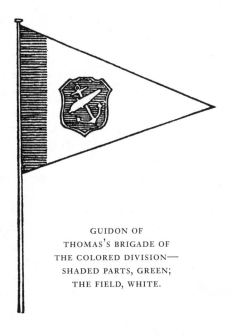

GUIDON OF
THOMAS'S BRIGADE OF
THE COLORED DIVISION—
SHADED PARTS, GREEN;
THE FIELD, WHITE.

We were then bivouacking on our arms in rear of our line, just behind the covered way leading to the mine. I returned to that bivouac dejected and with an instinct of disaster for the morrow. As I summoned and told my regimental commanders, their faces expressed the same feeling.

Any striking event or piece of news was usually eagerly discussed by the white troops, and in the ranks military critics were as plenty and perhaps more voluble than among the officers. Not so with the blacks; important news such as that before us, after the bare announcement, was usually followed by long silence. They sat about in groups, "studying," as they called it. They waited, like the Quakers, for the spirit to move; when the spirit moved, one of their singers would uplift a mighty voice, like a bard of old, in a wild sort of chant. If he did not strike a sympathetic chord in his hearers, if they did not find in his utterance the exponent of their idea, he would sing it again and again, altering sometimes the words, more often the music. If his changes met general acceptance, one voice after another would chime in; a rough harmony of three parts would add itself; other groups would join his, and the song would become the song of the command.

The night we learned that we were to lead the charge the news filled them too full for ordinary utterance. The joyous negro guffaw always breaking out about the camp-fire ceased. They formed circles in their company streets and were sitting on the ground intently and solemnly "studying." At last a heavy voice began to sing,

> "We-e looks li-ike me-en a-a-marchin' on,
> We looks li-ike men-er-war."

Over and over again he sang it, making slight changes in the melody. The rest listened to him intently; no sign of approval or disapproval escaped their lips or appeared on their faces. All at once, when his refrain had struck the right response in their hearts, his group took it up, and shortly half a thousand voices were upraised extemporizing a half dissonant middle part and bass. It was a picturesque scene—these dark men, with their white eyes and teeth and full red lips, crouching over a smoldering camp-fire, in dusky shadow, with only the feeble rays of the lanterns of the first sergeants and the lights of the candles dimly showing through the tents. The sound was as weird as the scene, when all the voices struck the low E (last note but one), held it, and then rose to A with a *portamento* as sonorous as it was clumsy. Until we fought the battle of the crater they sang this every night to the exclusion of all other songs. After that defeat they sang it no more.

About 3 A.M. the morning of the battle we were up after a short sleep under arms. Then came the soldiers' hasty breakfast. "Never fight on an empty stomach" was a proverb more honored in that army than any of Solomon; for the full stomach helps the wounded man to live through much loss of blood. This morning our breakfast was much like that on other mornings when we could not make fires: two pieces of hard-tack with a slice of raw, fat salt pork between—not a dainty meal, but solid provender to fight on. By good fortune I had a bottle of cucumber pickles. These I distributed to the officers about me. They were gratefully accepted, for nothing cuts the fat of raw salt pork like a pickle. We moistened our repast with black coffee from our canteens. The privates fared the same, barring the luxury of the pickle.

We had been told that the mine would be fired at 3:45 A.M. But 4 o'clock arrived, and all was quiet. Not long after that came a dull, heavy thud, not at all startling; it was a heavy, smothered sound, not nearly so distinct as a musket-shot. Could this be the mine? No; impossible. There was no charging, no yells—

SONG OF THE COLORED DIVISION BEFORE CHARGING INTO THE CRATER.

neither the deep-mouthed bass growl of the Union troops, nor the sharp, shrill, fox-hunting cry of the Confederates. Here was a mine blown up, making a crater from 150 to 200 feet long, 60 wide, and 30 deep, and the detonation and the concussion were so inconsiderable to us, not over a third of a mile away, that we could hardly believe the report of a staff-officer, back from the line, that the great mine had been exploded.

At about 5:30 A.M. a fairly heavy musketry fire from the enemy had opened. Shortly after, as we lay upon our arms awaiting orders, a quiet voice behind me said, "Who commands this brigade?" "I do," I replied. Rising, and turning toward the voice, I saw General Grant. He was in his usual dress: a broad-brimmed felt hat and the ordinary coat of a private. He wore no sword. Colonel Horace Porter, his aide-de-camp, and a single orderly accompanied him. "Well," said the general, slowly and thoughtfully, as if communing with himself rather than addressing a subordinate, "why are you not in?" Pointing to the First Brigade just in my front, I replied, "My orders are to follow that brigade." Feeling that golden opportunities might be slipping away from us, I added, "Will you give me the order to go in now?" After a moment's hesitation he answered in the same slow and ruminating manner, "No, you may keep the orders you have." Then, turning his horse's head, he rode away at a walk.

Fifteen minutes later an aide to the division commander gave us the order, and we moved into the covered way, my brigade following Sigfried's. This was about 6 A.M. For an hour or more we lay here inactive, the musketry growing quicker and sharper all the time. A heavy cannonading opened. We sat down at first, resting against the walls of the covered way. Soon, however, we had to stand to make room for the constantly increasing throng of wounded who were being brought past us to the rear. Some few, with flesh-wounds merely, greeted us with such jocularity as, "I'm all right, boys! This is good for a thirty days' sick-leave." Others were plucky and silent, their pinched faces telling the effort they were making to suppress their groans; others, with the ashy hue of death already gathering on their faces, were largely past pain. Many, out of their senses through agony, were moaning or bellowing like wild beasts. We stood there over an hour with this endless procession of wounded men passing. There could be no greater strain on the nerves. Every moment changed the condition from that of a forlorn hope to one of forlorn hopelessness. Unable to strike a blow, we were sickened with the contemplation of revolting forms of death and mutilation.

Finally, about 7:30 A.M., we got the order for the colored division to charge. My brigade followed Sigfried's at the double-quick. Arrived at the crater, a part of the First Brigade entered. The crater was already too full; that I could easily see. I swung my column to the right and charged over the enemy's rifle-pits connecting with the crater on our right. These pits were different from any in our lines—a labyrinth of bomb-proofs and magazines, with passages between. My brigade moved gallantly on right over the bomb-proofs and over the men of the First Division.[✣] As we mounted the pits, a deadly enfilade from eight guns on our right and a murderous cross-fire of musketry met us. Among the officers, the first to fall was the gallant Fessenden of the 23d Regiment. Ayres and Woodruff of the 31st dropped within a few yards of Fessenden, Ayres being killed, and Woodruff mortally wounded. Liscomb of the 23d then fell to rise no more; and then Hackhiser of the 28th and Flint and Aiken of the 29th. Major Rockwood of the 19th then mounted the crest and fell back dead, with a cheer on his lips. Nor were these all; for at that time hundreds of heroes "carved in ebony" fell. These black men commanded the admiration and respect of every beholder.

The most advantageous point for the purpose, about eight hundred feet from the crater, having been reached, we leaped from the works and endeavored to make a rush for the crest. Captain Marshall L. Dempey, and Lieutenant Christopher Pennell, of my staff, and four white orderlies with the brigade guidon accompanied me, closely followed by Lieutenant-Colonel Ross, leading the 31st Regiment. At the instant of leaving the works Ross was shot down; the next officer in rank, Captain Wright, was shot as he stooped over him. The men were largely without leaders, and their organization was destroyed. Two of my four orderlies were wounded: one, flag in hand; the remaining two sought shelter when Lieutenant Pennell, rescuing the guidon, hastened down the line outside the pits. With his sword uplifted in his right hand and the banner in his left, he sought to call out the men along the whole line of the parapet. In a moment, a musketry fire was focused upon him, whirling him round and round several times before he fell. Of commanding figure, his bravery was so conspicuous that, according to Colonel Weld's testimony, a number of his (Weld's) men were shot because, spell-bound, they forgot their own shelter in watching this superb boy, who was an only child of an old Massachusetts clergyman, and to me as Jonathan was to David. Two days later, on a flag of truce, I searched for his body in vain. He was doubtless shot literally to pieces, for the leaden hail poured for a long time almost incessantly about that spot, killing the wounded and mutilating the dead; and he probably sleeps among the unknown whom we buried in the long deep trench we dug that day.[✦]

The men of the 31st making the charge were being mowed down like grass, with no hope of any one reaching the crest, so I ordered them to scatter and run back. The fire was such that Captain Dempey and myself were the only officers

---

[✣]Major Van Buren's testimony, "Report of Committee on the Conduct of the War," Vol. I.

[✦]While the contemplation of one death so softens the heart, the sight of the myriad dead of a battle-field blunts the sensibilities. During the burial of the dead, a stretcher-bearer, seeing that the trousers-pocket of a soldier long dead contained tobacco, deliberately cut it out, and took a chew with an air of relish.
—H.G.T.

who returned, unharmed, of those who left the works for that charge.[†]

We were not long back within the honeycomb of passages and bomb-proofs near the crater before I received this order from the division commander: "Colonels Sigfried and Thomas, if you have not already done so, you will immediately proceed to take the crest in your front." My command was crowded into the pits, already too full, and were sandwiched, man for man, against the men of the First Division. They were thus partly sheltered from the fire that had reduced them coming up; but their organization was almost lost. I had already sent word to General Burnside by Major James L. Van Buren, of his staff, that unless a movement simultaneous with mine was made to the right, to stop the enfilading fire, I thought not a man would live to reach the crest; but that I would try another charge in about ten minutes, and I hoped to be supported. I then directed the commanders of the 23d, 28th, and 29th regiments to get their commands as much together and separated from the others as possible in that time, so that each could have a regimental following, for we were mixed up with white troops, and with one another to the extent of almost paralyzing any effort. We managed to make the charge, however, Colonel Bross of the 29th leading. The 31st had been so shattered, was so diminished, so largely without officers, that I got what was left of them out of the way of the charging column as much as possible. This column met the same fate in one respect as the former. As I gave the order, Lieutenant-Colonel John A. Bross, taking the flag into his own hands, was the first man to leap from the works into the valley of death below. He had attired himself in full uniform, evidently with the intent of inspiring his men. He had hardly reached the ground outside the works before he fell to rise no more. He was conspicuous and magnificent in his gallantry. The black men followed into the jaws of death, and advanced until met by a charge in force from the Confederate lines.

BREVET MAJOR-GENERAL HENRY G. THOMAS. FROM A PHOTOGRAPH.

The report of the Confederate General Bushrod R. Johnson (commanding

[†]My brigade guidon, which Lieutenant Pennell held when killed, was captured by Private John W. Niles, Company D, 41st Virginia, was stored in Richmond, and there retaken by our troops when we entered that city on April 3d, 1865, and is now stored in the War Department.—H.G.T.

UNION TROOPS.

CONFEDERATES CHARGING.

THE BATTLE OF THE CRATER. FROM AN OIL PAINTING.

the opposing forces at that point), to which I have had access, says that the Confederate troops in this charge were the First Brigade of Mahone's division, with the 25th and 49th North Carolina and the 26th and part of the 17th South Carolina regiments. It was no discredit to what was left of three regiments that they were repulsed by a force like that.

I lost in all 36 officers and 877 men,—total, 913. The 23d Regiment entered the charge with eighteen officers; it came out with seven. The 28th entered with eleven officers, and came out with four. The 31st had but two officers for duty that night.

Colonel Sigfried says in his official report:

"The First Brigade worked its way through the crater, and was halted behind the honeycomb of bomb-proofs. Here the 43d charged the intrenchments, but owing to the crowded condition of the bomb-proofs, it was impossible to get the rest of the brigade on. / Too much praise cannot be awarded to the bravery of officers and men; the former fearlessly led, while the latter as fearlessly followed, through a fire hot enough to cause the best troops to falter. But few of the field-officers escaped. Colonel Delevan Bates fell, shot in the face. Major Leeke stood, urging the men on, with the blood gushing from his mouth. Captain Wright of the 43d Regiment himself captured a Confederate stand of colors and five prisoners, and brought them in. Lieutenant-Colonel Wright, with two bullet wounds, retained the command of his regiment.... Had it not been for the almost impassable crowd of troops of the other divisions in the crater

/Brevet Brigadier-General H. Seymour Hall, who commanded the 43d United States colored troops, writes to the editors, under date of April 5th, 1868, as follows:

"After an inspection of the division by an officer of General Burnside's staff, the 43d was selected to lead the assault which was to follow the explosion of the mine, in the first plan of attack, and still had the advance when the division finally went into action. I drilled the command, and carefully inspected the ground over which we were to advance. When the order to lead out from the covered way was given me, we moved by the flank, scrambled, climbed, or jumped as best we could over our outer works double-quick, swept up the slope, already the center of a tornado of shot and shell, through which, leading my command directly to the crater, and mounting the crest of the débris, saw at once the utter hopelessness of passing the enemy's lines through and over the mass of soldiers in the yawning gulf. The 43d moved to our right around on the crest of the crater's rim, till within a few yards of the enemy's main line of intrenchments on our right, which was at that time fully manned by the rebel forces, who were concentrating upon us a deadly fire of musketry, and flaunting their colors defiantly almost in our very faces. Still at the double-quick, changing direction, to the right, leading the command in front of and parallel to the intrenchments held by the enemy, as soon as sufficient distance was taken I gave the command to march by the left flank, and as the line thus formed moved toward the enemy, gave the order to charge. Officers and men swept resistlessly on, over the enemy's intrenchments, without an instant's halt or waver, capturing nearly all the force in our immediate front, probably about one hundred prisoners, the stand of rebel colors mentioned, and recapturing a stand of national colors. All this occupied

LIEUTENANT CHRISTOPHER PENNELL.
FROM A PHOTOGRAPH.

and intrenchments, Cemetery Hill would have been ours without a falter on the part of my brigade."

Nor was the giving way a willing movement on the part of the colored troops. One little band, after my second charge was repulsed, defended the intrenchments we had won from the enemy, exhibiting fighting qualities that I never saw surpassed in the war. This handful stood there without the slightest organization of company or regiment, each man for himself, until the enemy's banners waved in their very faces. Then they made a dash for our own lines, and that at my order. Speaking of this stand, General Burnside says in his official report: "But not all of the colored troops retired; some held the pits behind which they had advanced, severely checking the enemy until they were nearly all killed."

The engagement was over. We had not only lost about forty per cent., but had been repulsed. The enemy having retaken their former lines, the troops, black and white, in the crater were cut off from our army. Squads there occasionally made a dash for our lines, but as many fell as reached them safely. By direction of officers in the crater the men began a deep trench toward our lines. Another, by direction of General Burnside, had been started from our lines to meet it. This was the situation when the enemy made their last charge on the crater. Its inmates had repelled three charges. They were weak, exhausted, and suffering from want of water. They succumbed, and most of them fell into the hands of the enemy. Of this last scene in the battle the Confederate General Bushrod R. Johnson says in his official report:

---

scarcely five minutes from the time we left the covered way, but we were exposed to the most terrific concentration of infantry and artillery fire it had ever been my lot to encounter.

"We had opened a gateway, but the crest of the ridge in rear of the mine, our objective, was not yet gained. Just as I was about to give the order to advance my right arm fell nerveless to my side, pierced and shattered near the shoulder by a musket-ball. Recovering my saber, which had dropped from my hand, I retired from the field to the amputating-table.

"The 43d had not more than 15 officers and 350 enlisted men present for duty. One officer and 28 men were killed, 10 officers and 94 men were wounded, 12 men missing.—total, 145. The colors were tattered, and the color-lance splintered and shivered into a dozen pieces by musket-balls."

—Editors.

"Between 11 and 12 A.M., a second unsuccessful charge having been made by Wright's brigade of Mahone's division, I proceeded to concert a combined movement on both flanks of the crater.... A third charge a little before 2 P.M. gave us entire possession of the crater and adjacent lines. This charge on the left [our right] and rear of the crater was made by Sanders's brigade of Mahone's division, the 61st North Carolina of Hoke's division, and the 17th South Carolina of this division.... These movements were all conducted by General Mahone, while I took the 22d and 23d South Carolina into the crater and captured three colors and 130 prisoners. Previous to this charge the incessant firing kept up by our troops on both flanks and in rear had caused many of the enemy to run the gauntlet of our cross-fires in front of the breach, but a large number still remained unable to advance, and perhaps afraid to retreat."

Thus ended in disaster what had at first promised to be a grand success. We were back within our old lines and badly cut up. We had inflicted a heavy, but by no means equal, loss on the enemy.

CHAPTER 8

Preparing for the Campaigns of '64.

Ulysses S. Grant, General, U.S.A.

My commission as lieutenant-general was given to me on the 9th of March, 1864. On the following day I visited General Meade, commanding the Army of the Potomac, at his headquarters, Brandy Station, north of the Rapidan. I had known General Meade slightly in the Mexican war, but had not met him since until this visit. I was a stranger to most of the Army of the Potomac; I might say to all except the officers of the regular army who had served in the Mexican war. There had been some changes ordered in the organization of that army before my promotion. One was the consolidation of five corps into three, thus throwing some officers of rank out of important commands. Meade evidently thought that I might want to make still one more change not yet ordered. He said to me that I might want an officer who had served with me in the West, mentioning Sherman especially, to take his place; if so, he begged me not to

HEADQUARTERS OF THE ARMY OF THE POTOMAC AT BRANDY STATION.
FROM A PHOTOGRAPH.

hesitate about making the change. He urged that the work before us was of such vast importance to the whole nation that the feeling or wishes of no one person should stand in the way of selecting the right men for all positions. For himself, he would serve to the best of his ability wherever placed. I assured him that I had no thought of substituting any one for him. As to Sherman, he could not be spared from the West.

This incident gave me even a more favorable opinion of Meade than did his great victory at Gettysburg the July before. It is men who wait to be selected, and not those who seek, from whom we may always expect the most efficient service.

Meade's position afterward proved embarrassing to me if not to him. For nearly a year previous to my taking command of all the armies he had been at the head of the Army of the Potomac, commanding an army independently. All other general officers occupying similar positions were independent in their commands so far as any one present with them was concerned. I tried to make General Meade's position as nearly as possible what it would have been if I had been in Washington or any other place away from his command. I therefore gave all orders for the movements of the Army of the Potomac to Meade to have them executed. To avoid the necessity of having to give orders direct, I established my headquarters near his, unless there were reasons for locating them elsewhere. This sometimes happened, and I had on occasions to give orders direct to the troops affected.

HEADQUARTERS FLAG, ARMY OF THE POTOMAC.

General Meade adopted solferino as the color of his headquarters flag, and a golden eagle in a silver wreath as the emblem, the latter having been in use as a badge for headquarters aides. It was a showy standard, and A. R. Wand, the war artist, remembers that General Grant, when he first saw it unfurled, as they broke camp for the Wilderness campaign, exclaimed: "What's this!—Is Imperial Cæsar anywhere about here!"—EDITORS.

On the 11th of March I returned to Washington, and on the day after orders were published by the War Department placing me in command of all the

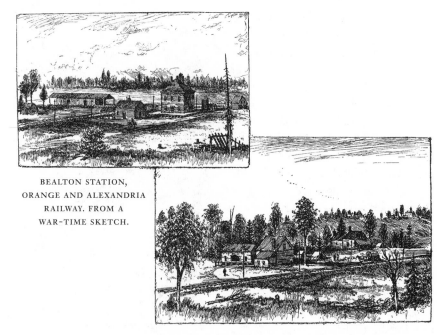

BEALTON STATION,
ORANGE AND ALEXANDRIA
RAILWAY. FROM A
WAR-TIME SKETCH.

BRANDY STATION, ORANGE AND ALEXANDRIA RAILWAY.
FROM A WAR-TIME SKETCH.

armies. I had left Washington the night before to return to my old command in the West and to meet Sherman, whom I had telegraphed to join me in Nashville.

Sherman assumed command of the Military Division of the Mississippi on the 18th of March, and we left Nashville together for Cincinnati. I had Sherman accompany me that far on my way back to Washington, so that we could talk over the matters about which I wanted to see him, without losing any more time from my new command than was necessary. The first point which I wished to discuss particularly was about the coöperation of his command with mine when the spring campaign should commence. There were also other and minor points,—minor as compared with the great importance of the question to be decided by sanguinary war,—the restoration to duty of officers who had been relieved from important commands, namely, McClellan, Burnside, and Frémont in the East, and Buell, McCook, Negley, and Crittenden in the West.

Some time in the winter of 1863–64 I had been invited by the general-in-chief to give my views of the campaign I thought advisable for the command under me—now Sherman's. General J. E. Johnston was defending Atlanta and the interior of Georgia with an army, the largest part of which was stationed at Dalton, about 38 miles south of Chattanooga. Dalton is at the junction of the railroad from Cleveland with the one from Chattanooga to Atlanta.

There could have been no difference of opinion as to the first duty of the armies of the Military Division of the Mississippi. Johnston's army was the first objective, and that important railroad center, Atlanta, the second. At the time I wrote General Halleck giving my views of the approaching campaign, and at the time I met General Sherman, it was expected that General Banks would be through with the campaign upon which he had been ordered[※] before my appointment to the command of all the armies, and would be ready to coöperate with the armies east of the Mississippi; his part in the programme being to move upon Mobile by land, while the navy would close the harbor and assist to the best of its ability. The plan, therefore, was for Sherman to attack Johnston and destroy his army if possible, to capture Atlanta and hold it, and with his troops and those of Banks to hold a line through to Mobile, or at least to hold Atlanta and command the railroad running east and west, and the troops from one or other of the armies to hold important points on the southern road, the only east-and-west road that would be left in the possession of the enemy. This would cut the Confederacy in two again, as our gaining possession of the Mississippi River had done before. Banks was not ready in time for the part assigned to him, and circumstances that could not be foreseen determined the campaign which was afterward made, the success and grandeur of which has resounded throughout all lands.

In regard to restoring to duty officers who had been relieved from important commands, I left Sherman to look after those who had been removed in the West, while I looked out for the rest. I directed, however, that he should make no assignment until I could speak to the Secretary of War about the matter. I shortly after recommended to the Secretary the assignment of General Buell to duty. I received the assurance that duty would be offered to him, and afterward the Secretary told me that he had offered Buell an assignment and that the latter declined it, saying that it would be a degradation to accept the assignment offered. I understood afterward that he refused to serve under either Sherman or Canby because he had ranked them both. Both were graduated before him, and ranked him in the old army. Sherman ranked him as brigadier-general. All of them ranked me in the old army, and Sherman and Buell did as brigadiers. The worst excuse a soldier can make for declining service is that he once ranked the commander he is ordered to report to.

On the 23d of March I was back in Washington, and on the 26th took up my headquarters at Culpeper Court House, a few miles south of the headquarters of the Army of the Potomac.

Although hailing from Illinois myself, the State of the President, I never met Mr. Lincoln until called to the capital to receive my commission as lieutenant-general. I knew him, however, very well and favorably from the accounts

---

[※]The Red River campaign.—Editors.

GENERAL MEADE'S HEADQUARTERS AT CULPEPER. FROM A WAR-TIME SKETCH.

given by officers under me at the West who had known him all their lives. I had also read the remarkable series of debates between Lincoln and Douglas a few years before, when they were rival candidates for the United States Senate. I was then a resident of Missouri, and by no means a "Lincoln man" in that contest; but I recognized then his great ability.

In my first interview with Mr. Lincoln alone he stated to me that he had never professed to be a military man or to know how campaigns should be conducted, and never wanted to interfere in them; but that procrastination on the part of commanders, and the pressure from the people at the North and from Congress, *which was always with him,* forced him into issuing his series of "Military Orders"—No. 1, No. 2, No. 3, etc. He did not know that they were not all wrong, and did know that some of them were. All he wanted, or had ever wanted, was some one who would take the responsibility and act, and call on him for all the assistance needed; he would pledge himself to use all the power of the Government in rendering such assistance. Assuring him that I would do the best I could with the means at hand, and avoid as far as possible annoying him or the War Department, our first interview ended.

The Secretary of War I had met once before only, but felt that I knew him better. While I had been commanding in west Tennessee we had held conversations over the wires at night. He and Halleck both cautioned me against giving the President my plans of campaign, saying that he was so kind-hearted, so averse to refusing anything asked of him, that some friend would be sure to get from him all he knew. I should have said that in our interview the President told me that he did not want to know what I proposed to do. But he submitted a plan of campaign of his own which he wanted me to hear and then dispose of as I pleased. He brought out a map of Virginia, on which he had evidently marked every position occupied by the Federal and Confederate armies up to that time. He pointed out on the map two streams which empty into the Potomac, and suggested that the army might be moved on boats and landed between the mouths of these streams. We would then have the Potomac to bring supplies, and the tributaries would protect our flanks while we moved out. I listened respectfully, but did not suggest that the same streams would protect Lee's flanks while he was shutting us up. I did not communicate my plans to the President or to the Secretary or to General Halleck.

On the 26th of March, with my headquarters at Culpeper, the work of preparing for an early campaign commenced.

. When I assumed command of all the armies the situation was about this: The Mississippi was guarded from St. Louis to its mouth; the line of the Arkansas was held, thus giving us all the North-west north of that river. A few points in Louisiana, not remote from the river, were held by the Federal troops, as was also the mouth of the Rio Grande. East of the Mississippi we held substantially all north of the Memphis and Charleston railroad as far east as Chattanooga, thence along the line of the Tennessee and Holston rivers, taking in nearly all of the State of Tennessee. West Virginia was in our hands, and also that part of old Virginia north of the Rapidan and east of the Blue Ridge. On the sea-coast we had Fort Monroe and Norfolk in Virginia; Plymouth, Washington, and New Berne in North Carolina; Beaufort, Folly and Morris islands, Hilton Head, and Port Royal, in South Carolina, and Fort Pulaski in Georgia; Fernandina, St. Augustine, Key West, and Pensacola in Florida. The remainder of the Southern territory, an empire in extent, was still in the hands of the enemy.

Sherman, who had succeeded me in the command of the Military Division of the Mississippi, commanded all the troops in the territory west of the Alleghanies and north of Natchez, with a large movable force about Chattanooga. His command was subdivided into four departments, but the commanders all reported to Sherman, and were subject to his orders. This arrangement, however, insured the better protection of all lines of communication through the acquired territory, for the reason that these different department commanders could act promptly in case of a sudden or unexpected raid within their respective jurisdictions, without waiting the orders of the division commander.

In the east the opposing forces stood in substantially the same relations toward each other as three years before, or when the war began; they were both between the Federal and Confederate capitals. It is true footholds had been secured by us on the sea-coast, in Virginia and North Carolina, but beyond that no substantial advantage had been gained by either side. Battles had been fought of as great severity as had ever been known in war, over ground from the James River and the Chickahominy, near Richmond, to Gettysburg and Chambersburg, in Pennsylvania, with indecisive results, sometimes favorable to the National army, sometimes to the Confederate army, but in every instance, I believe, claimed as victories for the South by the Southern press if not by the Southern generals. The Northern press, as a whole, did not discourage their claims; a portion of it always magnified rebel success and belittled ours, while another portion, most sincerely earnest in their desire for the preservation of the Union and the overwhelming success of the Federal arms, would nevertheless generally express dissatisfaction with whatever victories were gained because they were not more complete.

That portion of the Army of the Potomac not engaged in guarding lines of communication was on the northern bank of the Rapidan. The Army of Northern Virginia, confronting it on the opposite bank of the same river, was strongly intrenched and was commanded by the acknowledged ablest general in the Confederate army. The country back to the James River is cut up with many streams, generally narrow, deep, and difficult to cross except where bridged. The region is heavily timbered, and the roads are narrow and very bad after the least rain. Such an enemy was not, of course, unprepared with adequate fortifications at convenient intervals all the way back to Richmond, so that, when driven from one fortified position, they would always have another farther to the rear to fall back into. To provision an army, campaigning against so formidable a foe through such a country, from wagons alone, seemed almost impossible. System and discipline were both essential to its accomplishment.

The Union armies were now divided into nineteen departments, though four of them in the West had been concentrated into a single military division. The Army of the Potomac was a separate command, and had no territorial limits. There were thus seventeen distinct commanders. Before this time these various armies had acted separately and independently of each other, giving the enemy an opportunity, often, of depleting one command, not pressed, to reënforce another more actively engaged. I determined to stop this. To this end I regarded the Army of the Potomac as the center, and all west to Memphis, along the line described as our position at the time, and north of it, the right wing; the Army of the James, under General Butler,[1] as the left wing, and all the troops south as a force in rear of the enemy. Some of these last were occupying positions from which they could not render service proportionate to their numeri-

---

[1] From December 17th, 1862, when he was superseded in command of the Gulf Department by General Banks, General Butler was not in active service until November 11th, 1863, when he assumed command of the Department of Virginia and North Carolina (the Army of the James).—EDITORS.

cal strength. All such were depleted to the minimum necessary to hold their positions as a guard against blockade-runners; when they could not do this, their positions were abandoned altogether. In this way ten thousand men were added to the Army of the James from South Carolina alone, with General Gillmore in command./ It was not contemplated that Gillmore should leave his department; but as most of his troops were taken, presumably for active service, he asked to accompany them, and was permitted to do so. Officers and soldiers on furlough, of whom there were many thousands, were ordered to their proper commands; concentration was the order of the day, and the problem was to accomplish it in time to advance at the earliest moment the roads would permit.

As a reënforcement to the Army of the Potomac, or to act in support of it, the Ninth Army Corps, over twenty thousand strong, under General Burnside, had been rendezvoused at Annapolis, Maryland.✩ This was an admirable position for such a reënforcement. The corps could be brought at the last moment as a reënforcement to the Army of the Potomac, or it could be thrown on the sea-coast, south of Norfolk, to operate against Richmond from that direction. In fact, up to the last moment Burnside and the War Department both thought the Ninth Corps was intended for such an expedition.

My general plan now was to concentrate all the force possible against the Confederate armies in the field. There were but two such, as we have seen, east of the Mississippi River and facing north: the Army of Northern Virginia, General Robert E. Lee commanding, was on the south bank of the Rapidan, confronting the Army of the Potomac; the second, under General Joseph E. Johnston,‡ was at Dalton, Georgia, opposed to Sherman, who was still at Chattanooga. Besides these main armies, the Confederates had to guard the Shenandoah Valley—a great storehouse to feed their armies from—and their line of communications from Richmond to Tennessee. Forrest, a brave and intrepid cavalry general, was in the West, with a large force, making a larger command necessary to hold what we had gained in middle and west Tennessee. We could not abandon any territory north of the line held by the enemy, because it would lay the Northern States open to invasion. But as the Army of the Potomac was the principal garrison for the protection of Washington, even while it was moving on to Lee, so all the forces to the West, and the Army of the James, guarded

/These troops, the Tenth Corps, left the Department of the South during the month of April for rendezvous at Gloucester Point, Virginia.—EDITORS.

✩General Burnside had been relieved of the command of the Department of the Ohio on the 12th of December, by General J. G. Foster, and on the 7th of January, 1864, had been assigned to the command of the Ninth Corps. This corps left Knoxville, Tennessee, March 17th–23d, and was reorganized at Annapolis for the spring campaign, and received an addition to its strength of five cavalry and twelve infantry regiments and five batteries of artillery.—EDITORS.

‡General Johnston was relieved of the command of the Department of Tennessee by General Bragg, July 23d, 1863, and continued in command of the Department of Mississippi and East Louisiana. On December 27th, 1863, he assumed command of the Army of Tennessee, superseding Bragg.—EDITORS.

FROM A PHOTOGRAPH.

their special trusts when advancing from them as well as when remaining at them—better, indeed, for they forced the enemy to guard his own lines and resources, at a greater distance from ours and with a greater force, since small expeditions could not so well be sent out to destroy a bridge or tear up a few miles of railroad track, burn a storehouse, or inflict other little annoyances. Accordingly I arranged for a simultaneous movement all along the line.

Sherman was to move from Chattanooga, Johnston's army and Atlanta being his objective points. General George Crook, commanding in West Virginia,✢ was to move from the mouth of the Ganley River with a cavalry force and some artillery, the Virginia and Tennessee railroad to be his objective. Either the enemy would have to keep a large force to protect their communications or see them destroyed, and a large amount of forage and provisions, which they so much needed, would fall into our hands. Sigel,✦ who was in command in the valley of Virginia, was to advance up the valley, covering the North from an invasion through that channel as well while advancing as by remaining near Harper's Ferry. Every mile he advanced also gave us possession of stores on which Lee relied. Butler was to advance by the James River, having Richmond and Petersburg as his objective. Before the advance commenced I visited Butler at Fort Monroe. This was the first time I had ever met him. Before giving him any order as to the part he was to play in the approaching campaign I invited his views. They were very much such as I intended to direct, and as I did direct, in writing, before leaving.

General W. F. Smith, who had been promoted to the rank of major-general shortly after the battle of Chattanooga on my recommendation, had not yet been confirmed. I found a decided prejudice against his confirmation by a majority of the Senate, but I insisted that his services had been such that he should be rewarded. My wishes were now reluctantly complied with, and I assigned him to the command of one of the corps under General Butler. I was not long in finding out that the objections to Smith's promotion were well founded.❧

✢General Crook was transferred from the command of a cavalry division in the Army of the Cumberland and assumed command of an infantry division in the Department of West Virginia, February 15th, 1864.—EDITORS.

✦General Sigel succeeded General Benjamin F. Kelley in command of the Department of West Virginia on the 10th of March, 1864. After the second battle of Bull Run Sigel had been in command of the Eleventh Corps, the Reserve Grand Division of the Army of the Potomac, and the Lehigh District in Pennsylvania.—EDITORS.

❧After the appearance of General Grant's paper in "The Century" magazine for February, 1886, General William F. Smith made the following reply, which was printed in that magazine for May, 1886:

> "General Grant makes this general charge without assigning a reason for it or attempting to justify it by citing any instance in which I had failed in any duty I had been called upon to perform. This gives me the right to call General Grant himself as a witness in my own behalf, and to assert that the reasons which moved him to say that 'the objections to my confirmation were well founded' were of a personal, and not of a public nature.
>
> "The battle of Chattanooga ended on the 25th of November, 1863—my name was not

BREVET MAJOR-GENERAL M. C. MEIGS,
QUARTERMASTER-GENERAL, U.S.A.
FROM A PHOTOGRAPH.

In one of my early interviews with the President I expressed my dissatisfaction with the little that had been accomplished by the cavalry so far in the war, and the belief that it was capable of accomplishing much more than it had done if under a thorough leader. I said I wanted the very best man in the army for that command. Halleck was present and spoke up, saying: "How would Sheridan do?" I replied: "The very man I want."

The President said I could have anybody I wanted. Sheridan was telegraphed for that day, and on his arrival was assigned to the command of the cavalry corps with the Army of the Potomac. This relieved General Alfred Pleasonton. It was not a reflection on that officer, however, for as far as I knew he had been as efficient as any other cavalry commander.

---

sent to the Senate till the 15th of March, 1864. On the 18th it was returned to the President, with the request that the date of rank should conform to the date of nomination.

"On the 23d of the same month it was again sent to the Senate, and my nomination was confirmed on the same day. It was therefore nearly four months after the battle when my name was sent to the Senate for promotion, and in three days thereafter the Senate asked the President to make the date of rank conform to the date of nomination; and on the same day that my name was returned to the Senate my nomination was confirmed. The question of my confirmation therefore was settled on the 18th of March, when the request was made to have the date of rank conform to the date of nomination, and during this time and up to the time of my confirmation General Grant was not in the city of Washington.

"He left Washington on the night of the 11th of March for Nashville and did not return till some time during the 23d—the day on which the President returned my name to the Senate and upon which final action was taken. Shortly thereafter I was informed by a senator that my name had passed the Senate without having been referred to the Military Committee, which he stated to be a 'high compliment and one seldom paid by the Senate.' As to the fact whether this confirmation was made without a reference to the Military Committee, the records of the Senate will show.

"But much more important to me is the fact that this sweeping denunciation was not founded upon any failure on my part to perform the duty I owed to the country, then in its struggle for existence, and that no one knew this better than the general who was in command of its armies. On the 12th of November, 1863, General Grant had addressed the Secretary of War as follows:

"'I would respectfully recommend that Brigadier-General William F. Smith be placed first on the list for promotion to the rank of major-general. He is possessed of

Banks in the Department of the Gulf was ordered to assemble all his troops at New Orleans in time to join in the general move, Mobile to be his objective.

At this time I was not entirely decided as to whether I should move the Army of the Potomac by the right flank of the enemy or by his left. Each plan presented advantages. If by his right—my left—the Potomac, Chesapeake Bay, and tributaries would furnish us an easy line over which to bring all supplies to within easy hauling distance of every position the army could occupy from the Rapidan to the James River. But Lee, if he chose, could detach, or move his whole army north on a line rather interior to the one I would have to take in following. A movement by his left—our right—would obviate this; but all that was done would have to be done with the supplies and ammunition we started with. All idea of adopting this latter plan was abandoned when the limited quantity of supplies possible to take with us was considered. The country over which we would have to pass was so exhausted of all food or forage that we would be obliged to carry everything with us.

While these preparations were going on the enemy was not entirely idle. In the West, Forrest made a raid in west Tennessee up to the northern border, capturing the garrison of four or five hundred men at Union City, and followed it up by an attack on Paducah, Kentucky, on the banks of the Ohio. While he was able to enter the city, he failed to capture the forts or any part of the garrison. On the first intelligence of Forrest's raid I telegraphed Sherman to send all his

---

one of the clearest military heads in the army—is very practical and industrious—no man in the service is better qualified than he for our largest commands.'

"On July 1st, 1864, General Grant, from City Point, Virginia, addressed a letter to General Halleck, chief-of-staff, from which the following extracts are taken:

"'Mr. Dana, Assistant Secretary of War, has just returned. He informs me that he called attention to the necessity of sending General Butler to another field of duty.... I have feared that it might become necessary to separate him and General Smith. The latter is really one of the most efficient officers in the service, readiest in expedients, and most skillful in the management of troops in action. I would dislike removing him from his present command unless it was to increase it, but, as I say, I may have to do it if General Butler remains.... I would feel strengthened with Smith, Franklin, or J. J. Reynolds commanding the right wing of this army....'

"So that on the 1st of July, 1864, General Grant thought he would be strengthened with General Smith commanding the right wing of that army. On the strength of that letter I was placed in command of the troops in the field belonging to the Army of the James, and General Butler was ordered back to administrative duty at Fort Monroe.

"Being much out of health at this time, I had asked for a short leave of absence, to which this answer was returned:

" 'HEADQUARTERS, CITY POINT, JULY 2D, 1864.
" 'To MAJOR-GENERAL WILLIAM F. SMITH:

"Your application for leave of absence has just come to me. Unless it is absolutely necessary that you should leave at this time, I would much prefer not having you go.

cavalry against him, and not to let him get out of the trap he had put himself into. Sherman had anticipated me by sending troops against him before he got my order. Forrest, however, fell back rapidly, and attacked the troops at Fort Pillow, a station for the protection of the navigation of the Mississippi River. The garrison consisted of a regiment of colored infantry and a detachment of Tennessee cavalry. These troops fought bravely, but were overpowered. I will leave Forrest in his dispatches to tell what he did with them. "The river was dyed," he says, "with the blood of the slaughtered for two hundred yards.... The approximate loss was upward of 500 killed, but few of the officers escaping. My loss was about 20 killed and about 60 wounded.... It is hoped that these facts will demonstrate to the Northern people that negro soldiers cannot cope with Southerners." Subsequently Forrest made a report in which he left out the part which shocks humanity to read.

At the East, also, the rebels were busy. I had said to Halleck that Plymouth and Washington, North Carolina, were unnecessary to us, that it would be better to have the garrisons engaged there added to Butler's command. If success should attend our arms, both places, and others, would fall into our hands nat-

---

It will not be necessary for you to expose yourself in the hot sun, and if it should become necessary I can temporarily attach General Humphreys to your command.

" 'U. S. GRANT.'

"As my health did not improve I repeated my request for leave, and on the 9th of July I received the following from General Grant at City Point:

" 'General Ord can be assigned to the command of your corps during your absence if you think it advisable.'

"I left my command on that day, and City Point on the following day, and it is manifest General Grant up to that moment had not changed the opinion he had expressed in recommending my promotion. I returned to the army on the 19th of July, to find myself relieved from my command. During this absence of ten days, nothing connected with my military duties could have occurred to impair the confidence in me expressed in General Grant's communication of the 9th.

"I sought an explanation from him on the day of my return, and he was as reticent in assigning any cause for his action then as he was twenty-one years after, when, in preparing a contribution to the history of the war, he again passed sentence upon me without assigning a reason of any kind for his condemnation. I am to-day as ignorant of the causes for his action as I was then. That they were purely personal, and had not the remotest connection with my conduct as a soldier, I submit is proved by his own testimony, and it is upon this question alone that I care to defend myself."

In "The Century" magazine for September, 1886, Captain Joel B. Erhardt contributed the following extract from a letter that had never been made public:

"COLLEGE POINT, L. I., JULY 30TH, 1864.
"Hon. S. Foot.
"DEAR SENATOR:

"I am extremely anxious that my friends in my native State [Vermont] should not think that the reason of General Grant relieving me from duty was brought about by any miscon-

urally. These places had been occupied by Federal troops before I took command of the armies, and I knew that the executive would be reluctant to abandon them, and therefore explained my views; but before my views were carried out, the rebels captured the garrison at Plymouth. ⁄ I then ordered the abandonment of Washington, but directed the holding of New Berne at all hazards. This was essential, because New Berne was a port into which blockade-runners could enter.

General Banks had gone on an expedition up the Red River long before my promotion to general command. I had opposed the movement strenuously, but acquiesced because it was the order of my superior at the time.☆ By direction of Halleck I had reënforced Banks with a corps of about ten thousand men from Sherman's command. This reënforcement was wanted back badly before the forward movement commenced. But Banks had got so far that it seemed best that he should take Shreveport, on the Red River, and turn over the line of that river to Steele, who commanded in Arkansas, to hold instead of the line of the Arkansas. Orders were given accordingly, and with the expectation that the campaign would be ended in time for Banks to return A. J. Smith's command to where it belonged,‡ and get back to New Orleans himself in time to execute his part in the general plan. But the expedition was a failure. Banks did not get back in time to take part in the programme as laid down; nor was Smith returned until long after the movements of May, 1864, had been begun. The services of

---

duct of mine, and therefore I write to put you in possession of such facts in the case as I am aware of, and think will throw light upon the subject....

"On my return from a short leave of absence, on the 19th of July, General Grant sent for me to report to him, and then told me that he 'could not relieve General Butler,' and that as I had so severely criticised General Meade, he had determined to relieve me from the command of the Eighteenth Corps, and order me to New York City to await orders. The next morning the general gave some other reasons, such as an article in the 'Tribune' reflecting on General Hancock, which I had nothing in the world to do with, and two letters which I had written, before the campaign began, to two of General Grant's most devoted friends, urging upon them to try and prevent him from making the campaign he had just made....

"VERY TRULY YOURS.
"WILLIAM F. SMITH, MAJOR-GENERAL."

—EDITORS.

⁄The engagement at Plymouth extended from the 17th to the 20th of April, 1864. The garrison consisted of four regiments of infantry, with detachments of artillery and cavalry, under command of General H. W. Wessells. The principal reliance was the navy, which, however, was neutralized by the Confederate ram *Albemarle.* [See papers on the *Albemarle,* to follow.] After repulsing five charges General Wessells surrendered, with about 1500 men, to General R. F. Hoke.—EDITORS.

☆General Halleck's instructions for this movement were promulgated during January and February, 1864.—EDITORS.

‡The 10,000 troops under General A. J. Smith that had been thus detached belonged to the 16th and 17th corps (Sherman's army), at the time (March, 1864,) in the Mississippi Valley. Portions of these corps subsequently joined Sherman and Thomas.—EDITORS.

forty thousand veteran troops over and above the number required to hold all that was necessary in the Department of the Gulf were thus paralyzed. It is but just to Banks, however, to say that his expedition was ordered from Washington, and he was in no way responsible except for the conduct of it. I make no criticism on this point. He opposed the expedition.

By the 27th of April spring had so far advanced as to justify me in fixing a day for the great move. On that day Burnside left Annapolis to occupy Meade's position between Bull Run and the Rappahannock. Meade was notified and directed to bring his troops forward to his advance; on the following day Butler was notified of my intended advance on the 4th of May, and he was directed to move, the night of the same day, and get as far up the James River as possible by daylight, and push on from there to accomplish the task given him. He was also notified that reënforcements were being collected in Washington, which would be forwarded to him should the enemy fall back into the trenches at Richmond. The same day Sherman was directed to get his forces up ready to advance on the 5th. Sigel, at Winchester, was notified to move in conjunction with the others.

The criticism has been made by writers on the campaign from the Rapidan to the James River that all the loss of life could have been obviated by moving the army there on transports. Richmond was fortified and intrenched so perfectly that one man inside to defend was more than equal to five outside besieging or assaulting. To get possession of Lee's army was the first great object. With the capture of his army Richmond would necessarily follow. It was better to fight him outside of his stronghold than in it. If the Army of the Potomac had been moved bodily to the James River by water, Lee could have moved a part of his forces back to Richmond, called Beauregard from the South to reënforce it, and with the remainder moved on to Washington. Then, too, I ordered a move simultaneous with that of the Army of the Potomac up the James River, by a formidable army already collected at the mouth of the river.

While my headquarters were at Culpeper, from the 26th of March to the 4th of May, I generally visited Washington once a week to confer with the Secretary of War and the President. On the last occasion, a few days before moving, a circumstance occurred which came near postponing my part in the campaign altogether. Colonel John S. Mosby had for a long time been commanding a partisan corps, or regiment, which operated in the rear of the Army of the Potomac. On my return to the field on this occasion, as the train approached Warrenton Junction, a heavy cloud of dust was seen to the east of the road, as if made by a body of cavalry on a charge. Arriving at the junction, the train was stopped and inquiries were made as to the cause of the dust. There was but one man at the station, and he informed us that Mosby had crossed a few minutes before at full speed in pursuit of Federal cavalry. Had he seen our train coming, no doubt he would have let his prisoners escape to capture the train. I was on a special train, if I remember correctly, without any guard. Since

FROM A PHOTOGRAPH.

the close of the war I have come to know Colonel Mosby personally, and somewhat intimately. He is a different man entirely from what I had supposed. He is slender, not tall, wiry, and looks as if he could endure any amount of physical exercise. He is able, and thoroughly honest and truthful. There were probably

FROM A PHOTOGRAPH.

but few men in the South who could have commanded successfully a separate detachment, in the rear of an opposing army and so near the border of hostilities, as long as he did without losing his entire command.

On this same visit to Washington I had my last interview with the Presi-

dent before reaching the James River. He had, of course, become acquainted
with the fact that a general movement had been ordered all along the line, and
seemed to think it a new feature in war. I explained to him that it was necessary
to have a great number of troops to guard and to hold the territory we had captured, and to prevent incursions into the Northern States. These troops could
perform this service just as well by advancing as by remaining still; and by advancing they would compel the enemy to keep detachments to hold them back
or else lay his own territory open to invasion. "Oh! yes, I see that," he said. "As
we say out West, If a man can't skin he must hold a leg while somebody else
does."

The following correspondence closed the first chapter of my personal acquaintance with President Lincoln:

"EXECUTIVE MANSION, WASHINGTON, April 30, 1864.
"LIEUTENANT-GENERAL GRANT: Not expecting to see you again before
the Spring campaign opens, I wish to express in this way my entire satisfaction with what you have done up to this time, so far as I understand it.
The particulars of your plans I neither know or seek to know. You are vigilant and self-reliant; and, pleased with this, I wish not to obtrude any con-
straints or restraints upon you. While I am very anxious that any great
disaster, or the capture of our men in great numbers, shall be avoided, I
know these points are less likely to escape your attention than they would
be mine. If there is anything wanting which is within my power to give, do
not fail to let me know it. And now with a brave army, and a just cause,
may God sustain you.

"Yours very truly,
"A. LINCOLN."

"HEADQUARTERS, ARMIES OF THE UNITED STATES,
CULPEPER COURT HOUSE, VIRGINIA, May 1, 1864.
"THE PRESIDENT: Your very kind letter of yesterday is just received. The
confidence you express for the future and satisfaction for the past in my
military administration is acknowledged with pride. It shall be my earnest
endeavor that you and the country shall not be disappointed. From my
first entrance into the volunteer service of the country to the present day,
I have never had cause of complaint—have never expressed or implied a
complaint against the Administration or the Secretary of War, for throwing any embarrassment in the way of my vigorously prosecuting what appeared to be my duty. And since the promotion which placed me in
command of all the armies, and in view of the great responsibility and the
importance of success, I have been astonished at the readiness with which
everything asked for has been yielded, without even an explanation being

asked. Should my success be less than I desire and expect, the least I can say is, the fault is not with you.

> "Very truly, your obedient servant,
> "U. S. GRANT, LIEUTENANT-GENERAL."

Executive Mansion
Washington, April 30. 1864

Lieutenant General Grant.

    Not expecting to see you again before the Spring campaign opens, I wish to express, in this way, my entire satisfaction with what you have done up to this time, so far as I understand it. The particulars of your plans I neither know, or seek to know. You are vigilant and self-reliant; and, pleased with this, I wish not to obtrude any constraints or restraints upon you. While I am very anxious that any great disaster, or the capture of our men in great numbers, shall be avoided, I know these points are less likely to escape your attention than they would be mine — If there is anything wanting which is within my power to give, do not fail, to let me know it. And now with a brave Army, and a just cause, may God sustain you.

> Yours very truly
> A. Lincoln.

LINCOLN'S GOD-SPEED TO GRANT.
(FAC-SIMILE OF THE ORIGINAL, SLIGHTLY REDUCED IN SCALE.)

[This remarkable letter was received by General Grant on the 1st of May, three days before the Wilderness campaign began. He was always careless about his papers, and private or semi-official ones were often thrust into his pockets, where they remained for months. In some such way Mr. Lincoln's letter was mislaid. General Grant had forgotten its existence, until in 1866 I came across it in my researches for my history of his campaigns. He was so pleased at the discovery, or recovery, that he gave me the original letter at the time. It is my intention eventually to present it either to the Government or to the family of General Grant.

ADAM BADEAU.

NEW YORK, NOVEMBER 10, 1885.]

The armies were now all ready to move for the accomplishment of a single object. They were acting as a unit so far as such a thing was possible over such a vast field. Lee, with the capital of the Confederacy, was the main end to which all were working. Johnston, with Atlanta, was an important obstacle in the way of our accomplishing the result aimed at, and was therefore almost an independent objective. It was of less importance only because the capture of Johnston and his army would not produce so immediate and decisive a result in closing the rebellion as would the possession of Richmond, Lee and his army. All other troops were employed exclusively in support of these two movements. This was the plan; and I will now endeavor to give, as concisely as I can, the method of its execution, outlining first the operations of minor detached but coöperative columns.

As stated before, Banks failed to accomplish what he had been sent to do on the Red River, and eliminated the use of 40,000 veterans whose coöperation in the grand campaign had been expected—10,000 with Sherman and 30,000 against Mobile.

Sigel's record is almost equally brief. He moved out, it is true, according to programme; but just when I was hoping to hear of good work being done in the Valley I received instead the following announcement from Halleck: "Sigel is in full retreat on Strasburg. He will do nothing but run; never did anything else." The enemy had intercepted him about New Market and handled him roughly, capturing 6 guns and some 900 men out of 6000.

The plan had been for an advance of Sigel's forces in columns. Though the one under his immediate command failed ingloriously, the other proved more fortunate. Under Crook and Averell, his western column advanced from the Gauley in West Virginia at the appointed time, and with more happy results. They reached the Virginia and Tennessee railroad at Dublin, and destroyed a depot of supplies besides tearing up several miles of road and burning the bridge over New River. Having accomplished this, they recrossed the Alleghanies to Meadow Bluffs, and there awaited further orders.

Butler embarked at Fort Monroe with all his command, except the cavalry and some artillery which moved up the south bank of the James River. His steamers moved first up Chesapeake Bay and York River as if threatening the rear of Lee's army. At midnight they turned back, and by daylight Butler was far up the James River. He seized City Point and Bermuda Hundred early in the day, without loss, and no doubt very much to the surprise of the enemy.

This was the accomplishment of the first step contemplated in my instructions to Butler. He was to act from here, looking to Richmond as his objective point. I had given him to understand that I should aim to fight Lee between the Rapidan and Richmond if he would stand; but should Lee fall back into Richmond, I would follow up and make a junction of the armies of the Potomac and the James on the James River. He was directed to secure a footing as far up the south side of the river as he could at as early a date as possible.

By the 6th of May Butler was in position and had begun intrenching, and on the 7th he sent out his cavalry from Suffolk to cut the Weldon railroad. He also sent out detachments to destroy the railroads between Petersburg and Richmond, but no great success attended these latter efforts. He made no great effort to establish himself on that road, and neglected to attack Petersburg, which was almost defenseless. About the 11th he advanced slowly until he reached the works at Drewry's Bluff, about half-way between Bermuda Hundred and Richmond. In the meantime Beauregard[+] had been gathering reënforcements. On the 16th he attacked Butler with great vigor, and with such success as to limit very materially the further usefulness of the Army of the James as a distinct factor in the campaign. I afterward ordered a portion of it[‡] to join the Army of the Potomac, leaving a sufficient force with Butler to man his works, hold securely the footing he had already gained, and maintain a threatening front toward the rear of the Confederate capital.

The position which General Butler had chosen between the two rivers, the James and Appomattox, was one of great natural strength, and where a large area of ground might be thoroughly inclosed by means of a single intrenched line, and that a very short one in comparison with the extent of territory which it thoroughly protected. His right was protected by the James River, his left by the Appomattox, and his rear by their junction—the two streams uniting near by. The bend of the two streams shortened the line that had been chosen for intrenchment, while it increased the area which the line inclosed.

Previous to ordering any troops from Butler I sent my chief engineer, General Barnard, from the Army of the Potomac to that of the James, to inspect Butler's position and ascertain whether I could again safely make an order for General Butler's movement in coöperation with mine, now that I was getting so near Richmond; or, if I could not, whether his position was strong enough to justify me in withdrawing some of his troops and having them brought round by water to White House to join me and reënforce the Army of the Potomac. General Barnard reported the position very strong for defensive purposes, and that I could do the latter with great security; but that General Butler could not move from where he was, in coöperation, to produce any effect. He said that the general occupied a place between the James and Appomattox rivers which was of great strength, and where with an inferior force he could hold it for an indefinite length of time against a superior; but that he could do nothing offensively.

[+]On the 20th of April, 1864, General Beauregard was relieved of the command at Charleston, and on the 23d he assumed command of the Department of North Carolina, which on May 14th was extended to cover all of Virginia south of the James, including Drewry's Bluff.—EDITORS.
[‡]Smith's 18th Corps and two divisions of the 10th.

I then asked him why Butler could not move out from his lines and push across the Richmond and Petersburg railroad to the rear and on the south side of Richmond. He replied that it was impracticable because the enemy had substantially the same line across the neck of land that General Butler had. He then took out his pencil and drew a sketch of the locality, remarking that the position was like a bottle, and that Butler's line of intrenchments across the neck represented the cork; that the enemy had built an equally strong line immediately in front of him across the neck; and it was, therefore, as if Butler was in a bottle. He was perfectly safe against an attack; but, as Barnard expressed it, the enemy had corked the bottle, and with a small force could hold the cork in its place. This struck me as being very expressive of his position, particularly when I saw the hasty sketch which General Barnard had drawn; and in making my subsequent report I used that expression without adding quotation marks, never thinking that anything had been said that would attract attention, as this did, very much to the annoyance, no doubt, of General Butler, and I know very much to my own. I found afterward that this was mentioned in the notes of General Badeau's book, which, when they were shown to me, I asked to have stricken out; yet it was retained there, though against my wishes.☆

I make this statement here because, although I have often made it before, it has never been in my power until now to place it where it will correct history; and I desire to rectify all injustice that I may have done to individuals, particularly to officers who were gallantly serving their country during the trying period of the war for the preservation of the Union. General Butler certainly gave his very earnest support to the war; and he gave his own best efforts personally toward the suppression of the rebellion.

The further operations of the Army of the James can best be treated of in connection with those of the Army of the Potomac, the two being so intimately associated and connected as to be substantially one body in which the individuality of the supporting wing is merged. I will briefly mention Sheridan's first raid upon Lee's communications which, though an incident of the operations on the main line and not specifically marked out in the original plan, attained in its brilliant execution and results all the proportions of an independent campaign.

On the 8th of May, just after the battle of the Wilderness, and when we were moving on Spotsylvania, I directed Sheridan, verbally, to cut loose from

---

☆The words used in General Grant's report, dated July 22d, 1865, are these:

"His [Butler's] army, therefore, though in a position of great security, was as completely shut off from further operations directly before Richmond as if it had been in a bottle strongly corked.... The army sent to operate against Richmond having hermetically sealed itself up at Bermuda Hundred, the enemy was enabled to bring the most if not all of the reënforcements brought from the South by Beauregard against the Army of the Potomac."

—EDITORS.

the Army of the Potomac, pass around the left of Lee's army and attack his cavalry; to cut the two roads—one running west through Gordonsville, Charlottesville, and Lynchburg, the other to Richmond; and, when compelled to do
so for want of forage and rations, to move on to the James River and draw these
from Butler's supplies. This move took him past the entire rear of Lee's army.
These orders were also given in writing through Meade.

The object of this move was threefold: 1. If successfully executed—and it
was—he would annoy the enemy by cutting his lines of supplies and telegraphic communications, and destroy or get for his own use supplies in store in
the rear and coming up; 2. He would draw the enemy's cavalry after him, and
thus better protect our flanks, rear, and trains than by remaining with the army;
3. His absence would save the trains drawing his forage and other supplies from
Fredericksburg, which had now become our base. He started at daylight the
next morning, and accomplished more than was expected. It was sixteen days
before he got back to the Army of the Potomac.‡

Sheridan in this memorable raid passed entirely around Lee's army; encountered his cavalry in four engagements and defeated them in all; recaptured
four hundred Union prisoners and killed and captured many of the enemy; destroyed and used many supplies and munitions of war; destroyed miles of railroad and telegraph, and freed us from annoyance by the cavalry for more than
two weeks.

I fixed the day for Sherman to start when the season should be far enough
advanced, it was hoped, for the roads to be in a condition for the troops to

---

‡From "Personal Memoirs of U. S. Grant" (New York: C. L. Webster & Co.) we take this account of the
raid:

"The course Sheridan took was directly to Richmond. Before night Stuart, commanding the
Confederate cavalry, came on to the rear of his command. But the advance kept on, crossed
the North Anna, and at Beaver Dam, a station on the Virginia Central Railroad, recaptured
four hundred Union prisoners on their way to Richmond, destroyed the road, and used and
destroyed a large amount of subsistence and medical stores.

"Stuart, seeing that our cavalry was pushing toward Richmond, abandoned the pursuit
on the morning of the 10th, and by a detour and an exhausting march, interposed between
Sheridan and Richmond at Yellow Tavern, only about six miles north of the city. Sheridan
destroyed the railroad and more supplies at Ashland, and on the 11th arrived in Stuart's
front. A severe engagement ensued, in which the losses were heavy on both sides, but the
rebels were beaten, their leader mortally wounded, and some guns and many prisoners were
captured.

"Sheridan passed through the outer defenses of Richmond, and could, no doubt, have
passed through the inner ones; but, having no supports near, he could not have remained.
After caring for his wounded, he struck for the James River below the city, to communicate
with Butler, and to rest his men and horses as well as to get food and forage for them.

"He moved first between the Chickahominy and the James, but in the morning (the 12th)
he was stopped by batteries at Mechanicsville. He then turned to cross to the north side of
the Chickahominy by Meadow Bridge. He found this barred, and the defeated Confederate

march. General Sherman at once set himself to work preparing for the task which was assigned him to accomplish in the spring campaign.

The campaign to Atlanta was managed with the most consummate skill, the enemy being flanked out of one position after another all the way there. It is true this was not accomplished without a good deal of fighting, some of it very hard fighting, rising to the dignity of very important battles; neither were positions gained in a single day. On the contrary, weeks were spent at some; and about Atlanta more than a month was consumed.

Soon after midnight, May 3d–4th, the Army of the Potomac moved out from its position north of the Rapidan, to start upon that memorable campaign destined to result in the capture of the Confederate capital and the army defending it.

---

cavalry, reorganized, occupying the opposite side. The panic created by his first entrance within the outer works of Richmond having subsided, troops were sent out to attack his rear.

"He was now in a perilous position; one from which but few generals could have extricated themselves. The defenses of Richmond, manned, were to the right, the Chickahominy was to the left, with no bridge remaining, and the opposite bank guarded; to the rear was a force from Richmond. This force was attacked and beaten by Wilson's and Gregg's divisions, while Sheridan turned to the left with the remaining division and hastily built a bridge over the Chickahominy under the fire of the enemy, forced a crossing and soon dispersed the Confederates he found there. The enemy was held back from the stream by the fire of the troops not engaged in bridge-building.

"On the 13th Sheridan was at Bottom's Bridge, over the Chickahominy. On the 14th he crossed this stream, and on that day went into camp on the James River at Haxall's Landing. He at once put himself into communication with General Butler, who directed all the supplies he wanted to be furnished.

"Sheridan had left the Army of the Potomac at Spotsylvania, but did not know where either this or Lee's army was now. Great caution therefore had to be exercised in getting back. On the 17th, after resting his command for three days, he started on his return. He moved by the way of White House. The bridge over the Pamunkey had been burned by the enemy, but a new one was speedily improvised, and the cavalry crossed over it. On the 22d he was at Aylett's on the Mattapony, where he learned the position of the two armies. On the 24th he joined us on the march from North Anna to Cold Harbor, in the vicinity of Chesterfield."

CHAPTER 9

The Struggle for Atlanta.

Oliver O. Howard, Major-General, U.S.A.

The forces under General Grant after his appointment as general-in-chief were, the Army of the Potomac, under Meade; that of the Ohio, near Knoxville, under Schofield;‡ that of the Cumberland, under Thomas,Φ near Chattanooga; that of the Tennessee, under McPherson, scattered from Huntsville, Alabama, to the Mississippi; that of the Gulf, under Banks, in Louisiana; besides subordinate detachments, under Steele and others, in Arkansas and farther west.

Grant took the whole field into his thought. He made three parts to the long, irregular line of armies, which extended from Virginia to Texas. He gave to Banks the main work in the south-west; to Sherman the middle part, covering the hosts of McPherson, Thomas, Schofield, and Steele; and reserved to himself the remainder. The numbers were known, at least on paper; the plan, promptly adopted, was simple and comprehensive: To break and keep broken the connecting links of the enemy's opposing armies, beat them one by one, and unite for a final consummation. Sherman's part was plain. Grant's plan, flexible enough to embrace his own, afforded Sherman "infinite satisfaction." It looked like "enlightened war." He rejoiced at "this verging to a common center." "Like yourself," he writes to Grant, "you take the biggest load, and from me you shall have thorough and hearty coöperation."

Sherman made his calculations so as to protect most faithfully our line of supply which ran through Louisville, Nashville, and Chattanooga, guarding it against enemies within and without his boundaries, and against accidents. He segregated the men of all arms for this protection. Block-houses and intrench-

‡General John M. Schofield succeeded General John G. Foster in the command of the Department, and Army, of the Ohio, February 9th, 1864.—EDITORS.
ΦGeneral George H. Thomas succeeded General W. S. Rosecrans in command of the Department, and Army, of the Cumberland, October 19th, 1863.—EDITORS.

SAVING A GUN.

ments were put at bridges and tunnels along the railway. Locomotives and freight cars were gathered in, and a most energetic force of skilled railroad men was put at work or held in reserve under capable chiefs.

Besides an equal number of guards of his large depots and long line of supply, Sherman had an effective field force of 100,000,—50,000 with Thomas, 35,000 with McPherson, 15,000 with Schofield.

Sherman was gratified at the number of his force; for two years before, he had been held up as worthy of special distrust because he had declared to Secretary Cameron that before they were done with offensive operations on the line from the Big Sandy to Paducah, 200,000 men would be required.

A few changes of organization were made. Slocum's corps, the Twelfth, and mine, the Eleventh, were consolidated, making a new Twentieth, and Hooker was assigned to its command. I went at once to Loudon, east Tennessee, to take the Fourth Corps and relieve General Gordon Granger, to enable him to have a leave of absence. Slocum was sent to Vicksburg, Mississippi, to watch the great river from that quarter; while Hooker, Palmer, and myself, under Thomas, were to control the infantry and artillery of the Army of the Cumberland. In a few days I moved Wagner's (afterward Newton's) division and T. J. Wood's of my new corps to Cleveland, east Tennessee. Rations, clothing, transportation, and ammunition came pouring in with sufficient abundance, so that when orders arrived for the next movement, on the 3d of May, 1864, my division commanders, Stanley, Newton, and Wood, reported everything ready. This very day Schofield's column, coming from Knoxville, made its appearance at Cleveland. There was now the thrill of preparation, a new life everywhere. Soldiers and civilians alike caught the inspiration.

Ringgold and Catoosa Springs, Georgia, were the points of concentration for Thomas's three corps. We of his army were all in that neighborhood by the 4th of May. It took till the 7th for McPherson to get into Villanow, a few miles to the south of us. Schofield meanwhile worked steadily southward from Cleveland, east Tennessee, through Red Clay, toward Dalton, Georgia. The three railway lines uniting Chattanooga, Cleveland, and Dalton form an almost equilateral triangle. Dalton, its south-east vertex, was the center of the Confederate army, under Joseph E. Johnston. Pushing out from Dalton toward us at Catoosa Springs, Johnston occupied the famous pass through Taylor's Ridge, Buzzard-Roost Gap, and part of the ridge itself; and held, for his extreme outpost in our direction, Tunnel Hill, near which our skirmish-line and his first exchanged shots. His northern lines ran along the eastern side of the triangle, between Dalton and Red Clay.

Johnston, according to his official return for April, had a force of 52,992. At Resaca, a few days later, after the corps of Polk had joined him, it numbered 71,235. Our three field armies aggregated then, in officers and men, 98,797, with 254 pieces of artillery. The Confederate commander had about the same number of cannon. McPherson had thus far brought to Sherman but 24,465 men.

When the Army of the Cumberland was in line, facing the enemy, its left rested near Catoosa Springs, its center at Ringgold, the railway station, and its right at Leet's Tan-yard. My corps formed the left. Catoosa Springs was a Georgia watering-place, where there were several large buildings, hotel and boarding-houses, amid undulating hills, backed by magnificent mountain scenery. Here, on the morning of the 6th, I met Thomas and Sherman. Sherman had a habit of dropping in and explaining in a happy way what he purposed to do. At first he intended that Thomas and Schofield should simply breast the enemy and skirmish with him on the west and north, while McPherson, coming from Alabama, was to strike the Atlanta railroad at least ten miles below Resaca. McPherson, failing in getting some of his troops back from furlough, was not now deemed strong enough to operate alone; hence he was brought to Chattanooga instead, and sent thence to Villanow, soon after to pass through the Snake Creek Gap of Taylor's Ridge, all the time being kept near enough the other armies to get help from them in case of emergency. By this it was ardently hoped by Sherman that McPherson might yet succeed in getting upon Johnston's communications near Resaca. Thomas here urged his own views, which were to give Schofield and McPherson the skirmishing and demonstrations, while he (Thomas), with his stronger army, should pass through Snake Creek Gap and seize Johnston's communications. He felt sure of victory. Sherman, however, hesitated to put his main army twenty miles away beyond a mountain range on the enemy's line, lest he should thereby endanger his own. He could not yet afford an exchange of base. Still, in less than a week, as we shall see, he ran even a greater risk.

Early in the day, May 7th, the Fourth Corps, arranged for battle, was near a small farm-house in sight of Tunnel Hill. Two divisions, Stanley's and Newton's, abreast in long, wavy lines, and the other, Wood's, in the rear, kept on the *qui vive* to prevent surprises, particularly from the sweep of country to the

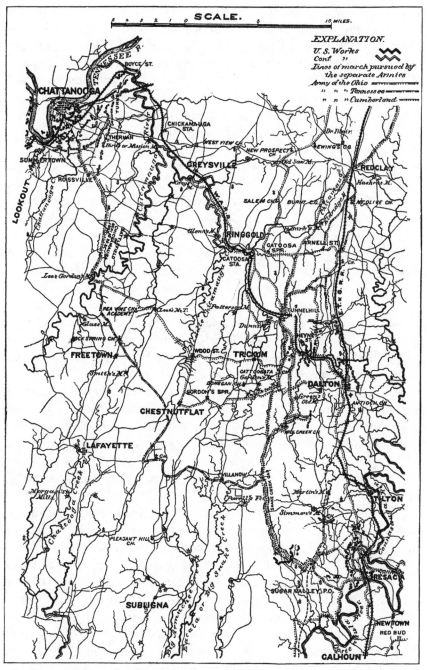

north of us. The front and the left of the moving men were well protected by infantry skirmishers. It was a beautiful picture—that army corps, with arms glistening in the morning light, ascending the slope. By 8 o'clock the few rifle-shots had become a continuous rattle. First we saw far off, here and there, puffs of smoke, and then the gray horsemen giving back and passing the crest. Suddenly there was stronger resistance, artillery and musketry rapidly firing upon our advance. At 9 o'clock the ridge of Tunnel Hill bristled with Confederates, mounted and dismounted. A closer observation from Stanley's field-glass showed them to be only horse artillery and cavalry supports. In a few moments Stanley's and Newton's men charged the hill at a run and cleared the ridge, and soon beheld the enemy's artillery and cavalry galloping away. "The ball is opened," Stanley called out, as I took my place by his side to study Taylor's Ridge and its "Rocky Face," which was now in plain sight. We beheld it, a craggy elevation of about five hundred feet, extending from a point not far north of us, but as far as the eye could reach southward. Its perpendicular face presented a formidable wall and afforded us no favorable door of entrance.

Thomas's three corps, Palmer occupying the middle and Hooker the right, were now marched forward till my men received rifle-shots from the heights, Palmer's a shower of them from the defenders of the gap, and Hooker's a more worrisome fusillade from spurs of the ridge farther south. Thomas could not sit down behind this formidable wall and do nothing. How could he retain before him the Confederate host? Only by getting into closer contact.

On the 8th I sent Newton some two miles northward, where the ascent was not so abrupt. He succeeded by rushes in getting from cover to cover, though not without loss, till he had wrested at least one-third of the "knife edge" from those resolute men of gray. Quickly the observers of this sharp contest saw the bright signal flags up there in motion. Stanley and Wood gave Newton all possible support by their marksmen and by their efforts to land shells on the ridge. The enemy's signals were near Newton. He tried hard to capture them, but failed. In the night two pieces of artillery, after much toil, reached the top, and soon cleared away a few hundred yards more of this territory in bloody dispute. On May 9th Thomas put forth a triple effort to get nearer his foe. First, Stanley's division reconnoitered Buzzard-Roost Gap into the very "jaws of death," till it drew the fire from newly discovered batteries, and set whole lines of Confederate musketry-supports ablaze. At this time I had a narrow escape. Stanley, Captain G. C. Kniffin of his staff, several other officers, and myself were in a group, watching a reconnoissance. All supposed there were no Confederate sharp-shooters near enough to do harm, when *whiz* came a bullet which passed through the group; Kniffin's hat was pierced, three holes were made in my coat, and a neighboring tree was struck.

Thomas now made a second effort. Palmer sent Morgan's brigade up one of the spurs south of the gap. It encountered the hottest fire, and suffered a considerable loss in killed and wounded. One regiment drove back the enemy's first line, and, like Newton's men, came within speaking distance of their opponents. Here arose the story to the effect that a witty corporal proposed to read to them the President's Emancipation Proclamation, and that they kept from firing while he did so. Still farther south, with Hooker's Twentieth Corps, and almost beyond our hearing, Thomas made his third push. In this action fifty were reported killed, and a larger number wounded; among them every regimental commander engaged. Similarly, but with easier approaches than ours, Schofield kept Johnston's attention at the east and north. Such was the demonstration, while McPherson was making his long détour through Villanow, Snake Creek Gap, and out into Sugar Valley. He found the gap unoccupied; and so, with Kilpatrick's small cavalry detachment ahead,⊉ followed closely by Dodge's Sixteenth Corps, with Logan's Fifteenth well closed up, he emerged from the mountains on the morning of the 9th, at the eastern exit.

Immediately there was excitement—the cavalry advance stumbled upon Confederate cavalry, which had run out from Resaca to watch this doorway. Our cavalry followed up the retreating Confederates with dash and persistency, till they found shelter behind the deep-cut works and guns at Resaca. In plain view of these works, though on difficult ground, Logan and Dodge pressed up their men, under orders from McPherson "to drive back the enemy and break the railroad." And pray, why were not these plain orders carried out? McPherson answers in a letter that night sent to Sherman: "They [probably Polk's men] displayed considerable force and opened on us with artillery. After skirmishing [among the gulches and thickets] till nearly dark, and finding that I could not succeed in cutting the railroad before dark, or in getting to it, I decided to withdraw the command and take up a position for the night between Sugar Valley

---

⊉Lieutenant James Oates wrote to the editors on July 8th, 1887, from Cincinnati, Ark., as follows:

"General Howard is in error in the above statement. On May 1st the 9th Illinois Mounted Infantry broke camp at Decatur, Alabama, to take part in the Atlanta campaign. On the afternoon of May 8th the regiment came up with General McPherson at Villanow. Lieutenant-Colonel J. J. Phillips, who was in command, received orders to take the advance of the Army of the Tennessee, and did so at once, Company 'K,' Lieutenant James Oates in command, taking the lead through Snake Creek Gap. We advanced down into the open country of Sugar Valley on the evening of May 8th. No part of General Kilpatrick's command was there when we passed through Snake Creek Gap. On the morning of the 9th of May our regiment took the advance without any other cavalry support. The infantry was a considerable distance in the rear. Very early in the morning we engaged the Confederate cavalry, losing several men in killed and wounded—among the latter, Lieutenant-Colonel Phillips. The infantry came up at double-quick to our support and ended the fight. Our regiment followed up the retreating Confederates 'with dash and persistency.' It was during the advance that day that we came in contact with the Georgia Cadets from the Military Institute at Marietta, who had come out from the woods at Resaca and formed their line behind a rail fence. After a volley from the Cadets, which killed several of our men, our regiment charged them and did not give up the chase until it ran against the works at Resaca."

and the entrance to the gap." At the first news Sherman was much vexed, and declared concerning McPherson's failure to break the enemy's main artery: "Such an opportunity does not occur twice in a single life,...still he was perfectly justified by his orders."

Our commander, believing that Johnston would now speedily fall back to Resaca, at once changed his purpose. Leaving me at Rocky Face with the Fourth Corps and Stoneman's small division of cavalry to hold our line of supply, Sherman pressed after McPherson the armies of Thomas and Schofield. But Johnston was not in a hurry. He terrified me for two days by his tentative movements, till our skirmishing amounted at times almost to a battle. But the night of the 12th of May he made off in one of his clean retreats. At dawn of the 13th the formidable Buzzard-Roost Gap was open and safe, and our men passed through. Stoneman rushed into the village of Dalton from the north, and the Fourth Corps, eager and rapid, kept close to the chasing cavalry. Not far south of Dalton we came upon a bothersome Confederate rear-guard, which made our marching all that long day slow and spasmodic, yet before dark my command had skirted the eastern slope of Taylor's Ridge for eighteen miles and joined skirmishers with Sherman, who was already, with McPherson, abreast of Resaca. Thus we ended the combats of Tunnel Hill and Dalton, and opened up Resaca.

As soon as Johnston reached the little town of Resaca he formed a horse-shoe-shaped line, something like ours at Gettysburg. He rested Polk's corps on

EXTREME LEFT (VIEW LOOKING SOUTH) OF THE CONFEDERATE LINES AT RESACA.
FROM A WAR-TIME PHOTOGRAPH.

The cluster of houses includes the railway station, the railway running generally parallel with the earth-works here seen, which in the distance descend to the Oostenaula River. The railway and wagon bridges mentioned in the notes on p. 266 are near the railway station.

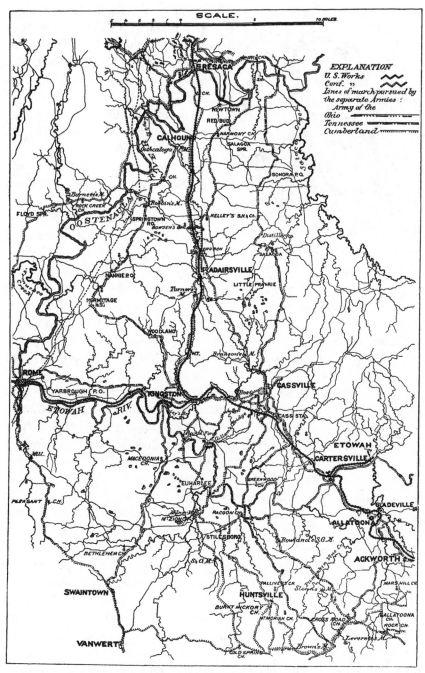

REPRODUCED FROM THE "MEMOIRS OF GENERAL WILLIAM T. SHERMAN"
(NEW YORK: D. APPLETON & CO.). BY PERMISSION OF AUTHOR AND PUBLISHER.

BREVET BRIGADIER-GENERAL BENJAMIN
HARRISON. FROM A PHOTOGRAPH.

the Oostenaula River; placed Hardee's next, running up Milk Creek; and then curved Hood's back to strike the Connasauga River. After the Confederates had thrown up the usual intrenchments, and put out one or two small advanced forts with cannon, the position was as strong as Marye's Heights had been against direct attack. We spent a part of the 14th of May creeping up among the bushes, rocks, and ravines.

Early that morning, while this was going on, Sherman, who had worked all night, was sitting on a log, with his back against a tree, fast asleep. Some men marching by saw him, and one fellow ended a slurring remark by: "A pretty way we are commanded!" Sherman, awakened by the noise, heard the last words. "Stop, my man," he cried; "while you were sleeping, last night, I was planning for you, sir; and now I was taking a nap." Thus, familiarly and kindly, the general gave reprimands and won confidence.

McPherson rested his right upon the Oostenaula River, opposite Polk. Thomas, with the corps of Palmer and Hooker, came next; and then that brave young officer, Cox, commanding the Twenty-third Corps, against a storm of bullets and shells swung his divisions round to follow the bend in the enemy's line. I watched the operation, so as to close upon his left. T. J. Wood's division moved up in a long line, with skirmishers well out, and then Stanley's carried us to the railway. Stanley's chief-of-artillery arranged two or three batteries to keep the enemy from walking around our unprotected left. The air was full of screeching shells and whizzing bullets, coming uncomfortably near, while line after line was adjusting itself for the deadly conflict. Our fighting at Resaca did not effect much. There might possibly have been as much accomplished if we had used skirmish-lines alone. In McPherson's front Logan had a battery well placed, and fired till he had silenced the troublesome foes on a ridge in his front; then his brave men, at a run, passed the ravine and secured the ridge. Here Logan intrenched his corps; and Dodge, abreast of him, did the same. Afterward, McPherson seized another piece of ground across Camp Creek, and held it. During the evening of the 14th a vigorous effort was made by Polk to regain this outpost, but he was repulsed with loss.

The detailed account gives great credit to Generals Charles R. Woods, Giles A. Smith, and J. A. J. Lightburn. One hundred prisoners and 1300 Confederates *hors de combat* were on Logan's list. This work forced Johnston to lay a new bridge over the Oostenaula. The divisions of Absalom Baird, R. W. Johnson, Jefferson C. Davis, and John Newton plunged into the thickets and worked their way steadily and bravely into the reëntrant angles on Hardee's front. Schofield's right division, under Judah, had a fearful struggle, losing six hundred men; the others, coming to its help, captured and secured a part of the enemy's intrenchments. Hood assailed my left after 3 P.M. The front attack was repulsed, but heavy columns came surging around Stanley's left. Everybody, battery men and supporting infantry, did wonders; still, but for help promptly rendered, Sherman's whole line, like the left of Wellington's at Waterloo, would soon have been rolled up and displaced. But Colonel Morgan of my staff, who had been sent in time, brought up Williams's division from Hooker's corps as quickly as men could march. Stanley's brave artillerymen were thus succored before they were forced to yield their ground, and Hood, disappointed, returned to his trenches. The next day, the 15th, came Hooker's attack. He advanced in a column of deployed brigades. Both armies watched with eager excitement this passage-at-arms. The divisions of Generals Butterfield, Williams, and Geary seized some trenches and cheered, but were stopped before a sort of lunette holding four cannon. The Confederates were driven from their trenches; but our men, meeting continuous and deadly volleys, could not get the guns till night. A color-bearer named Hess, of Colonel Benjamin Harrison's brigade, while his comrades were retiring a few steps for better cover, being chagrined at the defiant yell behind him, unfurled his flag and swung it to the breeze. He was instantly killed. A witness says: "There were other hands to grasp the flag, and it came back, only to return and wave from the very spot where its former bearer fell."

While the main battle was in progress, Dodge had sent a division under the one-armed Sweeny, to Lay's Ferry, a point below Resaca. Under the chief engineer, Captain Reese, he laid a bridge and protected it by a small force. Sweeny, being threatened by some Confederates crossing the river above him, and fearing that he might be cut off from the army, suddenly drew back about a mile beyond danger. On the 15th, however, he made another attempt and was more successful; formed a bridge-head beyond the river; threw over his whole force; and fought a successful battle against Martin's Confederate cavalry, before Walker's infantry, which was hastily sent against him from Calhoun, could arrive. Besides Sweeny's division, Sherman dispatched a cavalry force over the pontoons, instructing them to make a wider détour. The operations in this quarter being successful, there was nothing left to the Confederate commander but to withdraw his whole army from Resaca. This was effected during the night of the 15th, while our weary men were sound asleep. At the first peep of dawn Newton's skirmishers sprang over the enemy's intrenchments to find them abandoned.

In the ensuing pursuit, Thomas, crossing the river on a floating bridge, hastily constructed, followed directly with the Fourth and the Fourteenth corps.

Stanley had some sharp fighting with Stewart's Confederate division, which was acting as Johnston's rear-guard. It was, in fact, a running skirmish, that lasted till evening, at the close of which we encamped for the night near the enemy's empty works at Calhoun. Meanwhile McPherson had been marching on parallel roads to the right toward Rome, Georgia, Jefferson C. Davis's division from Thomas's army sweeping farther still to the right, and Schofield, accompanied by Hooker, to the left toward Cassville.

Our enemy, between these columns with his entire force, made a brief stand on the 17th of May at Adairsville, and fortified. About 4 P.M. Newton and Wood, of my corps, Wood on the right, found the resistance constantly increasing as they advanced, till Newton's skirmishers, going at double-time through clumps of trees, awakened a heavy opposing fire. A little after this, while I was watching the developments from a high point, Sherman with his staff and escort joined me. Our showy group immediately drew upon it the fire of a battery, shells bursting over our heads with indescribable rapidity. Colonel Morgan's horse was very badly lamed; Fullerton, the adjutant-general, was set afoot, and several horses of the escort were killed or crippled. Captain Bliss, of Newton's staff, had one shoulder-strap knocked off by a fragment, which bruised him badly. The skirmishing of Newton and Wood kept increasing. In fact, both parties, though desiring to avoid a general battle, nevertheless reënforced, till the firing amounted to an engagement. It was not till after 9 o'clock that the rattling of the musketry had diminished to the ordinary skirmish, and the batteries had ceased, except an occasional shot, as if each were trying to have the last gun. The losses in my command in this combat were about two hundred killed and wounded. The morning of the 18th found the works in front of Adairsville with few reminders that an army had been there the night before. Hooker and Schofield had done the work. Johnston's scouts during the night brought him word that a large Federal force was already far beyond his right near Cassville, threatening his main crossing of the Etowah; and also that McPherson was camping below him at McGuire's Cross-roads, and that our infantry (Davis's division) was already in sight of the little town of Rome, where, under a weak guard, were foundries and important mills. We began now to perceive slight evidences of our opponent's demoralization. I captured a regiment and quite a large number of detached prisoners. The whole number taken, including many commissioned officers, was about four thousand.

The rapidity with which the badly broken railroad was repaired seemed miraculous. We had hardly left Dalton before trains with ammunition and other supplies arrived. While our skirmishing was going on at Calhoun, the locomotive whistle sounded in Resaca. The telegraphers were nearly as rapid: the

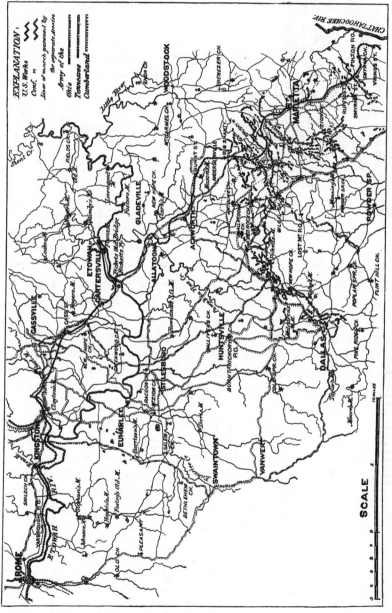

REPRODUCED FROM THE "MEMOIRS OF GENERAL WILLIAM T. SHERMAN" (NEW YORK: D. APPLETON & CO.).

BY PERMISSION OF AUTHOR AND PUBLISHER.

MAJOR-GENERAL JACOB D. COX.
FROM A PHOTOGRAPH.

lines were in order to Adairsville on the morning of the 18th. While we were breaking up the State arsenal at Adairsville, caring for the wounded and bringing in Confederate prisoners, word was telegraphed from Resaca that bacon, hard-bread, and coffee were already there at our service.

Johnston, by his speedy night-work, passed on through Kingston, and formed an admirable line of battle in the vicinity of Cassville, with his back to the Etowah River, protecting the selected crossing.

This was his final halt north of that river, so difficult with its mountain banks. Johnston remained here to obstruct and dispute our way one day only, for Schofield and Hooker had penetrated the forests eastward of him so far that Hood, still on Johnston's right, insisted that the Yankees were already beyond him and in force.

Upon this report, about which there has since been much controversy, Johnston ordered a prompt withdrawal. The morning of the 21st of May, bright and clear, showed us a country picturesque in its natural features, with farm and woodland as quiet and peaceful as if there had been no war. So Sherman, taking up his headquarters at Kingston, a little hamlet on the railway, gave his armies three days' rest./

A glance at the map shows the Etowah flowing nearly west thirty miles from Allatoona to Rome. Sherman's headquarters at Kingston were midway. While the armies were resting, the right (Davis's division) at Rome, the left (Schofield and Hooker) near Cartersville, and the remainder at Kingston, the railroad and telegraph lines were repaired to Kingston; baggage, temporarily abandoned, came back to officers and men; necessary supplies, at the hands of smiling quartermasters and commissaries, now found us. The dead were

/One of these days was Sunday. My friend E. P. Smith, of the Christian Commission, afterward Commissioner of Indian Affairs, was ringing the church bell at Kingston, when Sherman, being disturbed by the ringing, sent a guard to arrest the supposed "bummer."

Smith, in spite of his indignant protest, was marched to Sherman's anteroom and kept under guard for an hour. Then he was taken to Sherman, who looked up from his writing and asked abruptly:

"What were you ringing that bell for?"

"For service. It is Sunday, General," Smith replied.

"Oh! is it?" answered Sherman. "Didn't know it was Sunday. Let him go."—O.O.H.

buried, the sick and wounded were made more comfortable, and everybody got his mail and wrote letters. Meanwhile Sherman and his army commanders were endeavoring to find the location of their enemy.

Johnston was holding the region south of the Etowah, including the pass of Allatoona, and extended his army along the ridge of Allatoona Creek toward the south-west. He was picketing a parallel ridge in front of his line, along another creek, the Pumpkin Vine. This is substantially where we found this able and careful commander; but he pushed a little to the left and forward as we came on, till Hardee was at Dallas and Hood at New Hope Church. Our march was resumed on the morning of the 24th of May, Thomas crossing on his own pontoons south of Kingston; Hooker, contrary to the plan, went in advance of Schofield's column over a bridge at Milam's, east of Kingston; Davis, being at Rome, went straightforward from that place, and McPherson did the same from his position, laying his bridges so as to take the road to Van Wert. Stoneman's cavalry covered the left; Garrard's division was near McPherson and Davis, while McCook's cleared the front for the center. The whole country between the Etowah and the Chattahoochee presented a desolate appearance, with few openings and very few farms, and those small and poor; other parts were covered with trees and dense underbrush, which the skirmishers had great difficulty in penetrating. Off the ordinary "hog-backs" one plunged into deep ravines or ascended abrupt steeps. There was much loose, shifting soil on the hills, and many lagoons and small streams bordered with treacherous quicksands.

Very soon on May 24th the usual skirmishing with the cavalry began, but there was not much delay. Hooker, coming into Thomas's road the next morning, the 25th, led our column, taking the direct road toward Dallas. It was showery all day, and the weather and bad roads had a disheartening effect on men and animals. To relieve the situation as much as possible Thomas had my corps take advantage of country roads to the right, that would bring us into Dallas by the Van Wert route. McPherson and Davis had already come together at Van Wert. Now, suddenly, Geary's division found a bridge over Pumpkin Vine Creek on fire, and hostile cavalry behind it. The cavalry soon fled, and the bridge was repaired. Hooker, thinking there was more force in that quarter, pushed up the road toward New Hope Church. He had gone but a short distance before he ran upon one of Hood's brigades. It was an outpost of Stewart's division, put there to create delay. Hooker soon dislodged this outpost and moved on, driving back the brigade through the woods, till he came upon the enemy's main line.

The sound of cannon speedily drew Sherman to the point of danger. He immediately ordered the necessary changes. Williams's division, having passed on, faced about and came back. Butterfield's hastened up. The two divisions, each forming in parallel lines, promptly assaulted Hood's position. Again and again Hooker's brave men went forward through the forest only to run upon log-barricades thoroughly manned and protected by well-posted artillery. During these charges occurred a thunder-storm, the heaviest shower of the day. I turned to the left by the first opportune road, and deployed Newton's division to the right of Hooker by 6 P.M. The remainder of my command came up over roads deep with mud and obstructed by wagons. In the morning all the troops were at hand. On that terrible night the nearest house to the field was filled with the wounded. Torch-lights and candles lighted up dimly the incoming stretchers and the surgeons' tables and instruments. The very woods seemed to moan and groan with the voices of sufferers not yet brought in.

McPherson, with Davis for his left, took position at Dallas, having Logan on his right, and Garrard's cavalry still beyond. There must have been a gap of three miles between McPherson and us. Schofield was badly injured by the fall of his horse in that black forest while finding his way during the night to Sherman's bivouac, so that for a few days Cox took his command. Cox, with his Twenty-third Corps, and Palmer with the Fourteenth, swung in beyond me, as my men were moving up carefully into their usual positions in line of battle. Now the enemy kept strengthening his trench-barricades, which were so covered by thickets that at first we could scarcely detect them. As he did, so did we.

CONFEDERATE INTRENCHMENTS NEAR NEW HOPE CHURCH.
FROM A WAR-TIME PHOTOGRAPH.

No regiment was long in front of Johnston's army without having virtually as good a breastwork as an engineer could plan. There was a ditch before the embankment and a strong log revetment behind it, and a heavy "top-log" to shelter the heads of the men. I have known a regiment to shelter itself completely against musketry and artillery with axes and shovels, in less than an hour after it reached its position.

It would only weary the reader's patience to follow up the struggle step by step from New Hope Church to the Chattahoochee. Still, these were the hardest times which the army experienced. It rained continuously for seventeen days; the roads, becoming as broad as the fields, were a series of quagmires. And, indeed, it was difficult to bring enough supplies forward from Kingston to meet the needs of the army. Sherman began to pass his armies to the left. First, I was sent with two divisions to attempt to strike Johnston's right. I marched thither Wood's division, supported by R. W. Johnson's, and connected with the army by Cox on my right. At Pickett's Mill, believing I had reached the extreme of the Confederate line, at 6 P.M. of the 27th I ordered the assault. Wood encountered just such obstructions as Hooker had found at New Hope Church, and was similarly repulsed, suffering much loss. R. W. Johnson's division was hindered by a side-thrust from the hostile cavalry, so that we did not get the full benefit of his forward push. We believed that otherwise we should have lodged at least a brigade beyond Hindman's Confederate division. But we did what was most important: we worked our men all that weary night in fortifying. The Confederate commander was ready at daylight to take the offensive against us at Pickett's Mill, but he did not do so, because he found our position and works too strong to warrant the attempt. With a foot bruised by the fragment of a shell, I sat that night among the wounded in the midst of a forest glade, while Major Howard of my staff led regiments and brigades into the new position chosen for them. General R. W. Johnson had been wounded, Captain Stinson of my staff had been shot through the lungs, and a large number lay there, on a sideling slope by a faint camp-fire, with broken limbs or disfigured faces.

The next day, the 28th, McPherson made an effort to withdraw from Dallas, so as to pass beyond my left; but as Hardee at the first move quickly assailed him with great fury, he prudently advised further delay. This battle was the reverse of mine at Pickett's Mill. The enemy attacked mainly in columns of deployed regiments along the front of Dodge's and Logan's corps, and was repulsed with a dreadful loss, which Logan estimated at two thousand. Now, necessity pressing him in every direction, Sherman, mixing divisions somewhat along the line, gradually bore his armies to the left. The 1st of June put Stoneman into Allatoona, and on the 3d Schofield's infantry was across the railroad near Ackworth, having had a severe and successful combat *en route*.

Being now far beyond Johnston's right, and having seized and secured the Allatoona Creek from its mouth to Ackworth, Sherman was ready, from Alla-

UNION EARTH-WORKS IN FRONT OF BIG AND LITTLE KENESAW.
FROM A WAR-TIME PHOTOGRAPH.

toona as a new base, to push forward and strike a new and heavy blow, when, to his chagrin, in the night of the 4th of June Johnston abandoned his works and fell back to a new line. This line ran from Brush Mountain to Lost Mountain, with "Pine Top" standing out in a salient near the middle. He also held an outpost in front of Gilgal Church abreast of Pine Top. Slowly, with skirmishes and small combats, for the most part in dense woods, we continuously advanced. On my front we seized the skirmish-holes of the enemy, made epaulements for batteries there, and little by little extended our deep ditches or log-barricades close up to Johnston's. As we settled down to steady work again, McPherson was near Brush Mountain, having pushed down the railroad. F. P. Blair's corps (the Seventeenth) from Huntsville, Alabama, had now joined him, making up for our losses, which were already, from all causes, upward of nine thousand. This accession gave heart to us all. Thomas was next, advancing and bearing away toward Pine Top, and Schofield coming up against the salient angle near Gilgal Church. To tell the work of these two opposing hosts in their new position is a similar story to the last. There was gallant fighting here and there all along the lines. Here it was that my batteries, opening fire under the direct instruction of Sherman, drove back the enemy from the exposed intrenchments on Pine Top. It was at this time that General Polk was killed. McPherson, by overlapping Hood, skirmished heavily, and captured the 40th Alabama regiment entire. Schofield, brushing away the cavalry, penetrated between Lost Mountain and Gilgal Church, put his artillery on a prominent knoll, and, with rapid discharges, took Hardee in reverse.

That night, the 16th of June, Johnston again went back to a new line, already prepared, just behind Mud Creek. Our troops, being on the alert, followed at once with great rapidity. Just where the old lines joined the new (for Johnston's right wing was unchanged), I saw a feat the like of which never elsewhere fell under my observation. Baird's division, in a comparatively open field, put forth a heavy skirmish-line, which continued such a rapid fire of rifles as to keep down a corresponding hostile line behind its well-constructed trenches, while the picks and shovels behind the skirmishers fairly flew, till a good set of works was made four hundred yards distant from the enemy's and parallel to it. One of my brigades (Harker's), by a rush, did also a brave and unusual thing in capturing an intrenched and well-defended line of the enemy's works and taking their defenders captive. Again, another (Kirby's brigade), having lost Bald Hill in a skirmish, retook it by a gallant charge in line, under a hot fire of artillery and infantry, and intrenched and kept it.

Hood, who had been massed opposite McPherson, made a forced night-march, and suddenly appeared on the other flank fronting Schofield and Hooker. With his known method of charging and firing, he delivered there a desperate attack on the 22d of June. After a hard battle he was repulsed with heavy loss. This was the "Battle of Culp's Farm." Here it was that Hooker received a reproof from Sherman for an exaggerated dispatch, which inferentially, but wrongly, blamed Schofield.☆ Hooker was ever after incensed at Sherman.

Again, by the gradual pressure against Johnston's right and left, Sherman forced him to a new contraction of his lines. This time it was the famous Kenesaw position that he assumed. With his right still at Brush Mountain, he extended a light force over the crest of the Kenesaws, and placed a heavier one along the southern slope, reaching far beyond the Dallas and Marietta road. He drew back his left and fortified. The whole line was stronger in artificial contrivances and natural features than the cemetery at Gettysburg. The complete works, the slashings in front, and the difficulties of the slope toward us under a full sweep of cross-fire made the position almost impregnable.

For reasons similar to those which influenced Lee to strike twice for Little Round Top, Sherman ordered an assault here with the hope of carrying the southern slope of Kenesaw, or of penetrating Johnston's long front at some weak point. Schofield, well southward, advanced and crossed Olley's Creek, and kept up enough fire and effort to hold a large force in his front. McPherson, on the left, did the same, a serious engagement being sustained by Logan's corps

---

☆General Hooker signaled to General Sherman, on the evening of June 22d, that he [Hooker] was uneasy about his right flank, which Schofield had been ordered to protect.—EDITORS.

advancing straight against the mountain. Logan lost heavily from the trenches in his front, and from artillery that raked his men as they advanced. Seven regimental commanders fell, killed or wounded. But the dreadful battle, hard to describe, was left to Thomas. He commanded two attacks, one opposite the Confederate General Loring's‡ left, the other in front of Cheatham. Newton's division led my attack, and Davis that of Palmer. Like Pickett's charge at Gettysburg, the movement was preceded by a heavy cannonade. Then our skirmishers sprang forward and opened; and quickly the enemy's skirmish-line was drawn back to their main work. Harker, commanding one brigade, led his column rapidly over the open ground. Wagner did the same on Harker's left, and Kimball put his brigade in close support. The enemy's fire was terrific. Our men did not stop till they had gained the edge of the felled trees; a few penetrated, to fall close to the enemy's parapet; but most sought shelter behind logs and rocks, in rifle-holes, or depressions. Harker, moving with them, cheered on his men; when they were forced to stop, he rallied them again and made a second vigorous effort, in which he fell mortally wounded. Davis's effort was like Newton's; he met the same withering fire from rifle-balls and shells. But his men managed to make a shelter, which they kept, close up to the hostile works. Here they staid and intrenched. Among those who fell were brigade commanders Colonel Daniel McCook and Colonel O. F. Harmon. Our losses in this assault were heavy indeed, and our gain was nothing. We realized now, as never before, the futility of direct assaults upon intrenched lines already well prepared and well manned.

Plainly there was now nothing left for Sherman to do but to send his left army (McPherson's) to follow up the right (Schofield's) across Olley's Creek, and force his cavalry to Sandtown and the Chattahoochee far below Johnston's force. The first sign, namely, McPherson's starting, and Schofield's boldness, set the Confederates again in motion. On the morning of the 3d of July Sherman turned his spy-glass to the Kenesaw crest, and saw our pickets "crawling up the hill cautiously." The strong works were found vacant. Johnston had made new breastworks six miles below, at Smyrna Camp Ground, and another complete set, by the labor of slaves and new levies, where the railway crosses the Chattahoochee. Thomas, taking up the pursuit, followed his enemy through Marietta and beyond. My command skirmished up to the Smyrna works during the 3d. The next day Sherman paid us a Fourth of July visit. He could not at first believe that Johnston would make another stand north of the river. "Howard," he said to me, "you are mistaken; there is no force in your front; they are laughing

‡General Loring remained with his division in the Department of Mississippi and East Louisiana until the Atlanta campaign was fairly opened by Sherman's advance, when all the infantry in Mississippi was ordered to Johnston. Polk, with Loring's division, reached Resaca May 11th. June 14th, Polk having been killed, Loring succeeded temporarily to the command of the corps.—EDITORS.

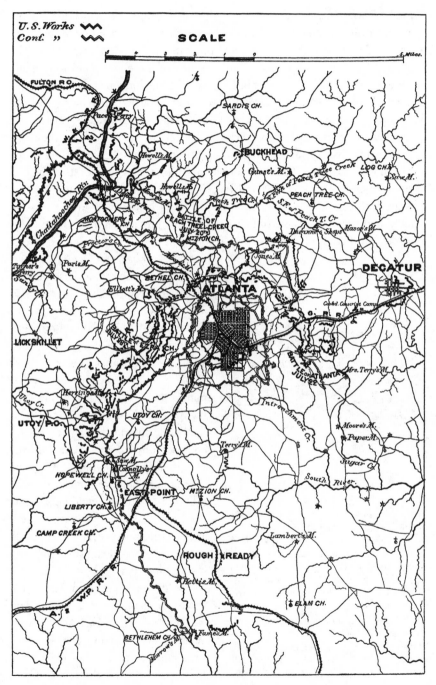

REPRODUCED FROM THE "MEMOIRS OF GENERAL WILLIAM T. SHERMAN"
(NEW YORK: D. APPLETON & CO.). BY PERMISSION OF AUTHOR AND PUBLISHER.

at you!" We were in a thinnish grove of tall trees, in front of a farm-house. "Well, General," I replied, "let us see." I called Stanley, whose division held the front. "General, double your skirmishers and press them." At once it was done. The lines sped forward, capturing the outlying pits of the enemy, and took many prisoners; but a sheet of lead instantly came from the hidden works in the edge of the wood beyond us, and several unseen batteries hurled their shot across our lines, some of them reaching our grove and forcing us to retire. Sherman, as he rode away, said that I had been correct in my report. While we kept the Confederates busy by skirmishing and battery firing, a set of demonstrations to the north and south of us finally resulted in gaining crossings of the river at Roswell, Soap Creek, Powers's and Paice's ferries. Schofield effected the first crossing by pushing out from Soap Creek boats loaded with men, crossing quickly, and surprising the Confederate cavalry and cannon in his front. This was done on the 9th of July. As soon as Johnston knew of it, he left his excellent works near the Chattahoochee, burned his bridges, and hastened his retreat to Atlanta. The weather had become good, and there was great animation and manifest joy on our side. It was gratifying to escape from such fastnesses and dismal forests as those which had hampered us for over a month, and we now firmly believed that the end of the campaign was sure.

GENERAL SHERMAN'S HEADQUARTERS
AT THE HOWARD HOUSE,
IN FRONT OF ATLANTA.
FROM A SKETCH MADE AT THE TIME.

In his "Memoirs" General Sherman says that on July 21st (the day before General McPherson was killed), while he (Sherman) was at the head of Schofield's troops, expecting that the enemy would evacuate, McPherson and his staff rode up. "We went back," he says, "to the Howard House, a double frame-building with a porch, and sat on the steps discussing the chances of battle, and Hood's general character. McPherson had also been of the same class at West Point with Hood, Schofield, and Sheridan. We agreed that we ought to be unusually cautious, and prepared at all times for sallies and for hard fighting, because Hood, though not deemed much of a scholar, or of great mental capacity, was undoubtedly a brave, determined, and rash man."—EDITORS.

Our armies made a right wheel—Thomas, on the pivot, taking the shortest line to Atlanta; McPherson, on the outer flank, coming by Roswell to Decatur, with Schofield between.

As the several columns were crossing the famous Peach Tree Creek my corps was divided. I was sent, with Stanley and Wood, to connect with Schofield, causing a gap of two miles. Newton remained on Thomas's left; on Newton's right was Ward; next, Geary; then, Williams; last, Palmer's corps; all, having crossed over, were stretched out along the creek. There was at that point but little open ground, mostly woodland, and very uneven with cross-ravines.

Just at this time, much to our comfort and to his surprise, Johnston was removed, and Hood placed in command of the Confederate army. Johnston had planned to attack Sherman at Peach Tree Creek, expecting just such a division between our wings as we made.

Hood endeavored to carry out the plan. A. P. Stewart now had Polk's corps, and Cheatham took Hood's. Hardee on the right and Stewart on his left, in lines that overlapped Newton's position, at 3 o'clock of the 20th of July, struck the blow. They came surging on through the woods, down the gentle slope, with noise and fury like Stonewall Jackson's men at Chancellorsville. As to our men, some of them were protected by piles of rails, but the most had not had time to barricade.

Stewart's masses advanced successively from his right, so Newton was first assailed. His rifles and cannon, firing incessantly and with utmost steadiness, soon stopped and repulsed the front attack; but whole battalions went far east of him into the gap before described. Thomas, behind the creek, was watching; he turned some reserved batteries upon those Confederate battalions, and fired his shells into the thickets that bordered the deep creek, sweeping the creek's valley as far as the cannon could reach. This was sufficient; in his own words, "it relieved the hitch." The hostile flankers broke back in confusion. In succession, Ward, Geary, Williams, and Palmer received the on-coming waves, and though their ranks were shaken in places, they each made a strong resistance, and soon rolled the Confederates back, shattered and broken. Hardee would have resumed the assault, but an order from Hood took away a whole division (Cleburne's), for McPherson was too rapidly approaching Cheatham and the defenses of Atlanta from the east.

The battle of the 20th did not end till Gresham's division, on McPherson's left, had gone diagonally toward Atlanta, sweeping the hostile cavalry of Wheeler before it past the Augusta railroad, and skirmishing up against an open knob denominated Bald Hill. General Gresham, a fine officer, was severely wounded during his brisk movement. Wheeler had made a desperate and successful stand here, and soon after, in the evening, the division (Cleburne's) which was taken from Newton's sorely handled front was brought hither and put into the trenches, in order to make secure the right of Hood's line. The Bald Hill was an important outpost.

The 21st, a fearfully hot day, was spent by all in readjustment. Thomas brought his three corps forward, near to the enemy. The gap in my lines was closed as we neared the city. Schofield filled the space between the Fourth (mine) and Logan's corps. McPherson, to get a better left, ordered Blair to seize Bald Hill. General Force, of Leggett's division, supported by Giles A. Smith, who now had Gresham's place, charged the hill and carried it, though with a heavy loss. No time ran to waste till this point was manned with batteries protected by thick parapets and well secured by infantry supports.

Atlanta appeared to us like a well-fortified citadel with outer and inner works. After Thomas had beaten him, Hood resolved to give up the Peach Tree line; so, after dark, he drew back two corps into those outer works.

Hardee, however, was destined to a special duty. About midnight he gathered his four divisions into Atlanta: Bate led the way; Walker came next; Cleburne, having now left the vicinity of Bald Hill (for he was soon to go beyond it), followed; then came Maney in rear. They pushed out far south and around Gresham's sleeping soldiers; they kept on eastward till Hardee's advance was within two miles of Decatur, and his rear was nearly past Sherman's extreme left. There, facing north, he formed his battle front; then he halted on rough ground, mostly covered by forest and thicket. He had made a blind night-march of fifteen miles; so he rested his men for a sufficient time, when, slowly and confidently, the well-disciplined Confederates in line took up their forward movement. Success was never more assured, for was not Sherman's cavalry well out of the

SCENE OF GENERAL MCPHERSON'S DEATH, ON THE BATTLE-FIELD OF JULY 22.
FROM WAR-TIME PHOTOGRAPHS.

A 32-pounder cannon, set upon a granite block, now marks the spot of General McPherson's death. A large pine stands within a few feet of the monument, which faces a partly improved roadway that is called McPherson Avenue.

MAJOR-GENERAL JAMES B. MCPHERSON, KILLED JULY 22, 1864. FROM A PHOTOGRAPH.

way, breaking a railroad and burning bridges at and beyond Decatur? And thus far no Yankee except a chance prisoner had discovered this Jacksonian march! The morning showed us empty trenches from Bald Hill to the right of Thomas. We quickly closed again on Atlanta, skirmishing as we went. McPherson's left was, however, near enough already, only a single valley lying between Blair's position and the outer defensive works of the city. The Sixteenth Corps (Dodge), having sent a detachment under General Sprague to hold Decatur, to support the cavalry and take care of sundry army wagons,—a thing successfully accomplished,—had marched, on the 21st, toward Atlanta. Dodge remained for the night with head of column a mile or more in rear of Blair's general line. Fuller's division was nearest Blair's left, and Sweeny's not far from the Augusta railroad, farther to the north. McPherson spent the night with Sweeny. His hospitals and main supply trains were between Sweeny and the front. About midday McPherson, having determined to make a stronger left, had set Dodge's men in motion. They marched, as usual, by fours, and were in long column pursuing their way nearly parallel to Hardee's battle front, which was hidden by the thick trees. Now danger threatened: at the first skirmish shots Dodge's troops halted and faced to the left and were in good line of battle. The Confederate divisions were advancing; fortunately for Dodge, after the firing began Hardee's approaching lines nearing him had to cross some open fields. McPherson was then paying a brief visit to Sherman near the Howard house. The attack was sudden, but Dodge's veterans, not much disturbed, went bravely to their work. It is easy to imagine the loud roar of artillery and the angry sounds of musketry that came to Sherman and McPherson when the sudden assault culminated and extended from Dodge to Blair's left. McPherson mounted, and galloped off toward the firing. He first met Logan and Blair near the railway; then the three separated, each to hasten to his place on the battle-line. McPherson went at once to Dodge; saw matters going well there; sent off aides and orderlies with dispatches, till he had but a couple of men left with him. He then rode forward to pass to Blair's left through the thick forest interval. Cheatham's division was just approaching. The call was made, "Surrender!" But McPherson, probably without a thought save to escape from such a trap, turned his horse toward his command. He was instantly slain, and fell from his horse. One of his orderlies was wounded and captured; the other escaped to tell the sad news. Our reënforcements were on the way, so that Cheatham was beaten back. While the battle raged, McPherson's body was brought to Sherman at the Howard house. I wrote next day: "We were all made sad yesterday by the death of General McPherson,—so young, so noble, so promising, already commanding a department!" I closed my report concerning him thus: "His death occasioned a profound sense of loss, a feeling that his place can never be completely filled. How valuable, how precious the country to us all, who have paid for its preservation

BATTLE OF ATLANTA, JULY 22, 1864—THE CONTEST ON BALD HILL: FOURTH DIVISION, FIFTEENTH CORPS, IN THE FOREGROUND. FROM THE PANORAMA OF "ATLANTA."

such a price!" Logan immediately took the Army of the Tennessee, giving his corps to Morgan L. Smith. As soon as Hood, from a prominent point in front of Atlanta, beheld Hardee's lines emerging from the thickets of Bald Hill, and knew by the smoke and sound that the battle was fully joined, he hurried forward Cheatham's division to attack Logan all along the east front of Atlanta. At the time, I sat beside Schofield and Sherman near the Howard house, and we looked upon such parts of the battle as our glasses could compass. Before long we saw the line of Logan broken, with parts of two batteries in the enemy's hands. Sherman put in a cross-fire of cannon, a dozen or more, and Logan organized an attacking force that swept away the bold Confederates by a charge in double-time. Blair's soldiers repulsed the front attack of Cheatham's and Maney's divisions, and then, springing over their parapets, fought Bate's and Maney's men from the other side. The battle continued till night, when Hood again yielded the field to Sherman and withdrew. The losses on both sides in this battle of Atlanta were probably nearly even—about four thousand each. Our gain was in morale.

Sherman now drew his half-circle closer and closer, and began to manœuvre with a view to get upon the railways proceeding southward. The Army of the Tennessee (late McPherson's) was assigned to me by the President, and I took command on the 27th of July, while it was marching around by the rear of Schofield and Thomas, in order to throw itself forward close to Atlanta on the south-west side, near Ezra Church. Skirmishing briskly, Dodge was first put into line facing the city; next Blair, beside him; last, Logan, on the right, making a large angle with Blair. He was not at night quite up to the crest of the ridge that he was to occupy. In the morning of the 28th he was moving slowly and steadily into position. About 8 o'clock Sherman was riding with me through the wooded region in rear of Logan's forces, when the skirmishing began to increase, and an occasional shower of grape cut through the tree-tops and struck the ground beyond us. I said: "General, Hood will attack me here." "I guess not—he will hardly try it again," Sherman replied. I said that I had known Hood at West Point, and that he was indomitable. As the signs increased, Sherman went back to Thomas, where he could best help me should I need reënforcement. Logan halted his line, and the regiments hurriedly and partially covered their front with logs and rails, having only a small protection while kneeling or lying down. It was too late for intrenching. With a terrifying yell, Hood's men charged through the forest. They were met steadily and repulsed. But in the impulse a few Confederate regiments passed beyond Logan's extreme right. To withstand them four regiments came from Dodge; Inspector-General Strong led thither two from Blair, armed with repeating-rifles; and my chief-of-artillery placed several batteries so as to sweep that exposed flank. These were brought in at the exact moment, and after a few rapid discharges, the repeating-rifles being remarkable in their execution, all the groups of

MAJOR-GENERAL JOHN A. LOGAN. FROM A PHOTOGRAPH.

flankers were either cut down or had sought safety in flight. This battle was prolonged for hours. We expected help from Morgan's division of Palmer's corps,
coming back from Turner's Ferry; but the Confederate cavalry kept it in check.
Our troops here exhibited nerve and persistency; Logan was cheerful and
hearty and full of enthusiasm. He stopped stragglers and sent them back, and
gave every needed order. Blair was watchful and helpful, and so was Dodge.
After the last charge had been repelled I went along my lines, and felt proud
and happy to be intrusted with such brave and efficient soldiers. Hood, having
again lost three times as many as we, withdrew within his fortified lines. Our
skirmishers cleared the field, and the battle of Ezra Church was won; and with
this result I contented myself. One officer, who was a little panic-stricken, ran
with the first stragglers to Sherman, and cried substantially, as I remember,
"You've made a mistake in McPherson's successor. Everything is going to
pieces!" Sherman said, "Is General Howard there?" "Yes; I suppose he is." "Well,
I'll wait before taking action till I hear from him!" So Sherman sustained and
trusted me, and I was content. Of General Logan, who has so recently gone
from us, I wrote, after this battle:

> "Major-General Logan was spirited and energetic, going at once to the
> point where he apprehended the slightest danger of the enemy's success.
> His decision and resolution animated and encouraged his officers and
> men to hold on at all hazards."

For a month Hood kept to a defensive attitude, and, like a long storm, the
siege operations set in. Sherman worked his right, with block after block, eastward and southward. Schofield and part of Thomas's command had passed beyond me, digging as they halted. Every new trench found a fresh one opposite.
The lines were near together. Many officers and men were slain and many were
wounded and sent back to the hospitals. Dodge, while reconnoitering, was
badly hurt; T.E.G. Ransom took his corps, and J. M. Corse a division in it.

Hooker, already vexed at Sherman, was incensed at my assignment, resigned, and went home. Slocum came from Vicksburg to command the Twentieth Corps. Palmer, having a controversy concerning his seniority, left the
Fourteenth Corps, and Jeff. C. Davis took his place. Hazen passed from a
brigade in the Fourth (Stanley's) to M. L. Smith's division of Logan's corps. F. P.
Blair, in a report, condensed the work of his corps in these words: "The command was occupied for 28 days in making approaches, digging rifle-pits, and
erecting batteries, being subjected day and night to a galling fire of artillery and
musketry."

Sherman now having his supplies well up, beginning on the night of the
25th of August, intrenched Slocum's strong corps across his railroad communi-

THE BATTLE OF EZRA CHURCH, JULY 28, 1864. FROM A SKETCH MADE AT THE TIME.

cation to defend it; then made another grand wheel of his armies. Schofield this time clung to the pivot. My command described an arc of 25 miles radius aiming at Jonesboro', while Thomas followed the middle course. Both southern railways were to be seized, and the stations and road destroyed.

Preceded by Kilpatrick, we made the march rapidly enough, considering the endless plague of the enemy's horse artillery supported by Wheeler's cavalry, and the time it took us to break up the West Point railroad. At Renfro Place we were to encamp on the night of the 30th of August. Finding no water there, and also hoping to secure the Flint River Bridge, six miles ahead, I called to Kilpatrick for a squadron. He sent me a most energetic young man, Captain Estes, and the horsemen needed. I asked Estes if he could keep the enemy in motion. He gave a sanguine reply, and galloped off at the head of his men. Wheeler's rear-guard was surprised, and hurried toward the river. Hazen's infantry followed, forgetting their fatigue in the excitement of pursuit. We reached the bridge as it was burning, extinguished the fire, crossed over in the dusk of the evening under an increasing fire from hostile cavalry and infantry, but did not stop till Logan had reached the wooded ridge beyond, near Jonesboro'. The command was soon put into position, and worked all night and during the next morning to intrench, and build the required bridges. Hood had sent Hardee by rail, with perhaps half of his command, to hold Jonesboro'. My Confederate classmate, S. D. Lee, who had had the immediate assault at Ezra Church, here appeared again, commanding Cheatham's corps. At 3 P.M. on the 31st the Confederates came on with the usual vigor, but were met by Logan and Ransom, and thoroughly repulsed. Hood now abandoned Atlanta, and united with

MAJOR-GENERAL JOHN M. CORSE,
WHO "HELD THE FORT" AT ALLATOONA.
FROM A PHOTOGRAPH.

Hardee in the vicinity of Jonesboro', near Lovejoy's Station. Thomas, joining my left flank, fought mainly the battle of September 1st. During the rest that followed, Blair and Logan went home on leave of absence; the field-force of the Army of the Tennessee was consolidated into two corps, Osterhaus temporarily commanding the Fifteenth, and Ransom the Seventeenth. Thomas went to Chattanooga to defend the communications with Sherman's army. Wagner's division was sent to Chattanooga, and Corse's division to Rome. Colonel John E. Tourtellotte had a detachment garrisoning the works at Allatoona Pass.

Hood had been threatening for some time to break Sherman's long line of communication and supply. Sherman could not divine where the blow would fall. He was already arranging for a campaign southward; but he wanted Grant's formal sanction, and he wished to make proper provision for Hood.

At last, on the 2d of October, Hood had passed on his way back beyond the Chattahoochee. Sherman had waited for this till he was sure that the first attempt against his line would be south of the Etowah. Now, leaving one corps, Slocum's, at Atlanta, he followed Hood with the remainder of his force. Hood stopped near Dallas, and sent French's division to take the garrison of Allatoona and the depots there. From the top of Kenesaw, Sherman communicated with Corse,‡ who had joined Tourtellotte at Allatoona, and taken command. The

‡On the 4th of October General John M. Corse, commanding the Fourth Division, Fifteenth Corps, stationed in observation at Rome, Georgia, was ordered by General Sherman to move by railway to Allatoona to assist the garrison at that point against a heavy force of Hood's army, which was moving north from Kenesaw Mountain. With a part of his command Corse reached Allatoona at 1 A.M. on the 5th. The battle which took place that day is described in his report as follows:

"The ammunition being unloaded, and the train sent back [to Rome] for reënforcements, accompanied by Colonel Tourtellotte, the post commandant. I rode around and inspected the ground and made such disposition of the troops as, in my judgment, was necessary to hold the place until daylight. I then learned from Colonel Tourtellotte that the garrison embraced the 4th Minnesota infantry, 450 men, Major J. C. Edson commanding; 93d Illinois infantry, 230 men, Major Fisher commanding; seven companies 18th Wisconsin infantry, 150 men, Lieutenant-Colonel Jackson commanding; 12th Wisconsin battery, six guns, Lieutenant Amaden commanding—furnishing a force of 890 men, commanded by Lieutenant-Colonel

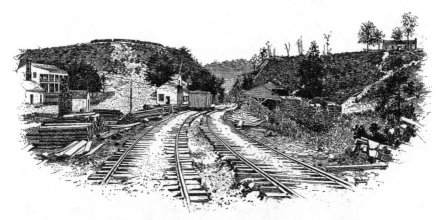

ALLATOONA PASS, LOOKING NORTH—CORSE'S FORT ON THE LEFT.
FROM A WAR-TIME PHOTOGRAPH.

popular hymn, "Hold the Fort," was based upon the messages between these chiefs and the noble defense that the garrison successfully made against a whole Confederate division. Sherman was coming, and French, several times repulsed with great loss, withdrew and joined Hood at New Hope Church.

Taking up his northward march, Hood avoided Rome and aimed for Resaca. Schofield was warned, and got ready to defend Chattanooga, while Sherman now made forced marches so as to overtake his enemy and force him to battle. Finding us on his heels, Hood, picking up two or three small garrisons,

---

J. E. Tourtellotte, 4th Minnesota Volunteer infantry. I took with me, of Rowett's brigade of this division, eight companies 39th Iowa infantry, 290 men, Lieutenant-Colonel James Redfield commanding; nine companies 7th Illinois infantry, 291 men, Lieutenant-Colonel Hector Perrin commanding; eight companies 50th Illinois infantry, 267 men, Lieut.-Colonel Wm. Hanna commanding; two companies 57th Illinois infantry, 61 men, Captain Vanstienburg commanding; detachment 12th Illinois, Adams brigade, 150 men, Capt. Koehler commanding; total, 1054—making an aggregate of 1944.... Under a brisk cannonade, kept up for near two hours, with sharp skirmishing on our south front and our west flank, the enemy pushed a brigade of infantry around north of us, cut the railroad and telegraph, severing our communications with Cartersville and Rome. The cannonading and musketry had not ceased when, at half-past 8 A.M., I received by flag of truce, which came from the north on the Cartersville road, the following summons to surrender:

" 'Around Allatoona, October 5th, 1864.
" 'Commanding Officer United States Forces, Allatoona.
" 'Sir: I have placed the forces under my command in such positions that you are surrounded, and to avoid a needless effusion of blood I call on you to surrender your forces at once and unconditionally. Five minutes will be allowed you to decide. Should you accede to this you will be treated in the most honorable manner as prisoners of war. I have the honor to be, very respectfully yours,

" 'S. G. French,
" 'Major-General Commanding Forces, Confederate States.'

THE BATTLE OF ALLATOONA, OCTOBER 5, 1864, FROM "THE MOUNTAIN CAMPAIGNS IN GEORGIA, OR WAR SCENES ON THE W.&A.," PUBLISHED BY THE WESTERN & ATLANTIC R.R. CO.

BREVET MAJOR-GENERAL T.E.G. RANSOM.
FROM A PHOTOGRAPH.

"To which I made the following reply:

" 'HEADQUARTERS, FOURTH DIVISION, FIFTEENTH ARMY CORPS, ALLATOONA, GEOR-
GIA, 8:30 A.M., OCTOBER 5TH, 1864.
" 'MAJOR-GENERAL S. G. FRENCH, Confederate States Army, etc.:

" 'Your communication demanding surrender of my command I acknowledge receipt
of, and respectfully reply that we are prepared for the "needless effusion of blood"
whenever it is agreeable to you. I am, very respectfully, your obedient servant,

" 'JOHN M. CORSE,
" 'Brigadier-General Commanding Forces, United States.'

"I then hastened to my different commands, informing them of the object of the flag, etc.,
my answer, and the importance and necessity of their preparing for hard fighting.... I had
hardly issued the incipient orders when the storm broke in all its fury.... The fighting up
to...about 11 A.M. was of the most extraordinary character.... About 1 P.M. I was wounded
by a rifle-ball, which rendered me insensible for some thirty or forty minutes, but managed
to rally on hearing some person or persons cry, 'Cease firing,' which conveyed to me the impression that they were trying to surrender the fort. Again I urged my staff, the few officers
left unhurt, and the men around me to renewed exertions, assuring them that Sherman
would soon be there with reënforcements. The gallant fellows struggled to keep their heads

above the ditch and parapet, had the advantage of the enemy, and maintained it with such success that they [the Confederates] were driven from every position, and finally fled in confusion, leaving the dead and wounded and our little garrison in possession of the field."...

Corse's entire loss, officially reported, was:

Garrison.	Killed.	Wounded.	Missing.	Total.
Officers	6	23	6	35
Men	136	330	206	672
Total	142	353	212	707

General Sherman, in his "Memoirs," says:

"We crossed the Chattahoochee River during the 3d and 4th of October, rendezvoused at the old battle-field of Smyrna Camp, and the next day reached Marietta and Kenesaw. The telegraph wires had been cut above Marietta, and learning that heavy masses of infantry, artillery, and cavalry had been seen from Kenesaw (marching north), I inferred that Allatoona was their objective point; and on the 4th of October I signaled from Vining's Station to Kenesaw, and from Kenesaw to Allatoona, over the heads of the enemy, a message for General Corse at Rome, to hurry back to the assistance of the garrison at Allatoona.... Reaching Kenesaw Mountain about 8 A.M. of October 5th (a beautiful day), I had a superb view of the vast panorama to the north and west. To the south-west, about Dallas, could be seen the smoke of camp-fires, indicating the presence of a large force of the enemy, and the whole line of railroad, from Big Shanty up to Allatoona (full fifteen miles), was marked by the fires of the burning railroad. We could plainly see the smoke of battle about Allatoona, and hear the faint reverberation of the cannon. From Kenesaw I ordered the Twenty-third Corps (General Cox) to march due west on the Burnt Hickory road, and to burn houses or piles of brush as it progressed, to indicate the head of column, hoping to interpose this corps between Hood's main army at Dallas and the detachment then assailing Allatoona. The rest of the army was directed straight for Allatoona, north-west, distant eighteen miles. The signal-officer on Kenesaw reported that since daylight he had failed to obtain any answer to his call for Allatoona; but, while I was with him, he caught a faint glimpse of the tell-tale flag through an embrasure, and after much time he made out these letters: 'C,' 'R,' 'S,' 'E,' 'H,' 'E,' 'R,' and translated the message, 'Corse is here.' It was a source of great relief, for it gave me the first assurance that General Corse had received his orders, and that the place was adequately garrisoned. I watched with painful suspense the indications of the battle raging there, and was dreadfully impatient at the slow progress of the relieving column, whose advance was marked by the smokes which were made according to orders, but about 2 P.M. I noticed with satisfaction that the smoke of battle about Allatoona grew less and less, and ceased altogether about 4 P.M. For a time I attributed this result to the effect of General Cox's march, but later in the afternoon the signal-flag announced the welcome tidings that the attack had been fairly repulsed, but that General Corse was wounded. The next day my aide, Colonel Dayton, received this characteristic dispatch:

" 'ALLATOONA, GEORGIA, OCTOBER 6TH, 1864, 2 P.M.
" 'CAPTAIN L. M. DAYTON, Aide-de-Camp:

" 'I am short a cheek-bone and an ear, but am able to whip all h——l yet! My losses are very heavy. A force moving from Stilesboro' to Kingston gives me some anxiety. Tell me where Sherman is.

" 'JOHN M. CORSE, Brigadier-General.

"Inasmuch as the enemy had retreated south-west, and would probably next appear at Rome, I answered General Corse with orders to get back to Rome with his troops as quickly as possible...."

but leaving untouched those that showed great pluck, like that of the resolute Colonel Clark R. Wever at Resaca,☦ rushed through Sugar Valley and Snake Creek Gap, choking it behind him with trees. My command, following rapidly through the pass (October 16th), cut away or threw the gap obstructions to the right and left, and camped close up to Hood's rear-guard. He again refused battle, and we pursued him beyond Gaylesville, Alabama. Between Rome and Gaylesville, General Ransom, the gallant and promising young officer before mentioned, died from over-work and exposure due to our forced marches. Taking advantage of a rich country, Sherman recuperated his men and moved slowly back to the Chattahoochee. Now, with the full consent of Grant, he hastened his preparations for his grand march to the sea.

"I esteemed this defense of Allatoona so handsome and important that I made it the subject of a general order, viz., No. 86, of October 7th, 1864:

"'The general commanding avails himself of the opportunity, in the handsome defense made at Allatoona, to illustrate the most important principle in war, that fortified posts should be defended to the last, regardless of the relative numbers of the party attacking and attacked.... The thanks of this army are due and are hereby accorded to General Corse, Colonel Tourtellotte, Colonel Rowett, officers, and men, for their determined and gallant defense of Allatoona, and it is made an example to illustrate the importance of preparing in time, and meeting the danger, when present, boldly, manfully, and well.

"'Commanders and garrisons of the posts along our railroad are hereby instructed that they must hold their posts to the last minute, sure that the time gained is valuable and necessary to their comrades at the front. By order of

"'MAJOR-GENERAL W. T. SHERMAN.

"'L. M. DAYTON, Aide-de-camp.'"

—EDITORS.

☦Hood had partly invested Resaca, and on the 12th of October he demanded the unconditional surrender of the garrison, which the commander, Colonel Wever, refused, saying, "In my opinion I can hold the post. If you want it, come and take it."—EDITORS.

CHAPTER 10

FARRAGUT AT MOBILE BAY.[†]

John Coddington Kinney, First Lieutenant, 13th Connecticut
Infantry, and Acting Signal Officer, U.S.A.

After the Mississippi was opened in July, 1863, by the capture of Vicksburg and the consequent surrender of Port Hudson, Admiral Farragut devoted a large share of his attention to the operations against Mobile Bay. He was aware that the Confederates were actively engaged in the construction of rams and iron-clads at Mobile and above, and it was his earnest desire to force the entrance into Mobile Bay and capture the forts that guarded it, before the more power-ful of the new vessels could be finished and brought down to aid in the defense. In January, 1864, he made a reconnoissance of Forts Gaines and Morgan, at which time no Confederate vessels were in the lower bay, except one transport. In letters to the Navy Department he urged that at least one iron-clad be sent to help his wooden fleet, and asked for the coöperation of a brigade of five thou-sand soldiers to enable him, after running into the bay, to reduce the forts at his leisure. It is easy to see now the wisdom of his plan. Had the operations against Mobile been undertaken promptly, as he desired, the entrance into the bay would have been effected with much less cost of men and materials, Mobile would have been captured a year earlier than it was, and the Union cause would have been saved the disaster of the Red River campaign of 1864. At this late day it is but justice to Farragut to admit the truth.

His position at the time was one of great anxiety. He saw the ease with which the forts could be captured if a few thousand troops could be obtained to coöperate with his fleet. He knew that the Confederates were bending all their energies to the construction of three or more powerful rams, to meet which he had until late in the summer nothing but wooden vessels. Every day was strengthening the Confederate situation and making his own position more

---

[†]Based upon the author's paper in "The Century" for May, 1881, entitled "An August Morning with Far-ragut," revised and extended for the present work.—EDITORS.

"GALENA"   "ITASCA."

THE "BROOKLYN" AFTER THE BATTLE OF MOBILE. FROM A SKETCH MADE AT THE TIME.

perilous. With the necessary coöperation he would run inside the bay, prevent any iron-clads from crossing Dog River bar (over which they had to be floated with "camels"), put a stop to the planting of torpedoes, effectually prevent blockade-running, and easily capture the garrisons of the forts.

But, much to his regret, the army under General Banks started up the Red River, and he was left alone with his little fleet to watch the operations he could not prevent. At last, about May 20th, the great ram *Tennessee* made her appearance in the lower bay. Just before she arrived, and when it was known that Admiral Buchanan was engaged in efforts to float the ram over the bar, eight miles up the bay, Farragut wrote to Secretary Welles:

> "I fully understand and appreciate my situation. The experience I had of the fight between the *Arkansas* and Admiral Davis's vessels on the Mississippi showed plainly how unequal the contest is between iron-clads and wooden vessels, in loss of life, unless you succeed in destroying the iron-clad. I therefore deeply regret that the department has not been able to give me *one* of the many iron-clads that are off Charleston and in the Mississippi. I have always looked for the latter, but it appears that it takes us twice as long to build an iron-clad as any one else. It looks as if the contractors and the fates were against us. While the rebels are bending their whole energies to the war our people are expecting the war to close by default; and if they do not awake to a sense of their danger soon it will be so. But be assured, sir, that the navy will do its duty, let the issue come when it may, or I am greatly deceived."

A few days later the *Tennessee* came down and anchored near Fort Morgan. From that time until the battle was fought, Farragut never left the *Hartford* except when making inspections. It was expected that the rebel admiral would attack the blockading fleet before the iron-clads arrived, and Farragut made his preparations accordingly, even arranging extemporized torpedoes to place himself in this respect on a par with the enemy. This he did very reluctantly, writing on May 25th:

> "Torpedoes are not so agreeable when used on both sides; therefore, I have reluctantly brought myself to it. I have always deemed it unworthy a chivalrous nation, but it does not do to give your enemy such a decided superiority over you."

In the same letter he speaks of the discouraging news just received of Banks's defeat, and adds:

> "I see by the rebel papers Buchanan is advertised to raise the blockade as soon as he is ready. As I have before informed the department, if I had the military force ... and one or two iron-clads, I would not hesitate to run in and attack him; but if I were to run in and in so doing get my vessels crippled, it would be in his power to retire to the shoal water with his iron-clads (in fact, all their vessels draw much less water than ours), and thus destroy us without our being able to get at him. But if he takes the offensive and comes out of port, I hope to be able to contend with him. The department has not yet responded to my call for the iron-clads in the Mississippi."

After the Red River disaster, General Grant decided that the majority of the fighting men of the army could be used to better advantage in Virginia, and the force in the Department of the Gulf was largely reduced. It was not until the latter part of July, 1864, that General Canby could make his arrangements to coöperate with Farragut at Mobile Bay. On the 3d of August a division of troops, under General Gordon Granger, landed on the west end of Dauphine Island and began preparations for a siege of Fort Gaines. Meantime, also, three monitors had arrived and a fourth was daily expected, and at last the time, for which Admiral Farragut had so long been praying, arrived.

On the morning of August 4th a detachment of army signal officers, under command of the late Major Frank W. Marston, arrived by tug from New Orleans. They were distributed among the principal vessels of the fleet, for the purpose of communicating with General Granger's force after the entrance into the bay had been effected, and it was the good fortune of the writer to be

THE "RICHMOND" AND THE "LACKAWANNA" STRIPPED FOR THE FIGHT.
FROM A WAR-TIME SKETCH.

assigned to duty on the *Hartford*. In the afternoon of the same day Admiral Farragut, with the commanding officers of the different vessels, made a reconnoissance on the steam-tender *Cowslip*, running inside of Sand Island, where the
three monitors were anchored, and within easy range of both the forts. On the
left, some three miles distant, was Fort Gaines, a small brick and earth work,
mounting a few heavy guns, but too far away from the ship channel to cause
much uneasiness to the fleet. Fort Morgan was on the right, one of the strongest
of the old brick forts, and greatly strengthened by immense piles of sand-bags,
covering every portion of the exposed front. The fort was well equipped with
three tiers of heavy guns, one of the guns, at least, of the best English make, imported by the Confederates. In addition, there was in front a battery of seven
powerful guns, at the water's edge on the beach. All the guns, of both fort and
water-battery, were within point-blank range of the only channel through
which the fleet could pass. The Confederates considered the works impregnable, but they did not depend solely upon them. Just around the point of land,
behind Fort Morgan, we could see that afternoon three saucy-looking gun-
boats and the famous ram *Tennessee*. The latter was then considered the
strongest and most powerful iron-clad ever put afloat. She looked like a great
turtle; her sloping sides were covered with iron plates six inches in thickness,
thoroughly riveted together, and she had a formidable iron beak projecting
under the water. Her armament consisted of six heavy Brooke rifles, each sending a solid shot weighing from 95 to 110 pounds—a small affair compared with
the heavy guns of the present time, but irresistible then against everything but
the turrets of the monitors. In addition to these means of resistance, the narrow
channel to within a few hundred yards of the shore had been lined with torpedoes. These were under the water, anchored to the bottom. Some of them were

FORT MORGAN. FROM WAR-TIME PHOTOGRAPHS.
1. Light-house, Mobile Point. 2. The south-east bastion. 3. The citadel, from the north side.

beer-kegs filled with powder, from the sides of which projected numerous little tubes containing fulminate, which it was expected would be exploded by contact with the passing vessels, but the greater part were tin cones fitted with caps.

Except for what Farragut had already accomplished on the Mississippi, it would have been considered a foolhardy experiment for wooden vessels to attempt to pass so close to one of the strongest forts on the coast; but when to the forts were added the knowledge of the strength of the ram and the supposed deadly character of the torpedoes, it may be imagined that the coming event impressed the person taking his first glimpse of naval warfare as decidedly hazardous and unpleasant. So daring an attempt was never made in any country but ours, and was never successfully made by any commander except Farragut, who, in this, as in his previous exploits in passing the forts of the Mississippi, proved himself one of the greatest naval commanders the world has ever seen. It was the confidence reposed in him, the recollection that he had not failed in his former attempts, and his manifest faith in the success of the projected movement, that inspired all around him.

The scene on the *Cowslip* that afternoon of the 4th of August was a notable one, as she steamed within range of the forts. The central figure was the grand old admiral, his plans all completed, affable with all, evidently not thinking of failure as among the possibilities of the morrow, and filling every one with his enthusiasm. He was sixty-three years old, of medium height, stoutly built, with a finely proportioned head and smoothly shaven face, with an expression combining overflowing kindliness with iron will and invincible determination, and with eyes that in repose were full of sweetness and light, but, in emergency, could flash fire and fury.

Next in prominence to the admiral was the tall, commanding form of Fleet-Captain Percival Drayton, the man of all men to be Farragut's chief-of-staff, gentlemanly and courteous to all, but thoughtful and reserved, a man of marked intellect and power, in whose death, a few years later, our navy lost one of its very brightest stars, and the cause of liberty and human rights a most devoted friend. I have digressed to this extent to pay my humble tribute to one of the bravest and most patriotic men I ever met, and to a native South Carolinian of bluest blood, and proud of his ancestry, who in his love of country had learned to look beyond State lines and to disregard the ties of kinship.

As we steamed slowly along inside Sand Island, inspecting every hostile point, a Confederate transport landed at Fort Gaines, and began discharging cargo. At a signal from the admiral, one of the monitors, by way of practice, opened fire at long range, and, as the huge fifteen-inch shell dropped uncomfortably near, the work of unloading was stopped, and the transport suddenly left—the last Confederate transport that ever crossed the bay.

After the reconnoissance the final council of war was held on board the *Hartford*, when the positions of the various vessels were assigned, and the order of the line was arranged. Unfortunately Captain (now Rear-Admiral) Thornton A. Jenkins was absent, his vessel, the *Richmond*, having been unavoidably delayed at Pensacola, whither she had gone for coal and to escort the monitor *Tecumseh*. Had he been present he certainly would have been selected to take the lead, in which event the perilous halt of the next day would not have occurred. Much against his own wish Admiral Farragut yielded to the unanimous advice of his

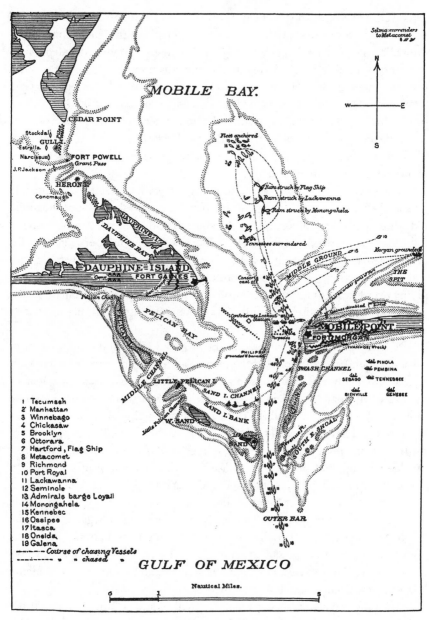

NOTE.—The *Tecumseh*, the leading monitor, moved from the position shown on the map under Fort Morgan, to the left toward the right of the line marked "Torpedoes," where she was blown up. The distance traversed by the *Metacomet*, after casting off from the *Hartford* and until she came up with the *Selma*, is estimated by Admiral Jouett at nine miles. The time elapsed, as noted in the various reports, sustains this estimate. Owing to the limited size of the page, the map fails to show this distance, but it indicates the direction of the course of the gun-boats. The capture of the *Selma*, as well as the grounding of the *Morgan*, occurred some distance to the north-east of the edge of the map.—EDITORS.

captains and gave up his original determination of placing his flagship in the advance, and, in the uncertainty as to the arrival of the *Richmond,* assigned the *Brooklyn,* Captain Alden, to that position.⊕

A few hours later, just before sunset, the *Richmond* arrived with the *Tecumseh,* and the cause of her delay was satisfactorily explained, but the admiral decided to make no change in the order of the line, which was settled upon as follows: *Brooklyn* and *Octorara, Hartford* and *Metacomet, Richmond* and *Port Royal, Lackawanna* and *Seminole, Monongahela* and *Kennebec, Ossipee* and *Itasca, Oneida* and *Galena.* The first-named of each pair was on the starboard or more exposed side.

The four monitors were to go a little in advance, and on the right flank of the wooden vessels. The *Tecumseh* and *Manhattan* were single-turreted, each with two 15-inch guns. The *Winnebago* and *Chickasaw* were of lighter draught, with two turrets each, and four 11-inch guns.

Before attempting to narrate the events of the next day, it may be well to give an idea of the situation. Mobile Bay gradually widens from the city to the gulf, a distance of thirty miles. The entrance is protected by a long, narrow arm of sand, with Fort Morgan on the extreme western point. Across the channel from Fort Morgan, and perhaps three miles distant, is Dauphine Island, a narrow strip of sand with Fort Gaines at its eastern end. Further to the west is little Fort Powell, commanding a narrow channel through which light-draught vessels could enter the bay. Between Dauphine Island and Fort Morgan, and in front of the main entrance to the bay, is Sand Island, a barren spot, under the lee of which three of our monitors were lying. The army signal officers were sent on board the fleet, not with any intention of having their services used in passing the forts, but in order to establish communication afterward between the fleet and the army, for the purpose of coöperating in the capture of the forts. The primary objects of Admiral Farragut in entering the bay were to close Mobile to the outside world, to capture or destroy the *Tennessee,* and to cut off all possible means of escape from the garrisons of the forts. Incidentally, also, he desired to secure the moral effect of a victory, and to give his fleet, which had been tossed on the uneasy waters of the Gulf for many months, a safe and quiet anchorage. There was no immediate expectation of capturing the city of Mobile, which was safe by reason of a solid row of piles and torpedoes across the river, three miles below the city. Moreover, the larger vessels of the fleet could not approach within a dozen miles of the city, on account of shallow water. But the lower bay offered a charming resting-place for the fleet, with the additional attraction of plenty of fish and oysters, and an occasional chance to forage on shore.

At sunset the last orders had been issued, every commander knew his duty,

⊕According to Admiral Farragut's report the *Brooklyn* was appointed to lead, because she had four chase-guns and apparatus for picking up torpedoes.—EDITORS.

and unusual quiet prevailed in the fleet. The sea was smooth, a gentle breeze relieved the midsummer heat, and the night came on serenely and peacefully, and far more quietly than to a yachting fleet at Newport. For the first hour after the candles were lighted below the stillness was almost oppressive. The officers of the *Hartford* gathered around the ward-room table, writing letters to loved ones far away, or giving instructions in case of death. As brave and thoughtful men, they recognized the dangers that they did not fear, and made provision for the possibilities of the morrow. But this occupied little time, and then, business over, there followed an hour of unrestrained jollity. Many an old story was retold and ancient conundrum repeated. Old officers forgot, for the moment, their customary dignity, and it was evident that all were exhilarated and stimulated by the knowledge of the coming struggle. There was no other "stimulation," for the strict naval rules prevented. Finally, after a half-hour's smoke under the forecastle, all hands turned in. The scene on the flag-ship was representative of the night before the battle throughout the fleet.

It was the admiral's desire and intention to get under way by daylight, to take advantage of the inflowing tide; but a dense fog came on after midnight and delayed the work of forming line.

It was a weird sight as the big ships "balanced to partners," the dim outlines slowly emerging like phantoms in the fog. The vessels were lashed together in pairs, fastened side by side by huge cables. All the vessels had been stripped for the fight, the top-hamper being left at Pensacola, and the starboard boats being

FORT GAINES.   "ONEIDA."   "ITASCA."   "CHICKASAW."   FORT MORGAN.
"GALENA."   "OSSIPEE."   "TENNESSEE."

THE BATTLE OF MOBILE. FROM A WAR-TIME SKETCH.

either left behind or towed on the port side. The admiral's steam-launch, the *Loyall*, named after his son,⁺ steamed alongside the flag-ship on the port side.

It was a quarter of six o'clock before the fleet was in motion. Meantime a light breeze had scattered the fog and left a clear, sunny August day. The line moved slowly, and it was an hour after starting before the opening gun was fired. This was a 15-inch shell from the *Tecumseh,* and it exploded over Fort Morgan. Half an hour afterward the fleet came within range and the firing from the starboard vessels became general, the fort and the Confederate fleet replying. The fleet took position across the entrance to the bay and raked the advance vessels fore and aft, doing great damage, to which it was for a time impossible to make effective reply. Gradually the fleet came into close quarters with Fort Morgan, and the firing on both sides became terrific. The wooden vessels moved more rapidly than the monitors, and as the *Brooklyn* came opposite the fort, and approached the torpedo line, she came nearly alongside the rear monitor. To have kept on would have been to take the lead, with the ram *Tennessee* approaching and with the unknown danger of the torpedoes underneath. At this critical moment the *Brooklyn* halted and began backing and signaling with the army signals. The *Hartford* was immediately behind and the following vessels were in close proximity, and the sudden stopping of the *Brooklyn* threatened to bring the whole fleet into collision, while the strong inflowing tide was likely to carry some of the vessels to the shore under the guns of the fort.

On the previous night the admiral had issued orders that the army signal officers were not to be allowed on deck during the fight, but were to go into the cockpit, on the lower deck, and assist the surgeons. The reason assigned was that these officers would not be needed during the passage of the forts, but would be wanted afterward to open communication with the army, and that therefore it would be a misfortune to have any of them disabled. The two army signal officers on the *Hartford* disrelished this order exceedingly, and, after consulting together, decided that in the confusion of the occasion their presence on deck would probably not be noticed, and that they would evade the command if possible. In this they were successful until shortly before passing Sand Island and coming within range of Fort Morgan. Then the executive officer, Lieutenant-Commander Lewis A. Kimberly, who never allowed anything to escape his attention, came to them very quietly and politely, and told them the admiral's order must be obeyed. We were satisfied from his manner that the surgeons had need of us, and, without endeavoring to argue the matter, made our way to the stifling hold, where Surgeon Lansdale and Assistant-Surgeon Commons, with their helpers, were sitting, with their paraphernalia spread out ready for use.

Nearly every man had his watch in his hand awaiting the first shot. To us, ignorant of everything going on above, every minute seemed an hour, and there

⁺Mrs. Farragut's maiden name was Loyall.—EDITORS.

"TENNESSEE."   "HARTFORD." "BROOKLYN."   SAND ISLAND LIGHT.
        FORT MORGAN.

THE BATTLE OF MOBILE, LOOKING SOUTH AND EASTWARD. FROM A WAR-TIME SKETCH.

was a feeling of great relief when the boom of the *Tecumseh*'s first gun was heard. Presently one or two of our forward guns opened, and we could hear the distant sound of the guns of the fort in reply. Soon the cannon-balls began to crash through the deck above us, and then the thunder of our whole broadside of nine Dahlgren guns kept the vessel in a quiver. But as yet no wounded were sent down, and we knew we were still at comparatively long range. In the intense excitement of the occasion it seemed that hours had passed, but it was just twenty minutes from the time we went below, when an officer shouted down the hatchway: "Send up an army signal officer immediately; the *Brooklyn* is signaling." In a moment the writer was on deck, where he found the situation as already described. Running on to the forecastle, he hastily took the *Brooklyn*'s message, which imparted the unnecessary information, "The monitors are right ahead; we cannot go on without passing them." The reply was sent at once from the admiral, "Order the monitors ahead and go on." But still the *Brooklyn* halted, while, to add to the horror of the situation, the monitor *Tecumseh,* a few hundred yards in the advance, suddenly careened to one side and almost instantly sank to the bottom, carrying with her Captain Tunis A. M. Craven and the greater part of his crew, numbering in all 114 officers and men.▮ The pilot, John Collins,

---

▮In Farragut's Supplementary General Order (No. 11) of July 29th, occurs the following:

"There are certain black buoys placed by the enemy from the piles on the west side of the channel across it towards Fort Morgan. It being understood that there are torpedoes and

and a few men who were in the turret jumped into the water and were rescued by a boat from the *Metacomet,* which, under charge of Acting Ensign Henry C. Nields, rowed up under the guns of the fort and through a deadly storm of shot and shell and picked them up./ Meantime the *Brooklyn* failed to go ahead, and the whole fleet became a stationary point-blank target for the guns of Fort Morgan and of the rebel vessels. It was during these few perilous moments that the most fatal work of the day was done to the fleet.

Owing to the *Hartford*'s position, only her few bow guns could be used, while a deadly rain of shot and shell was falling on her, and her men were being cut down by scores, unable to make reply. The sight on deck was sickening beyond the power of words to portray. Shot after shot came through the side, mowing down the men, deluging the decks with blood, and scattering mangled fragments of humanity so thickly that it was difficult to stand on the deck, so slippery was it. The old expressions of the "scuppers running blood," "the slippery deck," etc., give but the faintest idea of the spectacle on the *Hartford.* The bodies of the dead were placed in a long row on the port side, while the

---

other obstructions between the buoys, the vessels will take care to pass eastward of the easternmost buoy, which is clear of all obstructions."

The easternmost buoy was the famous red buoy which figures in all accounts of the battle. As the fleet approached, the *Tennessee* was lying in the rear of the torpedo obstructions, and therefore to the westward of the red buoy. When Craven, in the *Tecumseh,* drew near to the buoy, influenced by the narrowness of the channel to the eastward, as his remark to the pilot would indicate (Mahan, "Gulf and Inland Waters," p. 231), or by a desire to get at the *Tennessee* more quickly, as Parker suggests ("Battle of Mobile Bay," p. 26), he disregarded the instructions, and, shaping his course to the westward of the buoy, struck the torpedoes. His course crowded the main column to the westward, and left no choice to Alden and the fleet following in his wake, but to pass over the obstructions also. Of 114 officers and men on board the *Tecumseh,* 21 were saved. Of these two officers and five men escaped in one of the *Tecumseh*'s boats, four swam to Fort Morgan where they were made prisoners, and ten, including Ensign Zettick and John Collins, the pilot, were rescued by Acting-Ensign Nields. It is to the statement of Collins that the world is indebted for the account of that heroic act which will forever be associated with Craven's name. Commodore Parker thus tells the story:

"Craven and Mr. John Collins, the pilot of the *Tecumseh,* met, as their vessel was sinking beneath them, at the foot of the ladder leading to the top of the turret.... It may be, then, that Craven, in the nobility of his soul,—for all know he was one of nature's noble men,—it may be, I say, that, in the nobility of his soul, the thought flashed across him that it was through no fault of his pilot that the *Tecumseh* was in this peril; he drew back. 'After you, pilot,' said he, grandly. 'There was nothing after me,' relates Mr. Collins; 'when I reached the upmost round of the ladder, the vessel seemed to drop from under me.'"

—Editors.

/The gallantry of Nields's conduct was all the more striking in view of the fact that in pulling to the *Tecumseh*'s wreck it was necessary to pass around the stern and under the broadside of the *Hartford* and across the *Brooklyn*'s bow, thus placing the boat directly in the line of fire of the fleet as well as of the fort. In fact, as the boat at first carried no flag, Acting Ensign Whiting, in charge of the forecastle guns on board the *Hartford,* was about to fire at her, when some one standing by informed him of her character and errand. A moment later, Nields himself observed the omission, and took the flag from its case and shipped it. The rescued men were placed on board the *Winnebago,* and Nields and his boat's crew, unable to regain their ship, joined the *Oneida,* where they served during the remainder of the battle.—Editors.

wounded were sent below until the surgeons' quarters would hold no more. A solid shot coming through the bow struck a gunner on the neck, completely severing head from body. One poor fellow (afterward an object of interest at the great Sanitary Commission Fair in New York) lost both legs by a cannon-ball; as he fell he threw up both arms, just in time to have them also carried away by another shot. At one gun, all the crew on one side were swept down by a shot which came crashing through the bulwarks. A shell burst between the two forward guns in charge of Lieutenant Tyson, killing and wounding fifteen men. The mast upon which the writer was perched was twice struck, once slightly, and again just below the foretop by a heavy shell, from a rifle on the Confederate gun-boat *Selma.* Fortunately the shell came tumbling end over end, and buried itself in the mast, butt-end first, leaving the percussion-cap protruding. Had it come point first, or had it struck at any other part of the mast than in the reënforced portion where the heel of the topmast laps the top of the lower mast, this contribution to the literature of the war would probably have been lost to the world, as the distance to the deck was about a hundred feet. As it was, the sudden jar would have dislodged any one from the crosstrees had not the shell been visible from the time it left the *Selma,* thus giving time to prepare for it by an extra grip around the top of the mast. Looking out over the water, it was easy to trace the course of every shot, both from the guns of the *Hartford* and from the Confederate fleet. Another signal message from the *Brooklyn* told of the sinking of the *Tecumseh,* a fact known already, and another order to "go on" was given and was not obeyed.

Soon after the fight began, Admiral Farragut, finding that the low-hanging smoke from the guns interfered with his view from the deck, went up the rigging of the mainmast as far as the futtock-shrouds, immediately below the maintop. The pilot, Martin Freeman, was in the top directly overhead, and the fleet-captain was on the deck below. Seeing the admiral in this exposed position, where, if wounded, he would be killed by falling to the deck, Fleet-Captain Drayton ordered Knowles, the signal-quartermaster, to fasten a rope around him so that he would be prevented from falling.

Finding that the *Brooklyn* failed to obey his orders, the admiral hurriedly inquired of the pilot if there was sufficient depth of water for the *Hartford* to pass to the left of the *Brooklyn.* Receiving an affirmative reply, he said: "I will take the lead," and immediately ordered the *Hartford* ahead at full speed.☆ As he passed the *Brooklyn* a voice warned him of the torpedoes, to which he returned the contemptuous answer, "Damn the torpedoes." This is the current story, and may have some basis of truth. But as a matter of fact, there was never a moment when the din of the battle would not have drowned any attempt at conversation

---

☆In turning to clear the *Brooklyn'*s stern, the *Hartford* went ahead, while the *Metacomet* backed. —EDITORS.

between the two ships, and while it is quite probable that the admiral made the remark it is doubtful if he shouted it to the *Brooklyn*.‡

Then was witnessed the remarkable sight of the *Hartford* and her consort, the *Metacomet*, passing over the dreaded torpedo ground and rushing ahead far in advance of the rest of the fleet, the extrication of which from the confusion caused by the *Brooklyn's* halt required many minutes of valuable time.⁺ The *Hartford* was now moving over what is called the "middle ground," with shallow water on either side, so that it was impossible to move except as the channel permitted. Taking advantage of the situation, the Confederate gun-boat *Selma* kept directly in front of the flag-ship and raked her fore and aft, doing more damage in reality than all the rest of the enemy's fleet. The other gun-boats, the *Gaines* and the *Morgan*, were in shallow water on our starboard bow, but they received more damage from the *Hartford's* broadsides than they were able to inflict. Meanwhile the ram *Tennessee*, which up to this time had contented herself with simply firing at the approaching fleet, started for the *Hartford*, apparently with the intention of striking her amidships. She came on perhaps for half a mile, never approaching nearer than a hundred yards, and then suddenly turned and made for the fleet, which, still in front of the fort, was gradually getting straightened out and following the *Hartford*. This change of course on the part of the ram has always been a mystery. The captain of the ram, in papers published since the war, denies that any such move was made, but it was witnessed by the entire fleet, and is mentioned by both Admiral Farragut and Fleet-Captain Drayton in their official reports.

The *Hartford* had now run a mile inside the bay, and was suffering chiefly from the raking fire of the *Selma*, which was unquestionably managed more skillfully than any other Confederate vessel. Captain (now Admiral) Jouett, commanding the *Hartford's* escort, the *Metacomet*, repeatedly asked permission of the admiral to cut loose and take care of the *Selma*, and finally, at five minutes past eight, consent was given. In an instant the cables binding the two vessels

---

‡The period of delay between the halting of the *Brooklyn* and the decision of the admiral to take the lead could hardly have been less than ten minutes, and may have been longer. The first signal message from the *Brooklyn* was taken from the forecastle of the *Hartford*. Then the smoke from the *Hartford's* bow guns interfered, and I started up the foremast, intending to make a signal-station of the foretop. Finding a howitzer crew at work there I kept on to the foretop-gallant crosstrees, where I received and replied to two messages before the *Hartford* passed the *Brooklyn*. As I was not a sailor and had never before been so far up in the rigging of a ship, it could hardly have taken me less then five minutes to shift from the forecastle to the crosstrees. It was while going up the mast that I witnessed the sinking of the *Tecumseh*.
—J.C.K.

⁺Farragut, when he had altered his course, had every reason to suppose that there were torpedoes directly in his path. It was known that they had been placed west of the red buoy, the *Brooklyn* had seen them, and the fate of the *Tecumseh* was conclusive evidence. In fact the officers both of the *Hartford* and the *Richmond* heard the snapping of torpedo-primers under the bottom of the ships as they passed, but the torpedoes failed to explode, having probably been corroded by lying a long time in the water.
—Editors.

UNITED STATES STEAMSHIP "MONONGAHELA," SHOWING INJURIES RECEIVED
IN THE FIGHT. FROM A SKETCH MADE AFTER THE BATTLE OF MOBILE.

were cut, and the *Metacomet,* the fastest vessel in the fleet, bounded ahead. The *Selma* was no match for her, and, recognizing her danger, endeavored to retreat up the bay. But she was speedily overhauled, and when a shot had wounded her captain and killed her first lieutenant she surrendered. Before this the *Gaines* had been crippled by the splendid marksmanship of the *Hartford's* gunners, and had run aground under the guns of the fort, where she was shortly afterward set on fire, the crew escaping to the shore. The gun-boat *Morgan,* after grounding for a few moments on the shoals to the east of Navy Cove, retreated to the shallow water near the fort, whence she escaped the following night to Mobile. The *Hartford,* having reached the deep water of the bay, about three miles north of Dauphine Island, came to anchor.

Let us now return to the other vessels of the fleet, which we left massed in front of Fort Morgan by the remarkable action of the *Brooklyn* in stopping and refusing to move ahead. When the ram *Tennessee* turned away from the *Hartford,* as narrated, she made for the fleet, and in their crowded and confused condition it seemed to be a matter of no difficulty to pick out whatever victims the Confederate commander (Admiral Franklin Buchanan) might desire, as he had done in 1861 when commanding the *Merrimac* in Hampton Roads. Before he could reach them the line had become straightened, and the leading vessels had passed the fort. Admiral Jenkins, who commanded the *Richmond* during the fight, writing of this part of the fight, for the use of the present writer, says:

"During the delay under the guns of Fort Morgan and the water-battery by the backing of the *Brooklyn,* the vessels astern had remained apparently stationary, so that the nearest one to the *Richmond* was about half a mile off,

and some of them paid very dearly, for the men of the water-battery, who had been driven away from their guns and up the sand hills by the fire of the *Richmond* and *Chickasaw,* had time to return and attack them. When the *Hartford* 'cut adrift' from the *Brooklyn* and *Richmond*—the only safe thing possible to do—the *Tennessee* and the three gun-boats pursued her. That is, the *Tennessee,* after getting above the lines of torpedoes, turned into the main ship-channel and followed the *Hartford,* while the gun-boats were in shallow water to the northward, where our heavy vessels could not go after them. When the *Tennessee* was within probably half a mile of the *Hartford,* she suddenly turned her head toward the *Brooklyn* and *Richmond* (both close together). As she approached, every one on board the *Richmond* supposed that she would ram the *Brooklyn;* that, we thought, would be our opportunity, for if she struck the *Brooklyn* the concussion would throw her port side across our path, and being so near to us, she would not have time to 'straighten up,' and we would strike her fairly and squarely, and most likely sink her.

"The guns were loaded with solid shot and heaviest powder charge; the forecastle gun's crew were ordered to get their small-arms and fire into her gun-ports; and as previously determined, if we came in collision at any time, the orders were to throw gun charges of powder in bags from the fore and main yard-arms down her smoke-stack (or at least try to do so). To our great surprise, she sheered off from the *Brooklyn,* and at about one hundred yards put two shot or shells through and through the *Brooklyn*'s sides (as reported), doing much damage.

"Approaching, passing, and getting away from the *Richmond,* the ram received from us three full broadsides of 9-inch solid shot, each broadside being eleven guns. They were well aimed and all struck, but when she was examined next day, no other indications were seen than scratches. The musketry fire into the two ports prevented the leveling of her guns, and therefore two of her shot or shell passed harmlessly over the *Richmond,* except the cutting of a ratline in the port main-shroud, just under the feet of the pilot, while the other whistled unpleasantly close to Lieutenant Terry's head. The *Tennessee* passed toward the *Lackawanna,* the next vessel astern, and avoided her—wishing either to ram Captain Strong's vessel (*Monongahela*), or cross his bow and attack McCann's vessel (the *Kennebec,* Strong's consort). Strong was ready for her, and, anticipating her object, made at her, but the blow (by the quick manœuvring of the *Tennessee*) was a glancing one, doing very little damage to either Strong's or McCann's vessel. Thence the *Tennessee,* after firing two broadsides into the *Oneida,* proceeded toward the fort, and for a time entirely disappeared from our sight. During this time the three gun-boats were proceeding, apparently, up the bay, to escape. The *Hartford* was closely watched with our glasses, and soon after the *Tennessee* had left Strong the *Metacomet* (Jouett) was seen to cast off; and divining the purpose, the *Port Royal* (Gherardi) was ordered to cast off from the *Richmond* and go in chase of the enemy, pointing in the direction of the three gun-boats of the enemy. George Brown (in the *Itasca*) cast off from the *Ossipee* and (I believe) McCann did also, and steered for the enemy. By this time Jouett had come up with the *Selma,* and the fight commenced. A very few minutes after Gherardi had left the side of the *Richmond,* and the other small vessels had left their consorts, a thick mist, with light rain (just enough to wet the deck), passed over the *Richmond,* obscuring from sight every object outside the vessel; indeed, for a few minutes the bowsprit of the *Richmond* could not be seen from the poop-deck. This mist and rain, in a cloudless sunshiny day, were slowly wafted over the waters toward the fort and pilot town, enabling John W. Bennett, commanding one of the enemy's gun-boats, and George W. Harrison, commanding the other, to shape their courses for safety, in shoal water, and finally under Fort Morgan. Gherardi in the *Port Royal* (as soon as he could see) saw only the *Selma* and *Metacomet,* and continued his course for them."

Whatever damage was done by the *Tennessee* to the fleet in passing the fort was by the occasional discharge of her guns. She failed to strike a single one of

CAPTURE OF THE CONFEDERATE GUN-BOAT "SELMA" BY THE "METACOMET."
FROM A WAR-TIME SKETCH.

the Union vessels, but was herself run into by the *Monongahela,* Captain Strong, at full speed./ The captain says in his report:

> "After passing the forts I saw the rebel ram *Tennessee* head on for our line. I then sheered out of the line to run into her, at the same time ordering full speed as fast as possible. I struck her fair, and swinging around poured in a broadside of solid 11-inch shot, which apparently had little if any effect upon her."

This modest statement is characteristic of the gallant writer, now dead, as are so many others of the conspicuous actors in that day's work. The *Monongahela* was no match for the *Tennessee,* but she had been strengthened by an artificial iron prow, and being one of the fastest—or rather, *least slow*—of the fleet, was expected to act as a ram if opportunity offered. Captain Strong waited for no orders, but seeing the huge ram coming for the fleet left his place in the line and attacked her, as narrated. It was at this time that the *Monongahela*'s first lieutenant, Roderick Prentiss, a brave and gifted young officer, received his death wound, both legs being shattered.

At last all the fleet passed the fort, and while the ram ran under its guns the vessels made their way to the *Hartford* and dropped their anchors, except the *Metacomet, Port Royal, Kennebec,* and *Itasca.* After the forts were passed, the three last named had cut loose from their escorts and gone to aid the *Metacomet* in her struggle with the *Selma* and *Morgan.*☆

The thunder of heavy artillery now ceased. The crews of the various vessels had begun to efface the marks of the terrible contest by washing the decks and clearing up the splinters. The cooks were preparing breakfast, the surgeons were busily engaged in making amputations and binding arteries, and under canvas, on the port side of each vessel, lay the ghastly line of dead waiting the sailor's burial. As if by mutual understanding, officers who were relieved from immediate duty gathered in the ward-rooms to ascertain who of their mates were missing, and the reaction from such a season of tense nerves and excitement was just setting in when the hurried call to quarters came and the word passed around, "The ram is coming."

The *Tennessee,* after remaining near Fort Morgan while the fleet had made its way four miles above to its anchorage,—certainly as much as half an hour,—had suddenly decided to settle at once the question of the control of the bay.

/The *Tennessee,* after colliding with the *Monongahela,* grazed the bow of the *Kennebec,* injured slightly the latter's planking, and dropped one of her boats on the deck of the gun-boat.—EDITORS.

☆The *Oneida,* the last ship in the line, suffered more severely than any other of the fleet in the passage. One shell exploded in the boiler, another cut the wheel-ropes, and a third disabled the forward pivot-gun. The list of casualties was very large, Commander Mullany being among the wounded. The crippled vessel was carried on by her consort, the *Galena.*—EDITORS.

Single-handed she came on to meet the whole fleet, consisting now of ten wooden vessels and the three monitors. At that time the *Tennessee* was believed to be the strongest vessel afloat, and the safety with which she carried her crew during the battle proved that she was virtually invulnerable. Fortunately for the Union fleet she was weakly handled, and at the end fell a victim to a stupendous blunder in her construction—the failure to protect her rudder-chains. The spectacle afforded the Confederate soldiers, who crowded the ramparts of the two forts,—the fleet now being out of range,—was such as has very rarely been furnished in the history of the world. To the looker-on it seemed as if the fleet was at the mercy of the ram, for the monitors, which were expected to be the chief defense, were so destitute of speed and so difficult to manœuvre that it seemed an easy task for the *Tennessee* to avoid them and sink the wooden vessels in detail. Because of the slowness of the monitors, Admiral Farragut selected the fastest of the wooden vessels to begin the attack. While the navy signals for a general attack of the enemy were being prepared, the *Monongahela* (Captain Strong) and the *Lackawanna* (Captain Marchand) were ordered by the more rapid signal system of the army to "run down the ram," the order being immediately repeated to the monitors.

The *Monongahela*, with her prow already somewhat weakened by the previous attempt to ram, at once took the lead, as she had not yet come to anchor. The ram from the first headed for the *Hartford*, and paid no attention to her assailants, except with her guns. The *Monongahela*, going at full speed, struck the *Tennessee* amidships—a blow that would have sunk almost any vessel of the Union navy, but which inflicted not the slightest damage on the solid iron hull of the ram. (After the surrender it was almost impossible to tell where the attacking vessel had struck.) Her own iron prow and cutwater were carried away, and she was otherwise badly damaged about the stern by the collision. The *Lackawanna* was close behind and delivered a similar blow with her wooden bow, simply causing the ram to lurch slightly to one side. As the vessels separated the *Lackawanna* swung alongside the ram, which sent two shots through her and kept on her course for the *Hartford*, which was now the next vessel in the attack. The two flag-ships approached each other, bow to bow, iron against oak. It was impossible for the *Hartford*, with her lack of speed, to circle around and strike the ram on the side; her only safety was in keeping pointed directly for the bow of her assailant. The other vessels of the fleet were unable to do anything for the defense of the admiral except to train their guns on the ram, on which as yet they had not the slightest effect.

It was a thrilling moment for the fleet, for it was evident that if the ram could strike the *Hartford* the latter must sink. But for the two vessels to strike fairly, bows on, would probably have involved the destruction of both, for the ram must have penetrated so far into the wooden ship that as the *Hartford* filled and sank she would have carried the ram under water. Whether for this reason or for some other, as the two vessels came together the *Tennessee* slightly changed her course, the port bow of the *Hartford* met the port bow of the ram, and the ships grated against each other as they passed. The *Hartford* poured her whole port broadside against the ram, but the solid shot merely dented the side and bounded into the air. The ram tried to return the salute, but owing to defective primers only one gun was discharged. This sent a shell through the berth-deck, killing five men and wounding eight. The muzzle of the gun was so close to the *Hartford* that the powder blackened her side.

The admiral stood on the quarter-deck when the vessels came together, and as he saw the result he jumped on to the port-quarter rail, holding to the mizzen-rigging, a position from which he might have jumped to the deck of the ram as she passed. Seeing him in this position, and fearing for his safety, Flag-Lieutenant Watson slipped a rope around him and secured it to the rigging, so that during the fight the admiral was twice "lashed to the rigging," each time by devoted officers who knew better than to consult him before acting. Fleet-Captain Drayton had hurried to the bow of the *Hartford* as the collision was seen to be inevitable, and expressed keen satisfaction when the ram avoided a direct blow.

The *Tennessee* now became the target for the whole fleet, all the vessels of which were making toward her, pounding her with shot, and trying to run her down. As the *Hartford* turned to make for her again, we ran in front of the *Lackawanna*, which had already turned and was moving under full headway with the same object. She struck us on our starboard side, amidships, crushing half-way through, knocking two port-holes into one, upsetting one of the Dahlgren guns, and creating general consternation. For a time it was thought that we must sink, and the cry rang out over the deck: "Save the admiral! Save the admiral!" The port boats were ordered lowered, and in their haste some of the sailors cut the "falls," and two of the cutters dropped into the water wrong side up, and floated astern. But the admiral sprang into the starboard mizzen-rigging, looked over the side of the ship, and, finding there were still a few inches to spare above the water's edge, instantly ordered the ship ahead again at full speed, after the ram. The unfortunate *Lackawanna*, which had struck the ram a second blow, was making for her once more, and, singularly enough, again came up on our starboard side, and another collision seemed imminent. And now the admiral became a trifle excited. He had no idea of whipping the rebels to be himself sunk by a friend, nor did he realize at the moment that the *Hartford* was as much to blame as the *Lackawanna*. Turning to the writer he inquired, "Can you say 'For God's sake' by signal?" "Yes, sir," was the reply. "Then say to the *Lackawanna*, 'For God's sake get out of our way and anchor!'" In my haste to send the message, I brought the end of my signal flag-staff down with considerable violence upon the head of the admiral, who was standing nearer than I thought, causing him to wince perceptibly. It was a hasty message, for the fault was equally divided, each ship being too eager to reach the enemy, and it turned out all right, by a fortunate accident, that Captain Marchand never received it. The army signal officer on the *Lackawanna*, Lieutenant Myron Adams (now pastor of Plymouth Congregational Church in Rochester, N.Y.), had taken his station in the foretop, and just as he received the first five words, "For God's sake get out"— the wind flirted the large United States flag at the mast-head around him, so that he was unable to read the conclusion of the message.

The remainder of the story is soon told. As the *Tennessee* left the *Hartford* she became the target of the entire fleet, and at last the concentration of solid shot from so many guns began to tell. The flag-staff was shot away, the smoke-stack was riddled with holes, and finally disappeared. The monitor *Chickasaw*, Lieutenant-Commander Perkins, succeeded in coming up astern and began pounding away with 11-inch solid shot, and one shot from a 15-inch gun of the *Manhattan* crushed into the side sufficiently to prove that a few more such shots would have made the casemate untenable. Finally, one of the *Chickasaw*'s shots cut the rudder-chain of the ram and she would no longer mind her helm.† At this time, as Admiral Farragut says in his report, "she was sore beset. The *Chickasaw* was pounding away at her stern, the *Ossipee* was approaching her at full speed, and the *Monongahela, Lackawanna*, and this ship were bearing down upon her, determined upon her destruction." From the time the *Hartford* struck her she did not fire a gun. Finally the Confederate admiral, Buchanan, was severely wounded by an iron splinter or a piece of a shell, and just as the *Ossipee* was about to strike her the *Tennessee* displayed a white flag, hoisted on an improvised staff through the grating over her deck. The *Ossipee* (Captain Le Roy) reversed her engine, but was so near that a harmless collision was inevitable. Suddenly the terrific cannonading ceased, and from every ship rang out cheer after cheer, as the weary men realized that at last the ram was conquered and the day won.⍦ The *Chickasaw* took the *Tennessee* in tow and brought her to anchor near the *Hartford*. The impression prevailed at first that the *Tennessee* had been seriously injured by the ramming she had received and was sinking, and orders were signaled to send boats to assist her crew, but it was soon discovered that this was unnecessary. Admiral Buchanan surrendered his sword to Lieutenant Giraud, of the *Ossipee*, who was sent to take charge of the captured *Ten-*

---

†The admiral says in his report:

> "I cannot give too much praise to Lieutenant-Commander Perkins, who, though he had orders from the Department to return north, volunteered to take command of the *Chickasaw*, and did his duty nobly."

According to the pilot of the *Tennessee*, "the *Chickasaw* hung close under our stern. Move as we would, she was always there, firing the two 11-inch guns in her forward turret like pocket-pistols, so that she soon had the plates flying in the air."—EDITORS.

⍦The first gun of the day was fired at 6:47 A.M. The surrender of the ram occurred at 10 o'clock.
—EDITORS.

FIGHT BETWEEN THE "CHICKASAW" AND FORT POWELL, AUGUST 5, 1864.
FROM A WAR-TIME SKETCH.

The picture appears to represent the blowing up of Fort Powell, which did not occur until after 10 o'clock that night, when the fort was evacuated.—EDITORS.

nessee. Captain Heywood, of the Marine Corps, was sent on board the ram with a guard of marines. On meeting Admiral Buchanan he could not resist the temptation to inform him that they had met before under different circumstances, the captain having been on the frigate *Cumberland* when she was sunk in Hampton Roads by Buchanan in the *Merrimac.*↓

Late in the afternoon the *Metacomet* was sent to Pensacola with the

↓The casualties of the Union fleet, as reported by Admiral Farragut, were 52 killed and 170 wounded, as follows:

	Killed.	Wounded.
Hartford	25	28
Brooklyn	11	43
Lackawanna	4	35
Oneida	8	30
Monongahela	฿0	6
Metacomet	1	2
Ossipee	1	7
Richmond	0	2
Galena	0	1
Octorara	1	10
Kennebec	1	6

To the above should be added the casualties on board the *Tecumseh,* viz., 93 drowned and 4 captured, making the total losses 145 killed, 170 wounded and 4 captured.—EDITORS.

฿First-Lieutenant Roderick Prentiss died a day later, as already mentioned.

wounded of both sides, including Admiral Buchanan. In his report he accuses Captain Harrison of the *Morgan* of deserting the *Selma*. Captain Harrison in his report, on the other hand, charges Captain Murphy of the *Selma* with running away and with bad seamanship. Those who witnessed the fight at close quarters will not accept Captain Harrison's view, and the record of killed and wounded tells the story. On the *Morgan* one man was slightly wounded, on the *Selma* eight were killed and seven wounded; and there is no doubt that the *Selma* was better managed and did more harm to the Union fleet than the two other rebel gun-boats combined. Captain Murphy of the *Selma*, in his official report, written like those of Buchanan and Johnston from the Pensacola hospital, tells very briefly the story of his part in the fight and makes no insinuations or complaints against brother officers. The total casualties in the rebel fleet were 12 killed and 20 wounded, as follows:

	Killed.	Wounded.
Ram *Tennessee*	2	9
Gun-boat *Selma*	8	7
" *Gaines*	2	3
" *Morgan*	0	1
Total	12	20

[To the above should be added those captured on board the surrendered vessels, including, according to Farragut's report, 190 in the *Tennessee* and 90 in the *Selma*.—EDITORS.]

The *Gaines*, according to the official report of her captain, was disabled by a shot or shell from the *Hartford*, "which broke in the outer planking under the port quarter about the water-line, and which from the marks seemed to have glanced below in the direction of the stern-post." This caused a leak in the after-magazine that could not be stopped, and made it necessary to beach the vessel as already described. The captain succeeded in removing the ammunition, supplies, and small-arms to the shore, for the use of Fort Morgan, and during the next night made his escape with his crew to Mobile, pulling up the bay in six cutters, which in the darkness easily evaded the Union gun-boats that were on guard. The *Morgan* also succeeded in making her way through without difficulty, covering all her lights and running very slowly until she had passed the Union vessels. The writer of this sketch has never been able to understand why the *Morgan* and the boats belonging to the *Gaines* were not destroyed during the afternoon following the fight, as might have been done with ease and safety by any one of the monitors. This was supposed to have been the object of a little excursion of the *Winnebago* in the afternoon, which, however, aside from firing a few harmless and unnecessary shots at Fort Morgan, accomplished nothing. The *Chickasaw* (Lieutenant-Commander Perkins) at the same time shelled Fort Powell, which was evacuated about 10 P.M. that night, the officers and men escaping to the mainland. The *Chickasaw* also tackled Fort Gaines on the 6th, and speedily convinced the commanding officer that it would be folly to attempt to withstand a siege. The result was a surrender to the army and navy the next morning.

Fort Morgan was at once invested, and surrendered on the 23d of August.

CHAPTER 11

THE INVASION OF TENNESSEE.[†]

J. B. Hood, General, C.S.A.

Unless the army could be heavily reënforced, there was but one plan to be adopted: by manœuvres, to draw Sherman back into the mountains, then beat him in battle, and at least regain our lost territory. Therefore, after anxious reflection and consultation with the corps commanders, I determined to communicate with the President, and ascertain whether or not reënforcements could be obtained from any quarter.

The reply from His Excellency conveyed no hope of assistance:

> "RICHMOND, September 5th, 1864.
> "... The necessity for reënforcements was realized, and every effort made to bring forward reserves, militia, and detailed men for the purpose.... No other resource remains. It is now requisite that absentees be brought back, the addition required from the surrounding country be promptly made available, and that the means in hand be used with energy proportionate to the country's need.
>
> " 'JEFFERSON DAVIS."

I thereupon decided to operate at the earliest moment possible in the rear of Sherman, as I became more and more convinced of our inability successfully to resist an advance of the Federal army.

I recalled General Wheeler from Tennessee to join immediately the left of the army, whilst Colonel Presstman, of the engineer corps, made ready to move with the pontoon-train and a sufficient number of boats to meet any emergency.

[†]Taken by permission (and condensed) from General Hood's work, "Advance and Retreat," published by General G. T. Beauregard for the Hood Orphan Memorial Fund: New Orleans, 1880.

Upon the morning of the 18th the army began to move in the direction of the West Point Railroad, which the advance reached on the 19th. Upon the 20th, line of battle was formed, with the right east of the railroad, and the left resting near the river, with army headquarters at Palmetto.

On the 28th I issued instructions to commence the movement across the Chattahoochee at Pumpkin Town and Phillips's Ferry, and on the following morning I directed that our supplies from Newnan cross the river at Moore's Ferry. At noon I rode over the pontoon-bridge in advance of the infantry, and that night established my headquarters at Pray's Church, along with General W. H. Jackson, commanding the cavalry.

The morning of the 1st of October Brigadier-General Jackson advanced with the cavalry, sending a detachment at the same time to operate against the railroad between the Chattahoochee and Marietta. That night the army went into bivouac eight miles north of Pray's Church, after having effected an undisturbed and safe passage of the Chattahoochee. Information was here received that Kilpatrick's cavalry was north of the river, and that Garrard's cavalry had moved in the direction of Rome.

The night of the 2d the army rested near Flint Hill Church. On the morning of the 3d Lieutenant-General Stewart was instructed to move with his corps and take possession of Big Shanty; to send, if practicable, a detachment for the same purpose to Ackworth, and to destroy as great a portion of the railroad in the vicinity as possible; also to send a division to Allatoona to capture that place, if, in the judgment of the commanding officer, the achievement was feasible. The main body of the army in the meantime moved forward and bivouacked near Carley's house, within four miles of Lost Mountain.

On the 4th General Stewart captured, after a slight resistance, about 170 prisoners at Big Shanty, and at 9:30 A.M. the garrison at Ackworth, numbering 250 men, surrendered to General Loring. The forces under these officers joined the main body near Lost Mountain on the morning of the 5th, having, in addition, destroyed about ten or fifteen miles of the railroad.

I had received information that the enemy had in store at Allatoona large supplies which were guarded by two or three regiments. As one of the objects of the campaign was to deprive the enemy of provisions, Major-General French was ordered to move with his division, capture the garrison, if practicable, and gain possession of the supplies. Accordingly, on the 5th, at 10 A.M., after a refusal to surrender, he attacked the Federal forces at Allatoona, and succeeded in capturing a portion of the works; at that juncture he received intelligence that large reënforcements were advancing in support of the enemy, and fearing he would be cut off from the main body of the army, he retired and abandoned the attempt. Our soldiers fought with great courage; during the engagement Brigadier-General Young, a brave and efficient officer, was wounded and captured by the enemy. General Corse won my admiration by his gallant resistance, and not without reason the Federal commander complimented this officer, through a general order, for his handsome conduct in the defense of Allatoona.

Our presence upon his communications compelled Sherman to leave Atlanta in haste and cross the Chattahoochee on the 3d and 4th of October with, according to our estimate at that time, about 65,000 infantry and artillery and two divisions of cavalry. He left one corps to guard the city and the railway bridge across the river, and telegraphed to Grant he would attack me if I struck his road south of the Etowah.

On the 6th my army reached Dallas; our right rested at New Hope Church, where intelligence was received that the enemy was advancing from Lost Mountain. From Dallas we marched to Coosaville, ten miles south-west of Rome, via Van Wert, Cedartown, and Cave Spring. At the latter place Major-General Wheeler, with a portion of his command, joined me from Tennessee. We arrived at Coosaville on the 10th.

In a dispatch to General [Richard] Taylor, October 7th, I requested that Forrest be ordered to operate at once in Tennessee:

"Your dispatch of the 6th received. This army being in motion, it is of vital importance that Forrest should move without delay, and operate on the enemy's railroad. If he cannot break the Chattanooga and Nashville Railroad he can occupy their forces there and prevent damage being repaired on the other road. He should lose no time in moving."

On the 11th the army crossed the Coosa River, marched in the direction of Resaca and Dalton, and bivouacked that night fourteen miles above Coosaville and ten miles north-west of Rome. That same day Major-General Arnold Elzey, chief-of-artillery, was directed to move to Jacksonville with the reserve artillery and all surplus wagons, and General Jackson was instructed to retard the enemy as much as possible, in the event of his advance from Rome.

Having thus relieved the army of all incumbance, and made ready for battle, we marched rapidly to Resaca, and thence to Dalton, via Sugar Valley Post-Office. Lieutenant-General Lee moved upon Resaca, with instructions to display his forces and demand the surrender of the garrison, but not to attack unless, in his judgment, the capture could be effected with small loss of life. He decided not to assault the Federal works, and commenced at once the destruction of the railroad.

On the 13th I demanded the surrender of Dalton, which, in the first instance, was refused, but was finally acceded to at 4 P.M. The garrison consisted of about one thousand men. As the road between Resaca and Tunnel Hill had been effectually destroyed, the army was put in motion the next morning in the direction of Gadsden, and camped that night near Villanow.

From Villanow the army passed through the gaps in the mountains, and halted on the 15th at Cross Roads, in a beautiful valley about nine miles south of Lafayette. At this time I received intelligence that on the 13th Sherman had reached Snake Creek Gap, where the right of his line had rested in the early spring of this year; also that he was marching in our pursuit, whilst General Wheeler was endeavoring to retard his advance as much as possible. I here determined to advance no farther toward the Tennessee River, but to select a position and deliver battle, since Sherman, at an earlier date than anticipated, had moved as far north as I had hoped to allure him; moreover, I was again in the vicinity of the Alabama line, with the Blue Mountain Railroad in my rear, and I thought I had discovered that improvement in the morale of the troops which would justify me in delivering battle. In accordance with information received from our cavalry, Sherman had, however, made no further division of his forces after leaving Atlanta. I therefore estimated his strength to be about 65,000 effectives.

Upon the eve of action I considered it important to ascertain by personal inquiry and through the aid of officers of my staff,—not alone from corps commanders, but from officers of less rank,—whether or not my impressions after the capture of Dalton were correct, and I could rely upon the troops entering into battle at least hopeful of victory. I took measures to obtain likewise the views of Lieutenant-General S. D. Lee, who at this juncture was with his corps in rear, at or near Ship's Gap. He agreed with all the officers consulted; the opinion was unanimous that although the army had much improved in spirit, it was not in condition to risk battle against the numbers reported by General Wheeler.

The renouncement of the object for which I had so earnestly striven brought with it genuine disappointment; I had expected that a forward movement of one hundred miles would re-inspirit the officers and men in a degree to impart to them confidence, enthusiasm, and hope of victory, if not strong faith in its achievement.

I remained two days at Cross Roads in serious thought and perplexity. I could not offer battle while the officers were *unanimous* in their opposition. Neither could I take an intrenched position with likelihood of advantageous results, since Sherman could do the same, repair the railroad, amass a large army, place Thomas in my front in command of the forces he afterward assembled at Nashville, and then, himself, move southward; or, as previously suggested, he could send Thomas into Alabama, whilst he marched through Georgia, and left me to follow in his rear. This last movement upon our part would be construed by the troops into a retreat, and could but result in disaster. In this dilemma I conceived the plan of marching into Tennessee with the hope to establish our line eventually in Kentucky, and determined to make the campaign which followed, unless withheld by General Beauregard✢or the authorities at Richmond. I decided to make provision for twenty days' supply of rations in the haversacks and wagons; to order a heavy reserve of artillery to accompany the army, in order to overcome any serious opposition by the Federal gun-boats; to cross the Tennessee at or near Guntersville, and again destroy Sherman's communications at Stevenson and Bridgeport; to move upon Thomas and Schofield, and to attempt to rout and capture their army before it could reach Nashville. I intended then to march upon that city, where I would supply the army and reënforce it, if possible, by accessions from Tennessee. I was imbued with the belief that I could accomplish this feat, afterward march north-east, pass the Cumberland River at some crossing where the gun-boats, if too formidable at other points, were unable to interfere, then move into Kentucky, and take position with our left at or near Richmond, and our right extending toward Hazel Green, with Pound and Stony gaps in the Cumberland Mountains at our rear.

In this position I could threaten Cincinnati, and recruit the army from Kentucky and Tennessee; the former State was reported, at this juncture, to be more aroused and embittered against the Federals than at any other period of the war. While Sherman was debating between the alternatives of following our army or marching through Georgia, I hoped, by rapid movements, to achieve these results.

If Sherman should cut loose and move south—as I then believed he would do after I left his front *without previously worsting him in battle*—I would occupy at Richmond, Kentucky, a position of superior advantage, as Sherman, upon his arrival at the sea-coast, would be forced to go on board ship, and, after a long détour by water and land, repair to the defense of Kentucky and Ohio or march direct to the support of Grant. If he should return to confront my forces, or follow me directly from Georgia into Tennessee and Kentucky, I hoped then to be in condition to offer battle; and, if blessed with victory, to send reënforcements to General Lee, in Virginia, or to march through the gaps in the Cumberland Mountains and attack Grant in rear. This latter course I would pursue in the event of defeat or of inability to offer battle to Sherman. If, on the other hand, he should march to join Grant, I could pass through the Cumberland gaps to Petersburg, and attack Grant in rear at least two weeks before he, Sherman, could render him assistance. This move, I believed, would defeat Grant, and allow General Lee, in command of our combined armies, to march upon Washington or turn upon and annihilate Sherman.

Such is the plan which during the 15th and 16th, as we lay in bivouac near Lafayette, I maturely considered, and determined to carry out.

On the 17th the army resumed its line of march, and that night camped

---

✢On the 28th of September General Beauregard had been placed in control of the operations in the departments commanded by Generals Hood and Taylor.—EDITORS.

three miles from the forks of the Alpine, Gaylesville, and Summerville roads; thence it proceeded towards Gadsden. I proposed to move directly on to Guntersville and to take into Tennessee about one-half of Wheeler's cavalry (leaving the remainder to look after Sherman) and to have a depot of supplies at Tuscumbia in the event that I should meet with defeat in Tennessee.

Shortly after my arrival at Gadsden, General Beauregard reached the same point; I at once unfolded to him my plan, and requested that he confer apart with the corps commanders, Lieutenant-Generals Lee and Stewart and Major-General Cheatham. If after calm deliberation he deemed it expedient we should remain upon the Alabama line and attack Sherman, or take position, intrench, and finally follow on his rear when he should move south, I would of course acquiesce, albeit with reluctance. If, contrariwise, he should agree to my proposed plan to cross into Tennessee, I would move immediately to Guntersville, thence to Stevenson, Bridgeport, and Nashville.

This important question at issue was discussed during the greater part of one night, with maps before us. General Beauregard at length took the ground that, if I should engage in the projected campaign, it would be necessary to leave in Georgia all the cavalry at present with the army, in order to watch and harass Sherman in case he should move south, and to instruct Forrest to join me as soon as I should cross the Tennessee River. To this proposition I acceded. After he had held a separate conference with the corps commanders, we again debated several hours over the course of action to be pursued; and, during the interview, I discovered that he had gone to work in earnest to ascertain, in person, the true condition of the army; that he had sought information not only from the corps commanders, but from a number of officers, and had reached the same conclusion I had formed at Lafayette: that we were not competent to offer pitched battle to Sherman, nor could we follow him south without causing our retrograde movement to be construed by the troops into a *recurrence* of retreat, which would entail desertions and render the army of little or no use in its opposition to the enemy's march through Georgia. After two days' deliberation General Beauregard authorized me, on the evening of the 21st of October, to proceed to the execution of my plan of operations into Tennessee. General Beauregard's approval of a forward movement into Tennessee was soon made known to the army. The prospect of again entering that State created great enthusiasm, and from the different encampments arose at intervals that genuine Confederate shout so familiar to every Southern soldier, and which then betokened an improved state of feeling among the troops.

With twenty days' rations in the haversacks and wagons, we marched, on the 22d of October, upon all the roads leading from Gadsden in the direction of Guntersville, on the Tennessee River, and bivouacked that night in the vicinity of Bennettsville.

I here received information that General Forrest was near Jackson, Tennessee, and could not reach the middle portion of this State, as the river was too high. It would, therefore, be impossible for him to join me if I crossed at Guntersville; as it was regarded as essential that the whole of Wheeler's cavalry should remain in Georgia, I decided to deflect westward, effect a junction with Forrest, and then cross the river at Florence. General Beauregard sent orders to him to join me without delay, and also dispatched a messenger to hasten forward supplies to Tuscumbia.

The succeeding day the movement was continued toward Florence, in lieu of Guntersville as I had expected. Lieutenant-General Lee's corps reached the Tennessee, near Florence, on the 30th; [Edward] Johnson's division crossed the river and took possession of that town. My headquarters were during the 27th and 28th at the house of General Garth, near Decatur, where General Beauregard also stopped. While the army turned Decatur, I ordered a slight demonstration to be made against the town till our forces passed safely beyond, when I moved toward Tuscumbia, at which place I arrived on the 31st of October. Johnson's division, which held possession of Florence, was reënforced the same day by Clayton's division.

Thus the Confederate army rested upon the banks of the Tennessee one month after its departure from Palmetto. It had been almost continuously in motion during the interim; by rapid moves and manœuvres, and with only a small loss, it had drawn Sherman as far north as he stood in the early spring. The killed and wounded at Allatoona had been replaced by absentees who returned to ranks, and, as usual in such operations, the number of desertions became of no consequence.

Notwithstanding my request as early as the 9th of October that the railroad to Decatur be repaired, nothing had been done on the 1st of November toward the accomplishment of this important object. I had expected upon my arrival at Tuscumbia to find additional supplies, and to cross the river at once. Unfortunately, I was constrained to await repairs upon the railroad before a sufficient amount of supplies could be received to sustain the army till it was able to reach middle Tennessee.

General Beauregard remained two weeks at Tuscumbia and in its vicinity, during which interval the inaugurated campaign was discussed anew at great length. General Sherman was still in the neighborhood of Rome, and the question arose as to whether we should take trains and return to Georgia to oppose his movements south, or endeavor to execute the projected operations into Tennessee and Kentucky. I adhered to the conviction I had held at Lafayette and Gadsden, and a second time desired General Beauregard to consult the corps commanders, together with other officers, in regard to the effect a return to Georgia would produce upon the army. I also urged the consideration that Thomas would immediately overrun Alabama, if we marched to confront

Sherman. I had fixedly determined, unless withheld by Beauregard or the authorities at Richmond, to proceed, as soon as supplies were received, to the execution of the plan submitted at Gadsden.

At this juncture I was advised of the President's opposition to the campaign into Tennessee previous to a defeat of Sherman in battle.[+] The President was evidently under the impression that the army should have been equal to battle by the time it had reached the Alabama line, and was averse to my going into Tennessee. He was not, as were General Beauregard and myself, acquainted with its true condition. Therefore, a high regard for his views notwithstanding, I continued firm in the belief that the only means to checkmate Sherman, and coöperate with General Lee to save the Confederacy, lay in speedy success in Tennessee and Kentucky, and in my ability finally to attack Grant in rear with my entire force.

Although every possible effort was made to expedite the repairs upon the railroad, the work progressed slowly. Heavy rains in that section also interfered with the completion of the road. On the 13th I established my headquarters in Florence, upon the north branch of the Tennessee, and the following day General Forrest, with his command, reported for duty. On the 15th the remainder of Lee's corps crossed the river and bivouacked in advance also of Florence. Stewart's and Cheatham's corps were instructed to cross. About the time all necessary preparations verged to a completion, and I anticipated to move forward once more, heavy rains again delayed our supplies. Working parties were at once detailed and sent to different points on the railroad; wagons were also dispatched to aid in the transportation of supplies. The officer in charge was instructed to require the men to labor unceasingly for the accomplishment of this important object. In the meantime information had reached me that Sherman was advancing south, from Atlanta. He marched out of that fated city on the 16th. Thus were two opposing armies destined to move in opposite directions, each hoping to achieve glorious results.

[+] "RICHMOND, NOVEMBER 7TH, 1884.

"VIA MERIDIAN.

  "General J. B. Hood:

  "No troops can have been sent by Grant or Sheridan to Nashville. The latter has attempted to reënforce the former, but Early's movements prevented it. That fact will assure you as to their condition and purposes. The policy of taking advantage of the reported division of his [Sherman's] forces, where he cannot reunite his army, is too obvious to have been overlooked by you. I therefore take it for granted that you have not been able to avail yourself of that advantage during his march northward from Atlanta. Hope the opportunity will be offered before he is extensively recruited. If you keep his communications destroyed, he will most probably seek to concentrate for an attack on you. But if, as reported to you, he has sent a large part of his force southward, you may first beat him in detail, and, subsequently, without serious obstruction or danger to the country in your rear, advance to the Ohio River.

    "JEFFERSON DAVIS."

I well knew the delay at Tuscumbia would accrue to the advantage of Sherman, as he would thereby be allowed time to repair his railroad, and at least start to the rear all surplus material. I believed, however, that I could still get between Thomas's forces and Nashville, and rout them; furthermore, effect such manœuvres as to insure to our troops an easy victory. These convictions counterbalanced my regret that Sherman was permitted to traverse Georgia unopposed.

General Beauregard had moved in the direction of Georgia to assemble all available forces to oppose Sherman's advance.

On the 19th the cavalry was ordered to move forward. The succeeding day Lee's corps marched to the front about ten miles on the Chisholm road, between the Lawrenceburg and Waynesboro' roads. On the 20th of November, Stewart's corps having crossed the Tennessee and bivouacked several miles beyond on the Lawrenceburg road, orders were issued that the entire army move at an early hour the next morning. Lee's and Stewart's corps marched upon the Chisholm and the Lawrenceburg roads, and Cheatham's upon the Waynesboro' road. Early dawn of the 21st found the army in motion. I hoped by a rapid march to get in rear of Schofield's forces, then at Pulaski, before they were able to reach Duck River. That night headquarters were established at Rawhide, twelve miles north of Florence, on the Waynesboro' road. The march was resumed on the 22d and continued till the 27th, upon which date the troops, having taken advantage of every available road, reached Columbia, via Mount Pleasant. Forrest operated in our front against the enemy's cavalry, which he easily drove from one position to another.

The Federals at Pulaski became alarmed, and, by forced marches, reached Columbia, upon Duck River, in time to prevent our troops from cutting them off.

Colonel Presstman and his assistants laid the pontoons [over Duck River] during the night of the 28th, about three miles above Columbia; orders to move at dawn the following day having been issued to the two corps and the division above mentioned, I rode with my staff to Cheatham's right, passed over the bridge soon after daybreak, and moved forward at the head of Granbury's Texas brigade, of Cleburne's division, with instructions that the remaining corps and divisions follow, and at the same time keep well closed up during the march.

General Forrest had crossed, the evening previous, and moved to the front and right. I threw forward a few skirmishers who advanced at as rapid a pace as troops could possibly proceed.

During the march the Federal cavalry appeared on the hills to our left; not a moment, however, was lost on that account, as the army was marching by the right flank and was prepared to face at any instant in their direction. No attention, therefore, was paid to the enemy, save to throw out a few sharp-shooters in his front.⟩

Thus I led the main body of the army to within about two miles and in full view of the pike from Columbia to Spring Hill and Franklin. I here halted about 3 P.M., and requested General Cheatham, commanding the leading corps, and Major-General Cleburne to advance to the spot where, sitting upon my horse, I had in sight the enemy's wagons and men passing at double-quick along the Franklin pike. As these officers approached, I spoke to Cheatham in the following words, which I quote almost verbatim, as they have remained indelibly engraved upon my memory ever since that fatal day: "General, do you see the enemy there, retreating rapidly to escape us?" He answered in the affirmative. "Go," I continued, "with your corps, take possession of and hold that pike at or near Spring Hill. Accept whatever comes, and turn all those wagons over to our side of the house." Then, addressing Cleburne, I said, "General, you have heard the orders just given. You have one of my best divisions. Go with General Cheatham, assist him in every way you can, and do as he directs." Again, as a parting injunction to them, I added, "Go and do this at once. Stewart is near at hand, and I will have him double-quick his men to the front." ╱

They immediately sent staff-officers to hurry the men forward, and moved off with their troops at a quick pace in the direction of the enemy. I sent several of my staff with orders to Stewart and Johnson to make all possible haste. Meantime I rode to one side and looked on at Cleburne's division, followed by the remainder of Cheatham's corps, as it marched by, seemingly ready for battle.

Within about one-half hour from the time Cheatham left me skirmishing began with the enemy, when I rode forward to a point nearer the pike, and again sent a staff-officer to Stewart and Johnson to push forward. At the same time I dispatched a messenger to General Cheatham to lose no time in gaining pos-

---

⟩In the "Southern Bivouac" for April, 1885, General Cheatham, in an article dated November 30th, 1881, says, in reply to the above paragraph:

"General John C. Brown states that 'at or near Bear Creek the commanding general, apprehending an attack on our left flank, ordered your (Cheatham's) corps, in its march from that point, to move in two parallel columns, so that it could come instantly into action in two lines of battle.' General Brown's division marched 'five or six miles through fields and woods and over rough ground' some four hundred yards to the right of the road, necessarily causing more or less delay. General Brown further states that 'about the commencement of this movement, or soon afterward, by the orders of the commanding general in person, the whole of Gist's and about one-half of Strahl's brigade were detached for picket duty.'"—EDITORS.

╱"At the hour named, 3 P.M., there was no movement of 'wagons and men' in the vicinity of Spring Hill. Moreover, from the crossing at Duck River to the point referred to by General Hood, the turnpike was never in view, nor could it be seen until I had moved up to within three-quarters of a mile of Spring Hill. Only a mirage would have made possible the vision."

—GENERAL CHEATHAM, in the "BIVOUAC."

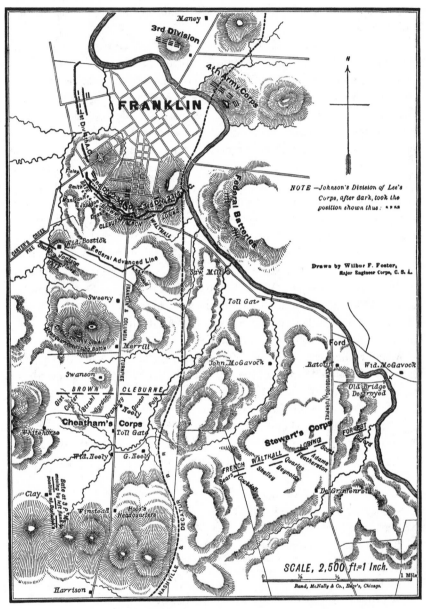

MAP OF THE BATTLE-FIELD OF FRANKLIN, TENNESSEE. FROM THE "BIVOUAC"
FOR JUNE, 1865.

session of the pike at Spring Hill. It was reported back that he was about to do so.☆

Listening attentively to the fire of the skirmishers in that direction I discovered there was no continued roar of musketry, and being aware of the quick approach of darkness, about 4 o'clock at that season of the year, I became somewhat uneasy, and again ordered an officer to go to General Cheatham, inform him that his supports were very near at hand; that he must attack at once, if he had not already so done, and take and hold possession of the pike. Shortly afterward I intrusted another officer with the same message, and, if my memory is not treacherous, finally requested the governor of Tennessee, Isham G. Harris, to hasten forward and impress upon Cheatham the importance of action without delay. I knew no large force of the enemy could be at Spring Hill, as couriers reported Schofield's main body still in front of Lee, at Columbia, up to a late hour in the day. I thought it probable that Cheatham had taken possession of Spring Hill without encountering material opposition, or had formed line across the pike, north of the town, and intrenched without coming in serious contact with the enemy, which would account for the little musketry heard in his direction. However, to ascertain the truth, I sent an officer to ask Cheatham if he held the pike, and to inform him of the arrival of Stewart, whose corps I intended to throw on his left, in order to assail the Federals in flank that evening or the next morning, as they approached and formed to attack Cheatham. At this juncture the last messenger returned with the report that the road had not been taken possession of. General Stewart was then ordered to proceed to the right of Cheatham and place his corps across the pike north of Spring Hill.

By this hour, however, twilight was upon us, when General Cheatham rode up in person. I at once directed Stewart to halt, and, turning to Cheatham, I exclaimed with deep emotion, as I felt the golden opportunity fast slipping from me, "General, why in the name of God have you not attacked the enemy and taken possession of that pike?" He replied that the line looked a little too long for him, and that Stewart should first form on his right.‡ I could hardly believe it possible that this brave old soldier, who had given proof of such courage and ability upon so many hard-fought fields, would even make such a report. After

---

☆"General Hood conveniently forgot to mention, in his account of this affair, the facts as to his orders to me at Rutherford's Creek. And he also forgot that, at the very moment he claims to have sent staff-officers to the rear with orders to Stewart and Johnson to make all possible haste, Stewart was forming line of battle on the south side of Rutherford's Creek, in pursuance of orders from him; nor did he remember that Stewart's corps was not ordered forward until about dusk."—GENERAL CHEATHAM, in the "BIVOUAC."

‡"Here, again, General Hood's memory proved treacherous. As to the preliminary statements of this paragraph, I refer to that portion of my account which covers the doings of the hours from 4 to 6 P.M., during most of which time General Hood was on the ground and in frequent personal communication with me. The dramatic scene with which he embellishes his narrative of the day's operations only occurred in the imagination of General Hood."—GENERAL CHEATHAM, in the "BIVOUAC."

leading him within full view of the enemy, and pointing out to him the Federals retreating in great haste and confusion along the pike, and then giving explicit orders to attack, I would as soon have expected midday to turn into darkness as for him to have disobeyed my orders. I then asked General Cheatham whether or not Stewart's corps, if formed on the right, would extend across the pike. He answered in the affirmative. Guides were at once furnished to point out Cheatham's right to General Stewart, who was ordered to form thereon, with his right extending across the pike. Darkness, however, which was increased by large shade-trees in that vicinity, soon closed upon us, and Stewart's corps, after much annoyance, went into bivouac for the night, near, but not across, the pike, at about 11 or 12 o'clock.

It was reported to me about this hour that the enemy was marching along the road, almost under the light of the camp-fires of the main body of the army. I sent anew to General Cheatham to know if at least a line of skirmishers could not be advanced, in order to throw the Federals in confusion, to delay their march, and allow us a chance to attack in the morning. Nothing was done. The Federals, with immense wagon-trains, were permitted to march by us the remainder of the night, within gunshot of our lines. I could not succeed in arousing the troops to action, when one good division would have sufficed to do the work. One good division, I reassert, could have routed that portion of the enemy which was at Spring Hill; could have taken possession of and formed line across the road; and thus could have made it an easy matter to Stewart's corps, Johnson's division, and Lee's two divisions, from Columbia, to have enveloped, routed, and captured Schofield's army that afternoon and the ensuing day. General Forrest gallantly opposed the enemy farther down to our right to the full extent of his power; beyond this effort nothing whatever was done, although never was a grander opportunity offered to utterly rout and destroy the Federal army. Had I dreamed for one moment that Cheatham would have failed to give battle, or at least to take position across the pike and force the enemy to assault him, I would myself have ridden to the front and led the troops into action.[ψ]

In connection with this grave misfortune, I must here record an act of candor and nobility upon the part of General Cheatham, which proves him to be equally generous-hearted and brave. I was, necessarily, much pained by the disappointment suffered, and, a few days later, telegraphed to Richmond, to withdraw my previous recommendation for his promotion, and to request that another be assigned to the command of his corps. Before the receipt of a reply,

[ψ]"The next order, in the shape of a suggestion that I had better have my pickets fire upon straggling troops passing along the pike in front of my left, was received and was immediately communicated to General Johnson, whose division was on my left and nearest the pike. This note from Major Mason, received about midnight, was the only communication I had from General Hood after leaving him at his quarters at Captain Thompson's."—GENERAL CHEATHAM, in the "BIVOUAC."

this officer called at my headquarters—then at the residence of Mr. Overton, six miles from Nashville—and, standing in my presence, spoke an honest avowal of his error, in the acknowledgment that he felt we had lost a brilliant opportunity at Spring Hill to deal the enemy a crushing blow, and that he was greatly to blame. I telegraphed and wrote to the War Department to withdraw my application for his removal, in the belief that, inspired with an ambition to retrieve his shortcoming, he would prove in the future doubly zealous in the service of his country. The following are the dispatches above referred to:

> "HEADQUARTERS,
> six miles from Nashville, on Franklin Pike,
> "December 7, 1864.
>
> "Hon. J. A. Seddon:
> "I withdraw my recommendation in favor of the promotion of Major-General Cheatham, for reasons which I will write more fully.
> "J. B. HOOD, General."

> "HEADQUARTERS,
> six miles from Nashville, on Franklin Pike,
> "December 8, 1864.
>
> "Hon. J. A. Seddon, Secretary of War;
> General G. T. Beauregard,
> "Macon, Ga.:
> "A good lieutenant-general should be sent here at once to command the corps now commanded by Major-General Cheatham. I have no one to recommend for the position.
> "J. B. HOOD, General."

> "HEADQUARTERS,
> six miles from Nashville, on Franklin Pike,
> "December 8, 1864.
>
> "Hon. J. A. Seddon:
> "Major-General Cheatham made a failure on the 30th of November which will be a lesson to him. I think it best he should remain in his position for the present. I withdraw my telegrams of yesterday and to-day on this subject.
> "J. B. HOOD, General."

On the 11th of December I wrote the Hon. Mr. Seddon:

"Major-General Cheatham has frankly confessed the great error of which he was guilty, and attaches much blame to himself. While his error lost so much to the country, it has been a severe lesson to him, by which he will profit in the future. In consideration of this, and of his previous conduct, I think that it is best that he should retain for the present the command he now holds."↓

The best move in my career as a soldier I was thus destined to behold come to naught. The discovery that the army, after a forward march of one hundred and eighty miles, was still, seemingly, unwilling to accept battle unless under the protection of breastworks, caused me to experience grave concern. In my inmost heart I questioned whether or not I would ever succeed in eradicating this evil. It seemed to me I had exhausted every means in the power of one man to remove this stumbling-block to the Army of Tennessee. On the morning of the 30th of November, Lee was on the march up the Franklin pike, when the main body of the army, at Spring Hill, awoke to find the Federals had disappeared.

I hereupon decided, before the enemy would be able to reach his stronghold at Nashville, to make that same afternoon another and final effort to overtake and rout him, and drive him into the Big Harpeth River at Franklin, since I could no longer hope to get between him and Nashville, by reason of the short distance from Franklin to that city, and the advantage which the Federals enjoyed in the possession of the direct road.

At early dawn the troops were put in motion in the direction of Franklin, marching as rapidly as possible to overtake the enemy before he crossed the Big

---

↓"In order to make clear what I have to say in this connection I will quote Governor Isham G. Harris:

" 'Governor James D. Porter.

" 'Dear Sir: . . . General Hood, on the march to Franklin, spoke to me, in the presence of Major [Lieut.-Colonel A. P.] Mason [Assistant Adjutant-General, Army of Tennessee], of the failure of General Cheatham to make the night attack at Spring Hill, and censured him in severe terms for his disobedience of orders. Soon after this, being alone with Major Mason, the latter remarked that "General Cheatham was not to blame about the matter last night. I did not send him the order." I asked if he had communicated the fact to General Hood. He answered that he had not. I replied that "it is due General Cheatham that this explanation should be made." Thereupon Major Mason joined General Hood and gave him the information. Afterward General Hood said to me that he had done injustice to General Cheatham, and requested me to inform him that he held him blameless for the failure at Spring Hill, and on the day following the battle of Franklin I was informed by General Hood that he had addressed a note to General Cheatham assuring him that he did not censure him with the failure to attack.

" 'Very respectfully,   Isham G. Harris.

" 'Memphis, Tennessee, May 20, 1877.'

"The first intimation made to me, from any source, that my conduct at Spring Hill, on the 29th of November, 1864, or during the night of that day, was the subject of criticism, was the receipt of a note from General Hood, written and received on the morning of the 3d of December. This is the communication referred to in the letter of Governor Harris, above

Harpeth, eighteen miles from Spring Hill. Lieutenant-General Lee had crossed Duck River after dark the night previous, and, in order to reach Franklin, was obliged to march a distance of thirty miles. The head of his column arrived at Spring Hill at 9 A.M. on the 30th, and, after a short rest, followed in the wake of the main body.

Stewart's corps was first in order of march; Cheatham followed immediately, and Lieutenant-General Lee in rear. Within about three miles of Franklin, the enemy was discovered on the ridge over which passes the turnpike. As soon as the Confederate troops began to deploy, and skirmishers were thrown forward, the Federals withdrew slowly to the environs of the town.

MAJOR-GENERAL PATRICK R. CLEBURNE, C.S.A., KILLED AT FRANKLIN, NOVEMBER 30, 1864. FROM A PHOTOGRAPH.

It was about 3 P.M. when Lieutenant-General Stewart moved to the right of the pike and began to establish his position in front of the enemy. Major-General Cheatham's corps, as it arrived in turn, filed off to the left of the road,

---

quoted. This note was read, so far as I know, by only four persons besides myself—my chief-of-staff, James D. Porter, Governor Isham G. Harris, Major J. F. Cumming, of Georgia, and John C. Burch. Not having been in the habit of carrying a certificate of military character, I attached no special value to the paper, and it was lost somewhere during the campaign in North Carolina. Governor Porter and Major Cumming agree with me that the following was the substance of the note:

" 'DECEMBER 3D, 1864.
" 'MY DEAR GENERAL:

"I do not censure you for the failure at Spring Hill. I am satisfied you are not responsible for it. I witnessed the splendid manner in which you delivered battle at Franklin on the 30th ult. I now have a higher estimate of you as a soldier than I ever had. You can rely upon my friendship.

"YOURS VERY TRULY, J. B. HOOD, GENERAL.

" 'To General B. F. Cheatham.'

"On the morning of the 4th of December I went to the headquarters of General Hood, and, referring to his note and the criticism of my conduct that had evidently been made by some one. I said to him: 'A great opportunity was lost at Spring Hill, but you know that I obeyed your orders there, as everywhere, literally and promptly.' General Hood not only did not dissent from what I said, but exhibited the most cordial manner, coupled with confidence and friendship. The subject was never again alluded to by General Hood to myself, nor, so far as I know, to any one. When he wrote, under date of December 11th, 1864, to Mr. Seddon,

and was also disposed in line of battle. The artillery was instructed to take no part in the engagement, on account of the danger to which women and children in the village would be exposed.‡ General Forrest was ordered to post cavalry on both flanks, and, if the assault proved successful, to complete the ruin of the enemy by capturing those who attempted to escape in the direction of Nashville. Lee's corps, as it arrived, was held in reserve, owing to the lateness of the hour and my inability, consequently, to post it on the extreme left. Schofield's position was rendered favorable for defense by open ground in front, and temporary intrenchments which the Federals had had time to throw up, notwithstanding the Confederate forces had marched in pursuit with all possible speed. At one or two points, along a short space, a slight abatis had been hastily constructed, by felling some small locust saplings in the vicinity.

Soon after Cheatham's corps was massed on the left, Major-General Cleburne came to me where I was seated on my horse in rear of the line, and asked permission to form his division in two, or, if I remember correctly, three lines for the assault. I at once granted his request, stating that I desired the Federals to be driven into the river in their immediate rear, and directing him to advise me as soon as he had completed the new disposition of his troops. Shortly afterward Cheatham and Stewart reported all in readiness for action, and received orders to drive the enemy from his position into the river *at all hazards*. About that time Cleburne returned, and, expressing himself with an enthusiasm which he had never before betrayed in our intercourse, said, "General, I am ready, and have more hope in the final success of our cause than I have had at any time since the first gun was fired." I replied, "God grant it!" He turned and moved at once toward the head of his division; a few moments thereafter he was lost to my sight in the tumult of battle. These last words, spoken to me by this brave and distinguished soldier, I have often recalled; they can never leave my memory, as within forty minutes after he had uttered them he lay lifeless upon or near the breastworks of the foe.

The two corps advanced in battle array at about 4 P.M., and soon swept away the first line of the Federals, who were driven back upon the main line. At this moment resounded a concentrated roar of musketry, which recalled to me some of the deadliest struggles in Virginia, and which now proclaimed that the possession of Nashville was once more dependent upon the fortunes of war. The conflict continued to rage with intense fury; our troops succeeded in

---

that 'Major-General Cheatham has frankly confessed the great error of which he was guilty, and attaches much blame to himself,' he made a statement for which there was not the slightest foundation."

—General Cheatham, in the "Bivouac."

‡General J. D. Cox has pointed out that the reports confirm his own observation that Hood's artillery was used in the battle.—Editors.

MAP OF
THE BATTLE-FIELD
OF NASHVILLE.
Dec. 15-16th, 1864.

Drawn by Wilbur F. Foster,
Major Engineer Corps, C. S. A.

FROM THE "BIVOUAC" FOR AUGUST, 1885.

breaking the main line at one or more points, capturing and turning some of the guns on their opponents.

Just at this critical moment of the battle, a brigade of the enemy, reported to have been Stanley's,⁄ gallantly charged, and restored the Federal line, capturing at the same time about one thousand of our troops within the intrenchments. Still the ground was obstinately contested, and at several points upon the immediate sides of the breastworks the combatants endeavored to use the musket upon one another, by inverting and raising it perpendicularly, in order to fire; neither antagonist, at this juncture, was able to retreat without almost a certainty of death. It was reported that soldiers were even dragged from one side of the breastworks to the other by men reaching over hurriedly and seizing their enemy by the hair or the collar.

Just before dark Edward Johnson's division of Lee's corps moved gallantly to the support of Cheatham; although it made a desperate charge and succeeded in capturing three stand of colors, it did not effect a permanent breach in the line of the enemy. Unfortunately, the two remaining divisions could not become engaged owing to the obscurity of night. The struggle continued with more or less violence until 9 P.M., when skirmishing and much desultory firing followed until about 3 A.M. the ensuing morning. The enemy then withdrew, leaving his dead and wounded upon the field. Thus terminated one of the fiercest conflicts of the war.

Nightfall, which closed in upon us so soon after the beginning of the battle, prevented the formation and participation of Lee's entire corps on the extreme left. This, it may safely be asserted, saved Schofield's army from destruction. I might, with equal assurance, assert that had Lieutenant-General Lee been in advance at Spring Hill the previous afternoon Schofield's army never would have passed that point.

Major-General Cleburne had been distinguished for his admirable conduct upon many fields, and his loss at this moment was irreparable. He was a man of equally quick perception and strong character, and was, especially in one respect, in advance of many of our people. He possessed the boldness and the wisdom earnestly to advocate, at an early period of the war, the freedom of the negro and the enrollment of the young and able-bodied men of that race. This stroke of policy and additional source of strength to our armies would, in my opinion, have given us our independence.

After the failure of my cherished plan to crush Schofield's army before it reached its strongly fortified position around Nashville, I remained with an effective force of only 23,053.✩ I was therefore well aware of our inability to attack

⁄Opdycke's brigade of Stanley's Fourth Corps, and the second line of Reilly's brigade of Cox's Twenty-third Corps.—EDITORS.

✩As shown by Colonel Mason's official report, made on the 10th of December, ten days after the battle,

the Federals in their new stronghold with any hope of success, although Schofield's troops had abandoned the field at Franklin, leaving their dead and wounded in our possession, and had hastened with considerable alarm into their fortifications—which latter information, in regard to their condition after the battle, I obtained through spies. I knew equally well that in the absence of the prestige of complete victory I could not venture with my small force to cross the Cumberland River into Kentucky, without first receiving reënforcements from the Trans-Mississippi Department. I felt convinced that the Tennesseans and Kentuckians would not join our forces,

MAJOR-GENERAL J. B. STEEDMAN.
FROM A PHOTOGRAPH.

since we had failed in the first instance to defeat the Federal army and capture Nashville. The President was still urgent in his instructions relative to the transference of troops to the Army of Tennessee from Texas, and I daily hoped to receive the glad tidings of their safe passage across the Mississippi River.

Thus, unless strengthened by these long-looked-for reënforcements, the only remaining chance of success in the campaign, at this juncture, was to take position, intrench about Nashville, and await Thomas's attack, which, if handsomely repulsed, might afford us an opportunity to follow up our advantage on the spot, and enter the city on the heels of the enemy.

I could not afford to turn southward, unless for the *special* purpose of forming a junction with the expected reënforcements from Texas, and with the avowed intention to march back again upon Nashville. In truth, our army was

---

our effective strength was: Infantry, 18,242; artillery, 2465; cavalry, 2306,—total, 23,053. This last number, subtracted from 30,000, the strength of the army at Florence, shows a total loss from all causes of 7547, from the 6th of November to the 10th of December, which period includes the engagements at Columbia, Franklin, and of Forrest's cavalry. The enemy's estimate of our losses, as well as of the number of Confederate colors captured, is erroneous, as will be seen by my telegram of December 15th to the Secretary of War:

> "The enemy claim that we lost thirty colors in the fight at Franklin. We lost thirteen, capturing nearly the same number. The men who bore ours were killed on or within the enemy's interior line of works."
>
> —J.B.H.

General J. D. Cox states in his "Franklin and Nashville" that the capture of 22 colors by Reilly and 10 by Opdycke was officially reported and verified at the time.—EDITORS.

in that condition which rendered it more judicious the men should face a decisive issue rather than retreat—in other words, rather than renounce the honor of their cause, without having made a last and manful effort to lift up the sinking fortunes of the Confederacy.

I therefore determined to move upon Nashville, to intrench, to accept the chances of reënforcements from Texas, and, even at the risk of an attack in the meantime by overwhelming numbers, to adopt the only feasible means of defeating the enemy with my own reduced numbers, viz., to await his attack, and, if favored by success, to follow him into his works. I was apprised of each accession to Thomas's army, but was still unwilling to abandon the ground as long as I saw a shadow of probability of assistance from the Trans-Mississippi Department, or of victory in battle; and, as I have just remarked, the troops would, I believed, return better satisfied even after defeat if, in grasping at the last straw, they felt that a brave and vigorous effort had been made to save the country from disaster. Such, at the time, was my opinion, which I have since had no reason to alter.

In accordance with these convictions I ordered the army to move forward on the 1st of December in the direction of Nashville; Lee's corps marched in advance, followed by Stewart's and Cheatham's corps, and the troops bivouacked that night in the vicinity of Brentwood. On the morning of the 2d the march was resumed, and line of battle formed in front of Nashville. Lee's corps was placed in the center and across the Franklin pike; Stewart occupied the left and Cheatham the right—their flanks extending as near the Cumberland as possible, whilst Forrest's cavalry filled the gap between them and the river.

General Rousseau occupied Murfreesboro' in rear of our right, with about eight thousand men, heavily intrenched. General Bate's division and Sears's and Brown's brigades were ordered, on the 5th, to report at that point to General Forrest, who was instructed to watch closely that detachment of the enemy. The same day information was received of the capture of 100 prisoners, two pieces of artillery, 20 wagons and teams by Forrest's cavalry at La Vergne; of the capture and destruction of three block houses on the Chattanooga Railroad by Bate's division; and of the seizure the day previous by Chalmers of two transports on the Cumberland River with 300 mules on board.

We had in our possession two engines and several cars, which ran as far south as Pulaski. Dispatches were sent to Generals Beauregard and Maury to repair the railroad from Corinth to Decatur, as our trains would be running in a day or two to the latter point. This means of transportation was of great service in furnishing supplies to the army. When we reached middle Tennessee our troops had an abundance of provisions, although sorely in need of shoes and clothing.

General Bate's division was ordered to return to the army; Forrest was instructed to direct Palmer's and Mercer's infantry brigades to thoroughly intrench on Stewart's Creek, or at La Vergne, according as he might deem more judicious, to constitute, with these troops and his cavalry, a force in observation of the enemy at Murfreesboro', and, lastly, to send a brigade of cavalry to picket the river at Lebanon.

The Federals having been reported to be massing cavalry at Edgefield, Forrest was instructed to meet and drive them back, if they attempted to cross the Cumberland. The same day, the 10th of December, Generals Stewart and Cheatham were directed to construct detached works in rear of their flanks, which rested near the river, in order to protect these flanks against an effort by the Federals to turn them. Although every possible exertion was made by these officers, the works were not completed when, on the 15th, the Federal army moved out and attacked both flanks, whilst the main assault was directed against our left. It was my intention to have made these defenses self-sustaining, but time was not allowed, as the enemy attacked on the morning of the 15th. Throughout that day they were repulsed at all points of the general line with heavy loss, and only succeeded toward evening in capturing the infantry outposts on our left, and with them the small force together with the artillery posted in these unfinished works. Finding that the main movement of the Federals was directed against our left, the chief engineer was instructed carefully to select a line in prolongation of the left flank; Cheatham's corps was withdrawn from the right during the night of the 15th and posted on the left of Stewart—Cheatham's left resting near the Brentwood Hills. The men were ordered to construct breastworks there during that same night.

The morning of the 16th found us with Lee's right on Overton's Hill. At an early hour the enemy made a general attack along our front, and were again and again repulsed at all points with heavy loss, especially in Lee's front. About 3:30 P.M. the Federals concentrated a number of guns against a portion of our line, which passed over a mound on the left of our center, and which had been occupied during the night. This point was favorable for massing troops for an assault under cover of artillery. Accordingly the enemy availed himself of the advantage presented, massed a body of men—apparently one division—at the base of this mound, and, under the fire of artillery, which prevented our men from raising their heads above the breastworks, made a sudden and gallant charge up to and over our intrenchments. Our line, thus pierced, gave way; soon thereafter it broke at all points, and I beheld for the first and only time a Confederate army abandon the field in confusion. I was seated upon my horse not far in rear when the breach was effected, and soon discovered that all hope to rally the troops was vain.

I did not, I might say, anticipate a break at that time, as our forces up to that moment had repulsed the Federals at every point, and were waving their colors in defiance, crying out to the enemy, "Come on, come on." Just previous to this fatal occurrence I had matured the movement for the next morning. The enemy's right flank, by this hour, stood in air some six miles from Nashville, and I had determined to withdraw my entire force during the night, and attack this exposed flank in rear. I could safely have done so, as I still had open a line of retreat.

The day before the rout, the artillery posted in the detached works had been captured; a number of guns in the main line were abandoned for the reason that the horses could not be brought forward in time to remove them. Thus the total number of guns captured amounted to fifty-four. We had fortunately still remaining a sufficient number of pieces of artillery for the equipment of the army, since, it will be remembered, I had taken with me at the outset of the campaign a large reserve of artillery to use against gun-boats. Our losses in killed and wounded in this engagement were comparatively small, as the troops were protected by breastworks.

Order among the troops was in a measure restored at Brentwood, a few miles in rear of the scene of disaster, through the promptness and gallantry of Clayton's division, which speedily formed and confronted the enemy, with Gibson's brigade and McKenzie's battery, of Fenner's battalion, acting as rearguard of the rear-guard. General Clayton displayed admirable coolness and courage that afternoon and the next morning in the discharge of his duties. Gibson, who evinced conspicuous gallantry and ability in the handling of his troops, succeeded, in concert with Clayton, in checking and staying the first and most dangerous shock which always follows immediately after a rout. The result was that even after the army passed the Big Harpeth, at Franklin, the brigades and divisions were marching in regular order.

General S. D. Lee displayed his usual energy and skill in handling his troops on the 17th, whilst protecting the rear of our army. Unfortunately, in the afternoon he was wounded and forced to leave the field. General C. L. Stevenson then assumed command of Lee's corps, and ably discharged his duties during the continuance of the retreat to and across the Tennessee River.

General Walthall, one of the most able division commanders in the South, was here ordered to form a rear-guard with eight picked brigades and Forrest's cavalry; the march was then resumed in the direction of Columbia, Stewart's corps moving in front, followed by those of Cheatham and Stevenson. The army bivouacked in line of battle near Duck River on the night of the 18th.

The following day we crossed the river and proceeded on different roads leading toward Bainbridge on the Tennessee. I entertained but little concern in regard to being further harassed by the enemy. I therefore continued to march leisurely, and arrived at Bainbridge on the 25th of December. The following day the march was continued in the direction of Tupelo, at which place Cheatham's corps, the last in the line of march, went into camp on the 10th of January, 1865.

On the 13th of January I sent the following dispatch to the Secretary of War: "I request to be relieved from the command of this army."

Upon General Beauregard's arrival at Tupelo, on the 14th of January, I informed him of my application to be relieved from the command of the army. I again telegraphed the authorities in Richmond, stating that the campaigns to the Alabama line and into Tennessee were my own conception; that I alone was responsible; that I had striven hard to execute them in such manner as to bring victory to our people, and at the same time repeated my desire to be relieved. The President finally complied with my request, and I bade farewell to the Army of Tennessee on the 23d of January, 1865, after having served with it somewhat in excess of eleven months, and having performed my duties to the utmost of my ability.

CHAPTER 12

SHERIDAN IN THE SHENANDOAH VALLEY.

Wesley Merritt, Major-General, U.S.V., Brigadier-General, U.S.A.

Up to the summer of 1864 the Shenandoah Valley had not been to the Union armies a fortunate place either for battle or for strategy. A glance at the map will go far toward explaining this. The Valley has a general direction from south-west to north-east. The Blue Ridge Mountains, forming its eastern barrier, are well defined from the James River above Lynchburg to Harper's Ferry on the Potomac. Many passes (in Virginia called "gaps") made it easy of access from the Confederate base of operations; and, bordered by a fruitful country filled with supplies, it offered a tempting highway for an army bent on a flank-

PART OF SHERIDAN'S WAGON TRAIN. FROM A WAR-TIME SKETCH.

ing march on Washington or the invasion of Maryland or Pennsylvania. For the Union armies, while it was an equally practicable highway, it led away from the objective, Richmond, and was exposed to flank attacks through the gaps from vantage-ground and perfect cover.

It was not long after General Grant completed his first campaign in Virginia, and while he was in front of Petersburg, that his attention was called to this famous seat of side issues between Union and Confederate armies. With quick military instinct he saw that the Valley was not useful to the Government for aggressive operations. He decided that it must be made untenable for either army. In doing this he reasoned that the advantage would be with us, who did not want it as a source of supplies, nor as a place of arms, and against the Confederates, who wanted it for both. Accordingly, instructions were drawn up for carrying on a plan of devastating the Valley in a way least injurious to the people. These instructions, which were intended for Hunter, were destined to be carried out by another, and how well this was accomplished it is my purpose to recount.

Hunter's failure to capture Lynchburg in the spring of 1864 and his retreat by a circuitous line opened the Valley to General Early, who had gone to the relief of Lynchburg. Marching down the Valley and taking possession of it without serious opposition, Early turned Harper's Ferry, which was held by a Union force under Sigel, and crossed into Maryland at Shepherdstown. The governors of New York, Pennsylvania, and Massachusetts were called on for hundred-days men to repel the invasion, and later the Army of the Potomac supplied its quota of veterans as a nucleus around which the new levies could rally. General Early marched on Washington, and on the 11th of July was in front of the gates of the capital. The following day, after a severe engagement in which the guns of Fort Stevens took part, he withdrew his forces through Rockville and Poolesville, and, crossing the Potomac above Leesburg, entered the Valley of Virginia through Snicker's Gap. Afterward, crossing the Shenandoah at the ferry of the same name, he moved to Berryville, and there awaited developments.

After the immediate danger to Washington had passed it became a question with General Grant and the authorities in Washington to select an

MAJOR-GENERAL WESLEY MERRITT.
FROM A PHOTOGRAPH.

officer who, commanding in the Valley, would prevent further danger from invasion. After various suggestions,‡ Major-General Philip H. Sheridan was selected temporarily for this command. His permanent occupation of the position was opposed by Secretary Stanton on the ground that he was too young for such important responsibility. On the 7th of August, 1864, Sheridan assumed command of the Middle Military Division and of the army for the protection of the Valley, afterward known as the "Army of the Shenandoah."

Naturally, on assuming command, Sheridan moved with caution. He was incited to this by his instructions, and inclined to it by his unfamiliarity with the country, with the command, and with the enemy he had to deal with. On the other hand, Early, who had nothing of these to learn, save the mettle of his new adversary, was aggressive, and at once manœuvred with a bold front, seemingly anxious for a battle. The movements of the first few days showed, however, that Early was not disposed to give battle unless he could do so on his own conditions.

On the morning of the 10th of August Sheridan, who had massed his army at Halltown, in front of Harper's Ferry, marched toward the enemy's communications, his object being to occupy Early's line of retreat and force him to fight before reënforcements could reach him. The march of my cavalry toward the Millwood-Winchester road brought us in contact with the enemy's cavalry on that road, and it was driven toward Kernstown. At the same time a brigade under Custer, making a reconnoissance on the Berryville-Winchester road, came on the enemy holding a defile of the highway while "his trains and infantry were marching toward Strasburg." As soon as the retreat of the enemy was known to General Sheridan the cavalry was ordered to pursue and harass him. Near White Post, Devin came upon a strongly posted force, which, after a sharp fight, he drove from the field, and the division took position on the Winchester–Front Royal pike. The same day my division had a severe affair with infantry near Newtown, in which the loss to my Second Brigade was considerable.

On the 12th of August, the enemy having retired the night before, the cavalry pursued to Cedar Creek, when it came up with Early's rear-guard and continued skirmishing until the arrival of the head of the infantry column. The day following, the reconnoissance of a brigade of cavalry discovered the enemy strongly posted at Fisher's Hill. About this time Early received his expected reënforcements. General Sheridan, being duly informed of this, made preparations to retire to a position better suited for defense and adapted to the changed conditions of the strength of the two armies.

‡On the 18th of July General Grant suggested Franklin for the command of the projected Middle Military Division, and, on this being objected to, proposed the assignment of Meade, with Hancock to command the Army of the Potomac and Gibbon for the Second Corps.—EDITORS.

On the 13th of August General Devin's brigade of the First Division was ordered to Cedarville on the Front Royal pike, and on the 14th I marched with the rest of my division to the same point, Gibbs taking position near Nineveh. On the arrival of his reënforcements Early had requested General R. H. Anderson, in command, to take station at Front Royal, it being a convenient point from which to make a flank movement in case of attack on Sheridan's command, which Early undoubtedly contemplated. At the same time it constituted a guard to the Luray Valley.

BREVET MAJOR-GENERAL DAVID A. RUSSELL, KILLED AT THE BATTLE OF WINCHESTER, SEPTEMBER 19, 1864. FROM A PHOTOGRAPH.

About 2 P.M. on the 16th an attack was made by this command on the First Cavalry Division, which resulted in the battle of Cedarville. A force of cavalry under Fitz Lee, supported by a brigade of Kershaw's division, made a descent on Devin's brigade. General Fitz Lee drove in the cavalry pickets and attacked Devin with great violence. This force was scarcely repulsed when a brigade of infantry was discovered moving on the opposite bank of the Shenandoah River toward the left of the cavalry position. One regiment of Custer's brigade, dismounted, was moved up to the crest of a hill near the river-bank to meet this force, while the rest of the brigade, mounted, was stationed to the right of the hill. At the same time the Reserve Brigade under General Gibbs was summoned to the field. The enemy advanced boldly, wading the river, and when within short carbine range was met by a murderous volley from the dismounted men, while the remainder of the command charged mounted. The Confederates were thrown into confusion and retreated, leaving 300 prisoners, together with two stands of colors. Anderson hurried reënforcements to his beaten

GENERAL PHILIP H. SHERIDAN. FROM A PHOTOGRAPH TAKEN IN 1864.

brigades, but no further attempt to cross the river was made. The loss to the Union cavalry was about 60 in killed and wounded. The loss to the enemy was not less than 500.

These affairs between the Union cavalry and the enemy's infantry were of more importance than might appear at first glance. They gave the cavalry increased confidence, and made the enemy correspondingly doubtful even of the ability of its infantry, in anything like equal numbers, to contend against our cavalry in the open fields of the Valley.

On the night of the 16th Sheridan withdrew toward his base, and on the following day the cavalry marched, driving all the cattle and live stock in the Valley before it, and burning the grain from Cedar Creek to Berryville. No other private property was injured, nor were families molested.

On the afternoon of the 17th the Third Division of cavalry, under General James H. Wilson, reported to General Torbert, chief-of-cavalry, who with it and Lowell's brigade and the Jersey brigade (Penrose's) of the Sixth Corps was ordered to cover the flank of the army which marched and took position near

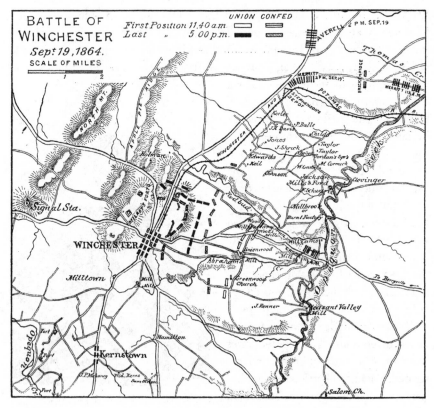

MAP OF THE BATTLE OF WINCHESTER, SEPTEMBER 19, 1864.

Berryville. General Early, who on the morning of the 17th discovered the withdrawal of Sheridan's force, pursued rapidly, Anderson advancing from Front Royal with his command. Early struck Torbert's force with such vigor and with such overwhelming numbers as completely to overthrow it, with considerable loss, and drive it from Winchester. In this affair Penrose's brigade lost about 300 men in killed, wounded, and prisoners, and Wilson's cavalry lost in prisoners some 50 men. At this time, information having reached Sheridan that the reënforcements that had come to Early under Anderson were only part of what might be expected, Sheridan concluded still further to solidify his lines. On the 21st of August Early moved with his army to attack Sheridan. His own command marched through Smithfield toward Charlestown, and Anderson on the direct road through Summit Point. Rodes's and Ramseur's infantry were advanced to the attack, and heavy skirmishing was continued for some time with a loss to the Sixth Corps, principally Getty's division, of 260 killed and wounded. In the meantime Anderson was so retarded by the Union cavalry that he did not reach the field, and night overtaking him at Summit Point, he there went into camp. That night Sheridan drew in the cavalry, and, carrying out the resolution already formed, withdrew his army to Halltown. During the three days following the Confederates demonstrated in front of Sheridan's lines, but to little purpose except to skirmish with Crook's and Emory's pickets. On the 25th, leaving Anderson's force in front of Sheridan, Early moved with his four divisions and Fitzhugh Lee's cavalry to Leetown, from which place he dispatched Lee toward Williamsport while he crossed the railroad at Kearneysville and moved toward Shepherdstown. Between Kearneysville and Leetown he was met by Torbert with the cavalry. A sharp fight followed, in the first shock of which Early's advance, consisting of Wharton's division, was driven back in confusion, but upon discovering the strength of the enemy, Torbert withdrew in good order, though Custer's brigade was pressed so closely that he was forced to cross the Potomac. A charge on the flank of the pursuing infantry relieved Custer from danger, and the next morning he returned, as ordered, via Harper's Ferry to the army at Halltown. Early's movement ended with this affair, and during the following two days he returned to the vicinity of Winchester.

During the absence of Early, R. H. Anderson's position was reconnoitered by Crook with two divisions and Lowell's cavalry brigade, who carried Anderson's lines, driving two brigades from their earth-works and capturing a number of officers and men, after which Anderson withdrew from Sheridan's front.

In a dispatch to Halleck Sheridan said: "I have thought it best to be prudent, everything considered." Grant commended Sheridan's conduct of affairs in general terms, and predicted the withdrawal from the Valley of all of Early's reënforcements. This the pressure of Grant's lines at Petersburg finally accomplished.

On the 28th of August Sheridan moved his army forward to Charlestown.

My division of cavalry marched to Leetown, and drove the enemy's cavalry to Smithfield and across the Opequon. The next day Early's infantry, in turn, drove my division from Smithfield; whereupon Sheridan, advancing with Ricketts's division, repulsed the enemy's infantry, which retired to the west bank of the Opequon. On this day the cavalry had some severe fighting with Early's infantry, but not until in hand-to-hand fighting the Confederate cavalry had been driven from the field.

On the 3d of September Rodes's Confederate division proceeded to Bunker Hill, and in conjunction with Lomax's cavalry made a demonstration which was intended to cover the withdrawal of Anderson's force from the Valley. But on marching toward the gap of the Blue Ridge, via Berryville, Anderson came upon Crook's infantry just taking station there. The meeting was a surprise to both commands and resulted in a sharp engagement which continued till nightfall. On the following morning Early moved with part of his infantry to Anderson's assistance, and demonstrating toward the right of Sheridan's lines, he made show of giving battle, but only long enough to extricate Anderson and his trains, when the entire command retired to the country near Winchester. On the 14th Anderson withdrew from Early's army, and this time unmolested pursued his march through the Blue Ridge to Culpeper Court House. Fitzhugh Lee's cavalry remained with Early.

About this time General Grant visited the Valley and found everything to his satisfaction. Sheridan was master of the situation, and he was not slow in showing it to his chief. On the 12th of September Sheridan had telegraphed Grant to the effect that it was exceedingly difficult to attack Early in his position behind the Opequon, which constituted a formidable barrier; that the crossings, though numerous, were deep, and the banks abrupt and difficult for an attacking force; and, in general, that he was waiting for the chances to change in his favor, hoping that Early would either detach troops or take some less defensible position. His caution was fortunate at this time, and his fearlessness and hardihood were sufficiently displayed thereafter. In the light of criticisms, then, it is curious that the world is now inclined to call Sheridan reckless and foolhardy.

At 2 A.M. of September 19th Sheridan's army was astir under orders to attack Early in front of Winchester. My cavalry was to proceed to the fords of the Opequon, near the railroad crossing, and, if opposed only by cavalry, was to cross at daylight and, turning to the left, attack Early's left flank. Wilson's division was to precede the infantry and clear the crossing of the Opequon, on the Berryville road,

FAC-SIMILE (REDUCED) OF
PRESIDENT LINCOLN'S LETTER
TO GENERAL SHERIDAN.

leading to Winchester. The infantry of the army, following Wilson, was to cross the Opequon, first Wright and then Emory, while Crook's command, marching across country, was to take position in reserve, or be used as circumstances might require. South of Winchester, running nearly east and emptying into the Opequon, is Abraham's Creek, and nearly parallel to it, on the north of Winchester, is Red Bud Creek. These two tributaries flanked the usual line of the Confederates, when in position, covering Winchester, and on this line, across the Berryville-Winchester road, Ramseur was stationed with his infantry, when Sheridan's forces debouched from the defile and deployed for attack. Sheridan's plan was to attack and overthrow this part of Early's force before the rest of the army, which a day or two before was known to be scattered to the north as far as Martinsburg, could come to its assistance. At daylight Wilson advanced across the Opequon, and carried the earth-work which covered the defile and captured part of the force that held it. The infantry followed—Wright's corps first, with Getty leading, and Emory next. Between two and three miles from the Opequon, Wright came up with Wilson, who was waiting in the earth-work he had captured. There the country was suitable for the deployment of the column, which commenced forming line at once. Ramseur, with the bulk of the Confederate artillery, immediately opened on Wright's troops, and soon the Union guns were in position to reply. Wilson took position on the left of the Sixth Corps. Then followed a delay that thwarted the part of the plan which contemplated the destruction of Early's army in detail. Emory's command was crowded off the road in its march, and so delayed by the guns and trains of the Sixth Corps that it was slow getting on the field, and it was hours before the lines were formed.♣ This delay gave the Confederates time to bring up the infantry of Gordon and Rodes. Gordon, who first arrived, was posted on Ramseur's left near the Red Bud, and when Rodes arrived with three of his four brigades, he was given the center. This change in the situation, which necessitated fighting Early's army in his chosen position, did not disconcert the Union commander. He had come out to fight, and though chafing at the unexpected delay, fight he would to the bitter end.

In the meantime the cavalry, which had been ordered to the right, had not

---

♣In an unpublished narrative, addressed to the Adjutant-General, and dated May 30th, 1872, Emory states that all the infantry was placed under command of Wright; that Wright ordered the column to march at 2 A.M., the Sixth Corps leading, followed by its train, the Nineteenth Corps next, followed by its train, then the Eighth Corps; that he (Emory) moved with the Nineteenth Corps at the appointed hour, and at the crossing of the Opequon was halted by General Wright in person, the head of the Sixth Corps not having passed yet; that the subsequent march was obstructed by the trains of the Sixth Corps [see above]; that, hearing a lively cannonade, after sending forward all his staff-officers in succession for instructions, he finally disregarded the order of march, and putting his corps in motion rode on to General Sheridan, who at once confirmed his action. The Sixth Corps was still engaged in crossing the Opequon. Owing to these delays, it was midday before the Nineteenth Corps reached its position.

—Editors.

THE BATTLE OF WINCHESTER—RICKETTS'S ADVANCE AGAINST RODES'S DIVISION ON THE MORNING OF SEPTEMBER 19, 1864.

been idle. Moving at the same time as did the rest of the army, my division reached the fords of the Opequon near the railroad crossing at early dawn. Here I found a force of cavalry supported by Breckinridge's infantry. After sharp skirmishing the stream was crossed at three different points, but the enemy contested every foot of the way beyond. The cavalry, however, hearing Sheridan's guns, and knowing the battle was in progress, was satisfied with the work it was doing in holding from Early a considerable force of infantry. The battle here continued for some hours, the cavalry making charges on foot or mounted according to the nature of the country, and steadily though slowly driving the enemy's force toward Winchester. Finally Breckinridge, leaving one brigade to assist the cavalry in retarding our advance, moved to the help of Early, arriving on the field about 2 P.M.

It was 11:30 A.M. before Sheridan's lines were ready to advance. When they moved forward Early, who had gathered all his available strength, met them with a front of fire, and the battle raged with the greatest fury. The advance was pressed in the most resolute manner, and the resistance by the enemy being equally determined and both sides fighting without cover, the casualties were very great. Wright's infantry forced Ramseur and Rodes steadily to the rear, while Emory on the right broke the left of the enemy's line and threw it into confusion. At this time the Confederate artillery opened with canister at short range, doing fearful execution. This, coupled with the weakening of the center at the junction between Emory and Wright, and with a charge delivered on this junction of the lines by a part of Rodes's command, just arrived on the field, drove back the Union center. At this critical moment Russell's division of Wright's corps moved into the breach on Emory's left, and, striking the flank of the Confederate troops who were pursuing Grover, restored the lines and stayed the Confederate advance.✦ The loss to both sides had been heavy. Gen-

---

✦General Emory, in his official narrative, says of the section on the right at this point:

"Grover's division was placed in line of battle on the right of the Sixth Corps, and Dwight's division was placed in échelon on the right of Grover's. Not many minutes elapsed before receiving orders to charge the enemy. I ordered Grover's division to charge, holding Dwight's in reserve. The charge was made with great bravery, dispersing the enemy's first line; but this first success seemed to throw our men off their guard, and give them too much confidence, and they rushed, without orders, with impetuosity upon the second line of the enemy, which had the protection of woods and stone walls, and they met with a bloody repulse.

"Simultaneously with this repulse, and a moment or two preceding it, I saw that the charge of the Sixth Corps, on my left, had been repulsed. Quickly drawing a brigade of Dwight's division from the right, I placed it on the line occupied by Grover's division, behind which that division rallied in good order, considering the terrible repulse they had met. The enemy rose from their sheltered position and charged in mass on our lines. A small point of woods projected at right angles from the right of my line; in this I posted Colonel Nicholas W. Day, 131st New York Volunteers, with his regiment, and as the enemy came down on our lines with loud yells they received the fire of this regiment in the flank and rear, and at the same time receiving a very spirited fire in front, they broke and fled."—EDITORS.

eral Russell of the Union army and Generals Rodes and Godwin of the Confederate were among the killed.

A lull in the battle now followed, which General Sheridan improved to restore his lines and to bring up Crook, who had not yet been engaged. It had been the original purpose to use Crook on the left to assist Wilson's cavalry in cutting off Early's retreat toward Newtown. But the stress of battle compelled Sheridan to bring his reserve in on the line, and accordingly Crook was ordered up on Emory's right, one brigade extending to the north of Red Bud Creek. At the same time Early re-formed his lines, placing Breckinridge's command in reserve. At this time Merritt, who with his cavalry had followed Breckinridge closely to the field, approached on the left rear of the Confederates, driving their flying and broken cavalry through the infantry lines. The cavalry then charged repeatedly into Early's infantry, first striking it in the rear, and afterward face to face as it changed front to repel the attack.⌡ These attacks were made by the cavalry without any knowledge of the state of the battle except what was apparent to the eye. First Devin charged with his brigade, returning to rally, with three battle-flags and over three hundred prisoners. Next Lowell charged with his brigade, capturing flags, prisoners, and two guns. After this the entire division was formed and charged to give the final coup.⌐

At the time of this last charge the Union infantry advanced along the entire line and the enemy fled in disorder from the field, and night alone (for it was now dark) saved Early's army from capture.

At daylight on the morning of the 20th the army moved rapidly up the

---

⌡"Breckinridge was scarcely in position before our cavalry on the left was discovered coming back in great confusion followed by the enemy's, and Breckinridge's force was ordered to the left to repel this cavalry force, which had gotten in rear of my left, and this with the assistance of the artillery he succeeded in doing. But as soon as the firing was heard in rear of our left flank the infantry commenced falling back along the whole line, and it was very difficult to stop them. I succeeded, however, in stopping enough of them in the old rifle-pits, constructed by General Johnston, to arrest the progress of the enemy's infantry, which commenced advancing again when confusion in our ranks was discovered, and would still have won the day if our cavalry would have stopped the enemy's; but so overwhelming was the latter, and so demoralized was the larger part of ours, that no assistance was received from it.

"The enemy's cavalry again charged around my left flank and the men began to give way again, so that it was necessary for me to retire through the town."

—Letter from General Early to General Lee, dated October 9th, 1864.

⌐An officer who was in this last charge, and who had the misfortune to fall into the hands of the enemy in consequence of the breaking of his bridle-curb, says: "The confusion, disorder, and actual rout produced by the successive charges of Merritt's division would appear incredible did not the writer actually witness them. To the right a battery with guns disabled and caissons shattered was trying to make to the rear, the men and horses impeded by broken regiments of cavalry and infantry; to the left, the dead and wounded, in confused masses, around their field-hospitals—many of the wounded, in great excitement, seeking shelter in Winchester; directly in front, an ambulance, the driver nervously clutching the reins, while six men in great alarm were carrying to it the body of General Rodes." General Torbert, chief of cavalry, also says in his report of the battle of Winchester: "This day the First Division (Brigadier-

main Valley road in pursuit of the enemy. Early had not stopped on the night of the battle until he reached the shelter of Fisher's Hill. This is admirably situated for defense for an army resisting a movement south. Here the Valley is obstructed by the Massanutten Mountains and its width virtually reduced to four or five miles. In this position Early's right was protected by impassable mountains and by the north fork of the Shenandoah, and he at once took means to protect his left artificially.

"On the evening of the 20th," reports Sheridan, "Wright and Emory went into position on the heights of Strasburg, Crook north of Cedar Creek, the cavalry on the right and rear of Emory, extending to the back road."

On the 21st Sheridan occupied the day in examining the enemy's lines and improving his own. Accompanied by General Wright, he directed changes in the lines of the Sixth Corps, so that it occupied the high lands to the north of Tumbling Run. Wright did not secure this vantage-ground without a severe struggle, in which Warner's brigade was engaged, finally holding the heights after a brilliant charge. Sheridan decided on turning Early's impregnable position by a movement on the Little North Mountain. On the night of the 21st he concealed Crook's command in the timber north of Cedar Creek. In making his disposition Sheridan did not attempt to cover the entire front, it being his intention to flank the enemy by Crook's march, and then, by advancing the right of Wright's and Emory's line, to form connection and make his line continuous. On the morning of the 22d, Crook, being still concealed, was marched to the timber near Little North Mountain and massed in it. Before this, Torbert, with his two divisions of cavalry, except one brigade (Devin's), was ordered via Front Royal into Luray Valley, with a view to reëntering the Valley of the Shenandoah at New Market. This design was not accomplished.✶

Not long before sundown Crook's infantry, which had not yet been discovered by the enemy, struck Early's left and rear so suddenly as to cause his army to break in confusion and flee. The rout was complete, the whole of Sheridan's troops uniting in the attack. That night, though the darkness made the marching difficult, Sheridan followed Early as far as Woodstock, some fifteen miles, and the following day up to Mount Jackson, where he drove the enemy, now to some extent reorganized, from a strong position on the opposite bank of the river. From this point the enemy retreated in line of battle. But every effort to make him fight failed. No doubt Sheridan in this pursuit regretted the absence

---

General Merritt) alone captured 775 prisoners, about 70 officers, seven battle-flags, and two pieces of artillery."—W.M.

✶It may be here remarked that Sheridan was, as a rule, opposed to combinations involving long marches. He had no faith in their successful accomplishment. It is therefore easy to believe that he looked upon this movement of the cavalry as a means of turning the Confederates out of the position at Fisher's Hill, provided his infantry was not successful in the present project.—W.M.

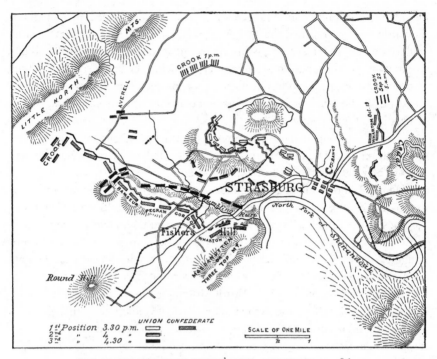

MAP OF THE BATTLE OF FISHER'S HILL, SEPTEMBER 22, 1864.

of his cavalry, which, with Torbert, was striving, by a circuitous and obstructed march, to reach the enemy's rear.

A few miles beyond New Market Early abandoned the main road, which leads on through Harrisonburg; turning to the east, he pursued the road that leads thence to Port Republic. This direction was taken to receive the reënforcements which were to reach him through one of the gaps of the Blue Ridge. For it appears that Kershaw and his command had not proceeded beyond Culpeper in his march to Lee's army before he was ordered to return to Early, the news of whose overthrow at Winchester, and afterward at Fisher's Hill, had reached the authorities at Richmond.

On the 25th of September Torbert with the cavalry rejoined General Sheridan, and was at once put to work doing what damage was possible to the Central Railway. After proceeding to Staunton and destroying immense quantities of army stores, Torbert moved to Waynesboro', destroying the railway track, and after burning the railway bridges toward the Blue Ridge, and on being threatened by Early's forces, which had moved thither to attack him, he retired to Bridgewater.

Naturally a question now arose between Sheridan, the authorities in Washington, and General Grant as to the future theater of the campaign and the line of operations. Sheridan was opposed to the proposition submitted by

THE REAR-GUARD—GENERAL CUSTER'S DIVISION RETIRING FROM MOUNT JACKSON,
OCTOBER 7, 1864. FROM A WAR-TIME SKETCH.

the others, which was to operate against Central Virginia from his base in the
Valley. The general reasons for his opposition were the distance from the base
of supplies, the lines of communication, which in a country infested by guerrillas it would take an army to protect, and the nearness, as the campaign progressed, if successful, to the enemy's base, from which large reënforcements
could easily and secretly be hurried and the Union army be overwhelmed.
But before the plan was finally adopted a new turn was given to affairs, and
the plan originally formed was delayed in its execution if not changed altogether.

When the army commenced its return march, the cavalry was deployed
across the Valley, burning, destroying, or taking away everything of value, or
likely to become of value, to the enemy. It was a severe measure, and appears
severer now in the lapse of time; but it was necessary as a measure of war. The
country was fruitful and was the paradise of bushwhackers and guerrillas. They
had committed numerous murders and wanton acts of cruelty on all parties
weaker than themselves. Officers and men had been murdered in cold blood on
the roads, while proceeding without a guard through an apparently peaceful
country. The thoughtless had been lured to houses only to find, when too late,
that a foe was concealed there, ready to take their lives if they did not surrender. It is not wonderful, then, that the cavalry sent to work the destruction contemplated did not at that time shrink from the duty. It is greatly to their credit

that no personal violence on any inhabitant was ever reported, even by their enemies. The Valley from Staunton to Winchester was completely devastated, and the armies thereafter occupying that country had to look elsewhere for their supplies. There is little doubt, however, that enough was left in the country for the subsistence of the people, for this, besides being contemplated by orders, resulted of necessity from the fact that, while the work was done hurriedly, the citizens had ample time to secrete supplies, and did so.

The movement north was conducted without interruption for two days, except that the enemy's cavalry, made more bold by the accession to its strength of a command under General T. L. Rosser, followed our cavalry, dispersed across the Valley as already described. On the 8th of October the enemy's cavalry harassed Custer's division on the back road during the day, taking from him some battery-forges and wagons. The cavalry also showed itself on the main road upon which Merritt was retiring, but dispersed upon being charged by a brigade which was sent to develop their strength. That night Sheridan gave orders to his chief-of-cavalry, Torbert, to attack and beat the enemy's cavalry the following day "or to get whipped himself," as it was expressed.

On the morning of the 9th Torbert's cavalry moved out to fight that of the enemy under Generals Rosser and Lomax. Merritt's division moved on the pike and extended across to the back road where Custer was concentrated. A stubborn cavalry engagement commenced the day, but it was not long before the Confederate cavalry was broken and routed, and from that time till late in the day it was driven a distance of twenty-six miles, losing everything on wheels, except one gun, and this at one time was in possession of a force too weak to hold it. At one time General Lomax was a prisoner, but made his escape by personally overthrowing his captor. In this affair the advantage of pluck, dash, and confidence, as well as of numbers, was on the Union side. From the time of the occupation of the Valley by Sheridan's force the cavalry had been the active part of his command. Scarcely a day passed that they were not engaged in some affair, and often with considerable loss, as is shown by the fact that in twenty-six engagements, aside from the battles, the cavalry lost an aggregate of 3205 men and officers.

In reporting the result of the cavalry battle of October 9th, Early says:

"This is very distressing to me, and God knows I have done all in my power to avert the disasters which have befallen this command; but the fact is the enemy's cavalry is so much superior to ours, both in numbers and equipment, and the country is so favorable to the operations of cavalry, that it is impossible for ours to compete with his."

He further says in this same connection:

"Lomax's cavalry is armed entirely with rifles and has no sabers, and the consequence is they cannot fight on horseback, and in this open country they cannot successfully fight on foot against large bodies of cavalry."

This is a statement on which those who think our cavalry never fought mounted and with the saber should ponder. The cavalry had scant justice done it in reports sent from the battle-field; and current history, which is so much made up of first reports and first impressions, has not to a proper extent been impressed with this record.

On the return of the army after the pursuit of the scattered remnants of Early's force, General Sheridan placed it in position on Cedar Creek north of the Shenandoah, Crook on the left, Emory in the center, and Wright in reserve. The cavalry was placed on the flanks. The occupation of Cedar Creek was not intended to be permanent; there were many serious objections to it as a position for defense. The approaches from all points of the enemy's stronghold at Fisher's Hill were through wooded ravines in which the growth and undulations concealed the movement of troops, and for this reason and its proximity to Fisher's Hill the pickets protecting its front could not be thrown, without danger of capture, sufficiently far to the front to give ample warning of the advance of the enemy. We have already seen how Sheridan took advantage of like conditions at Fisher's Hill. Early was now contemplating the surprise of his antagonist.

On the 12th of October Sheridan received a dispatch from Halleck saying that Grant wished a position taken far enough south to serve as a base for operations upon Gordonsville and Charlottesville. On the 13th and the 16th he received dispatches from the Secretary of War and from General Halleck pressing him to visit Washington for consultation.

On the 15th General Sheridan, taking with him Torbert with part of the cavalry, started for Washington, the design being to send the cavalry on a raid to Gordonsville and vicinity. The first camp was made near Front Royal, from which point the cavalry was returned to the army, it being considered safer to do so in consequence of a dispatch intercepted by our signal officers from the enemy's station on Three Top Mountain, and forwarded to General Sheridan by General Wright. This dispatch was as follows:

"To LIEUTENANT-GENERAL EARLY: Be ready to move as soon as my forces join you, and we will crush Sheridan.

—LONGSTREET, Lieutenant-General."

In sending back the cavalry General Sheridan wrote to General Wright, directing caution on his part, so that he might be duly prepared to resist the at-

THE SURPRISE AT CEDAR CREEK. FROM A WAR-TIME SKETCH.

The right of the picture shows the Confederate flanking column attacking the left of the Nineteenth Corps from the rear. The Union troops, after a determined resistance, took position on the outer side of their rifle-pits.

tack in case the above dispatch was genuine.‡ Sheridan continued to Washington, and the cavalry resumed its station in the line of defense at Cedar Creek. At this time everything was quiet—suspiciously so.

On the 16th Custer made a reconnoissance in his front on the back road,

‡General Wright wrote to General Sheridan, October 16th, inclosing Longstreet's intercepted message, and adding:

"If the enemy should be strongly reënforced in cavalry he might, by turning our *right,* give us a great deal of trouble.... I shall only fear an attack on my *right*."

To this Sheridan replied, the same day, from Front Royal:

"The cavalry is all ordered back to you.... Close in Colonel Powell, who will be at this point.... Look well to your ground, and be well prepared."

In his official report of the campaign General Sheridan says:

"During my absence the enemy had gathered all his strength,... striking Crook, who held the *left* of our line, in flank and rear, so unexpectedly and forcibly as to drive in his outposts, invade his camp, and turn his position. This surprise was owing, probably, to not closing in Powell, or that the cavalry divisions of Merritt and Custer were placed on the *right* of our line, where, it had always occurred to me, there was but little danger of attack."

The italics in these quotations are not in the originals.—EDITORS.

but found no enemy outside the lines at Fisher's Hill. This absence of the enemy's cavalry was accounted for the next morning just before daylight by the appearance of Rosser in the rear of Custer's picket line with his cavalry and one brigade of infantry. Rosser carrying the infantry behind his cavalry troopers had made a march of thirty-two miles to capture an exposed brigade of Custer's division on the right; but a change in the arrangements of the command (the return of Torbert) thwarted the scheme, and it resulted only in the capture of a picket guard. On the 18th reconnoissances on both flanks discovered no sign of a movement by the enemy.

The result of the destruction of supplies in the Valley was now being felt by Early's troops. About this time he writes: "I was now compelled to move back for want of provisions and forage, or attack the enemy in his position with the hope of driving him from it; and I determined to attack." From reports made by General Gordon and a staff-officer who ascended Three Top Mountain to reconnoiter the Union position, and the result of a reconnoissance made at the same time by General Pegram toward the right flank of the Union army, General Early concluded to attack by secretly moving a force to turn Sheridan's left flank at Cedar Creek.

The plan of this attack was carefully made; the routes the troops were to pursue, even after the battle had commenced, were carefully designated. [See General Early's article, p. 1,026.] The attack was made at early dawn. The surprise was complete. Crook's camp, and afterward Emory's, were attacked in

HILL AT CEDAR CREEK OCCUPIED BY SHERIDAN'S LEFT, OCTOBER 19, 1864,
AS SEEN FROM KERSHAW'S FORD. FROM A PHOTOGRAPH TAKEN IN 1865.

flank and rear and the men and officers driven from their beds, many of them not having the time to hurry into their clothes, except as they retreated half awake and terror-stricken from the overpowering numbers of the enemy. Their own artillery, in conjunction with that of the enemy, was turned on them, and long before it was light enough for their eyes, unaccustomed to the dim light, to distinguish friend from foe, they were hurrying to our right and rear intent only on their safety. Wright's infantry, which was farther removed from the point of attack, fared somewhat better, but did not offer more than a spasmodic resis-

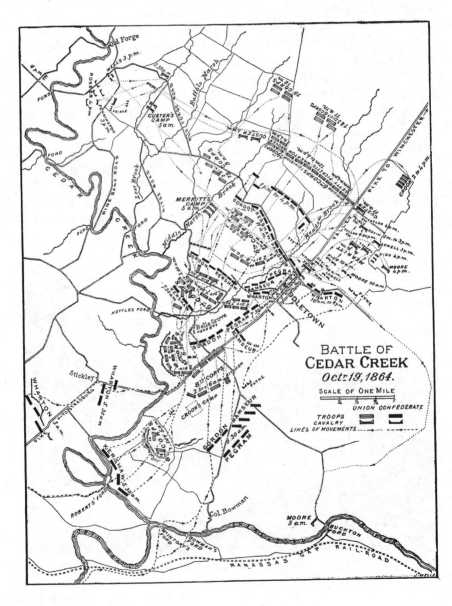

BATTLE OF
CEDAR CREEK
Oct. 19, 1864.

SCALE OF ONE MILE

UNION CONFEDERATE

TROOPS
CAVALRY
LINES OF MOVEMENTS

tance. The cavalry on the right was on the alert. The rule that in the immediate presence of the enemy the cavalry must be early prepared for attack resulted in the whole First Division being up with breakfast partly finished, at the time the attack commenced. A brigade sent on reconnoissance to the right had opened with its guns some minutes before the main attack on the left, for it had met the cavalry sent by Early to make a demonstration on our right.

The disintegration of Crook's command did not occupy many minutes. With a force of the enemy passing through its camp of sleeping men, and another powerful column well to their rear, it was not wonderful that the men as fast as they were awakened by the noise of battle thought first and only of saving themselves from destruction. The advance of Gordon deflected this fleeing throng from the main road to the rear, and they passed over to the right of the army and fled along the back road. Emory made an attempt to form line facing along the main road, but the wave of Gordon's advance on his left, and the thunders of the attack along the road from Strasburg, rendered the position untenable, and he was soon obliged to withdraw to save his lines from capture.[*]

At this time there were hundreds of stragglers moving off by the right to the rear, and all efforts to stop them proved of no avail. A line of cavalry was stretched across the fields on the right, which halted and formed a respectable force of men, so far as numbers were concerned, but these fled and disappeared to the rear as soon as the force which held them was withdrawn. By degrees the strength of the battle died away. The infantry of the Sixth Corps made itself felt on the advance of the enemy, and a sort of confidence among the troops which had not fled from the field was being restored. A brigade of cavalry was ordered to the left to intercept the enemy's advance to Winchester. Taylor's battery of artillery, belonging to the cavalry, moved to the south, and, taking position with the infantry which was retiring, opened on the enemy. The artillery with the cavalry was the only artillery left to the army. The other guns had either been captured or sent to the rear. This battery remained on the infantry lines and did much toward impeding the enemy's advance until the cavalry changed position to the Winchester-Strasburg road. This change took place by direction of General Torbert about 10 o'clock. In making it the cavalry marched through the broken masses of infantry direct to a point on the main road north-east of Middletown. The enemy's artillery fire was terrific. Not a man of the cavalry left the

---

[*]General Emory states in his "Narrative" that the Nineteenth Corps promptly repulsed the first attack on them but, the enemy having gained their rear through the capture of Crook's camps, then fell back about a mile and a half to a new line that "under the circumstances would have done honor to the best regular troops in the world." They were not again attacked, but by order of General Wright fell back in perfect order, about a mile, when "the Nineteenth Corps was again halted, and the men immediately facing about commenced throwing off their kits and stripping to renew the fight." About noon General Emory says he was again ordered by General Wright to retire to the position in which General Sheridan found the army on his arrival.—EDITORS.

ranks unless he was wounded, and everything was done with the precision and quietness of troops on parade. General Merritt informed Colonel Warner of Getty's division, near which the cavalry passed, and which was at that time following the general retreat of the army, of the point where the cavalry would take position and fight, and Warner promised to notify General Getty, and no doubt did so, for that division of the Sixth Corps advanced to the position on the cavalry's right. Then Devin and Lowell charged and drove back the advancing Confederates. Lowell dismounted his brigade and held some stone walls whose position was suited to defense. Devin held on to his advance ground. Here the enemy's advance was checked for the first time, and beyond this it did not go.

The enemy's infantry sheltered themselves from our cavalry attacks in the woods to the left, and in the inclosures of the town of Middletown. But they opened a devastating fire of artillery. This was the state of affairs when Sheridan arrived.

Stopping at Winchester over night on the 18th, on his way from Washington, General Sheridan heard the noise of the battle the following morning, and hurried to the field. His coming restored confidence. A cheer from the cavalry, which awakened the echoes of the valley, greeted him and spread the good news of his coming over the field.⁺

⁺In his "Personal Memoirs" (New York: C. L. Webster & Co., 1888), Vol. II., General Sheridan says that toward 6 A.M. of October 19th word was brought to him (at Winchester) of the artillery firing at Cedar Creek. Between half-past 8 and 9 o'clock, while he was riding along the main street of Winchester, toward Cedar Creek, the demeanor of the people who showed themselves at the windows convinced him that the citizens had received secret information from the battle-field, "and were in raptures over some good news." The narrative continues:

"For a short distance I traveled on the road, but soon found it so blocked with wagons and wounded men that my progress was impeded, and I was forced to take to the adjoining fields to make haste....

"My first halt was made just north of Newtown, where I met a chaplain digging his heels into the sides of his jaded horse, and making for the rear with all possible speed. I drew up for an instant, and inquired of him how matters were going at the front. He replied, 'Everything is lost; but all will be right when you get there;' yet, notwithstanding this expression of confidence in me, the parson at once resumed his breathless pace to the rear. At Newtown I was obliged to make a circuit to the left, to get around the village. I could not pass through it, the streets were so crowded, but meeting on this detour Major McKinley, of Crook's staff, he spread the news of my return through the motley throng there.

"When nearing the Valley pike, just north of Newtown, I saw about three-fourths of a mile west of the pike a body of troops, which proved to be Ricketts's and Wheaton's divisions of the Sixth Corps, and then learned that the Nineteenth Corps had halted a little to the right and rear of these; but I did not stop, desiring to get to the extreme front. Continuing on parallel with the pike, about midway between Newtown and Middletown I crossed to the west of it, and a little later came up in rear of Getty's division of the Sixth Corps. When I arrived, this division and the cavalry were the only troops in the presence of and resisting the enemy; they were apparently acting as a rear-guard at a point about three miles north of the line we held at Cedar Creek when the battle began. General Torbert was the first officer to meet me, saying as he rode up, 'My God! I am glad you've come....'

He rapidly made the changes necessary in the lines, and then ordered an advance. The cavalry on the left charged down on the enemy in their front, scattering them in all directions. The infantry, not to be outdone by the mounted men, moved forward in quick time and charged impetuously the lines of Gordon, which broke and fled.[b] It took less time to drive the enemy from the field than it had for them to take it. They seemed to feel the changed conditions in the Union ranks, for their divisions broke one after another and disappeared toward their rear. The cavalry rode after them and over them, until night fell and ended the fray at the foot of Fisher's Hill. Three battle-flags and twenty-

REDUCED FAC-SIMILE OF PRESIDENT LINCOLN'S CONGRATULATIONS TO GENERAL SHERIDAN ON THE BATTLE OF CEDAR CREEK.

"Jumping my horse over the line of rails, I rode to the crest of the elevation, and there, taking off my hat, the men rose up from behind their barricade with cheers of recognition.... I then turned back to the rear of Getty's division, and as I came behind it a line of regimental flags rose up out of the ground, as it seemed, to welcome me. They were mostly the colors of Crook's troops, who had been stampeded and scattered in the surprise of the morning. The color-bearers, having withstood the panic, had formed behind the troops of Getty. The line with the colors was largely composed of officers, among whom I recognized Colonel R. B. Hayes, since President of the United States, one of the brigade commanders. At the close of this incident I crossed the little narrow valley, or depression, in rear of Getty's line, and, dismounting on the opposite crest, established that point as my headquarters.... Returning to the place where my headquarters had been established, I met near them Ricketts's division, under General Keifer, and General Frank Wheaton's division, both marching to the front. When the men of these divisions saw me they began cheering and took up the double-quick to the front, while I turned back toward Getty's line to point out where these returning troops should be placed.

"All this had consumed a great deal of time, and I concluded to visit again the point to the east of the Valley pike, from where I had first observed the enemy, to see what he was doing. Arrived there, I could plainly see him getting ready for attack, and Major Forsyth now suggested that it would be well to ride along the line of battle before the enemy assailed us, for although the troops had learned of my return, but few of them had seen me. Following his suggestion I started in behind the men, but when a few paces had been taken I crossed to the front, hat in hand, passed along the entire length of the infantry line; and it is from this circumstance that many of the officers and men who then received me with such heartiness have since supposed that that was my first appearance on the field. But at least two hours had elapsed since I reached the ground, for it was after midday when this incident of riding down the front took place, and I arrived not later, certainly, than half-past ten o'clock."

—EDITORS.

[b] General Emory says in his "Narrative":

"This electric message from General Sheridan put every man on his feet.... Very soon the pickets came in, quickly followed by the enemy's infantry. Our first line [Grover] then rose

two guns were added to the trophies of the cavalry that day. Early lost almost all his artillery and trains, besides everything that was captured from the Union army in the morning.[a]

The victory was dearly bought. The killed or mortally wounded included General Bidwell and Colonels Thoburn and Kitching, besides many other officers and men. Among the killed in the final charge by the cavalry at Cedar Creek was Colonel Charles Russell Lowell. He had been wounded earlier in the day, but had declined to leave the field.

The battle of Cedar Creek has been immortalized by poets and historians. The transition from defeat, rout, and confusion to order and victory, and all this depending on one man, made the country wild with enthusiasm.

The victory was a fitting sequel to Winchester, a glorious prelude to Five Forks and Appomattox. In this battle fell mortally wounded on the Confederate side Major-General Stephen D. Ramseur, four years before a classmate of the writer at West Point. A Union officer—a friend—watched by his side in his last moments and conveyed to his southern home his last words of affection.

There is little more to record of events in the Valley. Part of the night after its defeat Early's army rested in the intrenchments on Fisher's Hill, but before dawn the next day it retreated to New Market. Rosser, with the Confederate cavalry, acted as rear-guard, and was driven by the Union cavalry beyond Woodstock. While Early remained at New Market reënforcements were sent him in the way of convalescents and one brigade from south-western Virginia. He contented himself, however, with remaining on the defensive.

The winter of 1864–65 was passed by Sheridan's command at Kernstown, where better protection could be given the troops and a short line of supplies secured. He moved to this position in November. About this time I moved under orders with my division of cavalry into Loudoun Valley and reduced it to a state of destitution, so far as supplies for the enemy were concerned, as had been done in other parts of the valley. On December 19th Torbert with two divisions of cavalry marched through Chester Gap in another raid on the Virginia Central Railway; but this attempt, like the others, was unsuccessful. The

---

up *en masse* and delivered their fire, and the enemy disappeared. There was not a sound of musket or gun for twenty minutes following. The First Division was deployed to the right of the Second, and the charge commenced.... The enemy resisted at every strong fence and ditch and other obstacle with great bravery, but still the line swept on. The First Brigade (Colonel Edwin P. Davis) of the First Division (Dwight's), which was on the extreme right, with unparalleled intrepidity and fleetness completely enveloped the enemy, so that one hour before the sun set ... the troops were in complete command ... of the camp they had occupied in the morning."

[a]It may be here remarked of this battle, as well as that at Winchester, that General Early speaks of the repulse of cavalry charges where no repulse occurred. Cavalry, even after successful charges, from the nature of the arm, is oftentimes obliged to retire and reform preparatory to making a new charge, or allowing other cavalry to charge.—W.M.

local troops and Valley cavalry succeeded in delaying Torbert until infantry was hurried by rail from Richmond, when he was forced to retire. As a diversion in favor of Torbert's expedition Custer's cavalry was moved up the Valley to engage the cavalry of Early. Near Harrisonburg he was attacked and surprised and was forced to retreat.

In making these expeditions the troops suffered intensely from cold, bad roads, and miserable camps. This was especially so with Torbert's column in crossing the mountains. It is difficult to imagine a more disagreeable duty for a mounted soldier than marching over sleety, slushy, snowy or icy roads in winter, and bivouacking without the means of protection. It is demoralizing to men and ruinous to horses.

After the failure of these expeditions no further movements were attempted in the Valley, and most of the infantry of Sheridan's army was sent either to the Army of the Potomac at Petersburg, or elsewhere where it was needed. In February Sheridan made arrangements to march from the Valley with the cavalry with a view to interrupting and destroying, as far as possible, the lines of supply through central Virginia. After accomplishing this it was intended that he should either move west of Richmond and join Sherman's army, or return to the Valley, or join Meade's army in front of Petersburg, as might be most practicable. February 27th the movement commenced, the command consisting of two superb divisions of cavalry which had been recruited and remounted during the winter, under myself, as chief-of-cavalry. The march to Staunton was made without noticeable opposition. On the morning of March 2d Early was found posted on a ridge west of Waynesboro'. The veteran soldier was full of pluck and made a bold front for a fight, but his troops were overcome, almost without even perfunctory resistance, by the advance regiments of the column, and Early, with a few general officers, barely escaped capture by flight. All Early's supplies, all transportation, all the guns, ammunition and flags, and most of the officers and men of the army were captured and sent to the rear.

From this point Sheridan moved unmolested to the Virginia Central Railroad, which was destroyed for miles, large bridges being wrecked, the track torn up, and the rails heated and bent. The command was divided and sent to the James River Canal, which was destroyed as effectually as the railroad. This done, the cavalry proceeded to White House, on the Pamunkey River, where it arrived on March 19th, 1865.

CHAPTER 13

REPELLING HOOD'S INVASION OF TENNESSEE.

Henry Stone, Brevet Colonel, U.S.V.,
Member of the Staff of General Thomas.

On September 28th, 1864, less than four weeks from the day the Union forces occupied Atlanta, General Sherman, who found his still unconquered enemy, General Hood, threatening his communications in Georgia, and that formidable raider, General Forrest, playing the mischief in west Tennessee, sent to the latter State two divisions—General Newton's of the Fourth Corps, and General J. D. Morgan's of the Fourteenth—to aid in destroying, if possible, that intrepid dragoon. To make assurance doubly sure, the next day he ordered General George H. Thomas, his most capable and experienced lieutenant, and the commander of more than three-fifths of his grand army, "back to Stevenson and Decherd...to look to Tennessee."

No order could have been more unwelcome to General Thomas. It removed him from the command of his own thoroughly organized and harmo-

DEFENDING AN EMBRASURE.

nious army of sixty thousand veterans, whom he knew and trusted, and who knew and loved him, and relegated him to the position of supervisor of communications. It also sent him to the rear just when great preparations were making for an advance. But, as often happens, what seemed an adverse fate opened the door to great, unforeseen opportunity. The task of expelling Forrest and reopening the broken communications was speedily completed, and on the 17th of October General Thomas wrote to General Sherman, "I hope to join you very soon." Sherman, however, had other views, and the hoped-for junction was never made. On the 19th he wrote to General Thomas:

> "I will send back to Tennessee the Fourth Corps, all dismounted cavalry, all sick and wounded, and all incumbrances whatever except what I can haul in our wagons.... I want you to remain in Tennessee and take command of all my [military] division not actually present with me. Hood's army may be set down at forty thousand (40,000) of all arms, fit for duty.... If you can defend the line of the Tennessee in my absence of three (3) months, it is all I ask."

With such orders, and under such circumstances, General Thomas was left to play his part in the new campaign.

General Hood, after a series of daring adventures which baffled all Sherman's calculations ("He can turn and twist like a fox," said Sherman, "and wear out my army in pursuit"), concentrated his entire force, except Forrest's cavalry, at Gadsden, Alabama, on the 22d of October, while General Sherman established his headquarters at Gaylesville,—a "position," as he wrote to General Halleck, "very good to watch the enemy." In spite of this "watch," Hood suddenly appeared on the 26th at Decatur, on the Tennessee River, seventy-five miles north-west of Gadsden. This move was a complete surprise, and evidently "meant business." The Fourth Corps, numbering about twelve thousand men, commanded by Major-General D. S. Stanley, was at once ordered from Gaylesville, to report to General Thomas. On the 1st of November its leading division reached Pulaski, Tennessee, a small town on the railroad, about forty miles north of Decatur, where it was joined four days later by the other two.

Making a slight though somewhat lengthened demonstration against Decatur, General Hood pushed on to Tuscumbia, forty-five miles west. Here he expected to find—what he had weeks before ordered—ample supplies, and the railroad in operation to Corinth. But he was doomed to disappointment. Instead of being in condition to make the rapid and triumphant march with which he had inflamed the ardor of his troops, he was detained three weeks, a delay fatal to his far-reaching hopes. Placing one corps on the north side of the river at Florence, he waited for supplies and for Forrest, who had been playing havoc throughout west Tennessee, from the line of the Mississippi border, northward to Kentucky, and was under orders to join him.

Convinced now of Hood's serious intentions, General Sherman also ordered the Twenty-third Corps, ten thousand men, under command of Major-General J. M. Schofield, to report to General Thomas. Reaching Pulaski, with one division, on the 14th of November, General Schofield, though inferior in rank to Stanley, assumed command by virtue of being a department commander. The whole force gathered there was less than 18,000 men; while in front

MAJOR-GENERAL GEORGE H. THOMAS. FROM A PHOTOGRAPH.

were some 5000 cavalry, consisting of a brigade of about 1500, under General Croxton, and a division of some 3500, under General Edward Hatch, the latter being fortunately intercepted while on his way to join Sherman.

The Confederate army in three corps (S. D. Lee's, A. P. Stewart's, and B. F. Cheatham's) began its northward march from Florence on the 19th of November, in weather of great severity. It rained and snowed and hailed and froze, and the roads were almost impassable. Forrest had come up, with about six thousand cavalry, and led the advance with indomitable energy. Hatch and Croxton made such resistance as they could; but on the 22d the head of Hood's column was at Lawrenceburg, some 16 miles due west of Pulaski, Tennessee, and on a road running direct to Columbia, where the railroad and turnpike to Nashville cross Duck River, and where there were less than 800 men to guard the bridges. The situation at Pulaski, with an enemy nearly three times as large fairly on the flank, was anything but cheering. Warned by the reports from General Hatch, and by the orders of General Thomas, who, on the 20th, had directed General Schofield to prepare to fall back to Columbia, the two divisions of General J. D. Cox and General George D. Wagner (the latter Newton's old division) were ordered to march to Lynnville—about half-way to Columbia—on the 22d. On the 23d the other two divisions, under General Stanley, were to follow with the wagon-trains. It was not a moment too soon. On the morning of the 24th General Cox, who had pushed on to within nine miles of Columbia, was roused by sounds of conflict away to the west. Taking a cross-road, leading south of Columbia, he reached the Mount Pleasant pike just in time to interpose his infantry between Forrest's cavalry and a hapless brigade, under command of Colonel Capron, which was being handled most unceremoniously.‡ In another

‡Major Henry C. Connelly, of the 14th Illinois cavalry, on August 8, 1887, wrote to the editors as follows:

"When General Hood advanced from the Tennessee River, General Capron's brigade was on the extreme right of our army, and from the 19th of November until the 24th, the day Columbia was reached, we fought Forrest's cavalry. I was with the rear-guard on the occasion referred to; it fell back and found the brigade in good position in line of battle. I rode to General Capron and expressed the opinion that he could not hold his position a moment against the troops pressing us in the rear and on the flanks, which we could easily see advancing rapidly to attack us. General Capron replied that he had been ordered to make a decided stand if it sacrificed every man in his brigade; that we must hold the advancing forces in check to enable the infantry to arrive and get in position. I replied, 'We are destroyed and captured if we remain here.' At this moment General Capron gave the order to retire. While passing through a long lane south of Columbia, Forrest's forces charged the brigade in rear and on both flanks with intrepid courage. Our command was confined to a narrow lane, with men and horses in the highest state of excitement. We were armed with Springfield rifles, which after the first volley were about as serviceable to a cavalryman thus hemmed in as a good club. The men could not reload while mounted, in the excitement of horses as well as soldiers. The only thing that could be done was to get out as promptly as possible, and before Forrest's forces should close in and capture the command.

"This was done successfully. The brigade was composed of the 14th and 16th Illinois cavalry and the 8th Michigan cavalry."

hour Forrest would have been in possession of the crossings of Duck River, and the only line of communication with Nashville would have been in the hands of the enemy. General Stanley, who had left Pulaski in the afternoon of the 23d, reached Lynnville after dark. Rousing his command at 1 o'clock in the morning, by 9 o'clock the head of his column connected with Cox in front of Columbia—having marched thirty miles since 2 o'clock of the preceding afternoon. These timely movements saved the little army from utter destruction.

When General Sherman had finally determined on his march to the sea, he requested General Rosecrans, in Missouri, to send to General Thomas two divisions, under General A. J. Smith, which had been lent to General Banks for the Red River expedition, and were now repelling the incursion of Price into Missouri. As they were not immediately forthcoming, General Grant had ordered General Rawlins, his chief-of-staff, to St. Louis, to direct, in person, their speedy embarkation. Thence, on the 7th of November, two weeks before Hood began his advance from Florence, General Rawlins wrote to General Thomas that Smith's command, aggregating nearly 14,000, would begin to leave that place as early as the 10th. No news was ever more anxiously awaited or more eagerly welcomed than this. But the promise could not be fulfilled. Smith had to march entirely across the State of Missouri; and instead of leaving St. Louis on the 10th, he did not arrive there until the 24th. Had he come at the proposed time, it was General Thomas's intention to place him at Eastport, on the Tennessee River, so as to threaten Hood's flank and rear if the latter advanced. With such disposition, the battles of Franklin and Nashville would have been relegated to the category of "events which never come to pass." But when Smith reached St. Louis, Hood was threatening Columbia; and it was an open question whether he would not reach Nashville before the reënforcements from Missouri.

As fast as the Union troops arrived at Columbia, in their hurried retreat from Pulaski, works were thrown up, covering the approaches from the south, and the trains were sent across the river. But the line was found to be longer than the small force could hold; and the river could easily be crossed, above or below the town. Orders were given to withdraw to the north side on the night of the 26th, but a heavy storm prevented. The next night the crossing was made, the railroad bridge was burned, and the pontoon boats were scuttled. This was an all-night job, the last of the pickets crossing at 5 in the morning. It was now the fifth day since the retreat from Pulaski began, and the little army had been exposed day and night to all sorts of weather except sunshine, and had been almost continually on the move. From deserters it was learned that Hood's infantry numbered 40,000, and his cavalry, under Forrest, 10,000 or 12,000. But the Union army was slowly increasing by concentration and the arrival of recruits. It now numbered at Columbia about 23,000 infantry and some 5000 cavalry—of whom only 3500 were mounted. General James H. Wilson, who had been ordered by General Grant to report to General Sherman,—and of whom General Grant wrote, "I believe he will add fifty per cent. to the effectiveness of your cavalry,"—had taken command personally of all General Thomas's cavalry, which was trying to hold the fords east and west of Columbia.

In spite of every opposition, Forrest succeeded in placing one of his divisions on the north side of Duck River before noon of the 28th, and forced back the Union cavalry on roads leading toward Spring Hill and Franklin. At 1 o'clock on the morning of the 29th General Wilson became convinced that the enemy's infantry would begin crossing at daylight, and advised General Schofield to fall back to Franklin. At 3:30 the same morning General Thomas sent him similar orders. Daylight revealed the correctness of Wilson's information. Before sunrise Cheatham's corps, headed by Cleburne's division,—a division unsurpassed for courage, energy, and endurance by any in the Confederate army,—was making its way over Duck River at Davis's Ford, about five miles east of Columbia. The weather had cleared, and it was a bright autumn morning, the air full of invigorating life. General Hood in person accompanied the advance.

When General Schofield was informed that the Confederate infantry were crossing, he sent a brigade, under Colonel P. Sidney Post, on a reconnoissance along the river-bank, to learn if the report was true. He also ordered General Stanley to march with two divisions, Wagner's and Kimball's, to Spring Hill, taking the trains and all the reserve artillery. In less than half an hour after receiving the order, Stanley was on the way. On reaching the point where Rutherford Creek crosses the Franklin Pike, Kimball's division was halted, by order of General Schofield, and faced to the east to cover the crossing against a possible attack from that quarter. In this position Kimball remained all day. Stanley, with the other division, pushed on to Spring Hill. Just before noon, as the head of his column was approaching that place, he met "a cavalry soldier who seemed to be badly scared," who reported that Buford's division of Forrest's cavalry was approaching from the east. The troops were at once double-quicked into the town, and the leading brigade, deploying as it advanced, drove off the enemy just as they were expecting, unmolested, to occupy the place. As the other brigades came up, they also were deployed, forming nearly a semicircle,—Opdycke's brigade stretching in a thin line from the railroad station north of the village to a point some distance east, and Lane's from Opdycke's right to the pike below. Bradley was sent to the front to occupy a knoll some three-fourths of a mile east, commanding all the approaches from that direction. Most of the artillery was placed on a rise south of the town. The trains were parked within the semicircle.

From Spring Hill roads radiate to all points, the turnpike between Columbia and Franklin being there intersected by turnpikes from Rally Hill and Mount Carmel, as well as by numerous country roads leading to the neighboring towns. Possession of that point would not only shut out the Union army from the road to Nashville, but it would effectually bar the way in every direction. Stanley's arrival was not a moment too soon for the safety of the army, and his prompt dispositions and steady courage, as well as his vigorous hold of all the ground he occupied, gave his little command all the moral fruits of a victory.

Hardly had the three brigades, numbering, all told, less than four thousand men, reached the positions assigned them, when Bradley was assailed by a force which the men declared fought too well to be dismounted cavalry. At the same time, at Thompson's Station, three miles north, an attack was made on a small wagon train heading for Franklin; and a dash was made by a detachment of the Confederate cavalry on the Spring Hill station, north-west of the town. It seemed as if the little band, attacked from all points, was threatened with destruction. Bradley's brigade was twice assaulted, but held its own, though with considerable loss, and only a single regiment could be spared to reënforce him. The third assault was more successful, and he was driven back to the edge of the village, Bradley himself receiving a disabling wound in rallying his men. While attempting to follow up this temporary advantage, the enemy, in crossing a wide corn-field, was opened upon with spherical case-shot from eight guns posted on the knoll, and soon scattered in considerable confusion. These attacks undoubtedly came from Cleburne's division, and were made under the eye of the corps commander, General Cheatham, and the army commander, General Hood. That they were not successful, especially as the other two divisions of the same corps, Brown's and Bate's, were close at hand, and Stewart's corps not far off, seems unaccountable. Except this one small division deployed in a long thin line to cover the wagons, there were no Union troops within striking distance; the cavalry were about Mount Carmel, five miles east, fully occupied in keeping Forrest away from Franklin and the Harpeth River crossings. The nearest aid was Kimball's division, seven miles south, at Rutherford Creek. The other three divisions of infantry which made up Schofield's force— Wood's, Cox's, and Ruger's (in part)—were still at Duck River. Thus night closed down upon the solitary division, on whose boldness of action devolved the safety of the whole force which Sherman had spared from his march to the sea to breast the tide of Hood's invasion. When night came, the danger increased rather than diminished. A single Confederate brigade, like Adams's or Cockrell's or Maney's,—veterans since Shiloh,—planted squarely across the pike, either south or north of Spring Hill, would have effectually prevented Schofield's retreat, and day-light would have found his whole force cut off from every avenue of escape by more than twice its numbers, to assault whom would have been madness, and to avoid whom would have been impossible.

Why Cleburne and Brown failed to drive away Stanley's one division before dark; why Bate failed to possess himself of the pike south of the town; why

CARTER HOUSE UNDER STEEPLES.　　GIN-HOUSE.　　ROPER'S KNOB.

THE BATTLE-FIELD OF FRANKLIN, TENNESSEE, LOOKING NORTH FROM GENERAL CHEATHAM'S HEADQUARTERS. FROM A PHOTOGRAPH.

MAJOR-GENERAL D. S. STANLEY.
FROM A PHOTOGRAPH.

Stewart failed to lead his troops to the pike at the north; why Forrest, with his audacious temper and his enterprising cavalry, did not fully hold Thompson's Station or the crossing of the West Harpeth, half-way to Franklin: these are to this day disputed questions among the Confederate commanders; and it is not proposed to discuss them here. The afternoon and night of November 29th, 1864, may well be set down in the calendar of lost opportunities. The heroic valor of the same troops the next day, and their frightful losses as they attempted to retrieve their mistake, show what might have been.

By 8 o'clock at night—two hours only after sunset, on a moonless night—at least two corps of Hood's army were in line of battle facing the turnpike, and not half a mile away. The long line of Confederate camp-fires burned bright, and the men could be seen standing around them or sauntering about in groups. Now and then a few would come almost to the pike and fire at a passing Union squad, but without provoking a reply. General Schofield, who had remained at Duck River all day, reached Spring Hill about 7 P.M., with Ruger's division and Whitaker's brigade. Leaving the latter to cover a cross-road a mile or two below the town, he started with Ruger about 9 P.M. to force a passage at Thompson's Station, supposed to be in the hands of the enemy. At 11 P.M. General Cox arrived with his division, and soon after Schofield returned to Spring Hill with the welcome news that the way was open. From Thompson's Station he sent his engineer officer, Captain William J. Twining, to Franklin, to telegraph the situation to General Thomas, all communication with whom had been cut off since early morning. Captain Twining's dispatch shows most clearly the critical condition of affairs: "The general says he will not be able to get farther than Thompson's Station to-night.... He regards his situation as extremely perilous.... Thinking the troops under A. J. Smith's command had reached Franklin, General Schofield directed me to have them pushed down to Spring Hill by daylight to-morrow." This was Tuesday. The day before, General Thomas had telegraphed to General Schofield that Smith had not yet arrived, but would be at Nashville in three days—that is, Thursday. The expectation of finding him at Franklin, therefore, was like a drowning man's catching at a straw.

Just before midnight Cox started from Spring Hill for Franklin, and was ordered to pick up Ruger at Thompson's Station. At 1 A.M. he was on the road, and the train, over five miles long, was drawn out. At the very outset it had to cross a bridge in single file. So difficult was this whole movement, that it was 5 o'clock in the morning before the wagons were fairly under way. As the head of the train passed Thompson's Station, it was attacked by the Confederate cavalry, and for a while there was great consternation. Wood's division, which had followed Cox from Duck River, was marched along to the east of the pike, to protect the train, and the enemy were speedily driven off. It was near daybreak when the last wagon left Spring Hill. Kimball's division followed Wood's, and at 4 o'clock Wagner drew in his lines, his skirmishers remaining till it was fairly daylight. The rear-guard was commanded by Colonel Emerson Opdycke, who was prepared, if necessary, to sacrifice the last man to secure the safety of the main body. So efficiently did his admirable brigade do its work, that, though surrounded by a cloud of the enemy's cavalry, which made frequent dashes at its lines, not a straggler nor a wagon was left behind. The ground was strewn with knapsacks cut from the shoulders of a lot of raw recruits weighed down with their unaccustomed burden.

The head of the column, under General Cox, reached the outskirts of Franklin about the same hour that the rear-guard was leaving Spring Hill. Here the tired, sleepy, hungry men, who had fought and marched, day and night, for nearly a week, threw up a line of earth-works on a slight eminence which guards the southern approach to the town, even before they made their coffee. Then they gladly dropped anywhere for the much-needed "forty winks." Slowly the rest of the weary column, regiment after regiment of worn-out men, filed into the works, and continued the line, till a complete bridge-head, from the river-bank above to the river-bank below, encircled the town. By noon of the 30th all the troops had come up, and the wagons were crossing the river, which was already fordable, notwithstanding the recent heavy rainfalls. The rear-guard was still out, having an occasional bout with the enemy.

The Columbia Pike bisected the works, which at that point were built just in front of the Carter house, a one-story brick dwelling west of the pike, and a large gin-house on the east side. Between the gin-house and the river the works were partly protected in front by a hedge of Osage orange, and on the knoll, near the railroad cut close to the bank, were two batteries belonging to the Fourth Corps. Near the Carter house was a considerable thicket of locust trees. Except these obstructions, the whole ground in front was entirely unobstructed and fenceless, and, from the works, every part of it was in plain sight. General Cox's division of three brigades, commanded that day, in order from left to right, by Colonels Stiles and Casement and General Reilly, occupied the ground between the Columbia Pike and the river above the town. The front line consisted of eight regiments, three in the works and one in reserve for each of the brigades of Stiles and Casement, while Reilly's brigade nearest the pike had but two regiments in the works, and two in a second line, with still another regiment behind that. West of the pike, reaching to a ravine through which passes a road branching from the Carter's Creek Pike, was Ruger's division of two brigades—the third, under General Cooper, not having come up from Johnsonville. Strickland's brigade, of four regiments, had two in the works and two in reserve. Two of these regiments, the 72d Illinois and 44th Missouri, belonged to A. J. Smith's corps, and had reported to General Schofield only the day before. A third, which was in reserve, the 183d Ohio, was a large and entirely new regiment, having been mustered into service only three weeks before, and having joined the army for the first time on the 28th. Moore's brigade, of six regiments, had four in the works and two in reserve. Beyond Ruger, reaching from the ravine to the river below, was Kimball's division of the Fourth Corps,—all veterans,—consisting of three brigades commanded by Generals William Grose and Walter C. Whitaker and Colonel Isaac M. Kirby. All the troops in the works were ordered to report to General Cox, to whom was assigned the command of the defenses.⁕ General Wood's division of the Fourth Corps had gone over the river with the trains; and two brigades of Wagner's division, which had so valiantly stood their ground at Spring Hill and covered the rear since, were halted on a slope about half a mile to the front. Opdycke had brought his brigade within the works, and held them massed, near the pike, behind the Carter house. Besides the guns on the knoll, near the railroad cut, there were six pieces in Reilly's works; four on Strickland's left; two on Moore's left, and four on Grose's left—in all, twenty-six guns in that part of the works, facing south, and twelve more in reserve, on or near the Columbia Pike.

As the bright autumn day, hazy with the golden light of an Indian summer atmosphere, wore away, the troops that had worked so hard looked hopefully forward to a prospect of ending it in peace and rest, preparatory either to a night march to Nashville, or to a reënforcement by Smith's corps and General Thomas. But about 2 o'clock, some suspicious movements on the hills a mile or two away—the waving of signal flags and the deployment of the enemy in line of battle—caused General Wagner to send his adjutant-general, from the advanced position where his two brigades had halted, to his commanding general, with the information that Hood seemed to be preparing for attack. In a very short time the whole Confederate line could be seen, stretching in battle array, from the dark fringe of chestnuts along the river-bank, far across the Columbia Pike, the colors gayly fluttering and the muskets gleaming brightly, and advanc-

---

⁕General D. S. Stanley, who commanded the Fourth Corps, takes exception to this statement. Some of his troops as they arrived were assigned to positions by General Cox. General Stanley, in the performance of his duty, went with General Schofield to the north side of the river, but returned when the firing began and assisted in rallying Wagner's brigades, of his corps, during which he was wounded. General Schofield said in his report of December 31st, 1864: "The troops were placed in position and intrenched under his [Cox's] immediate direction, and the greater portion of the line engaged was under his command during the battle."—EDITORS.

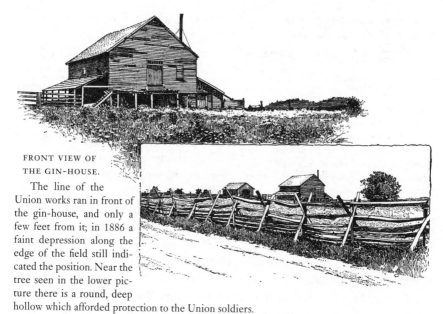

FRONT VIEW OF
THE GIN-HOUSE.

The line of the
Union works ran in front of
the gin-house, and only a
few feet from it; in 1886 a
faint depression along the
edge of the field still indicated the position. Near the
tree seen in the lower picture there is a round, deep
hollow which afforded protection to the Union soldiers.

VIEW OF THE GIN-HOUSE, FROM THE PIKE.

ing steadily, in perfect order, dressed on the center, straight for the works. Meantime General Schofield had retired to the fort, on a high bluff on the other side of the river, some two miles away, by the road, and had taken General Stanley with him. From the fort the whole field of operations was plainly visible. Notwithstanding all these demonstrations, the two brigades of Wagner were left on the knoll where they had been halted, and, with scarcely an apology for works to protect them, had waited until it was too late to retreat without danger of degenerating into a rout.

On came the enemy, as steady and resistless as a tidal wave. A couple of guns, in the advance line, gave them a shot and galloped back to the works. A volley from a thin skirmish-line was sent into their ranks, but without causing any delay to the massive array. A moment more, and with that wild "rebel yell" which, once heard, is never forgotten, the great human wave swept along, and seemed to ingulf the little force that had so sturdily awaited it.

The first shock came, of course, upon the two misplaced brigades of Wagner's division, which, through some one's blunder, had remained in their false position until too late to retire without disaster. They had no tools to throw up works; and when struck by the resistless sweep of Cleburne's and Brown's divisions, they had only to make their way, as best they could, back to the works. In that wild rush, in which friend and foe were intermingled, and the piercing "rebel yell" rose high above the "Yankee cheer," nearly seven hundred were

BRIDGE AT FRANKLIN OVER THE HARPETH
RIVER, LOOKING UP-STREAM.

The left of the picture is the north bank of the
stream; Franklin is upon the south bank. Fort
Granger, where General Schofield had his
headquarters, occupied the site of the buildings on the north bank.

made prisoners. But, worst of all for the Union side, the men of Reilly's and Strickland's brigades dared not fire, lest they should shoot down their own comrades, and the guns, loaded with grape and canister, stood silent in the embrasures. With loud shouts of "Let's go into the works with them," the triumphant Confederates, now more like a wild, howling mob than an organized army, swept on to the very works, with hardly a check from any quarter. So fierce was the rush that a number of the fleeing soldiers—officers and men—dropped exhausted into the ditch, and lay there while the terrific contest raged over their heads, till, under cover of darkness, they could crawl safely inside the intrenchments.

On Strickland's left, close to the Columbia Pike, was posted one of the new infantry regiments. The tremendous onset, the wild yells, the whole infernal din of the strife, were too much for such an undisciplined body. As they saw their comrades from the advance line rushing to the rear, they too turned and fled. The contagion spread, and in a few minutes a disorderly stream was pouring down the pike past the Carter house toward the town. The guns, posted on each side the Columbia Pike, were abandoned, and the works, for the space of more than a regimental front, both east and west of the pike, were deserted. Into the gap thus made, without an instant's delay, swarmed the jubilant Confederates, urged on by Cleburne and Brown, and took possession of both works and guns. For a moment it looked as though these two enterprising divisions, backed by the mass of troops converging toward the pike, would sweep down the works in both directions, and, taking Strickland and Reilly on the flank, drive them out, or capture them. Fortunately, there were at hand reserves of brave men who were not demoralized by the momentary panic. Colonel Emerson Opdycke, of Wagner's division, as already stated, had brought his brigade inside the works, and they were now massed near the Carter house, ready for any contingency. Two regiments of Reilly's brigade, the 12th and 16th Kentucky, which had reached Franklin about noon, had taken position a little in rear of the rest of the brigade, and thrown up works. As soon as the break was made in the lines all these reserves rushed to the front, and, after a terrific struggle, succeeded in regaining the works. Opdycke's brigade, deploying as it advanced, was involved in as fierce a hand-to-hand encounter as ever soldiers engaged in. The two Kentucky regiments joined in the fight with equal ardor and bravery. A large part of Conrad's and Lane's men, as they came in, though wholly disorganized, turned about and gave the enemy a hot reception. Opdycke's horse was shot under him, and he fought on foot at the head of his brigade. General Cox was everywhere present, encouraging and cheering on his men. General Stanley, who, from the fort where he had gone with General Schofield, had seen the opening clash, galloped to the front as soon as possible and did all that a brave man could until he was painfully wounded. Some of Opdycke's men manned the abandoned guns in Reilly's works; others filled the gap in Strickland's line. These timely movements first checked and then repulsed the assaulting foe, and soon the entire line of works was reoccupied, the enemy sullenly giving up the prize which was so nearly won. Stewart's corps, which was on Cheatham's right, filling the space to the river, kept abreast of its valiant companion, and, meeting no obstacle, reached the works near the Union left before Cheatham made the breach at the Columbia Pike. Owing to the peculiar formation of the field, the left of Stewart's line was thrown upon the same ground with the right of Cheatham's; the two commands there became much intermingled. This accounts for so many of General Stewart's officers and men being killed in front of Reilly's and Casement's regiments.

Where there was nothing to hinder the Union fire, the muskets of Stiles's and Casement's brigades made fearful havoc; while the batteries at the railroad cut plowed furrows through the ranks of the advancing foe. Time after time they came up to the very works, but they never crossed them except as prisoners. More than one color-bearer was shot down on the parapet. It is impossible to exaggerate the fierce energy with which the Confederate soldiers, that short November afternoon, threw themselves against the works, fighting with what seemed the very madness of despair. There was not a breath of wind, and the dense smoke settled down upon the field, so that, after the first assault, it was impossible to see at any distance. Through this blinding medium, assault after assault was made, several of the Union officers declaring in their reports that their lines received as many as thirteen distinct attacks. Between the gin-house and the Columbia Pike the fighting was fiercest, and the Confederate losses the greatest. Here fell most of the Confederate generals, who, that fateful afternoon, madly gave up their lives; Adams of Stewart's corps—his horse astride the works, and himself within a few feet of them. Cockrell and Quarles, of the same corps, were severely wounded. In Cheatham's corps, Cleburne and Granbury were killed near the pike. On the west of the pike Strahl and Gist were killed, and Brown was severely wounded. General G. W. Gordon was captured by Opdycke's brigade, inside the works. The heaviest loss in all the Union regiments was in the 44th Missouri, the advance guard of Smith's long-expected reënforcement, which had been sent to Columbia on the 27th, and was here stationed on the right of the raw regiment that broke and ran at the first onset of the enemy. Quickly changing front, the 44th held its ground, but with a loss of 34 killed, 37 wounded, and 92 missing, many of the latter being wounded. In the 72d Illinois, its companion, every field-officer was wounded, and the entire color-guard, of one sergeant and eight corporals, was shot down. Its losses were 10 killed, 66 wounded, and 75 missing.

While this infantry battle was going on, Forrest had crossed the river with his cavalry some distance east of the town, with the evident purpose of getting at Schofield's wagons. But he reckoned without his host. Hatch and Croxton, by General Wilson's direction, fell upon him with such vigor that he returned to the south side and gave our forces no further trouble. At nightfall the victory was complete on every part of the Union lines. But here and there on the Confederate side desultory firing was kept up till long after dark, though with little result.

At 3 o'clock in the afternoon, as the Confederate lines were forming for their great assault, General Schofield, in reply to a telegram from General Thomas, asking him if he could "hold Hood at Franklin for three days longer," replied, "I do not think I can.... It appears to me I ought to take position at Brentwood at once." Accordingly General Thomas, at 3:30, directed him to retire to Brentwood, which he did that night, bringing away all the wagons and other property in safety. Among the spoils of war were thirty-three Confederate colors, captured by our men from the enemy. The morning found the entire infantry force safe within the friendly shelter of the works at Nashville, where they also welcomed the veterans of A. J. Smith, who were just arriving from Missouri. Soon after, a body of about five thousand men came in from Chattanooga, chiefly of General Sherman's army, too late for their proper commands. These were organized into a provisional division under General J. B. Steedman, and were posted between the Murfreesboro' Pike and the river. Cooper's brigade also came in after a narrow escape from capture, as well as several regiments of colored troops from the railroad between Nashville and Johnsonville. Their arrival completed the force on which General Thomas was to rely for the task he now placed before himself—the destruction of Hood's army. It was an ill-assorted and heterogeneous mass, not yet welded into an army, and lacking a great proportion of the outfit with which to undertake an aggressive campaign. Horses, wagons, mules, pontoons, everything needed to mobilize an army, had to be obtained. At that time they did not exist at Nashville.

The next day Hood's columns appeared before the town and took up their positions on a line of hills nearly parallel to those occupied by the Union army, and speedily threw up works and prepared to defend their ground.

Probably no commander ever underwent two weeks of greater anxiety and distress of mind than General Thomas during the interval between Hood's arrival and his precipitate departure from the vicinity of Nashville. The story is too painful to dwell upon, even after the lapse of twenty-three years. From the 2d of December until the battle was fought on the 15th, the general-in-chief did not cease, day or night, to send him from the headquarters at City Point,

Va., most urgent and often most uncalled-for orders in regard to his operations, culminating in an order on the 9th relieving him, and directing him to turn over his command to General Schofield, who was assigned to his place—an order which, had it not been revoked, the great captain would have obeyed with loyal single-heartedness. This order, though made out at the Adjutant-General's office in Washington, was not sent to General Thomas, and he did not know of its existence until told of it some years later by General Halleck, at San Francisco. He felt, however, that something of the kind was impending. General Halleck dispatched to him, on morning of the 9th: "Lieutenant-General Grant expresses much dissatisfaction at your delay in attacking the enemy." His reply shows how entirely he understood the situation: "I feel conscious I have done everything in my power, and that the troops could not have been gotten ready before this. *If General Grant should order me to be relieved, I will submit without a murmur.*" As he was writing this,—2 o'clock in the afternoon of December 9th,—a terrible storm of freezing rain had been pouring down since daylight, and it kept on pouring and freezing all that day and a part of the next. That night General Grant notified him that the order relieving him—which he had divined—was suspended. But he did not know who had been designated as his successor. With this threat hanging over him; with the utter impossibility, in that weather, of making any movement; with the prospect that the labors of his whole life were about to end in disappointment, if not disaster,—he never, for an instant, abated his energy or his work of preparation. Not an hour, day and night, was he idle. Nobody—not even his most trusted staff-officers—knew the contents of the telegrams that came to him. But it was very evident that something greatly troubled him. While the rain was falling and the fields and roads were ice-bound, he would sometimes sit by the window for an hour or more, not speaking a word, gazing steadily out upon the forbidding prospect, as if he were trying to will the storm away. It was curious and interesting to see how, in this gloomy interval, his time was occupied by matters not strictly military.

Now, it was a visit from a delegation of the city government, in regard to some municipal regulation; again, somebody whose one horse had been seized and put into the cavalry; then, a committee of citizens, begging that wood might be furnished, to keep some poor families from freezing; and, of evenings, Governor Andrew Johnson—then Vice-President elect— would unfold to him, with much iteration, his fierce views concerning secession, rebels, and reconstruction.

HILL NEAR NASHVILLE FROM WHICH BATE'S CONFEDERATE DIVISION WAS DRIVEN ON DECEMBER 16. FROM A PHOTOGRAPH TAKEN IN 1884.

To all he gave a patient and kindly hearing, and he often astonished Governor Johnson by his knowledge of constitutional and international law. But, underneath all, it was plain to see that General Grant's dissatisfaction keenly affected him, and that only by the proof which a successful battle would furnish could he hope to regain the confidence of the general-in-chief.

So when, at 8 o'clock on the evening of December 14th, after having laid his plans before his corps commanders, and dismissed them, he dictated to General Halleck the telegram, "The ice having melted away to-day, the enemy will be attacked to-morrow morning," he drew a deep sigh of relief, and for the first time for a week showed again something of his natural buoyancy and cheerfulness. He moved about more briskly; he put in order all the little last things that remained to be done; he signed his name where it was needed in the letter-book, and then, giving orders to his staff-officers to be ready at 5 o'clock the next morning, went gladly to bed.

The ice had not melted a day too soon; for, while he was writing the telegram to General Halleck, General Logan was speeding his way to Nashville, with orders from General Grant that would have placed him in command of all the Union forces there assembled. General Thomas, fortunately, did not then learn this second proof of General Grant's lack of confidence; and General Logan, on reaching Louisville, found that the work intended for him was already done—and came no farther. At the very time when these orders were made out at Washington, in obedience to General Grant's directions, a large part of the cavalry was unmounted; two divisions were absent securing horses and proper outfit; wagons were unfinished and mules lacking or unbroken; pontoons unmade and pontoniers untrained; the ground was covered with a glare of ice which made all the fields and hillsides impassable for horses and scarcely passable for foot-men. The natives declared that the Yankees brought their weather as well as their army with them. Every corps commander in the army protested that a movement under such conditions would be little short of madness, and certain to result in disaster.

A very considerable reorganization of the army also took place during this enforced delay. General Stanley, still suffering from his wound, went North, and General T. J. Wood, who had been with it from the beginning, succeeded to the command of the Fourth Corps. General Ruger, who had commanded a division in the Twenty-third Corps, was also disabled by sickness, and was succeeded by General D. N. Couch, formerly a corps commander in the Army of the Potomac, and who had recently been assigned to duty in the Department of the Cumberland.⁺ General Wagner was retired from command of his divi-

---

⁺General Couch was in command of the Department of the Susquehanna from June 11th, 1863, to December 1st, 1864. On December 8th, 1864, he took command of the Second Division of the Twenty-third Corps.—EDITORS.

THE CAPITOL, NASHVILLE.

Strong works, set with cannon, inclosed the foundations of the Capitol. Cisterns within the building held a bountiful supply of water. Owing to its capacity and the massiveness of the lower stories, the Capitol was regarded as a citadel, in which a few thousand men could maintain themselves against an army.

sion, and was succeeded by General W. L. Elliott, who had been chief of cavalry on General Thomas's staff in the Atlanta campaign. General Kenner Garrard, who had commanded a cavalry division during the Atlanta campaign, was assigned to an infantry division in Smith's corps. In all these cases, except in that of General Wood succeeding to the command of the Fourth Corps, the newly assigned officers were entire strangers to the troops over whom they were placed.

On the afternoon of the 14th of December General Thomas summoned his corps commanders, and, delivering to each a written order containing a detailed plan of the battle, went with them carefully and thoroughly over the whole ground, answering all questions and explaining all doubts. Never had a commander a more loyal corps of subordinates or a more devoted army. The feeling in the ranks was one of absolute and enthusiastic confidence in their general. Some had served with him since his opening triumph at Mill Springs; some had never seen his face till two weeks before. But there was that in his bearing, as well as in the confidence of his old soldiers, which inspired the newcomers with as absolute a sense of reliance upon him as was felt by the oldest of his veterans.

The plan, in general terms, was for General Steedman, on the extreme left, to move out early in the morning, threatening the rebel right, while the cavalry, which had been placed on the extreme right, and A. J. Smith's corps were to make a grand left wheel with the entire right wing, assaulting and, if possible, overlapping the left of Hood's position. Wood was to form the pivot for this wheel, and to threaten and perhaps attack Montgomery Hill; while General Schofield was to be held in reserve, near the left center, for such use as the exigency might develop.

It was not daylight, on the morning of the 15th of December, when the army began to move. In most of the camps reveille had been sounded at 4 o'clock, and by 6 everything was ready. It turned out a warm, sunny, winter morning. A dense fog at first hung over the valleys and completely hid all movements, but by 9 o'clock this had cleared away. General Steedman, on the extreme left, was the first to draw out of the defenses, and to assail the enemy at their works between the Nolensville and Murfreesboro' pikes. It was not intended as a real attack, though it had that effect. Two of Steedman's brigades, chiefly colored troops, kept two divisions of Cheatham's corps constantly busy, while his third was held in reserve; thus one Confederate corps was disposed of. S. D. Lee's corps, next on Cheatham's left, after sending two brigades to the assistance of Stewart, on the Confederate left, was held in place by the threatening position of the garrison troops, and did not fire a shot during the day. Indeed, both Cheatham's and Lee's corps were held, as in a vise, between Steedman and Wood. Lee's corps was unable to move or to fight. Steedman maintained the ground he occupied till the next morning, with no very heavy loss.

When, about 9 o'clock, the sun began to burn away the fog, the sight from General Thomas's position was inspiring. A little to the left, on Montgomery Hill, the salient of the Confederate lines, and not more than six hundred yards distant from Wood's salient, on Lawrens Hill, could be seen the advance line of works, behind which an unknown force of the enemy lay in wait. Beyond, and along the Hillsboro' Pike, were stretches of stone wall, with here and there a detached earth-work, through whose embrasures peeped the threatening artillery. To the right, along the valley of Richland Creek, the dark line of Wilson's advancing cavalry could be seen slowly making its difficult way across the wet, swampy, stumpy ground. Close in front, and at the foot of the hill, its right joining Wilson's left, was A. J. Smith's corps, full of cheer and enterprise, and glad to be once more in the open field. Then came the Fourth Corps, whose left, bending back toward the north, was hidden behind Lawrens Hill. Already the skirmishers were engaged, the Confederates slowly falling back before the determined and steady pressure of Smith and Wood.

By the time that Wilson's and Smith's lines were fully extended and brought up to within striking distance of the Confederate works, along the Hillsboro' Pike, it was noon. Post's brigade of Wood's old division (now commanded by General Sam Beatty), which lay at the foot of Montgomery Hill, full of dash and spirit, had since morning been regarding the works at the summit with covetous eyes. At Post's suggestion, it was determined to see which party wanted them most. Accordingly, a charge was ordered—and in a moment the brigade was swarming up the hillside, straight for the enemy's advanced works. For almost the first time since the grand assault on Missionary Ridge, a year before, here was an open field where everything could be seen. From General Thomas's headquarters everybody looked on with breathless suspense, as the blue line, broken and irregular, but with steady persistence, made its way up the steep hillside against a fierce storm of musketry and artillery. Most of the shots, however, passed over the men's heads. It was a struggle to keep up with the colors, and, as they neared the top, only the strongest were at the front. Without a moment's pause, the color-bearers and those who had kept up with them, Post himself at the head, leaped the parapet. As the colors waved from the summit, the whole line swept forward and was over the works in a twinkling, gathering in prisoners and guns. Indeed, so large was the mass of the prisoners that a few minutes later was seen heading toward our own lines, that a number of officers at General Thomas's headquarters feared the assault had failed and the prisoners were Confederate reserves who had rallied and retaken the works. But the fear was only momentary; for the wild outburst of cheers that rang across the valley told the story of complete success.

Meanwhile, farther to the right, as the opposing lines neared each other, the sound of battle grew louder and louder, and the smoke thicker and thicker, until the whole valley was filled with the haze. It was now past noon, and, at every point the two armies were so near together that an assault was inevitable. Hatch's division of Wilson's cavalry, at the extreme right of the continuous line, was confronted by one of the detached works which Hood had intended to be "impregnable"; and the right of McArthur's division of A. J. Smith's infantry was also within striking distance of it. Coon's cavalry brigade was dismounted and ordered to assault the work, while Hill's infantry brigade received similar orders. The two commanders moved forward at the same time, and entered the work together, Colonel Hill falling dead at the head of his command. In a moment the whole Confederate force in that quarter was routed and fled to the rear, while the captured guns were turned on them.

With the view of extending the operations of Wilson's cavalry still farther to the right, and if possible gaining the rear of the enemy's left, the two divisions of the Twenty-third Corps that had been in reserve near Lawrens Hill were ordered to Smith's right, while orders were sent to Wilson to gain, if possible, a lodgment on the Granny White Pike. These orders were promptly obeyed, and Cooper's brigade on reaching its new position got into a handsome fight, in which its losses were more than the losses of the rest of the Twenty-third Corps during the two days' battle.

But though the enemy's left was thus rudely driven from its fancied security, the salient at the center, being an angle formed by the line along Hillsboro' Pike and that stretching toward the east, was still firmly held. Post's successful assault had merely driven out or captured the advance forces; the main line was intact. As soon as word came of the successful assault on the right, General Thomas sent orders to General Wood, commanding the Fourth Corps, to prepare to attack the salient. The staff-officer by whom this order was sent did not at first find General Wood; but seeing the two division commanders whose troops would be called upon for the work, gave them the instructions. As he was riding along the line he met one of the brigade commanders—an officer with a reputation for exceptional courage and gallantry—who, in reply to the direction to prepare for the expected assault, said, "You don't mean that we've got to go in here and attack the works on that hill?" "Those are the orders," was the answer. Looking earnestly across the open valley, and at the steep hill beyond, from which the enemy's guns were throwing shot and shell with uncomfortable frequency and nearness, he said, "Why, it would be suicide, sir; perfect suicide." "Nevertheless, those are the orders," said the officer; and he rode on to complete his work. Before he could rejoin General Thomas the assault was made, and the enemy were driven out with a loss of guns, colors, and prisoners, and their whole line was forced to abandon the works along the Hillsboro' Pike and fall back to the Granny White Pike. The retreating line was followed by the entire Fourth Corps (Wood's), as well as by the cavalry and Smith's troops; but night soon fell, and the whole army went into bivouac in the open fields wherever they chanced to be.

At dark, Hood, who at 12 o'clock had held an unbroken, fortified line from the Murfreesboro' to the Hillsboro' Pike, with an advanced post on Montgomery Hill and five strong redoubts along the Hillsboro' Pike, barely maintained his hold of a line from the Murfreesboro' Pike to the Granny White Pike, near which on two large hills the left of his army had taken refuge when driven out of their redoubts by Smith and Wilson. These hills were more than two miles to the rear of his morning position. It was to that point that Bate, who had started from Hood's right when the assault was first delivered on the redoubts, now made his way amidst, as he says, "streams of stragglers, and artillerists, and horses, without guns or caissons—the sure indications of defeat."

VIEW OF A PART OF THE UNION LINES AT NASHVILLE. FROM A PHOTOGRAPH.

General Hood, not daunted by the reverses which had befallen him, at once set to work to prepare for the next day's struggle. As soon as it was dusk Cheatham's whole corps was moved from his right to his left; Stewart's was retired some two miles and became the center; Lee's also was withdrawn and became the right. The new line extended along the base of a range of hills two miles south of that occupied during the day, and was only about half as long as that from which he had been driven. During the night the Confederates threw up works along their entire front, and the hills on their flanks were strongly fortified. The flanks were also further secured by return works, which prevented them from being left "in the air." Altogether, the position was naturally far more formidable than that just abandoned.

At early dawn the divisions of the Fourth Corps moved forward, driving out the opposing skirmishers. The men entered upon the work with such ardor that the advance soon quickened into a run, and the run almost into a charge. They took up their positions in front of the enemy's new line, at one point coming within 250 yards of the salient at Overton's Hill. Here they were halted, and threw up works, while the artillery on both sides kept up a steady and accurate fire. Steedman also moved forward and about noon joined his right to Wood's left, thus completing the alignment.

On his way to the front General Thomas heard the cannonading, and, as was his custom, rode straight for the spot where the action seemed heaviest. As

SOUTH-WEST FRONT OF THE CAPITOL AT NASHVILLE. FROM A PHOTOGRAPH.
The view is toward the battle-field. Near the base of the first column is seen in the distance the flag of Fort Negley.

he was passing a large, old-fashioned house, his attention was attracted by the noise of a window closing with a slam. Turning to see the cause, he was greeted by a look from a young lady whose expression at the moment was the reverse of angelic. With an amused smile, the general rode on, and soon forgot the incident in the excitement of battle. But this trifling event had a sequel. The young lady, in process of time, became the wife of an officer then serving in General Thomas's army,—though he did not happen to be a witness of this episode.

The ground between the two armies for the greater part of the way from the Franklin to the Granny White Pike is low, open, and crossed by frequent streams running in every direction, and most of the fields were either newly plowed or old corn-fields, and were heavy, wet, and muddy from the recent storms. Overton's Hill, Hood's right, is a well-rounded slope, the top of which was amply fortified, while hills held by the left of his line just west of the Granny White Pike are so steep that it is difficult to climb them, and their summits were crowned with formidable barricades, in front of which were abatis and masses of fallen trees. Between these extremities the works in many places consisted of stone walls covered with earth, with head-logs on the top. To their rear were ample woods, sufficiently open to enable troops to move through them, but thick enough to afford good shelter. Artillery was also posted at every available spot, and good use was made of it.

The morning was consumed in moving to new positions. Wilson's cavalry, by a wide détour, had passed beyond the extreme Confederate left, and secured a lodgment on the Granny White Pike. But one avenue of escape was now open for Hood—the Franklin Pike. General Thomas hoped that a vigorous assault by Schofield's corps against Hood's left would break the line there, and thus enable the cavalry, relieved from the necessity of operating against the rebel flank, to gallop down the Granny White Pike to its junction with the Franklin, some six or eight miles below, and plant itself square across the only remaining line of retreat. If this scheme could be carried out, nothing but capture or surrender awaited Hood's whole army.

Meantime, on the National left, Colonel Post, who had so gallantly carried Montgomery Hill the morning before, had made a careful reconnoissance of Overton's Hill, the strong position on Hood's right. As the result of his observation, he reported to General Wood, his corps commander, that an assault would cost dear, but he believed it could be made successfully; at any rate he was ready to try it. The order was accordingly given, and everything prepared. The brigade was to be supported on either side by fresh troops to be held in readiness to rush for the works the moment Post should gain the parapet. The bugles had not finished sounding the charge, when Post's brigade, preceded by a strong line of skirmishers, moved forward, in perfect silence, with orders to halt for nothing, but to gain the works at a run. The men dashed on, Post leading, with all speed through a shower of shot and shell. A few of the skirmishers reached the parapet; the main line came within twenty steps of the works, when, by a concentrated fire of musketry and artillery from every available point of the enemy's line, the advance was momentarily checked, and, in another instant, Post was brought down by a wound, at first reported as mortal. This slight hesitation and the disabling of Post were fatal to the success of the assault. The leader and animating spirit gone, the line slowly drifted back to its original position, losing in those few minutes nearly 300 men; while the supporting brigade on its left lost 250.

Steedman had promised to coöperate in this assault, and accordingly Thompson's brigade of colored troops was ordered to make a demonstration at the moment Post's advance began. These troops had never before been in action and were now to test their mettle. There had been no time for a reconnoissance, when this order was given, else it is likely a way would have been found to turn the enemy's extreme right flank. The colored brigade moved forward against the works east of the Franklin Pike and nearly parallel to it. As they advanced, they became excited, and what was intended merely as a demonstration was unintentionally converted into an actual assault. Thompson, finding his men rushing forward at the double-quick, gallantly led them to the very slope of the intrenchments. But, in their advance across the open field, the continuity of his line was broken by a large fallen tree. As the men separated to pass it, the enemy opened an enfilading fire on the exposed flanks of the gap thus created, with telling effect. In consequence, at the very moment when a firm and compact order was most needed, the line came up ragged and broken. Meantime Post's assault was repulsed, and the fire which had been concentrated on him was turned against Thompson. Nothing was left, therefore, but to withdraw as soon as possible to the original position. This was done without panic or confusion, after a loss of 467 men from the three regiments composing the brigade.

When it was seen that a heavy assault on his right, at Overton's Hill, was threatened, Hood ordered Cleburne's old division to be sent over to the exposed point, from the extreme left, in front of Schofield. About the same time General Couch, commanding one of the divisions of the Twenty-third Corps, told General Schofield that he believed he could carry the hill in his front, but doubted if he could hold it without assistance. The ground in front of General Cox, on Couch's right, also offered grand opportunities for a successful assault. Meantime the cavalry, on Cox's right, had made its way beyond the extreme left flank of the enemy, and was moving northward over the wooded hills direct to the rear of the extreme rebel left.

General Thomas, who had been making a reconnoissance, had no sooner reached Schofield's front than General McArthur, who commanded one of Smith's divisions, impatient at the long waiting, and not wanting to spend the second night on the rocky hill he was occupying, told Smith that he could carry the high hill in front of Couch,—the same that Couch himself had told

Schofield he could carry,—and would undertake it unless forbidden. Smith silently acquiesced, and McArthur set to work. Withdrawing McMillen's (his right) brigade from the trenches, he marched it by the flank in front of General Couch's position, and with orders to the men to fix bayonets, not to fire a shot and neither to halt nor to cheer until they had gained the enemy's works, the charge was sounded. The gallant brigade, which had served and fought in every part of the South-west, moved swiftly down the slope, across the narrow valley, and began scrambling up the steep hillside, on the top of which was the redoubt, held by Bate's division, and mounted also with Whitworth guns. The bravest onlookers held their breath as these gallant men steadily and silently approached the summit amid the crash of musketry and the boom of the artillery. In almost the time it has taken to tell the story they gained the works, their flags were wildly waving from the parapet, and the unmistakable cheer, "the voice of the American people," as General Thomas called it, rent the air. It was an exultant moment; but this was only a part of the heroic work of that afternoon. While McMillen's brigade was preparing for this wonderful charge, Hatch's division of cavalry, dismounted, had also pushed its way through the woods, and had gained the tops of two hills that commanded the rear of the enemy's works. Here, with incredible labor, they had dragged, by hand, two pieces of artillery, and, just as McMillen began his charge, these opened on the hill where Bate was, up the opposite slope of which the infantry were scrambling. At the same time Coon's brigade of Hatch's division with resounding cheers charged upon the enemy and poured such volleys of musketry from their repeating-rifles as I have never heard equaled. Thus beset on both sides, Bate's people broke out of the works, and ran down the hill toward their right and rear as fast as their legs could carry them. It was more like a scene in a spectacular drama than a real incident in war. The hillside in front, still green, dotted with the boys in blue swarming up the slope; the dark background of high hills beyond; the lowering clouds; the waving flags; the smoke slowly rising through the leafless tree-tops and drifting across the valleys; the wonderful outburst of musketry; the ecstatic cheers; the multitude racing for life down into the valley below,—so exciting was it all, that the lookers-on instinctively clapped their hands, as at a brilliant and successful transformation scene, as indeed it was. For, in those few minutes, an army was changed into a mob, and the whole structure of the rebellion in the South-west, with all its possibilities, was utterly overthrown. As soon as the other divisions farther to the left saw and heard the doings on their right, they did not wait for orders. Everywhere, by a common impulse, they charged the works in front, and carried them in a twinkling. General Edward Johnson and nearly all his division and his artillery were captured. Over the very ground where, but a little while before, Post's assault had been repulsed, the same troops now charged with resistless force, capturing fourteen guns and one thousand prisoners. Steedman's colored brigades also rallied and brought in their share of prisoners and other spoils of war. Everywhere the success was complete.

Foremost among the rejoicing victors was General Steedman, under whose command were the colored troops. Steedman had been a life-long Democrat and was one of the delegates, in 1860, to the Charleston convention, at which ultimately Breckinridge was nominated for President. As he rode over the field, immediately after the rout of the enemy, he asked, with a grim smile, as he pointed to the fleeing hosts, "I wonder what my Democratic friends over there would think of me if they knew I was fighting them with 'nigger' troops?"

I have not space to tell the story of the pursuit, which only ended, ten days later, at the Tennessee River. About a month before, General Hood had triumphantly begun his northward movement. Now, in his disastrous retreat, he was leaving behind him, as prisoners or deserters, a larger number of men than General Thomas had been able to place at Pulaski to hinder his advance—to say nothing of his terrific losses in killed at Franklin. The loss to the Union army, in all its fighting,—from the Tennessee River to Nashville and back again,—was less than six thousand killed, wounded, and missing. At so small a cost, counting the chances of war, the whole North-west was saved from an invasion that, if Hood had succeeded, would have more than neutralized all Sherman's successes in Georgia and the Carolinas; saved by the steadfast labors, the untiring energy, the rapid combinations, the skillful evolutions, the heroic courage and the tremendous force of one man, whose name will yet rank among the great captains of all time.

CHAPTER 14

EARLY'S MARCH TO WASHINGTON IN 1864.‡

Jubal A. Early, Lieutenant-General, C.S.A.

On the 12th of June, 1864, while the Second Corps (Ewell's) of the Army of Northern Virginia was lying near Gaines's Mill, in rear of Hill's line at Cold Harbor, I received orders from General Lee to move the corps, with two of the battalions of artillery attached to it, to the Shenandoah Valley; to strike Hunter's force in the rear and, if possible, destroy it; then to move down the valley, cross the Potomac near Leesburg, in Loudoun County, or at or above Harper's Ferry, as I might find most practicable, and threaten Washington city.↓ I was further directed to communicate with General Breckinridge, who would coöperate with me in the attack on Hunter and the expedition into Maryland.

The Second Corps now numbered a little over eight thousand muskets for duty. It had been on active and arduous service in the field for forty days. Divisions were not stronger than brigades ought to have been, nor brigades than regiments. On the morning of the 13th, at 2 o'clock, we commenced the march, and on the 16th arrived at the Rivanna River, near Charlottesville, having marched over eighty miles in four days. At Charlottesville I received a telegram from Breckinridge, dated at Lynchburg, informing me that Hunter was then in Bedford County about twenty miles from that place and moving on it. The railroad and telegraph between Charlottesville and Lynchburg had been, fortunately, but slightly injured by the enemy's cavalry, and had been repaired. I ordered all the trains of the two roads to be sent to me with all dispatch, for the purpose of transporting my troops to Lynchburg. The trains were not in readi-

---

‡Condensed from General Early's "Memoir of the Last Year of the War for Independence in the Confederate States of America" (Lynchburg: Published by Charles W. Button for the Virginia Memorial Association, 1867), here printed by permission of the author.

↓In a letter to the editors under date of November 23d, 1888, General Early says: "General Lee did not expect me to be able to enter Washington. His orders were merely to threaten the city, and when I suggested to him the idea of capturing it he said it would be impossible."

ness to take the troops on board until sunrise on the morning of the 17th, and then only enough were furnished to transport about half my infantry. I accompanied Ramseur's division, going on the front train; but the road and rolling stock were in such bad condition that I did not reach Lynchburg until about 1 o'clock in the afternoon, and the other trains were much later.

As General Breckinridge was in bed, suffering from an injury received near Cold Harbor, at his request General D. H. Hill, who happened to be in town, had made arrangements for the defense of the city with such troops as were at hand. Slight works had been hastily thrown up on College Hill, covering the turnpike and Forest roads from Liberty, manned by Breckinridge's infantry and the dismounted cavalry of the command [Jones's and Vaughn's brigades] which had been with Jones at Piedmont. The reserves, invalids from the hospitals, and the cadets from the Military Institute at Lexington occupied other parts of the line. My troops, as they arrived, had been ordered in front of the works to bivouac, and I immediately sent orders for them to move out on the turnpike, and two brigades of Ramseur's division arrived just in time to be thrown across the road at a redoubt about two miles from the city as Imboden's command was driven back by vastly superior numbers. These brigades, with two pieces of artillery in the redoubt, arrested the progress of the enemy, and Ramseur's other brigade, and the part of Gordon's division which had arrived, took position on the same line. The enemy opened a heavy fire of artillery on us, but as night soon came on he went into camp on our front.

Orders had been given for the immediate return of the trains for the rest of my infantry, but it did not get to Lynchburg until late in the afternoon of the 18th, and meanwhile I contented myself with acting on the defensive. There was artillery firing and skirmishing along the line, and in the afternoon an attack was made to the right of the turnpike, which was handsomely repulsed with considerable loss to the enemy. A demonstration of the enemy's cavalry on the Forest road was checked by part of Breckinridge's infantry under Wharton, and McCausland's cavalry. As soon as the remainder of my infantry arrived by the railroad, though none of my artillery had gotten up, arrangements were made for attacking Hunter at daylight on the 19th; but after midnight it was discovered that he was moving, and at light it was observed that he was in retreat, and pursuit commenced. The enemy's rear was overtaken at Liberty, twenty-five miles from Lynchburg, just before night, and driven through that place, after a brisk skirmish, by Ramseur's division. The day's march on the old turnpike, which was very rough, had been terrible. The pursuit was resumed early on the morning of the 20th, and the enemy was pursued into the mountains at Buford's Gap, but he had taken possession of the crest of the Blue Ridge, and put batteries in position commanding a gorge through which the road passes. On the 21st the pursuit was resumed very shortly after sunrise. The enemy had turned off from Salem toward Lewisburg, and McCausland had struck his column and captured ten pieces of artillery, but was compelled to fall back, carrying off, however, the prisoners and also a part of the artillery, and disabling the rest. As the enemy had got into the mountains, where nothing useful could be accomplished by pursuit, I did not deem it proper to continue it farther. A great part of my command had had nothing to eat for the last two days, except a little bacon which was obtained at Liberty. It had marched sixty miles in the three days' pursuit, over very rough roads. I determined, therefore, to rest on the 22d, so as to enable the wagons and artillery to get up, and prepare the men for the long march before them.§

At Lynchburg I had received a telegram from General Lee, directing me, after disposing of Hunter, either to return to his army or to carry out the original plan, as I might deem most expedient. After the pursuit had ceased I received another dispatch from him, submitting it to my judgment whether the condition of my troops would permit the expedition across the Potomac to be carried out, and I determined to take the responsibility of continuing it. On the 23d the march was resumed, and we reached Buchanan that night. On the 26th I reached Staunton in advance of the troops, and the latter came up next day, which was spent in reducing transportation and getting provisions from Waynesboro'. The official reports at this place showed about two thousand mounted men for duty in the cavalry, which was composed of four small brigades, to wit: Imboden's, McCausland's, Jackson's, and Jones's (now Johnson's). The official reports of the infantry showed ten thousand muskets for duty, including Vaughn's dismounted cavalry. Besides Breckinridge's own infantry division, under Elzey (now under Vaughn, afterward under Echols), Gordon's division of the Second Corps was assigned to General Breckinridge, in order to give him a command commensurate with his proper one. Nearly half the troops were barefoot, or nearly so, and shoes were sent for. But without waiting for them the march was resumed on the 28th, with five days' rations in the wagons and two days' in haversacks. Imboden was sent through Brock's Gap to the South

§Grant, in his report, says, "General Hunter, owing to a want of ammunition to give battle, retired from before the place" [Lynchburg]. This is a little remarkable, as it appears that this expedition had been long contemplated and was one of the prominent features of the campaign of 1864. Sheridan, with his cavalry, was to have united with Hunter at Lynchburg, and the two together were to have destroyed Lee's communications and depots of supplies, and then have joined Grant. Can it be believed that Hunter set out on so important an expedition with an insufficient supply of ammunition? Had Sheridan defeated Hampton at Trevilian's, he would have reached Lynchburg after destroying the railroad on the way, and I could not have reached there in time to do any good. But Hampton defeated Sheridan. Had Hunter moved on Lynchburg with energy, that place would have fallen before it was possible for me to get there.—J.A.E.

The notification of Secretary Stanton to General Stabel on the subject was as follows: "General Sheridan, who was sent by General Grant to open communication with General Hunter by way of Charlottesville, has just returned to York River without effecting his object. It is therefore very probable that General Hunter will be compelled to fall back into West Virginia."—EDITORS.

Branch of the Potomac to destroy the railroad bridge over that stream, and all the bridges on the Baltimore and Ohio Railroad from that point to Martinsburg. On the 2d of July we reached Winchester, and here I received a dispatch from General Lee, directing me to remain in the lower valley until everything was in readiness to cross the Potomac, and to destroy the Baltimore and Ohio Railroad and the Chesapeake and Ohio Canal as far as possible. This was in accordance with my previous determination, and its policy was obvious. My provisions were nearly exhausted, and if I had moved through Loudoun it would have been necessary for me to halt and thresh wheat and have it ground, as neither

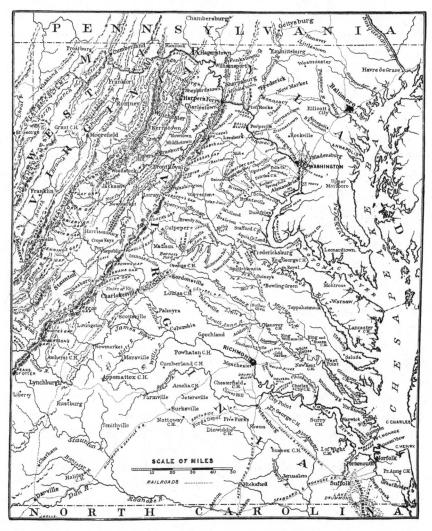

MAP OF THE VIRGINIA CAMPAIGNS OF 1864–5.

bread nor flour could be otherwise obtained; which would have caused much greater delay than was required on the other route, where we could take provisions from the enemy. Moreover, unless the Baltimore and Ohio Railroad was torn up the enemy would have been able to move troops from the West over that road to Washington.

On the morning of the 3d Sigel, with a considerable force, after slight skirmishing, evacuated Martinsburg, leaving considerable stores in our hands. McCausland burned the bridge over Back Creek, capturing the guard at North Mountain depot, and succeeded in reaching Hainesville; but Bradley T. Johnson, after driving Mulligan, with hard fighting at Leetown, across the railroad, was himself forced back, when Sigel united with Mulligan, upon Rodes's and Ramseur's divisions, which arrived at Leetown after a march of twenty-four miles. During the night Sigel retreated across the Potomac at Shepherdstown to Maryland Heights.

During the night of the 4th the enemy evacuated Harper's Ferry, burning the railroad and pontoon bridges across the Potomac. It was not possible to occupy the town of Harper's Ferry, except with skirmishers, as it was thoroughly commanded by the heavy guns on Maryland Heights; and the 5th was spent by Rodes's and Ramseur's divisions in demonstrating at that place. In the afternoon Breckinridge's command moved to Shepherdstown and crossed the Potomac, followed by Rodes's and Ramseur's divisions early on the 6th. Gordon's division advanced toward Maryland Heights, and drove the enemy into his works. Working parties were employed in destroying the aqueduct of the canal over the Antietam, and the locks and canal-boats. On the 7th Rodes moved through Rohrersville on the road to Crampton's Gap in South Mountain, and skirmished with a small force of the enemy, while Breckinridge demonstrated against Maryland Heights. McCausland had occupied Hagerstown and levied a contribution of $20,000, and Boonsboro' had been occupied by Johnson's cavalry. A letter from General Lee had informed me that an effort would be made to release the prisoners at Point Lookout, and directing me to take steps to unite them with my command. My desire had been to manœuvre the enemy out of Maryland Heights, so as to move directly to Washington; but he had taken refuge in his strongly fortified works, and I therefore determined to move through the gaps of South Mountain north of the Heights. On the 7th the greater portion of the cavalry was sent in the direction of Frederick; and that night the expected shoes arrived and were distributed.

Early on the morning of the 8th the whole force moved: Rodes through Crampton's Gap to Jefferson; Breckinridge through Fox's Gap; and Ramseur, with the trains, through Boonsboro' Gap, followed by Lewis's brigade, which had started from Harper's Ferry the night before, after burning the trestle-work on the railroad and the stores which had not been brought off. Early on the 9th Johnson, with his brigade of cavalry and a battery of horse artillery, moved to the north of Frederick, with orders to strike the railroads from Baltimore to Harrisburg and Philadelphia, burn the bridges over the Gunpowder, also to cut the railroad between Washington and Baltimore, and threaten the latter place; and then to move toward Point Lookout for the purpose of releasing the prisoners, if we should succeed in getting into Washington. The other troops also moved forward toward Monocacy Junction, and Ramseur's division passed through Frederick, driving a force of skirmishers before it.

The enemy in considerable force, under General Lew Wallace,/ was found strongly posted on the eastern bank of the Monocacy, near the junction, with an earth-work and

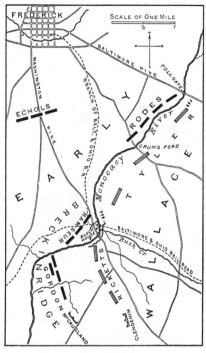

MAP OF THE BATTLE OF THE MONOCACY.

/In his "Personal Memoirs" (Vol. II., pp. 304–6), General Grant writes as follows of the battle of Monocacy and its effect:

"In the absence of Hunter, General Lew Wallace, with headquarters at Baltimore, commanded the department in which the Shenandoah lay. His surplus of troops with which to move against the enemy was small in number. Most of these were raw, and, consequently, very much inferior to our veterans and to the veterans which Early had with him; but the situation of Washington was precarious, and Wallace moved with commendable promptitude to meet the enemy at the Monocacy. He could hardly have expected to defeat him badly, but he hoped to cripple and delay him until Washington could be put into a state of preparation for his reception. I had previously ordered General Meade to send a division to Baltimore for the purpose of adding to the defenses of Washington, and he had sent Ricketts's division of the Sixth Corps (Wright's), which arrived in Baltimore on the 8th of July. Finding that Wallace had gone to the front with his command, Ricketts immediately took the cars and followed him to the Monocacy with his entire division. They met the enemy, and, as might have been expected, were defeated; but they succeeded in stopping him for the day on which the battle took place. The next morning Early started on his march to the capital of the nation, arriving before it on the 11th.

"Learning of the gravity of the situation, I had directed General Meade to also order Wright, with the rest of his corps, directly to Washington for the relief of that place, and the latter reached there the very day that Early arrived before it. The Nineteenth Corps, which had been stationed in Louisiana, having been ordered up to reënforce the armies about Richmond, had about this time arrived at Fortress Monroe, on their way to join us. I diverted

1864-5.
MAP OF THE
DEFENCES OF
WASHINGTON
SCALE OF MILES
1   2   3   4

two block-houses commanding both the railroad bridge and the bridge on the Georgetown pike. McCausland, crossing the river with his brigade, dis-

them from that point to Washington, which place they reached almost simultaneously with Wright, on the 11th. The Nineteenth Corps was commanded by Major-General Emory.

"Early made his reconnoissance with a view of attacking on the following morning, the 12th; but the next morning he found our intrenchments, which were very strong, fully manned. He at once commenced to retreat, Wright following. [The retreat began on the night of the 12th.—EDITORS.] There is no telling how much this result was contributed to by General Lew Wallace's leading what might well be considered almost a forlorn hope. If Early had been but one day earlier, he might have entered the capital before the arrival of the reënforcements I had sent. Whether the delay caused by the battle amounted to a day or not, General Wallace contributed on this occasion, by the defeat of the troops under him, a greater benefit to the cause than often falls to the lot of a commander of an equal force to render by means of a victory."

mounted his men and advanced rapidly against the enemy's left flank, which he threw into confusion, but he was then gradually forced back. McCausland's movement, which was very brilliantly executed, solved the problem for me, and orders were sent to Breckinridge to move up rapidly with Gordon's division to McCausland's assistance, and, striking the enemy's left, to drive him from the positions commanding the crossings in Ramseur's front, so that the latter might cross. This division crossed under the personal superintendence of General Breckinridge, and while Ramseur skirmished with the enemy in front, the attack was made by Gordon in gallant style, and with the aid of several pieces of King's artillery, which had been crossed over, and Nelson's artillery from the opposite side, he threw the enemy into great confusion and forced him from his position. Ramseur immediately crossed on the railroad bridge and pursued the enemy's flying forces, and Rodes crossed on the left and joined in the pursuit. Between 600 and 700 unwounded prisoners fell into their hands, and the enemy's loss in killed and wounded was very heavy. Our loss in killed and wounded was about 700. The action closed about sunset, and we had marched about fourteen miles before it commenced. All the troops and trains were crossed over the Monocacy that night, so as to resume the march early the next day. During the operations at Monocacy, a contribution of $200,000 in money was levied on the city of Frederick, and some much-needed supplies were obtained.

On the 10th the march was resumed at day-light, and we bivouacked four miles from Rockville, on the Georgetown pike, having marched twenty miles. McCausland, moving in front, drove a body of the enemy's cavalry before him,

FORT STEVENS, WASHINGTON. FROM A WAR-TIME PHOTOGRAPH.

and had a brisk engagement at Rockville, where he encamped after defeating and driving off the enemy.

We moved at daylight on the 11th, McCausland on the Georgetown pike, while the infantry, preceded by Imboden's cavalry under Colonel Smith, turned to the left at Rockville, so as to reach the 7th street pike which runs by Silver Springs into Washington. Jackson's cavalry moved on the left flank. The previous day had been very warm, and the roads were exceedingly dusty, as there had been no rain for several weeks. The heat during the night had been very oppressive, and but little rest had been obtained. This day was an exceedingly hot one, and there was no air stirring. While marching, the men were enveloped in a suffocating cloud of dust, and many of them fell by the way from exhaustion. Our progress was therefore very much impeded, but I pushed on as rapidly as possible, hoping to get into the fortifications around Washington before they could be manned. Smith drove a small body of cavalry before him into the works on the 7th street pike, and dismounted his men and deployed them as skirmishers. I rode ahead of the infantry, and arrived in sight of Fort Stevens on this road a short time after noon, when I discovered that the works were but feebly manned.

Rodes, whose division was in front, was immediately ordered to bring it into line as rapidly as possible, throw out skirmishers, and move into the works if he could. My whole column was then moving by flank, which was the only practicable mode of marching on the road we were on, and before Rodes's division could be brought up we saw a cloud of dust in the rear of the works toward Washington, and soon a column of the enemy filed into them on the right and left, and skirmishers were thrown out in front, while an artillery fire was opened on us from a number of batteries. This defeated our hopes of getting possession of the works by surprise, and it became necessary to reconnoiter.

Rodes's skirmishers were thrown to the front, driving those of the enemy to the cover of the works, and we proceeded to examine the fortifications in order to ascertain if it was practicable to carry them by assault. They were found to be exceedingly strong, and consisted of what appeared to be inclosed forts for heavy artillery, with a tier of lower works in front of each, pierced for an immense number of guns, the whole being connected by curtains with ditches in front, and strengthened by palisades and abatis. The timber had been felled within cannon range all around and left on the ground, making a formidable obstacle, and every possible approach was raked by artillery. On the right was Rock Creek, running through a deep ravine which had been rendered impassable by the felling of the timber on each side, and beyond were the works on the Georgetown pike which had been reported to be the strongest of all. On the left, as far as the eye could reach, the works appeared to be of the same impregnable character.✧ This reconnoissance consumed the balance of the day.

The rapid marching and the losses at Harper's Ferry, Maryland Heights, and Monocacy had reduced my infantry to about 8000 muskets.✦ Of these a very large number were greatly exhausted by the last two days' marching, some having fallen by sunstroke, and not more than one-third of my force could have been carried into action. I had about forty pieces of artillery, of which the largest were 12-pounder Napoleons, besides a few pieces of horse-artillery

---

✧General Barnard, in his "Defences of Washington," thus describes the works (see map, p. 1,032):

> "Every prominent point, at intervals of eight hundred to one thousand yards, was occupied by an inclosed field-fort; every important approach or depression of ground, unseen from the forts, swept by a battery for field-guns; and the whole connected by rifle-trenches which were in fact lines of infantry parapets, furnishing emplacement for two ranks of men, and affording covered communication along the line, while roads were opened wherever necessary, so that troops and artillery could be moved rapidly from one point of the immense periphery to another, or, under cover, from point to point along the line. The counterscarps were surrounded by abatis; bomb-proofs were provided in nearly all the forts; all guns not solely intended for distant fire placed in embrasures and well traversed. All commanding points on which an enemy would be likely to concentrate artillery to overpower that of one or two of our forts or batteries were subjected not only to the fire, direct and cross, of many points along the line, but also from heavy rifled guns from distant points unattainable by the enemy's field-guns. With all these developments, the lines certainly approximated to the maximum degree of strength which can be attained from unrevetted earth-works. Inadequately manned as they were, the fortifications compelled at least a concentration and an arraying of force on the part of the assailants, and thus gave time for the arrival of succor."

General Barnard gives this account of the local forces prior to the arrival of the Sixth and Nineteenth corps:

> "The effective forces were 1819 infantry, 1834 artillery, and 63 cavalry north of the Potomac, and 4064 infantry, 1772 artillery, and 51 cavalry south thereof. There were besides, in Washington and Alexandria, about 3900 effectives and about 4400 (six regiments) of Veteran Reserves. The foregoing constitutes a total of about 20,400 men. Of that number, however, but 9600, mostly perfectly raw troops, constituted the *garrison* of the defenses. Of the other troops, a considerable portion were unavailable, and the whole would form but an inefficient force for service on the lines."

Of the troops sent by Grant, Ricketts's division of the Sixth Corps was with Wallace at Baltimore; the other two divisions, under General Wright, and the first steamer-load, amounting to 800 men, of the Nineteenth Corps, reached Washington before 2 P.M. of the 11th. At 4:10 P.M. of that day Wright sent this dispatch to General Augur from Fort Stevens: "The head of my column has nearly reached the front." That night the Sixth Corps relieved the provisional forces on the picket line. The remainder of Emory's division of the Nineteenth Corps continued to come by installments.—EDITORS.

✦Writing on November 23d, 1888, General Early adds:

> "A considerable number of my men had broken down on the march, from exhaustion and want of shoes, and on my return to the Valley I found some 1800 or 2000 collected at Winchester by Colonel Goodwin, and others who had been temporarily disabled in the campaign from the Wilderness to Richmond also returned."

—EDITORS.

with the cavalry. McCausland reported the works on the Georgetown pike too strongly manned for him to assault. After dark on the 11th I held a consultation with Major-Generals Breckinridge, Rodes, Gordon, and Ramseur, in which I stated to them the necessity of doing something immediately, as the passes of South Mountain and the fords of the Upper Potomac would soon be closed against us. After interchanging views with them, I determined to make an assault on the enemy's works at daylight next morning. But during the night a dispatch was received from General Bradley T. Johnson from near Baltimore, that two corps had arrived from General Grant's army, and that his whole army was probably in motion. As soon as it was light enough to see, I rode to the front, and found the parapet lined with troops. I had, therefore, reluctantly to give up all hopes of capturing Washington, after I had arrived in sight of the dome of the Capitol, and given the Federal authorities a terrible fright.

Some of the Northern papers stated that, between Saturday and Monday, I could have entered the city; but on Saturday I was fighting at Monocacy, thirty-five miles from Washington, a force which I could not leave in my rear; and after disposing of that force and moving as rapidly as it was possible for me to move, I did not arrive in front of the fortifications until after noon on Monday, and then my troops were exhausted, and it required time to bring them up into line. I had then made a march, over the circuitous route by Charlottesville, Lynchburg, and Salem, down the valley and through the passes of the South Mountain, which, notwithstanding the delays in dealing with Hunter's, Sigel's, and Wallace's forces, is, for its length and rapidity, I believe, without a parallel in this or any other modern war. My small force had been thrown up to the very walls of the Federal capital, north of a river which could not be forded at any point within forty miles, and with a heavy force and the South Mountain in my rear—the passes through which mountain could be held by a small number of troops. A glance at the map, when it is recollected that the Potomac is a wide river, and navigable to Washington for the largest vessels, will cause the intelligent reader to wonder, not why I failed to take Washington, but why I had the audacity to approach it as I did, with the small force under my command. It was supposed by some, who were not informed of the facts, that I delayed in the lower valley longer than was necessary; but an examination of the foregoing narrative will show that not one moment was spent in idleness. I could not move across the Potomac and through the passes of the South Mountain, with any safety, until Sigel was driven from, or safely housed in, the fortifications at Maryland Heights.

After abandoning the idea of capturing Washington I determined to remain in front of the fortifications during the 12th, and retire at night. Johnson had burned the bridges over the Gunpowder, on the Harrisburg and Philadelphia roads, threatened Baltimore, and started for Point Lookout; but the attempt to release the prisoners was not made, as the enemy had received notice of it in some way. On the afternoon of the 12th a heavy reconnoitering force was sent out by the enemy, which, after severe skirmishing, was driven back by Rodes's division with but slight loss to us.ᴮ About dark we commenced retiring, and did so without molestation. Passing through Rockville and Poolesville, we crossed the Potomac at White's Ford, above Leesburg, in Loudoun County, on the morning of the 14th, bringing off the prisoners captured at Monocacy, and our captured beef cattle and horses, and everything else, in safety.⁄

ᴮGrant says: "On the 12th a reconnoissance was thrown out in front of Fort Stevens to ascertain the enemy's position and force. A severe skirmish ensued, in which we lost 280 in killed and wounded. The enemy's loss was probably greater. He commenced retiring during the night." The above is correct, with the exception of the estimate placed on our loss.—J.A.E.

⁄General Wright, with about 15,000 men of the Sixth and Nineteenth corps, followed by several thousand more, under Ricketts and Kenly, pursued General Early, who, however, after resting on the 14th and 15th at Leesburg, reached the Shenandoah Valley safely through Snicker's Gap, losing some loaded wagons at Purcellville to the cavalry of Hunter's field forces. These latter had returned from the Kanawha Valley to Harper's Ferry, and moved out under Crook against the flank of Early's column. Thoburn's division of Crook's command, crossing at Snicker's Gap, was repulsed by Early with a loss of 422 on the 18th of July. On the 20th Averell, with a mixed infantry and cavalry force, 2350 strong, attacked and defeated Ramseur's division near Winchester, inflicting a loss of about 400, and suffering a loss of 214. On July 22d General Early established himself at Strasburg.—EDITORS.

CHAPTER 15

SHERMAN'S ADVANCE FROM ATLANTA.

Oliver O. Howard, Major-General, U.S.A.

When Sherman decided to march south from Atlanta, he ordered to Thomas at Nashville Schofield with the Twenty-third Corps, Stanley with the Fourth Corps, all the cavalry, except Kilpatrick's division, all the detachments drawn back from the railway line, and such other troops, including A. J. Smith's, as Sherman's military division could furnish. Sherman reserved for his right wing my two corps, the Fifteenth and Seventeenth; and for his left wing the Fourteenth and Twentieth under Slocum. Mine, the Army of the Tennessee, numbered 33,000; Slocum's, the "Army of Georgia," 30,000; Kilpatrick's division of cavalry, 5000; so that the aggregate of all arms was 68,000 men. All surplus stores and trains were sent back to Tennessee. The railway south of the Etowah was next completely demolished. Under the efficient management of Colonel

MARCHING THROUGH GEORGIA.

O. M. Poe, Sherman's chief engineer, all that was of a public nature in Atlanta which could aid the enemy was destroyed. Wrecked engines, bent and twisted iron rails, blackened ruins and lonesome chimneys saddened the hearts of the few peaceful citizens who remained there.

HOOK USED BY GENERAL SHERMAN'S ARMY FOR TWISTING AND DESTROYING RAILROAD IRON.

Behold now this veteran army thus reorganized and equipped, with moderate baggage and a few days' supply of small rations, but with plenty of ammunition, ready to march anywhere Sherman might lead. Just before starting, Sherman had a muscular lameness in one arm that gave him great trouble. On a visit to him I found his servant bathing and continuously rubbing the arm. As I understood the general's ruling, I would command next to him, because I had from the President an assignment to an army and a department. I was therefore especially anxious to know fully his plans, and plainly told him so. While the rubbing went on he explained in detail what he proposed and pointed significantly to Goldsboro', North Carolina, on his map, saying, "I hope to get there." On November 15th we set forth in good earnest. Slocum, Sherman accompanying him, went by the Augusta Railroad, and passed on through Milledgeville. I followed the Macon Railroad, and for the first seven days had Kilpatrick with me.

Notwithstanding our reduction of the impedimenta, our wagon trains were still long, and always a source of anxiety. Pushing toward Macon, I found some resistance from General G. W. Smith's new levies. The crossing of the Ocmulgee, with its steep and muddy banks, was hard enough for the trains. I protected them by a second demonstration from the left bank against Macon. Smith crossed the river and gave us battle at Griswoldville. It was an affair of one division,—that of Charles R. Woods,—using mainly Walcutt's brigade. Smith was badly defeated, and during the *mêlée* our trains were hurried off to Gordon and parked there in safety.‡ Here, at Gordon, Sherman, from Milledgeville, came across to me. Slocum had enjoyed a fine march, having had but little resistance. The stories of the mock Legislature at the State capital, of the luxurious supplies enjoyed all along, and of the constant fun and pranks of "Sherman's bummers," rather belonged to that route than ours. Possibly we had more of the throngs of escaping slaves, from the baby in arms to the old negro hobbling painfully along the line of march—negroes of all sizes, in all sorts of patched costumes, with carts and broken-down horses and mules to match.

---

‡The Union loss at Griswoldville was 13 killed, 69 wounded, and 2 missing = 84. General C. C. Walcutt was among the wounded. The total Confederate loss was over 600.—EDITORS.

SHERMAN'S TROOPS DESTROYING RAILROADS AT ATLANTA. FROM A PHOTOGRAPH.

We brought along our wounded (over 200, I believe) in ambulances, and though they were jolted over corduroy roads and were much exposed to hardship, and participated in the excitements of the march, they all reached Savannah without the loss of a life. Our system of foraging was sufficiently good for the army, but the few citizens, women and children, who remained at home, suffered greatly. We marched our divisions on parallel roads when we could find them; but sometimes, using rails or newly cut poles, made our roads through swamps and soft ground, employing thousands of men. Arriving at the Oconee, Osterhaus found a wooded valley, with lagune bridges and a narrow causeway, on his road. A division of Hardee's, who himself had left Hood and gone to Savannah to command what Confederates he could hastily gather, had marched out to meet us and was intrenched on the east bank. Artillery and infantry fire swept our road. Osterhaus, excited by the shots, came to me shaking his head and asking how we would get any further. "Deploy your skirmishers more and more till there is no reply," I said. He did so. A half mile above he was able to send over among the cypresses a brigade in boats. The Confederate division gave way and fled. Then shortly our bridge was laid on the main road and we marched on. Blair, who had returned from his furlough before we left Atlanta, crossed and kept the left bank of the Ogeechee, and Sherman usually accompanied him. Blair's knowledge and hospitality attracted him. So the armies went on meeting an increased resistance, but were not much delayed till we got to the Savannah Canal. Captain Duncan from my cavalry escort had carried Sherman's messages down the Ogeechee in a boat past Confederate guards and

GENERAL SHERMAN SENDING HIS LAST TELEGRAM BEFORE CUTTING THE WIRES
AND ABANDONING ALL COMMUNICATION WITH THE NORTH.
FROM A SKETCH MADE AT THE TIME.

torpedoes, and gone out to sea. He was picked up by a United States vessel and
his message taken to the admiral. Hence navy and provision ships were waiting
off the headlands, uncertain just where Sherman would secure a harbor.

Owing to swamps and obstructed roads and Hardee's force behind them,
we could not enter Savannah. Our food was getting low. True, Sherman had
sent Kilpatrick to try and take Fort McAllister, a strong fort which held the
mouth of the Ogeechee. But as its capture was too much for the cavalry, I asked
Sherman to allow me to take that fort with infantry. Hazen's division was selected. My chief engineer, Reese, with engineers and pioneers and plenty of
men to help him, in three days repaired the burnt bridge, over 1000 feet long,
near King's house. Hazen, ready at the bridge, then marched over and took Fort
McAllister by assault,⚓ which Sherman and I witnessed from the rice mill, some
miles away on the other bank of the Ogeechee. Now we connected with the

⚓There seem to have been but 230 men in the work. Hazen's loss was 24 killed and 110 wounded.
—EDITORS.

SHERMAN'S ARMY LEAVING ATLANTA. FROM A SKETCH MADE AT THE TIME.

navy, and our supplies flowed in abundantly. Slocum soon put a force beyond the Savannah. Hardee, fearing to be penned up, abandoned his works and fled during the night before Slocum had seized his last road to the east. On December 23d the campaign culminated as Sherman entered Savannah. He sent the following dispatch to President Lincoln, which he received Christmas Eve: "I beg to present to you, as a Christmas gift, the city of Savannah, with one hundred and fifty heavy guns and plenty of ammunition, and also about twenty-five thousand bales of cotton."

CHAPTER 16

MARCHING THROUGH GEORGIA
AND THE CAROLINAS.

Daniel Oakey, Captain, 2d Massachusetts Volunteers.

To us of the Twelfth Corps who had gone West with the Eleventh Corps from the Army of the Potomac, the distant thunder of "the battle of the clouds" was the first sound of conflict in the new field. Some of our "Potomac airs," which had earned us the name of "Kid gloves and paper collars,"‡ began to wear away as we better understood the important work to be done by the great army organizing around us, and of which we were to form a considerable part. A most interesting feature of these preparations was the reënlistment of the old three-years regiments. The two Potomac corps were consolidated, and we of the Twelfth who wore "the bloody star" were apprehensive lest different insignia should be adopted; but the star became the badge of the new (Twentieth) corps, the crescent men amiably dropping their Turkish emblem.

General H. W. Slocum, who had commanded the Twelfth so long, was assigned to command at Vicksburg, but was recalled to succeed Hooker in the command of the Twentieth Corps when toward the end of August, 1864, Hooker asked to be relieved because Howard, who was his junior, had been placed at the head of the Army of the Tennessee to fill the vacancy made by the death of McPherson at Atlanta. This temporary separation from our commander was hard, as all will remember who crowded to his headquarters on the evening of April 7th, 1864. But the sorrow of the hour was dispelled by the gen-

---

‡The Twelfth Corps of the Army of the Potomac was named *"Kid gloves and paper collars"* by the Fourteenth Corps of the Western Army owing to the careful discipline of the Twelfth Corps. It was originally the Fifth Corps (March, 1862), then it became the Second Corps, Army of Virginia (June, 1862), then the Twelfth Corps (September, 1862). The basis of it was Banks's old division, and Banks was its first commander. Mansfield commanded the corps at Antietam, where he was killed and was succeeded by Slocum. The corps had as subordinate commanders such men as A. S. Williams, Charles S. Hamilton, John W. Geary, George H. Gordon, Ruger, Andrews, William Hawley, and the discipline they imparted continued to the end and affected other troops.—D.O.

CAMP OF THE 2D MASS., CITY HALL SQUARE, ATLANTA. FROM A WAR-TIME PHOTOGRAPH.

erous hospitality of his staff and his indulgent order to waive all rank for the occasion.

We observed in the Western troops an air of independence hardly consistent with the nicest discipline; but this quality appeared to some purpose at the battle of Resaca, where we saw our Western companions deliberately leave the line, retire out of range, clean their guns, pick up ammunition from the wounded, and return again to the fight. This cool self-reliance excited our admiration. On we went in a campaign of continual skirmishes and battles that ended in the capture of Atlanta. The morale of the troops had been visibly improved by this successful campaign.

On my way to army headquarters at Atlanta to call upon a staff friend, I met General Sherman, who acknowledged my salute with a familiar "How do you do, Captain." Scrutinizing the insignia on my cap, he continued, "Second Massachusetts? Ah, yes, I know your regiment; you have very fine parades over there in the park."

Sherman could be easily approached by any of his soldiers, but no one could venture to be familiar. His uniform coat, usually wide open at the throat, displayed a not very military black cravat and linen collar, and he generally wore low shoes and one spur. On the march he rode with each column in turn, and often with no larger escort than a single staff-officer and an orderly. In passing us on the march he acknowledged our salutations as if he knew us all, but hadn't time to stop. On "the march to the sea" a soldier called out to Sherman, "Uncle Billy, I guess Grant's waiting for us at Richmond." Sherman's acquaintance among his officers was remarkable, and of great advantage, for he learned the character of every command, even of regiments, and could assign officers to special duties, with knowledge of those who were to fill the vacancies so made. The army appreciated these personal relations, and every man felt in a certain sense that Sherman had his eye on him.

Before the middle of November, 1864, the inhabitants of Atlanta, by Sherman's orders, had left the place. Serious preparations were making for the march to the sea. Nothing was to be left for the use or advantage of the enemy. The sick were sent back to Chattanooga and Nashville, along with every pound of baggage that could be dispensed with. The army was reduced, one might say, to its fighting weight, no man being retained who was not capable of a long march. Our communications were then abandoned by destroying the railroad and telegraph. There was something intensely exciting in this perfect isolation.

The engineers had peremptory orders to avoid any injury to dwellings, but to apply gunpowder and the torch to public buildings, machine-shops, depots, and arsenals. Sixty thousand of us witnessed the destruction of Atlanta, while our post band and that of the 33d Massachusetts played martial airs and operatic selections. It was a night never to be forgotten. Our regular routine was a mere form, and there could be no "taps" amid the brilliant glare and excitement.

The throwing away of superfluous conveniences began at daybreak. The old campaigner knows what to carry and what to throw away. Each group of messmates decided which hatchet, stew-pan, or coffee-pot should be taken. The single wagon allowed to a battalion carried scarcely more than a grip-sack and blanket, and a bit of shelter tent about the size of a large towel, for each officer, and only such other material as was necessary for regimental business. Transportation was reduced to a minimum, and fast marching was to be the order of the day. Wagons to carry the necessary ammunition in the contingency of a battle, and a few days' rations in case of absolute need, composed the train of each army corps, and with one wagon and one ambulance for each regiment made very respectable "impediments," averaging about eight hundred wagons to a corps.

At last came the familiar "Fall in"; the great "flying column" was on the march, and the last regiment in Atlanta turned its back upon the smoking ruins. Our left wing (the Fourteenth and Twentieth corps under Slocum) seemed to threaten Macon, while the right wing (the Fifteenth and Seventeenth corps under Howard) bent its course as if for Augusta. Skirmishers were in advance, flankers were out, and foraging parties were ahead gathering supplies from the rich plantations. We were all old campaigners, so that a brush with the militia now and then or with Hardee's troops made no unusual delay; and Wheeler's cavalry was soon disposed of. We were expected to make fifteen miles a day; to corduroy the roads where necessary; to destroy such property as was designated by our corps commander, and to consume everything eatable by man or beast.

Milledgeville proved to be Sherman's first objective, and both wings came within less than supporting distance in and around the capital of the State. Our colored friends, who flocked to us in embarrassing numbers, told many stories about the fear and flight of the inhabitants at the approach of Sherman.

Cock-fighting became one of the pastimes of the "flying column." Many fine birds were brought in by our foragers. Those found deficient in courage and skill quickly went to the stew-pan in company with the modest barn-yard fowl, but those of redoubtable valor won an honored place and name, and were to be seen riding proudly on the front seat of an artillery caisson, or carried tenderly under the arm of an infantry soldier.

Our next objective was Savannah. Hazen's capture of Fort McAllister opened the gates of that beautiful city, while Hardee managed to escape with his little army; and Sherman, in a rather facetious dispatch, presented the city to Mr. Lincoln as a Christmas gift. Flushed with the success of our march, we settled down for a rest. Our uniforms were the worse for wear, but the army was in fine condition and fully prepared for the serious work ahead.

In the middle of December in the neighborhood of Savannah, after Hardee's troops had nearly exhausted the country, which was now mainly under water, there was little opportunity for the foragers to exercise their talents, and some of them returned to the ranks. The troops bivouacked here and there in comparatively dry spots, while picket duty had to be performed at many points in the water. In going from Sister's Ferry to Robertsville, where my regiment was in bivouac, I waded for a mile and a half in water knee-deep. At Purysburg the pickets were all afloat in boats and scows and on rafts, and the crestfallen foragers brought in nothing but rice, which became unpalatable when served three times a day for successive weeks. At length, when we left Savannah and launched cheerily into the untrodden land of South Carolina, the foragers began to assume their wonted spirit. We were proud of our foragers. They constituted a picked force from each regiment, under an officer selected for the command, and were remarkable for intelligence, spirit, and daring. Before daylight, mounted on horses captured on the plantations, they were in the saddle and away, covering the country sometimes seven miles in advance. Although I have said "in the saddle," many a forager had nothing better than a bit of carpet and a rope halter; yet this simplicity of equipment did not abate his power of carrying off hams and sweet-potatoes in the face of the enemy. The foragers were also important as a sort of advance guard, for they formed virtually a curtain of mounted infantry screening us from the inquisitive eyes of parties of Wheeler's cavalry, with whom they did not hesitate to engage when it was a question of a rich plantation.

When compelled to retire, they resorted to all the tricks of infantry skirmishers, and summoned reënforcements of foragers from other regiments to help drive the "Johnnies" out. When success crowned their efforts, the plantation was promptly stripped of live stock and eatables. The natives were accustomed to bury provisions, for they feared their own soldiers quite as much as they feared ours. These subterranean stores were readily discovered by the practiced "Yankee" eye. The appearance of the ground and a little probing with a ramrod or a bayonet soon decided whether to dig. Teams were improvised; carts and vehicles of all sorts were pressed into the service and loaded with provisions. If any antiquated militia uniforms were discovered, they were promptly donned, and a comical procession escorted the valuable train of booty to the point where the brigade was expected to bivouac for the night. The regimentals of the past, even to those of revolutionary times, were often conspicuous.

On an occasion when our brigade had the advance, several parties of foragers, consolidating themselves, captured a town from the enemy's cavalry, and

A BIVOUAC AMONG THE
GEORGIA PINES.

DESTROYING A RAILROAD.

occupied the neighboring plantations. Before the arrival of the main column hostilities had ceased; order had been restored, and mock arrangements were made to receive the army. Our regiment in the advance was confronted by a picket dressed in continental uniform, who waved his plumed hat in response to the gibes of the men, and galloped away on his bareback mule to apprise his comrades of our approach. We marched into the town and rested on each side of the main street. Presently a forager, in ancient militia uniform indicating high rank, debouched from a side street to do the honors of the occasion. He was mounted on a raw-boned horse with a bit of carpet for a saddle. His old plumed chapeau in hand, he rode with gracious dignity through the street, as if reviewing the brigade. After him came a family carriage laden with hams, sweet-potatoes, and other provisions, and drawn by two horses, a mule, and a cow, the two latter ridden by postilions.

At Fayetteville, North Carolina, the foragers as usual had been over the ground several hours before the heads of column arrived, and the party from my regiment had found a broken-down grist-mill. Their commander, Captain Parker, an officer of great spirit and efficiency, and an expert machinist, had the old wheel hoisted into its place and put the mill in working order. Several parties from other regiments had been admitted as working members, and teams of all sorts were busy collecting and bringing in corn and carrying away meal for distribution. This bit of enterprise was so pleasing to the troops that plenty of volunteers were ready to relieve the different gangs, and the demand was so great as to keep the mill at work all night by the light of pine-knot fires and torches.

The march through Georgia has been called a grand military promenade, all novelty and excitement. But its moral effect on friend and foe was immense. It proved our ability to lay open the heart of the Confederacy, and left the question of what we might do next a matter of doubt and terror. It served also as a preliminary training for the arduous campaign to come. Our work was incomplete while the Carolinas, except at a few points on the sea-coast, had not felt the rough contact of war. But their swamps and rivers, swollen and spread into lakes by winter floods, presented obstructions almost impracticable to an invading army, if opposed by even a very inferior force.

The task before us was indeed formidable. It involved exposure and indefatigable exertion. To succeed, our forward movement had to be continuous, for even the most productive regions would soon be exhausted by our 60,000 men and more, and 13,000 animals.

Although we were fully prepared, with our great trains of ammunition, to fight a pitched battle, our mission was not to fight, but to consume and destroy. Our inability to care properly for the wounded, who must necessarily be carried along painfully in jolting ambulances to die on the way from exhaustion and exposure, was an additional and very serious reason for avoiding collision

SHERMAN'S FORAGERS ON A GEORGIA PLANTATION.

with the enemy. But where he could not be evaded, his very presence across our path increased the velocity of our flying column. We repelled him by a decisive blow and without losing our momentum.

The beginning of our march in South Carolina was pleasant, the weather favorable, and the country productive. Sometimes at the midday halt a stray pig that had cunningly evaded the foragers would venture forth in the belief of having escaped "the cruel war," and would find his error, alas! too late, by encountering our column. Instantly an armed mob would set upon him, and his piercing shrieks would melt away in the scramble for fresh pork. But the midday sport of the main column and the happy life of the forager were sadly interrupted. The sun grew dim, and the rain came and continued. A few of our excellent foragers were reported captured by Wheeler's cavalry, while we sank deeper and deeper in the mud as we approached the Salkehatchie Swamp, which lay between us and the Charleston and Augusta railroad. As the heads of column came up, each command knew what it had to do. Generals Mower and G. A. Smith got their divisions across by swimming, wading, and floating, and effected lodgments in spite of the enemy's fire. An overwhelming mass of drenched and muddy veterans swept away the enemy, while the rest of our force got the trains and artillery over by corduroying, pontooning, and bridging. It seemed a grand day's work to have accomplished, as we sank down that night in our miry bivouac. The gallant General Wager Swayne lost his leg in this Salkehatchie encounter. Luckily for him and others we were not yet too far from our friends to send the wounded back, with a strong escort, to Pocotaligo.

We destroyed about forty miles of the Charleston and Augusta railroad, and, by threatening points beyond the route we intended to take, we deluded the enemy into concentrating at Augusta and other places, while we marched rapidly away, leaving him well behind, and nothing but Wade Hampton's cavalry, and the more formidable obstacle of the Saluda River and its swamps, between us and Columbia, our next objective. As the route of our column lay west of Columbia, I saw nothing of the oft-described and much-discussed burning of that city.

During the hasty removal of the Union prisoners from Columbia two Massachusetts officers managed to make their escape. Exhausted and almost naked, they found their way to my command. My mess begged for the privilege of caring for one of them. We gave him a mule to ride with a comfortable saddle, and scraped together an outfit for him, although our clothes were in the last stages. Our guest found the mess luxurious, as he sat down with us at the edge of a rubber blanket spread upon the ground for a table-cloth, and set with tin cups and platters. Stewed fighting-cock and bits of fried turkey were followed by fried corn-meal and sorghum. Then came our coffee and pipes, and we lay down by a roaring fire of pine-knots, to hear our guest's story of life in a rebel prison. Before daybreak the tramp of horses reminded us that our foragers were sallying forth. The red light from the countless camp-fires melted away as the dawn stole over the horizon, casting its wonderful gradations of light and color over the masses of sleeping soldiers, while the smoke from burning pine-knots befogged the chilly morning air. Then the bugles broke the impressive stillness, and the roll of drums was heard on all sides. Soon the scene was alive with blue coats and the hubbub of roll-calling, cooking, and running for water to the nearest spring or stream. The surgeons looked to the sick and footsore, and weeded from the ambulances those who no longer needed to ride.

It was not uncommon to hear shots at the head of the column. The foragers would come tumbling back, and ride alongside the regiment, adding to the noisy talk their account of what they had seen, and dividing among their comrades such things as they had managed to bring away in their narrow escape from capture. A staff-officer would gallop down the roadside like a man who had forgotten something which must be recovered in a hurry. At the sound of the colonel's ringing voice, silence was instant and absolute. Sabers flashed from their scabbards, the men brought their guns to the "carry," and the battalion swung into line at the roadside; cats, fighting-cocks, and frying-pans passed to the rear rank; officers and sergeants buzzed round their companies to see that the guns were loaded and the men ready for action. The color-sergeant loosened the water-proof cover of the battle-flag, a battery of artillery flew past on its way to the front, following the returning staff-officer, and we soon heard the familiar bang of shells. Perhaps it did not amount to much after all, and we were soon swinging into "route step" again.

At times when suffering from thirst it was hard to resist the temptation of crystal swamp water, as it rippled along the side of a causeway, a tempting sight for the weary and unwary. In spite of oft-repeated cautions, some contrived to drink it, but these were on their backs with malarial disease at the end of the campaign, if not sooner.

After passing Columbia there was a brief season of famine. The foragers worked hard, but found nothing. They made amends, however, in a day or two, bringing in the familiar corn-meal, sweet-potatoes, and bacon.

We marched into Cheraw with music and with colors flying. Stacking arms in the main street, we proceeded to supper, while the engineers laid the pontoons across the Pedee River. The railing of the town pump, and the remains of a buggy, said to belong to Mr. Lincoln's brother-in-law, Dr. Todd, were quickly reduced to kindling-wood to boil the coffee. The necessary destruction of property was quickly accomplished, and on we went. A mile from the Lumber River the country, already flooded ankle-deep, was rendered still more inhospitable by a steady down-pour of rain. The bridges had been partly destroyed by the enemy, and partly swept away by the flood. An attempt to carry heavy army wagons and artillery across this dreary lake might have seemed rather foolhardy, but we went to work without loss of time. The engineers were

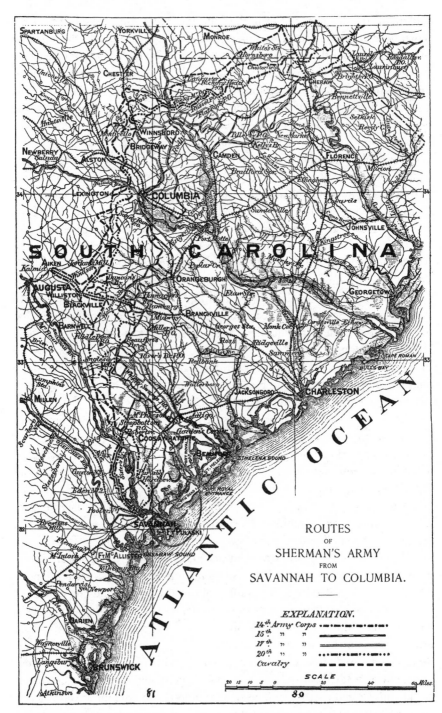

ROUTES
OF
SHERMAN'S ARMY
FROM
SAVANNAH TO COLUMBIA.

EXPLANATION.

14th Army Corps
15th   „   „
17th   „   „
20th   „   „
Cavalry

SCALE

REPRODUCED FROM THE "MEMOIRS OF GENERAL WILLIAM T. SHERMAN"
(NEW YORK: D. APPLETON & CO.), BY PERMISSION OF AUTHOR AND PUBLISHERS.

promptly floated out to the river, to direct the rebuilding of bridges, and the woods all along the line of each column soon rang with the noise of axes. Trees quickly became logs, and were brought to the submerged roadway. No matter if logs disappeared in the floating mud; thousands more were coming from all sides. So, layer upon layer, the work went bravely on. Soon the artillery and wagons were jolting over our wooden causeway.

As my regiment was the rear-guard for the day, we had various offices to perform for the train, and it was midnight before we saw the last wagon over the bridge by the light of our pine torches. It seemed as if that last wagon was never to be got over. It came bouncing and bumping along, its six mules smoking and blowing in the black, misty air. The teamster, mounted on one of the wheelers, guided his team with a single rein and addressed each mule by name, reminding the animal of his faults, and accusing him of having, among other peculiarities, "a black military heart." Every sentence of his oath-adorned rhetoric was punctuated with a dexterous whip-lash. At last, drenched to the skin and covered with mud, I took my position on the bridge, seated in a chair which one of my men had presented to me, and waited for the command to "close up."

As we passed the wagon camp, there was the deafening, indescribable chorus of mules and teamsters, besides the hoarse shouting of quartermasters and wagonmasters plunging about on horseback through the mud, to direct the arriving teams into their places. But it all died away in the distance as we marched on to find the oozy resting-place of the brigade. The army had been in bivouac some hours, and countless camp-fires formed a vast belt of fire that spread out into the black night.

As we advanced into the wild pine regions of North Carolina the natives seemed wonderfully impressed at seeing every road filled with marching troops, artillery, and wagon trains. They looked destitute enough as they stood in blank amazement gazing upon the "Yanks" marching by. The scene before us was very striking; the resin pits were on fire, and great columns of black smoke rose high into the air, spreading and mingling together in gray clouds, and suggesting the roof and pillars of a vast temple. All traces of habitation were left behind, as we marched into that grand forest with its beautiful carpet of pine-needles. The straight trunks of the pine-tree shot up to a great height, and then spread out into a green roof, which kept us in perpetual shade. As night came on, we found that the resinous sap in the cavities cut in the trees to receive it, had been lighted by "bummers" in our advance. The effect of these peculiar watch-fires on every side, several feet above the ground, with flames licking their way up the tall trunks, was peculiarly striking and beautiful. But it was sad to see this wanton destruction of property, which, like the firing of the resin pits, was the work of "bummers," who were marauding through the country committing every sort of outrage. There was no restraint except with the column or the regular foraging parties. We had no communications, and could

THE STORMING OF THE LITTLE SALKEHATCHIE RIVER BY WEVER'S BRIGADE
OF THE FIFTEENTH CORPS. FROM A WAR-TIME SKETCH.

have no safeguards. The country was necessarily left to take care of itself, and became a "howling waste." The "coffee-coolers" of the Army of the Potomac were archangels compared to our "bummers," who often fell to the tender mercies of Wheeler's cavalry, and were never heard of again, earning a fate richly deserved.

On arriving within easy distance of the Cape Fear River, where we expected to communicate with the navy, detachments were sent in rapid advance to secure Fayetteville. Our division, after a hard day of corduroying in various spots over a distance of twelve miles, went into camp for supper, and then, taking the plank-road for Fayetteville, made a moonlight march of nine miles in three hours, but our friends from the right wing arrived there before us.

Hardee retired to a good position at Averysboro', where Kilpatrick found him intrenched and too strong for the cavalry to handle unassisted. It was the turn of our brigade to do special duty, so at about 8 o'clock in the evening we were ordered to join the cavalry. We were not quite sure it rained, but everything was dripping. The men furnished themselves with pine-knots, and our weapons glistened in the torch-light, a cloud of black smoke from the torches floating back over our heads. The regimental wits were as ready as ever, and amid a flow of lively badinage we toiled on through the mud.

When the column was halted for a few minutes to give us an opportunity of drawing breath, I found Sergeant Johnson with one arm in the mud up to the elbow. He explained that he was trying to find his shoe. We floundered on for five miles, and relieved a brigade of Kilpatrick's men whom we found in some damp woods. There was a comfort in clustering round their camp-fires, while they retired into outer darkness to prepare for the morning attack. But the cavalry fireside was only a temporary refuge from the storm, for we also had to depart into the impenetrable darkness beyond, to await in wet line of battle the unforeseen. Those who were exhausted sank down in the mud to sleep, while others speculated on the future.

The clear wintry dawn disclosed a long line of blue-coats spread over the ground in motionless groups. This was the roaring torch-light brigade of the night before. The orders "Fall in!" "Forward!" in gruff tones broke upon the chilly air, and brought us shivering to our feet. We moved to the edge of the woods with the cavalry. The skirmish line, under Captain J. I. Grafton, had already disappeared into the opposite belt of woods, and evidently were losing no time in developing the enemy and ascertaining his force. They were drawing his fire from all points, indicating a force more than double that of our brigade. Dismounted cavalry were now sent forward to prolong the skirmish-line. Captain Grafton was reported badly wounded in the leg, but still commanding with his usual coolness. Suddenly he appeared staggering out of the wood into the open space in our front, bareheaded, his face buried in his hands, his saber hanging by the sword-knot from his wrist, one leg bound up with a handkerchief, his uniform covered with blood; in a moment he fell toward the colors. Officers clustered about him in silence, and a gloom spread through the brigade as word passed that Grafton was dead.

The main column was now arriving, and as the troops filed off to the right and left of the road, and the field-guns galloped into battery, we moved forward to the attack. The enemy gave us a hot reception, which we returned with a storm of lead. It was a wretched place for a fight. At some points we had to support our wounded until they could be carried off, to prevent their falling into the swamp water, in which we stood ankle-deep. Here and there a clump of thick growth in the black mud broke the line as we advanced. No ordinary troops were in our front. They would not give way until a division of Davis's corps was thrown upon their right, while we pressed them closely. As we passed over their dead and wounded, I came upon the body of a very young officer, whose handsome, refined face attracted my attention. While the line of battle swept past me I knelt at his side for a moment. His buttons bore the arms of South Carolina. Evidently we were fighting the Charleston chivalry. Sunset found us in bivouac on the Goldsboro' road, and Hardee in retreat.

As we trudged on toward Bentonville, distant sounds told plainly that the head of the column was engaged. We hurried to the front and went into action, connecting with Davis's corps. Little opposition having been expected, the distance between our wing and the right wing had been allowed to increase be-

SHERMAN'S "BUMMERS" CAPTURING FAYETTEVILLE COURT HOUSE, N.C.
FROM A SKETCH MADE AT THE TIME.

yond supporting distance in the endeavor to find easier roads for marching as well as for transporting the wounded. The scope of this paper precludes a description of the battle of Bentonville, which was a combination of mistakes, miscarriages, and hard fighting on both sides. It ended in Johnston's retreat, leaving open the road to Goldsboro', where we arrived ragged and almost barefoot. While we were receiving letters from home, getting new clothes, and taking our regular doses of quinine, Lee and Johnston surrendered, and the great conflict came to an end.

1865

Introduction

James I. Robertson, Jr.

The sun was setting on the Confederate States. By 1865, nothing could stop the approaching darkness of defeat. A Southern army still existed far across the Mississippi River, and small, isolated forces were at Mobile and elsewhere, but Tennessee and the great Western Theater were firmly in Union control. Sherman's 60,000 men stood poised at Savannah, to strike in any direction at their leisure. Grant had Lee's Army of Northern Virginia pinned in the trenches of Petersburg and Richmond, that once mighty fighting machine facing a slow death from the daily routine of attrition. All hope of foreign intervention was gone.

A Richmond diarist summed up common sentiment when she wrote at the turn of the year: "What calamities and sorrows crowd into ... this afflicted country of ours! God help us. ..."

Northern forces began strengthening for the death blows that had to be delivered. Southerners braced for the blows they had to endure. The beginning of the end came in January against Wilmington, North Carolina, the South's last operating seaport.

Guarding Wilmington at the mouth of the Cape Fear River was Fort Fisher, a well-designed, heavily armed series of sand dunes. It was the Confederacy's largest seacoast fortification. In December 1864, Union general Benjamin F. Butler had led a joint army-navy expedition against the place. Admiral David D. Porter's huge fleet did its work, but the inept Butler lost his nerve and retreated before making a land attack. A disgusted Porter told Grant that Fisher would fall whenever a competent general was sent to do the job.

Another amphibious combination arrived before Fisher the next month. Porter's fleet unleashed fifty thousand shells at the fortification in a bombardment one Confederate termed "without description." Tough General Alfred Terry sent 2,000 sailors and marines to assault Fisher's seaward face while half of his 8,000 army troops circled around and attacked the parapets in the rear. The 1,800 Confederate defenders waged an incredible fight. Hand-to-hand combat marked much of the January 15 action. With the 10 P.M. surrender of the fort, the South's last door to the outside world closed.

The sailors in the Union attack were armed only with cutlasses and pistols. They had to make a long charge down an open beach. At the first Confederate volley, one sailor wrote, "the whole mass of men went down like a row of falling bricks." A newspaper correspondent declared: "I never saw men fall so fast in my life."

In a wild retreat the seamen left three hundred of their comrades dead or wounded on the beach. Lieutenant Commander Thomas Oliver Selfridge, Jr., commanded part of the attacking force. Two decades later, when the Century Company began producing *Battles and Leaders of the Civil War,* the leading reconciliation compilation of the immediate postwar years, Selfridge wrote an article defending his men and their conduct. The essay is an attorney's brief more than a soldier's memoir.

The South was still reeling from the loss of Wilmington when Sherman and his hardened Union soldiers left Savannah and marched toward South Carolina, the "seedbed of secession." Stern, red-haired "Cump" Sherman openly declared his intention to destroy everything in his path, spread demoralization afar, and then join Grant in Virginia in a final showdown with Lee.

Sherman feinted one wing of his army toward the industrial city of Augusta, Georgia, and the other wing toward the port of Charleston. The Confederates rushed all available troops to both cities. The Federal army pushed straight northward in between the two, cutting railroad and communication lines. Augusta and Charleston, isolated and helpless, surrendered to delegations sent by Sherman.

Commanding one of the Union wings was General Henry Warner Slocum. A quiet, dependable soldier, Slocum did his duty without fanfare or ambition. His only published military accounts are the narratives of the Carolina campaign reprinted here. Written with the twenty-twenty perspective of hindsight and without the heated emotions of wartime, the Slocum narratives are calm and measured. Indeed, the first essay understates both the vigor of Sherman's soldiers on the northward march and the vengeance they unleashed on South Carolinians.

Opposition was all but nonexistent. Joseph E. Johnston had come out of retirement to take command of a hodgepodge force of second-class Confederate soldiers barely equal in number to Sherman's cavalry. "I can do no more than annoy him," Johnston wrote of Sherman, but he hoped that weather and swampy lowlands would impede the Union advance.

It did not. Most of Sherman's men were Midwestern frontiersmen accustomed to the challenges of nature. With ax and spade, they corduroyed roads, built bridges, forded icy rivers, and sometimes roosted in trees to escape the flooded ground. Johnston later remarked that no such army had existed since the legions of Julius Caesar.

A personal fury permeated the ranks as Union soldiers entered South Carolina. One Billy Yank put it succinctly: "Here is where treason began, and, by God, here is where it shall end!"

Marking the army's forty-five-mile-wide path were pillars of smoke by day and pillars of fire by night. Commercial buildings were leveled; homes were sacked and set afire; livestock were butchered; slaves were sent running, partly for freedom and partly from fear. One soldier wrote of the Savannah–Columbia march: "The country behind us is left a howling wilderness, in utter desolation."

Columbia, the state capital, caught the worst of the Union storm. Sherman's forces marched into the city on February 17, and by the next morning a third of Columbia was in ashes. Although the burning may have been accidental— a point still in dispute today—soldiers in the ranks asserted that if the accident had not taken place, they themselves would have burned the place.

Slocum attributed the destruction to Union soldiers provided too much whiskey by local citizenry. Why Carolinians would give alcohol to the human beings they most hated is a point Slocum did not explain.

The Union army entered North Carolina the first week of March. The Federals reverted back to good behavior. Whereas South Carolina has led the fight for secession, its northern neighbor had been among the last to leave the Union. It did not deserve a similar fate. In point of fact, there was no military need for another policy of destruction. The war was reaching its final stages.

When Sherman reached Fayetteville, he burned only an arsenal and machine shop. There he also established contact on the Cape Fear River with Union coastal forces. There, too, Sherman was finally able to rid himself of thousands of contrabands following in his wake. Ex-slaves were shuttled to Wilmington with promises of freedom. Now Sherman was ready for the final push toward Virginia.

Sixty miles northeast of Fayetteville, as the Union columns approached Goldsboro, Confederate resistance for the first time stiffened. A sharp fight ensued on March 16–17 at Averysboro. Then Johnston struck the exposed Union left wing (Slocum's) at Bentonville. But the Confederates were simply not strong enough to win a victory over half of Sherman's army. When Sherman dispatched reinforcements to the danger spot, the Southern offensive melted away. On March 23, Sherman reached Goldsboro. A Union corps under General John M. Schofield awaited his arrival. Sherman now had 80,000 veteran soldiers deep in the Carolinas behind Lee. The Federals could go anywhere they wanted to go without a thought of being stopped. "The Confederacy was being torn up by the roots," one observer noted, "including the ones that went deepest."

Lee's dwindling army, locked in earthworks at Petersburg and Richmond, was the one fixed point in the dissolving Southern nation. Yet it had suffered horribly during the war's coldest winter. Meanwhile, Grant had slowly stretched his massive forces in a semicircle that snaked thirty-five miles. This compelled Lee to extend his own thin numbers to vulnerable and dangerous lengths.

Lee made one effort to stop Grant's encirclement and possibly break the siege. In the predawn hours of March 25, a third of the Confederate army attacked Fort Stedman in the center of the Union line. Lee's gamble failed.

In command of that Union sector was General John Frederick Hartranft, an engineer and attorney who had won his general's star in the 1864 battle of Spotsylvania and would later in 1865 oversee the imprisonment and execution of the Lincoln assassination conspirators. Hartranft's brigade of Pennsylvania recruits was seeing its first action. It weathered a momentary breakthrough by the Confederates, then regrouped and slowly beat back the attackers. The battle was over by noon.

Hartranft's account of the action is pure military history. He delighted in showing the various regiments maneuvering in battle. Interestingly, the general mentioned a phenomenon known as an "acoustic shadow." This is a situation in which sound from nearby locations is not heard because of wind direction, terrain, and wetness of forests. Acoustic shadows affected other battles such as Shiloh, Perryville, and Chancellorsville.

Fort Stedman was Lee's last offensive action. It cost him 4,800 new casualties (most of them men taken prisoner). The next move was up to Grant, and it came quickly. Less than a week after Fort Stedman, Federal forces swept around Lee's extreme right flank and seized the vital road junction of Five Forks. The mismanagement of the Confederate commander, George E. Pickett, dulled the glamour of his reputation for boldness at Gettysburg.

Grant's all-out assaults on April 2 were expected and unstoppable. Federals poured over the Confederate lines like floodwaters engulfing a levee. The story of the breakthrough and of the pursuit of Lee's fragmenting brigades has been told many times. No observer on the Union side produced a more incisive account than Colonel Horace Porter, the most intellectual of Grant's aides. Porter's highly revealing articles for *Battles and Leaders* appeared a decade later in book form, under the title *Campaigning with Grant* (1897). The volume has been reprinted five times since.

As Grant started his pursuit of Lee's army in the darkness of April 2, a great glow filled the air. Confederate officials in Richmond had ordered warehouses loaded with tobacco and government property put to the torch. Strong winds turned the flames into a raging inferno. More than eight hundred buildings in the capital were gutted. Ironically, black soldiers in Union general Godfrey Weitzel's Twenty-fifth Corps finally brought the fires under control. The cremation of Richmond was a symbolic tragedy.

Two eyewitness accounts from opposite sides provide dramatic pictures of the abandonment of the city. A young Maryland captain, Clement Sulivane, commanded a company of local defense troops. His instructions were to assist in the city's evacuation and then to set fire to the major bridge spanning the James River. Sulivane's perspectives from the Southern side are unusually good for the utter chaos of April 2–3 in the capital.

One of Weitzel's aides, Thomas Graves, also penned his recollections while memories were still fresh. His narrative, which described President Abraham Lincoln arriving in Richmond while the city was still smoking, is even-tempered and conciliatory. Graves does stretch truth (and chronology) with his account of General Weitzel—who was removed from command on April 13—sending his wallet stuffed with greenbacks to help an old friend, Confederate general Fitzhugh Lee.

Like a wolf pack pursuing its wounded prey, Grant's overwhelming numbers slowly encircled the stumbling remnants of Lee's army. The end came on April 9 at Appomattox Court House. It was not grim old "Unconditional Surrender" Grant with whom Lee met to discuss terms. Instead, Lee found a sympathetic man who himself had known personal humiliation earlier in life. Grant's surrender proposals were generous. The Federal general set the tone for the future when he admonished Union soldiers for shouting joyfully. "Stop that cheering!" Grant ordered. "The Rebels are our countrymen again."

Colonel Charles Marshall was the only aide Lee took to the meeting with Grant. The next day the Virginia-born attorney had the heavy task of drafting Lee's farewell address to the fewer than 10,000 Confederate soldiers who remained. Marshall incorporated all of the correct phrases: "arduous service, marked by unsurpassed courage...the consciousness of duty faithfully performed...a grateful remembrance...."

When Lee read the document, a staff member noted, "the tears ran down the old hero's cheeks, and he gave way—for the first time that I ever knew him to do so since my connection with him."

The events after Lee's surrender were anticlimactic. In North Carolina, Johnston knew better than to try to continue the fight. Sherman had always been an advocate of hard war, but he was quick to offer a soft peace. On April 26, Johnston surrendered what was left of the Army of Tennessee.

Basil Wilson Duke was the brother-in-law of two Confederate generals, John Hunt Morgan and Ambrose Powell Hill. His account of final operations in southwestern Virginia and of President Jefferson Davis's "flight into oblivion" captured well the last breaths of the Southern Confederacy.

In the twilight of life, George Gibbs of the 18th Mississippi pondered: "I

look back now ... on those turbulent times, and wonder where I found the fortitude, patience and endurance to pass through so many trying experiences suffered during the four years of the war. In most cases I believe we gather
strength, courage and fortitude when circumstances are such as to require
them."

Those men of blue and gray performed with enough courage and honor to
give rise to legends that warmed the hearts of the old and embedded inspiration
into the hearts of the young.

CHAPTER 1

SHERMAN'S MARCH FROM SAVANNAH TO BENTONVILLE.

Henry W. Slocum, Major-General, U.S.V.

General Sherman's army commenced its march from "Atlanta to the Sea" on the morning of November 15th, and arrived in front of the defenses of Savannah on the 10th of December, 1864. No news had been received from the North during this interval except such as could be gleaned from Southern papers picked up by the soldiers on the line of our march. Our fleet was in Ossabaw Sound with supplies of food and clothing, and an immense mail, containing letters from home for nearly every one in the army, from the commanding general down to the private soldier. All that blocked our communication with the fleet was Fort McAllister on the Ogeechee River. This fort was captured by Hazen's division of the Fifteenth Corps on December 13th, and the 15th brought us our

ADVANCING UNDER DIFFICULTIES.

GENERAL WM. B. HAZEN.   GENERAL W. T. SHERMAN.   GENERAL HENRY W. SLOCUM.

GENERAL O. O. HOWARD.   GENERAL JOHN A. LOGAN.   GENERAL JEFF. C. DAVIS.   GENERAL J. A. MOWER.

FROM A PHOTOGRAPH.

mails and an abundant supply of food and ammunition, making this one of the happiest days experienced by the men of Sherman's army. Preparations were at once commenced for assaulting the Confederate works, and were nearly completed when the Confederates evacuated Savannah. Our troops entered the city before daybreak on the 21st of December. The fall of Fort McAllister placed General Sherman in communication with General Grant and the authorities at Washington. Prior to the capture of Savannah, the plan contemplated by General Grant involved the removal of the infantry of Sherman's army to City Point by sea. On December 6th General Grant wrote to Sherman:

"My idea now is that you establish a base on the sea-coast, fortify, and leave all your artillery and cavalry and enough infantry to protect them, and at the same time so threaten the interior that the militia of the South will have to be kept home. With the balance of your command come here with all dispatch."

In reply, under date of December 13th, Sherman said:

"I had expected, after reducing Savannah, instantly to march to Columbia, South Carolina, thence to Raleigh, and then to report to you."

The fall of Savannah resulted in the adoption of the plan which Sherman had contemplated. In a letter dated December 24th Sherman says:

"Many and many a person in Georgia asked me why I did not go to South Carolina, and when I answered that we were *en route* for that State, the invariable reply was, 'Well, if you will make those people feel the utmost severities of war we will pardon you for your desolation of Georgia.'"

About one month was spent in Savannah in clothing the men and filling the trains with ammunition and rations. Then commenced the movement which was to make South Carolina feel the severities of war.✣ The right wing, with the

---

✣At this time General Lee addressed the following letter to the Governor of South Carolina:

"HEADQUARTERS, ARMY N. VA., 27 JANUARY, '65.
"HIS EXCELLENCY A. G. MAGRATH, Governor of South Carolina, Columbia.
"SIR:

"I received to-day your letter of the 16th inst., and regret exceedingly to learn the present condition of affairs in the South. I infer from your letter that you consider me able to send an army to arrest the march of General Sherman. If such was the case I should not have waited for your application, for I lament as much as you do his past success, and see the injury that may result from his further progress. I have no troops except those within this department, within which my operations are confined. According to your statement of General Sherman's force, it would require this whole army to oppose him. It is now confronted by

exception of Corse's division of the Seventeenth Corps, moved via Hilton Head to Beaufort. The left wing with Corse's division and the cavalry moved up the west bank of the Savannah River to Sister's Ferry, distant about forty miles from Savannah. Sherman's plan was similar to that adopted on leaving Atlanta. When the army had started from Atlanta, the right wing had moved direct toward Macon and the left toward Augusta. Both cities were occupied by Confederate troops. The movements of our army had caused the Confederate authorities at each of these important cities to demand not only the retention of the troops at each place, but had induced them to demand help from every quarter. Sherman had had no thought of attacking either place, and at the proper time the movements of both wings of the army were so directed as to unite them and leave both cities in our rear, with little or no force in our front. On leaving Savannah our right wing threatened Charleston and the left again threatened Augusta, the two wings being again united in the interior of South Carolina, leaving the Confederate troops at Augusta with almost a certainty that Charleston must fall without a blow from Sherman. On the arrival of the left wing at Sister's Ferry on the Savannah, instead of finding, as was anticipated, a river a few yards in width which could be easily crossed, they found a broad expanse of water which was utterly impassable. The continuous rain-fall had caused the river to overflow, so that the lowland on the South Carolina side was covered with water, extending nearly half a mile from the river. We were delayed several days in vain efforts to effect a crossing, and were finally com-

---

General Grant with a far superior army. If it was transferred to South Carolina, I do not believe General Grant would remain idle on the James River. It would be as easy for him to move his army south as for General Sherman to advance north. You can judge whether the condition of affairs would be benefited by a concentration of the two large Federal armies in South Carolina, with the rest of the Confederacy stripped of defense. But should Charleston fall into the hands of the enemy, as grievous as would be the blow and as painful the result, I cannot concur in the opinion of your Excellency that our cause would necessarily be lost. Should our whole coast fall in the possession of our enemies, with our people true, firm, and united, the war could be continued and our purpose accomplished. As long as our armies are unsubdued and sustained, the Confederacy is safe. I therefore think it bad policy to shut our troops within intrenchments, where they can be besieged with superior forces, and prefer operating in the field. I recommend this course in South Carolina, and advise that every effort be made to prevent General Sherman reaching Charleston by contesting his advance. The last return made by General Hardee of his force which I have seen, gave his entire strength 20,500 of all arms; with 5000 South Carolina militia which he expected, and 1500 Georgia troops under General G. W. Smith, he would have 27,000. This is exclusive of Connor's brigade and Butler's division sent from this army, which ought to swell his force to 33,000. But I think it might be still further increased by a general turnout of all the men in Georgia and South Carolina, and that Sherman could be resisted until General Beauregard could arrive with reënforcements from the West. I see no cause for depression or despondency, but abundant reason for renewed exertion and unyielding resistance. With great respect, your Excellency's obedient servant, R. E. LEE, General." [Printed from the MS.]

—EDITORS.

RAILWAY DESTRUCTION AS A MILITARY ART.

pelled to await the falling of the waters. Our pontoon-bridge was finally con-structed and the crossing commenced. Each regiment as it entered South Car-olina gave three cheers. The men seemed to realize that at last they had set foot on the State which had done more than all others to bring upon the country the horrors of civil war. In the narrow road leading from the ferry on the South Carolina side torpedoes had been planted, so that several of our men were killed or wounded by treading upon them. This was unfortunate for that section of the State. Planting torpedoes for the defense of a position is legitimate war-fare, but our soldiers regarded the act of placing them in a highway where no contest was anticipated as something akin to poisoning a stream of water; it is not recognized as fair or legitimate warfare. If that section of South Carolina suffered more severely than any other, it was due in part to the blundering of people who were more zealous than wise.

About February 19th the two wings of the army were reunited in the vicin-ity of Branchville, a small village on the South Carolina Railroad at the point where the railroad from Charleston to Columbia branches off to Augusta. Here we resumed the work which had occupied so much of our time in Georgia, viz., the destruction of railroads.↓

↓A knowledge of the art of building railroads is certainly of more value to a country than that of the best means of destroying them; but at this particular time the destruction seemed necessary, and the time may again come when such work will have to be done. Lest the most effectual and expeditious method of destroying railroad tracks should become one of the lost arts, I will here give a few rules for the guid-ance of officers who may in future be charged with this important duty. It should be remembered that

SKIRMISHERS CROSSING THE NORTH EDISTO, S.C., ON A FLOATING FOOT-BRIDGE.
FROM A SKETCH MADE AT THE TIME.

Having effectually destroyed over sixty miles of railroads in this section, the army started for Columbia, the capital of South Carolina, each corps taking a separate road. The left wing (Slocum) arrived at a point about three miles from Columbia on the 16th, and there received orders to cross the Saluda River, at Mount Zion's Church. The Fourteenth Corps moved to the crossing, built a

---

these rules are the result of long experience and close observation. A detail of men to do the work should be made on the evening before operations are to commence. The number to be detailed being, of course, dependent upon the amount of work to be done, I estimate that one thousand men can easily destroy about five miles of track per day, and do it thoroughly. Before going out in the morning the men should be supplied with a good breakfast, for it has been discovered that soldiers are more efficient at this work, as well as on the battle-field, when their stomachs are full than when they are empty. The question as to the food to be given the men for breakfast is not important, but I suggest roast turkeys, chickens, fresh eggs, and coffee, for the reason that in an enemy's country such a breakfast will cause no unpleasantness between the commissary and the soldiers, inasmuch as the commissary will only be required to provide the coffee. In fact it has been discovered that an army moving through a hostile but fertile country, having an efficient corps of foragers (vulgarly known in our army as "bummers"), requires but few articles of food, such as hard-tack, coffee, salt, pepper, and sugar. Your detail should be divided into three sections of about equal numbers. I will suppose the detail to consist of three thousand men. The first thing to be done is to reverse the relative positions of the ties and iron rails, placing the ties up and the rails under them. To do this, Section No. 1, consisting of one thousand men, is distributed along one side of the track, one man at the end of each tie. At a given signal each man seizes a tie, lifts it gently till it assumes a vertical position, and then at another signal pushes it forward so that when it falls the ties will be over the rails. Then each man loosens his tie from the rail. This done, Section No. 1 moves forward to another portion of the road, and Section No. 2 advances and is distributed along the portion of the road recently occupied by Section No. 1. The duty of the second section is to collect the ties, place them in piles of about thirty ties each—place the rails on the top of these piles, the center of each rail being over the center of the pile, and then set fire to the ties. Section No. 2 then follows No. 1. As soon as the rails

bridge during the night, crossed the river next day, and was followed by the Twentieth Corps and Kilpatrick's cavalry. The right wing (Howard) moved direct to Columbia, the Fifteenth Corps moving through the city and camping outside on the Camden road. The Seventeenth Corps did not enter Columbia. During the night of February 17th the greater portion of the city of Columbia was burned. The lurid flames could easily be seen from my camp, many miles distant. Nearly all the public buildings, several churches, an orphan asylum, and many of the residences were destroyed. The city was filled with helpless women and children and invalids, many of whom were rendered houseless and homeless in a single night. No sadder scene was presented during the war. The suffering of so many helpless and innocent persons could not but move the hardest heart. The question as to who was immediately responsible for this disaster has given rise to some controversy. I do not believe that General Sherman countenanced or was in any degree responsible for it. I believe the immediate cause of the disaster was a free use of whisky (which was supplied to the soldiers by citizens with great liberality). A drunken soldier with a musket in one hand and a match in the other is not a pleasant visitor to have about the house on a dark, windy night, particularly when for a series of years you have urged him to come, so that you might have an opportunity of performing a surgical operation on him.

From Columbia the army moved toward Fayetteville—the left wing crossing the Catawba River at Rocky Mount. While the rear of the Twentieth Corps was crossing, our pontoon-bridge was swept away by flood-wood brought down the river, leaving the Fourteenth Corps on the south side. This caused a delay of three days, and gave rise to some emphatic instructions from Sherman to the commander of the left wing—which instructions resulted in our damming the flood-wood to some extent, but not in materially expediting the march.

On the 3d of March we arrived at Cheraw, where we found a large supply of stores sent from Charleston for safe-keeping. Among the stores was a large quantity of very old wine of the best quality, which had been kept in the cellars of Charleston many years, with no thought on the part of the owners that in its old age it would be drunk from tin cups by Yankee soldiers. Fortunately

---

are sufficiently heated Section No. 3 takes the place of No. 2; and upon this devolves the most important duty, viz., the effectual destruction of the rail. This section should be in command of an efficient officer who will see that the work is not slighted. Unless closely watched, soldiers will content themselves with simply bending the rails around trees. This should never be permitted. A rail which is simply bent can easily be restored to its original shape. No rail should be regarded as properly treated till it has assumed the shape of a doughnut; it must not only be bent but twisted. To do the twisting Poe's railroad hooks are necessary, for it has been found that the soldiers will not seize the hot iron bare-handed. This, however, is the only thing looking toward the destruction of property which I ever knew a man in Sherman's army to decline doing. With Poe's hooks a double twist can be given to a rail, which precludes all hope of restoring it to its former shape except by re-rolling.—H.W.S.

SHERMAN'S SOLDIERS GUARDING
THE PALMETTO MONUMENT, COLUMBIA.
FROM A SKETCH MADE AT THE TIME.

for the whole army the wine was discovered by the Seventeenth Corps and fell into the hands of the generous and chivalrous commander of that corps,—General Frank P. Blair,—who distributed it with the spirit of liberality and fairness characteristic of him. On the 6th we moved toward Fayetteville, where we arrived on the 10th. The march through South Carolina had been greatly delayed by the almost incessant rains and the swampy nature of the country. More than half the way we were compelled to corduroy the roads before our trains could be moved. To accomplish this work we had been supplied with axes, and the country was covered with saplings well suited to the purpose.

Three or four days prior to our arrival at Fayetteville General Sherman had received information that Wilmington was in possession of General Terry, and had sent two messengers with letters informing Terry when he would probably be at Fayetteville. Both messengers arrived safely at Wilmington, and on Sunday, the day after our arrival at Fayetteville, the shrill whistle of a steamboat floating the Stars and Stripes announced that we were once more in communication with our own friends. As she came up, the banks of the river were lined by our soldiers, who made the welkin ring with their cheers. The opening of communication with Wilmington not only brought us our mails and a supply of clothing, but enabled us to send to a place of safety thousands of refugees and contrabands who were following the army and seriously embarrassing it. We were dependent upon the country for our supplies of food and forage, and every one not connected with the army was a source of weakness to us. On several occasions on the march from Atlanta we had been compelled to drive thousands of colored people back, not from lack of sympathy with them, but simply as a matter of safety to the army. The refugee-train following in rear of the army was one of the most singular features of the march. Long before the war, the slaves of the South had a system of communication by which important information was transmitted from one section of the country to another. The advance of Sherman's army through a section never before visited by a Union

After Hood had been driven from Tennessee, Schofield was ordered to bring the Twenty-third Corps, General Cox, to Washington, whence it was sent to Fort Fisher, N.C. Schofield assumed command of the combined forces, and captured Wilmington, February 22d, 1865. Thence Cox was sent to New Berne; there he organized a provisional corps and moved via Kinston to Goldsboro', while the greater part of Schofield's forces advanced directly to that place.—EDITORS.

soldier was known far and wide many miles in advance of us. It was natural that these poor creatures, seeking a place of safety, should flee to the army, and endeavor to keep in sight of it. Every day, as we marched on we could see, on each side of our line of march, crowds of these people coming to us through roads and across the fields, bringing with them all their earthly goods, and many goods which were not theirs. Horses, mules, cows, dogs, old family carriages, carts, and

RAISING THE UNION FLAG OVER THE OLD STATE-HOUSE, COLUMBIA. FROM A SKETCH MADE AT THE TIME.

whatever they thought might be of use to them were seized upon and brought to us. They were allowed to follow in rear of our column, and at times they were almost equal in numbers to the army they were following. As singular, comical, and pitiable a spectacle was never before presented. One day a large family of slaves came through the fields to join us. The head of the family, a venerable negro, was mounted on a mule, and safely stowed away behind him in pockets or bags attached to the blanket which covered the mule were two little pickaninnies, one on each side. This gave rise to a most important invention, *i.e.,* "the best way of transporting pickaninnies." On the next day a mule appeared in column, covered by a blanket with two pockets on each side, each containing

CONTRABANDS IN THE WAKE OF SHERMAN'S ARMY.

a little negro. Very soon old tent-flies or strong canvas was used instead of the blanket, and often ten or fifteen pockets were attached to each side, so that nothing of the mule was visible except the head, tail, and feet, all else being covered by the black woolly heads and bright shining eyes of the little darkies. Occasionally a cow was made to take the place of the mule; this was a decided improvement, as the cow furnished rations as well as transportation for the babies. Old stages, family carriages, carts and lumber wagons filled with bedding, cooking-utensils and "traps" of all kinds, with men, women, and children loaded with bundles, made up the balance of the refugee-train which followed in our rear. As all the bridges were burned in front of us, our pontoon-trains were in constant use, and the bridges could be left but a short time for the use of the refugees. A scramble for precedence in crossing the bridge always oc-

VIEW FROM THE UNFINISHED CAPITOL.

VIEWS OF THE RUINS OF COLUMBIA. FROM PHOTOGRAPHS.

THE UNFINISHED CAPITOL, COLUMBIA.

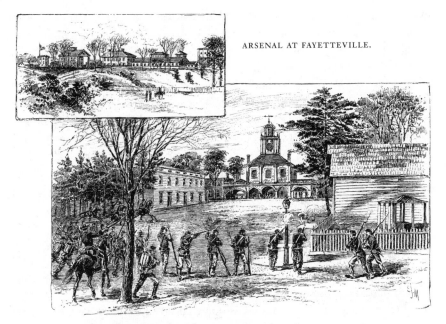

ARSENAL AT FAYETTEVILLE.

SHERMAN'S MEN DRIVING THE ENEMY OUT OF FAYETTEVILLE.
FROM A SKETCH MADE AT THE TIME.

curred. The firing of a musket or pistol in rear would bring to the refugees visions of guerrillas, and then came a panic. As our bridges were not supplied with guard-rails, occasionally a mule would be crowded off, and with its precious load would float down the river.

Having thoroughly destroyed the arsenal buildings, machine-shops, and foundries at Fayetteville, we crossed the Cape Fear River on the 13th and 14th and resumed our march. We were now entering upon the last stage of the great march which was to unite the Army of the West with that of the East in front of Richmond. If this march could be successfully accomplished the Confederacy was doomed. General Sherman did not hope or expect to accomplish it without a struggle. He anticipated an attack and made provision for it. He ordered me to send my baggage-trains under a strong escort by an interior road on my right, and to keep at least four divisions with their artillery on my left, ready for an attack.

During the 15th of March Hardee was retreating before us, having for his rear-guard a brigade composed of the troops which had garrisoned Charleston, commanded by Colonel Alfred Rhett. Kilpatrick's cavalry was in advance of the left wing, and during the day some of the skirmishers had come suddenly upon Colonel Rhett, accompanied by a few of his men, and had captured him. Rhett before the war had been one of the editors of the Charleston "Mercury," one of the strongest secession papers of the South. He was sent by Kilpatrick to General Sherman. Sherman while stationed in Charleston before the war had been acquainted with Rhett, and not wishing to have him under his immediate charge, he sent him to me. Rhett spent that night in my tent, and as I had also been stationed at Fort Moultrie in 1854 and '55, and had often met him, we had a long chat over old times and about common acquaintances in Charleston. The following morning Rhett was sent to the rear in charge of the cavalry. He was handsomely dressed in the Confederate uniform, with a pair of high boots beautifully stitched. He was deeply mortified at having been "gobbled up" without a chance to fight. One of my staff told me that he saw Rhett a few days later, trudging along under guard, but the beautiful boots were missing,—a soldier had exchanged a very coarse pair of army shoes for them. Rhett said that in all his troubles he had one consolation, that of knowing that no one of Sherman's men could get on those boots.

On the following morning Kilpatrick came upon the enemy behind a line of intrenchments. He moved his cavalry to the right, and Jackson's and Ward's divisions of the Twentieth Corps were deployed in front of the enemy's line. General Sherman directed me to send a brigade to the left in order to get in rear of the intrenchments, which was done, and resulted in the retreat of the enemy and in the capture of Macbeth's Charleston Battery and 217 of Rhett's men. The Confederates were found behind another line of works a short distance in rear of the first, and we went into camp in their immediate front. During the night Hardee retreated, leaving 108 dead for us to bury, and 68 wounded. We lost 12 officers and 65 men killed and 477 men wounded. This action was known as the battle of Averysboro'.

Our march to this point had been toward Raleigh. We now took the road

THE FOURTEENTH CORPS ENTERING FAYETTEVILLE.
FROM A SKETCH MADE AT THE TIME.

leading to Goldsboro.' General Sherman rode with me on the 18th and left me at 6 A.M. on the 19th to join General Howard, who was marching on roads several miles to our right. On leaving me General Sherman expressed the opinion that Hardee had fallen back to Raleigh, and that I could easily reach the Neuse River on the following day. I felt confident I could accomplish the task. We moved forward at 6 A.M., and soon met the skirmishers of the enemy. The resistance to our advance became very stubborn. Carlin's division was deployed and ordered to advance. I believed that the force in my front consisted only of cavalry with a few pieces of artillery. Fearing that the firing would be heard by General Sherman and cause the other wing of the army to delay its march, I sent Major E. W. Guindon of my staff to General Sherman, to tell him that I had met a strong force of cavalry, but that I should not need assistance, and felt confident I should be at the Neuse at the appointed time. Soon after the bearer of the message to General Sherman had left me, word came from Carlin that he had developed a strong force of the enemy in an intrenched position. About the same time one of my officers brought to me an emaciated, sickly appearing young man about twenty-two or twenty-three years of age, dressed in the Confederate gray. He had expressed great anxiety to see the commanding officer at once. I asked him what he had to say. He said he had been in the Union army, had been taken prisoner, and while sick and in prison had been induced to enlist in the Confederate service. He said he had enlisted with the intention of deserting when a good opportunity presented itself, believing he should die if he remained in prison. In reply to my questions he informed me that he formerly resided at Syracuse, New York, and had entered the service at the commencement of the war, in a company raised by Captain Butler. I had been a resident of Syracuse, and knew the history of his company and regiment. While I was talking with him one of my aides, Major William G. Tracy, rode up and at once recognized the deserter as an old acquaintance whom he had known at Syracuse before the war. I asked how he knew General Johnston was in command and what he knew as to the strength of his force. He said General Johnston rode along the line early that morning, and that the officers had told all the men that "Old Joe" had caught one of Sherman's wings beyond the reach of support, that he intended to *smash* that wing and then go for the other. The man stated that he had had no chance of escaping till that morning, and had come to me to warn me of my danger. He said, "There is a very large force immediately in your front, all under command of General Joe Johnston." While he was making his statement General Carlin's division with four pieces of artillery became engaged with the enemy. A line for defense was at once selected, and as the troops came up they were placed in position and ordered to collect fence-rails and everything else available for barricades. The men used their tin cups and hands as shovels, and needed no urging to induce them to work. I regretted that I had sent the message to General Sherman assuring him I needed no help, and saw the necessity of giving him information at once as to the situation. This information was carried to General Sherman by a young man, not then twenty years of age, but who was full of energy and activity and was always reliable. He was then the youngest member of my staff. He is now [1888] Governor of Ohio— Joseph B. Foraker. His work on this day secured his promotion to the rank of captain. Some years after the close of the war Foraker wrote to me calling my attention to some errors in a published account of this battle of Bentonville, and saying:

"Firing between the men on the skirmish-line commenced before Sherman had left us on the morning of the 19th, but it was supposed there was nothing but cavalry in our front. It was kept up steadily, and constantly increased in volume. Finally there was a halt in the column. You expressed some anxiety, and Major W. G. Tracy and I rode to the front to see what was going on. At the edge of open fields next to the woods in which the barricades were we found our skirmish-line halted.... In a few minutes it moved forward again. The enemy partly reserved their fire until it got half-way or more across the field. This induced Tracy and me to think there was but little danger, and so we followed up closely, until suddenly they began again a very spirited firing, in the midst of which we were sorry to find ourselves. I remember we hardly knew what to do—we could do no good by going on and none by remaining. To be killed under such circumstances would look like a waste of raw material, we thought. But the trouble was to get out. We didn't want to turn back, as we thought that would not look well. While we were thus hesitating a spent ball struck Tracy on the leg, giving him a slight but painful wound. Almost at the same moment our skirmishers charged and drove the rebels.... I rode back with Tracy only a very short distance, when we met you hurrying to the front. I found you had already been informed of what had been discovered, and that you had already sent orders to everybody to hurry to the front. I remember, too, that a little later Major Mosely, I think, though it may have been some other member of your staff, suggested that you ought to have the advance division charge and drive them out of the way; that it could not be possible that there was much force ahead of us, and that if we waited for the others to come up we should lose a whole day, and if it should turn out that there was nothing to justify such caution it would look bad for the left wing; to which you replied in an earnest manner, 'I can afford to be charged with being dilatory or over-cautious, but I cannot afford the responsibility of another Ball's Bluff affair.' Do you remember it? I presume not; but I was then quite young, and such remarks made a lasting impression. It excited my confidence and admiration, and was the first moment that I began to feel that there was really serious work before us.... You handed me a written message to take to General Sherman. The last words you spoke to me as I started were, 'Ride well to the right so as to keep clear of the enemy's left flank, and *don't spare horse-flesh.*' I reached General Sherman just about sundown. He was on the left side of the road on a sloping hillside, where, as I understood, he had halted only a few minutes before for the night. His staff were about him. I think General Howard was there, but I do not now remember seeing him,—but on the hillside twenty yards farther up Logan was lying on a blanket. Sherman saw me approaching and walked briskly toward me, took your message, tore it open, read it, and called out 'John Logan! where is Logan?' Just then Logan jumped up and started toward us. He too walked briskly, but before he had reached us Sherman had informed him of the situation and or-dered him to turn Hazen back and have him report to you. It was not yet dark when I rode away carrying an answer to your message. It was after midnight when I got back, the ride back being so much longer in point of time because the road was full of troops, it was dark, and my 'horse-flesh' was used up."

General Carlin's division of the Fourteenth Corps had the advance, and as the enemy exhibited more than usual strength, he had deployed his division and advanced to develop the position of the enemy. Morgan's division of the same corps had been deployed on Carlin's right. Colonel H. G. Litchfield, in-spector-general of the corps, had accompanied these troops. I was consulting with General Jeff. C. Davis, who commanded the Fourteenth Corps, when Colonel Litchfield rode up, and in reply to my inquiry as to what he had found in front he said, "Well, General, I have found something more than Dibrell's cavalry—I find infantry intrenched along our whole front, and enough of them to give us all the amusement we shall want for the rest of the day."

Foraker had not been gone half an hour when the enemy advanced in force, compelling Carlin's division to fall back. They were handled with skill and fell back without panic or demoralization, taking places in the line established. The Twentieth Corps held the left of our line, with orders to connect with the Four-teenth. A space between the two corps had been left uncovered, and Cogswell's brigade of the Twentieth Corps, ordered to report to General Davis, filled the gap just before the enemy reached our line.

The enemy fought bravely, but their line had become somewhat broken in advancing through the woods, and when they came up to our line, posted be-hind slight intrenchments, they received a fire which compelled them to fall back. The assaults were repeated over and over again until a late hour, each as-sault finding us better prepared for resistance. During the night Hazen reported to me, and was placed on the right of the Fourteenth Corps. Early on the next morning Generals Baird and Geary, each with two brigades, arrived on the

BENTONVILLE THE MORNING AFTER THE BATTLE—THE SMOKE IS FROM RESIN
THAT WAS FIRED BY THE CONFEDERATES. FROM A SKETCH MADE AT THE TIME.

field. Baird was placed in front of our works and moved out beyond the advanced position held by us on the preceding day. The 20th was spent in strengthening our position and developing the line of the enemy. On the morning of the 21st the right wing arrived. This wing had marched twenty miles over bad roads, skirmishing most of the way with the enemy. On the 21st General Johnston found Sherman's army united, and in position on three sides of him. On the other was Mill Creek. Our troops were pressed closely to the works of the enemy, and the entire day was spent in skirmishing. During the night of the 21st the enemy crossed Mill Creek and retreated toward Raleigh. The plans of the enemy to surprise us and destroy our army in detail were well formed and well executed, and would have been more successful had not the men of the Fourteenth and Twentieth corps been veterans, and the equals in courage and endurance of any soldiers of this or any other country.

CHAPTER 2

THE NAVY AT FORT FISHER.

Thomas O. Selfridge, Jr., Captain, U.S.N.

When the Secretary of the Navy, Mr. Welles, recognizing the importance of closing the port of Wilmington, urged upon President Lincoln to direct a coöperation of the army, General Grant was requested to supply the necessary force from the troops about Richmond. As Fort Fisher lay within the territorial jurisdiction of General Butler, commanding the Department of Virginia and North Carolina, the troops were detailed from his command, and in the first attack Butler, with General Weitzel in immediate command of the troops, had control of the land operations. The naval command of the expedition having been declined by Admiral Farragut, on account of ill-health, Rear-Admiral Porter, who had so successfully coöperated with the army in opening the Mississippi, was selected, and was allowed to bring with him five of his officers, of whom the writer was one, being detailed for the command of the gun-boat *Huron.* The Atlantic and Gulf coasts being almost entirely in our possession, the Navy Department was able to concentrate before Fort Fisher a larger force than had ever before assembled under one command in the history of the American navy—a total of nearly 60 vessels, of which five were iron-clads, including the *New Ironsides,* besides the three largest of our steam-frigates, viz., the *Minnesota, Colorado,* and *Wabash.*[†] The fleet arrived in sight of the fort on the morning of December 20th.

A novel feature of this first attack was the explosion of a powder-boat near the fort on the night of December 23d. The vessel was the *Louisiana,* an old gun-boat no longer serviceable. The more sanguine believed that Fort Fisher, with its garrison, guns, and equipment, would be leveled to the ground, while others were equally certain it would prove a fizzle. Commander A. C. Rhind, with a

---

[†]The total number of guns and howitzers in the fleet was over 600, and the total weight of projectiles at a single discharge of all the guns (both broadsides) was over 23 tons.—EDITORS.

INTERIOR VIEW OF THE FIRST SIX TRAVERSES ON THE SEA-FACE OF FORT FISHER.
FROM A PHOTOGRAPH.

crew of volunteers, successfully performed the perilous duty, and, applying the match at midnight, the crew rowed safely away to the *Wilderness,* a swift gunboat, in waiting. The whole fleet having moved off shore, under low steam, awaited the result in anxiety. A glare on the horizon and a dull report were the indications that the floating mine had been sprung. In the morning, when the fleet steamed in, all eyes were toward the fort. There it was, as grim as ever, apparently uninjured, with its flag floating as defiantly as before. In these days, with better electrical appliances, the explosion could have been made more nearly instantaneous, but I doubt if the general result would have been different.

The powder-boat proving an ignominious failure, the fleet stood in toward the fort in close order of divisions, the iron-clads leading. At 11:30 the signal was thrown out from the flag-ship *Malvern:* "Engage the enemy." The *Ironsides,* followed by the monitors, took position as close in as their draught would permit, engaging the north-east face. The *Ironsides* was followed by the *Minnesota, Colorado,* and *Wabash.* The enemy replied briskly, but when these frigates found the range and commenced firing rapidly nothing could withstand their broadsides of twenty-five 9-inch guns. It was a magnificent sight to see these frigates fairly engaged, and one never to be forgotten. Their sides seemed a sheet of flame, and the roar of their guns like a mighty thunderbolt.

CAPTAIN T. O. SELFRIDGE, JR.
FROM A PHOTOGRAPH.

THE BOMBARDMENT OF FORT FISHER, JANUARY 15, 1865. TAKEN FROM LITHOGRAPHS.

CAPTAIN K. R. BREESE.
FROM A PHOTOGRAPH.

Meanwhile all the other ships took positions as detailed, and so perfect were the plans of the admiral, and so well were they carried out by his captains, that not a mishap took place. Nothing could withstand such a storm of shot and shell as was now poured into this fort. The enemy took refuge in their bomb-proofs, replying sullenly with an occasional gun. The enemy's fire being silenced, signal was made to fire with deliberation, and attention was turned to the dismounting of the guns. So quickly had the guns of Fort Fisher been silenced[*] that not a man had been injured by their fire, though several ships had sustained losses by the bursting of their 100-pounder Parrott rifles. The *Mackinaw,* however, had had her boiler exploded by a shot, and several of her crew had been scalded, and the *Osceola* was struck by a shell near her magazine, but was saved from sinking by her captain, Commander Clitz.

During the bombardment the transports, with troops, arrived from Beaufort. On Christmas day, as agreed upon between Admiral Porter and General Butler, the smaller vessels were engaged in covering the disembarkation of the troops, while the iron-clads and frigates were sent in to resume the bombardment of the fort. The larger portion of the army was landed by the boats of the fleet and advanced with little or no opposition to within a short distance of the fort, the skirmish-line within fifty yards. Butler and Weitzel decided that it

[*]In a note to the editors Colonel Lamb says:

"The guns of Fort Fisher were not silenced. On account of a limited supply of ammunition, I gave orders to fire each gun not more than once in thirty minutes, except by special order, unless an attempt should be made to run by the fort, when discretion was given each gun commander to use his piece effectively. There were forty-four guns. On the 24th of December 672 shots were expended; a detailed report was received from each battery. Only three guns were rendered unserviceable, and these by the fire of the fleet disabling the carriages. On the 25th of December six hundred shots were expended, exclusive of grape and canister. Detailed reports were made. Five guns were disabled by the fire of the fleet, making eight in all. Besides, two 7-inch Brooke rifled guns exploded, leaving thirty-four heavy guns on Christmas night. The last guns on the 24th and 25th were fired by Fort Fisher on the retiring fleet. In the first fight the total casualties were 61, as follows: December 24th, mortally wounded, 1; seriously 3; slightly, 19 = 23. December 25th, killed, 3; mortally wounded, 2; severely, 7; slightly, 26. These included those wounded by the explosion of the Brooke rifled guns = 38."

could not be taken by assault. Orders were issued to reëmbark after being on shore but a few hours. Some seven hundred men were left on shore, the sea being too rough to get them off, but the demoralized enemy did not attempt to attack them. They were taken off in the morning, and the transports steamed away for Hampton Roads, the fleet returning to Beaufort. Thus ended the first attack upon Fort Fisher. Words cannot express the bitter feeling and chagrin of the navy. We all felt the fruit was ripe for plucking and with little exertion would have fallen into the hands of the army.

MAJOR GENERAL A. H. TERRY.
FROM A PHOTOGRAPH.

SECOND ATTACK UPON FORT FISHER.

Upon receiving Admiral Porter's dispatches, Mr. Welles again sought the coöperation of the army, to which General Grant at once acceded, sending back the same force of white troops, reënforced by two colored brigades under General Charles J. Paine, the whole under the command of Major-General Alfred H. Terry. While lying at Beaufort, Admiral Porter determined to assist in the land attack of the army by an assault upon the sea-face of Fort Fisher with a body of seamen. In a general order volunteers from the fleet were called for, and some two thousand officers and men offered themselves for this perilous duty.

General Terry arrived off Beaufort with his forces on the 8th of January, 1865, a plan of operations was agreed upon, and the 12th was fixed for the sailing of the combined force.

Upon the morning of the 13th the iron-clads were sent in to engage the fort. Going in much closer than before, the monitors were within twelve hundred yards of the fort. Their fire was in consequence much more effective.

The remainder of the fleet were occupied till 2 P.M. in landing the troops and stores. This particular duty, the provisioning of the army, and the protection of its flank was afterward turned over to the lighter gun-boats, whose guns were too small to employ them in the bombardment of the fort, the whole under the charge of Commander J. H. Upshur, commanding the gun-boat *A. D. Vance.*

On the afternoon of the 13th the fleet, excepting the iron-clads, which had

ASSAULT OF THE NAVAL COLUMN ON THE NORTH-EAST SALIENT OF FORT FISHER.

remained in their first positions close to the fort, steamed into the several positions assigned them and opened a terrific fire. By placing a buoy close to the
outer reef, as a guide, the leading ship, the *Minnesota,* was enabled to anchor
nearer, and likewise the whole battle-line was much closer and their fire more
effective, the best proof of which is the large number of guns upon the land-
face of the fort that was found to be destroyed or dismounted.[*] The weight of
fire was such that the enemy could make but a feeble reply. At nightfall the fleet
hauled off, excepting the iron-clads, which kept up a slow fire through the
night.

During the 14th a number of the smaller gun-boats carrying 11-inch guns
were sent in to assist in dismounting the guns on the land-face. Their fire was
necessarily slow, and the presence of these small craft brought the enemy out of
their bomb-proofs to open upon them, during which the *Huron* had her mainmast shot away. Upon seeing this renewal of fire, the *Brooklyn, Mohican,* and one
or two other vessels were ordered in by Porter, and with this reënforcement the
fire of the fort slackened. The bombardment from the smaller gun-boats and
iron-clads was kept up during the night. This constant duty day and night was
very hard upon these small vessels, and the officers and crew of my own vessel,
the *Huron,* were worn out.

Fort Fisher was at this time much stronger than at the first attack. The garrison had been reënforced by veteran troops, damages by the first bombardment had been repaired, and new defenses added; among which was a battery

[*]According to the report of General C. B. Comstock, General Terry's chief engineer, there were 21 guns
and 3 mortars on the land front; "of these three-fourths were rendered unserviceable." General H. L.
Abbot states ("Defence of the Sea Coast of the United States," p. 31), as a result of personal inspection
immediately after the capture, that out of 20 guns on the land-face "8 guns and 8 carriages (16 in all)
were disabled."—EDITORS.

of light pieces in a half-moon around the sally-port, from whose fire the sailors suffered heavily in their assault.[*]

It was arranged that the grand bombardment should begin on the morning of the 15th, and the separate assaults of soldiers and sailors should take place at 3 P.M. A code of signals was agreed upon between the two commanders, and the assault was to be signaled to the fleet by a blowing of steam-whistles, where-upon their fire would be directed to the upper batteries. After the assault of the sailors had failed the *Ironsides* used her 11-inch guns with great effect in firing into the traverses filled with Confederates resisting the advance of the Union forces. At 9 A.M. the fleet was directed by signal to move in three divisions, and each ship took its prescribed place as previously indicated to her commander; consequently there was no disorder.

All felt the importance of this bombardment, and while not too rapid to be ineffective such a storm of shell was poured into Fort Fisher, that forenoon, as I believe had never been seen before in any naval engagement. The enemy soon ceased to make any reply from their heavy guns, excepting the "Mound Battery," which was more difficult to silence, while those mounted on the land-face were by this time disabled. [See note, p. 1,086.]

Before noon the signal was made for the assaulting column of sailors and marines to land. From thirty-five of the sixty ships of the fleet boats shoved off, making, with their flags flying as they pulled toward the beach in line abreast, a most spirited scene. The general order of Admiral Porter required that the assaulting column of sailors should be armed with cutlasses and pistols. It was also intended that trenches or covered ways should be dug for the marines close to the fort and that our assault should be made under the cover of their fire; but it was impossible to dig such shelter trenches near enough to do much good under fire in broad daylight.

The sailors as they landed from their boats were a heterogeneous assembly, companies of two hundred or more from each of the larger ships, down to small parties of twenty each from the gun-boats. They had been for months confined on shipboard, had never drilled together, and their arms, the old-fashioned cutlass and pistol, were hardly the weapons to cope with the rifles and bayonets of the enemy. Sailor-like, however, they looked upon the landing in the light of a lark, and few thought the sun would set with a loss of one-fifth of their number.

After some discussion between the commander, Lieutenant-Commander

[*]Colonel Lamb, writing in December, 1868, says:

"There were never in Fort Fisher, including sick, killed, and wounded, over 1900 men. The sailors and marines, etc., captured from Battery Buchanan, and those captured in front of the work, while swelling the list of prisoners, cannot rightly be counted among the defenders of the work. No new defense was added to the face of the fort between the battles. The redoubt in front of the sally-port was there in December and had been used against Butler's skirmish-line."

K. R. Breese, and the senior officers, it was decided to form three divisions, each composed of the men from the corresponding division squadrons of the fleet; the first division, under the command of Lieutenant-Commander C. H. Cushman, the second under Lieutenant-Commander James Parker (who was Breese's senior but waived his rank, the latter being in command as the admiral's representative), the third under Lieutenant-Commander T. O. Selfridge, Jr.; a total of 1600 blue jackets, to which was added a division of 400 marines under Captain L. L. Dawson.

The whole force marched up the beach and lay down under its cover just outside rifle range, awaiting the movements of the army. We were formed by the flank, and our long line flying numerous flags gave a formidable appearance from the fort, and caused the Confederates to divide their forces, sending more than one-half to oppose the naval assault.

At a preconcerted signal the sailors sprang forward to the assault, closely following the water's edge, where the inclined beach gave them a slight cover. We were opened upon in front by the great mound battery, and in flank by the artillery of the half-moon battery, and by the fire of a thousand rifles. Though many dropped rapidly under this fire, the column never faltered, and when the angle where the two faces of the fort unite was reached the head halted to allow the rear to come up. This halt was fatal, for as the others came up they followed suit and lay down till the space between the parapet and the edge of the water was filled. As the writer approached with the Third Division he shouted to his men to come on, intending to lead them to where there was more space; but, looking back, he discovered that his whole command, with few exceptions, had stopped and joined their comrades. Making his way to the front, close to the palisade, he found several officers, among whom were Lieutenant-Commanders Parker and Cushman. The situation was a very grave one. The rush of the sailors was over; they were packed like sheep in a pen, while the enemy were crowding the ramparts not forty yards away, and shooting into them as fast as they could fire. There was nothing to reply with but *pistols.* Something must be done, and speedily. There were some spaces in the palisade where it was torn away by the fire of the fleet, and an attempt was made to charge through, but we found a deep, impassable ditch,╱ and those who got through were shot down. Flesh and blood could not long endure being killed in this slaughter-pen, and the rear of the sailors broke, followed by the whole body, in spite of all efforts to rally them. It was certainly mortifying, after charging for a mile,☆ under a most galling fire, to the very foot of the fort, to have the whole force retreat

╱Colonel Lamb says on this point: "There was no ditch, merely a dry depression in front of the berme where sand had been dug out to repair work."—EDITORS.

☆General Terry writes that the column of sailors was within 600 or 800 yards of the work before they began to charge; but Commander James Parker says that the column was under fire in marching to that point.—EDITORS.

down the beach. It has been the custom, unjustly in my opinion, to lay the blame on the marines for not keeping down the fire till the sailors could get in. But there were but 400 of them against 1200 of the garrison; the former in the open plain, and with no cover; the latter under the shelter of their ramparts.‡ The mistake was in expecting a body of sailors, collected hastily from different ships, unknown to each other, armed with swords and pistols, to stand against veteran soldiers armed with rifles and bayonets. Another fatal mistake was the stopping at the sea angle. Two hundred yards farther would have brought us to a low parapet without palisade or ditch, where, with proper arms, we could have intrenched and fought. Some sixty remained at the front, at the foot of the parapet, under cover of the palisade, until nightfall enabled them to withdraw. Among the number I remember Lieutenant-Commanders Breese, Parker, Cushman, Sicard; Lieutenants Farquhar, Lamson, S. W. Nichols, and Bartlett.

A loss of some three hundred in killed and wounded attests the gallant nature of the assault. Among these were several prominent officers, including Lieutenants Preston and Porter, killed; Lieutenant-Commanders C. H. Cushman, W. N. Allen, Lieutenant G. M. Bache, wounded.

After their repulse the sailors did good service with the marines by manning the intrenchments thrown up across the peninsula, which enabled General Terry to send Abbot's brigade and Blackman's (27th U.S.) colored regiment to the assistance of the troops fighting in the fort. Here they remained till morning, when they returned to their respective ships. When the assault of the naval column failed, the *Ironsides* and the monitors were directed to fire into the gun traverses in advance of the positions occupied by the army, and by doing so greatly demoralized the enemy. About 8 P.M. that night the fort fell into our hands after the hardest fighting by our gallant troops, and with its capture fell the last stronghold of the Southern Confederacy on the Atlantic coast.

I will not go so far as to say the army could not have stormed Fort Fisher without the diversion afforded by the naval assault, for no soldiers during the war showed more indomitable pluck than the gallant regiments that stormed the fort on that afternoon; but I do say our attack enabled them to get into the fort with far less loss than they would otherwise have suffered.

As a diversion the charge of sailors was a success; as an exhibition of courage it was magnificent; but the material of which the column was com-

‡Colonel Lamb, writing to the editors on the subject of the numbers defending the north-east salient, says:

"Five hundred effective men will cover all engaged in repulsing the naval column, and the destructive fire was from the three hundred, who, from the top of the ramparts and traverses, fired upon the assailants. The gallant navy need not exaggerate the number opposing them, assisted by the artillery. No apology or defense is necessary to excuse the repulse. The unorganized and improperly armed force failed to enter the fort, but their gallant attempt enabled the army to enter and obtain a foothold, which they otherwise could not have done."

posed, and the arms with which it was furnished, left no reasonable hope after the first onslaught had been checked that it could have succeeded.

While kept under the walls of the fort, I was an eye-witness to an act of heroism on the part of Assistant-Surgeon William Longshaw, a young officer of the medical staff, whose memory should ever be kept green by his corps, and which deserves more than this passing notice. A sailor too severely wounded to help himself had fallen close to the water's edge, and with the rising tide would have drowned. Dr. Longshaw, at the peril of his life, went to his assistance and dragged him beyond the incoming tide. At this moment he heard a cry from a wounded marine, one of a small group who, behind a little hillock of sand close to the parapet, kept up a fire upon the enemy. Longshaw ran to his assistance, and while attending to his wounds was shot dead. What made the action of this young officer even more heroic was the fact that on that very day he had received a leave of absence, but had postponed his departure to volunteer for the assault.

CHAPTER 3

The Recapture of Fort Stedman.[‡]

John F. Hartranft, Brevet Major-General, U.S.V.

Of the Union intrenchments in front of Petersburg, Fort Stedman, with Batteries X and IX on its right and Batteries XII and XI and Fort Haskell on its left, covered Meade's Station on the United States Military Railroad, the supply route of the Army of the Potomac. Meade's Station was the depot of the Ninth Army Corps. This part of the line—about a mile in length—was garrisoned principally by the Third Brigade of the First Division of the Ninth Corps, commanded by Colonel N. B. McLaughlen.

The First Division, commanded by General Willcox, was intrusted with the defense of the whole line from the Appomattox to somewhat beyond Fort Morton, and the Second Division (Potter's) continued the defense of the line about to Fort Alexander Hays. The Third Division, under my command, was in reserve to these two divisions. The division covered four miles, with headquarters at the Avery House, in the center, the right resting at the Friend House, a mile in rear of the works, north-east of Fort Stedman, and the left behind Fort Prescott.

From the Avery House a ravine ran northerly about two-thirds of a mile in rear of the works, to the Friend House, approaching Fort Stedman to within less than one-third of a mile. From this ravine the ground rose gently to the works on the west, and more sharply to a ridge of irregular hills, on the east, behind which ran the army railroad. About one hundred yards behind Fort Stedman, between the fort and the ravine, there was a slight rise in the slope, upon which was encamped the 57th Massachusetts, and to the left of this, some old works which the enemy had abandoned as our forces pressed upon the city. Between this camp and these works ran an old country road, somewhat sunken, from the rear of Stedman to Meade's Station. All the undergrowth and fences had long since disappeared, and the ground was generally open.

[‡]Condensed, with revisions by the author, from the "Philadelphia Press" for March 17th, 1886.

MAJOR-GENERAL JOHN G. PARKE.
FROM A PHOTOGRAPH.

Before dawn on the morning of March 25th, 1865, Major-General Gordon, of the Confederate Army, with his corps and two brigades, numbering probably 10,000 or 12,000 effectives, by a sudden and impetuous attack carried the line from Battery IX on the right to Fort Haskell on the left. This space included Fort Stedman and Batteries X, XI, and XII, and the bomb-proofs and covered ways connecting these works. It was, to a certain extent, a surprise, and the enemy captured some hundreds of prisoners, including Colonel McLaughlen. But before they were driven out of the works or captured, the troops inflicted considerable injury upon the enemy, and the attack upon Fort Haskell, made at the same time, was repulsed with heavy loss. Fortunately, upon the line taken, the enemy could not easily deploy for their farther advance upon Meade's Station and the railroad, the enfilading fires of Battery IX and Fort Haskell forcing their troops into the bomb-proofs of the captured lines to the right and left of Fort Stedman, which was thus the only opening for their columns to enter and deploy to the rear. Great credit is justly due to the garrisons of these two points for their steadiness in holding them in the confusion and nervousness of a night attack. If they had been lost the enemy would have had sufficient safe ground on which to recover and form their ranks, the reserves would have been overwhelmed and beaten in detail by a greatly superior force, and the destruction of the railroad and supplies of the army would have delayed its final movements for a long time. The tenacity with which these points were held, therefore, saved the Union army great loss of men, time, and materials.

The alarm of General Gordon's attack reached the headquarters of the division at 4:30 A.M., just before daybreak.

Upon receipt of this information, and of orders received from corps headquarters about 5 o'clock, the 208th Pennsylvania, the regiment nearest, was ordered to report to Colonel McLaughlen, and at the same time written orders were sent to Colonel J. A. Mathews, commanding the Second Brigade, to hold his brigade in readiness to move to the right, if needed.✣ On the way over to

---

✣General Hartranft's division was composed of the 200th, 208th, and 209th Pennsylvania, forming the First Brigade, under Lieutenant-Colonel W.H.H. McCall, and the 205th, 207th, and 211th Pennsylvania, forming the Second Brigade, under Colonel Joseph A. Mathews.—EDITORS.

General Willcox's headquarters, at the Friend House on the extreme right, I met the 209th Regiment moving *from* Meade's Station toward that point, and the 200th, drawn out of camp with its right resting on the Dunn House battery. These movements were by order of General Willcox, these regiments having instructions to obey orders direct from him in case of attack, to avoid delay in communicating through my headquarters, which were two miles away, owing to the great length of the line covered by my command. This movement apparently uncovered the objective point of the enemy's attack, viz., Meade's Station, and, although the détour of the 209th finally brought it into effective position on the extreme right, the 200th was, for the moment, the only regiment left in any position to strike the enemy.

While I was talking with General Willcox I called his attention to the puffs of smoke issuing from the wood in the rear and to the right and left of Fort Stedman. It was not yet light enough to see the enemy, nor could any sound be heard, owing to the direction of the wind, but the white puffs indicated musketry-firing, and, being in the rear of our lines, disclosed unmistakably an attack in force, and not a feint. It was a skirmish line followed by an assaulting column or a line of battle.[✦] It was equally evident that time must be gained, at any cost, to bring up the extended division in reserve to meet it. Requesting General Willcox to designate one of his staff-officers to conduct the 209th into position on the right, I rode down to Colonel W.H.H. McCall, of the 200th, as the one immediately in hand. A small body of the 57th Massachusetts, which had been driven from its camp, had rallied just in front of the 200th and were feebly replying to the enemy. This detachment was ordered forward to its old camp, and the 200th pushed forward to that point also without serious loss. Intending to force the fighting, no time was lost in feeling the enemy or fighting his skirmishers, but the regiment advanced in line of battle. This movement broke the enemy's line of skirmishers, and those directly in front were driven in; but in the old country road to Meade's Station, running from the rear of Fort Stedman, by the left of the camp, and in some old rebel works beyond the road on our left, the line was strong and the enemy was in force, while the guns of Fort Stedman just captured, turned against us, were on our right. Sending Major George Shorkley, of my staff, to hurry up the 209th to form connection on the right of the 200th, the latter was immediately led to the attack. It advanced bravely; but the enemy was too strong to be pushed, and the fire from the sup-

---

[✦]General Parke, in his report, calls these the enemy's skirmishers; General A. A. Humphreys, in "The Virginia Campaign of 1864–65," says: "Those whom General Parke calls skirmishers were probably the three detachments of Gordon's troops sent to capture the rear forts." General Gordon has since told me that he never heard from these detachments; not one of them returned to report. They must have been the ones who cut the telegraph lines to City Point, and I must have ridden on my way to General Willcox's headquarters, between them and the enemy in the forts. What the 200th attacked was, in my judgment, a heavy line and groups of skirmishers.—J.F.H.

ports and Fort Stedman was very severe. The momentum was lost a little beyond the camp, and after a momentary wavering the 200th was forced back through the camp and took shelter in an old line of works about forty yards in its rear and to the right. From horseback at this point the enemy's officers could now plainly be seen urging their men through Fort Stedman, and endeavoring to deploy them in the rear. To prevent or delay this would justify another attack, although the position of the enemy on the left, whose flag could be seen in the continuation of the old works on the other side of the road, not seventy yards away, and the supporting fire of the captured works on the front and right, plainly showed at what cost it must be made. It was better to attack than be attacked. The 200th was again led forward and responded gallantly. In the face of a galling fire in front and flanks it succeeded in reaching a fairly defensible position, and for a few moments the troops struggled tenaciously to hold it. Fighting under the eye of the general, every officer and man stood up nobly, and for twenty minutes struggled desperately to hold their own in the face of supporting batteries within a hundred yards and superior forces pressing on all sides.

This was the heaviest fighting of the day, and under a tremendous fire of small-arms and artillery the loss in twenty minutes was over one hundred killed and wounded. The regiment finally staggered and receded. But when its desperate grasp on the position was broken it fell back without confusion and ral-

INTERIOR OF FORT STEDMAN. FROM A PHOTOGRAPH.
The fort was named after Colonel Griffin A. Stedman, Jr., of the 11th Connecticut, who was mortally wounded in front of Petersburg on August 5, 1864.

lied and re-formed at the call of its officers and myself in the old works
from which it had advanced.

While the enemy was shaking off
these fierce assaults, the 209th had
been able to push its way to a good
position, its left resting on the old
works to which the 200th had fallen
back, with the right of which it now
connected and its right toward Battery IX, with which it was connected
by the 2d and 17th Michigan Volunteers, two small regiments of the First
Division, which also had thus had
time to come up and complete the
line. This information was brought to
me, while ordering the operations of

BREVET MAJOR-GENERAL JOHN F.
HARTRANFT. FROM A PHOTOGRAPH.

the 200th, by Captain L. C. Brackett, the staff-officer designated by General
Willcox, as requested, for that purpose—who also brought word of the wounding of Major Shorkley, of my staff, on the same errand. The 20th Michigan on
the line to the right of Battery IX had also been crowded forward into the work,
which was now fully manned, and had opened fire vigorously and effectively. A
solid line was thus formed against the advance of the enemy in this direction. A
ride around the line to Colonel McLaughlen's headquarters on the left showed
that a corresponding line had been formed on the south. While the enemy was
engaged with the 200th this had been done without interruption or difficulty.
Captain Prosper Dalien had succeeded in placing the 208th, which had been
ordered in the morning to report to Colonel McLaughlen, in a good position,
its left connected with Fort Haskell by about 200 men mostly from the 100th
Pennsylvania, and some few from the 3d Maryland, who had been driven from
Batteries XI and XII and were now formed on the left of the 208th. The 205th
and 207th regiments, which had promptly reported at division headquarters,
were conducted by Captain J. D. Bertolette, of my staff, by the right through the
ravine toward the road leading to Meade's Station. This he was doing in consequence of orders direct from corps headquarters to cover Meade's Station with
the Second Brigade. They were halted in continuation of the southern line,
when the left of the 207th connected with the 208th. The 211th, encamped
three miles from the field of action, had been notified and was rapidly approaching. The field-artillery, directed by Brevet Brigadier-General Tidball,
commanding the artillery brigade of the corps, had taken position on the hills
in the rear of Fort Stedman, and with Fort Haskell and Battery IX opened on
the captured works and the space around, driving the enemy to the bomb-

proofs and materially interfering with the deployment of a line of battle. There was still a distance of three hundred yards between the left of the 200th and the right of the 205th, through which ran the road to Meade's Station, uncovered. A short time before, Colonel Loring, of General Parke's staff, had delivered to me, on the way over from the right to the left, orders to put the Second Brigade in position on the hills directly covering Meade's Station. But the positions of the 205th and 207th of this brigade were so favorable, and the spirit of the order had been so effectually carried out, that it was unnecessary to obey it literally, and only the 211th, now at hand after a three-miles march, was ordered to deflect to the right and take post on the hills covering the station and in support of the artillery.

The time and opportunity to make these dispositions were due entirely to the stubborn courage of the 200th Regiment./ Its courage and steadiness undoubtedly saved that part of the army severe punishment; and although we did not know it at the time, and were apparently awaiting the attack of a superior force, it had recaptured Fort Stedman in its twenty-minutes fight.

Riding along on the other flank, the whole scene of operations on the opposite slope was spread out before me. On a semicircle of a mile and a half, five regiments and detachments, nearly 4000 men, were ready to charge.

At 7:30 o'clock the long line of the 211th lifted itself with cadenced step over the brow of the hill and swept down in magnificent style toward Fort Stedman. The success of the manœuvre was immediate and complete. The enemy, apparently taken by surprise and magnifying the mass pouring down the hill into the sweep of a whole brigade, began to waver, and the rest of the Third Division, responding to the signal, rose with loud cheers and sprang forward to the charge. So sudden and impetuous was the advance that many of the enemy's skirmishers and infantry in front of the works, throwing down their arms and rushing in to get out of the fire between the lines, looked in the distance like a counter-charge, and the rest were forced back into the works in such masses that the victors were scarcely able to deploy among the crowds of their prisoners. The 208th stormed Batteries XI and XII☆ and the lines to the fort; the 207th carried the west angle of Fort Stedman, the 205th and 211th the rear, the 200th the east angle, and the 209th Battery X and the remaining line to the right. These were taken almost simultaneously, and it is impossible to say which flag was first planted on the works. There was a momentary hand-to-hand struggle for the rebel flags in the batteries and fort. The substantial trophies of the vic-

/Officers and men of the 14th New York Heavy Artillery, who escaped from Fort Stedman, say that they formed a line at this point, fought, and captured prisoners. Major Mathews, commanding 17th Michigan, of the Second Brigade, makes a similar statement regarding his regiment.—EDITORS.

☆Lieutenant Stevenson's letter contains the statement that Company K, of the 100th Pennsylvania, was in possession of Battery XII when General Hartranft's men charged, having left Fort Haskell some time before.—EDITORS.

tory were some 1600 prisoners and a large number of small-arms. The prisoners were mostly passed through the lines to the rear, to be picked up and claimed by other commands, and all but one of the captured flags were claimed and taken from the soldiers by unknown officers.

Just as the 211th moved I received orders to delay the assault until the arrival of a division of the Sixth Army Corps, on its way to support me. As the movement was begun, it was doubtful whether the countermand would reach the regiments on the extreme right and left in time. Besides, I had no doubt of the result, and therefore determined to take the responsibility.

The losses in the assault were unexpectedly light. Then was reaped the full advantage of the work of the gallant 200th. This regiment lost in killed and wounded—mostly in its fight in the morning—122 out of a total loss for the division of 260.‡ The losses of the enemy must have been very heavy.ⱷ

‡A writer in "The Century" magazine for September, 1887, claims for the troops in Fort Haskell, reënforced by the 14th New York Heavy Artillery, the merit of recapturing Fort Stedman, and that the Third Division of Pennsylvanians merely advanced at 8 o'clock and re-occupied the positions. Such a claim is extravagantly absurd, and disproved at once by a reference to the official table of losses. The Ninth Corps lost 507 in killed and wounded; of these 260 were in the Third Division, 73 in the 100th Pennsylvania, and 37 in the 57th Massachusetts, of the First Division, and 37 in the Artillery Brigade,—in all, 407, showing conclusively who did the bulk of the fighting. The losses of the 14th New York were comparatively light in killed and wounded, the greater part happening in Fort Stedman, where 201 of them were captured. The veteran steadiness and good fighting of the 100th Pennsylvania saved Fort Haskell, as the reports and returns clearly indicate. Since the publication of the article in "The Century" I have seen General Gordon and his adjutant-general, Colonel Hy. Kyd. Douglas, who assure me that for the moment, whatever desultory attacks may have been made on Fort Haskell, they were paying no attention to that work, but were endeavoring to deploy their troops in the rear of the captured line and hurry over supports. [But see p. 1,093.] They ascribe their failure to the delay of the latter to come up, to the promptness with which the Third Division was assembled, and to the sudden attack of the 200th Pennsylvania.

In making this criticism and correction I do not wish to be understood as detracting from the merits of the garrison at Fort Haskell, to whose nerve in holding on, under trying circumstances, I had done full justice in the above article long before September, 1887.—J.F.H.

It should be noted that the losses of the several Union organizations, cited by General Hartranft, include those sustained before the movement to re-occupy the lines began.—EDITORS.

ⱷI transcribe the following receipt, found among the memoranda of the fight. It tells its own story:

"Received of Major Bertolette 120 dead and 15 wounded in the engagement of the 25th March, 1865.

"FOR MAJ.-GEN. GORDON,
"HY. KYD DOUGLAS, A.A. GEN."

If the same proportion held between their dead and wounded as between ours, their total loss would have been a little over four thousand. The ratio in our case was, however, unusually high. The Confederate loss was probably over three thousand. Two thousand (1949) of these were prisoners, the rest killed and wounded.—J.F.H.

CHAPTER 4

FIVE FORKS AND THE
PURSUIT OF LEE.

Horace Porter, Brevet Brigadier-General, U.S.A.

It was 9 o'clock in the morning of the 29th of March, 1865. General Grant and the officers of his staff had bidden good-bye to President Lincoln and mounted the passenger car of the special train that was to carry them from City Point to the front, and the signal was given to start; the train moved off, Grant's last campaign had begun. Since 3 o'clock that morning the columns had been in motion and the Union Army and the Army of Northern Virginia were soon locked in a death-grapple. The President remained at City Point, where he could be promptly informed of the progress of the movement.

The military railroad connecting headquarters with the camps south of Petersburg was about thirteen miles long, or would have been if it had been constructed on a horizontal plane, but as the portion built by the army was a surface road, up hill and down dale, if the rise and fall had been counted in, its length would have defied all ordinary means of measurement. Its undulations were so striking that a train moving along it looked in the distance like a fly crawling over a corrugated washboard. The general sat down near the end of the car, drew from his pocket the flint and slow-match that he always carried, which, unlike a match, never missed fire in a gale of wind, and was soon wreathed in the smoke of the inevitable cigar. I took a seat near him with several other officers of the staff, and he at once began to talk over his plans in detail. They had been discussed in general terms before starting out from City Point. It was his custom, when commencing a movement in the field, to have his staff-officers understand fully the objects he wished to accomplish, and what each corps of the army was expected to do in different emergencies, so that these officers, when sent to distant points of the line, might have a full comprehension of the general's intentions, and so that, when communication with him was impossible or difficult, they might be able to instruct the subordinate commanders intelligently as to the intentions of the general-in-chief.

MUSIC ON SHERIDAN'S LINE OF BATTLE.

For a month or more General Grant's chief apprehension had been that the enemy might suddenly pull out from his intrenchments and fall back into the interior, where he might unite with General Joe Johnston against Sherman and force our army to follow Lee to a great distance from its base. General Grant had been sleeping with one eye open and one foot out of bed for many weeks, in the fear that Lee would thus give him the slip. He did not dare delay his movements against the enemy's right until the roads became dry enough to permit an army to move comfortably, for fear Lee would himself take advantage of the good roads to start first. Each army, in fact, was making preparations for either a fight or a foot-race—or both. Sheridan, with his cavalry command, had been ordered to move out in the direction of Dinwiddie Court House, and to be ready to strike the enemy's right and rear. It was the intention, as soon as he could take up a good position for this purpose, to reënforce him with a corps of infantry, and cut off Lee's retreat in the direction of Danville, in case we should break through his intrenched lines in front of Petersburg, and force him from his position there.

The weather had been fair for several days, and the roads were getting in good condition for the movement of troops; that is, as good as could be expected, through a section of country in which the dust in summer was generally so thick that the army could not see where to move, and the mud in winter was so deep that it could not move anywhere. The general, in speaking of what was expected of Sheridan, said: "I had a private talk with Sheridan after I gave him his written instructions at City Point. When he read that part of them which directed him, in certain contingencies, to proceed south along the Danville railroad and coöperate with Sherman by operating in Joe Johnston's rear, he looked so unhappy that I said to him, as I followed him out of the tent, that that part of the instructions was put in only as a blind, so that if he did not meet with entire success the people of the North, who were then naturally restless and apt to become discouraged, might not look upon a temporary check as an entire defeat

UNION ARTILLERY AT PETERSBURG PROTECTED BY MAXTELETE.
FROM A WAR-TIME SKETCH.

of a definite plan,—and that what I really expected was that he would remain with the armies operating against Lee, and end matters right here. This made him happy, and he has started out perfectly confident of the success of the present movement." Referring to Mr. Lincoln, he said: "The President is one of the few visitors I have had who has not attempted to extract from me a knowledge of my plans. He not only never asked them, but says it is better he should not know them, and then he can be certain to keep the secret. He will be the most anxious man in the country to hear the news from us, his heart is so wrapped up in our success, but I think we can send him some good news in a day or two." I never knew the general to be more sanguine of victory than in starting out on this campaign.

When we reached the end of the railroad we mounted our horses, which had been carried on the same train, started down the Vaughan road, and went into camp for the night in a field just south of that road, close to Gravelly Run. That night (March 29th) the army was disposed in the following order from right to left: Weitzel in front of Richmond, with a portion of the Army of the James, Parke and Wright holding our works in front of Petersburg, Ord extending to the intersection of Hatcher's Run and the Vaughan road, Humphreys stretching beyond Dabney's Mill, Warren on the extreme left reaching as far as the junction of the Vaughan road and the Boydton plank-road, and Sheridan at Dinwiddie Court House. The weather had become cloudy, and toward evening rain began to fall. It fell in torrents during the night and continued with but little interruption all the next day. The country was densely wooded, and the ground swampy, and by evening of the 30th whole fields had become beds of quicksand in which horses sank to their bellies, wagons threatened to disappear altogether, and it seemed as if the bottom had fallen out of the roads. The men began to feel that if any one in after years should ask them whether they had been through Virginia, they could say, "Yes, in a number of places." The roads had become sheets of water; and it looked as if the saving of that army would require the services, not of a Grant, but of a Noah. Soldiers would call out to officers as they rode along: "I say, when are the gun-boats coming up?" The buoyancy of the day before was giving place to gloom, and some began to fear that the whole movement was premature.‡

While standing in front of the general's tent on the morning of the 30th, discussing the situation with several others on the staff, I saw General Sheridan turning in from the Vaughan road with a staff-officer and an escort of about a dozen cavalrymen, and coming toward our headquarters camp. He was riding his white pacer, a horse which had been captured from General Breckinridge's adjutant-general at Missionary Ridge. But, instead of striking a pacing gait now, it was at every step driving its legs knee-deep into the quicksand with the regularity of a pile-driver. As soon as Sheridan dismounted, he was asked with much eagerness about the situation on the extreme left. He took a decidedly cheerful view of matters, and entered upon a very animated discussion of the coming movements. He said he could drive in the whole cavalry force of the enemy with ease, and if an infantry force were added to his command he would strike out for Lee's right and either crush it or force him so to weaken his intrenched lines that the troops in front of them could break through and march into Petersburg. He warmed up with the subject as he proceeded, threw the whole energy of his nature into the discussion, and his cheery voice, beaming countenance, and impassioned language showed the earnestness of his convictions.

"How do you propose to supply your command with forage if this weather lasts?" he was asked by one of the group.

‡In his "Memoirs" (C. L. Webster & Co.) General Sheridan says that after the troops began to move he received the following letter from General Grant, whereupon he started at once for Grant's headquarters:

"'Headquarters, Armies of the United States, Gravelly Run, March 30th, 1865.
"'Major-General Sheridan:
"'The heavy rain of to-day will make it impossible for us to do much until it dries up a little, or we get roads around our rear repaired. You may, therefore, leave what cavalry you deem necessary to protect the left, and hold such positions as you deem necessary for that purpose, and send the remainder back to Humphreys's Station [on the military railroad], where they can get hay and grain. Fifty wagons loaded with forage will be sent you in the morning. Send an officer back to direct the wagons back to where you want them. Report to me the cavalry you will leave back, and the position you will occupy. Could not your cavalry go back by the way of Stoney Creek depot and destroy or capture the store of supplies there?—U.S. Grant, Lieutenant-General."

—Editors.

"Forage?" said Sheridan; "I'll get all the forage I want. I'll haul it out if I have to set every man in the command to corduroying roads, and corduroy every mile of them from the railroad to Dinwiddie. I tell you I'm ready to strike out tomorrow and go to smashing things." And, pacing up and down, he chafed like a hound in the leash. We told him this was the kind of talk we liked to listen to at headquarters, and while General Grant fully coincided in these views it would still further confirm him in his judgment to hear such words as had just been spoken; we urged Sheridan to go and talk in the same strain to the general-in-chief, who was in his tent with General Rawlins. Sheridan, however, objected to obtruding himself unbidden upon his commander. Then we resorted to a bit of strategy. One of us went into the general's tent and told him Sheridan had just come in from the left and had been telling us some matters of much interest, and suggested that he be invited in and asked to state them. This was assented to, and Sheridan was told the general wanted to hear what he had to say. Sheridan then went in and began to speak to General Grant as he had been speaking to the staff. Several persons soon after came into the tent, and General Sheridan stepped out and accompanied General Ingalls to the latter's tent. A few minutes later General Grant went to this tent, General Ingalls came out, and Grant and Sheridan fully discussed the situation. In spite of the opposition which had arisen in some quarters to continuing offensive operations, owing to the state of the weather and the deplorable condition of the roads, General Grant decided to press the movement against the enemy with all vigor.

After his twenty-minutes talk with Grant, Sheridan mounted his horse, and, waving us a good-bye with his hand, rode off to Dinwiddie. The next morning, the 31st, he reported that the enemy had been hard at work intrenching at Five Forks and to a point about a mile west of there. Lee had been as prompt as Grant to recognize that Five Forks was a strategic point of great importance, and, to protect his right, had sent Pickett there with a large force of infantry and nearly all the cavalry. The rain continued during the night of the 30th, and on the morning of the 31st the weather was cloudy and dismal.

General Grant had expected that Warren would be attacked that morning, and had warned him to be on the alert. Warren advanced his corps to ascertain with what force the enemy held the White Oak road and to try to drive him from it; but before he had gone far he met with a vigorous assault. When news came of the attack General Grant directed me to go to the spot and look to the situation of affairs there. I found Ayres's division had been driven in, and both he and Crawford were falling back upon Griffin. Miles, of Humphreys's corps, was sent to reënforce Warren, and by noon the enemy was checked. As soon as General Grant was advised of the situation, he directed General Meade to take the offensive vigorously. Miles made a movement to the left and attacked in flank the troops in front of Warren, and the enemy soon fell back. General Grant had now ridden out to the front, and hearing that he was at Mrs. Butler's house near the Boydton plank-road, I joined him there. It was then a little after 1 o'clock. He had in the meantime ordered the headquarters camp to be moved to Dabney's Mill, on a cross-road running from the Boydton plank to the Vaughan road, and about two miles from Meade's headquarters, which were near the crossing of the Vaughan road and Hatcher's Run. The general was becoming apprehensive lest the infantry force that had moved against Warren might turn upon Sheridan, who had only cavalry with which to resist, as the weather had rendered it impracticable thus far to send him a corps of infantry as intended, and the general-in-chief was urgent that a strong forward movement should be made by the Fifth Corps for the purpose of deterring the enemy from detaching infantry from that portion of his line. This advance was made later in the afternoon, and with decided success. When this movement had been decided upon, General Grant directed me to go to Sheridan and explain what was taking place in Warren's and in Humphreys's front, and have a full understanding with him as to further operations in his vicinity. I rode rapidly down the Boydton plank-road, and soon came to Gravelly Run. Hearing heavy firing in the direction of the Five Forks road, I hurried on in that direction. Crossing by the Brooks road from the Boydton plank to the Five Forks road, which runs north from Dinwiddie, I saw a portion of our cavalry moving eastward, pressed by a heavy force of the enemy, and it was found that Devin and Davies, after holding on tooth and nail for hours, had been driven in by the force of superior numbers and were falling back toward the Boydton plank-road. The brigades of Gibbs and J. I. Gregg had rushed in on the right and rear of the enemy, and got in some very good work, but were soon after compelled to fall back toward Dinwiddie. I turned the corner of the Brooks cross-road and the Five Forks road just as the rear of our cavalry was passing it, and encountered one of Sheridan's bands,[*] under a heavy fire, playing "Nellie Bly" as cheerily as if it were furnishing music for a country picnic.

I found Sheridan a little north of Dinwiddie Court House, and gave him an account of matters on the left of the Army of the Potomac. He said he had had one of the liveliest days in his experience, fighting infantry and cavalry with cavalry only, but that he was concentrating his command on the high ground just north of Dinwiddie, and would hold that position at all hazards. He did not stop here, but becoming more and more animated in describing the situation and stating his views and intentions, he declared his belief that with the corps of infantry he expected to be put under his command he could take the initiative the next morning and cut off the whole of the force that Lee had detached. He said: "This force is in more danger than I am—if I am cut off from the Army

---

[*]Sheridan's bands were generally mounted on gray horses, and instead of being relegated to the usual duty of carrying off the wounded and assisting the surgeons, they were brought out to the front and made to play the liveliest airs in their repertory, with great effect on the spirits of the men.—H.P.

of the Potomac, it is cut off from Lee's army, and not a man in it should ever be allowed to get back to Lee. We at last have drawn the enemy's infantry out of its fortifications, and this is our chance to attack it." He begged me to go to General Grant at once and again urge him to send him the Sixth Corps, because it had been under him in the battles in the Valley of Virginia, and knew his way of fighting. I told him, as had been stated to him before, that the Sixth Corps was next to our extreme right, and that the only one which could reach him by daylight was the Fifth. I started soon after for General Grant's headquarters at Dabney's Mill, a distance of about eight miles. I reached there at 7 o'clock P.M., and gave the general a full description of Sheridan's operations. He at once telegraphed the substance of my report to Meade, and preparations soon after began looking to the sending of the Fifth Corps to report to Sheridan. About 7:40 Captain M. V. Sheridan, of Sheridan's staff, brought still later news from Dinwiddie, saying that the cavalry had had more fighting but was holding its position.

It was finally decided that Warren should send Ayres down the Boydton plank and across by the Brooks road, and Griffin and Crawford by the Crump road, which runs from the White Oak road south to J. Boisseau's. Mackenzie's small division of cavalry was ordered to march to Dinwiddie and report to Sheridan. All haste was urged, in the hope that at daylight the enemy might be caught between Warren's two divisions of infantry on one side and Ayres's division and Sheridan's cavalry on the other, and be badly beaten. It was expected that the infantry would reach its destination in ample time to take the offensive at break of day, but now one delay after another was met with, and Grant, Meade, and Sheridan spent a painfully anxious night in hurrying forward the movement. Ayres had to rebuild a bridge over Gravelly Run, which took till 2 A.M. Warren, with his other two divisions, did not get started from their position on the White Oak road till 5 A.M., and the hope of crushing the enemy was hourly growing less. This proved to be one of the busiest nights of the whole campaign. Generals were writing dispatches and telegraphing from dark till daylight. Staff-officers were rushing from one headquarters to another, wading through swamps, penetrating forests, and galloping over corduroy roads, engaged in carrying instructions, getting information, and making extraordinary efforts to hurry up the movement of the troops.

The next morning, April 1st, General Grant said to me: "I wish you would spend the day with Sheridan's command, and send me a bulletin every half-hour or so, advising me fully as to the progress of his movements. You know my views, and I want you to give them to Sheridan fully. Tell him the contemplated movement is left entirely in his hands, and he must be responsible for its execution. I have every confidence in his judgment and ability. I hope there may now be an opportunity of fighting the enemy's infantry outside of its fortifications."

I set out with half a dozen mounted orderlies to act as couriers in transmitting field bulletins. Captain Peter T. Hudson, of our staff, went with me. After traveling again by way of the Brooks road, I met Sheridan, about 10 A.M., on the Five Forks road not far from J. Boisseau's house. Ayres had his division on this road, having arrived about daylight, and Griffin had reached J. Boisseau's between 7 and 8 A.M. I had a full conference with Sheridan. He told me the force in front of him had fallen back early in the morning, that he had pursued with his cavalry and had had several brushes with the enemy, and was driving him steadily back; that he had his patience sorely tried by the delays that had occurred in getting the infantry to him, but he was going to make every effort to strike a heavy blow with all the infantry and cavalry, as soon as he could get them into position, provided the enemy should make a stand behind his intrenchments at Five Forks, which seemed likely. General Warren, who had accompanied Crawford's division, arrived at 11 o'clock and reported in person to Sheridan.

A few minutes before noon Colonel (afterward General) Babcock, of General Grant's staff, came over from headquarters and said to Sheridan: "General Grant directs me to say to you, that if in your judgment the Fifth Corps would do better under one of the division commanders, you are authorized to relieve General Warren, and order him to report to General Grant, at headquarters." General Sheridan replied, in effect, that he hoped such a step as that might not become necessary, and then went on to speak of his plan of battle. We all rode on farther to the front, and soon met General Devin, who was considerably elated by his successes of the morning, and was loudly demanding to be permitted to make a general charge on the enemy. Sheridan told him he didn't believe he had enough ammunition, to which Devin replied: "I guess I've got enough to give 'em one surge more."

General Babcock now left us to return to headquarters. About 1 o'clock it was reported by the cavalry that the enemy was retiring to his intrenched position at Five Forks, which was just north of the White Oak road, and parallel to it, his earth-works running from a point about three-quarters of a mile east of Five Forks to a point a mile west, with an angle or crotchet about one hundred yards long thrown back at right angles to his left to protect that flank. Orders were at once given to the Fifth Corps to move up the Gravelly Run Church road to the open ground near the church, and form in order of battle, with Ayres on the left, Crawford on his right, and Griffin in rear as a reserve. The corps was to wheel to the left, and make its attack upon the "angle," and then, moving westward, sweep down in rear of the enemy's intrenched line. The cavalry, principally dismounted, was to deploy in front of the enemy's line and engage his attention, and, as soon as it heard the firing of our infantry, to make a vigorous assault upon his works.

The Fifth Corps had borne the brunt of the fighting ever since the army had moved out on the 29th, and the gallant men who composed it, and had per-

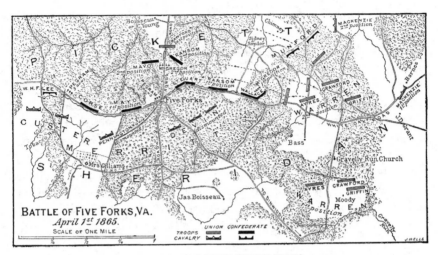

MAP OF THE BATTLE OF FIVE FORKS.

In his official report, General Fitzhugh Lee gives the following account of the battle of Five Forks from the Confederate point of view:

"Our position in the vicinity of Dinwiddie Court House [March 31st] brought us to the rear of the left of the infantry confronting the right of our line of battle at Burgess's Mills, and ascertaining during the night that that force, consisting of the Fifth Corps, had about-faced and was marching to the support of Sheridan and his discomfited cavalry, which would have brought them directly upon our left flank, at daylight on the 1st we commenced moving back to our former position at Five Forks, where Pickett placed his infantry in line of battle. W.H.F. Lee was on his right, one regiment of Munford's command on his left, uniting with the pickets of General Roberts's command, who

formed a conspicuous part in nearly every battle in which the Army of the Potomac had been engaged, seemed eager once more to cross bayonets with their old antagonists. But the movement was slow, the required formation seemed to drag, and Sheridan, chafing with impatience and consumed with anxiety, became as restive as a racer when he nears the score and is struggling to make the start. He made every possible appeal for promptness, he dismounted from his horse, paced up and down, struck the clinched fist of one hand into the palm of the other, and fretted like a caged tiger. He said at one time: "This battle must be fought and won before the sun goes down. All the conditions may be changed in the morning; we have but a few hours of daylight left us. My cavalry are rapidly exhausting their ammunition, and if the attack is delayed much longer they may have none left." And then another batch of staff-officers were sent out to gallop through the mud and hurry up the columns.

At 4 o'clock the formation was completed, the order for the assault was given, and the struggle for Pickett's intrenched line began. The Confederate infantry brigades were posted from right to left as follows: Terry, Corse, Steuart,

filled the gap between our position and the right of our main army, then at Burgess's Mills. Rosser was placed just in rear of the center as a reserve, Hatcher's Run intervening between him and our line. Everything continued quiet until about 3 P.M., when reports reached me of a large body of infantry marching around and menacing our left flank. I ordered Munford to go in person, ascertain the exact condition of affairs, hold his command in readiness, and, if necessary, order it up at once. He soon sent for it, and it reached its position just in time to receive the attack. A division of two small brigades of cavalry was not able long to withstand the attack of a Federal corps of infantry, and that force soon crushed in Pickett's left flank, swept it away, and before Rosser could cross Hatcher's Run the position at the Forks was seized and held, and an advance toward the railroad made. It was repulsed by Rosser. Pickett was driven rapidly toward the prolongation of the right of his line of battle by the combined attack of this infantry corps and Sheridan's cavalry, making a total of over 26,000 men, to which he was opposed with 7000 men of all arms. Our forces were driven back some miles, the retreat degenerating into a rout, being followed up principally by the cavalry, whilst the infantry corps held the position our troops were first driven from, threatening an advance upon the railroad, and paralyzing the force of reserve cavalry by necessitating its being stationary in an interposing position to check or retard such an advance.... I remained in position on Hatcher's Run, near Five Forks, during the night, and was joined by the cavalry which was driven back the previous afternoon, and by Lieutenant-General [R. H.] Anderson with Wise's and Gracie's brigades, who, leaving the position at Burgess's Mills, had marched by a circuitous route to our relief. Had he advanced up the direct road it would have brought him on the flank and rear of the infantry forming the enemy's right, which attacked our left at Five Forks, and probably changed the result of the unequal contest. Whilst Anderson was marching, the Fifth Corps was marching back, and was enabled to participate in the attack upon our lines the next day, whilst the services of the three infantry brigades (which General Anderson reënforced us by, too late for use) and the five with Pickett, by their absence, increased the disparity between the contending forces upon the next day for the possession of the lines circumvallating Petersburg."—Editors.

Ransom, and Wallace. General Fitzhugh Lee, commanding the cavalry, had placed W.H.F. Lee's two brigades on the right of the line, Munford's division on the left, and Rosser's in rear of Hatcher's Run to guard the trains. I rode to the front in company with Sheridan and Warren, with the head of Ayres's division, which was on the left. When this division became engaged, Warren took up a more central position with reference to his corps. Ayres threw out a skirmish-line and advanced across an open field, which sloped down gradually toward the dense woods, just north of the White Oak road. He soon met with a fire from the edge of this woods, a number of men fell, and the skirmish-line halted and seemed to waver. Sheridan now began to exhibit those traits that always made him such a tower of strength in the presence of an enemy. He put spurs to his horse and dashed along in front of the line of battle from left to right, shouting words of encouragement and having something cheery to say to every regiment. "Come on, men," he cried. "Go at 'em with a will. Move on at a clean jump or you'll not catch one of them. They're all getting ready to run now, and if you don't get on to them in five minutes, they'll every one get away from you!

Now go for them." Just then a man on the skirmish-line was struck in the neck; the blood spurted as if the jugular vein had been cut. "I'm killed!" he cried, and dropped on the ground. "You're not hurt a bit," cried Sheridan; "pick up your gun, man, and move right on to the front." Such was the electric effect of his words that the poor fellow snatched up his musket and rushed forward a dozen paces before he fell never to rise again. The line of battle of weather-beaten veterans was now moving right along down the slope toward the woods with a steady swing that boded no good for Pickett's command, earth-works or no earth-works. Sheridan was mounted on his favorite black horse "Rienzi" that had carried him from Winchester to Cedar Creek, and which Buchanan Read made famous for all time by his poem of "Sheridan's Ride." The roads were muddy, the fields swampy, the undergrowth dense, and "Rienzi," as he plunged and curveted, dashed the foam from his mouth and the mud from his heels. Had the Winchester pike been in a similar condition, he would not have made his famous twenty miles without breaking his own neck and Sheridan's too.

Mackenzie had been ordered up the Crump road with directions to turn east on the White Oak road and whip everything he met on that route. He met only a small cavalry command, and having whipped it according to orders, now came galloping back to join in the general scrimmage. He reported to Sheridan in person, and was ordered to strike out toward Hatcher's Run, then move west and get possession of the Ford road in the enemy's rear.

Soon Ayres's men met with a heavy fire on their left flank and had to change direction by facing more toward the west. As the troops entered the woods and moved forward over the boggy ground and struggled through the dense undergrowth, they were staggered by a heavy fire from the angle and fell back in some confusion. Sheridan now rushed into the midst of the broken lines, and cried out: "Where is my battle-flag?" As the sergeant who carried it rode up, Sheridan seized the crimson and white standard, waved it above his head, cheered on the men, and made heroic efforts to close up the ranks. Bullets were humming like a swarm of bees. One pierced the battle-flag, another killed the sergeant who had carried it, another wounded Captain A. J. McGonnigle in the side, others struck two or three of the staff-officers' horses. All this time Sheridan was dashing from one point of the line to another, waving his flag, shaking his fist, encouraging, threatening, praying, swearing, the very incarnation of battle. It would be a sorry soldier who could help following such a leader. Ayres and his officers were equally exposing themselves at all points in rallying the men, and soon the line was steadied, for such material could suffer but a momentary check. Ayres, with drawn saber, rushed forward once more with his veterans, who now behaved as if they had fallen back to get a "good-ready," and with fixed bayonets and a rousing cheer dashed over the earth-works, sweeping everything before them, and killing or capturing every man in their immediate front whose legs had not saved him.

Sheridan spurred "Rienzi" up to the angle, and with a bound the horse carried his rider over the earth-works, and landed in the midst of a line of prisoners who had thrown down their arms and were crouching close under their breastworks. Some of them called out, "Whar do you want us-all to go to?" Then Sheridan's rage turned to humor, and he had a running talk with the "Johnnies" as they filed past. "Go right over there," he said to them, pointing to the rear. "Get right along, now. Drop your guns; you'll never need them any more. You'll all be safe over there. Are there any more of you? We want every one of you fellows." Nearly 1500 were captured at the angle.

An orderly here came up to Sheridan and said: "Colonel Forsyth of your staff is killed, sir." "It's no such thing," cried Sheridan. "I don't believe a word of it. You'll find Forsyth's all right." Ten minutes after, Forsyth rode up. It was the gallant General Frederick Winthrop who had fallen in the assault and had been mistaken for him. Sheridan did not even seem surprised when he saw Forsyth, and only said: "There! I told you so." I mention this as an instance of a peculiar trait of Sheridan's character, which never allowed him to be discouraged by camp rumors, however disastrous.

The dismounted cavalry had assaulted as soon as they heard the infantry fire open. The natty cavalrymen, with tight-fitting uniforms, short jackets, and small carbines, swarmed through the pine thickets and dense undergrowth, looking as if they had been especially equipped for crawling through knot-

VIEW OF THE CONFEDERATE LINES COVERING PETERSBURG. FROM A PHOTOGRAPH.

holes. Those who had magazine guns created a racket in those pine woods that sounded as if a couple of army corps had opened fire.

The cavalry commanded by the gallant Merritt made a final dash, went over the earth-works with a hurrah, captured a battery of artillery, and scattered everything in front of them. Here Custer, Devin, Fitzhugh, and the other cavalry leaders were in their element, and vied with each other in deeds of valor. Crawford's division had advanced in a northerly direction, marching away from Ayres and leaving a gap between the two divisions. General Sheridan sent nearly all of his staff-officers to correct this movement, and to find General Warren, whom he was anxious to see.

After the capture of the angle I started off toward the right to see how matters were going there. I went in the direction of Crawford's division, passed around the left of the enemy's works, then rode due west to a point beyond the Ford road. Here I met Sheridan again, just a little before dark. He was laboring with all the energy of his nature to complete the destruction of the enemy's forces, and to make preparation to protect his own detached command from an attack by Lee in the morning. He said he had relieved Warren, directed him to report in person to General Grant, and placed Griffin in command of the Fifth Corps. I had sent frequent bulletins during the day to the general-in-chief, and now dispatched a courier announcing the change of corps commanders and giving the general result of the round-up.

Sheridan had that day fought one of the most interesting technical battles of the war, almost perfect in conception, brilliant in execution, strikingly dramatic in its incidents, and productive of immensely important results.

About half-past seven o'clock I started for general headquarters. The roads in places were corduroyed with captured muskets. Ammunition trains and ambulances were still struggling forward for miles; teamsters, prisoners, stragglers, and wounded were choking the roadway. The coffee-boilers had kindled their fires. Cheers were resounding on all sides, and everybody was riotous over the victory. A horseman had to pick his way through this jubilant condition of things as best he could, as he did not have the right of way by any means. I traveled again by way of the Brooks road. As I galloped past a group of men on the Boydton plank, my orderly called out to them the news of the victory. The only response he got was from one of them who raised his open hand to his face, put his thumb to his nose, and yelled: "No, you don't—April fool!" I then realized that it was the 1st of April. I had ridden so rapidly that I reached headquarters at Dabney's Mill before the arrival of the last courier I had dispatched. General Grant was sitting with most of the staff about him before a blazing camp-fire. He wore his blue cavalry overcoat, and the ever-present cigar was in his mouth. I began shouting the good news as soon as I got in sight, and in a moment all but the imperturbable general-in-chief were on their feet giving vent to wild demonstrations of joy. For some minutes there was a bewildering state of excitement, grasping of hands, tossing up of hats, and slapping of each other on the back. It meant the beginning of the end—the reaching of the "last ditch." It pointed to peace and home. Dignity was thrown to the winds. The general, as was expected, asked his usual question: "How many prisoners have been taken?" This was always his first inquiry when an engagement was reported. No man ever had such a fondness for taking prisoners. I think the gratification arose from the kindness of his heart, a feeling that it was much better to win in this way than by the destruction of human life. I was happy to report that the prisoners this time were estimated at over five thousand, and this was the only part of my recital that seemed to call forth a responsive expression from his usually impassive features. After having listened to the description of Sheridan's day's work, the general, with scarcely a word, walked into his tent, and by the light of a flickering candle took up his "manifold writer," a small book which retained a copy of the matter written, and after finishing several dispatches handed them

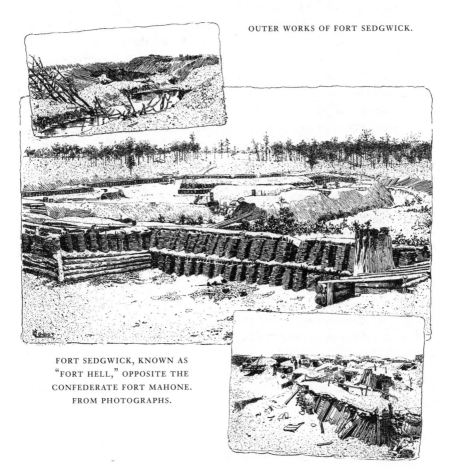

OUTER WORKS OF FORT SEDGWICK.

FORT SEDGWICK, KNOWN AS "FORT HELL," OPPOSITE THE CONFEDERATE FORT MAHONE. FROM PHOTOGRAPHS.

BOMB-PROOFS INSIDE FORT SEDGWICK.

to an orderly to be sent over the field wires, came out and joined our group at the campfire, and said as coolly as if remarking upon the state of the weather: "I have ordered an immediate assault along the lines." This was about 9 o'clock.

General Grant was anxious to have the different commands move against the enemy's lines at once, to prevent Lee from withdrawing troops and sending them against Sheridan. General Meade was all activity and so alive to the situation, and so anxious to carry out the orders of the general-in-chief, that he sent word that he was going to have the troops make a dash at the works without waiting to form assaulting columns. General Grant, at 9:30 P.M., sent a message saying he did not mean to have the corps attack without assaulting columns, but to let the batteries open at once and to feel out with skirmishers; and if the enemy was found to be leaving, to let the troops attack in their own way. The corps commanders reported that it would be impracticable to make a successful assault till morning, but sent back replies full of enthusiasm.

The hour for the general assault was now fixed at 4 the next morning. Miles was ordered to march with his division at midnight to reënforce Sheridan and enable him to make a stand against Lee, in case he should move westward in the night. The general had not been unmindful of Mr. Lincoln's anxiety. Soon after my arrival he telegraphed him: "I have just heard from Sheridan. He has carried everything before him. He has captured three brigades of infantry and a train of wagons, and is now pushing up his success." He had this news also communicated to the several corps commanders, in accordance with his invariable custom to let the different commands feel that they were being kept informed of the general movements, and to encourage them and excite their emulation by notifying them of the success of other commanders. A little after midnight the general tucked himself into his camp-bed, and was soon sleeping as peacefully as if the next day were to be devoted to a picnic instead of a decisive battle.

About 3 A.M. Colonel F. C. Newhall, of Sheridan's staff, rode up bespattered with more than the usual amount of Virginia soil. He had the latest report from Sheridan, and as the general-in-chief would, no doubt, want to take this opportunity of sending further instructions as to the morning's operations on the extreme left, he was wakened, and listened to the report from Newhall, who stood by the bedside to deliver it. The general told him of the preparations being made by the Army of the Potomac, and the necessity of Sheridan's looking out for a push in his direction by Lee, and then began his sleep again where he had left off. Newhall then started to take another fifteen-mile ride back to Sheridan. Every one at headquarters had caught as many cat-naps as he could, so as to be able to keep both eyes open the next day, in the hope of getting a sight of Petersburg, and possibly of Richmond. And now 4 o'clock came, but no assault. It was found that to remove abatis, climb over *chevaux de frise,* jump rifle-pits, and scale parapets, a little daylight would be of material assistance. At 4:45 there was a streak of gray in the heavens which soon revealed another streak of gray formed by Confederate uniforms in the works opposite, and the charge was ordered. The thunder of hundreds of guns shook the ground like an earthquake, and soon the troops were engaged all along the lines. The general awaited the result of the assault at headquarters, where he could be easily communicated with, and from which he could give general directions.

At a quarter past five a message came from Wright that he had carried the enemy's line and was pushing in. Next came news from Parke, that he had captured the outer works in his front, with 12 pieces of artillery and 800 prisoners. At 6:40 the general wrote a telegram with his own hand to Mr. Lincoln, as follows: "Both Wright and Parke got through the enemy's line. The battle now rages furiously. Sheridan with his cavalry, the Fifth Corps, and Miles's division of the Second Corps I sent to him since 1 this morning, is sweeping down from the west. All now looks highly favorable. Ord is engaged, but I have not yet heard the result on his part." A cheering dispatch was also sent to Sheridan, winding up with the words: "I think nothing is now wanting but the approach of your force from the west to finish up the job on this side."

Soon Ord was heard from, having broken through the intrenchments. Humphreys, too, had been doing gallant work; at half-past seven the line in his front was captured, and half an hour later Hays's division of his corps had carried an important earth-work, with three guns and most of the garrison. At 8:25 A.M. the general sat down to write another telegram to the President, summing up the progress made. Before he had finished it a dispatch was brought in from Ord saying some of his troops had just captured the enemy's works south of Hatcher's Run, and this news was added to the tidings which the general was sending to Mr. Lincoln.

The general and staff now rode out to the front, as it was necessary to give immediate direction to the actual movements of the troops, and prevent confusion from the overlapping and intermingling of the several corps as they pushed forward. He urged his horse over the works that Wright's corps had captured, and suddenly came upon a body of three thousand prisoners marching to the rear. His whole attention was for some time riveted upon them, and we knew he was enjoying his usual satisfaction in seeing them. Some of the guards told the prisoners who the general was, and they became wild with curiosity to get a good look at him. Next he came up with a division of the Sixth Corps flushed with success, and rushing forward with a dash that was inspiriting beyond description. When they caught sight of the leader, whom they had patiently followed from the Rapidan to the Appomattox, their cheers broke forth with a will and their enthusiasm knew no bounds. The general galloped along toward the right, and soon met Meade, with whom he had been in constant communication, and who had been pushing forward the Army of the Potomac with all vigor. Congratulations were quickly exchanged, and both went to pushing forward the work. General Grant, after taking in the situation, directed both

Meade and Ord to face their commands toward the east, and close up toward the inner lines which covered Petersburg. Lee had been pushed so vigorously that he seemed for a time to be making but little effort to recover any of his lost ground, but now he made a determined fight against Parke's corps, which was threatening his inner line on his extreme left and the bridge across the Appomattox. Repeated assaults were made, but Parke resisted them all successfully, and could not be moved from his position. Lee had ordered Longstreet from the north side of the James, and with these troops reënforced his extreme right. General Grant dismounted near a farm-house which stood on a knoll within a mile of the enemy's extreme line, and from which he could get a good view of the field of operations. He seated himself at the foot of a tree, and was soon busy receiving dispatches and writing orders to officers conducting the advance. The position was under fire, and as soon as the group of staff-officers was seen the enemy's guns began paying their respects. This lasted for nearly a quarter of an hour, and as the fire became hotter and hotter several of the officers, apprehensive of the general's safety, urged him to move to some less conspicuous position, but he kept on writing and talking without the least interruption from the shots falling around him, and apparently not noticing what a target the place was becoming. After he had finished his dispatches, he got up, took a view of the situation, and as he started toward the other side of the farm-house said, with a quizzical look at the group around him: "Well, they do seem to have the range on us." The staff was now sent to various points of the advancing lines, and all was activity in pressing forward the good work. By noon, nearly all the outer line of works was in our possession, except two strong redoubts which occupied a commanding position, named respectively Fort Gregg and Fort Whitworth. The general decided that these should be stormed, and about 1 o'clock three of Ord's brigades swept down upon Fort Gregg. The garrison of 300 [under Lieutenant-Colonel J. H. Duncan] with two rifled cannon made a desperate defense, and a most gallant contest took place. For half an hour after our men had gained the parapet a bloody hand-to-hand struggle continued, but nothing could stand against the onslaught of Ord's troops, flushed with their morning's victory. By half-past two 57 of the brave garrison lay dead, and about 250 had surrendered. Fort Whitworth was at once abandoned, but the guns of Fort Gregg were opened upon the garrison as they marched out, and the commander [Colonel Joseph M. Jayne] and sixty men were surrendered.

About this time Miles had struck a force of the enemy at Sutherland's Station on Lee's extreme right, and had captured two pieces of artillery and nearly a thousand prisoners. At 4:40 the general, who had been keeping Mr. Lincoln fully advised of the history that was so rapidly being made that day, sent him a telegram inviting him to come out the next day and pay him a visit. A prompt reply came back from the President, saying: "Allow me to tender you and all with you the nation's grateful thanks for the additional and magnificent success. At your kind suggestion, I think I will meet you to-morrow."

Prominent officers now urged the general to make an assault on the inner lines and capture Petersburg that afternoon, but he was firm in his resolve not to sacrifice the lives necessary to accomplish such a result. He said the city would undoubtedly be evacuated during the night, and he would dispose the troops for a parallel march westward, and try to head off the escaping army. And thus ended the eventful Sunday.

The general was up at daylight the next morning, and the first report brought in was that Parke had gone through the lines at 4 A.M., capturing a few skirmishers, and that the city had surrendered at 4:28 to Colonel Ralph Ely. A second communication surrendering the place was sent in to Wright. The evacuation had begun about 10 the night before, and was completed before 3 on the morning of the 3d. Between 5 and 6 A.M. the general had a conference with Meade, and orders were given to push westward with all haste. About 9 A.M. the general rode into Petersburg. Many of the citizens, panic-stricken, had escaped with the army. Most of the whites who remained staid indoors, a few groups of negroes gave cheers, but the scene generally was one of complete desertion. Grant rode along quietly with his staff until he came to a comfortable-looking brick house, with a yard in front, situated on one of the principal streets, and here he and the officers accompanying him dismounted and took seats on the piazza. A number of the citizens soon gathered on the sidewalk and gazed with eager curiosity upon the commander of the Yankee armies.

Soon an officer came with a dispatch from Sheridan, who had been reën-forced and ordered to strike out along the Danville railroad, saying he was already nine miles beyond Namosine Creek and pressing the enemy's trains. The general was anxious to move westward at once with the leading infantry columns, but Mr. Lincoln had telegraphed that he was on his way, and the general, though he had replied that he could not wait for his arrival, decided to prolong his stay until the President came up. Mr. Lincoln, accompanied by his little son "Tad," dismounted in the street and came in through the front gate with long and rapid strides, his face beaming with delight. He seized General Grant's hand as the general stepped forward to greet him, and stood shaking it for some time and pouring out his thanks and congratulations with all the fervor of a heart that seemed overflowing with its fullness of joy. I doubt whether Mr. Lincoln ever experienced a happier moment in his life. The scene was singularly affecting and one never to be forgotten. He then said:

"Do you know, General, I have had a sort of sneaking idea for some days that you intended to do something like this, though I thought some time ago that you would so manœuvre as to have Sherman come up and be near enough to coöperate with you."

"Yes," replied the general, "I thought at one time that Sherman's army might advance so far as to be in supporting distance of the Eastern armies when the spring campaign against Lee opened, but I have had a feeling that it is better to let Lee's old antagonists give his army the final blow and finish up the job. If the Western armies were even to put in an appearance against Lee's army, it might give some of our politicians a chance to stir up sectional feeling in claiming everything for the troops from their own section of country. The Western armies have been very successful in their campaigns, and it is due to the Eastern armies to let them vanquish their old enemy single-handed."

"I see, I see," said Mr. Lincoln, "but I never thought of it in that light. In fact, my anxiety has been so great that I didn't care where the help came from so the work was perfectly done."

"Oh," General Grant continued, "I do not suppose it would have given rise to much of the bickering I mentioned, and perhaps the idea would not have occurred to any one else. I feel sure there would have been no such feeling among the soldiers, but there might have been among our politicians. While I would not have risked the result of the campaign on account of any mere sentiment of this kind, I felt that our troops here are amply able to handle Lee."

Mr. Lincoln then began to talk about the civil complications that would follow the destruction of the Confederate armies in the field, and showed plainly the anxiety he felt regarding the great problems in statecraft that would soon be thrust upon him. He intimated very plainly, however, in a rambling talk of nearly half an hour, that thoughts of mercy and magnanimity were uppermost in his heart.

At 12:30 the general wrote a telegram to Weitzel at Richmond, asking news from him, and showed it to the President before sending it. The general hoped that he would hear before he parted with the President that Richmond was in our possession, but after the interview had lasted about an hour and a half, the general said he must ride on to the front and join Ord's column, and took leave of the President, who shook his hand cordially, and with great warmth of feeling wished him God-speed and every success.

The general and staff had ridden as far as Sutherland's Station, about nine miles, when a dispatch from Weitzel overtook him, which had come by a roundabout way. It read: "We took Richmond at 8:15 this morning. I captured many guns. Enemy left in great haste. The city is on fire in two places. Am making every effort to put it out." Although the news was expected, there were wild shouts of rejoicing from the group who heard it read. The general, who never manifested the slightest sign of emotion either in victories or defeats, merely said: "I am sorry I did not get this before we left the President. However, I suppose he has heard the news by this time," and then added: "Let the news be circulated among the troops as rapidly as possible."

Grant and Meade both went into camp at Sutherland's Station that evening, the 3d. The Army of the Potomac caught a few hours' sleep, and at 3 o'clock the next morning was again on the march. The pursuit had now become unflagging, relentless. Grant put a spur to the heel of every dispatch he sent. Sheridan "the inevitable," as the enemy had learned to call him, was in advance thundering along with his cavalry, followed by Griffin and the rest of the Army of the Potomac, while Ord was swinging along toward Burkeville to head off Lee from Danville, to which point it was naturally supposed he was pushing in order to unite with Joe Johnston's army. The 4th was another active day; the troops found that this campaign was to be won by legs, that the great walking-match had begun, and success would attend the army that should make the best distance record. General Grant marched this day with Ord's troops. Meade was sick, and had to take at times to an ambulance, but his loyal spirit never flagged, and his orders breathed the true spirit of the soldier. That night General Grant camped at Wilson's Station, on the South Side railroad, twenty-seven miles west of Petersburg. The next morning he sent a dispatch to Sherman in North Carolina, giving him an account of the situation and instructions as to his future movements, and winding up with the famous words, "Rebel armies are now the only strategic points to strike at." On the 5th he marched again with Ord's column, and at noon reached Nottoway Court House, about ten miles east of Burkeville, where he halted for a couple of hours. A young staff-officer here rode up to General Ord, in a state of considerable excitement, and said to him: "Is that a way-station?" This grim old soldier, who was always jocular, replied with great deliberation: "This is Nott-o-way Station." The staff collected around General Grant on the front porch of the old town tavern, and while we were examining maps and discussing movements, a dispatch came from Sheridan, saying he had captured six guns and some wagons, and had intercepted Lee's advance toward Burkeville, that Lee was in person at Amelia Court House, etc. This news was given to the passing troops, and lusty cheers went up from every throat. They had marched about fifteen miles already that day, and now struck out as if they were good for fifteen more, and swore they were going to beat the record of the cavalry. We continued to move along the road which runs parallel to the South Side railroad till nearly dark, and had reached a point about half-way between Nottoway and Burkeville. The road was skirted by a dense woods on the north side, the side toward the enemy. There was a sudden commotion among the headquarters escort, and on looking around I saw some of our men dashing up to a horseman in full rebel uniform, who had suddenly appeared in the road, and they were in the act of seizing him as a prisoner. I recognized him at once as one of Sheridan's scouts, who had before brought us important dispatches; said to him: "How do you do, Campbell?"; and told our men he was all right and was one of our own people. He told us he had had a hard ride from Sheridan's camp, and had brought a dispatch for General Grant. By this time the general had recognized him, and had

CAPTURE OF GUNS AND THE DESTRUCTION OF A CONFEDERATE WAGON-TRAIN
AT PAINEVILLE, APRIL 5, BY DAVIES'S CAVALRY BRIGADE OF CROOK'S DIVISION.
FROM A SKETCH MADE AT THE TIME.

The wagon-train was escorted by Gary's cavalry with five guns. General Humphreys, in "The Virginia Campaign," says it is believed that "the papers of General Robert E. Lee's headquarters, containing many valuable reports, copies of but few of which are now to be found, were destroyed by the burning of these wagons."

stopped in the road to see what he had brought. Campbell then took from his mouth a wad of tobacco, broke it open, and pulled out a little ball of tin-foil. Rolled up in this was a sheet of tissue paper on which was written the famous dispatch so widely published at the time, in which Sheridan described the situation at Jetersville, and added: "I wish you were here yourself."

The general said he would go at once to Sheridan, and dismounted from his black pony "Jeff Davis," which he had been riding, and called for his big bay horse "Cincinnati." He stood in the road and wrote a dispatch, using the pony's back for a desk, and then, mounting the fresh horse, told Campbell to lead the way. It was found we would have to skirt the enemy's lines, and it was thought prudent to take some cavalry with us, but there was none near at hand, and the general said he would risk it with our mounted escort of fourteen men. Calling upon me and two or three other officers to accompany him, he started off. It was now after dark, but there was enough moonlight to enable us to see the way without difficulty. After riding nearly twenty miles, following cross-roads through a wooded country, we struck Sheridan's pickets about half-past ten o'clock, and soon after reached his headquarters.

Sheridan was awaiting us, thinking the general would come after getting his dispatch. A good supper of coffee and cold chicken was spread out, and it was soon demonstrated that the night ride had not impaired any one's appetite.

When the general-in-chief had learned fully the situation in Sheridan's front, he first sent a message to Ord to watch the roads running south from Burkeville and Farmville, and then rode over to Meade's camp near by. Meade was still suffering from illness. His views differed somewhat from General Grant's regarding the movements of the Army of the Potomac for the next day, and the latter changed the dispositions that were being made so as to have the army unite with Sheridan's troops in swinging round toward the south, and heading off Lee in that direction. The next day, the 6th, proved a decided field-day in the pursuit. It was found in the morning that Lee had retreated during the night from Amelia Court House, and from the direction he had taken, and the information received that he had ordered rations to meet him at Farmville, it was seen that he had abandoned all hope of reaching Burkeville and was probably heading for Lynchburg. Ord was to try to burn the High Bridge and push on to Farmville. Sheridan's cavalry was to work around on Lee's left flank, and the Army of the Potomac was to make another forced march and strike the enemy wherever it could reach him.

I spent a portion of the day with Humphreys's corps, which attacked the enemy near Deatonville and gave his rear-guard no rest. I joined General Grant later and with him rode to Burkeville, getting there some time after dark.

Ord had pushed out to Rice's Station, and Sheridan and Wright had gone in against the enemy and had fought the battle of Sailor's Creek, capturing six general officers and about seven thousand men, and "smashing things" generally.

Ord had sent Colonel Francis Washburn, of the 4th Massachusetts Cavalry, with two infantry regiments to destroy High Bridge and return to Burkeville Station, but becoming apprehensive for their safety, owing to the movements of the enemy, he sent Colonel Theodore Read of his staff with eighty cavalrymen to recall the command. Read advanced as far as Farmville, and on his return found Washburn's troops confronting Lee's advance. The enemy were now between Ord and this little command of less than six hundred infantry and cavalry. Finding himself thus cut off, the gallant Read resolved to sacrifice the command in a heroic effort to delay Lee's march, and repeatedly charged the advancing columns. He was soon mortally wounded and not long after Washburn fell. Most of the men were killed or wounded, and the rest finally surrendered. Their heroic act had delayed Lee's advance long enough to be of material service in aiding his pursuers to capture a large part of his wagon trains. The next day, the 7th, Lee crossed the Appomattox at High Bridge and fired the bridge after his passage, but Humphreys arrived in time to extinguish the fire before it had made much progress, and followed Lee to the north side of the river.

THE CAPTURE OF EWELL'S CORPS, APRIL 6, 1865. FROM A SKETCH MADE AT THE TIME.

In his official report General Ewell gives the following account of the battle of Sailor's Creek and the capture of his corps:

"On crossing a little stream known as Sailor's Creek, I met General Fitzhugh Lee, who informed me that a large force of cavalry held the road just in front of General [R. H.] Anderson, and was so strongly posted that he had halted a short distance ahead. The trains were turned into the road nearer the river, while I hurried to General Anderson's aid. General [John B.] Gordon's corps turned off after the trains. General Anderson informed me that at least two divisions of cavalry were in his front, and suggested two modes of escape—either to unite our forces and break through, or to move to the right through the woods and try to strike a road which ran toward Farmville. I recommended the latter alternative, but as he knew the ground and I did not, and had no one who did, I left the dispositions to him. Before any were made the enemy appeared in rear of my column in large force preparing to attack. General Anderson informed me that he would make the attack in front, if I would hold in check those in the rear, which I did until his troops were broken and dispersed. I had no artillery, all being with the train. My line ran across a little ravine which leads nearly at right angles toward Sailor's Creek. General G.W.C. Lee was on the left with the Naval Battalion, under Commodore [John R.] Tucker, behind his right. Kershaw's division was on the right. All of Lee's and part of Kershaw's divisions were posted behind a rising ground that afforded some shelter from artillery. The creek was perhaps 300 yards in their front, with brush pines between and a cleared field beyond it. In this the enemy's artillery took a commanding position, and, finding we had none to reply, soon approached within 800 yards and opened a terrible fire. After nearly half an hour of this their infantry advanced, crossing the creek above and below us at the same time. Just as it attacked, General Anderson made his assault, which was repulsed in five minutes. I had ridden up near his lines with him to see the result, when a staff-officer, who had followed his troops in their charge, brought him word of its failure. General Anderson rode rapidly toward his command. I returned to mine to see if it were yet too late to try the other plan of escape. On riding past my left I came suddenly upon a strong line of the enemy's skirmishers advancing upon my left rear. This closed the only avenue of escape; as shells and even bullets were crossing each other from front and rear over my troops, and my right was completely enveloped, I surrendered myself and staff to a cavalry officer who came in by the same road General Anderson had gone out on. At my request he sent a messenger to General G.W.C. Lee, who was nearest, with a note from me telling him he was surrounded, General Anderson's attack had failed, I had surrendered, and he had better do so, too, to prevent useless loss of life, though I gave no orders, being a prisoner. Before the messenger reached him General [G.W.C.] Lee had been captured, as had General Kershaw, and the whole of my command. My two divisions numbered about 3000 each at the time of the evacuation; 2800 were taken prisoners, about 150 killed and wounded. The difference of over 3000 was caused mainly by the fatigue of four days' and nights' almost constant marching, the last two days with nothing to eat. Before our capture I saw men eating raw fresh meat as they marched in the ranks. I was informed at General Wright's headquarters, whither I was carried after my capture, that 30,000 men were engaged with us when we surrendered, namely, two infantry corps and Custer's and Merritt's divisions of cavalry."

General J. Warren Keifer, in a pamphlet on the battle of Sailor's Creek, says:

"General A. P. Hill, a corps commander in General Lee's army, was killed at Petersburg, April 2d, 1865, and this, or some other important reason, caused General Lee, while at Amelia Court House, to consolidate his army into two corps or wings, one commanded by Lieutenant-General Longstreet and the other by Lieutenant-General Ewell.

"The main body of the Confederate army had passed by toward Sailor's Creek. Pursuit with such troops as were up was promptly ordered by General Sheridan and conducted by General Horatio G. Wright, who commanded the Sixth Corps. The enemy's rear-guard fought stubbornly and fell back toward the stream. The Second Division of his corps, under General Frank Wheaton, arrived and joined the Third Division in the attack and pursuit. The main body of the cavalry, under General Merritt, was dispatched to intercept the Confederate retreat. General Merritt passed east and south of the enemy across Sailor's Creek, and again attacked him on the right rear. By about 5 P.M. the Confederate army was forced across the valley of Sailor's Creek, where it took up an unusually strong position on the heights immediately on the west bank of the stream. These heights, save on their face, were mainly covered with forests. There was a level bottom, wholly on the east bank of the creek, over which the Union forces would have to pass before reaching the stream, then swollen beyond its banks by recent rains, and which washed the foot of the heights on which General Ewell had rested the divisions of his army, ready for an attack if made, and with the hope that under cover of night the whole Confederate army might escape in safety to Danville.

"The pursuing troops were halted on the face of the hills skirting the valley, within the range of the enemy's guns, and lines were adjusted for an assault. Artillery was put in position on these hills, and a heavy fire was immediately opened. An effort was made to get up General G. W. Getty's division of the Sixth Corps, and a portion of the Second Brigade of the Third Division, which had been dispatched to attack a battery on the right, but the day was too far spent to await their arrival. After a few moments' delay, General Wright, as directed by General Sheridan, ordered an immediate assault to be made, by the infantry, under the cover of the artillery fire. Colonel Stagg's brigade of cavalry was, at the same time, ordered by General Sheridan to attack and, if possible, flank the extreme right of the enemy's position. General Merritt's cavalry divisions (First and Third) simultaneously attacked the Confederate army on its right and rear. Without waiting for reserves to arrive in sight, the two divisions of the Sixth Corps descended into the valley, and in single line of battle (First Division on the left and the Third on the right) moved steadily across the plain in the face of a destructive fire of the enemy, and, with shouldered guns and ammunition-boxes also, in most cases, over the shoulder, waded through the flooded stream. Though the water was from two to four feet deep, the stream was crossed without a halt or waver in the line. Many fell on the plain and in the water, and those who reached the west bank were in more or less disorder. The order to storm the heights was promptly given by the officers accompanying the troops, and it was at once obeyed. The infantry of the Sixth Corps began firing for the first time while ascending the heights, and when within only a few yards of the enemy. His advance line gave way, and an easy victory seemed about to be achieved by the Union forces. But before the crest of the heights was reached General Ewell's massed troops, in heavy column, made an impetuous charge upon and through the center of the assaulting line. The Union center was completely broken, and a disastrous defeat for the Union army was imminent. This large body of the Confederate infantry became, by reason of this success, exposed to the now renewed fire from General Wright's artillery remaining in position on the hills east of the stream.

"The right and left wings of the charging Union line met with better success, and each drove back all in its front, and, wholly disregarding the defeat of the center, persisted in advancing, each wheeling as upon a pivot, in the center of the line—then held by the Confederate masses. These masses were soon subjected to a terrible infantry fire upon both flanks as well as by the artillery in front. The swollen stream forbade a Confederate advance to attack the unguarded artillery. General Merritt and Colonel Stagg's cavalry, in a simultaneous attack, overthrew all before them on the right and rear. The Confederate officers gallantly struggled to avert disaster, and bravely tried to form lines to the right and left to repel the flank attacks. This latter proved impossible. The troops on the flanks were pushed up to within a few feet of the massed Confederates, which rendered any re-formation or change of direction by them out of the question, and speedily brought hopeless disorder. A few were bayoneted on each side. Flight was impossible, and nothing remained to put an end to the bloody slaughter but for them to throw down their arms and become captives. As the gloom of approaching night settled over the field, covered with dead and dying, the fire of artillery and musketry ceased, and General Ewell, together with eleven of his general officers [including Kershaw, G.W.C. Lee, Barton, Du Bose, Hunton, and Corse], and about all his gallant army that survived, were prisoners. Commodore Tucker and his Marine Brigade, numbering about 2000, surrendered to me a little later. They were under cover of a dense

CONFEDERATES DESTROYING THE RAILROAD FROM APPOMATTOX TOWARD LYNCHBURG, AND ARTILLERYMEN DESTROYING GUN-CARRIAGES, AT NIGHTFALL, SATURDAY, APRIL 8. FROM A SKETCH MADE AT THE TIME.

forest, and had been passed by in the first onset of the assault. Of the particular operations of the cavalry the writer of this, of his personal knowledge, knows little; but no less praise is due it than to the infantry. In this battle more men were captured in actual conflict without negotiation than on any other field in America."

General Grant started from Burkeville early the next morning, the 7th, and took the direct road to Farmville. The columns were crowding the roads, and the men, aroused to still greater efforts by the inspiring news of the day before, were sweeping along, despite the rain that fell, like trained pedestrians on a walking-track. As the general rode among them he was greeted with shouts and hurrahs, on all sides, and a string of sly remarks, which showed how familiar swords and bayonets became when victory furnishes the topic of their talk.

CHAPTER 5

THE FALL OF RICHMOND.

I. THE EVACUATION.

Clement Sulivane, Captain, C.S.A.

About 11:30 A.M. on Sunday, April 2d,[‡] a strange agitation was perceptible on the streets of Richmond, and within half an hour it was known on all sides that Lee's lines had been broken below Petersburg; that he was in full retreat on Danville; that the troops covering the city at Chaffin's and Drewry's Bluffs were on the point of being withdrawn, and that the city was forthwith to be abandoned. A singular security had been felt by the citizens of Richmond, so the news fell like a bomb-shell in a peaceful camp, and dismay reigned supreme.

All that Sabbath day the trains came and went, wagons, vehicles, and horsemen rumbled and dashed to and fro, and, in the evening, ominous groups of ruffians—more or less in liquor—began to make their appearance on the principal thoroughfares of the city. As night came on pillage and rioting and robbing took place. The police and a few soldiers were at hand, and, after the arrest of a few ringleaders and the more riotous of their followers, a fair degree of order was restored. But Richmond saw few sleeping eyes during the pandemonium of that night.

The division of Major-General G.W.C. Lee, of Ewell's corps, at that time rested in the trenches eight miles below Richmond, with its right on the James River, covering Chaffin's Bluff. I was at the time its assistant adjutant-general, and was in the city on some detached duty connected with the "Local Brigade" belonging to the division,—a force composed of the soldiers of the army, detailed on account of their mechanical skill to work in the arsenals, etc., and of clerks and other employés of the War, Treasury, Quartermaster, and other departments.

Upon receipt of the news from Petersburg I reported to General Ewell

[‡]Mr. Davis attended morning service at St. Paul's Church, where he received a dispatch, on reading which he left the church to prepare for the departure of the Government.—EDITORS.

THE RUINS OF RICHMOND BETWEEN THE CANAL BASIN AND CAPITOL SQUARE.
FROM A WAR-TIME PHOTOGRAPH.

(then in Richmond) for instructions, and was ordered to assemble and command the Local Brigade, cause it to be well supplied with ammunition and provisions, and await further orders. All that day and night I was engaged in this duty, but with small result, as the battalions melted away as fast as they were formed, mainly under orders from the heads of departments who needed all their employés in the transportation and guarding of the archives, etc., but partly, no doubt, from desertions. When morning dawned fewer than 200 men remained, under command of Captain Edward Mayo.

Shortly before day General Ewell rode in person to my headquarters and informed me that General G.W.C. Lee was then crossing the pontoon at Drewry's; that he would destroy it and press on to join the main army; that all the bridges over the river had been destroyed, except Mayo's, between Richmond and Manchester, and that the wagon bridge over the canal in front of Mayo's had already been burned by Union emissaries. My command was to hasten to Mayo's bridge and protect it, and the one remaining foot-bridge over the canal leading to it, until General Gary, of South Carolina, should arrive. I hurried to my command, and fifteen minutes later occupied Mayo's bridge, at the foot of 14th street, and made military dispositions to protect it to the last extremity. This done, I had nothing to do but listen for sounds and gaze on the terrible splendor of the scene. And such a scene probably the world has seldom witnessed. Either incendiaries, or (more probably) fragments of bombs from the arsenals, had fired various buildings, and the two cities, Richmond and Manchester, were like a blaze of day amid the surrounding darkness. Three high arched bridges were in flames; beneath them the waters sparkled and dashed and rushed on by the burning city. Every now and then, as a magazine exploded, a column of white smoke rose up as high as the eye could reach, instantaneously followed by a deafening sound. The earth seemed to rock and tremble as with the shock of an earthquake, and immediately afterward hundreds of shells would explode in air and send their iron spray down far below the bridge. As the immense magazines of cartridges ignited the rattle as of thousands of musketry would follow, and then all was still for the moment, except the dull roar and crackle of the fast-spreading fires. At dawn we heard terrific explosions about "The Rocketts," from the unfinished iron-clads down the river.

By daylight, on the 3d, a mob of men, women, and children, to the number of several thousands, had gathered at the corner of 14th and Cary streets and other outlets, in front of the bridge, attracted by the vast commissary depot at that point; for it must be remembered that in 1865 Richmond was a half-starved city, and the Confederate Government had that morning removed its guards and abandoned the removal of the provisions, which was impossible for the want of transportation. The depot doors were forced open and a demoniacal struggle for the countless barrels of hams, bacon, whisky, flour, sugar, coffee, etc., etc., raged about the buildings among the hungry mob. The gutters ran whisky, and it was lapped as it flowed down the streets, while all fought for a share of the plunder. The flames came nearer and nearer, and at last caught in the commissariat itself.

At daylight the approach of the Union forces could be plainly discerned. After a little came the clatter of horses' hoofs galloping up Main street. My infantry guard stood to arms, the picket across the canal was withdrawn, and the engineer officer lighted a torch of fat pine. By direction of the Engineer Department barrels of tar, surrounded by pine-knots, had been placed at intervals on the bridge, with kerosene at hand, and a lieutenant of engineers had reported for the duty of firing them at my order. The noisy train proved to be Gary's ambulances, sent forward preparatory to his final rush for the bridge. The muleteers galloped their animals about half-way down, when they were stopped by the dense mass of human beings. Rapidly communicating to Captain Mayo my instructions from General Ewell, I ordered that officer to stand firm at his post until Gary got up. I rode forward into the mob and cleared a lane. The ambulances were galloped down to the bridge, I retired to my post, and the mob closed in after me and resumed its wild struggle for plunder. A few minutes later a long line of cavalry in gray turned into 14th street, and sword in hand galloped straight down to the river; Gary had come. The mob scattered right and left before the armed horsemen, who reined up at the canal. Presently a single company of cavalry appeared in sight, and rode at headlong speed to the bridge. "My rear-guard," explained Gary. Touching his hat to me he called out, "All over, good-bye; blow her to h—ll," and trotted over the bridge. That was the first and last I ever saw of General Gary, of South Carolina.

In less than sixty seconds Captain Mayo was in column of march, and as he reached the little island about half-way across the bridge, the single piece of artillery, loaded with grape-shot, that had occupied that spot, arrived on the Manchester side of the river. The engineer officer, Dr. Lyons, and I walked leisurely to the island, setting fire to the provided combustible matter as we passed along, and leaving the north section of Mayo's bridge wrapped in flame and smoke. At the island we stopped to take a view of the situation north of the river, and saw a line of blue-coated horsemen galloping in furious haste up Main street. Across 14th street they stopped, and then dashed down 14th street to the flaming bridge. They fired a few random shots at us three on the island, and we retreated to Manchester. I ordered my command forward, the lieutenant of engineers saluted and went about his business, and myself and my companion sat on our horses for nearly a half-hour, watching the occupation of Richmond. We saw another string of horsemen in blue pass up Main street, then we saw a dense column of infantry march by, seemingly without end; we heard the very welkin ring with cheers as the United States forces reached Capitol Square, and then we turned and slowly rode on our way.

II. THE OCCUPATION.

Thomas Thatcher Graves, Aide-de-Camp on the Staff of Gen. Weitzel.

In the spring of 1865 the total length of the lines of the Army of the James before Richmond (under General Godfrey Weitzel, commanding the Twenty-fifth Corps) was about eleven miles, not counting the cavalry front, and extended from the Appomattox River to the north side of the James. The Varina and New Market turnpikes passed directly through the lines into the city, which was the center of all our efforts.

About 2 o'clock on the morning of April 3d bright fires were seen in the direction of Richmond. Shortly after, while we were looking at these fires, we heard explosions, and soon a prisoner was sent in by General Kautz. The prisoner was a colored teamster, and he informed us that immediately after dark the enemy had begun making preparations to leave, and that they were sending all of the teams to the rear. A forward movement of our entire picket-line corroborated this report. As soon as it was light General Weitzel ordered Colonel E. E. Graves, senior aide-de-camp, and Major Atherton H. Stevens, Jr., provost-marshal, to take a detachment of forty men from the two companies (E and H) of the 4th Massachusetts Cavalry, and make a reconnoissance. Slowly this little band of scouts picked their way in. Soon after we moved up the New Market road at a slow pace.

As we approached the inner line of defenses we saw in the distance divisions of our troops, many of them upon the double-quick, aiming to be the first in the city; a white and a colored division were having a regular race, the white troops on the turnpike and the colored in the fields. As we neared the city the fires seemed to increase in number and size, and at intervals loud explosions were heard.

On entering we found Capitol Square covered with people who had fled there to escape the fire and were utterly worn out with fatigue and fright. Details were at once made to scour the city and press into service every able-bodied man, white or black, and make them assist in extinguishing the flames. General Devens's division marched into the city, stacked arms, and went to work. Parsons's engineer company assisted by blowing up houses to check its advance, as about every engine was destroyed or rendered useless by the mob. In this manner the fire was extinguished and perfect order restored in an incredibly short time after we occupied the city.^Ψ There was absolutely no plundering upon the part of our soldiers; orders were issued forbidding anything to be taken without remuneration, and no complaints were made of infringement of these orders. General G. F. Shepley was placed on duty as military governor. He had occupied a similar position in New Orleans after its capture in 1862, and was eminently fitted for it by education and experience. As we entered the suburbs the general ordered me to take half a dozen cavalrymen and go to Libby Prison, for our thoughts were upon the wretched men whom we supposed were still confined within its walls. It was very early in the morning, and we were the first Union troops to arrive before Libby. Not a guard, not an inmate remained; the doors were wide open, and only a few negroes greeted us with, "Dey's all gone, massa!"

The next day after our entry into the city, on passing out from Clay street, from Jefferson Davis's house, I saw a crowd coming, headed by President Lincoln, who was walking with his usual long, careless stride, and looking about with an interested air and taking in everything. Upon my saluting he said: "Is it far to President Davis's house?" I accompanied him to the house, which was occupied by General Weitzel as headquarters. The President had arrived about 9 o'clock, at the landing called Rocketts, upon Admiral Porter's flag-ship, the *Malvern,* and as soon as the boat was made fast, without ceremony, he walked on shore, and started off uptown. As soon as Admiral Porter was informed of it he ordered a guard of marines to follow as escort; but in the walk of about two miles they never saw him, and he was directed by negroes. At the Davis house, he was shown into the reception-room, with the remark that the housekeeper had said that that room was President Davis's office. As he seated himself he remarked, "This must have been President Davis's chair," and, crossing his legs, he looked far off with a serious, dreamy expression. At length he asked me if the

---

^ΨAs one of our aides was riding through the streets, engaged in gathering together the able-bodied men to assist in extinguishing the fire, he was hailed by a servant in front of a house, toward which the fire seemed to be moving. The servant told him that his mistress wished to speak to him. He dismounted and entered the house, and was met by a lady, who stated that her mother was an invalid, confined to her bed, and as the fire seemed to be approaching she asked for assistance. The subsequent conversation developed the fact that the invalid was no other than the wife of General R. E. Lee, and the lady who addressed the aide was her daughter, Miss Lee. An ambulance was furnished by Colonel E. H. Ripley, of the 9th Vermont, and a corporal and two men guarded them until all danger was past.—T.T.G.

CITIZENS OF RICHMOND IN CAPITOL SQUARE DURING THE CONFLAGRATION.

housekeeper was in the house. Upon learning that she had left he jumped up and said, with a boyish manner, "Come, let's look at the house!" We went pretty much over it; I retailed all that the housekeeper had told me, and he seemed interested in everything. As we came down the staircase General Weitzel came, in breathless haste, and at once President Lincoln's face lost its boyish expression as he realized that *duty* must be resumed. Soon afterward Judge Campbell, General Anderson (Confederates), and others called and asked for an interview with the President. It was granted, and took place in the parlor with closed doors.

I accompanied President Lincoln and General Weitzel to Libby Prison and Castle Thunder, and heard General Weitzel ask President Lincoln what he (General Weitzel) should do in regard to the conquered people. President Lincoln replied that he did not wish to give any orders on that subject, but, as he expressed it, "If I were in your place I'd let 'em up easy, let 'em up easy."

A few days after our entry General R. E. Lee surrendered, and early one morning we learned that he had just arrived at his house in the city. General Weitzel called me into a private room, and, taking out a large, well-filled pocket-book, said, "Go to General Lee's house, find Fitzhugh Lee, and say that his old West Point chum Godfrey Weitzel wishes to know if he needs anything, and urge him to take what he may need from that pocket-book." Upon reaching General Lee's house I knocked, and General Fitzhugh Lee came to the door. He was dressed in a Confederate uniform. Upon introducing myself he asked me in, showing me into a parlor with double or folding doors, explaining that the servants had not returned. He was so overcome by Weitzel's message that for a moment he was obliged to walk to the other end of the room. He excused

PRESIDENT LINCOLN LEAVING THE DAVIS MANSION. FROM A SKETCH MADE AT THE TIME.

himself, and passed into the inner room, where I noticed General R. E. Lee sitting, with a tired, worn expression upon his face. Fitzhugh Lee knelt beside his general, as he sat leaning over, and placed a hand upon his knee.

After a few moments he came back, and in a most dignified and courteous manner sent his love to Godfrey Weitzel, and assured him that he did not require any loan of money, but if it would be entirely proper for *Godfrey* Weitzel to issue a pass for some ladies of General Lee's household to return to the city it would be esteemed a favor; but he impressed me to state that if this would embarrass *General* Weitzel, on no account would they request the favor. It is needless to state that the ladies were back in the house as soon as possible.

CHAPTER 6

THE SURRENDER AT APPOMATTOX COURT HOUSE.

Horace Porter, Brevet Brigadier-General, U.S.A.

A little before noon on the 7th of April, 1865, General Grant, with his staff, rode into the little village of Farmville, on the south side of the Appomattox River, a town that will be memorable in history as the place where he opened the correspondence with Lee which led to the surrender of the Army of Northern Virginia. He drew up in front of the village hotel, dismounted, and established headquarters on its broad piazza. News came in that Crook was fighting large odds with his cavalry on the north side of the river, and I was directed to go to his front and see what was necessary to be done to assist him. I found that he was being driven back, the enemy (Munford's and Rosser's cavalry divisions under Fitzhugh Lee) having made a bold stand north of the river. Humphreys was also on the north side, isolated from the rest of our infantry, confronted by a large portion of Lee's army, and having some very heavy fighting. On my return to general headquarters that evening Wright's corps was ordered to cross the river and move rapidly to the support of our troops there. Notwithstanding their long march that day, the men sprang to their feet with a spirit that made every one marvel at their pluck, and came swinging through the main street of the village with a step that seemed as elastic as on the first day of their toilsome tramp. It was now dark, but they spied the general-in-chief watching them with evident pride from the piazza of the hotel.

Then was witnessed one of the most inspiring scenes of the campaign. Bonfires were lighted on the sides of the street, the men seized straw and pine knots, and improvised torches; cheers arose from throats already hoarse with shouts of victory, bands played, banners waved, arms were tossed high in air and caught again. The night march had become a grand review, with Grant as the reviewing officer.

Ord and Gibbon had visited the general at the hotel, and he had spoken with them as well as with Wright about sending some communication to Lee

APPOMATTOX COURT HOUSE. FROM A WAR-TIME PHOTOGRAPH.

that might pave the way to the stopping of further bloodshed. Dr. Smith, formerly of the regular army, a native of Virginia and a relative of General Ewell, now one of our prisoners, had told General Grant the night before that Ewell had said in conversation that their cause was lost when they crossed the James River, and he considered that it was the duty of the authorities to negotiate for peace then, while they still had a right to claim concessions, adding that now they were not in condition to claim anything. He said that for every man killed after this somebody would be responsible, and it would be little better than murder. He could not tell what General Lee would do, but he hoped he would at once surrender his army. This statement, together with the news that had been received from Sheridan saying that he had heard that General Lee's trains of provisions which had come by rail were at Appomattox, and that he expected to capture them before Lee could reach them, induced the general to write the following communication:

> "HEADQUARTERS, ARMIES OF THE U.S.
> "5 P.M., April 7th, 1865.
>
> "GENERAL R. E. LEE, Commanding C.S.A.:
>
> "The results of the last week must convince you of the hopelessness of further resistance on the part of the Army of Northern Virginia in this struggle. I feel that it is so, and regard it as my duty to shift from myself the responsibility of any further effusion of blood by asking of you the surrender of that portion of the Confederate States army known as the Army of Northern Virginia.
>
> "U. S. GRANT, Lieutenant-General."

This he intrusted to General Seth Williams, adjutant-general, with directions to take it to Humphreys's front, as his corps was close up to the enemy's rear-guard, and have it sent into Lee's lines. The general decided to remain all night at Farmville and await the reply from Lee, and he was shown to a room in the hotel in which, he was told, Lee had slept the night before. Lee wrote the following reply within an hour after he received General Grant's letter, but it was brought in by rather a circuitous route and did not reach its destination till after midnight:

"APRIL 7TH, 1865.

"GENERAL: I have received your note of this date. Though not entertaining the opinion you express of the hopelessness of further resistance on the part of the Army of Northern Virginia, I reciprocate your desire to avoid useless effusion of blood, and therefore, before considering your proposition, ask the terms you will offer on condition of its surrender.

"R. E. LEE, General.

"LIEUTENANT-GENERAL U. S. GRANT,
Commanding Armies of the U.S."

The next morning before leaving Farmville the following reply was given to General Williams, who again went to Humphreys's front to have it transmitted to Lee:

"APRIL 8TH, 1865.

"GENERAL R. E. LEE, Commanding C.S.A.:

"Your note of last evening in reply to mine of the same date, asking the conditions on which I will accept the surrender of the Army of Northern Virginia, is just received. In reply I would say that, peace being my great desire, there is but one condition I would insist upon,—namely, that the men and officers surrendered shall be disqualified for taking up arms against the Government of the United States until properly exchanged. I will meet you, or will designate officers to meet any officers you may name for the same purpose, at any point agreeable to you, for the purpose of arranging definitely the terms upon which the surrender of the Army of Northern Virginia will be received.

"U. S. GRANT, Lieutenant-General."

There turned up at this time a rather hungry-looking gentleman in gray, in the uniform of a colonel, who proclaimed himself the proprietor of the hotel. He said his regiment had crumbled to pieces, he was the only man left in it, and he thought he might as well "stop off" at home. His story was significant as indicating the disintegrating process that was going on in the ranks of the enemy.

General Grant had been marching most of the way with the columns that were pushing along south of Lee's line of retreat; but expecting that a reply would be sent to his last letter and wanting to keep within easy communication with Lee, he decided to march this day with the portion of the Army of the Potomac that was pressing Lee's rear-guard. After issuing some further instructions to Ord and Sheridan, he started from Farmville, crossed to the north side of the Appomattox, conferred in person with Meade, and rode with his columns. Encouraging reports came in all day, and that night headquarters were established at Curdsville in a large white farm-house, a few hundred yards from Meade's camp. The general and several of the staff had cut loose from the headquarters trains the night he started to meet Sheridan at Jetersville, and had neither baggage nor camp-equipage. The general did not even have his sword with him. This was the most advanced effort yet made at moving in "light marching order," and we billeted ourselves at night in farm-houses, or bivouacked on porches, and picked up meals at any camp that seemed to have something to spare in the way of rations. This night we sampled the fare of Meade's hospitable mess and once more lay down with full stomachs.

General Grant had been suffering all the afternoon from a severe headache, the result of fatigue, anxiety, scant fare, and loss of sleep, and by night it was much worse. He had been induced to bathe his feet in hot water and mustard, and apply mustard plasters to his wrists and the back of his neck, but these remedies afforded little relief. The dwelling we occupied was a double house. The general threw himself upon a sofa in the sitting-room on the left side of the hall, while the staff-officers bunked on the floor of the room opposite to catch what sleep they could. About midnight we were aroused by Colonel Charles A. Whittier of Humphreys's staff, who brought another let-

THE VILLAGE OF APPOMATTOX COURT HOUSE, THE MCLEAN HOUSE ON THE RIGHT.
FROM A WAR-TIME SKETCH.

ter from Lee. Rawlins at once took it in to General Grant's room. It was as
follows:

"April 8th, 1865.

"General: I received at a late hour your note of to-day. In mine of
yesterday I did not intend to propose the surrender of the Army of Northern Virginia, but to ask the terms of your proposition. To be frank, I do not
think the emergency has arisen to call for the surrender of this army, but,
as the restoration of peace should be the sole object of all, I desired to
know whether your proposals would lead to that end. I cannot, therefore,
meet you with a view to surrender the Army of Northern Virginia; but as
far as your proposal may affect the Confederate States forces under my
command,‡ and tend to the restoration of peace, I should be pleased to
meet you at 10 A.M. to-morrow on the old stage road to Richmond, between the picket-lines of the two armies.

"R. E. Lee, General.

"Lieutenant-General U. S. Grant."

General Grant had been able to get but very little sleep. He now sat up and
read the letter, and after making a few comments upon it to General Rawlins
lay down again on the sofa.

About 4 o'clock on the morning of the 9th I rose and crossed the hall to ascertain how the general was feeling. I found his room empty, and upon going
out of the front door saw him pacing up and down in the yard holding both
hands to his head. Upon inquiring how he felt, he replied that he had had very
little sleep, and was still suffering the most excruciating pain. I said: "Well, there
is one consolation in all this, General: I never knew you to be ill that you did not
receive some good news. I have become a little superstitious regarding these
coincidences, and I should not be surprised if some good fortune overtook you
before night." He smiled and said: "The best thing that can happen to me to-day
is to get rid of the pain I am suffering." We were soon joined by some others of
the staff, and the general was induced to go over to Meade's headquarters with
us and get some coffee, in the hope that it would do him good. He seemed to
feel a little better now, and after writing the following letter to Lee and dispatching it he prepared to move forward. The letter was as follows:

"April 9th, 1865.

"General: Your note of yesterday is received. I have no authority to
treat on the subject of peace. The meeting proposed for 10 A.M. to-day

‡Since February 9th, 1865, Lee had been general-in-chief of all the Confederate armies, and, evidently,
was aiming here at a treaty of peace and general surrender.—Editors.

could lead to no good. I will state, however, that I am equally desirous for peace with yourself, and the whole North entertains the same feeling. The terms upon which peace can be had are well understood. By the South laying down their arms, they would hasten that most desirable event, save thousands of human lives, and hundreds of millions of property not yet destroyed. Seriously hoping that all our difficulties may be settled without the loss of another life, I subscribe myself, etc.,

"U. S. GRANT, Lieutenant-General.
"GENERAL R. E. LEE."

It was proposed to him to ride during the day in a covered ambulance which was at hand, instead of on horseback, so as to avoid the intense heat of the sun, but this he declined to do, and soon after mounted "Cincinnati" and struck off toward New Store. From that point he went by way of a cross-road to the south side of the Appomattox with the intention of moving around to Sheridan's front. While riding along the wagon road that runs from Farmville to Appomattox Court House, at a point eight or nine miles east of the latter place, Lieutenant Charles E. Pease of Meade's staff overtook him with a dispatch. It was found to be a reply from Lee, which had been sent in to our lines on Humphreys's front. It read as follows:

"APRIL 9TH, 1865.

"GENERAL: I received your note of this morning on the picket-line, whither I had come to meet you and ascertain definitely what terms were embraced in your proposal of yesterday with reference to the surrender of this army. I now ask an interview, in accordance with the offer contained in your letter of yesterday, for that purpose.

"R. E. LEE, General.
"LIEUTENANT-GENERAL U. S. GRANT."

Pease also brought a note from Meade, saying that at Lee's request he had read the communication addressed to General Grant and in consequence of it had granted a short truce.

The general, as soon as he had read these letters, dismounted, sat down on the grassy bank by the roadside, and wrote the following reply to Lee:

"APRIL 9TH, 1865.

"GENERAL R. E. LEE, Commanding C.S. Army:

"Your note of this date is but this moment (11:50 A.M.) received, in consequence of my having passed from the Richmond and Lynchburg road to the Farmville and Lynchburg road. I am at this writing about four miles west of Walker's Church, and will push forward to the front for the purpose of meeting you. Notice sent to me on this road where you wish the interview to take place will meet me.

"U. S. GRANT, Lieutenant-General."

He handed this to Colonel Babcock of the staff, with directions to take it to General Lee by the most direct route. Mounting his horse again the general rode on at a trot toward Appomattox Court House. When five or six miles from the town, Colonel Newhall, Sheridan's adjutant-general, came riding up from the direction of Appomattox and handed the general a communication. This proved to be a duplicate of the letter from Lee that Lieutenant Pease had brought in from Meade's lines. Lee was so closely pressed that he was anxious to communicate with Grant by the most direct means, and as he could not tell with which column Grant was moving he sent in one copy of his letter on Meade's front and one on Sheridan's. Colonel Newhall joined our party, and after a few minutes' halt to read the letter we continued our ride toward Appomattox. On the march I had asked the general several times how he felt. To the same question now he said, "The pain in my head seemed to leave me the moment I got Lee's letter." The road was filled with men, animals, and wagons, and to avoid these and shorten the distance we turned slightly to the right and began to "cut across lots"; but before going far we spied men conspicuous in gray, and it was seen that we were moving toward the enemy's left flank, and that a short ride farther would take us into his lines. It looked for a moment as if a very awkward condition of things might possibly arise, and Grant become a prisoner in Lee's lines instead of Lee in his. Such a circumstance would have given rise to an important cross-entry in the system of campaign bookkeeping. There was only one remedy—to retrace our steps and strike the right road, which was done without serious discussion. About 1 o'clock the little village of Appomattox Court House, with its half-dozen houses, came in sight, and soon we were entering its single street. It is situated on some rising ground, and beyond the country slopes down into a broad valley. The enemy was seen with his columns and wagon trains covering the low ground. Our cavalry, the Fifth Corps, and part of Ord's command were occupying the high ground to the south and west of the enemy, heading him off completely. Generals Sheridan and Ord, with a group of officers around them, were seen in the road, and as our party came up General Grant said: "How are you, Sheridan?" "First-rate, thank you; how are you?" cried Sheridan, with a voice and look that seemed to indicate that on his part he was having things all his own way. "Is Lee over there?" asked General Grant, pointing up the street, having heard a rumor that Lee was in that vicinity. "Yes, he is in that brick house," answered Sheridan. "Well, then, we'll go over," said Grant.

The general-in-chief now rode on, accompanied by Sheridan, Ord, and some others, and soon Colonel Babcock's orderly was seen sitting on his horse

MCLEAN'S HOUSE, APPOMATTOX COURT HOUSE. FROM A PHOTOGRAPH.

in the street in front of a two-story brick house, better in appearance than the rest of the houses. He said General Lee and Colonel Babcock had gone into this house a short time before, and he was ordered to post himself in the street and keep a lookout for General Grant, so as to let him know where General Lee was. Babcock told me afterward that in carrying General Grant's last letter he passed through the enemy's lines and found General Lee a little more than half a mile beyond Appomattox Court House. He was lying down by the roadside on a blanket which had been spread over a few fence rails on the ground under an apple-tree, which was part of an orchard. This circumstance furnished the only ground for the widespread report that the surrender occurred under an apple-tree. Babcock dismounted upon coming near, and as he approached on foot, Lee sat up, with his feet hanging over the roadside embankment. The wheels of the wagons in passing along the road had cut away the earth of this embankment and left the roots of the tree projecting. Lee's feet were partly resting on these roots. One of his staff-officers came forward, took the dispatch which Babcock handed him and gave it to General Lee. After reading it, the general rose and said he would ride forward on the road on which Babcock had come, but was apprehensive that hostilities might begin in the meantime, upon the termination of the temporary truce, and asked Babcock to write a line to

Meade informing him of the situation. Babcock wrote accordingly, requesting Meade to maintain the truce until positive orders from General Grant could be received. To save time it was arranged that a Union officer, accompanied by one of Lee's officers, should carry this letter through the enemy's lines. This route made the distance to Meade nearly ten miles shorter than by the roundabout way of the Union lines. Lee now mounted his horse and directed Colonel Charles Marshall, his military secretary, to accompany him. They started for Appomattox Court House in company with Babcock and followed by a mounted orderly. When the party reached the village they met one of its residents, named Wilmer McLean, who was told that General Lee wanted to occupy a convenient room in some house in the town. McLean ushered them into the sitting-room of one of the first houses he came to, but upon looking about and finding it quite small and meagerly furnished, Lee proposed finding something more commodious and better fitted for the occasion. McLean then conducted the party to his own house, about the best one in the town, where they awaited General Grant's arrival.

The house had a comfortable wooden porch with seven steps leading up to it. A hall ran through the middle from front to back, and on each side was a room having two windows, one in front and one in rear. Each room had two doors opening into the hall. The building stood a little distance back from the street, with a yard in front, and to the left was a gate for carriages and a roadway running to a stable in rear. We entered the grounds by this gate and dismounted. In the yard were seen a fine large gray horse, which proved to be General Lee's, and a good-looking mare belonging to Colonel Marshall. An orderly in gray was in charge of them, and had taken off their bridles to let them nibble the grass.

General Grant mounted the steps and entered the house. As he stepped into the hall Colonel Babcock, who had seen his approach from the window, opened the door of the room on the left, in which he had been sitting with General Lee and Colonel Marshall awaiting General Grant's arrival. The general passed in, while the members of the staff, Generals Sheridan and Ord, and some general officers who had gathered in the front yard, remained outside, feeling that he would probably want his first interview with General Lee to be, in a measure, private. In a few minutes Colonel Babcock came to the front door and, making a motion with his hat toward the sitting-room, said: "The general says, come in." It was then about half-past one of Sunday, the 9th of April. We entered, and found General Grant sitting at a marble-topped table in the center of the room, and Lee sitting beside a small oval table near the front window, in the corner opposite to the door by which we entered, and facing General Grant. Colonel Marshall, his military secretary, was standing at his left. We walked in softly and ranged ourselves quietly about the sides of the room, very much as people enter a sick-chamber when they expect to find the patient dan-

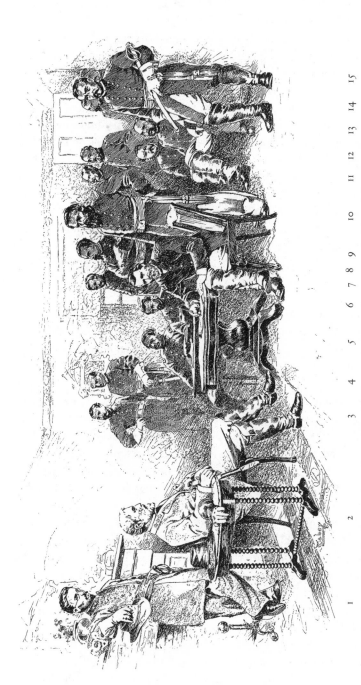

THE SURRENDER AT APPOMATTOX; BASED UPON THE LITHOGRAPH CALLED "THE DAWN OF PEACE." BY PERMISSION OF W. H. STELLE.

2. General Robert E. Lee. 1. Colonel Charles Marshall, of General Lee's Staff. 8. Lieutenant-General Ulysses S. Grant. 15. Major-General Philip H. Sheridan. 7. Major-General Edward O. C. Ord. 14. Brevet Major-General Rufus Ingalls. 10. Brigadier-General John A. Rawlins, Chief-of-Staff; other members of General Grant's Staff: 4. Major-General Seth Williams. 12. Brevet Major-General John G. Barnard. 9. Colonel Horace Porter. 3. Colonel Orville E. Babcock. 5. Colonel Ely S. Parker. 6. Colonel Theodore S. Bowers. 11. Colonel Frederick T. Dent. 13. Colonel Adam Badeau.

gerously ill. Some found seats on the sofa and the few chairs which constituted the furniture, but most of the party stood.

The contrast between the two commanders was striking, and could not fail to attract marked attention as they sat ten feet apart facing each other. General Grant, then nearly forty-three years of age, was five feet eight inches in height, with shoulders slightly stooped. His hair and full beard were a nut-brown, without a trace of gray in them. He had on a single-breasted blouse, made of dark-blue flannel, unbuttoned in front, and showing a waistcoat underneath. He wore an ordinary pair of top-boots, with his trousers inside, and was without spurs. The boots and portions of his clothes were spattered with mud. He had had on a pair of thread gloves, of a dark-yellow color, which he had taken off on entering the room. His felt "sugar-loaf" stiff-brimmed hat was thrown on the table beside him. He had no sword, and a pair of shoulder-straps was all there was about him to designate his rank. In fact, aside from these, his uniform was that of a private soldier.

Lee, on the other hand, was fully six feet in height, and quite erect for one of his age, for he was Grant's senior by sixteen years. His hair and full beard were a silver-gray, and quite thick, except that the hair had become a little thin in front. He wore a new uniform of Confederate gray, buttoned up to the throat, and at his side he carried a long sword of exceedingly fine workmanship, the hilt studded with jewels. It was said to be the sword that had been presented to him by the State of Virginia. His top-boots were comparatively new, and seemed to have on them some ornamental stitching of red silk. Like his uniform, they were singularly clean, and but little travel-stained. On the boots were handsome spurs, with large rowels. A felt hat, which in color matched pretty closely that of his uniform, and a pair of long buckskin gauntlets lay beside him on the table. We asked Colonel Marshall afterward how it was that both he and his chief wore such fine toggery, and looked so much as if they had turned out to go to church, while with us our outward garb scarcely rose to the dignity even of the "shabby-genteel." He enlightened us regarding the contrast, by explaining that when their headquarters wagons had been pressed so closely by our cavalry a few days before, and it was found they would have to destroy all their baggage, except the clothes they carried on their backs, each one, naturally, selected the newest suit he had, and sought to propitiate the god of destruction by a sacrifice of his second-best.

General Grant began the conversation by saying: "I met you once before, General Lee, while we were serving in Mexico, when you came over from General Scott's headquarters to visit Garland's brigade, to which I then belonged. I have always remembered your appearance, and I think I should have recognized you anywhere." "Yes," replied General Lee, "I know I met you on that occasion, and I have often thought of it and tried to recollect how you looked, but I have never been able to recall a single feature." After some further mention of

Mexico, General Lee said: "I suppose, General Grant, that the object of our present meeting is fully understood. I asked to see you to ascertain upon what terms you would receive the surrender of my army." General Grant replied: "The terms I propose are those stated substantially in my letter of yesterday,— that is, the officers and men surrendered to be paroled and disqualified from taking up arms again until properly exchanged, and all arms, ammunition, and supplies to be delivered up as captured property." Lee nodded an assent, and said: "Those are about the conditions which I expected would be proposed." General Grant then continued: "Yes, I think our correspondence indicated pretty clearly the action that would be taken at our meeting; and I hope it may lead to a general suspension of hostilities and be the means of preventing any further loss of life."

Lee inclined his head as indicating his accord with this wish, and General Grant then went on to talk at some length in a very pleasant vein about the prospects of peace. Lee was evidently anxious to proceed to the formal work of the surrender, and he brought the subject up again by saying:

"I presume, General Grant, we have both carefully considered the proper steps to be taken, and I would suggest that you commit to writing the terms you have proposed, so that they may be formally acted upon."

"Very well," replied General Grant, "I will write them out." And calling for his manifold order-book, he opened it on the table before him and proceeded to write the terms. The leaves had been so prepared that three impressions of the writing were made. He wrote very rapidly, and did not pause until he had finished the sentence ending with "officers appointed by me to receive them." Then he looked toward Lee, and his eyes seemed to be resting on the handsome sword that hung at that officer's side. He said afterward that this set him to thinking that it would be an unnecessary humiliation to require the officers to surrender their swords, and a great hardship to deprive them of their personal baggage and horses, and after a short pause he wrote the sentence: "This will not embrace the side-arms of the officers, nor their private horses or baggage." When he had finished the letter he called Colonel (afterward General) Ely S. Parker, one of the military secretaries on the staff, to his side and looked it over with him and directed him as they went along to interline six or seven words and to strike out the word "their," which had been repeated. When this had been done, he handed the book to General Lee and asked him to read over the letter. It was as follows:

"Appomattox Ct. H., Va.
"April 9, 1865.

"General R. E. Lee, Commanding C.S.A.:

"General: In accordance with the substance of my letter to you of the 8th inst., I propose to receive the surrender of the Army of Northern

FAC-SIMILE OF THE CONCLUSION OF A NOTE FROM GENERAL GRANT
TO MR. T. D. JEFFREES IN REPLY TO A QUESTION.

Virginia on the following terms, to wit: Rolls of all the officers and men to be made in duplicate, one copy to be given to an officer to be designated by me, the other to be retained by such officer or officers as you may designate. The officers to give their individual paroles not to take up arms against the Government of the United States until properly [exchanged], and each company or regimental commander to sign a like parole for the men of their commands. The arms, artillery, and public property to be parked, and stacked, and turned over to the officers appointed by me to receive them. This will not embrace the side-arms of the officers, nor their private horses or baggage. This done, each officer and man will be allowed to return to his home, not to be disturbed by the United States authorities so long as they observe their paroles, and the laws in force where they may reside. Very respectfully,

"U. S. Grant, Lieutenant-General."

Lee took it and laid it on the table beside him, while he drew from his pocket a pair of steel-rimmed spectacles and wiped the glasses carefully with his handkerchief. Then he crossed his legs, adjusted the spectacles very slowly and deliberately, took up the draft of the letter, and proceeded to read it attentively. It consisted of two pages. When he reached the top line of the second page, he looked up, and said to General Grant: "After the words 'until properly,' the word 'exchanged' seems to be omitted. You doubtless intended to use that word."

"Why, yes," said Grant; "I thought I had put in the word 'exchanged.'"

"I presumed it had been omitted inadvertently," continued Lee, "and with your permission I will mark where it should be inserted."

"Certainly," Grant replied.

Lee felt in his pocket as if searching for a pencil, but did not seem to be able to find one. Seeing this and happening to be standing close to him, I handed him my pencil. He took it, and laying the paper on the table noted the interlineation. During the rest of the interview he kept twirling this pencil in his fingers and occasionally tapping the top of the table with it. When he handed it back it was carefully treasured by me as a memento of the occasion. When Lee came to the sentence about the officers' side-arms, private horses, and baggage, he showed for the first time during the reading of the letter a slight change of countenance, and was evidently touched by this act of generosity. It was doubtless the condition mentioned to which he particularly alluded when he looked toward General Grant as he finished reading and said with some degree of warmth in his manner: "This will have a very happy effect upon my army."

General Grant then said: "Unless you have some suggestions to make in regard to the form in which I have stated the terms, I will have a copy of the letter made in ink and sign it."

"There is one thing I would like to mention," Lee replied after a short pause. "The cavalrymen and artillerists own their own horses in our army. Its organization in this respect differs from that of the United States." This expression attracted the notice of our officers present, as showing how firmly the conviction was grounded in his mind that we were two distinct countries. He continued: "I would like to understand whether these men will be permitted to retain their horses?"

"You will find that the terms as written do not allow this," General Grant replied; "only the officers are permitted to take their private property."

Lee read over the second page of the letter again, and then said:

"No, I see the terms do not allow it; that is clear." His face showed plainly that he was quite anxious to have this concession made, and Grant said very promptly and without giving Lee time to make a direct request:

"Well, the subject is quite new to me. Of course I did not know that any private soldiers owned their animals, but I think this will be the last battle of the war—I sincerely hope so—and that the surrender of this army will be followed soon by that of all the others, and I take it that most of the men in the ranks are small farmers, and as the country has been so raided by the two armies, it is doubtful whether they will be able to put in a crop to carry themselves and their families through the next winter without the aid of the horses they are now riding, and I will arrange it in this way: I will not change the terms as now written, but I will instruct the officers I shall appoint to receive the paroles to let all the men who claim to own a horse or mule take the animals home with them to work their little farms." (This expression has been quoted in various forms and has been the subject of some dispute. I give the exact words used.)

Lee now looked greatly relieved, and though anything but a demonstrative man, he gave every evidence of his appreciation of this concession, and said, "This will have the best possible effect upon the men. It will be very gratifying and will do much toward conciliating our people." He handed the draft of the terms back to General Grant, who called Colonel T. S. Bowers of the staff to him and directed him to make a copy in ink. Bowers was a little nervous, and he turned the matter over to Colonel (afterward General) Parker, whose handwriting presented a better appearance than that of any one else on the staff. Parker sat down to write at the table which stood against the rear side of the room. Wilmer McLean's domestic resources in the way of ink now became the subject of a searching investigation, but it was found that the contents of the conical-shaped stoneware inkstand which he produced appeared to be participating in the general breaking up and had disappeared. Colonel Marshall now came to the rescue, and pulled out of his pocket a small box-wood inkstand, which was put at Parker's service, so that, after all, we had to fall back upon the resources of the enemy in furnishing the stage "properties" for the final scene in the memorable military drama.

Lee in the meantime had directed Colonel Marshall to draw up for his signature a letter of acceptance of the terms of surrender. Colonel Marshall wrote out a draft of such a letter, making it quite formal, beginning with "I have the honor to reply to your communication," etc. General Lee took it, and, after reading it over very carefully, directed that these formal expressions be stricken out and that the letter be otherwise shortened. He afterward went over it again and seemed to change some words, and then told the colonel to make a final copy in ink. When it came to providing the paper, it was found we had the only supply of that important ingredient in the recipe for surrendering an army, so we gave a few pages to the colonel. The letter when completed read as follows:

"HEADQUARTERS,
Army of Northern Virginia
"April 9th, 1865.

"GENERAL: I received your letter of this date containing the terms of the surrender of the Army of Northern Virginia as proposed by you. As they are substantially the same as those expressed in your letter of the 8th inst., they are accepted. I will proceed to designate the proper officers to carry the stipulations into effect.

"R. E. LEE, General.
"LIEUTENANT-GENERAL U. S. GRANT."

While the letters were being copied, General Grant introduced the general officers who had entered, and each member of the staff, to General Lee. The General shook hands with General Seth Williams, who had been his adjutant when Lee was superintendent at West Point, some years before the war, and gave his hand to some of the other officers who had extended theirs, but to most of those who were introduced he merely bowed in a dignified and formal manner. He did not exhibit the slightest change of features during this ceremony until Colonel Parker of our staff was presented to him. Parker was a full-blooded Indian, and the reigning Chief of the Six Nations. When Lee saw his swarthy features he looked at him with evident surprise, and his eyes rested on him for several seconds. What was passing in his mind probably no one ever knew, but the natural surmise was that he at first mistook Parker for a negro, and was struck with astonishment to find that the commander of the Union armies had one of that race on his personal staff.

Lee did not utter a word while the introductions were going on, except to Seth Williams, with whom he talked quite cordially. Williams at one time referred in rather jocose a manner to a circumstance which occurred during their former service together, as if he wanted to say something in a good-natured way to break up the frigidity of the conversation, but Lee was in no mood for pleasantries, and he did not unbend, or even relax the fixed sternness of his features. His only response to the allusion was a slight inclination of the head. General Lee now took the initiative again in leading the conversation back into business channels. He said:

"I have a thousand or more of your men as prisoners, General Grant, a number of them officers whom we have required to march along with us for several days. I shall be glad to send them into your lines as soon as it can be arranged, for I have no provisions for them. I have, indeed, nothing for my own men. They have been living for the last few days principally upon parched corn, and we are badly in need of both rations and forage. I telegraphed to Lynchburg, directing several train-loads of rations to be sent on by rail from there, and when they arrive I should be glad to have the present wants of my men supplied from them."

At this remark all eyes turned toward Sheridan, for he had captured these trains with his cavalry the night before, near Appomattox Station. General Grant replied: "I should like to have our men sent within our lines as soon as possible. I will take steps at once to have your army supplied with rations, but I am sorry we have no forage for the animals. We have had to depend upon the country for our supply of forage. Of about how many men does your present force consist?"

"Indeed, I am not able to say," Lee answered after a slight pause. "My losses in killed and wounded have been exceedingly heavy, and, besides, there have been many stragglers and some deserters. All my reports and public papers, and, indeed, my own private letters, had to be destroyed on the march, to prevent them from falling into the hands of your people. Many companies are entirely without officers, and I have not seen any returns for several days; so that I have no means of ascertaining our present strength."

General Grant had taken great pains to have a daily estimate made of the enemy's forces from all the data that could be obtained, and, judging it to be about 25,000 at this time, he said: "Suppose I send over 25,000 rations, do you think that will be a sufficient supply?" "I think it will be ample," remarked Lee, and added with considerable earnestness of manner, "and it will be a great relief, I assure you."

General Grant now turned to his chief commissary, Colonel (now General) M. R. Morgan, who was present, and directed him to arrange for issuing the rations. The number of officers and men surrendered was over 28,000. As to General Grant's supplies, he had ordered the army on starting out to carry twelve days' rations. This was the twelfth and last day of the campaign.

Grant's eye now fell upon Lee's sword again, and it seemed to remind him of the absence of his own, and by way of explanation he said to Lee:

"I started out from my camp several days ago without my sword, and as I have not seen my headquarters baggage since, I have been riding about without any side-arms. I have generally worn a sword, however, as little as possible, only during the actual operations of a campaign." "I am in the habit of wearing mine most of the time," remarked Lee; "I wear it invariably when I am among my troops, moving about through the army."

General Sheridan now stepped up to General Lee and said that when he discovered some of the Confederate troops in motion during the morning, which seemed to be a violation of the truce, he had sent him (Lee) a couple of notes protesting against this act, and as he had not had time to copy them he would like to have them long enough to make copies. Lee took the notes out of the breast-pocket of his coat and handed them to Sheridan with a few words expressive of regret that the circumstance had occurred, and intimating that it must have been the result of some misunderstanding.

After a little general conversation had been indulged in by those present, the two letters were signed and delivered, and the parties prepared to separate. Lee before parting asked Grant to notify Meade of the surrender, fearing that fighting might break out on that front and lives be uselessly lost. This request was complied with, and two Union officers were sent through the enemy's lines as the shortest route to Meade,—some of Lee's officers accompanying them to prevent their being interfered with. At a little before 4 o'clock General Lee shook hands with General Grant, bowed to the other officers, and with Colonel Marshall left the room. One after another we followed, and passed out to the porch. Lee signaled to his orderly to bring up his horse, and while the animal was being bridled the general stood on the lowest step and gazed sadly in the direction of the valley beyond where his army lay—now an army of prisoners. He smote his hands together a number of times in an absent sort of a way; seemed not to see the group of Union officers in the yard who rose respectfully at his approach, and appeared unconscious of everything about him. All appreciated the sadness that overwhelmed him, and he had the personal sympathy of every one who beheld him at this supreme moment of trial. The approach of his horse seemed to recall him from his reverie, and he at once mounted. General Grant now stepped down from the porch, and, moving toward him, saluted him by raising his hat. He was followed in this act of courtesy by all our officers present; Lee raised his hat respectfully, and rode off to break the sad news to the brave fellows whom he had so long commanded.

General Grant and his staff then mounted and started for the headquarters camp, which, in the meantime, had been pitched near by. The news of the surrender had reached the Union lines, and the firing of salutes began at several points, but the general sent orders at once to have them stopped, and used these words in referring to the occurrence: "The war is over, the rebels are our countrymen again, and the best sign of rejoicing after the victory will be to abstain from all demonstrations in the field."

Mr. McLean had been charging about in a manner which indicated that the excitement was shaking his system to its nervous center, but his real trials did not begin until the departure of the chief actors in the surrender. Then the

GENERAL LEE AND COLONEL MARSHALL LEAVING MCLEAN'S HOUSE AFTER
THE SURRENDER. FROM A SKETCH MADE AT THE TIME.

relic-hunters charged down upon the manor-house and made various attempts to jump Mr. McLean's claims to his own furniture.✥ Sheridan set a good example, however, by paying the proprietor twenty dollars in gold for the table at which Lee sat, for the purpose of presenting it to Mrs. Custer, and handed it over to her dashing husband, who started off for camp bearing it upon his shoulder. Ord paid forty dollars for the table at which Grant sat, and afterward presented it to Mrs. Grant, who modestly declined it, and insisted that Mrs. Ord should become its possessor. Bargains were at once struck for all the articles in the room, and it is even said that some mementos were carried off for which no coin of the realm was ever exchanged.

Before General Grant had proceeded far toward camp he was reminded that he had not yet announced the important event to the Government. He dismounted by the roadside, sat down on a large stone, and called for pencil and paper. Colonel (afterward General) Badeau handed his order-book to the general, who wrote on one of the leaves the following message, a copy of which was sent to the nearest telegraph station. It was dated 4:30 P.M.:

> "HON. E. M. STANTON, Secretary of War, Washington: General Lee surrendered the Army of Northern Virginia this afternoon on terms proposed by myself. The accompanying additional correspondence will show the conditions fully.   U. S. GRANT, Lieut.-General."

Upon reaching camp he seated himself in front of his tent, and we all gathered around him, curious to hear what his first comments would be upon the crowning event of his life. But our expectations were doomed to disappointment, for he appeared to have already dismissed the whole subject from his mind, and turning to General Rufus Ingalls, his first words were: "Ingalls, do you remember that old white mule that so-and-so used to ride when we were in the city of Mexico?" "Why, perfectly," said Ingalls, who was just then in a mood to remember the exact number of hairs in the mule's tail if it would have helped to make matters agreeable. And then the general-in-chief went on to recall the antics played by that animal during an excursion to Popocatapetl [*sic*]. It was not until after supper that he said much about the surrender, when he talked freely of his entire belief that the rest of the rebel commanders would follow Lee's example, and that we would have but little more fighting, even of a partisan nature. He then surprised us by announcing his intention of starting to Washington early the next morning. We were disappointed at this, for we

---

✥It is a singular historical coincidence that McLean's former home was upon a Virginia farm, near the battle-ground of the first Bull Run, and his house was used for a time as the headquarters of General Beauregard. To avoid the active theater of war he removed to the quiet village of Appomattox, only to find himself again surrounded by contending armies. Thus the first and last great scenes of the war in Virginia were enacted upon his property.—H.P.

wanted to see something of the opposing army, now that it had become civil enough for the first time in its existence to let us get near it, and meet some of the officers who had been acquaintances in former years. The general, however, had no desire to look at the conquered, and but little curiosity in his nature, and he was anxious above all things to begin the reduction of the military establishment and diminish the enormous expense attending it, which at this time amounted to about four millions of dollars a day. When he considered, however, that the railroad was being rapidly put in condition and that he would lose no time by waiting till noon of the next day, he made up his mind to delay his departure.

That evening I made full notes of the occurrences which took place during the surrender, and from these the above account has been written.

There were present at McLean's house, besides Sheridan, Ord, Merritt, Custer, and the officers of Grant's staff, a number of other officers and one or two citizens who entered the room at different times during the interview.

About 9 o'clock on the morning of the 10th General Grant with his staff rode out toward the enemy's lines, but it was found upon attempting to pass through that the force of habit is hard to overcome, and that the practice which had so long been inculcated in Lee's army of keeping Grant out of his lines was not to be overturned in a day, and he was politely requested at the picket-lines to wait till a message could be sent to headquarters asking for instructions. As soon as Lee heard that his distinguished opponent was approaching, he was prompt to correct the misunderstanding at the picket-line, and rode out at a

UNION SOLDIERS SHARING THEIR RATIONS WITH THE CONFEDERATES.
FROM A SKETCH MADE AT THE TIME.

gallop to receive him. They met on a knoll that overlooked the lines of the two armies, and saluted respectfully, by each raising his hat. The officers present gave a similar salute, and then grouped themselves around the two chieftains in a semicircle, but withdrew out of ear-shot. General Grant repeated to us that evening the substance of the conversation, which was as follows:

Grant began by expressing a hope that the war would soon be over, and Lee replied by stating that he had for some time been anxious to stop the further effusion of blood, and he trusted that everything would now be done to restore harmony and conciliate the people of the South. He said the emancipation of the negroes would be no hindrance to the restoring of relations between the two sections of the country, as it would probably not be the desire of the majority of the Southern people to restore slavery then, even if the question were left open to them. He could not tell what the other armies would do or what course Mr. Davis would now take, but he believed it would be best for their other armies to follow his example, as nothing could be gained by further resistance in the field. Finding that he entertained these sentiments, General Grant told him that no one's influence in the South was so great as his, and suggested to him that he should advise the surrender of the remaining armies and thus exert his influence in favor of immediate peace. Lee said he could not take such a course without consulting President Davis first. Grant then proposed to Lee that he should do so, and urge the hastening of a result which was admitted to be inevitable. Lee, however, was averse to stepping beyond his duties as a soldier, and said the authorities would doubtless soon arrive at the same conclusion without his interference. There was a statement put forth that Grant asked Lee to see Mr. Lincoln and talk with him as to the terms of reconstruction, but this was erroneous. I asked General Grant about it when he was on his death-bed, and his recollection was distinct that he had made no such suggestion. I am of opinion that the mistake arose from hearing that Lee had been requested to go and see the "President" regarding peace, and thinking that this expression referred to Mr. Lincoln, whereas it referred to Mr. Davis. After the conversation had lasted a little more than half an hour and Lee had requested that such instructions be given to the officers left in charge to carry out the details of the surrender, that there might be no misunderstanding as to the form of paroles, the manner of turning over the property, etc., the conference ended. The two commanders lifted their hats and said good-bye. Lee rode back to his camp to take a final farewell of his army, and Grant returned to McLean's house, where he seated himself on the porch until it was time to take his final departure. During the conference Ingalls, Sheridan, and Williams had asked permission to visit the enemy's lines and renew their acquaintance with some old friends, classmates, and former comrades in arms who were serving in Lee's army. They now returned, bringing with them Cadmus M. Wilcox, who had been General Grant's groomsman when he was married; Longstreet, who had also been at his wedding; Heth, who had been a subaltern with him in Mexico, besides Gordon, Pickett, and a number of others. They all stepped up to pay their respects to General Grant, who received them very cordially and talked with them until it was time to leave. The hour of noon had now arrived, and General Grant, after shaking hands with all present who were not to accompany him, mounted his horse, and started with his staff for Washington without having entered the enemy's lines. Lee set out for Richmond, and it was felt by all that peace had at last dawned upon the land. The charges were now withdrawn from the guns, the camp-fires were left to smolder in their ashes, the flags were tenderly furled,—those historic banners, battle-stained, bullet-riddled, many of them but remnants of their former selves, with scarcely enough left of them on which to imprint the names of the battles they had seen,—and the Army of the Union and the Army of Northern Virginia turned their backs upon each other for the first time in four long, bloody years.

CHAPTER 7

General Lee's Farewell Address to His Army.‡

Charles Marshall, Colonel, C.S.A.

General Lee's order to the Army of Northern Virginia at Appomattox Court House was written the day after the meeting at McLean's house, at which the terms of the surrender were agreed upon. That night the general sat with several of us at a fire in front of his tent, and after some conversation about the army, and the events of the day, in which his feelings toward his men were strongly expressed, he told me to prepare an order to the troops.

The next day it was raining, and many persons were coming and going, so that I was unable to write without interruption until about 10 o'clock, when General Lee, finding that the order had not been prepared, directed me to get into his ambulance, which stood near his tent, and placed an orderly to prevent any one from approaching me.

I sat in the ambulance until I had written the order, the first draft of which (in pencil) contained an entire paragraph that was omitted by General Lee's direction. He made one or two verbal changes, and I then made a copy of the order as corrected, and gave it to one of the clerks in the adjutant-general's office to write in ink. I took the copy, when made by the clerk, to the general, who signed it, and other copies were then made for transmission to the corps commanders and the staff of the army. All these copies were signed by the general, and a good many persons sent other copies which they had made or procured, and obtained his signature. In this way many copies of the order had the general's name signed as if they were originals, some of which I have seen. The text of the order as issued was as follows:

‡From a letter dated September 27th, 1887, to General Bradley T. Johnson.

GENERAL LEE'S RETURN TO THE LINES AFTER THE SURRENDER.
FROM A WAR-TIME SKETCH.

In his "Memoirs of Robert E. Lee" (J. M. Stoddart & Co.), General A. L. Long says of this scene: "When, after his interview with Grant, General Lee again appeared, a shout of welcome instinctively ran through the army. But instantly recollecting the sad occasion that brought him before them, their shouts sank into silence, every hat was raised, and the bronzed faces of the thousands of grim warriors were bathed with tears. As he rode slowly along the lines hundreds of his devoted veterans pressed around the noble chief, trying to take his hand, touch his person, or even lay a hand upon his horse, thus exhibiting for him their great affection. The general then, with head bare and tears flowing freely down his manly cheeks, bade adieu to the army. In a few words he told the brave men who had been so true in arms to return to their homes and become worthy citizens."

"HEADQUARTERS,
Army of Northern Virginia
"April 10th, 1865.

"After four years of arduous service, marked by unsurpassed courage and fortitude, the Army of Northern Virginia has been compelled to yield to overwhelming numbers and resources. I need not tell the survivors of so many hard-fought battles, who have remained steadfast to the last, that I have consented to this result from no distrust of them, but, feeling that valor and devotion could accomplish nothing that could compensate for the loss that would have attended the continuation of the contest, I have determined to avoid the useless sacrifice of those whose past services have endeared them to their countrymen.

"By the terms of the agreement, officers and men can return to their homes, and remain there until exchanged. You will take with you the satisfaction that proceeds from the consciousness of duty faithfully performed; and I earnestly pray that a merciful God will extend to you his blessing and protection.

"With an increasing admiration of your constancy and devotion to your country, and a grateful remembrance of your kind and generous consideration of myself, I bid you an affectionate farewell.

"R. E. LEE, General."

CHAPTER 8

FINAL OPERATIONS
OF SHERMAN'S ARMY.

H. W. Slocum, Major-General, U.S.V.

From Bentonville [March 22d, 1865] we marched to Goldsboro', and in two or three days were in camp, busily engaged in preparing for another campaign. We had made the march from Savannah to Goldsboro', a distance of 430 miles, in seven weeks. We had constructed bridges across the Edisto, Broad, Catawba, Pedee, and Cape Fear rivers, and had destroyed all the railroads to the interior of South Carolina. We had subsisted mainly upon the country, and our men and animals were in better condition than when we left Savannah. All this was done in the winter season.

We found Goldsboro' already occupied by our troops, the Twenty-third Corps, under General Schofield, and the Tenth Corps, under General Terry, having captured Wilmington and arrived at Goldsboro' a day or two in advance of us.[✛] The railroad to New Berne was soon put in running order, and supplies of all kinds were pouring in upon us. Soon after we were settled in the vicinity of Goldsboro' General Sherman went to City Point, where he met President Lincoln and Lieutenant-General Grant, and the situation of affairs was discussed by them while on board the *River Queen,* a small steamer lying near the wharf at City Point. Both Grant and Sherman expressed to Mr. Lincoln their firm conviction that the end was near at hand. During the conversation something was said about the disposition to be made of the rebel leaders, particularly Mr. Davis. Sherman made no secret of the fact that he wished to have Davis escape arrest, get out of the country, and thus save our Government all

---

✛After the fall of Wilmington, Feb. 22d, 1865, General Schofield sent a column, under General J. D. Cox, to open the railway from New Berne to Goldsboro'. At Kinston, Cox encountered, March 8th, Bragg with Hoke's division and a portion of Hood's troops, under D. H. Hill. Fighting took place on the south side of the Neuse, March 8th to 10th. On the night of the 10th Bragg retreated toward Goldsboro', leaving a detachment at Kinston. Schofield occupied Kinston on the 14th, and reached Goldsboro' on the 21st.
—EDITORS.

VIEW OF GOLDSBORO, NORTH CAROLINA. FROM A WAR-TIME SKETCH.

embarrassment as to his case. Mr. Lincoln said that, occupying the position he did, he could not say that he hoped the leader of the great rebellion, which had brought so much misery upon the land, would escape, but that the situation reminded him of an anecdote. He said a man who had recently taken the temperance pledge was once invited to take a drink of spirits. He said, "No, I can't do it; I will take a glass of lemonade." When the lemonade was prepared, his friend suggested that its flavor would be improved by pouring in a little brandy. The man said, "If you could pour in a little of that stuff unbeknownst to me, I shouldn't get mad about it." If Mr. Davis had escaped from the country "unbeknownst" to Mr. Lincoln, he would not have grieved over it.

General Sherman soon returned, bringing with him an order constituting the left wing a distinct army under the title of the Army of Georgia, and assigning me to command.[+] The Tenth and Twenty-third corps had already been constituted an army known as the Army of the Ohio, with Schofield as commander.

On April 5th General Sherman issued a confidential order to the army and corps commanders and the chiefs of the staff departments. It stated that the next grand objective was to place his armies north of the Roanoke River, facing west, and in full communication with the Army of the Potomac. Everything was to be in readiness on April 10th, and the movement was to commence on the morning of the 11th. The Army of Georgia was to have the left, the Army of the Ohio the center, and the Army of the Tennessee the right in the movement. The roads to be taken by each command were indicated in the order. We went to bed that night happy in the belief that we were soon to be in front of Rich-

---

[+]On April 1st, 1865, General Sherman announced the organization of his army to be as follows: Right Wing (Army of the Tennessee), Maj.-Gen. O. O. Howard, commanding. Left Wing (Army of Georgia), Maj.-Gen. H. W. Slocum, commanding. Center (Army of the Ohio), Maj.-Gen. J. M. Schofield, commanding. Cavalry, Brevet Maj.-Gen. Judson Kilpatrick, commanding. Each of these commanders was authorized to exercise the powers prescribed by law for a general commanding a separate department or army in the field.—EDITORS.

mond, with our right connecting with the Army of the Potomac, and after having marched through the entire South from Chattanooga, via Atlanta, Savannah, and Columbia, we were to have the honor of taking part in the capture of Lee's army and the capital of the Confederacy. The next day brought us news which dispelled this happy vision. Richmond had fallen, and Lee's army was marching to make a junction with Johnston. The news was received with great joy by the men of Sherman's army. Bonfires, rockets, and a general jubilee kept the inhabitants of Goldsboro' from sleep that night. This event, however, caused Sherman to change his plans. He decided to move direct to Raleigh, hoping to meet Johnston either there or at Smithfield. We commenced our march on the 10th, arrived at Smithfield on the 11th, only to find that General Johnston had retreated to Raleigh. On the 12th, while on the march to Raleigh, some person on horseback came riding up the road crying to the men as he passed, "Grant has captured Lee's army!" Soon after, Sherman's Special Field Orders, No. 54, dated Smithfield, North Carolina, April 12th, 1865, was brought to me and published to the troops. It read as follows:

> "The general commanding announces to the army that he has official notice from General Grant that General Lee surrendered to him his entire army, on the 9th inst., at Appomattox Court House, Virginia. Glory to God and to our country, and all honor to our comrades in arms, toward whom we are marching! A little more labor, a little more toil on our part, and the great race is won, and our Government stands regenerated, after four long years of bloody war.
>
> "W. T. SHERMAN, Major-General Commanding."

It is useless to attempt to describe the effect of this news upon the men of Sherman's army. Instead of looking forward to another long campaign through the South in pursuit of the united armies of Lee and Johnston, the vision of every man now turned homeward. Thoughts of meeting wives, children, and friends from whom they had been so long separated by the bloody struggle, occupied the minds of all. A happier body of men never before surrounded their camp-fires than were to be found along the roads leading to Raleigh.

On the 13th we passed through Raleigh and encamped within three or four miles of the city. Kilpatrick's cavalry followed the retreating enemy about twenty-five miles beyond Raleigh and went into camp at Durham Station, on the road toward Hillsboro'. On the 14th Sherman ordered his army to move, with a view of preventing the retreat of Johnston in the direction of Salisbury and Charlotte. In this order, he said that in the hope of an early reconciliation no further destruction of railroads or private property would be permitted. We were authorized to take from the people forage and other necessary supplies, but were cautioned against stripping the poorer classes. On the morning of the day that this movement was to commence, General Sherman received from General Johnston a message requesting a cessation of hostilities with a view of negotiating terms of surrender. Sherman sent a reply at once, and arrangements were made for a personal interview on the 17th between the two commanders, at a point midway between our advance and the position held by the enemy.

As Sherman was entering a car on the morning of the 17th to attend this meeting, the telegraph operator stopped him and requested him to wait a few minutes, as he was just receiving an important dispatch, which he ought to see before he left. The dispatch was from Mr. Stanton announcing the assassination of Mr. Lincoln, and the attempt on the life of Mr. Seward and his son.⌐ General Sherman asked the operator if he had divulged the contents of the dispatch to any one, and being answered in the negative, he ordered him to keep it a secret until his return. Sherman and his staff met Johnston and Wade Hampton with a number of staff-officers at the house of Mrs. Bennett. None of the Confederate officers had heard of the assassination of Lincoln, and Sherman first made the fact known to them. They were much affected by the news, and apparently regretted it as much as did our own officers. In conversing as to the terms of surrender, Johnston suggested that they should be such as to embrace not only his army, but the armies under Dick Taylor and Kirby Smith in the Gulf States, and those under Maury, Forrest, and others. Sherman questioned Johnston's authority to negotiate the surrender of the other armies, and Johnston assured him that he could soon obtain the authority. A meeting was arranged for the following day.

Sherman returned to Raleigh and issued an order announcing the assassination of President Lincoln, which was published to the troops on the following morning. The men appreciated the generosity and nobleness of Mr. Lincoln's nature. The fact that he had carried us successfully through the great

⌐On Sunday, April 9th, President Lincoln reached Washington on his return from his visit to the field of operations on the James, having left Richmond on the 6th. On the night of Friday, the 14th, the President visited Ford's Theatre, where he was shot by John Wilkes Booth. The next morning about 7 o'clock Mr. Lincoln died. Booth escaped from the city, and, guided by some confederates, crossed the Potomac near Port Tobacco, Maryland, to Mathias Point, Virginia, on Saturday night, April 22d. On Monday, the 24th, he crossed the Rappahannock from Port Conway to Port Royal and took refuge in a barn, where he was found on Wednesday, the 26th, by a detachment of Company L, 16th New York Cavalry, and killed. The assassination of the President was the result of a conspiracy. Mr. Seward, the Secretary of State, was also attacked on the evening of April 14th by Lewis Payne, a fellow-conspirator, and was severely injured. The following persons were tried before a military commission convened at Washington, May 9th, 1865, on the charge of conspiracy to assassinate the President and other high officers of the Government: David E. Herold, G. A. Atzerodt, Lewis Payne, Michael O'Laughlin, Edward Spangler, Samuel Arnold, Mary E. Surratt, and Doctor Samuel A. Mudd. Herold, Atzerodt, Payne, and Mrs. Surratt were hanged; O'Laughlin, Arnold, and Mudd were imprisoned for life, and Spangler was imprisoned for six years.—Editors.

struggle caused them to feel toward him an attachment which the soldier always feels toward a great and successful leader. The startling news of his death was received with gloom and sadness.

On the following day General Sherman met General Johnston and negotiated with him a conditional treaty for the surrender of all the Confederates then under arms./ The condition was that it should first be approved by the President. Pending these negotiations, and after the proposed terms had been made known to the leading officers of Sherman's army, I conversed with nearly all these officers, among them Logan, Howard, and Blair, and heard no word of dissent from any of them. I can now recall to mind but one general officer who, at the time, questioned the wisdom of General Sherman's action, and that was General Carl Schurz. General Schurz was then serving temporarily as my chief-of-staff, and when I returned from Sherman's headquarters about 12 o'clock on the night of the 18th I found General Schurz sitting up, waiting for me. He was eager to learn the terms, and when I stated them to him he expressed regret and predicted just what subsequently happened. He said the

/Following is the text of the conditional treaty of April 18th:

"Memorandum, or Basis of Agreement, made this 18th day of April, A.D. 1865, near Durham's Station, in the State of North Carolina, by and between General Joseph E. Johnston, commanding the Confederate Army, and Major-General William T. Sherman, commanding the Army of the United States in North Carolina, both present:

"1. The contending armies now in the field to maintain the *status quo* until notice is given by the commanding general of any one to its opponent, and reasonable time—say forty-eight hours—allowed.

"2. The Confederate armies now in existence to be disbanded and conducted to their several State capitals, there to deposit their arms and public property in the State arsenal; and each officer and man to execute and file an agreement to cease from acts of war, and to abide the action of the State and Federal authority. The number of arms and munitions of war to be reported to the Chief of Ordnance at Washington City, subject to the future action of the Congress of the United States, and, in the meantime, to be used solely to maintain peace and order within the borders of the States respectively.

"3. The recognition by the Executive of the United States of the several State governments on their officers and legislatures taking the oaths prescribed by the Constitution of the United States, and where conflicting State governments have resulted from the war the legitimacy of all shall be submitted to the Supreme Court of the United States.

"4. The reëstablishment of all the Federal courts in the several States, with powers as defined by the Constitution of the United States and of the States respectively.

"5. The people and inhabitants of all the States to be guaranteed, so far as the Executive can, their political rights and franchises, as well as their rights of person and property, as defined by the Constitution of the United States and of the States respectively.

"6. The Executive authority of the Government of the United States not to disturb any of the people by reason of the late war, so long as they live in peace and quiet, abstain from acts of armed hostility, and obey the laws in existence at the place of their residence.

"7. In general terms—the war to cease; a general amnesty, so far as the Executive of the United States can command, on condition of the disbandment of the Confederate armies, the distribution of the arms, and the resumption of peaceful pursuits by the officers and men

public mind of the North would be inflamed by the assassination of Lincoln, and now that the armies of the Confederacy were virtually crushed, anything looking toward leniency would not be well received. The terms were not approved by President Johnson, and General Grant came to Raleigh.☆

His meeting with Sherman was a friendly one. He laid before Sherman a letter of instructions which he had received from Mr. Lincoln some time before the fall of Richmond, prohibiting him from embracing, in any negotiations he might have with General Lee, anything of a political nature. Had a copy of this letter been furnished General Sherman, his treaty with Johnston would not have been made. Sherman and all his officers were exceedingly anxious to prevent the Confederate armies from breaking up into guerrilla bands and roaming through the South, keeping the country in a disturbed condition for months, and perhaps for years. There never was the slightest justification for the

---

hitherto composing said armies. Not being fully empowered by our respective principals to fulfill these terms, we individually and officially pledge ourselves to promptly obtain the necessary authority, and to carry out the above programme.

"W. T. SHERMAN, MAJOR-GENERAL,
"COMMANDING ARMY OF THE UNITED STATES
"IN NORTH CAROLINA.
"J. E. JOHNSTON, GENERAL,
"COMMANDING CONFEDERATE STATES ARMY
"IN NORTH CAROLINA."

☆A copy of the memorandum of the 18th was sent to General Grant on the 20th. On the 24th Grant reached Sherman's headquarters, bringing the announcement of the Secretary of War that the negotiations were disapproved by President Johnson. Grant's own reply to Sherman was delivered at the same time as follows: "HEADQUARTERS, ARMIES OF THE UNITED STATES, WASHINGTON, D.C., April 21, 1865. Major-General W. T. SHERMAN, commanding Military Division of the Mississippi. GENERAL: The basis of agreement entered into between yourself and General J. E. Johnston, for the disbandment of the Southern army, and the extension of the authority of the General Government over all the territory belonging to it, sent for the approval of the President, is received. I read it carefully myself before submitting it to the President and Secretary of War, and felt satisfied that it could not possibly be approved. My reason for these views I will give you at another time, in a more extended letter.

"Your agreement touches upon questions of such vital importance that, as soon as read, I addressed a note to the Secretary of War, notifying him of their receipt, and the importance of immediate action by the President; and suggested, in view of their importance, that the entire Cabinet be called together, that all might give an expression of their opinions upon the matter. The result was a disapproval by the President of the basis laid down; a disapproval of the negotiations altogether—except for the surrender of the army commanded by General Johnston, and directions to me to notify you of this decision. I cannot do so better than by sending you the inclosed copy of a dispatch (penned by the late President, though signed by the Secretary of War)‡ in answer to me, on sending a letter received from General Lee, proposing to meet me for the purpose of submitting the question of peace to a convention of officers. Please notify General Johnston, immediately on receipt of this, of the termination of the truce, and resume hostilities against his army at the earliest moment you can, acting in good faith. Very respectfully, your obedient servant, U. S. GRANT, Lieutenant-General."

‡On the 2d of March, 1865, General R. E. Lee addressed a letter to General Grant suggesting a meeting between them to arrange "to submit the subjects of controversy between the belligerents to a convention,"

criticisms that were showered upon him for his course in this matter. On the 26th of April General Johnston surrendered his army upon the same terms that General Lee had received.[✛]

During our stay in Raleigh I witnessed a scene which to me was one of the most impressive of the war. It was the review by General Sherman of a division of colored troops. These troops passed through the principal streets of the city. They were well drilled, dressed in new and handsome uniforms, and with their bright bayonets gleaming in the sun they made a splendid appearance. The sides of the streets were lined with residents of the city and the surrounding country,—many of them, I presume, the former owners of some of these soldiers.

Soon after the surrender, orders were issued for the right and left wings to march to Washington via Richmond. On the evening before we left Raleigh the mails from the North arrived, and with them a large number of New York papers. On the following day, when we were about five miles from the city, my attention was called to a group of soldiers standing around a cart under which they had built a fire. The cart and its contents were being burned, while a young man in citizen's dress, with the mule that had been taken from the cart, was looking on. I sent a staff-officer to learn the meaning of it. He soon returned to me and said that a soldier, who seemed to be the leader of the party, said, "Tell General Slocum that cart is loaded with New York papers for sale to the soldiers. These papers are filled with the vilest abuse of General Sherman. We have followed Sherman through a score of battles and through nearly two thou-

---

etc. General Lee's letter was forwarded to the Secretary of War, and on the 4th of March the following was received in reply: "[Cipher.] Office United States Military Telegraph, Headquarters Armies of the United States. Lieutenant-General Grant: The President directs me to say to you that he wishes you to have no conference with General Lee, unless it be for the capitulation of Lee's army or on solely minor and purely military matters. He instructs me to say that you are not to decide, discuss, or confer upon any political question; such questions the President holds in his own hands, and will submit them to no military conferences or conventions. Meantime you are to press to the utmost your military advantages. Edwin M. Stanton, Secretary of War."—Editors.

[✛]General Grant advised General Sherman to accept Johnston's surrender on the same terms as those made with Lee. The meeting of Johnston and Sherman took place on the 26th, and the following was agreed upon and approved by General Grant:

"Terms of a Military Convention, entered into this 26th day of April, 1865, at Bennett's House, near Durham's Station, North Carolina, between General Joseph E. Johnston, commanding the Confederate Army, and Major-General W. T. Sherman, commanding the United States Army in North Carolina:

"1. All acts of war on the part of the troops under General Johnston's command to cease from this date.

"2. All arms and public property to be deposited at Greensboro', and delivered to an ordnance officer of the United States Army.

sand miles of the enemy's country, and we do not intend to allow these vile slanders against him to be circulated among his men." This was the last property that I saw destroyed by the men of Sherman's army, and I witnessed the scene with keener satisfaction than I had felt over the destruction of any property since the day we left Atlanta.

A march of three or four days brought us in sight of Richmond. There were men in the Twentieth Corps who had been near enough to that city, on a former occasion, to enable them to see the spires of her churches. Some had been in the first Bull Run, many more in the Seven Days' battles about Richmond, nearly all of them had been at Chancellorsville, Antietam, and Gettysburg. After the repulse at Chickamauga they had been detached from the Army of the Potomac and sent by rail with all possible speed to Nashville. Thence they had marched via Chattanooga, Atlanta, Savannah, Columbia, and Raleigh to the point which, during the first two years of the war, they had struggled so hard to reach by approaching it from the north side. They had swung around the circle,—the largest circle ever swung around by an army corps.

After resting a few days near Richmond we started for Washington over the battle-scarred route so familiar to the men who had fought under McDowell, McClellan, and subsequently under Grant, as well as to those who had served under Lee. The weather was pleasant and the march full of interest. On some of the fields where great battles had been fought we found the bodies of many Union soldiers lying unburied, apparently just as they had fallen on the field.

"3. Rolls of all the officers and men to be made in duplicate; one copy to be retained by the commander of the troops, and the other to be given to officer to be designated by General Sherman. Each officer and man to give his individual obligation in writing not to take up arms against the Government of the United States until properly released from this obligation.

"4. The side-arms of officers, and their private horses and baggage, to be retained by them.

"5. This being done, all the officers and men will be permitted to return to their homes, not to be disturbed by the United States authorities, so long as they observe their obligation and the laws in force where they may reside.

"W. T. SHERMAN, MAJOR-GENERAL,
"COMMANDING UNITED STATES FORCES IN NORTH CAROLINA.
"J. E. JOHNSTON, GENERAL,
"COMMANDING CONFEDERATE FORCES IN NORTH CAROLINA.
"APPROVED: U. S. GRANT, LIEUTENANT-GENERAL."

"SUPPLEMENTAL TERMS.

"1. The field transportation to be loaned to the troops for their march to their homes, and for subsequent use in their industrial pursuits. Artillery horses may be used in field transportation if necessary.

"2. Each brigade or separate body to retain a number of arms equal to one-seventh of its effective strength, which, when the troops reach the capitals of their States, will be disposed of as the general commanding the department may direct.

GRAND REVIEWING STAND IN FRONT OF THE WHITE HOUSE, WASHINGTON,
MAY 23–24, 1865. FROM A PHOTOGRAPH.

Parties were detailed to bury the dead, and subsequently a party was sent from Washington to complete the work.

We went into camp in the vicinity of Alexandria, my own headquarters being very near the place I had occupied during the first winter of the war,

---

"3. Private horses, and other private property of both officers and men, to be retained by them.

"4. The commanding general of the Military Division of West Mississippi, Major-General Canby, will be requested to give transportation by water from Mobile or New Orleans to the troops from Arkansas and Texas.

"5. The obligations of officers and soldiers to be signed by their immediate commanders.

"6. Naval forces within the limits of General Johnston's command to be included in the terms of this convention.

"J. M. SCHOFIELD, MAJOR-GENERAL,
"COMMANDING UNITED STATES FORCES IN NORTH CAROLINA.
"J. E. JOHNSTON, GENERAL,
"COMMANDING CONFEDERATE FORCES IN NORTH CAROLINA."

On leaving his army, General Johnston issued the following farewell order:

"COMRADES: In terminating our official relations, I earnestly exhort you to observe faithfully the terms of pacification agreed upon, and to discharge the obligations of good and peaceful citizens as well as you have performed the duties of thorough soldiers in the field. By such a course you will best secure the comfort of your families and kindred, and restore tranquility to our country.

"You will return to your homes with the admiration of our people, won by the courage and noble devotion you have displayed in this long war. I shall always remember with pride the loyal support and generous confidence you have given me.

"I now part with you with deep regret, and bid you farewell with feelings of cordial

when McClellan was organizing the Army of the Potomac. We were soon informed that the final scene of the war was to be a grand review of all the troops by the President and his Cabinet. All the foreign ministers resident in Washington, the governors of the States, and many other distinguished people had been invited to be present. The Eastern troops were to be reviewed on the 23d of May, and the Western on the day following. The leading officers of Sherman's command were invited to the stand to witness the review of the Army of the Potomac, and they gladly accepted the invitation. After the close of the review of that army, several of our officers assembled at Sherman's headquarters to discuss matters and prepare for the work to be done next day. In speaking of the review of the Army of the Potomac Sherman said: "It was magnificent. In dress, in soldierly appearance, in precision of alignment and marching we cannot beat those fellows." All present assented to this statement. Some one then suggested that we should not make the attempt, but should pass in review "as we went marching through Georgia"; that the foragers, familiarly known among us as "bummers," should form part of the column. This suggestion seemed to strike General Sherman favorably, and instructions were issued to carry it into effect. Early on the following morning the head of our column started up Pennsylvania Avenue and soon passed the reviewing stand, which was filled with distinguished people from all parts of the country. Sherman's men certainly presented a very soldierly appearance. They were proud of their achievements, and had the swing of men who had marched through half a dozen States. But the feature of the column which seemed to interest the spectators most was the attachments of foragers in rear of each brigade. At the review the men appeared "in their native ugliness" as they appeared on the march through Georgia and the Carolinas. Their pack-mules and horses, with rope bridles or halters, laden with supplies such as they had carried on the march, formed part of the column. It was a new feature in a grand review, but one which those who witnessed it will never forget.

Soon after the review the troops were ordered into various camps, where the paymaster paid them his last visit, and then they separated, never again to meet in large bodies, except on Memorial Day, the 30th of May, of each year,[+] when they meet to honor the memory of comrades who gave their lives for their

---

friendship, and with earnest wishes that you may have hereafter all the prosperity and happiness to be found in the world.

"Official.   J. E. JOHNSTON, General.

"Kinloch Falconer, A.A.G."

[+]Confederate Memorial Services are usually held at different dates in April and May. In some localities veterans on both sides participate in all memorial ceremonies. Of late years reunions of Union and Confederate veterans on battle-fields have become frequent.—EDITORS.

country, and at annual reunions of regimental associations, when they assemble
to renew the ties of comradeship[1] formed during the struggle of more than four
years' duration, which cost us hundreds of thousands of lives and thousands of
millions of treasure, but which has conferred, even upon the defeated South,
blessings that more than compensate the country for all her losses.

[1]The Grand Army of the Republic, dating from 1866, numbering in 1888 over 350,000 members, is the
largest veteran association in the country. Its membership is restricted to soldiers and sailors of the
Union army and navy, who served during the Civil War, whether honorably discharged or still in service. The Military Order of the Loyal Legion of the United States, numbering in 1888 about 6000 members (commissioned officers of the Union army and navy), was organized in 1865 to perpetuate the
memories of the war. There are also numerous Union veteran associations, either fraternal or provident,
or both; among them a national body of Naval Veterans, the societies of the Army of the Potomac, the
Army of the Cumberland, the Army of the Tennessee, the Army of the Ohio, and societies of the several army corps, forming parts of the societies of the main armies.—EDITORS.

CHAPTER 9

LAST DAYS OF THE CONFEDERACY.[†]

Basil W. Duke, Brigadier-General, C.S.A.

When General Lee began his retreat from Richmond and Petersburg Brigadier-General John Echols was in command of the Department of Southwestern Virginia.[ψ] Under him were General Wharton's division and the brigades of Colonels Trigg and Preston, between 4000 and 5000 infantry, and four brigades of cavalry, about 2200 men, commanded by Brigadier-Generals Vaughn and Cosby, Colonel Giltner, and myself. There was also attached to the departmental command Major Page's unusually well-equipped battalion of artillery. On the 2d day of April General Echols issued orders looking to a junction of his forces with those of General Lee. Marching almost constantly, by day and night, General Echols reached Christiansburg on the 10th, and concentrated his entire command there. He was confident that he would be able, within a few days, to join Lee somewhere to the south-west of Richmond, most probably in the vicinity of Danville. The command had halted for the night; General Echols and I were dismounted and standing upon the turnpike surrounded by the soldiers. Just then Lieutenant James B. Clay, who had been sent ahead three days before to gain information, galloped up and handed General Echols a dispatch. The latter's face flushed, and then grew deadly pale. The dispatch was from General Lomax, and in these words: "General Lee surrendered this morning at or near Appomattox Court House. I am trying with my own division and the remnants of Fitz Lee's and Rosser's divisions to arrange to make a junction with you."

After a brief conference we agreed that the news should be concealed from the men until the next day, if possible, and communicated that night only to the

---

[†]Condensed from "The Southern Bivouac," for August, 1886.—EDITORS.
[ψ]General Echols succeeded General Early in command of the department, March 30th, 1865.
—EDITORS.

brigade and regimental commanders. We hoped that some plan might be devised which would enable us to hold the troops together until we could learn what policy would be pursued by Mr. Davis, and whether it would be our duty to endeavor to join General Johnston. But to conceal such a fact when even one man was aware of it was impossible. Before we had concluded our brief conversation, we knew from the hum and stir in the anxious, dark-browed crowds nearest us, from excitement which soon grew almost to tumult, that the terrible tidings had gotten abroad. That night no man slept. Strange as the declaration may sound now, there was not one of the six or seven thousand then gathered at Christiansburg who had entertained the slightest thought that such an event could happen, and doubtless that feeling pervaded the ranks of the Confederacy. We knew that the heroic army which had so long defended Richmond was in retreat. We knew that its operations could no longer be conducted upon the methods which support regular warfare, and that everything necessary to maintain its efficiency was lost. We could hazard no conjecture as to what would be done; yet, that the Army of Northern Virginia, with Lee at its head, would ever surrender had never entered our minds. Therefore, the indescribable consternation and amazement which spread like a conflagration through the ranks when the thing was told can only be imagined by one who has had a similar experience.

During all that night officers and men were congregated in groups and crowds discussing the news, and it was curious to observe how the training and discipline of veteran soldiers were manifested even amid all this deep feeling and wild excitement. There was not one act of violence, not a harsh or insulting word spoken; the officers were treated with the same respect which they had previously received, and although many of the infantrymen who lived in that part of Virginia went off that night without leave and returned to their homes, none who remained were insubordinate or failed to obey orders with alacrity. Great fires were lighted. Every group had its orators, who, succeeding each other, spoke continuously. Every conceivable suggestion was offered. Some advocated a guerrilla warfare; some proposed marching to the trans-Mississippi, and thence to Mexico. The more practical and reasonable, of course, proposed that an effort to join General Johnston should immediately be made. Many, doubtless, thought of surrender, but I do not remember to have heard it mentioned.

On the next day General Echols convened a council of war composed of his brigade commanders. He proposed that the men of the infantry commands should be furloughed for sixty days, at the expiration of which time, if the Confederacy survived, they might possibly be returned to the service. The infantry commanders approved of this policy, and it was adopted. General Echols then requested the officers commanding the cavalry brigades to give expression to their views. General Cosby and Colonel Giltner frankly declared their conviction that further resistance was impossible, and that it was their duty to lose no time in making the best terms possible for their men. They expressed a determination to march to Kentucky and immediately surrender. General Vaughn and I believed that we were allowed no option in such a matter, but that, notwithstanding the great disaster of which we had just learned, we were not absolved from our military allegiance. We thought it clearly our duty to attempt to join General Johnston, and to put off surrender as long as the Confederate Government had an organized force in the field. We expressed ourselves ready to obey any order General Echols might issue. For my own part, I was convinced that all of the troops there would rather have their record protected than their safety consulted.

General Echols verbally notified each brigade commander of cavalry that he would be expected to take his brigade to General Johnston, and said that a written order to march that evening would be delivered to each. I received such an order. The infantry ostensibly was furloughed, virtually it was disbanded, in accord with this programme. The guns of Page's batteries were spiked and the carriages burned. The artillery horses and several hundred mules taken from the large wagon-train, which was also abandoned, were turned over to my brigade that I might mount my men, for our horses had mostly been sent to North Carolina for the winter, and had not been brought back. I had been joined at Christiansburg by a detachment of paroled prisoners of John Morgan's old command. I permitted as many of them as I could mount to accompany me, and armed them with rifles left by the disbanded infantrymen. I was compelled peremptorily to order a very considerable number of these paroled men to remain in a camp established in the vicinity of Christiansburg. They were anxious to follow on foot. Late on the evening of the 11th General Echols, at the head of Vaughn's brigade and mine, the latter on mule-back, began the march toward North Carolina, which was to close with the final surrender of the last Confederate organization east of the Mississippi River. The rain was pouring in torrents. On the next day ninety men of Colonel Giltner's brigade, under Lieutenant-Colonel George Dimond, overtook us. They had learned, after our departure, of the result of the conference, and of General Echols's determination to join General Johnston.

As we approached the North Carolina border, we heard frequent rumors that a large force of Federal cavalry was in the vicinity, prepared to contest our progress. The point at which it was supposed we would encounter them, and where collision would be most dangerous to us, was "Fancy Gap," which, however, we passed in safety.

On the second day after entering North Carolina we crossed the Yadkin River, and on the evening of the next day thereafter reached Statesville. Here General Echols left us in order to proceed more promptly to General Johnston, who was supposed to be at Salisbury. Vaughn marched in the direction of Morganton, and I set out for Lincolnton, where I expected to find my horses and the detail, under Colonel Napier, which I had sent in charge of them to their winter quarters in that vicinity. Crossing the Catawba River on the top of the covered railroad bridge I pushed on rapidly.

I had obtained credible information that the Federal cavalry under Stoneman were now certainly very near, and also marching in the direction of Lincolnton. I was very anxious to get there first, for I feared that if the enemy anticipated me the horses and guard would either be captured or driven so far away as to be entirely out of my reach. Early in the afternoon I discovered unmistakable indications that the enemy was close at hand, and found that he was moving upon another main road to Lincolnton, nearly parallel with that which I was pursuing, and some three miles distant. My scouts began fighting with his upon every by-road which connected our respective routes; and I learned, to my great chagrin and discomfort, that my men were not meeting with the success in that sort of combat to which they were accustomed, and which an unusual amount of experience in it might entitle them to expect. They were constantly driven in upon the column, and showed a reluctance to fight amounting almost to demoralization. Every man whom I questioned laid the blame in the most emphatic manner on his "d—d mule." All declared that these animals were prejudiced against advancing or standing in any decent fashion.

I sent a party of some twenty-five or thirty, mounted on horses and better equipped than the others, with instructions to get into Lincolnton before the enemy and communicate with Colonel Napier. However, when I had come within three miles of the place, about sunset, I met this party retiring before a very much larger body of Federals.

To countermarch would have destroyed the *morale* of the men; and if I had been attacked in rear my column would have dissolved in utter rout. Fortunately I had learned that a road, or rather trace, turned off to the left near this point, and led to other paths which conducted to the main road from Lincolnton to Charlotte. I turned into this road. Procuring guides, I marched some 15 miles and reached the Charlotte road late in the night.

At Charlotte, where we arrived the same day, we found General Ferguson's brigade of cavalry; the town was also crowded with paroled soldiers of Lee's army and refugee officials from Richmond.[+] On the next day Mr. Davis arrived,

[+]On Sunday, April 2d, on receipt of dispatches from General Lee that the army was about to evacuate the Petersburg and Richmond lines, Mr. Davis assembled his cabinet and directed the removal of the public archives, treasure, and other property to Danville, Virginia. The members of the Government left Richmond during the night of the 2d, and on the 5th Mr. Davis issued a proclamation stating that Virginia would not be abandoned. Danville was placed in a state of defense, and Admiral Raphael Semmes was appointed a brigadier-general in command of the defenses, with a force consisting of a naval brigade and two battalions of infantry. Upon the surrender of Lee and his army (April 9th), the Confederate

escorted by the cavalry brigades of General Dibrell, of Tennessee, and Colonel W.C.P. Breckinridge, of Kentucky.

In response to the greeting received from the citizens and soldiery, Mr. Davis made a speech which has been the subject of much comment, then and since. I heard it, and remember nothing said by him that could warrant much either of commendation or criticism. In the course of his remarks a dispatch was handed him by some gentleman in the crowd, who, I have been told since, was the mayor of Charlotte. It announced the assassination of Mr. Lincoln. Mr. Davis read it aloud, making scarcely any comment upon it at all. He certainly used no unkind language, nor did he display any feeling of exultation. The impression produced on my mind by his manner and few words was that he did not credit the statement.

General John C. Breckinridge, who was then Secretary of War, had not accompanied Mr. Davis to Charlotte, but had gone to General Johnston's headquarters at Greensboro', and was assisting in the negotiations between Johnston and Sherman.

When General Breckinridge reached Charlotte, about two days after Mr. Davis's arrival, he was under the impression that the cartel he had helped to frame would be ratified by the Federal Government and carried into effect. I saw him and had a long conversation with him immediately upon his arrival. He was in cheerful spirits, and seemed to think the terms obtained some mitigation of the sting of defeat and submission.

In the afternoon of that day General Johnston telegraphed that the authorities at Washington refused to recognize the terms upon which he and Sherman had agreed, that the armistice had been broken off, and that he would surrender, virtually, upon any terms offered him. Upon the receipt of this intelligence Mr. Davis resolved at once to leave Charlotte and attempt to march, with all the troops willing to follow him, to Generals Taylor and Forrest, who were somewhere in Alabama. He was accompanied by the members of his cabinet and his staff, in which General Bragg was included.[b] The brigades of Ferguson, Dibrell, Breckinridge, and mine composed his escort, the whole force under the command of General Breckinridge. We made not more than twelve or fifteen miles

---

Government was removed to Greensboro', North Carolina. On the 18th Mr. Davis and part of his cabinet and his personal staff, accompanied by a wagon-train containing the personal property of the members of the Government and the most valuable archives, started for Charlotte, North Carolina. On the 24th the terms of the convention [see p. 1,161] between Generals Johnston and Sherman were approved by Mr. Davis as President of the Confederate States.—EDITORS.

[b]In the party were General John C. Breckinridge, Secretary of War; Judah P. Benjamin, Secretary of State; S. R. Mallory, Secretary of the Navy; John H. Reagan, Postmaster General; General Samuel Cooper, Adjutant General; George Davis, Attorney General; Colonels John Taylor Wood, William Preston Johnston, and Frank R. Lubbock, staff-officers; and Colonel Burton N. Harrison, private secretary to Mr. Davis.—EDITORS.

daily. To the cavalry this slow progress was harassing, and a little demoralizing withal, as the men were inclined to construe such dilatoriness to mean irresolution and doubt on the part of their leaders. They were more especially of this opinion because a large body of Federal cavalry, the same which I had encountered at Lincolnton, were marching some ten or fifteen miles distant on our right flank, keeping pace with us, and evidently closely observing our movements. At Unionville I found Colonel Napier, with nearly all of the horses of my brigade and some seventy or eighty men.

Mr. Davis, General Breckinridge, Mr. Benjamin, and the other cabinet and staff officers mingled and talked freely with the men upon this march, and the effect was excellent. It was the general opinion that Mr. Davis could escape if he would, but that was largely induced by the knowledge that extraordinary efforts would be made to prevent his falling into the hands of the enemy. We all felt confident that General Breckinridge would not be made prisoner if duty permitted him to attempt escape. As Judge Reagan had been a frontiersman and, as we understood, a "Texas Ranger," the men thought his chances good; but all believed that Benjamin would surely be caught, and all deplored it, for he had made himself exceedingly popular. One morning he suddenly disappeared. When I next heard of him he was in England.⁄

At Abbeville, South Carolina, Mr. Davis held a conference with the officers in command of the troops composing his escort, which he himself characterized as a council of war, and which I may be justified, therefore, in so designating. It was, perhaps, the last Confederate council of war held east of the Mississippi River, certainly the last in which Mr. Davis participated. We had gone into camp in the vicinity of the little town, and, although becoming quite anxious to understand what was going to be done, we were expecting no immediate solution of the problem. We were all convinced that the best we could hope to do was to get Mr. Davis safely out of the country, and then obtain such terms as had been given General Johnston's army, or, failing in that, make the best of our way to the trans-Mississippi. The five brigade commanders [S. W. Ferguson, George G. Dibrell, J. C. Vaughn, Basil W. Duke, and W.C.P. Breckinridge] each received an order notifying him to attend at the private residence in Abbeville, where Mr. Davis had made his headquarters, about 4 o'clock of that afternoon. We were shown into a room where we found Mr. Davis and Generals Breckinridge and Bragg. No one else was present. I had never seen Mr. Davis look better or show to better advantage. He seemed in excellent spirits and humor; and the union of dignity, graceful affability, and decision, which made his manner usually so striking, was very marked in his reception of us. After some conversation of a general nature, he said: "It is time, that we adopt some

⁄Mr. Benjamin escaped through Florida to the sea-coast, thence to the Bahamas in an open boat.
—Editors.

definite plan upon which the further prosecution of our struggle shall be conducted. I have summoned you for consultation. I feel that I ought to do nothing now without the advice of my military chiefs." He smiled rather archly as he used this expression, and we could not help thinking that such a term addressed to a handful of brigadiers, commanding altogether barely three thousand men, by one who so recently had been the master of legions was a pleasantry, yet he said it in a way that made it a compliment.

After we had each given, at his request, a statement of the equipment and condition of our respective commands, Mr. Davis proceeded to declare his conviction that the cause was not lost any more than hope of American liberty was gone amid the sorest trials and most disheartening reverses of the Revolutionary struggle; but that energy, courage, and constancy might yet save all. "Even," he said, "if the troops now with me be all that I can for the present rely on, three thousand brave men are enough for a nucleus around which the whole people will rally when the panic which now afflicts them has passed away." He then asked that we should make suggestions in regard to the future conduct of the war.

We looked at each other in amazement and with a feeling a little akin to trepidation, for we hardly knew how we should give expression to views diametrically opposed to those he had uttered. Our respect for Mr. Davis approached veneration, and notwithstanding the total dissent we felt, and were obliged to announce, to the programme he had indicated, that respect was rather increased than diminished by what he had said.

I do not remember who spoke first, but we all expressed the same opinion. We told him frankly that the events of the last few days had removed from our minds all idea or hope that a prolongation of the contest was possible. The people were not panic-stricken, but broken down and worn out. We said that an attempt to continue the war, after all means of supporting warfare were gone, would be a cruel injustice to the people of the South. We would be compelled to live on a country already impoverished, and would invite its further devastation. We urged that we would be doing a wrong to our men if we persuaded them to such a course; for if they persisted in a conflict so hopeless they would be treated as brigands, and would forfeit all chance of returning to their homes.

He asked why then we were still in the field. We answered that we were desirous of affording him an opportunity of escaping the degradation of capture, and perhaps a fate which would be direr to the people than even to himself, in still more embittering the feeling between the North and South. We said that we would ask our men to follow us until his safety was assured, and would risk them in battle for that purpose, but would not fire another shot in an effort to continue hostilities.

He declared, abruptly, that he would listen to no suggestion which regarded only his own safety. He appealed eloquently to every sentiment and reminiscence that might be supposed to move a Southern soldier, and urged us to accept his views. We remained silent, for our convictions were unshaken; we felt responsible for the future welfare of the men who had so heroically followed us; and the painful point had been reached, when to speak again in opposition to all that he urged would have approached altercation. For some minutes not a word was spoken. Then Mr. Davis rose and ejaculated bitterly that all was indeed lost. He had become very pallid, and he walked so feebly as he proceeded to leave the room that General Breckinridge stepped hastily up and offered his arm.

I have undertaken to narrate very briefly what occurred in a conference which lasted for two or three hours. I believe that I have accurately given the substance of what was said; and that where I have put what was said by Mr. Davis in quotation marks, I have correctly reproduced it, or very nearly so.

Generals Breckinridge and Bragg took no part in the discussion. After Mr. Davis retired, both, however, assured us of their hearty approval of the position we had taken. They had forborne to say anything, because not immediately in command of the troops, and not supposed, therefore, to know their sentiments so well as we did. But they promised to urge upon Mr. Davis the necessity and propriety of endeavoring without further delay to get out of the country, and not permit other and serious complications to be produced by his capture and imprisonment, and perhaps execution.

It was determined that we should resume our march that night for Washington, Georgia, one or two days' march distant, and orders were issued by General Breckinridge to move at midnight. About 10 o'clock I received a message from General Breckinridge that he desired to see me immediately. I went to his quarters, and he informed me that the treasure which had been brought from Richmond was at the railroad station, and that it was necessary to provide for its removal and transportation. He instructed me to procure a sufficient number of wagons to remove it, and to detail a guard of fifty men under a field-officer for its protection. He further informed me that there was between five and six hundred thousand dollars in specie,—he did not know the exact amount,—the greater part gold. I must, he said, personally superintend its transfer from the cars to the wagons. This was not a very agreeable duty. I represented that if no one knew just what sum of money was there, it was rather an unpleasant responsibility to impose on the officer who was to take charge of it. I would have no opportunity to count it, nor any means of ascertaining whether the entire amount was turned over to me. He responded that all that had been considered, and bade me proceed to obey the order. I detailed fifty picked men as guard, and put them under command of Colonel Theophilus Steele and four of my best subalterns. I obtained six wagons, and began at once the task of removing the treasure. It was in charge of some of the former treasury clerks, and was packed in money-belts, shot-bags, a few small iron chests, and all sorts of boxes, some of them of the frailest description. In this shape I found it loaded in open box-cars. I stationed sentries at the doors, and rummaging through the cars by the faint light of a few tallow-candles gathered up all that was shown me, or that I could find. Rather more than an hour was consumed in making the transfer from the cars to the wagons, and after the latter had been started off and had gotten half a mile away, Lieutenant John B. Cole, one of the officers of the guard, rode up to me with a pine box, which may have held two or three thousand dollars in gold, on the pommel of his saddle. He had remained after the others had left, and ferreting about in a car which we thought we had thoroughly searched had discovered this box stuck in a corner and closely covered up with a piece of sacking. On the next day General Breckinridge directed me to increase the guard to two hundred men, and take charge of it in person. I suggested that instead of composing it entirely of men from my brigade, it should be constituted of details from all five. I thought this the best plan to allay any feeling of jealousy that might arise, and insure a more perfect vigilance, as I felt persuaded that these details would all carefully watch each other. My suggestion was adopted. Nearly the entire guard was kept constantly on duty, day and night, and a majority of the whole escort was usually about the wagons at every halt, closely inspecting the guard.

At the Savannah River, Mr. Davis ordered that the silver coin, amounting to one hundred and eight or ten thousand dollars, be paid to the troops in partial discharge of the arrears of pay due them. The quartermasters of the several brigades were engaged during the entire night in counting out the money, and until early dawn a throng of soldiers surrounded the little cabin where they were dividing "the pile" into their respective quotas. The sight of so much money seemed to banish sleep. My brigade received thirty-two dollars *per capita*, officers and men sharing alike. General Breckinridge was paid that sum, and, for the purpose, was borne on the roll of the brigade. On the next day, at Washington, Georgia, I turned over the residue of the treasure to Mr. M. H. Clarke, acting Treasurer of the Confederate States, and experienced a feeling of great relief.☆

Mr. Davis, having apparently yielded to the advice pressed upon him, that he should endeavor to escape, started off with a select party of twenty, commanded by Captain Given Campbell, of Kentucky, one of the most gallant and intelligent officers in the service. I knew nearly all of these twenty personally. Among them were Lieutenants Lee Hathaway and Winder Monroe of my brigade. Escort and commander had been picked as men who could be relied on in any emergency, and there is no doubt in my mind that, if Mr. Davis had really attempted to get away or reach the trans-Mississippi, this escort would

☆The treasure brought from Richmond included about $275,000 belonging to some Richmond banks.
—Editors.

have exhausted every expedient their experience could have suggested, and, if necessary, fought to the death to accomplish his purpose. I have never believed, however, that Mr. Davis really meant or desired to escape after he became convinced that all was lost. I think that, wearied by the importunity with which the request was urged, he seemingly consented, intending to put himself in the way of being captured. I am convinced that he quitted the main body of the troops that they might have an opportunity to surrender before it was too late for surrender upon terms, and that he was resolved that the small escort sent with him should encounter no risk in his behalf. I can account for his conduct upon no other hypothesis. He well knew—and he was urgently advised—that his only chance of escape was in rapid and continuous movement. He and his party were admirably mounted, and could easily have outridden the pursuit of any party they were not strong enough to fight. Therefore, when he deliberately procrastinated as he did, when the fact of his presence in that vicinity was so public, and in the face of the effort that would certainly be made by the Federal forces to secure his person, I can only believe that he had resolved not to escape.

Immediately after Mr. Davis's departure the greater portion of the troops were notified that their services would be no longer needed, and were given a formal discharge. Their officers made arrangements for their prompt surrender. General Breckinridge requested Colonel W.C.P. Breckinridge and myself to hold a body of our men together for two or three days, and, marching in a direction different from that Mr. Davis had taken, divert attention as much as possible from his movements.‡ We accordingly marched with 350 men of our respective brigades toward Woodstock, or Woodville,—I do not certainly remember the name. I moved upon one road; Colonel Breckinridge, with whom the general was, upon another. We were to meet at the point I have mentioned. I arrived first, and halted to await the others. I found that a considerable force of Federal cavalry was just to the west of the place, and not more than three miles distant. The officer in command notified me in very courteous terms that he would not attack unless I proceeded toward the west, in which event he said he would, very much to his regret, be compelled "to use violence." He said that he hoped I would think proper to surrender, as further bloodshed was useless and wrong; but that he would not undertake to hasten the matter. I responded that I appreciated his sentiments and situation, and that I would give the mat-

---

‡Jefferson Davis was captured on the 10th of May near Irwinsville, Georgia, by a detachment of the 4th Michigan Cavalry (belonging to General R.H.G. Minty's division of General James H. Wilson's cavalry corps), under Lieutenant-Colonel Benjamin D. Pritchard. Pritchard left Macon, Georgia, on the 7th, and was moving south along the west bank of the Ocmulgee when he crossed the route on which Mr. Davis and his party were moving with about twenty-four hours' start of their pursuers. A detachment of the 1st Wisconsin Cavalry (belonging to General John T. Croxton's division), under Lieutenant-Colonel Henry Harnden, was following Mr. Davis in the direct road to Irwinsville, and Pritchard, making a swift march on another road, came upon the fugitives in their camp, and arrested Mr. Davis just as the advance of Harnden's command reached the scene.—Editors.

ter of surrender immediate and careful consideration. That evening Colonel Breckinridge arrived. He had encountered a body of Federals, who had made to him almost the identical statement the officer in my front had addressed to me. He had parleyed with them long enough to enable General Breckinridge, with one or two officers who were to accompany him in his effort to escape, to get far enough away to elude pursuit,꙳ and then, telling them where he wished to go, was allowed to march by upon the same road occupied by the Federal column. The men of the previously hostile hosts cheered each other as they passed, and the "Yanks" shouted, "You rebs better go home and stop this nonsense; we don't want to hurt each other!" The colonel brought an earnest injunction from General Breckinridge that we should both surrender without delay. We communicated his message to our comrades, and for us the long agony was over.꙳

NOTES ON THE UNION AND CONFEDERATE ARMIES.

In a statistical exhibit of deaths in the Union Army, compiled (1885), under the direction of Adjutant-General Drum, by Joseph W. Kirkley, the causes of death are given as follows: Killed in action, 4142 officers, 62,916 men; died of wounds received in action, 2223 officers, 40,780 men, of which number 99 officers and 1973 men were prisoners of war; died of disease, 2795 officers and 221,791 men, of which 83 officers and 24,783 men were prisoners; accidental deaths (except drowned), 142 officers and 3972 men, of which 2 officers and 5 men were prisoners; drowned, 106 officers and 4838 men, of which 1 officer and 6 men were prisoners; murdered, 37 officers and 483 men; killed after capture, 14 officers and 90 men; committed suicide, 26 officers and 365 men; executed by United

---

꙳Among those who surrendered at the time, besides Mr. Davis's family and the guard, were Mr. Reagan and Colonels Lubbock, Johnston, and Harrison. General Breckinridge and Colonel Wood escaped, and made their way to Florida, whence they sailed to Cuba in an open boat.—EDITORS.

꙳On the 29th of May, 1865, President Johnson issued a proclamation of amnesty to all persons (with some notable exceptions) who had participated in the rebellion, and who should make oath to support the Constitution and the Union, and the proclamations and laws relating to emancipation. Among the exceptions, besides certain civil and diplomatic officers and agents, and others, were the officers of the Confederate service above the rank of colonel in the army and that of lieutenant in the navy, and those who had been educated at the United States Military and Naval Academies.

Amnesty was further extended by proclamations, on September 7th, 1867, and December 25th, 1868. In the first the military exceptions made in the amnesty of May 29th, 1865, were reduced to ex-Confederate officers above the rank of brigadier-general in the army, and of captain in the navy, and in the second all exceptions were removed and the pardon was unconditional and without the formality of any oath.

Mr. Davis was imprisoned at Fort Monroe immediately after his arrest, and was indicted on the charge of treason, by a Grand Jury in the United States Court for the District of Virginia, at Norfolk, May 8th, 1866. On May 13th, 1867, he was released on a bail-bond of $100,000, signed by Cornelius Vanderbilt, Gerrit Smith, and Horace Greeley, and in December, 1868, a *nolle prosequi* was entered in the case.—EDITORS.

States military authorities, 267 men; executed by the enemy, 4 officers and 60 men; died from sunstroke, 5 officers and 308 men, of which 20 men were prisoners; other known causes, 62 officers and 1972 men, of which 7 officers and 312 men were prisoners; causes not stated, 28 officers and 12,093 men, of which 9 officers and 2030 men were prisoners. Total, 9584 officers and 349,944 men, of which 219 officers and 29,279 men were prisoners. Grand aggregate, 359,528; aggregate deaths among prisoners, 29,498. Since 1885 the Adjutant-General has received evidence of the death in Southern prisons of 694 men not previously accounted for, which increases the number of deaths among prisoners to 30,192, and makes a grand aggregate of 360,222.

COMPARATIVE STATEMENT OF THE NUMBER OF MEN FURNISHED
THE UNITED STATES ARMY AND NAVY, AND OF THE DEATHS
IN THE ARMY, 1861–5.
Men furnished.

States, territories, etc.	White troops.	Sailors & marines.	Colored troops.	Total.	Aggregate of deaths.
Alabama	2,576			2,576	345
Arkansas	8,289			8,289	1,713
California	15,725			15,725	573
Colorado	4,903			4,903	323
Connecticut	51,937	2,163	1,764	55,864	5,354
Dakota	206			206	6
Delaware	11,236	94	954	12,284	882
Dist. of Columbia	11,912	1,353	3,269	16,534	290

NOTES TO THE TABLE ABOVE.

Figures in the column of deaths, opposite names of States, represent only such as occurred among *white troops* (losses among colored troops and Indians being given at the foot of the table). The table does not indicate losses among sailors and marines.

The colored soldiers organized under the authority of the General Government and not credited to any State were recruited as follows: In Alabama, 4969; Arkansas, 5526; Colorado, 93; Florida, 1044; Georgia, 3486; Louisiana, 24,052; Mississippi, 17,869; North Carolina, 5035; South Carolina, 5462; Tennessee, 20,133; Texas, 47; Virginia, 5723.

There were also 5896 negro soldiers enlisted at large, or whose credits are not specifically expressed by the records.

The number of officers and men of the Regular Army among whom the casualties herein noted occurred is estimated at 67,000; the number in the Veteran Reserve Corps was 60,508; and in Hancock's Veteran Corps, 10,883.

The other organizations of white volunteers, organized directly by the U.S. authorities, numbered about 11,000.

In 82 national cemeteries (according to the report of June 30th, 1888) 325,230 men are buried: 176,397 being known, and 148,833 unknown dead. These numbers include 1136 at Mexico City, most of whom lost their lives in the Mexican war; about 9500 Confederates; and about 8500 civilians.

States, territories, etc.	Men furnished.				Aggregate of deaths.
	White troops.	Sailors & marines.	Colored troops.	Total.	
Florida	1,290			1,290	215
Georgia					15
Illinois	255,057	2,224	1,811	259,092	34,834
Indiana	193,748	1,078	1,537	196,363	26,672
Iowa	75,797	5	440	76,242	13,001
Kansas	18,069		2,080	20,149	2,630
Kentucky	51,743	314	23,703	75,760	10,774
Louisiana	5,224			5,224	945
Maine	64,973	5,030	104	70,107	9,398
Maryland	33,995	3,925	8,718	46,638	2,982
Massachusetts	122,781	19,983	3,966	146,730	13,942
Michigan	85,479	498	1,387	87,364	14,753
Minnesota	23,913	3	104	24,020	2,584
Mississippi	545			545	78
Missouri	100,616	151	8,344	109,111	13,885
Nebraska*	3,157			3,157	239
Nevada	1,080			1,080	33
New Hampshire	32,930	882	125	33,937	4,882
New Jersey	67,500	8,129	1,185	76,814	5,754
New Mexico	6,561			6,561	277
New York	409,561	35,164	4,125	448,850	46,534
North Carolina	3,156			3,156	360
Ohio	304,814	3,274	5,092	313,180	35,475
Oregon	1,810			1,810	45
Pennsylvania	315,017	14,307	8,612	337,936	33,183
Rhode Island	19,521	1,878	1,837	23,236	1,321
Tennessee	31,092			31,092	6,777
Texas	1,965			1,965	141
Vermont	32,549	619	120	33,288	5,224
Virginia					42
Washington	964			964	22
West Virginia	31,872		196	32,068	4,017
Wisconsin	91,029	183	165	91,327	12,301
Indian Nations				*3,530	1,018

* Indians.

Colored Troops			99,337	[†]99,337	[‡]35,847
	2,494,392	101,207	178,975	2,778,304	

Veteran Reserve Corps	1,672
U.S. Veteran Volunteers (Hancock's Corps)	106
U.S. Volunteer Engineers and Sharp-shooters	552
U.S. Volunteer Infantry	243
General and general staff-officers, U.S. Volunt'rs	239
Miscellaneous U.S. Volunt'rs (brigade bands, etc.)	232
Regular Army	5,796
Grand aggregate	[§]359,528

[†] Number not credited to any State.
[‡] Includes losses in all colored organizations excepting three regiments from Massachusetts whose deaths aggregated 574.
[§] Increased by additional evidence since 1885 to 360,222.

ACKNOWLEDGMENTS

This ambitious and daunting project—so meticulously assembled and so beautifully published—would not have been possible without the generous commitment of the Modern Library, and its determination to mark the Civil War sesquicentennial by resurrecting an important, original classic and mining its most enduring gems for the benefit of a new generation of readers.

I am enormously grateful to former Modern Library editor John Flicker for welcoming the project to the Random House family, and to senior editor Jonathan Jao for so magnificently bringing it to fruition. Thanks also go to Jessie Waters, Tom Perry, and Richard Elman of Random House and all of the Random House designers and copy editors who worked so skillfully on the adaptation, particularly designer Chris Zucker and senior production editor Janet Wygal.

I could not have asked for a more distinguished and resourceful roster of contributors than the stellar list of friends and colleagues who joined me for this project. They not only provided chapter introductions but also supplied crucial advice on what material to include in the "best of" edition, which, despite its considerable length, necessarily omitted much material published in the multivolume nineteenth-century edition. Historians Craig Symonds, Stephen Sears, James McPherson, Joan Waugh, and "Bud" Robertson occupy the very top rank of Civil War scholars, and their commentary and analysis for this special edition of *Battles and Leaders* adds a level of expertise that even the veterans who wrote the original articles would have regarded with deep interest.

Thanks go, too, to the scholars who were unable to join the list of contributing editors but provided most useful advice on the material, especially Professor Gary Gallagher of the University of Virginia and William C. "Jack" Davis of Virginia Tech. For many years, at Civil War conferences and symposia across the country, I have enjoyed the pleasure of their company and the benefit of their expertise and counsel, and I particularly appreciate their advice on and enthusiasm for this project. I am grateful as well to my friends Frank J. Williams, chairman of the Lincoln Forum, and John M. Marszalek, reigning expert on Union Generals Henry Halleck and William T. Sherman, for their advice and inspiration. Likewise I thank my indomitable agent Geri Thoma for her great help with this and so many of my projects.

I could not have found the considerable time required for this book without the constant understanding and essential advice of my wife, Edith. With her unending support and encouragement, I have written and edited more than three hundred books and four hundred magazine articles over the years, but this book comes out as we mark our fortieth wedding anniversary, so it takes on special significance for us (even in the absence of the kind of long celebratory vacation that would have been possible absent my *Hearts Touched by Fire* deadlines). Thank you, Edith, for your patience and, of course, for Meg, Remy, and her husband, Adam, and for their magnificent Charlie.

Finally, this book was dedicated to a much-mourned friend who left us much too soon: Professor John Y. Simon, the longtime executive director of the Ulysses S. Grant Association and editor of the *Papers of Ulysses S. Grant*. For some forty years, John Y. was the undisputed authority on the Civil War's greatest general and one of the most knowledgeable, incisive—and certainly *the* most acerbic, irreverent, and hilarious—scholar of all the battles and leaders of the great conflict. I had the pleasure and honor of editing a previous book with John Y., and in that as with all professional endeavors, he demonstrated extraordinary mastery of the facts as well as a wonderful sense of humor.

I daresay all of the scholars who contributed to this project miss John Y. as much as I do. Had he lived, he would surely have added his wisdom to this book. The dedication to his memory hardly repays our debt to him for his friendship, knowledge, and service, but I hope it reminds readers of his contributions to both American history and American historians alike.

NOTES

1. Robert Underwood Johnson, *Remembered Yesterdays* (Boston: Little, Brown, 1927), 189.
2. Ibid.
3. The writers were, respectively, Alexander R. Boteler and F. B. Sanborn.
4. Johnson, *Remembered Yesterdays,* 190.
5. Ibid., 189, 194.
6. Robert Underwood Johnson and Clarence Clough Buel, eds., *Battles and Leaders of the Civil War, Being for the Most Part Contributions by Union and Confederate Officers. Based upon "The Century War Series,"* 4 vols. (New York: The Century Co., 1888), 1:x–xii.
7. Johnson, *Remembered Yesterdays,* 189.
8. Mark E. Neely, Jr., *The Abraham Lincoln Encyclopedia* (New York: McGraw-Hill, 1982), 142.
9. Mrs. Schuyler Van Rensselaer, "Richard Watson Gilder: Personal Memories," *The Outlook* 130 (March 8, 1922): 379. As the author put it: "Although his name never appeared in his magazine as that of its editor, every one in America knew that he was its editor and that it was his voice."
10. Quoted in Stephen Davis, "'A Matter of Sensational Interest': The Century 'Battles and Leaders' Series," *Civil War History* 27 (1981): 339. The editor gratefully acknowledges the extraordinary contributions made by historian Davis in his superbly researched articles on *Battles and Leaders.*
11. Van Rensselaer, "Richard Watson Gilder," 378.
12. Johnson, *Remembered Yesterdays,* 210; John Y. Simon, ed., *The Papers of Ulysses S. Grant,* 31 vols. (Carbondale, Ill.: Southern Illinois University Press, 1963–2009), 31:157–58; see also Adam Badeau, *Military History of Ulysses S. Grant, from April, 1861, to April, 1865* (New York: D. Appleton, 1881).
13. Johnson, *Remembered Yesterdays,* 202.
14. Ibid., 199.
15. Ibid., 192.

16. Davis, "'A Matter of Sensational Interest,'" 340.

17. Ibid.

18. Johnson, *Remembered Yesterdays,* 213–15.

19. Badeau obituary, *The New York Times,* March 21, 1895.

20. Simon, ed., *Papers of Ulysses S. Grant,* 31:170, 172, 175.

21. Ibid., 187–88.

22. Johnson, *Remembered Yesterdays,* 196, 199.

23. Ibid., 201.

24. See, for example, McClellan to his wife, October [29], 1862, in Stephen W. Sears, ed., *The Civil War Papers of George B. McClellan: Selected Correspondence, 1860–1865* (New York: Ticknor & Fields, 1989), 515.

25. Stephen Davis and J. Tracy Power, "Battles and Leaders of the Civil War," in Clyde N. Wilson, ed., *Dictionary of Literary Biography,* vol. 47: *American Historians, 1866–1912* (Detroit: Gale Publishing, 1986), 373.

26. Johnson, *Remembered Yesterdays,* 216, 219; Davis, "'A Matter of Sensational Interest,'" 340–41n8.

27. Davis, "'A Matter of Sensational Interest,'" 341.

28. Johnson, *Remembered Yesterdays,* 193–94, 196–97.

29. Ibid., 200.

30. Ibid., 196.

31. Buel to Sherman, March 13, 1884, in Simon, ed., *Papers of Ulysses S. Grant,* 31:189.

32. *Battles and Leaders,* 1:xi.

33. Ibid.; Johnson, *Remembered Yesterdays,* 203–4.

34. Davis and Power, "Battles and Leaders of the Civil War," 374.

35. Quoted in Davis, "'A Matter of Sensational Interest,'" 342–43.

36. Johnson, *Remembered Yesterdays,* 190. The editor further asserted that ten thousand items were cut from the index for space reasons.

37. *The Century War Book,* "Preface to the People's Pictorial Edition" (New York: The Century Co., 1894).

38. Davis, "'A Matter of Sensational Interest,'" 348.

39. *Battles and Leaders,* 1:ix.

INDEX

Note: Page numbers in *italics* refer to illustrations.

ABOUT THE CONTRIBUTORS

CRAIG L. SYMONDS was co-winner of the 2009 Lincoln Prize for his book *Lincoln and His Admirals: Abraham Lincoln, the U.S. Navy, and the Civil War*. Professor of History Emeritus at the U.S. Naval Academy, he later served as chief historian of the *USS Monitor* Center in Newport News, Virginia. The author of many books—notably biographies of Joseph E. Johnston, Patrick Cleburne, and Franklin Buchanan—he previously won the Theodore and Franklin Roosevelt Prize for the best book on naval history for his *Decision at Sea: Five Naval Battles That Shaped American History* (2005).

STEPHEN W. SEARS, a historian specializing in the Civil War, is the author of a number of acclaimed works, and is widely considered the leading authority on the controversial Union general George B. McClellan. His books include *Landscape Turned Red: The Battle of Antietam* (1983), *George B. McClellan: The Young Napoleon* (1988), *The Civil War Papers of George B. McClellan* (1989), *To the Gates of Richmond: The Peninsula Campaign* (1992), *Chancellorsville* (1996), and *Gettysburg* (2003). A graduate of Oberlin, he began his career as an editor at *American Heritage Magazine*.

JAMES M. McPHERSON, Professor of History Emeritus at Princeton University, has won two Lincoln Prizes, most recently as co-laureate for *Tried by War: Abraham Lincoln as Commander-in-Chief* (2008). McPherson earned the Pulitzer Prize for the 1988 classic *Battle Cry of Freedom: The Civil War Era* and recently authored the compelling brief biography *Abraham Lincoln* (2009). His many other books include *Drawn with the Sword: Reflections on the American Civil War* (1996), *For Cause and Comrades: Why Men Fought in the Civil War* (1997), and *Crossroads of Freedom: Antietam* (2002).

JOAN WAUGH is Professor of History at UCLA, where she specializes in Civil War and Reconstruction history. Her books include *Unsentimental Reformer: The Life of Josephine Shaw Lowell* (1998), *The Memory of the Civil War in American Culture* (co-author, 2004), and her latest book, the widely praised *U. S. Grant: American Hero, American Myth* (2009). She has organized several symposia at the Huntington Library in San Marino, California, has won UCLA's Distinguished Teaching Award, and has appeared on PBS's *American Experience* to discuss Ulysses S. Grant.

JAMES I. ROBERTSON, JR., a graduate of Emory University, is Alumni Distinguished Professor in History at Virginia Polytechnic Institute. After launching his career as the executive director of the Civil War Centennial (1961–65), he has published more than twenty widely respected books on the subject, including *General A. P. Hill* (1987), *Soldiers Blue and Gray* (1988), *Civil War! America Becomes One Nation* (1992), and *Stonewall Jackson: The Man, the Soldier, the Legend* (1997). He recently began serving as a member of Virginia's Civil War Sesquicentennial Commission.

About the Editor

HAROLD HOLZER is the author, co-author, or editor of more than thirty-five books on Abraham Lincoln and the Civil War, including *The Confederate Image* (1987), *The Union Image* (1990), *Eyewitness to War: The Civil War* (1996), *Prang's Civil War Pictures* (2001), and *In Lincoln's Hand* (2009). His many awards include a 2005 Lincoln Prize, the Bell I. Wiley Prize, and the National Humanities Medal, which was awarded to him by the president of the United States in 2008. From 2000 to 2010 he served as co-chair of the United States Lincoln Bicentennial Commission, lecturing widely and appearing frequently on television, including PBS, C-SPAN, and the History Channel. He is senior vice president for external affairs at the Metropolitan Museum of Art.

A Note on the Type

The principal text of this Modern Library edition
was set in a digitized version of Janson, a typeface that
dates from about 1690 and was cut by Nicholas Kis,
a Hungarian working in Amsterdam. The original matrices have
survived and are held by the Stempel foundry in Germany.
Hermann Zapf redesigned some of the weights and sizes for
Stempel, basing his revisions on the original design.